STATUTORY

INSTRUMENTS

1969

PART III
(in two Sections)

SECTION 2

Published by Authority

LONDON
HER MAJESTY'S STATIONERY OFFICE
1970

2a

© *Crown copyright* 1970

PRINTED AND PUBLISHED BY HER MAJESTY'S STATIONERY OFFICE

To be purchased from

49 High Holborn, LONDON, W.C.1
13a Castle Street, EDINBURGH, EH2 3AR   109 St. Mary Street, CARDIFF, CF1 1JW
Brazennose Street, MANCHESTER, M60 8AS   50 Fairfax Street, BRISTOL, BS1 3DE
258 Broad Street, BIRMINGHAM, 1   7 Linenhall Street, BELFAST, BT2 8AY

or through any Bookseller

1970

Price: £8 0s. 0d. the two Sections: the Volume, complete, £24 0s. 0d.

PRINTED IN ENGLAND

SBN 11 840046 0

HMSO
£8 (two vols)

Contents of the Volume

Contents of the Volume

PART I, Section 1

PART I, Section 2

PART II, Section 1

PART II, Section 2

PART III, Section 1

PART III, Section 2

STATUTORY INSTRUMENTS

1969 No. 1502

CARIBBEAN AND NORTH ATLANTIC TERRITORIES

The West Indies (Dissolution and Interim Commissioner) (Amendment) Order 1969

Made - - - -	*22nd October* 1969
Laid before Parliament	*24th October* 1969
Coming into Operation	*27th October* 1969

At the Court at Buckingham Palace, the 22nd day of October 1969

Present,

The Queen's Most Excellent Majesty in Council

Her Majesty, by virtue of the powers conferred upon Her by the West Indies Act 1962(a) and of all other powers enabling Her in that behalf, is pleased, by and with the advice of Her Privy Council, to order, and it is hereby ordered, as follows:—

1.—(1) This Order may be cited as the West Indies (Dissolution and Interim Commissioner) (Amendment) Order 1969 and shall be construed as one with the West Indies (Dissolution and Interim Commissioner) Order in Council 1962(b) (hereinafter referred to as "the principal Order"). *Citation, construction and commencement.*

(2) This Order shall come into operation on 27th October 1969.

2. Article 2(1) of the principal Order is amended by the deletion from the definition of " the Territories " of paragraph (j) (which specifies Saint Vincent). *Amendment of article 2 of principal Order.*

3. Nothing in this Order shall affect the operation in Saint Vincent, on and after the coming into operation of this Order, of any law having effect as part of the law of Saint Vincent immediately before the commencement of this Order by virtue of the provisions of articles 9, 15 or 16 of the principal Order. *Saving.*

W. G. Agnew.

EXPLANATORY NOTE

(*This Note is not part of the Order.*)

This Order removes Saint Vincent from the list of territories to which the West Indies (Dissolution and Interim Commissioner) Order in Council 1962 applies.

(a) 1962 c. 19.   (b) S.I. 1962/1084 (1962 II, p. 1220).

STATUTORY INSTRUMENTS

1969 No. 1503

SOLICITORS

The Overseas Solicitors (Admission) (Amendment) Order 1969

Made - - - - - *22nd October* 1969

At the Court at Buckingham Palace, the 22nd day of October 1969

Present,

The Queen's Most Excellent Majesty in Council.

Her Majesty, in pursuance of the powers conferred on Her, as regards England, by section 4 of the Solicitors Act 1957(**a**), as amended by section 3 of and Schedule 4 to the Solicitors Act 1965(**b**) and, as regards Scotland, by section 2 of the Colonial Solicitors Act 1900(**c**), and of all other powers thereunto Her enabling, is pleased, by and with the advice of Her Privy Council, to order, and it is hereby ordered, as follows:—

1.—(1) This Order may be cited as the Overseas Solicitors (Admission) (Amendment) Order 1969.

(2) The Interpretation Act 1889(**d**) shall apply with the necessary adaptations, for the purpose of interpreting this Order and otherwise in relation thereto as it applies for the purpose of interpreting and in relation to Acts of Parliament.

2. The following amendments shall be made to the Overseas Solicitors (Admission) Order 1964(**e**) as amended (**f**), namely:—

(*a*) after paragraph (i) of Article 3 shall be inserted the following paragraph:

" (ii) an applicant shall have passed such qualifying examination as is required by the laws or regulations in force in the territory specified in Schedule 1 to this Order in which he is a solicitor of a person applying for admission as a solicitor in that territory who has not qualified for admission in any other territory ; "

(*b*) paragraphs (ii) to (ix) of Article 3 shall be renumbered as paragraphs (iii) to (x) ;

(*c*) after sub-paragraph (*b*) of paragraph (iii) of Article 3 as so renumbered shall be inserted the following new sub-paragraph:

" (*c*) a certificate from the appropriate authority that he has passed the qualifying examination referred to in paragraph (ii) of this Article ; "

and sub-paragraph (*c*) of the said paragraph (iii) shall be relettered as sub-paragraph (*d*) ;

(**a**) 5 & 6 Eliz. 2. c. 27.　　(**b**) 1965. c. 31.　　(**c**) 63 & 64 Vict. c. 14.
(**d**) 52 & 53 Vict. c. 63.　(**e**) S.I. 1964/1848 (1964 III, p. 4026).
(**f**) S.I. 1965/1713 (1965 III, p. 4834).

(*d*) after paragraph (1) of the declaration in Schedule 2 shall be inserted:

"(2) I have passed the qualifying examination as required by the laws or regulations in force in
of a person applying for admission as a solicitor there who has not qualified for admission in any other territory."

and paragraphs (2) to (4) shall be renumbered as paragraphs (3) to (5);

(*e*) in paragraph (5) of the declaration as so renumbered for the words "The document" shall be substituted the words "The document now produced and shown to me and marked "B" is the certificate from the appropriate authority in   that I have passed the qualifying examination referred to in paragraph (2) of this declaration and the document"; for the letters "B", "C" and "D" in the said paragraph (5) shall be substituted the letters "C", "D" and "E" respectively.

W. G. Agnew.

EXPLANATORY NOTE

(*This Note is not part of the Order.*)

This Order amends the Overseas Solicitors (Admission) Order 1964 in respect of the admission as a solicitor in England or in Scotland of a solicitor of a Court of a part of the Commonwealth specified in Schedule 1 of that Order. Under the present Order, such a solicitor will need to have passed the qualifying examination required by the laws or regulations in that part of the Commonwealth of a person who is not qualified elsewhere.

STATUTORY INSTRUMENTS

1969 No. 1504

SOUTHERN RHODESIA

The Southern Rhodesia Act 1965 (Continuation) Order 1969

Laid before Parliament in draft

Made - - - - *22nd October* 1969

At the Court at Buckingham Palace, the 22nd day of October 1969

Present,

The Queen's Most Excellent Majesty in Council

Whereas a draft of the following Order has been laid before Parliament and approved by resolution of each House of Parliament:

Now, therefore, Her Majesty, in exercise of the powers conferred on Her by section 3(2) of the Southern Rhodesia Act 1965(a), is pleased, by and with the advice of Her Privy Council, to order, and it is hereby ordered, as follows:—

Continuation in force of s. 2 of Act of 1965

1. Section 2 of the Southern Rhodesia Act 1965 shall continue in force for a period of one year beginning with 16th November 1969.

Citation

2. This Order may be cited as the Southern Rhodesia Act 1965 (Continuation) Order 1969.

W. G. Agnew.

EXPLANATORY NOTE

(This Note is not part of the Order.)

This Order continues in force for a further year the powers conferred by section 2 of the Southern Rhodesia Act 1965 to make Orders in Council in relation to Southern Rhodesia.

(a) 1965 c. 76.

STATUTORY   INSTRUMENTS

1969 No. 1505

SUGAR

The Sugar (Rates of Surcharge and Surcharge Repayments) (No. 11) Order 1969

Made - - - -	*21st October* 1969
Laid before Parliament	*22nd October* 1969
Coming into Operation	*23rd October* 1969

The Minister of Agriculture, Fisheries and Food, in exercise of the powers conferred on him by sections 7(4), 8(6) and 33(4) of the Sugar Act 1956(a) having effect subject to the provisions of section 3 of, and Part II of Schedule 5 to, the Finance Act 1962(b), and section 58 of the Finance Act 1968(c) and of all other powers enabling him in that behalf, with the concurrence of the Treasury, on the advice of the Sugar Board, hereby makes the following order:—

1.—(1) This order may be cited as the Sugar (Rates of Surcharge and Surcharge Repayments) (No. 11) Order 1969; and shall come into operation on 23rd October 1969.

(2) The Interpretation Act 1889(d) shall apply for the interpretation of this order as it applies for the interpretation of an Act of Parliament.

2. Notwithstanding the provisions of Article 2 of the Sugar (Rates of Surcharge and Surcharge Repayments) (No. 10) Order 1969(e), the rates of surcharge payable under and in accordance with the provisions of section 7 of the Sugar Act 1956, having effect as aforesaid, in respect of sugar and invert sugar imported or home produced or used in the manufacture of imported composite sugar products shall on and after 23rd October 1969 be those rates specified in Schedule 1 to this order.

3. For the purpose of section 8(3)(b) of the Sugar Act 1956, having effect as aforesaid, the rates of surcharge repayments in respect of invert sugar produced in the United Kingdom from materials on which on or after 23rd October 1969 sugar duty has been paid or, by virtue of paragraph 1 of Part II of Schedule 5 to the Finance Act 1962, is treated as having been paid shall, notwithstanding the provisions of Article 3 of the Sugar (Rates of Surcharge and Surcharge Repayments) (No. 10) Order 1969 be those specified in Schedule 2 to this order.

(a) 1956 c. 48.   (b) 1962 c. 44.
(c) 1968 c. 44.   (d) 1889 c. 63.
(e) S.I. 1969/1426(1969 III, p. 4612).

In Witness whereof the Official Seal of the Minister of Agriculture, Fisheries and Food is hereunto affixed on 20th October 1969.

(L.S.)

R. P. Fraser,

Authorised by the Minister.

We concur.

21st October 1969.

E. G. Perry,
Joseph Harper,

Two of the Lords Commissioners of
Her Majesty's Treasury.

SCHEDULE 1

PART I

SURCHARGE RATES FOR SUGAR

Polarisation									Rate of Surcharge per cwt.
									s. d.
Exceeding—									
99° ...	...	...	...	...	...	...	...	...	23 4·0
98° but not exceeding 99° ...			...	...	...	...	...	...	22 0·0
97° „ „ „ 98°	...		...	...	...	...	...	...	21 5·6
96° „ „ „ 97°	...		...	...	...	...	...	...	20 10·8
95° „ „ „ 96°	...		...	...	...	...	...	...	20 4·1
94° „ „ „ 95°	...		...	...	...	...	...	...	19 9·4
93° „ „ „ 94°	...		...	...	...	...	...	...	19 2·7
92° „ „ „ 93°	...		...	...	...	...	...	...	18 8·0
91° „ „ „ 92°	...		...	...	...	...	...	...	18 1·2
90° „ „ „ 91°	...		...	...	...	...	...	...	17 6·5
89° „ „ „ 90°	...		...	...	...	...	...	...	16 11·8
88° „ „ „ 89°	...		...	...	...	...	...	...	16 5·1
87° „ „ „ 88°	...		...	...	...	...	...	...	15 11·5
86° „ „ „ 87°	...		...	...	...	...	...	...	15 5·9
85° „ „ „ 86°	...		...	...	...	...	...	...	15 0·8
84° „ „ „ 85°	...		...	...	...	...	...	...	14 7·8
83° „ „ „ 84°	...		...	...	...	...	...	...	14 2·8
82° „ „ „ 83°	...		...	...	...	...	...	...	13 9·7
81° „ „ „ 82°	...		...	...	...	...	...	...	13 5·2
80° „ „ „ 81°	...		...	...	...	...	...	...	13 0·8
79° „ „ „ 80°	...		...	...	...	...	...	...	12 8·3
78° „ „ „ 79°	...		...	...	...	...	...	...	12 3·8
77° „ „ „ 78°	...		...	...	...	...	...	...	11 11·3
76° „ „ „ 77°	...		...	...	...	...	...	...	11 6·8
Not exceeding 76°	...	...	...	...	...	...	...	...	11 3·0

PART II

SURCHARGE RATES FOR INVERT SUGAR

Sweetening matter content by weight	Rate of Surcharge per cwt.
	s. d.
70 per cent. or more	14 10
Less than 70 per cent. and more than 50 per cent.	10 8
Not more than 50 per cent.	5 2

SCHEDULE 2

SURCHARGE REPAYMENT RATES FOR INVERT SUGAR

Sweetening matter content by weight	Rate of Surcharge Repayment per cwt.
	s. d.
More than 80 per cent.	17 6
More than 70 per cent. but not more than 80 per cent.	14 10
More than 60 per cent. but not more than 70 per cent.	10 8
More than 50 per cent. but not more than 60 per cent.	8 5
Not more than 50 per cent. and the invert sugar not being less in weight than 14 lb. per gallon	5 2

EXPLANATORY NOTE

(*This Note is not part of the Order.*)

This order prescribes—

   (*a*) reductions equivalent to 2s. 4d. per cwt. of refined sugar in the rates of surcharge payable on sugar and invert sugar which become chargeable with surcharge on or after 23rd October 1969;

   (*b*) correspondingly reduced rates of surcharge repayment in respect of invert sugar produced in the United Kingdom from materials on which surcharge has been paid.

STATUTORY INSTRUMENTS

1969 No. 1506

SUGAR

The Composite Sugar Products (Surcharge and Surcharge Repayments—Average Rates) (No. 11) Order 1969

Made - - - -	*21st October* 1969
Laid before Parliament	*22nd October* 1969
Coming into Operation	*23rd October* 1969

Whereas the Minister of Agriculture, Fisheries and Food (hereinafter called " the Minister ") has on the recommendation of the Commissioners of Customs and Excise (hereinafter called " the Commissioners ") made an order(a) pursuant to the powers conferred upon him by sections 9(1) and 9(4) of the Sugar Act 1956(b), having effect subject to the provisions of section 3 of, and Part II of Schedule 5 to, the Finance Act 1962(c), to the provisions of section 52(2) of the Finance Act 1966(d), and to the provisions of Section 58 of the Finance Act 1968(e), providing that in the case of certain descriptions of composite sugar products surcharge shall be calculated on the basis of an average quantity of sugar or invert sugar taken to have been used in the manufacture of the products, and that certain other descriptions of composite sugar products shall be treated as not containing any sugar or invert sugar, and that in the case of certain descriptions of goods in the manufacture of which sugar or invert sugar is used, surcharge repayments shall be calculated on the basis of an average quantity of sugar or invert sugar taken to have been so used:

Now, therefore, the Minister, on the recommendation of the Commissioners and in exercise of the powers conferred upon him by sections 9(1), 9(4) and 33(4) of the Sugar Act 1956, having effect as aforesaid, and of all other powers enabling him in that behalf, hereby makes the following order:—

1.—(1) This order may be cited as the Composite Sugar Products (Surcharge and Surcharge Repayments—Average Rates) (No. 11) Order 1969; and shall come into operation on 23rd October 1969.

(2) The Interpretation Act 1889(f) shall apply for the interpretation of this order as it applies for the interpretation of an Act of Parliament.

2. Surcharge payable on or after 23rd October 1969 under and in accordance with the Sugar Act 1956, having effect as aforesaid, in respect of sugar and invert sugar used in the manufacture of the descriptions of imported composite sugar products specified in column 2 of Schedule 1 to this order shall, notwithstanding the provisions of the Sugar (Rates of Surcharge and Surcharge Repayments) (No. 11) Order 1969(g) andthe Composite Sugar Products (Surcharge and Surcharge Repayments—Average Rates) (No. 10) Order 1969(a), be calculated by reference to the weight or value, as the case may be, of the products at the rates specified in relation thereto in column 3 of the said Schedule.

(a) S.I. 1969/1427(1969 III, p. 4615).	(b) 1956 c. 48.	(c) 1962 c. 44.
(d) 1966 c. 18.	(e) 1968 c. 44.	(f) 1889 c. 63.
(g) S.I. 1969/1505(1969 III, p. 4891).		

3. Imported composite sugar products other than those of a description specified in Schedules 1 and 2 to this order shall be treated as not containing any sugar or invert sugar for the purposes of surcharge payable on or after 23rd October 1969.

4. Surcharge repayments payable on and after 23rd October 1969 under and in accordance with the provisions of section 8 of the Sugar Act 1956, having effect as aforesaid, in respect of sugar and invert sugar used in the manufacture of the descriptions of goods specified in column 1 of Schedule 3 to this order shall, notwithstanding the provisions of the Sugar (Rates of Surcharge and Surcharge Repayments) (No. 11) Order 1969(**a**) and the Composite Sugar Products (Surcharge and Surcharge Repayments—Average Rates) (No. 10) Order 1969(**b**), be calculated by reference to the quantity of the goods at the rates specified in relation thereto in column 2 of the said Schedule.

In Witness whereof the Official Seal of the Minister of Agriculture, Fisheries and Food is hereunto affixed on 21st October 1969.

(L.S.)   *R. P. Fraser,*
                                 Authorised by the Minister.

SCHEDULE 1

In this Schedule:—

" Tariff heading " means a heading or, where the context so requires, a subheading of the Customs Tariff 1959 (see paragraph (1) of Article 1 of the Import Duties (General) (No. 4) Order 1968(**c**)).

" Per cent." means, where it occurs in relation to any rate of surcharge, per cent. of the value for customs duty purposes of the product to which it relates.

Tariff heading	Description of Imported Composite Sugar Products	Rate of Surcharge
		per cwt. s. d.
04.02	Milk and cream, preserved, concentrated or sweetened, containing more than 10 per cent. by weight of added sweetening matter	10 4
17.02 (B) (2) and 17.05 (B)	Syrups containing sucrose sugar, whether or not flavoured or coloured, but not including fruit juices containing added sugar in any proportion:—	
	containing 70 per cent. or more by weight of sweetening matter	14 10
	containing less than 70 per cent., and more than 50 per cent., by weight of sweetening matter...	10 8
	containing not more than 50 per cent. by weight of sweetening matter	5 2

(a) S.I. 1969/1505 (1969 III, p. 4891).   (b) S.I. 1969/1427 (1969 III, p. 4615).
 (c) S.I. 1968/679 (1968 I, p. 1519).

Tariff heading	Description of Imported Composite Sugar Products	Rate of Surcharge
		per cwt. s. d.
17.02 (F) ...	Caramel:—	
	Solid	23 4
	Liquid	16 4
17.04	Sugar confectionery, not containing cocoa	19 0
18.06	Chocolate and other food preparations containing cocoa:—	
	Chocolate couverture not prepared for retail sale; chocolate milk crumb, liquid	10 4
	Chocolate milk crumb, solid	12 9
	Solid chocolate bars or blocks, milk or plain, with or without fruit or nuts; other chocolate confectionery consisting wholly of chocolate or of chocolate and other ingredients not containing added sugar, but not including such goods when packed together in retail packages with goods liable to surcharge at a higher rate	10 6
	Other	13 6
		per cent.
19.08	Pastry, biscuits, cakes and other fine bakers' wares containing added sweetening matter:—	
	Biscuits	5
	Other	3
20.01	Vegetables and fruit, prepared or preserved by vinegar or acetic acid, containing added sweetening matter	7
20.03	Fruit preserved by freezing, containing added sugar	2½
		per cwt. s. d.
20.04	Fruit, fruit-peel and parts of plants, preserved by sugar (drained, glacé or crystallised)	15 4
20.05	Jams, fruit jellies, marmalades, fruit purée and fruit pastes, being cooked preparations, containing added sweetening matter	14 8
		per cent.
20.06	Fruit otherwise prepared or preserved, containing added sweetening matter:—	
	Ginger	10
	Other	2½

SCHEDULE 2

Tariff heading	Description of Imported Composite Sugar Products
17.05 (A) and (B)	Sugar and invert sugar, flavoured or coloured.

SCHEDULE 3

Description of goods	Rate of surcharge repayment per bulk barrel of 36 gallons
Lager	11 ·7d.
All beer other than lager	10 ·4d.

EXPLANATORY NOTE

(This Note is not part of the Order.)

This order provides for reductions on and after 23rd October 1969 in the average rates of surcharge payable on imported composite sugar products of the descriptions specified in Schedule 1 and in the average rates of surcharge repayment in respect of exported goods of the descriptions specified in Schedule 3. These correspond to the reductions in surcharge rates effected by the Sugar (Rates of Surcharge and Surcharge Repayments) (No. 11) Order 1969 (S.I. 1969/1505). Provision is also made for certain imported composite sugar products to be treated as not containing any sugar or invert sugar.

STATUTORY INSTRUMENTS

1969 No. 1508

SOCIAL SECURITY

The National Insurance (Members of the Forces) Amendment Regulations 1969

Made - - - -	*14th October* 1969
Laid before Parliament	*30th October* 1969
Coming into Operation	*3rd November* 1969

The Secretary of State for Social Services, in exercise of his powers under section 4(6) and (7) of the National Insurance Act 1965(a), and the National Insurance Joint Authority, in conjunction with the Treasury, in exercise of the powers conferred by section 99 of that Act (as extended by section 1(1) of and Schedule 1 paragraph 9 to the National Insurance Act 1966(b)), in each case in exercise of all other powers enabling him or them in that behalf, hereby make the following regulations which contain no provisions other than such as are made in consequence of the National Insurance Act 1969(c) and which, accordingly, by virtue of the provisions of section 10(1)(*a*)(i) of the said Act of 1969, are exempt from the requirements of section 108 of the said Act of 1965 (preliminary draft of regulations to be submitted to the National Insurance Advisory Committee before the regulations are made):—

Citation, interpretation and commencement

1. These regulations, which may be cited as the National Insurance (Members of the Forces) Amendment Regulations 1969, shall be read as one with the National Insurance (Members of the Forces) Regulations 1968(d) (hereinafter referred to as "the principal regulations") and shall come into operation on the 3rd November 1969.

Amendment of regulation 5 of the principal regulations

2. In regulation 5 of the principal regulations (special provisions concerning graduated contributions), for paragraphs (3) and (4) there shall be substituted the following paragraph:—

"(3) As respects an employed person (being a serving member of the forces), the statutory provisions specified in column (1) of Schedule 4 to these regulations shall apply in relation to his employment as a serving member of the forces subject to the modifications shown in relation thereto in column (3) of that Schedule, so however that the said modifications shall be disregarded for the purposes of section 58 of the Act (payments in lieu of contributions)."

(a) 1965 c. 51.   (b) 1966 c. 6.
(c) 1969 c. 44.   (d) S.I. 1968/827 (1968 II, p. 2228).

Substitution of new Schedules for Schedules 3, 4 *and* 5 *to the principal regulations and insertion of additional Schedule*

3. For the provisions set out in Schedules 3 (reduction of weekly rates of flat-rate contributions), 4 (statutory provisions applying to graduated contributions which are modified in their application to employment as a serving member of the forces) and 5 (scale of graduated contributions) to the principal regulations, there shall respectively be substituted the provisions set out in Schedules 1, 2 and 3 to these regulations; and immediately after the said Schedule 5 as so substituted, there shall be inserted as Schedule 5A the Schedule set out in Schedule 4 to these regulations.

Signed by authority of the Secretary of State for Social Services.

David Ennals,
Minister of State,
Department of Health and Social Security.

10th October 1969.

Given under the Official Seal of the National Insurance Joint Authority.

(L.S.)

D. J. Carter,
Secretary,
National Insurance Joint Authority.

10th October 1969.

Walter Harrison,
Joseph Harper,

Two of the Lords Commissioners
of Her Majesty's Treasury.

14th October 1969.

SCHEDULE 1   Regulation 3

Schedule substituted for Schedule 3
to the National Insurance (*Members of the Forces*)
Regulations 1968

SCHEDULE 3   Regulation 4

Reduction of weekly rates of contributions

	Reduction of weekly rate of contributions	
Description of employed persons 1	Employed person 2	Employer 3
	s. d.	s. d.
Men over the age of 18	2 0	2 2
Women „ „ „ „ „	1 7	1 8
Boys under „ „ „ „ ...	1 2	1 3
Girls under „ „ „ „	1 0	1 0

Regulation 3

SCHEDULE 2

Schedule substituted for Schedule 4
to the National Insurance (Members of the Forces)
Regulations 1968

Regulation 5

SCHEDULE 4

Statutory Provisions applying to Graduated Contributions
which are modified in their application to employment as
a serving member of the Forces

(1) Provision	(2) Subject matter	(3) Modifications
National Insurance Act 1965 Section 4(1) (as amended by section 1(2) of the National Insurance Act 1969)	Graduated contributions by employed persons and employers	For paragraph (c), there shall be substituted the following paragraphs:— "(c) except where the employment is at the time of the payment a non-participating employment, the amount of the graduated contribution payable by each of them shall be the aggregate of— (i) 4½ per cent. of any amount, up to £9, by which that payment exceeds £9 (or of the equivalent amount for remuneration not paid weekly); and (ii) 2½ per cent. of any amount, up to £12, by which that payment exceeds £18 (or of the equivalent amount for remuneration not paid weekly); and (d) where the employment is at the time of the payment a non-participating employment, the amount of the graduated contribution payable by each of them shall be 2½ per cent. of any amount, up to £12, by which that payment exceeds £18 (or of the equivalent amount for remuneration not paid weekly)."
National Insurance (Assessment of Graduated Contributions) Regulations 1967	Equivalent amounts	For paragraph 2(a), there shall be substituted the following paragraph:— "(a) where the graduated contribution period is a week:

(1) Provision	(2) Subject matter	(3) Modifications
Regulation 2 (as amended by regulation 2 of the National Insurance (Assessment of Graduated Contributions) Amendment Regulations 1969(a))		(i) in the case where the employment is not at the time of the payment a non-participating employment, £9 and the amount, up to £9, by which the payment exceeds £9, and the amount, up to £12, by which the payment exceeds £18; (ii) in the case where the employment is at the time of the payment a non-participating employment, £18 and the amount, up to £12, by which the payment exceeds £18;" For paragraph (2)(c), there shall be substituted the following paragraph:— "(c) where the graduated contribution period is a month: (i) in the case where the employment is not at the time of the payment a non-participating employment, £39, and the amount, up to £39, by which the payment exceeds £39, and the amount, up to £52, by which the payment exceeds £78; (ii) in the case where the employment is at the time of the payment a non-participating employment, £78 and the amount, up to £52, by which the payment exceeds £78;".
Regulation 3 (as amended by regulation 3 of the National Insurance (Assessment of Graduated Contributions) Amendment Regulations 1969)	Calculation of graduated contributions	For the proviso to paragraph (3) there shall be substituted the following proviso:— "Provided that 4½ per cent. and 2½ per cent. of any amount (other than the amount of the graduated contribution), or of any equivalent amount, referred to in the provision substituted for section 4(1)(c) of the Act as

(a) S.I. 1969/1133 (1969 II, p. 3363).

(1) Provision	(2) Subject matter	(3) Modifications
Regulation 3 (as amended) etc. (*continued*)		amended by section 1(2) of the National Insurance Act 1969 by the first entry in column 3 of Schedule 4 to the National Insurance (Members of the Forces) Regulations 1968, or of the total of more than any one such amount or equivalent amount, may be calculated to the nearest penny, any amount of a halfpenny being disregarded." For paragraph (4), there shall be substituted the following paragraph:— "(4) In this regulation "appropriate Schedule" means Schedule 5 to the National Insurance (Members of the Forces) Regulations 1968 in the case of an employment which is not a non-participating employment and means Schedule 5A to those regulations in the case of a non-participating employment."

Regulation 3

SCHEDULE 3

*Schedule substituted for Schedule 5
to the National Insurance (Members of the Forces)
Regulations 1968*

Regulation 5

SCHEDULE 5

Employment which is not a non-participating employment

PART I

WEEKLY SCALE

Amount of payment	Amount of contribution
£ s. d.	s. d.
9 0 1	1
9 5 0	4
9 10 0	8
10 0 0	1 1
10 10 0	1 6

Amount of payment	Amount of contribution
£ s. d.	s. d.
11 0 0	1 11
11 10 0	2 4
12 0 0	2 9
12 10 0	3 2
13 0 0	3 7
13 10 0	4 0
14 0 0	4 6
14 10 0	4 11
15 0 0	5 4
15 10 0	5 9
16 0 0	6 2
16 10 0	6 7
17 0 0	7 0
17 10 0	7 5
18 0 0	7 11
19 0 0	8 5
20 0 0	8 11
21 0 0	9 5
22 0 0	9 11
23 0 0	10 5
24 0 0	10 11
25 0 0	11 5
26 0 0	11 11
27 0 0	12 5
28 0 0	12 11
29 0 0	13 5
30 0 0 or more	13 8

PART II

MONTHLY SCALE

Amount of payment	Amount of contribution
£ s. d.	£ s. d.
39 0 5	5
40 0 0	1 8
42 0 0	3 5
44 0 0	5 1
46 0 0	6 10
48 0 0	8 6
50 0 0	10 2
52 0 0	11 11
54 0 0	13 7
56 0 0	15 4
58 0 0	17 0
60 0 0	18 8
62 0 0	1 0 5
64 0 0	1 2 1
66 0 0	1 3 10
68 0 0	1 5 6
70 0 0	1 7 2
72 0 0	1 8 11
74 0 0	1 10 7
76 0 0	1 12 4
78 0 0	1 14 2
82 0 0	1 16 2
86 0 0	1 18 2
90 0 0	2 0 2
94 0 0	2 2 2

Amount of payment	Amount of contribution
£ s. d.	£ s. d.
98 0 0	2 4 2
102 0 0	2 6 2
106 0 0	2 8 2
110 0 0	2 10 2
114 0 0	2 12 2
118 0 0	2 14 2
122 0 0	2 16 2
126 0 0	2 18 2
130 0 0 or more	2 19 2

Regulation 3

SCHEDULE 4

Schedule added to the National Insurance (Members of the Forces) Regulations 1968

SCHEDULE 5A

Non-participating employment

PART I

WEEKLY SCALE

Amount of payment	Amount of contribution
£ s. d.	s. d.
18 0 3	3
19 0 0	9
20 0 0	1 3
21 0 0	1 9
22 0 0	2 3
23 0 0	2 9
24 0 0	3 3
25 0 0	3 9
26 0 0	4 3
27 0 0	4 9
28 0 0	5 3
29 0 0	5 9
30 0 0 or more	6 0

Part II

Monthly Scale

Amount of payment	Amount of contribution
£ s. d.	£ s. d.
78 1 0	1 0
82 0 0	3 0
86 0 0	5 0
90 0 0	7 0
94 0 0	9 0
98 0 0	11 0
102 0 0	13 0
106 0 0	15 0
110 0 0	17 0
114 0 0	19 0
118 0 0	1 1 0
122 0 0	1 3 0
126 0 0	1 5 0
130 0 0 or more	1 6 0

EXPLANATORY NOTE

(This Note is not part of the Regulations.)

These Regulations contain no provisions other than such as are made in consequence of the National Insurance Act 1969 and accordingly, by virtue of section 10(1) of that Act, they are exempt from reference to the National Insurance Advisory Committee and have not been referred to that Committee.

The Regulations amend the provisions of the National Insurance (Members of the Forces) Regulations 1968 relating to flat-rate and graduated contributions and for the first time graduated contributions in respect of non-participating employment as a serving member of the forces become payable. The rate of such contributions, however, as with the rate of graduated contributions in respect of employment as a serving member of the forces which is not non-participating employment and the rate of flat-rate contributions as a serving member of the forces, is a reduced rate.

STATUTORY INSTRUMENTS

1969 No. 1509

SUGAR

The Sugar (Surcharge Remission) (Amendment) Order 1969

Made - - -	*21st October* 1969
Laid before Parliament	*29th October* 1969
Coming into Operation	*30th October* 1969

The Minister of Agriculture, Fisheries and Food (hereinafter referred to as "the Minister") in exercise of the powers conferred upon him by section 58 of the Finance Act 1968(a) construed as one with the Sugar Act 1956(b), and of all other powers enabling him in that behalf, for the purpose of prescribing such goods as it appears to him to be expedient to prescribe for the purposes of subsection (1)(b) of that section in the interests of the national economy, hereby makes the following order:—

1.—(1) This order may be cited as the Sugar (Surcharge Remission) (Amendment) Order 1969, and shall come into operation on 30th October 1969.

(2) The Interpretation Act 1889(c) shall apply to the interpretation of this order as it applies to the interpretation of an Act of Parliament.

2. The Sugar (Surcharge Remission) Order 1968(d) shall be amended by adding to the Schedule thereto (which specifies the descriptions of goods which are prescribed for the purposes of subsection (1)(b) of section 58 of the Finance Act 1968) the following items:—

"Citric acid and its salts

Vitamin B12

Foundry sand bonding media

Enzyme solutions".

In Witness whereof the Official Seal of the Minister of Agriculture, Fisheries and Food is hereunto affixed on 21st October 1969.

(L.S.)   *Cledwyn Hughes,*
                          Minister of Agriculture, Fisheries and Food.

(a) 1968 c. 44.   (b) 1956 c. 48.
(c) 1889 c. 63.   (d) S.I.1968/2009 (1968 III, p. 5446).

EXPLANATORY NOTE

(This Note is not part of the Order.)

This order amends the Sugar (Surcharge Remission) Order 1968 by adding a number of items to the Schedule thereto which lists the descriptions of goods in respect of whose manufacture sugar surcharge may be remitted or repaid in accordance with the provisions of section 58(1)(*b*) of the Finance Act 1968.

STATUTORY INSTRUMENTS

1969 No. 1510 (C. 41)

TRANSPORT

The Transport (London) Act 1969
(Commencement No. 2) Order 1969

Made - - - *22nd October* 1969

The Minister of Transport in exercise of his powers under section 47 of the Transport (London) Act 1969(a) and of all other enabling powers hereby makes the following Order:—

1. This Order may be cited as the Transport (London) Act 1969 (Commencement No. 2) Order 1969.

2. The provisions of the Transport (London) Act 1969 (hereinafter referred to as "the Act") specified in the first column of Schedule 1 to this Order (which relate to the subject matter specified in the second column of that Schedule in relation to those provisions) shall come into force on the 30th October 1969, and the provisions of the Act specified in like manner in Schedule 2 to this Order and in the Appendix to that Schedule shall come into force on the 1st January 1970.

Sealed with the Official Seal of the Minister of Transport the 22nd October 1969.

(L.S.)

Fred Mulley,
Minister of Transport.

(a) 1969 c. 35.

SCHEDULE 1

PROVISIONS COMING INTO FORCE ON THE 30TH OCTOBER 1969

Provisions of the Act	Subject matter
Section 1	General duty of Greater London Council with respect to transport.
Section 2	Transport plans for Greater London.
Section 3	Power of Council to make grants.
Section 4	London Transport Executive.
Section 5	General duties of Executive and other bodies with respect to passenger transport services for Greater London.
Section 6	General powers of Executive.
Section 7	Financial duty of Executive.
Section 8	Borrowing by and loans to Executive.
Section 9	Provisions as to insurance by Executive.
Section 10	Accounts of Executive.
Section 11	Additional provisions as to control of Executive by Council.
Section 12	Minister's power to prevent improper conduct of sub-sidiary activities.
Section 13	Machinery for negotiation and consultation with staff.
Section 14	Users' consultative body.
Section 15	Annual report by Executive.
Section 18	Pensions functions.
Section 20	Power of Council to direct preparation of proposals for transfers of functions, etc.
Section 21	Schemes for transfers between Executive and Railways Board or Bus Company.
Section 22	Orders by Minister for transfers between Executive and Railways Board or Bus Company.
Section 23(1) to (5) and (7).	Regulation of services by public service vehicles in and around London.
Section 25	Railway closures in and around Greater London.
Section 26	Grants on refusal of Minister's consent to closure by Executive.
Section 37	Compensation for loss of employment, etc.
Section 38	Payments on termination of appointment of members of London Board.

SCHEDULE 1—contd.

Provisions of the Act	Subject matter
Section 39	Dissolution of London Board.
Section 40	Travel concessions.
Section 41 (in so far as it was not brought into force by the Transport (London) Act 1969 (Commencement No. 1) Order 1969(a)).	Approvals, consents and directions.
Section 42	Power to modify Act by order.
Section 44	Stamp duty.
Schedule 1	The London Transport Executive.
Schedule 2	Transfers under Section 16.
Schedule 4	Licences or consents for certain existing services by public service vehicles in and around London.

SCHEDULE 2

PROVISIONS COMING INTO FORCE ON THE 1ST JANUARY 1970

Provisions of the Act	Subject matter
Section 16	Transfer of property etc. of London Board.
Section 17	Disposal of London Board's statutory functions.
Section 23(6)	Functions of traffic commissioners in connection with Greater London.
Section 24	Functions of traffic commissioners in Metropolitan Traffic Area.

(a) S.I. 1969/1130 (1969 II, p. 3351).

SCHEDULE 2—contd.

Section 31	Powers of Council where obstruction of highway is greater or longer than necessary.
Section 33	Expenditure on arrangements for patrolling school crossings.
Section 34	Traffic signs.
Section 35	Operation of parking places on highways where charges are made.
Section 36	Control of off-street parking.
Section 47(2) (so far as it relates to those provisions of Schedule 6 to the Act specified in the Appendix to this Schedule).	Repeals.
Schedule 3	Disposal of certain statutory functions of London Board.
Schedule 5	Control of off-street parking.

APPENDIX TO SCHEDULE 2

REPEALS TAKING EFFECT ON THE 1ST JANUARY 1970

In Schedule 6, the following repeals:—

Chapter	Short title	Extent of Repeal
23 & 24 Geo. 5. c. 14.	The London Passenger Transport Act 1933.	Sections 16, 17, 25 and 26. In section 107(1), the definition of "Special Area". Parts II to IV of Schedule 7.
1 & 2 Geo. 6. c. xcii.	The London Passenger Transport Act 1938.	Section 66.
1 & 2 Eliz. 2. c. 33.	The Education (Miscellaneous Provisions) Act 1953.	Section 12(3).
5 & 6 Eliz. 2. c. 20.	The House of Commons Disqualification Act 1957.	In Part II of Schedule 1, and in the Part substituted therefor by Schedule 3, the entry "The London Transport Board".
8 & 9 Eliz. 2. c. 16.	The Road Traffic Act 1960.	In section 120, in subsection (1), the words "other than the Metropolitan Traffic Area", subsection (2), and in subsection (4) the words from "and references" onwards.

APPENDIX TO SCHEDULE 2—contd.

8 & 9 Eliz. 2. c. 16—contd.	The Road Traffic Act 1960—contd.	In section 121(1), the words "other than the Metropolitan Traffic Area".
		Section 122.
		In section 123(2), the words "the traffic commissioner for the Metropolitan Traffic Area", the word "other", the words "the said commissioner or" in the first place where they occur, and the words "said commissioner or" in the second place where they occur.
		In section 123(3), the words "traffic commissioner or" wherever they occur, and the words "traffic commissioner's or".
		In section 125(1), the words "to the traffic commissioner for the Metropolitan Traffic Area" and the word "other".
		In section 125(2), the words "or to the traffic commissioner for the Metropolitan Traffic Area".
		In section 126, the words from "(other than the Metropolitan Traffic Area)" onwards.
		In section 135(2), the words from "except" to "Area" where next occurring.
		In section 135(7), the words from "except" to "Area" where next occurring.
		In section 136(2), the words from "except" to "Area" where next occurring.
		Sections 141, 142, 153(5), 161(2) and 165(3).
		In section 193(1), the words from "or is" to "so constituted" and the words "or commissioner".
		In section 252(1), the words from "and references" onwards.
		In section 252(2), the words from the beginning to "special area".
		So much of Schedule 17 as amends section 16 or 17 of the London Passenger Transport Act 1933.

APPENDIX TO SCHEDULE 2—contd.

10 & 11 Eliz. 2. c. 46.	The Transport Act 1962.	In section 1(1), the word "four" and the words from "the London Transport" to "London Board". Sections 1(4), 3(2), 7 and 8. In section 13(3) the words from "or section" onwards. Sections 19(3)(ii), 58 and 59. In section 85(1) the words from "Before" where first occurring onwards. In section 92(1) the definitions of "the London Passenger Transport Area" and "the London Special Area". In Schedule 2, so much of Part I as relates to section 141 or 142 of the Road Traffic Act 1960.
10 & 11 Eliz. 2. c. 59.	The Road Traffic Act 1962.	In Schedule 4, so much of Part I as relates to section 135, 136 or 142 of the Road Traffic Act 1960.
1963 c. 33.	The London Government Act 1963.	In section 14(6)(d), the words "and 141(2) to (6)", the word "respectively", and the words from "and to" to "area". In Part I of Schedule 5, paragraph 26. In Schedule 17, paragraphs 7 and 26(c).
1966 c. 17.	The Transport Finances Act 1966.	Section 1(3).
1966 c. 27.	The Building Control Act 1966.	In the Schedule, the entry "The London Transport Board".
1966 c. 32.	The Selective Employment Payments Act 1966.	In Part I of Schedule 1, paragraph 10. In Part III of Schedule 1, the entry beginning "The London".
1966 c. 34.	The Industrial Development Act 1966.	In Schedule 2, the entry "The London Transport Board".
1967 c. 76.	The Road Traffic Regulation Act 1967.	Section 6(8)(b). In section 6(12), the words "the London special area and". Section 9(8)(b). Section 56(2).
1967 c. xxxvii.	The Dartford Tunnel Act 1967.	In section 71, in subsection (1) the words from the beginning to "1960" and the proviso, and in subsection (3)(a) the proviso.
1968 c. 32.	The Industrial Expansion Act 1968.	In Schedule 1, the entry "The London Transport Board".

APPENDIX TO SCHEDULE 2—contd.

1968 c. 73.	The Transport Act 1968.	Sections 24(3)(a), 33(2) and 41(6).
		In section 54(5)(d), the words "as the case may be the London Board and".
		Section 59(4).
		In section 138(3), the words "or the London Board".
		In section 145(2), the words "the traffic commissioner for the Metropolitan Traffic Area or", the word "other", and the words "any of".
		In section 159(1), in the definition of "the Boards", the words "the London Transport Board", and the definition of "the London Board".

EXPLANATORY NOTE

(This Note is not part of the Order.)

This Order brings into operation on either the 30th October 1969 or the 1st January 1970 all the provisions of the Transport (London) Act 1969 which were not brought into operation by the Transport (London) Act 1969 (Commencement No. 1) Order 1969, with the exception of section 19(1) to (7) (which relates to the transfer or extinguishment of the London Transport Board's debt to the Minister), sections 29 and 30 (which relate to metropolitan roads), section 32 (which relates to pedestrian crossings), and consequential repeals.

The Order specifies which provisions are to come into operation on the 30th October 1969 and which on the 1st January 1970, the latter date being the "vesting date" referred to in the Act.

STATUTORY INSTRUMENTS

1969 No. 1511

CORONERS

The Coroners' Records (Fees for Copies) Rules 1969

Made - - -	*21st October* 1969
Coming into Operation	*1st November* 1969

In pursuance of the powers conferred upon me by section 29(2) of the Coroners (Amendment) Act 1926**(a)**, I hereby make the following Rules:—

1.—(1) These Rules may be cited as the Coroners' Records (Fees for Copies) Rules 1969.

(2) The Interpretation Act 1889**(b)** shall apply for the interpretation of these Rules as it applies for the interpretation of an Act of Parliament.

(3) The Coroners' Records (Fees for Copies) Rules 1954**(c)** are hereby revoked.

(4) These Rules shall come into operation on 1st November 1969.

2. The fees payable to coroners or other persons for furnishing copies of inquisitions, depositions or other documents in their custody relating to an inquest shall be as follows:—

(*a*) for furnishing for a person charged by an inquisition with murder, manslaughter or infanticide a copy of the said inquisition or of the depositions of the witnesses at the inquest, 1d. for every folio or part of a folio of 60 words;

(*b*) for furnishing any such copy for the prosecution on the trial of any such person, 1s. 0d. for every folio or part of a folio of 90 words;

(*c*) for furnishing a copy of any document otherwise than as mentioned in the foregoing paragraphs—

  (i) for a copy which does not exceed 5 folios of 72 words each, 10s. 0d.;

  (ii) for a copy which exceeds 5 but does not exceed 20 folios of 72 words each, £1 1s. 0d.;

  (iii) for a copy which exceeds 20 folios of 72 words each, £1 1s. 0d. for the first 20 such folios and 1s. 0d. for each such folio or part thereof thereafter:

Provided that where a coroner or other person furnishing a copy as mentioned in this paragraph is satisfied that the person to whom the copy is being furnished is a properly interested person and by reason of his financial circumstances ought to be furnished with the copy at a lower rate, he shall fix such lower rate as may be appropriate to the circumstances of that person.

James Callaghan,
One of Her Majesty's Principal
Secretaries of State.

Home Office,
  Whitehall.
21st October 1969.

(a) 1926 c. 59.   **(b)** 1889 c. 63.
(c) S.I. 1954/14 (1954 I, p. 514).

EXPLANATORY NOTE

(This Note is not part of the Rules.)

These Rules replace the Coroners' Records (Fees for Copies) Rules 1954 and provide for an increase in the fees payable to coroners or other persons for furnishing copies of inquisitions, depositions or other documents in their custody relating to an inquest.

STATUTORY INSTRUMENTS

1969 No. 1513

COAL INDUSTRY

The Opencast Coal (Rate of Interest on Compensation) (No. 2) Order 1969

Made - - -	*22nd October* 1969
Laid before Parliament	*31st October* 1969
Coming into Operation	*1st November* 1969

The Treasury, in exercise of the powers conferred upon them by sections 35(8) and 49(4) of the Opencast Coal Act 1958(a) and of all other powers enabling them in that behalf, hereby make the following Order:—

1. This Order may be cited as the Opencast Coal (Rate of Interest on Compensation) (No. 2) Order 1969, and shall come into operation on 1st November 1969.

2. The Interpretation Act 1889(b) shall apply for the interpretation of this Order as it applies for the interpretation of an Act of Parliament.

3. The rate of interest for the purposes of section 35 of the Opencast Coal Act 1958 shall be 9¼ per cent. per annum.

4. The Opencast Coal (Rate of Interest on Compensation) Order 1969(c) is hereby revoked.

Joseph Harper,
E. G. Perry,
Two of the Lords Commissioners
of Her Majesty's Treasury.

22nd October 1969.

EXPLANATORY NOTE

(*This Note is not part of the Order.*)

Section 35 of the Opencast Coal Act 1958 provides that interest shall be payable in addition to compensation in certain circumstances. This Order increases the rate of interest from 8¾ per cent. to 9¼ per cent. per annum and revokes the Opencast Coal (Rate of Interest on Compensation) Order 1969.

(a) 1958 c. 69.   (b) 1889 c. 63.   (c) S.I. 1969/460 (1969 I, p. 1317).

STATUTORY INSTRUMENTS

1969 No. 1514

POLICE

The Special Constables (Pensions) (Amendment) (No. 2) Regulations 1969

Made - - - -	*23rd October* 1969
Laid before Parliament	*31st October* 1969
Coming into Operation	*3rd November* 1969

In exercise of the powers conferred on me by section 34 of the Police Act 1964(**a**) (read with section 1(2) of the Police Pensions Act 1961(**b**)), I hereby make the following Regulations :—

1. These Regulations may be cited as the Special Constables (Pensions) (Amendment) (No. 2) Regulations 1969 and shall come into operation on 3rd November 1969.

2. In these Regulations any reference to the Instrument of 1966 is a reference to the Special Constables (Pensions) Regulations 1966(**c**), as amended (**d**).

3.—(1) In the application of the Police Pensions Regulations 1966(**e**) to the calculation of the pension of the widow, or the allowance of a child, of a special constable under the Instrument of 1966, those Regulations shall apply as amended by the Police Pensions (Amendment) (No. 2) Regulations 1969(**f**) (which amendments relate to increases in widows' and children's awards).

(2) In accordance with paragraph (1) of this Regulation, for Regulation 15(1) of the Instrument of 1966 (which, as set out in the Special Constables (Pensions) (Amendment) Regulations 1969(**g**), defines the expression "the principal Regulations") there shall be substituted the following paragraph :—

'(1) In these Regulations the expression "the principal Regulations" means the Police Pensions Regulations 1966, as amended by the Police Pensions (Amendment) (No. 2) Regulations 1967(**h**), the Police Pensions (Amendment) Regulations 1968(**i**), the Police Pensions (Amendment) Regulations 1969 and the Police Pensions (Amendment) (No. 2) Regulations 1969.'

James Callaghan,

One of Her Majesty's Principal
Secretaries of State.

Home Office,
    Whitehall.

23rd October 1969.

(**a**) 1964 c. 48.   (**b**) 1961 c.35.
(**c**) S.I. 1966/1590 (1966 III, p. 5008).
(**d**) The relevant amending instrument is S.I. 1969/724 (1969 II, p. 1958).
(**e**) S.I. 1966/1582 (1966 III, p. 4894).   (**f**) S.I. 1969/1484.(1969 III, p. 4745).
(**g**) S.I. 1969/724 (1969 II, p. 1958).
(**h**) S.I. 1967/1500 (1967 III, p. 4204).   (**i**) S.I. 1968/530 (1968 I, p. 1269).

EXPLANATORY NOTE
(This Note is not part of the Regulations.)

These Regulations amend the Special Constables (Pensions) Regulations 1966 which give to special constables and their dependants certain pension benefits for which members of police forces and their dependants are eligible.

The Police Pensions (Amendment) (No. 2) Regulations 1969 provide that certain discretionary benefits payable to the dependants of members of police forces shall be increased.

These Regulations provide for similar increases in the discretionary benefits payable to the dependants of special constables.

STATUTORY INSTRUMENTS

1969 No. 1515 (S.120)

SEA FISHERIES

SEAL FISHERIES

The Grey Seals Protection (Suspension of Close Season) (Scotland) Order 1969

Laid before Parliament in draft

Made - - -	22nd October 1969
Coming into Operation	22nd October 1969

In exercise of the powers conferred upon me by section 1 of the Grey Seals Protection Act 1932(a), and of all other powers enabling me in that behalf, I hereby make the following order, a draft whereof has been laid before Parliament in accordance with section 1(4) of the said Act as read with section 6(2) of the Statutory Instruments Act 1946(b) :—

Citation

1. This order may be cited as the Grey Seals Protection (Suspension of Close Season) (Scotland) Order 1969.

Interpretation

2.—(1) In this order—

"the Act" means the Grey Seals Protection Act 1932 ;

"grey seal" means a seal of the species known as Halichoerus grypus ;

"the normal close season" means the period in each year in respect of which a close season for grey seals is established by section 1(1) of the Act (apart from any order made under the proviso thereto), that is to say the period extending from 1st September to 31st December ;

"the prescribed area" means Scotland other than the following areas— The islands of Haskeir Mor and Haskeir Beig in the Outer Hebrides and any place within 3 miles of any part of the said islands : and the following national nature reserves—

Rhum, St. Kilda, Sula Sgeir, North Rona, Hermaness (Unst, Shetland), Isle of May.

"the suspense period" means the period of 12 months next following the making of this order.

(a) 1932 c. 23. (b) 1946 c. 36.

(2) The Interpretation Act 1889(a) applies for the interpretation of this order as it applies for the interpretation of an Act of Parliament.

Suspension of close season for the prescribed area in 1969-70

3. The Secretary of State hereby directs that, notwithstanding anything (apart from the proviso) in section 1(1) of the Act, there shall be no close season in the prescribed area during the suspense period.

Regulations

4. The regulations contained in the Schedule to this order, being regulations providing for the grant and revocation of permits by the Secretary of State and prohibiting the killing of grey seals in the prescribed area during so much of the normal closes season as falls within the suspense period except by persons holding permits and in such manner and by means of such weapon or instrument as is specified in those regulations, shall have effect.

William Ross,
One of Her Majesty's Principal
Secretaries of State.

St. Andrew's House,
Edinburgh.

22nd October 1969.

Regulation 4

SCHEDULE

REGULATIONS

1. The killing of grey seals in the prescribed area during so much of the normal close season as falls within the suspense period except by a person holding a permit granted in accordance with these regulations, and except in such manner and by means of such weapon or instrument as is specified in these regulations, is hereby prohibited.

2.—(1) The Secretary of State may, if he thinks fit, grant to any person a permit under these regulations and he may revoke the permit at any time by giving notice to the person to whom it was granted.

(2) Any such permit shall specify—

    (*a*) the area within which the holder is authorised to kill grey seals, and

    (*b*) the manner of killing and the means which the holder may employ for that purpose, both of which shall be in accordance with regulation 3 of these regulations.

3. The only manner in which grey seals may be killed in the prescribed area by a person holding a permit, granted in accordance with these regulations, is by shooting in such a way that death is caused instantaneously. The only weapon to be employed for that purpose is a Webley ·32 humane killer or a rifle.

(a) 1889 c. 63.

EXPLANATORY NOTE

(This Note is not part of the Order.)

The Grey Seals Protection Act 1932 establishes an annual close season for grey seals extending from 1st September to 31st December. This order, made by the Secretary of State under section 1 of the Act, directs that there shall be no close season in Scotland other than in certain excepted areas during the period of 12 months next following the making of this order which was made on 22nd October 1969. The order will continue during the period of 12 months next following the making of the order the position created by the Grey Seals Protection (Scotland) (Suspension of Close Season) Order 1968.

In accordance with section 1(2) of the Act, the order contains regulations prohibiting the killing of grey seals during the period which would, apart from the provisions of this order, be the normal close season, except by persons holding permits granted by the Secretary of State. The regulations specify the conditions of permits generally and the means by which the seals are to be killed.

STATUTORY INSTRUMENTS

1969 No. 1516 (S.121)

PENSIONS

The Superannuation (Local Government and Jersey) Interchange (Scotland) Rules 1969

Made - - - -	*21st October* 1969
Laid before Parliament	*31st October* 1969
Coming into Operation	*1st November* 1969

ARRANGEMENT OF RULES

In exercise of the powers conferred on me by sections 2 and 15 of the Super-annuation (Miscellaneous Provisions) Act 1948(a) as amended by section 11(6) of the Superannuation (Miscellaneous Provisions) Act 1967(b), and of all other powers enabling me in that behalf, I hereby make the following rules:—

PART I
GENERAL

Citation and commencement

1. These rules may be cited as the Superannuation (Local Government and Jersey) Interchange (Scotland) Rules 1969 and shall come into operation on 1st November 1969.

Interpretation

2.—(1) In these rules, unless the context otherwise requires, the following expressions have the meanings hereby assigned to them—

"the Act" means the Superannuation (Miscellaneous Provisions) Act 1948;

"the Act of 1909" means the Asylums Officers' Superannuation Act 1909(c);

"the Act of 1937" means the Local Government Superannuation (Scotland) Act 1937(d);

"the Act of 1953" means the Local Government Superannuation Act 1953(e);

"the Acts of 1937 to 1953" means the Local Government Superannuation (Scotland) Acts 1937 to 1953(f);

"added years" means—

(a) in relation to a person in local government employment, any additional years of service reckonable by him under regulation 12 of the benefits regulations or any corresponding provision of a local Act scheme, and includes any additional years of service which, having been granted under any such provision or under any similar provision contained in any other enactment or scheme, have subsequently become and are reckonable under or by virtue of rules made under section 2 of the Act or any other enactment;

(b) in relation to a pensionable employee, any additional years of service of the nature of additional years of service referred to in paragraph (a) of this definition which have been granted in, or have otherwise become reckonable in, his employment;

"the benefits regulations" means the Local Government Superannuation (Benefits) (Scotland) Regulations 1954(g);

"contributory employee" has the same meaning as in the Act of 1937;

"employing authority", in relation to any pensionable employee, means the Board or Committee of the States of Jersey by which he is employed;

"local Act contributor" and "local Act scheme" have the same meaning as in the Act of 1937;

"local goverment employment" means employment by virtue of which the person employed is or is deemed to be a contributory employee or local Act contributor;

"national service", in relation to any person, means service which is relevant service within the meaning of the Reserve and Auxiliary Forces (Protection of Civil Interests) Act 1951(h), and any similar service immediately

---

(a) 1948 c. 33.   (b) 1967 c. 28.
(c) 1909 c. 48.   (d) 1937 c. 69.
(e) 1953 c. 25.   (f) 1937 c. 69; 1939 c. 18; 1953 c. 25.
(g) S.I. 1954/1059 (1954 II, p. 1632).   (h) 1951 c. 65.

following relevant serviçe entered into with the consent of the authority or person by whom he was employed before undertaking that service or, in the case of a person who holds an appointment to an office and is not employed under a contract of employment, with the consent of the authority by whom he was appointed;

"pensionable employee" means a person employed in the pensionable employment of the States of Jersey either in the civil service, police force, fire service or prison service, or as a manual worker whose terms of employment are governed by the Manual Workers Joint Council, or who is employed, other than as a civil servant, by the Telephones Committee;

"the relevant Jersey Rules", in relation to a pensionable employee, means the rules governing the superannuation scheme applicable to him in his employment;

"the transfer value regulations" means the Local Government Superannuation (Transfer Value) (Scotland) Regulations 1954(a);

"voluntary contributions" means—

(a) in relation to a person who has become employed as a pensionable employee after leaving local government employment, payments made voluntarily by him while in local government employment or in overseas employment within the meaning of the Superannuation (Local Government and Overseas Employment) Interchange (Scotland) Rules 1958(b) for the purpose of securing benefits for his widow, children or other dependants and payments (other than completed payments, that is to say, payments made in respect of a liability which has been wholly discharged) of any of the following categories—

(i) additional contributory payments of the kind referred to in subsections (3) and (4) of section 2 of the Act of 1953;

(ii) any similar payments made under a local Act scheme as a condition of reckoning any period of employment as service or as a period of contribution for the purposes of the scheme or, where the local Act scheme provides for the reckoning of non-contributing service, as contributing service for the purposes of the scheme;

(iii) any payments made for the purpose of increasing the length at which any period of service or of contribution would be reckonable for the purpose of calculating a benefit under a local Act scheme;

(iv) any payments made in respect of added years; and

(b) in relation to a person who has entered local government employment after ceasing to be employed as a pensionable employee, any payment similar in character to any such payments as aforesaid for which provision was made under the relevant Jersey Rules.

(2) References in these rules to the provisions of any enactment, rules or regulations shall be construed, unless the context otherwise requires, as references to those provisions as amended, applied or re-enacted by any subsequent enactment, rules or regulations.

(3) The Superannuation (Local Government and Overseas Employment) Interchange (Scotland) Rules 1958 shall not apply in relation to any change of employment to which Part II of these rules applies.

(4) The Interpretation Act 1889(c) shall apply for the interpretation of these rules as it applies for the interpretation of an Act of Parliament.

(a) S.I. 1954/1256 (1954 II, p. 1736).   (b) S.I. 1958/1402 (1958 II, p. 1857).
(c) 1889 c. 63.

Part II

Transfer from Local Government Employment to Pensionable Employment in the Island of Jersey

Persons to whom Part II of the rules applies

3.—(1) This Part of these rules shall apply to any person who—

(a) either—

    (i) becomes a pensionable employee within 12 months after leaving local government employment, or

    (ii) having become engaged in national service immediately after leaving local government employment becomes employed as a pensionable employee within 6 months after the termination of such national service; and

(b) has not become entitled to any benefit in respect of his local government employment other than a return of contributions or, if he has become so entitled, has not received payment of such a benefit; and

(c) within 3 months after the date on which he becomes a pensionable employee or within 6 months after the date of the coming into operation of these rules, whichever period last expires, notifies in writing the employing authority that he desires these rules to apply to him, and furnishes the employing authority with particulars of any national service in which he has been engaged since he left the previous employment; and

(d) if he has received any payment by way of a return of contributions (other than voluntary contributions) in respect of his local government employment, pays a sum equal to such payment to the employing authority together with any further sum required by way of interest under paragraph (4) of this rule within 3 months after the date on which he becomes employed as a pensionable employee or within 6 months after the date of the coming into operation of these rules, whichever period last expires, or within such longer period as the employing authority may in any particular case allow; and

(e) is not a person in respect of whom a transfer value has been paid by the authority maintaining the superannuation fund to which he was a contributor since he left his local government employment.

(2) The reference in paragraph (1)(a) of this rule to a period of 12 months after the date on which a person leaves local government employment shall be construed in relation to a person to whom section 6 of the Act (which makes special provision as to local government superannuation during periods of emergency) applies as a reference to a period of 5 years after that date, or such longer period as the Secretary of State may in any particular case allow.

(3) Without prejudice to the provisions of the last preceding paragraph, any period mentioned in paragraph (1)(a) or (c) of this rule may in any particular case be extended by the employing authority with the consent of the authority maintaining the superannuation fund to which the person was a contributor.

(4) Where a person becomes or became a pensionable employee more than 12 months after leaving local government employment the authority maintaining the superannuation fund to which he was a contributor may require him to make a payment by way of compound interest on any sum paid to him by way of

return of contributions (other than voluntary contributions) on or after leaving that employment at a rate of 3% per annum with half-yearly rests for a period beginning either with the date 12 months after the date on which he left that employment or, where this is later, the date on which he received such sum, and ending with the date on which he notified in writing his desire that these rules should apply to him:

Provided that the interest so payable shall not exceed a sum equal to one-half of the difference between the transfer value payable under these rules and the transfer value which would be payable if calculated by reference to the person's age on leaving local government employment.

(5) This Part of these rules shall apply to such a person as aforesaid and shall be deemed always to have applied to him even though he left local government employment or became a pensionable employee before the commencement of these rules:

Provided that—

> (a) the authority maintaining the superannuation fund to which he was a contributor consents; and
>
> (b) if he has ceased to be employed as a pensionable employee before the commencement of these rules, the employing authority consents.

(6) This rule shall not apply to any person all of whose rights in relation to his previous local government employment have been forfeited by a direction under section 17(3) of the Act of 1953 or under the corresponding provision of a local Act scheme.

Transfer values payable by local authorities

4.—(1) Subject to the provisions of this rule, the authority maintaining the superannuation fund to which a person to whom this Part of the rules has become applicable was a contributor shall pay out of the fund the like transfer value to the employing authority as would have been payable under the transfer value regulations had the person become a contributory employee in the circumstances described in section 24 of the Act of 1937 less an amount equal to any sum which the authority maintaining the fund may become liable to pay by way of income tax in respect of the amount transferred by way of transfer value and an amount equal to any sum required by way of interest under rule 3(4) of these rules and the like particulars of the person's previous pensionable service shall be furnished to the employing authority and the person as would have been given to the person if instead of becoming a pensionable employee he had become a contributory employee:

Provided that—

> (i) the transfer value payable in respect of a person who ceased to hold his former employment more than 12 months before the date of the commencement of these rules shall be calculated by reference to his age at that date;
>
> (ii) the transfer value payable in respect of a person who becomes a pensionable employee after the commencement of these rules and more than 12 months after leaving local government employment shall be calculated by reference to his age on the date on which he becomes a pensionable employee;
>
> (iii) the transfer value payable in respect of a person who had been an established officer or servant within the meaning of the Act of 1909 shall be calculated as if paragraph (c) had been omitted from the

definition of "service" in paragraph 1 of the first schedule to the transfer value regulations;

(iv) the transfer value payable for a person who has forfeited some of his rights in relation to his previous local government employment by a direction under section 17(3) of the Act of 1953 or under the corresponding provision of a local Act scheme shall be calculated by reference only to the service the rights in relation to which have not been forfeited.

(2) Where—

(a) a transfer value is payable under this rule in respect of a person who before entering local government employment had been subject to the Act of 1909, and

(b) the body by whom he was last employed while subject to that Act would, if he had become entitled to a superannuation allowance on leaving local government employment, have been liable to contribute to that allowance,

that body shall pay to the authority maintaining the fund a sum equal to the transfer value which that body would have been liable to pay to the Secretary of State under regulation 52(4) of the National Health Service (Scotland) (Superannuation) Regulations 1950(a) if that regulation had become applicable to the person on the date on which he became a pensionable employee; and where that body would have had in respect of any such contribution a right of contribution from any other body, that other body shall pay to the authority maintaining the fund a sum equal to the transfer value which that other body would have been liable to pay to the Secretary of State under paragraph (5) of the said regulation 52 if that regulation had become applicable to the person when he became a pensionable employee.

(3) Where any body referred to in the last preceding paragraph has been dissolved or has ceased to exercise functions as such, references to that body shall be construed as references to the appropriate authority as defined in paragraph (15) of the regulation mentioned therein.

Exercise by local authority of discretionary powers to increase benefits

5.—(1) Where a person becomes or became a pensionable employee after leaving local government employment and these rules have become applicable to him, the authority or body by whom he was employed may, within 6 months after the date on which they are informed by the employing authority of his notification that he desires these rules to apply to him, exercise any discretion which, with a view to increasing the benefits payable to him, it would have been open to them to exercise at the time when he left their employment if he had then retired and had been entitled to a retirement pension under regulation 5 of the benefits regulations, or (if that regulation was not applicable to him) to any corresponding benefit provided under the superannuation provisions which were applicable to him in his former employment.

(2) A decision in the exercise of any discretion under the last preceding paragraph shall be subject to the limitations and restrictions (if any) and to the right of appeal (if any) to which it would have been subject if the discretion had been exercised on the person's retirement in the circumstances aforesaid.

(3) Where a discretion has been exercised under paragraph (1) of this rule the service reckonable immediately before he left his former employment by the

(a) S.I. 1950/498 (1950 I, p. 1458).

person in whose favour the discretion has been exercised shall be deemed to have been correspondingly increased and the transfer value payable in respect of that person shall be calculated accordingly.

(4) Any increase in service, if attributable to a decision under this rule to increase the benefits payable to the person otherwise than by any notional increase or extension of the service reckonable for the purpose of calculating those benefits, or by treating any specified period of non-contributing service as contributing service or, under a local Act scheme, by similarly converting service of one category to service of another category, shall be ascertained by converting a higher rate of benefit into years of contributing service or service for the purposes of the relevant local Act scheme in the manner in which fractions of remuneration are converted into years of contributing service under section 2(4) of the Act of 1953.

(5) Where the amount of any transfer value payable under the last preceding rule is increased in consequence of the exercise by an authority or body of any power conferred upon them by paragraph (1) of this rule, that authority or body shall repay the amount of the said increase to the superannuation fund out of which the transfer value is payable.

PART III

TRANSFER FROM PENSIONABLE EMPLOYMENT IN THE ISLAND OF JERSEY TO LOCAL GOVERNMENT EMPLOYMENT

Persons to whom Part III of the rules applies

6.—(1) This Part of these rules shall apply to any person who—

(a) enters local government employment within 12 months after ceasing to be employed as a pensionable employee;

(b) has not become entitled to any benefit in respect of his pensionable employment other than a return of contributions or, if he has become so entitled, has not received payment of such a benefit; and

(c) within 3 months after the date on which he enters local government employment or within 6 months after the date of the coming into operation of these rules, whichever period last expires, notifies in writing the local authority maintaining the superannuation fund to which he is then a contributor or, if he has left local government employment, the local authority maintaining the fund to which he was last a contributor that he desires these rules to apply to him.

(2) Any period mentioned in paragraph (1)(a) or (c) of this rule may in any particular case be extended by the authority mentioned in the said paragraph (1)(c) with the consent of the employing authority.

(3) This Part of these rules shall apply to such person as aforesaid and shall be deemed always to have applied to him notwithstanding that he ceased to be employed as a pensionable employee or entered local government employment before the commencement of these rules:

Provided that—

(a) he has been in local government employment without a break of more than 12 months at any one time from the date when he ceased to be employed as a pensionable employee until the commencement of these rules or, if he left local government employment before such date, until the date when he ceased to be in such employment; and (*b*) if he left local government employment before the commencement of these rules, the local authority maintaining the superannuation fund to which he was last a contributor consent.

Reckoning of previous service

7.—(1) Subject as hereinafter provided, if the authority maintaining the superannuation fund to which he becomes or first became a contributor receive from the employing authority a transfer value of an amount equal to the transfer value which would have been payable under the transfer value regulations if the person, instead of having ceased to be a pensionable employee, had ceased to be a contributory employee in the circumstances described in section 24 of the Act of 1937, the period of his service which for the purposes of the relevant Jersey Rules was reckonable as service in the capacity of a pensionable employee shall be reckoned as contributing service for the purposes of the Act of 1937, or as service or as a period of contribution for the purposes of the local Act scheme, as the case may be; and any period of service of which account would have been taken for the purpose of determining whether he has served for the minimum period prescribed by the relevant Jersey Rules as necessary for any pension to be paid to or in respect of him shall, to the same extent, be reckonable for the purpose of determining whether any benefit is payable to or in respect of him as a contributory employee or local Act contributor:

Provided that—

    (*a*) in relation to any person who, before entering local government employ-ment was employed in the fire service, police force or prison service of the States of Jersey, the period of his service which for the purposes of the relevant Jersey Rules was reckonable as service in the capacity of a pensionable employee shall, if the transfer value payable as aforesaid is correspondingly increased, be increased by one-third;

    (*b*) if any part of the service which he would become entitled to reckon as contributing service by virtue of the preceding provisions of this rule is attributable to service which, before he became a pensionable employee, was non-contributing service under the Act of 1937 or under a local Act scheme, that service shall be reckonable in his new employment as non-contributing service unless payments with a view to that service being reckoned as contributing service or as service or as a period of contribution under a local Act scheme had been completed while he was a pensionable employee;

    (*c*) where the 12 months period mentioned in rule 6(1)(*a*) of these rules is extended by virtue of rule 6(2) of these rules, the provision of this rule requiring payment of a transfer value calculated in accordance with the transfer value regulations shall be read as requiring payment of a transfer value calculated as if the person were ceasing to be in local government employment and entering the employment of the employing authority under these rules.

  (2) A person to whom this Part applies shall not be entitled under section 12(2) of the Act of 1937 or any corresponding provision of a local Act scheme to reckon as service any local government employment prior to the date on which he became a pensionable employee if a transfer value has been paid in respect of that local government employment under rule 4 of these rules or under the corresponding provision of any other rules made under section 2 of the Act.

Continuation of payments made with a view to adding to, or enhancing the value of, previous service

8.—(1) Where any person to whom rule 6 of these rules has become applicable was, at the time when he ceased to be employed as a pensionable employee, in the course of making payments (other than those to which paragraph (2) of this rule applies) by way of—

(*a*) instalments in discharge of a fixed sum or

(*b*) contributions of a fraction or percentage of emoluments,

as a condition of being entitled to reckon the service in relation to which those payments were being made as a period of reckonable service for the purposes of the relevant Jersey Rules, or as a condition of increasing the length at which the said service would be reckonable for the purpose of calculating a benefit under those rules, he shall be entitled, if he forthwith repays to his last employing authority or pays to the authority maintaining the superannuation fund to which he is a contributor in his new employment a sum equal to any sum paid to him by way of return of such payments on or after ceasing to be employed as a pensionable employee, to make payments and, in respect of the service in respect of which the payments were being made, shall enjoy rights and be subject to liabilities as if in his previous employment he had been, instead of a pensionable employee, a local Act contributor.

(2) Where any person to whom rule 6 of these rules has become applicable was in the course of making payments in respect of added years he shall be entitled, if he forthwith repays to his last employing authority or pays to the authority maintaining the superannuation fund to which he is a contributor in his new employment a sum equal to any sum paid to him by way of return of such payments as aforesaid on or after ceasing to be employed as a pensionable employee, to pay the outstanding payments in the manner in which they would have been payable if he had remained in his employment as a pensionable employee and, in respect of the added years in respect of which those payments are made, shall enjoy rights and be subject to liabilities as if those years were added years in respect of which payments are being made in his new employment under regulation 12 of the benefits regulations or, if in his new employment he is subject to a local Act scheme, under such provisions corresponding to the said regulation 12, or to regulation 5 of the Local Government Superannuation (Reckoning of Service on Transfer) (Scotland) Regulations 1954(a) as are contained in that scheme.

PART IV

MISCELLANEOUS PROVISIONS

Cessation of entitlement to payment out of superannuation fund

9. Notwithstanding anything in the Act of 1937 or any local Act scheme, when these rules become applicable to a person who has ceased to be in employment in which he was a contributing employee or local Act contributor, he shall cease to be entitled to any payment out of the superannuation fund to which he contributed while in that employment in respect of any service of which account was taken in calculating the transfer value payable under rule 4 of these rules, other than a payment by way of return of voluntary contributions.

Computation of contributions of a person to whom rule 6 has become applicable

10.—(1) Where a person to whom rule 6 of these rules has become applicable—

(*a*) ceases to be in local government employment in the circumstances mentioned in section 10(1) of the Act of 1937; or

(*b*) dies in the circumstances mentioned in section 10(3) of the Act of 1937; or

---

(a) S.I. 1954/1241 (1954 II, p. 1680).

(c) ceases (by reason of permanent ill-health or infirmity of mind or body) to be in local government employment, or dies, in circumstances in which there is payable to or in respect of him a benefit which falls to be calculated by reference to the amount of his contributions (with or without interest),

he shall be deemed to have made to the appropriate superannuation fund, on becoming a contributor to such fund, contributions in respect of the period of his employment as a pensionable employee before 1st January 1968 of an aggregate amount equal to three-eightieths of the annual salary and emoluments of his office multiplied by the number of completed years of his service as a pensionable employee during that period:

Provided that—

(a) in the case of a person who did not exercise any option open to him to participate in the contributory pension scheme established by the Public Employees (Contributory Retirement Scheme) (Jersey) Regulations 1967(a), any period of employment as a pensionable employee on and after 1st January 1968 shall also be taken into account, and shall be aggregated with any period of employment before that date;

(b) in the case of a sum payable on the death of any person this paragraph shall apply only if the last pensionable employment of that person before he entered local government employment was in the Jersey civil service.

(2) Where a person to whom rule 6 of these rules has become applicable and who was a participant in the contributory pension scheme established by the Public Employees (Contributory Retirement Scheme) (Jersey) Regulations 1967, leaves local government employment or dies in circumstances in which under the relevant superannuation provisions there is payable to or in respect of him an amount by way of a return of contributions (with or without interest) or a benefit which falls to be calculated by reference to any such amount then, for the purposes of the relevant superannuation provisions, the amount of his contributions shall be taken to include in respect of any period of service on and after 1st January 1968 which by virtue of these rules has become reckonable as service for the purposes of the Act of 1937 or the relevant local Act scheme an amount equal to the amount which would have been payable by way of a return of contributions in respect of his employment as a pensionable employee during that period, if on his ceasing to hold that employment, he had been entitled to receive an amount by way of return of contributions without interest.

(3) Where under the relevant superannuation provisions the amount payable by way of return of contributions or by way of benefit is a sum which is equal to, or falls to be calculated by reference to, the amount of his contributions with interest thereon, interest shall also be payable in respect of the amount by which those contributions are increased under the last preceding paragraph, calculated—

(a) as respects the period ending immediately before the date on which he entered local government employment at the rate at which it would have been calculated in respect of his employment as a pensionable employee if on leaving that employment he had been entitled to a return of contributions together with interest thereon; and

(b) as respects the period beginning on his date of entering local government employment, in accordance with the provisions of section 10 of the Act of 1937 or, as the case may be, the corresponding provision of the relevant local Act scheme.

(a) No. 5010.

(4) Notwithstanding anything in this rule, the sum by which the contributions payable under the Act of 1937 are increased under paragraphs (2) and (3) of this rule shall not include—

(a) any amount in respect of payments made voluntarily for the purpose of securing benefits for a widow, children or other dependant;

(b) any sum in respect of contributions which, on or after the person's leaving pensionable employment, were returned to and retained by him; or

(c) any amount in respect of voluntary contributions described in rule 8 which have not been continued in pursuance of that rule.

(5) In this rule "the annual salary and emoluments of his office" means the average annual amount of the pensionable salary and emoluments of his office during the 3 years ending with the last day of his service as a pensionable employee, or, where his service during that period is less than 3 years, the average annual amount of his pensionable salary and emoluments during the actual period of his said service.

Rights of former insured persons to whom rule 6 has become applicable

11. Where any person to whom rule 6 of these rules has become applicable was in his employment as a pensionable employee an insured person within the meaning of the Insular Insurance (Jersey) Law 1950**(a)** then—

(a) if he had been excepted from the operation of any provision (hereinafter called "the modification provision") modifying his benefits under the relevant Jersey Rules, the provisions of the National Insurance (Modification of Local Government Superannuation Schemes) (Scotland) Regulations 1947**(b)**, and the provisions of any other regulations or of any scheme replacing wholly or in part the provisions of the first-mentioned regulations, shall not apply to him;

(b) if he had not been so excepted the provisions of any such regulations or scheme as aforesaid applicable to him in his new employment shall apply to him as if any service which he becomes entitled to reckon under rule 6 of these rules, being service of which account would have been taken under the modification provision for the purpose of reducing any benefit to which the person might have become entitled under the relevant Jersey Rules had he continued to be subject thereto, were service rendered on or after the 5th July 1948.

Application of section 30 of the Act of 1937

12. The provisions of section 30 of the Act of 1937 shall have effect in relation to a person who becomes a contributory employee or a person who is deemed to be a contributory employee in circumstances in which these rules apply as if the reference in the said section to regulations made under that Act included a reference to these rules.

William Ross,
One of Her Majesty's
Principal Secretaries of State.

St. Andrew's House,
Edinburgh.
21st October 1969.

(a) Recueil des Lois, Tome 1949-1950, p. 497.
(b) S.R. & O. 1947/1697 (Rev. XVI, p. 286: 1947 I, p. 1509).

EXPLANATORY NOTE
(This Note is not part of the Rules.)

These Rules provide for the preservation of the superannuation rights of persons who, after leaving pensionable employment in local government in Scotland, enter within the prescribed time limit (generally 12 months) pensionable employment in various public services (other than the teaching service) in the Island of Jersey, or who, after leaving pensionable employment in those services, enter (within the same time limit) pensionable employment in local government in Scotland.

The Rules extend to changes of employment which have taken place before the commencement of the Rules, but only where the person concerned has been employed in Jersey since the date his Jersey employment became pensionable. The Rules are given this limited retrospective operation under the express authority of, and subject to the safeguards required by, section 2(5) of the Superannuation (Miscellaneous Provisions) Act 1948.

STATUTORY INSTRUMENTS

1969 No. 1517

CONSTABULARY, IRELAND

The Royal Irish Constabulary (Widows' Pensions) Regulations 1969

Made	-	-	-	*24th October* 1969
Laid before Parliament				*31st October* 1969
Coming into Operation				*3rd November* 1969

In exercise of the powers conferred on me by section 1 of the Royal Irish Constabulary (Widows' Pensions) Act 1954(a) (read with Article 2(1) of the Minister for the Civil Service Order 1968(b)), I hereby, with the consent of the Minister for the Civil Service, make the following Regulations:—

1. These Regulations may be cited as the Royal Irish Constabulary (Widows' Pensions) Regulations 1969 and shall come into operation on 3rd November 1969.

2. In Regulations 1 and 2 of the Royal Irish Constabulary (Widows' Pensions) Regulations 1958(c), as amended (d), for the words "ninety shillings", wherever they occur, there shall be substituted the words "one hundred shillings".

James Callaghan,
One of Her Majesty's Principal
Secretaries of State.

24th October 1969.

Consent of the Minister for the Civil Service given under his Official Seal on 24th October 1969.

(L.S.)

K. H. McNeill,
Authorised by the
Minister for the Civil Service.

(a) 1954 c. 17.
(b) S.I. 1968/1656 (1968 III, p. 4485).
(c) S.I. 1958/101 (1958 I, p. 354).
(d) S.I. 1961/402, 1963/920, 1965/500, 1967/1501 (1961 I, p. 584; 1963 II, p. 1547; 1965 I, p. 1249; 1967 III, p. 4208).

EXPLANATORY NOTE

(This Note is not part of the Regulations.)

Under the Royal Irish Constabulary (Widows' Pensions) Regulations 1958 there may be paid to certain widows of former members of the Royal Irish Constabulary a pension or an allowance supplementary to an existing pension. A pension or allowance is not payable under the 1958 Regulations (as amended in 1961, 1963, 1965 and 1967) unless the rate of any state insurance benefit received by the widow is less than 90s. 0d. a week, and (subject to a minimum rate of 5s. 0d. a week in the case of a pension) it is to be at such rate as will secure that the combined rate of the Royal Irish Constabulary awards and the widow's state insurance benefit, if any, is equal to 90s. 0d. a week; for this purpose state insurance benefit means any benefit or pension under the National Insurance Act 1965 (c. 51) or the National Insurance (Industrial Injuries) Act 1965 (c. 52) or similar benefit or pension paid out of public funds in Northern Ireland, any of the Channel Islands, the Isle of Man or the Republic of Ireland. The present Regulations substitute 100s. 0d. for 90s. 0d. in the 1958 Regulations.

STATUTORY INSTRUMENTS

1969 No. 1518

AGRICULTURE

The Price Stability of Imported Products (Rates of Levy No. 22) Order 1969

Made	-	-	-	*24th October* 1969
Coming into Operation		-		*25th October* 1969

The Minister of Agriculture, Fisheries and Food, in exercise of the powers conferred upon him by section 1(2), (4), (5), (6) and (7) of the Agriculture and Horticulture Act 1964(**a**) and of all other powers enabling him in that behalf, hereby makes the following order:—

1. This order may be cited as the Price Stability of Imported Products (Rates of Levy No. 22) Order 1969, and shall come into operation on 25th October 1969.

2.—(1) In this order—

" the Principal Order " means the Price Stability of Imported Products (Levy Arrangements) Order 1966 (*b*) as amended (*c*) and as amended by any subsequent order, and if any such order is replaced by any subsequent order the expression shall be construed as a reference to such subsequent order;

AND other expressions have the same meaning as in the Principal Order.

(2) The Interpretation Act 1889(**d**) shall apply to the interpretation of this order as it applies to the interpretation of an Act of Parliament and as if this order and the orders hereby revoked were Acts of Parliament.

3. In accordance with and subject to the provisions of Part II of the Principal Order (which provides for the charging of levies on imports of certain specified commodities)—

(*a*) the rate of general levy for such imports into the United Kingdom of any specified commodity as are described in column 2 of Part I of the Schedule to this order in relation to a tariff heading indicated in column 1 of that Part shall be the rate set forth in relation thereto in column 3 of that Part;

(*b*) the rate of country levy for such imports into the United Kingdom of any specified commodity as are described in column 2 of Part II of the Schedule to this order in relation to a tariff heading indicated in column 1 of that Part shall be the rate set forth in relation thereto in column 3 of that Part.

(a) 1964 c. 28.
(c) S.I. 1969/758 (1969 II, p. 2137).
(b) S.I. 1966/936 (1966 II, p. 2271).
(d) 1889 c. 63.

4. The Price Stability of Imported Products (Rates of Levy No. 20) Order 1969(a) and the Price Stability of Imported Products (Rates of Levy No. 21) Order 1969(b) are hereby revoked.

In Witness whereof the Official Seal of the Minister of Agriculture, Fisheries and Food is hereunto affixed on 24th October 1969.

(L.S.)   *W. C. Tame,*
Authorised by the Minister.

SCHEDULE

PART I

1. Tariff Heading	2. Description of Imports	3. Rate of General Levy
		per ton £ s. d.
	Imports of:—	
10.01	Denatured wheat	15 0
10.01	Any wheat (other than seed wheat the value of which is not less than £34 per ton, denatured wheat, durum wheat and wheat which has been grown in and consigned to the United Kingdom from the Hungarian People's Republic) for which a minimum import price level is prescribed	15 0
10.03	Barley	2 10 0
11.01	Wheat flours	15 0

11.02	Cereal meals—
	     of barley .. ..
	     of maize .. ..
		
		7 5 0
		1 0 0

11.02	Rolled, flaked, crushed or bruised cereals— barley	 5 15 0

(a) S.I. 1969/1294 (1969 III, p. 3838).   (b) S.I. 1969/1329 (1969 III, p. 3956).

PART II

1. Tariff Heading	2. Description of Imports	3. Rate of Country Levy
		per ton £ s. d.
10.01	Imports of:— Denatured wheat which has been grown in and consigned to the United Kingdom from Belgium, the French Republic or the Kingdom of the Netherlands	15 0
10.01	Any wheat (other than seed wheat the value of which is not less than £34 per ton, denatured wheat and durum wheat) for which a minimum import price level is prescribed and which has been grown in and consigned to the United Kingdom from Belgium or the French Republic	10 0
10.03	Barley which has been grown in and consigned to the United Kingdom from— the Kingdom of the Netherlands .. .. the French Republic .. .. Canada	2 0 0 2 5 0 2 10 0

EXPLANATORY NOTE

(*This Note is not part of the Order.*)

This order, which comes into operation on 25th October 1969, supersedes the Price Stability of Imported Products (Rates of Levy No. 20) Order 1969 and the Price Stability of Imported Products (Rates of Levy No. 21) Order 1969. It:—

(*a*) increases to 15*s*. per ton the general levy on imports of wheat (other than seed wheat the value of which is not less than £34 per ton, denatured wheat, durum wheat and wheat which has been grown in and consigned to the United Kingdom from Hungary);

(*b*) removes the exemption from general levy of imports of wheat which has been grown in and consigned to the United Kingdom from the U.S.S.R.; and

(*c*) reimposes unchanged the other rates of general and country levy in force immediately before the commencement of the order.

STATUTORY INSTRUMENTS

1969 No. 1519

CUSTOMS AND EXCISE

The Import Duties (Temporary Exemptions) (No. 8) Order 1969

Made - - - -	*27th October* 1969
Laid before the House of Commons -	*31st October* 1969
Coming into Operation	*6th November* 1969

The Lords Commissioners of Her Majesty's Treasury, by virtue of the powers conferred on them by sections 3(6) and 13 of the Import Duties Act 1958(a), and of all other powers enabling them in that behalf, on the recommendation of the Board of Trade hereby make the following Order:—

1.—(1) This Order may be cited as the Import Duties (Temporary Exemptions) (No. 8) Order 1969.

(2) The Interpretation Act 1889(b) shall apply for the interpretation of this Order as it applies for the interpretation of an Act of Parliament.

(3) This Order shall come into operation on 6th November 1969.

2.—(1) Until the beginning of 1st January 1970, any import duty which is for the time being chargeable on goods of a heading of the Customs Tariff 1959 specified in Schedule 1 to this Order shall not be chargeable in respect of goods of any description there specified in relation to that heading.

(2) The period for which the goods of the headings of the Customs Tariff 1959 and the descriptions specified in Schedule 2 to this Order are exempt from import duty shall be extended until the beginning of 1st January 1970.

(3) Any entry in column 2 in Schedule 1 or 2 to this Order is to be taken to comprise all goods which would be classified under an entry in the same terms constituting a subheading (other than the final subheading) in the relevant heading in the Customs Tariff 1959.

(4) For the purposes of classification under the Customs Tariff 1959, in so far as that depends on the rate of duty, any goods to which paragraph (1) or (2) above applies shall be treated as chargeable with the same duty as if this Order had not been made.

> *Joseph Harper,*
> *E. G. Perry,*
> Two of the Lords Commissioners
> of Her Majesty's Treasury.

27th October 1969

(a) 1958 c. 6.	(b) 1889 c. 63.

SCHEDULE 1

GOODS TEMPORARILY EXEMPT FROM IMPORT DUTY

Tariff Heading	*Description*
12.05	Dried chicory root
29.04	3,6-Dimethyloctan-3-ol
29.06	o-Cresol
29.14	Phenylacetic acid
29.15	Fumaric acid
29.17	1-isoButyl-4-ethyloctyl sodium sulphate
29.25	3,4,4'-Trichloro-NN'-diphenylurea
29.33	4-Chloromercuribenzoic acid of a purity of not less than 98 per cent. and a melting point of not less than 278° centigrade
29.36	Sulphanilamide
29.38	Calciferol
29.44	Sodium cephalothin
39.02	Acrylic sheet, transparent, colourless, of a thickness not less than 1·5 millimetres and not greater than 17·0 millimetres, which, when kept for 24 hours at a temperature of 110° centigrade, undergoes a linear shrinkage of not more than 10 per cent., and which, when kept for 24 hours at a temperature of 145° centigrade, undergoes a linear shrinkage of not less than 40 per cent.
81.04	Zirconium alloy ingots, surface trimmed, containing not less than 1·0 per cent. by weight nor more than 2·0 per cent. by weight of tin as the major alloying element, of circular cross section of a diameter of not less than 17 inches and not more than 21 inches, and of a length of not less than 40 inches and not more than 50 inches

SCHEDULE 2

GOODS FOR WHICH EXEMPTION FROM IMPORT DUTY EXTENDED

Tariff Heading	*Description*
10.05	Flat white maize
25.19	Magnesite, dead-burned, containing (a) not less than 90 per cent. by weight of magnesium compounds expressed as MgO, (b) a total of not more than 1·0 per cent. by weight of aluminium compounds and iron compounds expressed as Al_2O_3 and Fe_2O_3, (c) a total of not less than 2·5 per cent. by weight and not more than 5·0 per cent. by weight of calcium compounds and silicon compounds expressed as CaO and SiO_2, and in which the weight of calcium compounds expressed as CaO is not less than 1·5 times the weight of silicon compounds expressed as SiO_2
28.18	Magnesium oxide, dead-burned but not fused, of a purity not less than 96 per cent., containing (a) a total of not more than 1·0 per cent. by weight of aluminium compounds and iron compounds expressed as Al_2O_3 and Fe_2O_3, (b) a total of not more than 3·5 per cent. by weight of calcium compounds and silicon compounds expressed as CaO and SiO_2, the weight of silicon compounds being not less than 1·5 times and not more than 3·0 times the weight of calcium compounds; and (c) of which not less than 50 per cent. by weight is retained by a sieve having a nominal width of aperture of 3/16 inch
	Magnesium oxide, dead-burned but not fused, of a purity not less than 96 per cent., which contains (a) not more than 0·05 per cent. by weight of boron compounds expressed as B_2O_3, (b) a total of not more than 0·5 per cent. by weight of aluminium compounds and iron compounds expressed as Al_2O_3 and Fe_2O_3, and (c) a total of not less than 1·0 per cent. by weight and not more than 3·5 per cent. by

Tariff Heading	*Description*
	weight of calcium compounds and silicon compounds expressed as CaO and SiO_2, the weight of calcium compounds being not less than $1 \cdot 5$ times and not more than $2 \cdot 5$ times the weight of silicon compounds; and (d) of which not less than 35 per cent. by weight is retained by a sieve having a nominal width of aperture cf 3/16 inch
29.04	2,3-Dibromopropan-1-ol containing not more than $0 \cdot 1$ per cent. by weight of 1,2,3-tribromopropane
	Tridecyl alcohol, mixed isomers
29.06	2-secButylphenol
29.07	2,4,5-Trichlorophenol
29.15	Maleic anhydride
29.22	1,2-Diaminoethane
	Diethylenetriamine
	Tetraethylenepentamine
	Triethylenetetramine
29.25	Procainamide hydrochloride
29.35	N-tertButylbenzothiazole-2-sulphenamide
	mesoInositol hexanicotinate
	Phenothiazine of a purity not less than 98 per cent., which contains not more than $0 \cdot 0035$ per cent. by weight of total iodine, and which yields not more than $0 \cdot 05$ per cent. by weight of sulphated ash
73.06	Iron or steel ingots, blocks, lumps and similar forms, other than those manufactured entirely from pig iron smelted wholly with charcoal
73.07	Iron or steel blooms, billets, slabs and sheet bars
73.08	Iron or steel coils for re-rolling
73.15	Single strand alloy steel wire coated with niobium alloy containing tin and with an outer coating of silver
73.19	Hot rolled seamless circular steel tubes of an outside diameter of not less than $19\frac{1}{2}$ inches and not more than $24\frac{1}{2}$ inches, and of a wall thickness of not less than 7/16 inch and not more than 5/8 inch
81.04	Wrought titanium of a purity exceeding 99.6 per cent. titanium, in the form of slabs of a thickness of not less than $4\frac{1}{2}$ inches nor more than 6 inches, of a width of not less than 36 inches nor more than 48 inches, in random lengths
	Wrought titanium alloy containing not less than 3 per cent. nor more than 5 per cent. by weight of vanadium, not less than 5 per cent. nor more than 7 per cent. by weight of aluminium, the balance being mainly titanium, in the form of billets of not less than 4 inches nor more than 7 inches in diameter, or not less than 4 inches nor more than 7 inches square, in random lengths
90.01	Photographic process screens of the contact type, consisting of a base of cellulose acetate or of poly(ethylene terephthalate) on which is a regularly spaced pattern of grey-coloured or magenta-coloured dots

EXPLANATORY NOTE

(*This Note is not part of the Order.*)

This Order provides that the goods listed in Schedule 1 shall be temporarily exempt from import duty, and those listed in Schedule 2 shall continue to be exempt from import duty, both until 1st January 1970.

STATUTORY INSTRUMENTS

1969 No. 1523

INDUSTRIAL TRAINING

The Industrial Training Levy (Hotel and Catering)

Order 1969

Made	-	-	-	*24th October* 1969
Laid before Parliament				*6th November* 1969
Coming into Operation			*19th November* 1969

The Secretary of State after approving proposals submitted by the Hotel and Catering Industry Training Board for the imposition of a further levy on employers in the hotel and catering industry and in exercise of her powers under section 4 of the Industrial Training Act 1964(a) and of all other powers enabling her in that behalf hereby makes the following Order :—

Title and commencement

1. This Order may be cited as the Industrial Training Levy (Hotel and Catering) Order 1969 and shall come into operation on 19th November 1969.

Interpretation

2.—(1) In this Order unless the context otherwise requires :—

(*a*) "an appeal tribunal" means an industrial tribunal established under section 12 of the Industrial Training Act 1964 ;

(*b*) "assessment" means an assessment of an employer to the levy ;

(*c*) "the Board" means the Hotel and Catering Industry Training Board ;

(*d*) "emoluments" means all emoluments assessable to income tax under Schedule E (other than pensions), being emoluments from which tax under that Schedule is deductible, whether or not tax in fact falls to be deducted from any particular payment thereof ;

(*e*) "employer" means a person who is an employer in the hotel and catering industry at any time in the third levy period ;

(*f*) "establishment" (except in sub-paragraph (*g*) or (*h*) of this paragraph) means an establishment comprising catering activities or a hotel and catering establishment ;

(*g*) "establishment comprising catering activities" means an establishment in Great Britain at or from which persons were employed in the third base period in the supply of food or drink to persons for immediate consumption, but does not include—

    (i) a hotel and catering establishment ; or

    (ii) an establishment in which the employer supplied for immediate consumption light refreshments to persons employed at or from the same where the employer was not otherwise engaged at or from the establishment in any activities to which paragraph 1 of the Schedule to the industrial training order applies or in the manufacture of any chocolate or flour confectionery so supplied as light refreshments;

(a) 1964 c. 16.

(*h*) "hotel and catering establishment" means an establishment in Great Britain that was engaged in the third base period wholly or mainly in the hotel and catering industry ;

(*i*) "hotel and catering industry" means any one or more of the activities which, subject to the provisions of paragraph 2 of the Schedule to the industrial training order, are specified in paragraph 1 of that Schedule as the activities of the hotel and catering industry ;

(*j*) "the industrial training order" means the Industrial Training (Hotel and Catering Board) Order 1969(**a**) ;

(*k*) "the levy" means the levy imposed by the Board in respect of the third levy period ;

(*l*) "notice" means a notice in writing ;

(*m*) "the supply of food or drink to persons for immediate consumption" means such a supply either by way of business or by a person carrying on a business to persons employed in the business ;

(*n*) "the third base period" means the period of twelve months that commenced on 6th April 1968 ;

(*o*) "the third levy period" means the period commencing with the day upon which this Order comes into operation and ending on 31st March 1970 ;

(*p*) other expressions have the same meaning as in the industrial training order.

(2) In the case where an establishment is taken over (whether directly or indirectly) by an employer in succession to, or jointly with, another person, a person employed at any time in the third base period at or from the establishment shall be deemed, for the purposes of this Order, to have been so employed by the employer carrying on the said establishment on the day upon which this Order comes into operation, and any reference in this Order to persons employed by an employer in the third base period at or from an establishment shall be construed accordingly.

(3) Any reference in this Order to an establishment that ceases to carry on business shall not be taken to apply where the location of the establishment is changed but its business is continued wholly or mainly at or from the new location, or where the suspension of activities is of a temporary or seasonal nature.

(4) The Interpretation Act 1889(**b**) shall apply to the interpretation of this Order as it applies to the interpretation of an Act of Parliament.

Imposition of the Levy

3.—(1) The levy to be imposed by the Board on employers in respect of the third levy period shall be assessed in accordance with the provisions of this and the next following Article.

(2) Subject to the provisions of the next following Article, the levy shall be assessed by the Board separately in respect of each establishment of an employer (not being an employer who is exempt from the levy by virtue of paragraph (3) of this Article), but in agreement with the employer one assessment may be made in respect of any number of hotel and catering establish-

---

(**a**) S.I. 1969/1405 (1969 III, p. 4132).   (**b**) 1889 c. 63.

ments or of establishments comprising catering activities, in which case such establishments shall be deemed for the purposes of the assessment to constitute one establishment.

(3) There shall be exempt from the levy an employer in whose case the sum of the emoluments of all the persons employed by him in the third base period' in the hotel and catering industry at or from the establishment or establishments of the employer was less than £4,000.

Assessment of the Levy

4.—(1) Subject to the provisions of this Article, the levy assessed in respect of an establishment shall be an amount equal to one per cent. of the sum of the emoluments of the following persons, being persons employed by the employer at or from the establishment in the third base period, that is to say—

(*a*) in the case of a hotel and catering establishment, all such persons ;

(*b*) in the case of an establishment comprising catering activities, all such persons employed wholly or mainly in the supply of food or drink to persons for immediate consumption.

(2) In the case of one establishment only of an employer, the sum of the emoluments determined in accordance with the last foregoing paragraph shall be treated for the purpose of the assessment of the levy in respect of that establishment as if that sum were reduced by £2,000.

(3) For the purposes of the application of the provisions of the last foregoing paragraph, the Board shall, if necessary—

(*a*) select the establishment in relation to which the provisions of the said paragraph are to apply ; or

(*b*) aggregate the sum total of the emoluments of the persons employed at or from any two or more establishments of the employer (each sum first being determined separately in accordance with paragraph (1) of this Article) in which case the said establishments shall be deemed for the purposes of the assessment thereof to constitute one establishment.

(4) The amount of the levy imposed in respect of an establishment that ceases to carry on business in the third levy period shall be in the same proportion to the amount that would otherwise be due under the foregoing provisions of this Article as the number of days between the commencement of the said levy period and the date of cessation of business (both dates inclusive) bears to the number of days in the said levy period.

(5) For the purposes of this Article, no regard shall be had to the emoluments of any person employed as follows—

(*a*) wholly in the supply (except at or in connection with an hotel, restaurant, café, snack bar, canteen, mess room or similar place of refreshment) of—

(i) ice cream, chocolate confectionery, sugar confectionery or soft drink ;

(ii) shellfish or eels ; or

(iii) food or drink by means of an automatic vending machine ;

(*b*) otherwise than wholly in the supply of food or drink to persons for immediate consumption, where the employment is at or from an establishment engaged mainly in any activities of an industry specified in column 1 of the Schedule to this Order by virtue of the relevant industrial training order specified in column 2 of that Schedule or in any activities of two or more such industries;

2c

(c) as a member of the crew of an aircraft, or as the master or a member of the crew of a ship or, in the case of a person ordinarily employed as a seaman, in or about a ship in port by the owner or charterer thereof on work of a kind ordinarily done by a seaman on a ship while it is in port;

(d) by a local authority in any activities mentioned in sub-paragraph (d) or (e) of paragraph 1 of the Schedule to the industrial training order, not being activities mentioned in head (ii) or head (iv) of paragraph 3(1) of that Schedule; or

(e) in any activities mentioned in sub-paragraph (b), (c)(ii), (d) or (e) of paragraph 1 of the Schedule to the industrial training order when carried out by—

(i) a harbour authority while acting in that capacity;

(ii) the Electricity Council, the Central Electricity Generating Board or an Area Electricity Board;

(iii) the North of Scotland Hydro-Electric Board or the South of Scotland Electricity Board;

(iv) the Gas Council or an Area Gas Board;

(v) statutory water undertakers within the meaning of the Water Act 1945(a) or regional water boards or water development boards within the meaning of the Water (Scotland) Act 1967(b), being the activities of such undertakers or boards in the exercise of their powers or duties as such;

(vi) the British Airports Authority, the British European Airways Corporation, the British Overseas Airways Corporation, BEA Helicopters Limited or B.O.A.C. Associated Companies Limited;

(vii) a marketing board; or

(viii) the United Kingdom Atomic Energy Authority.

Assessment Notices

5.—(1) The Board shall serve an assessment notice on every employer assessed to the levy, but one notice may comprise two or more assessments.

(2) An assessment notice shall state the Board's address for the service of a notice of appeal or of an application for an extension of time for appealing.

(3) An assessment notice may be served on the person assessed to the levy either by delivering it to him personally or by leaving it, or sending it to him by post, at his last known address or place of business in the United Kingdom or, if that person is a corporation, by leaving it, or sending it by post to the corporation, at such address or place of business or at its registered or principal office.

Payment of the Levy

6.—(1) Subject to the provisions of this Article and of Articles 7 and 8, the amount of each assessment appearing in an assessment notice served by the Board shall be due and payable to the Board one month after the date of the notice.

(2) The amount of an assessment shall not be recoverable by the Board until there has expired the time allowed for appealing against the assessment by Article 8(1) of this Order and any further period or periods of time that the

---

(a) 1945 c. 42.   (b) 1967 c. 78.

Board or an appeal tribunal may have allowed for appealing under paragraph (2) or (3) of that Article or, where an appeal is brought, until the appeal is decided or withdrawn.

Withdrawal of Assessment

7.—(1) The Board may, by a notice served on the person assessed to the levy in the same manner as an assessment notice, withdraw an assessment notice if that person has appealed against an assessment contained therein under the provisions of Article 8 of this Order and the appeal has not been entered in the Register of Appeals kept under the appropriate Regulations specified in paragraph (5) of that Article, and such withdrawal shall apply to each assessment appearing in the assessment notice.

(2) The withdrawal of an assessment notice shall be without prejudice to the power of the Board to serve a further assessment notice in respect of any establishment to which the first mentioned notice related.

Appeals

8.—(1) A person assessed to the levy may appeal to an appeal tribunal against the assessment within one month from the date of the service of the assessment notice or within any further period or periods of time that may be allowed by the Board or an appeal tribunal under the following provisions of this Article.

(2) The Board by notice may for good cause allow a person assessed to the levy to appeal to an appeal tribunal against the assessment at any time within the period of four months from the date of the service of the assessment notice or within such further period or periods as the Board may allow before such time as may then be limited for appealing has expired.

(3) If the Board shall not allow an application for extension of time for appealing, an appeal tribunal shall upon application made to the tribunal by the person assessed to the levy have the like powers as the Board under the last foregoing paragraph.

(4) In the case of an establishment that ceases to carry on business in the third levy period on any day after the date of the service of the relevant assessment notice, the foregoing provisions of this Article shall have effect as if for the period of four months from the date of the service of the assessment notice mentioned in paragraph (2) of this Article there were substituted the period of six months from the date of the cessation of business.

(5) An appeal or an application to an appeal tribunal under this Article shall be made in accordance with the Industrial Tribunals (England and Wales) Regulations 1965(a) as amended by the Industrial Tribunals (England and Wales) (Amendment) Regulations 1967(b) except where the establishment to which the relevant assessment relates is wholly in Scotland in which case the appeal or application shall be made in accordance with the Industrial Tribunals (Scotland) Regulations 1965(c) as amended by the Industrial Tribunals (Scotland) (Amendment) Regulations 1967(d).

(6) The powers of an appeal tribunal under paragraph (3) of this Article may be exercised by the President of the Industrial Tribunals (England and Wales) or by the President of the Industrial Tribunals (Scotland) as the case may be.

Evidence

9.—(1) Upon the discharge by a person assessed to the levy of his liability under an assessment the Board shall if so requested issue to him a certificate to that effect.

(a) S.I. 1965/1101 (1965 II, p. 2805).   (b) S.I. 1967/301 (1967 I, p. 1040).
(c) S.I. 1965/1157 (1965 II, p. 3266).   (d) S.I. 1967/302 (1967 I, p. 1050).

(2) The production in any proceedings of a document purporting to be certified by the Secretary of the Board to be a true copy of an assessment or other notice issued by the Board or purporting to be a certificate such as is mentioned in the foregoing paragraph of this Article shall, unless the contrary is proved, be sufficient evidence of the document and of the facts stated therein. 24th October 1969.

Barbara Castle,
First Secretary of State and
Secretary of State for Employment and Productivity.

SCHEDULE

THE INDUSTRIES REFERRED TO IN ARTICLE 4(5)(*b*) OF THIS ORDER

Column 1	Column 2
The wool, jute and flax industry	The Industrial Training (Wool Industry Board) Order 1964 as amended by the Industrial Training (Wool, Jute and Flax Board) Order 1968(a)
The iron and steel industry	The Industrial Training (Iron and Steel Board) Order 1964 as amended by the Industrial Training (Iron and Steel Board) Order 1969(b)
The construction industry	The Industrial Training (Construction Board) Order 1964 as amended by the Industrial Training (Construction Board) Order 1967(c)
The engineering industry	The Industrial Training (Engineering Board) Order 1964 as amended by the Industrial Training (Engineering Board) Order 1968 and the Industrial Training (Engineering Board) Order 1968 (Amendment) Order 1969(d)
The shipbuilding industry	The Industrial Training (Shipbuilding Board) Order 1964 as amended by the Industrial Training (Shipbuilding Board). Order 1968(e)
The electricity supply industry	The Industrial Training (Electricity Supply Board) Order 1965(f)
The gas industry	The Industrial Training (Gas Industry Board) Order 1965(g)
The water supply industry	The Industrial Training (Water Supply Board, Order 1965(h)
The ceramics, glass and mineral products industry	The Industrial Training (Ceramics, Glass and Mineral Products Board) Order 1965 as amended by the Industrial Training (Ceramics, Glass and Mineral Products Board) Order 1969(i)
The furniture and timber industry	The Industrial Training (Furniture and Timber Industry Board) Order 1965 as amended by the Industrial Training (Furniture and Timber Industry Board) Order 1969(j)
The man-made fibres producing industry	The Industrial Training (Man-made Fibres Producing Industry Board) Order 1966 as amended by the Industrial Training (Man-made Fibres Producing Industry Board) Order 1969(k)

(a) S.I. 1964/907, 1968/898 (1964 II, p. 1928; 1968 II, p. 2376).
(b) S.I. 1964/949, 1969/884 (1964 II, p. 2127; 1969 II, p. 2517).
(c) S.I. 1964/1079, 1967/924 (1964 II, p. 2384; 1967 II, p. 2757).
(d) S.I. 1964/1086, 1968/1333, 1969/1376 (1964 II, p. 2402; 1968 II, p. 3694; 1969 III, p. 4103).
(e) S.I. 1964/1782, 1968/1614 (1964 III, p. 3928; 1968 III, p. 4432).
(f) S.I. 1965/1256 (1965 II, p. 3548).
(g) S.I. 1965/1257 (1965 II, p. 3552).
(h) S.I. 1965/1258 (1965 II, p. 3556).
(i) S.I. 1965/1391, 1969/689 (1965 II, p. 4062; 1969 II, p. 1860).
(j) S.I. 1965/2028, 1969/1290 (1965 III, p. 5998; 1969 III, p. 3820).
(k) S.I. 1966/143, 1969/1210 (1966 I, p. 257; 1969 II, p. 3545).

Column 1	Column 2
The carpet industry	The Industrial Training (Carpet Board) Order 1966 as amended by the Industrial Training (Carpet Board) Order 1968(a)
The knitting, lace and net industry	The Industrial Training (Knitting, Lace and Net Industry Board) Order 1966(b)
The cotton and allied textiles industry	The Industrial Training (Cotton and Allied Textiles Board) Order 1966(c)
The agricultural, horticultural and forestry industry	The Industrial Training (Agricultural, Horticultural and Forestry Board) Order 1966(d)
The road transport industry	The Industrial Training (Road Transport Board) Order 1966 as amended by the Industrial Training (Road Transport Board) Order 1969(e)
The civil air transport industry	The Industrial Training (Civil Air Transport Board) Order 1967(f)
The petroleum industry	The Industrial Training (Petroleum Board) Order 1967(g)
The rubber and plastics processing industry	The Industrial Training (Rubber and Plastics Processing Board) Order 1967(h)
The chemical and allied products industry	The Industrial Training (Chemical and Allied Products Board) Order 1967(i)
The paper and paper products industry	The Industrial Training (Paper and Paper Products Board) Order 1968(j)
The printing and publishing industry	The Industrial Training (Printing and Publishing Board) Order 1968(k)
The distributive industry	The Industrial Training (Distributive Board) Order 1968(l)
The food, drink and tobacco industry	The Industrial Training (Food, Drink and Tobacco Board) Order 1968(m)
The footwear, leather and fur skin industry	The Industrial Training (Footwear, Leather and Fur Skin Board) Order 1968(n)
The clothing and allied products industry	The Industrial Training (Clothing and Allied Products Board) Order 1969(o)

(a) S.I. 1966/245, 1968/1882 (1966 I, p. 499; 1968 III, p. 5017).
(b) S.I. 1966/246 (1966 I, p. 506).
(c) S.I. 1966/823 (1966 II, p. 1907).
(d) S.I. 1966/969 (1966 II, p. 2333).
(e) S.I. 1966/1112, 1969/879 (1966 III, p. 2712; 1969 II, p. 2495).
(f) S.I. 1967/263 (1967 I, p. 968).
(g) S.I. 1967/648 (1967 I, p. 2032).
(h) S.I. 1967/1062 (1967 II, p. 3151).
(i) S.I. 1967/1386 (1967 III, p. 4049).
(j) S.I. 1968/787 (1968 II, p. 2194).
(k) S.I. 1968/786 (1968 II, p. 2185).
(l) S.I. 1968/1032 (1968 II, p. 2709).
(m) S.I. 1968/1033 (1968 II, p. 2721).
(n) S.I. 1968/1763 (1968 III, p. 4785).
(o) S.I. 1969/1375 (1969 III, p. 4094).

EXPLANATORY NOTE
(*This Note is not part of the Order.*)

This Order gives effect to proposals submitted by the Hotel and Catering Industry Training Board to the Secretary of State for Employment and Productivity for the imposition of a further levy upon employers in the hotel and catering industry for the purpose of raising money towards the expenses of the Board.

The levy is to be imposed in respect of the third levy period commencing with the day upon which this Order comes into operation and ending on 31st March 1970. The levy will be assessed by the Board and there will be a right of appeal against an assessment to an industrial tribunal.

STATUTORY   INSTRUMENTS

1969 No. 1527

SUGAR

The Sugar (Rates of Surcharge and Surcharge Repayments) (No. 12) Order 1969

Made - - - -	*28th October* 1969
Laid before Parliament	*30th October* 1969
Coming into Operation	*31st October* 1969

The Minister of Agriculture, Fisheries and Food, in exercise of the powers conferred on him by sections 7(4), 8(6) and 33(4) of the Sugar Act 1956(a) having effect subject to the provisions of section 3 of, and Part II of Schedule 5 to, the Finance Act 1962(b), and section 58 of the Finance Act 1968(c) and of all other powers enabling him in that behalf, with the concurrence of the Treasury, on the advice of the Sugar Board, hereby makes the following order:—

1.—(1) This order may be cited as the Sugar (Rates of Surcharge and Surcharge Repayments) (No. 12) Order 1969; and shall come into operation on 31st October 1969.

(2) The Interpretation Act 1889(d) shall apply for the interpretation of this order as it applies for the interpretation of an Act of Parliament.

2. Notwithstanding the provisions of Article 2 of the Sugar (Rates of Surcharge and Surcharge Repayments) (No. 11) Order 1969(e), the rates of surcharge payable under and in accordance with the provisions of section 7 of the Sugar Act 1956, having effect as aforesaid, in respect of sugar and invert sugar imported or home produced or used in the manufacture of imported composite sugar products shall on and after 31st October 1969 be those rates specified in Schedule 1 to this order.

3. For the purpose of section 8(3)(b) of the Sugar Act 1956, having effect as aforesaid, the rates of surcharge repayments in respect of invert sugar produced in the United Kingdom from materials on which on or after 31st October 1969 sugar duty has been paid or, by virtue of paragraph 1 of Part II of Schedule 5 to the Finance Act 1962, is treated as having been paid shall, notwithstanding the provisions of Article 3 of the Sugar (Rates of Surcharge and Surcharge Repayments) (No. 11) Order 1969 be those specified in Schedule 2 to this order.

(a) 1956 c. 48.   (b) 1962 c. 44.
(c) 1968 c. 44.   (d) 1889 c. 63.
(e) S.I. 1969/1505 (1969 III, p. 4891).

In Witness whereof the Official Seal of the Minister of Agriculture, Fisheries and Food is hereunto affixed on 27th October 1969.

(L.s.)

R. P. Fraser,

Authorised by the Minister.

We concur.

28th October 1969.

Joseph Harper,
Ernest Armstrong,

Two of the Lords Commissioners of
Her Majesty's Treasury.

SCHEDULE 1

PART I

SURCHARGE RATES FOR SUGAR

Polarisation										Rate of Surcharge per cwt.
										s. d.
Exceeding—										
99°	...	...	...	...	...	...	...	...	...	21 0·0
98° but not exceeding 99°	...	...	...	...	...	...	...	19 9·6
97° ,, ,, ,,	98°	...	...	...	...	...	...	...	19 3·8
96° ,, ,, ,,	97°	...	...	...	...	...	..	...	18 9·7
95° ,, ,, ,,	96°	...	...	...	...	...	...	...	18 3·7
94° ,, ,, ,,	95°	...	...	...	...	...	...	...	17 9·6
93° ,, ,, ,,	94°	...	...	...	...	...	...	...	17 3·6
92° ,, ,, ,,	93°	...	...	...	...	...	...	...	16 9·6
91° ,, ,, ,,	92°	...	...	...	...	...	...	...	16 3·5
90° ,, ,, ,,	91°	...	...	...	...	...	...	...	15 9·5
89° ,, ,, ,,	90°	...	...	...	...	...	...	...	15 3·4
88° ,, ,, ,,	89°	...	...	...	...	...	...	...	14 9·4
87° ,, ,, ,,	88°	...	...	...	...	...	...	...	14 4·3
86° ,, ,, ,,	87°	...	...	...	...	...	...	...	13 11·3
85° ,, ,, ,,	86°	...	...	...	...	...	...	...	13 6·7
84° ,, ,, ,,	85°	...	...	...	...	...	...	...	13 2·2
83° ,, ,, ,,	84°	...	...	...	...	...	...	...	12 9·7
82° ,, ,, ,,	83°	...	...	...	...	...	...	...	12 5·1
81° ,, ,, ,,	82°	...	...	...	...	...	...	...	12 1·1
80° ,, ,, ,,	81°	...	...	...	...	...	...	...	11 9·1
79° ,, ,, ,,	80°	...	...	...	...	...	...	...	11 5·0
78° ,, ,, ,,	79°	...	...	...	...	...	...	...	11 1·0
77° ,, ,, ,,	78°	...	...	...	...	...	...	...	10 9·0
76° ,, ,, ,,	77°	...	...	...	...	...	...	...	10 4·9
Not exceeding 76°	...	...	...	...	...	...	...	...	10 0·9

PART II

SURCHARGE RATES FOR INVERT SUGAR

Sweetening matter content by weight	Rate of Surcharge per cwt.
	s. d.
70 per cent. or more	13 4
Less than 70 per cent. and more than 50 per cent.	9 7
Not more than 50 per cent.	4 8

SCHEDULE 2

SURCHARGE REPAYMENT RATES FOR INVERT SUGAR

Sweetening matter content by weight	Rate of Surcharge Repayment per cwt.
	s. d.
More than 80 per cent.	15 9
More than 70 per cent. but not more than 80 per cent.	13 4
More than 60 per cent. but not more than 70 per cent.	9 7
More than 50 per cent. but not more than 60 per cent.	7 7
Not more than 50 per cent. and the invert sugar not being less in weight than 14 lb. per gallon	4 8

EXPLANATORY NOTE

(*This Note is not part of the Order.*)

This order prescribes—

(*a*) reductions equivalent to 2s. 4d. per cwt. of refined sugar in the rates of surcharge payable on sugar and invert sugar which become chargeable with surcharge on or after 31st October 1969;

(*b*) correspondingly reduced rates of surcharge repayment in respect of invert sugar produced in the United Kingdom from materials on which surcharge has been paid.

STATUTORY INSTRUMENTS

1969 No. 1528

SUGAR

The Composite Sugar Products (Surcharge and Surcharge Repayments—Average Rates) (No. 12) Order 1969

Made - - - -	28*th October* 1969
Laid before Parliament	30*th October* 1969
Coming into Operation	31*st October* 1969

Whereas the Minister of Agriculture, Fisheries and Food (hereinafter called " the Minister ") has on the recommendation of the Commissioners of Customs and Excise (hereinafter called " the Commissioners ") made an order(a) pursuant to the powers conferred upon him by sections 9(1) and 9(4) of the Sugar Act 1956(b), having effect subject to the provisions of section 3 of, and Part II of Schedule 5 to, the Finance Act 1962(c), to the provisions of section 52(2) of the Finance Act 1966(d), and to the provisions of Section 58 of the Finance Act 1968(e), providing that in the case of certain descriptions of composite sugar products surcharge shall be calculated on the basis of an average quantity of sugar or invert sugar taken to have been used in the manufacture of the products, and that certain other descriptions of composite sugar products shall be treated as not containing any sugar or invert sugar, and that in the case of certain descriptions of goods in the manufacture of which sugar or invert sugar is used, surcharge repayments shall be calculated on the basis of an average quantity of sugar or invert sugar taken to have been so used:

Now, therefore, the Minister, on the recommendation of the Commissioners and in exercise of the powers conferred upon him by sections 9(1), 9(4) and 33(4) of the Sugar Act 1956, having effect as aforesaid, and of all other powers enabling him in that behalf, hereby makes the following order:—

1.—(1) This order may be cited as the Composite Sugar Products (Surcharge and Surcharge Repayments—Average Rates) (No. 12) Order 1969; and shall come into operation on 31st October 1969.

(2) The Interpretation Act 1889(f) shall apply for the interpretation of this order as it applies for the interpretation of an Act of Parliament.

2. Surcharge payable on or after 31st October 1969 under and in accordance with the Sugar Act 1956, having effect as aforesaid, in respect of sugar and invert sugar used in the manufacture of the descriptions of imported composite sugar products specified in column 2 of Schedule 1 to this order shall, notwithstanding the provisions of the Sugar (Rates of Surcharge and Surcharge Repayments) (No. 12) Order 1969(g) andthe Composite Sugar Products (Surcharge and Surcharge Repayments—Average Rates) (No. 11) Order 1969(a), be calculated by reference to the weight or value, as the case may be, of the products at the rates specified in relation thereto in column 3 of the said Schedule.

(a) S.I. 1969/1506 (1969 III, p. 4894). (b) 1956 c. 48.   (c) 1962 c. 44.
(d) 1966 c. 18.   (e) 1968 c. 44.   (f) 1889 c. 63.
(g) S.I. 1969/1527 (1969 III, p. 4953).

3. Imported composite sugar products other than those of a description specified in Schedules 1 and 2 to this order shall be treated as not containing any sugar or invert sugar for the purposes of surcharge payable on or after 31st October 1969.

4. Surcharge repayments payable on and after 31st October 1969 under and in accordance with the provisions of section 8 of the Sugar Act 1956, having effect as aforesaid, in respect of sugar and invert sugar used in the manufacture of the descriptions of goods specified in column 1 of Schedule 3 to this order shall, notwithstanding the provisions of the Sugar (Rates of Surcharge and Surcharge Repayments) (No. 12) Order 1969(a) and the Composite Sugar Products (Surcharge and Surcharge Repayments—Average Rates) (No. 11) Order 1969(b), be calculated by reference to the quantity of the goods at the rates specified in relation thereto in column 2 of the said Schedule.

In Witness whereof the Official Seal of the Minister of Agriculture, Fisheries and Food is hereunto affixed on 28th October 1969.

(L.S.)   *R. P. Fraser,*
                                      Authorised by the Minister.

SCHEDULE 1

In this Schedule:—

" Tariff heading " means a heading or, where the context so requires, a subheading of the Customs Tariff 1959 (see paragraph (1) of Article 1 of the Import Duties (General) (No. 4) Order 1968(c)).

" Per cent." means, where it occurs in relation to any rate of surcharge, per cent. of the value for customs duty purposes of the product to which it relates.

Tariff heading	Description of Imported Composite Sugar Products	Rate of Surcharge
		per cwt. s. d.
04.02	Milk and cream, preserved, concentrated or sweetened, containing more than 10 per cent. by weight of added sweetening matter	9 4
17.02 (B) (2) and 17.05 (B)	Syrups containing sucrose sugar, whether or not flavoured or coloured, but not including fruit juices containing added sugar in any proportion:— containing 70 per cent. or more by weight of sweetening matter	13 4
	containing less than 70 per cent., and more than 50 per cent., by weight of sweetening matter...	9 7
	containing not more than 50 per cent. by weight of sweetening matter	4 8

(a) S.I. 1969/1527 (1969 III, p. 4953). (b) S.I. 1969/1506 (1969 III, p. 4894).
(c) S.I. 1968/679 (1968 I, p. 1519).

Tariff heading	Description of Imported Composite Sugar Products	Rate of Surcharge
		per cwt. s. d.
17.02 (F) ...	Caramel:—	
	Solid	21 0
	Liquid	14 8
17.04	Sugar confectionery, not containing cocoa	17 1
18.06	Chocolate and other food preparations containing cocoa:—	
	Chocolate couverture not prepared for retail sale; chocolate milk crumb, liquid	9 4
	Chocolate milk crumb, solid	11 6
	Solid chocolate bars or blocks, milk or plain, with or without fruit or nuts; other chocolate confectionery consisting wholly of chocolate or of chocolate and other ingredients not containing added sugar, but not including such goods when packed together in retail packages with goods liable to surcharge at a higher rate	9 5
	Other	12 2
		per cent.
19.08	Pastry, biscuits, cakes and other fine bakers' wares containing added sweetening matter:—	
	Biscuits	$4\frac{1}{2}$
	Other	$2\frac{7}{10}$
20.01	Vegetables and fruit, prepared or preserved by vinegar or acetic acid, containing added sweetening matter	$6\frac{3}{10}$
20.03	Fruit preserved by freezing, containing added sugar	$2\frac{1}{4}$
		per cwt. s. d.
20.04	Fruit, fruit-peel and parts of plants, preserved by sugar (drained, glacé or crystallised)	13 10
20.05	Jams, fruit jellies, marmalades, fruit purée and fruit pastes, being cooked preparations, containing added sweetening matter	13 2
		per cent.
20.06	Fruit otherwise prepared or preserved, containing added sweetening matter:—	
	Ginger	9
	Other	$2\frac{1}{4}$

SCHEDULE 2

Tariff heading	Description of Imported Composite Sugar Products
17.05 (A) and (B)	Sugar and invert sugar, flavoured or coloured.

SCHEDULE 3

Description of goods	Rate of surcharge repayment per bulk barrel of 36 gallons
Lager	10·5d.
All beer other than lager	9·4d.

EXPLANATORY NOTE

(*This Note is not part of the Order.*)

This order provides for reductions on and after 31st October 1969 in the average rates of surcharge payable on imported composite sugar products of the descriptions specified in Schedule 1 and in the average rates of surcharge repayment in respect of exported goods of the descriptions specified in Schedule 3. These correspond to the reductions in surcharge rates effected by the Sugar (Rates of Surcharge and Surcharge Repayments) (No. 12) Order 1969 (S.I. 1969/1527). Provision is also made for certain imported composite sugar products to be treated as not containing any sugar or invert sugar.

STATUTORY INSTRUMENTS

1969 No. 1529 (S. 122)

POLICE

The Special Constables (Pensions) (Scotland) Amendment (No. 2) Regulations 1969

Made - - -	*27th October* 1969
Laid before Parliament	*31st October* 1969
Coming into Operation	*3rd November* 1969

In exercise of the powers conferred on me by section 26 of the Police (Scotland) Act 1967(a) (as read with section 1(2) of the Police Pensions Act 1961(b)), and of all other powers enabling me in that behalf, and after consultation with the Joint Central Committee and such bodies and associations as are mentioned in section 26(9) (b) of the said Act of 1967, I hereby make the following regulations:—

1. These regulations may be cited as the Special Constables (Pensions) (Scotland) Amendment (No. 2) Regulations 1969 and shall come into operation on 3rd November 1969.

2. In these regulations any reference to the Instrument of 1966 is a reference to the Special Constables (Pensions) (Scotland) Regulations 1966(c), as amended (d).

3.—(1) In the application of the Police Pensions Regulations 1966(e) to the calculation of the pension of the widow, or the allowance of a child, of a special constable under the Instrument of 1966, those regulations shall apply as amended by the Police Pensions (Amendment) (No.2) Regulations 1969(f) (which amendments relate to increases in widows' and children's awards).

(2) In accordance with paragraph (1) of this regulation, for regulation 2(1) of the Instrument of 1966 (which, as set out in the Special Constables (Pensions) (Scotland) Amendment Regulations 1969(g), defines the expression "the principal regulations") there shall be substituted the following paragraph:—

'(1) In these regulations the expression "the principal regulations" means the Police Pensions Regulations 1966, as amended by the Police Pensions (Amendment) (No. 2) Regulations 1967(h), the Police Pensions (Amendment) Regulations 1968(i), the Police Pensions (Amendment) Regulations 1969 and the Police Pensions (Amendment) (No. 2) Regulations 1969.'.

William Ross,
One of Her Majesty's Principal
Secretaries of State.

St. Andrew's House,
Edinburgh.

27th October 1969.

(a) 1967 c. 77.   (b) 1961 c. 35.   (c) S.I. 1966/1625 (1966 III, p. 5066).
(d) The relevant amending instruments are S.I. 1967/1553, 1968/1995, 1969/989 (1967 III, p. 4315; 1968 III, p. 5425; 1969 II, p. 2903).
(e) S.I. 1966/1582 (1966 III, p. 4894).   (f) S.I. 1969/1484 (1969 III, p. 4745).
(g) S.I. 1969/989 (1969 II, p. 2903).
(h) S.I. 1967/1500 (1967 III, p. 4204).
(i) S.I. 1968/530 (1968 I, p. 1269).

EXPLANATORY NOTE
(*This Note is not part of the Regulations.*)

These Regulations amend the Special Constables (Pensions) (Scotland) Regulations 1966 which give to special constables and their dependants certain pension benefits for which members of police forces and their dependants are eligible.

The Police Pensions (Amendment) (No. 2) Regulations 1969 provide that certain discretionary benefits payable to the dependants of members of police forces shall be increased.

These Regulations provide for similar increases in the discretionary benefits payable to the dependants of special constables.

STATUTORY INSTRUMENTS

1969 No. 1532

TOWN AND COUNTRY PLANNING, ENGLAND AND WALES

The Town and Country Planning (Control of Advertisements) Regulations 1969

Made - - - -	*29th October* 1969
Laid before Parliament	*7th November* 1969
Coming into Operation	*1st January* 1970

ARRANGEMENT OF REGULATIONS

PART I

CITATION, COMMENCEMENT, INTERPRETATION, APPLICATION AND REVOCATION

PART II

GENERAL PROVISIONS

PART III

ADVERTISEMENTS THE DISPLAY OF WHICH MAY BE UNDERTAKEN WITHOUT EXPRESS CONSENT

PART IV

APPLICATIONS FOR EXPRESS CONSENT

PART V
SPECIAL CASE

PART VI
REVOCATION AND MODIFICATION OF EXPRESS CONSENT

PART VII
AREAS OF SPECIAL CONTROL

PART VIII
MISCELLANEOUS

SCHEDULES

The Minister of Housing and Local Government in exercise of his powers under sections 34, 126 and 217 of the Town and Country Planning Act 1962(a), and section 63 of that Act as amended by section 101 and Schedule 8 to the Town and Country Planning Act 1968(b), and of all other powers enabling him in that behalf, hereby makes the following regulations:—

PART I

CITATION, COMMENCEMENT, INTERPRETATION, APPLICATION AND REVOCATION

Citation and Commencement

1. These regulations may be cited as the Town and Country Planning (Control of Advertisements) Regulations 1969, and shall come into operation on 1st January 1970.

(a) 1962 c. 38.   (b) 1968 c. 72.

Interpretation

2.—(1) In these regulations—

"the Act" means the Town and Country Planning Act 1962;

"advertisement" means any word, letter, model, sign, placard, board, notice, device or representation, whether illuminated or not, in the nature of, and employed wholly or partly for the purposes of, advertisement, announcement or direction (excluding any such thing employed wholly as a memorial or as a railway signal), and (without prejudice to the preceding provisions of this definition) includes any hoarding or similar structure used, or adapted for use, for the display of advertisements, and references to the display of advertisements shall be construed accordingly;

"advertiser" means a person who himself, or by his servant or agent, undertakes or maintains the display of an advertisement;

"area of special control" means an area defined under regulation 26 as an area of special control in respect of the display of advertisements;

"building" includes any structure or erection and any part of a building as so defined;

"business premises" has the meaning assigned to it by regulation 14(3);

"the Common Council" means the Common Council of the City of London;

"enactment" includes an enactment in any local or private Act of Parliament and an order, rule, regulation, byelaw or scheme made under an Act of Parliament;

"illuminated advertisement" means an advertisement which is designed or adapted to be illuminated by artificial lighting, directly or by reflection, and which is so illuminated for the purposes of advertisement, announcement or direction at any time after the date on which these regulations come into operation;

"land" includes buildings, and land covered with water;

"local authority" means the council of a county, county borough or county district, the Common Council, the Greater London Council, the council of a London borough and any other authority (except the Receiver for the Metropolitan Police District) who are a local authority within the meaning of the Local Loans Act 1875(a), and includes any drainage board and any joint board or joint committee if all the constituent authorities are such local authorities as aforesaid;

"local planning authority" means, for each county or county borough, the council of that county or county borough, for each London borough, the council of that London borough, for the City of London, the Common Council, and for any united district established by the Minister under section 2 of the Act, means the joint planning board constituted for that district, and references to the local planning authority in these regulations shall, in relation to the exercise of any functions delegated by the local planning authority in accordance with regulations made under section 3 of the Act, be construed as references to the authority to whom those functions are for the time being delegated;

"the Minister", as respects Wales and Monmouthshire, means the Secretary of State, and otherwise means the Minister of Housing and Local Government;

"owner" in relation to any land, has the meaning assigned to it by section 221(1) of the Act;

(a) 1875 c. 83.

"site", in relation to an advertisement, means any land, or any building other than an advertisement as herein defined, on which an advertisement is displayed;

"specified classes" means the classes of advertisements specified in regulation 14(1);

"standard conditions" means the standard conditions set out in Schedule 1 to these regulations;

"statutory undertakers" means persons authorised by any enactment to carry on any railway, light railway, tramway, road transport, water transport, canal, inland navigation, dock, harbour, pier or lighthouse undertaking, or any undertaking for the supply of electricity, gas, hydraulic power or water, and "statutory undertaking" shall be construed accordingly, and, in relation to the display of advertisements of descriptions specified in Class I in regulation 14(1), shall be deemed to include any undertaking carried on by the National Coal Board for the winning or supply of coal, and any undertaking carried on by the British Airports Authority or by the Post Office for the purposes of their respective functions.

(2) Reference in these regulations to the person displaying an advertisement shall be construed as reference to the advertiser, and shall be deemed to include—

(a) the owner and occupier of the land on which the advertisement is displayed; and

(b) any person to whose goods, trade, business or other concerns publicity is given by the advertisement.

(3) A regulation or schedule referred to only by number in these regulations means the regulation or schedule so numbered in these regulations.

(4) The Interpretation Act 1889(a) shall apply to the interpretation of these regulations as it applies to the interpretation of an Act of Parliament.

Application

3.—(1) These regulations shall apply to the display on land in England and Wales of all advertisements, except any advertisement—

(a) displayed on enclosed land, and not readily visible from land outside the enclosure wherein it is displayed or from any part of such enclosure over which there is a public right of way or to which there is public right of access;

(b) displayed within a building, other than an advertisement of a description specified in regulation 12;

(c) displayed on or in a vehicle;

(d) incorporated in, and forming part of, the fabric of a building, other than a building used principally for the display of such advertisements or a hoarding or similar structure;

(e) displayed on an article for sale or on the package or other container in which an article is sold, or displayed on the pump, dispenser or other container from which an article is sold; being an advertisement wholly with reference to the article for sale, which is not an illuminated advertisement and does not exceed 0·1 square metre in area;

(2) For the purposes of this regulation—

(a) "article" includes a gas or liquid;

(a) 1889 c. 63.

(b) the expression "enclosed land" means land which is wholly or for the most part enclosed within a hedge, fence, or wall or similar screen or structure, and shall be deemed to include any railway station (and its yards) or bus station, together with their forecourts, whether enclosed or not; but shall not include any public park, public garden or other land held for the use or enjoyment of the public, or (save as hereinbefore specified) any enclosed railway land normally used for the carriage of passengers or goods by rail;

(c) "vehicle" means a vehicle normally employed as a moving vehicle on any highway or railway, or a vessel normally employed as a moving vessel on any inland waterway; but shall not include any such vehicle or vessel during any period when it is used primarily for the display of advertisements;

(d) no advertisement shall be deemed to be displayed within a building unless there is access to the advertisement from inside the building;

(e) no advertisement shall be deemed to form part of the fabric of a building by reason only of being affixed to, or painted on, the building.

Revocation

4. The Town and Country Planning (Control of Advertisements) Regulations 1960(a) and the Town and Country Planning (Control of Advertisements) (Amendment) Regulations 1965(b) are hereby revoked; without prejudice however to the validity of anything done thereunder before the date of the coming into operation of these regulations: and any order, claim or application made, consent granted, direction given or notice served before the said date, shall, if in force immediately before that date, continue in force and have effect as if made, granted, given or served, under the corresponding provision of these regulations or, if there is no corresponding provision, shall continue in force and have effect as if these regulations had not been made and as if the regulations hereby revoked had not been revoked.

PART II

GENERAL PROVISIONS

Control of advertisements to be exercised in the interests of amenity and public safety

5.—(1) The powers conferred by these regulations with respect to the grant or refusal of consent for the display of advertisements, the revocation or modification of such consent, and the discontinuance of the display of advertisements with consent deemed to be granted, shall be exercisable only in the interests of amenity and public safety.

(2) When exercising such powers a local planning authority,

(a) shall, in the interests of amenity, determine the suitability of the use of a site for the display of advertisements in the light of the general characteristics of the locality, including the presence therein of any feature of historic, architectural, cultural or similar interest; and when assessing the general characteristics of a locality the authority may disregard any advertisements therein being displayed;

(b) shall, in the interests of public safety, have regard to the safety of persons who may use any road, railway, waterway (including any coastal waters), dock, harbour or airfield affected or likely to be affected by any display

---

(a) S.I. 1960/695 (1960 III, p. 3253).   (b) S.I. 1965/555 (1965 I, p. 1722).

of advertisements; and shall in particular consider whether any such display is likely to obscure, or hinder the ready interpretation of, any road traffic sign, railway signal, or aid to navigation by water or air; but without prejudice to their power to have regard to any other material factor.

(3) In the determination of an application for consent for the display of advertisements, or where the revocation or modification of a consent is under consideration, regard may be had to any material change in circumstances likely to occur within the period for which the consent is required or granted.

(4) Save as hereinafter provided, and subject to the provisions of these regulations, express consent for the display of advertisements shall not contain any limitation or restriction relating to any particular subject matter or class of subject matter or to the content or design of any subject matter to be displayed, but shall take effect as consent to the use of a site for the purpose of displaying advertisements in the manner authorised by the consent whether by the erection of structures on the site or otherwise as the case may be:

Provided that where an application for consent relates to the display of a particular advertisement the local planning authority may have regard to the effect on amenity and public safety of the display of such advertisement.

Consent required for the display of advertisements

6.—(1) No advertisement may be displayed without consent granted by the local planning authority or by the Minister on an application in that behalf (referred to in these regulations as "express consent"), or deemed to be granted under paragraph (2) below.

(2) Consent shall be deemed to be granted for the display of any advertisement displayed in accordance with any provision of these regulations whereby advertisements of that description may be displayed without express consent; and where the display of such advertisements is allowed subject to the power of the local planning authority to require the discontinuance of the display under regulation 16, the consent so deemed to be granted shall be consent limited until such time as a notice served under regulation 16 takes effect; without prejudice however to the provisions of regulation 27 as respects the removal of advertisements which are being displayed in an area of special control.

(3) In so far as the nature of the consent permits, consent for the display of advertisements shall enure for the benefit of the land to which the consent relates and of all persons for the time being interested in that land; without prejudice however to the provisions of these regulations as respects the revocation or modification of an express consent.

(4) Save only as hereinafter excepted, it shall be a condition (whether expressly imposed or not) of every consent granted by or under these regulations that before any advertisement is displayed on land in pursuance of the consent the permission of the owner of that land or other person entitled to grant permission in relation thereto shall be obtained; except where an advertisement of the description specified in regulation 9(1)(b) is required to be displayed notwithstanding that such permission is not obtained.

The standard conditions

7. Without prejudice to the power of the local planning authority to impose additional conditions upon a grant of consent under these regulations, the standard conditions set out in Schedule 1 shall, subject to the provisions of these regulations, apply without further notice—

(a) in the case of the conditions set out in Part I of that schedule, to the display of all advertisements; and

(b) in the case of the condition set out in Part II of that schedule, only to advertisements being displayed with consent deemed to be granted by these regulations, or granted under regulation 23.

Contravention of regulations

8.—(1) A person displaying an advertisement in contravention of these regulations shall be liable on summary conviction of an offence under section 63(2) of the Act to a fine of one hundred pounds and, in the case of a continuing offence, five pounds for each day during which the offence continues after conviction.

(2) Failure to observe any condition relating to the maintenance of an advertisement or of the site used for the display thereof, or to the satisfactory removal of an advertisement, shall not be a contravention of these regulations for the purposes of section 63(2) of the Act in so far as concerns any person who is only deemed by virtue of section 63(3) of the Act to display the advertisement, unless such person has failed to comply with a notice served on him by the local planning authority under this paragraph requiring him to comply with the condition within such period (not being less than twenty-eight days after the service thereof) as may be specified in the notice.

PART III

ADVERTISEMENTS THE DISPLAY OF WHICH MAY BE UNDERTAKEN WITHOUT EXPRESS CONSENT

Election notices, statutory advertisements and traffic signs

9.—(1) The display of advertisements of the following descriptions may be undertaken without express consent:—

(a) any advertisement relating specifically to a pending parliamentary or local government election, not being an advertisement to which sub-paragraph (b) of this paragraph applies;

(b) advertisements required to be displayed by an enactment for the time being in force, or by Standing Orders of either House of Parliament, including (but without prejudice to the generality hereof) advertisements the display of which is so required as a condition of the valid exercise of any other power, or proper performance of any function, given or imposed by an enactment;

(c) advertisements which are traffic signs employed wholly for the control, guidance or safety of traffic, and displayed by a local highway traffic or police authority in accordance with regulations and general directions made by the Minister of Transport and Secretary of State acting jointly, or in accordance with an authorisation and any relevant directions given by either of them.

(2) Consent deemed to be granted by virtue of these regulations for the display of advertisements of the foregoing descriptions shall be subject to the following conditions in addition to the standard conditions:—

(a) Where advertisements of the description specified in paragraph 1(b) above could, apart from this regulation be displayed as advertisements of a specified class, they shall conform with any provision of regulation 14 as respects size, number or height in relation to the display of advertisements of that class, and otherwise shall not exceed in those respects what may reasonably be considered necessary to achieve the purpose for which the display is required; without prejudice, however, to the express requirements in regard to size, number or height as aforesaid of any enactment or Standing Orders under which such advertisements are displayed.

(b) An advertisement of the description specified in paragraph (1)(a) above shall be removed within fourteen days after the close of the poll in the election to which the advertisement relates; and any other advertisement displayed for a temporary purpose in accordance with this regulation shall be removed as soon as may be after the expiry of the period during which such advertisement is required or authorised to be displayed, or, if no such period is specified, shall be removed within a reasonable time after the purpose for which such advertisement was required or authorised to be displayed is satisfied.

(3) With respect to the display of advertisements of the description specified in paragraph 1(a) above standard condition 1 shall not apply.

Display of advertisements by local planning authorities

10.—(1) Subject to this regulation, a local planning authority may without express consent display advertisements on land in their area; but shall not display in an area of special control any advertisement for the display of which they could not, by virtue of the provisions of regulation 27, grant express consent.

(2) Consent deemed to be granted for the display of advertisements to which this regulation relates shall be subject to service of a notice by the Minister, under regulation 16, requiring the discontinuance of the display.

Advertisements displayed on 1st August 1948

11.—(1) Advertisements displayed on 1st August 1948 may continue to be displayed without express consent, subject to the power of the local planning authority to require the discontinuance of the display under regulation 16.

(2) Nothing in this regulation shall restrict the exercise by a local planning authority of any power hereinafter conferred on them to decide an application voluntarily made to them or to take action in respect of any contravention of these regulations.

(3) Reference in this regulation to the display of advertisements shall be construed as reference also to the use of a site for the display of advertisements.

Provided that consent deemed in consequence to be granted for the continued use for the purpose of displaying advertisements of any site which was being used for that purpose on 1st August 1948 shall be subject to the following conditions and limitations—

(a) there shall be no substantial increase in the extent, or substantial alteration in the manner, of the use of the site for that purpose on that date;

(b) where a building or structure on which advertisements were being displayed on that date is required under any enactment to be removed, consent under this regulation shall not extend to the erection of any building or structure on which to continue the display of such advertisements without substantial alteration in the manner of the display.

Control of advertisements displayed within buildings

12.—(1) Without prejudice to the provisions of regulation 3, the display of an advertisement within a building so as to be visible from outside that building shall, if the advertisement is—

(a) an illuminated advertisement, or

(b) an advertisement displayed within any building used principally for the display of advertisements, or

(c) an advertisement any part of which is within a distance of one metre from any external door, window or other opening, through which the advertisement is visible from outside the building,

be subject to these regulations.

(2) Any advertisement the display of which is made subject to these regulations by paragraph (1) above, may be displayed without express consent, subject, except where the advertisement is of a description specified in regulation 9, to the power of the local planning authority to require the discontinuance of the display under regulation 16.

(3) For the purpose of the exercise of any of the powers conferred by the provisions of these regulations, the display of any advertisement made subject to these regulations by paragraph (1) above shall be treated as if it were the display in accordance with the provisions of regulation 14 of an advertisement of a specified class.

Display of advertisements after the expiration of express consent

13.—(1) Except where the local planning authority when granting express consent impose a condition to the contrary, or where the renewal of consent is applied for and is refused, advertisements displayed with express consent granted under these regulations may on the expiration of the consent continue to be displayed without express consent, subject to the power of the local planning authority to require the discontinuance of the display under regulation 16.

(2) Consent deemed by virtue of regulation 6(2) to be granted in respect of the continuance of such display shall be subject to the like conditions as those to which the immediately preceding express consent was subject, and, unless previously brought to an end under these regulations, shall expire when the site ceases to be used for such display.

The specified classes

14.—(1) Advertisements of the following classes may be displayed without express consent, subject to the provisions of this regulation and to the power of the local planning authority to require the discontinuance of the display under regulation 16:—

CLASS I—Functional advertisements of local authorities, statutory undertakers and public transport undertakers.

Advertisements employed wholly for the purposes of announcement or direction in relation to any of the functions of a local authority or to the operation of a statutory undertaking or of a public transport undertaking engaged in the carriage of passengers in a manner similar to that of a statutory undertaking, being advertisements which are reasonably required to be displayed in the manner in which they are displayed in order to secure the safe or efficient performance of those functions, or operation of that under-taking, and which cannot be displayed as such, or in such a manner, under the provisions of this regulation relating to advertisements of any other of the specified classes.

CLASS II—Miscellaneous advertisements relating to premises on which they are displayed.

(a) Advertisements for the purpose of identification, direction or warning with respect to the land or buildings on which they are displayed, and not exceeding 0·2 square metre in area in the case of any such advertisement.

(b) Advertisements relating to any person, partnership or company separately carrying on a profession, business or trade at the premises where any such advertisement is displayed; limited to one advertisement, not exceeding 0·3 square metre in area, in respect of each such person, partnership or company, or, in the case of premises with entrances on different road frontages, one such advertisement at each of two such entrances.

(c) Advertisements relating to any institution of a religious, educational, cultural, recreational or medical or similar character, or to any hotel, inn or public house, block of flats, club, boarding house or hostel situate on the land on which any such advertisement is displayed; limited to one advertisement, not exceeding 1·2 square metres in area, in respect of each such premises or, in the case of premises with entrances on different road frontages, two such advertisements displayed on different road frontages of the premises.

CLASS III—Certain advertisements of a temporary nature.

(a) Advertisements relating to the sale or letting of the land on which they are displayed; limited, in respect of each such sale or letting, to one advertisement consisting of a board (whether or not attached to a building) not exceeding 2 square metres in area, or of two conjoined boards, together not exceeding 2·3 square metres in area; no such advertisement, when displayed on a building, to project further than one metre from the face of the building.

(b) Advertisements announcing a sale of goods or livestock, and displayed on the land where such goods or livestock are situated or where such sale is held, not being land which is normally used, whether at regular intervals or otherwise, for the purpose of holding such sales; limited to one advertisement not exceeding 1·2 square metres in area at each place where such advertisements may be displayed.

(c) Advertisements relating to the carrying out of building or similar work on the land on which they are displayed, not being land which is normally used, whether at regular intervals or otherwise, for the purpose of carrying out such work; limited to one advertisement (on each road frontage of the land) in respect of each separate development project, being an advertisement not exceeding, in aggregate, in the case of an advertisement referring to one person, 2 square metres, or, in the case of an advertisement referring to more than one person, 2 square metres together with an additional 0·4 square metre in respect of each additional person referred to, and, in either case, together with 0·2 of the area permitted above for the name, if any, of the particular development project:

Provided that where such an advertisement is displayed more than

10 metres from a highway, there shall be substituted for the references to 2 square metres references to 3 square metres, and for the reference to 0·4 square metre a reference to 1·6 square metres;

And provided also that any person carrying out such work may, if an advertisement displayed in accordance with the preceding provisions of this paragraph does not refer to him, display a separate advertisement which does so, not exceeding 0·5 square metre in area, for a period not exceeding three months, on each road frontage of the land.

(d) Advertisements announcing any local event of a religious, educational, cultural, political, social or recreational character, and advertisements relating to any temporary matter in connection with an event or local activity of such a character, not in either case being an event or local activity promoted or carried on for commercial purposes; limited to a display of advertisements occupying an area not exceeding a total of 0·6 square metre on any premises.

(e) Advertisements relating to any demonstration of agricultural methods or processes on the land on which they are displayed; limited, in respect of each such demonstration to a display of advertisements occupying an area not exceeding a total of 1·2 square metres, no one of which exceeds 0·4 square metre in area, the maximum period of display for any demonstration to be six months in any period of twelve months.

CLASS IV—Advertisements on business premises.

Advertisements displayed on business premises wholly with reference to all or any of the following matters: the business or other activity carried on, the goods sold or services provided, and the name and qualifications of the person carrying on such business or activity or supplying such goods or services, on those premises:

Provided that—

(a) no such advertisement may be displayed on the wall of a shop, unless the wall contains a shop window;

(b) no such advertisement may be displayed so that the highest part of the advertisement is above the level of the bottom of any first-floor window in the wall on which it is displayed;

(c) the space which may be occupied by such advertisements on any external face of a building in an area of special control shall not exceed 0·1 of the overall area of that face up to a height of 3·6 metres from ground level; and the area occupied by any such advertisement shall, notwithstanding that it is displayed in some other manner, be computed as if the advertisement as a whole were displayed flat against the face of the building.

CLASS V—Advertisements on the forecourts of business premises.

Advertisements displayed on any forecourt of business premises wholly with reference to all or any of the matters specified in Class IV above; limited as respects the aggregate area of the advertisements displayed under this class on any such forecourt to 4·5 square metres:

Provided that a building with a forecourt on two or more frontages shall be treated as having a separate forecourt on each of those frontages.

CLASS VI—Flag advertisements.

Any advertisement in the form of a flag which is attached to a single flagstaff fixed in an upright position on the roof of a building, and which bears no inscription or emblem other than the name or device of a person or persons occupying the building.

(2) Consent deemed to be granted by virtue of these regulations for the display of advertisements of the foregoing classes shall be subject to the following conditions in addition to the standard conditions—

(a) no such advertisements, other than an advertisement of Class I, shall contain letters, figures, symbols, emblems or devices of a height exceeding 0·75 metre or, in an area of special control, 0·31 metre until 31st December 1972, and thereafter, save as respects advertisements first displayed on or before that date, 0·3 metre;

(b) no such advertisement, other than an advertisement of Class I, or Class VI shall be displayed so that the highest part of the advertisement is above 4·6 metres from ground level, or, in an area of special control, above 3·6 metres from ground level:

Provided that an advertisement of Class III(a) relating to the sale or letting of part of a building above such height limit may be displayed on or below that part of the building at the lowest level above that limit at which it is reasonably practicable to display the advertisement.

(c) No such advertisement shall be illuminated except as follows—

(i) advertisements of Class I, illuminated in a manner reasonably required to achieve the purpose of the advertisement;

(ii) advertisements of Class II or Class IV for the purpose of indicating that medical or similar services or supplies are available at the premises on which they are displayed; and illuminated in a manner reasonably required for that purpose;

(d) save as hereinafter provided, no advertisement of Class III relating to a sale or other matter which is due to start or take place on a specified date shall be displayed earlier than twenty-eight days before that date, and every advertisement of that class shall be removed within fourteen days after the conclusion of the event or other matter to which it relates.

Provided that an advertisement of Class III relating to the carrying out on land of building or similar works may be displayed only while such works are in progress.

(3) In this regulation the following expressions have the meaning hereinafter respectively assigned to them, namely:—

(a) "business premises" means, save as hereinafter provided, any building normally used for the purpose of carrying on therein any professional, commercial or industrial undertaking, or any building (other than an institution in respect of which advertisements of Class II(c) may be displayed) normally used for the purpose of providing therein services to members of the public or of any association, and includes public restaurants, licensed premises and places of public entertainment; but, in the case of any building normally used only partly for such purposes, means only the part of the building normally used for such purposes: Provided that the expression shall not include—

(i) any building designed for use as one or more separate dwellings, unless the building was normally used immediately before 1st September 1949 for the purpose of carrying on therein any such undertaking or providing therein any such services as aforesaid, or unless the building has been, or is at any time, adapted for use as business premises by the construction of a shop front or the making of a material alteration of a similar kind to the external appearance of the building,

(ii) any forecourt or other land forming part of the curtilage of a building;

(iii) any fence, wall or similar screen or structure, unless it forms part of the fabric of a building constituting business premises.

(b) in relation to Class V "forecourt" includes any fence, wall or similar screen or structure enclosing a forecourt and not forming part of the fabric of a building constituting business premises.

(c) in relation to the display of advertisements on any building, "ground level" means the ground-floor level of that building;

(d) "recreational" in relation to an institution shall not apply to any institution for the carrying on of sports, games or physical training primarily as a commercial undertaking.

(4) On the determination of an application for express consent made in respect of an advertisement of a specified class, the provisions of this regulation whereby advertisements may be displayed without express consent shall cease to apply with respect to that advertisement; and, in the event of refusal of consent, or of the grant of consent subject to conditions in the nature of restrictions as to the site on which, or the manner in which, the display may be undertaken, or both, the provisions of this regulation whereby the display of advertisements may be undertaken without express consent shall not apply to the subsequent display on the same land of any advertisement in contravention of that refusal or of those conditions, by, or on behalf of, the person whose application was so refused or granted subject to conditions.

(5) The conditions and limitations in this regulation apply only to the display without express consent of advertisements of the description therein mentioned, and shall not restrict the powers of a local planning authority in regard to the determination in accordance with these regulations of any application for express consent.

Power to exclude application of regulation 14

15.—(1) If the Minister is satisfied, whether upon representations made to him by the local planning authority or otherwise, that the display of advertisements of a class or description specified in regulation 14 should not be undertaken in any particular area or in any particular case without express consent, he may direct that the provisions of that regulation shall not apply to the display of such advertisements in that area or in that case.

(2) Notice of any direction given by the Minister under this regulation with respect to an area shall be published by the local planning authority in at least one newspaper circulating in the locality in which the area is situate, and, unless the Minister otherwise directs, on the same or a subsequent date in the London Gazette; and such notice shall contain a concise statement of the effect of the direction and name a place or places in that locality where a copy thereof and of a map defining the area to which it relates may be seen at all reasonable hours.

(3) Notice of any direction given by the Minister under this regulation in a particular case shall be served by the local planning authority on the owner and on any occupier of the land to which the direction relates, and on any other person who, to the knowledge of the authority, proposes to display on such land an advertisement of the class or description referred to in the direction.

(4) A direction given under this regulation with respect to an area shall come into force on the date specified in the notice relating thereto, being a date not less than fourteen, and not more than twenty-eight days after the first

publication of the notice; and a direction given under this regulation in a particular case shall come into force on the date on which notice thereof is served on the occupier, or if there is no occupier, on the owner of the land.

Power to require the discontinuance of the display of advertisements displayed with deemed consent

16.—(1) Subject to these regulations, the local planning authority, if they consider it expedient to do so in the interests of amenity or public safety, may serve a notice under this regulation (referred to in these regulations as a "discontinuance notice") requiring the discontinuance of the display of an advertisement with consent deemed to be granted under these regulations, other than an advertisement of a description specified in regulation 9:

Provided that, in relation to the display in accordance with the provisions of regulation 14 of an advertisement of a specified class, the authority shall not serve a discontinuance notice unless they are satisfied that the service of such a notice is required to remedy a substantial injury to the amenity of the locality or a danger to members of the public.

(2) Where the local planning authority serve a discontinuance notice, the notice—

(*a*) shall be served on the advertiser and on the owner and occupier of the land on which the advertisement is displayed, and

(*b*) may, if the local planning authority think fit, also be served on any other person displaying the advertisement.

(3) A discontinuance notice shall—

(*a*) specify the advertisement to the display of which it relates,

(*b*) specify a period within which the display is to be discontinued, and

(*c*) contain a full statement of the reasons why the authority consider it expedient in the interests of amenity and public safety that the display should be discontinued.

(4) Subject to paragraph (5) below, a discontinuance notice shall take effect at the end of such period (not being less than one month after the service thereof) as may be specified in the notice:

Provided that if an appeal is made to the Minister under regulation 22 the notice shall be of no effect pending the final determination or withdrawal of the appeal.

(5) The local planning authority by a notice served on the advertiser may withdraw a discontinuance notice at any time before it takes effect or may where no appeal to the Minister is pending under regulation 22 from time to time vary a discontinuance notice by extending the period specified therein for the taking effect of the notice: and on any such variation the period for appeal to the Minister under regulation 22(2) shall be enlarged by the number of days by which the period specified was extended or further extended.

(6) The local planning authority shall on serving on the advertiser a notice of withdrawal or variation under paragraph (5) above send a copy thereof to every other person who was served with the discontinuance notice.

(7) Notwithstanding the provisions of paragraph (1) above, but without prejudice thereto, a discontinuance notice may require the discontinuance of the use of land for the display of advertisements with consent deemed to be granted under these regulations, other than advertisements of a description specified in regulation 9; and in relation to a notice served in pursuance of this paragraph

there shall be substituted for references in these regulations to the display of advertisements references to the use of land for the display of advertisements.

PART IV

APPLICATIONS FOR EXPRESS CONSENT

How to apply

17.—(1) Subject to this regulation an application to a local planning authority for consent to display advertisements shall be made on a form issued by the local planning authority and obtainable from that authority or from the council with whom the application is to be lodged, and shall include such particulars and shall be accompanied by such plans, together with such additional number of copies (not exceeding two) of the form and plans, as may be required by the directions of the local planning authority printed on the form.

(2) The application shall be lodged—

(a) where the land to which the application refers is in the City of London, with the Common Council;

(b) where the land is in a London borough, with the council of that London borough;

(c) where the land is outside Greater London, with the council of the county borough or county district in which the land is situate and the council of a county district with whom an application is lodged shall, where necessary, transmit it to the local planning authority to whom it is made.

(3) On receipt of the application the local planning authority shall send an acknowledgement in writing to the applicant and may by a direction addressed to him in writing require such information, in addition to that given in the application, as may be requisite to enable them to determine the matter in respect of which the application is made, to be given to them, or such evidence as they may reasonably call for to verify any particulars of information given to them to be produced to an officer of the authority.

(4) The Minister may restrict, by direction given either generally or in any particular case or class of case, the amount of particulars, plans or information which an applicant may be required to furnish under this regulation.

(5) The provisions of paragraph (1) above shall be without prejudice to the acceptance by a local planning authority of an application in writing made otherwise than on the form therein referred to, in any case in which the information provided is sufficient to enable the authority to determine the application.

Duty to consult with respect to an application

18.—(1) A local planning authority shall, before granting consent for any display of advertisements, consult with the following authorities, persons, or bodies, namely:—

(a) with any neighbouring local planning authority whose area, or any part thereof, appears likely to be affected by the display of advertisements to which the application relates;

(b) with the council of any county district in whose area land to which the application relates is situate; except where consultation concerning any application or class of application is agreed by the local planning authority and such council to be unnecessary;

(c) where it appears to the local planning authority that the display of advertisements to which the application relates may affect the safety of persons using—

  (i) any trunk road as defined in section 295 of the Highways Act 1959(a) being a trunk road which is in England, with the Minister of Transport;

  (ii) any railway, waterway (including any coastal waters), dock, harbour or airfield, with the British Transport Commission, or other authority, statutory undertaker, body or person responsible for the operation thereof, and, in the case of any coastal waters, the Corporation of Trinity House;

(d) with such authorities, persons or bodies as the Minister may direct under regulation 28.

(2) The local planning authority shall give to any authority, person or body with whom they are required to consult as aforesaid, not less than fourteen days' notice that an application is to be taken into consideration and shall, in determining the application, take into account any representation made by such authority, person or body.

Power of local planning authority to deal with applications

19.—(1) Subject to the provisions of these regulations, where application for consent for the display of advertisements is made to the local planning authority, that authority may grant consent subject to the standard conditions specified in Part I of Schedule 1 and to such additional conditions (if any) as they think fit, or may refuse consent:

Provided that where the application relates to the display in accordanc: with the provisions of regulation 14 of an advertisement of a specified class the authority shall not refuse consent, or impose a condition more restrictive in effect than any provision of regulation 14 in relation to advertisements of that class, unless they are satisfied that such refusal or condition is required to prevent or remedy a substantial injury to the amenity of the locality or a danger to members of the public.

(2) Without prejudice to the generality of paragraph (1) above and subject always to the provisions of regulation 5, conditions may be imposed on the grant of consent hereunder—

  (a) for regulating the display of advertisements to which the consent relates, or the use of land by the applicant for the display of advertisements (whether or not it is land in respect of which the application was made), or requiring the carrying out of works on any such land, so far as appears to the local planning authority to be expedient for the purposes of or in connection with the display of advertisements authorised by the consent;

  (b) for requiring the removal of any advertisement authorised by the consent, or the discontinuance of any use of land so authorised, at the expiration of a specified period, and the carrying out of any works required for the reinstatement of land at the expiration of that period.

(3) Consent under this regulation may be—

  (a) for the display of any particular advertisement or advertisements with or without illumination, as the application requires, or

  (b) for the use of certain land for the display of advertisements in a specified manner, whether by reference to the number, siting, size or illumi-

(a) 1959 c. 25.

nation of advertisements or structures intended for such display, or the design or appearance of any such structure, or otherwise.

(4) The power to grant consent for the display of advertisements under these regulations shall include power to grant consent for the retention on land of any advertisement being displayed thereon before the date of the application or for the continuance of any use of land for the display of advertisements begun before that date; and reference in these regulations to consent for the display of advertisements and to applications for such consent shall be construed accordingly.

Consent to be limited

20.—(1) Every grant of express consent shall be for a fixed period which shall not be longer than five years from the date of grant of consent without the approval of the Minister, or shorter than five years unless so required by the application or considered expedient by the authority in the light of the provisions of regulation 5; and if no period is specified the consent shall have effect as consent for five years.

(2) Where the authority grant consent for a period shorter than five years they shall (unless the application required such a consent) state in writing their reasons for doing so, and the limitation in respect of time shall for the purposes of these regulations be deemed to be a condition imposed upon the granting of consent.

(3) Provision may be made, in granting consent, for the term thereof to run from the subsequent inception of the display to which the consent relates or from a subsequent date not later than six months after the date on which the consent is granted, whichever is the earlier.

(4) At any time within a period of six months before the expiry of a consent granted under these regulations, application may be made for the renewal thereof, and the provisions of these regulations relating to applications for consent and to the determination thereof shall apply where application is made for such renewal.

Notification of local planning authority's decision

21.—(1) The grant or refusal by a local planning authority of consent for the display of advertisements shall be in writing and, where the authority decide to grant consent subject to conditions in addition to the standard conditions, or to refuse consent, the reasons for their decision shall be stated in writing.

(2) The local planning authority shall, within two months from the date of receipt of the application, give notice to the applicant of their decision or, if the application has been referred to the Minister in accordance with directions given by him under regulation 28, shall within two months as aforesaid notify the applicant accordingly:

Provided that such period of two months may, at any time before the expiration thereof, be extended by agreement in writing made between the authority and the applicant.

Appeals to the Minister

22.—(1) Where, on application being made for consent under these regulations, consent is refused by the local planning authority or is granted by them subject to conditions, the applicant may appeal to the Minister:

Provided that the Minister shall not be required to entertain an appeal under this regulation if it appears to him having regard to the provisions of these regulations, that consent for the display of advertisements in respect of which application was made could not have been granted by the local planning authority, or could not have been granted otherwise than subject to the conditions imposed by them.

(2) Any person who desires to appeal under this regulation shall give notice of appeal in writing to the Minister within one month from the receipt of notification of the local planning authority's decision or such longer period as the Minister may allow, and shall within one month from giving notice of appeal or such longer period as the Minister may allow send to the Minister a copy of each of the following documents:—

    (i) the application made to the local planning authority;

    (ii) all relevant plans and particulars submitted to them;

    (iii) the notice of the decision, if any;

    (iv) all other relevant correspondence with the authority.

(3) The Minister may, if he thinks fit, require the applicant or the local planning authority to submit within a specified period a further statement in writing in respect of any of the matters to which the appeal relates, and if, after considering the grounds of the appeal and any such further statement, the Minister is satisfied that he is sufficiently informed for the purpose of reaching a decision as to the matters to which the appeal relates, he may decide the appeal without further investigation; but otherwise the Minister shall, if either party so desire, afford to each of them an opportunity of appearing before and being heard by a person appointed by the Minister for the purpose.

(4) Where an appeal is brought under this regulation from a decision of the local planning authority the Minister may allow or dismiss the appeal or may reverse or vary any part of the decision of the local planning authority, whether or not the appeal relates to that part, and deal with the application as if it had been made to him in the first instance.

(5) Where the local planning authority fail to notify the applicant as required by regulation 21 within two months from receipt of the application, or within such extended period as is agreed between them, the provisions of paragraphs (1) and (2) above shall apply in relation to the application as if consent had been refused by the local planning authority and as if notification of their decision had been received by the applicant at the expiration of the said period of two months or the extended period agreed upon as aforesaid, as the case may be.

(6) Subject as hereinafter provided, where the local planning authority serve a discontinuance notice on any person under regulation 16, the provisions of paragraphs (1) and (2) above shall apply as if that person had made an application for consent for the display or the use of land for the display of advertisements to which the notice relates and the local planning authority had refused consent for the reasons stated in the notice, and as if the notice constituted notification of the authority's decision as required by regulation 21:

Provided that paragraph (2) above shall apply subject to the provisions of regulation 16(5) and as if the following sub-paragraphs were substituted for sub-paragraphs (i) to (iv) thereof:—

    "(i) the discontinuance notice;

    (ii) any notice of variation thereof;

    (iii) any relevant correspondence with the authority.".

(7) On the determination of an appeal under this regulation made by virtue

of paragraph (6) above, the Minister shall give such directions as may be necessary for giving effect to his determination, including, where appropriate, directions for quashing the discontinuance notice or for varying the terms of the discontinuance notice in favour of the appellant.

(8) The decision of the Minister on an appeal under this regulation shall be final and shall otherwise have effect as if it were a decision of the local planning authority.

PART V

SPECIAL CASE

Advertisements relating to travelling circuses and fairs

23.—(1) On application in that behalf being made to them, a local planning authority may grant consent for the temporary display, on unspecified sites in their area, of placards, posters or bills relating to the visit of a travelling circus, fair or similar travelling entertainment to any specified place in the district; and for the purposes of this regulation the expression "in the district" means in the area of the local planning authority to whom application for such consent is made or in the area of any neighbouring local planning authority.

(2) Consent granted under this regulation shall be subject to the following conditions in addition to the standard conditions set out in Parts I and II of Schedule 1:—

(*a*) no such advertisement shall exceed 0·6 square metre in area or be displayed above 3·6 metres from ground level;

(*b*) no such advertisement shall be displayed earlier than fourteen days before the first performance or opening of the circus, fair or other entertainment in the district, at a place specified in the advertisement, and every such advertisement shall be removed within seven days after the last performance or closing of the circus, fair or other entertainment in the district at a place specified in the advertisement,

and it shall be the duty of the local planning authority, when granting consent for the display of such advertisements, to inform the applicant that consent does not extend to the display of any advertisement on land without the prior permission of the owner of that land or other person entitled to grant permission in relation thereto.

(3) Without prejudice to the right to apply under Part IV of these regulations for consent to display advertisements of the foregoing description on specified sites, the provisions of that part shall not apply to an application for consent under this regulation, and the decision of a local planning authority on any such application shall be final.

PART VI

REVOCATION AND MODIFICATION OF EXPRESS CONSENT

Revocation and modification of consent

24.—(1) Subject to the provisions of regulation 5 and of this regulation, if it appears to the local planning authority that it is expedient that any express consent for the display of advertisements should be revoked or modified, they may by order revoke or modify the consent to such extent as appears to them to be expedient as aforesaid:

Provided that no such order shall take effect unless it is confirmed by the Minister, and the Minister may confirm any order submitted to him for the purpose either without modification or subject to such modifications as he considers expedient.

(2) Where a local planning authority submit an order to the Minister for his confirmation under this regulation, that authority shall serve notice on the person on whose application the consent was granted, on the owner and on the occupier of the land affected, and on any other person who in their opinion will be affected by the order; and if within such period as may be specified in that behalf in the notice (not being less than twenty-eight days from the service thereof) any person on whom the notice is served so requires, the Minister shall, before confirming the order, afford to him and to the local planning authority an opportunity of appearing before and being heard by a person appointed by the Minister for the purpose.

(3) The power conferred by this regulation to revoke or modify consent for the display of advertisements may be exercised—

(a) where the consent relates to a display which involves the carrying out of building or similar operations, at any time before those operations have been completed;

(b) where the consent relates to a display which involves no such operations as aforesaid, at any time before the display is begun:

Provided that the revocation or modification of consent for a display which involves the carrying out of building or similar operations shall not affect so much of those operations as has been previously carried out.

Supplementary provisions as to revocation and modification

25.—(1) Where consent for the display of advertisements is revoked or modified by an order made under the last foregoing regulation then if, on a claim made to the local planning authority in writing and served in the manner indicated in paragraph (3) below within six months after confirmation of the order, it is shown that any person has incurred expenditure in carrying out, in connection with the display in question, work which is rendered abortive by the revocation or modification, or has otherwise sustained loss or damage which is directly attributable to the revocation or modification, that authority shall pay to that person compensation in respect of that expenditure, loss or damage:

Provided that no compensation shall be payable under this paragraph in respect of loss or damage consisting of the depreciation in value of any interest in the land by virtue of the revocation or modification.

(2) For the purposes of this regulation, any expenditure incurred in the preparation of plans for the purposes of any work or upon other similar matters preparatory thereto shall be deemed to be included in the expenditure incurred in carrying out that work, but except as aforesaid no compensation shall be paid under this regulation in respect of any work carried out before the grant of the consent which is revoked or modified, or in respect of any other loss or damage arising out of anything done or omitted to be done before the grant of that consent.

(3) A claim for compensation made to a local planning authority under paragraph (1) above shall be served on that authority by delivering it at the offices of the authority addressed to the Clerk thereof or by sending it by pre-paid post addressed as aforesaid.

PART VII

AREAS OF SPECIAL CONTROL

Definition of areas of special control

26.—(1) Every local planning authority shall from time to time consider whether any part, or any additional part, of their area should be defined as an area of special control, and whether, in the light of circumstances then obtaining, any order under this regulation in force in relation to land in their area should be modified or revoked:

Provided that, except as respects any such order in force before the date on which these regulations come into operation, every local planning authority shall consider the matters mentioned in the preceding provisions of this paragraph at least once in every five years after the date on which these regulations come into operation; and, as respects any such order in force before the date on which these regulations come into operation, they shall consider, within two years from that date or, if longer, within five years from the date when the order came into force, whether, in the light of the circumstances obtaining, the order should be modified or revoked, and after such consideration shall consider the same matters at least once in every five years while the order remains in force.

(2) By virtue of section 34(3) of the Act rural areas or areas other than rural areas which appear to the Minister to require special protection on grounds of amenity may be defined by order as areas of special control; and the provisions of regulation 5(2)(a) shall apply with respect to the exercise by a local planning authority of their powers under this regulation as if those provisions related to the display in any such area of advertisements in general and to the general characteristics of such an area.

(3) In the selection of areas under this regulation a local planning authority shall consult—

  (a) where it appears to them that the order is likely to affect any part of the area of a neighbouring local planning authority, with that authority;

  (b) with the council of any county district in whose area any land they propose to define as aforesaid is situate;

  (c) with such authorities, associations or persons as the Minister may direct under regulation 28.

(4) An area of special control shall be defined by an order made by the local planning authority and approved by the Minister in accordance with the provisions of Schedule 2 and any such order may be revoked or varied by a subsequent order made and approved in the like manner.

Display of advertisements in areas of special control

27.—(1) No display of advertisements may be undertaken in an area of special control except in the case of—

  (a) advertisements of the classes and descriptions specified in regulations 9, 12, 14 and 23;

  (b) advertisements of the descriptions specified in the next following paragraph.

(2) Without prejudice to the provisions of these regulations with respect to advertisements of the descriptions referred to in paragraph (1)(a) above, advertisements of the following descriptions may be displayed in an area

of special control with express consent granted in accordance with these regulations—

    (a) hoardings or similar structures to be used only for the display of notices relating to local events, activities or entertainments;

    (b) any advertisement for the purpose of announcement or direction in relation to buildings or other land in the locality, being an advertisement which, in the opinion of the local planning authority, or of the Minister on appeal, is reasonably required having regard to the nature and situation of such buildings or other land;

    (c) any advertisement which, in the opinion of the local planning authority or of the Minister on appeal, is required in the interests of public safety to be displayed, and which is not an advertisement of any other description specified in this regulation;

    (d) any advertisement which could be displayed as an advertisement of a specified class but for some non-compliance with a condition or limitation as respects size, height from the ground, number or illumination imposed by regulation 14 in relation to the display thereunder of advertisements of that class, being an advertisement which, in the opinion of the local planning authority or of the Minister on appeal, may in all the circumstances reasonably be allowed to be displayed otherwise than in accordance with that condition or limitation.

(3) The power conferred on local planning authorities by regulation 19 to grant consent for the display of advertisements shall, in relation to the display of advertisements in an area of special control, be limited to advertisements of the descriptions mentioned in paragraphs (1) and (2) above, including illuminated advertisements of those descriptions.

(4) On the coming into force of an order defining an area of special control, advertisements then being displayed in accordance with these regulations in the area may continue to be displayed as follows:—

    (a) advertisements of the descriptions specified in regulations 9, 12 and 23 may continue to be displayed in accordance with the provisions of those regulations respectively;

    (b) advertisements of the specified classes and advertisements of the description specified in paragraph 2(d) above may continue to be displayed with or without express consent, subject, after the term of any express consent has expired, to the power of the local planning authority to require the discontinuance of the display of any such advertisement under regulation 16.

    (c) any other advertisement may continue to be displayed

        (i) for a period of six months from the date on which the order defining the area comes into force or for the remainder of the term of any express consent, whichever is the longer, or.

        (ii) where no such consent has been granted, for a period of six months from the date on which the order defining the area comes into force,

and then, in every case, for a further two months within which the advertisement shall without further notice be removed, unless express consent is granted for the continued display thereof in accordance with this regulation.

(5) Nothing in the foregoing provisions of this regulation shall—

    (a) affect a notice served under regulation 16 before the coming into force of the order defining an area of special control;

(*b*) override any condition attached to a consent, whereby an advertisement is required to be removed;

(*c*) restrict the powers of a local planning authority, or of the Minister, in regard to any contravention of these regulations;

(*d*) restrict the power of the local planning authority, or of the Minister, to consent to the display in an area of special control of advertisements of the specified classes in respect of which a direction under regulation 15 is in force.

PART VIII

MISCELLANEOUS

Powers of the Minister

28.—(1) If it appears expedient to the Minister so to do he may give directions to any local planning authority, or to local planning authorities generally, requiring them—

(*a*) to refer to him for his decision any particular application for consent under these regulations or any class or description of such applications;

(*b*) to furnish him with such information as he may require for the purpose of exercising any of his functions under these regulations;

(*c*) to consult, in the exercise of their functions under these regulations, with any, or any class of, persons, bodies or authorities;

and, without prejudice to the generality of the foregoing, such directions may be given as respects any particular area or class of area.

(2) Where an application is referred to the Minister under this regulation the provisions of regulation 19 and of regulation 22(3) shall apply, with such modifications as may be necessary, to the determination of the application by the Minister.

(3) If it appears to the Minister, after consultation with the local planning authority, to be expedient that an order should be made under regulation 26 defining an area of special control, or revoking or varying such an order, or that a notice should be served under regulation 16, he may give directions to the local planning authority requiring them to make such an order, or to serve such a notice, as the case may be, or may himself make the order or serve the notice; and any reference in these regulations to the power of the local planning authority under regulation 16 shall be deemed to include a reference to the power of the Minister.

(4) Where the Minister proposes to make an order under regulation 26 he shall prepare a draft of the order in the form in which he proposes to make it, defining an area by reference to a map, and in all other respects the provisions of Schedule 2 shall apply, with such modifications as may be necessary, to the making of the order by the Minister as they apply to the making of such an order by the local planning authority.

(5) The decision of the Minister on any application referred or submitted to him under the provisions of this regulation shall be final and shall otherwise have effect as if it were a decision of the local planning authority.

Extension of time

29.—(1) Subject to the provisions of the Act and of these regulations—

(a) the Minister may for special reasons, in any particular case, extend the time within which anything is required under these regulations to be done, or within which any objection, representation or claim for compensation may be made thereunder;

(b) the local planning authority may, on reasonable cause being shown to them, extend the time within which an application for consent is required to be, or may be, made to them under these regulations,

and any such extension may be granted either unconditionally or subject to such conditions as the Minister or the local planning authority, as the case may be, think fit to impose.

(2) The power conferred by this regulation to grant extensions of time shall not apply to—

(a) the time within which the local planning authority is required, under regulation 21, to notify an applicant of the manner in which his application had been dealt with, save as expressly provided in that regulation;

(b) any period specified by these regulations during which an advertisement may be displayed without express consent.

Recovery of compensation under section 126 of the Act

30.—(1) Where, for the purpose of complying with these regulations, works are carried out by any person—

(a) for removing an advertisement which was being displayed on 1st August 1948, or

(b) for discontinuing the use for the display of advertisements of a site used for that purpose on the last-mentioned date,

and that person desires to recover compensation under section 126 of the Act in respect of any expenses reasonably incurred by him in that behalf, he shall submit a claim in writing to the local planning authority within six months after the completion of those works; and that claim shall contain sufficient information to enable the local planning authority to give proper consideration thereto.

(2) If the local planning authority consider that the information furnished by any claimant under this regulation is insufficient to enable them properly to determine the claim, they may call for such further particulars as they require for that purpose.

Register of applications

31.—(1) Every local planning authority shall keep a register containing the following information in respect of all land within their area namely:—

(a) particulars of any application made to them for consent for the display of advertisements on any such land, including the name and address of the applicant, the date of the application, and brief particulars of the type of advertisements forming the subject of the application;

(b) particulars of any direction given under these regulations in respect of the application;

(c) the decision (if any) of the local planning authority in respect of the application and the date of such decision;

(d) the date and effect of any decision of the Minister in respect of the application whether on appeal or on a reference to him under regulation 28.

(2) Such register shall include an index, which shall be in the form of a map,

unless the Minister approves some other form, for enabling a person to trace any entry in the register.

(3) Such register shall be kept at the office of the local planning authority:

Provided that, where the authority is a county council, so much of the register as relates to land in a county district may be kept at a place within or convenient to that district.

(4) Every entry in such register consisting of particulars of an application shall be made within fourteen days of the receipt of such application.

Directions and notices

32.—(1) Any power conferred by these regulations to give a direction shall be construed as including power to cancel or vary that direction by a subsequent direction.

(2) Any notice to be served or given under these regulations may be served or given in the manner prescribed by section 214 of the Act and by regulation 20 of the Town and Country Planning General Regulations 1969(a).

Provisions of the Act applied

33.—(1) The provisions of the Act specified in the first column of Schedule 4 hereto are applied, subject to adaptations and modifications, in the regulations specified respectively in the second column of that schedule.

(2) Section 19(4) and (5) of the Act shall apply in relation to applications for consent under these regulations:

Provided that section 19(4) of the Act shall apply as if for the words "a development order" there were substituted the words "regulations under section thirty-four of this Act", and as if for the words "planning permission" there were substituted the words "consent for the display of advertisements".

Other statutory obligations unaffected

34. Without prejudice to section 35 of the Act, nothing in these regulations, or in a consent granted under these regulations, shall operate so as to affect any obligation or liability imposed or incurred under any other enactment in relation to anything involved in the display of advertisements.

Regulation 7   **SCHEDULE 1**

THE STANDARD CONDITIONS

PART I

Conditions attaching to all consents save as otherwise provided in the regulations

1. All advertisements displayed, and any land used for the display of advertisements, shall be maintained in a clean and tidy condition to the reasonable satisfaction of the local planning authority.

2. Any hoarding or similar structure, or any sign, placard, board or device erected or used principally for the purpose of displaying advertisements shall be maintained in a safe condition to the reasonable satisfaction of the local planning authority.

_____

(a) S.I. 1969/286 (1969 I, p. 766).

3. Where any advertisement is required under these regulations to be removed, the removal thereof shall be carried out to the reasonable satisfaction of the local planning authority.

PART II

Conditions attaching to consent deemed to be granted, or granted under regulation 23

4. An advertisement for which consent is deemed to be granted, or is granted under regulation 23 of the foregoing regulations, shall not be sited or displayed so as to obscure, or hinder the ready interpretation of, any road traffic sign, railway signal or aid to navigation by water or air, or so as otherwise to render hazardous the use of any highway, railway, waterway (including any coastal waters) or airfield.

SCHEDULE 2   Regulation 26

PROCEDURE FOR DEFINING AREAS OF SPECIAL CONTROL

1. Where a local planning authority propose to define an area of special control they shall make an order, defining an area by reference to a map annexed thereto, either with or without descriptive matter (which, in the case of any discrepancy with the map, shall prevail except in so far as may be otherwise provided by the order).

2. As soon as may be thereafter the authority shall submit the order with map and any descriptive matter annexed thereto to the Minister for approval, and shall send therewith to the Minister two certified copies of the order, map and descriptive matter (if any), and a statement of their reasons for proposing that the area to which the order relates should be defined as an area of special control. Where it appears expedient to the Minister in any particular case so to do, he may direct the authority to send to him an additional certified copy of the order, map and any descriptive matter.

3. The authority shall forthwith publish in the London Gazette, and in each of two successive weeks in one or more newspapers circulating in the locality in which the area is situate, a notice in the appropriate form prescribed in Schedule 3, or in a form substantially to the like effect, describing the area, stating that an order defining it as an area of special control for the purpose of these regulations has been submitted to the Minister, naming a place or places where a copy of the order and of the map and any descriptive matter annexed thereto and of the statement of reasons mentioned in paragraph 2 above may be seen at all reasonable hours without payment of fee and specifying the time, not being less than 28 days from the first local advertisement, within which objections or representations with respect to the order may be sent in writing to the Minister.

4. If any objection is duly made as aforesaid and is not withdrawn the Minister shall, before approving the order, either cause a public local inquiry to be held or afford to the person making such objection an opportunity of appearing before and being heard by a person appointed by the Minister for the purpose, and if any such person avails himself of the opportunity of being heard, the Minister shall afford to the local planning authority, and to any other person to whom it appears to the Minister expedient to afford it, an opportunity of being heard on the same occasion.

5. After considering any representation or objection duly made and not withdrawn and the report of the person by whom any inquiry or hearing was held, the Minister may approve the order with or without modifications:
Provided that if the Minister proposes to approve the order subject to a modification involving the inclusion therein of any area of land not included in the order as submitted he shall publish prior notice of his intention so to do and

shall afford opportunity for the making of objections and representations with respect to the proposed modification, and for such further hearing as may appear to him in the light of any such objections or representations, to be necessary or expedient.

6. As soon as may be after the order has been approved, the local planning authority shall publish in the London Gazette, and in each of two successive weeks in one or more newspapers circulating throughout the locality in which the area is situate, a notice in the appropriate form prescribed in Schedule 3, or a form substantially to the like effect, stating that the order has been approved and naming a place or places where a copy or copies thereof and of the map and any descriptive matter annexed thereto may be seen at all reasonable hours without payment of fee ; and any such order shall come into force on the date on which notice of the approval thereof is published in the London Gazette.

SCHEDULE 3

FORMS OF NOTICES

FORM 1

Form of notice of submission for approval of an order defining an area of special control

TOWN AND COUNTRY PLANNING ACT 1962

Town and Country Planning (Control of Advertisements) Regulations 1969

Notice is hereby given that the (1)   in exercise of their powers under regulation 26 of the Town and Country Planning (Control of Advertisements) Regulations 1969 have submitted for the approval of the [Minister of Housing and Local Government] [Secretary of State] (2) an order defining as an area of special control for the purposes of the said regulations an area of land situate at   and described in the schedule hereto, which land is shown coloured   on the map accompanying the order, and that the order is about to be considered by the [Minister] [Secretary of State] (2).

A copy of the order and of the map referred to [and of the descriptive matter annexed thereto] (2) and of a statement of reasons submitted therewith have been deposited at   and will be available for inspection free of charge between the hours of   .

Any objection to the order must be made in writing, stating the grounds of the objection, and addressed to the Secretary, [Ministry of Housing and Local Government, Whitehall, S.W.1] [Welsh Office, Summit House, Windsor Place, Cardiff, CF1 3BX] (2) before (3) 19   .

Schedule

(Here insert description of the lands comprised in the order.)

19   .   (Signature)

Directions for completing this Form

(1) Insert name of authority.

(2) Delete words in square brackets where inapplicable.

(3) Insert a date not less than 28 days from the first date of local advertisement.

FORM 2

Form of notice of the approval of an order defining an area of special control

TOWN AND COUNTRY PLANNING ACT 1962

Town and Country Planning (Control of Advertisements) Regulations 1969

Notice is hereby given that the [Minister of Housing and Local Government] [Secretary of State] (1) in exercise of his powers under section 34 of the Town and Country Planning Act 1962 and regulation 26 of the Town and Country Planning (Control of Advertisements) Regulations 1969, has approved [with modifications] (1) an order defining as an area of special control for the purposes of those regulations an area of land situate at and described in the schedule hereto, which land is shown coloured   on the map referred to in the order.

The order comes into force on   19   . (2)

A copy of the approved order and of the map [and of the descriptive matter annexed thereto] (1) have been deposited at   and will be available for inspection free of charge between the hours of

Schedule

(Here insert description of the lands comprised in the order.)

19   .   (Signature)

IMPORTANT

Attention is drawn to regulation 27 of the above regulations under which advertisements being displayed in an area defined as an area of special control are in certain circumstances required to be removed without further notice within two months after expiry of a specified period, not being less than six months from the date on which the order defining the area comes into force.

Directions for completing this Form

(1) Delete words in square brackets where inapplicable.

(2) Insert date of publication in the London Gazette.

Regulation 33(1)   SCHEDULE 4

PROVISIONS OF THE ACT APPLIED

Provision applied	Regulation in which applied
Section 17(1).	Regulation 19(1).
Section 18(1).	Regulation 19(2).
Section 22.	Regulation 28.
Sections 23 and 24.	Regulation 22.
Section 20(1) and (2).	Regulation 19(4).
Section 21(1).	Regulation 6(3).
Section 27.	Regulation 24.
Section 118.	Regulation 25.

Given under the official seal of the Minister of Housing and Local Government on 29th October 1969.

(L.S.)

Anthony Greenwood,
Minister of Housing and
Local Government.

EXPLANATORY NOTE

(This Note is not part of the Regulations.)

These regulations, made by the Minister of Housing and Local Government after consultation with the Secretary of State for Wales, consolidate, with amendments, the Town and Country Planning (Control of Advertisements) Regulations 1960 and the Town and Country Planning (Control of Advertisements) (Amendment) Regulations 1965.

The regulations provide for the control of the display of advertisements in England and Wales.

References to the Town and Country Planning Act 1962 have been substituted for references to the Town and Country Planning Act 1947 and account has been taken of certain amendments of the 1962 Act effected by the Town and Country Planning Act 1968. The regulations have been re-arranged to facilitate their use. The principal changes of substance are as follows:—

    (i) certain small advertisements displayed on or in relation to articles for sale have been exempted from control;

    (ii) the penalties for contravening the regulations have been increased to the maximum permitted by section 63 of the 1962 Act, as amended by the 1968 Act;

    (iii) the control of advertisements displayed within buildings has been extended;

    (iv) the specified classes have been amended in certain respects, and a new class relating to advertisements displayed on the forecourts of business premises has been included;

    (v) a power to require the discontinuance of the display of advertisements displayed with deemed consent has been substituted for the power to require the making of an application for express consent for the display of such advertisements;

    (vi) local planning authorities are required to review the use of their powers as respects the definition etc. of areas of special control within specified periods;

    (vii) the regulations no longer contain powers as respects the service of enforcement notices and related matters.

STATUTORY INSTRUMENTS

1969 No. 1534

MINISTERS OF THE CROWN

The Transfer of Functions (Monopolies, Mergers and Restrictive Trade Practices) Order 1969

Made - - - - -	*29th October* 1969
Laid before Parliament - -	*29th October* 1969
Coming into Operation - -	*30th October* 1969

At the Court at Buckingham Palace, the 29th day of October 1969

Present,

The Queen's Most Excellent Majesty in Council

Her Majesty, in pursuance of section 1 of the Ministers of the Crown (Transfer of Functions) Act 1946(a) and section 4 of the Ministers of the Crown Act 1964(b), is pleased, by and with the advice of Her Privy Council, to order, and it is hereby ordered, as follows:—

Citation, interpretation and commencement

1.—(1) This Order may be cited as the Transfer of Functions (Monopolies, Mergers and Restrictive Trade Practices) Order 1969.

(2) The Interpretation Act 1889(c) applies for the interpretation of this Order as it applies for the interpretation of an Act of Parliament.

(3) This Order shall come into operation on 30th October 1969.

Transfer of functions, and consequential transfer of rights and liabilities

2.—(1) The following functions of the Board of Trade, that is to say,—

(*a*) the functions under the Monopolies and Mergers Acts 1948 and 1965(d), together with any functions under section 40(3) of the Patents Act 1949(e); and

---

(a) 9 & 10 Geo. 6 c. 31.   (b) 1964 c. 98.   (c) 52 & 53 Vict. c. 63.
(d) 11 & 12 Geo. 6 c. 66 and 1965 c. 50, together with Part III of 4 & 5 Eliz. 2 c. 68, in part.
(e) 12, 13 & 14 Geo. 6 c. 87.

(b) the functions under Part I and section 31(1) of the Restrictive Trade Practices Act 1956(a) and functions under the Restrictive Trade Practices Act 1968(b) other than those as a competent authority for the purposes of section 2 of that Act;

are hereby transferred to the Secretary of State, and there are also transferred to him all rights and liabilities to which the Board of Trade is entitled or subject in connection with those functions at the coming into operation of this Order.

(2) In so far as any functions of the Board of Trade expressed to be transferred by this Article to the Secretary of State are, apart from the operation of this Order, exercisable concurrently with him, they shall cease to be exercisable by the Board of Trade; and references in this Order to functions transferred shall be construed accordingly.

(3) This Article as it applies to functions under section 40(3) of the Patents Act 1949 shall apply to any such functions of a competent authority other than the Board of Trade and the Secretary of State as it applies to functions of the Board of Trade, and in relation to those functions references in this Order to the Board of Trade shall apply also to any such competent authority.

Consequential amendments and repeal

3.—(1) In accordance with Article 2 above (but subject to Article 4 below)—

(a) in the Patents Act 1949, in section 40(3), for the words " a competent authority within the meaning of the said Act of 1948 " there shall be substituted the words " the Secretary of State "; and

(b) in the Agriculture Act 1967(c), in section 9(11), for the words " the President of the Board of Trade " there shall be substituted the words " the Secretary of State for Employment and Productivity "; and

(c) in the Restrictive Trade Practices Act 1968, in section 3(3), (4) and (6), for the words " Board of Trade or other competent authority " there shall be substituted the words " Secretary of State or other competent authority ".

(2) In the Monopolies and Mergers Act 1965(d), in Schedule 1, so much of paragraph 6 as follows sub-paragraph (b) is hereby repealed.

Supplemental

4.—(1) This Order shall not affect the validity of anything done by or in relation to the Board of Trade before the coming into operation of the Order; and anything which at the coming into operation of the Order is in process of being done by or in relation to the Board of Trade (including in particular any legal proceedings to which the Board is a party) may, if it relates to any functions, rights or liabilities transferred by this Order, be continued by or in relation to the Secretary of State.

(2) Any authorisation given (by way of approval or otherwise), requirement imposed or appointment made by the Board of Trade in connection with any functions transferred by this Order shall, if in force at the coming into operation of this Order, have effect as if given, imposed or made by the Secretary of State in so far as that is required for continuing its effect after the coming into operation of this Order.

(a) 4 & 5 Eliz. 2 c. 68. (b) 1968 c. 66. (c) 1967 c. 22.
(d) 1965 c. 50.

(3) Subject to any express amendment or repeal made by this Order, any enactment or instrument passed or made before the coming into operation of this Order shall have effect, so far as may be necessary for the purpose or in consequence of the transfers effected by this Order, as if any reference to the Board of Trade or to the department or an officer of the Board (including any reference which is to be construed as such a reference) were or included a reference to the Secretary of State or to his department or an officer of his, as the case may require.

W. G. Agnew.

EXPLANATORY NOTE

(This Note is not part of the Order.)

This Order transfers to the Secretary of State the functions of the Board of Trade relating to monopolies, mergers and restrictive trade practices.

STATUTORY INSTRUMENTS

1969 No. 1536 (S.123)

COURT OF SESSION, SCOTLAND

Act of Sederunt (Sessions of Court Amendment) 1969

Made - - -		*24th October* 1969
Coming into Operation		*1st January* 1970

The Lords of Council and Session, by virtue of the powers conferred upon them by section 2 of the Administration of Justice (Scotland) Act 1948(a), do hereby enact and declare as follows:—

1. The Act of Sederunt (Sessions of Court) 1969(b) is hereby repealed.

2. The Ordinary sessions of the Court of Session during 1970 shall be as follows:—

From Tuesday, 6th January to Thursday, 26th March;

From Tuesday, 28th April to Saturday, 18th July;

From Thursday, 1st October to Saturday, 19th December.

3. This Act of Sederunt may be cited as the Act of Sederunt (Sessions of Court Amendment) 1969 and shall come into operation on 1st January 1970.

And the Lords appoint this Act of Sederunt to be inserted in the Books of Sederunt.

J. L. Clyde,
I.P.D.

Edinburgh
24th October 1969.

EXPLANATORY NOTE

(This Note is not part of the Act of Sederunt.)

This Act of Sederunt prescribes amended dates for the ordinary sessions of the Court of Session during 1970.

(a) 12, 13 & 14 Geo. 6. c. 10.   (b) S.I. 1969/39 (1969 I, p. 114).

STATUTORY INSTRUMENTS

1969 No. 1537 (S. 124)

SHERIFF COURT, SCOTLAND

Act of Sederunt (Betting and Gaming Appeals No. 2) 1969

Made - - -	*24th October* 1969
Coming into Operation	*25th October* 1969

The Lords of Council and Session, under and by virtue of the powers conferred upon them by paragraph 24 of Schedule 1 and paragraph 7 of Schedule 6 to the Betting, Gaming and Lotteries Act 1963(a), do hereby enact and declare as follows:—

1. Paragraphs 1, 2 and 3 of the Act of Sederunt (Betting, Gaming and Lotteries Act Appeals) 1965(b) are hereby repealed.

2. This Act of Sederunt may be cited as the Act of Sederunt (Betting and Gaming Appeals No. 2) 1969, and shall come into operation on 25th October 1969.

And the Lords appoint this Act of Sederunt to be inserted in the Books of Sederunt.

J. L. Clyde,
I.P.D.

Edinburgh
24th October 1969

EXPLANATORY NOTE

(*This Note is not part of the Act of Sederunt.*)

This Act of Sederunt effects the repeal of certain provisions superseded by the Act of Sederunt (Betting and Gaming Appeals and Fees of Clerks to Licensing Authorities) 1969 (S.I. 1969/1452).

(a) 1963 c. 2. (b) S.I. 1965/1168 (1965 II, p. 3301).

STATUTORY INSTRUMENTS

1969 No. 1541

INCOME TAX

The Capital Allowances (Relevant Grants) (No. 2) Order 1969

Made - - - *30th October* 1969

The Treasury in pursuance of powers conferred on them by section 83(4) of the Capital Allowances Act, 1968(**a**), as amended by section 3(2) of the Transport (London) Act, 1969(**b**), do hereby make the following Order :-

1. Any grant made under section 3 of the Transport (London) Act, 1969, is hereby declared to be relevant for the purposes of the withholding or withdrawal of investment and initial allowances.

2. This Order may be cited as the Capital Allowances (Relevant Grants) (No. 2) Order 1969.

Joseph Harper,

Neil McBride,

Two of the Lords Commissioners
of Her Majesty's Treasury.

Dated 30th October 1969.

EXPLANATORY NOTE

(This Note is not part of the Order.)

Section 83(4) of the Capital Allowance Act, 1968, entitles the Treasury to prescribe grants as "relevant" with the consequence that capital expenditure in respect of which the grant is paid will be disqualified from investment and initial allowances for tax purposes. This instrument so prescribes grants made by the Greater London Council under section 3 of the Transport (London) Act, 1969, to the London Transport Executive or to the British Railways Board.

(a) 1968 c. 3. (b) 1969 c. 35.

STATUTORY INSTRUMENTS

1969 No. 1543

INDUSTRIAL TRAINING

The Industrial Training Levy (Wool, Jute and Flax) Order 1969

Made	-	-	-	30th October 1969
Laid before Parliament				10th November 1969
Coming into Operation				19th November 1969

The Secretary of State after approving proposals submitted by the Wool, Jute and Flax Industry Training Board for the imposition of a further levy on employers in the wool, jute and flax industry and in exercise of her powers under section 4 of the Industrial Training Act 1964(**a**) and of all other powers enabling her in that behalf hereby makes the following Order :—

Title and commencement

1. This Order may be cited as the Industrial Training Levy (Wool, Jute and Flax) Order 1969 and shall come into operation on 19th November 1969.

Interpretation

2.—(1) In this Order unless the context otherwise requires :—

(*a*) "an appeal tribunal" means an industrial tribunal established under section 12 of the Industrial Training Act 1964 ;

(*b*) "assessment" means an assessment of an employer to the levy ;

(*c*) "the Board" means the Wool, Jute and Flax Industry Training Board ;

(*d*) "business" means any activities of industry or commerce ;

(*e*) "emoluments" means all emoluments assessable to income tax under Schedule E (other than pensions), being emoluments from which tax under that Schedule is deductible, whether or not tax in fact falls to be deducted from any particular payment thereof ;

(*f*) "employer" means a person who is an employer in the wool, jute and flax industry at any time in the fifth levy period ;

(*g*) "the fifth base period" means the period of twelve months that commenced on 6th April 1968 ;

(*h*) "the fifth levy period" means the period commencing with the day upon which this Order comes into operation and ending on 5th April 1970 ;

(*i*) "the industrial training order" means the Industrial Training (Wool, Jute and Flax Board) Order 1968(**b**) ;

(*j*) "the levy" means the levy imposed by the Board in respect of the fifth levy period ;

(*k*) "notice" means a notice in writing ;

(**a**) 1964 c. 16.   (**b**) S.I. 1968/898 (1968 II, p. 2376).

(*l*) "wool, jute and flax establishment" means an establishment in Great Britain engaged in the fifth base period wholly or mainly in the wool, jute and flax industry for a total of twenty-seven or more weeks or, being an establishment that commenced to carry on business in the fifth base period, for a total number of weeks exceeding one-half of the number of weeks in the part of the said period commencing with the day on which business was commenced and ending on the last day thereof, but does not include an establishment in the case of which the sum of the emoluments of all persons employed in the fifth base period at or from the establishment by the employer carrying on the same is £5,000 or less ;

(*m*) "the wool, jute and flax industry" means any one or more of the activities which, subject to the provisions of paragraph 2 of the Schedule to the industrial training order, are specified in paragraph 1 of that Schedule as the activities of the wool, jute and flax industry.

(2) In the case where a wool, jute and flax establishment is taken over (whether directly or indirectly) by an employer in succession to, or jointly with, another person, a person employed at any time in the fifth base period at or from the establishment shall be deemed, for the purposes of this Order, to have been so employed by the employer carrying on the said establishment on the day upon which this Order comes into operation, and any reference in this Order to persons employed by an employer at or from a wool, jute and flax establishment in the fifth base period shall be construed accordingly.

(3) Any reference in this Order to an establishment that commences to carry on business or that ceases to carry on business shall not be taken to apply where the location of the establishment is changed but its business is continued wholly or mainly at or from the new location, or where the suspension of activities is of a temporary or seasonal nature.

(4) The Interpretation Act 1889(**a**) shall apply to the interpretation of this Order as it applies to the interpretation of an Act of Parliament.

Imposition of the Levy

3.—(1) The levy to be imposed by the Board on employers in respect of the fifth levy period shall be assessed in accordance with the provisions of this Article and of the Schedule to this Order.

(2) The levy shall be assessed by the Board separately in respect of each wool, jute and flax establishment of an employer, but in agreement with the employer one assessment may be made in respect of any number of such establishments, in which case those establishments shall be deemed for the purposes of that assessment to constitute one establishment.

Assessment Notices

4.—(1) The Board shall serve an assessment notice on every employer assessed to the levy, but one notice may comprise two or more assessments.

(2) An assessment notice shall state the amount of the levy payable by the person assessed to the levy, and that amount shall be equal to the total amount (rounded down where necessary to the nearest £1) of the levy assessed by the Board under this Order in respect of each establishment included in the notice.

(**a**) 1889 c. 63.

(3) An assessment notice shall state the Board's address for the service of a notice of appeal or of an application for an extension of time for appealing.

(4) An assessment notice may be served on the person assessed to the levy either by delivering it to him personally or by leaving it, or sending it to him by post, at his last known address or place of business in the United Kingdom or, if that person is a corporation, by leaving it, or sending it by post to the corporation, at such address or place of business or at its registered or principal office.

Payment of the Levy

5.—(1) Subject to the provisions of this Article and of Articles 6 and 7, the amount of the levy payable under an assessment notice served by the Board shall be due and payable to the Board one month after the date of the notice.

(2) The amount of an assessment shall not be recoverable by the Board until there has expired the time allowed for appealing against the assessment by Article 7(1) of this Order and any further period or periods of time that the Board cr an appeal tribunal may have allowed for appealing under paragraph (2) or (3) of that Article or, where an appeal is brought, until the appeal is decided or withdrawn.

Withdrawal of Assessment

6.—(1) The Board may, by a notice served on the person assessed to the levy in the same manner as an assessment notice, withdraw an assessment if that person has appealed against that assessment under the provisions of Article 7 of this Order and the appeal has not been entered in the Register of Appeals kept under the appropriate Regulations specified in paragraph (5) of that Article.

(2) The withdrawal of an assessment shall be without prejudice—

(*a*) to the power of the Board to serve a further assessment notice in respect of any establishment to which that assessment related ; or

(*b*) to any other assessment included in the original assessment notice, and such notice shall thereupon have effect as if any assessment withdrawn by the Board had not been included therein.

Appeals

7.—(1) A person assessed to the levy may appeal to an appeal tribunal against the assessment within one month from the date of the service of the assessment notice or within any further period or periods of time that may be allowed by the Board or an appeal tribunal under the following provisions of this Article.

(2) The Board by notice may for good cause allow a person assessed to the levy to appeal to an appeal tribunal against the assessment at any time within the period of four months from the date of the service of the assessment notice or within such further period or periods as the Board may allow before such time as may then be limited for appealing has expired.

(3) If the Board shall not allow an application for extension of time for appealing, an appeal tribunal shall upon application made to the tribunal by the person assessed to the levy have the like powers as the Board under the foregoing paragraph.

(4) In the case of an establishment that ceases to carry on business in the

fifth levy period on any day after the date of the service of the relevant assessment notice, the foregoing provisions of this Article shall have effect as if for the period of four months from the date of the service of the assessment notice mentioned in paragraph (2) of this Article there were substituted the period of six months from the date of the cessation of business.

(5) An appeal or an application to an appeal tribunal under this Article shall be made in accordance with the Industrial Tribunals (England and Wales) Regulations 1965(**a**) as amended by the Industrial Tribunals (England and Wales) (Amendment) Regulations 1967(**b**) except where the establishment to which the relevant assessment relates is wholly in Scotland in which case the appeal or application shall be made in accordance with the Industrial Tribunals (Scotland) Regulations 1965(**c**) as amended by the Industrial Tribunals (Scotland) (Amendment) Regulations 1967(**d**).

(6) The powers of an appeal tribunal under paragraph (3) of this Article may be exercised by the President of the Industrial Tribunals (England and Wales) or by the President of the Industrial Tribunals (Scotland) as the case may be.

Evidence

8.—(1) Upon the discharge by a person assessed to the levy of his liability under an assessment the Board shall if so requested issue to him a certificate to that effect.

(2) The production in any proceedings of a document purporting to be certified by the Secretary of the Board to be a true copy of an assessment or other notice issued by the Board or purporting to be a certificate such as is mentioned in the foregoing paragraph of this Article shall, unless the contrary is proved, be sufficient evidence of the document and of the facts stated therein.

Signed by order of the Secretary of State.
30th October 1969.

Edmund Dell,
Minister of State,
Department of Employment and Productivity.

Article 3

SCHEDULE

1.—(1) In this Schedule unless the context otherwise requires—

    (*a*) "the appropriate percentage" means, in relation to the emoluments of persons employed at or from a wool, jute and flax establishment that was engaged wholly or mainly in any one or more of the activities comprised in one of the thirteen groups of activities specified in the first and second columns of the Appendix to this Schedule, the percentage specified in relation to that group in the third column of that Appendix ;

    (*b*) "arranging for the carrying out on commission" in relation to any activities mentioned in the Appendix to this Schedule means arranging for the carrying out by another person in pursuance of a contract of work or

---

(**a**) S.I. 1965/1101 (1965 II, p. 2805).   (**b**) S.I. 1967/301 (1967 I, p. 1040).
(**c**) S.I. 1965/1157 (1965 II, p. 3266).   (**d**) S.I. 1967/302 (1967 I, p. 1050).

labour (with or without the provision of materials) of those activities wholly or mainly upon or from materials owned in the course of his business by the person for whom such activities are to be carried out ;

(c) "production" in relation to any yarn or fabric includes any of the processes mentioned in sub-paragraphs (d), (e), (f) and (g) of paragraph 1 of the Schedule to the industrial training order ;

(d) "related or administrative activities" means activities of a kind to which paragraph 1(r) of the Schedule to the industrial training order applies ;

(e) other expressions have the meanings assigned to them respectively by paragraph 3 or 4 of the Schedule to the industrial training order or by Article 2 of this Order.

(2) The activities in any Group (other than Group 1) specified in the first and second columns of the Appendix to this Schedule include the activities of arranging either directly or through another person for the carrying out on commission of any activities comprised in that Group, and the activities comprised in any such Group (including Group 1) include any related or administrative activities undertaken in relation to any activities comprised in such Group.

(3) In reckoning any sum of emoluments for the purposes of this Schedule no regard shall be had to the emoluments of any person engaged wholly in the supply of food or drink for immediate consumption.

2. Subject to the provisions of this Schedule, the amount of the levy imposed on an employer in respect of a wool, jute and flax establishment shall be equal to the appropriate percentage of the sum (less £5,000) of the emoluments of all persons employed by the employer at or from the establishment in the fifth base period.

3. The amount of the levy imposed in respect of a wool, jute and flax establishment that ceases to carry on business in the fifth levy period shall be in the same proportion to the amount that would otherwise be due in accordance with the foregoing provisions of this Schedule as the number of days between the commencement of the said levy period and the date of cessation of business (both dates inclusive) bears to the number of days in the said levy period.

APPENDIX

Group No.	Description of Activities	Appropriate Percentage
1.	Dealing in—	0·2
	(a) fleeces, textile fibres (not being jute, flax, hemp or similar fibres) or tops ; or	
	(b) yarn not consisting of jute, flax, hemp or similar fibres.	
2.	The activities following or any of them—	0·55
	(a) sorting, packing, or warehousing fleeces not being the property of the British Wool Marketing Board ;	
	(b) sorting, packing, re-packing or warehousing textile fibres, tops or yarn.	
3.	The activities following (not being activities comprised in Group 4, 6, 8, 11 or 13 of this Appendix) or any of them—	0·6
	(a) treating (other than dyeing), using or consuming textile fibres (not being jute, flax, hemp or similar fibres) or tops ;	

Group No.	Description of Activities	Appropriate Percentage

(b) treating (other than dyeing) rags or reducing into a fibrous form rags or yarn or, when carried out by an employer engaged in any such process, the ripping of rags.

4. The activities following (not being activities comprised in Group 6, 8 or 13 of this Appendix) or any of them—   0·65

     (a) the manufacture of needle felt ;

     (b) hackling, carding, combing or re-combing any textile fibres or the conversion, for use in making rovings or spinning yarn, of any textile fibres or tow (other than jute, flax, hemp or similar fibres or tow made therefrom) into tops, hank tops, bumps or slivers.

5. The manufacture of pressed felt.   0·8

6. The production (other than burling and finished mending) of woven fabric, being production in a textile factory from any textile fibres or from continuous filament and, in either case, by a system of manufacture commonly employed in the production of woollen yarn or woollen fabric or by a system similar thereto.   0·95

7. The activities following or any of them—   1·0

     (a) the production of—

         (i) yarn from jute ;

         (ii) any woven fabric from such yarn ; or

         (iii) any other yarn or woven fabric, being production in a textile factory from any textile fibres or from continuous filament and, in either case, by a system of manufacture commonly employed in the production of jute yarn or jute fabric or by a system similar thereto ;

     (b) dyeing textile fibres, tops or yarn or any woven fabric containing textile fibres other jute, flax, hemp or similar fibres or yarn or any woven fabric made therefrom) ;

     (c) any process of dyeing, flame-proofing, moth-proofing, rot-proofing, water-proofing, tarring, bleaching, shrinking, printing, calendering, finishing, milling, tentering, raising, whipping, binding, tabbing, perching. assessing or cloth examination of any woven fabric containing textile fibres other than jute, flax, hemp or similar fibres.

8. The activities following or any of them—   1·1

     (a) burling and finished mending of any woven fabric ;

     (b) the production of woven fabric being production in a textile factory from any textile fibres or from continuous filament and, in either case, by a system of manufacture

Group No.	Description of Activities	Appropriate Percentage

commonly employed in the production of worsted yarn or worsted fabric or by a system similar thereto ;

(c) making up yarn for the purpose of hand knitting in the form of hanks, skeins, balls or the like of a kind normally sold by retail, when neither the employer engaged in such making up nor an associated company of the employer, being a company, is engaged in the production of woollen or worsted yarn.

9.   Any activities of the wool, jute and flax industry, not being activities comprised in any other Group in this Appendix.   1·25

10.   The making or re-making of rope, cord, core for wire ropes, lines, twine, string or similar articles, not being fancy cords.   1·35

11.   Making rovings, from textile fibres or tops, or spinning yarn or twisting, doubling, folding, winding, warping, warp dressing, beaming, reeling, curling, sizing or any other process (not being dyeing) in the preparation of yarn for further processing, being processes carried out—   1·65

(a) from or upon textile fibres, tops, yarn or continuous filament produced in a textile factory by a system of manufacture commonly employed in the production of worsted yarn or by a system similar thereto ; and

(b) by an employer who is not engaged in making up the yarn in the form of hanks, skeins, balls or the like of a kind normally sold by retail and none of whose associated companies (if any) are so engaged.

12.   The production of—   1·7

(a) yarn from flax ;

(b) any woven fabric from such yarn ; or

(c) any other yarn or woven fabric, being production in a textile factory from any textile fibres or from continuous filament and, in either case, by a system of manufacture commonly employed in the production of flax yarn or flax fabric or by a system similar thereto.

13.   The production (other than dyeing) of woollen or worsted yarn for the purpose of hand knitting, when the employer engaged in the production of such yarn (or an associated company of the employer, being a company) is engaged, at the same establishment or elsewhere and either directly or through another person on commission, in making up such yarn in the form of hanks, skeins, balls or the like of a kind normally sold by retail.   2·0

EXPLANATORY NOTE

(*This Note is not part of the Order.*)

This Order gives effect to proposals submitted to the Secretary of State for Employment and Productivity by the Wool, Jute and Flax Industry Training Board for the imposition of a further levy upon employers in the wool, jute and flax industry for the purposes of raising money towards the expenses of the Board.

The levy is to be imposed in respect of the fifth levy period commencing with the day upon which this Order comes into operation and ending on 5th April 1970. The levy will be assessed by the Board and there will be a right of appeal to an industrial tribunal.

STATUTORY INSTRUMENTS

1969 No. 1547 (L.26)

COUNTY COURTS

The County Court Funds (Amendment No. 2) Rules 1969

Made - - - -	*30th October* 1969
Laid before Parliament	*10th November* 1969
Coming into Operation	*1st December* 1969

The Lord Chancellor, with the concurrence of the Treasury and in pursuance of the powers contained in section 168 of the County Courts Act 1959(a), as amended by section 9 of the Administration of Justice Act 1965(b), hereby makes the following Rules:—

1. These Rules may be cited as the County Court Funds (Amendment No. 2) Rules 1969 and shall come into operation on 1st December 1969.

2. The County Court Funds Rules 1965(c), as amended(d), shall have effect subject to the amendments set out in the Schedule to these Rules.

Dated 27th October 1969.

Gardiner, C.

We concur

Dated 30th October 1969.

Ernest Armstrong,
Joseph Harper,
Two of the Lords Commissioners
of Her Majesty's Treasury.

(a) 1959 c. 22.
(c) S.I. 1965/1500 (1965 II, p.4343).
(b) 1965 c. 2.
(d) There are no relevant amendments.

SCHEDULE

AMENDMENTS TO COUNTY COURT FUNDS RULES 1965

1. The following amendments shall be made in the Arrangement of Rules:—

   (*a*) in Part IV, after the words "By post" and "By cheque", where they respectively occur, there shall be added the words "or through the National Giro"; and

   (*b*) in the heading to Part X, for the words "Post Office Register", there shall be substituted the words "National Savings Stock Register".

2. In rule 2(1) (which relates to the interpretation of terms)—

   (*a*) after the definitions of "the bank", "court" and "deposit account" respectively, there shall be inserted the following definitions:—

   ' "central control account" means the Accountant-General's county court account opened with the National Giro';

   ' "court's Giro account" means the account opened with the National Giro on behalf of a court and subsidiary to the central control account';

   ' "Director of Savings" means the person appointed as such in pursuance of section 93(1) of the Post Office Act 1969(**a**)'; and

   (*b*) the definition of "Controller" shall be omitted.

3. For rule 3 (which relates to the payment of suitors' money into court), there shall be substituted the following rule:—

   "3. Suitors' money to be paid into court may be so paid either—

   (*a*) through the National Giro, or

   (*b*) by post or otherwise into the office of the registrar, in which case payment may be made during office hours on any day on which the office is open and the registrar shall give a receipt therefor".

4. For rule 4 (which relates to suitors' money paid into court), there shall be substituted the following rule:—

   "4. Money received pursuant to the last preceding rule which is not required for making authorised payments shall be paid by the registrar into the bank to the credit of his official account (or into the court's Giro account, as the registrar may determine) on the day of receipt or, if that is not practicable, on the next working day".

5. In rule 6 (which relates to the transmission of money from one court to another), after the word "transmitted", where it appears for the second time, there shall be inserted the words:—

   "through the National Giro or".

6. The following amendments shall be made to rule 8 (which relates to the payment of suitors' money out of court):—

   (*a*) in paragraph (3), after the words "crossed cheque", there shall be inserted the words "or through the National Giro"; and

   (*b*) paragraph (4) shall be omitted.

7. The following amendments shall be made to rule 10 (which relates to the transmission of suitors' money by post):—

   (*a*) at the end of paragraph (1), there shall be inserted the words "or through the National Giro";

   (*b*) in paragraph (2)(*b*), after the words "crossed cheque", there shall be inserted the words "or through the National Giro";

(**a**) 1969 c. 48.

(c) in paragraph 2(c), after the words "sufficiently stamped", there shall be inserted the words "for the return of the proof of title and, where appropriate,";

(d) in paragraph (3), for the words "forward the money", there shall be substituted the words "pay the money through the National Giro or forward it".

8. At the end of rule 11 (which relates to payment of suitors' money out of court), there shall be inserted the words "or pay that sum through the National Giro".

9. In rule 12(1) (which relates to the payment of funds into court), after subparagraph (a), there shall be inserted the following subparagraph:—

"(aa) transmit the money through the National Giro, or".

10. In rule 13 (which relates to the transfer of funds from one court to another), for paragraph (1)(a), there shall be substituted the following subparagraph:—

"(a) in the case of stock on the National Savings Stock Register, through the Director of Savings;".

11. For rule 14 (which relates to the duties of registrars), there shall be substituted the following rule:—

"14—(1) All funds paid into court or transferred from a District Registry shall be paid by the registrar into the bank to the credit of his official account (or into the court's Giro account, as the registrar may determine) on the day of receipt or, if that is not practicable, on the next working day.

(2) The registrar shall, at such intervals as the Lord Chancellor may direct, give to the Accountant-General written notice of the total payments made by him in pursuance of paragraph (1), above.

(3) The registrar shall, whenever convenient, transfer to the court's Giro account any sum standing to the credit of his official account at the bank which is surplus to his requirements and shall, at such intervals as the Lord Chancellor may in the case of any court authorise, transfer to the central control account any sum then standing to the credit of the court's Giro account.

(4) All securities deposited with the registrar shall be kept in the office safe or placed in the custody of the bank".

12. The following amendments shall be made to paragraph (2) of rule 16 (which relates to the opening of deposit accounts):—

(a) in subparagraph (a), the words "and shall transmit that amount to the Accountant-General, and" shall be omitted;

(b) at the end of subparagraph (b) there shall be added the word "and"; and

(c) after subparagraph (b) there shall be inserted the following subparagraph:—

"(c) at such intervals as the Lord Chancellor may direct, give to the Accountant-General written notice of the total of the amounts paid in."

13. In rule 26 (which relates to the payment of funds out of court)—

(a) for paragraph (2), there shall be substituted the following paragraph:—

"(2) If the cash in hand and in the bank is insufficient to make the payment, the registrar shall (save where he makes the payment through the National Giro) transfer the sum required from the court's Giro account (irrespective of the amount, if any, standing to the credit of that account) to his bank account"; and

(b) after the words "crossed cheque" in paragraph (4), there shall be inserted the words "or through the National Giro".

14. In rule 28 (which relates to the duties of the Accountant-General), for the words

"by registrars for making payments out of court", there shall be substituted the words "for payment into the central control account so as to enable him to keep courts' Giro accounts in balance".

15. In the heading to Part X (which relates to funds invested in stock on the Post Office Register), for the words "*Post Office Register*", there shall be substituted the words "*National Savings Stock Register*" and, in rules 33 and 35, for the word "Controller", wherever it appears, there shall be substituted the words "Director of Savings".

EXPLANATORY NOTE

(*This Note is not part of the Rules*.)

These Rules amend the County Court Funds Rules 1965 by providing for the payment of money into, or out of, a county court through accounts opened with the National Giro. The new rule substituted for rule 14 requires each registrar, at intervals to be specified by the Lord Chancellor, to transfer to the Accountant-General's central account with the Giro any sum standing to the credit of the court's Giro account, while the amendment to rule 28 requires the Accountant-General to make payments into the central account so as to enable him to keep courts' Giro accounts in balance. The Rules also make minor verbal amendments consequential on the coming into force of the Post Office Act 1969.

The Rules come into operation on 1st December 1969.

STATUTORY INSTRUMENTS

1969 No. 1549

SOCIAL SECURITY

The National Insurance (Modification of the Superannuation Acts) (Amendment) Regulations 1969

Made - - -	31*st October* 1969	
Laid before Parliament	7*th November* 1969	
Coming into Operation	8*th November* 1969	

The Minister for the Civil Service, having determined under section 110(1) of the National Insurance Act 1965(a) and article 2(2) of the Minister for the Civil Service Order 1968(b) that he is the appropriate Minister of the Crown in relation to the scheme for the provision of pensions established by the Superannuation Acts 1965 and 1967(c), and in exercise of the powers conferred on him by the said section 110(1) and of all other powers enabling him in that behalf, hereby makes the following Regulations :—

1. These Regulations may be cited as the National Insurance (Modification of the Superannuation Acts) (Amendment) Regulations 1969, and shall come into operation on 8th November 1969.

2. The Interpretation Act 1889(d) shall apply for the interpretation of these Regulations as it applies for the interpretation of an Act of Parliament, and as if these Regulations and the Regulations hereby revoked were Acts of Parliament.

3. The National Insurance (Modification of the Superannuation Acts) Regulations 1960(e), as amended (f), shall be further amended by substituting for paragraph (3) of Regulation 4 thereof the following paragraph :—

"(3) In calculating for the purposes of paragraphs (1)(c) and (2) of this Regulation the number of units of a person's graduated contributions, no account shall be taken of so much of any contributions calculated in accordance with section 4(1)(c) or (d) of the National Insurance Act 1965 as is attributable to the amendment of section 4(1) of that Act by section 1(2) of the National Insurance Act 1966(g) or section 1(2) of the National Insurance Act 1969(h)."

(a) 1965 c. 51. (b) S.I. 1968/1656 (1968 III, p. 4485).
(c) 1965 c. 74; 1967 c. 28. (d) 1889 c. 63.
(e) S.I. 1960/1270 (1960 II, p. 2297).
(f) The relevant amending instrument is S.I. 1966/952 (1966 II, p. 2299).
(g) 1966 c. 6. (h) 1969 c. 44.

4. The National Insurance (Modification of the Superannuation Acts) (Amendment) Regulations 1966(**a**) are hereby revoked.

Given under the official seal of the Minister for the Civil Service on 31st October 1969.

(L.S.)

K. H. McNeill,
Authorised by the Minister
for the Civil Service.

EXPLANATORY NOTE
(This Note is not part of the Regulations.)

Regulation 4 of the National Insurance (Modification of the Superannuation Acts) Regulations 1960 provides for the reduction of the superannuation allowance payable during any period after age 65 (60 for women) to an established civil servant who is entitled to a graduated National Insurance pension, where any of the graduated pension is attributable to service in the civil service which is reckonable for determining the amount of his superannuation allowance.

These Regulations amend the Regulations of 1960 so as to provide that graduated pension which accrues by virtue of the additional contributions for earnings-related short-term benefits introduced by the National Insurance Act 1966 or by virtue of the new graduated contributions introduced by the National Insurance Act 1969 shall be disregarded when such reductions are calculated.

The Regulations revoke and replace the National Insurance (Modification of the Superannuation Acts) (Amendment) Regulations 1966, which contained similar provisions in relation only to those additional contributions which were introduced by the National Insurance Act 1966.

(**a**) S.I. 1966/952 (1966 II, p. 2299).

STATUTORY   INSTRUMENTS

1969 No. 1550

AGRICULTURE

The Price Stability of Imported Products (Rates of Levy No. 23) Order 1969

Made - - - -		*3rd November* 1969
Coming into Operation -		*4th November* 1969

The Minister of Agriculture, Fisheries and Food, in exercise of the powers conferred upon him by section 1(2), (4), (5), (6) and (7) of the Agriculture and Horticulture Act 1964(a) and of all other powers enabling him in that behalf, hereby makes the following order:—

1. This order may be cited as the Price Stability of Imported Products (Rates of Levy No. 23) Order 1969, and shall come into operation on 4th November 1969.

2.—(1) In this order—

" the Principal Order " means the Price Stability of Imported Products (Levy Arrangements) Order 1966(b) as amended(c) and as amended by any subsequent order, and if any such order is replaced by any subsequent order the expression shall be construed as a reference to such subsequent order;

AND other expressions have the same meaning as in the Principal Order.

(2) The Interpretation Act 1889(d) shall apply to the interpretation of this order as it applies to the interpretation of an Act of Parliament and as if this order and the orders hereby revoked were Acts of Parliament.

3. In accordance with and subject to the provisions of Part II of the Principal Order (which provides for the charging of levies on imports of certain specified commodities)—

(*a*) the rate of general levy for such imports into the United Kingdom of any specified commodity as are described in column 2 of Part I of the Schedule to this order in relation to a tariff heading indicated in column 1 of that Part shall be the rate set forth in relation thereto in column 3 of that Part;

(*b*) the rate of country levy for such imports into the United Kingdom of any specified commodity as are described in column 2 of Part II of the Schedule to this order in relation to a tariff heading indicated in column 1 of that Part shall be the rate set forth in relation thereto in column 3 of that Part.

(a) 1964 c. 28. (b) S.I. 1966/936 (1966 II, p. 2271).
(c) S.I. 1969/758 (1969 II, p. 2137). (d) 1889 c. 63.

4. The Price Stability of Imported Products (Rates of Levy No. 22) Order 1969(a) is hereby revoked.

In Witness whereof the Official Seal of the Minister of Agriculture, Fisheries and Food is hereunto affixed on 3rd November 1969.

(L.S.)

J. A. Barrah,
Assistant Secretary.

SCHEDULE

PART I

1. Tariff Heading	2. Description of Imports	3. Rate of General Levy
		per ton £ s. d.
	Imports of:—	
10.01	Denatured wheat	10 0
10.01	Any wheat (other than seed wheat the value of which is not less than £34 per ton, denatured wheat, durum wheat and wheat which has been grown in and consigned to the United Kingdom from the Union of Soviet Socialist Republics or the Hungarian People's Republic) for which a minimum import price level is prescribed	5 0
10.03	Barley	2 10 0
11.01	Wheat flours	15 0
11.02	Cereal meals— of barley .. .. of maize	7 5 0 1 0 0
11.02	Rolled, flaked, crushed or bruised cereals— barley	5 15 0

(a) S.I. 1969/1518(1969 III, p.4939).

PART II

1. Tariff Heading	2. Description of Imports	3. Rate of Country Levy
		per ton £ s. d.
10.01	Imports of:— Denatured wheat which has been grown in and consigned to the United Kingdom from Belgium, the French Republic or the Kingdom of the Netherlands	10 0
10.01	Any wheat (other than seed wheat the value of which is not less than £34 per ton, denatured wheat and durum wheat) for which a minimum import price level is prescribed and which has been grown in and consigned to the United Kingdom from Belgium or the French Republic	5 0

10.03	Barley which has been grown in and consigned to the United Kingdom from—
	    the Kingdom of the Netherlands .. ..
	    the French Republic .. ..
	    Canada .. ..
		2 0 0
		2 5 0
		2 10 0

EXPLANATORY NOTE

(*This Note is not part of the Order.*)

This order, which comes into operation on 4th November 1969, supersedes the Price Stability of Imported Products (Rates of Levy No. 22) Order 1969. It:—

(*a*) reduces to 10*s.* per ton both the general levy on denatured wheat and the country levy on denatured wheat grown in and consigned to the United Kingdom from Belgium, France or the Netherlands;

(*b*) reduces to 5*s.* per ton the general levy on imports of wheat (other than seed wheat the value of which is not less than £34 per ton, denatured wheat, durum wheat and wheat which has been grown in and consigned to the United Kingdom from the U.S.S.R. or Hungary);

(*c*) removes from general levy imports of wheat grown in and consigned to the United Kingdom from the U.S.S.R.;

(*d*) reduces to 5*s.* per ton the country levy on imports of wheat (other than seed wheat the value of which is not less than £34 per ton, denatured wheat and durum wheat) which has been grown in and consigned to the United Kingdom from Belgium or France; and

(*e*) reimposes unchanged the other rates of general and country levy in force immediately before the commencement of the order.

STATUTORY INSTRUMENTS

1969 No. 1551 (C. 42)

SEA FISHERIES

The Sea Fisheries Act 1968 (Commencement No. 1) Order 1969

Made - - -	31*st October* 1969
Laid before Parliament	11*th November* 1969
Coming into Operation	24*th November* 1969

The Minister of Agriculture, Fisheries and Food and the Secretaries of State for Scotland and the Home Department (being the Secretaries of State respectively concerned with the sea-fishing industry in Scotland and Northern Ireland) in exercise of the powers conferred on them by section 23 of the Sea Fisheries Act 1968(a) (hereinafter referred to as "the Act") and of all other powers enabling them in that behalf hereby make the following Order:—

1. This Order may be cited as the Sea Fisheries Act 1968 (Commencement No. 1) Order 1969 and shall come into operation on the 24th November 1969.

2. The following provisions of the Act shall come into force:—

Section 5 (regulation of conduct of fishing operations)

Section 6 (restriction on fishing within the fishery limits of the British Islands)

Section 7 (sea-fishery officers)

Section 8 (general powers of British sea-fishery officers)

Section 9 (powers of sea-fishery officers to enforce conventions)

Section 10 (miscellaneous provisions as to sea-fishery officers)

Section 11 (evidence)

Section 12 (recovery of fines imposed on master, etc. or crew)

Section 13 (compensation for damage caused by offence)

Section 14 (jurisdiction to try offences)

Part II of Schedule 1 (minor and consequential amendments)

Part II of Schedule 2 (enactments repealed) with the exception of the following provisions:—

The Sea Fisheries Act 1883(b) Sections 1 to 5, 11, 12, 14 to 22, in Section 25 the words "this Act shall apply to the whole of the British Islands as defined by this Act and to the seas surrounding the same whether within or without the fishery limits of the British Islands", sections 26, 28 and 31 and Articles XIII to XXIII and XXX, XXXI and XXXIII of the First Schedule.

The Sea Fisheries (Scotland) Act 1885(c) section 5

The Illegal Trawling (Scotland) Act 1934(d) section 3

The Sea Fisheries Act 1951(e) section 25

The Sea Fish Industry Act 1962(f) section 18

The Fishery Limits Act 1964(g) section 3(2)

(a) 1968 c. 77.   (b) 1883 c. 22.
(c) 1885 c. 70.   (d) 1934 c. 18.
(e) 1951 c. 30.   (f) 1962 c. 31.
(g) 1964 c. 72.

In Witness whereof the Official Seal of the Minister of Agriculture, Fisheries and Food is hereunto affixed on 23rd October 1969.

(L.S.)

Cledwyn Hughes,
Minister of Agriculture,
Fisheries and Food.

Given under the Seal of the Secretary of State for Scotland on 27th October 1969.

(L.S.)

William Ross,
Secretary of State for Scotland.

Given under the Hand of the Secretary of State for the Home Department on 31st October 1969.

James Callaghan,
Secretary of State for the Home
Department.

EXPLANATORY NOTE

(This Note is not part of the Order.)

This Order brings into force on 24th November 1969 those provisions of the Sea Fisheries Act 1968 which are not already in operation except the repeal of certain provisions of the Sea Fisheries Act 1883 and of certain other enactments related to that Act.

STATUTORY INSTRUMENTS

1969 No. 1552 (C.43)

CHILDREN AND YOUNG PERSONS

The Children and Young Persons Act 1969 (Commencement No. 1) Order 1969

Made	-	-	-	*3rd November* 1969

In exercise of the powers conferred upon me by section 73(2) of the Children and Young Persons Act 1969(a), I hereby make the following Order:—

Citation

1. This Order may be cited as the Children and Young Persons Act 1969 (Commencement No. 1) Order 1969.

Interpretation

2. In this Order "the Act" means the Children and Young Persons Act 1969.

Day appointed for coming into force of certain provisions of the Act

3. The provisions of the Act specified in column 1 of the Schedule to this Order (which relate to the matters specified in column 2 thereof) shall come into operation on 16th November 1969.

James Callaghan,
One of Her Majesty's Principal
Secretaries of State.

Home Office,
Whitehall.
3rd November 1969.

(a) 1969 c. 54.

SCHEDULE

PROVISIONS COMING INTO FORCE ON 16TH NOVEMBER 1969

Provisions of the Act	Subject matter of provisions
Section 69	Orders and regulations etc.
Section 70	Interpretation and ancillary provisions.
Section 72(3), so far as it relates to paragraphs 63, 64(1), 69, 73, 75 and 76 of Schedule 5	Minor and consequential amendments.
Section 72(4), so far as it relates to the repeal set out in the Appendix to this Schedule	Repeals.
Section 73	Citation, commencement and extent.
Paragraphs 63, 64(1), 69, 73, 75 and 76 of Schedule 5	Amendment of sections 90(1) and 94(1) of the Social Work (Scotland) Act 1968 and of paragraph 1(1) (a) of Schedule 7 and paragraphs 17(1), 51(1) and 54 of Schedule 8 thereto.
Schedule 6, so far as it relates to the repeal set out in the Appendix to this Schedule	Repeals.

APPENDIX TO SCHEDULE

REPEAL TAKING EFFECT FROM 16TH NOVEMBER 1969

Chapter	Short title	Extent of repeal
1968 c. 49.	The Social Work (Scotland) Act 1968.	In section 90(1) the words "or to prescribe any matter".

EXPLANATORY NOTE

(This Note is not part of the Order.)

This Order brings into force the provisions of the Children and Young Persons Act 1969 specified in the Schedule to the Order on 16th November 1969.

STATUTORY INSTRUMENTS

1969 No. 1564

AGRICULTURE

The Price Stability of Imported Products (Levy Arrangements) (Amendment No. 2) Order 1969

Made - - -	*4th November* 1969
Laid before Parliament	*13th November* 1969
Coming into Operation	*17th November* 1969

The Minister of Agriculture, Fisheries and Food and the Secretaries of State respectively concerned with agriculture in Scotland and Northern Ireland, acting jointly in exercise of the powers conferred upon them by section 1(2), (3), (4), (6) and (7) of the Agriculture and Horticulture Act 1964(a) and of all other powers enabling them in that behalf, with the approval of the Treasury, hereby make the following order:—

1. This order may be cited as the Price Stability of Imported Products (Levy Arrangements) (Amendment No. 2) Order 1969, and shall come into operation on 17th November 1969.

2. The Price Stability of Imported Products (Levy Arrangements) Order 1966(b) as amended (c) shall be further amended by adding to the countries named in Schedule 2 thereto the following entries:—

"The Union of Soviet Socialist Republics
The Hungarian People's Republic".

In Witness whereof the Official Seal of the Minister of Agriculture, Fisheries and Food is hereunto affixed on 9th October 1969.

(L.S.)   *Cledwyn Hughes,*
                Minister of Agriculture, Fisheries and Food.

Given under the Seal of the Secretary of State for Scotland on 14th October 1969.

(L.S.)   *William Ross,*
                      Secretary of State for Scotland.

Given under the hand of the Secretary of State for the Home Department on 31st October 1969.

                                     James Callaghan,
               Secretary of State for the Home Department.

Approved, 4th November 1969.

                                     Neil McBride,
                                    Joseph Harper,
                 Two of the Lords Commissioners of
                              Her Majesty's Treasury.

(a) 1964 c. 28.   (b) S.I. 1966/936 (1966 II, p. 2271).
(c) The amending order is not relevant to the subject matter of this order.

EXPLANATORY NOTE

(This Note is not part of the order.)

This order amends the Price Stability of Imported Products (Levy Arrangements) Order 1966, as amended, by adding the U.S.S.R. and Hungary to the list of co-operating countries. The original order provides for exemption from any general levy for imports from co-operating countries.

STATUTORY INSTRUMENTS

1969 No. 1565 (C.44)

CHILDREN AND YOUNG PERSONS

The Children and Young Persons Act 1969
(Commencement No. 2) Order 1969

Made - - - -   *6th November* 1969

In exercise of the powers conferred on me by section 73(2) and (3) of the Children and Young Persons Act 1969(a), I hereby make the following Order:—

Citation

1. This Order may be cited as the Children and Young Persons Act 1969 (Commencement No. 2) Order 1969.

Interpretation and extent

2.—(1) In this Order "the Act" means the Children and Young Persons Act 1969.

(2) Nothing in this Order shall bring into force, in their application to Scotland, any provisions of paragraph 54 of Schedule 5 to the Act and, accordingly, the references to the said provisions in Schedule 1 to this Order shall not include references thereto in their application to Scotland.

Days appointed for coming into force of certain provisions of the Act

3. The provisions of the Act specified in column 1 of each of the first two Schedules to this Order (which relate to the matters specified in column 2 thereof) shall, subject to Article 2(2) of this Order, come into force on the day specified in the heading to that Schedule.

Transitional provisions

4. The transitional provisions contained in Schedule 3 to this Order shall have effect in connection with the provisions brought into force by this Order which are referred to in that Schedule.

James Callaghan,
One of Her Majesty's Principal
Secretaries of State.

Home Office,
  Whitehall.
6th November 1969.

(a) 1969 c. 54.

SCHEDULE 1

PROVISIONS COMING INTO FORCE ON 1ST DECEMBER 1969

Provisions of the Act	Subject matter of provisions
Section 33(1), so far as it relates to paragraph 6 of Schedule 1.	Legal aid.
Section 35	Regional planning of accommodation for children in care.
Section 36	Regional plans for community homes.
Section 37	Approval and variation of regional plans.
Section 38	Provision of community homes by local authorities.
Section 39	Instruments of management for assisted and controlled community homes.
Section 40	Supplementary provisions as to instruments of management and trust deeds.
Section 41	Management of controlled community homes.
Section 42	Management of assisted community homes.
Section 43	Control of premises used for, and conduct of, community homes.
Section 44	Controlled and assisted community homes exempted from certain provisions as to voluntary homes.
Section 45	Determination of disputes relating to controlled and assisted community homes.
Section 46, except subsection (2) so far as it relates to paragraphs 3, 4 and 8 of Schedule 3.	Discontinuance of approved schools etc. on establishment of community homes.
Section 47	Discontinuance by voluntary organisation of controlled or assisted community home.
Section 48	Financial provisions applicable on cessation of controlled or assisted community home.
Section 49	Provision of accommodation and maintenance for children in care.

5022   CHILDREN AND YOUNG PERSONS

Sch. 1 (*contd.*)

Provisions of the Act	Subject matter of provisions
Section 50	Accommodation of persons over school age in convenient community home.
Section 58	Inspection of children's homes etc. by persons authorised by Secretary of State.
Section 59	Powers of entry supplemental to section 58.
Section 60	Extradition offences.
Section 62(2)	Contributions in respect of children and young persons in care.
Section 63	Returns of information and presentation of reports etc. to Parliament.
Section 64	Expenses of Secretary of State in providing homes offering specialised facilities.
Section 65	Grants to voluntary organisations etc.
Section 66	Increase of rate support grants.
Section 67	Administrative expenses.
Section 68	Compulsory acquisition of land.
Section 71	Application to Isles of Scilly.
Section 72(1), so far as it relates to paragraphs 13 and 14 of Schedule 4.	Transitional provisions.
Section 72(3), so far as it relates to the provisions of Schedule 5 specified in Appendix A to this Schedule.	Minor and consequential amendments.
Section 72(4), so far as it relates to the repeals set out in Appendix B to this Schedule.	Repeals.
In Schedule 1, paragraph 6	Modifications of Part IV of Criminal Justice Act 1967(a).
Schedule 2	Children's regional planning committees.
Schedule 3, except paragraphs 3, 4 and 8	Approved schools and other institutions.
In Schedule 4, paragraphs 13 and 14	Transitional provisions and savings.
In Schedule 5, the provisions specified in Appendix A to this Schedule.	Minor and consequential amendments of enactments.

(a) 1967 c. 80.

Sch. 1 *(contd.)*

Provisions of the Act	Subject matter of provisions
Schedule 6, so far as it relates to the repeals set out in Appendix B to this Schedule.	Repeals.

APPENDIX A TO SCHEDULE 1

AMENDMENTS TAKING EFFECT FROM 1ST DECEMBER 1969

Provisions of Schedule 5	Enactments amended
Paragraph 4	Section 46 of the Children and Young Persons Act 1933(a).
Paragraphs 14, 15, 18, 19, 20(2), 21(1) and 21(3).	Sections 4(3), 20(1), 39(1), 43(1), 51(3) and 54(3) and (5) of the Children Act 1948(b).
In paragraph 20(1), the following provision:— 'In subsection (1) of section 51 of the said Act of 1948, for the words from "homes" to "this Act" there shall be substituted the words "community homes provided by them or in controlled community homes".'	Section 51(1) of the Children Act 1948.
Paragraph 37	Section 9 of the Mental Health Act 1959(c).
Paragraphs 51 and 52	Sections 45(1) and 49(1) of the Children and Young Persons Act 1963(d).
In paragraph 54(2), the following provision:— 'for the words from "5(1)" to "1956" there shall be substituted the words "13(2) of the Children Act 1948".'	Section 11(2) of the Family Allowances Act 1965(e).
Paragraph 54(3)	Section 11(3) of the Family Allowances Act 1965.
Paragraphs 65(2) and 66	Sections 97(1) and 98 of the Social Work (Scotland) Act 1968(f).

(a) 1933 c. 12.	(b) 1948 c. 43.
(c) 1959 c. 72.	(d) 1963 c. 37.
(e) 1965 c. 53	(f) 1968 c. 49.

APPENDIX B TO SCHEDULE 1

REPEALS TAKING EFFECT FROM 1ST DECEMBER 1969

Chapter	Short title	Extent of repeal
1894 c. 60.	The Merchant Shipping Act 1894.	In section 183(3), the proviso.
1918 c. 57.	The War Pensions (Administrative Provisions) Act 1918.	Section 9(4).
1920 c. 23.	The War Pensions Act 1920.	Section 9.
1933 c. 12.	The Children and Young Persons Act 1933.	Sections 76(2) and 77(1). Section 94.
1948 c. 43.	The Children Act 1948	Section 3(3) to (5). In section 4(3), the proviso. Sections 7, 15 and 16. Section 39(1)(e). Section 51(2). Section 54(1) and (2).
1956 c.50.	The Family Allowances and National Insurance Act 1956.	Section 5.
1958 c. 65.	The Children Act 1958.	In Schedule 2 the entry relating to section 54 of the Children Act 1948.
1963 c. 37.	The Children and Young Persons Act 1963.	Section 1(4).
1968 c. 49.	The Social Work (Scotland) Act 1968.	In Schedule 8, paragraph 18.

SCHEDULE 2

PROVISIONS COMING INTO FORCE ON 1ST JANUARY 1970

Provisions of the Act	Subject matter of provisions
Section 51	Modification of general duty of local authorities with respect to foster children.
Section 52	Amendments of definitions of "foster child" and "protected child".
Section 53	Modification of duty of persons maintaining foster children to notify local authority.
Section 54	Inspection of premises in which foster children are kept.
Section 55	Imposition of requirements and prohibitions relating to the keeping of foster children.
Section 56, except subsection (1)(a).	Extension of disqualification for keeping foster children.

Sch. 2 *(contd.)*

Provisions of the Act	Subject matter of provisions
Section 57	Modifications of provisions as to offences.
Section 72(3), so far as it relates to the provisions of Schedule 5 specified in Appendix A to this Schedule.	Minor and consequential amendments.
Section 72(4), so far as it relates to the repeals set out in Appendix B to this Schedule.	Repeals.
Section 72(5), except so far as it relates to sections 2(4) and 6(1)(*b*) of the Children Act 1958.	Sections 1 to 6 and 14 of the Children Act 1958(a), as amended.
In Schedule 5, the provisions specified in Appendix A to this Schedule.	Minor and consequential amendments.
Schedule 6, so far as it relates to the repeals set out in Appendix B to this Schedule.	Repeals.
Schedule 7, except so far as it relates to sections 2(4) and 6(1)(*b*) of the Children Act 1958.	Sections 1 to 6 and 14 of the Children Act 1958, as amended.

APPENDIX A TO SCHEDULE 2

AMENDMENTS TAKING EFFECT FROM 1ST JANUARY 1970

Provisions of Schedule 5	Enactments amended
Paragraphs 30 and 31	Sections 9 and 12(1) of the Children Act 1958.
Paragraph 35	Section 37(2) of the Adoption Act 1958(b).

(a) 1958 c. 65.
(b) 1958(7 & 8 Eliz. 2)c. 5.

APPENDIX B TO SCHEDULE 2

REPEALS TAKING EFFECT FROM 1ST JANUARY 1970

Chapter	Short title	Extent of repeal
1958 c. 65.	The Children Act 1958.	In section 2, in subsection (1) the words from "for reward" to "one month", in subsection (2) the words from "by" in the first place where it occurs to "or" where that word first subsequently occurs, and subsections (6) and (7).
		In section 3, in subsection (4), the words from "or is removed" to "maintaining him" and the words from "or removal" onwards, in subsection (5) the words "need not give a notice under subsection (4) of this section but", and subsection (6).
1958 c. 5 (7 & 8 Eliz. 2)	The Adoption Act 1958.	In section 37, in subsection (1) the words "but is not a foster child within the meaning of Part 1 of the Children Act 1958", in subsection (2) the words from "by reason" to "subsection nor".

SCHEDULE 3

TRANSITIONAL MODIFICATIONS OF PARAGRAPHS 20 AND 37 OF SCHEDULE 5 TO THE ACT

So long as section 15 of the Children Act 1948 continues to apply to a local authority by virtue of paragraph 13 of Schedule 4 to the Act then, in relation to that authority, paragraphs 20 and 37 of Schedule 5 to the Act shall have effect as if they provided that section 51 of the said Act of 1948, as amended by the said paragraph 20, and section 9 of the Mental Health Act 1959, as amended by the said paragraph 37, should have effect as if a home provided by the local authority under the said section 15 were a community home so provided under the Act.

EXPLANATORY NOTE

(*This Note is not part of the Order.*)

This Order brings certain provisions of the Children and Young Persons Act 1969 into force (subject, in the case of two provisions, to transitional modifications contained in Schedule 3 to the Order).

The provisions specified in Schedule 1 to the Order are brought into force on 1st December 1969 and those specified in Schedule 2 on 1st January 1970.

STATUTORY INSTRUMENTS

1969 No. 1569 (C.45) (S.127)

TOWN AND COUNTRY PLANNING, SCOTLAND

The Town and Country Planning (Scotland) Act 1969

(Commencement No. 1) Order 1969

Made - - - -   30*th October* 1969

In exercise of the powers conferred on me by section 104 of the Town and Country Planning (Scotland) Act 1969**(a)**, I hereby make the following order:—

1.—(1) This order may be cited as the Town and Country Planning (Scotland) Act 1969 (Commencement No. 1) Order 1969.

(2) In this order:—

"the Act" means the Town and Country Planning (Scotland) Act 1969;

"the 1945 Act" means the Town and Country Planning (Scotland) Act 1945**(b)**;

"the 1947 Act" means the Town and Country Planning (Scotland) Act 1947**(c)**;

"the 1959 Act" means the Town and Country Planning (Scotland) Act 1959**(d)**.

2. The provisions of the Act specified in column 1 of Schedule 1 to this order (which relate to the matters specified in column 2 thereof) shall come into operation in the whole of Scotland on 8th December 1969.

3. The transitional provisions contained in Schedule 2 to this order shall have effect in connection with the provisions brought into force by this order

William Ross,
One of Her Majesty's Principal
Secretaries of State.

St. Andrew's House,
Edinburgh.
30th October 1969.

(a) 1969 c. 30.   (b) 1945 c. 33.
(c) 1947 c. 53.   (d) 1959 c. 70.

SCHEDULE I   Article 2

PROVISIONS COMING INTO OPERATION ON 8th DECEMBER 1969

Provisions of the Act	Subject matter of Provisions
Section 13	Regulations and directions as to structure and local plans, and provision for their operation.
Section 14	Proceedings for questioning validity of structure plans, etc.
Section 15	New provision as to enforcement notices.
Section 16	Appeal against enforcement notice.
Section 17	Enforcement notice to have effect against subsequent development.
Part IV (except section 35 and section 36 in so far as it relates to section 35).	Acquisition and disposal of land.
Section 61	Constitution of Planning Inquiry Commissions.
Section 62	References to a Planning Inquiry Commission.
Section 63	Procedure on reference to a Planning Inquiry Commission.
Section 64	Commissions to inquire into planning matters affecting Scotland and England.
Section 65	Delegation of planning functions to officers of local authorities.
Section 66	Limit of duration of planning permissions past and future.
Section 67	Outline planning permissions.
Section 68	Provisions supplementary to sections 66 and 67.
Section 69	Termination of planning permission by reference to time limit.
Section 70	New provision as to what is "operational land" of statutory undertakers.
Section 71	Planning applications and appeals by statutory undertakers.
Section 72	Restrictions on entitlement of statutory undertakers to compensation for adverse planning decisions.
Section 73	Modifications of section 24 of the 1945 Act.
Section 74	Notice for same purposes as section 24 of the 1945 Act but given by statutory undertakers to developing authority.

Provisions of the Act	Subject matter of Provisions
Section 75	Expansion of building below ground to constitute development.
Section 76	Modification of transitory exemptions based on pre-1948 use.
Section 78	Extension of section 12 of the 1947 Act with respect to development affecting trunk and special roads.
Section 79	Information regarding, and local register of, planning applications.
Section 80	Reference to Secretary of State of application for approval under outline planning permission.
Section 83	Notice by Secretary of State to planning authority when exercising default powers.
Section 84	Partial abrogation of dual control of office development.
Section 85	Modification of section 7 of Control of Office and Industrial Development Act 1965(a).
Section 86	Restriction on creation of office premises in building altered or extended.
Section 87	Corresponding restriction on planning permission for erection of several buildings.
Section 88	Provisions supplementary to sections 84 to 87.
Section 89	Procedure for making orders for stopping-up and diverting highways.
Section 90	New powers to authorise stopping-up and diversion of highways.
Section 93	Powers for local planning authorities analogous to section 46 of the 1947 Act.
Section 94	Extinguishment of footpaths etc. over land held for planning purposes.
Section 95	Confirmation, validity, etc. of orders under sections 93 and 94.
Section 96	Miscellaneous amendments of section 46 of, and Schedule 6 to, the 1947 Act.
Section 97	Grants for research, etc.
Section 98	Exchequer contributions in connection with town development.

(a) 1965 c. 33.

Provisions of the Act	Subject matter of Provisions
Section 99	Agreements of Crown Estate Commissioners.
Section 100	Increase of certain penalties under the 1947 Act and the 1959 Act.
Section 101	Offences by corporations.
Section 102	Expenses.
Section 103	Interpretation.
Section 104	Commencement.
Section 105	Adaptation, amendment and modification of enactments so far as it relates to those paragraphs of Schedule 9 to the Act specified below.
Section 106	Transitional provisions and savings so far as it relates to those paragraphs of Schedule 10 to the Act specified below.
Section 107	Repeals so far as relating to those provisions of Schedule 11 to the Act specified below.
Section 108	Short title, citation and extent.
Schedule 2	General vesting declarations for land compulsorily acquired.
Schedule 5	Construction of references in sections 62 and 63 to 'the responsible Minister or Ministers.'
Schedule 6	Joint Planning Inquiry Commissions.
Schedule 7	Procedure in connection with orders relating to footpaths and bridleways.
Schedule 8	Increase of penalties under the 1947 Act and the 1959 Act.
In Schedule 9, paragraph 5	Provisions as to references in other legislation to acquisition of land under Part III of the 1947 Act.
In Schedule 9, paragraph 7	Saving for specific provisions of Part II of Schedule 9 and for Schedule 10 to the Act in construing Part I of Schedule 9.
In Schedule 9, paragraph 8	Amendment of section 18(4) of the 1945 Act (cases where the Secretary of State's consent is needed for the disposal of land held for planning purposes) consequential on the provisions of sections 28 and 29(1) of the Act.

Provisions of the Act	Subject matter of Provisions
In Schedule 9, paragraph 9	Amendment of section 18(5) of the 1945 Act (special provisions as to land comprised in or contiguous or adjacent to areas of comprehensive development) consequential on the provisions of sections 28 and 29(1) of the Act.
In Schedule 9, paragraph 10	Provision as to references in the 1947 Act to section 35 of the Act.
In Schedule 9, paragraph 11	Amendment of section 12 of the 1947 Act (application to local planning authorities for planning permission) as to duration of planning permissions granted under the section and as to directions restricting the grant of planning permission,
In Schedule 9, paragraph 12	Amendment of section 17 of the 1947 Act (obligation to purchase land on refusal of planning permission in certain cases) as to deemed confirmation of purchase notices and as to hearings in connection with purchase notices.
In Schedule 9, paragraph 13	Amendment of section 22 of the 1947 Act (supplementary provisions as to enforcement) substituting for a reference to the sheriff a reference to the Secretary of State and introducing references to breach of planning control.
In Schedule 9, paragraph 14	Approval of the Secretary of State to agreements under section 23 of the 1947 Act to be dispensed with.
In Schedule 9, paragraph 16	Extension of provisions of section 29 of the 1947 Act (power to provide by regulations for enforcement of advertisement control) to include Part II of the Act.
In Schedule 9, paragraph 17	Power to define areas of special advertisement control by reference to the provisions of a development plan to cease to have effect.
In Schedule 9, paragraph 18	Substitution of 16th August 1948 for previous provision as to dates of display of advertisement qualifying for compensation under section 30 of the 1947 Act.
In Schedule 9, paragraph 19	Extension to Part II of the Act of section 32 of the 1947 Act (enforcement in relation to local planning authorities).
In Schedule 9, paragraph 21	Amendment of section 39(1) of the 1947 Act (appropriation of open spaces etc.) as to the purpose for which appropriation may be authorised.
In Schedule 9, paragraph 22	Amendment of section 42(1) of the 1947 Act (objections to compulsory purchase orders) consequential on the provisions of section 28 of the Act.

Provisions of the Act	Subject matter of Provisions
In Schedule 9, paragraph 23	Application to section 73(2) of the 1947 Act (authorisation of existing development) of the provisions of Part II of the Act.
In Schedule 9, paragraph 24	Application of section 78(1) of the 1947 Act (power to modify that Act in relation to minerals) to the provisions of the Act.
In Schedule 9, paragraph 25(a) in relation to the references to sections 24, 26 and 31 of the 1947 Act and section 15 of the Act; and paragraph 25(c) so far as it relates to enforcement notices under section 15 of the Act.	Amendment of provisions as to service of enforcement notices in respect of Crown land.
In Schedule 9, paragraph 26	Power to apply sections 70 to 72 of the Act to the National Coal Board.
In Schedule 9, paragraph 27 so far as it relates to Part II of the Act.	Extension of power in section 93 of the 1947 Act (for Ministers to make contributions towards compensation paid by local authorities) to decisions under Part II of the Act.
In Schedule 9, paragraph 28 so far as it relates to Part II of the Act.	Extension of power under section 94 of the 1947 Act (for local authorities or statutory undertakers to make contributions towards expenses incurred by other authorities) to expenses in performing functions under Part II of the Act.
In Schedule 9, paragraph 29	Application of section 95(2) of the 1947 Act (expenses of local authorities) to the provisions of the Act.
In Schedule 9, paragraph 30 except so far as it relates to enforcement notices under section 44 of the Act.	Default powers of the Secretary of State under section 96 of the 1947 Act to apply to enforcement notices under section 15 of the Act or under the provisions of that section as applied by regulations made under section 29 of the 1947 Act, to stop notices under section 20 of the Act, to completion notices under section 69 of the Act, and to orders requiring steps to be taken for the acquisition of land under section 29 of the Act.
In Schedule 9, paragraph 31 except so far as it relates to listed buildings and buildings proposed to be listed	Rights of entry under the 1947 Act to apply in connection with notices under Part II of the Act, claims for compensation under any provision of the Act and acquisitions of land by local authorities or Ministers authorised to acquire land under section 29 or 30 of the Act.
In Schedule 9, paragraph 32 except so far as it relates to Part V of the Act	Extension of provision (in section 105 of the 1947 Act) as to determination of claims for compensation, to claims under Part II or section 91 of the Act.

Provisions of the Act	Subject matter of Provisions
In Schedule 9, paragraph 33	Insertion in the 1947 Act of definition of the Act ("the Act of 1969").
In Schedule 9, paragraph 35 except so far as it relates to Part V of the Act.	Extension of provision (in paragraph 1 of Schedule 4 to the 1947 Act) as to compensation for depreciation in the value of land, to compensation under section 91 of the Act (conversion of highway into footpath or bridleway).
In Schedule 9, paragraph 36	Amendments of paragraph 1 of Schedule 5 to the 1947 Act (determination of applications etc. by statutory undertakers in respect of operational land) as to applications deemed to be made under section 16(7) or 19(5) of the Act.
In Schedule 9, paragraph 38(a) so far as it relates to the following orders:— (f) any order under section 22 of the 1945 Act (g) any order under section 26 of the 1945 Act (h) any order under section 46 of the 1947 Act (i) any order under section 90 of the Act (j) any order under section 91 of the Act (k) any order under section 93 or 94 of the Act.	Extension of section 31 of the 1959 Act (orders and actions which are the subject of special provisions as to challenge) to orders concerning extinguishment of right of way, relief for statutory undertakers, stopping-up and diversion of highways, conversion of highway into footpath or bridleway and stopping-up and extinguishment of footpaths etc.
In Schedule 9, paragraph 38(b) so far as it relates to the following decisions under the Act:— (f) any decision of the Secretary of State on an appeal to him under section 14 of the Civic Amenities Act 1967(a). (g) any decision of the Secretary of State on an appeal to him under section 16(1)(a), (f), or (g); (h) any decision of the Secretary of State on an application for an established use certificate referred to him under section 19(1); (i) any decision of the Secretary of State on an appeal under section 19(2);	Extension of section 31 of the 1959 Act (orders and actions which are the subject of special provisions as to challenge) to decisions concerning enforcement notices, established use certificates and completion notices.

(a) 1967 c. 69.

Provisions of the Act	Subject matter of Provisions
(k) any decision of the Secretary of State to confirm a completion notice under section 69	
In Schedule 9, paragraph 38(c)	Extension of section 31(5)(b) of the 1959 Act (power of Court of Session to quash orders or actions) to the provisions of the Act.
In Schedule 9, paragraph 39	Amendment of section 35 of the 1959 Act (publication of notices of applications for planning permission) as to determination of applications of which notice is required to be published under the section.
In Schedule 9, paragraph 40	Amendments of section 36 of the 1959 Act (notification of applications for planning permissions to owners and agricultural tenants) as to the form of certificates to be furnished under the section.
In Schedule 9, paragraph 41	Amendment of section 17 of the Control of Office and Industrial Development Act 1965(a) (application to Scotland) consequential on the amendment of that Act by the Town and Country Planning Act 1968(b).
In Schedule 9, paragraph 42	Amendment of section 24 of the Industrial Development Act 1966(c) (provisions as to conditions of industrial development certificates) consequential on the replacement of section 46 of the Town and Country Planning Act 1962(d) and section 21 of the 1947 Act by section 16 of the Town and Country Planning Act 1968 and section 16 of the Act respectively.
In Schedule 9, paragraph 46	Application of the Act to Conservation Areas under section 1 of the Civic Amenities Act 1967(e).
In Schedule 9, paragraph 50	Amendment of section 14 of the Civic Amenities Act 1967 (default powers and appeals in relation to replacement of trees) consequential on the replacement of section 21 of the 1947 Act by section 16 of the Act.
In Schedule 9, paragraph 52	Consequential amendment to definitions in the Civic Amenities Act 1967.
In Schedule 10, paragraphs 1 to 15	Transitional provisions in relation to development plans, enforcement of planning control and acquisition of land.
In Schedule 10, paragraph 19	Savings for existing regulations under section 86(1) of the 1947 Act.

(a) 1965 c. 33. (b) 1968 c. 72.
(c) 1966 c. 34. (d) 1962 c. 38.
(e) 1967 c. 69.

Provisions of the Act	Subject matter of Provisions
In Schedule 11, the entries relating to the 1945 Act; the 1947 Act, sections 7, 21, 23(1), 29(4), 34 to 36, 37, 39, 42, 83(2)(a), 84, 107(4), Schedule 5, Schedule 6, and Schedule 10; the Post Office Act 1953(a); the Electricity Act 1957(b); the Land Powers (Defence) Act 1958(c); the 1959 Act, in section 31 the proviso to subsection (9), section 38, section 42(5), and Schedule 5; the Post Office Act 1961(d); the Land Compensation (Scotland) Act 1963(e); the Housing (Scotland)Act 1966 (f); the Land Commission Act 1967(g); the New Towns (Scotland) Act 1968(h); and the Town and Country Planning Act 1968(i) in Schedule 9, paragraph 66(b).	Repeals consequential upon the bringing into operation of the foregoing provisions of the Act.

SCHEDULE 2   Article 3

TRANSITIONAL PROVISIONS

1. The substitution of section 14 of the Act for section 9 of the 1947 Act shall not prejudice the continued operation of that section as originally enacted in relation to development plans approved or made under Part II of the 1947 Act whether before or after 8th December 1969.

2. The bringing into operation of the repeal of Schedule 6 to the 1945 Act and sections 36 and 42 of, and Schedule 6 to, the 1947 Act shall not affect the operation of any direction included in a compulsory purchase order confirmed before 8th December 1969 that those provisions shall apply to the order.

3. The bringing into operation of the repeal of section 176 of the Housing (Scotland) Act 1966 and of sections 15 to 17 of, and Schedule 7 to, the New Towns (Scotland) Act 1968 shall not affect the operation of any direction included in a compulsory purchase order confirmed before 8th December 1969 that those provisions shall apply to the order.

EXPLANATORY NOTE
(This Note is not part of the Order.)

This Order brings into force for the whole of Scotland the provisions of the Town and Country Planning (Scotland) Act 1969 which are set out in Schedule 1 to this Order, subject to the transitional provisions contained in Schedule 2.

(a) 1953 c. 36.	(b) 1957 c. 48.	(c) 1958 c. 30.
(d) 1961 c. 15.	(e) 1963 c. 51.	(f) 1966 c. 49.
(g) 1967 c. 1.	(h) 1968 c. 16.	(i) 1968 c. 72.

STATUTORY INSTRUMENTS

1969 No. 1570 (S.128)

ACQUISITION OF LAND

The Compulsory Purchase of Land (General Vesting Declaration) (Scotland) Regulations 1969

Made - - -	*30th October* 1969
Laid before Parliament	*17th November* 1969
Coming into Operation	*8th December* 1969

In exercise of the powers conferred on me by section 107 of the Town and Country Planning (Scotland) Act 1947(**a**) and sections 31 and 103 of, and paragraphs 1, 2 and 4 of Schedule 2 to, the Town and Country Planning (Scotland) Act 1969(**b**), and of all other powers enabling me in that behalf, I hereby make the following regulations:—

Citation and commencement

1. These regulations may be cited as the Compulsory Purchase of Land (General Vesting Declaration) (Scotland) Regulations 1969 and shall come into operation on 8th December 1969.

Interpretation

2.—(1) In these regulations :—

"the Act" means the Town and Country Planning (Scotland) Act 1969 ;

"acquiring authority" has the meaning assigned to it by section 31(2) of the Act ;

"general vesting declaration" has the meaning assigned to it by paragraph 1 of Schedule 2 to the Act ;

"charge" includes any such feu-duty, ground annual or rent, or other payment or incumbrance as is mentioned in the words introductory to sections 107 to 111 of the Lands Clauses Consolidation (Scotland) Act 1845(**c**) ;

"Lands Tribunal" means the Lands Tribunal for Scotland :

Provided that until sections 1 to 3 of the Lands Tribunal Act 1949(**d**) come into force as regards Scotland, for any reference in these regulations to the Lands Tribunal there shall be substituted a reference to an official arbiter appointed under Part I of the Land Compensation (Scotland) Act 1963(**e**) and sections 3 and 5 of that Act shall apply, subject to any necessary modifications, in relation to the determination of any question under these regulations by an arbiter so appointed.

(2) The Interpretation Act 1889(**f**) shall apply for the interpretation of these regulations as it applies for the interpretation of an Act of Parliament.

(**a**) 1947 c. 53.	(**b**) 1969 c. 30.
(**c**) 1845 c. 19.	(**d**) 1949 c. 42.
(**e**) 1963 c. 51.	(**f**) 1889 c. 63.

General Vesting Declarations

3.—(1) For the purposes of paragraph 1 of Schedule 2 to the Act (by virtue of which an acquiring authority may execute a general vesting declaration in respect of land which they are authorised to acquire by a compulsory purchase order), a general vesting declaration shall be in the form specified in Part I of Schedule 1 to these regulations or in a form substantially to the like effect.

(2) For the purposes of paragraph 4 of Schedule 2 to the Act, a notice specifying the land specified in a general vesting declaration and stating the effect of the declaration (which notice is required by that paragraph to be served by an acquiring authority on the persons referred to in sub-paragraphs (a) and (b) thereof as soon as may be after the authority have executed a general vesting declaration) shall be in the form specified in Part II of Schedule 1 to these regulations or in a form substantially to the like effect.

4. For the purposes of sub-paragraph (1) of paragraph 2 of Schedule 2 to the Act (which requires an acquiring authority, before making a general vesting declaration, to publish or serve a statement of the effect of paragraphs 1 to 8 of that Schedule and a notification inviting interested persons to give information to them with respect to their interest in the relevant land) the statement set out in Part I of Schedule 2 to these regulations, or a statement substantially to the like effect, shall be the statement prescribed under sub-paragraph (1)(a), and the form set out in Part II of the said Schedule 2, or a form substantially to the like effect, shall be the form prescribed under sub-paragraph (1)(b) of the said paragraph 2.

William Ross,
One of Her Majesty's Principal
Secretaries of State.

St. Andrew's House.
Edinburgh.
30th October 1969.

Regulation 3   SCHEDULE 1

PART I

FORM OF GENERAL VESTING DECLARATION

We (1)...in exercise of the powers conferred on
us by section 30 of the Town and Country Planning (Scotland) Act 1969, and the
authorisation given to us by*[the Confirmation by (2)..on
....19 of] the (3)...............................Compulsory
Purchase Order 19 , recorded in the division of the General Register of Sasines
applicable to the County of...............................on...19 ,
HEREBY DECLARE that the land described in the Schedule hereto, together with the
right to enter upon and take possession of the same shall vest in us on (4).................
...............................being the end of a period which meets the requirements of
paragraphs 4 and 8 of Schedule 2 to the Town and Country Planning (Scotland) Act
1969.

                              Signature.....................................
                              *Secretary/Town Clerk/County Clerk
Place

Date

                    *Delete where appropriate

                    (5) SCHEDULE

Notes

(1) Name of authority

(2) Name of confirming authority (if any)

(3) Give citation of order

(4) Insert a date not less than 28 days after the date on which service of the notices required
by paragraph 4 of Schedule 2 to the Town and Country Planning (Scotland) Act 1969 is completed and which, in a case where a short tenancy or a long tenancy about to expire exists,
also meets the requirements of paragraph 8 of the said Schedule 2

(5) By paragraph 1(2) of the said Schedule 2 a particular description of the lands affected
or a description by reference in the manner provided by section 61 of the Conveyancing
(Scotland) Act 1874(a) is required, and where appropriate the description should refer to a
map annexed to the *general vesting declaration/compulsory purchase order.

PART II

FORM OF NOTICE STATING EFFECT OF GENERAL VESTING DECLARATION
TOWN AND COUNTRY PLANNING (SCOTLAND) ACT 1969

        The   Compulsory Purchase Order 19

To:

of:

NOTICE IS HEREBY GIVEN that the
(hereinafter called "the Authority") on   19   made a general
vesting declaration under section 31 of the Town and Country Planning (Scotland)
Act 1969 (hereinafter called "the Act") vesting the land described in the Schedule to
this notice (hereinafter called "the said land") in themselves as from the end of the
period of   days from the date on which the service of notices required by
paragraph 4 of Schedule 2 to the Act is completed. (Paragraph 4 of Schedule 2 to the
Act requires notice to be served on every occupier of any of the land specified in the

_____

                    (a) 1874 c. 94.

declaration (other than land in which there subsists a "short tenancy" or a "long tenancy which is about to expire"—these expressions are defined in Appendix A to this notice) and on every other person who has given information to the Authority with respect to any of that land in consequence of the invitation published and served under paragraph 2(1) of Schedule 2 to the Act.)

The Authority will in due course specify in a certificate the date on which the service of the said notices is completed.

The effect of the general vesting declaration is as follows:—

On the date of vesting (as determined in accordance with the first paragraph of this notice) the said land, together with the right to enter upon and take possession of it, will vest in the Authority as if the Authority had on that date exercised their powers under the Lands Clauses Consolidation (Scotland) Act 1845 to expede a notarial instrument (whether for vesting land or any interest in land in themselves or for extinguishing the whole or part of any feu-duty, ground annual or rent, or other payment or incumbrance).

Also, on the date of vesting, the Acts providing for compensation will apply as if, on the date on which the general vesting declaration was made (namely 19) a notice to treat had been served on every person on whom the Authority could have served such a notice (other than any person entitled to an interest in the land in respect of which such a notice had actually been served before that date and any person entitled to a short tenancy or a long tenancy which is about to expire).

If the land includes any land in which there is a short tenancy or a long tenancy which is about to expire, the right of entry will not be exercisable in respect of that land unless, after serving a notice to treat in respect of that tenancy, the Authority have served on every occupier of any of the land in which the tenancy subsists a notice stating that, at the end of a specified period (not being less than fourteen days) from the date of service of the notice they intend to enter upon and take possession of the land specified in the notice, and that period has expired: the vesting of the land will then be subject to the tenancy until that period expires, or the tenancy comes to an end, whichever happens first.

Schedule 3 to the Land Commission Act 1967(a) as applied by the Act contains supplementary provisions as to general vesting declarations executed under the Act. These provisions as so applied are set out in Appendix B to this notice.

A copy of the general vesting declaration to which this notice refers and of the plan annexed to the declaration can be inspected at and may be seen there at all reasonable hours.

Signature.....................................
Secretary/Town Clerk/County Clerk

Place

Date

THE SCHEDULE above referred to
[Description of the land vested in the
Authority by the general vesting
declaration]

APPENDIX A
[Here set out paragraph 17 of Schedule
2 to the Town and Country Planning
(Scotland) Act 1969]

APPENDIX B
[Here set out Schedule 3 to the Land
Commission Act 1967 as applied by
paragraph 9 of Schedule 2 to the Town
and Country Planning (Scotland) Act
1969]

(a) 1967 c. 1.

Regulation 4 **SCHEDULE 2**

PART I

STATEMENT OF THE EFFECT OF PARAGRAPHS 1 TO 8 OF SCHEDULE 2 TO THE TOWN AND COUNTRY PLANNING (SCOTLAND) ACT 1969 FOR THE PURPOSES OF PARAGRAPH 2(1)(*a*) OF THAT SCHEDULE

Power to make a general vesting declaration

1. The [insert the name of the acquiring authority] (hereinafter called "the Authority") may acquire any of the land to which this notice relates (hereinafter called "the relevant land") by making a general vesting declaration under section 31 of the Town and Country Planning (Scotland) Act 1969, which has the effect, subject to paragraph 4 below, of vesting the land in the Authority at the end of the period mentioned in paragraph 2 below. Generally a declaration may not be made before the end of the period of two months from the order becoming operative; but the order may prescribe a longer period. In either case, the Authority may make a declaration before the end of the period with the consent of every occupier of the land affected.

Notice, etc preliminary to general vesting declaration

2. If the Authority make a general vesting declaration, they must serve notice of it on every occupier of any of the land affected (except land where there is one of the tenancies described in paragraph 3 below) and on every person who gives them information relating to the land in consequence of the invitation contained in this or any similar notice. When the service of notices of the general vesting declaration is completed, an intermediate period before vesting begins to run. This period, which must not be less than 28 days, will be specified in the declaration. At the end of the period the land described in the declaration will, subject to paragraph 4 below, vest in the Authority together with the right to enter on the land and take possession of it. At the same time every person on whom the Authority could have served a notice to treat in respect of his interest in the land (other than a tenant under one of the tenancies described in paragraph 3 below) will be entitled to compensation for the acquisition of his interest in the land and to interest on the compensation from the date of vesting.

Tenancies with only a short time to run

3. Where a person's interest arises under a tenancy which has only a short time to run, the position stated above is subject to modification. For the modifications to apply the tenancy must be either a "short tenancy", i.e., a tenancy for a year or from year to year or any lesser interest, or a "long tenancy which is about to expire". The latter expression means a tenancy granted for an interest greater than a short tenancy but having at the date of the general vesting declaration a period still to run which is not more than the period specified in the declaration for this purpose (which must be more than a year). In calculating how long a tenancy has to run where any option to renew or to terminate it is available to either party, it is assumed that the landlord will take every opportunity open to him to terminate the tenancy while the tenant will use every opportunity to retain or extend his interest.

Notice of entry

4. The Authority may not exercise the right of entry referred to in paragraph 2 above in respect of land subject to one of the tenancies described in paragraph 3 above unless they first serve notice to treat in respect of the tenancy and then serve every occupier of the land with a notice of their intention to enter and take possession after the period (not less than 14 days) specified in the notice. The right of entry will be exercisable at the end of that period. The effect of the general vesting declaration will be subject to the tenancy until it comes to an end.

Severance

5. If the effect of the general vesting declaration will be to sever a house, building or factory, or a park or garden belonging to a house, by vesting part of it in the Authority and leaving part of it with the person who is entitled to, and is in a position to sell, the whole, that person may serve on the Authority a notice of objection to severance. A notice of objection to severance, in order to be effective, must be served by that

person within 28 days of the service on him by the Authority of the notice of the general vesting declaration referred to in paragraph 2 above (save in the exceptional cases referred to in paragraph 13 of Schedule 3 to the Land Commission Act 1967, as applied by paragraph 9 of Schedule 2 to the Town and Country Planning (Scotland) Act 1969). This (save in those exceptional cases) stops the objector's interest from vesting in the Authority until his rights in the matter have been settled. The Authority have (save in those exceptional cases) three courses open to them:

(1) they may serve the objector with a notice which in effect excludes the objector's land from the scope of the declaration (and, if he receives no notice from the Authority under one of the other two alternatives within three months after he has served them with his notice of objection to severance, they will be treated as having done this); or

(2) they may serve him with notice that the declaration shall have effect in relation to the whole of the land (in which case the declaration will take effect in accordance with the notice); or

(3) they may refer the objection to the Lands Tribunal and give him notice that they have done so.

Powers of the Lands Tribunal in severance cases

6. If the Lands Tribunal determine that the part of the objector's property comprised in the declaration can be taken without material detriment (where the objection concerns the taking of part of a house, building or factory) or (where the objection concerns the taking of part of a park or garden) can be taken without seriously affecting the amenity or convenience of the house, the notice of objection ceases to have effect, so that the land affected, i.e., the part of the property comprised in the declaration, will vest in the Authority. If the Lands Tribunal do not decide in that way, they must decide what part (if any) of the objector's land the Authority ought to be required to take in addition to the part comprised in the declaration. The declaration will then take effect as if both these parts had been comprised in the declaration.

Apportionment of charge

7. If any of the relevant land forms part of property subject to a charge, and the charge is apportioned between the relevant land and the remainder of the property by agreement or under section 109 of the Lands Clauses Consolidation (Scotland) Act 1845, the part apportioned to the relevant land will be treated as extinguished on the vesting of that land in the Authority, and after that the owner of the land will only be liable to pay the part apportioned to the remainder of the property. Compensation for the extinguishment will be payable to the person entitled to the charge, and may be settled by agreement between him and the Authority or determined by the Lands Tribunal. Alternatively the owner of the land and the person entitled to the charge may agree that the part of the property which is comprised in the relevant land shall be released from the charge and that the whole charge shall be charged on the remainder of the property. This will operate to release the relevant land from the charge and to charge the whole charge on the remainder of the property.

Apportionment of rent

8. Where any of the relevant land forms part of property subject to a tenancy, the rent will be apportioned between the relevant land and the remainder of the property on the vesting in the Authority of the tenancy of the relevant land. After that, the tenant will only be liable for that part of the rent which is apportioned to the remainder of the property. Any compensation to which he may be entitled for severance of his property will be assessed with reference to the severance caused by that vesting.

PART II

FORM FOR THE GIVING OF INFORMATION TO AN ACQUIRING AUTHORITY IN RESPONSE TO
AN INVITATION REQUIRED TO BE NOTIFIED UNDER PARAGRAPH 2(1)(*b*) OF SCHEDULE 2
TO THE TOWN AND COUNTRY PLANNING (SCOTLAND) ACT 1969

TOWN AND COUNTRY PLANNING (SCOTLAND) ACT 1969

The   Compulsory Purchase Order 19

To: (*a*)

[I] [We]* being [a person] [persons]* who, if a general vesting declaration were made
under paragraph 1 of Schedule 2 to the Town and Country Planning (Scotland)
Act 1969 in respect of all the land comprised in the compulsory purchase order cited
above in respect of which notice to treat has not been given, would be entitled to claim
compensation in respect of [all] [part of]* that land, hereby give you the following
information, in terms of the provisions of paragraph 2(1)(*b*) of the said Schedule 2:—

1. Name and address..(*b*)
   of claimant(s) ....

2. Land in which an...(*c*)
   interest is held by..
   claimant(s) ....
   ....

3. Nature of interest...(*d*)
   (including parti-...
   culars of any mort-..
   gage or charge..
   thereon) ....

                         Signed...

                         [On behalf of...]*

                         Date ....

NOTES

(*a*) Insert name of acquiring authority.

(*b*) In the case of a joint interest, insert the names and addresses of all the claimants.

(*c*) The land should be described as concisely as possible.

(*d*) If the interest is under a lease, the date of commencement and length of term should
     be given.   Charges include feuduties and other ground burdens.

*Delete where inappropriate

EXPLANATORY NOTE

(This Note is not part of the Regulations.)

These regulations prescribe the form of general vesting declaration which may be made by an acquiring authority under the Town and Country Planning (Scotland) Act 1969 and the form of other documents required to be published or served before or after the making of such a declaration.

Regulation 3, with Schedule 1, prescribes the form of general vesting declaration, and the form of notice stating the effect thereof, for the purposes of paragraphs 1 and 4 of Schedule 2 to the Act, under which an acquiring authority may by means of such a declaration vest in themselves land which they are authorised to acquire by a compulsory purchase order.

Paragraph 2(1)(*a*) of Schedule 2 to the Act requires an acquiring authority, before they make a general vesting declaration. to include in the notice which they give of the making or confirmation of the relevant compulsory purchase order (or in a notice given subsequently) a statement of the effect of paragraphs 1 to 8 of that Schedule. Such a statement is set out in Part I of Schedule 2 to these Regulations.

Paragraph 2(1)(*b*) of Schedule 2 to the Act requires the same notice also to contain an invitation to any person who will be entitled to compensation if a general vesting declaration is made, to inform the acquiring authority of his name and address and his interest in any land affected by the declaration: the giving of this information then entitles him under paragraph 4 of the Schedule to receive notice of the making of any general vesting declaration so that he may make a claim for compensation. Part II of Schedule 2 to these Regulations sets out the form in which the information is to be given.

STATUTORY INSTRUMENTS

1969 No. 1575 (S. 129)

CINEMATOGRAPHS AND CINEMATOGRAPH FILMS

The Cinematograph (Safety) (Scotland) (Amendment) Regulations 1969

Made - - -	*5th November* 1969
Laid before Parliament	*18th November* 1969
Coming into Operation	*19th November* 1969

In exercise of the powers conferred on me by section 1 of the Cinematograph Act 1909(a) as amended by section 8 of and the Schedule to the Cinematograph Act 1952(b) and of sections 1 and 2(1)(*a*) of the said Act of 1952, I hereby make the following regulations:—

1.—(1) These regulations may be cited as the Cinematograph (Safety) (Scotland) (Amendment) Regulations 1969, and shall come into operation on 19th November 1969.

(2) The Interpretation Act 1889(c), applies to the interpretation of these regulations as it applies to an Act of Parliament.

(3) These regulations shall extend only to Scotland.

(4) In these regulations the expression "principal regulations" means the Cinematograph (Safety) (Scotland) Regulations 1955(d).

2. Paragraphs (2)(*c*) and (3) of regulation 8 of the principal regulations (which relate to the metal shutters to cover the openings in the front face of a projection room) shall be omitted.

3. After regulation 31 of the principal regulations there shall be inserted the following regulation:—

"*Projection room shutters*

31A.—(1) The openings in the front face of a projection room in which inflammable film is used shall be fitted with metal shutters so constructed that—

(*a*) they can be closed from a point within the projection room near the projectors and also from a point outside the projection and rewinding rooms which is accessible to members of the staff;

(*b*) they can, if required, be closed simultaneously; and

(*c*) when closed, they fit closely over the openings.

(2) The shutters aforesaid and the mechanism for closing them shall be tested on each day on which there is a cinematograph exhibition, and before the public are admitted to the premises".

William Ross,
One of Her Majesty's Principal
Secretaries of State.

St. Andrew's House,
Edinburgh.
5th November 1969.

(a) 1909 c. 30.   (b) 1952 c. 68.
(c) 1889 c. 63.   (d) S.I. 1955/1125 (1955 I, p. 326).

EXPLANATORY NOTE

(*This Note is not part of the Regulations.*)

These Regulations amend the Cinematograph (Safety) (Scotland) Regulations 1955 so that the requirements as regards metal shutters to cover the windows in the front of a projection room shall apply only where inflammable film is used.

STATUTORY INSTRUMENTS

1969 No. 1579 (C.46)

ROAD TRAFFIC

The Vehicle and Driving Licences Act 1969 (Commencement No. 3) Order 1969

Made - - -	*7th November* 1969
Laid before Parliament	*18th November* 1969
Coming into Operation	*19th November* 1969

The Minister of Transport hereby makes this Order in exercise of his powers under section 38(2) of the Vehicle and Driving Licences Act 1969(**a**) and of all other enabling powers.

1. This Order may be cited as the Vehicle and Driving Licences Act 1969 (Commencement No. 3) Order 1969.

2. Section 2(3) and (4) of the Vehicle and Driving Licences Act 1969 shall come into operation on the 19th November 1969.

Given under the Official Seal of the Minister of Transport the 7th November 1969.

(**L.S.**)

Fred Mulley,
Minister of Transport.

EXPLANATORY NOTE
(This Note is not part of the Order.)

This Order brings into operation on the 19th November 1969 the following provisions of the Vehicle and Driving Licences Act 1969:—

Section 2(3), which empowers the Minister of Transport to make regulations providing for compensation for persons who suffer loss as a result of the transfer of functions envisaged by section 1.

Section 2(4), which protects certain superannuation rights of local government employees who, as a result of the transfer of functions envisaged by section 1, either:—

(*a*) lose their employment with a local authority and subsequently transfer to other specified superannuable employment, or

(*b*) remain employed by the local authority concerned but at a reduced rate of remuneration.

(**a**) 1969 c. 27.

STATUTORY INSTRUMENTS

1969 No. 1581

NATIONAL HEALTH SERVICE, ENGLAND AND WALES

The National Health Service (Executive Councils and Dental Estimates Board) Financial Regulations 1969

Made - - - - -	*7th November* 1969
Laid before Parliament	*19th November* 1969
Coming into Operation	*1st December* 1969

The Secretary of State for Social Services, in exercise of his powers under sections 40(2), 54 and 55 of the National Health Service Act 1946(a), sections 28 and 29 of, and paragraph 6 of Schedule 1 to, the Health Services and Public Health Act 1968(b), and of all other powers enabling him in that behalf and with the approval of the Treasury, hereby makes the following regulations:—

PART I

GENERAL

Citation, commencement and interpretation

1. These regulations may be cited as the National Health Service (Executive Councils and Dental Estimates Board) Financial Regulations 1969 and shall come into operation on 1st December 1969.

2.—(1) In these regulations, unless the context otherwise requires—

"the Act" means the National Health Service Act 1946;

"the Act of 1968" means the Health Services and Public Health Act 1968;

"auditor" means an auditor appointed by the Secretary of State under section 55(2) of the Act;

"Council" means the Executive Council constituted for any area;

"finance committee" means the finance committee appointed under regulation 15 of the National Health Service (Executive Councils) Regulations 1969(c);

"financial officer" means the clerk or other officer appointed by the Council under regulation 4 of these regulations;

"financial year" means the period of twelve months ending on 31st March.

(2) The Interpretation Act 1889(d) applies to the interpretation of these regulations as it applies to the interpretation of an Act of Parliament.

(a) 1946 c. 81. (b) 1968 c. 46.
(c) S.I. 1969/352 (1969 I, p. 980). (d) 1889 c. 63.

PART II

EXECUTIVE COUNCILS

Finance committee

3. The functions of the finance committee of a Council shall include—

   (*a*) advising the Council on the financial aspects of all matters within the scope of the functions of the Council;

   (*b*) ensuring that proper financial control is maintained in all matters for which the Council are responsible;

   (*c*) issuing Standing Financial Instructions;

   (*d*) ensuring the proper maintenance of such financial records as the Secretary of State may specify;

   (*e*) submitting to the Council financial estimates specified by the Council or by the Secretary of State.

Duties of the financial officer

4. The Council shall appoint the clerk, or another of their officers approved by the Secretary of State, as financial officer, whose duties shall include—

   (*a*) the giving of information and advice on financial matters to the Council or any of their committees;

   (*b*) the continuous oversight of the arrangements for financial control;

   (*c*) the preparation and completion of all financial estimates and returns specified by the Council, or by the Secretary of State;

   (*d*) the maintenance of a system of balancing double entry ledger accounts for recording the receipts and payments of the Council, stores records, and such other records as the Secretary of State may specify;

   (*e*) the proper collection of all moneys due to, the safe custody and the prompt payment into the bank of all moneys received by, and the prompt disbursement of all payments authorised by, the Council.

Annual and supplementary estimates

5.—(1) The Council shall submit to the Secretary of State in such form and under such heads of account and by such date in each financial year as he may specify an estimate (hereinafter referred to as the "annual estimate") of the receipts and payments of the Council during the succeeding financial year and a revised estimate of receipts and payments during the current financial year.

(2) If at any time it appears to the Council that there will be receipts or payments under any head of account in respect of which the Secretary of State has required the submission of an annual estimate, and provision for such receipts or payments has not been included in the Council's annual estimate, the Council shall prepare and submit to the Secretary of State as soon as may be an estimate of such additional receipts or payments (hereinafter referred to as a "supplementary estimate"), unless the Secretary of State has notified the Council that because of the nature of the additional receipts or payments it is not necessary to submit such a supplementary estimate.

(3) No expenditure under any head of account which has been specified under paragraph (1) above shall be incurred by or on behalf of the Council unless provision for such expenditure has been included in an annual estimate, or in a supplementary estimate, or the Secretary of State has notified the Council that it is not necessary to submit a supplementary estimate in respect of that expenditure.

Advances of funds by the Secretary of State

. **6.** The Council shall furnish to the Secretary of State such periodic estimates of sums required for the purpose of discharging their functions under the Act and the Act of 1968 and such additional information in connection therewith as he may specify, and the Secretary of State shall advance to the Council at such times, and in such manner as the Treasury under section 54(6) of the Act may direct, such amounts as appear to him to be necessary to meet payments which will fall due.

Authorisation of payments

7. No payments shall be made by or on behalf of the Council unless authorised in such manner as the Secretary of State may, by direction given under section 29(2) of the Act of 1968, require.

Auditors

8. An auditor shall have the right of access at all reasonable times to the relevant books, accounts, vouchers and other documents of the Council and their officers. He may by writing under his hand require the production before him of such books and documents, and shall be entitled to require from any member or officer, or former member or officer, of the Council such information relating to the affairs of the Council as he may consider necessary for the purpose of his duty under section 55(2) of the Act, as amended by section 28 of the Act of 1968.

Annual accounts

9.—(1) After the close of a financial year the financial officer shall prepare annual accounts in such form as the Secretary of State, with the approval of the Treasury, may from time to time direct under section 55(3) of the Act, as amended by section 28(3) of the Act of 1968. After certifying them as correct, the financial officer shall submit them to the Council for approval, and the Council shall submit them to the Secretary of State by such date as he may specify.

(2) The annual accounts shall be audited by an auditor who shall certify the accounts, with or without reservation, and shall transmit the audited accounts with his report thereon to the Secretary of State.

Losses and claims

10. Where a Council suffer a loss of public cash or property or where a claim which may result in the payment of damages or compensation is made against the Council, the Council shall follow such procedure, maintain such records and make such returns as the Secretary of State may specify.

Part III

Dental Estimates Board

11. The provisions of Part II of these regulations shall apply to the Dental Estimates Board in the same way as they apply to Executive Councils with the following modifications:—

(1) The word "Board" shall be substituted for the word "Council".

(2) References to the finance committee of a Council shall be references to the Board but regulation 3(*a*) and (*e*) shall not apply.

PART IV

REVOCATION

12. The National Health Service (Executive Councils and Dental Estimates Board) Financial Regulations 1948(a) are hereby revoked, but this revocation shall not affect any approval subsisting at the date on which these regulations come into operation.

R. H. S. Crossman,

Secretary of State for Social Services.

6th November 1969.

We approve these regulations.

E. G. Perry,

Walter Harrison,

Two of the Lords Commissioners cf

Her Majesty's Treasury.

7th November 1969.

EXPLANATORY NOTE

(This Note is not part of the Regulations.)

These Regulations (which supersede the National Health Service (Executive Councils and Dental Estimates Board) Financial Regulations 1948) govern the internal financial arrangements and systems of financial control of Executive Councils and make provision for the audit of their accounts.

The principal matters dealt with in the regulations include—

(*a*) the functions of the finance committee of an Executive Council (regulation 3) and the duties of the financial officer (regulation 4);

(*b*) the submission of financial estimates by Councils (regulation 5);

(*c*) the advancing of funds to Councils to meet expenditure incurred for the purpose of discharging their functions (regulation 6);

(*d*) the prohibition of payments by Councils unless authorised in such manner as required by a direction under section 29(2) of the Health Services and Public Health Act 1968 (regulation 7);

(*e*) the rights of auditors of access to, and production of, relevant documents (regulation 8);

(*f*) annual accounts (regulation 9);

(*g*) losses and claims (regulation 10).

The regulations are applied, with minor modifications, to the Dental Estimates Board constituted under section 40(2) of the National Health Service Act 1946.

(a) S.I. 1948/1239 (Rev. XV, p. 716: 1948 II, p. 2076).

STATUTORY INSTRUMENTS

1969 No. 1582

NATIONAL HEALTH SERVICE, ENGLAND AND WALES

HOSPITAL AND SPECIALIST SERVICES

The National Health Service (Hospital Accounts and Financial Provisions) Regulations 1969

Made - - - -	*7th November* 1969
Laid before Parliament	*19th November* 1969
Coming into Operation	*1st December* 1969

The Secretary of State for Social Services, in exercise of his powers under sections 54 and 55 of the National Health Service Act 1946(a) (as amended by sections 27 and 28 of the Health Services and Public Health Act 1968(b)), paragraph 2 of Part IV of Schedule 3 to the said Act of 1946, section 29 of the Health Services and Public Health Act 1968, and of all other powers enabling him in that behalf and with the approval of the Treasury, hereby makes the following regulations:—

Citation, commencement and interpretation

1. These regulations may be cited as the National Health Service (Hospital Accounts and Financial Provisions) Regulations 1969 and shall come into operation on 1st December 1969.

2.—(1) In these regulations, unless the context otherwise requires—

"the Act" means the National Health Service Act 1946;

"the Act of 1968" means the Health Services and Public Health Act 1968;

"auditor" means an auditor appointed by the Secretary of State under section 55(2) of the Act;

"Board" means a Regional Hospital Board or a Board of Governors, as the case may be;

"Board of Governors" means a Board of Governors of a teaching hospital;

"capital expenditure" means expenditure of a hospital authority on works of construction, reconstruction or alteration and associated purchases of furniture and equipment, after the deduction of direct credits;

"chief financial officer" means the treasurer or other officer appointed by a Board or a Hospital Management Committee under regulation 4 of these regulations;

"direct credit" means an item of income offset for accounting purposes against the expenditure of a hospital authority;

(a) 1946 c. 81.   (b) 1968 c. 46.

"financial year" means the period of twelve months ending on 31st March;

"hospital authority" means a Regional Hospital Board, Board of Governors or Hospital Management Committee, as the case may be;

"revenue expenditure" means expenditure, other than capital expenditure, of a hospital authority, after the deduction of direct credits.

(2) The Interpretation Act 1889(a) applies to the interpretation of these regulations as it applies to the interpretation of an Act of Parliament.

Finance committee and sub-committee

3.—(1) A Board shall appoint a finance committee and a Hospital Management Committee shall appoint a finance sub-committee and such committee or sub-committee shall, notwithstanding anything contained in regulation 4(i) of the National Health Service (Regional Hospital Boards etc.) Regulations 1947(b), as amended(c), consist wholly of members of the appointing body.

(2) The functions of the finance committee or finance sub-committee shall include—

(a) advising the hospital authority on the financial aspects of all matters within the scope of the functions of that authority;

(b) ensuring that proper financial control is maintained in all matters for which the hospital authority are responsible;

(c) issuing Standing Financial Instructions;

(d) ensuring the proper maintenance of such financial records as the Secretary of State may specify;

(e) submitting to the hospital authority financial estimates specified by that authority, or, as the case may be, by the Regional Hospital Board or by the Secretary of State.

Duties of chief financial officer

4. A hospital authority shall appoint a chief financial officer whose duties shall include—

(a) the giving of information and advice on financial matters to the authority or any of their committees;

(b) the continuous oversight of the arrangements for financial control;

(c) the preparation and completion of all financial estimates and returns specified by the hospital authority, or, as the case may be, by the Regional Hospital Board or by the Secretary of State;

(d) the maintenance of a system of balancing double entry ledger accounts for recording the income and expenditure of the authority, a system of cost accounts, stores, stocktaking records, and such other records as the Secretary of State may specify;

(e) the proper collection of all moneys due to, the safe custody and the prompt payment into the bank of all moneys received by, and the prompt disbursement of all payments authorised by, the hospital authority.

(a) 1889 c. 63.
(b) S.R. & O. 1947/1298 (Rev. XV, p. 538: 1947 I, p. 1355).
(c) The amending regulations are not relevant to the subject matter of these regulations.

Control of capital expenditure

5.—(1) Each Board shall submit to the Secretary of State in such form and by such dates in each financial year as he may specify—

(*a*) an estimate of capital expenditure for the next succeeding financial year and a revised estimate of capital expenditure for the current financial year; and

(*b*) annual programmes showing capital schemes for which the Board propose the start of works on site in such financial years as the Secretary of State may specify.

(2) Subject to regulation 5(3) of these regulations the Secretary of State may approve the estimates submitted under regulation 5(1)(*a*) and, for such financial years as he may specify, annual programmes of proposed capital schemes submitted under regulation 5(1)(*b*).

(3) The Secretary of State may approve such estimates or programmes with or without modification or subject to conditions, and may at any time prior to or during any financial year approve variations of an approved estimate or programme, but any such approval shall be without prejudice to any requirement for the consent of the Secretary of State to a specific scheme under the National Health Service (Functions of Regional Hospital Boards, etc.) Regulations 1969**(a)**.

Control of revenue expenditure

6.—(1) Each Hospital Mangement Committee shall submit to the Regional Hospital Board, in such form and by such date in each financial year as the Board may specify, forecasts of revenue expenditure for such subsequent financial years as the Board may specify.

(2) The Board shall examine the forecasts of revenue expenditure submitted to them as aforesaid and after making such modification as they think fit shall submit to the Secretary of State, in such form and by such date as he may specify, in respect of the Regional Hospital Board and their Hospital Management Committees, forecasts of revenue expenditure for such subsequent financial years as he may specify.

(3) Each Board of Governors shall submit to the Secretary of State, in such form and by such date in each financial year as he may specify, forecasts of revenue expenditure for such subsequent financial years as he may specify.

(4) The Secretary of State shall notify each Board of the total revenue expenditure which may be incurred by the Board in such subsequent financial years as he may specify, subject to such conditions as he may think fit.

(5) A Regional Hospital Board shall notify each Hospital Management Committee in their area of the total revenue expenditure which may be incurred by the Committee in the subsequent financial year, subject to such conditions as they may think fit.

7.—(1) Each Hospital Management Committee shall submit to the Regional Hospital Board in such form and under such heads of account and by such dates as the Board may specify:—

(*a*) an estimate of the revenue expenditure to be incurred in a financial year not being in excess of the sum notified to the Committee in respect of that year under regulation 6(5) of these regulations; and

(*b*) a revised estimate of revenue expenditure for the current financial year.

(a) S.I. 1969/297 (1969 I, p. 809).

(2) Each Regional Hospital Board shall examine the estimates of revenue expenditure submitted to them by Hospital Management Committees as aforesaid and after making such modifications as they think fit shall submit to the Secretary of State in such form and under such heads of account and by such dates as he may specify in respect of the Regional Hospital Board and their Hospital Management Committees—

(a) estimates of the revenue expenditure to be incurred in a financial year not being in excess of the sum notified to the Board in respect of that year under regulation 6(4) of these regulations; and

(b) a revised estimate of revenue expenditure for the current financial year.

(3) Each Board of Governors shall submit to the Secretary of State in such form and under such heads of account and by such dates as he may specify—

(a) an estimate of revenue expenditure for a financial year not being in excess of the sum notified to the Board in respect of that year under regulation 6(4) of these regulations; and

(b) a revised estimate of revenue expenditure for the current financial year.

(4) The Secretary of State may approve the estimates of a Board, with or without modification or subject to conditions, and shall notify the Board of the revenue expenditure approved under section 54(1) of the Act for such financial year as he may specify.

(5) A Regional Hospital Board may approve the estimates of each Hospital Management Committee, with or without modification or subject to conditions, and shall notify each Hospital Management Committee of the revenue expenditure approved under section 54(2) of the Act, as amended by section 27 of the Act of 1968, for such financial year as they may specify.

8. Where in accordance with the provisions of regulation 7(4) and (5) of these regulations estimates of revenue expenditure have been approved under separate heads of account, a Board shall obtain the approval of the Secretary of State, and a Hospital Management Committee shall obtain the approval of the Regional Hospital Board, to the application of savings or expected savings under one head of account towards any excess of expenditure under another head of account.

9. The Secretary of State may at any time prior to or during any financial year vary the estimate approval under regulation 7(4) of these regulations of revenue expenditure which may be incurred by a Board, or the conditions under which it was approved, and a Regional Hospital Board may at any time prior to or during any financial year vary the estimate approved under regulation 7(5) of these regulations of revenue expenditure which may be incurred by a Hospital Management Committee, or the conditions under which it was approved, and the approved estimates shall be reduced or increased accordingly.

Advances of funds

10.—(1) A Board shall furnish to the Secretary of State such periodic estimates of sums necessary to defray the expenditure approved by him under section 54(1) of the Act and such additional information in connection therewith as he may specify, and the Secretary of State shall advance to each Board, at such times and in such manner as the Treasury under section 54(6) of the Act may direct, such amounts as appear to him to be necessary to meet the expenses of the Board.

(2) A Hospital Management Committee shall furnish to the Regional Hospital Board such periodic estimates of sums necessary to defray the expenditure approved by the Board under section 54(2) of the Act, as amended by section 27(1) of the Act of 1968, and such additional information in connection therewith as the Board may specify and the Board shall advance to the Committee at such intervals as the Board think fit such amounts as appear to the Board to be necessary to meet the expenses of the Committee.

Authorisation of payments

11. No payments shall be made by or on behalf of a hospital authority unless authorised in such manner as the Secretary of State may, by direction given under section 29(2) of the Act of 1968, require.

Auditors

12. An auditor shall have the right of access at all reasonable times to the relevant books, accounts, vouchers and other documents of a hospital authority and their officers. He may by writing under his hand require the production before him of such books and documents, and shall be entitled to require from any member or officer, or former member or officer, of the hospital authority such information relating to the affairs of the authority as he may consider necessary for the purpose of his duty under section 55(2) of the Act.

Annual accounts

13.—(1) After the close of a financial year the chief financial officer shall prepare annual accounts in such form as the Secretary of State ,with the approval of the Treasury, may from time to time direct under section 55(3) of the Act, as amended by section 28(3) of the Act of 1968. After certifying them as correct, the chief financial officer shall submit them to the hospital authority for approval, and that authority shall submit them to the Secretary of State by such dates as he may specify, and in the case of a Hospital Management Committee shall also transmit a copy to the Regional Hospital Board.

(2) The annual accounts shall be audited by an auditor who shall certify the accounts, with or without reservation, and shall transmit the audited accounts with his report thereon to the Secretary of State.

Annual cost statements

14.—(1) After the close of a financial year the chief financial officer of a Board of Governors shall prepare and the Board shall submit to the Secretary of State such annual cost statements by such date as he may specify in respect of the hospital, or any part of the hospital, or any service for which the Board are responsible.

(2) After the close of a financial year the chief financial officer of a Hospital Management Committee shall prepare such annual cost statements by such date as the Secretary of State may specify in respect of any hospital or any part of a hospital, or any service for which the Committee are responsible, and the Committee shall transmit copies of the statements to the Regional Hospital Board who shall submit to the Secretary of State copies of the statements or summaries of the statements in such form as he may specify.

Losses and claims

15. Where a hospital authority suffers a loss of public cash or property or where a claim which may result in the payment of damages or compensation is made against a hospital authority, that authority shall follow such procedure, maintain such records and make such returns as the Secretary of State may specify.

Trust funds

16. Only regulations 2, 3, (except 3(2)(*a*)), 4, 12 and 13 of these regulations (and regulation 5, if a hospital authority proposes to incur capital expenditure from trust funds on property vested in the Secretary of State) shall apply to property or liabilities held, acquired or incurred by a hospital authority under sections 7, 59 and 60 of the Act. The annual accounts required to be submitted in accordance with regulation 13(1) of these regulations in respect of such property and liabilities shall be acompanied by a statement of balances at the end of the financial year.

Revocation

17. The National Health Service (Hospital Accounts and Financial Provisions) Regulations 1948**(a)** are hereby revoked, but this revocation shall not affect any approval subsisting at the date on which these regulations come into operation.

R. H. S. Crossman,
Secretary of State for Social Services.

6th November 1969.

We approve these regulations.

E. G. Perry,
Walter Harrison,
Two of the Lords Commissioners
of Her Majesty's Treasury.

7th November 1969.

(a) S.I. 1948/1414 (Rev. XV, p. 734: 1948 I, p. 2083).

EXPLANATORY NOTE

(This Note is not part of the Regulations.)

These Regulations (which supersede the National Health Service (Hospital Accounts and Financial Provisions) Regulations 1948) govern the internal financial arrangements and systems of financial control of the hospital service and make provision for the audit of hospital authorities' accounts.

The principal matters dealt with in the regulations include—

(*a*) the appointment of finance committees or finance sub-committees and the responsibility of hospital authorities for proper financial control (regulation 3) and the role of the chief financial officer in this respect (regulation 4);

(*b*) the control and approval of expenditure (regulations 5 to 9);

(*c*) the advancing of funds to hospital authorities in respect of approved expenditure (regulation 10);

(*d*) the prohibition of payments by hospital authorities unless authorised in such manner as required by a direction under section 29(2) of the Health Services and Public Health Act 1968 (regulation 11);

(*e*) the rights of auditors of access to, and production of, relevant documents (regulation 12);

(*f*) annual accounts and cost statements (regulations 13 and 14);

(*g*) losses and claims (regulation 15);

(*h*) hospital trust funds (regulation 16).

STATUTORY INSTRUMENTS

1969 No. 1585 (S. 130)

PENSIONS

The Pensions Appeal Tribunals (Scotland) (Amendment) Rules 1969

Made - - -	*5th November* 1969
Laid before Parliament	*19th November* 1969
Coming into Operation	*20th November* 1969

The Lord President of the Court of Session, in exercise of the powers conferred upon him by paragraph 5(4) of the Schedule to, as read along with section 13 of, the Pensions Appeal Tribunals Act 1943(a), and after consultation with the Council on Tribunals in accordance with section 8 of the Tribunals and Inquiries Act 1958(b), hereby makes the following Rules:—

1. These Rules may be cited as the Pensions Appeal Tribunals (Scotland) (Amendment) Rules 1969 and shall come into operation on 20th November 1969.

2. The Pensions Appeal Tribunals (Scotland) Rules 1946(c) as amended (d) shall be further amended as follows:—

For Part I of Schedule 2 (which relates to subsistence allowances payable to appellants, etc.), there shall be substituted the following:—

"PART I

Subsistence Allowances to Appellants, etc.

1. The maximum allowance payable under paragraph (1) of Rule 26 to an appellant or other person absent from home for the purpose of attending the Tribunal or undergoing a medical examination shall be—

    (*a*) for a period of two and a half hours or more but less than five hours consecutively, 3s. 0d., or for a period of five hours or more but less than ten hours consecutively, 5s. 6d., or for a period of ten hours or more consecutively, 11s. 6d.;

    (*b*) for a night, 36s. 0d. in addition to any sum payable under paragraph (*a*).

2. When the appellant or other person is absent from home for more than twenty-four hours he shall be entitled to a further allowance calculated in accordance with the foregoing provisions for periods of absence during each successive period of twenty-four hours."

Edinburgh, 5th November 1969.   *J. L. Clyde.*

(a) 1943 c. 39.   (b) 1958 c. 66.

(c) S.R. & O. 1946/1709 (Rev. XVII, p. 752: 1946 I, p. 1331).

(d) The relevant amending instruments are: S.I. 1949/2239, 1957/1972, 1962/2522, 1965/2017, 1967/27 (1949 I, p. 3010; 1957 II, p. 1834; 1962 III, p. 3400; 1965 III, p. 5946; 1967 I, p. 78).

EXPLANATORY NOTE

(*This Note is not part of the Rules.*)

These Rules further amend the Pensions Appeal Tribunals (Scotland) Rules 1946, so as to increase the subsistence allowances payable to appellants and their attendants.

STATUTORY INSTRUMENTS

1969 No. 1586 (S. 131)

POLICE

The Police (Scotland) Amendment (No. 4) Regulations 1969

Made - - -	*4th November* 1969
Laid before Parliament	*20th November* 1969
Coming into Operation	*21st November* 1969

In exercise of the powers conferred on me by section 26 of the Police (Scotland) Act 1967(**a**), and of all other powers enabling me in that behalf, and after consulting the Police Council for Great Britain in accordance with section 26(8) of the said Act of 1967, I hereby make the following regulations:—

1.—(1) These regulations may be cited as the Police (Scotland) Amendment (No. 4) Regulations 1969.

(2) These regulations shall come into operation on 21st November 1969 and shall have effect as from 1st September 1969.

2. In these regulations any reference to the principal regulations is a reference to the Police (Scotland) Regulations 1968(**b**).

3. In Schedule 5 of the principal regulations (which relates to refreshment, subsistence and lodging allowances) for the table in paragraph 1 there shall be substituted the following table:—

TABLE

Description of Allowance	Super-intendents	Inspectors, Sergeants and Constables
	s. d.	s. d.
Refreshment Allowance:		
(i) for one meal	8 3	7 6
(ii) for two meals	12 0	10 9
Subsistence Allowance:		
Period of retention or engagement on duty—		
(i) over 5 hours and not exceeding 8 hours ...	12 0	10 9
(ii) over 8 hours and not exceeding 12 hours ...	17 6	15 9
(iii) over 12 hours and not exceeding 24 hours ...	30 0	26 0
(iv) over 24 hours—at the rate under (iii) above for each complete period of 24 hours' retention or engagement, together with whichever is the appropriate amount under the preceding provisions of this Table for any excess over the aggregate of such complete periods.		
Lodging Allowance—for each night	54 0	42 0

(**a**) 1967 c. 77.　　　　　　　　　(**b**) S.I. 1968/716 (1968 II, p. 2024).

William Ross,

One of Her Majesty's Principal
Secretaries of State.

St. Andrew's House,
Edinburgh.
4th November 1969.

EXPLANATORY NOTE

(This Note is not part of the Regulations.)

These Regulations amend the Police (Scotland) Regulations 1968 to provide for increases in the rates of refreshment, subsistence and lodging allowances with effect from 1st September 1969.

STATUTORY INSTRUMENTS

1969 No. 1587

BUILDING SOCIETIES

The Building Societies (Accounts and Annual Return etc.) (Amendment) Regulations 1969

Made - - -	11*th November* 1969
Laid before Parliament	19*th November* 1969
Coming into Operation	21*st November* 1969

The Chief Registrar of Friendly Societies, with the consent of the Treasury, in exercise of the powers conferred upon him by sections 78(2), 88(3) and 91(2) of the Building Societies Act 1962(a), and of all other powers enabling him in that behalf, hereby makes the following Regulations:—

1.—(1) These Regulations may be cited as the Building Societies (Accounts and Annual Return etc.) (Amendment) Regulations 1969, and shall come into operation on 21st November 1969.

(2) The Interpretation Act 1889(b) shall apply to the interpretation of these Regulations as it applies to the interpretation of an Act of Parliament.

2. The Building Societies (Accounts and Annual Return etc.) Regulations 1968(c) as they apply to the Revenue and Appropriation Account and annual return of a building society relating to a financial year ending on or after 31st December 1969 shall be amended as follows:—

(*a*) After regulation 6, insert the following regulation:—

"6A(1) Where any share or deposit holding is related to a linked life insurance scheme and is required to be included in the entries to be made in item 3 of Schedule No. 2 to the annual return, the number of such holdings and the total amount shall be shown in that item as separate entries.

(2) For the purposes of the preceding paragraph the expression "a linked life insurance scheme" means an arrangement entered into between a building society and an insurance company under which the company invests with the society some or all of the money received by the company in respect of premiums paid on life policies issued by the company pursuant to the arrangement."

(*b*) At the end of paragraph (*b*) of regulation 7, add the following sub-paragraph:—

"(iv) Schedule No. 10."

(*c*) In the forms of Revenue and Appropriation Account set out in Parts I and II of the Schedule, after the item relating to Proposed Interest to Shareholders, insert the following item:—

"Provision for bonus under Contractual Savings Scheme."

(a) 1962 c. 37.   (b) 1889 c. 63.
(c) S.I. 1968/1954 (1968 III, p. 5332).

(*d*) In the form of annual return set out in Part II of the Schedule:—

    (i) before the Revenue and Appropriation Account, insert the words:—
"The society *has/has not an arrangement with an Insurance Company to receive share or deposit holdings related to a linked life insurance scheme (*Delete as appropriate)";

    (ii) in item 3 of Schedule No. 2, for the words in brackets which follow the words "exceeding £10,000" substitute the words "(excluding (*a*) holdings under a contractual savings scheme under section 53 of the Finance Act 1969 and (*b*) holdings where the aggregate holding of a husband and his wife does not exceed £20,000)";

    (iii) in item 5 of Schedule No. 2, for the words "Details of any changes in normal interest rates made during the financial year", substitute the words:—
"Details of any changes made during the financial year in normal interest rates for shares, deposits and loans, and mortgages.";

    (iv) after Schedule No. 9, add the following Schedule:—

"
SCHEDULE No. 10
Contractual Savings Scheme under Section 53 of the Finance Act 1969.

Number of accounts where members were contributing at end of financial year	....

Number of accounts where contributions stopped during the year:
    (*a*) because of death   ..   ..
    (*b*) for other reasons   ..   ..
	
	....
	....

Total	....
Amount contributed during year	£.................
Amount included in Balance Sheet under heading "Due to Investing Shareholders"	£................. "

S. D. Musson,
Chief Registrar of Friendly Societies.

Dated 11th November 1969.

We consent to these Regulations.

Neil McBride,
E. G. Perry,
Two of the Lords Commissioners of
Her Majesty's Treasury.

Dated 11th November 1969.

EXPLANATORY NOTE

(This Note is not part of the Regulations.)

These Regulations amend the form of Revenue and Appropriation Account which is required to be laid before the annual general meeting of a building society. They also amend the form of annual return which a building society is required to make to the Chief Registrar of Friendly Societies.

The main amendments require a building society to furnish in its annual return information regarding any linked life insurance scheme or contractual savings scheme operated by it.

STATUTORY INSTRUMENTS

1969 No. 1588 (C.47)

TRANSPORT

The Transport (London) Act 1969 (Commencement No. 3) Order 1969

Made - - - *11th November* 1969

The Minister of Transport in exercise of his powers under section 47 of the Transport (London) Act 1969(a) and of all other enabling powers hereby makes the following Order :—

1. This Order may be cited as the Transport (London) Act 1969 (Commencement No. 3) Order 1969.

2. Section 19(1)(a) of the Transport (London) Act 1969 (which relates to the extinguishment of the London Transport Board's debts to the Minister of Transport) shall come into force on the 19th November 1969.

Sealed with the Official Seal of the Minister of Transport the 11th November 1969.

(L.S.)

J. Garlick,
An Under Secretary of the
Ministry of Transport.

(a) 1969 c. 35.

STATUTORY INSTRUMENTS

1969 No. 1589

ROAD TRAFFIC

The Road Vehicles (Registration and Licensing) (Amendment) (No. 2) Regulations 1969

Made - - -	*6th November* 1969
Laid before Parliament	*19th November* 1969
Coming into Operation	*1st January* 1970

The Minister of Transport in exercise of his powers under subsection (3) of section 8 of the Vehicles (Excise) Act 1962(**a**), as substituted by section 147 of the Transport Act 1968(**b**), under subsections (1) to (5) of section 12 of the said Act of 1962, as substituted by section 6(2) of the Finance Act 1969(**c**), under section 16(2) of the said Act of 1962 as amended by paragraph 3 in Part II of Schedule 12 to the said Act of 1969, under section 23 of the said Act of 1962, and of all other enabling powers, hereby makes the following Regulations:—

1.—(1) These Regulations shall come into operation on the 1st January 1970 and may be cited as the Road Vehicles (Registration and Licensing) (Amendment) (No. 2) Regulations 1969.

(2) The Interpretation Act 1889(**d**) shall apply for the interpretation of these Regulations as it applies for the interpretation of an Act of Parliament.

2. The Road Vehicles (Registration and Licensing) Regulations 1964(**e**), as amended(**f**), shall be further amended in accordance with the following provisions of these Regulations.

3. Regulation 2 (Transitional provisions etc.) and Regulation 3(1) (Interpretation) shall have effect as though any references therein to a limited trade licence book, general trade licence or limited trade licence were omitted.

4. Regulation 7 (Surrender of licences) shall have effect as though the words "a limited trade licence or" and the word "general" in both places where it occurs were omitted.

5. For Part V—Trade Licences, there shall be substituted the following Part:—

"PART V—TRADE LICENCES

Applications for trade licences

32. For the purposes of section 12 of the Act the prescribed manner for—
(*a*) a motor trader to make an application to take out a licence under that section for all mechanically propelled vehicles which are from

---

(**a**) 10 & 11 Eliz. 2. c. 13.
(**b**) 1968 c. 73.
(**c**) 1969 c. 32.
(**d**) 52 & 53 Vict. c. 63.
(**e**) S.I. 1964/1178 (1964 II, p. 2722).
(**f**) There is no relevant amending instrument.

time to time temporarily in his possession in the course of his business as a motor trader and all recovery vehicles kept by him for the purpose of dealing with disabled vehicles in the course of that business, or

　(b) a vehicle tester to make an application to take out a licence under the said section for all mechanically propelled vehicles which are from time to time submitted to him for testing in the course of his business as a vehicle tester,

shall be to furnish the prescribed particulars and to make the prescribed declaration to the council of the county in which his business premises are situated.

Form of trade licences

33. Each trade licence issued by a council shall contain the following particulars:—

　(a) the name and business address of the person to whom the licence is issued;

　(b) the general registration mark assigned to that person;

　(c) the date of expiry of the licence;

　(d) the amount of duty paid;

　(e) the serial number of the licence;

　(f) the date stamp of the office of issue.

Notification of change of address etc.

34. If the holder of a trade licence changes the name of his business or his business address he shall notify this fact and the new name or address forthwith to the council by which the licence was issued and shall at the same time send to that council the licence for any necessary amendment.

Issue of trade plates and replacements therefor

35.—(1) A council shall issue to every holder of a trade licence in respect of that licence two plates (in these Regulations referred to as "trade plates") appropriate to the class of vehicles on which they will be used showing the general registration mark assigned to the holder of the licence, and one of the plates so issued shall contain means whereby the licence may be fixed thereto:

Provided that where the holder of a trade licence satisfies the council by which it was issued that the vehicles which he will use by virtue of the licence include vehicles which would otherwise be liable to duty under Schedule 1 to the Act and other vehicles he shall be entitled to be issued free of charge with two additional trade plates in respect of the vehicles first mentioned in this proviso.

(2) Each trade plate shall remain the property of the council by which it was issued, and shall be returned forthwith to the council if the person to whom it was issued no longer holds a trade licence which is in force or if that person ceases to be a motor trader or a vehicle tester.

(3) If a trade plate issued by a council to the holder of a trade licence is lost, destroyed, mutilated or defaced or the figures and particulars thereon have become illegible or the colour of the plate has become altered by fading or otherwise, the holder shall apply to the council by which the plate was issued for the issue to him of a replacement for that plate, and the council upon being satisfied as to such loss, destruction, mutilation, defacement,

illegibility or alteration as aforesaid and, upon the receipt of the plate except where the plate has been lost or destroyed, shall issue a replacement for the plate on payment of a fee of eighteen shillings if the plate was issued in respect of vehicles otherwise liable to duty under Schedule 1 to the Act or a fee of twenty-seven shillings in any other case, and the replacement so issued shall have the same effect as the plate which it replaces:

Provided that where the council are satisfied that the figures or particulars have become illegible or the colour of the plate has become altered by fading or otherwise without any act or neglect on the part of the holder of the trade licence they shall issue a replacement free of charge.

(4) In the case of the loss of any trade plate, if at any time after the issue of a replacement the original plate is found, the holder of the trade licence if the plate is in his possession, shall forthwith return it to the council which issued the replacement therefor, or if it is not in his possession but he becomes aware that it is found, shall take all reasonable steps to obtain possession of it and if successful shall forthwith return it to the said council so, however, that if possession is not obtained, such fact shall be notified to the council by the holder of the licence.

Alteration of trade plates and similar offences

36.—(1) No person shall alter, deface, mutilate or add anything to any trade plate or exhibit upon any mechanically propelled vehicle any trade plate which has been altered, defaced, mutilated or added to as aforesaid or upon which the figures or particulars have become illegible or the colour has become altered by fading or otherwise.

(2) No person shall exhibit on any mechanically propelled vehicle anything which could be mistaken for a trade plate.

Exhibition of trade plates and licences

37. No person shall use a vehicle on a public road by virtue of a trade licence except in accordance with the following provisions:—

(a) there shall be fixed to and displayed on the vehicle the trade plates issued by the council which issued the trade licence in such a manner that, if the trade plates contained a registration mark assigned to the vehicle, the provisions of Regulations 22 and 23 would be complied with, notwithstanding the vehicle may not have been first registered on or after 1st October 1938 or it is a works truck;

(b) where in accordance with the provisions of the preceding paragraph a trade plate is required to be fixed to the front of a vehicle, the trade plate so fixed shall be that containing means for fixing the licence thereto, and the trade licence shall be fixed to the vehicle by means of that plate and exhibited on that plate so as to be at all times clearly visible by daylight.

Restriction on use of trade plates and licences

38. No person, not being the holder of a trade licence, shall use on a public road a vehicle on which there is displayed a trade plate or a trade licence, so however, that nothing in this Regulation shall apply so as to prevent a person with the consent of the holder of the trade licence from driving a vehicle when the vehicle is being used on a public road by virtue of a trade licence and by the holder thereof.

Purposes for which a vehicle may be used

39.—(1) In this Regulation, "business purpose", in relation to a motor trader means—

(*a*) a purpose connected with his business as a manufacturer or repairer of or dealer in mechanically propelled vehicles, or

(*b*) a purpose connected with his business as a manufacturer or repairer of or dealer in trailers carried on in conjunction with his business as a motor trader.

(2) For the purposes of sub-paragraphs (*a*) to (*k*) of paragraph (4) of this Regulation, where a mechanically propelled vehicle is used on a public road by virtue of a trade licence and that vehicle is drawing a trailer, the vehicle and trailer shall be deemed to constitute a single vehicle.

(3) No person, being a motor trader and the holder of a trade licence, shall use any mechanically propelled vehicle on a public road by virtue of that licence unless it is a vehicle which is temporarily in his possession in the course of his business as a motor trader or a recovery vehicle kept by him for the purpose of dealing with disabled vehicles in the course of that business.

(4) Without derogation from the provisions of the last preceding paragraph of this Regulation, no person, being a motor trader and the holder of a trade licence, shall use any mechanically propelled vehicle on a public road by virtue of that licence for a purpose other than a business purpose and other than one of the following purposes:—

(*a*) for its test or trial or the test or trial of its accessories or equipment in the ordinary course of construction or repair or immediately after completion in either such case;

(*b*) for proceeding to or from a public weighbridge for ascertaining its unladen weight or to or from any place for its registration or inspection by a council;

(*c*) for its test or trial for the benefit of a prospective purchaser, for proceeding at the instance of a prospective purchaser to any place for the purpose of such test or trial, or for returning after such test or trial;

(*d*) for its test or trial for the benefit of a person interested in promoting publicity in regard to it, for proceeding at the instance of such a person to any place for the purpose of such test or trial, or for returning after such test or trial;

(*e*) for delivering it to the place where the purchaser intends to keep it;

(*f*) for demonstrating its operation or the operation of its accessories or equipment when being handed over to the purchaser;

(*g*) for delivering it from one part of his premises to another part of his premises, or for delivering it from his premises to the premises of, or between parts of premises of, another manufacturer or repairer of or dealer in mechanically propelled vehicles or removing it from the premises of another manufacturer or repairer of or dealer in mechanically propelled vehicles direct to his own premises;

(*h*) for proceeding to or returning from a workshop in which a body or a special type of equipment or accessory is to be or has been fitted to it or in which it is to be or has been painted or repaired;

(*i*) for proceeding from the premises of a manufacturer or repairer of or dealer in mechanically propelled vehicles to a place from which it is to be transported by train, ship or aircraft or for proceeding to the premises of such a manufacturer, repairer or dealer from a place to which it has been so transported;

(*j*) for proceeding to or returning from any garage, auction room or other place at which vehicles are usually stored or usually or periodically offered for sale and at which the vehicle is to be or has been stored or is to be or has been offered for sale as the case may be;

(*k*) for proceeding to or returning from a place where it is to be or has been tested, or for proceeding to a place where it is to be broken up or otherwise dismantled; or

(*l*) in the case of a recovery vehicle—

    (i) for proceeding to or returning from a place where assistance is to be, or has been, rendered to a disabled vehicle; or

    (ii) for carrying a disabled vehicle, or for towing such a vehicle (whether with the assistance of a trailer or not), from the place where it has broken down or from such other place where it is subsequently for the time being situated to a place for repair or storage or breaking up.

40. No person, being a vehicle tester and the holder of a trade licence, shall use any mechanically propelled vehicle on a public road by virtue of that licence for any purpose other than testing it or any trailer drawn thereby or any of the accessories or equipment on such vehicle or trailer in the course of his business as a vehicle tester.

Conveyance of goods or burden

41.—(1) No person, being a motor trader and the holder of a trade licence, shall use a mechanically propelled vehicle on a public road by virtue of that licence for the conveyance of goods or burden of any description other than—

(*a*) a load which is carried by a vehicle being used for a relevant purpose and is carried solely for the purpose of testing or demonstrating the vehicle or any of its accessories or equipment and which is returned to the place of loading without having been removed from the vehicle except for such last mentioned purpose or in the case of accident:

    In this sub-paragraph "relevant purpose" means a purpose mentioned in Regulation 39(4)(*a*), (*c*), (*d*) and (*f*) of these Regulations; or

(*b*) in the case of a recovery vehicle, being used for a relevant purpose, any such load as is referred to in the definition of such a vehicle contained in section 12(10) of the Act or a load consisting of a disabled vehicle:

    In this sub-paragraph "relevant purpose" means a purpose mentioned in Regulation 39(4)(*l*) of these Regulations; or

(*c*) any load built in as part of the vehicle or permanently attached thereto; or

(*d*) a load consisting of parts, accessories or equipment designed to be fitted to the vehicle and of tools for so fitting them, the vehicle being used for a relevant purpose:

    In this sub-paragraph "relevant purpose" means a purpose mentioned in Regulation 39(4)(*g*) or (*h*) of these Regulations; or

(*e*) a load consisting of a trailer, the vehicle carrying the trailer being used for a relevant purpose:

    In this sub-paragraph "relevant purpose" means a purpose mentioned in Regulation 39(4)(*e*), (*h*) or (*i*) of these Regulations.

(2) For the purposes of this Regulation and the next succeeding Regulation, where a vehicle is so constructed that a trailer may by partial superimposition be attached to the vehicle in such a manner as to cause a substantial part of

the weight of the trailer to be borne by the vehicle, the vehicle and the trailer shall be deemed to constitute a single vehicle.

42. No person, being a vehicle tester and the holder of a trade licence, shall use a mechanically propelled vehicle on a public road by virtue of that licence for the conveyance of goods or burden of any description other than—

(a) a load which is carried solely for the purpose of testing or demonstrating the vehicle or any of its accessories or equipment and which is returned to the place of loading without having been removed from the vehicle except for such purpose or in the case of accident;

(b) any load built in as part of the vehicle or permanently attached thereto.

Carriage of passengers

43.—(1) No person, being the holder of a trade licence, shall use a mechanically propelled vehicle on a public road by virtue of that licence for carrying any person on the vehicle or on any trailer drawn thereby other than—

(a) the driver of the vehicle, being the holder of the licence, an employee of the holder, or any other person driving with the consent of the holder while (except in the case of a vehicle which is constructed to carry only one person) accompanied by the holder or an employee of his;

(b) any person required to be on the vehicle or trailer by, or by virtue of, the Road Traffic Act 1960(a);

(c) any person carried for the purpose of fulfilling his statutory duties in connection with an inspection of the vehicle or trailer;

(d) any person in a disabled vehicle being towed;

(e) the holder of the trade licence or an employee of his, if in either case his presence is necessary for the purpose for which the vehicle is being used;

(f) an employee of the holder of the trade licence proceeding to a place for the purpose of driving vehicles on behalf of the holder of the trade licence in the course of his business as a motor trader;

(g) a prospective purchaser or his servant or agent or any person requested to accompany the said prospective purchaser, or in the case of a vehicle being used for the purpose mentioned in Regulation 39(4)(f) of these Regulations, the purchaser or his servant or agent or any person requested to accompany the said purchaser;

(h) a person mentioned in Regulation 39(4)(d) of these Regulations.

(2) Where a person coming within sub-paragraph (g) or (h) of the preceding paragraph is carried he shall be accompanied (except in the case of a vehicle which is constructed to carry only one person) by the holder of the trade licence or an employee of his.".

Given under the Official Seal of the Minister of Transport the 6th November 1969.

(**L.S.**)

Fred Mulley,
Minister of Transport.

(a) 8 & 9 Eliz. 2. c. 16.

EXPLANATORY NOTE

(This Note is not part of the Regulations.)

These Regulations further amend the Road Vehicles (Registration and Licensing) Regulations 1964. The principal change is to introduce into the 1964 Regulations regulations, namely, Regulations 32 to 43 containing new provisions relating to trade licences issued to motor traders and vehicle testers. These new provisions are consequent upon the amendments made as from 1st January 1970 in the Vehicles (Excise) Act 1962 by section 6(2) of the Finance Act 1969, which amendments were designed, *inter alia*, to restrict the vehicles which may be used under a trade licence and the purposes for which they may be used, and to substitute for general trade licences and limited trade licences a single type of trade licence. The main changes made by the new Regulations are as follows:—

1. Regulation 32 deals with applications for trade licences by virtue of which motor traders may use, *inter alia*, "recovery vehicles" a term defined in paragraph 2 in Part II of Schedule 12 to the Finance Act 1969.

2. Regulation 38 makes it an offence for a person other than the holder of a trade licence to use on roads a vehicle on which there is displayed a trade plate or trade licence.

3. Regulations 39 and 40 make more stringent provision restricting the purposes for which vehicles may be used by virtue of a trade licence.

4. Regulations 41 and 42 prohibit the conveyance of goods on vehicles used by virtue of a trade licence, subject to specified exceptions.

5. Regulation 43 contains changes as respects persons who may be carried on vehicles when used under trade licences.

STATUTORY INSTRUMENTS

1969 No. 1594

LOCAL GOVERNMENT, ENGLAND AND WALES
TOWN AND COUNTRY PLANNING, ENGLAND AND WALES

The Town and Country Planning (Grants) (Amendment) Regulations 1969

Made - - - -	12*th November* 1969
Laid before Parliament	19*th November* 1969
Coming into Operation	1*st December* 1969

The Minister of Housing and Local Government, with the consent of the Treasury and after consultation with the associations of local authorities appearing to him to be concerned and the local authority with whom consultation appeared to him to be desirable, in exercise of the powers conferred on him by sections 186 and 221 of the Town and Country Planning Act 1962(**a**) and section 7 of the Local Government Act 1966(**b**) and of all other powers enabling him in that behalf, hereby makes the following regulations :—

1.—(1) These regulations may be cited as the Town and Country Planning (Grants) (Amendment) Regulations 1969 and shall come into operation on 1st December 1969.

(2) The Interpretation Act 1889(**c**) shall apply for the interpretation of these regulations as it applies for the interpretation of an Act of Parliament.

2. At the end of paragraph (4) of regulation 5 of the Town and Country Planning (Grants) Regulations 1968(**d**) there shall be added the following sub-paragraph—

"(*d*) section 28 of the Town and Country Planning Act 1968(**e**)".

Given under the official seal of the Minister of Housing and Local Government on 12th November 1969.

(L.S.)

Anthony Greenwood,
Minister of Housing and Local Government.

We consent to the making of these regulations.

Joseph Harper,
Neil McBride,

Two of the Lords Commissioners of Her Majesty's Treasury on 12th November 1969.

(**a**) 1962 c. 38.   (**b**) 1966 c. 42.   (**c**) 1889 c. 63.
(**d**) S.I. 1968/189 (1968 I, p. 539).   (**e**) 1968 c. 72.

EXPLANATORY NOTE

(This Note is not part of the Regulations.)

These regulations amend the Town and Country Planning (Grants) Regulations 1968 to take account of the effect of the Town and Country Planning Act 1968.

The regulations of 1968 determine the basis and method of calculation of grants payable by the Minister of Housing and Local Government and the Secretary of State for Wales to local authorities in respect of expenditure by them on the acquisition and clearing of land for the development and redevelopment of any area as a whole and for associated purposes.

Such grants are payable only in respect of land acquired under certain enactments specified in regulation 5(4) of the regulations of 1968, which regulation specifies, among others, section 68 (compulsory acquisition of land for development) of the Town and Country Planning Act 1962. That section has been superseded by section 28 (compulsory acquisition of land in connection with development and for other planning purposes) of the Town and Country Planning Act 1968, and these regulations add the latter section to the enactments specified in regulation 5(4) of the regulations of 1968.

STATUTORY INSTRUMENTS

1969 No. 1597 (S.132)

CRIMINAL PROCEDURE, SCOTLAND
The Act of Adjournal (Probation Orders) 1969

Made - - -	*7th November* 1969
Coming into Operation	*17th November* 1969

ACT OF ADJOURNAL
Relative to Probation Orders

AT EDINBURGH, the SEVENTH day of NOVEMBER, Nineteen hundred and sixty nine years.

Present:

The Right Honourable The Lord Justice-General
The Right Honourable The Lord Justice-Clerk
The Honourable Lord Guthrie
The Honourable Lord Migdale
The Honourable Lord Cameron.
The Honourable Lord Johnston

The Lord Justice-General, Lord Justice-Clerk and Lords Commissioners of Justiciary, by virtue of the powers conferred upon them by section 2(2) of the Criminal Justice (Scotland) Act, 1949(a), as substituted by section 95(1) of, and paragraph 22(1) of Schedule 8 to, the Social Work (Scotland) Act, 1968(b), and of all other powers competent to them in that behalf, do hereby enact and declare as follows:—

1. A probation order shall be as nearly as may be in the form set forth in the Schedule hereto.

2. This Act of Adjournal may be cited as the Act of Adjournal (Probation Orders) 1969, and shall come into operation on 17th November 1969.

And the Lords appoint this Act of Adjournal to be recorded in the Books of Adjournal, and to be published in the EDINBURGH GAZETTE.

J. L. Clyde,
I.P.D.

(a) 1949 c. 94.   (b) 1968 c. 49.

SCHEDULE
FORM OF PROBATION ORDER

In the   Court at   on

The Court, [being satisfied that the accused (here insert name and address) has committed the offence with which he is charged] (or as the case may be) [in view of the conviction of the accused (here insert name and address)], and being of the opinion that having regard to the circumstances, including the nature of the offence and the character of the said (name), it is expedient to make a probation order under the Criminal Justice (Scotland) Act 1949 containing the under-noted requirements:

And the Court having explained to the said (name) the effect of the order (including the requirements set out below), and that, if he fails to comply with the order, he may be brought before the Court by his supervising officer for a breach of probation and may be sentenced for the original offence, and that, if he commits another offence during the period of the probation order, he may be dealt with likewise:

And the said (name) having expressed his willingness to comply with the requirements of the order;

The Court therefore orders that for a period of   from the date hereof the said (name) who [resides] [is to reside] in the local authority area of   shall be under the supervision of an officer [of that local authority allocated for the purpose] [allocated for the purpose as required by the Court at   in the said local authority area]; that the said (name) shall be notified in writing by the Clerk of Court of the name and official address of the officer who is to supervise him and similarly if at any time such supervision is to be undertaken by another officer of the local authority allocated for the purpose; and that the said (name) shall comply with the following requirements, namely—

1. to be of good behaviour;
2. to conform to the directions of the supervising officer;
3. to inform the supervising officer at once if he/she changes his/her [residence or] (delete if inappropriate) [place of employment];
4. (here insert any additional requirements).

(Signature)

Date,

EXPLANATORY NOTE
(This Note is not part of the Act of Adjournal.)

This Act of Adjournal prescribes the form of a probation order.

STATUTORY INSTRUMENTS

1969 No. 1598 (C. 48)

HEARING AID COUNCIL

The Hearing Aid Council Act (Commencement) Order 1969

Made - - - 13*th November* 1969

The Board of Trade, in pursuance of the power conferred upon them by section 15 of the Hearing Aid Council Act 1968(a), hereby make the following Order:—

1. This Order may be cited as the Hearing Aid Council Act (Commencement) Order 1969.

2. The Hearing Aid Council Act 1968 shall come into force on 29th December 1969.

Gwyneth Dunwoody,
Parliamentary Secretary
to the
13th November 1969 **Board of Trade.**

(a) 1968 c. 50.

Under section 108(4) *of the National Insurance Act* 1965 *these Provisional Regulations will not continue in force for longer than three months after the receipt by the Secretary of State for Social Services of the Report of the National Insurance Advisory Committee on the preliminary draft thereof submitted to them in accordance with the said section* 108.

STATUTORY INSTRUMENTS

1969 No. 1603

SOCIAL SECURITY

The National Insurance and Industrial Injuries (Stamps) Provisional Regulations 1969

Made - - -	*14th November* 1969
Laid before Parliament	*17th November* 1969
Coming into Operation	*18th November* 1969

The Secretary of State for Social Services hereby certifies under subsection (4) of section 108 of the National Insurance Act 1965(**a**) that on account of urgency the following regulations should come into operation without delay, and, in exercise of powers under section 14(2) of the said Act of 1965 (as amended by section 121 of the Post Office Act 1969(**b**)) and under section 67(2) of the National Insurance (Industrial Injuries) Act 1965(**c**) and in exercise of all other powers enabling him in that behalf, after submitting a preliminary draft to the National Insurance Advisory Committee, hereby makes the following regulations as provisional regulations :—

Adaptation of Enactments

1. Those provisions of the Stamp Duties Management Act 1891(**d**) (as amended by any subsequent enactment), and of section 63 of the Post Office Act 1953(**e**) (as so amended) which, with the necessary adaptations for applying them to stamps prepared and issued for the purposes of the National Insurance Act 1965 and the National Insurance (Industrial Injuries) Act 1965, are set out in the Schedule hereto, shall apply to the said stamps.

Provided that the provisions of section 13 of the Stamp Duties Management Act 1891, which are printed in italics in the said Schedule, shall only apply in Scotland.

Revocation

2. The National Insurance and Industrial Injuries (Stamps) Regulations 1967(**f**) and the National Insurance and Industrial Injuries (Stamps) Regulations 1969(**g**) are hereby revoked.

(**a**) 1965 c. 51. (**b**) 1969 c. 48.
(**c**) 1965 c. 52. (**d**) 1891 c. 38.
(**e**) 1953 c. 36. (**f**) S.I. 1967/488 (1967 II, p. 1553).
(**g**) S.I. 1969/1132 (1969 II, p. 3353).

Commencement and Citation

3. These Regulations shall come into operation on 18th November 1969 and may be cited as The National Insurance and Industrial Injuries (Stamps) Provisional Regulations 1969.

Interpretation

4. The Interpretation Act 1889(**a**) applies to the interpretation of these Regulations as it applies to the interpretation of an Act of Parliament.

Signed by authority of the Secretary of State for Social Services.

David Ennals,

Minister of State,

Department of Health and Social Security.

14th November 1969.

SCHEDULE

STAMP DUTIES MANAGEMENT ACT 1891

Section of Act	Subject matter	Adapted provisions
3	Power to grant licences to deal in stamps.	(1) The Secretary of State may in his discretion grant a licence to any person to deal in stamps in such places and subject to such conditions as the Secretary of State may approve.
		. . . .
		(4) One licence only shall be required for any number of persons in partnership, and the licence may at any time be revoked by the Secretary of State.
4	Penalty for unauthorised dealing in stamps etc.	(1) If any person who is not duly appointed to sell and distribute stamps deals in any manner in stamps, without being licensed so to do . . . . he shall for every such offence incur a fine of twenty pounds.
		(2) If any person who is not duly appointed to sell and distribute stamps, or duly licensed to deal in stamps, has, or puts upon his premises either in the inside or on the outside thereof, or upon any board or any material whatever exposed to public view, and whether the same be affixed to his premises or not, any letters importing or intending to import that he deals in stamps, or is licensed so to do, he shall incur a fine of ten pounds.

(**a**) 1889 c. 63.

Section of Act	Subject matter	Adapted provisions
5	Provisions as to determination of licence.	(1) If the licence of any person to deal in stamps expires or is revoked, or if any person licensed to deal in stamps dies or becomes bankrupt, and any such person at the expiration or revocation of his licence, or at the time of his death or bankruptcy, has in his possession any stamps, such person, or his executor or administrator, or the receiver or trustee or official assignee under his bankruptcy, may, within six months after the expiration or revocation of the licence, or after the death or bankruptcy, as the case may be, bring or send the stamps to the Secretary of State.
		(2) The Secretary of State may in any such case pay to the person bringing or sending stamps the amount of the duty thereon if proof to his satisfaction is furnished that the same were actually in the possession of the person whose licence has expired or been revoked, or so dying or becoming bankrupt, for the purpose of sale, at the time of the expiration or revocation of the licence, or of his death or bankruptcy, and that the stamps were purchased or procured by that person from the Secretary of State, or from some person duly appointed to sell and distribute stamps, or duly licensed to deal in stamps.
6	Penalty for hawking stamps.	(1) If any person, whether licensed to deal in stamps or not, hawks or carries about for sale or exchange any stamps, he shall, in addition to any other fine or penalty to which he may be liable, incur a fine of twenty pounds.
		(2) In default of payment of the fine, on summary conviction the offender shall be imprisoned for any term not exceeding two months.
		(3) All stamps which are found in the possession of the offender shall be forfeited, and shall be delivered to the Secretary of State to be disposed of as he thinks fit.
		(4) Any person may arrest a person found committing an offence against this section, and take him before a justice having jurisdiction where the offence is committed, who shall hear and determine the matter.

Section of Act	Subject matter	Adapted provisions
9	Procedure for obtaining allowance.	Subject to such regulations as the Secretary of State may think proper to make, and to the production of such evidence by statutory declaration or otherwise as the Secretary of State may require, allowance is to be made by the Secretary of State for stamps spoiled in the case hereinafter mentioned (that is to say):— .... (2) Any stamp which has been inadvertently and undesignedly spoiled or rendered unfit for use and has not in the opinion of the Secretary of State been affixed to any material ; .... Provided as follows:— (a) That the application for relief is made within two years after the stamp has been spoiled or become useless. ....
11	Allowance, how to be made.	In any case in which allowance is made for spoiled or misused stamps the Secretary of State may give in lieu thereof other stamps of the same denomination and value, or if required, and he thinks proper, stamps of any other denomination to the same amount in value, or in his discretion, the same value in money.
12	Stamps not wanted may be re-purchased.	When any person is possessed of a stamp which has not been spoiled or rendered unfit or useless for the purpose intended, but for which he has no immediate use, the Secretary of State may, if he thinks fit, repay to him the value of the stamp in money, upon his delivering up the stamp to be cancelled, and proving to the satisfaction of the Secretary of State that it was purchased by him.... from some person duly appointed to sell and distribute stamps or duly licensed to deal in stamps, within the period of two years next preceding the application and with a bona-fide intention to use it.
13	Certain offences in relation to stamps.	Every person who does, or causes or procures to be done, or knowingly aids, abets or assists in doing any of the acts following, that is to say:— (1) *Forges a die or stamp ;* (2) *Prints or makes an impression upon any material with a forged die ;* (3) Fraudulently prints or makes an impression upon any material from a genuine die ;

Section of Act	Subject matter	Adapted provisions
13	Certain offences in relation to stamps.—contd.	(4) Fraudulently cuts, tears, or in any way removes from any material any stamp, with intent that any use should be made of such stamp or of any part thereof ;
		(5) Fraudulently mutilates any stamp, with intent that any use should be made of any part of such stamp ;
		(6) Fraudulently fixes or places upon any material or upon any stamp, any stamp or part of a stamp which, whether fraudulently or not, has been cut, torn, or in any way removed from any other material, or out of or from any other stamp ;
		(7) Fraudulently erases or otherwise either really or apparently removes from any stamped material any name, sum, date or other matter or thing whatsoever thereon written, with intent that any use should be made of the stamp upon such material ;
		(8) Knowingly sells or exposes for sale or utters or uses *any forged stamp or* any stamp which has been fraudulently printed or impressed from a genuine die ;
		(9) Knowingly, and without lawful excuse (the proof whereof shall lie on the person accused) has in his possession *any forged die or stamp or* any stamp which has been fraudulently printed or impressed from a genuine die, or any stamp or part of a stamp which has been fraudulently cut, torn, or otherwise removed from any material, or any stamp which has been fraudulently mutilated or any stamped material out of which any name, sum, date or other matter or thing has been fraudulently erased or otherwise either really or apparently removed,
		shall be guilty of an offence and shall on conviction be liable to be imprisoned for any term not exceeding fourteen years.
16	Proceedings for detection of forged dies, etc.	On information given before a justice upon oath that there is just cause to suspect any person of being guilty of any of the offences aforesaid, such justice may, by warrant under his hand, cause every house, room, shop, building or place belonging to or occupied by the suspected person, or where he is suspected of being or having been in any way engaged or concerned in the commission of any such offence, or of secreting any machinery, implements or utensils applicable to the commission of any such offence, to be searched, and if upon any such search any of the said several matters and things are

Section of Act	Subject matter	Adapted provisions
16	Proceedings for detection of forged dies, etc.—contd.	found, the same may be seized and carried away, and shall afterwards be delivered over to the Secretary of State.
17	Proceedings for detection of stamps stolen or obtained fraudulently.	(1) Any justice having jurisdiction in the place where any stamps are known or supposed to be concealed or deposited may, upon reasonable suspicion that the same have been stolen or fraudulently obtained, issue his warrant for the seizure thereof and for apprehending and bringing before himself or any other justice within the same jurisdiction the person in whose possession or custody the stamps may be found, to be dealt with according to law.
		(2) If the person does not satisfactorily account for the possession of the stamps, or it does not appear that the same were purchased by him.... from some person duly appointed to sell and distribute stamps or duly licensed to deal in stamps, the stamps shall be forfeited and shall be delivered over to the Secretary of State.
		(3) Provided that if at any time within six months after the delivery any person makes out to the satisfaction of the Secretary of State that any stamps so forfeited were stolen or otherwise fraudulently obtained from him, and that the same were purchased by him....from some person duly appointed to sell or distribute stamps, or duly licensed to deal in stamps, such stamps may be delivered up to him.
18	Licensed person in possession of forged stamps.	(1) If any forged stamps are found in the possession of any person appointed to sell and distribute stamps, or being or having been licensed to deal in stamps, that person shall be deemed and taken, unless the contrary is satisfactorily proved, to have had the same in his possession knowing them to be forged and with intent to sell, use or utter them, and shall be liable to the punishment imposed by law upon a person selling, using, uttering or having in possession forged stamps knowing the same to be forged.
		(2) If the Secretary of State has cause to suspect any such person of having in his possession any forged stamps, he may by warrant under his hand authorise any person to enter between the hours of nine in the morning and seven in the evening into

Section of Act	Subject matter	Adapted provisions

18	Licensed person in possession of forged stamps.—contd.	any house, room, shop or building of or belonging to the suspected person, and if on demand of admittance, and notice of the warrant, the door of the house, room, shop or building, or any inner door thereof, is not opened, the authorised person may break open the same and search for and seize any stamps that may be found therein or in the custody or possession of the suspected person.
		
		(3) All officers of the peace are hereby required, upon request of any person so authorised, to aid and assist in the execution of the warrant.
		
		(4) Any person who—
		  (a) Refuses to permit any such search or seizure to be made as aforesaid, or
		  (b) Assaults, opposes, molests or obstructs any person so authorised in the due execution of the powers conferred by this section or any person acting in his aid or assistance,
		
		and any officer of the peace who, upon any such request as aforesaid, refuses or neglects to aid or assist any person so authorised in the due execution of his powers shall incur a fine of fifty pounds.

19	Mode of proceeding where stamps are seized.	Where stamps are seized under a warrant, the person authorised by the warrant shall, if required, give to the person in whose custody or possession the stamps are found an acknowledgment of the number, particulars and amount of the stamps, and permit the stamps to be marked before the removal thereof.
20	As to defacement of adhesive stamps.	Every person who by any writing in any manner defaces any stamp before it is used shall incur a penalty of five pounds. Provided that any person may, with the express sanction of the Secretary of State and in conformity with the conditions which the Secretary of State may prescribe, write upon or otherwise appropriate a stamp before it is used for the purpose of identification thereof.
24	Declarations, how to be made.	Any statutory declaration, affidavit or oath to be made in pursuance of or for the purpose of this or any other Act for the time being in force relating to stamps may be made before the Secretary of State or any officer or person authorised by him in that behalf,

Section of Act	Subject matter	Adapted provisions
24	Declarations, how to be made.—contd.	or before any commissioner for oaths or any justice or any notary public in any part of Great Britain, or at any place out of Great Britain before any person duly authorised to administer oaths there.
25	Mode of granting licences.	Any licence or certificate to be granted by the Secretary of State under this or any other Act for the time being in force relating to stamps may be granted by such officer or person as the Secretary of State may authorise in that behalf.
26	Recovery of fines.	All fines imposed by this Act or by any Act for the time being in force relating to stamps may be proceeded for and recovered in the same manner, and in the case of summary proceedings with the like power of appeal as any fine or penalty under any Act relating to the Excise.
27	Definitions.	In the provisions of this Act, unless the context otherwise requires:—
		The expression "Secretary of State" means Secretary of State for Social Services.
		. . . .
		The expression "duty" includes any contribution payable under the National Insurance (Industrial Injuries) Act 1965, or the National Insurance Act 1965, and directed to be made by means of stamps.
		The expression "material" includes every sort of material upon which words or figures can be expressed.
		. . . .
		The expression "die" includes any plate, type, tool or implement whatever used under the direction of the Secretary of State for expressing, or denoting any duty, or rate of duty, or the fact that any duty or rate of duty. . . . has been paid. . . . or for denoting any fee, and also any part of any such plate, type, tool or implement.
		The expressions "forge" and "forged" include counterfeit and counterfeited. The expression "stamp" means in relation to stamps prepared and issued for the purposes of the National Insurance Act 1965 an adhesive stamp, and, in relation to stamps prepared and issued for the purposes of the National Insurance (Industrial Injuries) Act 1965 an adhesive stamp or a stamp impressed by means of a die.

Section of Act	Subject matter	Adapted provisions
27	Definitions—contd.	The expression "stamped" is applicable as well to instruments and material impressed with stamps by means of a die as to instruments and material having adhesive stamps affixed thereto. The expression "justice" means justice of the peace.

POST OFFICE ACT 1953

Section of Act	Subject matter	Adapted provisions
63	Prohibition of fictitious stamps.	(1) A person shall not:— (a) make, knowingly utter, deal in or sell any fictitious stamp ; (b) have in his possession unless he shows a lawful excuse, any fictitious stamp ; or (c) make or, unless he shows a lawful excuse, have in his possesion any die, plate, instrument or materials for making any fictitious stamp. (2) A person shall not knowingly use for the purposes of payment of contributions under the National Insurance (Industrial Injuries) Act 1965, or the National Insurance Act 1965, any fictitious stamp. (3) If any person acts in contravention of the foregoing provisions of this section he shall be liable on summary conviction to a fine not exceeding twenty pounds. (4) Any stamp, die, plate, instrument or materials found in the possession of any person in contravention of subsection (1) of this section may be seized and shall be forfeited. (5) The importation into the United Kingdom (a) of any facsimile, imitation or representation, whether on paper or otherwise, of any stamp ; or (b) of any die, plate, instrument or materials for making such a facsimile, imitation or representation, is hereby prohibited.

Section of Act	Subject matter	Adapted provisions
		(6) In this section (*a*) the expression "fictitious stamp" means any facsimile, imitation or representation, whether on paper or otherwise, of any stamp, and (*b*) the expression "stamp" means in relation to stamps prepared and issued for the purposes of the National Insurance Act 1965, an adhesive stamp and, in relation to stamps prepared and issued for the purposes of the National Insurance (Industrial Injuries) Act 1965, an adhesive stamp or a stamp impressed by means of a die. . . . .

EXPLANATORY NOTE

(This Note is not part of the Regulations.)

These Provisional Regulations made by the Secretary of State for Social Services replace, with necessary adaptations, the National Insurance and Industrial Injuries (Stamps) Regulations 1967 which were made by the Postmaster General. They are made necessary by the passing of the Post Office Act 1969 which transferred to the Secretary of State the control of the system of distribution of national insurance stamps.

The regulations apply the provisions of the Stamp Duties Management Act 1891 (as amended by subsequent enactments) and section 63 of the Post Office Act 1953 to national insurance stamps. These are stamps by means of which contributions under the National Insurance Act 1965 and the National Insurance (Industrial Injuries) Act 1965 are paid.

STATUTORY INSTRUMENTS

1969 No. 1605

BETTING AND GAMING

The Dog Racecourse Totalisator (Percentage) Order 1969

Made - - - - 12*th November* 1969

Coming into Operation 8*th December* 1969

In pursuance of paragraph 3 of Schedule 5 to the Betting, Gaming and Lotteries Act 1963(**a**) as amended by section 1 of the Betting, Gaming and Lotteries (Amendment) Act 1969(**b**), I hereby make the following Order:—

1. This Order may be cited as the Dog Racecourse Totalisator (Percentage) Order 1969 and shall come into operation on 8th December 1969.

2. A percentage of twelve and a half per cent. is hereby specified for the purposes of sub-paragraph (*a*) of paragraph 3 of Schedule 5 to the Betting, Gaming and Lotteries Act 1963 as amended by section 1 of the Betting, Gaming and Lotteries (Amendment) Act 1969.

James Callaghan,
One of Her Majesty's Principal
Secretaries of State.

Home Office,
Whitehall.
12th November 1969.

EXPLANATORY NOTE

(*This Note is not part of the Order.*)

This Order permits the operator of a totalisator on a dog racecourse to specify up to 12½ % (instead of the 6 % mentioned in paragraph 3(*a*) of Schedule 5 to the Betting, Gaming and Lotteries Act 1963) as the percentage he will deduct from the amounts staked.

(**a**) 1963 c. 2.   (**b**) 1969 c. 17.

STATUTORY INSTRUMENTS

1969 No. 1607 (C.49)

SUPREME COURT OF JUDICATURE, ENGLAND

MENTAL HEALTH

The Administration of Justice Act 1969 (Commencement No. 1) Order 1969

Made - - - 14*th November* 1969

The Lord Chancellor, in exercise of the power conferred on him by section 36(5) of the Administration of Justice Act 1969(**a**), hereby makes the following Order :—

1.—(1) This Order may be cited as the Administration of Justice Act 1969 (Commencement No. 1) Order 1969.

(2) In this Order, "the Act" means the Administration of Justice Act 1969.

(3) The Interpretation Act 1889(**b**) applies to this Order as it applies to an Act of Parliament.

2. The provisions of the Act specified in Schedule 1 to this Order shall come into operation on 1st December 1969.

3. The provisions of the Act specified in Schedule 2 to this Order shall come into operation on 1st January 1970.

Dated 14th November 1969.

Gardiner, C.

SCHEDULE 1

PROVISIONS COMING INTO OPERATION ON 1ST DECEMBER 1969

Provisions of the Act	Subject matter of provisions
Section 6	General ancillary jurisdiction of county court.
Section 7	Right of audience.
Section 8	Assessors.
Section 9, except subsection (1)	County court rules.
Section 11	Miscellaneous amendments of County Courts Act 1959(**c**).
Part III (Sections 17-19)	Power to make wills and codicils for mentally disordered persons.
Section 23	Power of Lord Chancellor to assign any particular jurisdiction of the High Court to two or more Divisions concurrently.
Section 24	Appeal Tribunals under Patents Act 1949(**d**) and Registered Designs Act 1949(**e**).

(**a**) 1969 c. 58.   (**b**) 1889 c. 63.   (**c**) 1959 c. 22.   (**d**) 1949 c. 87.   (**e**) 1949 c. 88.

Provisions of the Act	Subject matter of provisions
Section 25	Clerks to registrars of Chancery Division.
Section 26	Provisions as to other employments in Supreme Court.
Section 29	Reduction of period of apprenticeship for public notaries in London.
Section 31	Further provisions as to pension rights and related matters.
Section 32	Transfer of liability for stipend and fees of Chancellor of County Palatine of Durham.
Section 33	Extension of legislative power of Parliament of Northern Ireland with respect to grand juries and indictments.
Section 34	Interpretation, application to Crown, and provisions as to orders.
Section 35 (except as provided below with regard to Schedules 1 and 2 to the Act)	Minor and consequential amendments and repeals.
Section 36	Short title, extent and commencement.
Schedule 1, except so far as it relates to the Settled Land Act 1925(a), the Solicitors Act 1957(b), the County Courts Act 1959, and the Northern Ireland Act 1962(c).	Enactments amended.
Schedule 2, except so far as it relates to the Probates and Letters of Administration (Ireland) Act 1857(d), section 153 of the Supreme Court of Judicature (Consolidation) Act 1925(e), section 47 of the County Courts Act 1959, the Northern Ireland Act 1962 and the County Courts Jurisdiction Order 1965(f).	Repeals.

(a) 1925 c. 18.   (b) 1957 c. 27.   (c) 1962 c. 30.
(d) 1857 c. 79.   (e) 1925 c. 49.   (f) S.I. 1965/2141 (1965 III, p. 6290).

SCHEDULE 2

PROVISIONS COMING INTO OPERATION ON 1ST JANUARY 1970

Provisions of the Act	Subject matter of provisions
Part II (Sections 12-16)	Appeals from High Court to House of Lords.
Section 20	Orders for interim payment.
Section 21	Powers of court exercisable before commencement of action.
Section 22	Interest on damages.
Section 27	Records of grants of probate and grants of administration.
Section 28	Second and subsequent grants of probate and administration.
Section 30	Superannuation benefits in respect of certain judicial offices.
Section 35 (to the extent provided below with regard to Schedules 1 and 2 to the Act).	Minor and consequential amendments and repeals.
Schedule 1, so far as it relates to the Northern Ireland Act 1962.	Enactments amended.
Schedule 2, so far as it relates to the Probates and Letters of Administration (Ireland) Act 1857, section 153 of the Supreme Court of Judicature (Consolidation) Act 1925 and the Northern Ireland Act 1962.	Repeals.

EXPLANATORY NOTE

(*This Note is not part of the Order.*)

This Order brings most of the provisions of the Administration of Justice Act 1969 into operation on either 1st December 1969 or 1st January 1970. The only provisions not brought into operation are sections 1 to 5, 9(1) and 10 (which amend the law relating to the jurisdiction of the county court), and the amendments and repeals consequential upon those sections.

STATUTORY INSTRUMENTS

1969 No. 1609 (C.50) (S.133)

EVIDENCE

The Law Reform (Miscellaneous Provisions) (Scotland) Act 1968 (Commencement No. 2) Order 1969

Made - - - - - 12*th November* 1969

In exercise of the powers conferred on me by section 22(5) of the Law Reform (Miscellaneous Provisions) (Scotland) Act 1968(a) and of all other powers enabling me in that behalf, I hereby make the following order:—

1. Sections 13, 14 and 15 of the Law Reform (Miscellaneous Provisions) (Scotland) Act 1968 shall come into operation on 1st December 1969.

2. This Order may be cited as the Law Reform (Miscellaneous Provisions) (Scotland) Act 1968 (Commencement No. 2) Order 1969.

William Ross,
One of Her Majesty's
Principal Secretaries of State.

St. Andrew's House,
Edinburgh.

12th November 1969.

EXPLANATORY NOTE

(This Note is not part of the Order.)

This Order brings into force on 1st December 1969 those provisions of the Law Reform (Miscellaneous Provisions) (Scotland) Act 1968 which make a statement contained in a document produced by a computer admissible as evidence in civil proceedings and which set down the conditions to be complied with and the procedure to be followed before such a statement can be admitted as evidence.

(a) 1968 c. 70.

STATUTORY INSTRUMENTS

1969 No. 1611 (S.135)

NATIONAL HEALTH SERVICE, SCOTLAND

The National Health Service (Hospital Accounts and Financial Provisions) (Scotland) Regulations 1969

Made - - - -	14*th November* 1969
Laid before Parliament	24*th November* 1969
Coming into Operation	1*st December*1969

In exercise of the powers conferred upon me by sections 54 and 55 of, and Schedule 4 to, the National Health Service (Scotland) Act 1947(a) (as amended by sections 27 and 28 of the Health Services and Public Health Act 1968(b)) and by section 29 of the said Act of 1968, and of all other powers enabling me in that behalf and with the approval of the Treasury I hereby make the following regulations:—

Citation and commencement

1. These regulations may be cited as the National Health Service (Hospital Accounts and Financial Provisions) (Scotland) Regulations 1969 and shall come into operation on 1st December 1969.

Interpretation

2.—(1) In these regulations, unless the context otherwise requires:—

"the Act" means the National Health Service (Scotland) Act 1947;

"the Act of 1968" means the Health Services and Public Health Act 1968;

"auditor" means an auditor appointed by the Secretary of State under section 55(2) of the Act;

"Board" means a Regional Hospital Board or Board of Management constituted under section 11 of the Act;

"capital expenditure" means expenditure of a Board on works of construction, reconstruction or alteration and associated purchases of furniture and equipment after the deduction of direct credits;

"chief financial officer" means, in the case of a Regional Hospital Board, the Regional Treasurer; and in the case of a Board of Management, the Secretary and Treasurer;

"direct credit" means an item of income of a class determined by the Secretary of State with the approval of the Treasury as proper to be offset against the expenditure of a hospital authority;

"financial year" means the period of twelve months ending on 31st March;

"revenue expenditure" means the expenditure, other than capital expenditure, of a Board after the deduction of direct credits.

(2) The Interpretation Act 1889(c) applies for the interpretation of these regulations as it applies for the interpretation of an Act of Parliament.

(a) 1947 c. 27. **(b)** 1968 c. 46. **(c)** 1889 c. 63.

Finance Committee

3.—(1) For the supervision and control of their financial affairs each Board shall appoint a finance committee which, notwithstading anything contained in regulation 10 of the National Health Service (Regional Hospital Boards and Boards of Management) (Scotland) Regulations 1947(a) shall consist wholly of members of the appointing body.

(2) The functions of the Finance Committee shall include:—

(*a*) advising the Board on the financial aspects of all matters which are within the scope of the functions of that Board;

(*b*) ensuring that proper financial control is maintained in all matters for which the Board are responsible, and that standing financial instructions are issued;

(*c*) ensuring the proper maintenance of such financial records as the Secretary of State may specify;

(*d*) submitting of financial estimates required by the Board.

Duties of the Chief Financial Officer

4. The duties of the chief financial officer of a Board shall include:—

(*a*) giving information and advice on financial matters to the Board and to their Finance Committee;

(*b*) the continuous oversight and review of the arrangements for financial control;

(*c*) the preparation and completion of all financial estimates and returns required by his Board;

(*d*) the maintenance of a system of balancing double entry ledger accounts for recording the income and expenditure of the Board, of a system of cost accounts integrated therewith, and of such other financial records as the Secretary of State may specify;

(*e*) the proper collection of all moneys due to, the safe custody and the prompt payment into the bank of all moneys received by, and the prompt disbursement of all payments due by the Board.

Control of Capital Expenditure

5.—(1) Each Regional Hospital Board shall submit to the Secretary of State in such form and by such dates in each financial year as the Secretary of State may specify:—

(*a*) an estimate of capital expenditure for the next succeeding financial year and a revised estimate of capital expenditure for the current financial year;

(*b*) annual programmes showing capital schemes for which the Board propose the start of works on site in such financial years as the Secretary of State may specify.

(a) S.R.&O. 1947/2261 (Rev. XV p. 837: 1947 I p. 1366).

(2) The Secretary of State may approve the estimates and, for such financial years as he may specify, annual programmes of proposed capital schemes with or without modification or subject to conditions and may at any time prior to or during any financial year approve variations of an approved estimate or programme, but any such approval shall be without prejudice to any requirement for the consent of the Secretary of State to a specific scheme under the National Health Service (Functions of Regional Hospital Boards) (Scotland) Regulations 1948(a) as amended(b).

Control of Revenue Expenditure

6.—(1) Each Board of Management shall submit to the appropriate Regional Hospital Board, in such form and by such date in each financial year as the Regional Hospital Board may specify, forecasts of revenue expenditure for such subsequent financial years as the Regional Hospital Board may specify.

(2) The Regional Hospital Board shall examine the forecasts of revenue expenditure submitted to them as aforesaid and after making such modification as they think fit shall submit to the Secretary of State, in such form and by such date as he may specify in respect of the area of the Regional Hospital Board as a whole, forecasts of revenue expenditure for such subsequent financial years as he may specify.

(3) As soon as possible before the beginning of each financial year the Secretary of State shall notify each Regional Hospital Board of the total revenue expenditure which may be incurred by the Board in that year; and may subsequently revise the amounts so approved.

(4) A Regional Hospital Board shall notify each Board of Management in their area of the total revenue expenditure which may be incurred by that Board in each financial year, and may subsequently revise the amounts so approved.

Cash requirements

7.—(1) A Regional Hospital Board shall furnish to the Secretary of State such periodic estimates of cash requirements arising from expenditure approved by the Secretary of State for the purposes of section 54(1) of the Act and such additional information in connection therewith as he may specify, and the Secretary of State shall advance to each Board at such times and in such manner as the Treasury under section 54(4) of the Act may direct such amounts as appear to him to be necessary to meet the expenses of the Board.

(2) A Board of Management shall furnish to the Regional Hospital Board concerned such periodic estimates of cash requirements arising from expenditure approved by the Regional Hospital Board and such additional information in connection therewith as the Regional Hospital Board may specify and the Regional Hospital Board shall advance to the Board of Management at such intervals as they think fit such amounts as appear to them to be necessary to meet the expenses of the Board of Management.

Authorisation of Payments

8. No payments shall be made by or on behalf of a Board unless authorised in such manner as the Secretary of State may direct.

(a) S.I. 1948 No. 594 (Rev. XV p. 841; 1948 I p. 2449).
(b) The relevant amending instruments are S.I. 1963/993 (1963 II p. 1633) and S.I. 1969/437 (1969 I, p. 1290).

Auditors

9. An auditor shall have the right of access at all reasonable times to all books, accounts and other records of a Board. He may require their production before him and shall be entitled to require from any member or officer, or former member or officer of the Board such information relating to the affairs of the Board as he may deem necessary for the purpose of his audit.

Annual Accounts

10.—(1) As soon as may be after the close of a financial year the chief financial officer shall prepare annual accounts in such form as the Secretary of State, with the approval of the Treasury may direct. After certifying them as correct the chief financial officer shall submit them to the Board for approval. The Board shall thereafter transmit them to the auditor and, in the case of a Board of Management, shall also transmit a copy to the Regional Hospital Board, by such date as the Secretary of State may specify.

(2) The annual accounts shall be audited by the auditor who shall certify them with or without reservation. The auditor shall thereafter transmit them with his report thereon to the Secretary of State and shall also transmit a copy of each to the Regional Hospital Board.

Losses and Claims

11. Where a Board suffer a loss of public cash or property or where a claim which may result in the payment of damages or compensation is made against a Board, that Board shall follow such procedure, maintain such records and make such returns as the Secretary of State may specify.

Application of Regulations

12. These regulations shall apply to all accounts kept by a Board under section 55(2) of the Act, as amended by Section 28(3) of the Act of 1968.

Revocation of Regulations

13.—(1) The National Health Service (Hospital Accounts and Financial Provisions) (Scotland) Regulations 1948(a), are hereby revoked.

(2) Section 38 of the Interpretation Act 1889 shall apply as if these regulations were an Act of Parliament and as if any regulations revoked by these regulations were Acts of Parliament repealed by an Act of Parliament.

William Ross,
One of Her Majesty's Principal
Secretaries of State.

St. Andrew's House,
   Edinburgh, 1.
   12th November 1969.

We approve.

E. S. Perry,
Joseph Harper,
Two of the Lords Commissioners of
Her Majesty's Treasury.

14th November 1969.

(a) S.I. 1948/2038 (Rev. XV p. 1003; 1948 I p 2336).

EXPLANATORY NOTE

(This Note is not part of the Regulations.)

These Regulations which supersede the National Health Service (Hospital Accounts and Financial Provisions (Scotland) Regulations 1948) govern the internal financial arrangements and systems of financial control of the hospital service and make provisions for the audit of Hospital Board accounts.

The principal matters dealt with in the Regulations include—

(*a*) the appointment of finance committees and the responsibility of a Board for proper financial control (regulation 3) and the role of the chief financial officer in this respect (regulation 4);

(*b*) the control and approval of expenditure (regulations 5 and 6);

(*c*) the making of cash advances to Boards in respect of approved expenditure (regulation 7);

(*d*) the authorisation of payments by Boards (regulation 8);

(*e*) the rights of auditors of access to, and production of, records (regulation 9);

(*f*) annual accounts (regulation 10);

(*g*) losses and claims (regulation 11).

The Regulations also prescribe some of the circumstances in which the Secretary of State may issue directions under Sections 28(3) and 29(2) of the Health Services and Public Health Act 1968.

STATUTORY INSTRUMENTS

1969 No. 1612 (S. 136)

NATIONAL HEALTH SERVICE, SCOTLAND

The National Health Service (Executive Councils and Scottish Dental Estimates Board) (Scotland) Financial Regulations 1969

Made - - -	14*th November* 1969
Laid before Parliament	24*th November* 1969
Coming into Operation	1*st December* 1969

In exercise of the powers conferred on me by sections 39, 54 and 55 of, and Schedule 6 to, the National Health Service (Scotland) Act 1947(a) and by sections 28 and 29 of the Health Services and Public Health Act 1968(b) and of all other powers enabling me in that behalf and with the approval of the Treasury, I hereby make the following regulations:—

PART I

Citation and commencement

1. These regulations may be cited as the National Health Service (Executive Councils and Scottish Dental Estimates Board) (Scotland) Financial Regulations 1969 and shall come into operation on 1st December 1969.

Interpretation

2.—(1) In these regulations, unless the context otherwise requires:—

"the Act" means the National Health Service (Scotland) Act 1947;

"the Act of 1968" means the Health Services and Public Health Act 1968;

"auditor" means an auditor appointed by the Secretary of State under section 55(2) of the Act;

"Council" means the Executive Council constituted for any area;

"finance officer" means the Clerk appointed by the Council under regulation 10(1) of the National Health Service (Executive Councils) (Scotland) Regulations 1954(c);

"financial year" means the period of twelve months ending on 31st March;

"Ophthalmic Services Committee" means a Joint Ophthalmic Services Committee established under the National Health Service (Joint Ophthalmic Services Committees) (Scotland) Order 1948(d).

(2) The Interpretation Act 1889(e) applies for the interpretation of these regulations as it applies for the interpretation of an Act of Parliament.

(a) 1947 c. 27. (b) 1968 c. 46. (c) S.I. 1954/461 (1954 I, p. 1370)

(d) S.I. 1948/1452 (Rev. XV, p. 977; (1948 I, p. 2425) (e) 1889 c. 63.

PART II

EXECUTIVE COUNCILS

Finance committee

3. The functions of the finance committee of a Council shall include:—

(a) advising the Council on the financial aspects of all matters within the scope of the functions of that Council;

(b) ensuring that proper financial control is maintained in all matters for which the Council are responsible, and that standing financial instructions are issued;

(c) ensuring the proper maintenance of such financial records as the Secretary of State may specify;

(d) submitting to the Council financial estimates specified by the Council or by the Secretary of State.

Duties of the finance officer

4. The duties of the finance officer shall include:—

(a) the giving of information and advice on financial matters to the Council or any of their Committees;

(b) the continuous oversight and review of the arrangements for financial control;

(c) the preparation and completion of all financial estimates and returns specified by the Council, or by the Secretary of State;

(d) the maintenance of a system of balancing double entry ledger accounts for recording the receipts and payments by the Council, and such other records as the Secretary of State may specify;

(e) the proper collection of all moneys due to, the safe custody and the prompt payment into the bank of all moneys received by, and the prompt disbursement of all payments due by the Council.

Annual and supplementary estimates

5.—(1) The Council shall submit to the Secretary of State, in such form and under such heads of account and by such date in each financial year, as he may specify, an estimate (hereinafter referred to as the "annual estimate") of the receipts and payments of the Council during the succeeding financial year and a revised estimate of receipts and payments during the current financial year.

(2) If at any time it appears to the Council that there will be receipts or payments under any head of account in respect of which the Secretary of State has required the submission of an annual estimate, and provision for such receipts or payments has not been included in the Council's annual estimate, the Council shall prepare and submit to the Secretary of State as soon as may be an estimate of such additional receipts or payments (hereinafter referred to as a "supplementary estimate"), unless the Secretary of State has notified the Council that because of the nature of the additional receipts or payments it is not necessary to submit such a supplementary estimate.

(3) No expenditure under any head of account which has been specified under sub-paragraph (1) above shall be incurred by or on behalf of the Council unless provision for such expenditure has been included in an annual estimate, or in a supplementary estimate, or the Secretary of State has notified the Council that it is not necessary to submit a supplementary estimate in respect of that expenditure.

Cash requirements

6. The Council shall furnish to the Secretary of State such periodic estimates of cash requirements arising from expenditure approved by the Secretary of State for the purposes of section 54(1) of the Act and such additional information in connection therewith as he may specify, and the Secretary of State shall advance to the Council at such times and in such manner as the Treasury under section 54(4) of the Act may direct, such amounts as appear to him to be necessary to meet the expenses of the Council, including the expenses of an Ophthalmic Services Committee acting on behalf of the Council.

Authorisation of payments

7. No payments shall be made by or on behalf of the Council unless authorised in such manner as the Secretary of State may direct.

Auditors

8. An auditor shall have the right of access at all reasonable times to all books, accounts, and other records of a Council. He may require their production before him, and shall be entitled to require from any member or officer, or former member or officer of the Council such information relating to the affairs of the Council as he may deem necessary for the purpose of his audit.

Annual accounts

9.—(1) After the close of a financial year the finance officer shall prepare annual accounts in such form as the Secretary of State with the approval of the Treasury may direct. After certifying them as correct, the finance officer shall submit them to the Council for approval, and the Council shall thereafter submit them to the Secretary of State by such date as he may specify.

(2) The annual accounts shall be audited by an auditor who shall certify the accounts, with or without reservation, and shall transmit the audited accounts with his report thereon to the Secretary of State.

Losses and claims

10. Where a Council suffer a loss of public cash or property or where a claim which may result in the payment of damages or compensation is made against the Council, the Council shall follow such procedure, maintain such records and make such returns as the Secretary of State may specify.

PART III

SCOTTISH DENTAL ESTIMATES BOARD

11. The provisions of Part II of these regulations shall apply to the Scottish Dental Estimates Board in the same way as they apply to Executive Councils with the following modifications:—

(1) The word "Board" shall be substituted for the word "Council".

(2) References to the finance committee of a Council shall be construed as references to the Board but regulations 3(*a*) and (*d*) shall not apply.

(3) References to the Ophthalmic Services Committee shall be omitted.

PART IV

REVOCATION

12.—(1) The National Health Service (Finance of Executive Councils and Scottish Dental Estimates Board) (Scotland) Regulations 1948(a) are hereby revoked.

(a) S.I. 1948/1494 (Rev. XV, p. 996; (1948 I, p. 2328)

(2) Section 38 of the Interpretation Act 1889 shall apply as if these regulations were an Act of Parliament and as if any regulations revoked by these regulations were Acts of Parliament repealed by an Act of Parliament.

William Ross,
One of Her Majesty's Principal
Secretaries of State.

St. Andrew's House,
    Edinburgh.
12th November 1969.

We approve.

E. G. Perry,
Joseph Harper,
Two of the Lords Commissioners of
Her Majesty's Treasury.

14th November 1969.

EXPLANATORY NOTE

(This Note is not part of the Regulations.)

These Regulations (which supersede the National Health Service (Finance of Executive Councils and Scottish Dental Estimates Board) (Scotland) Regulations 1948) govern the internal financial arrangements and systems of financial control of Executive Councils and make provision for the audit of their accounts. The principal matters dealt with in the Regulations include—

(a) the functions of the finance committee of an Executive Council (regulation 3) and the duties of the finance officer (regulation 4);

(b) the submission of financial estimates by Councils (regulation 5);

(c) the making of cash advances to Councils to meet expenditure incurred for the purpose of discharging their functions (regulation 6);

(d) the authorisation of payments by Councils (regulation 7);

(e) the rights of auditors of access to, and production of, relevant documents (regulation 8);

(f) annual accounts (regulation 9);

(g) losses and claims (regulation 10).

The Regulations also include some of the circumstances in which the Secretary of State may issue directions under sections 28(3) and 29(2) of the Health Services and Public Health Act 1968.

The Regulations are applied, with minor modifications, to the Scottish Dental Estimates Board constituted under section 39(2) of the National Health Service (Scotland) Act 1947.

STATUTORY INSTRUMENTS

1969 No. 1613 (C.51)

TRANSPORT

The Transport Act 1968 (Commencement No. 3) Order 1969

Made - - - *17th November* 1969

The Minister of Transport hereby makes this Order in exercise of his powers under section 166 of the Transport Act 1968(a) and of all other enabling powers:—

1. This Order may be cited as the Transport Act 1968 (Commencement No. 3) Order 1969.

2.—(1) In this Order "the Act" means the Transport Act 1968.

(2) The Interpretation Act 1889(b) shall apply for the interpretation of this Order as it applies for the interpretation of an Act of Parliament.

3.—(1) On the 20th November 1969 there shall come into force—

(a) the provisions of the Act specified in column 1 of Schedule 1 to this Order; and

(b) the provisions thereof specified in columns 2, 3 and 4 of the said Schedule 1 to the extent and for the purposes respectively specified in the headings to those columns in relation to those provisions.

(2) The provisions specified in columns 1 and 2 of Schedule 2 to this Order shall come into force for the purposes specified for those provisions in that Schedule in relation to the persons specified in column 1 of Schedule 3 to this Order—

(a) on the dates specified in relation to those persons in column 2 of Schedule 3 in the case of the provisions in Part I of Schedule 2; and

(b) on the dates specified in relation to those persons in column 3 of Schedule 3 in the case of the provisions in Part II of Schedule 2.

Sealed with the Official Seal of the Minister of Transport the 17th November 1969.

G. R. W. Brigstocke,
An Under Secretary of the
Ministry of Transport

(a) 1968 c. 73. (b) 1889 c. 63.

SCHEDULE 1

PROVISIONS COMING INTO FORCE ON THE 20TH NOVEMBER 1969

Column 1	Column 2	Column 3	Column 4
Provisions coming into force for all purposes:	Provisions coming into force for the purpose only of enabling regulations to be made:	Provisions coming into force for the purpose only of enabling regulations relating to operators' licensing to be made:	Provisions coming into force only in so far as they relate to operators' licensing:
Section 59	Section 60(2) and (4)		
Section 61	Section 63(1), (3) and (4)		
	Section 67(2)		
Section 69(4)		Section 71(6)	Section 85
		Section 86	
		Section 87(4)	Section 88
	Section 89(1)		Section 90
			Section 91
			Section 92
Section 95			
Section 98			
Section 101			
Section 102			
Section 103(1) to (7) and (9)			

SCHEDULE 2

Provisions Coming into Force in Relation to the Persons
Specified in Column 1 of Schedule 3 to This Order
on the Dates Respectively Specified in Columns 2 and 3 of
the Said Schedule 3 in Relation to Them

Column 1 Provisions coming into force so far as not brought into force by Schedule 1 to this Order:	Column 2 Provisions coming into force so far as not brought into force by Schedule 1 to this Order and in so far as they relate to operators' licensing:
Part I	
Section 62 Section 63 Section 64(1) to (4) Section 66 Section 67 Section 68 Section 69 Section 70 Section 82(4) and (5)	
	Section 84 Section 86 Section 87 Section 89
Section 94(1), (2) and (7)	
In Schedule 10 *to the Act*	
Part I	
Part II	
Section 60	Section 71(6)

SCHEDULE 3

Description of Persons in Relation to whom the Provisions
Specified in Part I of Schedule 2 come into Force on the Dates Specified
in Column 2 of this Schedule, and the Provisions Specified in Part II of
Schedule 2 come into Force on the Dates Specified in
Column 3 of this Schedule

Column 1 Description of persons:	Column 2 Date on which the provisions specified in Part I of Schedule 2 come into force in relation to the persons specified in the same entry in Column 1:	Column 3 Date on which the provisions specified in Part II of Schedule 2 come into force in relation to the persons specified in the same entry in Column 1:

1.—(1) Any person (other than the Post Office) who—
   (a) proposes to use a goods vehicle (other than a farmer's goods vehicle) on a road for the carriage of goods for hire or reward or for or in connection with any trade or business carried on by him, not being a use for which an operator's licence is not required by virtue of section 60(2) of the Act, and
   (b) does not hold a carrier's licence or holds a carrier's licence of Class A or B in relation to any vehicle.
 	
   (2) Any person who holds a carrier's licence of any Class which has been granted or has effect as if granted to him under Regulation 13 (simplified procedure for the grant, etc. of carriers' licences in respect of Northern Ireland or foreign goods vehicles temporarily in Great Britain) of the Goods Vehicles (Carriers' Licences) (Temporary Use in Great Britain) Regulations 1969(a).
	1st December 1969	1st March 1970

2. Any person (except the Post Office) who holds a carrier's licence of Class C, the number whereof ends with figures between 000 and 333 inclusive, in relation to any vehicles.	1st March 1970	1st June 1970
3. Any person (except the Post Office) who holds a carrier's licence of Class C, the number whereof ends with figures between 334 and 666 inclusive, in relation to any vehicles.	1st June 1970	1st September 1970
4. Any person (except the Post Office) who holds a carrier's licence of Class C, the number whereof ends with figures between 667 and 999 inclusive, in relation to any vehicles.	1st September 1970	1st December 1970

(a) S.I. 1969/1423 (1969 III, p. 4596).

INTERPRETATION

1. In this Schedule—

"carrier's licence" means a licence granted under Part IV of the Road Traffic Act 1960(**a**);

"farmer's goods vehicle" has the same meaning as in paragraph 7(1) of Schedule 4 to the Vehicles (Excise) Act 1962(**b**); and

"Post Office" means the Post Office established by section 6 of the Post Office Act 1969(**c**).

2. If any person qualifies under more than one of the descriptions in Column 1 of this Schedule the earlier or earliest of such descriptions in that column shall be treated as the only description applying to him.

EXPLANATORY NOTE
(*This Note is not part of the Order.*)

This Order brings into operation, on the various dates specified in it, those provisions of Part V of the Transport Act 1968 relevant to operators' licensing. It also brings into operation those provisions of Part VI of the Act necessary to enable Regulations to be made about the keeping of drivers' record books.

(**a**) 1960 c. 16. (**b**) 1962 c. 13. (**c**) 1969 c. 48.

STATUTORY INSTRUMENTS

1969 No. 1614

ROAD TRAFFIC

The Motor Vehicles (Driving Licences) (Amendment) (No. 2) Regulations 1969

Made - - -	14*th November* 1969
Laid before Parliament	25*th November* 1969
Coming into Operation	26*th November* 1969

The Minister of Transport in exercise of his powers under sections 102 and 113 of the Road Traffic Act 1960(**a**) and of all other enabling powers and after consultation with representative organisations in accordance with section 260(2) of that Act, hereby makes the following Regulations :—

1.—(1) These Regulations shall come into operation on the 26th November 1969, and may be cited as the Motor Vehicles (Driving Licences) (Amendment) (No. 2) Regulations 1969.

(2) The Interpretation Act 1889(**b**) shall apply for the interpretation of these Regulations as it applies for the interpretation of an Act of Parliament.

2. The Motor Vehicles (Driving Licences) Regulations 1963(**c**), as amended (**d**), shall have effect as though for paragraph (2)(*a*) of Regulation 7 there were substituted the following :—

> "(*a*) is undergoing a test or a test of competence to drive heavy goods vehicles under Part V of the Act of 1960 ; or"

3. The provisions of Regulation 7 of the Motor Vehicles (Driving Licences) Regulations 1963, as amended by these Regulations, shall apply in relation to a provisional licence granted before the date of coming into force of these Regulations, and in force on that date, as they apply in relation to a provisional licence granted on or after that date.

Given under the Official Seal of the Minister of Transport the 14th November 1969.

(L.S.)

Fred Mulley,
Minister of Transport.

(**a**) 1960 c. 16. (**b**) 1889 c. 63.
(**c**) S.I. 1963/1026 (1963 II, p. 1730).
(**d**) There is no amendment which relates expressly to the subject matter of these regulations.

EXPLANATORY NOTE
(*This Note is not part of the Regulations.*)

These Regulations amend the Motor Vehicles (Driving Licences) Regulations 1963 by permitting the holder of a provisional licence granted under Part II of the Road Traffic Act 1960 to drive a heavy goods vehicle otherwise than under the supervision of a qualified driver when undergoing a test of competence under Part V of that Act.

1969 No. 1621 (S.138)

JUVENILE COURTS AND OFFENDERS

The Children's Panels and Children's Panel Advisory Committees (Travelling Allowances, etc.) (Scotland) Regulations 1969

Made - - -	13*th November* 1969
Laid before Parliament	20*th November* 1969
Coming into Operation	21*st November* 1969

In exercise of the powers conferred on me by paragraph 8 of Schedule 3 to the Social Work (Scotland) Act 1968(a) I hereby make the following regulations:—

Citation and commencement

1. These regulations may be cited as the Children's Panels and Children's Panel Advisory Committees (Travelling Allowances, etc.) (Scotland) Regulations 1969 and shall come into operation on 21st November 1969.

Interpretation

2.—(1) In these regulations, unless the context otherwise requires:
"the Act" means the Social Work (Scotland) Act 1968;
"children's panel" means a panel formed under section 33(1) of the Act;
"Children's Panel Advisory Committee" means a committee formed under paragraph 3 of Schedule 3 to the Act;
"local authority" means the local authority responsible for the payment of allowances under paragraph 8 of Schedule 3 to the Act;
"member" includes any person appointed in accordance with the provisions of Schedule 3 to the Act to serve as a member of a children's panel or a Children's Panel Advisory Committee, and any person who has made application or has been suggested for appointment as a member of a children's panel and has been required to incur expenses under arrangements made by a Children's Panel Advisory Committee in pursuance of their duty under paragraph 5(*a*) or (*b*) of Schedule 3 to the Act or by the Secretary of State or a local authority in pursuance of their powers to arrange training under paragraphs 6 and 7 of the said Schedule 3.

(2) The Interpretation Act 1889(b) shall apply for the interpretation of these regulations as it applies for the interpretation of an Act of Parliament.

(3) In these regulations unless the context otherwise requires references to any enactment or regulation shall be construed as references to that enactment or regulation as amended by any subsequent enactment or regulation or to any enactment or regulation substituted for that enactment or regulation.

Allowances

3. The rates of travelling, subsistence and financial loss allowances payable to a member in respect of expenditure necessarily incurred by him shall be the rates set out in Schedules 1, 2 and 3 to these regulations respectively.

(a) 1968 c. 49.　　　　　　(b) 1889 c. 63.

4. A member who claims payment of any of the said allowances shall complete and submit to the local authority an application in the form set out in Schedule 4 to these regulations or in a form substantially to the like effect.

5. A local authority shall keep a record of every payment made by it under these regulations, showing the amount and nature of the payment and the name of the member to whom it was paid.

William Ross,
One of Her Majesty's Principal
Secretaries of State.

St. Andrew's House,
Edinburgh.
13th November 1969.

Regulation 3

SCHEDULE 1
RATES OF TRAVELLING ALLOWANCE

1. The rate for travel by public service shall not exceed the amount of the ordinary, or any available cheap, fare, and where more than one class of fare is available the rate shall be determined, in the case of travel by ship, by reference to first class fares, and in any other case by reference to second class fares, unless the local authority determines, either generally or specially, that first class fares shall be substituted:

Provided that the said rate may be increased by supplementary allowances not exceeding expenditure actually incurred—

    (*a*) on Pullman car or similar supplements, reservation of seats, and deposit or porterage of luggage; and

    (*b*) on sleeping accommodation engaged by a member for an overnight journey, subject, however, to reduction by one third of any subsistence allowance payable to him for that night.

2. The rate for travel by taxi-cab or cab—

    (*a*) in cases of urgency or where no public service is reasonably available shall not exceed the amount of the actual fare and any reasonable gratuity paid; and

    (*b*) in any other case, shall not exceed the amount of the fare for travel by an appropriate public service.

3. The rate for travel by a member's own private motor vehicle—

    (*a*) in circumstances which in the opinion of the local authority involve a substantial saving in his time or are otherwise reasonable, shall not exceed such rate as may from time to time be prescribed in paragraph 3 of Schedule 1 to the Local Government (Travelling Allowances, etc.) (Scotland) Regulations 1954(**a**), as amended (**b**), as the maximum rate for travel by a member's own private motor vehicle where in the opinion of the local authority it is reasonable that he should so travel rather than by public service; and

    (*b*) in circumstances other than those mentioned in sub-paragraph (*a*) of this paragraph, shall not exceed the maximum rate prescribed from time to time in the said paragraph 3, as it may be amended, for travel by a member's own private motor vehicle in circumstances other than those mentioned in the said sub-paragraph (*a*).

4. The rate for travel by a hired motor vehicle other than a taxi-cab or cab shall not exceed the rate which would have been applicable had the vehicle belonged to the member who hired it:

Provided that where the authority so approves, the rate may be increased to an amount not exceeding the actual cost of the hiring.

(a) S.I. 1954/265 (1954 I, p. 1159).   (b) S.I. 1962/1834 (1962 II, p. 2172).

5. The rate for travel by air shall not exceed the rate applicable to travel by appropriate alternative means of transport together with an allowance equivalent to the amount of any saving in financial loss allowance and subsistence allowance consequent on travel by air:

Provided that, where the local authority resolves, either generally or specially, that the saving in time is so substantial as to justify payment of the fare for travel by air, there may be paid an amount not exceeding—

(a) the ordinary, or any available cheap, fare for travel by regular air service; or

(b) where no such service is available or in case of urgency, the fare actually paid by the member.

Regulation 3

SCHEDULE 2

RATES OF SUBSISTENCE ALLOWANCE

The rates of subsistence allowance payable to a member shall not exceed such rates, and shall be subject to such conditions, as may from time to time be prescribed in Schedule 2 to the Local Government (Travelling Allowances, etc.) (Scotland) Regulations 1954(a), as amended (b):

Provided that in the application to members of the said Schedule, the proviso to paragraph 2 shall be of no effect.

Regulation 3

SCHEDULE 3

RATES OF FINANCIAL LOSS ALLOWANCE

The payment which a member shall be entitled to receive by way of financial loss allowance shall not exceed such payment, and shall be subject to the same conditions, as may from time to time be prescribed in Schedule 3 to the Local Government (Travelling Allowances, etc.) (Scotland) Regulations 1954(c), as amended (d).

(a) S.I. 1954/265 (1954 I, p. 1159).
(b) The relevant amending instrument is S.I. 1965/196 (1965 I, p. 501).
(c) S.I. 1954/265 (1954 I, p. 1159).
(d) The relevant amending instrument is S.I. 1966/899 (1966 II, p. 2152).

SCHEDULE 4

FORM OF APPLICATION FOR TRAVELLING AND SUBSISTENCE ALLOWANCES

Regulation 4

Date	Place and time of departure	Place and time of return	Description of approved duties	Mode and class of travel	No. of miles travelled by private motor vehicle, other than taxi-cab or cab, and rate applicable	Fares and other authorised payments	Travelling allowance claimed	Subsistence allowance claimed
(1)	(2)	(3)	(4)	(5)	(6)	(7)	(8)	(9)
					TOTALS ...	...	...	...

Particulars of amounts received or claimed by way of travelling or subsistence allowance from other authorities or bodies.

Amounts now claimed ...

I declare that I have actually and necessarily incurred expenditure on travelling and subsistence for the purpose of enabling me to perform approved duties in relation to membership of.., that I have actually paid the fares and made the other payments, shown above, and that the amounts claimed are strictly in accordance with the rates determined by..

I declare that the statements above are correct. Except as shown above I have not made, and will not make, any claim under any enactment for travelling or subsistence expenses or allowances in connection with the duties indicated above.

Date.. Signature...

FORM OF APPLICATION FOR FINANCIAL LOSS ALLOWANCE

Date (1)	Place and time of departure (2)	Place and time of return (3)	Description of approved duties (4)	Amount claimed (5)

Particulars of amounts received or claimed by way of financial loss allowance from other authorities or bodies.

Amount now claimed   ...   ...

I declare that I have actually and necessarily—

(a) suffered loss of earnings which I should otherwise have made; or

(b) incurred additional expense, other than expense on account of travelling or subsistence,

for the purpose of enabling me to perform approved duties in relation to membership of...and that the amount of such loss and expense is not less than the sum claimed.

I declare that the statements above are correct. Except as shown above I have not made, and will not make, any claim under any enactment for financial loss allowance in connection with the duties indicated above.

Date.. Signature...

EXPLANATORY NOTE

(This Note is not part of the Regulations.)

These Regulations prescribe, in pursuance of paragraph 8 of Schedule 3 to the Social Work (Scotland) Act 1968, the rates of travelling, subsistence and financial loss allowances payable to members of Children's Panel Advisory Committees and to members and possible members of children's panels.

STATUTORY INSTRUMENTS

1969 No. 1622 (S.139)

RESIDENTIAL ESTABLISHMENTS, SCOTLAND

The Registration of Establishments (Scotland) Order 1969

Made - - - -	13*th November* 1969
Coming into Operation	18*th November* 1969

In exercise of the powers conferred on me by section 62(2) of the Social Work (Scotland) Act 1968(a), I hereby make the following Order:—

Citation and Commencement

1. This Order may be cited as the Registration of Establishments (Scotland) Order 1969 and shall come into operation on 18th November 1969.

Interpretation

2.—(1) In this Order the following expressions shall have the meanings hereby respectively assigned to them:—

"the Act" means the Social Work (Scotland) Act 1968;

"establishment" means any establishment within the meaning of section 61(1) of the Act.

(2) The Interpretation Act 1889(b) applies to the interpretation of this Order as it applies to the interpretation of an Act of Parliament.

Form of Application for Registration

3. Application for registration of any person carrying on or intending to carry on an establishment shall be in the form set out in the Schedule to this Order, or in a form to the like effect, and shall contain such information as is requested therein.

Revocation

4. The Voluntary Homes (Registration) (Scotland) Regulations 1948(c), the National Assistance (Registration of Homes) (Scotland) Regulations 1949(d) and the National Assistance (Registration of Homes) (Scotland) (Amendment) Regulations 1962(e) are hereby revoked.

William Ross,
One of Her Majesty's Principal
Secretaries of State.

St. Andrew's House,
Edinburgh.
13th November 1969.

(a) 1968 c. 49.	(b) 1889 c. 63.
(c) S.I. 1948/ 2595 (Rev. III, p. 806).	(d) S.I. 1949/1668 (1949 I, p. 2582).
(e) S.I. 1962/2489 (1962 III, p. 3368).	

SCHEDULE

Application for registration of a person carrying on or intending to carry on an establishment within the meaning of section 61(1) of the Social Work (Scotland) Act 1968 (see Notes below).

1. Full name, postal address and telephone number of applicant. (If application is made by an organisation, the address to be given is that of the registered or principal office. In addition the full names and addresses of the chairman and secretary must be given.)	
2. Name, postal address and telephone number of premises in respect of which application is made.	
3. Please state purposes of establishment and category or categories of persons to be received.	

4. Numbers of places:	Residents		By day only	
	M	F	M	F
(1) Maximum number				
(2) Age range				

5. General description of services and facilities to be provided.	
6.—(1) If children of school age are to be received in the establishment, is full-time education and/or training to be provided for 5 or more of them on the premises? (2) If so, is it intended that the children concerned should be only those who have been reported to the local authority as unsuitable for education or training in school?	
7. Names, ages, qualifications and experience of persons to be engaged in the management of the establishment. Please indicate in each case whether resident or non-resident.	
8. Number and types of other staff to be engaged in running the establishment.	

9. If a Firemaster's Report has been obtained in relation to the proposed use of the premises, please state the date of the report and whether action has been taken to implement the recommendations contained in it.

10. Date on which establishment is to be open for the reception of persons for whom it is to be provided or, in the case of a change of user, the date on which the change is to take effect.

If the establishment was already open at 17th November 1969, or if application for registration is being made in respect of a change of user, please state the authority, if any, with which the establishment was previously registered and the date of that registration.

11. Is the establishment carried on or to be carried on for financial reward?

12. Is the establishment intended to be used for purposes other than those of the Act? If so, please indicate these purposes.

I hereby make application for registration in respect of the above-mentioned premises which I am carrying on   * as an establishment within the meaning of section
            I intend to carry on
61(1) of the Social Work (Scotland) Act 1968.

Signature of applicant.............................

Designation ....

Full postal address ....

....

Date ....

*Delete as appropriate

NOTES

Note 1: *Meaning of "establishment"*

An establishment within the meaning of section 61(1) of the Act is "any residential or other establishment the sole or main object of which is to accommodate persons for the purposes of this Act, whether for reward or not, not being premises controlled or managed by a Government department or by a local authority, or required to be registered, or premises in respect of which a person is required to be registered, with a Government department or a local authority under any other enactment". (Until the commencement of Part III of the Act the expression "establishment" will not include an approved school; but following the commencement of Part III it will include any establishment which immediately before that date was an approved school and is not controlled or managed by a local authority.)

Note 2: *Registration authority to which application is to be made*

An application for registration in respect of an establishment is to be made to the county, city or large burgh within whose area the establishment is situated.

Note 3: *Right to require further information and to refuse application*

The registration authority to whom this application is made may require such further information as they may consider necessary to enable them to decide whether the requirements of registration are fulfilled. In terms of section 62(3) of the Act an application for registration may be refused if the registration authority are satisfied—

    (a) that the applicant or any person employed or proposed to be employed by him in the management of the establishment or any part thereof is not a fit person whether by reason of age or otherwise, to carry on or to be so employed at an establishment of such a description as the establishment named in the application; or

    (b) that for reasons connected with situation, construction, state of repair, accommodation, staffing or equipment, the establishment or any premises used in connection therewith are not fit to be used for an establishment of such a description as aforesaid; or

    (c) that the way in which it is proposed to conduct the establishment is such as not to provide services or facilities reasonably required by persons resorting to such an establishment.

Note 4: *Appeal against refusal of application*

Section 64 of the Act lays down the machinery for appeals against refusal of an application for registration. The registration authority are obliged to give the applicant not less than 14 days notice of their intention to refuse an application for registration and to state the grounds on which they propose to do so. If the applicant wishes to show cause why his application should not be refused, the authority must give him an opportunity to do so either in person or by representative before the application is refused. A person whose application for registration is refused may, within 21 days of the date of the notice of refusal, appeal to a tribunal established under Schedule 5 of the Act.

Note 5: *Planning permission etc.*

Registration under the Act does not obviate the need to obtain any necessary planning permission and/or approval under the relevant Building Standards (Scotland) Regulations.

EXPLANATORY NOTE

(This Note is not part of the Order.)

This Order prescribes the form in which an application for registration in respect of any esablishment within the meaning of section 61(1) of the Social Work (Scotland) Act 1968 is to be made and the information which is to be provided to the registration authority by the applicant.

STATUTORY INSTRUMENTS

1969 No. 1624

EXCHANGE CONTROL

The Exchange Control (Authorised Dealers and Depositaries) (Amendment) (No. 4) Order 1969

Made - - -	18*th November* 1969	
Coming into Operation	27*th November* 1969	

The Treasury, in exercise of the powers conferred upon them by sections 36(5) and 42(1) of the Exchange Control Act 1947(a), hereby make the following Order:—

1.—(1) This Order may be cited as the Exchange Control (Authorised Dealers and Depositaries) (Amendment) (No. 4) Order 1969, and shall come into operation on 27th November 1969.

(2) The Interpretation Act 1889(b) shall apply for the interpretation of this Order as it applies for the interpretation of an Act of Parliament.

2. Schedule 2 to the Exchange Control (Authorised Dealers and Depositaries) Order 1969(c), as amended(d), shall be further amended as follows:—

(a) by deleting the words "National Provincial & Rothschild (International) Ltd.";

(b) by inserting the words "Northern Trust Company, The." after the words "Northern Bank Ltd."; and

(c) by inserting the words "Rothschild Intercontinental Bank Ltd." after the words "Rothschild & Sons (C.I.) Ltd., N.M."

3. This Order shall extend to the Channel Islands, and any reference in this Order to the Exchange Control Act 1947 includes a reference to that Act as extended by the Exchange Control (Channel Islands) Order 1947(e).

Neil McBride,

Walter Harrison,

Two of the Lords Commissioners
18th November 1969. of Her Majesty's Treasury.

EXPLANATORY NOTE

(This Note is not part of the Order.)

This Order amends the list of persons authorised by the Treasury under the Exchange Control Act 1947 to act as dealers in gold and foreign currencies and as depositaries for the purpose of the deposit of securities.

(a) 1947 c. 14.	(b) 1889 c. 63.
(c) S.I. 1969/517 (1969 I, p. 1432).	(d) S.I. 1969/1414 (1969 III, p. 4475).
(e) S.R. & O. 1947/2034 (Rev. VI, p. 1001: 1947 I, p. 660).	

STATUTORY INSTRUMENTS

1969 No. 1626

HOUSING, ENGLAND AND WALES
HOUSING, SCOTLAND

The Assistance for House Purchase and Improvement (Increase of Subsidy) Order 1969

Laid before the House of Commons in draft

Made - - -	19*th November* 1969
Coming into Operation	1*st December* 1969

The Minister of Housing and Local Government, the Secretary of State for Wales and the Secretary of State for Scotland, acting jointly in exercise of their powers under subsections (3) and (4) of section 28 of the Housing Subsidies Act 1967(**a**) (added to that section by section 78 of the Housing Act 1969(**b**)) and of all other powers enabling them in that behalf, with the approval of the Treasury, hereby make the following order in the terms of a draft approved by resolution of the Commons House of Parliament :—

1. This order may be cited as the Assistance for House Purchase and Improvement (Increase of Subsidy) Order 1969 and shall come into operation on 1st December 1969.

2.—(1) In this order "the Act" means the Housing Subsidies Act 1967.

(2) The Interpretation Act 1889(**c**) shall apply for the interpretation of this order as it applies for the interpretation of an Act of Parliament.

3. This order does not apply to any contract requiring repayment of a loan subsidised under Part II of the Act at any time when the rate of interest applicable thereunder does not exceed seven per cent. per annum.

4. Where the rate of interest applicable for the time being under a contract requiring repayment of a loan subsidised under Part II of the Act falls within one of the limits set out in column (1) of the Schedule to this order, then with respect to interest payable for any period beginning on or after 1st January 1970, the calculation required by subsection (1)(*b*) of section 28 of the Act shall be made as if—

(**a**) 1967 c. 29. (**b**) 1969 c. 33. (**c**) 1889 c. 63.

(*a*) in the case of a loan where by virtue of the said subsection (1)(*b*) the rate is two per cent., there were substituted the higher percentage specified in column (2) of the said Schedule opposite that limit ; and

(*b*) in the case of a loan where by virtue of subsection (2) of the said section 28 the rate is one and three-quarters per cent., there were substituted the higher percentage specified in column (3) of the said Schedule opposite that limit.

SCHEDULE

(1) Rate of Interest	(2) Higher percentage	(3) Higher percentage
Exceeding 7 per cent. per annum but not exceeding 7⅞ per cent. per annum.	2¼ per cent.	2 per cent.
Exceeding 7⅞ per cent. per annum but not exceeding 8¾ per cent. per annum.	2½ per cent.	2¼ per cent.
Exceeding 8¾ per cent. per annum but not exceeding 9⅝ per cent. per annum.	2¾ per cent.	2½ per cent.
Exceeding 9⅝ per cent. per annum.	3 per cent.	2¾ per cent.

Given under the official seal of the Minister of Housing and Local Government on 19th November 1969.

(L.S.)   *Anthony Greenwood,*
                    Minister of Housing and Local Government.

Given under my hand on 19th November 1969.

George Thomas,
Secretary of State for Wales.

Given under the Seal of the Secretary of State for Scotland on 19th November 1969.

(L.S.)   *William Ross,*
                    Secretary of State for Scotland.

We approve,

Neil McBride,
Walter Harrison,
Two of the Lords Commissioners of
Her Majesty's Treasury.

19th November 1969.

EXPLANATORY NOTE

(This Note is not part of the Order.)

By this order the three Ministers specify two scales of percentages higher than and to replace, in most cases, the two per cent. and the one and three-quarters per cent. mentioned respectively in section 28(1) and (2) of the Housing Subsidies Act 1967 (aggregate amount of subsidy for option mortgages). Subsidy is thus increased for option mortgages where the rate of interest applicable for the time being under the contract requiring repayment of the loan (the "repayment contract") exceeds seven per cent. per annum. The order does not apply to option mortgages where the rate of interest applicable for the time being under the repayment contract does not exceed seven per cent. per annum. The scale of higher percentages in column (2) of the Schedule to the order applies where the periodical payments consist partly of repayment of capital and partly of interest on the loan. The scale of higher percentages in column (3) of the Schedule applies to periodical payments of interest on capital where, under the repayment contract, no repayment of capital is required to be made by those periodical payments. Each scale varies according to the rate of interest applicable for the time being under the repayment contract. The increase of subsidy will be paid with respect to interest payable for a period beginning on or after 1st January 1970.

STATUTORY INSTRUMENTS

1969 No. 1632 (S.143)

POLICE

The Police (Appeals) (Scotland) Rules 1969

Made - - -	13*th November* 1969
Laid before Parliament	27*th November* 1969
Coming into Operation	1*st December* 1969

In exercise of the powers conferred on me by paragraph 5 of Schedule 3 to the Police (Scotland) Act 1967(**a**) and after consultation with the Council on Tribunals in terms of section 7A of the Tribunals and Inquiries Act 1958(**b**) I hereby make the following rules :—

1.—(1) These rules may be cited as the Police (Appeals) (Scotland) Rules 1969 and shall come into operation on 1st December 1969.

(2) In these rules, which shall apply to all appeals by constables of a police force in Scotland under section 30 of the Police (Scotland) Act 1967, the expressions "appellant" and "respondent" shall have the same meanings respectively as in the last mentioned Act.

(3) The Interpretation Act 1889(**c**) shall apply for the interpretation of these rules as it applies for the interpretation of an Act of Parliament.

Notice of Appeal

2.—(1) Notice of Appeal to the Secretary of State shall be given in the form set out in the Schedule to these rules or in a form to the like effect.

(2) The Notice of Appeal shall be sent to the Secretary of State within 21 days from the date on which the appellant received notification of the decision against which he desires to appeal.

Provided that where the Secretary of State is satisfied, on the application of the appellant, that by reason of the special circumstances of the case it is just and right that an appeal should be entertained after the expiration of the period aforesaid, the Notice of Appeal shall be sent to the Secretary of State by such date as he may fix.

(3) The Notice of Appeal sent to the Secretary of State shall be accompanied by

    (*a*) a statement setting out fully on what grounds the appeal is made ; and

    (*b*) any documentary evidence which the appellant may desire to submit.

(a) 1967 c. 77.   (b) 1958 c. 66.
(c) 1889 c. 63.

(4) The appellant shall send to the respondent at the time of lodging the appeal a copy of the Notice of Appeal, of the relative statement and of any documentary evidence submitted.

Statement by respondent

3.—(1) The respondent shall, within 21 days of the date of receipt of the copy of the Notice of Appeal and relative statement and documentary evidence referred to in rule 2(4) of these rules, send to the Secretary of State a statement, signed and dated, saying whether or not the appeal is opposed.

Provided that where the Secretary of State is satisfied, on the application of the respondent, that there is good reason why the statement cannot be submitted within 21 days, it shall be sent to the Secretary of State by such date as he may fix.

(2) If the appeal is opposed the statement by the respondent shall

    (*a*) set out fully on what grounds it is opposed ;

    (*b*) contain any representations which the respondent may desire to submit with regard to the information furnished by the appellant ; and

    (*c*) contain a list of any documents which may accompany it in terms of paragraph (4) of this rule.

(3) A copy of the statement by the respondent and of any documents which may accompany it of which the appellant does not already possess a copy shall be sent to the appellant, and the statement shall contain a declaration that a full and true copy of the statement and of such accompanying documents has been sent to the appellant.

(4) The statement sent by the respondent to the Secretary of State shall be accompanied by

    (*a*) any documentary evidence which the respondent may desire to submit ;

    (*b*) a transcript of the verbatim record of the proceedings at the disciplinary hearing which led to the punishment or finding and punishment against which the appeal is made ;

    (*c*) a certified copy of the personal record of the appellant as provided for in the Police (Scotland) Regulations 1968(**a**), and

    (*d*) a certified copy of the discipline form as provided for in the Police (Discipline) (Scotland) Regulations 1967(**b**).

Documents to be sent to the Sheriff

4. Unless the Secretary of State decides that an inquiry shall not be held, he shall send to the sheriff the Notice of Appeal, the statements by the appellant and respondent and the other documents referred to in rules 2 and 3 of these rules, and the appellant and respondent shall be informed when this has been done.

Procedure

5. The sheriff, if he considers it necessary or expedient, may appoint the parties to revise and finally adjust their respective statements before proceeding to hold the inquiry.

(**a**) S.I. 1968/716 (1968 II, p. 2024).   (**b**) S.I. 1967/1021 (1967 II, p. 3091).

6.—(1) The sheriff shall, by Interlocutor, appoint a day, time and place for the holding of the inquiry and shall ordain the parties to intimate in writing to the Sheriff Clerk specified in the Interlocutor, not later than 5 days before the date of the inquiry the names of any witnesses or havers whom they wish to be required to attend or to produce documents in their possession. The sheriff shall cause a copy of the Interlocutor to be sent to the appellant, the respondent and the Secretary of State not less than 14 days before the date of the inquiry.

(2) The sheriff may proceed with the inquiry in the absence of either the appellant or the respondent, whether represented or not, if it appears to him to be just and proper to do so, and may adjourn the inquiry from time to time as may appear necessary for the due hearing of the appeal.

(3) Subject to these rules, the procedure at an inquiry shall be determined by the sheriff who shall have power to hear any new evidence, and to rehear the evidence given at the disciplinary hearing, and to specify by Interlocutor the procedure to be followed at the inquiry and the party who shall lead evidence first.

Withdrawal of Appeal

7. The appellant may withdraw his appeal at any time prior to its decision by giving notice in writing to the Secretary of State.

Representation at inquiry

8. The appellant shall have the right to be assisted in presenting his appeal and to be represented at the inquiry by a constable or by counsel or a solicitor.

9. The respondent shall have the right to be assisted in opposing the appeal and to be represented at the inquiry by a constable or by the clerk or other officer of the police authority, or by counsel or a solicitor.

Inquiry to be in private

10. Unless the sheriff otherwise directs, the inquiry shall be held in private but without prejudice to this generality the sheriff may allow such person or persons as he considers appropriate to attend the whole or such part of the inquiry as he thinks fit.

Record of evidence at inquiry

11. Unless the Secretary of State otherwise directs, a verbatim record of the evidence given at the inquiry shall be taken.

Report of the Sheriff

12. The sheriff shall include in his report, with reasons for his opinions and recommendations

    (a) a statement of the facts admitted or found to be proved ;

    (b) a statement of his opinion as to whether the punishment awarded was a just and proper one warranted by the facts and, if not, what other punishment (if any) ought to have been awarded ;

    (c) when the appeal is against punishment by dismissal, by being required to resign, or by reduction in rank, a recommendation as to the extent (if any) that the appellant, if he were reinstated in the force or in his rank, should be deemed for the purposes of pay to have served in the force or in that rank, as the case may be, continuously from the date of the decision appealed from to the date of his reinstatement and, if he was suspended for a period immediately preceding the date of the decision, as to the provision dealing with the suspension which should be included in the determination ; and

(d) a recommendation as to whether the appellant should be required to pay any, and if so what part, or the whole, of his own expenses of the appeal.

13. The report of the inquiry, and four copies thereof, shall be submitted to the Secretary of State as early as may be after the termination of the inquiry, together with the verbatim record of evidence, the transcription thereof, the Notice of Appeal, the statements by the appellant and respondent, and the other documents referred to in Rules 2 and 3 of these rules.

Further investigation by the Sheriff

14. Where the Secretary of State remits a case for further investigation by the sheriff in accordance with paragraph 3(5) of Schedule 3 to the Police (Scotland) Act 1967, these rules shall apply, subject to any necessary modification, in relation to that further investigation as they apply in relation to an inquiry.

Services of documents

15. Where any notice, statement or other document is required by these rules to be sent by or to the Secretary of State or other person or authority, it shall be a sufficient compliance with these rules if such notice, statement or other document is posted, within such time (if any) as is prescribed by these rules, in a letter for recorded delivery service directed, in the case of a letter to the Secretary of State, to the Secretary, Scottish Home and Health Department, St. Andrew's House, Edinburgh, EH1 3DE and in any other case to the person for whom it is intended at his usual office or other ordinary address.

Determination of questions

16. If any question arises as to the proper compliance with any provision of these rules it shall be determined by the Secretary of State whose decision shall be final.

Revocation

17. The Police (Appeals) (Scotland) Rules 1964(a) are hereby revoked in respect of any punishment imposed after 30th November 1969.

William Ross,
One of Her Majesty's Principal
Secretaries of State.

St. Andrew's House,
Edinburgh.
13th November 1969.

(a) S.I. 1964/1216 (1964 II, p. 2836).

SCHEDULE

FORM OF NOTICE OF APPEAL TO THE SECRETARY OF STATE

I, ...on... Give name
..............................19......, while holding the rank of........................... and number.
in the..police force was punished
by being... Insert the
punishment
on the ground that.. awarded.

....

.... Here state the
charge or
.... charges under
the Discipline
.... Code.

....

   I received notification of the decision on..
and acknowledged having received the decision on.......................................

   I appeal against the said $\dfrac{\text{finding and punishment}}{\text{punishment}}$ on the grounds fully set

out in the accompanying statement.

   This Notice of Appeal is accompanied by the following documentary evidence Omit if
which I desire to submit:— unnecessary.

   (1) .... Give brief
particulars,
   (2) .... e.g. "letter of
10th August
   (3) .... from Chief
Constable".

   At the date on which I was so punished I was in receipt of pay at the rate of Omit if there
was a period of
£   :   :   a year of suspension
immediately
prior to the
punishment.

   Before being so punished I was suspended on... Omit if there
was no period
....19......, at which date I was in receipt of pay at the of suspension
immediately
rate of £   :   :   a year. After being suspended I $\dfrac{\text{was}}{\text{was not}}$ prior to the
punishment.

notified that my period of suspension would be deducted in reckoning my
approved service for the purposes of pension.

   I declare that a full and true copy of this Notice of Appeal, of the accompanying Give address
to which sent.
statement setting out fully on what grounds the appeal is made and of the Give dates on
documentary evidence was sent to... which sent.
as or on behalf of the respondent, on..

                  Signature..

                  Address..

                  ....

Date...........................19.   ....

EXPLANATORY NOTE

(This Note is not part of the Rules.)

These rules relate to the procedure to be followed on police disciplinary appeals, and at inquiries in connection with appeals, under the Police (Scotland) Act 1967. They replace the Police (Appeals) (Scotland) Rules 1964 with certain amendments, of which the most important are as follows.

Rule 2(2) extends the time in which an appeal may be lodged to 21 days and Rule 3(1) makes a similar extension of time for submission of the respondent's statement and provides for late submision of the statement subject to the Secretary of State's approval.

Rule 6 sets out in more detail the arrangements for determining the procedure at an inquiry.

Rule 7 makes it clear that an appeal may be withdrawn at any time prior to its decision.

Rule 10 makes it clear that the Sheriff has discretion to permit such persons as he thinks fit to attend the whole or part of an inquiry.

STATUTORY INSTRUMENTS

1969 No. 1633

FACTORIES

The Fees of Appointed Factory Doctors Order 1969

Made - - -	*19th November* 1969	
Coming into Operation	*1st December* 1969	

The Secretary of State by virtue of her powers under section 152 of the Factories Act 1961(**a**) and of all other powers enabling her in that behalf, hereby makes the following Order:—

Citation and commencement

1. This Order may be cited as the Fees of Appointed Factory Doctors Order 1969 and shall come into operation on 1st December 1969.

Revocation

2. The Fees of Appointed Factory Doctors Order 1968(**b**), the Fees of Appointed Factory Doctors (Amendment) Order 1968(**c**) and the Fees of Appointed Factory Doctors (Amendment) Order 1969(**d**) are hereby revoked.

Interpretation

3.—(1) The Interpretation Act 1889(**e**) shall apply to the interpretation of this Order as it applies to the interpretation of an Act of Parliament, and as if this Order and the Orders hereby revoked were Acts of Parliament.

(2) For the purposes of this Order, unless the context otherwise requires, the following expressions have the meanings hereby assigned to them respectively, that is to say:—

"the appointed factory doctor's central point" means a place fixed by the Chief Inspector for the purpose of calculating the mileage or, where no place is so fixed, the residence of the appointed factory doctor;

"the principal Act" means the Factories Act 1961 as amended by or under any other Act;

"section" means section of the principal Act.

Fees of Appointed Factory Doctors

4.—(1) Subject to the provisions of Article 5 of this Order, the Secretary of State hereby determines that the fees payable by occupiers of factories to appointed factory doctors for the carrying out of such of their duties under the principal Act as are specified in paragraphs (2), (3), (4) and (5) of this Article shall be of the amounts respectively so specified.

(2) For examinations of young persons under section 99(4) or under section 118, or after the service by an inspector on the occupier of a notice

---

(a) 1961 c. 34.　　　　　　　　　　　(b) S.I. 1968/937 (1968 II, p. 2445).
(c) S.I. 1968/1771 (1968 III, p. 4799).　(d) S.I. 1969/813 (1969 II, p. 2316).
(e) 1889 c. 63.

under section 119 as to the employment of a young person in a factory, the fees shall be as follows, that is to say:—

(a) when the examination is at the factory—seventeen shillings and threepence for the first and ten shillings and threepence for each other person examined on the occasion of any one visit to the factory, and in addition, if the distance (measured by the shortest route by which the appointed factory doctor can travel by road) between the appointed factory doctor's central point and the factory exceeds two miles, two shillings for each complete mile by which that distance exceeds two miles;

(b) when the examination is not at the factory but at the residence of the appointed factory doctor or at some other place appointed by him for the purpose and approved by the Chief Inspector—ten shillings and threepence for each person examined.

(3) For examinations of persons for the purposes of the undermentioned Regulations the fees shall (wherever the examinations take place) be as follows, that is to say:—

(a) in the case of the Work in Compressed Air Special Regulations 1958(a), forty-two shillings and sixpence for the first examination of any person for the purposes of those Regulations and fourteen shillings for any other examination of that person for the purposes of those Regulations;

(b) in the case of the Diving Operations Special Regulations 1960(b), fifty-seven shillings and sixpence for the first examination of any person for the purposes of those Regulations and twenty-eight shillings and ninepence for any other examination of that person for the purposes of those Regulations;

(c) in the case of the Carcinogenic Substances Regulations 1967(c), twenty-seven shillings for the first examination of any person for the purposes of those Regulations and thirteen shillings and sixpence for any other examination of that person for the purposes of those Regulations;

(d) in the case of the Ionising Radiations (Unsealed Radioactive Substances) Regulations 1968(d), fifty-seven shillings and sixpence for the first examination of any person for the purposes of those Regulations and twenty-eight shillings and ninepence for any other examination of that person for the purposes of those Regulations; and

(e) in the case of the Ionising Radiations (Sealed Sources) Regulations 1969(e), fifty-seven shillings and sixpence for the first examination of any person for the purposes of those Regulations and twenty-eight shillings and ninepence for any other examination of that person for the purposes of those Regulations;

and in addition, if the distance (measured as aforesaid) between the appointed factory doctor's central point and the place of the examination exceeds two miles, two shillings for each complete mile by which that distance exceeds two miles.

(4) For examinations of employed persons for the purposes of section 75 or of any Regulations under section 76 (other than the Regulations specified in paragraph (3) of this Article), the fees shall be as follows, that is to say:—

(a) S.I. 1958/61 (1958 I, p. 1115).
(b) S.I. 1960/688 (1960 II, p. 1410).
(c) S.I. 1967/879 (1967 II, p. 2619).
(d) S.I. 1968/780 (1968 II, p. 2153).
(e) S.I. 1969/808 (1969 II, p. 2296).

(a) when the examination is at the factory or other place of employment—seventeen shillings and threepence for the first and six shillings for each other person examined on the occasion of any one visit to the factory or place, and in addition, if the distance (measured as aforesaid) between the appointed factory doctor's central point and the factory exceeds two miles, two shillings for each complete mile by which that distance exceeds two miles;

(b) when the examination is not at the factory or other place of employment but at the residence of the appointed factory doctor or at some other place appointed by him for the purpose and approved by the Chief Inspector—six shillings for each person examined.

(5) For an examination or part of an examination consisting, in either case, of a haemoglobin estimation made in pursuance of the Lead Processes (Medical Examinations) Regulations 1964(a) the fees shall be as follows, that is to say:—

(a) in respect of the first or only person examined on any one occasion—eighteen shillings;

(b) in respect of the second to the tenth person examined on any one occasion—eight shillings and ninepence for each person; and

(c) in respect of the eleventh and each subsequent person examined on any one occasion—six shillings for each person.

Inclusions and exclusions

5. The fees specified in this Order—

(a) are subject to any agreement between the appointed factory doctor and the occupier of a factory;

(b) include payment for the making of entries in registers, the issuing or refusal of certificates and the carrying out of other duties as may be required in connection with the examinations;

(c) do not cover, in the case of the fees specified in Article 4(2) and (4) of this Order, any special examinations of the blood, microscopical examinations of urine, X-ray examinations, serological tests or other special investigations undertaken in connection with examinations of employed persons on particular occasions or in particular instances (and this Order shall be without prejudice to the making of arrangements between the appointed factory doctor and the occupier of a factory for the carrying out of such special investigations); and

(d) do not cover, in the case of the fees specified in Article 4(3) of this Order, any examination of the blood or any other special examination required in pursuance of Regulation 29(1) of the Ionising Radiations (Sealed Sources) Regulations 1969 or Regulation 32(1) of the Ionising Radiations (Unsealed Radioactive Substances) Regulations 1968, or any chest examination by radiography required in pursuance of Regulation 9 of the Diving Operations Special Regulations 1960.

Signed by order of the Secretary of State.

19th November 1969.

K. Barnes,
Deputy Under Secretary of State,
Department of Employment and Productivity.

(a) S.I. 1964/1728 (1964 III, p. 3846).

EXPLANATORY NOTE
(*This Note is not part of the Order.*)

This Order determines the amount of fees payable by occupiers of factories to appointed factory doctors for various services required under the Factories Act 1961. It increases the fees determined by the Fees of Appointed Factory Doctors Order 1968 as amended. The said Order, the Fees of Appointed Factory Doctors (Amendment) Order 1968 and the Fees of Appointed Factory Doctors (Amendment) Order 1969 are revoked. The fees determined by this Order can be varied by agreement between the appointed factory doctor and the occupier of a factory.

STATUTORY INSTRUMENTS

1969 No. 1634

INDUSTRIAL TRAINING
The Industrial Training (Hairdressing and Allied Services Board) Order 1969

Made - - - -	*19th November* 1969
Laid before Parliament	*1st December* 1969
Coming into Operation	*10th December* 1969

The Secretary of State after consultation with organisations and associations of organisations appearing to be representative respectively of substantial numbers of employers engaging in the activities hereinafter mentioned and of substantial numbers of persons employed in those activities and in exercise of her powers under section 1 of, and paragraphs 1 and 7 of the Schedule to, the Industrial Training Act 1964(a) (hereinafter referred to as "the Act") and of all other powers enabling her in that behalf hereby makes the following Order:—

Citation, commencement and interpretation

1.—(1) This Order may be cited as the Industrial Training (Hairdressing and Allied Services Board) Order 1969 and shall come into operation on 10th December 1969.

(2) The Interpretation Act 1889(b) shall apply to the interpretation of this Order as it applies to the interpretation of an Act of Parliament.

Establishment of Industrial Training Board

2. An industrial training board to be known as the Hairdressing and Allied Services Industry Training Board (hereinafter referred to as "the Board") is hereby established to exercise in relation to the activities specified in Schedule 1 to this Order as the activities of the hairdressing and allied services industry the functions conferred on industrial training boards by the Act.

Membership and proceedings of the Board

3. The provisions of Schedule 2 to this Order shall have effect in relation to the Board.

19th November 1969.

Barbara Castle,
First Secretary of State and
Secretary of State for Employment and Productivity.

(a) 1964 c. 16.   (b) 1889 c. 63.

Article 2

SCHEDULE 1

The Hairdressing and Allied Services Industry

1. Subject to the provisions of this Schedule, the activities of the hairdressing and allied services industry are the following activities in so far as they are carried out by way of business in Great Britain:-

    (a) hairdressing ;

    (b) wig making or fitting ;

    (c) beauty treatment ;

    (d) the provision of facilities for taking turkish, sauna or other steam or dry heat baths ;

    (e) giving instruction in any of the activities above mentioned in this paragraph ;

    (f) any activities (other than those above mentioned), being—

        (i) related activities incidental or ancillary to principal activities of the hairdressing and allied services industry ; or

        (ii) activities undertaken in the administration, control or direction of one or more establishments, being establishments engaged wholly or mainly in principal activities of that industry, in related activities incidental or ancillary thereto, or in the administration, control or direction of one or more other establishments engaged in such principal or related activities ;

and carried out, in either case, by the employer engaged in those principal activities or, where that employer is a company, by the company or by an associated company of the company ;

    (g) any activities of industry or commerce (other than hairdressing and allied services activities) carried out at or from an establishment mainly engaged—

        (i) in hairdressing and allied services activities; or

        (ii) in hairdressing and allied services activities and in activities described in the Appendix to this Schedule, but to a greater extent in hairdressing and allied services activities than in activities described in that Appendix in relation to any one industry.

2. Notwithstanding anything contained in this Schedule, there shall not be included in the activities of the hairdressing and allied services industry :-

    (a) the activities of any establishment engaged—

        (i) mainly in activities not being hairdressing and allied services activities or activities described in the Appendix to this Schedule; or

        (ii) to a less extent in hairdressing and allied services activities than in activities described in that Appendix in relation to any one industry ;

    (b) the activities of any establishment engaged wholly or mainly in related activities, being activities—

        (i) incidental or ancillary to the activities of one or more establishments (in this sub-paragraph hereafter referred to as "the principal establishment") engaged wholly or mainly in any activities not being principal activities of the hairdressing and allied services industry ; and

        (ii) carried out by the employer carrying on the principal establishment or, where that employer is a company, by the company or by an associated company of the company ;

    (c) the activities of any hospital, nursing home, convalescent home or similar establishment providing treatment or accommodation for the sick, infirm or mentally disordered, including the activities of any person employed therein as a nursing assistant, nursing auxiliary or nursing cadet ;

(*d*) any activities undertaken personally in the exercise of his profession as such by a person who is registered as a dentist, dispensing or ophthalmic optician, medical practitioner or pharmaceutical chemist or who is registered—

    (i) with a Board established under the Professions Supplementary to Medicine Act 1960(**a**) ;

    (ii) as a member of the Institute of Trichologists (Incorporated) ; or

    (iii) as an osteopath by the General Council and Register of Osteopaths ;

(*e*) any activities undertaken personally in the exercise of his profession as such by a person who is—

    (i) registered as a nurse with the General Nursing Council ;

    (ii) enrolled on the roll of nurses of the General Nursing Council ;

    (iii) included in the list of student and pupil nurses maintained by the General Nursing Council ;

    (iv) a midwife holding the certificate of the Central Midwives Board ;

    (v) included in the list of pupil midwives maintained by the Central Midwives Board ;

    (vi) under training for, or holding, the diploma or certificate in orthopaedic nursing of the Joint Examination Board of the British Orthopaedic Association and the Central Council for the Care of the Disabled ;

    (vii) under training for, or holding, the diploma of ophthalmic nursing of the Ophthalmic Nursing Board ;

    (viii) under training for, or holding, the thoracic nursing certificate of the British Tuberculosis Association ; or

    (ix) holding the certificate of the Royal Medico-Psychological Association ;

(*f*) any activities when carried out by the master or a member of the crew of a ship or by a person ordinarily employed as a seaman who is employed in or about a ship in port by the owner or charterer thereof on work of a kind ordinarily done by a seaman on a ship while it is in port ; or

(*g*) the supply of food or drink for immediate consumption.

3. In this Schedule unless the context otherwise requires—

(a) "beauty treatment" means any treatment that is designed to enhance the appearance of the human face or body and, without prejudice to the generality of this definition, includes in particular—

    (i) the application of beauty packs ;

    (ii) the application of cosmetics ;

    (iii) eyebrow shaping or colouring ;

    (iv) manicure ;

    (v) massage ;

    (vi) the removal from the skin of superfluous hair ;

(b) "business" means a trade or business carried on for the purposes of gain ;

(c) "Central Midwives Board" means the Central Midwives Board for England and Wales or for Scotland, as the case may be ;

(d) "company" includes any body corporate, and "subsidiary" has the same meaning as by virtue of section 154 of the Companies Act 1948(**b**) it has for the purposes of that Act ;

(e) "General Nursing Council" means the General Nursing Council for England and Wales or for Scotland, as the case may be ;

(f) "hairdressing" means shaving, cutting, shampooing, tinting, dyeing, bleaching, waving, curling, straightening, setting, or dressing of the hair, upon the scalp or face, with or without the aid of any apparatus or appliance, preparation or substance, and includes the hand or vibro massage of the scalp or face ;

(g) "hairdressing and allied services activities" means any one or more of the principal activities of the hairdressing and allied services industry and the activities included in that industry by virtue of paragraph 1(f) of this Schedule ;

(h) "office premises" has the same meaning as in section 1(2) of the Offices, Shops and Railway Premises Act 1963(**a**) ;

(i) "principal activities of the hairdressing and allied services industry" means activities which, subject to the provisions of paragraph 2 of this Schedule, are specified in paragraph 1, other than sub-paragraphs (f) and (g) thereof, as activities of the hairdressing and allied services industry ;

(j) "related activities" means any of the following activities, that is to say—

(i) research, development, design or drawing ;

(ii) buying, selling, letting out on hire, testing, advertising, packing, distribution, transport or any similar operations ;

(iii) operations of a kind performed at office premises or laboratories ;

(iv) operations of a kind performed at stores, warehouses or similar places ;

(v) cleaning, washing or garaging vehicles or carrying out running repairs or minor adjustments thereto ;

(vi) training of employees and apprentices ;

(k) "wig making" means the making of wigs or hair pieces from any material, or the weaving of hair pieces into growing hair, and includes the cleaning and dressing of wigs or hair pieces.

4. For the purposes of this Schedule, two companies shall be taken to be associated companies if one is a subsidiary of the other or both are subsidiaries of a third company, and "associated company" shall be construed accordingly.

(**a**) 1963 c. 41.

APPENDIX

The activities that would be included in an industry specified in Column 1 hereof by virtue of the industrial training order specified in the corresponding entry in Column 2, if the provisions specified in Column 3 were omitted from that order.

Column 1	Column 2	Column 3
The wool, jute and flax industry	The Industrial Training (Wool Industry Board) Order 1964 as amended by the Industrial Training (Wool, Jute and Flax Board) Order 1968(a)	Schedule 1 Paragraph 1(s)
The iron and steel industry	The Industrial Training (Iron and Steel Board) Order 1964 as amended by the Industrial Training (Iron and Steel Board) Order 1969(b)	Schedule 1 Paragraph 1(k)
The construction industry	The Industrial Training (Construction Board) Order 1964 as amended by the Industrial Training (Construction Board) Order 1967(c)	Schedule 1 Paragraph 1(l)
The engineering industry	The Industrial Training (Engineering Board) Order 1964 as amended by the Industrial Training (Engineering Board) Order 1968 and the Industrial Training (Engineering Board) Order 1968 (Amendment) Order 1969(d)	Schedule 1 Paragraph 1(m)
The shipbuilding industry	The Industrial Training (Shipbuilding Board) Order 1964 as amended by the Industrial Training (Shipbuilding Board) Order 1968(e)	Schedule 1 Paragraph 1(g)
The ceramics, glass and mineral products industry	The Industrial Training (Ceramics, Glass and Mineral Products Board) Order 1965 as amended by the Industrial Training (Ceramics, Glass and Mineral Products Board) Order 1969(f)	Schedule 1 Paragraph 1(p)
The furniture and timber industry	The Industrial Training (Furniture and Timber Industry Board) Order 1965 as amended by the Industrial Training (Furniture and Timber Industry Board) Order 1969(g)	Schedule 1 Paragraph 1(x)
The man-made fibres producing industry	The Industrial Training (Man-made Fibres Producing Industry Board) Order 1966 as amended by the Industrial Training (Man-made Fibres Producing Industry Board) Order 1969(h)	Schedule 1 Paragraph 1(e)

(a) S.I. 1964/907, 1968/898 (1964 II, p. 1928; 1968 II, p. 2376).
(b) S.I. 1964/949, 1969/884 (1964 II, p. 2127; 1969 II, p. 2517).
(c) S.I. 1964/1079, 1967/924 (1964 II, p. 2384; 1967 II, p. 2757).
(d) S.I. 1964/1086, 1968/1333, 1969/1376 (1964 II, p. 2402; 1968 II, p. 3694; 1969 III, p. 4103).
(e) S.I. 1964/1782, 1968/1614 (1964 III, p. 3928; 1968 III, p. 4432).
(f) S.I. 1965/1391, 1969/689 (1965 II, p. 4062; 1969 II, p. 1860).
(g) S.I. 1965/2028, 1969/1290 (1965 III, p. 5998; 1969 III, p. 3820).
(h) S.I. 1966/143, 1969/1210 (1966 I, p. 257; 1969 II, p. 3545).

Column 1	Column 2	Column 3
The carpet industry	The Industrial Training (Carpet Board) Order 1966 as amended by the Industrial Training (Carpet Board) Order 1968(a)	Schedule 1 Paragraph 1(f)
The knitting, lace and net industry	The Industrial Training (Knitting, Lace and Net Industry Board) Order 1966(b)	Schedule 1 Paragraph 1(j)
The cotton and allied textiles industry	The Industrial Training (Cotton and Allied Textiles Board) Order 1966(c)	Schedule 1 Paragraph 1(p)
The agricultural, horticultural and forestry industry	The Industrial Training (Agricultural, Horticultural and Forestry Board) Order 1966(d)	Schedule 1 Paragraph 1(m)
The road transport industry	The Industrial Training (Road Transport Board) Order 1966 as amended by the Industrial Training (Road Transport Board) Order 1969(e)	Schedule 1 Paragraph 1(p)
The hotel and catering industry	The Industrial Training (Hotel and Catering Board) Order 1966 as amended by the Industrial Training (Hotel and Catering Board) Order 1969(f)	Schedule 1 Paragraph 1(e)
The civil air transport industry	The Industrial Training (Civil Air Transport Board) Order 1967(g)	Schedule 1 Paragraph 1(h)
The petroleum industry	The Industrial Training (Petroleum Board) Order 1967(h)	Schedule 1 Paragraph 1(h)
The rubber and plastics processing industry	The Industrial Training (Rubber and Plastics Processing Board) Order 1967(i)	Schedule 1 Paragraph 1(k)
The chemical and allied products industry	The Industrial Training (Chemical and Allied Products Board) Order 1967(j)	Schedule 1 Paragraph 1(s)
The paper and paper products industry	The Industrial Training (Paper and Paper Products Board) Order 1968(k)	Schedule 1 Paragraph 1(j)
The printing and publishing industry	The Industrial Training (Printing and Publishing Board) Order 1968(l)	Schedule 1 Paragraph 1(n)
The distributive industry	The Industrial Training (Distributive Board) Order 1968(m)	Schedule 1 Paragraph 1(h)
The food, drink and tobacco industry	The Industrial Training (Food, Drink and Tobacco Board) Order 1968(n)	Schedule 1 Paragraph 1(q)
The footwear, leather and fur skin industry	The Industrial Training (Footwear, Leather and Fur Skin Board) Order 1968(o)	Schedule 1 Paragraph 1(v)
The clothing and allied products industry	The Industrial Training (Clothing and Allied Products Board) Order 1969(p)	Schedule 1 Paragraph 1(j)

(a) S.I. 1966/245, 1968/1882 (1966 I, p. 499; 1968 III, p. 5017).
(b) S.I. 1966/246 (1966 I, p. 506).
(c) S.I. 1966/823 (1966 II, p. 1907).
(d) S.I. 1966/969 (1966 II, p. 2333).
(e) S.I. 1966/1112, 1969/879 (1966 III, p. 2712; 1969 II, p. 2495).
(f) S.I. 1966/1347, 1969/1405 (1966 III, p. 3669; 1969 III, p. 4132).
(g) S.I. 1967/263 (1967 I, p. 968).
(h) S.I. 1967/648 (1967 I, p. 2032).
(i) S.I. 1967/1062 (1967 II, p. 3151).
(j) S.I. 1967/1386 (1967 III, p. 4049).
(k) S.I. 1968/787 (1968 II, p. 2194).
(l) S.I. 1968/786 (1968 II, p. 2185).
(m) S.I. 1968/1032 (1968 II, p. 2709).
(n) S.I. 1968/1033 (1968 II, p. 2721).
(o) S.I. 1968/1763 (1968 III, p. 4785).
(p) S.I. 1969/1375 (1969 III, p. 4094).

SCHEDULE 2

MEMBERSHIP

1. The appointment of a member of the Board shall be for such term as the Secretary of State may determine and, subject to the provisions of this Schedule, a member shall hold and vacate office in accordance with the terms of the instrument appointing him to be a member.

2. A person who has held office as a member of the Board shall be eligible for reappointment.

3. A member of the Board may resign his office by notice in writing to the Secretary of State and the resignation shall have effect on such date as the Secretary of State shall appoint.

4. If a member of the Board—

   (a) is absent from meetings of the Board for more than six months consecutively unless his absence is due to illness or some other reason approved by the Secretary of State ; or

   (b) becomes in the opinion of the Secretary of State unfit to continue in office or incapable of performing his duties ;

the Secretary of State may declare the office of that member to be vacant and shall notify the fact in such manner as she shall think fit, and thereupon the office of the member shall become vacant.

PROCEEDINGS AND MEETINGS

5. At a meeting of the Board one-third of the members shall be the quorum, or if the number so ascertained includes a fraction the nearest higher whole number of members.

6. The chairman or if absent the deputy chairman (if any) shall preside at all meetings of the Board at which he shall be present, but if at any meeting the said chairman and any deputy chairman be not present within 10 minutes of the time appointed for holding the meeting the members present shall choose some one of their number to be chairman of the meeting.

7. At a meeting of the Board a resolution put to the vote on any matter not relating to the imposition of a levy shall be decided on a show of hands of the members present and voting; each member shall have one vote and if the votes are equally divided the chairman of the meeting shall have a second or casting vote.

8.—(1) If at a meeting of the Board a resolution relating to the imposition of a levy is put to the vote of the members appointed as mentioned in paragraph 3(a) of the Schedule to the Act, each such member shall have one vote, and the resolution shall be decided on a show of hands of those members present and voting unless a poll is demanded by any such member (before or on the declaration of the result of the show of hands) in which case the poll shall be taken forthwith and the votes may be given either personally or by proxy.

(2) The instrument appointing a proxy shall be in writing under the hand of the appointor, and the proxy shall be a member of the Board appointed as mentioned in paragraph 3(a) of the Schedule to the Act.

(3) An instrument appointing a proxy shall be in the following form or a form as near thereto as circumstances admit :—

I..........of............in the county of...........being a member of the Hairdressing and Allied Services Industry Training Board appointed as mentioned in paragraph 3(a) of the Schedule to the Industrial Training Act 1964, hereby appoint........of..........or failing him........of........ as my proxy to vote for me on my behalf on any matter relating to the imposition of a levy at the meeting of the said Board to be held on the.......... day of............19...... and at any adjournment thereof.

        Signed this..............day of..........19......

(4) A vote given in accordance with the terms of an instrument of proxy shall be valid notwithstanding the previous death or insanity of the principal or revocation of the proxy, provided that no intimation in writing of any such death, insanity or revocation shall have been received by the Board at its office before the commencement of the meeting or adjourned meeting at which the proxy is used.

9. Minutes shall be kept of the proceedings of the Board and any such minutes shall, if signed by any person purporting to have acted as chairman of the meeting or at a meeting at which they were read, be evidence of the proceedings at the first-mentioned meeting, and a meeting to which any such minutes relate shall, unless the contrary is proved, be taken to have been regularly convened and constituted.

10. The Board shall have an office at which communications and notices will at all times be received and shall notify to the Secretary of State the address of that office and any change of that address.

EXECUTION AND ISSUE OF INSTRUMENTS

11. The seal of the Board shall be authenticated by the signature of the chairman of the Board or some other member of the Board authorised by the Board to act in that behalf and of the secretary or some other person authorised by the Board so to act.

12. Every document purporting to be a document duly executed or issued either under the seal of the Board authenticated in the manner provided by this Schedule or on behalf of the Board, or purporting to be signed by the secretary or any other person, being a member, officer or servant of the Board authorised to act in that behalf, shall, until the contary be proved, be deemed to be a document so executed or issued or so signed as the case may be.

EXPLANATORY NOTE

(This Note is not part of the Order.)

This Order, which is made under the Industrial Training Act 1964, establishes an industrial training board to be known as the Hairdressing and Allied Services Industry Training Board, and defines the industry to which it relates. Provision is made as to the membership of the Board and its meetings and proceedings.

STATUTORY INSTRUMENTS

1969 No. 1636

ROAD TRAFFIC

The Goods Vehicles (Operators' Licences) Regulations 1969

Made - - -	*20th November* 1969
Laid before Parliament	*28th November* 1969
Coming into Operation	*1st December* 1969

ARRANGEMENT OF REGULATIONS

PART I

GENERAL

PART IV

MISCELLANEOUS FURTHER PROVISIONS WITH RESPECT TO OPERATORS' LICENCES

PART V

SUPPLEMENTARY

SCHEDULES

The Minister of Transport, in exercise of his powers under sections 60(2) and (4), 63(1), (3) and (4), 67(2), 69(4), 71(6), 85, 86, 87(4) and 91(1), (2) and (5) of the Transport Act 1968(a) and all other enabling powers, and after consultation with representative organisations in accordance with section 91(8) of the said Act of 1968, and with the Council on Tribunals in accordance with the requirements of section 8 of the Tribunals and Inquiries Act 1958(b), hereby makes the following Regulations :—

(a) 1968 c. 73. (b) 1958 c. 66.

Part I

General

Commencement and Citation

1. These Regulations shall come into operation on the 1st December 1969 and may be cited as the Goods Vehicles (Operators' Licences) Regulations 1969.

Interpretation

2.—(1) In these Regulations, unless the context otherwise requires, the following expressions have the meanings hereby respectively assigned to them, that is to say :—

"the Act" means the Transport Act 1968 ;

"application" means an application for an operator's licence, or for the variation of an operator's licence by a direction under section 68 of the Act ;

"Applications and Decisions" means the statement issued by the licensing authority under Regulation 7 of these Regulations ;

"the holder of an operator's licence" means the person to whom the licence was granted ;

"identity disc" means a disc issued to the holder of an operator's licence in respect of a motor vehicle specified in the licence for the purpose of enabling the vehicle to be identified as a specified vehicle ;

"notifiable application" means an application of which publication is required by sections 63(1) or 68(4) of the Act ;

and any expression not defined above which is also used in Part V of the Act has the same meaning as in that Part of the Act.

(2) Any reference in these Regulations to any enactment or instrument shall be construed, unless the context otherwise requires, as a reference to that enactment or instrument as amended by any subsequent enactment or instrument.

(3) The Interpretation Act 1889(a) shall apply for the interpretation of these Regulations as it applies for the interpretation of an Act of Parliament.

Part II

Cases in which an Operator's Licence is not Required

Cases in which an operator's licence is not required

3. Section 60(1) of the Act (Users of certain goods vehicles to hold operators' licences) shall not apply to the use of a vehicle of any class specified in Schedule 1 to these Regulations.

(a) 1889 c. 63.

PART III

THE GRANT AND VARIATION OF OPERATORS' LICENCES

Applications for the grant or variation of operators' licences

4.—(1) A separate application for the grant of an operator's licence shall be made in respect of each traffic area in which the applicant has an operating centre but no operator's licence, only one application for the grant of an operator's licence shall be made in respect of all the operating centres of the applicant in any one traffic area, and no such application (except an application for an interim licence under section 67(5) of the Act) shall be made in any traffic area whilst another such application in that traffic area has not been disposed of.

(2) Every application shall be made on the appropriate form obtainable from the licensing authority.

(3) An applicant shall not include in any application—

    (*a*) a vehicle specified in a current operator's licence, unless the application is for an operator's licence to replace the operator's licence in which the vehicle is specified or is for the purpose of having the vehicle deleted from one operator's licence and added to another ;

    (*b*) a vehicle specified in an operator's licence issued to him which has been suspended under section 69 of the Act during the period of such suspension, a vehicle removed from an operator's licence issued to him which has been curtailed under that section during the period of such curtailment, or a vehicle specified in an operator's licence issued to him which has been revoked before the date when such revoked licence is expressed to expire ; or

    (*c*) a vehicle specified in another application which is still under consideration by any licensing authority, unless the applications are for the purpose of having the vehicle deleted from one operator's licence and added to another.

(4) Every application shall be signed—

    (*a*) if made by a body corporate, by a person duly authorised in that behalf by such body corporate ;

    (*b*) if made by a partnership, by one of the partners ; and

    (*c*) in any other case, by the applicant.

Date of submission of applications

5.—(1) Every application shall be sent to the licensing authority so as to reach him not less than 9 weeks before the date on which it is desired that the licence or variation of the licence shall take effect.

(2) The licensing authority may accept and deal with any application notwithstanding that the requirement of paragraph (1) of this Regulation has not been complied with.

Copies of applications and operators' licences available for inspection

6.—(1) A copy of the information given in respect of every notifiable application shall be available for inspection by any person authorised in writing in that behalf by a local authority, a chief officer of police or a trade union or association specified in Regulation 8 of these Regulations at the office of the licensing authority until the application has been determined by the licensing authority and during the currency of any licence granted or varied in respect of the application.

(2) A copy of every licence shall be available for inspection at the office of the licensing authority during the currency of the licence by any person who appears to the licensing authority to have reasonable ground for desiring to inspect it.

Statement to be issued by the licensing authority

7.—(1) The licensing authority shall cause to be issued as occasion may require a statement called "Applications and Decisions" which shall contain (unless previously notified therein)—

(*a*) as regards applications under section 94(1) of the Act and notifiable applications—

    (i) notices of notifiable applications ;

    (ii) the dates on which and the places at which he proposes to hold inquiries and the applications which he proposes to consider at those inquiries ; and

    (iii) the licensing authority's decisions on applications under section 94(1) of the Act which have been refused wholly or in part, and on notifiable applications, other than decisions to grant interim licences under section 67(5) of the Act ; and

(*b*) any direction to revoke, suspend or curtail a licence given under section 69 of the Act.

(2) The publication of the date of any inquiry in "Applications and Decisions" shall not prevent the licensing authority from adjourning from time to time the consideration of any application and in particular any inquiry held or proposed to be held in connection with the application, notwithstanding that the date of any such inquiry may have been published in "Applications and Decisions".

(3) Copies of "Applications and Decisions" may be inspected at the office of the licensing authority by whom it was issued and at such other places (if any) as he may determine and copies shall be supplied to any person requiring them, on payment of the prescribed fee.

Trade unions and associations which may object to the grant or variation of an operator's licence

8.—(1) This Regulation applies to the following trade unions and associations, that is to say :—

(*a*) The Freight Transport Association ;

(*b*) The General and Municipal Workers' Union ;

(*c*) The National Union of Railwaymen ;

(*d*) The Road Haulage Association ;

(*e*) The Scottish Commercial Motormen's Union ;

(*f*) The Transport & General Workers' Union ;

(*g*) The Union of Shop, Distributive and Allied Workers ; and

(*h*) The United Road Transport Union.

(2) Each of the trade unions and associations to which this Regulation applies may object under section 63(3) of the Act, or under that section as applied by section 68(4) of the Act, to the grant of a notifiable application.

Notice of objections

9.—(1) Every objection in respect of an application shall be in writing in the form set out in Schedule 2 to these Regulations and shall be signed in the case of an objection by a trade union or association by a duly authorised officer thereof, and in any other case by the objector or by a person duly authorised in that behalf by the objector.

(2) Every such objection shall be sent to the licensing authority so as to reach him not later than 3 weeks after notice of the application has appeared in "Applications and Decisions" and a copy of every such objection shall be sent by the objector to the applicant at the same time as it is sent to the licensing authority.

(3) The licensing authority may consider objections notwithstanding that all or any of the requirements of paragraphs (1) and (2) of this Regulation have not been complied with.

Procedure at inquiries

10.—(1) An inquiry or any part of an inquiry held by a licensing authority in connection with an application, being an inquiry or part of an inquiry into the financial resources which are or are likely to be available to the applicant, shall be held in private if the licensing authority so directs at the request of the applicant, but a member of the Council on Tribunals or its Scottish Committee shall be entitled to attend the hearing in his capacity as such member.

(2) An applicant for or for the variation of an operator's licence, any person who in pursuance of section 63(3) of the Act has objected to the grant or variation of an operator's licence, and any person who in pursuance of section 69(9) of the Act has requested a licensing authority to hold an inquiry shall be entitled to appear at any relevant inquiry and may be heard in person or be represented by counsel or solicitor or, with the leave of the licensing authority, by any other person.

(3) Where a licensing authority refuses an application for, or for the variation of, an operator's licence or grants such an application otherwise than in the terms applied for it shall be his duty to furnish to the applicant and any objector a statement, either written or oral, of the reasons for his decision.

(4) Subject to the provisions of the Act and these Regulations a licensing authority may regulate the procedure of any inquiry which he holds under section 69(9) or 87 of the Act in connection with operators' licences.

PART IV

MISCELLANEOUS FURTHER PROVISIONS WITH RESPECT TO OPERATORS' LICENCES

Identification of specified vehicles

11.—(1) The licensing authority shall, before an operator's licence comes into force in respect of any motor vehicle specified in the licence, issued to the holder of the licence an identity disc in respect of each such vehicle.

(2) The holder of an operator's licence shall during such time as any motor vehicle is specified in the licence and whether or not for the time being the vehicle is being used for the purpose for which a licence is required, cause a valid identity disc appropriate to the vehicle to be affixed to that vehicle in a waterproof container—

(a) in the case of a vehicle used under a licence which has been issued in respect of that vehicle under the Vehicles (Excise) Act 1962(a) and is affixed to the vehicle in accordance with the requirements of the Road Vehicles (Registration and Licensing) Regulations 1964(b), in a place on the vehicle adjacent to that licence ; and

(b) in any other case, in or adjacent to the place on the vehicle where a licence issued in respect of that vehicle under the last mentioned Act would be required to be affixed in accordance with the requirements of the last mentioned Regulations.

(3) At all times while an identity disc is affixed to a vehicle in accordance with the requirements of paragraph (2) of this Regulation the person for the time being in control of that vehicle shall keep that disc readily legible.

Temporary addition of a specified vehicle

12. Where—

(1) a motor vehicle specified in an operator's licence (hereinafter in this Regulation referred to as "the specified vehicle") has been rendered unfit for service, or withdrawn from service for overhaul or repair, and the holder of the licence informs the licensing authority of his desire to have a variation of the licence specifying, until it is rendered fit for service again, a motor vehicle in his possession or to be hired without a driver (hereinafter in this Regulation referred to as "the additional vehicle") or

(2) the specified vehicle has been rendered fit for service again, and the holder of the licence informs the licensing authority of his desire to have a variation of the licence whereby the additional vehicle will cease to be specified in the licence,

the provisions of Regulations 4(2) and 5 shall not apply and the holder of the licence shall return to the licensing authority the identity disc for the specified vehicle, or the additional vehicle, as the case may be.

Notification of change of address

13. If during the currency of an operator's licence the holder thereof changes his business address for the service of notices as notified in his application or as subsequently notified under this Regulation he shall within 3 weeks from the date of such change notify such change to the licensing authority by whom the licence was granted.

Production of operators' licences for examination

14.—(1) The holder of an operator's licence shall produce it for examination if required to do so by any police constable, by any certifying officer or examiner or by any person duly authorised by the licensing authority in that

---

(a) 1962 c. 13.   (b) S.I. 1964/1178 (1964 II, p. 2722).

behalf and may elect whether to produce it at his operating centre, head office or principal place of business within the traffic area of the licensing authority by whom the licence was granted.

(2) In this Regulation—

"certifying officer" means a certifying officer appointed under section 128 of the Road Traffic Act 1960(a) or whose appointment has effect as if made under that section ; and

"examiner" means an examiner appointed under section 183 of the Road Traffic Act 1960 or whose appointment has effect as if made under that section.

Issue of copies of operators' licences and identity discs

15.—(1) If an operator's licence or an identity disc has during the currency thereof been lost, destroyed or defaced, the holder thereof shall forthwith notify in writing the licensing authority by whom such licence or disc was granted or issued.

(2) If—

(a) the licensing authority is satisfied that an operator's licence or identity disc has been lost, destroyed or defaced during the currency thereof, and

(b) in the case of any such licence or disc which has been defaced, such licence or disc is surrendered to the licensing authority,

the licensing authority shall issue a copy (so marked) which shall have effect as the original licence or disc.

(3) Where a licence or disc has been lost and after a copy has been issued the lost licence or disc is found by the holder of the licence, or is found by some other person and comes into the possession of the holder of the licence, the holder of the licence shall forthwith return the original licence or disc to the licensing authority.

Return of operators' licences and identity discs to the licensing authority

16.—(1) If during the currency of an operator's licence the holder thereof ceases to be the user of any vehicle specified in it he shall within 3 weeks notify the licensing authority by whom the licence was granted and return to that licensing authority the licence for variation and the identity disc relating to the vehicle.

(2) If an operator's licence is varied under section 68 of the Act, the holder of the licence shall, when required by the licensing authority so to do, return the licence and, if the number of vehicles specified in the licence has been reduced, the identity discs relating to those vehicles, to the licensing authority.

(3) If an operator's licence is revoked or for some other reason ceases to have effect otherwise than by the effluxion of time, or is suspended or curtailed, or if a licensing authority has given a direction in respect of a licence under section 69(2) of the Act, the holder of the licence shall within 5 days after a notice to that effect has been delivered to him personally or sent to him by the recorded delivery service at the address shown in his application or last notified in accordance with Regulation 13 of these Regulations send or deliver to the licensing authority by whom the licence was granted the licence together

---

(a) 1960 c. 16.

with the identity discs relating to such of the vehicles specified in the licence as the licensing authority may specify, for cancellation, retention during the time of suspension, or alteration as the case may be.

Expiry of operators' licences

17. The dates for the expiration of operators' licences for the purposes of section 67(2) of the Act shall be the 24th March and the last day of every other month.

PART V

SUPPLEMENTARY

Definition of "relevant plated weight"

18. The relevant plated weight of a vehicle, for the purposes of section 60(4) of the Act (definition of small goods vehicle) and section 71(6) of the Act (definition of large goods vehicle), so far as that subsection relates to the subsequent provisions of Part V of the Act relating to operators' licensing, is the gross weight not to be exceeded in Great Britain of the vehicle as shown on a Ministry plate as defined in Regulation 118 of the Motor Vehicles (Construction and Use) Regulations 1969(a), or, if no such plate has been issued in respect of that vehicle, the maximum gross weight of the vehicle as shown on a plate affixed to the vehicle by virtue of Regulation 30 of the said Regulations of 1969.

Death, bankruptcy, etc. of the holder of an operator's licence

19.—(1) Where owing to the death, incapacity, bankruptcy, or liquidation of the holder of an operator's licence or the sequestration of his estate or to the appointment of a receiver or manager or trustee in relation to his trade or business, he ceases to be the user of the vehicles authorised to be used by him under the licence the person carrying on the trade or business of the holder shall be deemed to be the holder of the licence if—

(a) within 2 months notice that the holder has ceased to be the user of those vehicles and of the reason therefor, and of the name of the person by whom the trade or business is being carried on, is sent to the licensing authority by whom the licence was granted, and

(b) within one month of the sending of such notice an application for a new licence is made.

(2) The period during which a person shall be deemed to be the holder of a licence under paragraph (1) of this Regulation shall in no case extend beyond the date on which the licence would have expired but for the occurrence of the relevant event and shall terminate immediately the application for a new licence is disposed of.

Holding companies and subsidiaries

20.—(1) A holding company may apply to the licensing authority for any traffic area—

(a) if it does not already hold an operator's licence in respect of that area, or if it desires to replace its existing licence in respect of that area with a new licence, for the grant of an operator's licence, or

---

(a) S.I. 1969/321 (1969 I, p. 829).

(b) if it already holds an operator's licence in respect of that area and does not desire to replace such licence with a new licence, for the variation of its operator's licence by a direction under section 68(1)(a) of the Act.

which would have the effect, if the application is granted, of including in the licence to be issued to, or already held by, the holding company, goods vehicles belonging to or in the possession of a subsidiary of that company specified in the application.

(2) An application by a holding company under paragraph (1) of this Regulation shall, unless the subsidiary is not the holder of an operator's licence, or the licence or variation applied for by the holding company will not take effect until any operator's licence held by the subsidiary has expired by effluxion of time, be accompanied by an application by the subsidiary for the variation of the licence held by the subsidiary by a direction under section 68(1)(b) of the Act for the removal therefrom of all or some of the vehicles authorised to be used thereunder, being the vehicles to which the application of the holding company relates.

(3) Where a holding company, on an application under paragraph (1) of this Regulation, signifies to the licensing authority its desire that the provisions of this Regulation should have effect as respects a subsidiary of that company, then, in relation to the application and to any licence granted to the holding company, or held by the holding company and varied, on that application, and to the use of any vehicles authorised to be used under any such licence, Part V of the Act and these Regulations shall have effect subject to the modifications specified in Schedule 3 to these Regulations.

(4) The provisions of this Regulation shall cease to have effect as respects a holding company and its subsidiary—

(a) if the holding company gives notice to the licensing authority who granted or varied its licence that it desires that this Regulation should, as from any date, cease to apply to the holding company and that subsidiary, as from that date ; or

(b) as from the date on which that subsidiary ceases to be a subsidiary of that holding company.

(5) Where by virtue of the provisions of paragraphs (1) to (3) of this Regulation a holding company holds an operator's licence which includes goods vehicles belonging to or in the possession of a subsidiary of that company, and the holding company gives notice under sub-paragraph (a) of paragraph (4) of this Regulation, then in relation to any application by the subsidiary for the grant of an operator's licence in respect of all or any of those vehicles, section 63 of the Act shall have effect as if for subsection (1) there were substituted the following subsection : —

"(1) The licensing authority may publish in the prescribed manner notice of any application to the authority for an operator's licence made by a company or other body corporate in pursuance of regulations made under section 85 of this Act."

(6) Where the provisions of this Regulation cease to have effect as respects a holding company and its subsidiary by virtue of sub-paragraph (b) of paragraph (4) of this Regulation, the company which was the holding company shall within 3 weeks of the event which caused the subsidiary to cease to be a

subsidiary of that company notify the licensing authority by whom the licence was granted, supply all material details of the event, and return to the licensing authority the licence and the identity discs relating to the vehicles authorised to be used thereunder.

(7) In this Regulation and Schedule 3 to these Regulations "holding company" means a holding company as defined by section 154 of the Companies Act 1948(a).

Computation of time

21. In all cases in which any period of time is prescribed by these Regulations, the same shall be reckoned exclusively of the first day and inclusively of the last day, unless the last day shall happen to fall on a Sunday, Christmas day, New Year's Day or Good Friday, or any day appointed by law to be a bank-holiday, or a day appointed for a public fast or thanksgiving, in which case the time shall be reckoned exclusively of that day also.

Offences

22. It is hereby declared that any contravention of or failure to comply with a provision of Regulations 11(2) and (3), 13, 14, 15(1) and (3), 16 and 20(6) of these Regulations is an offence and accordingly by virtue of section 91(6) of the Act a person who contravenes or fails to comply with such a provision is liable on summary conviction to a fine not exceeding £20.

Given under the Official Seal of the Minister of Transport the 20th November 1969.

(L.S.)   *Fred Mulley,*

                                         Minister of Transport.

(a) 1948 c. 38.

SCHEDULE 1 (See Regulation 3)

CASES IN WHICH AN OPERATOR'S LICENCE IS NOT REQUIRED

1. Any such vehicle (including a trailer drawn thereby) as is mentioned in paragraph 2(1) of Part I of Schedule 3 to the Vehicles (Excise) Act 1962(a) whilst being used solely for the haulage of such objects as are referred to in sub-paragraphs (a) to (e) of that paragraph.

2. A dual-purpose vehicle (as defined in Regulation 3(1) of the Motor Vehicles (Construction and Use) Regulations 1969(b)), and any trailer drawn thereby.

3. A vehicle used on a road only in passing from one part of any private premises to another or to other private premises in the immediate neighbourhood belonging (except in the case of a vehicle so used only in connection with excavation or demolition) to the same person, provided that the distance travelled on a road by any such vehicle does not exceed in the aggregate six miles in any one week.

4. A public service vehicle which is being used in pursuance of a public service vehicle licence granted under Part III of the Road Traffic Act 1960(c), and any trailer drawn thereby.

5. A motor vehicle constructed solely for the carriage of not more than fifteen passengers exclusive of the driver and their effects when adapted to draw or drawing a trailer, and any trailer drawn thereby.

6. A hackney carriage within the meaning of the Vehicles (Excise) Act 1962 which is being used as such a carriage.

7. A vehicle which is being used for the purposes of funerals.

8. A vehicle which is being used for police, fire brigade or ambulance purposes.

9. A vehicle which is being used under the provisions of section 72 of the Mines and Quarries Act 1954(d) (which makes provision as to fire-fighting and rescue operations at mines.)

10. A vehicle upon which no permanent body has been constructed, which is being used only for carrying burden which either is carried solely for the purpose of test or trial, or consists of articles and equipment which will form part of the completed vehicle when the body is constructed.

11. As from the 1st January 1970 a vehicle which is being used under a trade licence within the meaning of section 12 of the Vehicles (Excise) Act 1962 as amended by section 6(2) of and Schedule 12 to the Finance Act 1969(e).

12. A vehicle in the service of a visiting force or of a headquarters and a vehicle while hired, whether directly or through a contractor, by the Secretary of State for Defence or any Territorial Auxiliary and Volunteer Reserve Association, for naval, military or air force purposes or by the naval, military or air force authorities of a visiting force or headquarters for the purposes of a visiting force or headquarters in connection with the manning of any war stations in anticipation of enemy attack, or the mobilisation of the fighting services or of a visiting force or headquarters, or in connection with manoeuvres, exercises or training.

For the purposes of this paragraph, where a vehicle is so hired, the period of hire shall be deemed to include its journey to and from the war station or the area where the mobilisation, manoeuvres, exercises or training take place.

In this paragraph "visiting force", "headquarters" and "vehicle in the service of a visiting force or of a headquarters" have the same respective meanings as in the Visiting Forces and International Headquarters (Application of Law) Order 1965(f).

(a) 1962 c. 13   (b) S.I. 1969/321 (1969 I, p. 829).

(c) 1960 c. 16.   (d) 1954 c. 70.

(e) 1969 c. 32.   (f) S.I. 1965/1536 (1965 II, p. 4462).

13. A trailer not constructed primarily for the carriage of goods but which is being used incidentally for that purpose in connection with the construction, maintenance or repair of roads.

14. A road roller and any trailer drawn thereby.

15. A vehicle while being used under the direction of H.M. Coastguard or of the Royal National Lifeboat Institution for the carriage of life-boats, life-saving appliances or crew.

16. A vehicle fitted with a machine, appliance, apparatus or other contrivance which is a permanent or essentially permanent fixture, provided that the only goods carried on the vehicle are such as are required for use in connection with the machine, appliance, apparatus or contrivance or the running of the vehicle.

17. A vehicle while being used by a local authority : —

(1) for road cleansing, road watering, snow-clearing or the collection or disposal of refuse, night-soil or the contents of cess-pools, or for the purposes of the enactments relating to weights and measures or the sale of food and drugs ; or

(2) for the distribution of grit, salt or other materials on frosted, icebound or snow-covered roads or for going to or from the place where it is to be used for the said purposes or for any other purpose directly connected with those purposes.

18. A vehicle while being used by a local authority as defined in section 9 of the Civil Defence Act 1948(a) in the discharge of any function conferred on or exercisable by that authority under Regulations made under the said Act.

19. A vehicle while being used by a highway authority for the purposes of sections 224 and 261 of the Road Traffic Act 1960.

20. A tower wagon or trailer drawn by a tower wagon, provided in each case the only goods carried on the vehicle are such as are required for use in connection with the work on which the tower wagon is ordinarily used as such.

21. A vehicle while being used for the carriage of goods within an aerodrome within the meaning of section 23(1) of the Airports Authority Act 1965(b).

22. An electrically propelled vehicle.

23. A showman's vehicle and any trailer drawn thereby.

In this paragraph "showman's vehicle" means a vehicle registered under the Vehicles (Excise) Act 1962 in the name of a person following the business of a travelling showman and used solely by him for the purposes of his business and for no other purpose.

SCHEDULE 2 (see Regulation 9)

NOTICE OF OBJECTION

TRANSPORT ACT 1968

OPERATORS' LICENSING

NOTICE OF OBJECTION

To the LICENSING AUTHORITY, ... TRAFFIC AREA. I/We, being an objector under Section 63(3) of the Transport Act 1968, hereby give notice of objection to the application for/the variation of an operator's

(a) 12, 13 & 14 Geo. 6. c. 5.   (b) 1965 c. 16.

licence made by .... and numbered ....

in Applications and Decisions dated .... and numbered

........................on the following grounds:—

*(a) that the applicant is not a fit person to hold an operator's licence having regard to relevant activities of himself or others before the making of the application and/or relevant convictions of himself or others during the 5 years preceding the making of the application.

Details are as follows:— ....

.... ;

*(b) that the applicant will not make satisfactory arrangements for securing that Part VI of the Transport Act 1968 (i.e. the provisions relating to the statutory limits on drivers' hours) will be complied with.

Details are as follows:— ....

.... ;

*(c) that the applicant will not make satisfactory arrangements for securing that his vehicles will not be overloaded.

Details are as follows:— ....

.... ;

*(d) that the applicant will not provide satisfactory facilities and arrangements for maintaining his vehicles in a fit and serviceable condition.

Details are as follows:— ....

.... ;

*(e) that the provision of satisfactory maintenance facilities and arrangements by the applicant will be prejudiced by reason of his having insufficient financial resources for that purpose.

Details are as follows:— ....

.... ;

A copy of this objection has been sent to the applicant.

Body or person by whom objection is made ....

Signature of [person authorised by*] the above-named objector.

....

Position held by signatory ....

Address of objector ....

....

Date...

*Delete if not applicable. In each case where a ground of objection is included, give reasons.

SCHEDULE 3 (see Regulation 20)

MODIFICATIONS OF PART V OF THE ACT AND THESE REGULATIONS IN RELATION TO HOLDING COMPANIES AND SUBSIDIARIES

1. Part V of the Act and these Regulations shall have effect as if any reference in a provision thereof (except in this Schedule) to a provision which is modified by this Schedule were a reference to that provision as so modified.

2. Part V of the Act shall have effect : —

(a) as if goods vehicles belonging to, or in the possession of, the subsidiary, belonged to, or were in the possession of, the holding company ;

(b) as if, where a goods vehicle is used in circumstances in which, but for the provisions of Regulation 20 of these Regulations, the subsidiary would be deemed to be the user thereof, the holding company were the user thereof ;

(c) as if a trade or business carried on by the subsidiary were carried on by the holding company ;

(d) as if the subsidiary were an applicant for the grant or variation of the licence ;

(e) as if any operating centre of the subsidiary were an operating centre of the holding company ;

(f) as if any person who is a director of the subsidiary were a director of the holding company ;

(g) as if any person who is an employee of the subsidiary were an employee of the holding company ;

(h) as if for section 63(1) there were substituted the following subsection : —

"(1) The licensing authority may publish in the prescribed manner notice of any application to the authority for an operator's licence made by a company or other body corporate in pursuance of regulations made under section 85 of this Act" ;

(i) as if in section 66(1) the reference in paragraph (b) to persons holding shares in the company included a reference to persons holding shares in the subsidiary, and the reference in paragraph (c) to the holder of the licence included a reference to the subsidiary ;

(j) as if in section 67(4) for the words "by the holder of that licence for the grant to him of a new licence in substitution therefor, the existing licence" there were substituted the words "by a company or other body corporate in respect of a subsidiary of that company or other body corporate in pursuance of regulations made under section 85 of this Act, for the grant of a licence to take effect when a licence held by that subsidiary has expired by effluxion of time, the existing licence held by the subsidiary" ;

(k) as if in section 68(4) for the words from "Except in the following cases" to "the licensing authority shall publish" there were substituted the words "In the case of an application for a direction under subsection (1)(a) of this section made by a company or other body corporate in pursuance of regulations made under section 85 of this Act, the licensing authority may publish" ;

(l) as if in section 69(1) the references in paragraphs (a), (c), (d) and (e) to the holder of the licence included references to the subsidiary ;

(m) as if in section 69(4) the references to the holder of the licence or any servant or agent of his included references to the subsidiary or any servant or agent of it, and as if the reference in paragraph (h) to a vehicle of which the holder of the licence was the owner included a reference to a vehicle of which the subsidiary was the owner ;

(n) as if in section 69(5) the reference to the holder of the licence included a reference to the subsidiary ;

(*o*) as if in section 69(6) after sub-paragraph (ii) there were inserted the following sub-paragraph : —

"(iii) a company which is a subsidiary of such a company as aforesaid ; or";

(*p*) as if in section 69(7) for the words "where that person was a company, in relation to any director of that company," there were substituted the words "where that person is a company or other body corporate which is the holder of the licence in respect of a subsidiary of that company or other body corporate in pursuance of regulations made under section 85 of this Act, in relation to any director of that company or other body corporate or of that subsidiary"; and

(*q*) as if in section 94(1) the reference to a person who is the holder of a carrier's licence in respect of vehicles in relation to which section 60 of the Act comes into force included a reference to a holding company making an application in respect of a subsidiary of that company in pursuance of regulations under section 85 of this Act and in relation to vehicles all or any of which are authorised under a carrier's licence held by that subsidiary.

3. These Regulations shall have effect—

(*a*) as if in Regulation 4(1) the reference to an operating centre of the applicant included a reference to an operating centre of the subsidiary ;

(*b*) as if in Regulation 14 the reference to the holder of the licence included a reference to the subsidiary.

EXPLANATORY NOTE

(This Note is not part of the Regulations.)

These Regulations provide for various matters necessary for the introduction of operators' licensing of goods vehicles used for hire or reward or on own account under Part V of the Transport Act 1968.

Regulation 3 and Schedule 1 prescribe exemptions from the requirement to have an operator's licence.

Regulations 4 to 10 and Schedule 2 prescribe various matters relating to the procedure for granting and varying operators' licences. In particular, Regulation 8 prescribes the trade unions and associations which may object to applications for the grant or variation of an operator's licence.

Regulations 11 to 22 and Schedule 3 prescribe various miscellaneous and supplemental matters relating to operators' licensing. In particular, Regulation 20 and Schedule 3 make provision for a body corporate which has a subsidiary to hold an operator's licence for the subsidiary's vehicles.

STATUTORY INSTRUMENTS

1969 No. 1637 (C.52)

ROAD TRAFFIC

The Vehicle and Driving Licences Act 1969 (Commencement No. 4) Order 1969

Made - - -	19*th November* 1969	
Laid before Parliament	3*rd December* 1969	
Coming into Operation	1*st February* 1970	

The Minister of Transport hereby makes this Order in exercise of his powers under section 38(2) of the Vehicle and Driving Licences Act 1969(**a**) and of all other enabling powers.

1. This Order may be cited as the Vehicle and Driving Licences Act 1969 (Commencement No. 4) Order 1969.

2. Sections 9, 10, 16(2) (in so far as it relates to paragraphs 6, 8, 9, 10, 11 and 12 of Schedule 2), 16(6), 22, 25, 26, 28(1), (2)(*a*), (2)(*c*), (4), (5) and (6), 30, 31, 32 and 35 (in so far as the latter two sections relate to section 22) and 37 (in so far as it relates to the repeal of section 19(1) and (3) of the Vehicles (Excise) Act 1962(**b**)) of the Vehicle and Driving Licences Act 1969 shall come into operation on 1st February 1970.

Given under the Official Seal of the Minister of Transport the 19th November 1969.

(L.S.)

Fred Mulley,
Minister of Transport.

EXPLANATORY NOTE

(*This Note is not part of the Order.*)

This Order brings into operation on the 1st February 1970 the following provisions of the Vehicle and Driving Licences Act 1969 :—

Section 9, which provides that for the purposes of provisions relating to vehicles excise a person keeps a mechanically propelled vehicle on a road if he causes it to be on a road for any period however short when it is not in use there.

Section 10, which restricts the use which may be made of a vehicle in connection with vehicle testing when it is unlicensed.

Section 16(2), which amends the Road Traffic Act 1960 in accordance with Schedule 2 to the Act of 1969. The relevant amendments in the Schedule are:—

(**a**) 1969 c. 27.　　　　　　(**b**) 1962 c. 13.

paragraph 6, which amends sections 225(1)(*d*) and 226(2) (power of police to require production of driving licences and to obtain names and addresses from persons accompanying learner drivers),

paragraph 8, which amends section 232(2)(*a*) (power to require the owner of a vehicle to identify the driver of it who is alleged to have committed certain offences),

paragraph 9, which amends section 233(1) (which specifies the documents of which, among other things, the forgery or misuse is an offence under that section),

paragraph 10, which amends section 241(2)(*c*)(ii) and (4)(*a*) (which relate to the service of notices of intended prosecution),

paragraph 11, which amends section 244 (which specifies the time for bringing summary proceedings for certain offences),

paragraph 12, which amends section 247 (which relates to the destination of fines).

Section 16(6), which amends section 85(2)(*a*) of the Road Traffic Regulation Act 1967 (power to require the owner of a vehicle to identify the driver of it who is alleged to have committed certain offences).

Section 22, which makes provision for obtaining information as to a person's date of birth and sex.

Section 25, which relates to the institution and conduct of proceedings in England and Wales.

Section 26, which relates to the institution and conduct of proceedings in Scotland.

Section 28(1), (2)(*a*), (2)(*c*), (4), (5) and (6), which make alterations to penalties and offences and the application of sums under the Vehicles (Excise) Act 1962.

Section 30, which makes provision for ascertaining the amount payable in respect of back-duty on a plea of guilty by an absent accused to an offence under section 7 of the Vehicles (Excise) Act 1962.

Section 31, which relates to appeals against the conduct of a driving test.

Section 32 (in so far as it relates to section 22), which provides a maximum penalty of £50 for an offence under section 22.

Section 35 (in so far as it relates to section 22), which provides for the service of notices under section 22(6).

Section 37, which makes a repeal in the Vehicles (Excise) Act 1962 consequential on sections 25 and 26 of the Act of 1969.

STATUTORY INSTRUMENTS

1969 No. 1638

ROAD TRAFFIC

The Goods Vehicles (Licences and Prohibitions) (Amendment) (No. 2) Regulations 1969

Made - - -	19*th November* 1969	
Laid before Parliament	28*th November* 1969	
Coming into Operation	1*st December* 1969	

The Minister of Transport in exercise of his powers under sections 179 and 190 of the Road Traffic Act 1960(**a**) as amended by section 22 of the Road Traffic Act 1962(**b**), and of all other enabling powers, and after consultation with representative organisations in accordance with the provisions of section 260(2) of the said Act of 1960, and with the Council on Tribunals in accordance with the requirements of section 8 of the Tribunals and Inquiries Act 1958(**c**) hereby makes the following Regulations :—

1.—(1) These Regulations shall come into operation on the 1st December 1969 and may be cited as the Goods Vehicles (Licences and Prohibitions) (Amendment) (No. 2) Regulations 1969.

(2) The Interpretation Act 1889(**d**) shall apply for the interpretation of these Regulations as it applies for the interpretation of an Act of Parliament.

2. The Goods Vehicles (Licences and Prohibitions) Regulations 1960(**e**), as amended (**f**), shall have effect as though—

(1) in Regulation 4,
   (*a*) paragraph (2) were omitted ; and
   (*b*) in paragraph (5), before the words "be accompanied" there were inserted the words "if so required by the licensing authority" ;

(2) in Regulation 8, in sub-sub-paragraph (1)(*a*)(ii), the words "(no date unless the licensing authority for special reasons otherwise determines being within 14 days of the issue of statement)" were omitted ;

(3) in Regulation 9, for the words "fourteen days", there were substituted the words "3 weeks" ;

(4) For Regulation 14 there were substituted the following Regulation :—
   "Temporary replacement of Authorised Vehicles
   14.—(1) Where a motor vehicle specified in an A or a B licence (hereinafter referred to as "the specified vehicle") has been destroyed, rendered unfit for service, or withdrawn from service for overhaul or repair and the holder of the licence desires a licence authorising, until it is replaced or rendered fit for service again, the use in its place of a motor vehicle or an articulated combination (as defined in section 92(1)

(**a**) 1960 c. 16.
(**c**) 1958 c. 66.
(**e**) S.I. 1960/1505 (1960 III, p. 3020).

(**b**) 1962 c. 59.
(**d**) 1889 c. 63.
(**f**) There is no relevant amending instrument.

of the Transport Act 1968) in his possession or to be hired without a driver (hereinafter referred to as "the substituted vehicle or combination") which vehicle or combination he is not authorised to use under his existing licence. the provisions of paragraphs (4) and (5) of Regulation 4 and of Regulations 6 and 7 shall not apply and the application for such licence shall be accompanied by the identity certificate for the specified vehicle.

(2) If on consideration of such an application the licensing authority decides to grant a licence authorising the use of the substituted vehicle or combination and, for such special reasons as aforesaid, determines under the provisions of section 169(2) of the Act that such licence shall expire on the prescribed date next ensuing after the expiration of 3 months from the date of such grant, the following provisions shall have effect : —

> (a) notwithstanding the provisions of Regulation 13 no fee shall be charged for the licence ; and

> (b) the identity certificate for the specified vehicle shall be returned to the holder of the licence when he surrenders to the licensing authority the licence authorising the use of the substituted vehicle or combination and the relative identity certificate or certificates." ;

(5) in Regulation 16, for the words "seven days", there were substituted the words "3 weeks" ;

(6) in Regulation 18 the words "on payment of the prescribed fee" were omitted ;

(7) in Regulation 20, for the words "five days", there were substituted the words "3 weeks" ;

(8) in Regulation 21, in paragraph (a), for the words "one month", there were substituted the words "2 months" ; and

(9) in Schedule 2,

> (a) in Form GV5, item 5 were omitted in the case of an application which is not required by the licensing authority to be accompanied by the licence fee.

> (b) in Form GV7, item 5 were omitted.

Given under the Official Seal of the Minister of Transport the 19th November 1969.

(L.S.)

Fred Mulley,
Minister of Transport.

EXPLANATORY NOTE
(This Note is not part of the Regulations.)

These Regulations make minor amendments to The Goods Vehicles (Licences and Prohibitions) Regulations 1960 so as to make the procedures for applying for and varying carriers' licences under Part IV of the Road Traffic Act 1960 similar to the procedures for applying for and varying operators' licences under Part V of the Transport Act 1968.

STATUTORY INSTRUMENTS

1969 No. 1641 (S. 144)

NATIONAL HEALTH SERVICE, SCOTLAND

The National Health Service (Drug Accounts Committee) (Scotland) Amendment Order 1969

Made - - -	18*th November* 1969
Coming into Operation	1*st December* 1969

The Secretary of State, in exercise of the powers conferred on him by sections 32 and 73(4) of the National Health Service (Scotland) Act 1947(a) and of all other powers enabling him in that behalf, hereby makes the following order:—

1.—(1) This order may be cited as the National Health Service (Drug Accounts Committee) (Scotland) Amendment Order 1969 and shall come into operation on 1st December 1969.

(2) The Interpretation Act 1889(b) shall apply for the interpretation of this order as it applies for the interpretation of an Act of Parliament.

2. The National Health Service (Drug Accounts Committee) (Scotland) Order 1948(c) as amended (d) shall be further amended as follows:—

    (1) For article 10(1) (Procedure) there shall be substituted the following:—

        "The provisions of regulations 10 (Officers), 11 (Committees), 12 (Meetings), 13 (Minutes) and 14 (Power to make standing orders) of the National Health Service (Executive Councils) (Scotland) Regulations 1954(e) shall apply for the purposes of this order as if for any reference therein to a Council there were substituted a reference to the Committee and as if for any reference to a committee of a Council there were substituted a reference to a sub-committee."

    (2) Articles 13 (Application of the National Health Service (Finance of Executive Councils and Scottish Dental Estimates Board) (Scotland) Regulations 1948(f)), 14 (Annual and Supplementary Estimates), 15 (Books and Accounts) and 16 (Audit) shall cease to have effect.

3. The provisions of the National Health Service (Executive Councils and Scottish Dental Estimates Board) (Scotland) Financial Regulations 1969(g) shall apply to the Drug Accounts Committee as they apply to Executive Councils subject to the following modifications:—

    (*a*) the word "Committee" shall be substituted for the word "Council";

(a) 1947 c. 27.
(b) 1889 c. 63.
(c) S.I. 1948/1596 (Rev. XV, p. 989; 1948 I, p. 2321).
(d) S.I. 1950/577 (1950 I, p. 1438).
(e) S.I. 1954/461 (1954 I, p. 1370).
(f) S.I. 1948/1494 (Rev. XV, p. 996; 1948 I, p. 2328).
(g) S.I. 1969/1612 (1969 III, p. 5098).

(b) references to the finance committee shall be construed as references to the finance sub-committee; and

(c) references to the Ophthalmic Services Committee shall be omitted.

Given under the Seal of the Secretary of State for Scotland.

A. T. F. Ogilvie,
Assistant Secretary.

St. Andrew's House,
Edinburgh.

18th November 1969.

EXPLANATORY NOTE

(This Note is not part of the Order.)

This Order amends the National Health Service (Drug Accounts Committee) (Scotland) Order 1948 which constituted a Joint Committee to carry out the duties of the Executive Councils in Scotland with respect to the checking and pricing of the prescriptions for drugs, medicines and appliances supplied as pharmaceutical services under section 40 of the National Health Service (Scotland) Act 1947. This Order applies to the Drug Accounts Committee the provisions of the National Health Service (Executive Councils and Scottish Dental Estimates Board) (Scotland) Financial Regulations 1969 in place of certain provisions of the National Health Service (Finance of Executive Councils and Scottish Dental Estimates Board) (Scotland) Regulations 1948 which the regulations of 1969 replace.

STATUTORY INSTRUMENTS

1969 No. 1642 (S.145)

PENSIONS

The Superannuation (Local Government and Overseas Employment) Interchange (Scotland) Rules 1969

Made - - -	*14th November* 1969
Laid before Parliament	*28th November* 1969
Coming into Operation	*1st December* 1969

ARRANGEMENT OF RULES

Part I

Preliminary

Part II

Transfer from Local Government Employment to Overseas Employment

Part III

Re-Entry into Local Government Employment

PART IV

GENERAL

12. Effect of payment of transfer value.

13. Entry into further overseas employment.

14. Return of contributions.

15. Right of appeal.

16. Revocations and transitional provisions.

SCHEDULES

Schedule 1. Reduction of benefits.

Schedule 2. Surrender of part of superannuation benefit.

In exercise of the powers conferred on me by sections 2 and 15 of the Superannuation (Miscellaneous Provisions) Act 1948(**a**) as amended by section 11(6) of the Superannuation (Miscellaneous Provisions) Act 1967(**b**), and of all other powers enabling me in that behalf, I hereby make the following rules :—

PART I

PRELIMINARY

Title and commencement

1. These rules may be cited as the Superannuation (Local Government and Overseas Employment) Interchange (Scotland) Rules 1969, and shall come into operation on 1st December 1969.

Interpretation

2.—(1) In these rules, unless the context otherwise requires—

"the Act of 1937" means the Local Government Superannuation (Scotland) Act 1937(**c**) ;

"the Act of 1948" means the Superannuation (Miscellaneous Provisions) Act 1948 ;

"the Act of 1953" means the Local Government Superannuation Act 1953(**d**) ;

"added years" means any additional years of service reckonable under regulation 12 of the benefits regulations, and includes any additional years of service which, having been granted under any enactment, have subsequently become and are reckonable under or by virtue of an enactment ;

"benefit" means any superannuation benefit payable to or in respect of a person ;

"the benefits regulations" means the Local Government Superannuation (Benefits) (Scotland) Regulations 1954(**e**) :

(a) 1948 c. 33.   (b) 1967 c. 28.
(c) 1937 c. 69.   (d) 1953 c. 25.
(e) S.I. 1954/1059 (1954 II, p. 1632).

"contributing service", "contributory employee", "designated employee" and "disqualifying break of service" have the same meanings as in the Act of 1937 ;

"enactment" includes any instrument made under an enactment ;

"first fund authority" means the local authority administering the super-annuation fund to which a person last contributed before entering overseas employment ;

"injury allowance" means an injury allowance (however named) to which a person becomes entitled in the capacity of contributory employee ;

"local Act contributor" and "local authority" have the same meanings as in the Act of 1937 ;

"local government employment" means employment by virtue of which a person is or is deemed to be a contributory employee ;

"national service", in relation to any person, means service which is relevant service within the meaning of the Reserve and Auxiliary Forces (Protection of Civil Interests) Act 1951(a), and any similar service imme-diately following relevant service, entered into with the consent of the authority or person by whom he was employed before undertaking that service or, in the case of a person who holds an appointment to an office and is not employed under a contract of employment, with the consent of the authority by whom he was appointed ;

"non-contributing service" has the same meaning as in the Act of 1937 ;

"overseas country" means any country other than a country within the United Kingdom ;

"overseas employment" means employment in the service of—

(a) the central or local government of an overseas country or a govern-ment constituted for two or more overseas countries or any Authority established for the purpose of providing or administering services which are common to, or relate to matters of common interest to, two or more overseas countries ;

(b) a university or college in an overseas country ;

(c) a public institution or other organisation engaged in health, welfare, research or educational services in an overseas country ;

(d) an organisation receiving grants from Her Majesty's Government in connection with functions overseas ;

(e) the United Nations Organisation or any of its specialised agencies or any other inter-governmental organisation to which Her Majesty's Government may be party ; or

(f) the Ministry of Overseas Development for service overseas ;
being employment which is either pensionable employment within the mean-ing of section 17(1) of the Act of 1948 or employment undertaken with the approval of the first fund authority ;

"prescribed period" has the meaning assigned to it by rule 3 ;

"retirement pension" means any retirement pension (however named) to which a person becomes entitled in the capacity of contributory employee ;

(a) 1951 c. 65.

"the rules of 1958" means the Superannuation (Local Government and Overseas Employment) Interchange (Scotland) Rules 1958(**a**) ;

"the rules of 1961" means the Superannuation (Local Government and Overseas Employment) Interchange (Scotland) Amendment Rules 1961(**b**) ;

"second fund authority" means the local authority administering the superannuation fund to which a person contributes on re-entering local government employment after ceasing to hold overseas employment ;

"the transfer value regulations" means the Local Government Superannuation (Transfer Value) (Scotland) Regulations 1954(**c**) ;

"voluntary contributions" means payments made voluntarily by a contributory employee for the purpose of securing benefits for his widow, children or other dependants and payments (other than payments made in respect of a liability which has been wholly discharged) of any of the following categories—

(*a*) additional contributory payments of the kind referred to in section 2(3) and (4) of the Act of 1953 ;

(*b*) any similar payments made under a local Act scheme as a condition of reckoning any period of employment as service or as a period of contribution for the purposes of the scheme or, where the local Act scheme provides for the reckoning of non-contributing service, as contributing service for the purposes of the scheme ;

(*c*) any payments made for the purpose of increasing the length at which any period of service or of contribution would be reckonable for the purpose of calculating a benefit under a local Act scheme ;

(*d*) any payments made in respect of added years ;

"war service" means war service within the meaning of the Local Government Staffs (War Service) Act 1939(**d**), but in the case of a person who before the termination of his war service made a claim under section 10 of the Act of 1937 for the return of contributions, does not include any part of his war service after the date on which the claim was made.

(2) Any references in these rules to a person as a contributory employee, or to contributing service, or to the Act of 1937, the Act of 1953, the benefits regulations, or any provision in any of those enactments in their application to that person shall be deemed to include references to a person as a local Act contributor within the meaning of the Act of 1937 and to a person entitled to participate in the benefits of a superannuation fund maintained under a local Act scheme, or to service for the purposes of a local Act scheme, or to any corresponding local Act or scheme or provision therein in their application to that person.

(3) References in these rules to a numbered rule or schedule shall, unless the reference is to a rule of or a schedule to a specified enactment, be construed as references to the rule or schedule bearing that number in these rules.

(4) References in these rules to the provisions of any enactment shall, unless the context otherwise requires, be construed as references to those provisions as amended, extended, modified, applied or re-enacted by any subsequent enactment.

(5) The Interpretation Act 1889(**a**) shall apply for the interpretation of these rules as it applies for the interpretation of an Act of Parliament, and as if these rules and the rules revoked by rule 16(1) were Acts of Parliament.

Meaning of "prescribed period"

3.—(1) Subject to the provisions of this rule, the expression "prescribed period" in these rules means a period of 12 months after the date on which a person left local government employment or, as the case may be, overseas employment, and in the case of a person who immediately after leaving such employment became engaged in national service, a period of 6 months after the termination of that service.

(2) The reference in paragraph (1) of this rule to a period of 12 months shall be construed in relation to a person to whom section 6 of the Act of 1948 applies (which makes special provisions as to local government superannuation during periods of emergency) as a reference to a period of 5 years or such longer period as the Secretary of State may in any particular case allow.

(3) Without prejudice to paragraph (2) of this rule, the first fund authority may—

> (*a*) in respect of a person who has left local government employment, extend either of the periods referred to in paragraph (1) ;
>
> (*b*) in respect of a person who has left one overseas employment and entered further overseas employment, extend the period of 12 months referred to in paragraph (1) ;
>
> (*c*) in respect of a person who has left overseas employment and re-entered local government employment, extend the period of 12 months referred to in paragraph (1), if—
>
>> (i) the person notifies the second fund authority that he desires rule 11 to apply to him, and
>>
>> (ii) the second fund authority consent.

PART II

TRANSFER FROM LOCAL GOVERNMENT EMPLOYMENT TO OVERSEAS EMPLOYMENT

Persons to whom Part II applies

4.—(1) Subject to the provisions of these rules and to the conditions specified in rule 5 being satisfied, this Part of these rules shall apply—

> (*a*) to a person who on or after the commencement of these rules enters overseas employment within the prescribed period after leaving local government employment, and
>
> (*b*) if the first fund authority consent, to a person who before the commencement of these rules entered overseas employment within the prescribed period, having left local government employment on or after 4th February 1948.

(2) This Part of these rules shall not apply to any person who has become entitled to any benefit (other than a return of contributions) in respect of his local government employment.

(**a**) 1889 c. 63.

Conditions for application of Part II

5.—(1) The conditions referred to in rule 4(1) are that the person shall, before or within 6 months after entering overseas employment or, if he entered that employment before the commencement of these rules, within 6 months after their commencement—

(*a*) notify the first fund authority in writing that he desires these rules to apply to him;

(*b*) furnish that authority with particulars in writing of any national service in which he has been engaged since leaving local government employment; and

(*c*) pay to that authority an amount equal to any sum paid to him by way of return of contributions (other than voluntary contributions) on or after leaving local government employment.

(2) The first fund authority may extend the period for compliance with any condition specified in this rule.

Rights in respect of entry into overseas employment

6.—(1) Where a person ceases to hold overseas employment in such circumstances, including that of his age and the length of his service (taking into account the period of overseas employment), as had they obtained when he ceased to hold his local government employment would have entitled him to any benefit (other than an injury allowance) under the Act of 1937, he shall be entitled, as from the date on which he ceases to hold the overseas employment, to receive that benefit out of the superannuation fund of the first fund authority, calculated as if he had become entitled thereto at the date on which he ceased to hold his local government employment.

(2) Where a person ceases to hold overseas employment and has attained the age of 60 years, or any lesser age at which under the conditions of service applicable to him in the overseas employment he is required by reason of age to retire from that employment, but by reason of his not having attained some greater age and served for a correspondingly longer period he does not qualify for a benefit under the provisions of the preceding paragraph, he shall be entitled on attaining such greater age to receive the like benefits as he would have received under the preceding paragraph if he had attained that age at the date when he ceased to hold the overseas employment and had held that employment for a correspondingly longer period.

(3) Where a person dies in any of the following circumstances, that is to say—

(*a*) while in overseas employment;

(*b*) within 12 months after leaving overseas employment;

(*c*) after ceasing to be in overseas employment in the circumstances mentioned in paragraph (2) of this rule and before attaining such greater age as is therein mentioned; or

(*d*) after having become entitled to a benefit under paragraph (1) or (2) of this rule,

there shall be paid in respect of him out of the superannuation fund of the first fund authority the like benefits (if any), except any benefit for which the requisite voluntary contributions have not been maintained during the period of overseas employment, as would have been paid—

(i) in any of the three first-mentioned circumstances, if he had died immediately before ceasing to hold his local government employment and there had been reckonable for the purpose of determining whether any benefit might have become payable to or in respect of him under the Act of 1937, in addition to any service reckonable under the said Act, a period of service equal in length to the period of overseas employment and, if he was a person to whom paragraph (2) applied, the period between the date of his ceasing to hold that employment and the date of his death, and

(ii) in the last-mentioned circumstance, if he had become entitled to the said benefit under the said Act.

(4) Where a person ceases to hold overseas employment in the circumstances mentioned in paragraph (2) of this rule, the first fund authority shall, if within 6 months after ceasing to hold the overseas employment he so requests, pay to him in lieu of the benefits to which he would otherwise later become entitled under the said paragraph (2), those benefits reduced, according to his age at the date on which he ceased to be employed in the overseas employment, by the percentages shown in the appropriate columns of the Tables set out in Schedule 1 so, however, that any such reduction shall be disregarded in the calculation of any widow's pension which may become payable in respect of the person under paragraph (3) of this rule.

(5) Where a person to whom this rule applies became engaged in national service after ceasing to hold his local government employment, that service shall for the purposes of calculating any benefit payable to or in respect of him under this rule be reckonable as contributing service if that service would have been so reckonable had the person returned to his local government employment at the date on which he entered overseas employment, or, if it would not have been so reckonable as aforesaid by reason of the fact that the person had not complied with any condition as to the payment of contributions, if immediately after he entered the overseas employment or immediately after he notified the first fund authority, whichever is the later, he paid to the first fund authority the like sum as he would have been required to pay in order to comply with the said condition had he returned to his local government employment.

Restrictions on calculation of benefits

7.—(1) Where a benefit becomes payable to or in respect of a person by virtue of rule 6(1) or (3), any provision of any enactment applicable to him prescribing a minimum benefit or a method of calculating the benefit otherwise than by reference to the amount of his contributions or the service reckonable by him or the amount of the pension which, calculated by reference to that service was, or would in certain given circumstances have become, payable to him, shall be disregarded.

(2) Where a benefit becomes payable to or in respect of a person to whom rule 11 has become applicable and the amount of that benefit falls to be calculated under any provision of any enactment applicable to him prescribing a minimum benefit or a method of calculating the benefit otherwise than by reference to the amount of the person's contributions or the service reckonable by him or the amount of the pension which, calculated by reference to that service, was, or would in certain circumstances have become, payable to him, then, if the number of years of service reckonable by the person under the provisions of that enactment is less than any minimum number of years of qualifying service prescribed for the receipt of the said benefit, the amount of the said benefit, in so far as it is obtained by reference to the said provision, shall be the amount which bears the same proportion to the sum otherwise payable as the number of years of service so reckonable as aforesaid bears to the minimum number of years of qualifying service.

Exercise of discretionary powers on a person's entry into overseas employment

8.—(1) Where a person has entered overseas employment and these rules have become applicable in relation to him, the authority or body by whom he was employed may, within 6 months after the date on which they receive notification from him (or, if the employing authority are not the first fund authority, from the first fund authority) of his election that these rules shall apply to him, exercise in relation to him any discretion which, with a view to increasing the benefits payable to him, it would have been open to them to exercise at the time when he left their employment if he had then retired and had been entitled to a retirement pension.

(2) A decision made in the exercise of any discretion under this rule shall be subject to the limitations and restrictions (if any) and to the right of appeal (if any) to which it would have been subject if the discretion had been exercised on the person's retirement in the circumstances aforesaid.

(3) Where a discretion has been exercised under this rule, the service reckonable immediately before he left his local government employment by the person in whose favour the discretion has been exercised shall be deemed to have been correspondingly increased, and any transfer value that may become payable by virtue of rule 11 shall be calculated accordingly.

(4) Any increase in service, if attributable to a decision under this rule to increase the benefits payable to the person otherwise than by any notional increase or extension of the service reckonable for the purpose of calculating those benefits, or by treating any specified period of non-contributing service as contributing service or, under a local Act scheme, by similarly converting service of one category to service of another category, shall be ascertained by converting the service in respect of which the higher rate of benefit is payable into contributing service in the manner in which non-contributing service is converted into contributing service under section 2(4) of the Act of 1953.

(5) Where the amount of any benefit to which a person becomes entitled under rule 6, or the amount of any transfer value payable in pursuance of rule 11, is increased in consequence of the exercise by an authority or body of any power conferred upon them by this rule, that authority or body shall repay the amount of the increase to the superannuation fund out of which the benefit or transfer value is payable.

Additional contributory payments and added years

9.—(1) Where a person in respect of whom a benefit may become payable under rule 6 was, at the time when he ceased to be a contributory employee, in the course of making payments (other than those to which paragraph (2) of this rule applies) by way of—

    (*a*) instalments in discharge of a fixed sum or

    (*b*) contributions of a fraction or percentage of emoluments additional to the percentage payable in respect of current service,

as a condition of being entitled to reckon any period of service as a period of contributing service for the purposes of the Act of 1937 or as a condition of increasing the length at which the said service would be reckonable for the purpose of calculating a benefit under the said Act, he shall be entitled, if on electing under rule 5 that these rules shall apply to him he repays forthwith to the first fund authority a sum equal to any sums repaid to him by way of a return of such payments on or after ceasing to hold his local government employment, to pay the outstanding payments to that authority in the manner in which he would have been liable to pay them if, on the date when he entered overseas employment, he had entered employment in which he was a contributory employee, and—

    (i) if he continues the payments, the service in respect of which they are made shall be reckonable for the purposes of the Act of 1937 in the manner in which it would have been reckonable if, immediately before he ceased to hold his local government employment, he had been under no further liability in respect of such payments;

    (ii) if he does not continue the payments, then for the purposes of the Act of 1937 account shall be taken of the service in respect of which the payments were being made only to the extent (if any) to which account would have been taken of that service if he had not been in the course of making such payments as aforesaid in respect thereof at the time when he left his former employment.

(2) Subject to the provisions of rule 11, where a person in respect of whom a benefit may become payable under rule 6 was in the course of making payments in respect of added years at the time when he left his local government employment, those years shall not be reckonable for any purpose of these rules.

Allocation of part of superannuation benefit to spouse or dependant

10. A person who becomes entitled under rule 6 to a benefit by way of annual amounts or who would become so entitled if he were to retire and who would have been entitled to surrender a part thereof had he become entitled to receive that benefit under the Act of 1953 on his retirement as an employee of the authority or body whose employment he left before entering overseas employment may surrender a part of that allowance in consideration of the grant of a pension to his spouse or any dependant on his death, subject to and in accordance with the provisions of Schedule 2.

PART III

RE-ENTRY INTO LOCAL GOVERNMENT EMPLOYMENT

Re-entry into local government employment

11.—(1) Subject to the provisions of this rule, where a person to whom Part II of these rules applies ceases to hold overseas employment and within the prescribed period thereafter re-enters local government employment, then—

    (*a*) he shall be entitled to be treated as if he had done so within 12 months after leaving local government employment, and

    (*b*) he shall be entitled to reckon his period of overseas employment for the purpose of determining whether he is entitled to a benefit under the Act of 1937, but for no other purpose.

(2) This rule shall not apply to a person who has received a return of contributions from the first fund authority on or after ceasing to hold his last overseas employment unless he pays to the second fund authority—

    (*a*) an amount equal to the returned contributions (other than voluntary contributions) and

    (*b*) any interest which he may be required to pay under paragraph (5) of this rule.

2j

(3) Where there is a break of 12 months or more between the date on which a person leaves and the date on which he re-enters local government employment, he shall not be entitled—

    (i) to enjoy rights under sections 6 and 26 of the Act of 1937 as a designated employee in respect of service rendered without a disqualifying break of service;

    (ii) to exercise an option under regulation 17(1)(c) of the benefits regulations;

    (iii) to enjoy the rights which he previously enjoyed by virtue of having exercised an option under regulation 17(1) of the benefits regulations; or

    (iv) to make in his new local government employment any such payments as are mentioned in rule 9(1) or (2) in respect of any amount which was outstanding at the time when he ceased to be subject to the Act of 1937, other than any such payments as are mentioned in rule 9(1) which under these rules he has continued to make but has not completed in his overseas employment.

(4) The amount of any transfer value which may become payable under the transfer value regulations in respect of a person to whom this rule applies shall be calculated by reference to his age on the date on which he again enters local government employment:

Provided that—

    (a) where such date is earlier than the commencement of these rules, the transfer value shall be calculated by reference to his age at the commencement of these rules; and

    (b) where interest is required to be paid under paragraph (5) of this rule, the transfer value shall be reduced by an amount equivalent to the interest paid.

(5) Where a person re-enters or re-entered local government employment more than 12 months after ceasing to hold his last overseas employment and the period of 12 months is extended pursuant to rule 3(3)(c), the first fund authority may require him to pay compound interest on any sum paid to him by way of return of contributions (other than voluntary contributions) on or after leaving his overseas employment at a rate of 3% per annum with half-yearly rests for a period beginning either with the date 12 months after the date on which he left overseas employment or, where this is later, the date on which he received such sum, and ending with the date on which he notified his desire under rule 3(3)(c) for this rule to apply to him.

(6) The interest payable under this rule shall not exceed a sum equal to one-half of the difference between the transfer value payable under paragraph (4) of this rule (or where the superannuation fund concerned is the same in the case of both employments, the transfer value which would have been payable had he transferred to the employment of an authority whose contributory employees participate in a different fund) and the transfer value which would be payable if calculated by reference to the person's age on ceasing to hold his last overseas employment.

PART IV
GENERAL

Effect of payment of transfer value

12. Where a person to whom Part II of these rules applies ceases to hold overseas employment, and enters other employment in such circumstances that the first fund authority pay a transfer value in respect of him under interchange rules made under section 2 of the Act of 1948 the said Part II shall cease to apply to him.

Entry into further overseas employment

13. Where a person to whom Part II of these rules applies ceases to hold overseas employment in such circumstances that no benefit becomes payable under rule 6, the said Part shall continue to apply to him if—

(a) he enters further overseas employment within the prescribed period after leaving his former overseas employment and

(b) before or within 6 months after entering the further overseas employment he notifies the first fund authority in writing that he desires these rules to continue to apply to him and pays to that authority an amount equal to any sum paid to him by that authority by way of return of contributions (other than voluntary contributions) on or after ceasing to hold his former overseas employment.

Return of contributions

14. Notwithstanding anything in the Act of 1937, no payment shall be made thereunder by way of a return of contributions (other than voluntary contributions) to any person who enters overseas employment in which Part II of these rules has become applicable to him unless and until he ceases to hold that employment in circumstances in which he does not become entitled to a benefit under these rules.

Right of appeal

15. The provisions of section 30 of the Act of 1937 (which provides for decision of questions and appeals to the Secretary of State), shall have effect in relation to a person who has ceased to be a contributory employee and to whom these rules have become applicable as if the reference therein to an employee of a local authority included a reference to such a person and as if the reference to regulations made under that Act included a reference to these rules:

Provided that this rule shall not apply in relation to a person who has ceased to be a local Act contributor.

Revocations and transitional provisions

16.—(1) The rules of 1958 and the rules of 1961 are hereby revoked but, subject to the provisions of paragraph (2) of this rule, shall continue to apply in relation to any person to whom they applied before the commencement of these rules or who has before that date given notice of his election that they should apply.

(2) Where a person to whom the rules hereby revoked continue to apply by virtue of the preceding paragraph either

(a) transfers, or has transferred, to further employment which is not overseas employment for purposes of those rules but would be overseas employment for purposes of these rules or

(b) re-enters or has re-entered local government employment twelve months or more after leaving overseas employment, he may apply to the first fund authority for consent that these rules should apply to him; and if that authority consent, he shall be treated as a person to whom Part II of these rules applies and as if any thing done by or in relation to him under the rules hereby revoked had been duly done under the corresponding provision of these rules.

William Ross,
One of Her Majesty's Principal
Secretaries of State.

St. Andrew's House,
Edinburgh.
14th November 1969.

SCHEDULE 1

REDUCTION OF BENEFITS

TABLE I

Superannuation Allowance or Retirement Pension

Age of person at date of ceasing to hold overseas employment:—	Percentage reduction to be made under rule 6(4) by reference to the under-mentioned minimum age at which the person would have been entitled to a retirement pension in the circumstances therein mentioned:—										
	55	56	57	58	59	60	61	62	63	64	65
30 and under	74	76	77	79	80	81	82	84	85	86	87
31 „ „	72	74	76	77	79	80	81	83	84	85	86
32 „ „	71	73	75	76	78	79	80	82	83	84	85
33 „ „	70	72	74	75	77	78	79	81	82	84	85
34 „ „	68	70	72	74	75	77	78	80	82	83	84
35 „ „	67	69	71	73	74	76	77	79	81	82	83
36 „ „	65	68	70	72	73	75	76	78	80	81	82
37 „ „	63	66	68	70	72	74	75	77	79	80	82
38 „ „	62	64	66	69	71	73	74	76	78	80	81
39 „ „	60	62	65	67	70	72	73	75	77	79	80
40 „ „	58	61	63	66	68	70	72	74	76	78	79
41 „ „	56	59	61	64	66	69	71	73	75	77	78
42 „ „	54	57	59	62	65	67	69	71	73	75	77
43 „ „	51	54	57	60	63	66	68	70	72	74	76
44 „ „	49	52	55	58	61	64	67	69	71	73	75
45 „ „	46	50	53	56	59	62	65	67	69	71	73
46 „ „	43	47	51	54	57	60	63	65	67	70	72
47 „ „	40	44	48	51	55	58	61	63	65	68	71
48 „ „	36	41	45	48	52	56	59	61	63	66	69
49 „ „	32	37	42	45	49	53	56	59	61	64	67
50 „ „	28	33	38	42	46	50	53	56	59	62	65
51 „ „	23	29	34	38	43	47	50	53	57	60	63
52 „ „	18	24	30	34	39	43	47	50	54	58	61
53 „ „	13	19	25	30	35	39	44	47	51	55	58
54 „ „	7	13	20	25	31	35	40	44	48	52	55
55 „ „	—	7	14	20	26	31	36	41	45	49	52
56 „ „	—	—	7	14	20	26	31	37	41	46	49
57 „ „	—	—	—	7	14	20	26	32	37	42	46
58 „ „	—	—	—	—	7	14	20	27	32	38	42
59 „ „	—	—	—	—	—	7	14	21	27	33	38
60 „ „	—	—	—	—	—	—	7	15	21	28	33
61 „ „	—	—	—	—	—	—	—	8	15	22	28
62 „ „	—	—	—	—	—	—	—	—	8	16	23
63 „ „	—	—	—	—	—	—	—	—	—	9	17
64 „ „	—	—	—	—	—	—	—	—	—	—	9

TABLE II

Lump Sum or Retirement Grant

Age of person at date of ceasing to hold overseas employ- ment:—	55	56	57	58	59	60	61	62	63	64	65
	Percentage reduction to be made under rule 6(4) by reference to the undermentioned minimum age at which the person would have been entitled to a lump sum or a retirement grant in the circumstances therein mentioned:—										
30 and under	58	60	61	63	64	65	66	67	69	70	71
31 ,, ,,	56	58	60	61	63	64	65	66	67	69	70
32 ,, ,,	55	57	59	60	61	63	64	65	66	68	69
33 ,, ,,	53	55	57	59	60	61	62	64	65	66	68
34 ,, ,,	51	53	55	57	59	60	61	62	64	65	67
35 ,, ,,	50	52	54	56	58	59	60	61	62	64	66
36 ,, ,,	48	50	52	54	56	57	59	60	62	63	65
37 ,, ,,	46	48	50	52	54	56	58	60	61	62	64
38 ,, ,,	45	47	49	51	53	55	57	58	60	61	63
39 ,, ,,	43	45	47	49	51	53	55	57	59	61	62
40 ,, ,,	41	44	46	48	50	52	54	56	58	60	61
41 ,, ,,	39	42	44	46	48	50	52	54	56	58	59
42 ,, ,,	37	40	42	45	47	49	51	53	55	57	58
43 ,, ,,	35	38	41	43	45	47	49	51	53	55	57
44 ,, ,,	33	36	39	41	43	45	47	49	51	53	55
45 ,, ,,	31	33	36	38	41	43	45	47	50	52	54
46 ,, ,,	28	31	34	36	39	41	43	45	48	50	52
47 ,, ,,	25	28	31	34	37	39	41	44	46	48	50
48 ,, ,,	23	26	29	32	35	37	39	42	44	46	49
49 ,, ,,	20	23	26	29	32	35	37	40	42	45	47
50 ,, ,,	17	20	23	26	29	32	35	38	40	43	45
51 ,, ,,	14	18	21	24	27	30	33	35	38	41	43
52 ,, ,,	11	14	18	21	24	27	30	33	36	39	41
53 ,, ,,	8	11	15	18	22	25	28	31	34	36	39
54 ,, ,,	4	8	11	15	19	22	25	28	31	34	37
55 ,, ,,	—	4	8	12	15	19	22	26	29	32	35
56 ,, ,,	—	—	4	8	12	15	19	23	26	29	32
57 ,, ,,	—	—	—	4	8	12	16	20	23	26	29
58 ,, ,,	—	—	—	—	4	8	12	16	20	23	26
59 ,, ,,	—	—	—	—	—	4	8	12	16	20	23
60 ,, ,,	—	—	—	—	—	—	4	9	13	16	20
61 ,, ,,	—	—	—	—	—	—	—	5	9	13	17
62 ,, ,,	—	—	—	—	—	—	—	—	5	9	14
63 ,, ,,	—	—	—	—	—	—	—	—	—	5	10
64 ,, ,,	—	—	—	—	—	—	—	—	—	—	5

SCHEDULE 2   *Rule* 10

SURRENDER OF PART OF SUPERANNUATION BENEFIT

1. For the purpose of the exercise by a person of the right conferred by rule 10 to surrender part of a benefit, the Local Government Superannuation (Surrender of Superannuation Allowance) (Scotland) Rules 1954(a) shall apply, subject to the modifications made by this Schedule and any other necessary modifications.

2. Rules 3(1) and (2) and 4(1) and (2) of the said rules shall not apply.

3. A person to whom paragraph (2) of rule 6 applies shall, for the purpose of the rules applied by paragraph 1 of this Schedule, be deemed to cease to hold his employment at the date when he attains the greater age mentioned in that paragraph.

4.—(1) A person who may become entitled to exercise and may desire to exercise as a retiring employee within the meaning of the said rules such right as is mentioned in paragraph 1 of this Schedule may give 6 months' notice in writing to the first fund authority of the date, or probable date, on which the benefit will become payable, and that he may desire to exercise such right and shall inform them of any alteration in any date so notified.

(2) Where a person to whom this Schedule applies has not given a notice under sub-paragraph (1) of this paragraph but has become entitled to exercise and may desire to exercise such right as aforesaid, he shall within 1 month after ceasing to hold his overseas employment notify the first fund authority in writing that he may desire to exercise such right as aforesaid, and of the date on which he ceased to hold that employment.

(3) A person who may become entitled to exercise and may desire to exercise as an eligible employee within the meaning of the said rules such right as is mentioned in paragraph 1 of this Schedule may give 6 months' notice in writing to the first fund authority of the date on which he expects to become so entitled and that he may desire to exercise such right and shall inform them of any alteration in any date so notified.

(4) Upon receipt of the notice from a person under any of the preceding sub-paragraphs of this paragraph, the first fund authority shall treat the notice as if it were an application made under rule 3 of the said rules and shall accordingly furnish the person with the documents referred to in the said rule 3, the provisional estimate referred to in that rule being calculated in the case of an eligible employee as at the date on which he is expected to become an eligible employee.

(5) Not more than 1 month after receipt of the documents mentioned in the last preceding sub-paragraph (or in the case of an eligible employee at any time allowed by the said rules) the person may notify his desire to surrender a part of the benefit which is or may become payable to him by completing the form provided for the purpose and sending it to the first fund authority.

(6) Where the first fund authority are satisfied that owing to circumstances beyond the control of the person it has not been reasonably practicable for him to notify his desire to surrender a part of a benefit within the time limit imposed by this paragraph, they may at their discretion extend that limit to a date not more than 6 months after the date on which he ceases to hold his overseas employment.

(a) S.I. 1954/888 (1954 II, p. 1709).

EXPLANATORY NOTE

(This Note is not part of the Rules.)

The Rules replace, and extend, the Superannuation (Local Government and Overseas Employment) Interchange (Scotland) Rules 1958 and 1961. These enable pensionable employees of local authorities who take up certain overseas appointments of a public nature to preserve the benefit of the pension rights which accrued during their local government employment. These rights are, in effect, frozen during the overseas employment. Advantage may be taken of them as follows:—

(i) when the person concerned retires from his overseas appointment, he can receive a local government pension (but at a reduced rate if he retires and claims his pension before the appropriate retiring age in local government);

(ii) if he returns to local government pensionable employment, from his overseas appointment, he can reckon his previous local government service for pension purposes as though there had been no break in his local government employment;

(iii) if he becomes disabled or dies before becoming entitled to his local government pension under the Rules, payment can be made of a disability pension, widow's pension or death benefit.

The principal changes from the previous Rules are these—

(a) the definition of "overseas employment" has been widened to include employment with the Ministry of Overseas Development, and an organisation receiving grants, for overseas functions, from Her Majesty's Government;

(b) the permissible length of any break between employments and the time limits for compliance with certain conditions can be extended by the authority or authorities concerned;

(c) a person who proceeds overseas and later returns to local government employment can in certain circumstances be required to pay interest on any returned contributions held by him in the meantime.

The Rules are given limited retrospective operation under the authority of, and subject to the safeguards required by, section 2(5) of the Superannuation (Miscellaneous Provisions) Act 1948.

STATUTORY   INSTRUMENTS

1969 No. 1643 (S.146)

SHERIFF COURT, SCOTLAND

Act of Sederunt (Computer Evidence in the Sheriff Court) 1969

Made	-	-	-	18*th November* 1969
Coming into operation				1*st December* 1969

The Lords of Council and Session, by virtue of the powers conferred upon them by section 34 of the Administration of Justice (Scotland) Act 1933(a) and section 15(6) of the Law Reform (Miscellaneous Provisions) (Scotland) Act 1968(b), do hereby enact and declare as follows : —

1. A party to any civil proceedings who wishes to rely on a statement contained in a document produced by a computer shall, not later than the date of closing the Record, send to every other party to the proceedings a copy of the statement together with a notice in writing—

(*a*) intimating that the party intends to rely on the statement ;

(*b*) stating that the statement is contained in a document produced by a computer ; and

(*c*) informing the party to whom it is addressed that he may give a counter-notice in terms of the next following paragraph ;

and the party so giving notice may within fourteen days thereafter lodge in process a certificate in terms of section 13(4) of the Law Reform (Miscellaneous Provisions) (Scotland) Act 1968(b) relating to the document.

2. When a certificate in terms of section 13(4) of the Law Reform (Miscellaneous Provisions) (Scotland) Act 1968(b) shall have been lodged in process, a copy thereof shall be sent to every other party to the proceedings within fourteen days after the date of the notice referred to in paragraph 1 hereof.

3. Any party who receives such a notice as is mentioned in paragraph 1 hereof may, within twenty-one days thereafter, by counter-notice in writing addressed to the party who served the notice, require him, within twenty-one days, to furnish him in writing with all or any of the following information—

(*a*) any such information as might have been the subject of a certificate under section 13(4) of the Law Reform (Miscellaneous Provisions) (Scotland) Act 1968(b), except in so far as such information is the subject of a certificate lodged in process as aforesaid ;

(*b*) the name, occupation, business address and place of residence of a person occupying at the material time a responsible position in relation to each of (i) the operation of the device involved in the production of the document, (ii) the management of the activities for the purposes of which the computer was used to store or process information, (iii) the supply of information to the computer, (iv) the operation of the computer, and (v) the operation of any equipment by means of which the document containing the statement was produced by the computer ; and

---

(a) 1933 c. 41.   (b) 1968 c. 70.

(c) the name, occupation, business address and place of residence of the person who signed any certificate lodged in process in terms of section 13(4) of the Law Reform (Miscellaneous Provisions) (Scotland) Act 1968(a).

4. Subject to the provisions of section 15(8) of the Law Reform (Miscellaneous Provisions) (Scotland) Act 1968(a), a party upon whom a counter-notice has been served in terms of paragraph 3 hereof shall not be entitled to rely upon the statement in the document to which the notice under paragraph 1 hereof related, unless the counter-notice shall have been withdrawn by the party who gave it or unless the Court shall be satisfied that the counter-notice was complied with so far as was reasonably possible.

5. Any party to whom information is furnished under a counter-notice by virtue of paragraph 3 hereof may, not later than twenty-eight days before the date of the proof or trial, by notice in writing require that the party wishing to rely on the statement in the document produced by a computer should call as a witness any person of whom particulars were furnished under sub-paragraph (b) or (c) of paragraph 3 hereof.

6. (i) Subject to the provisions of section 15(8) of the Law Reform (Miscellaneous Provisions) (Scotland) Act 1968(a) a party who has been required to call any person as a witness in terms of paragraph 5 hereof shall not be entitled to rely upon the statement in the document to which the notice under paragraph 1 hereof related unless the notice requiring that person to be called as a witness shall have been withdrawn by the party who gave it, or unless that person shall be adduced as a witness, or unless the Court shall be satisfied that such person is dead, or beyond the seas, or unfit by reason of his bodily or mental condition to attend as a witness, or cannot with reasonable diligence be identified or found, or cannot reasonably be expected (having regard to the passage of time and to all the circumstances) to have any recollection of matters relevant to the accuracy or otherwise of the statement in the document.

(ii) In the event that such person is not to be adduced as a witness for any reason aforesaid, the party wishing to rely on the statement in the document produced by a computer shall give notice in writing to every other party to the proceedings that such witness is not to be adduced and the reason therefor.

(iii) The notice referred to in sub-paragraph (ii) hereof shall be given not later than fourteen days after the date of the notice under paragraph 5 hereof or, if such reason could not reasonably have become known to him within that period, immediately such reason shall become known.

7. This Act of Sederunt shall apply to all civil proceedings in the Sheriff Court.

8. This Act of Sederunt may be cited as the Act of Sederunt (Computer Evidence in the Sheriff Court) 1969, and shall come into operation on 1st December 1969.

And the Lords appoint this Act of Sederunt to be inserted in the Books of Sederunt.

J. L. Clyde,
I.P.D.

Edinburgh,
18th November, 1969.

(a) 1968 c. 70.

EXPLANATORY NOTE

(This Note is not part of the Act of Sederunt.)

This Act of Sederunt prescribes certain procedure for the admission as evidence in civil proceedings in the Sheriff Court of statements produced by computers.

STATUTORY INSTRUMENTS

1969 No. 1644 (S.147)

COURT OF SESSION, SCOTLAND

Act of Sederunt (Computer Evidence in the Court of Session) 1969

Made - - - -	18*th November* 1969
Coming into Operation	1*st December* 1969

The Lords of Council and Session, by virtue of the powers conferred upon them by section 16 of the Administration of Justice (Scotland) Act 1933(**a**) and section 15(6) of the Law Reform (Miscellaneous Provisions) (Scotland) Act 1968(**b**), do hereby enact and declare as follows : —

1. A party to any civil proceedings who wishes to rely on a statement contained in a document produced by a computer shall, not later than the date of closing the Record, send to every other party to the proceedings a copy of the statement together with a notice in writing—

(*a*) intimating that the party intends to rely on the statement ;

(*b*) stating that the statement is contained in a document produced by a computer ; and

(*c*) informing the party to whom it is addressed that he may give a counter-notice in terms of the next following paragraph ;

and the party so giving notice may within fourteen days thereafter lodge in process a certificate in terms of section 13(4) of the Law Reform (Miscellaneous Provisions) (Scotland) Act 1968(**b**) relating to the document.

2. When a certificate in terms of section 13(4) of the Law Reform (Miscellaneous Provisions) (Scotland) Act 1968(**b**) shall have been lodged in process, a copy thereof shall be sent to every other party to the proceedings within fourteen days after the date of the notice referred to in paragraph 1 hereof.

3. Any party who receives such a notice as is mentioned in paragraph 1 hereof may, within twenty-one days thereafter, by counter-notice in writing addressed to the party who served the notice, require him, within twenty-one days, to furnish him in writing with all or any of the following information—

(*a*) any such information as might have been the subject of a certificate under section 13(4) of the Law Reform (Miscellaneous Provisions) (Scotland) Act 1968(**b**), except in so far as such information is the subject of a certificate lodged in process as aforesaid ;

(*b*) the name, occupation, business address and place of residence of a person occupying at the material time a responsible position in relation to each of (i) the operation of the device involved in the production of the document, (ii) the management of the activities for the purposes of which the computer was used to store or process information, (iii) the supply of information to the computer, (iv) the operation of the computer, and (v) the operation of any equipment by means of which the document containing the statement was produced by the computer ; and

(*c*) the name, occupation, business address and place of residence of the person who signed any certificate lodged in process in terms of section 13(4) of the Law Reform (Miscellaneous Provisions) (Scotland) Act 1968(**a**).

(a) 1933 c. 41.   (b) 1968 c. 70.

4. Subject to the provisions of section 15(8) of the Law Reform (Miscellaneous Provisions) (Scotland) Act 1968(a), a party upon whom a counter-notice has been served in terms of paragraph 3 hereof shall not be entitled to rely upon the statement in the document to which the notice under paragraph 1 hereof related, unless the counter-notice shall have been withdrawn by the party who gave it or unless the Court shall be satisfied that the counter-notice was complied with so far as was reasonably possible.

5. Any party to whom information is furnished under a counter-notice by virtue of paragraph 3 hereof may, not later than twenty-eight days before the date of the proof or trial, by notice in writing require that the party wishing to should call as a witness any person of whom particulars were furnished under sub-paragraph (*b*) or (*c*) of paragraph 3 hereof.

6. (i) Subject to the provisions of section 15(8) of the Law Reform (Miscellaneous Provisions) (Scotland) Act 1968(a), a party who has been required to call any person as a witness in terms of paragraph 5 hereof shall not be entitled to rely upon the statement in the document to which the notice under paragraph 1 hereof related unless the notice requiring that person to be called as a witness shall have been withdrawn by the party who gave it, or unless that person shall be adduced as a witness, or unless the Court shall be satisfied that such person is dead, or beyond the seas, or unfit by reason of his bodily or mental condition to attend as a witness, or cannot with reasonable diligence be identified or found, or cannot reasonably be expected (having regard to the passage of time and to all the circumstances) to have any recollection of matters relevant to the accuracy or otherwise of the statement in the document.

(ii) In the event that such person is not to be adduced as a witness for any reason aforesaid, the party wishing to rely on the statement in the document produced by a computer shall give notice in writing to every other party to the proceedings that such witness is not to be adduced and the reason therefor.

(iii) The notice referred to in sub-paragraph (ii) hereof shall be given not later than fourteen days after the date of the notice under paragraph 5 hereof or, if such reason could not reasonably have become known to him within that period, immediately such reason shall become known.

7. This Act of Sederunt shall apply to all civil proceedings in the Court of Session.

8. This Act of Sederunt may be cited as the Act of Sederunt (Computer Evidence in the Court of Session) 1969, and shall come into operation on 1st December 1969.

And the Lords appoint this Act of Sederunt to be inserted in the Books of Sederunt.

Edinburgh.

18th November 1969.

J. L. Clyde,
I.P.D.

EXPLANATORY NOTE

(This Note is not part of the Act of Sederunt.)

This Act of Sederunt prescribes certain procedure for the admission as evidence in civil proceedings in the Court of Session of statements produced by computers.

(a) 1968 c. 70.

STATUTORY INSTRUMENTS

1969 No. 1645

WAGES COUNCILS

The Wages Regulation (Aerated Waters) (Scotland)

(No. 2) Order 1969

Made - - - -	20*th November* 1969
Coming into Operation	12*th December* 1969

Whereas the Secretary of State has received from the Aerated Waters Wages Council (Scotland) the wages regulation proposals set out in the Schedule hereto;

Now, therefore, the Secretary of State in exercise of her powers under section 11 of the Wages Councils Act 1959(a), and of all other powers enabling her in that behalf, hereby makes the following Order:—

1. This Order may be cited as the Wages Regulation (Aerated Waters) (Scotland) (No. 2) Order 1969.

2.—(1) In this Order the expression "the specified date" means the 12th December 1969, provided that where, as respects any worker who is paid wages at intervals not exceeding seven days, that date does not correspond with the beginning of the period for which the wages are paid, the expression "the specified date" means, as respects that worker, the beginning of the next such period following that date.

(2) The Interpretation Act 1889(b) shall apply to the interpretation of this Order as it applies to the interpretation of an Act of Parliament and as if this Order and the Order hereby revoked were Acts of Parliament.

3. The wages regulation proposals set out in the Schedule hereto shall have effect as from the specified date and as from that date the Wages Regulation (Aerated Waters) (Scotland) Order 1969(c) shall cease to have effect.

Signed by order of the Secretary of State.
20th November 1969.

A. A. Jarratt,
Deputy Under Secretary of State,
Department of Employment and Productivity.

(a) 1959 c. 69.   (b) 1889 c. 63.
(c) S.I. 1969/546 (1969 I, p. 1471).

Article 3

SCHEDULE

The following minimum remuneration shall be substituted for the statutory minimum remuneration fixed by the Wages Regulation (Aerated Waters) (Scotland) Order 1969 (Order A.S. (67)).

STATUTORY MINIMUM REMUNERATION

PART I

GENERAL

1. The minimum remuneration payable to a worker to whom this Schedule applies for all work except work to which a minimum overtime rate applies under Part III, is—

   (1) in the case of a time worker, the hourly general minimum time rate payable to the worker under Part II of this Schedule;

   (2) in the case of a worker employed on piece work, piece rates each of which would yield, in the circumstances of the case, to an ordinary worker at least the same amount of money as the hourly general minimum time rate which would be payable to the worker under Part II of this Schedule if he were a time worker.

PART II

GENERAL MINIMUM TIME RATES

ALL WORKERS EXCEPT WORKERS IN THE ORKNEY OR SHETLAND ISLANDS

2. The general minimum time rates payable to all workers except workers in the Orkney or Shetland Islands are as follows:—

	Per hour		Per week of 41 hours	
	s.	d.	s.	d.
(1) Male workers aged:—				
21 years or over	5	5	222	1
20 and under 21 years	4	6	184	6
19 ,, ,, 20 ,,	4	1	167	5
18 ,, ,, 19 ,,	3	5¼	142	8
17 ,, ,, 18 ,,	3	0	123	0
16 ,, ,, 16 ,,	2	5¼	101	8
Under 16 years	2	0¼	82	11
(2) Female workers aged:—				
19 years or over	4	1	167	5
18 and under 19 years	3	5¼	142	8
17 ,, ,, 18 ,,	3	0	123	0
16 ,, ,, 17 ,,	2	5¼	101	8
Under 16 years	2	0¼	82	11

WORKERS IN THE ORKNEY OR SHETLAND ISLANDS

3. The general minimum time rates payable to male or female workers in the Orkney or Shetland Islands are, in each case, 1d. per hour less than the general minimum time rates specified in paragraph 2.

Part III

OVERTIME AND WAITING TIME
MINIMUM OVERTIME RATES

4.—(1) Minimum overtime rates are payable to a worker to whom this Schedule applies as follows:—

(a) on a Sunday or a customary holiday, for all time worked...   DOUBLE TIME

(b) in any week, exclusive of any time in respect of which an overtime rate is payable under the provisions of (a) of this sub-paragraph, for all time worked in excess of 41 hours   ...   TIME-AND-A-HALF

(2) In this Part of this Schedule—

(a) the expressions "time-and-a-half" and "double time" mean respectively:—

(i) in the case of a time worker, one and a half times and twice the hourly general minimum time rate otherwise payable to the worker;

(ii) in the case of a worker employed on piece work, one and a half times and twice the piece rates otherwise payable to the worker under paragraph 1(2);

(b) the expression "customary holiday" means—

1st and 2nd January (or, if either of these days falls on a Sunday, 3rd January shall be substituted for such day); the local Spring holiday, the local Summer holiday and the local Autumn holiday, each to be allowed on a Monday fixed by the employer and notified to the worker not less than three weeks before the holiday; and Christmas Day (or, if Christmas Day falls on a Sunday, 26th December shall be substituted).

WAITING TIME

5.—(1) A worker is entitled to payment of the minimum remuneration specified in this Schedule for all time during which he is present on the premises of his employer unless he is present thereon in any of the following circumstances:—

(a) without the employer's consent, express or implied;

(b) for some purpose unconnected with his work and other than that of waiting for work to be given to him to perform;

(c) by reason only of the fact that he is resident thereon;

(d) during normal meal times in a room or place in which no work is being done, and he is not waiting for work to be given to him to perform.

(2) The minimum remuneration payable under sub-paragraph (1) of this paragraph to a piece worker when not engaged on piece work is that which would be applicable if he were a time worker.

Part IV

APPLICABILITY OF STATUTORY MINIMUM REMUNERATION

6. This Schedule applies to workers in relation to whom the Aerated Waters Wages Council (Scotland) operates, that is to say, workers employed in Scotland in the trade specified in the Schedule to the Trade Boards (Aerated Waters Trade, Scotland) (Constitution and Proceedings) Regulations 1939(a), namely:—

The manufacture, wherever carried on, of mineral or aerated waters, non-alcoholic cordials, flavoured syrups, unfermented sweet drinks, and other similar beverages, and the manufacture in unlicensed premises of brewed liquors, including:—

(a) the operations of bottle washing, bottling and filling, and all other operations preparatory to the sale of any of the aforesaid liquors in bottles, jars, syphons, casks, or other similar receptacles;

(a) S.R. & O. 1939/1367 (1939 II, p.3178).

and including also:—

    (b) the operations of bottle washing, bottling and filling, and all subsidiary operations preparatory to the sale in bottles, jars or other similar receptacles of cider, ale, stout, porter and other alcoholic beers, where all or any of such last-mentioned operations are, or is, conducted or carried on in association with or in conjunction with all or any of the operations specified under (a) above so as to form a common or interchangeable form of employment for workers, and whether the two sets of operations or any of them are, or is, carried on simultaneously or not.

EXPLANATORY NOTE

(This Note is not part of the Order.)

This Order, which has effect from 12th December 1969, sets out the statutory minimum remuneration payable in substitution for that fixed by the Wages Regulation (Aerated Waters) (Scotland) Order 1969 (Order A.S. (67)), which Order is revoked.

New provisions are printed in italics.

STATUTORY INSTRUMENTS

1969 No. 1646

SOCIAL SECURITY

The National Insurance (Industrial Injuries) (Colliery Workers Supplementary Scheme) Amendment (No. 2) Order 1969

Laid before Parliament in draft

Made - -		*20th November* 1969
Coming into operation		*2nd December* 1969

Whereas the National Committee for the time being constituted in accordance with the Supplementary Scheme set out in Schedule 1 to the National Insurance (Industrial Injuries) (Colliery Workers Supplementary Scheme) Amendment and Consolidation Order 1963(**a**) as subsequently varied and amended(**b**) is the body charged with the administration of that Scheme and has requested the Secretary of State to vary and amend the provisions of the said Supplementary Scheme in manner set out in the following Order:—

Now, therefore, the Secretary of State, in exercise of his powers under section 47(1)(*a*)(ii) of the National Insurance Act 1965(**c**) as applied by section 82(2) of the National Insurance (Industrial Injuries) Act 1965(**d**) and of all other powers enabling him in that behalf, hereby makes the following Order, a draft of which has been laid before Parliament and has been approved by resolution of each House of Parliament:—

Citation, commencement and interpretation

1.—(1) This Order, which may be cited as the National Insurance (Industrial Injuries) (Colliery Workers Supplementary Scheme) Amendment (No. 2) Order 1969, shall come into operation on 2nd December 1969.

(2) In this Order "the Scheme" means the Supplementary Scheme set out in Schedule 1 to the National Insurance (Industrial Injuries) (Colliery Workers Supplementary Scheme) Amendment and Consolidation Order 1963 as varied and amended.

Amendment of Article 12 *of the Scheme*

2.—(1) In paragraph (3) of Article 12 of the Scheme for the words "or any other Act or Regulations, increasing such rate or amount, which may be passed or made after 3rd June 1969 and come into force or operation before 3rd December 1969", there shall be substituted the words " or any subsequent Act or Regulations increasing such rate or amount".

(a) S.I. 1963/934 (1963 II, p. 1559).
(b) The relevant amending instruments are S.I. 1967/1550, 1968/83, 1896, 1969/716 (1967 III, p. 4313; 1968 I, p. 266; III, p. 5039; 1969 II, p. 1947).
(c) 1965 c. 51.   (d) 1965 c. 52.

(2) In paragraph (4)(*a*) of Article 12 of the Scheme for the date "2nd December 1969" there shall be substituted the date "2nd June 1970".

Signed by authority of the Secretary of State for Social Services.

David Ennals,
Minister of State,

20th November 1969.   Department of Health and Social Security.

EXPLANATORY NOTE

(*This Note is not part of the Order.*)

This Order amends the provisions of the National Insurance (Industrial Injuries) Colliery Workers Supplementary Scheme by extending until 2nd June 1970 the period during which the rates of certain supplementary benefits that are calculated by reference to benefits payable under the National Insurance (Industrial Injuries) Act 1965 are not affected by any increase in such benefits payable under the said Act under or by virtue of the National Insurance Act 1967 or any subsequent legislation.

STATUTORY INSTRUMENTS

1969 No. 1647

ROAD TRAFFIC

The Road Vehicles (Headlamps) Regulations 1969

Made - - -		*18th November* 1969
Laid before Parliament		*4th December* 1969
Coming into Operation		*1st January* 1970

The Minister of Transport in exercise of his powers under section 5(1) of the Road Transport Lighting Act 1957(a), sections 15 and 16(3) of the Road Traffic Act 1962(b) and of all other enabling powers, and after consultation with representative organisations in accordance with the provisions of section 13 of the Road Transport Lighting Act 1957, as amended by section 264 of, and Schedule 17 to, the Road Traffic Act 1960(c) and as applied by section 15(5) of the said Act of 1962 hereby makes the following Regulations :—

Commencement and Citation

1. These Regulations shall come into operation on 1st January 1970 and may be cited as the Road Vehicles (Headlamps) Regulations 1969.

Revocation

2. The Road Vehicles (Headlamps) Regulations 1967(d) and the Road Vehicles (Headlamps) Regulations 1968(e) are hereby revoked.

Interpretation

3.—(1) In these Regulations, except where the context otherwise requires, the following expressions have the meanings hereby assigned to them respectively, that is to say—

"the 1964 Regulations" means the Road Vehicles Lighting Regulations 1964(f) as amended (g) ;

"dipped beam" means a beam of light emitted by a headlamp, being a beam which is deflected downwards or both downwards and to the left to such an extent that it is at all times incapable of dazzling any person who is on the same horizontal plane as the vehicle at a greater distance than 25 feet from the lamp whose eye-level is not less than 3 feet 6 inches above that plane ;

(a) 1957 c. 51. (b) 1962 c. 59.
(c) 1960 c. 16. (d) S.I. 1967/1933 (1967 III, p. 5382).
(e) S.I. 1968/1930 (1968 III, p. 5239). (f) S.I. 1964/205 (1964 I, p. 345).
(g) There is no relevant amending instrument.

"fog lamp" means a lamp on a vehicle which is designed, when lit, to illuminate the road in front of the vehicle, and which is used only in conditions of fog or whilst snow is falling ;

"headlamp" means a lamp on a vehicle which is designed, when lit, to illuminate the road in front of the vehicle, and which is not a fog lamp ;

"industrial tractor" means a tractor, not being a land tractor, which—

(a) has an unladen weight not exceeding $7\frac{1}{4}$ tons,

(b) is designed and used primarily for work off roads, or for work on roads in connection only with road construction or maintenance (including any such tractor when fitted with an implement or implements designed primarily for use in connection with such work, whether or not any such implement is of itself designed to carry a load), and

(c) which is so constructed as to be incapable of exceeding a speed of 20 miles per hour on the level under its own power ;

"matched pair of headlamps", in relation to a vehicle, means a pair of headlamps, one on each side of the vertical plane passing through the longitudinal axis of the vehicle (disregarding, for the purpose of ascertaining such axis, any side-car attached thereto) in respect of which the following conditions are satisfied, namely :—

(a) each lamp in the pair is at the same height above the ground ; and

(b) the distances between the centre of each lamp in the pair and the said vertical plane passing through the longitudinal axis of the vehicle does not vary by more than 25 millimetres ;

"matched pair of obligatory headlamps", in relation to a vehicle, means a matched pair of headlamps required to be carried by the vehicle by virtue of Regulation 5 or 6 of these Regulations ;

"main beam" means a beam of light emitted by a headlamp, being a beam which is not a dipped beam ;

"moped" means a motor bicycle whereof the cylinder capacity of the engine does not exceed 50 cubic centimetres, being a bicycle equipped with pedals by means whereof it is capable of being propelled ;

"motor bicycle" means a bicycle propelled by mechanical power ;

"motor vehicle" has the meaning assigned to it in section 253 of the Road Traffic Act 1960 ;

"obligatory headlamp" means any headlamp required to be carried by a vehicle by Regulation 5 or 6 of these Regulations ;

"obligatory side lamp" has the meaning assigned to the expression "obligatory front lamp" in Regulation 3(1) of the 1964 Regulations ;

"outermost part" has the meaning assigned to it in Regulation 3(1) of the 1964 Regulations ;

"public service vehicle" shall be construed in accordance with sections 117 and 118 of the Road Traffic Act 1960 ;

"sealed beam lamp" means a lamp unit comprising a reflector system, a lens system and one or more electrical filaments, which has been sealed in the course of manufacture and which cannot be dismantled without rendering the unit unusable as a lamp ;

"supplementary main beam" means a main beam which is emitted by an obligatory headlamp which can also emit a dipped beam and which can only be used in conjunction with a main beam from another obligatory headlamp on the same side of the vertical plane passing through the longitudinal axis of the vehicle ;

"agricultural implement", "engineering plant", "road clearance vehicle" and "works truck" have the meanings respectively assigned to them in Regulation 3(1) of the 1964 Regulations ; and

"land locomotive", "land tractor" and "overall width" have the meanings respectively assigned to them in Regulation 3(1) of the Motor Vehicles (Construction and Use) Regulations 1969(**a**).

(2) For the purposes of these Regulations, in determining when a motor vehicle is first used, the date of such first use shall be taken to be the date which is prescribed as the date of first use by Regulation 3(2) of the Motor Vehicles (Construction and Use) Regulations 1969 for the purposes of those Regulations.

(3) Any reference in these Regulations to a vehicle having any number of wheels is a reference to a vehicle having that number of wheels the tyres or rims of which are in contact with the ground when the vehicle is in motion on a road, and any two such wheels shall be treated as one wheel if the distance between the centres of the area of contact between them and the road surface is less than 18 inches.

(4) For the purposes of these Regulations a vehicle so constructed that it can be divided into two parts both of which are vehicles and one of which is a motor vehicle shall (when not so divided) be treated as that motor vehicle with the other part attached as a trailer.

(5) For the purposes of these Regulations the unladen weight of a motor vehicle shall be calculated in accordance with section 255 of the Road Traffic Act 1960.

(6) Any reference in these Regulations to any enactment or instrument shall be construed, unless the context otherwise requires, as a reference to that enactment or instrument as amended by any subsequent enactment or instrument.

(7) The Interpretation Act 1889(**b**) shall apply for the interpretation of these Regulations as it applies for the interpretation of an Act of Parliament, and as if for the purposes of section 38 of that Act these Regulations were an Act of Parliament and the Regulations revoked by Regulation 2 of these Regulations were Acts of Parliament thereby repealed.

Application and exemptions

4.—(1) Except as provided by paragraph (2) of this Regulation, these Regulations apply to every motor vehicle—

    (*a*) the whole of the weight of which is transmitted to the road surface by means of wheels ;

    (*b*) the obligatory side lamp or lamps of which are electrically operated ; and

    (*c*) which is on a road.

(**a**) S.I. 1969/321 (1969 I, p. 829).   (**b**) 1889 c. 63.

(2) These Regulations do not apply—

(a) to a vehicle first used before 1st January 1931 ; or

(b) to a vehicle controlled by a pedestrian and not constructed or adapted for use or used for the carriage of a driver or passengers ; or

(c) to an agricultural implement, a land locomotive, a land tractor, a works truck, or a road roller ; or

(d) to a vehicle which is so constructed as to be incapable of exceeding a speed of 6 miles per hour on the level ; or

(e) to a vehicle brought temporarily into Great Britain by a person resident outside the United Kingdom provided that it complies in every respect with the requirements as to lighting equipment and reflectors relating thereto contained in Part II of Annex 6 to the Convention on Road Traffic concluded at Geneva on the 19th September 1949(a) ; or

(f) to a vehicle owned by or in the service of the naval, military or air forces of Her Majesty raised in the United Kingdom and used for naval, military or air force purposes ; or

(g) to a vehicle used for the purposes of any such body, contingent or detachment of the forces of any country as is a visiting force for the purposes of any of the provisions of the Visiting Forces Act 1952(b), or used for the purposes of any headquarters or organisation designated by an Order in Council under section 1 of the International Headquarters and Defence Organisations Act 1964(c) ; or

(h) (i) to an electrically propelled goods vehicle which is so constructed as to be incapable of exceeding a speed of 15 miles per hour on the level ; or

(ii) until 1st January 1974 to an electrically propelled goods vehicle which has two or three wheels, which is first used before 1st January 1972 and which is so constructed as to be capable of exceeding a speed of 15 miles per hour on the level ; and

(iii) until 1st October 1971 to an electrically propelled goods vehicle which has four or more wheels, which is first used before 1st October 1969 and which is so constructed as to be capable of exceeding a speed of 15 miles per hour on the level.

Headlamps to be carried by vehicles with two wheels and some vehicles with three wheels

5.—(1) This Regulation applies to a motor vehicle to which these Regulations apply and which—

(a) has two wheels ; or

(b) has three wheels and is first used before 1st January 1972 ; or

(c) has three wheels, is first used on or after 1st January 1972 and except in the case of a motor bicycle with a side-car attached thereto has an unladen weight of not more than 400 kilogrammes and an overall width of not more than 1.30 metres.

(a) Cmnd. 7997 and also Treaty Series No. 49 (1958).
(b) 1952 c. 67.   (c) 1964 c. 5.

(2) Every vehicle to which this Regulation applies shall carry—

(*a*) one headlamp in the vertical plane passing through the longitudinal axis of the vehicle (disregarding, for the purpose of ascertaining such axis, any side-car attached thereto) which either—

(i) in the case of a moped with or without a side-car attached thereto and first used before 1st January 1972 or in the case of any vehicle which is so constructed as to be incapable of exceeding a speed of 25 miles per hour on the level, can only emit a dipped beam ; or

(ii) in the case of any vehicle, is wired to a device the operation of which at the will of the driver can cause to be emitted from it either a main beam or a dipped beam ; or

(*b*) a matched pair of headlamps, both headlamps in the pair being wired to a device the operation of which at the will of the driver can cause to be emitted from them at the same time either—

(i) in the case of any vehicle which is so constructed as to be incapable of exceeding a speed of 25 miles per hour on the level, only dipped beams ; or

(ii) in the case of any vehicle, either main beams or dipped beams.

(3) Every beam emitted by any lamp required to be carried by this Regulation shall be derived from the filament or filaments of an electric bulb or bulbs, or from the filament or filaments of a sealed beam lamp, the rating of such filament or at least one of such filaments not being less than—

(*a*) 10 watts in the case of a main or dipped beam emitted by a lamp carried by a moped with or without a side-car attached thereto which was first used before 1st January 1970 and which is so constructed as to be incapable of exceeding a speed of 25 miles per hour on the level ;

(*b*) 15 watts in the case of a main or dipped beam emitted by a lamp carried by—

(i) a moped with or without a side-car attached thereto which is first used on or after 1st January 1970 and which is so constructed as to be incapable of exceeding a speed of 25 miles per hour on the level ; or

(ii) a moped with or without a side-car attached thereto which is first used before 1st January 1972 and which is so constructed as to be capable of exceeding a speed of 25 miles per hour on the level ; or

(iii) a motor bicycle (not being a moped) with or without a side-car attached thereto, which was first used before 1st January 1970 and whereof the cylinder capacity of the engine is not more than 250 cubic centimetres ;

(*c*) 18 watts in the case of a main or dipped beam emitted by a lamp carried by—

(i) a moped with or without a side-car attached thereto which is first used on or after 1st January 1972 and which is so constructed as to be capable of exceeding a speed of 25 miles per hour on the level ; or

(ii) a motor bicycle (not being a moped) with or without a side-car attached thereto, which is first used on or after 1st January 1970, and whereof the cylinder capacity of the engine is not more than 250 cubic centimetres ;

(*d*) 24 watts in the case of a dipped beam emitted by a lamp carried by any other vehicle ; and

(*e*) 30 watts in the case of a main beam emitted by a lamp carried by any other vehicle.

(4) Where any vehicle carries a matched pair of headlamps in accordance with the requirements of this Regulation, each of the lamps in the pair shall, except in the case of lamps carried by a vehicle which is engineering plant, an industrial tractor or a motor bicycle with or without a side-car attached thereto, be so positioned on one side of the vehicle that no part of its illuminated area is less than 300 millimetres from any part of the illuminated area of the other lamp in the pair.

Headlamps to be carried by some vehicles with three wheels and by vehicles with four or more wheels

6.—(1) This Regulation applies to a motor vehicle to which these Regulations apply and which—

(*a*) has three wheels, is not a motor bicycle with a side-car attached thereto, is first used on or after 1st January 1972 and has an unladen weight of more than 400 kilogrammes or an overall width of more than 1.30 metres ; or

(*b*) has four or more wheels.

(2) Every vehicle to which this Regulation applies shall carry—

(*a*) a matched pair of headlamps, both headlamps in the pair being wired to a device the operation of which at the will of the driver can cause to be emitted from them at the same time either—

(i) in the case of any vehicle which is so constructed as to be incapable of exceeding a speed of 25 miles per hour on the level, only dipped beams ; or

(ii) in the case of any vehicle, either main beams or dipped beams ; or

(*b*) two or more matched pairs of headlamps, the headlamps being arranged so that—

(i) they form two groups of headlamps, one on each side of the vertical plane passing through the longitudinal axis of the vehicle ;

(ii) the headlamps in one of the matched pairs, which are at least as far away from the vertical plane passing through the longitudinal axis of the vehicle as any other headlamps in another matched pair of headlamps, can each emit a dipped beam without at the same time emitting a main beam, and so that every other headlamp can emit a main beam ; and

(iii) all the headlamps in both groups are wired to a device the operation of which at the will of the driver can at the same time extinguish every main beam emitted by every headlamp in both groups, and cause either to be emitted or to continue to be emitted the dipped beams from the two headlamps in the matched pair which are at least as far away from the vertical plane passing through the longitudinal axis of the vehicle as any other headlamps in another matched pair of headlamps :

Provided that in the case of a public service vehicle first used before 1st October 1969 or, until 1st April 1970, in the case of a road clearance vehicle first used before 1st January 1955 it shall be a sufficient compliance with the requirements of this paragraph if the vehicle carries a matched pair of head-lamps one of which can emit a dipped beam without either lamp at the same time emitting a main beam.

(3) Every main or dipped beam emitted by any lamp required to be carried by this Regulation shall be derived from the filament or filaments of an electric bulb or bulbs or from the filament or filaments of a sealed beam lamp the rating of such filament or at least one of such filaments not being less than 30 watts.

(4) Every headlamp which emits a dipped beam carried by a vehicle in accordance with the requirements of this Regulation shall, except in the case of a lamp carried by a vehicle which is engineering plant or an industrial tractor, be so positioned on one side of the vehicle that—

(a) no part of its illuminated area is, in the case of a vehicle first used before 1st October 1969, less than 350 millimetres, or, in the case of a vehicle first used on or after that date, less than 600 millimetres, from any part of the illuminated area of any such lamp on the other side ; and

(b) in the case of a vehicle first used on or after 1st January 1972 the outer-most part of the illuminated area of the lamp is not more than 400 milli-metres from the outermost part of the vehicle on the side on which the lamp is placed.

Single units for side and head lamps

7.—(1) In the case of a vehicle which carries one obligatory side lamp and one obligatory headlamp, such lamps may be combined so as to form a single unit.

(2) In the case of a motor bicycle with a side-car attached thereto, being a vehicle which carries two obligatory side lamps and one obligatory headlamp, one of the obligatory side lamps may be combined with the obligatory head-lamp so as to form a single unit.

(3) In the case of a vehicle which carries two obligatory side lamps they may be combined—

(a) in the case of a vehicle which has only two obligatory headlamps, with such lamps, or

(b) with the two obligatory headlamps in the matched pair which are at least as far away from the vertical plane passing through the longi-tudinal axis of the vehicle as any other obligatory headlamps in another matched pair of obligatory headlamps,

so as to form two single units each comprising an obligatory headlamp and an obligatory side lamp.

Requirements for every obligatory headlamp

8. Every obligatory headlamp carried by any vehicle shall comply with the following conditions, namely :—

(1) it shall be securely fixed to the vehicle ;

(2) it shall be so constructed and maintained that the direction of the beam of light emitted therefrom can be adjusted whilst the vehicle is stationary

so that the lamp when lit emits the type of beam which it is required to be capable of emitting by these Regulations ; and

(3) it shall be kept in a clean and efficient condition.

Requirements for every matched pair of obligatory headlamps

9. Every matched pair of obligatory headlamps carried on any vehicle to which these Regulations apply shall comply with the following conditions, namely :—

(1) both lamps in the pair shall, except in the case of lamps carried by a public service vehicle first used before 1st October 1969, have the same area and shape when illuminated ;

(2) both lamps in the pair shall, except in the case of lamps carried by a public service vehicle first used before 1st October 1969 or, until 1st April 1970, by a road clearance vehicle first used before 1st January 1955, have their wiring arranged so that—

(*a*) if they can emit either main beams or dipped beams, the beams which they can emit can only be switched on or off together ;

(*b*) if they can emit both main and dipped beams, the dipped beams can only be switched on or off together and the main beams can only be switched on or off together;

(*c*) if they can emit supplementary main beams, such beams can only be switched on or off together with the main beams emitted by another pair of obligatory headlamps ; and

(3) both lamps in the pair shall, when lit, emit beams of the same colour light.

Colour of headlamp beams

10. Every main or dipped beam emitted by any headlamp or fog lamp carried on any vehicle to which these Regulations apply shall be a beam of white or yellow light.

Requirements as to use of headlamps

11.—(1) This Regulation applies to every motor vehicle to which Regulation 6 of these Regulations applies and which has four or more wheels.

(2) This Regulation applies to every length of road, except that it does not apply to a length of road—

(*a*) on which there is provided a system of street lighting furnished by means of lamps placed not more than two hundred yards apart, and

(*b*) while such lamps are lit.

(3) When any motor vehicle to which these Regulations apply is in motion during the hours of darkness on a length of road to which this Regulation applies a matched pair of obligatory headlamps carried by the vehicle shall be kept lit :

Provided that this paragraph shall not apply—

(i) in conditions of fog or whilst snow is falling to a vehicle which carries two permitted lamps, if both such permitted lamps are kept lit ;

(ii) to a public service vehicle first used before 1st October 1969, or until 1st April 1970 to a road clearance vehicle first used before 1st January 1955, if one obligatory headlamp carried by the vehicle is kept lit, or, in conditions of fog or whilst snow is falling, and if the vehicle carries a fog lamp, if that lamp is kept lit ;

(iii) to a vehicle being drawn by another vehicle ; or

(iv) to a vehicle while being used to propel in front thereof a snow plough.

(4) In this Regulation "two permitted lamps" means two fog lamps or one fog lamp and one headlamp (not being an obligatory headlamp), being lamps which comply with the following conditions, namely :—

(a) the two lamps shall be fixed one on each side of the vertical plane passing through the longitudinal axis of the vehicle ;

(b) the centres of both lamps shall be at the same height above the ground ;

(c) the distances between the centre of each lamp and the vertical plane passing through the longitudinal axis of the vehicle shall be the same ; and

(d) each lamp shall be so positioned that—

(i) in the case of a vehicle first used before 1st January 1971 no part of the illuminated area of one lamp is less than 350 millimetres from any part of the illuminated area of the other lamp ; and

(ii) in the case of a vehicle first used on or after 1st January 1971 the outermost part of the illuminated area of either lamp is not more than 400 millimetres from the outermost part of the vehicle on the side on which the lamp is placed.

Given under the Official Seal of the Minister of Transport the 18th November 1969.

(L.S.)

Fred Mulley,
Minister of Transport.

EXPLANATORY NOTE

(This Note is not part of the Regulations.)

These Regulations consolidate with modifications the Road Vehicles (Head-lamps) Regulations 1967 and 1968 which required most vehicles with four or more wheels to carry headlamps and contained requirements as to the use of such lamps by such vehicles moving at night.

The principal changes are:—

(1) The previous requirement that most motor vehicles having four or more wheels must carry headlamps is extended to most motor vehicles having two or more wheels. These Regulations impose requirements for the headlamps now required to be carried by most motor vehicles with two or three wheels, including requirements as to their wiring, their position on the vehicle and the wattage of their bulbs or filaments, and a require-ment that every matched pair of these lamps shall emit beams of the same colour light. (Regulations 5, 6 and 9).

(2) Motor vehicles not capable of exceeding a speed of 25 miles per hour need only carry headlamps which can only emit dipped beams. (Regu-lations 5(2)(b)(i) and 6(2)(a)(i)).

(3) The previous requirement that the beam of light emitted by any head-lamp must be a beam of white or yellow light is extended to fog lamps. (Regulation 10).

STATUTORY INSTRUMENTS

1969 No. 1654

INDUSTRIAL ASSURANCE

The Industrial Assurance (Collecting Societies' Deposits) Regulations 1969

Made	- - -	24th November 1969
Laid before Parliament		3rd December 1969
Coming into Operation		5th December 1969

The Industrial Assurance Commissioner, pursuant to the powers conferred on him by section 20(1) of the Insurance Companies Act 1958(a), as amended by sections 14(3) and 17(1) of, and Schedule 1 to, the Administration of Justice Act 1965(b), as applied by section 7(1) of the Industrial Assurance Act 1923(c), as amended by section 99 of, and Part II of Schedule 6 to, the Companies Act 1967(d), and of all other powers enabling him in that behalf, hereby makes the following Regulations :—

1. These Regulations may be cited as the Industrial Assurance (Collecting Societies' Deposits) Regulations 1969 and shall come into operation on 5th December 1969.

2.—(1) In these Regulations, except where the context otherwise requires, the following expressions have the meanings hereby respectively assigned to them :—

"the Act" means the Industrial Assurance Act 1923 ;

"the Accountant General" means the Accountant General of the Supreme Court ;

"the Bank" has the meaning assigned to it by rule 3 of the Supreme Court Fund Rules 1927(e) as amended (f) ;

"the Commissioner" means the Industrial Assurance Commissioner ;

"the court" means the High Court ;

"the depositor" has the meaning assigned to it by regulation 3 of these Regulations.

"long-term investment account" and "short-term investment account" have the same meanings as in section 6(1)(a) of the Administration of Justice Act 1965 ;

"principal society" and "subsidiary society" have the meanings assigned to them by section 7(5) of the Act ;

"society" means a collecting society within the meaning of section 1(1A) of the Act.

(a) 1958 c. 72.   (b) 1965 c. 2.
(c) 1923 c. 8.   (d) 1967 c. 81.
(e) S.R. & O. 1927/1184 (1927 p. 1638).
(f) The relevant amending instrument is S.I. 1965/1608 (1965 II, p. 4621).

(2) Other words and phrases used in these Regulations shall, except where the context otherwise requires, have the meanings assigned to them in the Act.

(3) The Interpretation Act 1889(a) shall apply to the interpretation of these Regulations as it applies to the interpretation of an Act of Parliament.

3. Where a society is required to deposit with the Accountant General the sum of £20,000 in pursuance of section 7 of the Act the society, or the persons applying for the registration thereof, may apply to the Commissioner for a warrant which shall be a sufficient authority for the Accountant General to issue a directive for the payment into the Bank to the credit of his account by the society named in the warrant (hereinafter referred to as "the depositor") of the said sum of £20,000, which shall be credited in the books of the Accountant General to an account entitled ex parte the depositor, in respect of Industrial Assurance business.

Provided that in lieu, wholly or in part, of the deposit of money the depositor may deposit an equivalent amount of securities in which cash under the control of or subject to the order of the court may for the time being be invested (the value thereof being taken at a price as near as may be to, but not exceeding, the current market price) and in that case the Commissioner shall vary his warrant accordingly.

4.—(1) The court may, on the application of the depositor, make an order for dealing with any money which has been deposited in court by its placement to a short-term or long-term investment account or by its investment in any securities in which cash under the control of or subject to the order of the court may for the time being be invested, or for the variation of any existing investment by way of sale and re-investment, or otherwise, and for the payment of the interest, dividends or income accruing due on such investment.

(2) Any interest, dividend or income accruing due on money or securities deposited with the court shall, subject to any order of the court, be paid to the depositor at its request.

(3) Any money which has been deposited with the court may be placed to a short-term investment account at the request of the depositor.

5. The court may, on the application of the depositor (of which application notice shall be served on the Commissioner), in any case where it may be just and equitable to do so, and in particular where the depositor has ceased altogether to carry on industrial assurance business, order any money or securities deposited in court to be paid or transferred out of court to the depositor or otherwise as the court may direct.

6. A company into which the depositor has converted itself under section 71 of the Friendly Societies Act 1896(b), or a society with which the depositor has amalgamated, or a society or company to which the depositor has transferred its engagements under section 70 of that Act as modified by section 36 of the Act, may apply in writing to the Commissioner for a certificate under the following regulation.

7. If on an application under the preceding regulation the Commissioner is satisfied that by reason of the conversion, amalgamation or transfer of engagements as the case may be the depositor has ceased altogether to carry on industrial assurance business he shall send to the Accountant General a certificate in the form set out in the Schedule hereto and shall notify the applicant accordingly ; and on receipt of such notification the applicant may apply in

---

(a) 1889 c. 63.   (b) 1896 c. 25.

writing to the Accountant General for the money or securities standing to the credit of the depositor to be paid out or transferred in accordance with the certificate, which certificate shall be sufficient authority for the Accountant General to make such payment out or transfer.

8. Where a deposit is made under section 7(5) of the Act by a principal society.

> (*a*) the application to the Commissioner for his warrant and any application to the court under these Regulations may be made by the principal society ;
>
> (*b*) the Commissioner's warrant shall state that the principal society is authorised to make the deposit on behalf of the subsidiary society and the Accountant General shall so record it in his books ;
>
> (*c*) interest, dividends or income from time to time accruing on the deposit, whether made under these or any preceding Rules or Regulations, shall be paid to the principal society and not to the subsidiary society.

9. Regulations 4 to 7 of these Regulations and, subject to regulations 3 to 8 of these Regulations, the relevant provisions of the Rules for the time being in force under section 7 of the Administration of Justice Act 1965 (Rules as to funds in Supreme Court), shall apply to deposits made in pursuance of section 7 of the Act whether under these or any preceding Rules or Regulations.

10. The Industrial Assurance (Deposits etc.) Rules 1950(**a**) are hereby revoked.

S. D. Musson,
Industrial Assurance Commissioner.
24th November 1969.

SCHEDULE

Certificate under regulation 7 of the Industrial Assurance
(Collecting Societies' Deposits) Regulations 1969

Name of Society :

I hereby certify that on................a special resolution was registered for

> (i) conversion of the above-named society into a company ; *or*
>
> (ii) amalgamation of the above-named society with the................
>
> ...., *or*
>
> (iii) transfer of the engagements of the above-named society to the......
>
> ....society/company,

and as I am satisfied that by reason thereof the society has ceased altogether to carry on industrial assurance business and is no longer required to keep a deposit in court, I hereby authorise the payment out/transfer of the money/securities deposited in court and standing to its credit to the (name of company) *or* to the (name of society).

Industrial Assurance Commissioner

(**a**) S.I. 1950/1544 (1950 I, p. 1102).

EXPLANATORY NOTE

(This Note is not part of the Regulations.)

These Regulations prescribe the manner in which collecting societies may make the deposit required by section 7 of the Industrial Assurance Act 1923 and provide for the investment and withdrawal of such deposits. They supersede the Industrial Assurance (Deposits etc.) Rules 1950 (S.I. 1950/1544).

STATUTORY INSTRUMENTS

1969 No. 1658

CUSTOMS AND EXCISE

The Import Duty Drawbacks (No. 2) Order 1969

Made - - - -	24*th November* 1969
Laid before the House of Commons - - -	28*th November* 1969
Coming into operation -	4*th December* 1969

The Lords Commissioners of Her Majesty's Treasury, by virtue of the powers conferred on them by sections 9 and 13 of, and Schedule 5 to, the Import Duties Act 1958(a), and of all other powers enabling them in that behalf, on the recommendation of the Board of Trade hereby make the following Order:—

1.—(1) This Order may be cited as the Import Duty Drawbacks (No. 2) Order 1969.

(2) The Interpretation Act 1889(b) shall apply for the interpretation of this Order as it applies for the interpretation of an Act of Parliament.

(3) This Order shall come into operation on 4th December 1969.

2. In Schedule 1 to the Import Duty Drawbacks (No. 10) Order 1968(c) (which relates to the drawbacks to be allowed on the exportation of imported articles or goods incorporating them), the entry relating to heading 09.02 of the Customs Tariff 1959 (tea) shall be omitted.

3. In Schedule 2 to the said Order of 1968 (which relates to the drawbacks to be allowed on the exportation of goods produced or manufactured from imported articles), in column 3 of the entry relating to shuttlecocks and shuttlecock skirts, for " 0·021d. per gramme " there shall be substituted " 0·0252d. per gramme ".

Joseph Harper,
Walter Harrison,
Two of the Lords Commissioners
of Her Majesty's Treasury

28*th November* 1969

EXPLANATORY NOTE

(*This Note is not part of the Order.*)

This Order—

(1) revokes the provisions for the allowance of drawback of import duty on tea; and

(2) increases the rate of drawback of import duty on shuttlecocks and shuttlecock skirts manufactured from imported poly (11-aminoundecanoic acid) granules.

(a) 1958 c. 6.   (b) 1889 c. 63.   (c) S.I. 1968/1881 (1968 III p. 4969).

STATUTORY INSTRUMENTS

1969 No. 1659

INDUSTRIAL TRAINING

The Industrial Training Levy (Footwear, Leather and Fur Skin) Order 1969

Made - - -		*24th November* 1969
Laid before Parliament		*3rd December* 1969
Coming into Operation		*17th December* 1969

The Secretary of State after approving proposals submitted by the Footwear, Leather and Fur Skin Industry Training Board for the imposition of a levy on employers in the footwear, leather and fur skin industry and in exercise of her powers under section 4 of the Industrial Training Act 1964(a) and of all other powers enabling her in that behalf hereby makes the following Order :—

Title and commencement

1. This Order may be cited as the Industrial Training Levy (Footwear, Leather and Fur Skin) Order 1969 and shall come into operation on 17th December 1969.

Interpretation

2.—(1) In this Order unless the context otherwise requires :—

(a) "an appeal tribunal" means an industrial tribunal established under section 12 of the Industrial Training Act 1964 ;

(b) "assessment" means an assessment of an employer to the levy ;

(c) "the Board" means the Footwear, Leather and Fur Skin Industry Training Board ;

(d) "business" means any activities of industry or commerce ;

(e) "emoluments" means all emoluments assessable to income tax under Schedule E (other than pensions), being emoluments from which tax under that Schedule is deductible, whether or not tax in fact falls to be deducted from any particular payment thereof ;

(f) "employer" means a person who is an employer in the footwear, leather and fur skin industry at any time in the first levy period ;

(g) "the first base period" means the period of twelve months that commenced on 6th April 1968 ;

(h) "the first levy period" means the period commencing with the day upon which this Order comes into operation and ending on 5th April 1971 ;

(a) 1964 c. 16.

(*i*) "footwear, leather and fur skin establishment" means an establishment in Great Britain engaged in the first base period wholly or mainly in the footwear, leather and fur skin industry for a total of twenty-seven or more weeks or, being an establishment that commenced to carry on business in the first base period, for a total number of weeks exceeding one half of the number of weeks in the part of the said period commencing with the day on which business was commenced and ending on the last day thereof ;

(*j*) "footwear, leather and fur skin industry" means any one or more of the activities which, subject to the provisions of paragraph 2 of Schedule 1 to the industrial training order, are specified in paragraph 1 of that Schedule as the activities of the footwear, leather and fur skin industry ;

(*k*) "the industrial training order" means the Industrial Training (Footwear, Leather and Fur Skin Board) Order 1968(**a**) ;

(*l*) "the levy" means the levy imposed by the Board in respect of the first levy period ;

(*m*) "notice" means a notice in writing.

(2) In the case where a footwear, leather and fur skin establishment is taken over (whether directly or indirectly) by an employer in succession to, or jointly with, another person, a person employed at any time in the first base period at or from the establishment shall be deemed, for the purposes of this Order, to have been so employed by the employer carrying on the said establishment on the day upon which this Order comes into operation, and any reference in this Order to persons employed by the employer at or from a footwear, leather and fur skin establishment in the first base period shall be construed accordingly.

(3) Any reference in this Order to an establishment that commences to carry on business or that ceases to carry on business shall not be taken to apply where the location of the establishment is changed but its business is continued wholly or mainly at or from the new location, or where the suspension of activities is of a temporary or seasonal nature.

(4) The Interpretation Act 1889(**b**) shall apply to the interpretation of this Order as it applies to the interpretation of an Act of Parliament.

Imposition of the Levy

3.—(1) The levy to be imposed by the Board on employers in respect of the first levy period shall be assessed in accordance with the provisions of this Article.

(2) Subject to the provisions of this Article, the levy shall be assessed by the Board in respect of each employer and the amount thereof shall be equal to 0.175 per cent. of the sum (less £1,000) of the emoluments of all the persons employed by the employer at or from the footwear, leather and fur skin establishment or establishments of the employer in the first base period.

(3) Where the sum of the emoluments of the persons mentioned in the last foregoing paragraph is less than £1,000 the employer shall be exempt from the levy.

(4) Where any persons whose emoluments are taken into account for the purposes of this Article were employed at or from an establishment that ceases to carry on business in the first levy period, the sum of the emolu-

---

(**a**) S.I. 1968/1763 (1968 III, p. 4785).   (**b**) 1889 c. 63.

ments of those persons shall be reduced in the same proportion as the number of days between the commencement of the said levy period and the date of cessation of business (both dates inclusive) bears to the number of days in the said levy period.

(5) For the purposes of this Article no regard shall be had to the emoluments of a person engaged wholly in the supply of food or drink for immediate consumption.

Assessment Notices

4.—(1) The Board shall serve an assessment notice on every employer assessed to the levy.

(2) The amount of an assessment shall be rounded down to the nearest £1.

(3) An assessment notice shall state the Board's address for the service of a notice of appeal or of an application for an extension of time for appealing.

(4) An assessment notice may be served on the person assessed to the levy either by delivering it to him personally or by leaving it, or sending it to him by post, at his last known address or place of business in the United Kingdom or, if that person is a corporation, by leaving it, or sending it by post to the corporation, at such address or place of business or at its registered or principal office.

Payment of the Levy

5.—(1) Subject to the provisions of this Article and of Articles 6 and 7, the amount of the levy payable under an assessment notice served by the Board shall be due and payable to the Board one month after the date of the notice.

(2) The amount of an assessment shall not be recoverable by the Board until there has expired the time allowed for appealing against the assessment by Article 7(1) of this Order and any further period or periods of time that the Board or an appeal tribunal may have allowed for appealing under paragraph (2) or (3) of that Article or, where an appeal is brought, until the appeal is decided or withdrawn.

Withdrawal of Assessment

6.—(1) The Board may, by a notice served on the person assessed to the levy in the same manner as an assessment notice. withdraw an assessment if that person has appealed against that assessment under the provisions of Article 7 of this Order and the appeal has not been entered in the Register of Appeals kept under the appropriate Regulations specified in paragraph (5) of that Article.

(2) The withdrawal of an assessment shall be without prejudice to the power of the Board to serve a further assessment notice on the employer.

Appeals

7.—(1) A person assessed to the levy may appeal to an appeal tribunal against the assessment within one month from the date of the service of the assessment notice or within any further period or periods of time that may be allowed by the Board or an appeal tribunal under the following provisions of this Article.

(2) The Board by notice may for good cause allow a person assessed to the levy to appeal to an appeal tribunal against the assessment at any time within the period of four months from the date of the service of the assess-

ment notice or within such further period or periods as the Board may allow before such time as may then be limited for appealing has expired.

(3) If the Board shall not allow an application for extension of time for appealing, an appeal tribunal shall upon application made to the tribunal by the person assessed to the levy have the like powers as the Board under the last foregoing paragraph.

(4) In the case of an assessment that has reference to an establishment that ceases to carry on business in the first levy period on any day after the date of the service of the assessment notice the foregoing provisions of this Article shall have effect as if for the period of four months from the date of the service of the assessment notice mentioned in paragraph (2) of this Article there were substituted the period of six months from the date of the cessation of business.

(5) An appeal or an application to an appeal tribunal under this Article shall be made in accordance with the Industrial Tribunals (England and Wales) Regulations 1965(a) as amended by the Industrial Tribunals (England and Wales) (Amendment) Regulations 1967(b), except where the assessment relates to persons employed at or from an establishment which is wholly in Scotland and to no other persons, in which case the appeal or application shall be made in accordance with the Industrial Tribunals (Scotland) Regulations 1965(c) as amended by the Industrial Tribunals (Scotland) (Amendment) Regulations 1967(d).

(6) The powers of an appeal tribunal under paragraph (3) of this Article may be exercised by the President of the Industrial Tribunals (England and Wales) or by the President of the Industrial Tribunals (Scotland) as the case may be.

Evidence

8.—(1) Upon the discharge by a person assessed to the levy of his liability under an assessment the Board shall if so requested issue to him a certificate to that effect.

(2) The production in any proceedings of a document purporting to be certified by the Secretary of the Board to be a true copy of an assessment or other notice issued by the Board or purporting to be a certificate such as is mentioned in the foregoing paragraph of this Article shall, unless the contrary is proved, be sufficient evidence of the document and of the facts stated therein.

24th November 1969.

Barbara Castle,

First Secretary of State and Secretary of State for Employment and Productivity.

(a) S.I. 1965/1101 (1965 II, p. 2805).   (b) S.I. 1967/301 (1967 I, p. 1040).
(c) S.I. 1965/1157 (1965 II, p. 3266).   (d) S.I. 1967/302 (1967 I, p. 1050).

EXPLANATORY NOTE

(This Note is not part of the Order.)

This Order gives effect to proposals submitted by the Footwear, Leather and Fur Skin Industry Training Board to the Secretary of State for Employment and Productivity for the imposition of a levy upon employers in the footwear, leather and fur skin industry for the purpose of raising money towards the expenses of the Board.

The levy is to be imposed in respect of the first levy period commencing on the day upon which this Order comes into operation and ending on 5th April 1971. The levy will be assessed by the Board and there will be a right of appeal against an assessment to an industrial tribunal.

STATUTORY INSTRUMENTS

1969 No. 1664

SUGAR

The Sugar (Rates of Surcharge and Surcharge Repayments) (No. 13) Order 1969

Made - - - -	*25th November* 1969
Laid before Parliament	*27th November* 1969
Coming into Operation	*28th November* 1969

The Minister of Agriculture, Fisheries and Food, in exercise of the powers conferred on him by sections 7(4), 8(6) and 33(4) of the Sugar Act 1956(a) having effect subject to the provisions of section 3 of, and Part II of Schedule 5 to, the Finance Act 1962(b), and section 58 of the Finance Act 1968(c) and of all other powers enabling him in that behalf, with the concurrence of the Treasury, on the advice of the Sugar Board, hereby makes the following order:—

1.—(1) This order may be cited as the Sugar (Rates of Surcharge and Surcharge Repayments) (No. 13) Order 1969; and shall come into operation on 28th November 1969.

(2) The Interpretation Act 1889(d) shall apply for the interpretation of this order as it applies for the interpretation of an Act of Parliament.

2. Notwithstanding the provisions of Article 2 of the Sugar (Rates of Surcharge and Surcharge Repayments) (No. 12) Order 1969(e), the rates of surcharge payable under and in accordance with the provisions of section 7 of the Sugar Act 1956, having effect as aforesaid, in respect of sugar and invert sugar imported or home produced or used in the manufacture of imported composite sugar products shall on and after 28th November 1969 be those rates specified in Schedule 1 to this order.

3. For the purpose of section 8(3)(b) of the Sugar Act 1956, having effect as aforesaid, the rates of surcharge repayments in respect of invert sugar produced in the United Kingdom from materials on which on or after 28th November 1969 sugar duty has been paid or, by virtue of paragraph 1 of Part II of Schedule 5 to the Finance Act 1962, is treated as having been paid shall, notwithstanding the provisions of Article 3 of the Sugar (Rates of Surcharge and Surcharge Repayments) (No. 12) Order 1969 be those specified in Schedule 2 to this order.

(a) 1956 c. 48.   (b) 1962 c. 44.
(c) 1968 c. 44.   (d) 1889 c. 63.
(e) S.I. 1969/1527 (1969 III, p. 4953).

In Witness whereof the Official Seal of the Minister of Agriculture, Fisheries and Food is hereunto affixed on 25th November 1969.

(L.S.)   *R. P. Fraser,*

Authorised by the Minister.

We concur.

25th November 1969.

Walter Harrison,

Ernest Armstrong,

Two of the Lords Commissioners of
Her Majesty's Treasury.

SCHEDULE 1

PART I

SURCHARGE RATES FOR SUGAR

Polarisation										Rate of Surcharge per cwt.	
										s.	d.
Exceeding—											
99°	...	...	...	...	...	...	...	...	...	23	4·0
98° but not exceeding 99°	...	...	...	...	...	...	...	22	0·0		
97°	,,	,,	,,	98°	...	...	...	...	...	21	5·6
96°	,,	,,	,,	97°	...	...	...	...	...	20	10·8
95°	,,	,,	,,	96°	...	...	...	...	...	20	4·1
94°	,,	,,	,,	95°	...	...	...	...	...	19	9·4
93°	,,	,,	,,	94°	...	...	...	...	...	19	2·7
92°	,,	,,	,,	93°	...	...	...	...	...	18	8·0
91°	,,	,,	,,	92°	...	...	...	...	...	18	1·2
90°	,,	,,	,,	91°	...	...	...	...	...	17	6·5
89°	,,	,,	,,	90°	...	...	...	...	...	16	11·8
88°	,,	,,	,,	89°	...	...	...	...	...	16	5·1
87°	,,	,,	,,	88°	...	...	...	...	...	15	11·5
86°	,,	,,	,,	87°	...	...	...	...	...	15	5·9
85°	,,	:,	,,	86°	...	...	...	...	...	15	0·8
84°	,,	,,	,,	85°	...	...	...	...	...	14	7·8
83°	,,	,,	,,	84°	...	...	...	...	...	14	2·8
82°	,,	,,	,,	83°	...	...	...	...	...	13	9·7
81°	,,	,,	,,	82°	...	...	...	...	...	13	5·2
80°	,,	,,	,,	81°	...	...	...	...	...	13	0·8
79°	,,	,,	,,	80°	...	...	...	...	...	12	8·3
78°	,,	,,	,,	79°	...	...	...	...	...	12	3·8
77°	,,	,,	,,	78°	...	...	...	...	...	11	11·3
76°	,,	,,	,,	77°	...	...	...	...	...	11	6·8
Not exceeding 76°	...	...	...	...	...	...	...	...	11	3·0

PART II
SURCHARGE RATES FOR INVERT SUGAR

Sweetening matter content by weight	Rate of Surcharge per cwt.
	s. d.
70 per cent. or more	14 10
Less than 70 per cent. and more than 50 per cent.	10 8
Not more than 50 per cent.	5 2

SCHEDULE 2
SURCHARGE REPAYMENT RATES FOR INVERT SUGAR

Sweetening matter content by weight	Rate of Surcharge Repayment per cwt.
	s. d.
More than 80 per cent.	17 6
More than 70 per cent. but not more than 80 per cent.	14 10
More than 60 per cent. but not more than 70 per cent.	10 8
More than 50 per cent. but not more than 60 per cent.	8 5
Not more than 50 per cent. and the invert sugar not being less in weight than 14 lb. per gallon	5 2

EXPLANATORY NOTE
(This Note is not part of the Order.)

This order prescribes—

(a) increases equivalent to 2s. 4d. per cwt. of refined sugar in the rates of surcharge payable on sugar and invert sugar which become chargeable with surcharge on or after 28th November 1969;

(b) correspondingly increased rates of surcharge repayment in respect of invert sugar produced in the United Kingdom from materials on which surcharge has been paid.

STATUTORY INSTRUMENTS

1969 No. 1665

SUGAR

The Composite Sugar Products (Surcharge and Surcharge Repayments—Average Rates) (No. 13) Order 1969

Made - - - - -	*25th November* 1969
Laid before Parliament	*27th November* 1969
Coming into Operation	*28th November* 1969

Whereas the Minister of Agriculture, Fisheries and Food (hereinafter called " the Minister ") has on the recommendation of the Commissioners of Customs and Excise (hereinafter called " the Commissioners ") made an order(a) pursuant to the powers conferred upon him by sections 9(1) and 9(4) of the Sugar Act 1956(b), having effect subject to the provisions of section 3 of, and Part II of Schedule 5 to, the Finance Act 1962(c), to the provisions of section 52(2) of the Finance Act 1966(d), and to the provisions of Section 58 of the Finance Act 1968(e), providing that in the case of certain descriptions of composite sugar products surcharge shall be calculated on the basis of an average quantity of sugar or invert sugar taken to have been used in the manufacture of the products, and that certain other descriptions of composite sugar products shall be treated as not containing any sugar or invert sugar, and that in the case of certain descriptions of goods in the manufacture of which sugar or invert sugar is used, surcharge repayments shall be calculated on the basis of an average quantity of sugar or invert sugar taken to have been so used:

Now, therefore, the Minister, on the recommendation of the Commissioners and in exercise of the powers conferred upon him by sections 9(1), 9(4) and 33(4) of the Sugar Act 1956, having effect as aforesaid, and of all other powers enabling him in that behalf, hereby makes the following order:—

1.—(1) This order may be cited as the Composite Sugar Products (Surcharge and Surcharge Repayments—Average Rates) (No. 13) Order 1969; and shall come into operation on 28th November 1969.

(2) The Interpretation Act 1889(f) shall apply for the interpretation of this order as it applies for the interpretation of an Act of Parliament.

2. Surcharge payable on or after 28th November 1969 under and in accordance with the Sugar Act 1956, having effect as aforesaid, in respect of sugar and invert sugar used in the manufacture of the descriptions of imported composite sugar products specified in column 2 of Schedule 1 to this order shall, notwithstanding the provisions of the Sugar (Rates of Surcharge and Surcharge Repayments) (No. 13) Order 1969(g) and the Composite Sugar Products (Surcharge and Surcharge Repayments—Average Rates) (No. 12) Order 1969(a), be calculated by reference to the weight or value, as the case may be, of the products at the rates specified in relation thereto in column 3 of the said Schedule.

(a) S.I. 1969/1528 (1969 III, p. 4956).   (b) 1956 c. 48.   (c) 1962 c. 44.
(d) 1966 c. 18.   (e) 1968 c. 44.   (f) 1889 c. 63.
(g) S.I. 1969/1664 (1969 III, p. 5210).

3. Imported composite sugar products other than those of a description specified in Schedules 1 and 2 to this order shall be treated as not containing any sugar or invert sugar for the purposes of surcharge payable on or after 28th November 1969.

4. Surcharge repayments payable on and after 28th November 1969 under and in accordance with the provisions of section 8 of the Sugar Act 1956, having effect as aforesaid, in respect of sugar and invert sugar used in the manufacture of the descriptions of goods specified in column 1 of Schedule 3 to this order shall, notwithstanding the provisions of the Sugar (Rates of Surcharge and Surcharge Repayments) (No. 13) Order 1969(a) and the Composite Sugar Products (Surcharge and Surcharge Repayments—Average Rates) (No. 12) Order 1969(b), be calculated by reference to the quantity of the goods at the rates specified in relation thereto in column 2 of the said Schedule.

In Witness whereof the Official Seal of the Minister of Agriculture, Fisheries and Food is hereunto affixed on 25th November 1969.

(L.S.)

R. P. Fraser,
Authorised by the Minister.

SCHEDULE 1

In this Schedule:—

" Tariff heading " means a heading or, where the context so requires, a subheading of the Customs Tariff 1959 (see paragraph (1) of Article 1 of the Import Duties (General) (No. 4) Order 1968(c)).

" Per cent." means, where it occurs in relation to any rate of surcharge, per cent. of the value for customs duty purposes of the product to which it relates.

Tariff heading	Description of Imported Composite Sugar Products	Rate of Surcharge
		per cwt. s. d.
04.02	Milk and cream, preserved, concentrated or sweetened, containing more than 10 per cent. by weight of added sweetening matter	10 4
17.02 (B) (2) and 17.05 (B)	Syrups containing sucrose sugar, whether or not flavoured or coloured, but not including fruit juices containing added sugar in any proportion:—	
	containing 70 per cent. or more by weight of sweetening matter	14 10
	containing less than 70 per cent., and more than 50 per cent., by weight of sweetening matter...	10 8
	containing not more than 50 per cent. by weight of sweetening matter	5 2

(a) S.I. 1969/1664 (1969 III, p. 5210). (b) S.I. 1969/1528 (1969 III, p. 4956).
(c) S.I. 1968/679 (1968 I, p. 1519).

Tariff heading	Description of Imported Composite Sugar Products	Rate of Surcharge
		per cwt. s. d.
17.02 (F) ...	Caramel:—	
	Solid	23 4
	Liquid	16 4
17.04	Sugar confectionery, not containing cocoa	19 0
18.06	Chocolate and other food preparations containing cocoa:—	
	Chocolate couverture not prepared for retail sale; chocolate milk crumb, liquid	10 4
	Chocolate milk crumb, solid	12 9
	Solid chocolate bars or blocks, milk or plain, with or without fruit or nuts; other chocolate confectionery consisting wholly of chocolate or of chocolate and other ingredients not containing added sugar, but not including such goods when packed together in retail packages with goods liable to surcharge at a higher rate	10 6
	Other	13 6
		per cent.
19.08	Pastry, biscuits, cakes and other fine bakers' wares containing added sweetening matter:—	
	Biscuits	5
	Other	3
20.01	Vegetables and fruit, prepared or preserved by vinegar or acetic acid, containing added sweetening matter	7
20.03	Fruit preserved by freezing, containing added sugar	2½
		per cwt. s. d.
20.04	Fruit, fruit-peel and parts of plants, preserved by sugar (drained, glacé or crystallised)	15 4
20.05	Jams, fruit jellies, marmalades, fruit purée and fruit pastes, being cooked preparations, containing added sweetening matter	14 8
		per cent.
20.06	Fruit otherwise prepared or preserved, containing added sweetening matter:—	
	Ginger	10
	Other	2½

SCHEDULE 2

Tariff heading	Description of Imported Composite Sugar Products
17.05 (A) and (B)	Sugar and invert sugar, flavoured or coloured.

SCHEDULE 3

Description of goods	Rate of surcharge repayment per bulk barrel of 36 gallons
Lager	11·7d.
All beer other than lager	10·4d.

EXPLANATORY NOTE

(*This Note is not part of the Order.*)

This order provides for increases on and after 28th November 1969 in the average rates of surcharge payable on imported composite sugar products of the descriptions specified in Schedule 1 and in the average rates of surcharge repayment in respect of exported goods of the descriptions specified in Schedule 3. These correspond to the increases in surcharge rates effected by the Sugar (Rates of Surcharge and Surcharge Repayments) (No. 13) Order 1969 (S.I. 1969/1664). Provision is also made for certain imported composite sugar products to be treated as not containing any sugar or invert sugar.

STATUTORY INSTRUMENTS

1969 No. 1674

NURSES AND MIDWIVES

The Enrolled Nurses Rules, Approval Instrument 1969

Made - - -	26th *November* 1969
Laid before Parliament	9th *December* 1969
Coming into Operation	12th *December* 1969

The Secretary of State for Social Services, in exercise of his powers under section 32 of the Nurses Act 1957(**a**), and of all other powers enabling him in that behalf, hereby approves the rules made by the General Nursing Council for England and Wales as set out in the Schedule hereto.

This instrument may be cited as the Enrolled Nurses Rules, Approval Instrument 1969, and shall come into operation on 12th December 1969.

SCHEDULE

THE GENERAL NURSING COUNCIL FOR ENGLAND AND WALES

The Nurses Acts 1957 to 1969

The General Nursing Council for England and Wales, in exercise of the powers conferred on them by the following sections of the Nurses Act 1957, namely, section 2(1) (as substituted by section 1(1) of the Nurses Act 1969(**b**)), section 3 (as amended by section 14 of, and paragraph 7 of Schedule 1 to, the Nurses (Amendment) Act 1961(**c**), and as extended by section 1 of the Nurses Act 1964(**d**), and section 7(1) of the Nurses Act 1969) and sections 7, 10, 30 and 32, and of all other powers enabling them in that behalf, hereby make the following rules:—

PART I

Citation and interpretation

1. These Rules may be cited as the Enrolled Nurses Rules 1969.

2.—(1) In these Rules, unless the context otherwise requires, the following expressions have the meaning hereby respectively assigned to them:—

"the Act of 1957" means the Nurses Act 1957;

"the Act of 1969" means the Nurses Act 1969;

"approved training institution" means an institution approved by the Council for the purpose of these Rules as a training school or as part of a training school for admission to the roll;

(a) 1957 c. 15.	(b) 1969 c. 47.
(c) 1961 c. 14.	(d) 1964 c. 44.

"the Council" means the General Nursing Council for England and Wales;

"the Education Committee" means the Standing Education Committee of the Council;

"enrolled general nurse" means a nurse who is enrolled in the general part of the roll;

"enrolled mental nurse" means a nurse who is enrolled in the part of the roll containing the names of nurses trained in the nursing and care of persons suffering from mental disorder other than severe subnormality or subnormality;

"enrolled nurse" means a nurse whose name is on the roll;

"enrolled nurse for the mentally subnormal" means a nurse who is enrolled in the part of the roll containing the names of nurses trained in the nursing and care of persons suffering from severe subnormality or subnormality;

"experience under supervision" means practical experience in the nursing of the sick acquired under the supervision of registered nurses in an approved training institution;

"introductory training course" means a course of training carried out in an approved training institution for the purpose of introducing a pupil nurse to the subjects included in her training for a part of the roll prior to her training in wards or departments.

"person qualified in ophthalmic nursing" means a person who is qualified (except for the qualification of registration by the Council) to receive the diploma of ophthalmic nursing of the Ophthalmic Nursing Board by virtue of ophthalmic nursing training;

"person qualified in orthopaedic nursing" means a person who is qualified (except for the qualification of registration by the Council) to receive the orthopaedic nursing certificate of the British Orthopaedic Association and the Central Council for the Care of the Disabled; or the orthopaedic nursing diploma of the Joint Examination Board of those bodies based on orthopaedic training commenced on or after 1st September 1969;

"person qualified in thoracic nursing" means a person who holds the thoracic nursing certificate of the British Tuberculosis Association;

"pupil nurse" means a person who is for the time being undergoing training for admission to any part of the roll, prior to passing the examination prescribed by these Rules;

"the register" means the register of nurses maintained by the Council;

"registered mental nurse" means a nurse who is registered in the part of the register containing the names of nurses trained in the nursing and care of persons suffering from mental disorder, other than severe subnormality or subnormality;

"registered nurse for the mentally subnormal" means a nurse who is registered in the part of the register containing the names of nurses trained in the nursing and care of persons suffering from severe subnormality or subnormality;

"the Registrar" means the person for the time being appointed to act as Registrar of the Council under paragraph 12 of Schedule 1 to the Act of 1957, and includes any person duly authorised to act and acting on her behalf;

"the Registration and Enrolment Committee" means the Standing Registration and Enrolment Committee of the Council;

"the roll" means the roll of nurses maintained by the Council;

"student nurse" means a person who is for the time being undergoing training for admission to any part of the register;

"training" means training in an approved training institution and in the case of training in a part of a training school in accordance with a scheme of training approved by the Council; and in accordance with a syllabus contained in Schedule 2 to these Rules;

"training for the register" means training for admission to the register in a training institution approved by the Council under rule 5 of the Nurses Rules 1969(a) and any reference to training for a particular part of the register is a reference to training in accordance with the syllabus of training prescribed in Schedules 3 and 4 to those rules for the examinations qualifying a person to be admitted to that part of the register.

(2) The Interpretation Act 1889(b), applies to the interpretation of these Rules as it applies to the interpretation of an Act of Parliament, and in these Rules words importing the feminine gender include the masculine, unless the contrary intention appears.

3. The Enrolled Nurses Rules 1961(c), except Part V of those Rules, and The Enrolled Nurses (Amendment) Rules 1964(d) and The Enrolled Nurses (Amendment) Rules 1966(e), are hereby revoked and Part V of the Enrolled Nurses Rules 1961 shall be revoked on 22nd September 1970:

Provided that—

(a) such revocation shall not affect any right, privilege, obligation or liability acquired, accrued, or incurred, or anything duly done or suffered under those Rules; and

(b) such revocation shall not affect any application, appointment, certificate, decision, inquiry or notice made, prepared, issued or given under the rules so revoked, and every such application, appointment, certificate, decision, inquiry or notice shall, so far as it could have been made, prepared, issued or given under these Rules have effect as if it had been so made, prepared, issued or given;

(c) such revocation shall not affect proceedings for the removal of the name of a nurse from the roll where judgment has been postponed and such proceedings shall be resumed under the provisions of these Rules.

PART II

Formation and maintenance of the roll

4.—(1) The roll shall contain the particulars set forth in Schedule 1 to these Rules.

(2) Each person admitted to the roll shall be assigned an enrolment number in the part or parts of the roll in which her name is included.

(3) An enrolled nurse shall notify to the Registrar every permanent change of address, and for the purpose of these Rules the address last so notified shall be deemed to be her registered address.

(4) An enrolled nurse shall notify to the Registrar a change of her surname whether occasioned by marriage or otherwise.

(5) It shall be the duty of the Council to cause to be removed from the roll any entry which has been incorrectly made.

(a) Scheduled to S.I. 1969/1675. (b) 1889 c. 63.
(c) Scheduled to S.I. 1961/1519 (1961 II, p. 3105).
(d) Scheduled to S.I. 1964/1851 (1964 III, p. 4034).
(e) Scheduled to S.I. 1966/545 (1966 II, p. 1122).

PART III

Approval of training institutions

5.—(1) For the purposes of section 3(1)(*b*) of the Act of 1957, an institution shall be approved by the Council either—

 (*a*) as a training school capable of providing a complete training qualifying for admission to the roll; or

 (*b*) as a part of a training school comprising two or more parts capable of providing in association under a scheme of training such complete training as aforesaid; and in approving a training institution to take part in a scheme of training provided by a group of such institutions, the Council shall direct what proportion of the training period shall be spent in each of the participating institutions. The Council may, if they think fit, approve the same institution both as a training school and as a part of a training school for admission to the roll.

(2) The Council shall prepare and keep lists of institutions which are for the time being approved by the Council as training schools under the following headings:—

training schools for enrolled general nurses.

training schools for enrolled mental nurses.

training schools for enrolled nurses for the mentally subnormal.

(3) The Council shall also prepare and keep lists of the institutions for the time being approved by the Council as parts of training schools, and such lists shall be kept so far as necessary under headings corresponding to those relating to training schools.

(4) Subject to paragraph (5) of this rule, in respect of every institution, other than an institution vested in the Secretary of State for Social Services or the Secretary of State for Wales, for which application is made to the Council for approval under paragraph (1) of this rule, there shall be paid to the Council by the persons responsible for its management, the following fees:—

 (*a*) in all cases on the making of the application, a fee of £5 5s. 0d. which shall be retained by the Council whether or not approval of the institution is granted;

 (*b*) in the case of institutions at which pupil nurses may spend more than 26 weeks of their training, an additional fee of £5 5s. 0d. in respect of the first year, which fee shall be payable on receipt of notice of approval, and an annual fee of £10 10s. 0d. in respect of each subsequent year during which the approval of the Council is continued, which fee shall be payable at the commencement of such year;

 (*c*) in the case of institutions at which pupil nurses may spend not more than 26 weeks of their training, an annual fee of £5 5s. 0d. in respect of each year after the first year during which the approval of the Council is continued, which fee shall be payable at the commencement of such year.

(5) Where an institution, other than an institution vested in the Secretary of State for Social Services or the Secretary of State for Wales was approved by the Council prior to 1st May 1950, there shall be paid to the Council by the persons responsible for its management on each anniversary of the date of such approval, in respect of the ensuing year, during the period in which approval is continued, a fee of:—

(a) £10 10s. 0d. where the institution is one at which pupil nurses may spend more than 26 weeks of their training, or

(b) £5 5s. 0d. where the institution is one at which pupil nurses may spend not more than 26 weeks of their training.

PART IV

Training and examination

6. The training for a person training for the roll shall be training in accordance with this part of these Rules.

7. A person shall enter an introductory training course at an approved training school provided that she has attained the age of 18 years or will have attained that age by the last day of a period of 30 days beginning with the day she entered the course.

8. Within 30 days of commencement of training for the roll a pupil nurse, other than a pupil nurse who has discontinued training as a student nurse or a pupil nurse who is already enrolled in a part of the roll, shall send to the Council such fee as is for the time being determined by the Council with the approval of the Secretary of State for Social Services under section 3(1) of the Act of 1957, as amended by section 7 of the Act of 1969.

9.—(1) Where an applicant has been admitted to an approved training institution as a pupil nurse, the institution shall submit to the Council within 30 days of the commencement of her training, or in the case of a person who is entitled under these Rules to enter for the examination for the roll by virtue of training for the register, before her name is entered for the examination, the following particulars: her full name, evidence of age, the date of commencement of training or other particulars of her training for the register as appropriate and any other particulars which the Council may reasonably require.

(2) If a pupil nurse for any reason discontinues her training, the approved training institution concerned shall report the fact to the Council; and if she has at the time of such discontinuance completed not less than 26 weeks training, the institution shall send the Council a statement showing the training undergone by her.

10. The Council shall keep an index of pupil nurses and shall, on being satisfied that a pupil nurse has been admitted to an introductory training course in accordance with the provisions of rule 7 of these Rules and upon receipt of the fee required by rule 8 of these Rules, include her name in the index of pupil nurses.

11.—(1) Subject to rule 12 of these Rules, the training required for persons for the general part of the roll shall be that provided in paragraph (2) or paragraph (3) of this rule.

(2) A person—

(a) must have completed not less than 104 weeks training in accordance with the syllabus of training prescribed in Part 1 of Schedule 2 to these Rules in an approved training institution for enrolled general nurses; and

(b) except for a person who has completed not less than 104 weeks training for the register and passed the practical part of the appropriate examination for the register, must have passed the examination held by the

Council in accordance with rule 19 of these Rules for which she may enter, subject to the provisions of rules 17 and 18 of these Rules, at the following times:—

    (i) in the case of a person who has completed not less than 104 weeks training for the register, at any time,

    (ii) in the case of a person whose training has been reduced under these Rules, not earlier than 13 weeks before the end of her reduced period of training, and

    (iii) in every other case, after the completion of not less than 78 weeks training.

(3) The person—

    (a) must have served or must have been qualified to serve in the Royal Navy as a naval nursing leading rate or in the Army as an army nurse class I (or army male nurse class I); and

    (b) must have been admitted to an approved training institution within a period of 6 months following her discharge from the service of the Admiralty Board or the Army Board, as the case may be, of the Defence Council and must have acquired at least 3 months' experience of geriatric nursing in the institution.

12. The period of training for the general part of the roll shall be reduced by:—

    (a) 78 weeks in the case of a person who has undergone not less than 104 weeks training for the parts of the register for registered mental nurses or registered nurses for the mentally subnormal; or

    (b) 52 weeks in the case of a person who has undergone not less than 52 weeks training for any part of the register or who is qualified in ophthalmic nursing, orthopaedic nursing or thoracic nursing or who is an enrolled mental nurse or enrolled nurse for the mentally subnormal; or

    (c) 26 weeks in case of a person who is a certified midwife; or

    (d) 104 weeks in the case of a person who has completed 104 weeks training for the general part of the register or for the part of the register for registered sick children's nurses.

13.—(1) Subject to rule 14 of these Rules, the training required for persons for the part of the roll for enrolled mental nurses shall be as provided in paragraph (2) of this rule.

(2) A person—

    (a) must have completed not less than 104 weeks training in accordance with the syllabus of training prescribed in Part 2 of Schedule 2 to these Rules in an approved training institution for enrolled mental nurses; and

    (b) must comply with the conditions relating to the passing of an examination which are prescribed for a person training for the general part of the roll in rule 11(2)(b) of these Rules.

14. The period of training for the part of the roll for mental nurses shall be reduced by:—

    (a) 78 weeks in the case of a person who has undergone not less than 104 weeks training for any part of the register other than the part for registered mental nurses; or

(b) 52 weeks in the case of a person who has undergone not less than 52 weeks training for any part of the register, or who is an enrolled general nurse; or

(c) 104 weeks in the case of a person who has completed 104 weeks training for the part of the register for registered mental nurses; or

(d) 65 weeks in the case of a person who is an enrolled nurse for the mentally subnormal.

15.—(1) Subject to rule 16 of these Rules, the training required for persons for the part of the roll for enrolled nurses for the mentally subnormal shall be as provided in paragraph (2) of this rule.

(2) A person—

(a) must have completed not less than 104 weeks training in accordance with the syllabus of training prescribed in Part 3 of Schedule 2 to these Rules in an approved training institution for enrolled nurses for the mentally subnormal; and

(b) must comply with the conditions relating to the passing of an examination which are prescribed for a person training for the general part of the roll in rule 11(2)(b) of these Rules.

16. The period of training for the part of the roll for the mentally subnormal shall be reduced by:—

(a) 78 weeks in the case of a person who has undergone not less than 104 weeks training for any part of the register other than the part for registered nurses for the mentally subnormal; or

(b) 52 weeks in the case of a person who has undergone not less than 52 weeks training for any part of the register, or who is an enrolled general nurse; or

(c) 104 weeks in the case of a person who has completed 104 weeks training for the part of the register for registered nurses for the mentally subnormal; or

(d) 65 weeks in the case of a person who is an enrolled mental nurse.

17. Subject to rule 18 of these Rules a person who is trained in accordance with rules 11, 13 and 15 of these Rules shall be entitled to enter for the appropriate examination for a part of the roll held under rule 19 of these Rules if she complies with the following conditions:—

(a) her name is in the index of pupil nurses; and

(b) she is of good character and her conduct has been satisfactory during the period of training under supervision; and

(c) she has or will have completed by the last day of the month in which the examination is held the period of training prescribed in her case in rule 11(2)(b) of these Rules and has received instruction in each of the subjects contained in the appropriate syllabus on which the examination is based; and

(d) she has deposited with the Registrar a certificate signed by the senior nurse or other officer acceptable to the Council of the institution or institutions in which she was trained verifying that the requirements specified in this paragraph have been satisfied:

Provided that if a candidate fails an examination for a second time she may be required to undergo further training for such period not exceeding 13 weeks, as the Education Committee may decide, before being permitted to enter again for that examination.

18. Should it come to the notice of the Council that a candidate for entry to any of the Council's examinations has been guilty of a criminal offence or has been guilty of conduct which, had she been an enrolled nurse, would in the opinion of the Council have rendered her liable to disciplinary action under these Rules, the Council may, after giving the candidate the opportunity of stating her case orally or in writing as she may wish, and making such other reasonable investigations as may be necessary, refuse to admit her to the examination in question.

19.—(1) The Council shall hold examinations for the parts of the roll at such times and subject to such conditions as they may from time to time determine.

(2) The examinations held under this rule shall be based on the subjects prescribed in the appropriate syllabus contained in Part 1, Part 2 or Part 3 of Schedule 2 to these rules:

(3) The examination shall consist of a simple written test together with a test of practical efficiency and shall be held in an approved training institution.

(4) Any fee payable to the Council under the provisions of section 3(3) of the Act of 1957 in respect of an application to be examined shall be paid to the Council by the applicant before the Council enters her name for the examination.

Breaks and transfers during training

20.—(1) In this rule a break in training means an absence from training of 12 weeks or more and in calculating the length of a break in training for the purposes of this rule no account shall be taken of an aggregate of 14 days' absence on sick leave, maternity leave or compassionate leave in the period of training or 4 weeks' annual leave in each 52 week period of training or of such appropriately reduced periods of absence on sick leave, maternity leave, compassionate leave or annual leave as the periods of training are reduced under rules 12, 14 or 16 of these Rules.

(2) Subject to paragraphs (3) and (5) of this rule, where a person has a break in training of not less than 12 consecutive weeks and not more than 5 years she shall be required to do an additional period of training of one week for every 4 weeks of the break; but in no case shall additional training required under this paragraph exceed 11 weeks.

(3) Where a break in training occurs by reason of sick leave, the Council may reduce the period of additional training required under paragraph (2) of this rule as they think fit.

(4) Without prejudice to paragraphs (2) and (5) of this rule, where a person at any time during her training transfers from one training institution to another she may be required to do such an additional period of training of not more than 13 weeks as the Council may determine.

(5) Where a person—

    (*a*) has a break in training of more than 5 years, or

    (*b*) following a break in training or a transfer from one training institution to another the Council are satisfied, as a result of a report in respect of her, that she has been convicted of a criminal offence or has been guilty of conduct which had she been an enrolled nurse might, in the opinion of the Council, have rendered her liable to disciplinary action under these Rules,

the Council may require that person—
(i) to begin her training again or
(ii) to do such period of additional training of not less than 11 weeks and, when added to the remainder of her period of training following the break, not more than 104 weeks, as the Council may determine.

(6) The Council, on receipt of a report under paragraph 5(*b*) of this rule may make such investigations as they think necessary and shall not require a pupil nurse to start her training again or do such additional period as may have been determined under that paragraph unless they have given her an opportunity of stating her case to them either orally or in writing as she may wish.

(7) Where additional periods of training are required of a person under paragraphs (2) and (4) of this rule they shall be cumulative.

(8) This rule shall apply *mutatis mutandis* to persons who have transferred from a training institution in Scotland or Northern Ireland to a training institution in England and Wales as if they were transferring between two training institutions in England and Wales.

PART V

Conditions of admission to the roll and certificate of admission to the roll

21.—(1) A person shall, subject to the provisions of the next following paragraphs, be entitled to be admitted to the appropriate part or parts of the roll and be issued with a certificate or certificates to that effect if she complies with the following conditions:—
(*a*) she is over the age of 20 years;
(*b*) she has completed the appropriate training and passed any appropriate examination in accordance with Part IV of these Rules or complies with the conditions of admission required by rules 25 and 28 of these Rules;
(*c*) she is of good character and her conduct has been satisfactory during the period of her training under supervision;
(*d*) she has deposited with the Registrar a certificate signed by the senior nurse or other officer acceptable to the Council of the institution or institutions in which she was trained verifying that the requirements specified in this paragraph have been satisfied.

(2) Should it come to the notice of the Council that an applicant for enrolment has either before or since the date on which she sat for the appropriate examination been convicted of a criminal offence or has been guilty of conduct which, had she been an enrolled nurse would, in the opinion of the Council, have rendered her liable to disciplinary action under these Rules, the Council may, after giving the applicant the opportunity of stating her case orally or in writing as she may wish and making such other reasonable investigations as may be necessary, refuse to admit her to the roll.

22.—(1) Where before 1st May 1950, the name of an enrolled nurse was removed from the roll in consequence of the failure of the said nurse to apply for the retention of her name on the roll in accordance with Rules then in force, or where between 1st May 1950 and 1st May 1952, the name of an enrolled nurse was removed for failure to pay the retention fee due under section 15(1) of the Nurses Act 1949(**a**), such person shall be entitled to apply to have her name restored to the roll.

(**a**) 1949 c. 73.

(2) An application for restoration shall be made on a form to be supplied by the Council and shall include an explanation of the applicant's failure to apply for retention of her name on the roll. The applicant shall send to the Council together with her application form the fee in respect of restoration to the roll which is prescribed in paragraph (4) of this rule.

(3) If the Council are satisfied with the explanation offered by the applicant and any references which they may reasonably require are satisfactory, they shall restore her name to the roll. If the Council are not so satisfied with the explanation offered, they shall, before reaching their decision, refer the matter to the Registration and Enrolment Committee who shall, before reporting thereon to the Council, afford to the applicant, if she wishes, an opportunity of being heard by them and of adducing further evidence.

(4) The fee payable by a person upon restoration to the roll under this rule in respect of the retention of her name on the roll without limit of time shall be a fixed sum of £4 4s. 0d. and an additional sum of an amount determined by the age of the person on the date on which her application form for restoration is received by the Council in accordance with the following scale:—

Age of person on date of receipt of application form					Additional sum
Over 55 years ...	...	...	...	...	£1 1s. 0d.
Over 50 years and less than 55 years			...		£2 2s. 0d.
Over 45 years and less than 50 years			...		£3 3s. 0d.
Over 40 years and less than 45 years			...		£4 4s. 0d.
Less than 40 years	...	...	...	...	£5 5s. 0d.

23. Where subsequent to her enrolment, the name of an enrolled nurse has been or is included in the register, her name may be removed from the roll at her request.

24.—(1) Any person whose name is entered on the roll kept by the General Nursing Council for Scotland or by the Joint Nursing and Midwives Council for Northern Ireland who makes application to the Registrar on a form to be supplied by the Council, pays any fee in respect of such application for enrolment due under section 3(3) of the Act of 1957 and produces a certificate issued by the Registrar of the Council on whose roll her name is entered to that effect and a complete copy of such entry shall be admitted to the appropriate part of the roll.

(2) The provisions of paragraph (1) of this rule shall not apply to a person whose name has been removed by the Disciplinary Committee from the roll under Part VI of these Rules.

Conditions of admission to the part of the roll for enrolled mental nurses or to the part of the roll for enrolled nurses for the mentally subnormal by practice, knowledge and experience of nursing of persons suffering from mental disorder

25. A person shall be entitled to be admitted to the part of the roll for enrolled mental nurses or to the part of the roll for enrolled nurses for the mentally subnormal as the case may be on proving to the satisfaction of the Council:—

(a) that she has before 1st December 1967 and after attaining the age of 18 years been bona fide engaged in practice as a nurse in attendance on persons suffering from mental disorder or on persons suffering from severe subnormality or subnormality for the periods and under the conditions specified in the next following rule; and

(b) that she has such knowledge and experience of nursing as to justify her admission to the roll.

26.—(1) Subject to the next following rule, the periods of practice, and the conditions of practice for the purpose of rule 25(a) shall be:—

(a) not less than 2 years' whole-time practice under the supervision of a registered mental nurse or registered nurse for the mentally subnormal as the case may be carried out in a hospital, mental nursing home or other institution acceptable to the Council; or

(b) not less than 5 years' whole-time practice under the supervision of a registered mental nurse or registered nurse for the mentally subnormal as the case may be.

(2) For the purposes of this rule, a person shall be deemed to have carried out a period of whole-time practice required under paragraph (1) of this rule if she carried out periods of practice, whether whole-time or part-time, which in the aggregate amount to the required period of whole-time practice.

27. A person who on the date of making application for admission to the roll is engaged in nursing but who has failed by 1st December 1967 to complete a period of practice prescribed in rule 26(1) may nevertheless be enrolled if—

(a) she has carried out since 1st December 1962 a period of practice under the conditions specified in paragraph (a) of that rule; or since 1st December 1960 a period of practice under the conditions specified in paragraph (b) of that rule; and

(b) the length of time by which she has failed to complete a prescribed period of practice is so short as in the view of the Council not materially to affect her fitness for enrolment.

Conditions of admission to the general part of the roll by knowledge and experience acquired either before 17th March 1943 or before 1st January 1949

28. A person shall be entitled to be admitted to the general part of the roll on proving to the satisfaction of the Council that she is engaged in nursing and that she has since attaining the age of 17½ years acquired knowledge and experience of nursing in the manner specified in the next following rule.

29. The knowledge and experience of nursing entitling a person to be enrolled under rule 28 shall have been acquired in one of the following ways:—

(a) by not less than 2 years' whole-time training or experience in the nursing of the sick undergone or acquired, as the case may be, before 17th March 1943 under the supervision of trained nursing staff in a hospital or institution; or

(b) by not less than 3 years' whole-time bona fide practice in the nursing of the sick carried out before 17th March 1943, including not less than 6 months' whole-time training or experience under the supervision of trained nursing staff in a hospital or institution; or

(c) in the case of a person who before 17th March 1943, was a state certified midwife, by not less than 3 years' whole-time training or experience in the nursing of the sick or midwifery undergone or acquired, as the case may be, before that date, including not less than 6 months' whole-time training or experience in the nursing of the sick under the supervision of trained nursing staff in a hospital or institution; or

(d) by 5 years' whole-time bona fide practice in the nursing of the sick carried out before 17th March 1943, including such nursing experience recently acquired before that date as would have been considered adequate by the Council; or

(e) by not less than 2 years' whole-time training or experience in the nursing of the sick undergone or acquired, as the case may be, before 1st January 1949, under the supervision of trained nursing staff in a hospital or institution of which not less than 1 year was spent in the employment of one hospital or institution or in one or more hospitals or institutions under one authority; or

(f) in the case of a person who before 1st January 1947, was a state certified midwife, by not less than 2 years and 6 months' whole-time training in the nursing of the sick or midwifery, undergone before that date, including not less than 6 months' whole-time training in the nursing of the sick under the supervision of trained nursing staff in a hospital or institution.

References

30.—(1) For the purposes of rules 25 and 28 the applicant shall furnish to the Registrar the name and address of a person willing and able to give evidence of her character. The person shall be a householder not being a relation of the applicant who has known the applicant for not less than 3 years.

(2) For the purposes of rules 25(a) and 28 evidence of the applicant's date of birth shall be sufficient if given to the Council by the applicant in the form of a birth certificate or a statutory declaration stating the date of birth.

(3) For the purposes of rules 25 and 28, an applicant shall furnish to the Registrar the names and addresses of the persons under whom the applicant has worked for not less than 3 months specified in sub-paragraph (a) or (b) of this paragraph as appropriate in her case who are willing to send to the Council a certificate relating to the professional efficiency of the applicant, that is to say—

(a) in the case of an applicant whose period of practice entitling her to enrolment has been carried out in a hospital or mental nursing home or other institution, any 2 persons, such persons being a senior nurse or other senior nursing officer of a hospital or mental nursing home or other institution in which she has been employed or a registered medical practitioner; and

(b) in the case of an applicant whose period of practice entitling her to enrolment has been carried out other than as in (a) above, a registered nurse and a registered medical practitioner under whose supervision she has worked.

31. Every nurse admitted to the roll shall be granted a certificate stating that her name has been enrolled, and the date of her enrolment, and such certificate shall be sealed with the seal of the Council.

32. In the event of a certificate becoming lost or accidentally destroyed, the holder may apply to the Council for a fresh certificate, and the Council may, if they think fit, grant such fresh certificate upon payment by the applicant of a fee of £1 1s. 0d. A certificate issued under this rule shall be marked "Duplicate".

33. Any person shall be entitled, upon payment to the Registrar of a fee of £1 1s. 0d. to be furnished with a certificate under the seal of the Council certifying that a person is, or was at any date, or is not, or was not at any date, duly enrolled.

PART VI

REMOVAL FROM AND RESTORATION TO THE ROLL

Interpretation

34. This part of the Rules shall not have effect until 22nd September 1970.

35. For the purpose of this part of these Rules, the following expressions have the meanings hereby respectively assigned to them except where the content otherwise requires:—

"Committee" means the Disciplinary Committee as constituted under the Nurses Rules 1969(**a**);

"complainant" means a body or person by whom a complaint has been made to the Council alleging that an enrolled nurse has been convicted of a crime or been guilty of misconduct or alleging that the entry of the name of an enrolled nurse in the roll has been procured by fraud and who, where the case has been referred by the Investigating Committee in their discretion under rule 36 of these Rules to the Committee, wishes to be a party to the proceedings;

"crime" means a criminal offence and includes an offence committed outside England and Wales which if committed in England and Wales would be a criminal offence;

"legal assessor" means a person appointed to be assessor under the provisions of section 10 of the Nurses (Amendment) Act 1961(**b**);

"respondent" means any enrolled nurse who is alleged to be liable to have her name removed from the roll or in respect of whom a question has arisen whether the entry of her name in the roll has been procured by fraud;

"solicitor" means the person who for the time being holds the office of solicitor to the Council or his deputy appointed by the Council.

Investigating Committee

36.—(1) When it is brought to the notice of the Council that an enrolled nurse has been convicted of a crime, or where she is alleged to have been guilty of any misconduct, during the period in which her name is in the roll or during any period in which her name has for any reason been excluded from the roll, or where a question arises whether an entry in the roll was procured by fraud, the Registrar, after making such further inquiries relative thereto as she thinks necessary, shall invite the respondent to furnish any written statement or explanation which she may desire to offer and shall lay the matter before the Investigating Committee.

(2) The Investigating Committee shall consider the matter and may at any stage of the case take the advice of the solicitor, and may instruct him to obtain proofs of evidence in support of the allegations against the respondent, and may, in such cases as they think fit, decline to proceed with the matter.

(3) Where the Investigating Committee decide that the case is one in which the nurse shall be cited to appear before the Committee they shall refer the

---

(**a**) Scheduled to S.I. 1969/1675.　　　　(**b**) 1961 c. 14.

case to the Committee and may direct the solicitor to take all necessary steps for verifying the evidence to be submitted to the Committee and for obtaining the necessary documents and the attendance of witnesses.

Notice of inquiry before Committee

37.—(1) Where a case has been referred by the Investigating Committee to the Committee under the provisions of rule 36 of these Rules, the Registrar shall send to the respondent a notice of inquiry in writing in the form set out in Schedule 3 to these Rules, specifying the nature and particulars of the charge against her, and informing her of the time and place of the meeting of the Committee at which the case will be heard, and requiring her to send or deliver to the Registrar her certificate of enrolment and badge, if any, not later than the date on which the hearing takes place. Such notice shall be sent by registered post to the registered address of the respondent contained in the roll or, if the Registrar has reason to believe that that address is not her present address, then to any later address which may be known to the Registrar, and shall be posted so as to allow at least twenty-one days to elapse between the day on which the notice is posted and the date fixed for the hearing.

(2) In any case in which there is a complainant, the Registrar shall send him a copy of the notice of inquiry and a copy of the Rules.

(3) Upon application by any party to the inquiry, the Registrar shall send to that party copies of any statutory declaration, explanation, admission or other similar statement or communication sent to the Council by any party to the inquiry.

(4) Any party to the inquiry may appear in person or be represented at the hearing by a friend, or by counsel or solicitor, provided that a complainant may be represented only by counsel or solicitor or, in the case of a corporate body being a complainant, by a member or officer duly appointed by them for the purpose.

Postponement or cancellation of inquiry

38.—(1) The chairman of the Committee, of her own motion or upon the application of any party thereto, may postpone the hearing of an inquiry, or may refer the matter to the Investigating Committee for further consideration as to whether an inquiry should be held;

Provided that, where the complainant, if any, has intimated his intention of participating in the proceedings, the Investigating Committee shall not in a case referred back to them direct that an inquiry should not be held except with the agreement of the complainant.

(2) Where before the inquiry opens it appears to the chairman of the Committee, or at any stage of the proceedings it appears to the Committee, that a notice of inquiry is defective, she or they shall cause the notice to be amended unless it appears that the required amendment cannot be made without injustice, or, if she or they consider that the circumstances in which an amendment is made require it, she or they may direct that the inquiry shall be postponed or shall not be held.

(3) The Registrar shall, as soon as may be, give to all parties to whom a notice of inquiry has been sent notification of any decision to postpone or not hold an inquiry, informing them of the date fixed for the hearing of a postponed inquiry.

The reading of the charge

39.—(1) The charge shall be read in the presence of the parties:

Provided that if the respondent does not appear but the Committee nevertheless decide that the inquiry shall proceed the charge shall be read in her absence.

(2) As soon as the charge has been read the respondent may, if she so desires, object to the charge, or to any part of it, in point of law, and any other party may reply to any such objection; and if any such objection is upheld no further proceedings shall be taken on that charge or on that part of the charge.

Proof of conviction

40.—(1) In cases arising out of a complaint or information from which it appears that an enrolled nurse has been convicted of a crime (referred to in these Rules as cases relating to conviction) the following order of proceedings shall be observed concerning proof of the convictions alleged in the charge:—

(*a*) the complainant, or, if no complainant appears, the solicitor shall adduce evidence of each conviction, and a certificate of a competent officer of the Court in which the proceedings took place that the respondent was convicted of a crime shall be sufficient for this purpose;

(*b*) if no evidence is adduced concerning any particular conviction, the chairman of the Committee shall thereupon announce that that conviction has not been proved;

(*c*) if the respondent appears, then the chairman shall ask her concerning each conviction of which evidence is so adduced whether she admits the conviction; and if she admits it the chairman shall thereupon announce that the conviction has been proved.

(2) If, where the respondent appears, she does not admit all the convictions, she may then adduce evidence, concerning any conviction which she has not admitted, on the question whether she was convicted as alleged, and may address the Committee on that question:

Provided that only one address may be made under this sub-paragraph and, where the respondent adduces evidence, that address shall be made either before that evidence is begun or after it is concluded.

(3) Where evidence is adduced under the last foregoing sub-paragraph, the complainant, or, where no complainant appears, the solicitor may adduce evidence to rebut such evidence.

(4) On the conclusion of proceedings under the last foregoing paragraph, the Committee shall consider every conviction of which evidence has been adduced and shall determine whether or not it has been proved; and the chairman shall announce their determination in such terms as they may approve.

(5) After the Committee have determined that any conviction has been proved, the validity of that conviction shall not be questioned either by the Committee or by any party to the inquiry.

Proof of the facts in cases of alleged misconduct

41.—(1) In cases arising out of a complaint or information from which it appears that a question arises whether an enrolled nurse has been guilty of misconduct the following order of proceedings shall be observed as respects proof of the charge or charges:—

(a) if the respondent appears the chairman shall ask her whether she admits the facts alleged in the charge or charges;

(b) if the respondent does not appear and has not admitted by letter the facts alleged in the charge or charges, or if she appears and does not admit all the facts alleged, the complainant (if any appears) or the solicitor shall open the case and adduce evidence of the facts alleged;

(c) if no evidence is adduced concerning any particular charge on which there has been no admission of the facts alleged, the Committee, subject to their right in such a case to order the adjournment of the inquiry, shall record and the chairman shall announce a finding that the respondent is not guilty of misconduct in respect of the matters to which that charge relates.

(2) Where the respondent appears the following further order of proceedings shall be observed:—

(a) at the close of the case against her the respondent may, if she so desires, make either or both of the following submissions relating to any charge concerning which evidence has been adduced, namely—

(i) that no sufficient evidence has been adduced upon which the Committee could find that the facts alleged in that charge have been proved;

(ii) that the facts alleged in the charge are not such as to constitute misconduct,

and where such a submission is made, any other party may reply thereto;

(b) if a submission is made under the last foregoing sub-paragraph, the Committee shall consider and determine whether it should be upheld; and if the Committee determine to uphold it they shall record and the chairman shall announce their finding that, in relation to the matters to which that charge relates, the respondent is not guilty of misconduct;

(c) the respondent may adduce evidence in answer to any charge concerning which evidence has been adduced and, whether she adduces evidence or not, may address the Committee. Except with the leave of the Committee only one address may be made under this sub-paragraph and, where the respondent adduces evidence, shall be made either before that evidence is begun or after it is concluded;

(d) at the close of the case for the respondent the complainant or the solicitor, as the case may be, may, with the leave of the Committee, adduce evidence to rebut any evidence adduced by the respondent; and if he does so, the respondent may make a further address limited to the rebutting evidence;

(e) the complainant or the solicitor, as the case may be, may address the Committee by way of reply to the respondent's case—

(i) if oral evidence (not being evidence as to character) other than that of the respondent herself has been given on the respondent's behalf; or

(ii) with the leave of the Committee, where no such evidence has been given;

(f) without prejudice to the last foregoing sub-paragraph if the respondent has made a submission to the Committee on a point of law any other party shall have a right of reply limited to that submission.

(3) On the conclusion of the aforesaid proceedings, the Committee shall consider and determine as respects each charge which remains outstanding

which, if any, of the facts alleged in the charge have been proved to their satisfaction.

(4) If under the last foregoing paragraph the Committee determine as respects any charge, either that none of the facts alleged in the charge has been proved to their satisfaction, or that such facts as have been so proved would be insufficient to support a finding of misconduct the Committee shall record a finding that the respondent is not guilty of misconduct in respect of the matters to which that charge relates and the chairman shall announce the finding of the Committee.

Procedure upon proof of conviction or of the facts in cases of alleged misconduct

42.—(1) Where the Committee have found that a conviction has been proved the chairman shall invite the complainant or the solicitor, as the case may be, to address the Committee, and to adduce evidence as to the circumstances leading up to the conviction and as to the previous history of the respondent. The chairman shall then invite the respondent to address the Committee by way of mitigation and the respondent may adduce evidence as aforesaid, and as to character.

(2) Where in a case of alleged misconduct the Committee have found that the facts or any of them alleged in any charge have been proved to their satisfaction (and have not on those facts recorded a finding of not guilty) the Committee shall forthwith consider and determine whether in relation to the facts found proved as aforesaid the respondent is guilty of misconduct. If they determine that she is not guilty of misconduct in relation to some or any of such facts they shall record a finding to that effect and the chairman shall announce it. If they determine that she is guilty of misconduct in relation to all or any of such facts the chairman shall invite the complainant or the solicitor, as the case may be, to address the Committee and to adduce evidence as to circumstances leading up to the facts in question and as to the previous history of the respondent. The chairman shall then invite the respondent to address the Committee by way of mitigation and the respondent may adduce evidence as aforesaid, and as to character.

(3) Except where (in a case of alleged misconduct) the respondent has been found not guilty on all charges the Committee shall next consider and determine whether they should postpone judgment.

(4) If the Committee determine to postpone judgment, the judgment of the Committee shall stand postponed until such future meeting of the Committee as they may determine; and the chairman of the Committee shall announce their determination in such terms as the Committee shall have approved.

(5) If the Committee determine not to postpone judgment, they shall determine whether by reason of the conviction or convictions proved against the respondent or of her misconduct the Registrar should be directed to remove her name from the roll, and the chairman shall announce their determination in such terms as they shall have approved.

Procedure in cases relating both to conviction and to misconduct

43. Where in any case it is alleged against the respondent both that she has been convicted and that she has been guilty of misconduct, the Committee shall proceed upon the charge or charges of each kind separately under rule 40 or rule 41 of these Rules according as the charge relates to a conviction or to alleged misconduct and shall then proceed under so much of rule 42 of these

Rules as may be applicable either upon the charge or charges of each kind separately or upon the charges of both kinds concurrently, according as the circumstances of the case may require.

Procedure upon postponement of judgment

44.—(1) Where under any of the foregoing provisions of these Rules the judgment of the Committee in any case stands postponed, the following shall be the procedure:—

(a) the Registrar shall, not later than six weeks before the date fixed for the resumption of the proceedings, send to the respondent a notice which shall—

(i) specify the day, time and place at which the proceedings are to be resumed and invite her to appear thereat;

(ii) invite the respondent to furnish to the Registrar, not less than three weeks before the day fixed for the resumption of the proceedings, the names and addresses of at least two suitable persons with knowledge of the facts found against her who are able and willing to identify the respondent and give evidence as to her character and the nature of her employment since the adjourned hearing, and such other evidence as the Committee may reasonably require;

(b) a copy of the notice shall be sent to the complainant, if any, and he may in turn, if he so desires, send to the Registrar a statement or statutory declaration, whether made by himself or not concerning any matter relating to the conduct of the respondent since the previous hearing;

(c) at the meeting at which the proceedings are resumed the chairman shall first invite the solicitor to recall, for the information of the Committee, the position in which the case stands and the Committee may then receive further oral or documentary evidence in relation to the case, or to the conduct of the respondent since the previous hearing, and shall hear any other party to the proceedings who desires to be heard;

(d) the Committee shall then consider and determine whether they should further postpone their judgment on the charges on which their judgment was previously postponed; and if the Committee determine further to postpone judgment, the judgment of the Committee shall stand postponed until such future meeting of the Committee as they may determine; and the chairman of the Committee shall announce their determination in such terms as the Committee may approve. The provisions of this rule shall apply to any case in which judgment is further postponed;

(e) if the Committee determine that judgment shall not be further postponed paragraph (5) of rule 42 of these Rules shall apply.

(2) At any resumed proceedings any new charge alleged against the respondent in accordance with these Rules shall first be dealt with in accordance with such of rules 39 to 41 of these Rules and so much of rule 42 of these Rules as may be applicable and if the Committee determine not to postpone judgment in respect of any such new charge, the Committee may apply paragraph (5) of rule 42 of these Rules simultaneously to the new charge and the charge in respect of which they had postponed judgment.

(3) Nothing in the last foregoing paragraph shall prevent the Committee from receiving evidence at any resumed proceedings of any conviction recorded against the respondent which has not been made the subject of a charge under these Rules.

(4) The validity of any resumed proceedings shall not be called into question by reason only that members of the Committee who were present at any former

meeting were not present at the resumed meeting or that members present at the resumed meeting were not present at any former meeting.

Cases relating to entries in roll alleged to have been procured by fraud

45.—(1) Where any question whether an entry in the roll has been procured by fraud is referred to the Committee the Registrar shall send to the respondent a notice of inquiry specifying the nature of the fraud alleged, stating the day, time and place at which the Committee will hold an inquiry into the question, inviting her attendance at such inquiry, and containing such further information as the nature of the case may require. The provisions of rule 37 of these Rules shall apply as though such a notice were a notice of inquiry such as is mentioned in that rule.

(2) A copy of the notice shall be sent to any person who is alleged to have been a party to the fraud alleged and to such other persons (if any) as the chairman may direct. Any such person may with the leave of the chairman appear at the inquiry as an additional party thereto.

(3) The inquiry shall proceed as though the question were a charge contained in a notice of inquiry in a case relating to misconduct and the provisions of rule 41 of these Rules shall accordingly apply thereto so far as may be.

(4) If the Committee determine that the entry has been proved to their satisfaction to have been procured by fraud, they shall make an order in writing, under the hand of the chairman, that the entry, having been proved to the satisfaction of the Committee to have been procured by fraud, shall be removed from the roll; and the chairman shall announce the determination in such terms as the Committee may approve.

(5) Whether or not the Committee proceed to determine that an entry has been proved to their satisfaction to have been procured by fraud, they may, if they are satisfied that the entry has been incorrectly made, cause the entry to be amended.

(6) Where an inquiry relates to two or more entries, the Committee may proceed under the foregoing provisions of this rule in respect of those entries either separately or taken together, as the Committee may think fit; and where an inquiry relates to an entry specifying two or more particulars, the Committee may proceed thereunder in respect of so much of the entry as specifies each of those particulars as if it were a separate entry.

Procedure where there is more than one respondent

46. Nothing in this part of these Rules shall prevent one inquiry being held into charges against two or more respondents; and where such an inquiry is held the foregoing rules shall apply with the necessary adaptions and subject to any directions given by the Committee as to the order in which proceedings shall be taken under any of those rules by or in relation to the several respondents, so however that any of the rights ensured to a respondent under those rules shall be exercised separately by each of the respondents who desires to invoke that right.

Restoration of name to the roll

47.—(1) Where the name of an enrolled nurse has been removed from the roll for disciplinary reasons, any application for its restoration to the roll shall be made in writing addressed to the Registrar and signed by the applicant, stating the grounds on which the application is made.

(2) The application shall contain the names and addresses of two or more persons, with knowledge of the facts found against her, of whom two shall be justices of the peace, ministers of religion, registered medical practitioners, registered nurses, or such other persons as the Council may approve, able and willing to identify the applicant and give evidence as to her character, and the nature of her employment since the date of the removal of her name, and, where practicable, before that date.

(3) The Committee may invite the applicant to amplify her application by making a statement in writing in relation to any facts which the Committee consider to be material in making their decision.

(4) The Committee may require the applicant to verify by statutory declaration any statement made in her application or on the invitation of the Committee.

(5) Unless the Committee decide to restore the name of an applicant without a hearing, they shall afford to her if she wishes an opportunity of being heard by them and of adducing evidence.

(6) Subject to the foregoing provisions of this rule and to those of rules 51 to 53 of these Rules, the procedure of the Committee shall be such as they may determine.

48. Upon consideration of the application and of the evidence furnished in support of it, the Committee shall reach their decision and the Registrar shall forthwith communicate it to the applicant by registered post. Where the Committee have decided that the name of the applicant shall be restored to the roll then, upon payment by the applicant of the undermentioned fee or fees, her name shall be restored to the part or parts of the roll from which it was removed and a new certificate or certificates of enrolment shall be issued to her:—

(a) in all cases a fee of £4 4s. 0d. shall be payable;

(b) where the name of the applicant was removed for disciplinary reasons from the roll prior to 1st May 1950 or where in the case of an applicant whose name was removed for disciplinary reasons between 1st May 1950 and 1st May 1952, the applicant had not paid the retention fee due under section 15(1) of the Nurses Act 1949, there shall be payable an additional fee calculated in accordance with the scale contained in rule 22(4) of these Rules in respect of her age on the date her application for restoration under this rule was received by the Council.

49. In the event of the restoration of the name of a person to the roll under this part of these Rules, notification of the fact shall forthwith be sent by the Registrar to the General Nursing Council for Scotland and/or the Joint Nursing and Midwives Council for Northern Ireland, if the Council are aware that the name of such person is or was also enrolled in Scotland and/or Northern Ireland.

50. In the event of notice being received by the Council from the General Nursing Council for Scotland and/or the Joint Nursing and Midwives Council for Northern Ireland that they have restored to their roll the name of a person whose name they had removed from their roll for disciplinary reasons, if the Registrar shall find that the name of such person was removed from the roll, it shall be the duty of the Registrar to lay the matter before the Committee. The Committee shall then consider the matter, and if necessary make inquiries and may, if they think fit, having regard to all the circumstances and at their discretion, restore the name of such person to the roll, if she applies under and conforms to such of the provisions of this part of these Rules as the Committee shall require. Unless the Committee decide to restore the name of the applicant without a hearing they shall afford to her, if she wishes, an opportunity of being heard by them and of adducing evidence: in the event of the Committee restoring the name of a nurse to the roll under this rule, the Registrar shall as soon as possible notify the fact of such restoration to the General Nursing Council for Scotland and/or the Joint Nursing and Midwives Council for Northern Ireland.

Hearing and adjournment

51.—(1) The Committee may deliberate in camera (with or without the legal assessor) at any time and for any purpose during or after the hearing of any proceedings.

(2) Save as aforesaid all proceedings before the Committee shall take place in the presence of all parties thereto who appear therein and shall be held in public except as provided by the following paragraph hereof.

(3) Where in the interests of justice it appears to the Committee that the public should be excluded from any proceedings or part thereof, the Committee may direct that the public shall be so excluded; but a direction under this paragraph shall not apply to the announcement in pursuance of any of these Rules of a determination of the Committee.

(4) The Committee may adjourn their proceedings from time to time as they think fit.

Evidence

52.—(1) Where any respondent or applicant has supplied to the Committee or to the Registrar on their behalf the name of any person to whom reference may be made confidentially as to her character or conduct the Committee may consider any information received from such person in consequence of such reference without disclosing the same to the respondent or applicant.

(2) The Committee may receive oral, documentary or other evidence of any fact which appears to them relevant to the inquiry into the case before them:

Provided that, where a fact which it is sought to prove or the form in which any evidence is tendered is such that it would not be admissible in criminal proceedings in an English court, the Committee shall not receive evidence of that fact or in that form, unless after consultation with the legal assessor they are satisfied that it is desirable in the interests of justice to receive it having regard to the difficulty and expense of obtaining evidence which would be so admissible.

(3) A witness including the respondent (if she gives evidence) shall first be examined by the person calling him and may then be cross-examined and re-examined. Questions may be put to any witness by the Committee through the chairman or by the legal assessor with the leave of the chairman.

(4) The Committee may cause any person to be called as a witness in any proceedings before them whether or not the parties consent thereto.

Voting

53.—(1) Any question put to the vote shall be put in the form of a motion. The chairman shall call upon the members present to vote for or against the motion by raising their hands and shall declare that the motion appears to her to have been carried or not carried as the case may be.

(2) Where the result so declared is challenged by any member, the chairman shall call upon the Registrar to read the roll and as her name is read every member present including the chairman (who shall be called last) shall say "For" or "Against" according as her vote is given for or against the motion. The chairman shall thereupon declare the number of members who have voted for and the number who have voted against the motion and whether the motion has been carried or not carried.

(3) Where on any of the questions the votes are equal, the question shall be deemed to have been resolved in favour of the respondent or applicant, as the case may be, and for the purpose of this paragraph a decision to postpone judgment shall be taken to be in favour of the respondent or applicant unless she indicates to the Committee that she is opposed to postponement.

Communication of decision of Committee in disciplinary cases

54.—(1) The Registrar shall forthwith communicate with the respondent by registered post informing her of the decision of the Committee.

(2) The Registrar shall in the case of the removal of the respondent's name from the roll retain the respondent's certificate of enrolment and badge, if any, and shall remove her name from the part or parts of the roll in which it is included.

(3) Where the respondent's name has been removed from the roll and the respondent has failed to deliver her certificate and badge, if any, to the Registrar prior to or during the proceedings for removal, the Registrar shall, on notifying her of the Committee's decision, request her to deliver the said certificate and badge, and warn her of her liability to proceedings if she fails to comply with the request.

55. In the event of the removal of the name of a nurse from any part of the roll under this part of these Rules, notification of the facts shall forthwith be sent by the Registrar to the General Nursing Council for Scotland and/or to the Joint Nursing and Midwives Council for Northern Ireland, if the Council are aware that the name of such nurse is or was also enrolled in Scotland and/or in Northern Ireland.

56. In the event of the Council receiving a notification from the General Nursing Council for Scotland and/or the Joint Nursing and Midwives Council for Northern Ireland, that the name of any nurse enrolled by either or both of these Councils has been removed from the roll in Scotland or Northern Ireland by reason of a finding by such Council that such nurse has been guilty of a crime, or any misconduct, if the Registrar shall find that the name of the nurse is also entered on any part of the roll, she shall inform her by registered post that the Council have received such notification, and shall inquire of her whether she desires to show cause why her name should not also be removed from the roll. If no answer is received by the Registrar within twenty-eight days after the despatch of such letter, or such longer period as the Committee may allow if they are satisfied that there is sufficient reason for an extension of time, or if the nurse replies that she does not desire to show cause as aforesaid, then the Committee shall at their next convenient meeting direct the Registrar to remove the nurse's name from the roll. If the nurse replies that she does desire to show cause as aforesaid, the Registrar shall lay the matter before the

Committee who shall thereupon proceed to deal with the matter by way of a fresh hearing under this part of these Rules, as if the complaint had been originally made to the Council. The action of the Committee shall in due course be notified to the General Nursing Council for Scotland and/or the Joint Nursing and Midwives Council for Northern Ireland, as the case may be.

57. If any question arises as to the meaning or effect of this part of these Rules, or if any question or matter shall arise which is not provided for by this part of these Rules, such question or matter shall be decided by the Committee.

PART VII

Rules with respect to the uniform and badge which may be worn by enrolled nurses

58. The uniform and badge of an enrolled nurse shall be that described in Schedule 4 to these Rules.

59. The uniform in all its detail shall be strictly adhered to, and no alteration or embellishment of any kind shall be permitted. No unauthorised letters or devices, and no trimmings, lace or jewellery shall be worn on any part of the uniform, provided that this prohibition shall not apply to the wearing of the badge or of the ribbon or other insignia of any order, decoration or medal conferred by the Sovereign, or of any foreign order, decoration or medal accepted by permission of the Sovereign.

60. The wearing of the uniform by enrolled nurses shall not be compulsory:

Provided that an enrolled nurse who wears the uniform shall wear the whole uniform and not a portion thereof only.

61. No enrolled nurse shall wear the uniform without a permit from the Registrar, which shall be issued free by the Council to every enrolled nurse, at the time of her enrolment.

62. In the event of loss of, or damage to, the original permit, an enrolled nurse desirous of obtaining a duplicate permit shall make application to the Registrar on a form to be supplied by the Council and shall pay a fee of 2s. 6d. or on or after 15th February 1971 13p. with her application. The fee payable for any further permit shall be 5s. 0d.

63. A uniform shall be obtained only from a firm authorised by the Council to supply uniforms, and the permit from the Registrar shall be produced at the time of the order.

64. The material for a uniform shall be obtained only from a firm authorised by the Council to supply material which shall be of the kind, weight and colour laid down by the Council, and the uniform shall be made in accordance with the designs approved by the Council.

65. An enrolled nurse shall not dispose of her uniform unless all distinguishing features have been previously removed therefrom.

66. The badge shall be issued by the Council to every enrolled nurse at the time of her enrolment and shall remain the property of the Council. In the event of loss of, or damage to, a badge, application for a duplicate badge on payment of a sum of 10s. 6d. or on or after 15th February 1971 53p. may be made to the Registrar on a form to be supplied by the Council.

67. The badge may be worn with or without uniform, and shall, when worn by female enrolled nurses, be affixed to the right side of the person.

Rule 4   SCHEDULE 1

                              FORM OF ROLL

Each part of the roll shall show in respect of each enrolled nurse admitted the following particulars:—

(1) enrolment number,

(2) full names and, if married, maiden name,

(3) permanent address,

(4) date of enrolment,

(5) qualifications. Under this heading shall appear the qualification in each case for admission to the roll (including certificate of training, if any), the dates of obtaining such qualification, and the hospital or hospitals in which the qualifying training or experience has been received.

Rules, 11, 13 and 15   SCHEDULE 2

                    TRAINING FOR ADMISSION TO THE ROLL

           Part 1. Syllabus of training for the general part of the roll

                                 Part A

                     Principles and practice of nursing

Introduction: development of nursing.
An outline of the National Health Service, and the nurse's place within it.
Principles and practice of nursing.
First aid.

                                 Part B

                       The human individual and his care

An elementary knowledge of:—
    Personal development of the individual.
    Promotion of individual and communal health.
    The structure and function of the human body, including nutrition.

                                 Part C

           Outline of the causes, course and treatment of disease

An elementary knowledge of the causes of disease and principles of treatment as a background to understanding the nursing care given to patients.

        Part 2. Syllabus of training for the part of the roll for enrolled mental nurses

                                 Part A

                             Mental nursing

Introduction: development of nursing.
Outline of Mental Health Services.
An elementary knowledge of the legal and administrative aspects of mental disorder.
A general outline of mental illness.
A general understanding of the nursing care and management of mentally ill patients, including short stay and long stay patients and disturbed and physically sick patients.
General principles of occupational therapy, social therapy, and after care.
First aid.

Part B

The human individual and his care

An elementary knowledge of:—
Personal development of the individual.
The promotion of individual and communal health.
The structure and function of the human body, including nutrition.

Part C

Care of patients who are ambulant and patients confined to bed

Part 3. Syllabus of training for the part of the roll for enrolled nurses for the mentally subnormal

Part A

Mental subnormality nursing

Introduction: development of nursing.
Outline of Mental Health Services.
An elementary knowledge of the legal and administrative aspects of mental disorder.
A general outline of mental subnormality.
A general understanding of the nursing care and management of mentally subnormal patients, including children, adolescents, and adults and those who are physically handicapped and in the education and training of these patients.
General principles of occupational therapy, social therapy, and after-care.
First aid.

Part B

The human individual and his care

An elementary knowledge of:—
Personal development of the individual.
The promotion of individual and communal health.
The structure and function of the human body, including nutrition.

Part C

Care of patients who are ambulant and patients confined to bed

SCHEDULE 3   Rule 37

FORM OF NOTICE

THE GENERAL NURSING COUNCIL FOR ENGLAND AND WALES DISCIPLINARY COMMITTEE

Nurses Acts 1957 to 1969

To ....

of ....

Take notice that the charge (or charges) against you, particulars of which are set
forth below ——— has been brought to the notice of the Council, and that the Disciplinary
have
Committee of the Council propose to investigate such charge(s) at a meeting to be
held at the offices of the Council, 23 Portland Place, London, W1A 1BA at
a.m.
.... ——— on .... the .... 19.....,
p.m.
and to determine whether your name should be removed from the roll.

PARTICULARS OF CHARGE(S)

You are hereby required to attend before the Disciplinary Committee of the Council at the time and place mentioned above and to answer such charge(s), bringing with you all papers and documents in your possession relevant to the matter and any persons whose evidence you wish to lay before the Disciplinary Committee.

The following points should be carefully noted:—

(a) You are entitled to be represented at the hearing before the Disciplinary Committee by a friend, or by counsel or a solicitor, but if you propose to employ counsel or a solicitor, you should give written notice to the Registrar at the address mentioned above at least seven days before the hearing.

(b) It is imperative that you should either send to the Registrar before the date fixed for the hearing, or bring with you to the hearing your certificate of enrolment (and badge).

A copy of the Enrolled Nurses Rules 1969, is enclosed, and your attention is directed to Part VI of those Rules.

Date.. Registrar of the Council.

Rule 58 **SCHEDULE 4**

Part 1

DESCRIPTION OF UNIFORM, BADGE AND LETTERING FOR
FEMALE ENROLLED NURSES

1. The basic colours shall be dark green, apple green, and bronze.

2. The outdoor uniform shall consist of:—

(a) An overcoat (lightweight or heavyweight); or approved raincoat; and/or costume worn with approved blouse; and

(b) A peaked cap with embroidered device in front; or beret with cockade and embroidered device; or double-crowned felt hat with cockade and embroidered device; or tricorn shape felt hat with cockade and embroidered device; or a white peaked crash helmet made in accordance with the specification of the British Standards Institution for protective helmets for motor cyclists.

With any of the above uniforms there shall be worn brown shoes, brown stockings and brown gloves; a handbag, if carried, shall be of brown leather.

3. The indoor uniform shall consist of:—

(a) A washing frock to be worn with or without an approved apron, or

(b) a mess frock.

With either of the above uniforms there shall be worn brown shoes and brown stockings.

4. The badge shall be made of bronze and apple green enamel, and its size and design shall be as follows:—

Diameter: 3.6 centimetres.
Outer edge: 5 petals of Tudor Rose. Between each petal a small Tudor Rose.
Centre: Figure of Hygeia with rose and daffodil design on either side, encircled by garter bearing the words, "The General Nursing Council for England and Wales".

5. The embroidered device shall consist of the appropriate letters of designation worked in gold wire on a dark green background.

6. The metal letters on epaulettes shall consist of bronze plated metal letters of designation indicating the part or parts of the roll in which the nurse is enrolled:—

Enrolled general nurse—S.E.N.
Enrolled mental nurse—S.E.N.(M)
Enrolled nurse for the mentally subnormal—S.E.N.(M.S.)

Part 2

DESCRIPTION OF UNIFORM, BADGE AND LETTERING FOR
MALE ENROLLED NURSES

1. The basic colours shall be dark brown, apple green, and bronze.

2. The outdoor uniform shall consist of:—

   (a) An overcoat (lightweight or heavyweight); or approved raincoat; and

   (b) A dark brown lounge suit worn with white shirt, and dark green tie; and

   (c) A dark brown peaked cap with embroidered device in front; or dark brown beret with embroidered device in front; or dark brown forage cap with two small regulation buttons in front and embroidered device or a white peaked crash helmet made in accordance with the specification of the British Standards Institution for protective helmets for motor cyclists.

3. The indoor uniform shall consist of:—

   A washing duty coat.

   With any of the above uniforms there shall be worn:—

   Dark brown socks, brown boots or shoes and, with the outdoor uniform, dark brown or chamois gloves.

4. The badge, embroidered device and metal letters shall be identical with those prescribed for female enrolled nurses.

(L.S.)   *G. E. Watts,*
Chairman of the Council.

The seal of the General Nursing Council for England and Wales was hereunto affixed on 25th November 1969.

M. Henry,
Registrar.

Signed by authority of the Secretary of State for Social Services.

Serota,
Minister of State,
Department of Health and Social Security.

26th November 1969.

EXPLANATORY NOTE

(This Note is not part of the Instrument.)

The Rules approved by this Instrument consolidate with amendments the Enrolled Nurses Rules 1961, the Enrolled Nurses (Amendment) Rules 1964 and the Enrolled Nurses (Amendment) Rules 1966. The amendments include in particular:-

(*a*) provision for enrolment in, and a separate training for the three parts of the roll established under the Nurses Act 1969;

(*b*) the hearing of disciplinary cases by the Disciplinary Committee of the General Nursing Council instead of the Enrolled Nurses Committee after 22nd September 1970;

(*c*) provision for fees to be paid by pupil nurses on entering training;

(*d*) additional periods of training in certain circumstances where a break in training or a transfer from one training institution to another occurs.

STATUTORY INSTRUMENTS

1969 No. 1675

NURSES AND MIDWIVES

The Nurses Rules, Approval Instrument 1969

Made - - - -	26th November 1969
Laid before Parliament	9th December 1969
Coming into Operation	12th December 1969

The Secretary of State for Social Services, in exercise of his powers under section 32 of the Nurses Act 1957(a), and of all other powers enabling him in that behalf, hereby approves the rules made by the General Nursing Council for England and Wales as set out in the Schedule hereto.

This instrument may be cited as the Nurses Rules, Approval Instrument 1969 and shall come into operation on 12th December 1969.

SCHEDULE

THE GENERAL NURSING COUNCIL FOR ENGLAND AND WALES

The Nurses Acts 1957 to 1969

The General Nursing Council for England and Wales, in exercise of the powers conferred on them by the following sections of the Nurses Act 1957, namely section 2(1) (as substituted by section 1(1) of the Nurses Act 1969(b)), section 3 (as extended by section 7(1) of the Nurses Act 1969), section 4(1) (as extended by section 7(2) of the Nurses Act 1969), sections 6, 7 and 10, section 17 (as substituted by section 1 of the Teachers of Nursing Act 1967(c)), and sections 20, 30 and 32, and under paragraphs 11 and 12 of Schedule 1 to that Act, and of all other powers enabling them in that behalf, hereby make the following rules:—

PART I

Citation and interpretation

1. These Rules may be cited as the Nurses Rules 1969.

2.—(1) In these Rules, unless the context otherwise requires—

"the Act of 1957" means the Nurses Act 1957;

"the Act of 1969" means the Nurses Act 1969;

"approved training institution" means an institution approved by the Council for the purpose of these Rules as a training school or as part of a training school for admission to the register;

"the certificate of the Royal Medico-Psychological Association" means a certificate issued by that Association certifying that the person named thereon, having been duly trained, has, after examination by the Association, shown that she has attained proficiency in mental nursing or in the nursing of the mentally subnormal, as the case may be;

(a) 1957 c. 15.   (b) 1969 c. 47.
(c) 1967 c. 16.

"certified midwife" means a woman whose name is on the roll of certified midwives kept by the Central Midwives Board;

"the Council" means the General Nursing Council for England and Wales;

"enrolled general nurse" means a nurse whose name is on the general part of the roll;

"enrolled mental nurse" means a nurse who is enrolled in the part of the roll containing the names of nurses trained in the nursing and care of persons suffering from mental disorder, other than severe subnormality or subnormality.

"enrolled nurse" means a nurse whose name is on the roll;

"enrolled nurse for the mentally subnormal" means a nurse who is enrolled in the part of the roll containing the names of nurses trained in the nursing and care of persons suffering from severe subnormality or subnormality;

"introductory training course" means a course of training carried out in an approved training institution for the purpose of introducing a student nurse to the subjects included in her training for a part of the register prior to her training in wards or departments;

"the list" means the list of nurses maintained by the Council under section 5 of the Act of 1957;

"person qualified in ophthalmic nursing" means a person who is qualified (except for the qualification of registration by the Council) to receive the diploma of ophthalmic nursing of the Ophthalmic Nursing Board by virtue of ophthalmic nursing training carried out after 1st January 1963, in an institution which in the opinion of the Council is satisfactory for the purpose, and which training included not less than 8 weeks' experience in the operating theatre and not less than 6 weeks' experience of day duty in an out-patient department or a casualty department and experience in the wards;

"person qualified in orthopaedic nursing" means a person who is qualified (except for the qualification of registration by the Council) to receive the orthopaedic nursing certificate of the British Orthopaedic Association and the Central Council for the Care of the Disabled by virtue of training carried out after 1st January 1963, in an institution which in the opinion of the Council is satisfactory for the purpose and who in her second year of orthopaedic nursing training acquired not less than 8 weeks' experience in the operating theatre or in an out-patient department;

"person qualified in thoracic nursing" means a person who holds the thoracic nursing certificate of the British Tuberculosis Association by virtue of training carried out after 1st January 1963, in an institution which in the opinion of the Council is satisfactory for the purpose;

"the register" means the register of nurses maintained by the Council;

"registered fever nurse" means a nurse who is registered in the part of the register containing the names of nurses trained in the nursing of persons suffering from infectious diseases;

"registered general nurse" means a nurse who is registered in the general part of the register;

"registered mental nurse" means a nurse who is registered in the part of the register containing the names of nurses trained in the nursing and care of persons suffering from mental disorder other than severe subnormality or subnormality;

"registered nurse" means a nurse whose name is in the register;

"registered nurse for the mentally subnormal" means a nurse who is registered in the part of the register containing the names of nurses trained in the nursing and care of persons suffering from severe subnormality or subnormality;

"registered sick children's nurse" means a nurse who is registered in the part of the register containing the names of nurses trained in the nursing of sick children;

"the Registrar" means the person for the time being appointed to act as Registrar of the Council under paragraph 12 of Schedule 1 to the Act of 1957, and includes any person duly authorised to act and acting on her behalf;

"the roll" means the roll of nurses maintained by the Council;

"the Secretary of State" means the Secretary of State for Social Services;

"student nurse" means a person who is for the time being undergoing training for admission to any part of the register;

"training" means training—

(a) in an approved training institution, and in the case of training in a part of a training school in accordance with a scheme of training approved by the Council; and

(b) in accordance with the appropriate syllabus contained in Schedules 3 and 4 to these Rules.

(2) The Interpretation Act 1889(a), applies to the interpretation of these Rules as it applies to the interpretation of an Act of Parliament, and in these Rules words importing the feminine gender include the masculine, unless the contrary intention appears.

3. The rules named in Schedule 6 to these Rules are hereby revoked:
Provided that—

(a) such revocation shall not affect any right, privilege, obligation or liability acquired, accrued or incurred, or anything duly done or suffered under those rules;

(b) such revocation shall not affect any application, appointment, certificate, decision, delegation of powers, inquiry or notice made, prepared, issued or given under the rules so revoked, and every such application, appointment, certificate, decision, delegation of powers, inquiry or notice shall, so far as it could have been made, prepared, issued or given under these Rules have effect as if it had been so made, prepared, issued or given;

(c) such revocation shall not affect proceedings for the removal of the name of a nurse from the register where judgment has been postponed by the Council, and such proceedings shall be resumed before the Disciplinary Committee under the provisions of these Rules; and

(d) where a notice that the Council propose to investigate a charge has been served on a nurse under the provisions of those rules such notice shall have effect as if it had been a notice of inquiry under these Rules, and the inquiry shall proceed before the Disciplinary Committee under the provisions of these Rules.

PART II

Formation and maintenance of the register

4.—(1) The Council shall in addition to the parts of the register prescribed in section 2(1) of the Act of 1957 (as substituted by the Act of 1969) maintain for

---

(a) 1889 c. 63.

so long as any names are contained therein a part of the register for nurses trained in the nursing of persons suffering from infectious diseases.

(2) The register shall contain the particulars set forth in Schedule 1 to these Rules.

(3) Each person admitted to the register shall be assigned a registration number in the part or parts of the register in which her name is included.

(4) A registered nurse shall notify to the Registrar every permanent change of address, and for the purpose of these Rules the address last so notified shall be deemed to be her registered address.

(5) A registered nurse shall notify to the Registrar a change of her surname whether occasioned by marriage or otherwise.

(6) It shall be the duty of the Council to cause to be removed from the register any entry which has been incorrectly made.

PART III

Approval of training institutions

5.—(1) For the purposes of section 3(1)(*b*) of the Act of 1957, an institution shall be approved by the Council either:—

(*a*) as a training school capable of providing a complete training qualifying for admission either to the general part of the register or to any other part of the register; or

(*b*) as a part of a training school comprising two or more parts capable of providing, in association under a scheme of training, such a complete training; and in approving a training institution to take part in a scheme of training provided by a group of such institutions the Council shall direct what proportion of the training period shall be spent in each of the participating institutions. The Council may, if they think fit, approve the same institution both as a training school and as a part of a training school.

(2) The Council shall prepare and keep a list of institutions which are for the time being approved by the Council as training schools under the following headings:—

training schools for registered general nurses

training schools for registered mental nurses

training schools for registered nurses for the mentally subnormal

training schools for registered sick children's nurses.

(3) The Council shall also prepare and keep lists of the institutions for the time being approved by the Council as parts of training schools, and such lists shall be kept so far as necessary under headings corresponding to those relating to training schools.

(4) Subject to paragraph (5) of this rule, in respect of every institution, other than an institution vested in the Secretary of State or the Secretary of State for Wales, for which application is made to the Council for approval under paragraph (1) of this rule, there shall be paid to the Council by the persons responsible for its management the following fees:—

(*a*) in all cases on the making of the application, a fee of £5 5s. 0d. which shall be retained by the Council whether or not approval of the institution is granted;

(*b*) in the case of institutions at which student nurses may spend more than 26 weeks of their training, an additional fee of £5 5s. 0d. in respect of the first year, which fee shall be payable on receipt of notice of approval, and an annual fee of £10 10s. 0d. in respect of each subsequent year during which the approval of the Council is continued, which fee shall be payable at the commencement of such year;

(c) in the case of institutions at which student nurses may spend not more than 26 weeks of their training, an annual fee of £5 5s. 0d. in respect of each year after the first year during which the approval of the Council is continued, which fee shall be payable at the commencement of such year.

(5) Where an institution, other than an institution vested in the Secretary of State or the Secretary of State for Wales was approved by the Council prior to 24th March 1950, there shall be paid to the Council by the persons responsible for its management on each anniversary of the date of such approval, in respect of the ensuing year, during the period in which approval is continued, a fee of:—

(a) £10 10s. 0d. where the institution is one at which student nurses may spend more than 26 weeks of their training, or

(b) £5 5s. 0d. where the institution is one at which student nurses may spend not more than 26 weeks of their training.

PART IV

Training and examination of nurses

6. The training for a person training for the register shall be training in accordance with this part of these Rules.

7.—(1) Training for the register shall include an introductory training course which, subject to the provisions of paragraph (2) of this rule, a person may enter if she fulfils the following conditions:—

(a) she has attained the age of 18 years or will have attained that age by the last day of a period of 30 days beginning with the day she entered the introductory training course; and

(b) she complies with one of the following educational requirements:—

(i) she holds the General Certificate of Education at ordinary level or the Certificate of Secondary Education at the level of a Grade I pass in two subjects, of which one shall be English (or Welsh) language, or English (or Welsh) literature or history and has since attaining the age of 11 years completed in the aggregate at least 5 years' full-time education in school or in school and in an establishment for further education, and has during such period studied at least 5 additional subjects of general education; or

(ii) she holds a General Certificate of Education at ordinary level or a certificate of Secondary Education at the level of a Grade I pass in at least 3 subjects, of which one shall be English (or Welsh) language or English (or Welsh) literature or history; or

(iii) she holds an equivalent overseas educational certificate acceptable to the Council and has since attaining the age of 11 years completed in the aggregate at least 5 years' full-time education in school or in school and in an establishment for further education; or

(iv) she holds such other qualification as may be acceptable to the Council; or

(v) she has passed an educational test set by the Council.

(2) A person shall not enter an introductory training course more than 3 times for any part of the register.

8. Within 30 days of commencement of training for the register a student nurse, other than a student nurse who is already registered in a part of the register, shall send to the Council such fee as is for the time being determined by the Council with the approval of the Secretary of State under section 3(1) of the Act of 1957 as amended by section 7 of the Act of 1969.

9.—(1) The senior nurse of an approved training institution, or such other officer as the Council may authorise in that behalf, shall within 30 days of the admission of a student nurse to an introductory training course notify the Council in writing of the full name of the student nurse, her age, her educational qualifications and the date on which she commenced her training and such other particulars as the Council may reasonably require and shall send to the Council with the notification any evidence of the age and educational qualifications of the student nurse that the Council may require.

(2) The senior nurse of an approved training institution, or such other officer as the Council may authorise in that behalf, shall, if a student nurse being trained in that institution discontinues her training, notify the Council of the fact and of the reason for the discontinuation and if the student nurse has completed not less than 26 weeks' training shall at the same time send to the Council a statement giving particulars of the training completed. No person shall be able to enter an introductory training course more than three times for training for admission for any one part of the register.

10. The Council shall keep an index of student nurses and shall, on being satisfied that a student nurse has been admitted to an introductory training course in accordance with the provisions of rule 7 of these Rules and on receipt of the fee required by rule 8 of these Rules include her name in the index of student nurses.

11.—(1) The Council shall at such times, at such places and subject to such conditions as the Council may from time to time determine hold examinations for all parts of the register.

(2) Any fee payable to the Council under the provisions of section 3(3) of the Act of 1957 in respect of an application to be examined shall be paid to the Council by the applicant before the Council enters her name for the examination.

12.—(1) A student nurse may enter for the intermediate examination for the part of the register for mental nurses and for the part of the register for nurses for the mentally subnormal, if she complies with the following conditions:—

(a) she has, subject to the provisions of paragraph (2) of this rule, completed not less than 52 weeks' training in an approved training institution including an introductory training course for mental nurses or for nurses for the mentally subnormal, or is due to complete such training by the last day of the month in which the examination is held; and

(b) she has attended a course of lectures on the subjects included in the syllabus of training on which the examination for which she is entering is based set out in Schedule 3 to these Rules and has undergone practical instruction in the wards; and

(c) she is honest and of good character and her conduct has been satisfactory during the period of her training;

(d) she has deposited with the Registrar a certificate signed by the senior nurse or other officer acceptable to the Council of the approved training institution or institutions in which she has been trained or instructed verifying that the requirements of sub-paragraphs (a), (b) and (c) of this paragraph have been satisfied; and

(e) her name is included in the index of student nurses.

(2) The requirements of sub-paragraph (1)(a) of this rule as to the completion of 52 weeks' training shall not apply to an enrolled nurse who has proved to the satisfaction of the Council that she has completed not less than 39 weeks' training in an approved training institution or is due to complete such training by the end of the month in which the examination is completed and has applied through the senior nurse or other officer acceptable to the Council of that institution for and has received permission from the Council to undergo a reduced period of training.

13. Subject to rule 14 of these Rules, the training required of a person entering for the final examination for the general part of the register shall be not less than 156 weeks' training in accordance with the syllabus of training prescribed in Part 1 of Schedule 4 to these Rules in an approved training institution for registered general nurses or in accordance with the syllabus of training prescribed in Part 1 of Schedule 4 to these Rules in the service of the Admiralty Board, Army Board or Air Force Board of the Defence Council.

14. The period of training for the final examination for the general part of the register shall be reduced by:—

(a) 78 weeks in the case of a person who when starting the training is a registered nurse; or

(b) 52 weeks in the case of an enrolled general nurse with specified practical experience provided that such a person shall have attained the standard required by the approved training institution after having completed not less than 39 weeks after commencing such training; or

(c) by 26 weeks in the case of a person who is an enrolled general nurse without specified practical experience, or an enrolled nurse for the mentally subnormal, an enrolled mental nurse, a certified midwife or a person who when starting the training is qualified in ophthalmic or orthopaedic nursing provided that such a person shall have attained the standard required by the approved training institution after have completed not less than 39 weeks after commencing such training; or

(d) by 13 weeks in the case of a person who when starting the training is qualified in thoracic nursing.

15. Subject to rule 16 of these Rules the training required of a person entering for the final examination for the part of the register for mental nurses shall be not less than 156 weeks' training in accordance with the syllabus of training prescribed in Part 2 of Schedule 4 to these Rules in an approved training institution for registered mental nurses.

16. The period of training for the final examination for the part of the register for mental nurses shall be reduced by:—

(a) 104 weeks in the case of a registered nurse for the mentally subnormal; or

(b) 78 weeks in the case of a person who when starting the training is a registered nurse other than a registered nurse for the mentally subnormal; or

(c) 52 weeks in the case of an enrolled mental nurse or an enrolled nurse for the mentally subnormal provided that such a person shall have passed the appropriate intermediate examination held under rule 11 of these Rules; or (*d*) 26 weeks in the case of an enrolled general nurse provided that such a person shall have attained the standard required by the approved training institution after having completed not less than 39 weeks after commencing such training.

17. Subject to rule 18 of these Rules, the training required of a person entering for the final examination for the part of the register for nurses for the mentally subnormal shall be not less than 156 weeks' training in accordance with the syllabus of training prescribed in Part 3 of Schedule 4 to these Rules in an approved training institution for registered nurses for the mentally subnormal.

18. The period of training for the final examination for the part of the register for nurses for the mentally subnormal shall be reduced by:—

(*a*) 104 weeks in the case of a registered mental nurse; or

(*b*) 78 weeks in the case of a person who when starting the training is a registered nurse other than a registered mental nurse; or

(*c*) 52 weeks in the case of an enrolled mental nurse or an enrolled nurse for the mentally subnormal provided that such a person shall have passed the appropriate intermediate examination held under rule 11 of these Rules; or

(*d*) 26 weeks in the case of an enrolled general nurse provided that such a person shall have attained the standard required by the approved training institution after having completed not less 39 weeks after commencing such training.

19. Subject to rule 20 of these Rules, the training required of a person entering for the final examination for the part of the register for sick children's nurses shall be not less than 156 weeks' training in accordance with the syllabus of training prescribed in Part 4 of Schedule 4 to these Rules in an approved training institution for registered sick children's nurses.

20. The period of training for the final examination for the part of the register for sick children's nurses shall be reduced by:—

(*a*) 78 weeks in the case of a person who when starting the training is a registered nurse; or

(*b*) 52 weeks in the case of an enrolled general nurse with specified practical experience provided that such a person shall have attained the standard required by the approved training institution after having completed not less than 39 weeks after commencing such training; or

(*c*) 26 weeks in the case of an enrolled general nurse without specified practical experience or an enrolled mental nurse or an enrolled nurse for the mentally subnormal provided that such a person shall have attained the standard required by the approved training institution after having completed not less than 30 weeks after commencing such training.

21. Should it come to the notice of the Council that a candidate for entry to any of the Council's examinations has been convicted of a criminal offence or has been guilty of conduct which, had she been a registered nurse, would in the opinion of the Council have rendered her liable to disciplinary action under these Rules, the Council may, after giving the candidate the opportunity of stating her case orally or in writing as she may wish, and making such other reasonable investigations as may be necessary, refuse to admit her to the examinations in question.

22.—(1) Subject to the provisions of paragraph (2) of this rule, a person may enter for the final examination for a part of the register if she complies with the following conditions:—

(a) she has attained, or will have attained by the last day of the month in which the examination is completed, the age of 21 years; and

(b) she fulfils the following requirements:—

(i) she is on the index of student nurses; and

(ii) she has reached the standard required by the approved training institution; or

(iii) where she is a person training for entry for the parts of the register for mental nurses and nurses for the mentally subnormal she has passed the intermediate examination held under rule 11 of these Rules; or she is already registered in a part of the register; and

(c) she has completed, or is due to complete by the last day of the month in which the examination is completed (or in the case of a candidate referred to in rule 14(a) or rule 16(b) or rule 18(c) or rule 20(a), the last day of the month following that month), the training appropriate to her case specified in rules 13, 15, 17 and 19 of these Rules for candidates for the final examination for which she is entering and if she has failed 3 times to pass that final examination at least 6 months' further training since her third failure; and

(d) she has undergone systematic instruction in each of the subjects included in the syllabus of training prescribed in Schedule 4 to these Rules for the final examination for which she is entering; and

(e) she is honest and of good character and her conduct has been satisfactory during the period of training; and

(f) she has deposited with the Registrar certificates signed by the senior nurse or other officer acceptable to the Council of the institution or institutions in which she was trained or instructed, verifying that the requirements specified in this paragraph have been satisfied.

(2) No person shall enter for the final examination for a part of the register if she has failed 4 times to pass the final examination for that part.

Breaks and transfers during training

23.—(1) In this rule a break in training means an absence from training of 12 weeks or more and in calculating the length of a break in training no account shall be taken of an aggregate of 21 days absence on sick leave, maternity leave or compassionate leave in the period of training or 4 or 5 weeks' annual leave in each 52 week period of training or of such appropriately reduced periods of absence on sick leave, maternity leave or compassionate leave as the periods of training are reduced under rules 14, 16, 18 and 20 of these Rules.

(2) Subject to paragraphs (3) and (5) of this rule, where a person has a break in training of not less than 12 consecutive weeks and not more than 5 years she shall be required to do an additional period of training of one week for every 4 weeks of the break; but in no case shall additional training required under this paragraph exceed 16 weeks.

(3) Where a break in training occurs by reason of sick leave, the Council may reduce the period of additional training required under paragraph (2) of this rule as they think fit.

(4) Without prejudice to paragraphs (2) and (5) of this rule, where a person at any time during her training transfers from one training institution to another

she may be required to do such an additional period of training of not more than 26 weeks as the Council may determine.

(5) Where a person—

    (a) has a break in training of more than 5 years; or

    (b) following a break in training or a transfer from one training institution to another the Council are satisfied, as a result of a report in respect of her, that she has been convicted of a criminal offence or has been guilty of conduct which had she been a registered nurse might, in the opinion of the Council, have rendered her liable to disciplinary action under these Rules,

the Council may require that person—

    (i) to begin her training again; or

    (ii) to do such period of additional training of not less than 16 weeks and, when added to the remainder of her period of training following the break, not more than 156 weeks, as the Council may determine.

(6) The Council, on receipt of a report under paragraph 5(b) of this rule may make such investigations as they think necessary and shall not require a student nurse to start her training again or do such additional period as may have been determined under that paragraph unless they have given her an opportunity of stating her case to them either orally or in writing as she may wish.

(7) Where additional periods of training are required of a person under paragraphs (2) and (4) of this rule they shall be cumulative.

(8) This rule shall apply *mutatis mutandis* to persons who have transferred from a training institution in Scotland or Northern Ireland to a training institution in England and Wales as if they were transferring between two training institutions in England and Wales.

PART V

Conditions of admission to the register and certificate of admission to the register

24.—(1) A person shall, subject to paragraph (2) of this rule, be entitled to be admitted to a part of the register and be issued with a certificate to that effect if she complies with the following conditions:—

    (a) she is over 21 years; and

    (b) she has completed the training and passed the final examination for that part of the register, or she complies with the conditions of admission to the register required by rules 27, 28, 29 or 30 of these Rules.

(2) Should it come to the notice of the Council that an applicant for registration has either before or since the date on which she sat for a final examination been convicted of a criminal offence or has been guilty of conduct which, had she been a registered nurse, would in the opinion of the Council have rendered her liable to disciplinary action under these Rules, the Council may, after giving the applicant the opportunity of stating her case orally or in writing as she may wish, and making such other reasonable investigations as may be necessary, refuse to admit her to the register.

25.—(1) Where before 24th March 1950, the name of a nurse was removed from the register in consequence of the failure of the said nurse to apply for the retention of her name in the register in accordance with Rules then in force, or where between 24th March 1950, and 1st January 1952, the name of a nurse was removed for failure to pay the retention fee due under section 15(1) of the Nurses Act 1949(a), such person may apply to have her name restored to any part of the register from which it was removed.

(a) 1949 c. 73.

(2) An application for restoration to the register except for an application under Part VII of these Rules shall be made on a form to be supplied by the Council and shall include an explanation of the applicant's failure to apply for the retention of her name on the register. The applicant shall send to the Council together with her application form the fee appropriate to her case which is prescribed in paragraph (4) of this rule.

(3) If the Council are satisfied with the explanation offered by an applicant, and any references which they may reasonably require are satisfactory, they shall restore her name to the appropriate part or parts of the register. If the Council are not so satisfied they shall, before reaching their decision, refer the matter to the Registration and Enrolment Committee who shall, before reporting thereon to the Council, afford to the applicant, if she wishes, an opportunity of being heard by them and of adducing further evidence.

(4) The fee payable by a person upon restoration to the register under this rule in respect of the retention of her name on the register without limit of time shall be a fixed sum of £5 5s. 0d. and an additional sum in respect of each part of the register to which the person is restored, of an amount determined by the age of the person on the date on which her application form for restoration is received by the Council in accordance with the following scales:—

Age of person on the date of receipt of application form						Additional sum
55 years and over	...	...	...	...	...	£1 1s. 0d.
50 years and over and less than 55 years		...	...	...	£2 2s. 0d.
45 years and over and less than 50 years		...	...	...	£3 3s. 0d.
40 years and over and less than 45 years		...	...	...	£4 4s. 0d.
Less than 40 years	...	...	...	...	...	£5 5s. 0d.

26. The provisions of rule 25 of these Rules shall apply *mutatis mutandis* to restoration to the list as they apply to restoration to the register with the exception that the fixed sum in respect of restoration to the list shall be £5 5s. 0d. and the additional sum in respect of restoration to each part of the list shall in every case be £1 1s. 0d.

Conditions of admission of persons holding the certificate of the Royal Medico-Psychological Association to the parts of the register for mental nurses and for nurses for the mentally subnormal

27. A person holding the certificate of the Royal Medico-Psychological Association who deposits the certificate with the Registrar, or produces to the Registrar such other evidence as the Council may require that she is the holder of such a certificate, shall:—

(a) if the certificate indicates her proficiency in mental nursing be qualified to be admitted to the part of the register for mental nurses, or

(b) if the certificate indicates her proficiency in the nursing of the mentally subnormal, be qualified to be admitted to the part of the register for nurses for the mentally subnormal:

Provided that a person who on the date of the making of her application for registration is not employed in a hospital or institution shall not be so qualified until she satisfies the Council by the production of references that she is of good character, and until she satisfies the Council by the production of up-to-date references that her proficiency in mental nursing or the nursing of the mentally subnormal, as the case may be, remains satisfactory.

Conditions of admission of persons trained prior to July 1925

28.—(1) Any person whose name is included in a part of the list, who makes application to the Registrar on a form to be supplied by the Council, shall be admitted to the corresponding part of the register upon payment at the time of application of a registration fee of £2 2s. 0d. In the case of an applicant who applies to be admitted to more than one part of the register, an additional fee of £1 1s. 0d. shall be payable at the time of such application in respect of admission to any second or subsequent part of the register:

Provided that every applicant who has already paid a fee for the retention of her name in the list shall be credited with the amount of such fee in respect of her application for admission to the corresponding part or parts of the register.

(2) Any person who not being included in the list, holds a certificate issued by an institution which appears to the Council to be satisfactory for the purposes of the provisions of section 5(1) of the Act of 1957, stating that she completed before the beginning of July 1925, a course of training in nursing in that institution, and who satisfies the Council that she is of good character and has adequate knowledge and experience of nursing, shall be admitted to the appropriate part of the register after making application to the Registrar, on a form to be supplied by the Council, and on paying at the time of such application a registration fee of £3 3s. 0d. In the case of an applicant who applies to be admitted to more than one part of the register, an additional fee of £1 11s. 6d. or on or after 15th February 1971 £1.57 shall be payable at the time of such application in respect of admission to any second or subsequent part of the register.

Conditions of admission of persons registered in Scotland and Northern Ireland

29.—(1) Any person whose name is included in any part or parts of the register kept by the General Nursing Council for Scotland or by the Joint Nursing and Midwives Council for Northern Ireland, who produces a certificate issued by the Registrar of the Council in whose register her name is entered to that effect and a complete copy of that entry, shall be qualified to be admitted to the corresponding part or parts of the register.

(2) The provisions of paragraph (1) of this rule shall not apply to a person whose name is for the time being removed from the register by direction of the Disciplinary Committee of the Council under Part VII of these Rules.

Conditions of admission of persons trained outside the United Kingdom

30. Any person who desires to be registered in any part of the register appearing to the Council to be appropriate to her case, under the provisions of section 4 of the Act of 1957, shall make application to the Registrar, on a form to be supplied by the Council and shall pay a fee of £3 0s. 0d. to the Council at the time of making such application, for registration in the appropriate part or parts of the register. There shall be payable at the time of registration a registration fee of £9 9s. 0d. in respect of each part of the register.

31. In the event of a certificate becoming lost or accidentally destroyed, the holder may apply to the Council for a fresh certificate, and the Council may, if they think fit, grant such fresh certificate upon payment by the applicant of a fee of £1 1s. 0d. A certificate issued under this rule shall be marked "Duplicate".

32. Any person shall be entitled upon payment to the Registrar of a fee of £1 1s. 0d. to be furnished with a certificate under the seal of the Council certifying that a person is, or was at any date, or is not, or was not at any date, duly registered.

33. Any person making any application under this part of these Rules to be registered shall at the time of making her application pay any fee due under the provisions of Section 3(3) of the Act of 1957.

34. Every nurse admitted to the register shall be granted a certificate stating in which part her name has been registered, and the date of registration, and such certificate shall be sealed with the seal of the Council.

PART VI

Qualifications of teachers of nurses

35. The Council shall give a certificate as a teacher of nurses (hereinafter referred to as "the Council's Certificate") to a registered nurse or a person whose name is included in the list who satisfies the requirements of rule 36 of these Rules.

36.—(1) The requirements for qualification as a teacher of nurses shall in the case of a nurse tutor be as follows:—

(*a*) she has undergone a course of training (for the time being approved by the Council) conducted under the auspices of a University at an institution which course was of at least one year's duration and included training in teaching methods with particular application to the teaching of nursing which will entitle her to the award of a diploma or a certificate as the case may be, of that University; or

(*b*) she has successfully completed a course of training which is for the time being recognised by the Secretary of State for Education and Science as entitling her to be a qualified teacher for the purpose of regulations made, or having effect as if made, under section 4(2) of the Local Government Act 1966(**a**) and has had since registration not less than three years experience in nursing of which:—

(i) not less than one year has been spent as a person in charge of a ward or department of an approved training institution in which pupil or student nurses are regularly trained, and

(ii) not less than one year has been spent in other clinical nursing acceptable to the Council for the purposes of this paragraph, and

(iii) not less than one year has been spent in the teaching of nursing at an approved training institution under the supervision of a person who holds the Council's certificate under this paragraph of this rule; or

(*c*) her name is included in any roll of teachers for the time being maintained by the Council for the Training of Health Visitors and she has had since her registration—

(i) not less than 2 year's experience in nursing in charge of a ward or department of an approved training institution in which pupil or student nurses are regularly trained; or

(ii) not less than 1 year of such experience and one years' experience as a health visitor; or

(*d*) in any particular case she appears to the Council and the Secretary of State to be qualified for the teaching of nursing otherwise than as mentioned in the preceding provisions of this rule.

(2) The requirements for qualification as a teacher of nurses shall, in the case of a clinical teacher be as follows:—

(*a*) she has undergone a course of training (for the time being approved by the Council) conducted by an institution which course included training in teaching methods with particular application to the teaching of nursing which will entitle her to the award of a certificate as a teacher of pupil nurses, or a clinical instructor certificate as the case may be of that institution; or

---

(a) 1966 c. 42.

(b) she has completed not less than 2 years' post-registration experience in a post of responsibility in an approved training institution and possesses one of the following qualifications—

(i) Diploma of Nursing in Clinical Teaching of the University of London

(ii) Midwifery Tutor's Diploma

(iii) Teacher's Certificate of the City and Guilds No. 394 or 395; or

(c) she must have completed, on or before 31st December 1970, not less than 3 years' post-registration experience in a post of responsibility in an approved training institution and she must have been, for not less than 2 years of those 3 years, engaged in clinical instruction or in the teaching of pupil nurses, and she shall have carried out teaching in the clinical situation amounting to not less than 20 hours per week over a period of 2 years; or

(d) in any particular case she appears to the Council and the Secretary of State to be qualified for the teaching of nursing otherwise than as mentioned in the preceding provisions of this rule.

37. A fee of £5 5s. 0d. shall be payable on the granting of the Council's certificate. In the event of such certificate becoming lost or accidentally destroyed, the holder may apply to the Council for a fresh certificate, and the Council may, if they think fit, grant such fresh certificate upon payment by the applicant of a fee of £1 1s. 0d.; and a certificate so issued shall be marked "Duplicate".

38. The Council's certificate shall be sealed with the seal of the Council and the granting of the Council's certificate shall be indicated by means of a distinguishing mark placed against the entry relating to the holder in the register or list. The Council's certificate shall be valid only so long as the holder is so registered or her name appears on the list, as the case may be, but validity shall be retored on re-inclusion of the holder's name in the register or list.

39. Any registered nurse who holds a certificate of registration as a nurse tutor or clinical instructor granted by the General Nursing Council for Scotland or the Joint Nursing and Midwives Council for Northern Ireland shall, on making application to the Registrar and on paying a fee of 10s. 6d. or on or after 15th February 1971 53p. and on producing the certificate granted by the General Nursing Council for Scotland or the Joint Nursing and Midwives Council for Northern Ireland, be granted the Council's certificate.

40. Any person shall be entitled, upon payment of a fee of £1 1s. 0d. to be furnished with a certificate under the seal of the Council certifying that on a specified date, or during a specified period, a person is or was, or is not or was not, registered as a teacher of nurses as defined by these Rules.

PART VII
REMOVAL FROM AND RESTORATION TO THE REGISTER

Interpretation

41. For the purpose of this part of these Rules, the following expressions have the meaning hereby respectively assigned to them except where the content otherwise requires:—

"Committee" means the Disciplinary Committee;

"complainant" means a body or person by whom a complaint has been made to the Council alleging that a registered nurse has been convicted of a crime or been guilty of misconduct or alleging that the entry of the name of a registered nurse in the register has been procured by fraud and who, where the case has been referred by the Investigating Committee in their discretion under rule 42 of these Rules to the Committee, wishes to be a party to the proceedings;

"crime" means a criminal offence and includes an offence committed outside England and Wales, which if committed in England and Wales would be a criminal offence;

"legal assessor" means a person appointed to be assessor under the provisions of section 10 of the Nurses (Amendment) Act 1961(a);

"respondent" means any registered nurse who is alleged to be liable to have her name removed from the register or in respect of whom a question has arisen whether the entry of her name in the register has been procured by fraud;

"solicitor" means the person who for the time being holds the office of Solicitor to the Council or his deputy appointed by the Council.

Investigating Committee

42.—(1) When it is brought to the notice of the Council that a registered nurse has been convicted of a crime, or where she is alleged to have been guilty of any misconduct, during the period in which her name is in the register or during any period in which her name has for any reason been excluded from the register, or where a question arises whether an entry in the register was procured by fraud, the Registrar, after making such further inquiries relative thereto as she thinks necessary, shall invite the respondent to furnish any written statement or explanation which she may desire to offer and shall lay the matter before the Investigating Committee.

(2) The Investigating Committee shall consider the matter and may at any stage of the case take the advice of the solicitor, and may instruct him to obtain proofs of evidence in support of the allegations against the respondent, and may, in such cases as they think fit, decline to proceed with the matter.

(3) Where the Investigating Committee decide that the case is one in which the nurse shall be cited to appear before the Committee they shall refer the case to the Committee and may direct the solicitor to take all necessary steps for verifying the evidence to be submitted to the Committee and for obtaining the necessary documents and the attendance of witnesses.

Notice of inquiry before Committee

43.—(1) Where a case has been referred by the Investigating Committee to the Committee under the provisions of rule 42 of these Rules, the Registrar shall send to the respondent a notice of inquiry in writing in the form set out in Schedule 2 to these Rules, specifying the nature and particulars of the charge against her, and informing her of the time and place of the meeting of the Committee at which the case will be heard, and requiring her to send or deliver to the Registrar her certificate of registration and badge, if any, not later than the date on which the hearing takes place. Such notice shall be sent by registered post to the registered address of the respondent contained in the register or, if the Registrar has reason to believe that that address is not her present address, then to any later address which may be known to the Registrar, and shall be posted so as to allow at least twenty-one days to elapse between the day on which the notice is posted and the date fixed for the hearing.

(a) 1961 c. 14.

(2) In any case in which there is a complainant, the Registrar shall send him a copy of the notice of inquiry and a copy of the Rules.

(3) Upon application by any party to the inquiry, the Registrar shall send to that party copies of any statutory declaration, explanation, admission or other similar statement or communication sent to the Council by any party to the inquiry.

(4) Any party to the inquiry may appear in person or be represented at the hearing by a friend, or by counsel or solicitor, provided that a complainant may be represented only by counsel or solicitor or, in the case of a corporate body being a complainant, by a member or officer duly appointed by them for the purpose.

Postponement or cancellation of inquiry

44.—(1) The chairman of the Committee, of her own motion or upon the application of any party thereto, may postpone the hearing of an inquiry, or may refer the matter to the Investigating Committee for further consideration as to whether an inquiry should be held:

Provided that where the complainant, if any, has intimated his intention of participating in the proceedings the Investigating Committee shall not in a case referred back to them direct that an inquiry should not be held except with the agreement of the complainant.

(2) Where before the inquiry opens it appears to the chairman of the Committee, or at any stage of the proceedings it appears to the Committee, that a notice of inquiry is defective she or they shall cause the notice to be amended unless it appears that the required amendment cannot be made without injustice, or, if she or they consider that the circumstances in which an amendment is made require it, she or they may direct that the inquiry shall be postponed or shall not be held.

(3) The Registrar shall, as soon as may be, give to all parties to whom a notice of inquiry has been sent notification of any decision to postpone or not to hold an inquiry, informing them of the date fixed for the hearing of a postponed inquiry.

The reading of the charge

45.—(1) The charge shall be read in the presence of the parties:

Provided that if the respondent does not appear but the Committee nevertheless decide that the inquiry shall proceed the charge shall be read in her absence.

(2) As soon as the charge has been read the respondent may, if she so desires, object to the charge, or to any part of it, in point of law, and any other party may reply to any such objection; and, if any such objection is upheld, no further proceedings shall be taken on that charge or on that part of the charge.

Proof of conviction

46.—(1) In cases arising out of a complaint or information from which it appears that a registered nurse has been convicted of a crime (referred to in these Rules as cases relating to conviction) the following order of proceedings shall be observed concerning proof of the convictions alleged in the charge:—

(a) the complainant, or, if no complainant appears, the solicitor shall adduce evidence of each conviction, and a certificate of a competent officer of the Court in which the proceedings took place that the respondent was convicted of a crime shall be sufficient for this purpose;

(b) if no evidence is adduced concerning any particular conviction, the chairman of the Committee shall thereupon announce that that conviction has not been proved;

(c) if the respondent appears, then the chairman shall ask her concerning each conviction of which evidence is so adduced whether she admits the conviction; and if she admits it the chairman shall thereupon announce that the conviction has been proved.

(2) If, where the respondent appears, she does not admit all the convictions she may then adduce evidence, concerning any conviction which she has not admitted, on the question whether she was convicted as alleged, and may address the Committee on that question:

Provided that only one address may be made under this paragraph and, where the respondent adduces evidence, that address shall be made either before that evidence is begun or after it is concluded.

(3) Where evidence is adduced under the last foregoing paragraph, the complainant, or, where no complainant appears, the solicitor may adduce evidence to rebut such evidence.

(4) On the conclusion of proceedings under the last foregoing paragraph, the Committee shall consider every conviction of which evidence has been adduced and shall determine whether or not it has been proved; and the chairman shall announce their determination in such terms as they may approve.

(5) After the Committee have determined that any conviction has been proved, the validity of that conviction shall not be questioned either by the Committee or by any party to the inquiry.

Proof of the facts in cases of alleged misconduct

47.—(1) In cases arising out of a complaint or information from which it appears that a question arises whether a registered nurse has been guilty of misconduct the following order of proceedings shall be observed as respects proof of the charge or charges:—

(a) if the respondent appears the chairman shall ask her whether she admits the facts alleged in the charge or charges;

(b) if the respondent does not appear and has not admitted by letter the facts alleged in the charge or ·charges, or if she appears and does not admit all the facts alleged, the complainant (if any appears) or the solicitor shall open the case and adduce evidence of the facts alleged;

(c) if no evidence is adduced concerning any particular charge on which there has been no admission of the facts alleged, the Committee, subject to their right in such a case to order the adjournment of the inquiry, shall record and the chairman shall announce a finding that the respondent is not guilty of misconduct in respect of the matters to which that charge relates.

(2) Where the respondent appears the following further order of proceedings shall be observed:—

(a) at the close of the case against her the respondent may, if she so desires, make either or both of the following submissions relating to any charge concerning which evidence has been adduced, namely—

(i) that no sufficient evidence has been adduced upon which the Committee could find that the facts alleged in that charge have been proved;

(ii) that the facts alleged in the charge are not such as to constitute misconduct;
and where such a submission is made, any other party may reply thereto;

(b) if a submission is made under the last foregoing sub-paragraph, the Committee shall consider and determine whether it should be upheld; and if the Committee determine to uphold it they shall record and the chairman shall announce their finding that, in relation to the matters to which that charge relates, the respondent is not guilty of misconduct;

(c) the respondent may adduce evidence in answer to any charge concerning which evidence has been adduced and, whether she adduces evidence or not, may address the Committee. Except with the leave of the Committee only one address may be made under this sub-paragraph and, where the respondent adduces evidence, shall be made either before that evidence is begun or after it is concluded;

(d) at the close of the case for the respondent, the complainant or the solicitor, as the case may be, may, with the leave of the Committee, adduce evidence to rebut any evidence adduced by the respondent; and if he does so the respondent may make a further address limited to the rebutting evidence;

(e) the complainant or the solicitor, as the case may be, may address the Committee by way of reply to the respondent's case—

(i) if oral evidence (not being evidence as to character) other than that of the respondent herself has been given on the respondent's behalf; or

(ii) with the leave of the Committee, where no such evidence has been given;

(f) without prejudice to the last foregoing sub-paragraph, if the respondent has made a submission to the Committee on a point of law any other party shall have a right of reply limited to that submission.

(3) On the conclusion of the aforesaid proceedings, the Committee shall consider and determine as respects each charge which remains outstanding which, if any, of the facts alleged in the charge have been proved to their satisfaction.

(4) If under the last foregoing paragraph the Committee determine as respects any charge, either that none of the facts alleged in the charge has been proved to their satisfaction, or that such facts as have been so proved would be insufficient to support a finding of misconduct, the Committee shall record a finding that the respondent is not guilty of misconduct in respect of the matters to which that charge relates and the chairman shall announce the findings of the Committee.

Procedure upon proof of conviction or of the facts in cases of alleged misconduct

48.—(1) Where the Committee have found that a conviction has been proved the chairman shall invite the complainant or the solicitor, as the case may be, to address the Committee, and to adduce evidence as to the circumstances leading up to the conviction and as to the previous history of the respondent. The chairman shall then invite the respondent to address the Committee by way of mitigation and the respondent may adduce evidence as aforesaid, and as to character.

(2) Where in a case of alleged misconduct the Committee have found that the facts or any of them alleged in any charge have been proved to their satisfaction (and have not on those facts recorded a finding of not guilty) the Committee

shall forthwith consider and determine whether in relation to the facts found proved as aforesaid the respondent is guilty of misconduct. If they determine that she is not guilty of misconduct in relation to some or any of such facts they shall record a finding to that effect and the chairman shall announce it. If they determine that she is guilty of misconduct in relation to all or any of such facts the chairman shall invite the complainant or the solicitor, as the case may be, to address the Committee and to adduce evidence as to circumstances leading up to the facts in question and as to the previous history of the respondent. The chairman shall then invite the respondent to address the Committee by way of mitigation and the respondent may adduce evidence as aforesaid, and as to character.

(3) Except where (in a case of alleged misconduct) the respondent has been found not guilty on all charges the Committee shall next consider and determine whether they should postpone judgment.

(4) If the Committee determine to postpone judgment, the judgment of the Committee shall stand postponed until such future meeting of the Committee as they may determine; and the chairman of the Committee shall announce their determination in such terms as the Committee shall have approved.

(5) If the Committee determine not to postpone judgment, they shall determine whether by reason of the conviction or convictions proved against the respondent or of her misconduct the Registrar should be directed to remove her name from the register, and the chairman shall announce their determination in such terms as they shall have approved.

Procedure in cases relating both to conviction and to misconduct

49. Where in any case it is alleged against the respondent both that she has been convicted and that she has been guilty of misconduct, the Committee shall proceed upon the charge or charges of each kind separately under rule 46 or rule 47 of these Rules according as the charge relates to a conviction or to alleged misconduct and shall then proceed under so much of rule 48 of these Rules as may be applicable either upon the charge or charges of each kind separately or upon the charges of both kinds concurrently, according as the circumstances of the case may require.

Procedure upon postponement of judgment

50.—(1) Where under any of the foregoing provisions of these Rules the judgment of the Committee in any case stands postponed, the following shall be the procedure:—

(a) the Registrar shall, not later than six weeks before the day fixed for the resumption of the proceedings, send to the respondent a notice, which shall—

(i) specify the day, time and place at which the proceedings are to be resumed and invite her to appear thereat; and

(ii) invite the respondent to furnish to the Registrar, not less than three weeks before the day fixed for resumption of the proceedings, the names and addresses of at least two suitable persons with knowledge of the facts found against her who are able and willing to identify the respondent and give evidence as to her character and the nature of her employment since the adjourned hearing, and such other evidence as the Committee may reasonably require;

(b) a copy of the notice shall be sent to the complainant, if any, and he may in turn, if he so desires, send to the Registrar a statement or statutory declaration, whether made by himself or not, concerning any matter relating to the conduct of the respondent since the previous hearing;

(c) at the meeting at which the proceedings are resumed the chairman shall first invite the solicitor to recall, for the information of the Committee, the position in which the case stands and the Committee may then receive further oral or documentary evidence in relation to the case, or to the conduct of the respondent since the previous hearing, and shall hear any other party to the proceedings who desires to be heard;

(d) the Committee shall then consider and determine whether they should further postpone their judgment on the charges on which their judgment was previously postponed; and if the Committee determine further to postpone judgment, the judgment of the Committee shall stand postponed until such future meeting of the Committee as they may determine; and the chairman of the Committee shall announce their determination in such terms as the Committee may approve. The provisions of this rule shall apply to any case in which judgment is further postponed;

(e) if the Committee determine that judgment shall not be further postponed paragraph (5) of rule 48 of these Rules shall apply.

(2) At any resumed proceedings any new charge alleged against the respondent in accordance with these Rules shall first be dealt with in accordance with such of rules 45 to 47 of these Rules and so much of rule 48 of these Rules as may be applicable and if the Committee determine not to postpone judgment in respect of any such new charge the Committee may apply paragraph (5) of rule 48 of these Rules simultaneously to the new charge and the charge in respect of which they had postponed judgment.

(3) Nothing in the last foregoing paragraph shall prevent the Committee from receiving evidence at any resumed proceedings of any conviction recorded against the respondent which has not been made the subject of a charge under these Rules.

(4) The validity of any resumed proceedings shall not be called into question by reason only that members of the Committee who were present at any former meeting were not present at the resumed meeting or that members present at the resumed meeting were not present at any former meeting.

Cases relating to entries in register alleged to have been procured by fraud

51.—(1) Where any question whether an entry in the register has been procured by fraud is referred to the Committee the Registrar shall send to the respondent a notice of inquiry specifying the nature of the fraud alleged, stating the day, time and place at which the Committee will hold an inquiry into the question, inviting her attendance at such inquiry, and containing such further information as the nature of the case may require. The provisions of rule 43 of these Rules shall apply as though such notice were a notice of inquiry such as is mentioned in that rule.

(2) A copy of the notice shall be sent to any person who is alleged to have been a party to the fraud alleged and to such other persons (if any) as the chairman may direct. Any such person may with the leave of the chairman appear at the inquiry as an additional party thereto.

(3) The inquiry shall proceed as though the question were a charge contained in a notice of inquiry in a case relating to misconduct and the provisions of rule 47 of these Rules shall accordingly apply thereto so far as may be.

(4) If the Committee determine that the entry has been proved to their satisfaction to have been procured by fraud, they shall make an order in writing,

under the hand of the chairman, that the entry, having been proved to the satisfaction of the Committee to have been procured by fraud, shall be removed from the register; and the chairman shall announce the determination in such terms as the Committee may approve.

(5) Whether or not the Committee proceed to determine that an entry has been proved to their satisfaction to have been procured by fraud, they may, if they are satisfied that the entry has been incorrectly made, cause the entry to be amended.

(6) Where an inquiry relates to two or more entries, the Committee may proceed under the foregoing provisions of this rule in respect of those entries either separately or taken together, as the Committee may think fit; and where an inquiry relates to an entry specifying two or more particulars, the Committee may proceed thereunder in respect of so much of the entry as specifies each of those particulars as if it were a separate entry.

Procedure where there is more than one respondent

52. Nothing in this part of these Rules shall prevent one inquiry being held into charges against two or more respondents; and where such an inquiry is held the foregoing rules shall apply with the necessary adaptations and subject to any directions given by the Committee as to the order in which proceedings shall be taken under any of those rules by or in relation to the several respondents, so however that any of the rights ensured to a respondent under those rules shall be exercised separately by each of the respondents who desires to invoke that right.

Restoration of name to the register

53.—(1) Where the name of a registered nurse has been removed from the register for disciplinary reasons, any application for its restoration to the register shall be made in writing addressed to the Registrar and signed by the applicant, stating the grounds on which the application is made.

(2) The application shall contain the names and addresses of two or more persons with knowledge of the facts found against her of whom two shall be justices of the peace, ministers of religion, registered medical practitioners, registered nurses or such other persons as the Council may approve, able and willing to identify the applicant and give evidence as to her character, and the nature of her employment since the date of the removal of her name and, where practicable, before that date.

(3) The Committee may invite the applicant to amplify her application by making a statement in writing in relation to any facts which the Committee consider to be material in making their decision.

(4) The Committee may require the applicant to verify by statutory declaration any statement made in her application or on the invitation of the Committee.

(5) Unless the Committee decide to restore the name of an applicant without a hearing, they shall afford to her, if she wishes, an opportunity of being heard by them and of adducing evidence.

(6) Subject to the foregoing provisions of this rule and to those of rules 57 to 59 of these Rules, the procedure of the Committee shall be such as they may determine.

54. Upon consideration of the application and of the evidence furnished in support of it, the Committee shall reach their decision and the Registrar shall forthwith communicate it to the applicant by registered post. Where the Committee have decided that the name of the applicant shall be restored to the register then, upon payment by the applicant of the undermentioned fee or fees, her name shall be restored to the part or parts of the register from which it was removed and a new certificate or certificates of registration shall be issued to her:—

    (*a*) in all cases a fee of £5 5s. 0d. shall be payable;

    (*b*) where the name of the applicant was removed for disciplinary reasons from the register prior to 24th day of March 1950, or where in the case of an applicant whose name was removed for disciplinary reasons between 24th day of March 1950, and 1st day of January 1952, the applicant had not paid the retention fee due under section 15(1) of the Nurses Act 1949(**a**), there shall be payable an additional fee calculated in accordance with the scale contained in rule 25(4) of these Rules in respect of her age on the date her application for restoration under this rule was received by the Council.

55. In the event of the restoration of the name of a nurse to any part of the register under this part of these Rules, notification of the fact shall be forthwith sent by the Registrar to the General Nursing Council for Scotland and/or the Joint Nursing and Midwives Council for Northern Ireland, if the Council are aware that the name of such nurse is or was also registered in Scotland and/or Northern Ireland.

56. In the event of notice being received by the Council from the General Nursing Council for Scotland and/or the Joint Nursing and Midwives Council for Northern Ireland that they have restored to their register the name of a nurse whose name they had removed from their register, if the Registrar shall find that the name of such nurse was removed from the register, it shall be the duty of the Registrar to lay the matter before the Committee. The Committee shall then consider the matter, and if necessary make inquiries and may, if they think fit, having regard to all the circumstances and at their discretion, restore the name of such nurse to the register, if she applies under and conforms to such of the provisions of this part of these Rules as the Committee shall require. Unless the Committee decide to restore the name of an applicant without a hearing they shall afford to her, if she wishes, an opportunity of being heard by them and of adducing evidence. In the event of the Committee restoring the name of a nurse to the register under this rule, the Registrar shall as soon as possible notify the fact of such restoration to the General Nursing Council for Scotland and/or the Joint Nursing and Midwives Council for Northern Ireland.

Hearing and adjournment

57.—(1) The Committee may deliberate in camera (with or without the legal assessor) at any time and for any purpose during or after the hearing or any proceedings.

(2) Save as aforesaid all proceedings before the Committee shall take place in the presence of all parties thereto who appear therein and shall be held in public except as provided by the following paragraph hereof.

(3) Where in the interests of justice it appears to the Committee that the public should be excluded from any proceedings or part thereof, the Committee may direct that the public shall be so excluded; but a direction under this paragraph shall not apply to the announcement in pursuance of any of these Rules of a determination of the Committee.

(4) The Committee may adjourn their proceedings from time to time as they think fit.

Evidence

58.—(1) Where any respondent or applicant has supplied to the Committee or to the Registrar on their behalf the name of any person to whom reference may be made confidentially as to her character or conduct the Committee may consider any information received from such person in consequence of such reference without disclosing the same to the respondent or applicant.

(2) The Committee may receive oral, documentary, or other evidence of any fact which appears to them relevant to the inquiry into the case before them; provided that, where a fact which it is sought to prove or the form in which any evidence is tendered is such that it would not be admissible in criminal proceedings in any English court, the Committee shall not receive evidence of that fact or in that form, unless after consultation with the legal assessor they are satisfied that it is desirable in the interests of justice to receive it having regard to the difficulty and expense of obtaining evidence which would be so admissible.

(3) A witness including the respondent (if she gives evidence) shall first be examined by the person calling him and may then be cross-examined and re-examined. Questions may be put to any witness by the Committee through the chairman or by the legal assessor with the leave of the chairman.

(4) The Committee may cause any person to be called as a witness in any proceedings before them whether or not the parties consent thereto.

Voting

59.—(1) Any question put to the vote shall be put in the form of a motion. The chairman shall call upon the members present to vote for or against the motion by raising their hands and shall declare that the motion appears to her to have been carried or not carried as the case may be.

(2) Where the result so declared is challenged by any member, the chairman shall call upon the Registrar to read the roll and as her name is read every member present including the chairman (who shall be called last) shall say "For" or "Against" according as her vote is given for or against the motion. The chairman shall thereupon declare the number of members who have voted for and the number who have voted against the motion and whether the motion has been carried or not carried.

(3) Where on any of the questions the votes are equal, the question shall be deemed to have been resolved in favour of the respondent or applicant, as the case may be, and for the purposes of this paragraph a decision to postpone judgment shall be taken to be in favour of the respondent or applicant unless she indicates to the Committee that she is opposed to postponement.

Communication of decision of committee in disciplinary cases

60.—(1) The Registrar shall forthwith communicate with the respondent by registered post informing her of the decision of the Committee.

(2) The Registrar shall in the case of the removal of the respondent's name from the register, retain the respondent's certificate of registration and badge, if any, and shall delete her name from the part or parts of the register in which it is included.

2m

(3) Where the respondent's name has been removed from the register and the respondent has failed to deliver her certificate and badge, if any, to the Registrar prior to or during the proceedings for removal, the Registrar shall, on notifying her of the Committee's decision, request her to deliver the said certificate and badge, and warn her of her liability to proceedings if she fails to comply with that request.

61. In the event of the removal of the name of a nurse from any part of the register under this part of these Rules, notification of the fact shall forthwith be sent by the Registrar to the General Nursing Council for Scotland and/or the Joint Nursing and Midwives Council for Northern Ireland, if the Council are aware that the name of such nurse is or was also registered in Scotland and/or Northern Ireland.

62. In the event of the Council receiving a notification from the General Nursing Council for Scotland and/or the Joint Nursing and Midwives Council for Northern Ireland that the name of any nurse registered by either or both of those Councils has been removed from the register in Scotland or Northern Ireland by reason of a finding by such Council that such nurse has been guilty of a crime, or any misconduct, if the Registrar shall find that the nurse is also registered in any part of the register, she shall inform her by registered post that the Council have received such notification, and shall inquire of her whether she desires to show cause why her name should not also be removed from the register. If no answer is received by the Registrar within twenty-eight days after the despatch of such letter, or such longer period as the Committee may allow if they are satisfied that there is sufficient reason for an extension of time, or if the nurse replies that she does not desire to show cause as aforesaid, then the Committee shall at their next convenient meeting direct the Registrar to remove the nurse's name from the register. If the nurse replies that she does desire to show cause as aforesaid, the Registrar shall lay the matter before the Committee, who shall thereupon proceed to deal with the matter by way of a fresh hearing under this part of these Rules, as if the complaint had been originally made to the Council. The action of the Committee shall in due course be notified to the General Nursing Council for Scotland and/or the Joint Nursing and Midwives Council for Northern Ireland, as the case may be.

63. If any question arises as to the meaning or effect of this part of these Rules, or if any question or matter shall arise which is not provided for by this part of these Rules, such question or matter shall be decided by the Committee.

PART VIII

Procedure of Council and Committees

64.—(1) At the ordinary meeting of the Council in the month of September in each year the Council shall appoint from their members a chairman and vice-chairman, who shall hold office until a chairman and vice-chairman have been appointed at the ordinary meeting in the month of September in the following year.

(2) If the office of chairman or of vice-chairman becomes vacant during the year, it shall be filled at such next meeting of the Council as may be convenient, and the member appointed shall hold office for the remainder of the term of office of the person in whose place she is appointed.

(3) In the event of two or more persons being nominated for the office of chairman, or of vice-chairman, the voting shall be by ballot, and there shall be as many ballots as are necessary to reduce the final ballot to two candidates

for the office in question. After each ballot the name of the candidate receiving the lowest number of votes shall be struck out and the next ballot shall be between the remaining candidates, and so on until the final ballot is between two candidates.

(4) In the event of neither the chairman nor the vice-chairman being present at any meeting of the Council, the Council shall appoint a chairman to preside at that meeting.

65.—(1) The Council shall meet not less than four times a year and, except for one meeting which shall be held in September, meetings shall, subject to the provision of this rule, be held at such times as the Council may decide.

(2) The chairman may at any time convene a meeting of the Council, and the Registrar shall within fourteen days convene a meeting, if required to do so by any six members of the Council by writing under their hands.

(3) Every member of the Council attending a meeting of the Council shall sign her name in a book kept for the purpose.

(4) Not less than ten days' notice of any meeting shall be given to each member of the Council, directed to such address as she shall from time to time furnish to the Registrar.

(5) The quorum of the Council shall be twelve.

66. The Registrar shall act as secretary of the Council.

67. Minutes of the proceedings of the Council shall be taken by the Registrar, and shall be duly entered in a book provided for the purpose. A draft of the minutes shall be circulated to the members of the Council, together with the notice of the meeting at which they are to be submitted for confirmation.

68. Except in cases where the presiding chairman on the ground of urgency or convenience otherwise directs, the following order of business shall be observed:—

(1) minutes of the last meeting.

(2) adjourned business.

(3) correspondence.

(4) reports of Committees.

(5) notices of motion.

(6) any other business.

(7) date of next meeting.

69. No business which is not upon the agenda paper shall be discussed at any meeting of the Council (except routine business), unless the presiding chairman declare such business to be of an urgent nature, and is supported by two-thirds of the members present and voting.

70. Every question, the manner of voting on which is not otherwise specified in these Rules, shall be decided on a show of hands by a majority of members present and voting, but any member may call for a division, in which case the names of members for and against and of those who abstained from voting shall be taken down in writing and entered in the minutes. In the case of an equality of votes, the presiding chairman shall have a second or casting vote.

71. Every motion or amendment shall be moved and seconded, and shall be reduced to writing and handed to the presiding chairman, and shall be read before it is further discussed or put to the meeting.

72.—(1) Every notice of motion shall be in writing, shall be signed by the member giving the notice, and shall be given or sent to the Registrar.

(2) The Registrar shall insert in the agenda paper of the next ordinary meeting of the Council all notices of motion which she may have received not less than one clear day prior to the day on which the agenda paper is sent out to members, in the order in which they have been received by her.

73. No resolution of the Council shall be altered or rescinded at a subsequent meeting, except upon a notice of motion on which a copy has been sent out to members by the Registrar ten clear days before such meeting.

74.—(1) In addition to the Mental Nurses Committee referred to in rule 75 of these Rules and to the Finance Committee referred to in rule 76 of these Rules, there shall be the following Standing Committees of the Council:—

    (*a*) a Standing Committee consisting of the whole Council

    (*b*) a Registration and Enrolment Committee

    (*c*) an Education Committee

    (*d*) a Disciplinary Committee

    (*e*) an Investigating Committee

(2) At the ordinary meeting of the Council in the month of September in each year, the Council shall appoint the members of the Registration and Enrolment Committee, the Education Committee, the Investigating Committee and the Disciplinary Committee, who shall hold office until their successors have been appointed at the ordinary meeting of the Council in the month of September in the following year.

(3) Any casual vacancy which occurs on any of these Committees shall be filled by the Council at such next meeting of the Council as may be convenient and the person appointed to fill the casual vacancy shall hold office for the remainder of the term of office of the person in whose place she is appointed.

(4) The Registration and Enrolment Committee shall consist of eight members of the Council together with the chairman and vice-chairman of the Council, as ex-officio members; and a quorum shall be four. The Education Committee shall consist of eighteen members of the Council one of whom shall be the enrolled general nurse who was elected to the Council by enrolled general nurses, together with the chairman and vice-chairman as ex-officio members; and a quorum shall be six.

(5) The Disciplinary Committee shall consist of the chairman of the Council and eleven other members of the Council other than the vice-chairman thereof, at least two of whom shall not be nurses; and a quorum shall be six.

(6) The Investigating Committee shall consist of the vice-chairman of the Council and seven other members of the Council, none of whom shall be members of the Disciplinary Committee; and a quorum shall be three.

75.—(1) Pursuant to section 18 of the Act of 1957, as substituted by section 4 of the Act of 1969, the Council shall appoint to the Mental Nurses Committee eleven members of the Council of whom:—

(a) three shall be registered mental nurses elected to the Council,

(b) one shall be a registered nurse for the mentally subnormal elected to the Council,

(c) two shall be registered nurses appointed to the Council engaged in the training of pupil nurses in the psychiatric field,

(d) one shall be an enrolled mental nurse or enrolled nurse for the mentally subnormal elected to the Council.

(2) The quorum of the Mental Nurses Committee shall be four.

(3) At the ordinary meeting of the Council in the month of September in each year, the Council shall appoint the members of the Mental Nurses Committee, who shall hold office until their successors have been appointed at the ordinary meeting of the Council in the month of September in the following year.

(4) Any casual vacancy which occurs on the Committee shall be filled by the Council at such next meeting of the Council as may be convenient. The person appointed to fill the casual vacancy shall hold office for the remainder of the term of office of the person in whose place she is appointed.

(5) The chairman of the Mental Nurses Committee shall be a member of the Council.

76.—(1) Pursuant to section 20 of the Act of 1957, the Council shall appoint a Finance Committee which shall consist of ten members of the Council, including the chairman and vice-chairman thereof who shall be ex-officio members, and of such persons other than members of the Council (not exceeding two in number) as may be nominated by the Secretary of State after consultation with the Council. The quorum shall be four.

(2) At the ordinary meeting of the Council in the month of September in each year, the Council shall appoint the members of the Finance Committee, who shall hold office until their successors have been appointed at the ordinary meeting of the Council in the month of September in the following year.

(3) Any casual vacancy which occurs on the Committee shall be filled by the Council at such next meeting of the Council as may be convenient. The persons appointed to fill the casual vacancy shall hold office for the remainder of the term of office of the person in whose place she is appointed.

(4) The chairman of the Finance Committee shall be a member of the Council.

77.—(1) The Council may delegate to any Standing Committee, with such restrictions and qualifications, if any, as they think fit, all or any of their powers (other than in respect of the matters required by the Nurses Acts 1957 to 1969 or by these Rules or by the Enrolled Nurses Rules 1969(**a**) to be referred to a specific Committee).

(2) The chairman of the Council or such deputy as shall be appointed by the Disciplinary Committee to act in her absence shall be the chairman of the Disciplinary Committee; save as aforesaid, each committee shall elect its own chairman. In the absence of the chairman of any committee, the committee shall appoint a chairman to preside at the meeting.

(3) Each committee shall report its proceedings to the Council. Any recommendations which a committee may make shall, so far as is practicable, be in the form of resolutions to be considered by the Council. Every report from a committee other than a report of proceedings under Part VII of these Rules

(**a**) Scheduled to S.I. 1969/1674.

or under Part VI of the Enrolled Nurses Rules 1969, shall be submitted by the chairman of the committee (if present) who shall move that it shall be received by the Council, and on the motion being carried, the chairman or any other member of the committee may move to agree with the resolution of the committee and such resolutions shall be considered seriatim. The motion that the report (if necessary as amended) be now approved shall be put from the chair, and no debate shall be allowed thereon.

(4) Except by special permission of the Council, no report of a committee shall be discussed by the Council unless it has been sent to the members of the Council at least three days before the meeting of the Council at which it is to be presented.

78.—(1) All bills and claims shall be examined by the Registrar or other official as authorised by the Council and laid by her before the Finance Committee, who shall report thereon to the Council, and such bills and claims as are allowed shall be initialled by the presiding chairman.

(2) All payments made by or on behalf of the Council shall be made by cheque or other order drawn on the bankers of the Council, except in the case of sums not exceeding £10 or of such greater amount as the Council may from time to time determine, or in cases of urgency.

(3) Subject to the provisions of the following paragraph, all cheques or other authorities for payment of money by the bankers of the Council shall be signed by two members of the Finance Committee nominated by the Council and counter-signed by the Registrar or her deputy.

(4) The Council shall have power to open a special account or special accounts with their bankers and to authorise the Registrar or her deputy, or other official of the Council, to draw thereon up to such amounts and subject to such conditions as the Council may from time to time prescribe.

79. At every meeting of the Council, the Registrar or other official as authorised by the Council shall present a statement in writing from the Finance Committee showing receipts and expenditure by the Council for the current year up to the date of such meeting, and showing the existing balances, if any, to the credit of the Council.

80. The presiding chairman of the Council shall decide upon any point of order or procedure and her decision shall be final.

81. The foregoing rules of procedure for the Council shall, so far as they are capable of application, apply to the procedure of committees appointed by the Council.

82. All minutes, registers and records shall be open to the inspection of members of the Council during the Registrar's business hours.

PART IX

Rules with respect to the uniform and badge which may be worn by registered nurses

83. The uniform and badge of a registered nurse shall be that described in Schedule 5 to these Rules.

84. The uniform in all its details shall be strictly adhered to, and no alteration or embellishment of any kind shall be permitted. No unauthorised letters or devices, and no trimmings, lace or jewellery shall be worn on any part of the uniform, provided that this prohibition shall not apply to the wearing of the badge or of the ribbon or other insignia of any order, decoration or medal conferred by the Sovereign or of any foreign order, decoration or medal accepted by permission of the Sovereign.

85. The wearing of the uniform by registered nurses shall not be compulsory, provided that a registered nurse who wears the uniform shall wear the whole uniform and not a portion thereof.

86. No registered nurse shall wear the uniform without a permit from the Registrar, which shall be issued free by the Council to every nurse at the time of her registration.

87. In the event of loss of, or damage to, the original permit, a registered nurse desirous of obtaining a duplicate permit shall make application to the Registrar on a form to be supplied by the Council, and shall pay a fee of 5s. 0d. with her application. The fee payable for any further permit shall be 10s. 0d.

88. A uniform shall be obtained only from a firm authorised by the Council to supply uniforms, and the permit from the Registrar shall be produced at the time of the order.

89. The material for a uniform shall be obtained only from a firm authorised by the Council to supply material which shall be of the kind, weight and colour laid down by the Council, and the uniform shall be made in accordance with the designs approved by the Council.

90. A registered nurse shall not dispose of her uniform unless all distinguishing features have been previously removed therefrom.

91. The badge shall be issued by the Council to every nurse at the time of her registration and shall remain the property of the Council. In the event of loss of, or damage to, a badge, application for a duplicate badge on payment of the sum of £1 1s. 0d. may be made to the Registrar on a form to be supplied by the Council.

92. The badge may be worn with or without uniform, and shall, when worn by female registered nurses, be affixed to the right side of the person.

PART X
Miscellaneous

93. The Council shall be at liberty to request any member or members of the Council to visit any place or places for the purpose of explaining the Nurses Acts, 1957 to 1969 and to sanction the payment of all proper expenses incurred by such member or members in connection with such visit.

94. The authentication of the seal of the Council shall be the signature (including a facsimile of a signature by whatever process reproduced) of the chairman of the Council or of the Registrar. The seal shall be and remain in the custody of the Registrar, who shall be responsible therefor. The Registrar shall have possession of one set of keys of the seal, and the chairman of the Council, or a member of the Council nominated by her, shall have possession of the other set. A record shall be kept by the Registrar, and signed by the chairman, of the occasions on which, and the purposes for which, the seal of the Council has been affixed.

95. Where under these Rules a date is to be announced by the Council, such announcement shall appear in such journals as, in the opinion of the Council, will be best calculated to bring the matter to the notice of the nursing profession.

Rule 4

SCHEDULE 1
FORM OF REGISTER

Each part of the register shall show in respect of each nurse admitted the following particulars:—

(1) Registration number.

(2) Full names and, if married, maiden name.

(3) Permanent address.

(4) Date of registration.

(5) Qualifications. Under this heading shall appear the qualification in each case for admission to the register (including certificate of training, if any), the dates of obtaining such qualification, and the hospital or hospitals in which the qualifying training has been received.

(6) The granting of a certificate of registration as a teacher of nurses, (either as a nurse tutor or as a clinical teacher) where appropriate.

Rule 43

SCHEDULE 2
FORM OF NOTICE

GENERAL NURSING COUNCIL FOR ENGLAND AND WALES
DISCIPLINARY COMMITTEE

Nurses Acts, 1957 *to* 1969

To ....

of ....

Take notice that the charge (or charges) against you, particulars of which are set forth below, $\frac{has}{have}$ been brought to the notice of the Council, and that the Disciplinary Committee of the Council propose to investigate such charge(s) at a meeting to be held at the offices of the Council, 23 Portland Place, London, W1A 1BA at................ $\frac{a.m.}{p.m.}$ on................

the .... 19.. and to determine whether your name should be removed from the register.

PARTICULARS OF CHARGE(S)

You are hereby required to attend before the Disciplinary Committee of the Council at the time and place mentioned above and to answer such charges, bringing with you all papers and documents in your possession relevant to the matter and any persons whose evidence you wish to lay before the Disciplinary Committee.

The following points should be carefully noted:—

(a) you are entitled to be represented at the hearing before the Disciplinary Committee by a friend, or by counsel or a solicitor, but if you propose to employ counsel or a solicitor, you should give written notice to the Registrar at the address mentioned above at least seven days before the hearing.

(b) it is imperative that you should either send to the Registrar before the date fixed for the hearing, or bring with you to the hearing your certificate of registration (and badge).

A copy of the Nurses Rules 1969 is enclosed, and your attention is directed to Part VII of those Rules.

....
Registrar of the Council.

Date..

SCHEDULE 3　　　　　　　　　　Rule 12

SYLLABUS OF TRAINING FOR THE INTERMEDIATE EXAMINATION

1. For candidates for the part of the register for mental nurses the preliminary study, practice and experience of the following subjects.

Human development and human behaviour within the family and society.

Introduction to psychological concepts.

　Human biology.

　Psycho-physical disturbances and physical illness.

　Human behaviour in relation to illness.

　Principles and practice of psychiatric nursing including—

　　first aid;

　　psychopathology, psychiatry and psychiatric treatment; and

　　legal and administrative aspects of the nursing of the mentally ill.

2. For candidates for the part of the register for nurses for the mentally subnormal the preliminary study, practice and experience of the following subjects.

Human development and human behaviour within the family and society.

Introduction to psychological concepts.

　Human biology.

　Psycho-physical disturbances and physical illness.

　Human behaviour in relation to illness.

　Principles and practice of the nursing of the mentally subnormal including—

　　first aid;

　　concept and nature of mental subnormality;

　　training and treatment of the mentally subnormal; and

　　legal and administrative aspects of the nursing of the mentally subnormal.

Rules 13, 15, 17 and 19   SCHEDULE 4

SYLLABUS OF TRAINING FOR THE FINAL EXAMINATIONS

Part 1. For candidates for the general part of the register.

    Principles and practice of nursing.

    First aid, including treatment of emergencies.

    Ward organisation and preparation for management.

    Study of the human individual.

    Concepts of the nature and causes of diseases, including applied anatomy and physiology.

    Investigations and treatment.

    Nursing care.

    Social aspects.

    Rehabilitation.

Part 2. For candidates for the part of the register for mental nurses.

    Human development and human behaviour within the family and society.

    Introduction to psychological concepts.

    Human biology.

    Psycho-physical disturbances and physical illness.

    Human behaviour in relation to illness.

    Principles and practices of psychiatric nursing including—

        first aid;

        psychopathology, psychiatry and psychiatric treatment; and

        legal and administrative aspects of the nursing of the mentally ill.

Part 3. For candidates for the part of the register for the mentally subnormal.

    Human development and human behaviour within the family and society.

    Introduction to psychological concepts.

    Human biology.

    Psycho-physical disturbances and physical illness.

    Human behaviour in relation to illness.

    Principles and practice of the nursing of the mentally subnormal including—

        first aid;

        concept and nature of mental subnormality;

        training and treatment of the mentally subnormal; and

        legal and administrative aspects of the nursing of the mentally subnormal.

Part 4. For candidates for the part of the register for sick children's nurses the study of the following subjects in relation to the child;

    Principles and practice of nursing.

    First aid, including treatment of emergencies.

    Ward organisation and preparation for management.

    Study of the human individual.

    Concepts of the nature and causes of diseases, including applied anatomy and physiology.

    Investigations and treatment.

    Nursing care.

    Social aspects.

    Rehabilitation.

SCHEDULE 5

PART 1

DESCRIPTION OF UNIFORM, BADGE AND LETTERING FOR FEMALE REGISTERED NURSES

1. The basic colours shall be navy blue, Cambridge blue, and silver.

2. The outdoor uniform shall consist of:—

   (*a*) an overcoat (lightweight or heavyweight); or raincoat; and/or costume worn with blouse; or lightweight summer uniform; and

   (*b*) a peaked cap with embroidered device in front; or beret with cockade and embroidered device; or shallow double-crowned felt hat with cockade and embroidered device; or tricorne-shape hat with cockade and embroidered device made in felt, straw, or material to match the lightweight summer uniform; or a white peaked crash-helmet made in accordance with the specification of the British Standards Institution for protective helmets for motor cyclists.

With any of the above uniforms there shall be worn navy or black shoes, coloured stockings and navy, black or chamois gloves; a handbag, if carried, shall be of navy leather.

3. The indoor uniform shall consist of:—

   (*a*) a washing frock to be worn with or without an apron, or

   (*b*) a mess frock.

With any of the above uniform there shall be worn navy or black shoes with coloured stockings.

4. The badge shall be made of silver or chromium plated metal and blue enamel, and its size and design shall be as follows:—

   Diameter: 3.6 centimetres.

   Outer edge: 5 petals of Tudor Rose.

   Between each petal a small Tudor Rose.

   Centre: Figure of Hygeia with rose and daffodil design on either side, encircled by garter bearing the words: "The General Nursing Council for England and Wales".

5. The embroidered device shall consist of the appropriate letters of designation worked in silver colour on a navy blue background.

6. The metal letters on epaulettes shall consist of the plated metal letters of designation indicating the part or parts of the register in which the nurse is registered:—

   General Nurses—SRN

   Mental Nurses—RMN

   Nurses for the Mentally Subnormal—RNMS

   Sick Children's Nurses—RSCN

   Fever Nurses—RFN

PART 2

DESCRIPTION OF UNIFORM, BADGE AND LETTERING FOR MALE REGISTERED NURSES

1. The basic colours shall be navy blue, Cambridge blue, and silver.

2. The outdoor uniform shall consist of:—

(a) An overcoat (lightweight or heavyweight); or raincoat; and

(b) A navy blue lounge suit worn with Air Force blue shirt, black tie; and

(c) A navy blue peaked cap with embroidered device in front; or navy blue beret with embroidered device in front; or navy blue forage cap with two small regulation buttons in front and embroidered device; or white peaked crash-helmet made in accordance with the specification of the British Standards Institution for protective helmets for motor cyclists.

3. The indoor uniform shall consist of:—

A washing duty coat.

With any of the above uniforms there shall be worn:—

Navy or black socks, black boots or shoes and with the outdoor uniform, dark brown or chamois gloves.

4. The badge, embroidered device and metal letters shall be identical with those prescribed for female registered nurses.

Rule 3   SCHEDULE 6

Rules Revoked

The Nurses Rules 1961, scheduled to the Nurses Rules, Approval Instrument 1961(a).

The Nurses (Amendment) Rules 1965, scheduled to the Nurses Rules, Approval Instrument 1965(b).

The Nurses (Amendment) Rules 1966, scheduled to the Nurses Rules, Approval Instrument 1966(c).

The Nurses (Amendment) Rules 1967, scheduled to the Nurses Rules, Approval Instrument 1967(d).

(L.S.)   *G. E. Watts,*

Chairman of the Council.

The seal of the General Nursing Council for England and Wales was hereunto affixed on 25th November 1969.

M. Henry,

Registrar.

Signed by authority of the Secretary of State for Social Services.

Serota,

Minister of State,

Department of Health and Social Security.

26th November 1969.

(a) S.I. 1961/1520 (1961 II, p. 3127).   (b) S.I. 1965/1485 (1965 II, p. 4324).
(c) S.I. 1966/255 (1966 I, p. 659).   (d) S.I. 1967/1704 (1967 III, p. 4629).

EXPLANATORY NOTE

(This Note is not part of the Instrument.)

The Rules approved by this Instrument consolidate with amendments the Rules specified in Schedule 6 to these Rules. The amendments include in particular:—

    (*a*) provision for fees to be paid by student nurses on entering training and by nurses trained abroad on applying for registration by the Council;

    (*b*) additional periods of training in certain circumstances where a break in training or a transfer from one training institution to another occurs;

    (*c*) the granting of a certificate as a teacher of nurses to persons trained in clinical instruction;

    (*d*) abolition of the preliminary examination for registered general and sick children's nurses;

    (*e*) the transfer of the functions of the Enrolled Nurses Committee, following its abolition under the 1969 Act, to the standing committees of the Council.

STATUTORY INSTRUMENTS

1969 No. 1676

NURSES AND MIDWIVES

The General Nursing Council (Election Scheme) Rules, Approval Instrument 1969

Made - - -	26th November 1969
Laid before Parliament	9th December 1969
Coming into Operation	12th December 1969

The Secretary of State for Social Services, in exercise of his powers under section 32 of the Nurses Act 1957(**a**), and of all other powers enabling him in that behalf, hereby approves the rules made by the General Nursing Council for England and Wales in the form set out in the Schedule hereto.

This instrument may be cited as the General Nursing Council (Election Scheme) Rules, Approval Instrument 1969 and shall come into operation on 12th December 1969.

SCHEDULE

THE GENERAL NURSING COUNCIL FOR ENGLAND AND WALES

The Nurses Acts 1957 *to* 1969.

The General Nursing Council for England and Wales in exercise of the powers conferred on them by sections 30 and 32 of the Nurses Act 1957 and paragraph 4 of Schedule 1 to that Act as amended by section 4 of the Nurses (Amendment) Act 1961(**b**) and all other powers enabling them in that behalf, hereby make the following rules:—

1. These Rules may be cited as the General Nursing Council (Election Scheme) Rules 1969.

2. The Interpretation Act 1889(**c**) applies to the interpretation of these Rules as it applies to the interpretation of an Act of Parliament.

3. The General Nursing Council (Election Scheme) Rules 1964(**d**), the Enrolled Nurses Committee (Election Scheme) Rules 1962(**e**) and the Mental Nurses Committee (Election Scheme) Rules 1964(**f**) are hereby revoked:

Provided that such revocation shall not affect any right, privilege, obligation or liability acquired, accrued or incurred, or anything duly done or suffered, under those Rules.

4. The members of the General Nursing Council for England and Wales, who are required by the provisions of paragraph 1(*a*) of Schedule 1 to the Nurses Act 1957 as amended by section 2(1) of the Nurses Act 1969(**g**), to be elected in accordance with the provisions of sub-paragraphs (1) and (2) of paragraph (2) of that Schedule as substituted respectively by subsections (2) and (3) of section 2 of the Nurses Act 1969, shall be elected in accordance with the Scheme set out in the Schedule to these Rules.

(**a**) 1957 c. 15.　　　　　　　(**b**) 1961 c. 14.　　　　　　(**c**) 1889 c. 63.
(**d**) Scheduled to S.I. 1964/1971 (1964 III, p. 4453).
(**e**) Scheduled to S.I. 1962/1504 (1962 II, p. 1630).
(**f**) Scheduled to S.I. 1964/1972 (1964 III, p. 4466).　　　(**g**) 1969 c. 47.

SCHEDULE TO THE RULES

Interpretation

1.—(1) Unless the context otherwise requires expressions used in this Scheme have the same meanings as in the Nurses Rules 1969(a), and the feminine shall include the masculine.

(2) The expression "area" means one of the 15 areas into which England and Wales is divided for the purposes of the election, as determined by the Secretary of State for Social Services under paragraph 2(2) of Schedule 1 to the Nurses Act 1957 as substituted by section 2(3) of the Nurses Act 1969.

Returning Officer

2.—(1) The Council shall at least 6 months before the date on which their elected members cease to hold office appoint a person, not being a member of the Council, or of any committee thereof, to be the Returning Officer for the ensuing election.

(2) The Returning Officer shall appoint a Deputy Returning Officer, not being a member of the Council, or of any committee thereof, to act for him in the event of his absence or inability to act, and the expression "Returning Officer" in this Scheme includes the Deputy Returning Officer so acting.

(3) The Returning Officer shall have power, subject to the approval of the Council, to employ and pay for out of the monies received from the Council, the staff and equipment necessary for the conduct of the election.

(4) Subject to the provisions of this Scheme, the Returning Officer shall be responsible for the conduct of the election.

Qualifications of candidates and electors

3.—(1) The numbers and qualifications of the several classes of persons to be elected are specified in the 1st and 2nd columns of the following table, and the qualifications of the persons entitled to nominate and to take part in the election of candidates of each of those classes are specified in the 3rd column of the table.

(a) Scheduled to S.I. 1969/1675 (1969 III, p. 5245).

TABLE

QUALIFICATIONS OF CANDIDATES AND ELECTORS

Number of persons to be elected	Qualifications of persons to be elected	Qualifications of persons entitled to nominate and take part in election
15 (one from each of the 15 areas determined by the Secretary of State being the Regional Hospital Areas* for the purposes of the National Health Service Act 1946(a)), viz:— 1. Newcastle 2. Leeds 3. Sheffield 4. East Anglian 5. North West Metropolitan 6. North East Metropolitan 7. South East Metropolitan 8. South West Metropolitan 9. Oxford 10. South Western 11. Welsh 12. Birmingham 13. Manchester 14. Liverpool 15. Wessex	Registered general nurses who, on the date fixed for the purpose of the election as the last date for the receipt of nomination papers, are engaged in the area for which they are candidates for election in work for which the employment of a registered nurse is requisite or for which a registered nurse is commonly employed.	Registered general nurses and registered fever nurses.
3	Registered mental nurses who, on the date fixed for the purpose of the election as the last date for receipt of nomination papers, are engaged in work for which the employment of a registered nurse is requisite or for which a registered nurse is commonly employed.	Registered mental nurses.

*See the National Health Service (Regional Hospital Areas) Order 1965 (S.I. 1965/527 (1965 I, p. 1382)) as amended by S.I. 1969/451 (1969 I, p. 1297).

(a) 1946 c. 81.

Number of persons to be elected	Qualifications of persons to be elected	Qualifications of persons entitled to nominate and take part in election
1	Registered nurse for the mentally subnormal who, on the date fixed for the purpose of the election as the last date for receipt of nomination papers, is engaged in work for which the employment of a registered nurse is requisite or for which a registered nurse is commonly employed.	Registered nurses for the mentally subnormal.
1	Registered sick children's nurse who, on the date fixed for the purpose of the election as the last date for receipt of nomination papers, is engaged in work for which the employment of a registered nurse is requisite or for which a registered nurse is commonly employed.	Registered sick children's nurses.
1	Enrolled general nurse who, on the date fixed for the purpose of the election as the last date for receipt of nomination papers, is engaged in work for which the employment of an enrolled nurse is requisite or for which an enrolled nurse is commonly employed.	Enrolled general nurses.
1	Enrolled mental nurse or enrolled nurse for the mentally subnormal who, on the date fixed for the purpose of the election as the last date for receipt of nomination papers, is engaged in work for which the employment of an enrolled nurse is requisite or for which an enrolled nurse is commonly employed.	Enrolled mental nurses and enrolled nurses for the mentally subnormal.

(2) In order to be eligible for election under this Scheme or to be entitled to nominate for and take part in the election, a person must have the requisite qualifications on the date fixed by the Returning Officer under rule 4 of this Scheme as the last day on which nomination papers are to be received.

Publication of notice of election

4. The Returning Officer shall fix the last day on which nomination papers are to be received, and at least 28 clear days before the day so fixed shall cause a notice of the election to be published, specifying the number and description of persons to be elected, the place to which the nomination papers are to be sent, and the last day on which they are to be received. The notice shall be published in 2 or more newspapers circulating in England and Wales, Scotland and Northern Ireland, and shall as nearly as may be, be in the form marked A in the Appendix to this Scheme.

Nomination

5.—(1) Each candidate for election shall be nominated on a separate nomination paper signed by not fewer than 6 persons having the requisite qualifications for nominating the candidate and no person may nominate more than the number of persons to be elected.

(2) Each nomination paper shall contain the name, address and requisite qualifications of the person nominated, and also the addresses and requisite qualifications of each person signing such paper, and shall be, as nearly as may be, in the appropriate form marked B(i) or B(ii) or B(iii) or B(iv) in the Appendix to this Scheme.

(3) Every nomination paper shall, before 12 noon on the last day fixed for the receipt of nomination papers, be delivered by post or otherwise, to the Returning Officer, General Nursing Council for England and Wales, 23 Portland Place, London W1A 1BA, and shall be accompanied by a declaration in writing, signed by the person nominated, in the appropriate form marked C(i) or C(ii) in the Appendix to this Scheme or to the like effect, acknowledging that such person consents to be nominated.

(4) Nomination papers shall be invalid if either:—

(i) they are not received by the Returning Officer before 12 noon on the last day fixed for the receipt of nomination papers, or

(ii) any requirement of this Scheme has not been complied with provided that no misnomer or inaccurate or incomplete description of any person or place named in any nomination paper shall invalidate that paper if, in the opinion of the Returning Officer, the description of the person or place is such as to be commonly understood.

(5) Where, in the opinion of the Returning Officer, a nomination of any candidate is, by virtue of paragraph (4)(ii) of this rule, invalid, the Returning Officer shall forthwith notify the candidate to that effect and within one week after the publication of the list of the duly nominated candidates under paragraph (9) of this rule the candidate may, either personally or by her agent, appointed in writing, notify in writing to the Returning Officer that she considers her nomination valid.

(6) If after further consideration of the contention disclosed in such notice, and after taking such legal advice as he thinks fit the Returning Officer is satisfied that the nomination paper was valid he shall cause the name of the candidate to be included in the list of duly nominated candidates.

(7) If after further consideration of the contention disclosed in the notice the Returning Officer is satisfied that the nomination was invalid he shall forthwith so certify. In that event he shall forward a copy of his certificate to the candidate for nomination, who may within 7 days of receiving such copy, appeal to the Secretary of State for Social Services and notify the Returning Officer accordingly.

(8) The Secretary of State shall consider any appeal made under sub-paragraph (7) hereof and the Returning Officer shall forthwith forward to the Secretary of State a copy of his certificate given under sub-paragraph (7) hereof together with any comments he wishes to make and the Secretary of State's decision as to whether the appellant was validly nominated shall be final. In the event of the Secretary of State deciding that the appellant was validly nominated and in the event that the election shall have taken place a fresh election in respect of that area or class shall take place.

(9) As soon as possible after the time fixed for the receipt of nomination papers has expired and notwithstanding any notifications under paragraph (5) of this rule the Returning Officer shall publish at the offices of the Council a list of the duly nominated candidates and on the same day shall send a copy of that list by registered post to each of them. Before 12 noon on the 7th day from the date of publication of the list, a candidate may withdraw from the poll by delivering by post or otherwise to the Returning Officer a written notice of withdrawal and on receipt thereof the Returning Officer shall expunge the name of such candidate from the list. No notice of withdrawal received after 12 noon on the 7th day from the date of publication of the list shall be valid.

(10) After the period for withdrawal has expired under paragraph (9) of this rule, should there be no valid nomination or insufficient valid nominations in respect of any area or class, the Returning Officer shall publish at the offices of the Council a list of the areas or classes for which there are no duly nominated candidates and the Returning Officer shall allow one further period, until noon on the 14th day after publication of that list, for the receipt of nomination papers in respect of such areas or classes.

(11) The provisions of paragraphs (1) to (9) of this rule shall apply to the nomination of a candidate under paragraph (10) as they apply to the nomination of candidates under the preceding paragraphs of this rule.

Conduct of election

6.—(1) The election of the 15 registered general nurses shall be conducted in the manner set out in the following paragraphs of this rule.

(2) If the number of duly nominated candidates in respect of any one area does not exceed 1, the Returning Officer shall forthwith declare such candidate to be elected.

(3) If the number of duly nominated candidates in respect of any one area exceeds 1, the Returning Officer shall cause ballot papers and identification envelopes to be prepared. Ballot papers shall contain the names, addresses and requisite qualification or qualifications of all the persons who have been nominated and whose names have not been expunged from the list and shall state the last day on which ballot papers may be received, and the place to which they are to be returned. The identification envelope shall bear a declaration of identity. Ballot papers and identification envelopes shall be, as nearly as may be, in the forms marked D and E in the Appendix to this Scheme.

(4) The Returning Officer shall, 21 clear days at least before the last day fixed for the receipt of ballot papers, cause a ballot paper to be forwarded by post to each person qualified to vote in the election at her registered address, together with an identification envelope. Each elector shall be entitled to receive 1 ballot paper and 1 identification envelope and no more, and votes shall not be given except upon the ballot papers provided by the Returning Officer.

(5) Each elector shall mark the ballot paper delivered to her with a X against the name or names of the person or persons (not exceeding the number of persons to be elected), for whom she votes and shall not mark the ballot paper in any other way; she shall then place her ballot paper in the identification envelope, and securely fasten the same. The elector shall sign the declaration printed on the said envelope, place it inside a covering envelope, and send it by post or otherwise to the Returning Officer at the place named in the ballot paper as the place to which it is to be returned. Every ballot paper in respect of which any requirement of this Scheme has not been complied with, or which is not received by the Returning Officer before 12 noon on the last day fixed for the receipt of ballot papers, shall be invalid.

(6) The Returning Officer, immediately after the last day fixed for the receipt of ballot papers, shall cause the validity of the votes to be ascertained by an examination of the identification envelopes and by such other evidence, if any, as he may think necessary, and shall cause such of the identification envelopes as are found to be valid to be opened, and the ballot papers withdrawn, and placed in a ballot box. When all

the ballot papers have been transferred to the ballot box they shall be examined and counted, and the number of valid votes given for each candidate shall be ascertained. Any candidate, or agent appointed by her in writing to represent her, may be present during the examination of the identification envelopes and the counting of the ballot papers and accordingly the Returning Officer shall notify each candidate of the time and place of the examination and counting.

(7) In each of the 15 areas, the candidate having the greatest number of votes shall be declared elected for that area by the Returning Officer. If an equality of votes is found to exist between any of the candidates, in any one of the areas and the addition of a vote would entitle any of such candidates to be declared elected, the Returning Officer shall determine by lot which of the candidates whose votes are equal shall be declared elected.

7. The foregoing provisions with regard to the conduct of the election of registered general nurses shall apply with the necessary modifications to the election of registered mental nurses, registered nurses for the mentally subnormal, registered sick children's nurses, enrolled general nurses, enrolled mental nurses and enrolled nurses for the mentally subnormal.

Powers of Returning Officer

8. Subject to any decision given by the Secretary of State on an appeal made to him under rules 5 or 11 of these Rules any question arising with regard to the validity of a nomination or ballot paper, or otherwise in connection with any election held under this Scheme, shall be determined by the Returning Officer.

Notice of result of election

9. The Returning Officer shall forthwith give to every candidate whose name has not been expunged from the list written notice of the result of the election, and shall furnish the Council with a list of the persons certified by him to have been duly elected, showing the number of votes cast for each of such persons.

Secrecy of ballot

10. The Returning Officer, and every officer, clerk, or servant employed in connection with the election shall maintain, and aid in maintaining the secrecy of the ballot, and shall not communicate to any person any information as to the manner in which any elector has recorded her vote.

Validity of election

11.—(1) Any candidate unsuccessful at the poll may either personally or by her agent appointed in writing notify the Returning Officer within 14 days after the declaration of the result of the election that she contests the validity of that part of the election in respect of which she was unsuccessful on the grounds of non-compliance with the provisions of this Scheme, or of any misdescription or miscount, or of the non-delivery, loss or miscarriage of any document.

(2) If after consideration of the contention disclosed in the notice, the Returning Officer is satisfied in respect of that part that the election was conducted substantially in accordance with the provisions of this Scheme and that any non-compliance, misdescription, miscount, non-delivery, loss or miscarriage did not affect the result of that part of the election, he may, within 14 days of receiving such notice, so certify. In that event he shall forward a copy of his certificate to the unsuccessful candidate, who may within 7 days of receiving such copy, appeal to the Secretary of State for Social Services.

(3) Where the Returning Officer does not so certify, he shall not later than the 15th day after receiving the notice forward a copy thereof to the Secretary of State for Social Services together with such comments as he shall think fit.

(4) The Secretary of State shall consider any appeal made under paragraph (2) or any

notice received under paragraph (3) of this rule and his decision as to whether the result of the relevant part of the election was affected by any non-compliance, misdescription, miscount, non-delivery, loss or miscarriage, shall be final. In the event of the Secretary of State deciding that the result of the relevant part of the election was so affected, a fresh election in respect of the seat in that part of the election shall take place.

APPENDIX

FORM A (*Notice of election*)

Nurses Acts 1957 *to* 1969

Notice is hereby given that pursuant to the *Nurses Acts* 1957 to 1969 an election of 22 members of the General Nursing Council for England and Wales, 20 to represent the nurses registered upon the register of that Council and 2 to represent the nurses enrolled upon the roll of that Council, is about to be held.

The following table shows the numbers and qualifications of the persons to be elected, and the qualifications of the persons entitled to nominate and take part in the election of each class of candidate.

TABLE

QUALIFICATIONS OF CANDIDATES AND ELECTORS

Number of persons to be elected	Qualifications of persons to be elected	Qualifications of persons entitled to nominate and take part in election
15 (one from each of the 15 areas determined by the Secretary of State being the Regional Hospital Areas* for the purposes of the National Health Service Act 1946(a)), viz:— 1. Newcastle 2. Leeds 3. Sheffield 4. East Anglian 5. North West Metropolitan 6. North East Metropolitan 7. South East Metropolitan 8. South West Metropolitan 9. Oxford 10. South Western 11. Welsh 12. Birmingham 13. Manchester 14. Liverpool 15. Wessex	Registered general nurses who, on the date fixed for the purpose of the election as the last date for the receipt of nomination papers, are engaged in the area for which they are candidates for election in work for which the employment of a registered nurse is requisite or for which a registered nurse is commonly employed.	Registered general nurses and registered fever nurses.
3	Registered mental nurses who, on the date fixed for the purpose of the election as the last date for receipt of nomination papers, are engaged in work for which the employment of a registered nurse is requisite or for which a registered nurse is commonly employed.	Registered mental nurses.

* See the National Health Service (Regional Hospital Areas) Order 1965 (S.I. 1965/527 (1965 I, p. 1382)) as amended by S.I. 1969/451 (1969 I, p. 1297).

(a) 1946 c. 81.

Number of persons to be elected	Qualifications of persons to be elected	Qualifications of persons entitled to nominate and take part in election
1	Registered nurse for the mentally subnormal who, on the date fixed for the purpose of the election as the last date for receipt of nomination papers, is engaged in work for which the employment of a registered nurse is requisite or for which a registered nurse is commonly employed.	Registered nurses for the mentally subnormal.
1	Registered sick children's nurse who, on the date fixed for the purpose of the election as the last date for receipt of nomination papers, is engaged in work for which the employment of a registered nurse is requisite or for which a registered nurse is commonly employed.	Registered sick children's nurses.
1	Enrolled general nurse who, on the date fixed for the purpose of the election as the last date for receipt of nomination papers, is engaged in work for which the employment of an enrolled nurse is requisite or for which an enrolled nurse is commonly employed.	Enrolled general nurses.
1	Enrolled mental nurse or enrolled nurse for the mentally subnormal who, on the date fixed for the purpose of the election as the last date for receipt of nomination papers, is engaged in work for which the employment of an enrolled nurse is requisite or for which an enrolled nurse is commonly employed.	Enrolled mental nurses and enrolled nurses for the mentally subnormal.

In order to be eligible for election under this Scheme or to be entitled to nominate for and take part in the election, a person must have the requisite qualifications on 19 ,* and no person may nominate in any part of the election more than the number of persons to be elected in that part. Each candidate must be nominated on a separate nomination paper.

Every nomination paper must contain the name, address and requisite qualifications of the candidate nominated; it must be signed by not fewer than 6 persons having the requisite qualifications for nominating the candidate; and the address and requisite qualification of each one so signing must be appended to her signature.

The nomination paper must be accompanied by a declaration in writing, signed by the person nominated, acknowledging that she consents to be nominated, and must be delivered by post or otherwise, before the hour of 12 noon on 19 ,* addressed to the Returning Officer, The General Nursing Council for England and Wales, 23 Portland Place, London, W1A 1BA. Forms of nomination papers may, on application by post or otherwise, be obtained from the Returning Officer at the above address; in making such application it should be clearly stated for what part of the election the nomination form or forms are required; i.e. for nurses registered in the general part of the register, for registered nurses for the mentally subnormal, for registered mental nurses, for registered sick children's nurses, for enrolled general nurses or for enrolled mental nurses and for enrolled nurses for the mentally subnormal.

Every nomination paper which is not received at the address given above before the hour of 12 noon on 19 ,* will be invalid.

Returning Officer.

(Date)

FORM B

FORM B (i) (*Form of nomination paper for registered general nurses*)

We, the undersigned, being nurses registered in the general part of the register for England and Wales, or in the part of the register for fever nurses hereby nominate
(1)
of (2)
who is registered in the general part of the register and whose registration number is
(3)
and who is employed at (4)
where he or she is engaged in work for which the employment of a registered nurse is requisite or for which a registered nurse is commonly employed, that is to say as
(5)
in the area in respect of which he or she is nominated, i.e. area (6)
as a proper person to be elected to the General Nursing Council for England and Wales by the nurses registered in the general part of the register, and in the part of the register for fever nurses.

---

*This will be the date fixed by the Returning Officer as the last day for the receipt of nomination papers.

We declare that we have signed no other nomination paper in respect of this area.

Signatures of Nominators	Address	Registered Qualification and Number

(Date)

(1) Here insert full name, including forenames, of candidate.
(2) Here insert candidate's address.
(3) Here insert candidate's registration number.
(4) Here insert candidate's place of employment, and its postal address.
(5) Here insert candidate's present post.
(6) Here insert description of area as determined for election purposes.

N.B.—Only a nurse registered in the general part of the register may be nominated as a candidate, but a nurse registered in the general part of the register or in the part of the register for fever nurses may sign the nomination paper as a nominator.

FORM B (ii)   (*Form of nomination paper for registered mental nurses, registered nurses for the mentally subnormal and registered sick children's nurses*)

We, the undersigned, being nurses registered in the   (1)
for England and Wales
hereby nominate   (2)
of   (3)
who is registered in the   (1)
and whose registration number is   (4)
and who is employed at   (5)
where he or she is engaged in work for which the employment of a registered nurse is requisite or for which a registered nurse is commonly employed, that is to say as
     (6)
as a proper person to be elected to the General Nursing Council for England and Wales by the nurses registered in the   (1)

We declare that we have signed no nomination papers in excess of the number of persons to be elected in this part of the election.

Signatures of Nominators	Address	Registered Qualification and Number

(Date)

    (1) Here insert the words "part of the register for mental nurses", or "part of the register for nurses for the mentally subnormal", or "part of the register for sick children's nurses", as the case may be.

    (2) Here insert full name, including forenames, of candidate.

    (3) Here insert candidate's address.

    (4) Here insert candidate's registration number.

    (5) Here insert candidate's place of employment, and its postal address.

    (6) Here insert candidate's present post.

N.B.—A nurse cannot nominate a candidate for election by the nurses registered in a particular part of the register unless she is herself registered in that particular part.

FORM B(iii)   (*Form of nomination paper for enrolled general nurses*)

We, the undersigned, being nurses enrolled in the general part of the roll for England and Wales hereby nominate (1)
of (2)
who is enrolled in the general part of the roll
and whose enrolment number is (3)
and who is employed at (4)
where he or she is engaged in work for which the employment of an enrolled nurse is requisite or for which an enrolled nurse is commonly employed, that is to say as (5)
as a proper person to be elected to the General Nursing Council for England and Wales by the nurses enrolled in the general part of the roll.

We declare that we have signed no other nomination paper in respect of this part of the election.

Signatures of Nominators	Address	Enrolled Qualification and Number

(Date)

    (1) Here insert full name, including forenames, of candidate.

    (2) Here insert candidate's address.

    (3) Here insert candidate's enrolment number.

    (4) Here insert candidate's place of employment, and its postal address.

    (5) Here insert candidate's present post.

N.B.—Only an enrolled general nurse may sign the nomination paper as a nominator.

FORM B(iv) (*Form of nomination paper for enrolled mental nurses and enrolled nurses for the mentally subnormal*)

We, the undersigned, being nurses enrolled in the (1)
for England and Wales
hereby nominate (2)

of (3)
who is enrolled in the (1)
and whose enrolment number is (4)
and who is employed at (5)
where he or she is engaged in work for which the employment of an enrolled nurse is requisite or for which an enrolled nurse is commonly employed, that is to say as
(6)
as a proper person to be elected to the General Nursing Council for England and Wales by the nurses enrolled in the parts of the roll for mental nurses and for nurses for the mentally subnormal.

We declare that we have signed no other nomination paper in respect of this part of the election.

Signatures of Nominators	Address	Enrolled Qualification and Number

(Date)

    (1) Here insert the words "part of the roll for mental nurses" or "part of the roll for nurses for the mentally subnormal", as the case may be.
    (2) Here insert full name, including forenames, of candidate.
    (3) Here insert candidate's address.
    (4) Here insert candidate's enrolment number.
    (5) Here insert candidate's place of employment, and its postal address.
    (6) Here insert candidate's present post.

N.B.—An enrolled mental nurse or an enrolled nurse for the mentally subnormal may nominate a candidate enrolled either in the part of the roll for mental nurses or in the part of the roll for nurses for the mentally subnormal, but she may not nominate more than one candidate in this part of the election.

FORM C *(Form of declaration to be issued with the nomination papers for return by the candidate nominated)*

ELECTION OF DIRECT REPRESENTATIVES TO THE GENERAL NURSING COUNCIL FOR ENGLAND AND WALES

Form C(i) *(Form of declaration for registered nurses)*

(Date)

    I consent to be nominated as a candidate for election as a representative of the nurses registered in the (1)
to serve on the General Nursing Council for England and Wales. I declare that the statements in the nomination paper with regard to my qualifications are correct.

Name

Address

Registration Number

(1) Here insert "general part of the register and the part of the register for fever nurses", or "part of the register for mental nurses", or "part of the register for nurses for the mentally subnormal", or "part of the register for sick children's nurses", as the case may be.

FORM C(ii) (*Form of declaration for enrolled nurses*)

(Date)

I consent to be nominated as a candidate for election as a representative of the nurses enrolled in the (1)
to serve on the General Nursing Council for England and Wales. I declare that the statements in the nomination paper with regard to my qualifications are correct.

Name

Address

Enrolment Number

(1) Here insert "general part of the roll" or "part of the roll for mental nurses and the part of the roll for nurses for the mentally subnormal", as the case may be.

FORM D

Election to the General Nursing Council for England and Wales by nurses registered in the general part of the register and in the part of the register for fever nurses

BALLOT PAPER I
Election of 15 registered general nurses

Area	Name of Candidate Nominated	Present post and address of Candidate Nominated	Registered Qualification and Number	Elector's Mark X

N.B.—Nurses registered in the general part of the register, or in the part of the register for fever nurses are entitled to vote for candidates in this ballot paper. The elector must put a mark thus, X, against the name or names of the candidate or candidates for whom he or she votes. The elector must not vote for more than one candidate in respect of each area.

The elector may vote for fewer candidates than are to be elected.

The elector must not place any mark on this ballot paper other than the X or Xs for the vote or votes cast.

This paper must be placed in the identification envelope, which must be signed by the elector in the place marked for that purpose, securely fastened and placed in a covering envelope, which must then be sent by post or otherwise to the Returning Officer, General Nursing Council for England and Wales, 23 Portland Place, London, W1A IBA and must be received there before the hour of 12 noon on
19   .*

---

* This will be the date fixed by the Returning Officer as the last day for the receipt of ballot papers.

Failure to comply with any of these requirements will render the ballot paper null and void.

Election to the General Nursing Council for England and Wales by nurses registered in the part of the register for mental nurses.

BALLOT PAPER II

Election of 3 nurses registered in the part of the register for mental nurses.

Name of Candidate Nominated	Present post and address of Candidate Nominated	Registered Qualification and Number	Elector's Mark X

N.B.—The registered mental nurse voting must put a mark thus, X, against the name or names of the candidate or candidates for whom he or she votes.

The elector must not vote for more than 3 mental nurses. The elector must not place any mark on this ballot paper other than the X or Xs. for the vote or votes cast.

This paper must be placed in the identification envelope, which must be signed by the elector in the place marked for that purpose, securely fastened and placed in a covering envelope, which must then be sent by post or otherwise to the Returning Officer, General Nursing Council for England and Wales, 23 Portland Place, London, W1A 1BA and must be received there before the hour of 12 noon on   , 19   .*

Failure to comply with any of these requirements will render the ballot paper null and void.

Election to the General Nursing Council for England and Wales by nurses registered in the part of the register for nurses for the mentally subnormal

BALLOT PAPER III

Election of one registered nurse for the mentally subnormal.

Name of Candidate Nominated	Present post and address of Candidate Nominated	Registered Qualification and Number	Elector's Mark X

* This will be the date fixed by the Returning Officer as the last day for the receipt of ballot papers.

N.B.—The registered nurse for the mentally subnormal voting must put a mark thus, X, against the name of the candidate for whom he or she votes.

One only of the above-named candidates is to be elected.

The elector must not vote for more than one candidate or place any mark on this ballot paper other than the X for the vote cast.

This paper must be placed in the identification envelope, which must be signed by the elector in the place marked for that purpose, securely fastened and placed in a covering envelope, which must then be sent by post or otherwise to the Returning Officer, General Nursing Council for England and Wales, 23 Portland Place, London, W1A 1BA and must be received there before the hour of 12 noon on ,
19 .*

Failure to comply with any of these requirements will render the ballot paper null and void.

Election to the General Nursing Council for England and Wales by nurses registered in the part of the register for sick children's nurses

BALLOT PAPER IV

Election of 1 nurse registered in the part of the register for sick children's nurses.

Name of Candidate Nominated	Present post and address of Candidate Nominated	Registered Qualification and Number	Elector's Mark X

N.B.—The registered sick children's nurse voting must put a mark thus, X, against the name of the candidate for whom she votes.

One only of the above-named candidates is to be elected. The elector must not vote for more than 1 candidate or place any mark on this ballot paper other than the X for the vote cast.

This paper must be placed in the identification envelope, which must be signed by the elector in the place marked for that purpose, securely fastened and placed in a covering envelope, which must then be sent by post or otherwise to the Returning Officer, General Nursing Council for England and Wales, 23 Portland Place, London, W1A 1BA and must be received there before the hour of 12 noon on ,
19 .*

Failure to comply with any of these requirements will render the ballot null and void.

* This will be the date fixed by the Returning Officer as the last day for the receipt of ballot papers.

Election to the General Nursing Council for England and Wales by nurses enrolled in the general part of the roll

BALLOT PAPER V.

Election of 1 nurse enrolled in the general part of the roll.

Name of Candidate Nominated	Present post and address of Candidate Nominated	Enrolled Qualification and Number	Elector's Mark X

N.B.—The enrolled general nurse voting must put a mark thus, X, against the name or names of the candidate for whom he or she votes.

One only of the above named candidates is to be elected.

The elector must not vote for more than one candidate or place any mark on this ballot paper other than the X for the vote cast.

This paper must be placed in the identification envelope, which must be signed by the elector in the place marked for that purpose, securely fastened and placed in a covering envelope, which must then be sent by post or otherwise to the Returning Officer, General Nursing Council for England and Wales, 23 Portland Place, London, W1A 1BA and must be received there before the hour of 12 noon on　　　　　　　　　　,
19　.*

Failure to comply with any of these requirements will render the ballot paper null and void.

Election to the General Nursing Council for England and Wales by nurses enrolled in the parts of the roll for mental nurses and nurses for the mentally subnormal

BALLOT PAPER VI

Election of one nurse enrolled in the part of the roll for mental nurses or in the part of the roll for nurses for the mentally subnormal.

Name of Candidate Nominated	Present post and address of Candidate Nominated	Enrolled Qualification and Number	Elector's Mark X

* This will be the date fixed by the Returning Officer as the last day for the receipt of ballot papers.

N.B.—The enrolled mental nurse or enrolled nurse for the mentally subnormal voting must put a mark thus, X, against the name of the candidate for whom she votes.

One only of the above-named candidates is to be elected. The elector must not vote for more than 1 candidate or place any mark on this ballot paper other than the X for the vote cast.

This paper must be placed in the identification envelope, which must be signed by the elector in the place marked for that purpose, securely fastened and placed in a covering envelope, which must then be sent by post or otherwise to the Returning Officer, General Nursing Council for England and Wales, 23 Portland Place, London, W1A 1BA and must be received there before the hour of 12 noon on   ,
19   .*

Failure to comply with any of these requirements will render the ballot paper null and void.

FORM E (*Form of identification envelope*)

Identification envelope I

(Identification Envelope)

_____

TO
    I, the undersigned, hereby declare that I am the person to whom the enclosed ballot paper is addressed as above, that I am a nurse registered in the   part of the register and that I have not marked any other ballot paper in this part of the election.

(Signature)

Identification envelope II

(Identification Envelope)

TO
    I, the undersigned, hereby declare that I am the person to whom the enclosed ballot paper is addressed as above, that I am a nurse enrolled in the   part of the roll, and that I have not marked any other ballot paper in this part of the election.

(Signature)

(L.S.)   *G. E. Watts*,
Chairman of the Council.

The seal of the General Nursing Council for England and Wales was hereunto affixed on 25th November 1969.

M. Henry,
Registrar.

Signed by authority of the Secretary of State for Social Services.

Serota,
Minister of State,
Department of Health and Social Seurity.

26th November 1969.

_____

* This will be the date fixed by the Returning Officer as the last day for the receipt of ballot papers.

EXPLANATORY NOTE

(This Note is not part of the Instrument.)

The Rules approved by this instrument supersede the General Nursing Council (Election Scheme) Rules 1964. The changes made take into account the alteration of the constitution of the Council under the Nurses Act 1969.

A right of appeal is introduced for candidates who wish to contest the rejection of their nomination paper.

STATUTORY INSTRUMENTS

1969 No. 1677

AGRICULTURE

The Price Stability of Imported Products (Rates of Levy No. 24) Order 1969

Made	-	-	-	*26th November* 1969
Coming into Operation		-		*27th November* 1969

The Minister of Agriculture, Fisheries and Food, in exercise of the powers conferred upon him by section 1(2), (4), (5), (6) and (7) of the Agriculture and Horticulture Act 1964(a) and of all other powers enabling him in that behalf, hereby makes the following order:—

1. This order may be cited as the Price Stability of Imported Products (Rates of Levy No. 24) Order 1969, and shall come into operation on 27th November 1969.

2.—(1) In this order—

" the Principal Order " means the Price Stability of Imported Products (Levy Arrangements) Order 1966(b) as amended(c) and as amended by any subsequent order, and if any such order is replaced by any subsequent order the expression shall be construed as a reference to such subsequent order;

AND other expressions have the same meaning as in the Principal Order.

(2) The Interpretation Act 1889(d) shall apply to the interpretation of this order as it applies to the interpretation of an Act of Parliament and as if this order and the order hereby revoked were Acts of Parliament.

3. In accordance with and subject to the provisions of Part II of the Principal Order (which provides for the charging of levies on imports of certain specified commodities)—

(a) the rate of general levy for such imports into the United Kingdom of any specified commodity as are described in column 2 of Part I of the Schedule to this order in relation to a tariff heading indicated in column 1 of that Part shall be the rate set forth in relation thereto in column 3 of that Part;

(b) the rate of country levy for such imports into the United Kingdom of any specified commodity as are described in column 2 of Part II of the Schedule to this order in relation to a tariff heading indicated in column 1 of that Part shall be the rate set forth in relation thereto in column 3 of that Part.

(a) 1964 c. 28. (b) S.I. 1966/936 (1966 II, p. 2271).
(c) S.I. 1969/758, 1564 (1969 II, p. 2137; III, p. 5018). (d) 1889 c. 63.

4. The Price Stability of Imported Products (Rates of Levy No. 23) Order 1969(a) is hereby revoked.

In Witness whereof the Official Seal of the Minister of Agriculture, Fisheries and Food is hereunto affixed on 26th November 1969.

(L.S.)

R. J. E. Taylor,
Assistant Secretary.

SCHEDULE

PART I

1. Tariff Heading	2. Description of Imports	3. Rate of General Levy
		per ton £ *s. d.*
	Imports of:—	
10.01	Denatured wheat	5 0
10.03	Barley	2 10 0
11.01	Wheat flours	1 0 0
11.02	Cereal meal— of barley	7 5 0
11.02	Rolled, flaked, crushed or bruised cereals— barley	5 15 0

PART II

1. Tariff Heading	2. Description of Imports	3. Rate of Country Levy
		per ton £ *s. d.*
	Imports of:—	
10.01	Denatured wheat which has been grown in and con-signed to the United Kingdom from Belgium, the French Republic or the Kingdom of the Nether-lands	5 0
10.03	Barley which has been grown in and consigned to the United Kingdom from— the Kingdom of the Netherlands .. .. the French Republic .. .. Canada	 2 0 0 2 5 0 2 10 0

(a) S.I. 1969/1550 (1969 III, p. 5011).

EXPLANATORY NOTE

(This Note is not part of the Order.)

This order, which comes into operation on 27th November 1969, supersedes the Price Stability of Imported Products (Rates of Levy No. 23) Order 1969. It:—

(*a*) reduces to 5*s.* per ton both the general levy on denatured wheat and the country levy on denatured wheat grown in and consigned to the United Kingdom from Belgium, France or the Netherlands;

(*b*) removes from general levy imports of wheat (other than denatured wheat) and of maize meal;

(*c*) removes from country levy imports of wheat (other than denatured wheat) grown in and consigned to the United Kingdom from Belgium or France;

(*d*) increases to 20*s.* per ton the general levy on imports of wheat flours; and

(*e*) reimposes unchanged the other rates of general and country levy in force immediately before the commencement of the order.

STATUTORY INSTRUMENTS

1969 No. 1679 (S. 149)

POLICE

The Police Federation (Scotland) Amendment Regulations 1969

Made - - -	18*th November* 1969
Laid before Parliament	9*th December* 1969
Coming into Operation	10*th December* 1969

In exercise of the powers conferred on me by section 44 of the Police Act 1964(a), and of all other powers enabling me in that behalf, and after consultation with the three Central Committees of the Police Federation for Scotland sitting together as a Joint Committee, I hereby make the following regulations:—

1. These regulations may be cited as the Police Federation (Scotland) Amendment Regulations 1969 and shall come into operation on 10th December 1969.

2. The Police Federation (Scotland) Regulations 1966(b) (hereinafter referred to as "the principal regulations") as amended (c), shall have effect subject to the amendments specified in regulations 3 and 4 of these regulations.

3. In regulation 11(2) of the principal regulations as amended (which relates to central committees) there shall be inserted at the end the words "but subject always to the provisions of paragraph 4(2) of Schedule 2."

4. For paragraph 4 of Schedule 2 of the principal regulations (which relates to the procedure to be followed when there is an equality of votes between candidates at any election to any branch board, each central conference and each central committee) there shall be substituted the following provisions:—

"4.—(1) Where at any election to any branch board and each central conference an equality of votes is found to exist between any candidates and the addition of a vote would entitle any of those candidates to be declared elected, the decision between those candidates shall be reached by lot and the candidate on whom the lot falls shall be declared elected.

(2) Where at any election to any central committee an equality of votes is found to exist between any candidates and the addition of a vote would entitle any of those candidates to be declared elected a further ballot shall be held, and if equality still exists, then all the delegates from all the areas to the inspectors', sergeants', or as the case may be, constables' central conference shall each have the right to cast a vote to determine the elected candidate, and in the event of an equality of votes still being found then the decision between those candidates shall be reached by lot and the candidate on whom the lot falls shall be declared elected."

William Ross,
One of Her Majesty's Principal
Secretaries of State.

St. Andrew's House,
Edinburgh.
18th November 1969.

(a) 1964 c. 48.　(b) S.I. 1966/132 (1966 I, p. 241).　(c) S.I. 1968/590 (1968 I, p. 1360).

EXPLANATORY NOTE

(This Note is not part of the Regulations.)

These Regulations amend the procedure to be followed where at any election to any central committee an equality of votes is found to exist between any candidates.

STATUTORY INSTRUMENTS

1969 No. 1682

DEFENCE
The Air Force Act 1955 (Continuation) Order 1969

Laid before Parliament in draft

Made - - - 28*th November* 1969

At the Court at Buckingham Palace, the 28th day of November 1969

Present,

The Queen's Most Excellent Majesty in Council

Whereas a draft of the following Order in Council has been laid before Parliament and approved by resolution of each House of Parliament:

Now, therefore, Her Majesty, in pursuance of section 1(2) of the Armed Forces Act 1966(a), is pleased, by and with the advice of Her Privy Council, to order, and it is hereby ordered, as follows:—

1. The Air Force Act 1955(b) shall continue in force for a period of twelve months beyond the 31st December 1969, that date being the date on which it would otherwise expire.

2. This Order may be cited as the Air Force Act 1955 (Continuation) Order 1969.

W. G. Agnew.

(a) 1966 c. 45.   (b) 1955 c. 19.

STATUTORY INSTRUMENTS

1969 No. 1683

DEFENCE

The Army Act 1955 (Continuation) Order 1969

Laid before Parliament in draft

Made - - - - 28*th November* 1969

At the Court at Buckingham Palace, the 28th day of November 1969

Present,

The Queen's Most Excellent Majesty in Council

Whereas a draft of the following Order in Council has been laid before Parliament and approved by resolution of each House of Parliament:

Now, therefore, Her Majesty, in pursuance of section 1(2) of the Armed Forces Act 1966(**a**), is pleased, by and with the advice of Her Privy Council, to order, and it is hereby ordered, as follows: —

1. The Army Act 1955(**b**) shall continue in force for a period of twelve months beyond the 31st December 1969, that date being the date on which it would otherwise expire.

2. This Order may be cited as the Army Act 1955 (Continuation) Order 1969.

W. G. Agnew.

(**a**) 1966 c. 45.   (**b**) 1955 c. 18.

STATUTORY   INSTRUMENTS

1969 No. 1685

TANZANIA

The Colonial Probates Act (Application to Tanganyika) Order 1969

Made - - - -	28th November 1969
Laid before Parliament	4th December 1969
Coming into Operation	5th December 1969

At the Court at Buckingham Palace, the 28th day of November 1969

Present,

The Queen's Most Excellent Majesty in Council

Her Majesty, by virtue and in exercise of the powers vested in Her by section 3(4) of the Tanganyika Independence Act 1961(a) is pleased, by and with the advice of Her Privy Council, to order, and it is hereby ordered, as follows : —

1.—(1) This Order may be cited as the Colonial Probates Act (Application to Tanganyika) Order 1969.

(2) This Order shall come into operation on 5th December 1969.

(3) The Interpretation Act 1889(b) shall apply, with the necessary adaptations, for the purpose of interpreting this Order and otherwise in relation thereto as it applies for the purpose of interpreting and in relation to Acts of Parliament.

2. The Colonial Probates Act 1892(c) shall have effect as if the Act had been applied to Tanganyika by an Order made under section 1 thereof in respect of the period beginning on 9th December 1961 and ending immediately before 26th April 1964.

W. G. Agnew.

EXPLANATORY NOTE

(This Note is not part of the Order.)

Section 3(4) of the Tanganyika Independence Act 1961 provides that Her Majesty may by Order in Council make such adaptations in any Act of Parliament passed before that Act as appear to Her necessary in consequence of section 1 of that Act and that any such Order may be made so as to have effect from 9th December 1961 (on which day, under section 1, Tanganyika

---

(a) 1961 c. 1 (10 & 11 Eliz. 2).   (b) 1889 c. 63.   (c) 1892 c. 6.

became part of Her Majesty's dominions and Her Majesty's Government in the United Kingdom ceased to have responsibility for the government of Tanganyika). This Order makes provision in pursuance of section 3(4) of the Act of 1961 for the application of the Colonial Probates Act 1892 to Tanganyika in respect of the period between 9th December 1961 and 26th April 1964 when Tanganyika entered into a union with Zanzibar.

The Colonial Probates Act (Application to Tanganyika) Order 1965

Made	—	—	26th November 1965
Laid before Parliament		6th December 1965
Coming into Operation		9th December 1965

At the Court at Buckingham Palace, the 26th day of November 1965

Present,

The Queen's Most Excellent Majesty in Council

Her Majesty, by virtue and in exercise of the powers vested in Her by section 3(4) of the Tanganyika Independence Act 1961(a) is pleased, by and with the advice of Her Privy Council, to order, and it is hereby ordered, as follows:—

1.—(1) This Order may be cited as the Colonial Probates Act (Application to Tanganyika) Order 1965.

(2) This Order shall come into operation on 9th December 1965.

(3) The Interpretation Act 1889(b) shall apply, with the necessary adaptations, for the purpose of interpreting this Order and otherwise in relation thereto as it applies for the purpose of interpreting and in relation to Acts of Parliament.

2. The Colonial Probates Act 1892(c) shall have effect as if the Act had been applied to Tanganyika by an Order made under section 1 thereof in respect of the period beginning on 9th December 1961 and ending immediately before 26th April 1964.

W. G. Agnew.

EXPLANATORY NOTE

(This Note is not part of the Order)

STATUTORY INSTRUMENTS

1969 No. 1686

SOCIAL SECURITY

The National Insurance and Industrial Injuries (Bermuda) Order 1969

Made - - - *28th November* 1969

At the Court at Buckingham Palace, the 28th day of November 1969

Present,

The Queen's Most Excellent Majesty in Council

Whereas an Agreement between the Government of the United Kingdom of Great Britain and Northern Ireland and the Government of Bermuda on social security (which Agreement is set out in the Schedule hereto) was signed on behalf of those Governments:

And Whereas by Article 23 of the said Agreement it was provided that (subject to the provisions of paragraphs (1) and (2) of that Article) the Agreement should enter into force on 1st November 1969:

And Whereas by section 105(1) of the National Insurance Act 1965(a) and section 84(1) of the National Insurance (Industrial Injuries) Act 1965(b) it is provided that Her Majesty may, by Order in Council, make provision for modifying or adapting the said Acts of 1965 in their application to cases affected by agreements with other governments providing for reciprocity in matters specified in those sections:

Now, therefore, Her Majesty, in pursuance of the said section 105(1) and the said section 84(1), and of all other powers enabling Her in that behalf, is pleased, by and with the advice of Her Privy Council, to order, and it is hereby ordered, as follows:—

Citation and interpretation

1.—(1) This Order may be cited as the National Insurance and Industrial Injuries (Bermuda) Order 1969.

(2) The rules for the construction of Acts of Parliament contained in the Interpretation Act 1889(c) shall apply in relation to this Order as they apply in relation to an Act of Parliament.

Modification of Acts

2. The provisions contained in the Agreement set out in the Schedule to this Order shall have full force and effect, so far as the same relate to England, Wales and Scotland and provide by way of agreement with the Government of Bermuda for reciprocity with the said Government in any matters specified in either section 105(1) of the National Insurance Act 1965 or section 84(1) of the National Insurance (Industrial Injuries) Act 1965 ; and the National Insurance Acts 1965 to 1969 and the National Insurance (Industrial Injuries) Acts 1965 to 1969 shall have effect subject to such modifications as may be required therein for the purpose of giving effect to any such provisions.

W. G. Agnew.

(a) 1965 c. 51.   (b) 1965 c. 52.
(c) 1889 c. 63.

SCHEDULE

AGREEMENT ON SOCIAL INSURANCE BETWEEN THE GOVERNMENT OF THE UNITED KINGDOM OF GREAT BRITAIN AND NORTHERN IRELAND AND THE GOVERNMENT OF BERMUDA

The Government of the United Kingdom of Great Britain and Northern Ireland and the Government of Bermuda have agreed as follows:

PART I—DEFINITIONS AND SCOPE

ARTICLE 1

For the purposes of this Agreement, unless the context otherwise requires—

(a) "benefit" means any pension, allowance, or other benefit payable under the legislation of one (or the other) Contracting Party, and includes any increase payable for a dependant;

(b) "competent authority" means, in relation to the United Kingdom, the Secretary of State for Social Services, the Ministry of Health and Social Services for Northern Ireland, the Isle of Man Board of Social Services, the Social Security Committee of the States of Jersey or the States of Guernsey Insurance Authority, as the case may require, and, in relation to Bermuda, the Insurance Officer of Bermuda;

(c) "dependant" means a person for whom an increase of benefit is payable under the legislation which is being applied;

(d) "legislation" means, according to the context, the legislation specified in Article 2 in force in any part of the territory of one (or the other) Party;

(e) "old age pension" means, in relation to the United Kingdom, a retirement pension or old age pension payable under the legislation of the United Kingdom, and, in relation to Bermuda, a contributory old age pension payable under the legislation of Bermuda;

(f) "territory" means, in relation to the United Kingdom, England, Scotland, Wales, Northern Ireland, the Isle of Man, and the Islands of Jersey, Guernsey, Alderney, Herm and Jethou, and, in relation to Bermuda, the Bermudas or Somers Islands;

(g) "widow's benefit" means, in relation to the United Kingdom, widow's benefit payable under the legislation of the United Kingdom, and, in relation to Bermuda, a widow's allowance payable under the legislation of Bermuda.

ARTICLE 2

(1) The provisions of this Agreement shall apply—

(a) in relation to the United Kingdom, to—

(i) the National Insurance Act 1965, the National Insurance Act (Northern Ireland) 1966, the National Insurance (Isle of Man) Act 1948, and the legislation which was consolidated by, or repealed by legislation consolidated by, those Acts;

(ii) the National Insurance (Industrial Injuries) Act 1965, the National Insurance (Industrial Injuries) Act (Northern Ireland) 1966 and the National Insurance (Industrial Injuries) (Isle of Man) Act 1948;

(iii) the Insular Insurance (Jersey) Law 1950; and

(iv) the Social Insurance (Guernsey) Law 1964;

(b) in relation to Bermuda, to the Workmen's Compensation Act 1965 and the Contributory Pensions Act 1967.

(2) Subject to the provisions of paragraph (3) of this Article, the Agreement shall apply also to any law, order or regulation which amends, supplements or consolidates the legislation specified in paragraph (1) of this Article.

(3) The Agreement shall apply, only if the Contracting Parties so agree, to laws, orders or regulations, which amend or supplement the legislation specified in paragraph (1) of this Article for the purpose of giving effect to any reciprocal agreement on social security between one (or the other) Party and a third party.

PART II—CONTRIBUTIONS

ARTICLE 3

(1) An employed person shall be subject, in relation to his employment, to the legislation of only one Contracting Party.

(2) If an insured person is liable to pay contributions as an employed person for any period under the legislation of one Party, he shall not be liable to pay contributions as a self-employed person or as a non-employed person for that period under the legislation of the other Party.

ARTICLE 4

(1) Subject to the provisions of paragraphs (2) and (3) of this Article, where a person is employed in the territory of one Party, the legislation of that Party shall apply to him, even if he resides in the territory of the other Party or if his employer's principal place of business is in that territory.

(2) Where a person, who is insured under the legislation of one Party and is employed by an employer who has a place of business in the territory of that Party is sent by that employer to the territory of the other Party, that legislation shall continue to apply to him as if he were employed in the territory of the former Party, provided that his employment in the territory of the latter Party is not expected to last for more than twelve months or such longer period as may be agreed by the competent authorities of the two Parties in any particular case.

(3) The provisions of paragraphs (1) and (2) of this Article shall not apply to members of Her Majesty's regular forces or to any person to whom any of the provisions of Articles 5, 6 and 7 of this Agreement apply.

ARTICLE 5

(1) Where a person, employed in the Government service of one Contracting Party and insured under the legislation of that Party, is sent to the territory of the other Party, the legislation of the former Party shall continue to apply to him as if he were employed in its territory.

(2) Where a person in the Government service of one Party is employed in the territory of the other Party, having been engaged for that employment in that territory, the legislation of the latter Party shall apply to him.

(3) The competent authorities of the Parties may provide by agreement that, where a person, employed by a public corporation or official body of one Party and insured under the legislation of that Party, is sent to the territory of the other Party, the legislation of the former Party shall apply to him as if he were employed in its territory.

ARTICLE 6

If a person is employed as master or a member of the crew of any ship or vessel belonging to Her Majesty which is stationed in Bermuda and he is not a member of any of the naval, military or air forces of the Crown, he shall be insured in relation to that employment—

(a) under the legislation of the United Kingdom if he is ordinarily resident in the United Kingdom;

(b) under the legislation of Bermuda if he is ordinarily resident in Bermuda.

ARTICLE 7

(1) For the purpose of this Article, "ship" means, in relation to a Contracting Party, a ship or vessel (other than a ship or vessel belonging to Her Majesty) which is owned in the territory of that Party, or any other ship or vessel which is registered in that territory and not owned in the territory of the other Party ; and a ship or vessel shall be deemed to be owned in one (or the other) territory if the owner or, where there is more than one owner, the managing owner or manager resides or has his principal place of business in that territory.

(2) Subject to the provisions of paragraphs (3) and (4) of this Article, if a person, ordinarily resident in the territory of one Party, is employed on board a ship of the other Party, then, in relation to that employment, the legislation of the latter Party shall apply to him as if he were ordinarily resident in the territory of that Party.

(3) If a person, ordinarily resident in the territory of one Party, is employed as master or a member of the crew of a ship of the other Party which is registered in the territory of the former Party or calls regularly at ports of that Party, then, in relation to that employment, the legislation of the former Party shall apply to him as if he were employed as master or a member of the crew of a ship of the former Party.

(4) If a person, ordinarily resident in the territory of one Party, is employed on board a ship of the other Party, and is in the service of an employer having a place of business in the territory of the former Party and not being the owner of the ship, then, in relation to that employment, the legislation of the former Party shall apply to him as if he were employed on board a ship of that Party.

ARTICLE 8

Where a person ordinarily resident in Bermuda is employed as a member of the crew of an aircraft registered in the United Kingdom, the legislation of the United Kingdom shall apply to him as if any conditions relating to residence or domicile in the United Kingdom were satisfied in his case.

PART III—BENEFIT

Benefit of one Contracting Party payable in the territory of the other

ARTICLE 9

(1) The provisions of this Article shall apply only to old age pensions and widow's benefit, payable under the legislation of one (or the other) Contracting Party.

(2) Where a person would be entitled to receive benefit under the legislation of one Party if he were in the territory of that Party, he shall be entitled to receive that benefit while he is in the territory of the other Party, provided that, if he is not ordinarily resident in the territory of the former Party, then, subject to the provisions of paragraph (3) of this Article, the rate of his benefit shall be determined in accordance with any provisions of that legislation which concern the payment of benefit to persons who are not ordinarily resident in the territory of the former Party.

(3) Any increase of benefit rates which, after the entry into force of this Agreement, is awarded under the legislation of one Party to beneficiaries in the territory of that Party shall apply also to beneficiaries who are ordinarily resident in the territory of the other Party.

(4) Where a person who is entitled to receive benefit under the legislation of one Party would be entitled to receive an increase of that benefit if a dependant of his were in the territory of that Party, he shall be entitled to receive that increase if the dependant is in the territory of the other Party.

ARTICLE 10

(1) Where a person would be entitled to receive any benefit under the legislation of one Contracting Party in respect of an industrial accident or an industrial disease if he were in the territory of that Party, he shall be entitled to receive that benefit while he is in the territory of the other Party.

(2) The provisions of paragraph (1) of this Article shall apply also to any increase of the benefit specified in that paragraph and any additional allowance payable therewith, other than a special hardship allowance payable under the legislation of the United Kingdom.

(3) Where a person who is entitled to receive benefit under the legislation of one Party in respect of an industrial accident or an industrial disease would be entitled to receive an increase of that benefit if a dependant of his were in the territory of that Party, he shall be entitled to receive that increase if the dependant is in the territory of the other Party.

Old Age Pensions

ARTICLE 11

(1) If a person has been insured under the legislation of both Contracting Parties, then—

(a) for the purpose of determining whether he is entitled to receive an old age pension under the legislation of one Party, any contribution paid by him or credited to him under the legislation of the other Party shall be treated as if it were a contribution, respectively, paid by him or credited to him under the legislation of the former Party ; and

(b) if he is entitled to receive an old age pension under the legislation of the former Party, the rate of that pension shall be a part of the rate of the pension which would have been payable to him under that legislation if every contribution paid by him or credited to him under the legislation of the latter Party had been a contribution, respectively, paid by him or credited to him under the legislation of the former Party, namely, that part which bears the same relation to the whole as the number of contributions paid by him or credited to him under the legislation of the former Party bears to the total number of contributions paid by him or credited to him under the legislation of both Parties.

(2) For the purpose of applying the provisions of paragraph (1) of this Article—

(a) no account shall be taken of any graduated contributions paid under the legislation of the United Kingdom or of any graduated retirement benefit payable under that legislation, but any such benefit which is payable by virtue of such contributions shall be paid in addition to the old age pension which is calculated in accordance with those provisions ;

(b) in those cases where, under the legislation of one (or the other) Party, the person concerned is—

(i) a woman claiming an old age pension by virtue of her husband's insurance ; or

(ii) a woman whose husband's contributions are taken into account in determining her right to receive an old age pension by virtue of her own insurance, her marriage having been terminated by the death of her husband or otherwise ;

any reference to a contribution paid by a person or credited to a person shall be construed, for the purpose of ascertaining her husband's yearly average of contributions, as including a reference to a contribution paid by her husband or credited to him ;

(c) where a person has reached pensionable age, as prescribed in his case under the legislation of the United Kingdom, no account shall be taken under that legislation of any subsequent contributions which he pays under the legislation of Bermuda or has credited to him under that legislation.

(3) For the purpose of determining, in accordance with the provisions of paragraph (1) of this Article, whether a person is entitled to receive benefit under the legislation of Bermuda and for the purpose of determining, in accordance with those provisions, what benefit would have been payable under that legislation if every contribution paid by a person or credited to him under the legislation of the United Kingdom had been a contribution respectively paid by him or credited to him under the legislation of Bermuda, no account shall be taken of any contribution paid or credited under the legislation of the United Kingdom for any week before the week beginning on 5th August 1968.

(4) For the purpose of applying the provisions of sub-paragraph (b) of paragraph (1) of this Article, no account shall be taken of any contribution which a person has paid or had credited to him under the legislation of the United Kingdom if, in the calculation of the yearly average of contributions paid by him or credited to him under that legislation, no account is taken of that contribution.

(5) The provisions of the foregoing paragraphs of this Article shall not apply in relation to the legislation of one (or the other) Party in any case where a person qualifies for an old age pension under that legislation solely by virtue of contributions paid or credited under that legislation.

Widow's Benefit
ARTICLE 12

(1) The provisions concerning old age pensions contained in Article 11 of this Agreement shall apply (with such modifications as the differing nature of the benefit shall require) to claims for widow's benefit under the legislation of one (or the other) Contracting Party.

(2) Where, under the legislation of one Party, a woman would be entitled to receive widow's benefit if a child or young person were in the territory of that Party, she shall be entitled to receive that benefit while the child or young person is in the territory of the other Party.

(3) Where a woman is receiving widow's benefit for any period under the legislation of one (or the other) Party in accordance with the provisions of paragraph (1) of this Article and her benefit has been calculated under the provisions of paragraphs (1), (2) and (4) of Article 11 of the Agreement, contributions shall be credited to her under that legislation only for the part of that period which bears the same relation to the whole as that specified in respect of her claim under that legislation in sub-paragraph (b) of paragraph (1) of that Article.

Non-Contributory Old Age Pensions in Bermuda
ARTICLE 13

(1) Subject to the provisions of paragraphs (2) and (3) of this Article, where a person who is resident in Bermuda claims a non-contributory old age pension under the legislation of Bermuda, any period during which he has been ordinarily resident in the United Kingdom shall be treated, for the purposes of his claim, as a period during which he has been ordinarily resident in Bermuda.

(2) Where a person is entitled to receive a retirement pension under the legislation of the United Kingdom and would be entitled, but for the provisions of this paragraph, to receive also a non-contributory old age pension under the legislation of Bermuda, he shall not receive more by way of the latter pension than any amount by which the former pension is less than the standard rate of the latter pension.

(3) The provisions of paragraph (2) of this Article shall not apply to anyone who, before 5th August 1973, qualifies for a non-contributory old age pension under the legislation of Bermuda, otherwise than by virtue of the provisions of paragraph (1) of this Article.

Accidents outside the territory of the Contracting Party whose legislation is applicable

ARTICLE 14

(1) Where a person is employed in the territory of one Contracting Party and the legislation of the other Party applies to him in accordance with any of the provisions of Articles 4 and 5 of this Agreement, he shall be treated for the purpose of any right to receive benefit under that legislation for an accident happening or an industrial disease contracted in the course of that employment as if the accident had happened or the disease had been contracted in the territory of the latter Party.

(2) If an accident happens to an employed person after he leaves the territory of one Party to go, in the course of his employment, to the territory of the other Party and before he arrives in the latter territory, then, for the purpose of any claim to receive benefit in respect of that accident—

(a) the accident shall be treated as if it had happened in the territory of the Party whose legislation was expected to apply to him in the latter territory ; and

(b) his absence from the territory of either Party shall be disregarded in determining whether that legislation applied to him at the time of the accident.

Overlapping Benefits

ARTICLE 15

(1) Where, but for the provisions of this Article, a person would have been entitled to receive benefits under the legislation of both Contracting Parties for the same period, an adjustment shall be made, subject to the provisions of this Article, under the legislation of one Party, namely—

(a) that Party—

(i) in whose territory he is at the beginning of the period ; or

(ii) in whose territory he is ordinarily resident, if he is not in the territory of either Party at that time ; or

(iii) in whose territory he was last ordinarily resident before that time, if at that time he is not in or ordinarily resident in the territory of either Party ; or

(b) if the competent authorities so agree, the other Party.

(2) For the purpose of the adjustment specified in paragraph (1) of this Article, the benefit which would otherwise have been payable under the legislation of the Party specified in that paragraph shall be reduced by any amount by which the sum of the two benefits exceeds the amount which would have been payable under that legislation if the benefit payable under the legislation of the other Party had been the corresponding benefit payable under the legislation of the former Party.

(3) The provisions of paragraph (1) of this Article shall not apply in any case—

(a) where one of the benefits is a non-contributory old age pension payable under the legislation of Bermuda ;

(b) where one of the benefits is an old age pension payable to a woman by virtue of her husband's insurance and the other is widow's benefit ;

(c) where both the benefits are old age pensions payable to a man ;

(d) where both the benefits are old age pensions payable to a woman by virtue of her own insurance ; or

(e) where both the benefits are widow's benefits.

PART IV—MISCELLANEOUS PROVISIONS

ARTICLE 16

The competent authorities—

(a) shall make such administrative arrangements as may be required for the application of this Agreement ;

(b) shall communicate to each other information regarding any measure taken by them for the application of the Agreement ;

(c) shall furnish assistance to one another with regard to any matter relating to the application of the Agreement ;

(d) shall communicate to each other, as soon as possible, information regarding any change in their legislation which may affect the application of the Agreement.

ARTICLE 17

Where, under the provisions of this Agreement, any benefit is payable by the competent authority of one Contracting Party to a person who is in the territory of the other Party, the payment may, at the request of that authority, be made by the competent authority of the latter Party as agent for the competent authority of the former Party.

ARTICLE 18

No benefit paid under the legislation of one Contracting Party by virtue of this Agreement shall be reimbursed out of any fund established under the legislation of the other Party.

ARTICLE 19

Where a person becomes entitled, under the legislation of one Contracting Party, to receive arrears of benefit for any period, the competent authority responsible for the payment of these arrears may, at the request of a competent authority of the other Party, deduct from these arrears any amount by which the latter authority has paid sums by way of benefit for that period under the legislation of the latter Party in excess of the benefit which was actually due to the person for that period under that legislation, and may transmit this amount to the latter authority.

ARTICLE 20

Any exemption from, or reduction of, legal dues, charges and fees, provided for in the legislation of one Contracting Party in connection with the issue of any certificate or document required to be produced for the purposes of that legislation, shall be extended to certificates and documents required to be produced for the purposes of the legislation of the other Party.

ARTICLE 21

Any claim, notice or appeal which should, for the purposes of the legislation of one Contracting Party, have been presented within a prescribed period to a competent authority of that Party, but which is in fact presented within the same period to the corresponding authority of the other Party, shall be treated as if it had been presented to the authority of the former Party. In such cases, the authority of the latter Party shall, as soon as possible, arrange for the claim, notice or appeal to be sent to the competent authority of the former Party.

ARTICLE 22

In the event of the termination of this Agreement, any right acquired by a person in accordance with its provisions shall be maintained, and negotiations shall take place for the settlement of any rights then in course of acquisition by virtue of those provisions.

ARTICLE 23

(1) No provision of this Agreement shall diminish any rights which a person has acquired under the legislation of either Contracting Party before the date of the entry into force of the Agreement.

(2) The provisions of this Agreement, in so far as they modify the legislation of either Party concerning industrial injuries insurance or workmen's compensation, shall have effect only from a date to be agreed by the competent authorities of the two Parties after the entry into force of the Agreement.

(3) Subject to the provisions of paragraphs (1) and (2) of this Article, the Agreement shall enter into force on 1st November 1969 and shall remain in force for a period of one year from that date. Thereafter, it shall continue in force from year to year unless notice of termination is given in writing by either Party at least three months before the expiry of any such yearly period.

In witness whereof the undersigned, duly authorised thereto by their respective Governments, have signed this Agreement.

Done in duplicate and signed at London on the 13th day of October 1969 and at Hamilton on the 23rd day of October 1969.

For the Government of the   For the Government
United Kingdom of Great Britain   of Bermuda:
and Northern Ireland:

                                     H. J. TUCKER.

     R. H. S. CROSSMAN.

EXPLANATORY NOTE

(This Note is not part of the Order.)

This Order gives effect in England, Wales and Scotland to the Agreement (set out in the Schedule) made between the Governments of the United Kingdom and of Bermuda in so far as it relates to the matters for which provision is made by the National Insurance Acts 1965 to 1969 and the National Insurance (Industrial Injuries) Acts 1965 to 1969.

STATUTORY INSTRUMENTS

1969 No. 1688 (C.53)

CIVIL AVIATION

The Tokyo Convention Act 1967 (Commencement No. 2) Order 1969

Made - - - *28th November* 1969

At the Court at Buckingham Palace, the 28th day of November 1969

Present,

The Queen's Most Excellent Majesty in Council

Her Majesty, in exercise of the powers conferred upon Her by section 9(3) of the Tokyo Convention Act 1967(a) and of all other powers enabling Her in that behalf, is pleased, by and with the advice of Her Privy Council, to order, and it is hereby ordered, as follows:

1. Section 2 of the Tokyo Convention Act 1967 shall come into force on 4th December 1969.

2. This Order may be cited as the Tokyo Convention Act 1967 (Commencement No. 2) Order 1969.

W. G. Agnew.

EXPLANATORY NOTE

(*This Note is not part of the Order.*)

The Tokyo Convention Act 1967, except section 2 (which makes provisions as to extradition), was brought into force on 1st April 1968 by the Tokyo Convention Act 1967 (Commencement) Order 1968 (S.I. 1968/469). This Order brings section 2 into force on 4th December 1969, the date notified by the International Civil Aviation Organisation, in pursuance of Article 26 of the Convention on Offences and certain other Acts Committed on board Aircraft (Cmnd. 2261) signed in Tokyo on 14th September 1963, as the date on which that Convention comes into force. The Convention has been ratified by the United Kingdom.

(a) 1967 c. 52.

STATUTORY INSTRUMENTS

1969 No. 1689 (L.27)

SUPREME COURT OF JUDICATURE, ENGLAND

PROCEDURE

The Non-Contentious Probate (Amendment) Rules 1969

Made - - -	26th November 1969
Laid before Parliament	4th December 1969
Coming into Operation	1st January 1970

The President of the Probate Division, in exercise of the powers conferred on him by section 100 of the Supreme Court of Judicature (Consolidation) Act 1925(**a**), and with the concurrence of the Lord Chancellor and the Lord Chief Justice, hereby makes the following Rules:—

1.—(1) These Rules may be cited as the Non-Contentious Probate (Amendment) Rules 1969 and shall come into operation on 1st January 1970.

(2) The Interpretation Act 1889(**b**) shall apply to the interpretation of these Rules as it applies to the interpretation of an Act of Parliament.

2. The amendments set out in the Schedule to these Rules shall be made to the Non-Contentious Probate Rules 1954(**c**), as subsequently amended(**d**).

Dated 24th November 1969.

J. E. S. Simon, P.

We concur

Dated 26th November 1969.

Gardiner, C.

Dated 24th November 1969.

Parker of Waddington, C.J.

SCHEDULE

AMENDMENTS TO NON-CONTENTIOUS PROBATE RULES 1954

1. In the definition of "Registrar" in rule 2(2) (which relates to interpretation), for the words "the registry in question", there shall be substituted the words "a district probate registry".

2. In rule 3(1) (which relates to applications for grants made through solicitors), the words "Subject to section 153 of the Act (which prescribes the places where applications for second and subsequent grants may be made)" shall be omitted.

(**a**) 1925 c. 49. (**b**) 1889 c. 63.
(**c**) S.I. 1954/796 (1954 II, p. 2202).
(**d**) The only relevant amending instruments are S.I. 1967/748, 1968/1675 (1967 II, p. 2225; 1968 III, p. 4505).

3. The following amendments shall be made in rule 21 (which relates to the order of priority for a grant in case of intestacy):—

(a) in paragraph (1)(ii), the words in parentheses shall be omitted;

(b) in paragraph (1)(iii), the words from "or, in the case of" to the end of the subparagraph shall be omitted;

(c) in subparagraph (iv) of paragraph (1) and in subparagraphs (i), (iii) and (iv) of paragraph (2), the words "during the lifetime of the deceased" shall be omitted; and

(d) for paragraph (6) there shall be substituted the following paragraph:—

"(6) In this rule references to children of the deceased include references to his illegitimate, legitimated and adopted children and 'father or mother of the deceased' shall be construed accordingly".

4. In rule 38(6) (which relates to administration bonds), the words "or sub-registry" shall be inserted after the word "registry".

EXPLANATORY NOTE

(This Note is not part of the Rules.)

These Rules make amendments to the Non-Contentious Probate Rules 1954, most of which are consequential upon the coming into force on 1st January 1970 of section 14 of the Family Law Reform Act 1969 which gives to illegitimate children and their parents rights to succeed on each others' intestacies: as amended, rule 21 will afford to illegitimate children and their parents the same priorities for the purposes of grants of administration as are afforded to legitimate children and their parents.

In addition, the amendment to rule 2 makes it possible for the registrar of one district probate registry to dispose of applications relating to grants issuing from another district probate registry. The Rules also make miscellaneous minor, drafting and consequential amendments. They come into force on 1st January 1970.

STATUTORY INSTRUMENTS

1969 No. 1695

TRANSPORT

PENSIONS AND COMPENSATION

The British Transport (Closed Railway Pension Scheme) Order 1969

Made - - -		*25th November* 1969
Laid before Parliament		*9th December* 1969
Coming into Operation		*10th December* 1969

The Minister of Transport, in exercise of his powers under section 74 of the Transport Act 1962(a) and of all other enabling powers, hereby makes the following Order:—

Commencement, citation and interpretation

1.—(1) This Order shall come into operation on the 10th December 1969 and may be cited as the British Transport (Closed Railway Pension Scheme) Order 1969.

(2) In this Order unless the context otherwise requires—

"the closed pension scheme" means the London and North Western Railway Provident Society for providing Pensions for Widows and Orphans of the Salaried Staff;

"existing", in relation to the terms of the closed pension scheme, means existing immediately before the provisions of this Order have effect as respects that scheme;

"management committee", in relation to the closed pension scheme, means the Committee of Management constituted pursuant to the existing terms of the scheme and charged by those terms with the management thereof;

"the Minister" means the Minister of Transport;

"the Railways Board" means the British Railways Board;

"term", in relation to the closed pension scheme, includes any rule or provision of the scheme, or of any statutory provision relating to the scheme, or of any trust deed or other instrument made for the purposes of the scheme.

(3) The Interpretation Act 1889(b) shall apply for the interpretation of this Order as it applies for the interpretation of an Act of Parliament.

Application of the Order

2. The closed pension scheme shall be construed and have effect as if the provisions of this Order were terms of the scheme, any other term thereof, whether express or implied, to the contrary notwithstanding.

(a) 1962 c. 46.   (b) 1889 c. 63.

Alterations to the terms of the closed pension scheme

3. The following alterations shall be made to the terms of the closed pension scheme:—

(a) the functions of the management committee of the scheme shall be transferred to and exercised by the Railways Board;

(b) any existing terms of the scheme relating to the holding of meetings of participants in order to elect or appoint members of the management committee, or otherwise relating to the election, appointment or tenure of office of such members, shall cease to have effect;

(c) the audit of the funds of the scheme shall be carried out by a single auditor from time to time appointed for the scheme by the Railways Board (the terms of the appointment being determined by the Railways Board) and the existing terms of the scheme relating to the appointment or election of auditors by the employer or by the participants shall cease to have effect.

Disposal of surplus on winding up

4. If after the death, or other cessation of entitlement to benefit, of the last remaining person entitled to receive benefit from the closed pension scheme, and after provision has been made for the payment of all costs, charges and expenses of winding up the scheme, there remain any surplus funds subject to the trusts of the scheme, then, in so far as no provision is made by the existing terms of the scheme for the application of such surplus funds, the same shall be transferred and added to the funds of such one or more other pension schemes of the Railways Board (and if more than one, in such proportions) as the Railways Board may, with the approval of the Minister, determine.

Sealed with the Official Seal of the Minister of Transport the 25th November 1969.

(L.S.)

Fred Mulley,
Minister of Transport.

EXPLANATORY NOTE
(*This Note is not part of the Order.*)

The Order provides for the functions of the management committee of the London and North Western Railway Provident Society for providing Pensions for Widows and Orphans of the Salaried Staff to be transferred to and exercised by the British Railways Board (Article 3(a)). Existing provisions of the scheme relating to the election or appointment of members of the management committee are to cease to have effect and the audit of the funds of the scheme is to be carried out by auditors appointed by the British Railways Board (Article 3(b) and (c)). Provision is also made for the disposal of surplus funds on the winding up of the scheme (Article 4).

STATUTORY INSTRUMENTS

1969 No. 1696

SOCIAL SECURITY

The National Insurance (Contributions) Regulations 1969

Made - - -	*27th November* 1969
Laid before Parliament	*8th December* 1969
Coming into Operation	*9th December* 1969

ARRANGEMENT OF REGULATIONS

Part IV

Provisions Relating to Contributions which are not Paid or Paid after the Due Date

23. Treatment for the purpose of benefit of late paid or unpaid contributions where there was no consent, connivance or negligence by the insured person.
24. Treatment for the purpose of any benefit of contributions paid late through ignorance or error.
25. Treatment for the purpose of unemployment or sickness benefit of late paid contributions.
26. Treatment for the purpose of maternity benefit of late paid contributions.
27. Treatment for the purpose of widow's benefit, child's special allowance or retirement pension of late paid contributions.
28. Treatment for the purpose of increase of rate of retirement pension of late paid contributions.
29. Treatment for the purpose of death grant of late paid contributions.
30. Treatment for the purpose of any benefit of late paid graduated contributions and payments in lieu of contributions.

Part V

Provisions Relating to Contributions which Persons are Entitled, but not Liable, to Pay

31. Treatment for the purpose of any benefit of contributions which persons are entitled, but not liable, to pay.
32. Contributions not paid within prescribed periods.
33. Payments after death.
34. Revocation and general savings.

SCHEDULES

SCHEDULE 1—Conditions attaching to exception from liability to pay, and to the crediting of, contributions.

SCHEDULE 2—Regulations revoked.

The Secretary of State for Social Services, in exercise of powers under sections 1(1), 8(1), 8(6), 9, 10 (as amended by section 1(1)(d) of the National Insurance Act 1967(a)), 11, 14(1) and 103 of, and paragraph 18 of Schedule 11 to, the National Insurance Act 1965(b), and the National Insurance Joint Authority, in exercise of powers under sections 18(1) and 114(5) of the said Act of 1965, in either case in conjunction with the Treasury so far as relates to matters with regard to which the Treasury have so directed, and in exercise of all other powers enabling them in that behalf and for the purpose only of consolidating the regulations hereby revoked, hereby make the following regulations:—

Part I

General

Citation, commencement and interpretation

1.—(1) These regulations may be cited as the National Insurance (Contributions) Regulations 1969, and shall come into operation on 9th December 1969.

(2) In these regulations, unless the context otherwise requires:—
   "the Act" means the National Insurance Act 1965;
   "the Secretary of State" means the Secretary of State for Social Services;

(a) 1967 c. 73.   (b) 1965 c. 51.

"the Industrial Injuries Act" means the National Insurance (Industrial Injuries) Act 1965(a);

"the Classification Regulations" means the National Insurance (Classification) Regulations 1948(b);

"the Collection of Contributions Regulations" means the National Insurance and Industrial Injuries (Collection of Contributions) Regulations 1948(c);

"the General Benefit Regulations" means the National Insurance (General Benefit) Regulations 1948(d);

"the Married Women Regulations" means the National Insurance (Married Women) Regulations 1948(e);

"the Overlapping Benefits Regulations" means the National Insurance (Overlapping Benefits) Regulations 1948(f);

"the Residence and Persons Abroad Regulations" means the National Insurance (Residence and Persons Abroad) Regulations 1948(g);

"the Unemployment and Sickness Benefit Regulations" means the National Insurance (Unemployment and Sickness Benefit) Regulations 1967(h);

"certificate of exception" means, except in relation to regulation 9, a certificate issued for the purposes of the provisions of section 10(1)(a)(iii) of the Act;

"contribution" has the same meaning as in the Act save that it does not include a graduated contribution;

"contribution year" and "benefit year" have the same meanings as in the General Benefit Regulations;

"due date" in Part IV of these regulations means in relation to any contribution (including any graduated contribution) the date on which that contribution was due to be paid, and in relation to any payment in lieu of contributions, the date on which that payment became due;

"employment exchange" includes any office or place appointed by the Secretary of State for the purpose of claiming unemployment benefit;

"an employed contributor's employment" includes, in relation to regulations 2 and 3 only, any employment before 5th July 1948 which would have been treated as employed contributor's employment if the Act and the regulations made thereunder had been in operation during that employment;

"personal benefit", "Personal Injuries Scheme", "Service Pensions Instrument" and "1914–1918 War Injuries Scheme" have the same meanings as in the Overlapping Benefits Regulations;

"week" means contribution week;

and other expressions have the same meanings as in the Act or, as the case may require, the Industrial Injuries Act.

(3) References in these regulations to any enactment or regulations shall, except in so far as the context otherwise requires, be construed as references to such enactments or regulations as amended or extended by or under any other enactment, order or regulations and as including references to any enactment or regulations thereby consolidated.

(a) 1965 c. 52.
(b) S.I. 1948/1425 (Rev. XVI, p. 95: 1948 I, p. 2738).
(c) S.I. 1948/1274 (Rev. XVI, p. 148: 1948 I, p. 3037).
(d) S.I. 1948/1278 (Rev. XVI, p. 179: 1948 I, p. 2626).
(e) S.I. 1948/1470 (Rev. XVI, p. 123: 1948 I, p. 2795).
(f) S.I. 1948/2711 (Rev. XVI, p. 196: 1948 I, p. 2657).
(g) S.I. 1948/1275 (Rev. XVI, p. 88: 1948 I, p. 2864).
(h) S.I. 1967/330 (1967 I, p. 1131).

(4) The rules for the construction of Acts of Parliament contained in the Interpretation Act 1889(a) shall apply in relation to this instrument (including any instrument read as one therewith) and in relation to any revocation effected thereby as if this instrument, the regulations revoked by it and any regulations revoked by the regulations so revoked were Acts of Parliament, and as if each revocation were a repeal.

PART II
EXCEPTIONS AND CREDITS

Unemployment

2.—(1) Subject to the provisions of paragraph (2) of this regulation, and paragraphs (1), (3), (4) and (5) of regulation 5—

   (*a*) an insured person shall be excepted from liability to pay a contribution under the Act for any week of unemployment if Condition I or Condition II of Schedule 1 to these regulations has been satisfied, and a contribution as an employed person shall be credited to him for that week:

   Provided that if the said Condition II is not satisfied, it shall be deemed to be satisfied if the insured person proves to the satisfaction of the Secretary of State that he has become unemployed following employment in an employed contributor's employment and that he will normally rely upon such employment for his livelihood;

   (*b*) (and subject to the other provisions of these regulations) an insured person shall not be excepted from any liability to pay a contribution under the Act for any week of unemployment not being a week of unemployment in respect of which a contribution is credited under sub-paragraph (*a*) of this paragraph.

(2) It shall be a condition of a person's right to be credited with a contribution for any week under paragraph (1) above that he shall attend at an employment exchange on every working day in that week for which he does not claim unemployment benefit and, if directed to do so, shall sign a register kept there for that purpose and that he shall so attend at such time, if any, as the Secretary of State may direct:

Provided that—

   (*a*) a person shall—

   (i) if he resides at a distance of more than two miles and not more than four miles from the employment exchange nearest or most convenient to his place of residence be required to attend only on alternate days; or

   (ii) if he resides at a distance of more than four miles from such employment exchange be required to attend on only one day in the week;

   (*b*) the Secretary of State may in any case—

   (i) dispense with the foregoing requirements of this paragraph; or

   (ii) vary the said requirements by permitting any person to attend at longer intervals; and

   (iii) impose the further or alternative requirement upon any person that he furnish within a specified time such evidence or such further evidence as the Secretary of State may direct that any day or days for which he has not claimed unemployment benefit was a day or were days of unemployment for the purposes of paragraph (1) above.

(a) 1889 c. 63.

(3) "Working day" for the purposes of paragraph (2) above means every day other than—

(a) Sunday; and

(b) any day which in the case of any person falls to be treated as a day of unemployment by virtue of head (i) of the proviso to regulation 5(5); and

(c) any day upon which a person is incapable of work but is treated as unemployed by virtue of regulation 5(4).

Incapacity for work

3.—(1) Subject to the provisions of this regulation and paragraphs (2) to (5) of regulation 5—

(a) an insured person shall be excepted from liability to pay a contribution under the Act for any week of incapacity for work if any one of the Conditions contained in Schedule 1 to these regulations has been satisfied, and a contribution shall be credited to him for that week as follows:—

(i) if Condition I or Condition II of the said Schedule has been satisfied, a contribution as an employed person:

Provided that if the said Condition II is not satisfied, it shall be deemed to be satisfied by the insured person if he proves to the satisfaction of the Secretary of State that he became incapable of work following employment in an employed contributor's employment, and that he will normally rely upon such employment for his livelihood;

(ii) if Condition III or Condition IV of the said Schedule has been satisfied (but not Condition I or Condition II thereof), a contribution as a self-employed person:

Provided that if the said Condition IV is not satisfied, it shall be deemed to be satisfied by the insured person if he proves to the satisfaction of the Secretary of State that he became incapable of work following employment in an employed contributor's employment or as a self-employed person, and that he will normally rely upon any such employment for his livelihood;

(b) (and subject to the other provisions of these regulations) an insured person shall not be excepted from any liability to pay a contribution under the Act for any week of incapacity for work if none of the Conditions contained in the said Schedule has been satisfied.

(2) Notwithstanding anything contained in the foregoing provisions of this regulation, where industrial injury benefit is payable to an insured person under the Industrial Injuries Act in respect of a week of incapacity for work, that person shall be excepted from liability to pay a contribution under the Act, and a contribution as an employed person shall be credited to him for that week.

(3) It shall be a condition of a person's right to be credited with a contribution for any week, other than a week in respect of which he has claimed sickness benefit, under paragraph (1) above that he shall furnish to the Secretary of State notice in writing of the grounds on which a contribution should be so credited before the end of the benefit year immediately following the contribution year in which the week in question falls, or within such longer period as the Secretary of State may in a particular case allow.

Payment of contributions by persons excepted from liability under regulation 2 or regulation 3

4. Where an insured person is excepted from liability to pay a contribution for any week under the provisions of regulation 2 or of regulation 3 he may, for any such week, pay a contribution as a non-employed person.

Provisions determining days of unemployment or incapacity for work

5.—(1) For the purposes of regulation 2 and subject to the provisions of this regulation—

(*a*) a day shall not be a day of unemployment unless on that day the person concerned is capable of work and is, or is deemed in accordance with the Unemployment and Sickness Benefit Regulations to be, available for employment in an employed contributor's employment;

(*b*) the occupation of a person in employment on any day in a week shall be disregarded, and that day shall not by reason only of that occupation be treated as not being a day of unemployment if—

(i) the employment is one in which that person, being available for full time employment in some employed contributor's employment, is occupied on any day or days in that week for not more than eight hours in the aggregate (including any occupation in an employment which by virtue of Schedule 1, Part III of the Classification Regulations, as amended(**a**), or, being employment in Her Majesty's Forces, by virtue of regulation 3 of the National Insurance (Members of the Forces) Regulations 1968(**b**), is to be disregarded) and the occupation in which he is so employed is consistent with that full time employment and, if he is following that occupation under a contract of service, it is not his usual main occupation; or

(ii) the employment (not being employment which falls within head (i) above) is one in respect of which, by virtue of paragraph 10 of Part II of Schedule 1 to the Classification Regulations, as amended(**c**), (which relates to employment in which a person renders part-time service) he is treated as a self-employed person or would be so treated but for the said Schedule 1, Part III and in which he is occupied on one day only in that week:

Provided that, where in the same week a person is occupied in employment which falls within head (i) and in employment which falls within head (ii) of this sub-paragraph, the provisions of this sub-paragraph shall not apply if he is occupied in such employments for more than eight hours in the aggregate in that week.

(2) For the purposes of regulation 3 and subject to the provisions of this regulation—

(*a*) a day shall not be a day of incapacity for work unless on that day the person concerned is, or is deemed in accordance with the Unemployment and Sickness Benefit Regulations to be, incapable of work by reason of some specific disease or bodily or mental disablement;

(*b*) any period in respect of which a person is disqualified under, or by virtue of regulations made under, section 31 of the Industrial Injuries Act for receiving industrial injury benefit (other than a period in respect of which a person is so disqualified for failure to make a claim for benefit within the prescribed time) shall not be a period of incapacity for work.

(3) For the purposes of regulations 2 and 3, and subject to the provisions of this regulation—

(a) The relevant amending instruments are S.I. 1950/765, 830, 1951/993, 1952/1024, 1454, 1954/585, 1957/2175 (1950 II, pp. 10, 12; 1951 I, p. 1454; 1952 II, pp. 2137, 2139; 1954 I, p. 1407; 1957 I, p. 1623).
(b) S.I. 1968/827 (1968 II, p. 2228).
(c) The relevant amending instruments are S.I. 1957/2175, 1968/1684 (1957 I, p. 1623; 1968 III, p. 4578).

(a) a day which is in accordance with the Unemployment and Sickness Benefit Regulations treated as a day of unemployment or incapacity for work for the purposes of unemployment benefit and sickness benefit shall be a day of unemployment or incapacity for work, as the case may be, for the purposes of this regulation, but any day which under the said Regulations is treated as not being such a day shall not be a day of unemployment or incapacity for work for those purposes:

Provided that:—

(i) subject to the provisions of head (ii) of this proviso any day which is treated as not being a day of unemployment by reason only of the provisions of regulation 7(1)(j) of the Unemployment and Sickness Benefit Regulations (which relates to days on which a person is on holiday), shall be a day of unemployment for the purposes of this regulation if it is a day of recognised or customary holiday in connection with that person's employment in a week which contains not more than three days of such holiday, and is a day in a period during which that employment is suspended, unless it is a day in respect of which remuneration is deemed to be paid under the provisions of regulation 11 of the Collection of Contributions Regulations, as amended(a) (which relates to the payment of contributions in respect of weeks of holiday); and

(ii) no day in any week shall fail to be a day of unemployment by reason that a person receives or is entitled to receive any remuneration which is, or which if his employment had not terminated would have been, deemed not to be remuneration paid in respect of any day in that week under the provisions of regulation 10A of the last mentioned regulations, as amended(a) (which relates to the payment of contributions in respect of weeks in respect of which no services are rendered and remuneration does not exceed the specified amount); and

(iii) any Sunday which is treated as not being a day of unemployment under regulation 7(1)(f) of the Unemployment and Sickness Benefit Regulations shall be a day of unemployment for the purposes of this regulation if any day in the week in which that Sunday occurs will fall to be treated as a day of unemployment by virtue of head (i) of the proviso to paragraph (5) of this regulation.

(b) Any period which would in respect of any person be a period of unemployment or incapacity for work by virtue of the provisions of this regulation but for the provisions of section 48 of the Act (claims and notices) or of regulations made under section 49(3) of the Act (disqualification for failure to claim benefit within the prescribed time) shall be treated as a period of unemployment or incapacity for work, as the case may be.

(c) Any period in respect of which a person—

(i) is disqualified under section 22(1) of the Act (trade disputes) or section 49(1)(a) thereof (absence from Great Britain) for receiving unemployment or sickness benefit; or

(ii) is, or would if he had otherwise had a right thereto have been, disqualified under subsection (2) or regulations made under subsection (3)

(a) The relevant amending instruments are S.I. 1959/207, 1969/1362 (1959 II, p. 1893; 1969 III, p. 4069).

of the said section 22 (which subsections relate to various grounds of disqualification) for receiving either such benefit; or

(iii) is unable to satisfy any additional conditions with respect to the receipt of unemployment benefit or sickness benefit imposed in his case by regulations made under subsection (4) of the said section 22, other than the Married Women Regulations or the National Insurance (Seasonal Workers) Regulations 1950(a);

shall not be a period of unemployment or incapacity for work, as the case may be:

Provided that, for the purposes of head (i) of this sub-paragraph where the disqualification is under the said section 49(1)(a), any day in respect of which industrial injury benefit is payable to an insured person under the Industrial Injuries Act shall be treated as a day of incapacity for work.

(4) For the purposes of regulation 2 and regulation 3, where in any week a person is for part of that week unemployed and for the remainder of that week incapable of work, he shall be treated as if unemployed for the whole of that week, if Condition I or Condition II of Schedule 1 to these regulations has been satisfied, and, if neither of those Conditions has been satisfied but Condition III or Condition IV of that Schedule has been satisfied, he shall be treated as if incapable of work for the whole of that week, and the said regulations shall be construed accordingly:

Provided that for the purposes only of this paragraph a person shall not in respect of any week be treated as being unemployed on any day or days by virtue of paragraph (1)(b) of this regulation unless—

(i) Condition I or Condition II of Schedule 1 to these regulations has been satisfied, and

(ii) in respect of any day to which head (ii) of the said paragraph (1)(b) applies, he is unemployed on at least one other day in that week.

(5) For the purposes of regulation 2 and regulation 3, where under the foregoing provisions of this regulation any week would be a week of unemployment or a week of incapacity in respect of any person if the Sunday occurring in that week were a day of unemployment or a day of incapacity for work, as the case may be, that Sunday shall be treated as such a day unless on it that person does any work as an employed or self-employed person other than such work as is referred to in regulation 7(1)(h) of the Unemployment and Sickness Benefit Regulations (which relates to work undertaken as part of medical treatment and certain work as a non-employed person):

Provided that—

(i) in the case of any person who objects on religious grounds to working on a specific day in each week other than Sunday and does not so object to working on Sunday, the said day shall be substituted for Sunday for the purposes of the foregoing provisions of this paragraph; and

(ii) no day in any week shall be treated by virtue of the provisions of this paragraph as a day of incapacity for work unless some other day in that week is or but for the provisions of paragraph (4) of this regulation would be such a day.

Persons over pensionable age

6.—(1) A person who is over pensionable age shall be excepted from liability to pay a contribution for any week of unemployment or incapacity to which

---

(a) S.I. 1950/1220 (1950 II, p. 29).

regulation 2 or regulation 3 of these regulations applies, notwithstanding that the conditions for exception from such liability under either of those regulations are not satisfied in his case.

(2) Subject to the provisions of paragraph (4) of this regulation, any person who on attaining pensionable age does not satisfy the contribution conditions for a retirement pension specified in paragraph 4 of Schedule 2 to the Act shall be excepted from liability to pay a contribution as an insured person for any week after attaining that age:

Provided that for the purposes of this paragraph a person who satisfies the condition as to contributions specified in regulation 7(1) of the National Insurance (Widow's Benefit and Retirement Pensions) Regulations 1948(a), as amended(b), (under which a person may be entitled to a retirement pension if the yearly average of contributions paid or credited is not less than thirteen) shall be deemed to satisfy the condition specified in paragraph 4(1)(b) of the said Schedule (which provision requires that the said yearly average shall not be less than fifty).

(3) Subject to the provisions of paragraph (4) of this regulation, a woman who on attaining pensionable age is married and is not by virtue of paragraph (1) of this regulation excepted from liability to pay a contribution as an insured person for any week thereafter shall nevertheless be excepted from the said liability if she fails to satisfy the further conditions for a retirement pension specified in section 33(2) of the Act (which requires that contributions have been paid or credited to her for not less than one-half of the number of contribution weeks since the date of her marriage or that the period between that date and her attaining pensionable age is less than 3 years).

(4) Any person who but for the provisions of paragraphs (2) and (3) of this regulation would be liable to pay a contribution as an insured person for any week after attaining pensionable age may elect to be liable to pay such a contribution.

(5) Any election under paragraph (4) of this regulation—

    (a) shall be made by giving notice in writing to the Secretary of State and shall be operative from the beginning of the week in which the notice was given, or from such earlier date as the Secretary of State may allow; and

    (b) may be cancelled by giving notice in writing to the Secretary of State to that effect, and such cancellation shall be operative from the beginning of the week in which the notice was given, or from such earlier date as the Secretary of State may allow:

Provided that the employer of an employed person who makes such an election shall not be liable to pay a contribution on behalf of that person for any week unless before the expiry of the time prescribed by regulation 6 of the Collection of Contributions Regulations for payment he is informed of the said person's election to be liable to pay such a contribution.

Imprisonment or detention in legal custody

7.—(1) For any week during the whole of which an insured person is undergoing imprisonment or detention in legal custody he—

    (a) shall be excepted from liability to pay a contribution as a self-employed or non-employed person, if by reason of his imprisonment or detention he

---

(a) S.I. 1948/1261 (Rev. XVI, p. 207: 1948 I, p. 2704).
(b) There is no amendment which relates expressly to the subject matter of these Regulations.

is, or if he had otherwise had a right thereto would have been, disqualified for receiving sickness benefit for that week or if he would for the said reason have been so disqualified but for the provisions of regulation 6(3) of the General Benefit Regulations, as amended(a); but

(b) shall not, save as provided in paragraph (3) of this regulation, have any contribution credited to him under these regulations if by reason of his imprisonment or detention he is, or if he had otherwise had a right to sickness benefit would have been, so disqualified.

(2) A person who under the provisions of the last foregoing paragraph is excepted from liability to pay a contribution as a self-employed or non-employed person, and who is not liable to pay a contribution as an employed person, for any week of imprisonment or detention in legal custody, may if he so desires pay therefor, at any time before the end of the sixth contribution year following the contribution year in which the period of imprisonment or detention in legal custody terminated, a contribution as a non-employed person or alternatively, if immediately before the commencement of that period he was a self-employed person, a contribution as a self-employed person.

(3) Notwithstanding that a person is undergoing imprisonment or detention in legal custody and by reason thereof is, or if he had otherwise had a right thereto would have been, disqualified for receiving sickness benefit for any week—

(i) the provisions of regulation 10, if he is detained in a remand home or an approved school or if he is liable to be detained in a hospital or similar institution to which he has been transferred from a remand home or from an approved school; and

(ii) the provisions of regulation 16;

shall have effect in all respects as if paragraph (1) of this regulation did not apply to him.

Unemployability supplement

8.—(1) An insured person shall be excepted from liability to pay a contribution as a non-employed person for any week in respect of which he is receiving an unemployability supplement, but contributions shall not be credited in respect of any such week under this provision, although, if he so desires, the insured person may for any such week pay a contribution as a non-employed person.

(2) For the purposes of this regulation the expression "unemployability supplement" means—

(a) a payment by way of unemployability supplement under the provisions of section 13 or section 81 of the Industrial Injuries Act;

(b) a supplement on account of unemployability payable by virtue of any Service Pensions Instrument, Personal Injuries Scheme or 1914–1918 War Injuries Scheme;

(c) an increase of an allowance on account of unemployability payable under the provisions of Article 7 of the Pneumoconiosis, Byssinosis and Miscellaneous Diseases Benefit Scheme 1966(b).

Widows

9.—(1) A widow who but for the provisions of this paragraph would be liable to pay a contribution as an insured person, shall be entitled but shall not

(a) The relevant amending instrument is S.I. 1960/1282 (1960 II, p. 2154).
(b) S.I. 1966/164 (1966 I, p. 303).

be liable to pay such a contribution, and if she is an employed person her employer shall not be liable to pay such a contribution on her behalf unless before the expiry of the time prescribed by regulation 6 of the Collection of Contributions Regulations for payment he is informed of her desire to pay it—

(a) for the week in which the death of her husband occurs and each of the twenty-six succeeding weeks; and

(b) if at the end of that period there is pending a claim or application, made by her or on her behalf as a widow, for any benefit or specified benefit referred to in paragraph (2) or paragraph (3) of this regulation other than a widow's basic pension or a contributory old age pension, for each week during any part of which that claim or application remains pending.

(2) A woman who is a non-employed person shall be entitled but shall not be liable to pay a contribution as a non-employed person for any week for the whole or any part of which widow's benefit (not being a widows' basic pension within the meaning of the National Insurance (Pensions, Existing Beneficiaries and Other Persons) (Transitional) Regulations 1948(a)) is payable to her as the widow of her husband.

(3) A woman who is an employed or self-employed person shall not be liable to pay a contribution as an employed or self-employed person, as the case may be, for any such week as is specified in paragraph (2) of this regulation or for any week for the whole or any part of which a retirement pension by virtue of her husband's insurance (not being a contributory old age pension within the meaning of the last-mentioned regulations) is payable to her as the widow of her husband or as a woman to whom regulation 8C(2) of the Married Women Regulations, as amended(b), applies or would be so payable but for the provisions of section 30(7) of the Act (which subsection relates to the reduction, based on earnings, of retirement pensions) and a woman shall not be liable to pay a contribution as an insured person for any week for the whole or any part of which any of the specified benefits as defined in regulation 2 of the Overlapping Benefits Regulations, as amended(c), is payable to her as a widow at a weekly rate which is not less than the weekly rate of widow's pension specified in Column 2 of Schedule 3 to the Act, if (in each case) it is a week to which a certificate of exception issued or deemed to have been issued by the Secretary of State pursuant to this regulation relates.

(4) Where such a certificate has been, or is deemed to have been, issued to a woman to whom any of the said specified benefits was payable as a widow at a weekly rate not less than the weekly rate of widow's pension aforesaid, any subsequent increase in the weekly rate of widow's pension under the Act shall, so long as she remains a widow, be disregarded for the purpose of the application to her of the provisions of the last foregoing paragraph.

(5) The following provisions shall apply in relation to the issue and operation of certificates of exception pursuant to this regulation:—

(a) A woman desiring the issue of such a certificate shall apply to the Secretary of State therefor and the Secretary of State shall issue a certificate if he is satisfied that she is, or that if she were an employed or self-employed person she would be, entitled subject to the issue thereof to exception from liability to pay contributions.

(a) S.I. 1948/55 (Rev. XVI, p. 36: 1948 I, p. 2822).
(b) The relevant amending instrument is S.I. 1957/1322 (1957 I, p. 1681).
(c) The relevant amending instruments are S.I. 1952/422, 526, 1959/1290 (1952 II, pp. 2194, 2196; 1959 II, p. 1875).

(*b*) The period to which the certificate relates shall commence—

    (i) if application for the certificate is made not later than thirteen weeks after the applicant's being notified of the award to her of any benefit or specified benefit by virtue whereof she is entitled to such a certificate, at the beginning of the week in which she was so notified; and

    (ii) if application for the certificate is not so made, at the beginning of the week in which the application is made:

Provided that if in any case it appears to the Secretary of State that the making of application for the certificate has been delayed by reason of an error on the part of the applicant as to her right to exception from liability to pay contributions or to apply for a certificate, or as to the effect upon her rights under the Act of obtaining or failing to obtain such a certificate or of paying or failing to pay contributions, he may direct that the period to which the certificate relates shall commence at the beginning of such earlier week as he considers appropriate in the circumstances.

(*c*) Where a woman entitled by virtue of paragraph (3) of this regulation, subject to the issue of a certificate, to exception from liability to pay contributions was, immediately before the death of her husband occurring on or after the 26th February 1962, an employed person who had elected not to be liable to pay contributions as an employed person, or a self-employed or non-employed person who had not elected to be liable to pay contributions as a self-employed or non-employed person—

    (i) a certificate shall be deemed to have been issued to her by the Secretary of State pursuant to this regulation and to relate to the period commencing at the beginning of the week in which the death of her husband occurs; and

    (ii) any certificate of election not to pay contributions as an employed person issued to her as a married woman shall be treated for the purposes of this regulation as a certificate of exception issued pursuant to this regulation;

unless she notifies the Secretary of State that she does not wish to be excepted from liability to pay contributions.

(*d*) A person to whom a certificate is issued pursuant to this regulation shall produce it without delay to any employer who may employ her while it is in operation.

(*e*) A person to whom a certificate is issued or deemed to be issued pursuant to this regulation—

    (i) may give notice to the Secretary of State at any time that she desires it to be cancelled, in which event the certificate shall cease to be in operation from such date as the Secretary of State may determine;

    (ii) upon giving such notice shall surrender to the Secretary of State any certificate issued to her pursuant to this regulation or issued to her under other provisions and deemed to have been issued pursuant to this regulation; and

    (iii) if she is an employed person shall inform her employer forthwith of any cancellation of her certificate and of the date from which it ceased to be in operation.

(6) For the purposes of regulation 20—

(*a*) any contribution paid by a woman excepted from liability to pay that contribution by virtue of any of the provisions of this regulation shall be treated as a contribution paid under the erroneous belief that it was payable if it was paid in error and the error was of a description specified in the proviso to paragraph (5)(*b*) of this regulation; and

(*b*) an application for the return of any contribution so treated shall be deemed to be made within the appropriate time specified in paragraph (4) of the said regulation 20 if it was made within six years from the date on which the said woman discovered her error.

Full-time education, unpaid apprenticeship and training

10.—(1) In this regulation "education" means full-time education, "apprenticeship" means full-time unpaid apprenticeship, "training" means full-time training at a course approved by the Secretary of State, and "national service" means whole-time service within the meaning of Part I of the National Service Act 1948(**a**), and the provisions of this regulation shall have effect in relation to any person who has not attained the age of eighteen as if any week in a period not exceeding thirteen weeks from and including the week in which the termination of education, apprenticeship or training occurs and ending immediately before the first week thereafter in respect of which a contribution is payable by him as an employed or self-employed person or the week in which he attains the age of eighteen, whichever first occurs, were a week of education, apprenticeship or training, as the case may be.

(2) For any week of education, apprenticeship or training a person—

(*a*) shall be excepted from liability to pay a contribution as a non-employed person or, for a week of education or training, as a self-employed person in respect of any employment undertaken in the course of and for the purpose only of such education or training; and

(*b*) may, if he so desires and is not entitled to be credited with a contribution for that week under paragraph (4) of this regulation, pay a contribution as a non-employed person, and payment thereof may be made at any time before the end of the sixth contribution year following the contribution year in which the education, apprenticeship or training terminated.

(3) Any contribution paid by a person as a non-employed person in accordance with the preceding paragraph shall be treated as equivalent to a contribution of the appropriate class in relation to unemployment and sickness benefit if in respect of the period of three years, disregarding any period of national service, immediately preceding the commencement of the education, apprenticeship or training he had paid or had credited to him not less than one hundred and four contributions as an employed or self-employed person.

(4) To persons excepted from liability to pay contributions under paragraph (2) of this regulation, contributions shall be credited as follows:—

(*a*) to any person who has not attained the age of eighteen years there shall be credited for any week of education, apprenticeship or training a contribution of the class specified in relation to his case in sub-paragraph (*c*) of this paragraph;

(*b*) to any person who has attained the age of eighteen years there shall be credited for any week of training a contribution of the class specified in relation to his case in the succeeding sub-paragraph if—

(i) the training was not, at its commencement, intended to continue for more than one year or, in the case of a person undergoing a course of training provided under the Disabled Persons (Employment) Act 1944(**b**), such longer period as the Secretary of State may in such case think fit, and

---

(a) 1948 c. 64.   (b) 1944 c. 10.

(ii) he has, unless the Secretary of State is of the opinion that in the circumstances of his case it is reasonable to dispense with this condition, paid or had credited to him not less than one hundred and four contributions as an employed or self-employed person in respect of the three years, disregarding any period of national service, preceding the commencement of the training, and

(iii) immediately before the commencement of the training there were, in the opinion of the Secretary of State, having regard to his particular circumstances and the industrial conditions in the district in which he ordinarily resides, reasonable grounds for believing that unless he underwent training he would become, or remain, unemployed.

(c) Contributions specified for the purposes of the two preceding sub-paragraphs are—

(i) in the case of a person who satisfies Condition I or Condition II of Schedule 1 to these regulations, a contribution as an employed person;

(ii) in the case of a person who satisfies Condition III or Condition IV of the said Schedule (but not Condition I or Condition II thereof), a contribution as a self-employed person;

(iii) in the case of a person who satisfies none of the Conditions of the said Schedule, a contribution as a non-employed person.

(5) For the purposes of unemployment and sickness benefit only—

(a) a person who—

(i) has made a claim for unemployment or sickness benefit after the termination of education, apprenticeship or training; and

(ii) has paid twenty-six contributions of the appropriate class, excluding contributions paid in respect of him for any period of national service, since his entry into insurance under the Act;

shall, subject to the following provisions of this paragraph, be credited with a contribution of the appropriate class for any week of education, apprenticeship or training, being education, apprenticeship or training which commenced before he paid the twenty-sixth contribution referred to in head (ii) of this sub-paragraph;

(b) a contribution shall not be credited to any person under this paragraph in respect of any week—

(i) for which a contribution of the appropriate class is payable; or

(ii) which occurred before the beginning of the contribution year immediately preceding the benefit year which includes the period for which benefit is claimed.

(6) For the purposes of regulations 2 and 3 of these regulations, when a person has in any benefit year made a claim for unemployment or sickness benefit (as the case may be) and such claim has been allowed by reason of his having been credited with contributions under the preceding paragraph, he shall be deemed to have satisfied Condition I of Schedule 1 to these regulations in respect of any week in that benefit year other than a week commencing before the first day in that year for which he made such claim.

Insured women who have been confined

11.—(1) An insured woman shall be excepted from liability to pay a contribution as a self-employed or non-employed person for any week in which she is confined, and for each of the three succeeding weeks, and, subject to the provisions of paragraph (3) of this regulation, if one of the following conditions is satisfied, a contribution shall be credited to her for that week as follows, provided a contribution as an employed person is not payable for that week:—

> (a) if not less than twenty-six contributions as an employed person have been paid by or credited to the insured woman in respect of the last complete contribution year before the benefit year which includes the date of the confinement, a contribution as an employed person;

> (b) if not less than twenty-six contributions, whether as an employed person or self-employed person, have been paid by or credited to the insured woman in respect of the last complete contribution year before the benefit year which includes the date of the confinement, a contribution as a self-employed person.

(2) A woman who, but for the provisions of the foregoing paragraph, would be liable to pay a contribution as a self-employed or non-employed person for any week and to whom a contribution is not be to credited for that week in accordance with those provisions may, if she so desires, pay for that week the contribution which, but for the said provisions, she would be liable to pay.

(3) It shall be a condition of a woman's right to be credited with a contribution for any week, other than a week in respect of which she has claimed maternity benefit, under paragraph (1) above that she shall furnish to the Secretary of State notice in writing of the grounds on which a contribution should be so credited before the end of the benefit year immediately following the contribution year in which the week in question falls, or within such longer period as the Secretary of State may in a particular case allow.

Maternity allowance

12. An insured woman shall be excepted from liability to pay a contribution for any week in respect of which a maternity allowance is payable to her, and a contribution shall be credited to her for that week as follows:—

> (a) if not less than twenty-six contributions as an employed person were paid by or credited to her in respect of the fifty-two weeks in respect of which the contribution conditions for the allowance (being either the relevant contribution conditions or those conditions as modified by regulations in their application to cases falling within section 24(6) of the Act) were required to have been satisfied, a contribution as an employed person;

> (b) in any other case, a contribution as a self-employed person.

Applications for, and duration and cancellation of, certificates of exception

13.—(1) A person who desires to be excepted from liability to pay contributions by virtue of the provisions of section 10(1)(a)(iii) of the Act (which relates to the exception from such liability on grounds of small income) shall make an application for that purpose to the Secretary of State who, if he grants the application, shall issue to the applicant a certificate of exception.

(2) Any such application and certificate shall be in such form as may for the time being be approved by the Secretary of State.

(3) An applicant for, and a holder of, a certificate of exception shall furnish to the Secretary of State such information and evidence relating to his income as the Secretary of State may require on the making of the application and from time to time thereafter.

(4) A certificate of exception shall be in force for such period as may be specified therein, being a period commencing not earlier than the date on which the application therefor was made:

Provided that—

(a) if any condition attached to the issue, or continuation in force, of the certificate is not, or ceases to be fulfilled, the certificate shall cease to be in force as from the date of such non-fulfilment or cessation, and the holder shall forthwith notify the Secretary of State to that effect;

(b) the period specified in the certificate may, at the discretion of the Secretary of State, commence on such date not earlier than thirteen weeks before the application therefor was made as the Secretary of State may consider appropriate to the circumstances of the case.

(5) The holder of a certificate of exception—

(a) shall, when called upon to do so by an officer of the Department of Health and Social Security, produce the certificate for the officer's inspection;

(b) may at any time give notice to the Secretary of State that he desires the certificate to be cancelled, whereupon the certificate shall cease to be in force from such date as the Secretary of State may determine.

Income for the purposes of certificates of exception

14.—(1) Where an applicant for a certificate of exception is in receipt of an income exceeding £312 a year by reason only of the inclusion therein of any one or more of the following items, he shall be deemed for the purposes of section 10(1)(a)(iii) of the Act not to be in receipt of an income exceeding £312 a year:—

(a) any sum received by way of benefit under the Ministry of Social Security Act 1966(a);

(b) any sum received on account of the death of any person by way of pension or allowances payable to or in respect of any child (within the meaning of the instrument authorising the payment) or by way of a rent allowance payable to a widow or other dependant, being in either case a sum which

(i) is payable by the Secretary of State under the War Orphans Act 1942(b) or under a Service Pensions Instrument or a Personal Injuries Scheme; or

(ii) is payable under any enactment, scheme, ordinance, regulation or other instrument whatsoever promulgated or made in any place outside the United Kingdom or under the law of any such place, and in the opinion of the Secretary of State is analogous to any payment falling within sub-paragraph (i) above; or

(iii) is payable under a 1914–1918 War Injuries Scheme;

(c) any sum received on account of an allowance under the Family Allowances Act 1965(c);

(d) any sum received by way of guardian's allowance, child's allowance, child's special allowance or orphan's pension under the Act;

(e) any sum received by way of death benefit in respect of a child under the Industrial Injuries Act;

(a) 1966 c. 20.   (b) 1942 c. 8.   (c) 1965 c. 53.

(*f*) any one of the following payments or parts of payments up to the amount of thirty shillings a week or, if the applicant is in receipt of more than one such payment, up to the said amount in the aggregate:

(i) the first fifteen shillings a week of any payment of sick pay received from a friendly society or trade union;

(ii) the first fifteen shillings a week of any superannuation payment or superannuation payments in respect of previous service or employment from which the applicant has retired or resigned (whether payable by a former employer or not);

(iii) any payment by way of maternity allowance under section 24 of the Act;

(iv) any payment in respect of retired pay or pension to which section 380 of the Income Tax Act 1952(a) applies, including any such payment in respect of a dependants' allowance attached to such a pension;

(v) any payment in respect of a disablement pension awarded under the Personal Injuries (Emergency Provisions) Act 1939(b), including an increase in such a pension in respect of dependants;

(vi) any weekly payment by way of compensation under any enactment relating to workmen's compensation;

(vii) any payment by way of disablement benefit under section 12 of the Industrial Injuries Act.

(2) Where an applicant for a certificate of exception is in receipt of an income which, after the deduction therefrom of such, if any, of the items specified in paragraph (1) above as are included therein, exceeds £312 a year by an amount not greater than the amount of the contributions which he would be liable to pay in a year if he were not excepted, he shall be deemed for the purposes of section 10(1)(*a*)(iii) of the Act, not to be in receipt of an income exceeding £312 a year.

Certificates of exception—exception from liability for, and payment and crediting of, contributions

15.—(1) An insured person shall be excepted from liability to pay a contribution as a self-employed person or a non-employed person for any week during the whole of which a certificate of exception is in force in relation to him.

(2) A person to whom paragraph (1) above is applicable may, if he so desires, pay a contribution as, or as if he were, a non-employed person for any week during the whole of which the certificate is in force and during which he is either a self-employed person or a non-employed person.

(3) Contributions shall not be credited to a person, in respect of whom a certificate of exception has been granted, while the certificate remains in force, but any such person, in respect of whom at the time of the issue of the certificate less than twenty-six contributions as an employed person had been paid in respect of him since his entry into insurance under the Act shall, nevertheless, upon the first occasion on which such a certificate ceases to be in force in his case, be entitled, for the purposes only of unemployment and sickness benefit in respect of periods occurring after the certificate has ceased to be in force, to have a contribution credited as an employed person in respect of every week (not being a week in respect of which a contribution as an employed person is payable) during which the certificate was in force, subject to the following provisions, namely:—

(a) 1952 c. 10.   (b) 1939 c. 82.

(*a*) the question of crediting any such contributions shall not be determined unless and until the next following sub-paragraph is satisfied and thereafter the person concerned makes his first claim for any such benefit;

(*b*) contributions shall not be credited to such a person until twenty-six contributions, whether as an employed or self-employed person, have been paid in respect of him for weeks commencing not earlier than the week in which the certificate ceased to be in force;

(*c*) notwithstanding the provisions of the foregoing sub-paragraph, any such contributions so credited shall not be taken into account for the purposes of unemployment benefit until twenty-six contributions as an employed person have been paid in respect of him for weeks commencing not earlier than the week in which the said certificate ceases to be in force;

(*d*) contributions shall not be credited for any period earlier than the beginning of the contribution year immediately preceding the benefit year which includes the period for which benefit is claimed.

(4) Nothing in these regulations shall preclude a person from receiving benefit, while a certificate of exception is in force, by virtue of contributions paid by or credited to him in respect of any period before the day on which the certificate commenced to be in force.

Pre-entry credits

16.—(1) Subject to the provisions of paragraph (3) of this regulation, contributions as an employed person shall be credited to a person for the period between the beginning of the contribution year last preceding that in which he became an insured person and his entry into insurance under the Act:

Provided that, in the case of a person who by reason of having at some time been outside Great Britain did not enter insurance until after he had attained the age of sixteen, the number of contributions so credited shall not, for the purpose of calculating the yearly average of the contributions paid by or credited to him, exceed the number of contributions (of whatever class) which would have been credited to him under the provisions of paragraph (3) of this regulation in respect of the period between the beginning of the contribution year in which he attained the age of sixteen and his attainment of that age if throughout that period he had been an insured person who would have been liable to pay a contribution as a non-employed person but for the provisions of section 9 of the Act (which provides that a person shall not be liable to pay a contribution as a non-employed person before attaining the age of sixteen) and of regulations made under section 103 of the Act (which provides for the modification of the Act in relation to insured persons outside Great Britain).

(2) Contributions credited in respect of a person in accordance with paragraph (1) above shall not be taken into account for the purpose of the Conditions mentioned in Schedule 1 to these regulations, unless, in the case of Condition I or Condition II, twenty-six contributions as an employed person have been paid by or in respect of him since his entry into insurance, or, in the case of Condition III or Condition IV, twenty-six contributions, whether as an employed person or self-employed person, have been so paid since such entry, and shall not be taken into account for the purposes of maternity allowance.

(3) A contribution shall be credited to a person who on his entry into insurance is under the age of sixteen for the week in which he enters insurance and for any subsequent week ending before he attains the age of sixteen, being, in either case, a week for which he would have been liable to pay a contribution as a non-employed person but for the provisions of section 9 of the Act or, in

the case of a period of absence from Great Britain, but for the provisions of that section and of regulations made under section 103 of the Act, and the contribution so credited for any such week shall be—

(a) in the case of a person who but for the said provisions would for that week have been excepted from liability for a contribution under the Act and entitled to have a contribution credited to him as an employed or self-employed person by virtue of any of these regulations, a contribution as an employed person or a self-employed person as if that regulation applied to his case; and

(b) in any other case, a contribution as a non-employed person.

Contributions to be taken into account

17. Where by virtue of these regulations more than one contribution is credited to any person for any week or a contribution is credited to him for a week in respect of which a contribution is paid in respect of him, not more than one such contribution shall be taken into account for any purpose.

Provisions relating to Schedule 1

18.—(1) Any contributions which under regulation 10(3) of these regulations or under any regulations which provide for treating contributions as a non-employed person as equivalent to contributions of the appropriate class for the purpose of a maternity allowance, are treated as equivalent to contributions of another class shall for the purpose of Schedule 1 to these regulations be treated as contributions of that other class.

(2) In determining whether a person shall be excepted from liability for, and credited with, contributions under regulation 2 of these regulations and for no other purpose, the provisions of paragraph (1) above shall apply to any contributions which under the provisions of regulation 2 of the National Insurance (Seasonal Workers) (No. 2) Regulations 1950(a), as amended(b), are treated as equivalent to contributions of another class.

(3) Any contribution as a non-employed or self-employed person which under the provisions of the Unemployment and Sickness Benefit Regulations is treated as equivalent to a contribution of another class for the purposes of unemployment benefit or sickness benefit shall be treated as a contribution of that other class for the purposes of the application of Schedule 1 hereto to the provisions of regulation 2 or regulation 3 of these regulations:

Provided that—

(a) any such contribution which is so treated as equivalent to a contribution of another class for the purposes only of unemployment benefit shall be treated as a contribution of that other class for the purposes only of the application of Schedule 1 to regulation 2 of these regulations; and

(b) any such contribution which is so treated as equivalent to a contribution of another class for the purposes only of sickness benefit shall be treated as a contribution of that other class for the purposes only of the application of Schedule 1 to regulation 3 of these regulations.

(a) S.I. 1950/1915 (1950 II, p. 32).
(b) There is no amendment which relates expressly to the subject matter of these Regulations.

PART III

MISCELLANEOUS PROVISIONS RELATING TO CONTRIBUTIONS

Disposal of contributions improperly paid

19.—(1) Where contributions are paid under the Act which are of the wrong class or at the wrong rate, the Secretary of State may treat them as paid on account of the contributions properly payable or on account of contributions under the Industrial Injuries Act, and where contributions are paid under the Industrial Injuries Act which are not payable, he may, notwithstanding anything in that Act, treat them as paid on account of contributions under the Act.

(2) In this regulation references to "contributions" include references to graduated contributions and to payments in lieu of contributions.

Return of contributions paid in error

20.—(1) Subject to the provisions of regulation 19 and of this regulation, any contributions paid by a person or his employer (if any) under the erroneous belief that the contributions were payable by, or in respect or on behalf of, that person under the provisions of the Act shall be returned by the Secretary of State to that person or his employer, as the case may require, if application to that effect is made in writing to the Secretary of State within the appropriate time specified in paragraph (4) of this regulation.

(2) In calculating the amount of any repayment to be made under this regulation to such a person or employer, there shall be deducted—

> (*a*) in the case of employers' contributions and contributions as an insured person, the amount of any contributions paid under the said erroneous belief which have under the provisions of regulation 19 been treated as paid on account of other contributions; and

> (*b*) in the case of contributions as an insured person, the amount, if any, paid to that person (and to any other person on the basis of that erroneous belief) by way of benefit which would not have been paid had the contributions (in respect of which an application for their return is duly made in accordance with paragraph (4) of this regulation) not been paid in the first instance.

(3) Contributions erroneously paid by an employer on behalf of any person and not recovered from him may be repaid to the employer instead of to that person, but if so recovered may be repaid to that person, or, with his consent in writing, to his employer.

(4) A person desiring to apply for the return of any contribution paid under the said erroneous belief shall make the application in such form and in such manner as the Secretary of State may from time to time determine, and—

> (*a*) if the contribution was paid at the due date, within two years from the date on which that contribution was paid; or

> (*b*) if the contribution was paid at a later date than the due date, within two years from the due date or within twelve months from the date of actual payment of the contribution, whichever period ends later.

(5) In this regulation the expression "due date" means the date on which the contribution, if it had been payable, would have been due to be paid.

(6) The provisions of this regulation apply to graduated contributions and to payments in lieu of contributions as they apply to contributions subject to the following rules, namely:—

(a) the time within which a person desiring to apply for the return of any graduated contribution paid under the said erroneous belief shall make the application is six years from the end of the income tax year in which the payment of remuneration was made on which that contribution was based, or such longer time as the Secretary of State may allow if he is satisfied that that person had good cause for not applying within those six years;

(b) the time within which a person desiring to apply for the return of any payment in lieu of contributions made under the said erroneous belief shall make the application is six years from the date on which the payment was made, or such longer time as the Secretary of State may allow if he is satisfied that that person had good cause for not applying within those six years;

(c) for the purposes of paragraph (2) and paragraph (3) of this regulation one half of the amount of any payment in lieu of contributions made in respect of any person shall be treated as an employer's contribution and the other half thereof shall be treated as a contribution as an insured person paid on behalf of that person, and any sum recovered or retained by virtue of the provisions of section 60 of the Act (which relates to an employer's right to recovery where a refund is payable to or in respect of an insured person under a recognised superannuation scheme) shall be treated as a sum recovered from that person;

(d) the provision of this paragraph shall apply to any part of a graduated contribution or of a payment in lieu of contributions as they apply to that contribution or that payment respectively; and

(e) for the purposes of this regulation, where the graduated contributions paid by a person, in respect of his remuneration from two or more employments in any income tax year, exceed the amount prescribed under section 4(4) of the Act, the excess shall be treated as representing contributions paid under the erroneous belief that they were payable by that person under the Act.

Employment to be disregarded

21. There shall be disregarded for the purposes of subsections (3) to (5) of section 8 of the Act (which relates to the number and class of contributions for any week) any employment in which a person who is under pensionable age engages or continues to be engaged solely or mainly for the purposes of acquiring or preserving a right or a larger right to benefit.

Calculation of weekly rate of remuneration

22. Where a person is employed for less than forty hours a week, the rate of his remuneration for the purpose of Part I and Part II of Schedule 1 to the Act shall be deemed to be that sum a week which bears the same proportion to his actual remuneration as forty hours bears to the number of hours for which he is employed.

PART IV

PROVISIONS RELATING TO CONTRIBUTIONS WHICH ARE NOT PAID

OR ARE PAID AFTER THE DUE DATE

Treatment for the purpose of any benefit of late paid or unpaid contributions where there was no consent, connivance or negligence by the insured person

23.—(1) Where a contribution payable by an employer on behalf of an insured person is paid after the due date or is not paid, and the delay or failure in making payment thereof is shown to the satisfaction of the Secretary of State not to have been with the consent or connivance of, or attributable to any negligence on the part of the insured person, the contribution shall, for the purpose of any right to benefit, be treated as paid on the date due.

(2) The provisions of this regulation apply to a graduated contribution and to a payment in lieu of contributions as they apply to a contribution and as if, in the case of a payment in lieu of contributions, that payment were payable by the employer on behalf of the person in respect of whom it is payable:

Provided that where by virtue of this paragraph any graduated contribution falls to be treated as paid on the due date, the amount to be so treated shall not exceed such amount as is shown to the satisfaction of the Secretary of State to have been payable.

(3) The following provisions of these regulations shall, in their application to a contribution payable by an employer on behalf of an insured person, have effect subject to the provisions of this regulation.

Treatment for the purpose of any benefit of contributions paid late through ignorance or error

24. In the case of a contribution paid after the due date, where—

    (*a*) the contribution is paid after the time when it would, under the following provisions of these regulations, have been treated as paid for the purposes of the right to a benefit; and

    (*b*) the failure to pay the contribution before that time is shown to the satisfaction of the Secretary of State to be attributable to ignorance or error on the part of the insured person which was not due to any failure on his part to exercise due care and diligence;

the Secretary of State may direct that for the purposes of the following provisions of this Part of these regulations the contribution shall be treated as having been paid on such earlier day as he may consider appropriate in the circumstances and those provisions shall have effect subject to any such direction.

Treatment for the purpose of unemployment or sickness benefit of late paid contributions

25.—(1) For the purpose of any right to unemployment or sickness benefit, a contribution paid after the due date shall, in determining whether the relevant contribution conditions are satisfied as respects the number of contributions paid in respect of the period between entry into insurance and the day for which the benefit is claimed, be treated—

    (*a*) for the purpose of the right to any such benefit in respect of any day before the date on which payment of the contribution is made—as not paid; and

    (*b*) for the purpose of the right to any such benefit in respect of any other day—as paid on the date on which payment of the contribution is made.

(2) For the purpose aforesaid, in determining whether the relevant contribution conditions are satisfied in whole or in part as respects the number of contributions paid or credited in respect of the last complete contribution year before the beginning of the benefit year which includes the day for which unemployment or sickness benefit is claimed, a contribution paid after the due date shall be treated—

    (*a*) if paid before the beginning of the said benefit year—as paid on the due date;

(*b*) if paid during the said benefit year—as not paid in relation to the right to either of the said benefits in respect of any day before the expiry of a period of 42 days (including Sundays) from and including the date on which payment of that contribution is made and as paid at the expiry of that period in relation to the right to either of the said benefits in respect of any other day;

(*c*) if paid after the end of the said benefit year—as not paid.

Treatment for the purpose of maternity benefit of late paid contributions

26.—(1) For the purpose of any right to maternity allowance, a contribution paid after the due date shall be treated—

(*a*) if paid before the expiry of the maternity allowance period or the period of four weeks after the date on which the claim for allowance is made (whichever period ends later)—as paid on the due date;

(*b*) if paid after the expiry of whichever of the said periods ends later—as not paid;

and, for the purposes of this paragraph, the expression "the maternity allowance period" means the period mentioned in subsection (2) of section 24 of the Act or, in a case in relation to which that subsection is modified in accordance with regulations made under subsection (6) of that section, the period mentioned in the said subsection (2) as so modified.

(2) For the purpose of any right to a maternity grant, a contribution paid after the due date shall be treated—

(*a*) if paid before the expiry of the period of three months after the date of confinement—as paid on the due date;

(*b*) if paid after the expiry of the said period of three months—as not paid.

Treatment for the purpose of widow's benefit, child's special allowance or retirement pension of late paid contributions

27.—(1) For the purpose of any right to widow's benefit, to child's special allowance or to a retirement pension, a contribution paid after the due date and before the relevant time shall be treated—

(*a*) if paid before the end of the sixth contribution year following the contribution year which includes the contribution week in respect of which it is payable—as paid on the due date;

(*b*) if paid at any other time—as not paid.

(2) For the purpose aforesaid, a contribution paid after the due date and after the relevant time shall, if it is a contribution—

(*a*) payable in respect of a week

(i) commencing before the relevant time in the contribution year which includes that time; or

(ii) in the contribution year immediately preceding that year; and

(*b*) paid before the end of the period of one year from the relevant time; be treated as paid on the due date and any other contribution paid after the due date and after the relevant time shall be treated as not paid:

Provided that a contribution payable in respect of a week commencing after the relevant time shall for the said purpose be treated as paid on the date on which payment of the contribution is made.

(3) In this regulation the expression "relevant time" has the same meaning as in paragraph 4 of Schedule 2 to the Act.

Treatment for the purpose of increase of rate of retirement pension of late paid contributions

28. For the purpose of section 31(1) of the Act (which provides for the increase of the weekly rate of retirement pension where contributions are paid in respect of the period after the attainment of pensionable age) and for the purpose of section 34(1) of the Act (which relates to women's retirement pensions), a contribution paid after the due date shall be treated—

(a) if paid before the end of the period of one year beginning immediately after the end of the contribution year which includes the contribution week in respect of which it is payable—as paid on the due date;

(b) if not paid before the end of the said period—as not paid.

Treatment for the purpose of death grant of late paid contributions

29.—(1) For the purpose of any right to a death grant, a contribution paid after the due date shall, subject to the provisions of the next following paragraph, be treated as not paid if—

(a) the grant is claimed in respect of the death of the relevant person and the contribution is paid after the date of that death;

(b) the grant is claimed in respect of the death of a person dying during the life time of the relevant person and the contribution is paid after the date of such death;

(c) the relevant person has predeceased the person in respect of whose death the grant is claimed and the contribution (not being a contribution which by virtue of regulation 27(2) has been treated as paid on the due date for the purpose of a claim for widow's benefit or for retirement pension) is paid after the date of the death of the relevant person;

and in any other case shall, subject as aforesaid, be treated as paid on the due date.

(2) For the purpose aforesaid and notwithstanding the provisions of the last foregoing paragraph, in determining whether the relevant contribution conditions are satisfied in whole or in part as respects the yearly average of contributions paid or credited to any person—

(a) a contribution paid after the due date and before the relevant time shall be treated—

(i) if paid before the end of the sixth contribution year following the contribution year which includes the contribution week in respect of which it is payable—as paid on the due date;

(ii) if paid at any other time—as not paid;

(b) a contribution paid after the due date and after the relevant time, being a contribution payable in respect of any week in the contribution year immediately preceding the contribution year which includes the relevant time, shall be treated as paid on the due date.

(3) In this regulation the expressions "relevant person" and "relevant time" have the same meanings as in paragraph 5 of Schedule 2 to the Act.

Treatment for the purpose of any benefit of late paid graduated contributions and payments in lieu of contributions

30.—(1) For the purpose of any right to benefit (including any increase in the amount of benefit under section 36(4) of the Act where a person does not retire from regular employment on attaining pensionable age) a graduated contribution paid after the due date shall be treated—

(a) if paid before the end of the sixth income tax year following the income tax year in which the payment of remuneration was made on which that contribution was based—as paid on the due date;

(b) if paid at any other time—as not paid.

(2) For the purpose aforesaid, a payment in lieu of contributions made after the due date shall be treated—

(a) if made before before the end of the sixth income tax year following the income tax year in which it became due—as made on the due date;

(b) if made at any other time—as not made.

PART V

PROVISIONS RELATING TO CONTRIBUTIONS WHICH PERSONS ARE ENTITLED, BUT NOT LIABLE, TO PAY

Treatment for the purpose of any benefit of contributions which persons are entitled, but not liable, to pay

31.—(1) Subject to the following provisions of this regulation, the provisions of Part IV of these regulations shall apply to contributions which persons are entitled, but not liable, to pay as if each such contribution were due to be paid on the last day in the contribution week in respect of which it is paid.

(2) For the purpose of any right to widow's benefit, to child's special allowance, to a retirement pension or to a death grant, a contribution which a person is entitled, but not liable, to pay in accordance with the provisions of regulation 7(2) or regulation 10 of these regulations or regulation 5 of the Residence and Persons Abroad Regulations, as amended(a), (which regulation contains special provisions for payment of contributions in respect of periods abroad), shall, if it is paid before the relevant time and within the period within which it may be paid under any of the said provisions, be treated as paid on the due date.

(3) In the preceding paragraph of this regulation, the expression "the relevant time" has the same meaning as in paragraph 4 or paragraph 5, as the case may require, of Schedule 2 to the Act.

Contributions not paid within prescribed periods

32.—(1) Where a person was entitled to pay a contribution under any of the provisions of the regulations referred to in regulation 31(2) of these regulations (imprisonment or detention in legal custody, full-time education, unpaid apprenticeship and training, and periods abroad) but he failed to pay that contribution in the period provided for payment in the said provision applicable and his failure is shown to the satisfaction of the Secretary of State to be attributable to ignorance or error on his part which was not due to any failure on his part to exercise due care and diligence, that contribution may be paid within such further period as the Secretary of State may direct.

(2) Where a person was entitled to pay a contribution under the provisions of regulation 6(b) of the Residence and Persons Abroad Regulations, as amended(c), (which made special provision for payment of contributions by persons returning to Great Britain after 5th July 1948) but he failed to pay that contribution in the period provided for payment in those provisions and his failure so to pay is shown to the satisfaction of the Secretary of State to be attributable to ignorance or error on his part which was not due to any

---

(a) The relevant amending instruments are S.I. 1950/1946, 1956/2021 (1950 II, p. 27; 1956 I, p. 1687).

(b) Revoked with effect from 22nd December 1956 by S.I. 1956/2021 (1956 I, p. 1687), regulation 3.

(c) The relevant amending instrument is S.I. 1950/1946 (1950 II, p. 27).

failure on his part to exercise due care and diligence, that contribution may be paid within such further period as the Secretary of State may direct.

(3) Where a person returning to Great Britain more than three years after 5th July 1948 would have been entitled to pay contributions under the said regulation 6 if the power of the Minister of National Insurance or of the Minister of Pensions and National Insurance had been exercised thereunder to determine that in the particular case a period exceeding three years should apply, the Secretary of State may, having regard to the circumstances of the case, determine that the provisions of paragraph (2) of this regulation shall apply as if the said period had been extended so as to include the date of that person's return to Great Britain.

(4) Where contributions are paid for any period in respect of a person by virtue of the provisions of paragraphs (2) or (3) of this regulation, that person shall be deemed to have been an insured person for that period.

Payments after death

33. If a person dies, any contributions which, immediately before his death, he was entitled, but not liable, to pay, if he so desired, may be paid notwithstanding his death, subject, however, to the same provisions with respect to the time for payment as were applicable to that person.

Revocation and general savings

34.—(1) The regulations specified in column 1 of Schedule 2 to these regulations are hereby revoked to the extent mentioned in column 3 of that Schedule.

(2) Anything whatsoever done under or by virtue of any regulation revoked by these regulations shall be deemed to have been done under or by virtue of the corresponding provision of these regulations, and anything whatsoever begun under any such regulation may be continued under these regulations as if begun under these regulations.

(3) So much of any document as refers expressly or by implication to any regulation revoked by these regulations shall, if and so far as the context permits, be construed as referring to the corresponding provision of these regulations.

(4) Nothing in paragraphs (2) and (3) of this regulation shall be taken as affecting the general application by regulation 1(4) of these regulations of the rules for the construction of Acts of Parliament contained in section 38 of the Interpretation Act 1889 (effect of repeal) with regard to the effect of revocations.

Signed by authority of the Secretary of State for Social Services.

David Ennals,
Minister of State,
Department of Health and Social Security.

25th November 1969.
Given under the Official Seal of the National Insurance Joint Authority.

(L.S.) *D. J. Carter,*
Secretary,
National Insurance Joint Authority.

25th November 1969.

Neil McBride,
E. G. Perry,
Two of the Lords Commissioners of
Her Majesty's Treasury.

27th November 1969.

SCHEDULE 1

CONDITIONS ATTACHING TO EXCEPTION FROM LIABILITY TO PAY, AND TO THE CREDITING OF, CONTRIBUTIONS

Condition I

That not less than twenty-six contributions as an employed person have been paid by or credited to the insured person in respect of the contribution year immediately preceding the benefit year which includes the relevant week.

Condition II

That not less than ten contributions as an employed person have been paid by or credited to the insured person in respect of the thirteen weeks immediately preceding the relevant week.

Condition III

That not less than twenty-six contributions, whether as an employed person or a self-employed person, have been paid by or credited to the insured person in respect of the contribution year immediately preceding the benefit year which includes the relevant week.

Condition IV

That not less than ten contributions, whether as an employed person or a self-employed person, have been paid by or credited to the insured person in respect of the thirteen weeks immediately preceding the relevant week.

In this Schedule the expression "the relevant week" means the week in respect of which a question arises under these regulations either in relation to exception from liability to pay, or to the crediting of, a contribution.

SCHEDULE 2   Regulation 34(1)

1 Regulations Revoked	2 References	3 Extent of Revocation
The National Insurance (Contributions) Regulations 1948	S.I. 1948/1417 (Rev. XVI p. 164: 1948 I, p. 2767).	The whole regulations
The National Insurance (Contributions) Amendment Regulations 1950	S.I. 1950/330 (1950 II, p. 15).	The whole regulations
The National Insurance (Contributions) Amendment (No. 2) Regulations 1950	S.I. 1950/1947 (1950 II, p. 20).	The whole regulations
The National Insurance (Contributions) Amendment Regulations 1952	S.I. 1952/1393 (1952 II, p. 2140).	The whole regulations

Schedule 2—*cont.*

1 Regulations Revoked	2 References	3 Extent of Revocation
The National Insurance (Contributions) Amendment Regulations 1953	S.I. 1953/495 (1953 I, p. 1371).	The whole regulations
The National Insurance (Contributions) Amendment (No. 2) Regulations 1953	S.I. 1953/1544 (1953 I, p. 1372).	The whole regulations
The National Insurance (Maternity Benefit and Miscellaneous Provisions) Regulations 1954	S.I. 1954/189 (1954 I, p. 1387).	Regulation 20 and Parts VI to VIII of Schedule 1
The National Insurance (Contributions) Amendment Regulations 1955	S.I. 1955/1602 (1955 I, p. 1629).	The whole regulations
The National Insurance (Contributions) Amendment Regulations 1956	S.I. 1956/2020 (1956 I, p. 1639).	The whole regulations
The National Insurance (Child's Special Allowance) Regulations 1957	S.I. 1957/1835 (1957 I, p. 1523).	In the Schedule the entry relating to the National Insurance (Contributions) Amendment Regulations 1956
The National Insurance (Contributions) Amendment Regulations 1957	S.I. 1957/1299 (1957 I, p. 1635).	The whole regulations
The National Insurance (Contributions) Amendment (No. 2) Regulations 1957	S.I. 1957/2176 (1957 I, p. 1642).	The whole regulations
The National Insurance (Contributions) Amendment Regulations 1959	S.I. 1959/847 (1959 II, p. 1882).	The whole regulations
The National Insurance (Contributions) Amendment (No. 2) Regulations 1959	S.I. 1959/1803 (1959 II, p. 1891).	The whole regulations

Schedule 2—*cont.*

1 Regulations Revoked	2 References	3 Extent of Revocation
The National Insurance (Contributions) Amendment Regulations 1960	S.I. 1960/782 (1960 II, p. 2228).	The whole regulations
The National Insurance (Graduated Contributions and Non-participating Employments—Miscellaneous Provisions) Regulations 1960	S.I. 1960/1210 (1960 II, p. 2234).	Part IV
The National Insurance (Contributions) Amendment (No. 2) Regulations 1960	S.I. 1960/1285 (1960 II, p. 2230).	The whole regulations
The National Insurance (Consequential Provisions) Regulations 1962	S.I. 1962/12 (1962 I, p. 10).	Regulation 6 and Schedule 4
The National Insurance (Contributions) Amendment Regulations 1962	S.I. 1962/300 (1962 I, p. 289).	The whole regulations
The National Insurance (Contributions) Amendment (No. 2) Regulations 1962	S.I. 1962/987 (1962 II, p. 1112).	The whole regulations
The National Insurance (Contributions) Amendment Regulations 1963	S.I. 1963/501 (1963 I, p. 575).	The whole regulations
The National Insurance (Miscellaneous Consequential Amendments and Transitional Provisions) Regulations 1966	S.I. 1966/1010 (1966 II, p. 2407).	Regulation 4
The National Insurance (Increase of Benefit and Miscellaneous Provisions) Regulations 1967	S.I. 1967/1265 (1967 II, p. 3673).	Item 7 in Schedule L
The National Insurance (Contributions) Amendment Regulations 1967	S.I. 1967/1468 (1967 III, p. 4154).	The whole regulations

EXPLANATORY NOTE

(This Note is not part of the Regulations.)

These Regulations are made for the purpose only of consolidating Regulations hereby revoked and accordingly, by virtue of section 108(9)(*c*) of the National Insurance Act 1965, no reference of them has been made to the National Insurance Advisory Committee.

The Regulations consolidate the regulations hitherto in force relating to contributions under the National Insurance Act 1965. Part II of the Regulations deals with the circumstances in which persons are excepted from liability to pay contributions and in which they are either credited with contributions or permitted to pay them. The Regulations also contain (in Part III) provisions relating to the disposal and return of contributions which have been paid in error and (in Parts IV and V) provisions relating to the treatment for benefit purposes of contributions which are paid after the due date or not paid.

The National Insurance (Contributions) Amendment (No. 2) Regulations 1960	S.I. 1960/1285 (1960 I, p. 2230)	The whole regulations
The National Insurance (Consequential Provisions) Regulations 1960	S.I. 1962/12 (1962 I, p. 10)	Regulations 6 and Schedule 4
The National Insurance (Contributions) Amendment Regulations 1962	S.I. 1962/300 (1962 I, p. 391)	The whole regulations
The National Insurance (Insurance) (Contributions) Amendment (No. 2) Regulations 1962	S.I. 1962/989 (1962 I, p. 1172)	The whole regulations
The National Insurance (Contributions) Amendment Regulations 1963	S.I. 1963/500 (1963 I, p. 871)	The whole regulations
The National Insurance (Miscellaneous Consequential Amendments and Transitional Provisions) Regulations 1966	S.I. 1966/1016 (1966 II, p. 2607)	Regulation 4
The National Insurance (Increase of Benefit and Miscellaneous Provisions) Regulations 1967	S.I. 1967/1265 (1967 II, item 7 in Schedule 1, p. 3632)	item 7 in Schedule 1
The National Insurance (Contributions) Amendment Regulations 1967	S.I. 1967/1168 (1967 III, p. 4150)	The whole regulations

STATUTORY INSTRUMENTS

1969 No. 1699

SAVINGS BANKS

The Savings Banks (Ordinary Deposits) (Limits) (Amendment) Order 1969

Laid before Parliament in draft

Made	-	-	-	28*th November* 1969
Coming into Operation			29*th November* 1969

The Treasury, in exercise of the powers conferred on them by section 4 of the Post Office Savings Bank Act 1954(a), as amended by section 94(2) of and Part I of Schedule 6 to the Post Office Act 1969(b), section 16(1) of and paragraph 5 of Schedule 4 to the Trustee Investments Act 1961(c), and section 14(1) of the Trustee Savings Banks Act 1969(d), and of all other powers enabling them in that behalf, hereby make the following Order :—

1. This Order may be cited as the Savings Banks (Ordinary Deposits) (Limits) (Amendment) Order 1969, and shall come into operation on 29th November 1969.

2. The Interpretation Act 1889(e) shall apply for the interpretation of this Order as it applies for the interpretation of an Act of Parliament.

3. The Savings Banks (Ordinary Deposits) (Limits) Order 1969(f) shall have effect as if—

    (a) for references to the Postmaster General, there were substituted references to the Director of Savings ;

    (b) for references to the Post Office Savings Bank, there were substituted references to the National Savings Bank ;

    (c) for the reference in article 3(2) thereof to the Post Office Register, there were substituted a reference to the National Savings Stock Register.

4. This Order shall not affect the validity of any approval of the Postmaster General given before the coming into operation of this Order under article 4 of the Savings Banks (Ordinary Deposits) (Limits) Order 1969 or having effect as if given under that article ; and for the purposes of article 4(2) of that

---

(a) 1954 c. 62.
(c) 1961 c. 62.
(e) 1889 c. 63.

(b) 1969 c. 48.
(d) 1969 c. 50.
(f) S.I. 1969/939 (1969 II, p. 2829).

Order any such approval shall be deemed to be an approval given by the Director of Savings.

Neil McBride,
Joseph Harper,
Two of the Lords Commissioners
of Her Majesty's Treasury.

28th November 1969.

EXPLANATORY NOTE

(This Note is not part of the Order.)

The Post Office Act 1969 transfers the functions of the Postmaster General in relation to the Post Office Savings Bank to the Director of Savings, and changes the name of that Bank to the National Savings Bank. This Order makes the necessary consequential amendments to the Savings Banks (Ordinary Deposits) (Limits) Order 1969.

STATUTORY INSTRUMENTS

1969 No. 1700

SAVINGS BANKS

The Trustee Savings Banks (Amendment) Regulations 1969

Laid before Parliament in draft

| Made | - | - | - | 28th November 1969 |
| Coming into Operation | | | | 29th November 1969 |

The Treasury, in exercise of the powers conferred upon them by sections 28 and 86 of the Trustee Savings Banks Act 1969(a), and of all other powers enabling them in that behalf, with the concurrence of the National Debt Commissioners, hereby make the following Regulations:—

1. These Regulations may be cited as the Trustee Savings Banks (Amendment) Regulations 1969, and shall come into operation on 29th November 1969.

2. The Interpretation Act 1889(b) shall apply for the interpretation of these Regulations as it applies for the interpretation of an Act of Parliament.

3. The Trustee Savings Banks Regulations 1929(c), as amended (d), shall have effect as if—

(a) in Regulation 2 thereof, in the definition of "Government Stock", for the words "Post Office Register" there were substituted the words "National Savings Stock Register";

(b) in Regulation 16 thereof, for the words "Post Office Savings Bank", in both places where they occur, there were substituted the words "National Savings Bank";

(c) in Regulation 29 thereof, as substituted by Regulation 1 of the Trustee Savings Banks (Amendment) (No. 2) Regulations 1956(e), and as amended by the Trustee Savings Banks (Amendment) Regulations 1965(f), in paragraph (1), for the figures "£1,500", there were substituted the figures "£3,000"; in paragraph (2), for the words "Post Office Register", there were substituted the words "National Savings Stock Register"; and after sub-paragraph (b) there were added the following sub-paragraph:—

"(c) the total amount (including any bonus or interest) which would have been repayable (if repayment had been demanded) at the date of the death of the depositor in respect of all savings contracts entered into by him and registered by the trustees of the savings bank under a contractual savings scheme certified by the Treasury in accordance with section 53(2) of the Finance Act 1969(g)";

(a) 1969 c. 50.   (b) 1889 c. 63.
(c) S.R. & O. 1929/1048 (Rev. XX, p. 584; 1929, p. 1282).
(d) The relevant amending instruments are S.I. 1956/1179 and 1965/573 (1956 II, p. 2195; 1965 I, p. 1794).
(e) S.I. 1956/1179 (1956 II, p. 2195).   (f) S.I. 1965/573 (1965 I, p. 1794).
(g) 1969 c. 32.

and in paragraph (3), for the words "the last preceding sub-paragraph", there were substituted the words "sub-paragraph (*b*) of paragraph (2) of this Regulation"; and for the words "Post Office Register", there were substituted the words "National Savings Stock Register".

Neil McBride,
Joseph Harper,
Two of the Lords Commissioners
of Her Majesty's Treasury.

28th November 1969.

I concur.

I. de Lisle Radice,
On behalf of the National Debt
Commissioners.

28th November 1969.

EXPLANATORY NOTE

(This Note is not part of the Regulations.)

The Post Office Act 1969 (c. 48) changes the name of the Post Office Register to the National Savings Stock Register, and of the Post Office Savings Bank to the National Savings Bank. These Regulations make the necessary consequential amendments to the Trustee Savings Banks Regulations 1929. They also amend Regulation 29 of the Regulations of 1929 (as substituted by the Trustee Savings Banks (Amendment) (No. 2) Regulations 1956), which in certain circumstances requires the production of a statement as to payment of death duties where the aggregate value of the specified assets (as defined in the Regulation) exceeds a limit of £1,500. The Regulations substitute a new limit of £3,000 and provide for the inclusion in the specified assets of any amounts repayable in respect of savings contracts.

STATUTORY INSTRUMENTS

1969 No. 1701

SAVINGS BANKS

The Post Office Savings Bank (Investment Deposits) (Limits) (Amendment) Order 1969

Laid before Parliament in draft

Made - - -	28*th November* 1969
Coming into Operation	29*th November* 1969

The Treasury, in exercise of the powers conferred on them by section 4 of the Post Office Savings Bank Act 1954(a), as amended by section 94(2) of and Part I of Schedule 6 to the Post Office Act 1969(b), section 16(1) of and paragraph 5 of Schedule 4 to the Trustee Investments Act 1961(c), and section 7(1) of the Post Office Savings Bank Act 1966(d), and of all other powers enabling them in that behalf, hereby make the following Order :—

1. This Order may be cited as the Post Office Savings Bank (Investment Deposits) (Limits) (Amendment) Order 1969, and shall come into operation on 29th November 1969.

2. The Interpretation Act 1889(e) shall apply for the interpretation of this Order as it applies for the interpretation of an Act of Parliament.

3. The Post Office Savings Bank (Investment Deposits) (Limits) Order 1969(f) shall have effect as if, for the reference to the Postmaster General, there were substituted a reference to the Director of Savings, and as if, for references to the Post Office Savings Bank, there were substituted references to the National Savings Bank.

Neil McBride,

Joseph Harper,

Two of the Lords Commissioners
of Her Majesty's Treasury.

28th November 1969.

(a) 1954 c. 62.	**(b)** 1969 c. 48.
(c) 1961 c. 62.	**(d)** 1966 c. 12.
(e) 1889 c. 63.	**(f)** S.I. 1969/940 (1969 II, p. 2832).

EXPLANATORY NOTE

(*This Note is not part of the Order.*)

The Post Office Act 1969 transfers the functions of the Postmaster General in relation to the Post Office Savings Bank to the Director of Savings, and changes the name of that Bank to the National Savings Bank. This Order makes the necessary consequential amendments to the Post Office Savings Bank (Investment Deposits) (Limits) Order 1969.

STATUTORY INSTRUMENTS

1969 No. 1702 (S.150)

COURT OF SESSION, SCOTLAND

Act of Sederunt (Rules of Court Amendment No. 3) 1969

Made - - -		*25th November* 1969
Coming into Operation		*26th November* 1969

The Lords of Council and Session, under and by virtue of the powers conferred upon them by section 2 of the Courts of Law Fees (Scotland) Act 1895(a) and section 16 of the Administration of Justice (Scotland) Act 1933(b) and of all other powers competent to them in that behalf, with the approval of the Treasury for the exercise of the said powers under section 2 of the Courts of Law Fees (Scotland) Act 1895(a), do hereby enact and declare as follows :—

1. The Act of Sederunt (Rules of Court Amendment No. 2) 1969(c) shall apply to procedure following upon summonses lodged prior to 1st April 1969, or upon petitions lodged prior to 1st April 1969, and to proceedings commenced prior to the said date by a Minute lodged in a process in which leave to apply to the Court has been reserved by the Court or by virtue of an Act of Parliament, and to actions commenced prior to the said date, but only in respect of anything done on or after 1st April 1969, as if such summonses, petitions, proceedings and actions had been lodged or commenced on or after 1st April 1969.

2. Section 1 of Rule 346 of the Rules of Court (d) shall continue to apply in respect of anything done on or after 1st April 1969 as if the Act of Sederunt (Rules of Court Amendment No. 2) 1969(c) had not been made.

3. This Act of Sederunt may be cited as the Act of Sederunt (Rules of Court Amendment No. 3) 1969, and shall come into operation on 26th November 1969.

And the Lords appoint this Act of Sederunt to be inserted in the Books of Sederunt.

J. L. Clyde,
I. P. D.

Edinburgh,
25th November 1969.

(a) 1895 c. 14.   (b) 1933 c. 41.
(c) S.I. 1969/475 (1969 I, p. 1362).
(d) S.I. 1965/321 (1965 I, p. 803).

EXPLANATORY NOTE

(This Note is not part of the Act of Sederunt.)

This Act of Sederunt applies the table of Fee-fund dues in the Court of Session to actions in court before 1st April 1969. It also makes provision for Fee-fund dues in the Accountant of Court's Department in respect of proceedings on or after 1st April 1969.

STATUTORY INSTRUMENTS

1969 No. 1703 (S.151)

COURT OF SESSION, SCOTLAND

Act of Sederunt (Rules of Court Amendment No. 4) 1969

Made - - -	*26th November* 1969	
Coming into Operation	*6th January* 1970	

The Lords of Council and Session, under and by virtue of the powers conferred upon them by section 16 of the Administration of Justice (Scotland) Act 1933(a) and of all other powers competent to them in that behalf, do hereby enact and declare as follows :—

1. The Table of Witnesses' Fees, contained in Chapter II of Rule 347 of the Rules of Court **(b)** as substituted by the Act of Sederunt (Rules of Court Amendment No. 1) 1966(c), shall be amended by the deletion of section (*a*) and the following words of section (*b*) namely "(*b*) Witnesses whose attendance entails loss of wages or payment of substitutes" ; and by the substitution therefor of the following :—

"(*a*) Professional persons, persons in managerial or like executive positions, and officers in H.M. Services or in the Mercantile Marine, per day Such sum not exceeding £26 5/- as the Auditor may determine, plus, in the case of a witness in the medical profession, such expenses (if any) as the Auditor may determine to have been necessarily incurred by the witness in employing a substitute or substitutes.

"(*b*) Witnesses whose attendance entails loss of wages or payment of substitutes (except the payment of a substitute to a witness to whom a fee is allowed under section (*a*) hereof)."

2. This Act of Sederunt may be cited as the Act of Sederunt (Rules of Court Amendment No. 4) 1969, and shall come into operation on 6th January 1970.

And the Lords appoint this Act of Sederunt to be inserted in the Books of Sederunt.

J. L. Clyde,
I. P. D.

Edinburgh,
26th November 1969.

(**a**) 1933 c. 41   (**b**) S.I. 1965/321 (1965 I, p. 803).
(**c**) S.I. 1966/335 (1966 I, p. 778).

EXPLANATORY NOTE

(This Note is not part of the Act of Sederunt.)

This Act of Sederunt revises the Table of Witnesses' Fees in the Court of Session so far as it relates to professional and certain other persons.

STATUTORY INSTRUMENTS

1969 No. 1704

LANDLORD AND TENANT

The Agriculture (Calculation of Value for Compensation) Regulations 1969

Made - - - -	27th November 1969
Laid before Parliament	9th December 1969
Coming into Operation	1st January 1970

The Minister of Agriculture, Fisheries and Food, in exercise of the powers conferred upon him by section 51(1) of the Agricultural Holdings Act 1948(a) and of all other powers enabling him in that behalf, and with the advice of the Committee appointed under the provisions of section 79 of the Act, hereby makes the following Regulations:—

1. These Regulations may be cited as the Agriculture (Calculation of Value for Compensation) Regulations 1969, and shall come into operation on 1st January 1970.

2.—(1) In these Regulations, unless the context otherwise requires,—

"the Act" means the Agricultural Holdings Act 1948;

"roots" means the produce of any root crop of a kind normally grown for consumption on the holding;

"tenant" means the outgoing tenant;

"year" means a period of twelve consecutive calendar months.

(2) The Interpretation Act 1889(b) applies for the interpretation of these Regulations as it applies for the interpretation of an Act of Parliament.

3. Subject to subsections (2) and (3) of section 51 of the Act and to regulation 4 below, the compensation for any improvement or other matter specified in a numbered paragraph of Schedule 4 to the Act shall, where the tenancy of the tenant claiming such compensation terminates on or after the coming into operation of these Regulations, be calculated in accordance with the paragraph so numbered in Schedule 1 to these Regulations.

4.—(1) Where any work in relation to an improvement or other matter has not been carried out in the most efficient and economical manner practicable in the circumstances, or any improvement or other matter has been adversely affected by—

(a) any breach by the tenant of the rules of good husbandry, or

(b) any other act or omission of the tenant, whether intentional or negligent,

the compensation for that improvement or other matter shall be reduced so as not to exceed the value to an incoming tenant, but no reduction shall be made for any adverse effects of seasonal conditions which the tenant could not reasonably have been expected to guard against or mitigate.

(a) 1948 c. 63.   (b) 1889 c. 63.

(2) Where—

    (*a*) any hay, fodder crops, straw, roots, manure or compost are destroyed by fire or otherwise, or, after the giving of a notice to quit by the tenant or the landlord and without the landlord's written consent, are sold by the tenant or removed by him from the holding, and

    (*b*) but for the destruction, sale or removal, compensation would have been payable to the tenant under paragraph 8 of Schedule 4 to the Act in respect of the produce destroyed, sold or removed,

the compensation which would otherwise be payable to the tenant under these Regulations shall be reduced by an amount equal to the reasonable cost to an incoming tenant of replacing on the holding produce similar in all respects to that which has been destroyed, sold or removed, less the value of the replaced produce itself, calculated under these Regulations as if it had been on the holding when the tenant quitted at the termination of the tenancy.

(3) Paragraphs 8 to 10 of Part II of Schedule 1 to these Regulations do not apply to crops or produce grown, seeds sown, cultivations, fallows or acts of husbandry performed or pasture laid down in contravention of the terms of a written contract of tenancy unless either—

    (*a*) the tenant shows that the terms contravened were inconsistent with the fulfilment of the tenant's responsibilities to farm the holding in accordance with the rules of good husbandry, or

    (*b*) the contravention was reasonably necessary in consequence of the giving of a direction under the Agriculture Act 1947(**a**).

5. The instruments mentioned in Schedule 2 to these Regulations (of which those numbered 1 to 4 in that Schedule are spent) are hereby revoked, but without prejudice to the application, in relation to tenancies terminating before the coming into operation of these Regulations, of the instruments numbered 5 and 6 in that Schedule.

In witness whereof the Official Seal of the Minister of Agriculture, Fisheries and Food is hereunto affixed on 27th November 1969.

           (L.S.)   *Cledwyn Hughes,*
                                Minister of Agriculture, Fisheries and Food.

Regulation 3   SCHEDULE 1

PART I

1. *Mole drainage and works carried out to secure the efficient functioning thereof*

(1) (*a*) Where the moles discharge into a piped main drain, the value shall (subject to sub-paragraph (2) below) be the reasonable cost of the work less one-sixth for each year since the work was completed;

    (*b*) Where the moles discharge direct into an open ditch (whether the outfalls are piped or not), the value shall (subject to sub-paragraph (2) below) be the reasonable cost of the work less one-third for each year since the work was completed.

(2) The value of any work, calculated in accordance with sub-paragraph (1) above, shall be reduced so as not to exceed the value to an incoming tenant, in any case where—

    (*a*) plans on a suitable scale, made at the time when the work was done, and showing the position of all moles, mains and outfalls, are not made available to the landlord; or

---

(**a**) 1947 c. 48.

(*b*) moles were not drawn at a proper depth, having regard to the nature of the soil and subsoil; or

(*c*) any ditches into which the outfalls discharge have not been maintained clean, free from obstruction and at a proper depth since the work was done; or

(*d*) deep cultivation or other work interfering with the efficient functioning of the drains has been done on the land since the drainage work was completed; or

(*e*) the land is not of consistently suitable slope or soil texture for mole drainage to be effective; or

(*f*) the drainage scheme was not a proper one, having regard to all the conditions, or was not efficiently carried out; or

(*g*) for any other reason, the drainage system does not function efficiently.

2. *Protection of fruit trees against animals*

The value shall be the reasonable cost of the protection, whether around each tree or around the perimeter of the orchard or both, reduced where necessary according to—

(*a*) the existing condition of the protection;

(*b*) the existing condition of the fruit trees;

(*c*) the further period for which protection is likely to be necessary.

3. *Chalking of land*

The same as paragraph 5 below (Liming of land).

4. *Clay burning*

The value shall be the reasonable cost of the work, less one quarter for each growing season since the work was completed.

5. *Liming of land (also Chalking of land)*

(1) The value shall be the reasonable cost of the lime (or chalk) as applied to the land (including the cost of delivery and application), reduced by not less than one-eighth and not more than one-quarter for each growing season since application.

(2) For the purposes of sub-paragraph (1) above, the reasonable cost shall not be regarded as exceeding the estimated cost (including the cost of delivery and application) of the equivalent in burnt lime or ground limestone (as the case may be) of forty hundredweight per acre pure calcium oxide (CaO), unless in the circumstances of the case a heavier dressing was economic, and of benefit to the incoming tenant.

6. *Application to land of purchased manure (including artificial manure)*

(1) Where no crop has been taken from the land since the manure was applied, the value shall be the reasonable cost of the manure as applied to the land (including the cost of delivery and spreading).

(2) Where one crop or more has been taken from the land since the manure was applied, the value shall be:—

(*a*) in the case of inorganic manure other than basic slag, the amount calculated in accordance with Table 1 below for each unit of nitrogen (N), phosphoric acid (P₂O₅) and potash (K₂O) contained in the manure as stated in the relevant statutory statement given under the Fertilisers and Feeding Stuffs Act 1926(a);

___
(a) 1926 c. 45.

(b) in the case of basic slag, the amount calculated in accordance with Table 2 below for each unit of phosphoric acid (P_2O_5) contained in the manure as stated in the relevant statutory statement given under the Fertilisers and Feeding Stuffs Act 1926, the amount of phosphoric acid insoluble in citric acid being found by subtracting the amount of phosphoric acid stated to be soluble in citric acid from the stated total amount of phosphoric acid:

Provided that the amount shall in no case exceed—

    (i) after one crop has been taken from the land, two-thirds of the reasonable cost of the basic slag as applied to the land, including the cost of delivery and spreading;

    (ii) after two crops have been taken from the land, one-third of such reasonable cost as aforesaid; and

    (iii) after three crops have been taken from the land, one-sixth of such reasonable cost as aforesaid;

(c) in the case of purchased stable or farmyard manure, two-fifths of the reasonable cost as aforesaid after one crop only has been taken from the land since the manure was applied, reduced to nil after more than one crop has been so taken;

(d) in the case of other organic manure, where there is a statutory statement under the Fertilisers and Feeding Stuffs Act 1926, or other certificate of analysis relating to the manure, the amount calculated in accordance with Table 3 below for each unit of nitrogen (N) and phosphoric acid (P_2O_5) contained in the manure as stated in the said statement or certificate, and (whether or not there is any such statement or certificate), in the case of shoddy and similar bulky organic manure where not more than two crops have been taken from the land since the manure was applied, an amount in respect of residual mechanical value not exceeding—

    (i) ten shillings for each ton of manure applied, where not more than one crop has been taken from the land since the manure was applied;

    (ii) five shillings for each ton of manure applied, where two crops have been so taken;

so, however, that the total amount payable in respect of shoddy and similar bulky organic manure shall not exceed the reasonable cost of the manure as applied to the land, including the cost of delivery and spreading.

(3) The value per ton of bracken, moss litter, peat, bean-straw and other similar materials, purchased for the purpose of absorbing plant food from urine, increasing the bulk of farmyard manure, or improving the physical condition of the soil, shall be:

    (a) where no crop has been taken from the land since application, twelve shillings;

    (b) where one crop has been taken from the land since application, six shillings;

    (c) where more than one crop has been taken from the land since application, nil.

(4) For the purposes of sub-paragraphs (1), (2) and (3) above and Tables 1, 2 and 3 below—

    (a) the value of any manure or material applied by the tenant to a crop for which the tenant is to be paid on the basis of the face value of the crop, shall be calculated as if that crop had been taken from the land;

    (b) the reasonable cost of any manure and of its delivery and spreading, or the residual mechanical value, shall not exceed:

        (i) the reasonable cost, or the residual mechanical value, of such quantity of manure as was reasonably necessary to be applied to the land, having regard to the rules of good husbandry, the type of farming practised on the holding, and sound economic practice; and

        (ii) the reasonable cost of delivering and spreading such amount as aforesaid.

TABLE 1

UNIT VALUES OF 1% OF A TON OF MANURE

	After one crop has been taken from the land	After two crops have been taken from the land	After three crops have been taken from the land	After four crops have been taken from the land
	s. d.	s. d.	s d	s d
Nitrogen:				
(a) Inorganic N and urea	Nil	Nil	Nil	Nil
Phosphoric acid:				
(b) P$_2$O$_5$ soluble in water or in citric acid ...	11 4	5 8	2 10	Nil
(c) P$_2$O$_5$ insoluble in water or of unspecified solubility	5 8	2 10	1 5	Nil
Potash:				
(d) Total K$_2$O	4 6	2 3	Nil	Nil

Notes— (i) The unit values in this Table are inclusive of the cost of delivery and spreading.
   (ii) Unit values per ton may be calculated to the nearest shilling.

TABLE 2

UNIT VALUES OF 1% OF A TON OF BASIC SLAG

	After one crop has been taken from the land	After two crops have been taken from the land	After three crops have been taken from the land	After four crops have been taken from the land
	s. d.	s. d.	s. d.	s. d.
Phosphoric acid:				
(a) P$_2$O$_5$ soluble in citric acid	11 4	5 8	2 10	Nil
(b) P$_2$O$_5$ insoluble in citric acid	5 8	2 10	1 5	Nil

Notes— (i) The unit values in this Table are inclusive of the cost of delivery and spreading.
   (ii) Unit values per ton may be calculated to the nearest shilling.

TABLE 3

UNIT VALUES OF 1% OF A TON OF MANURE

	After one crop has been taken from the land	After two crops have been taken from the land	After three crops have been taken from the land	After four crops have been taken from the land
	s. d.	s. d.	s. d.	s. d.
Nitrogen:				
(a) N in dried blood ...	Nil	Nil	Nil	Nil
(b) Organic N other than in dried blood and urea ...	8 6	4 3	Nil	Nil
Phosphoric acid:				
(c) Total P_2O_5 in bone products	8 6	4 3	2 2	Nil
(d) Total P_2O_5 in other materials	5 8	2 10	1 5	Nil

Notes— (i) The unit values in this Table are inclusive of the cost of delivery and spreading.

(ii) Unit values per ton may be calculated to the nearest shilling.

7. *Consumption on the holding of corn (whether produced on the holding or not) or of cake or other feeding stuff not produced on the holding by (a) horses, cattle, sheep or pigs, or (b) poultry folded on the land as part of a system of farming practised on the holding*

(1) The values per ton of feeding stuff consumed set out in Table 4 below shall apply in all cases where feeding stuffs are fed to dairy cattle in cowhouses, or to other stock in open yards, under satisfactory conditions which provide:

(a) that the urine is conserved;

(b) that the dung is well made and protected from loss in the heap; and

(c) that both urine and dung are effectively used, and that there is sufficient land with the farm to allow adequate returns from the manure made.

(2) Where sub-paragraph (1) above is not applicable, the values set out in the said Table 4 shall be adjusted in accordance with Table 5 hereunder.

(3) Poultry folded on the land as part of a system of farming practised on the holding shall be treated as "stock other than milking cows".

(4) Where manure is applied to land in the form of slurry, then subject to a maximum of six pounds per acre of the land so treated and to the provisions of sub-paragraph (5) below, the values per ton of feeding stuff consumed shall be as set out in Table 6 below.

(5) Where—

(a) slurry has been applied at the wrong time of year, or

(b) slurry has been applied to arable land, and too long a period has elapsed between its application and the cultivation of the land, or

(c) urine has not been adequately conserved, or

(d) conditions are otherwise unsatisfactory,

the compensation calculated in accordance with paragraph (4) above shall be reduced accordingly.

(6) Where more than one crop has been taken from the land, the values set out in Tables 4 and 6 below shall be reduced to nil.

TABLE 4

	Value per ton of feedingstuffs consumed	
	Before one crop has been taken from the land	After one crop has been taken from the land
	£ s. d.	£ s. d.
1. Decorticated cotton cake ...	3 1 0	1 10 6
2. Undecorticated cotton cake (Egyptian)	2 2 0	1 1 0
3. Undecorticated cotton cake (Bombay)	2 0 0	1 0 0
4. Linseed cake	2 1 0	1 0 6
5. Linseed	1 15 0	17 6
6. Soya bean cake	2 15 0	1 7 6
7. Palmnut cake	1 4 0	12 0
8. Coconut cake	1 16 0	18 0
9. Decorticated earthnut cake	2 9 0	1 4 6
10. Rape cake	2 10 0	1 5 0
11. Meat meal	5 1 0	2 10 6
12. Fish meal	5 14 0	2 17 0
13. Beans	1 11 0	15 6
14. Peas	1 7 0	13 6
15. Wheat	18 0	9 0
16. Barley	15 0	7 6
17. Oats	16 0	8 0
18. Maize	15 0	7 6
19. Rice meal	1 10 0	15 0
20. Locust beans	17 0	8 6
21. Malt	18 0	9 0
22. Malt culms	2 1 0	1 0 6
23. Bran and other offals of wheat	1 18 0	19 0
24. Brewers' grains (dried) ...	1 5 0	12 6
25. Brewers' grains (wet) ...	9 0	4 6
26. Clover hay	1 3 0	11 6
27. Meadow hay	17 0	8 6
28. Dried grass and meal ...	1 1 0	10 6
29. Mangolds	4 0	2 0
30. Swedes	3 0	1 6
31. Turnips	3 0	1 6
32. Sugar beet pulp (dried) ...	10 0	5 0
33. Sugar beet pulp (wet) ...	2 0	1 0
34. Potatoes	6 0	3 0
35. Straw, pea straw and pods	16 0	8 0
36. Compound cakes and meal: For each 1 % of albuminoids (proteins)	9	4
For phosphates and potash	12 0	6 0
Thus:—18 % albuminoids ...	1 5 6	12 0
24 % albuminoids ...	1 10 0	14 0
30 % albuminoids ...	1 14 6	16 0

NOTE:—In the case of straw mechanical value has been taken into account.

TABLE 5

	Feedingstuffs fed to Milking Cows	Feedingstuffs fed to stock other than Milking Cows
(a) Feedingstuffs fed directly on the land ...	As Table 4	Add one-third
(b) Feedingstuffs fed under cover under satisfactory conditions	As Table 4	Add one-third
(c) Feedingstuffs fed in open yards under satisfactory conditions	Subtract one-third	As Table 4
(d) Conditions unsatisfactory	Subtract up to two-thirds	Subtract up to one-half

TABLE 6

VALUE PER TON OF FEEDING STUFFS CONSUMED AND
APPLIED TO LAND AS SLURRY

| | Before one crop has been taken from the land | | | | After one crop has been taken from the land | | | |
| | Closed Storage | | | Open Storage | | | Closed Storage | | | Open Storage | | |
	£	s.	d.	£	s.	d.	£	s.	d.	£	s.	d.
1. Decorticated cotton cake ...	3	1	0	2	14	0	1	6	0	1	3	0
2. Undecorticated cotton cake (Egyptian)	2	2	0	1	18	0		18	0		17	0
3. Undecorticated cotton cake (Bombay)	2	0	0	1	16	0		17	0		16	0
4. Linseed cake	2	1	0	1	15	0		17	0		15	0
5. Linseed	1	15	0	1	10	0		14	0		13	0
6. Soya bean cake ...	2	15	0	2	7	0	1	2	0		19	0
7. Palmnut cake	1	4	0	1	0	0		10	0		9	0
8. Coconut cake	1	16	0	1	12	0		15	0		14	0
9. Decorticated earthnut cake	2	9	0	2	1	0		19	0		16	0
10. Rape cake	2	10	0	2	4	0	1	1	0		19	0
11. Meat meal	5	1	0	4	9	0	2	3	0	1	19	0
12. Fish meal	5	14	0	5	2	0	2	9	0	2	6	0
13. Beans	1	11	0	1	6	0		12	0		11	0
14. Peas	1	7	0	1	3	0		11	0		10	0
15. Wheat		18	0		15	0		7	0		7	0
16. Barley		15	0		13	0		6	0		6	0
17. Oats...		16	0		14	0		7	0		6	0
18. Maize		15	0		13	0		6	0		6	0
19. Rice meal	1	10	0	1	8	0		14	0		13	0
20. Locust beans		17	0		14	0		6	0		5	0
21. Malt		18	0		16	0		8	0		7	0
22. Malt culms	2	1	0	1	17	0		18	0		16	0
23. Bran and other offals of wheat	1	18	0	1	15	0		17	0		16	0
24. Brewers' grains (dried) ...	1	5	0	1	2	0		10	0		9	0
25. Brewers' grains (wet) ...		9	0		7	0		3	0		3	0
26. Clover hay	1	3	0	1	1	0		10	0		9	0
27. Meadow hay		17	0		16	0		8	0		7	0
28. Dried grass and meal ...	1	1	0		19	0		9	0		8	0
29. Mangolds		4	0		3	0		2	0		2	0
30. Swedes		3	0		3	0		1	0		1	0
31. Turnips		3	0		2	0		1	0		1	0
32. Sugar beet pulp (dried) ...		10	0		9	0		4	0		4	0
33. Sugar beet pulp (wet) ...		2	0		2	0		1	0		1	0
34. Potatoes		6	0		5	0		3	0		2	0
35. Straw, pea straw and pods		10	0		9	0		4	0		4	0
36. Compound cakes and meal:												
For each 1% of albuminoids (proteins) ...			9			6			3			2
For phosphates and potash		12	0		12	0		6	0		6	0

PART II

8. *Growing crops and severed or harvested crops and produce, being in either case crops or produce grown on the holding in the last year of the tenancy, but not including crops or produce which the tenant has a right to sell or remove from the holding*

(1) Growing crops:—

The value shall be the reasonable cost of seeds sown, and cultivations, fallows and acts of husbandry performed, calculated in accordance with the provisions of paragraph 9 below.

(2) Severed or harvested crops and produce:—

The value shall be the average market value on the holding during that season of hay, fodder crops, straw, roots and other crops or produce of good quality, less the manurial value thereof calculated in accordance with Table 4 above, on the basis that no crop has been taken from the land:

Provided that the value so calculated shall be reduced so as not to exceed the value to an incoming tenant in any case where—

(*a*) the crops or produce are of inferior quality; or

(*b*) the quantity of any kind of crops or produce exceeds the quantity reasonably required for the system of farming practised on the holding; or

(*c*) the crops or produce are not left in convenient or proper places on the farm; or

(*d*) any hay or straw is not properly stacked and thatched or otherwise protected.

(3) The value of farmyard manure or compost made on the farm shall be the reasonable expenditure incurred by the tenant in loading, carting, heaping and spreading such manure or compost on land from which no crop has been taken.

9. *Seeds sown and cultivations, fallows and acts of husbandry performed on the holding at the expense of the tenant*

(1) The value shall be the reasonable cost of seeds sown and of cultivations, fallows and acts of husbandry performed, taking into account—

(*a*) normal current costs, having regard to the current agricultural wage, the cost of horse and tractor operations, the size and shape of the fields, and other relevant conditions;

(*b*) reasonable costs of hired tractor cultivations;

(*c*) increased costs over normal tractor rates, where owing to the size of the farm or fields, the shape of the fields, or to other special circumstances, it was reasonable to use horse labour;

but leaving out of account any expenditure incurred by the tenant up to and including the removal from the land of the last preceding crop and any rent paid by the tenant.

(2) For the purposes of sub-paragraph (1) above, the reasonable cost shall not be regarded as reduced merely because more than one operation was carried out by the tenant at the same time.

(3) Nothing in sub-paragraph (1) above shall be taken to limit the operation of this paragraph to any particular method of sowing nor to cultivations, fallows or acts of husbandry performed in any particular way.

10. *Pasture laid down with clover, grass, lucerne, sainfoin or other seeds, being either—*

　　(a) *pasture laid down at the expense of the tenant otherwise than in compliance with an obligation imposed on him by an agreement in writing to lay it down to replace temporary pasture comprised in the holding when the tenant entered thereon which was not paid for by him; or*

　　(b) *pasture paid for by the tenant on entering on the holding*

(1) Where no crop has been removed either by mowing or by grazing, the value shall be the reasonable cost of seeds sown, and cultivations, fallows and acts of husbandry performed, calculated in accordance with paragraph 9 above, but also taking into account any expenditure incurred solely for the benefit of the pasture before the removal of any crop in or with which the pasture was sown.

(2) Where one crop or more has been removed either by mowing or by grazing, the value shall be the face value of the pasture, taking into account:—

　　(a) present condition;

　　(b) management since sowing;

　　(c) situation on the holding;

　　(d) fencing;

　　(e) water supply;

　　(f) any other circumstances appearing to be relevant.

11. *Acclimatisation, hefting or settlement of hill sheep on hill land*

(1) The value of hill sheep on hill land shall include such amount (if any) as represents the value attributable to the acclimatisation, hefting or settlement of the sheep on such land, but the said amount shall not in any case exceed a sum of thirty shillings per sheep.

(2) Any amount which may be included in the value of hill sheep under the provisions of the last foregoing sub-paragraph shall be apportioned and separately shown by the person carrying out the valuation as being attributable to the value of acclimatisation, hefting or settlement of such sheep.

SCHEDULE 2	Regulation 5
Regulations revoked	References
1. The Agriculture (Calculation of Value for Compensation) Regulations 1948.	S.I. 1948/185 (Rev. I, p. 821: 1948 I, p. 57).
2. The Agriculture (Calculation of Value for Compensation) Amendment Regulations 1952.	S.I. 1952/170 (1952 I, p. 40).
3. The Agriculture (Calculation of Value for Compensation) Amendment (No. 2) Regulations 1952.	S.I. 1952/1617 (1952 I, p. 41).
4. The Agriculture (Calculation of Value for Compensation) Amendment Regulations 1953.	S.I. 1953/456 (1953 I, p.2).
5. The Agriculture (Calculation of Value for Compensation) Regulations 1959.	S.I. 1959/496 (1959 I, p. 1528).
6. The Agriculture (Calculation of Value for Compensation) Amendment Regulations 1968.	S.I. 1968/378 (1968 I, p. 1034).

EXPLANATORY NOTE

(This Note is not part of the Regulations.)

These Regulations consolidate with amendments the provisions previously made for calculating the compensation payable to the outgoing tenant of an agricultural holding in respect of the short-term improvements and other matters comprised in Schedule 4 to the Agricultural Holdings Act 1948. The amendments, other than drafting amendments, are as follows:—

(1) Compensation for the liming and chalking of land (paragraph 5 of Schedule 1 to the Regulations) may be reduced by as much as one quarter for each growing season since application (the previous standard reduction of one-eighth is now the minimum).

(2) New Tables 1, 2, 3 and 4 are provided (paragraphs 6 and 7).

(3) An additional Table 6 for calculating the value of slurry applications is provided (sub-paragraphs (4) to (6) of paragraph 7).

(4) Steam cultivations are no longer provided for (paragraph 9).

(5) The new maximum allowance in respect of settled hill sheep is thirty shillings per sheep (paragraph 11).

The regulations apply (except so far as excluded, in relation to the matters in Part II of Schedule 1 to the Regulations, by a written contract of tenancy) wherever the tenancy of the tenant claiming compensation terminates on or after the date of their coming into operation; in relation to tenancies terminating before that date, the Agriculture (Calculation of Value for Compensation) Regulations 1959, as amended, continue to apply with a similar exception.

STATUTORY INSTRUMENTS

1969 No. 1706

PATENTS

The Patents (Amendment No. 2) Rules 1969

Made - - -	*1st December* 1969
Laid before Parliament	*8th December* 1969
Coming into Operation	*9th December* 1969

The Board of Trade, in pursuance of the powers conferred upon them by sections 94 and 99 of the Patents Act 1949(a), as amended by the Patents Act 1957(b), the Patents and Designs (Renewals, Extensions and Fees) Act 1961(c) and the Patents (Fees Amendment) Order 1961(d), and of all other powers enabling them in that behalf, and with the consent of the Treasury, hereby make the following Rules:—

1. These Rules may be cited as the Patents (Amendment No. 2) Rules 1969 and shall come into operation on 9th December 1969.

2. The Interpretation Act 1889(e) shall apply to the interpretation of these Rules as it applies to the interpretation of an Act of Parliament.

3. Subject to Rule 4 of these Rules, the fee payable by virtue of Rule 3 of the Patents Rules 1968(f), as amended (g), in respect of any of the items specified in the Schedule hereto shall be the appropriate fee so specified and, accordingly, for items 3, 21 and 25 in Schedule 1 to the said Patents Rules there shall be substituted the items specified in the Schedule hereto.

4. Where an application is made before 1st February 1970 for a certificate of payment of a patent renewal fee in respect of any year beginning before that date, the fee payable upon such application by virtue of Rule 3 of the said Patents Rules shall be that which would have been payable if these Rules had not been made.

Gwyneth Dunwoody,

Parliamentary Secretary to the
Board of Trade.

1st December 1969.

We consent to the making of these Rules.

Ernest Armstrong,

E. G. Perry,

Two of the Lords Commissioners of
Her Majesty's Treasury.

1st December 1969.

(a) 1949 c. 87.
(b) 1957 c. 13.
(c) 1961 c. 25.
(d) S.I. 1961/1499 (1961 II, p. 3050).
(e) 1889 c. 63.
(f) S.I. 1968/1389 (1968 II, p. 3958).
(g) The relevant amending instrument is S.I. 1969/482 (1969 I, p. 1374).

SCHEDULE

	£ s. d.	Corresponding Form
3. On filing specification:—		
Provisional	—	Patents Form No. 2.
Complete	15 0 0	Patents Form No. 3.
21. On a request for sealing of a patent ..	6 0 0	Patents Form No. 20.
25. †On application for certificate of payment of renewal fee:—		
Before the expiration of the 4th year from the date of the patent and in respect of the 5th year	11 0 0	Patents Form No. 24.
Before the expiration of the 5th year from the date of the patent and in respect of the 6th year	12 0 0	,, ,, ,,
Before the expiration of the 6th year from the date of the patent and in respect of the 7th year	13 0 0	,, ,, ,,
Before the expiration of the 7th year from the date of the patent and in respect of the 8th year	14 0 0	,, ,, ,,
Before the expiration of the 8th year from the date of the patent and in respect of the 9th year	16 0 0	,, ,, ,,
Before the expiration of the 9th year from the date of the patent and in respect of the 10th year	18 0 0	,, ,, ,,
Before the expiration of the 10th year from the date of the patent and in respect of the 11th year	20 0 0*	,, ,, ,,
Before the expiration of the 11th year from the date of the patent and in respect of the 12th year	22 0 0*	,, ,, ,,
Before the expiration of the 12th year from the date of the patent and in respect of the 13th year	24 0 0*	,, ,, ,,
Before the expiration of the 13th year from the date of the patent and in respect of the 14th year	26 0 0*	,, ,, ,,
Before the expiration of the 14th year from the date of the patent and in respect of the 15th year	28 0 0*	,, ,, ,,
Before the expiration of the 15th year from the date of the patent and in respect of the remainder of the term of the patent	30 0 0*	,, ,, ,,

†One half only of these fees payable on patents endorsed "Licences of Right".

EXPLANATORY NOTE

(This Note is not part of the Rules.)

These Rules further amend the Patents Rules 1968.

With the exceptions indicated by asterisk the fees payable under the Patents Rules 1968, in respect of the matters specified in the Schedule to these Rules, are increased. Renewal fees are not, however, increased in the case of an application made before 1st February 1970 in respect of a year beginning before that date.

STATUTORY INSTRUMENTS

1969 No. 1707

THERAPEUTIC SUBSTANCES

The Therapeutic Substances (Manufacture of Antibiotics) Amendment Regulations 1969

Made - - -		*1st December* 1969
Laid before Parliament		*8th December* 1969
Coming into Operation		*1st January* 1970

The Joint Committee constituted by section 4(1) of the Therapeutic Substances Act 1956(a), as amended by article 2(2) of and Schedule 1 to the Transfer of Functions (Wales) Order 1969(b), in exercise of the powers conferred on them by sections 1 and 5 of the said Act, after consultation with the Advisory Committee constituted under section 4(2) of the said Act, hereby make the following regulations :—

Citation, commencement and interpretation

1.—(1) These regulations may be cited as the Therapeutic Substances (Manufacture of Antibiotics) Amendment Regulations 1969 and shall come into operation on 1st January 1970.

(2) The Therapeutic Substances (Manufacture of Antibiotics) Regulations 1966 to 1968(c) and these regulations may be cited together as the Therapeutic Substances (Manufacture of Antibiotics) Regulations 1966 to 1969.

(3) The Interpretation Act 1889(d) shall apply to the interpretation of these regulations as it applies to the interpretation of an Act of Parliament.

Amendment of the Therapeutic Substances (Manufacture of Antibiotics) Regulations 1966

2. The Therapeutic Substances (Manufacture of Antibiotics) Regulations 1966, as amended, shall be further amended as follows :—

(*a*) in the regulations mentioned in column 1 of the schedule to these regulations (which relate to the strength of substances specified in that column) the number of units of potency shown opposite each regulation in column 3 of the said schedule shall be substituted for the number of units of potency shown in column 2 of the said schedule ;

(*b*) at the end of regulation 48(1) (which relates to the strength of Erythromycin) there shall be added the words "calculated with reference to the anhydrous material".

(a) 1956 c. 25.   (b) S.I. 1969/388 (1969 I, p. 1070).
(c) S.I. 1966/505, 1967/1195, 1968/906 (1966 I, p. 1049; 1967 II, p. 3498; 1968 II, p. 2389).
(d) 1889 c. 63.

SCHEDULE

Regulation	Existing number of Units per milligram	Number of Units per milligram substituted
(1)	(2)	(3)
19 (streptomycin)	700	720
25 (tetracycline)	930	950
32(1) (polymyxin B sulphate)	6,400	6,500
32(2) (colistin sulphate)	14,700	17,500
37 (viomycin)	685	700
43 (bacitracin)	54	55
48 (erythromycin)	880	920
60 (vancomycin)	880	900
71 (neomycin sulphate)	640	650

These regulations were made by the aforesaid Joint Committee on 1st December 1969.

W. K. Fitzsimmons,
William Ross,
George Thomas,
R. H. S. Crossman,
Members of the Joint Committee.

L. H. Hayward,
Clerk to the Joint Committee.

EXPLANATORY NOTE

(This Note is not part of the Regulations.)

These Regulations made under Part I of the Therapeutic Substances Act 1956, increase the minimum potency values prescribed for the antibiotics referred to in the Schedule.

STATUTORY INSTRUMENTS

1969 No. 1708

PRICES AND INCOMES

The Awards and Settlements (Temporary Continuation of Standstill) (No. 3) Order 1969

Made - - -	*1st December* 1969
Laid before Parliament	*5th December* 1969
Coming into Operation	*6th December* 1969

Whereas by virtue of a Reference to the National Board for Prices and Incomes under section 2(1) of the Prices and Incomes Act 1966(a) (the text whereof was published on 8th August 1969 in the London Gazette) the implementation of the agreement described in Article 2 hereof relating to the pay of certain workers employed by members of the Association of Film Laboratory Employers in technical, clerical and general grades was forbidden by section 15(2) of that Act;

And whereas before the said implementation ceased to be so forbidden a Report of the Board on the said reference was published on 6th November 1969(b) with a recommendation adverse to the implementation of the said agreement;

And whereas by virtue of the said recommendation and subsections (1) and (2) (*a*) of section 1 of the Prices and Incomes Act 1967(c) the said section 15(2) continued to apply to the implementation of the said agreement as it applied up to the date of publication of the said Report:

Now, therefore, the Secretary of State, having given notice under section 1(2) (*a*) of the said Act of 1967 within a period of ten days after the date of the said publication, of a proposal to make this Order, and having taken into considera-tion representations duly made in pursuance of the said notice, in exercise of the powers conferred on her by section 1(2) (*b*) of the said Act of 1967, as amended by section 3(2) of the Prices and Incomes Act 1968(d) and of all other powers enabling her in that behalf, hereby makes the following Order:

1.—(1) This Order, which may be cited as the Awards and Settlements (Temporary Continuation of Standstill) (No. 3) Order 1969, shall come into operation on 6th December 1969.

(2) The Interpretation Act 1889(e) shall apply for the interpretation of this Order as it applies for the interpretation of an Act of Parliament.

2. The Secretary of State hereby directs that section 15(2) of the Prices and Incomes Act 1966 shall continue to forbid the implementation up to and including 7th February 1970 of the undermentioned agreement, that is to say:

(a) 1966 c. 33.   (b) Report No. 131 entitled "Pay of certain employees in the Film Processing Industry" (Cmnd. 4185).   (c) 1967 c. 53.   (d) 1968 c. 42.   (e) 1889 c. 63.

the agreement made on or about 20th July 1969 between the Association of Film Laboratory Employers and the Association of Cinematograph, Television and Allied Technicians providing, with effect from 1st July 1969, for, amongst other things, increases in the minimum weekly rates of pay applicable to workers employed by members of the Association of Film Laboratory Employers in technical, clerical and general grades.

1st December 1969.

Barbara Castle,
First Secretary of State and Secretary of State
for Employment and Productivity.

EXPLANATORY NOTE
(This Note is not part of the Order.)

This Order, which has effect from 6th December 1969, provides for the further continuation until 7th February 1970 of the standstill on the implementation of an agreement relating to the pay of certain workers employed by members of the Association of Film Laboratory Employers in technical, clerical and general grades.

STATUTORY INSTRUMENTS

1969 No. 1709 (C.55)

LEGAL AID AND ADVICE, ENGLAND

The Legal Aid and Advice Act 1949 (Commencement No. 12) Order 1969

Made - - - *1st December* 1969

The Lord Chancellor, in exercise of the powers conferred on him by section 17(2) of the Legal Aid and Advice Act 1949(a) hereby makes the following Order:—

1.—(1) The Interpretation Act 1889(b) shall apply to the interpretation of this Order as it applies to the interpretation of an Act of Parliament.

(2) This Order may be cited as the Legal Aid and Advice Act 1949 (Commencement No. 12) Order 1969.

2. The provisions of Part I of the Legal Aid and Advice Act 1949 shall come into operation on 1st January 1970 for the purpose of making legal aid available in connection with proceedings in the House of Lords in the exercise of its jurisdiction in relation to appeals from the High Court in England under Part II of the Administration of Justice Act 1969(c).

Dated 1st December 1969.

Gardiner, C.

EXPLANATORY NOTE

(*This Note is not part of the Order.*)

This Order brings the provisions of Part I of the Legal Aid and Advice Act 1949 into operation on 1st January 1970 so as to make legal aid available in respect of appeals from the High Court to the House of Lords under Part II of the Administration of Justice Act 1969.

(a) 1949 c. 51.   (b) 1889 c. 63.   (c) 1969 c. 58.

STATUTORY INSTRUMENTS

1969 No. 1710 (L.28)

MAGISTRATES' COURTS

PROCEDURE

The Magistrates' Courts (Forms) (Amendment) Rules 1969

Made - - -	*28th November* 1969
Laid before Parliament	*9th December* 1969
Coming into Operation	*1st February* 1970

The Lord Chancellor, in exercise of the power conferred on him by section 15 of the Justices of the Peace Act 1949(a), as extended by section 122 of the Magistrates' Courts Act 1952(b), after consultation with the Rule Committee appointed under the said section 15, hereby makes the following Rules:—

1. These Rules may be cited as the Magistrates' Courts (Forms) (Amendment) Rules 1969 and shall come into operation on 1st February 1970.

2. Form 29 in the Schedule to the Magistrates' Courts (Forms) Rules 1968(c) shall be amended as follows:—

(*a*) by the insertion before the final sentence of the first paragraph of the words "[If you write as mentioned, you are required to include a statement of your date of birth and sex.]*";

(*b*) by the insertion of the following paragraph after the fourth paragraph:—

"*[A notice from the vehicle licensing authority is also served herewith. This notice states that in the event of your being convicted it will be alleged that an order falls to be made requiring you to pay the amount specified in the notice (being the amount calculated to be the duty payable in respect of the period during which the vehicle was unlicensed). If you send in a written plea of guilty, you may nevertheless include in it a statement that the amount so specified is inappropriate (e.g. because you were not the keeper of the vehicle for the whole of the period during which the vehicle was unlicensed or because the vehicle was not kept or used on a public road during the whole of that period). If you do not include a statement that the amount is inappropriate, the Court will proceed on the assumption that the amount is correctly calculated. If you do include such a statement and you decide to appear in person and dispute the amount, you should arrange to have at Court any witnesses or documents which may help you to prove that the amount is inappropriate.]".

(a) 1949 c. 101.   (b) 1952 c. 55.   (c) S.I. 1968/1919 (1968 III, p. 5075).

3. In the said Schedule, after Form 98, there shall be inserted the form contained in the Schedule to these Rules.

Dated 28th November 1969.

Gardiner, C.

Rule 3 SCHEDULE

98A

Notice of order to give information of date of birth and sex
(*Vehicle and Driving Licences Act* 1969, *s.* 22; *M.C. Rules* 1968, *r.* 88*A.*)

In the [county of . Petty Sessional
Division of].

To A.B. of

Take notice that this Court, having [this day] convicted you of (*state shortly particulars of offence*) and [ordered that your driving licence be endorsed] [imposed an interim disqualification for holding or obtaining a driving licence], ordered that you inform the Court in writing of your [date of birth] [and] [sex]. Failure to provide this information will render you liable to a fine not exceeding £50.

Dated the day of , 19 .

J.C.,
Clerk of the Court.

EXPLANATORY NOTE
(*This Note is not part of the Rules.*)

Rule 2 amends Form 29 of the Magistrates' Courts (Forms) Rules 1968 (Notice to defendant: plea of guilty in absence)—

(*a*) to enable a defendant who decides to plead guilty in writing of an offence involving endorsement of a driving licence or disqualification to be informed that he is required (by section 22(2) of the Vehicle and Driving Licences Act 1969 (c. 27)) to include a statement of his date of birth and sex, and

(*b*) to enable a defendant who is alleged to have used or kept an unlicensed vehicle on the road to be informed, in accordance with section 30 of the Act, that if he is convicted, the court may order him to pay any unpaid duty.

Rule 3 and the Schedule to the Rules prescribe the form of notice to be given to a person in whose case the court has ordered endorsement of a driving licence or disqualification, informing him that the court has ordered him under section 22 of the Act to state his date of birth or sex or both.

1969 No. 1711 (L.29)

MAGISTRATES' COURTS

PROCEDURE

The Magistrates' Courts (Amendment) Rules 1969

Made - - -	*28th November* 1969
Laid before Parliament	*9th December* 1969
Coming into Operation	*1st February* 1970

The Lord Chancellor, in exercise of the power conferred on him by section 15 of the Justices of the Peace Act 1949(a), as extended by section 122 of the Magistrates' Courts Act 1952(b), after consultation with the Rule Committee appointed under the said section 15, hereby makes the following Rules:—

1.—(1) These Rules may be cited as the Magistrates' Courts (Amendment) Rules 1969 and shall come into operation on 1st February 1970.

(2) The Interpretation Act 1889(c) applies for the interpretation of these Rules as it applies for the interpretation of an Act of Parliament.

2. In Rule 16(1) of the Magistrates' Courts Rules 1968(d)—

(a) at the end of sub-paragraph (*d*) the word "and" shall be omitted;

(b) at the end of sub-paragraph (*e*) there shall be added the word "and" and the following sub-paragraph:—

"(*f*) if the court imposes under section 56(8) of the Criminal Justice Act 1967(e) an interim disqualification for holding or obtaining a licence under Part II of the Road Traffic Act 1960(f), a statement of the date of birth and sex of the offender.".

3. At the end of Rule 28 of the said Rules there shall be added the following paragraph:—

"(2) Where a magistrates' court orders that the licence of an offender be endorsed as mentioned in paragraph (1) of this Rule or imposes an interim disqualification as mentioned in Rule 16(1) (*f*) of these Rules and the clerk of the court knows or is informed of the date of birth and sex of the offender, the clerk shall send the information to the licensing authority which granted the licence.".

4. After Rule 88 of the said Rules there shall be inserted the following Rule:—

"*Notice of order under s.22 of Vehicle and Driving Licences Act* 1969

88A.—(1) Where a magistrates' court makes an order under section 22 of the Vehicle and Driving Licences Act 1969(g) that an offender shall inform the court of his date of birth or sex or both and the offender is not present in court, the clerk of the court shall serve notice in writing of the order on the offender.

(2) A notice under this Rule shall be served by delivering it to the offender or by sending it to him by post in a letter addressed to him at his last known or usual place of abode.".

Dated 28th November 1969.   *Gardiner*, C.

(a) 1949 c. 101.	(b) 1952 c. 55.
(c) 1889 c. 63.	(d) S.I. 1968/1920 (1968 III, p. 5175).
(e) 1967 c. 80.	(f) 1960 c. 16.
(g) 1969 c. 27.	

EXPLANATORY NOTE

(This Note is not part of the Rules.)

These Rules amend the Magistrates' Courts Rules 1968.

Section 22 of the Vehicle and Driving Licences Act 1969 enables a court which orders that the driving licence of an offender be endorsed or that he be temporarily disqualified for holding a driving licence, to order also that his date of birth and sex be supplied to the court.

Rule 2 requires the clerk of a magistrates' court which commits an offender for sentence and orders that he be temporarily disqualified for holding a driving licence, to inform the court to which he is committed of his date of birth and sex.

Rule 3 requires the clerk of a magistrates' court which orders that the driving licence of an offender be endorsed or that he be temporarily disqualified for holding a driving licence, to inform the licensing authority of his date of birth and sex.

Rule 4 requires the clerk of a magistrates' court which orders an offender who is not present in court to give his date of birth or sex, to notify the offender of the order.

STATUTORY INSTRUMENTS

1969 No. 1713

EDUCATION, ENGLAND AND WALES

The Remuneration of Teachers (Further Education) Order 1969

Made - - - -	*1st December* 1969
Coming into Operation	*2nd December* 1969

Whereas—

(1) in pursuance of section 2(2) of the Remuneration of Teachers Act 1965(a) (hereinafter referred to as "the Act") the Committee constituted under section 1 of the Act for the purpose of considering the remuneration of teachers in establishments for further education (other than farm institutes) maintained by local education authorities (hereinafter referred to as "the Committee") transmitted to the Secretary of State for Education and Science (hereinafter referred to as "the Secretary of State") certain recommendations agreed on by them with respect to the remuneration of such teachers;

(2) in pursuance of section 3(1) of the Act certain other matters in respect of which agreement had not been reached in the Committee were referred to arbitration;

(3) in pursuance of sections 2(3) and 4(1) of the Act, the Secretary of State has prepared a draft document setting out the scales and other provisions required for determining the remuneration of teachers of the description aforesaid in the form in which, in his opinion, those scales and provisions should be so as to give effect to the recommendations of the Committee and of the arbitrators;

(4) the Secretary of State, as required by section 2(4) of the Act, has consulted the Committee with respect to the draft document and made such modifications thereof as were requisite for giving effect to representations made by the Committee; and

(5) the Secretary of State has arranged for a document setting out the requisite scales and other provisions in the form of the draft as modified as aforesaid to be published by Her Majesty's Stationery Office on 28th November 1969 under the title "SCALES OF SALARIES FOR TEACHERS IN ESTABLISHMENTS FOR FURTHER EDUCATION, ENGLAND AND WALES, 1969".

Now therefore the Secretary of State, in pursuance of sections 2(4) and 4(1) of the Act, hereby orders as follows:—

Citation and Commencement

1. This Order may be cited as the Remuneration of Teachers (Further Education) Order 1969 and shall come into operation on 2nd December 1969.

Interpretation

2. The Interpretation Act 1889(b) shall apply for the interpretation of this Order as it applies for the interpretation of an Act of Parliament.

(a) 1965 c. 3.   (b) 1889 c. 63.

Remuneration of Teachers

3. The remuneration payable from 1st April 1969 to full-time teachers in establishments for further education (other than farm institutes) maintained by local education authorities shall be determined in accordance with the scales and other provisions set out in the document published by Her Majesty's Stationery Office as aforesaid.

Revocation

4. The Remuneration of Teachers (Further Education) Order 1968(a) and the Remuneration of Teachers (Further Education) (Amendment) Order 1968(b) are hereby revoked and section 38(2) of the Interpretation Act 1889 (which relates to the effect of repeals) shall have effect in relation to those Orders as if they were enactments repealed by an Act.

Given under the Official Seal of the Secretary of State for Education and Science on 1st December 1969.

(L.S.)

Alice Bacon,
Minister of State for Education and Science.

EXPLANATORY NOTE

(This Note is not part of the Order.)

This Order brings into operation the scales and other provisions relating to the remuneration of full-time teachers in establishments for further education (other than farm institutes) maintained by local education authorities contained in a document published by Her Majesty's Stationery Office. This document gives effect both to agreed recommendations made by the Committee for the consideration of the remuneration of such teachers and, subject to certain modifications agreed by the Committee, to an arbitration award.

The Order has effect from 1st April 1969 by virtue of section 7(3) of the Remuneration of Teachers Act 1965.

(a) S.I. 1968/197 (1968 I, p. 548).　　　　(b) S.I. 1968/1798 (1968 III, p. 4811).

STATUTORY INSTRUMENTS

1969 No. 1714

WAGES COUNCILS

The Wages Regulation (Road Haulage) Order 1969

Made	- - -	*1st December* 1969
Coming into Operation		*23rd January* 1970

Whereas the Secretary of State has received from the Road Haulage Wages Council the wages regulation proposals set out in the Schedule hereto ;

Now, therefore, the Secretary of State in exercise of her powers under section 11 of the Wages Councils Act 1959(**a**), and of all other powers enabling her in that behalf, hereby makes the following Order :—

1. This Order may be cited as the Wages Regulation (Road Haulage) Order 1969.

2.—(1) In this Order the expression "the specified date" means the 23rd January 1970, provided that where, as respects any worker who is paid wages at intervals not exceeding seven days, that date does not correspond with the beginning of the period for which the wages are paid, the expression "the specified date" means, as respects that worker, the beginning of the next such period following that date.

(2) The Interpretation Act 1889(**b**) shall apply to the interpretation of this Order as it applies to the interpretation of an Act of Parliament and as if this Order and the Order hereby revoked were Acts of Parliament.

3. The wages regulation proposals set out in the Schedule hereto shall have effect as from the specified date and as from that date the Wages Regulation (Road Haulage) Order 1968(**c**) shall cease to have effect.

Signed by order of the Secretary of State.

1st December 1969.

A. A. Jarratt,
Deputy Under Secretary of State,
Department of Employment and Productivity.

(**a**) 1959 c. 69.   (**b**) 1889 c. 63.
(**c**) S.I. 1968/1130 (1968 II, p. 3101).

ARRANGEMENT OF SCHEDULE

MINIMUM REMUNERATION AND HOLIDAYS

PART I

PART II

PART III

PART IV

PART V

PART VI

PART VII

Article 3

SCHEDULE

The following minimum remuneration and provisions as to holidays and holiday remuneration shall be substituted for the statutory minimum remuneration and provisions as to holidays and holiday remuneration set out in the Wages Regulation (Road Haulage) Order 1968 (hereinafter referred to as "Order R.H.(88)").

STATUTORY MINIMUM REMUNERATION

PART I

REGULAR WORKERS OTHER THAN MILK WORKERS

This Part of this Schedule applies to regular workers (as defined in paragraph 39) other than milk workers (as defined in paragraph 44).

1. Subject to the provisions of this Part and of Parts III and V of this Schedule, the minimum remuneration of regular workers other than milk workers shall be as follows:—

(1) All workers except those employed on the Carriage of Indivisible Loads to whom sub-paragraph (2) of this paragraph applies:—

Occupation	Carrying capacity of vehicle (as defined in paragraph 35)	Age of worker	Remuneration per week	
			Workers whose home depot is situated in the London Area (as defined in para. 36)	Workers whose home depot is situated outside the London Area (as defined in para. 36)
			s. d.	s. d.
(a) Drivers of vehicles other than (i) tractors not exceeding two tons unladen weight used exclusively for furniture removal work and (ii) tractors which operate from a depot in the London Area (as defined in paragraph 36).	Of 1 ton or less	Under 19 years ... 19 and under 21 years 21 years or over ...	158 6 189 9 233 6	156 6 187 9 228 6
	Over 1 ton and up to and including 5 tons " 5 tons " " " " " 10 " " 10 " " " " " 15 " " 15 " " " " " 18 " " 18 " " " " " 21 " " 21 "	All ages	233 6 242 9 250 6 259 6 271 3 281 0	228 6 237 9 245 6 254 9 266 3 276 0
(b) Drivers of tractors not exceeding two tons unladen weight used exclusively for furniture removal work.	—	All ages	233 6	228 6

Occupation	Carrying capacity of vehicle (as defined in paragraph 35)	Age of worker	Remuneration per week	
			Workers whose home depot is situated in the London Area (as defined in para. 36)	Workers whose home depot is situated outside the London Area (as defined in para. 36)
			s. d.	s. d.
(c) Drivers of tractors, other than tractors not exceeding two tons unladen weight used exclusively for furniture work, which operate from a depot in the London Area (as defined in paragraph 36).	Up to and including 8 tons ... ... Over 8 tons and up to and including 12 tons ... Over 12 tons	All ages	244 0 252 3 261 0	— — —
(d) Workers in the Furniture Warehousing and Removing Industry employed as: Foremen Removal packers Porters	—	21 years or over ...	 232 6 225 6 223 0	 228 0 223 0 220 6
(e) Statutory attendants	—	Under 18 years ...	134 6	131 9
(f) Other road haulage workers		Under 16 years ... 16 and under 17 years 17 " " 18 " 18 " " 19 " 19 " " 20 " 20 " " 21 " 21 years or over ...	90 9 99 0 107 9 145 0 158 0 174 6 225 6	88 6 96 9 106 6 142 3 154 3 170 3 222 6

(2) Workers employed on the Carriage of Indivisible Loads.

   (a) Workers on vehicles whilst used in connection with the movement of loads, other than live or dead cattle, which by reason of indivisibility require mechanical loading or unloading equipment carried on the vehicle and operated upon the responsibility of the driver, or

   (b) Workers employed on vehicles authorised for the carriage of abnormal indivisible loads as defined in the Motor Vehicles (Authorisation of Special Types) General Order 1969(a):—

Occupation	Class of Vehicle	Carrying capacity of vehicle (as defined in paragraph 35)	Remuneration per week	
			Workers whose home depot is situated in the London Area (as defined in para. 36)	Workers whose home depot is situated outside the London Area (as defined in para. 36)
			s. d.	s. d.
Drivers ...	Vehicles referred to in (a) above	Over 6 tons and up to and including 10 tons	251 0	247 0
		" 10 " " 16 "	261 6	257 6
	Vehicles referred to in (b) above	" 16 " " 20 "	277 0	273 0
		" 20 " " 25 "	283 3	279 3
		" 25 " " 45 "	290 0	286 0
		" 45 " " 65 "	322 6	318 6
		" 65 "	337 6	333 6
Mates ...	Vehicles referred to in (a) above	Over 6 tons and up to and including 16 tons	225 6	222 6
	Vehicles referred to in (b) above	" 16 " " 20 "	227 9	224 9
		Over 20 tons ...	234 6	231 6
Heavy brakesmen and steersmen (as defined in paragraph 42).	Vehicles referred to in (b) above	—	251 3	248 3

A worker who on any day is employed in the circumstances specified in this sub-paragraph shall be paid at the rate appropriate to the vehicle for all hours worked by him on that day notwithstanding that he may be employed on other work during some part of that day.

(a) S.I. 1969/344 (1969 I, p. 947).

COMPUTATION OF HOURS OF WORK

2. The following provisions shall apply to regular workers, other than milk workers, to whom the guaranteed weekly remuneration provisions apply:—

(1) a five-day worker who works on any day other than Saturday or Sunday shall be deemed to have worked for 8 hours on any such day notwithstanding that he was employed for less than 8 hours;

(2) a six-day worker who works on any day other than Sunday shall, subject to the provisions of paragraph 25 and the proviso to paragraph 45(1)(a), be deemed to have worked for 7¼ hours on any day Monday to Thursday, for 7 hours on Friday and for 4 hours on Saturday notwithstanding that he was employed for less than 7¼, 7 or 4 hours respectively:

Provided that a worker who is instructed to report for duty and presents himself for duty but does not commence work shall be deemed to have commenced work.

OVERTIME

3. Subject to the provisions of paragraphs 24, 25 and 45 the following shall be regarded as overtime:—

(1) Time worked in excess of 7¼ hours on any day Monday to Thursday and 7 hours on Friday (subject to the proviso to paragraph 45(1)(a)) in the case of a six-day worker and in excess of 8 hours on any day Monday to Friday in the case of a five-day worker.

(2) Time worked on Saturdays:—

    (a) in the case of a six-day worker, in excess of 4 hours, provided that all time worked after 12.30 p.m. by a worker other than a film transport worker shall be regarded as overtime;

    (b) in the case of a five-day worker, all time worked, provided that a five-day worker who works for less than 4 hours shall be deemed to have worked for 4 hours.

(3) Time worked on Sunday.

A worker who works for less than 5½ hours on Sunday shall be deemed to have worked for 5½ hours:

Provided that a worker whose hours entail a spell of duty commencing on Saturday and finishing on Sunday before 5.30 a.m. or commencing on Sunday after 6.30 p.m. and finishing on Monday, shall not, unless the Sunday duty is less than 3 hours, be deemed to have worked on Sunday in excess of the hours actually worked. If the Sunday duty is less than 3 hours he shall be deemed to have worked 3 hours on Sunday:

Provided also that a worker commencing work on Saturday who finishes work between midnight and 1 a.m. on Sunday shall be deemed to have worked one hour on Sunday.

(4) Time worked in any week in excess of 40 hours.

4.—(1) In determining the time to be regarded as overtime, time worked shall include time deemed to have been worked under the provisions of paragraphs 2, 3(3) and 24.

(2) Time worked on a customary holiday in accordance with paragraph 27(2)(b) or paragraph 28(2)(b) or on a day in the circumstances set out in the proviso to paragraph 27(4)(a) or paragraph 28(4)(a), paragraph 27(3) or paragraph 28(3) shall not be included in the calculation of overtime.

(3) When a worker's hours of duty or any part thereof entail employment between 9 p.m. and 6 a.m., a day shall, for the purpose of paragraph 3(1) and paragraph 3(2), be deemed to be any period of 24 hours commencing at 12 noon.

PAYMENT FOR OVERTIME

5. The following are the rates payable for overtime:—

in any week (exclusive of Sunday)	...	...	...	...	...	...	time-and-a-half
on Sunday	...	...	...	...	...	...	double time

PART II
MILK WORKERS

This Part of this Schedule applies to milk workers (as defined in paragraph 44)

6. Subject to the provisions of this Part and of Parts III and V of this Schedule, the minimum remuneration of milk workers shall be as follows:—

Occupation	Carrying capacity of vehicle (as defined in paragraph 35)	Age of worker	Remuneration per week	
			Workers whose home depot is situated in the London Area (as defined in para. 36)	Workers whose home depot is situated outside the London Area (as defined in para. 36)
			s. d.	s. d.
(1) Drivers of vehicles other than tractors which operate from a depot in the London Area (as defined in paragraph 36).	Of 1 ton or less...	Under 19 years ... 19 and under 21 years 21 years or over ...	158 6 189 9 233 6	156 6 187 9 228 6
	Over 1 ton and up to and including 5 tons ,, 5 tons ,, ,, ,, ,, ,, 10 ,, ,, 10 ,, ,, ,, ,, ,, 15 ,, ,, 15 ,, ,, ,, ,, ,, 18 ,, ,, 18 ,, ,, ,, ,, ,, 21 ,, ,, 21 ,, ...	All ages	233 6 242 9 250 6 259 9 271 3 281 0	228 6 237 9 245 6 254 9 266 3 276 0
(2) Drivers of tractors which operate from a depot in the London Area (as defined in paragraph 36).	Up to and including 8 tons ... ... Over 8 tons and up to and including 12 tons Over 12 tons	All ages	244 0 252 3 261 0	— — —
(3) Statutory attendants	—	Under 18 years ...	134 6	131 9
(4) Other road haulage workers	—	Under 16 years ... ... 16 and under 17 years 17 ,, ,, 18 ,, 18 ,, ,, 19 ,, 19 ,, ,, 20 ,, 20 ,, ,, 21 ,, 21 years or over ...	90 9 99 0 107 9 145 0 158 0 174 6 225 6	88 6 96 9 106 6 142 3 154 3 170 3 222 6

SUNDAY WORK

7. A milk worker shall be paid time-and-a-half for 6 hours 40 minutes for any time worked or deemed to have been worked not exceeding 6 hours 40 minutes on Sunday not being the worker's normal day of rest and, thereafter, in accordance with paragraph 11.

COMPUTATION OF HOURS OF WORK

8. A milk worker to whom the guaranteed weekly remuneration provisions apply who works on any day shall be deemed to have worked for 6 hours 40 minutes notwithstanding that he was employed for less than 6 hours 40 minutes:

Provided that a milk worker who is instructed to report for duty and presents himself for duty but does not commence work shall be deemed to have commenced work.

OVERTIME

9. Subject to the provisions of paragraphs 25 and 45 the following shall be regarded as overtime:—

(1) Time worked in excess of 6 hours 40 minutes on any day other than the milk worker's normal day of rest, and all time worked on the milk worker's day of rest.

(2) Time worked in any week in excess of 40 hours.

10.—(1) In determining the time to be regarded as overtime, time worked shall include time deemed to have been worked under the provisions of paragraphs 8 and 24.

(2) Time worked on a customary holiday in accordance with paragraph 27(2)(b) or paragraph 28(2)(b) or on a day in the circumstances set out in the proviso to paragraph 27(4)(a) or paragraph 28(4)(a), paragraph 27(3) or paragraph 28(3) shall not be included in the calculation of overtime.

(3) When a worker's hours of duty or any part thereof entail employment between 9 p.m. and 6 a.m., a day shall, for the purpose of paragraph 9(1), be deemed to be any period of 24 hours commencing at 12 noon.

PAYMENT FOR OVERTIME

11. The following are the rates payable for overtime:—

in any week exclusive of the milk worker's normal day of rest and Sunday	time-and-a-half
on Sunday not being the milk worker's normal day of rest—	
for all time worked in excess of 6 hours 40 minutes ...	double time
on the milk worker's normal day of rest—	
for any time worked not exceeding 6 hours 40 minutes ...	double time for 6 hours 40 minutes
for all time worked in excess of 6 hours 40 minutes ...	double time.

PART III

REGULAR WORKERS INCLUDING MILK WORKERS

This Part of this Schedule applies to regular workers including milk workers.

WORKERS TEMPORARILY TRANSFERRED

12. A worker who is temporarily transferred away from his normal home depot and stationed in another locality (beyond reasonable daily travelling distance from his home) for more than one week shall be paid either the rates of wages appropriate to the locality in which his normal home depot is situated, or those appropriate to the new locality in which he has been stationed, whichever is more favourable to the worker.

HOURLY RATE

13. For the purpose of calculating the hourly rates of regular workers, the rates of wages specified in paragraphs 1 and 6 shall be divided by 40.

GUARANTEED WEEKLY REMUNERATION

14.—(1) Notwithstanding the provisions of the other paragraphs of this Schedule, where in any week a worker has performed some road haulage work for the employer and the total remuneration payable for time worked and time deemed to have been worked (excluding overtime and special payments as defined in sub-paragraph (4) of this paragraph is less than the guaranteed weekly remuneration provided under this paragraph, the minimum remuneration payable to that worker for that week shall, subject to the provisions of this paragraph, be that guaranteed weekly remuneration with the addition of any amount which may be payable in respect of overtime and by way of special payments.

(2) The guaranteed weekly remuneration is the pay for 40 hours, reduced by any time not reckonable by reason of sub-paragraph (3) of this paragraph and excluding special payments, calculated as follows:—

(a) for the time worked and time deemed to have been worked at the rate or rates applicable to such work (but excluding overtime) and

(b) for the remaining time at the time rate normally applicable to the worker.

(3) In calculating the guaranteed weekly remuneration no account shall be taken of

(a) *any time during which the worker is at his own request absent from work with leave of the employer, is absent without leave of the employer or on account of sickness or*

(b) any time during which the worker is suspended from work following the expiry of any notice given to him in any of the following manners and circumstances:—

(i) flood, snow, ice or other climatic conditions of such a nature as to preclude the operation of the vehicle, provided that not less than 24 hours' notice of the suspension of work shall be given individually to the worker and by the posting of a notice in the depot or other mutually convenient place;

(ii) where the employer is unable to carry on his business by reason of a strike or lock-out, provided that not less than 4 days' notice of such inability is given to the worker;

(iii) where the employer is unable to operate a vehicle or vehicles owing to the restriction of his fuel supply under any enactment or regulation made thereunder, provided that not less than 24 hours' notice of such inability is given to the worker or workers concerned:

Provided that the foregoing notices shall not be given when the worker is away from his home depot, and the suspension shall not operate until the required notice has been given to the worker on his return to his home depot.

(4) For the purposes of sub-paragraphs (1) and (2) of this paragraph:—

(a) in addition to any time deemed to have been worked under the other provisions of this Schedule;

(i) where a worker is allowed a day as a customary holiday or in lieu of a customary holiday or an annual holiday he shall be deemed to have worked the number of hours (excluding overtime) ordinarily worked by him on that day of the week;

(ii) where a worker is required to work on a day of customary holiday he shall be deemed to have worked the number of hours (excluding overtime) ordinarily worked by him on that day of the week notwithstanding that he was employed for less than that number of hours:

Provided that if a worker works on a customary holiday in accordance with the provisions of paragraph 27(2)(b) or paragraph 28(2)(b) or on a day in the circumstances set out in the proviso to paragraph 27(4)(*a*) or paragraph 28(4)(*a*) he shall be deemed only to have worked double the number of hours worked by him on that day (part of an hour being counted as an hour).

(*b*) "Special payments" means the following amounts:—

(i) Any additional payment for night work payable under paragraph 21.

(ii) Any amount payable under paragraph 23 (payment for telephoning for instructions whilst off duty).

(iii) Any subsistence allowance (other than payment for hours during which the worker is deemed to be on duty) payable under paragraph 24.

(iv) Any amount payable in respect of customary holidays occurring on the worker's weekly half-holiday or, in the case of a five-day worker, on a Saturday, or, in the case of a milk worker, on his normal day of rest, under provisos (*a*) (*b*) and (*c*) of paragraph 27(1) or under provisos (i), (ii) and (iii) of paragraph 28(1).

(5) The provisions of this paragraph shall not apply to a worker whose normal employment in the service of the employer substantially includes other work as well as road haulage work. Such a worker shall be paid in respect of the road haulage work at the appropriate rate for the time actually spent on such work.

A worker not normally a road haulage worker, but who occasionally performs road haulage work, shall be paid the rates of wages appropriate to a road haulage worker for the time actually spent on such work.

GUARANTEED MINIMUM REMUNERATION

15.—(1) Where in any week a worker has worked, or under the provisions of paragraphs 2, 3(3), 8, 14(4)(*a*) and 24 is deemed to have worked, on road haulage work for the employer for not less than 40 hours and the total remuneration payable to that worker for that week for time worked and time deemed to have been worked (including overtime but excluding special payments as defined in paragraph 14(4)(*b*)) is not less than the guaranteed weekly remuneration provided for by sub-paragraph (2) of paragraph 14 but is less than *320s. 0d.*, then, notwithstanding anything contained in this Schedule, the minimum remuneration payable to that worker shall be the guaranteed minimum remuneration provided for by sub-paragraph (2) of this paragraph, with the addition of any amount which may be payable by way of special payments.

(2) The guaranteed minimum remuneration shall be the total remuneration increased by the amount provided for either in (*a*) or (*b*) of this sub-paragraph whichever is the lesser:—

(*a*) (i) by *forty shillings* in the case of a worker aged 21 years or over or whose rate of remuneration per week is not related to his age;

(ii) by *thirty-five shillings* in the case of a worker aged under 21 years of age and whose rate of remuneration per week is related to his age;

(*b*) by an amount equal to the difference between the total remuneration and *320s. 0d.*

PART IV

WORKERS OTHER THAN REGULAR WORKERS

This Part of this Schedule applies to workers other than regular workers.

16. Subject to the provisions of this Part and of Part V of this Schedule, the minimum remuneration of workers other than regular workers shall be the hourly rates applicable to regular workers under Part I or Part II of this Schedule increased by 4d. per hour.

GUARANTEED DAY

17. Subject to the provisions of paragraph 25 (relating to the alternative weekly half-holiday) and sub-paragraphs (6) and (7) of paragraphs 27 and 28 (relating to

work on customary holidays), a worker other than a regular worker shall be paid not less than the wages due for 7¼ hours in respect of work done, or deemed to have been done, by him on any day Monday to Thursday, for 7 hours in respect of work done, or deemed to have been done, on Friday, and not less than the wages due for 4 hours in respect of work done, or deemed to have been done, by him on Saturday:

Provided that—

(1) where a spell of duty commences before midnight and continues thereafter, a worker shall not be entitled, by that fact alone, to two guaranteed payments in respect of that spell of duty;

(2) a worker who is engaged for a day of not less than 7¼ hours on any day Monday to Thursday, of not less than 7 hours on Friday, or for not less than 4 hours on Saturday, for work other than road haulage work, but who may perform some road haulage work, shall be paid for the time actually spent on road haulage work at the hourly rate or rates, calculated in accordance with the provisions of paragraph 16; and

(3) a worker who is instructed to report for duty, and presents himself for duty but does not commence work, shall be deemed to have commenced work.

Subject to the provisions relating to overtime, a worker other than a regular worker shall, when the number of hours worked or payable under the guarantee provided in this paragraph, is 7¼ on any day Monday to Thursday, 7 on Friday or 4 on Saturday, be paid the wages applicable to a regular worker for 7¼ hours, 7 hours or 4 hours as the case may be, plus 2s. 8d.

In all other circumstances, he shall be paid at an hourly rate, which is 4d. per hour above the hourly rate applicable to a regular worker.

OVERTIME

18. Subject to the provisions of paragraphs 24 and 25, the following shall be regarded as overtime:—

(1) Time worked in excess of 7¼ hours on any day Monday to Thursday, in excess of 7 hours on Friday and in excess of 4 hours on Saturday.

(2) Time worked on Sunday.

A worker who works for less than 5½ hours on Sunday shall be deemed to have worked for 5½ hours:

Provided that a worker whose hours entail a spell of duty commencing on Saturday and finishing on Sunday before 5.30 a.m. or commencing on Sunday after 6.30 p.m. and finishing on Monday, shall not, unless the Sunday duty is less than 3 hours, be deemed to have worked on Sunday in excess of the hours actually worked. If the Sunday duty is less than 3 hours he shall be deemed to have worked 3 hours on Sunday:

Provided also that a worker commencing work on Saturday who finishes work between midnight and 1 a.m. on Sunday shall be deemed to have worked one hour on Sunday.

19.—(1) In determining the time to be regarded as overtime, time worked shall include time deemed to have been worked under the provisions of paragraphs 18(2) and 24.

(2) Time worked on a customary holiday in accordance with paragraph 27(2)(b) or paragraph 28(2)(b) or on a day in the circumstances set out in the proviso to paragraph 27(4)(a) or paragraph 28(4)(a) shall not be included in the calculation of overtime.

(3) When a worker's hours of duty or any part thereof entail employment between 9 p.m. and 6 a.m., a day shall, for the purpose of paragraph 18(1), be deemed to be any period of 24 hours commencing at 12 noon.

PAYMENT FOR OVERTIME

20. The following are the rates payable for overtime:—

on any day (other than Sunday) ... ... time-and-a-half
on Sunday ... ... double time.

PART V

ALL WORKERS—ADDITIONAL PROVISIONS

This Part of this Schedule applies to all workers except where otherwise stated.

NIGHT WORK

21. A worker whose hours of duty or any part thereof entail employment between 7 p.m. and 6 a.m. shall be paid the appropriate rates of wages specified in paragraph 1, paragraph 6, or paragraph 16 and, in addition, in each spell of duty, *1s. 0d. for each hour, or part of an hour*, worked between 7 p.m. and 6 a.m. provided that where a spell of duty commences before 7 p.m. and finishes not later than 9 p.m. the additional payment shall not be payable. Where overtime is payable in respect of hours worked between 7 p.m. and 6 a.m., this additional payment remains payable but is not to be included for the purpose of calculating the overtime rate payable in respect of those hours.

TRAVELLING

22. When a worker is required to travel in, or on, or to accompany a vehicle for the purpose of doing road haulage work he shall, in determining the wages payable, be deemed to be engaged on the road haulage work usually performed by him.

TELEPHONING FOR INSTRUCTIONS WHILE OFF DUTY

23.—(1) If a worker during the period between two spells of duty is required to telephone for instructions he shall be paid the wages due for one hour:

Provided that this provision shall not apply when the telephone call is made immediately following a spell of duty.

(2) On each subsequent occasion, during the same period between two spells of duty, on which the worker is required to telephone for instructions he shall be paid the wages due for 4 hours:

Provided that if when telephoning on any such occasion the worker is instructed to commence work within one hour of so telephoning, he shall be paid for one hour instead of the said 4 hours.

(3) The payments to be made under sub-paragraphs (1) and (2) of this paragraph shall be at the rate normally applicable to the worker and shall be in addition to the weekly wages otherwise due to him.

SUBSISTENCE

24.—(1)(a) When a worker's period of rest occurs away from his home depot he shall be paid *25s. 0d.* in respect of each period of rest not exceeding 15 hours' continued duration. Subject to the provisions of sub-paragraph (1)(b) of this paragraph, when any such period of rest exceeds 15 hours the worker shall be deemed to be on duty and shall be entitled to be paid (in addition to the *25s. 0d.*) at the time rate which would be payable if he were actually at work for the period he is resting in excess of 15 hours but not in excess of 24 hours or 23 hours according to whether he is a five- or six-day worker. If the period of rest exceeds 24 or 23 hours, as the case may be, these arrangements will continue to apply until the worker resumes actual duty;

(b) Where, following the first 15 hours of a period of rest for which subsistence is payable, deemed duty or actual duty commences on a Sunday, the worker shall be entitled (in addition to the *25s. 0d.*) in respect of any deemed and any actual duty performed on the Sunday to not less than the wages due for 9 hours or 8 hours at double time, according to whether he is a five- or six-day worker.

(2) Notwithstanding the provisions of sub-paragraph (1) of this paragraph the following provisions shall apply in the case of a worker who is temporarily transferred away from his normal home depot and stationed in another locality (beyond reasonable daily travelling distance from his home) for more than one week:—

(a) after payment in respect of the first week in accordance with the provisions of sub-paragraph (1) of this paragraph a worker shall, in respect of the second and subsequent weeks, be paid a weekly subsistence allowance of *122s. 6d.* (*i.e. 17s. 6d. per day*);

(*b*) if a worker already on temporary transfer is temporarily transferred to another new station beyond reasonable travelling distance from his home he shall (after payment in respect of the first week at such other new station in accordance with sub-paragraph (1) of this paragraph) be paid, in respect of the second and subsequent weeks, a weekly subsistence allowance of *122s. 6d.* (*i.e. 17s. 6d. per day*);

(*c*) for any period of rest occurring away from a new station and from his home, he shall be paid in accordance with the provisions of sub-paragraph (1) of this paragraph and, in respect of any day for which payment is made to the worker under the provisions of that sub-paragraph, the subsistence allowances of *17s. 6d. per day* (specified in (*a*) and (*b*) above) shall be reduced to *13s. 6d. per day.*

ALTERNATIVE WEEKLY HALF-HOLIDAY

25. Where it is the established practice of any section of the industry to allow the weekly half-holiday on any weekday other than a Saturday, and that day is in the case of a six-day worker substituted for Saturday as the worker's weekly half-holiday the provisions of paragraphs 2, 3(1) and (2), 14, 17, 18(1) and 45, shall apply as if in these provisions that day were substituted for "Saturday" and "Saturday" for that day.

MEAL TIMES

26. The hours of work specified are, except for the purpose of paragraph 24, exclusive of meal times.

CUSTOMARY HOLIDAYS—ENGLAND AND WALES

27.—(1) Subject to the provisions of this paragraph, an employer in England and Wales shall allow the following days as holidays to regular workers to whom paragraphs 1 and 6 apply and who were in his employment on the day immediately prior to the day of holiday:—Christmas Day (or, if Christmas Day falls on a Sunday, such weekday as may be prescribed by national proclamation, or the next following Tuesday), Boxing Day, Good Friday, Easter Monday, Whit Monday (or where another day is substituted therefor by national proclamation, that day), August Bank Holiday and all nationally proclaimed holidays. Where in any place it is not the custom or practice to observe such days as holidays, other days (not fewer in number) may, by agreement between the employer and the worker, be substituted for the above-mentioned days. Each such day (i.e., one of the days specified above or a day substituted therefor—hereafter in this paragraph referred to as a "customary holiday") taken as a holiday shall be paid for on the basis of the wages due for the number of hours (excluding overtime) ordinarily worked by the worker on that day of the week at the time rate normally applicable to the worker:

Provided that—

(*a*) in addition to the foregoing, in the case of a six-day worker, other than a milk worker, where the customary holiday falls on the worker's weekly half-holiday he shall be paid in respect of that day a sum equivalent to the wages due for 4 hours' work at the rate normally applicable to him;

(*b*) in the case of a five-day worker, where the customary holiday falls on a Saturday he shall be paid in respect of that day a sum equivalent to the wages due for 8 hours' work at the rate normally applicable to him;

(*c*) in the case of a milk worker, where the customary holiday falls on the worker's normal day of rest he shall be paid in respect of that day a sum equivalent to the wages due for 6 hours 40 minutes' work at the rate normally applicable to him.

(2) Notwithstanding the foregoing provisions of this paragraph, a regular worker may work for the employer on a customary holiday:—

(*a*) where by reason of the necessity of maintaining essential services the allowing of a customary holiday is rendered impracticable; or

(*b*) where the worker will work on the customary holiday for not more than 3 hours during a spell of duty commencing on the day before the customary holiday or ending on the day after the holiday:

Provided that this sub-paragraph shall not apply to women and young persons in whose cases work on the customary holiday would be illegal.

(3)(a) Where a worker works on a customary holiday by virtue of sub-paragraph (2)(a) of this paragraph he shall be paid for work on that day at not less than double the rate appropriate to such work for all time worked by him thereon or for the basic hours for that worker, whichever amount is the greater. For the purpose of this sub-paragraph basic hours means in the case of a milk worker 6 hours 40 minutes, and, in the case of any other worker, the number of hours (excluding overtime) ordinarily worked by him on the day of the week on which the customary holiday falls.

(b) Where a worker works on a customary holiday by virtue of sub-paragraph (2)(b) of this paragraph he shall be paid for work on that day at not less than double the rate appropriate to such work (part of an hour being counted as an hour) and, in addition, an amount equal to the holiday remuneration to which he would have been entitled under the provisions of this order if he had been allowed a customary holiday on that day.

(4)(a) Where a regular worker works on a customary holiday by virtue of the provisions of sub-paragraph (2)(a) of this paragraph he shall, within the period of eight weeks immediately following the customary holiday, be allowed a day's holiday (hereafter referred to as "a day in lieu of a customary holiday") on a weekday (other than a weekly half-holiday) on which the worker normally works for the employer:

Provided that if on a weekday which is not a customary holiday or a weekly half-holiday within the said period of eight weeks the worker works for the employer for not more than 3 hours during a spell of duty commencing on the immediately preceding day or ending on the following day and the worker is paid for such work remuneration not less than the remuneration provided for work on a customary holiday under sub-paragraph (3)(b) of this paragraph, an employer is not required to allow to a worker a day in lieu of a customary holiday.

(b) For each day in lieu of a customary holiday allowed to a worker he shall be paid not less than the holiday remuneration to which he would have been entitled under the provisions of this Schedule if the day had been a customary holiday.

(c) For the purposes of this paragraph in the case of a worker who is employed on spells of duty which start before midnight and continue for more than 3 hours after midnight the day in lieu of a customary holiday shall include any period of 24 consecutive hours beginning and ending at noon on a weekday (other than a weekly half-holiday) on which the worker normally works.

(5) The holiday remuneration for a customary holiday or a day in lieu of a customary holiday shall be paid by the employer to the worker not later than the day on which the wages for the first working day following the customary holiday or day in lieu of the customary holiday are paid.

(6) Except as specified in sub-paragraph (7) of this paragraph a worker, other than a regular worker, who is employed on a customary holiday shall be paid for such work at double the rate otherwise appropriate thereto, and, notwithstanding that he may work for less than 7¼ hours on any such day, he shall be paid not less than twice the amount due, under the provisions of paragraph 17, for a guaranteed day of 7¼ hours.

(7) Where a worker, other than a regular worker, works for the employer on a customary holiday for not more than 3 hours during a spell of duty commencing on the immediately preceding day or ending on the following day, he shall be paid for such work at double the rate appropriate to such work, part of an hour being counted as an hour.

CUSTOMARY HOLIDAYS—SCOTLAND

28.—(1) Subject to the provisions of this paragraph, an employer in Scotland shall allow the following days as holidays to regular workers to whom paragraphs 1 and 6 apply and who were in his employment on the day immediately prior to the day of holiday:—

(*a*) New Year's Day (or the following day if New Year's Day falls on a Sunday) the local Spring Holiday, the local Autumn Holiday, and all nationally proclaimed holidays;

(*b*) Three other days in the course of a calendar year, to be fixed by the employer and notified to the workers not less than 21 days before the holiday;

(*c*) Where in any place it is not the custom or practice to observe the days mentioned in (*a*) above as holidays, other days (not fewer in number) may, by agreement between the employer and the worker, be substituted for the abovementioned days.

Each such day (i.e., one of the days specified above or a day substituted therefor —hereafter in this paragraph referred to as a "customary holiday") taken as a holiday shall be paid for on the basis of the wages due for the number of hours (excluding overtime) ordinarily worked by the worker on that day of the week at the time rate normally applicable to the worker:

Provided that—

(i) in addition to the foregoing, in the case of a six-day worker other than a milk worker, where the customary holiday falls on the worker's weekly half-holiday he shall be paid in respect of that day a sum equivalent to the wages due for 4 hours' work at the rate normally applicable to him;

(ii) in the case of a five-day worker, where the customary holiday falls on a Saturday he shall be paid in respect of that day a sum equivalent to the wages due for 8 hours' work at the rate normally applicable to him;

(iii) in the case of a milk worker, where the customary holiday falls on the worker's normal day of rest he shall be paid in respect of that day a sum equivalent to the wages due for 6 hours 40 minutes' work at the rate normally applicable to him.

(2) Notwithstanding the foregoing provisions of this paragraph, a regular worker may work for the employer on a customary holiday:—

(*a*) where by reason of the necessity of maintaining essential services the allowing of a customary holiday is rendered impracticable; or

(*b*) where the worker will work on the customary holiday for not more than 3 hours during a spell of duty commencing on the day before the customary holiday or ending on the day after the holiday:

Provided that this sub-paragraph shall not apply to women and young persons in whose cases work on the customary holiday would be illegal.

(3)(*a*) Where a worker works on a customary holiday by virtue of sub-paragraph (2)(*a*) of this paragraph he shall be paid for work on that day at not less than double the rate appropriate to such work for all time worked by him thereon or for the basic hours for that worker, whichever amount is the greater. For the purpose of this sub-paragraph basic hours means, in the case of a milk worker, 6 hours 40 minutes and, in the case of any other worker, the number of hours (excluding overtime) ordinarily worked by him on the day of the week on which the customary holiday falls.

(*b*) Where a worker works on a customary holiday by virtue of sub-paragraph (2)(*b*) of this paragraph he shall be paid for work on that day at not less than double the rate appropriate to such work (part of an hour being counted as an hour) and, in addition, an amount equal to the holiday remuneration to which he would have been entitled under the provisions of this order if he had been allowed a customary holiday on that day.

(4)(*a*) Where a regular worker works on a customary holiday by virtue of the provisions of sub-paragraph (2)(*a*) of this paragraph he shall, within the period of eight weeks immediately following the customary holiday, be allowed a day's holiday (hereafter referred to as "a day in lieu of a customary holiday") on a weekday (other than a weekly half-holiday) on which the worker normally works for the employer:

Provided that if on a weekday which is not a customary holiday or a weekly half-holiday within the said period of eight weeks the worker works for the employer for not more than 3 hours during a spell of duty commencing on the immediately preceding day or ending on the following day and the worker is paid for such work remuneration not less than the remuneration provided for work on a customary holiday under sub-paragraph (3)(b) of this paragraph an employer is not required to allow a worker a day in lieu of a customary holiday.

(b) For each day in lieu of a customary holiday allowed to a worker he shall be paid not less than the holiday remuneration to which he would have been entitled under the provisions of this Schedule if the day had been a customary holiday.

(c) For the purposes of this paragraph in the case of a worker who is employed on spells of duty which start before midnight and continue for more than 3 hours after midnight the day in lieu of a customary holiday shall include any period of 24 consecutive hours beginning and ending at noon on a weekday (other than a weekly half-holiday) on which the worker normally works.

(5) The holiday remuneration for a customary holiday or a day in lieu of a customary holiday shall be paid by the employer to the worker not later than the day on which the wages for the first working day following the customary holiday or day in lieu of a customary holiday are paid.

(6) Except as specified in sub-paragraph (7) of this paragraph, a worker, other than a regular worker, who is employed on any of the days mentioned in sub-paragraph (1)(a) of this paragraph shall be paid for such work at double the rate otherwise appropriate thereto, and, notwithstanding that he may work for less than 7¼ hours on any such day, he shall be paid not less than twice the amount due, under the provisions of paragraph 17, for a guaranteed day of 7¼ hours.

(7) Where a worker, other than a regular worker, works for the employer on a customary holiday for not more than 3 hours during a spell of duty commencing on the immediately preceding day or ending on the following day, he shall be paid for such work at double the rate appropriate to such work, a part of an hour being counted as an hour.

ANNUAL HOLIDAY, *ADDITIONAL ANNUAL HOLIDAY* AND HOLIDAY REMUNERATION

29.—(1) In addition to the holidays provided for in paragraphs 27 and 28 (and subject to the provisions of sub-paragraphs (3) and (6) of this paragraph) an employer shall between 1st May 1970 and 15th October 1970, and in each succeeding year between 1st May and 15th October allow a holiday (hereinafter referred to as an "annual holiday") to every worker in his employment for whom statutory minimum remuneration has been fixed under paragraphs 1, 6 or 16 and who was during the 12 months immediately preceding the commencement of the holiday season in that year (hereinafter referred to as the "qualifying period") in his employment for any of the periods of employment specified below, and the duration of a worker's annual holiday shall be related to the period of his employment during the qualifying period as follows:—

Six-day workers		Five-day workers	
Period of employment	Duration of annual holiday	Period of employment	Duration of annual holiday
At least 48 weeks	12 days	At least 48 weeks	10 days
,, ,, 44 ,,	11 ,,	,, ,, 43 ,,	9 ,,
,, ,, 40 ,,	10 ,,	,, ,, 38 ,,	8 ,,
,, ,, 36 ,,	9 ,,	,, ,, 33 ,,	7 ,,
,, ,, 32 ,,	8 ,,	,, ,, 28 ,,	6 ,,
,, ,, 28 ,,	7 ,,	,, ,, 24 ,,	5 ,,
,, ,, 24 ,,	6 ,,	,, ,, 19 ,,	4 ,,
,, ,, 20 ,,	5 ,,	,, ,, 14 ,,	3 ,,
,, ,, 16 ,,	4 ,,	,, ,, 9 ,,	2 ,,
,, ,, 12 ,,	3 ,,	,, ,, 4 ,,	1 day
,, ,, 8 ,,	2 ,,		
,, ,, 4 ,,	1 day		

(2) For the purpose of calculating a period of employment in respect of annual holiday and accrued holiday remuneration "employment" means employment on road haulage work specified in paragraphs 46 and 47 and also employment partly on that work and partly on work other than such road haulage work, and a worker shall be treated as in the employment of the employer when absent from work in any of the following circumstances:—

(a) absences of the worker arising from suspension in accordance with paragraph 14(3)(b);

(b) absences of the worker owing to proved illness or accident up to but not exceeding 16 weeks in the aggregate during the qualifying period;

(c) suspension from employment owing to shortage of work or mechanical breakdown up to but not exceeding 16 weeks in the aggregate during the qualifying period;

(d) absences of the worker arising from the allowance of holidays provided for in paragraph 27 or paragraph 28 and annual holiday allowed under the provisions of this paragraph;

(e) other absences with reasonable cause during the qualifying period;

(f) absence for not more than 7 days during the qualifying period for reasons other than those specified in (a) to (e) above.

(3) Notwithstanding the provisions of sub-paragraphs (1) and (2) of this paragraph, a worker who has been absent for more than 7 days during the qualifying period for reasons other than those specified in (a) to (e) of sub-paragraph (2) of this paragraph shall not be entitled to any annual holiday in respect of such period.

(4) In this Schedule the expression "holiday season" means in relation to an annual holiday during the year 1970, the period commencing on 1st May 1970 and ending on 15th October 1970, and in relation to each subsequent year, the period commencing on 1st May and ending on 15th October in that year.

(5) Notwithstanding the provisions of sub-paragraphs (1) and (4) of this paragraph, where before 1st October in any holiday season, at the written request of a worker his employer has agreed in writing that the worker shall be allowed after the end of the holiday season and before 1st May in the following year, the annual holiday, or any part thereof, for which he has qualified under this paragraph, any such days of annual holiday may, subject to the provisions of paragraph 34, be allowed in accordance with the agreement and if so allowed shall be treated for the purposes of this Schedule as having been allowed during the holiday season.

30.—(1) *Subject to the provisions of this paragraph and in addition to the holidays provided for in paragraphs 27, 28 and 29, an employer shall allow to every worker in his employment for whom statutory minimum remuneration has been fixed under paragraphs 1, 6 or 16 a further annual holiday (hereinafter referred to as an "additional annual holiday") amounting to 6 days in the case of a six-day worker or 5 days in the case of a five-day worker and the additional annual holiday to be allowed shall depend on the duration of the worker's continuous employment with the employer as follows:—*

(a) *during the 12 months commencing on 1st May 1970—not less than 5 years' continuous employment immediately preceding 1st May 1970;*

(b) *during the 12 months commencing on 1st May 1971—not less than 4 years' continuous employment immediately preceding 1st May 1971; and*

(c) *during the 12 months commencing on 1st May 1972 and on 1st May in each succeeding year—not less than 3 years' continuous employment immediately preceding 1st May 1972 and 1st May in each succeeding year.*

(2) *Days of additional annual holiday, which need not be consecutive, shall be allowed on days on which the worker is normally called upon to work for the employer and during the relevant period of 12 months commencing on 1st May at any time either—*

(a) *on dates agreed between the employer and the worker or his representative at any time before 6th April in that period; or*

(b) *during the remaining days of that period.*

31.—(1) In respect of an annual holiday allowed under paragraph 29, holiday re-muneration shall be paid as follows:—

Period of annual holiday Column 1	Holiday remuneration for—		Column 4
	Six-day workers Column 2	Five-day workers Column 3	
12 days	Twice the amount in Col. 4	—	The amount which the worker would be entitled to receive from his employer at the date of the annual holiday for 40 hours' work (exclusive of overtime) at the time rate normally applicable to him under this Schedule, together with an addition, in the case of a regular worker, where the amount so calculated is less than *320s. 0d.* of whichever of the following amounts is the lesser:— (a) the difference between the amount so calculated and *320s. 0d.* OR (b) (i) *forty shillings* in the case of a worker aged 21 years or over or whose rate of remuneration per week is not related to his age: (ii) *thirty-five shillings* in the case of a worker aged under 21 years of age and whose rate of remuneration per week is related to his age.
11 days	One and five-sixths times the amount in Col. 4	—	
10 days	One and two-thirds times the amount in Col. 4	Twice the amount in Col. 4	
9 days	One and a half times the amount in Col. 4	One and four-fifths times the amount in Col. 4	
8 days	One and one-third times the amount in Col. 4	One and three-fifths times the amount in Col. 4	
7 days	One and one-sixth times the amount in Col. 4	One and two-fifths times the amount in Col. 4	
6 days	The amount in Col. 4	One and one-fifth times the amount in Col. 4	
5 days	Five-sixths of the amount in Col. 4	The amount in Col. 4	
4 days	Two-thirds of the amount in Col. 4	Four-fifths of the amount in Col. 4	
3 days	One-half of the amount in Col. 4	Three-fifths of the amount in Col. 4	
2 days	One-third of the amount in Col. 4	Two-fifths of the amount in Col. 4	
1 day	One-sixth of the amount in Col. 4	One-fifth of the amount in Col. 4	

(2) A worker entitled to be allowed an additional annual holiday under paragraph 30 shall be paid by his employer in respect thereof the amount specified in Column 4 of the preceding table.

(3) Holiday remuneration shall be paid on the last pay day preceding an annual holiday or additional annual holiday as the case may be.

Provided that,

(a) (i) *where in accordance with the proviso to paragraph 34(1) an annual holiday is allowed in two or three periods; or*

(ii) *where an additional annual holiday is allowed in more than one period, holiday remuneration shall be apportioned accordingly;*

(b) *where an additional annual holiday is allowed in more than one period as a day or as days within a week in which the worker also works for the employer, holiday remuneration in respect of that day or those days shall be paid not later than the day on which the wages for the first working day following the day or days of additional annual holiday are paid.*

32. Where any accrued holiday remuneration has been paid by the employer to the worker under paragraph 33(1) in respect of any period of employment in the qualifying period preceding the holiday season current when the annual holiday is allowed, the amount to be paid in respect of the period of such holiday is the appropriate amount payable under paragraph 31 less the accrued holiday remuneration previously paid as aforesaid.

33.—(*1*) *Subject to the provisions of this paragraph, where a worker ceases to be employed, the employer shall immediately on the termination of employment (hereinafter referred to as "the termination date") pay to him as accrued holiday remuneration:*—

(*a*) *in respect of employment in the 12 months up to 30th April preceding the termination date, a sum equal to the holiday remuneration which would be payable for any days of annual holiday for which he has qualified (except days of annual holiday which he has been allowed or has become entitled to be allowed before the said date) if they were allowed at the time of leaving the employment;*

(*b*) *in respect of employment up to 30th April preceding the termination date, a sum equal to the holiday remuneration which would be payable for any days of additional annual holiday for which he has qualified (except days of additional annual holiday which he has been allowed or has become entitled to be allowed before the said date) if they were allowed at the time of leaving the employment;*

(*c*) *in respect of any employment since 30th April preceding the termination date, of not less than four weeks duration, a sum equal to the holiday remuneration which would have been payable to him if he could have been allowed an annual holiday in respect of that employment at the termination date.*

(2) The amount of any accrued holiday remuneration payable in respect of any period of employment shall be reduced by the amount of any previous payment of accrued holiday remuneration in respect of that period made by the employer to the worker under the provisions of this Schedule or of Order R.H. (88).

(3) Accrued holiday remuneration shall not be payable to a worker in respect of a qualifying period during which he was absent for more than seven days for reasons other than those specified in (*a*) to (*e*) of paragraph 29(2).

34.—(1) An annual holiday under paragraph 29 shall be allowed on consecutive working days being days upon which the worker is normally called upon to work, and days of holiday shall be treated as consecutive notwithstanding that a Sunday or any of the holidays allowed under paragraph 27 or paragraph 28 intervenes:—

Provided that where the duration of an annual holiday for which a worker is qualified exceeds the period of his normal working week, the holiday may, at the written request of the worker and with the agreement of the employer, be allowed in two or three periods, one of which shall be not less than the period of his normal working week.

(2) An employer shall give to a worker reasonable notice of the commencing date or dates and of the duration of his annual holiday *or additional annual holiday if not agreed between them.* Such notice may be given individually to a worker or by the posting of a notice in the worker's home depot.

PART VI

DEFINITIONS

Carrying capacity

35.—(1) The carrying capacity of a vehicle is the weight of the maximum load normally carried by the vehicle, and such carrying capacity when so established shall not be affected either by variations in the weight of the load resulting from collections or deliveries or emptying of containers during the course of the journey, or by the fact that on any particular journey a load greater or less than the established carrying capacity is carried.

(2) Where a trailer is attached to the vehicle, the load shall be the loads of the vehicle and trailer combined.

LONDON AREA

36. London Area means the localities named below, and these localities are, unless the context otherwise requires, those defined for local government purposes as at 1st August 1964.

Locality	Local Authority	Locality	Local Authority
City of London		Rainham (see Hornchurch UD)	Parish
Dartford	Borough	Romford	Borough
Dartford—Only Parish of Stone	Rural District	Stone (see Dartford RD) ...	Parish
		Swanscombe	Urban District
Gravesend	Borough		
Hornchurch—Only Parishes of Rainham, Wennington, and such other parts as are within 2 miles, in a straight line, of the north bank of the River Thames	Urban District	Thurrock—Only that part which is within 2 miles, in a straight line, of the north bank of the River Thames, except those parts which were, prior to 1st April 1936, known as the Parishes of Corringham, Fobbing, Mucking, Stanford-le-Hope, in the Rural District of Orsett	Urban District
Metropolitan Police District as existing on 1st August 1964— Except that part of the Borough of Watford which is included therein, and except the UD of Bushey...	—		
Northfleet	Urban District	Wennington (see Hornchurch UD)	Parish

Note: In case of doubt as to the grading applicable to a particular depot, an enquiry should be addressed to the Clerk of the appropriate Local Authority as to the title of the Local Government administrative area, as it existed on 1st August 1964, in which the depot is situated.

Overtime expressions

37. The expressions time-and-a-half and double time mean respectively one and a half times and twice the rate of wages otherwise applicable.

Vehicle

38. Vehicle means a mechanically driven goods vehicle.

Regular worker

39. A regular worker is a worker employed by the week or longer period.

Driver

40. A driver is a worker employed in driving a vehicle and in performing when so required any other road haulage work.

Foremen and removal packers in the Furniture Warehousing and Removing Industry

41.—(1) A foreman in the Furniture Warehousing and Removing Industry is a worker who has charge of a removal and who has authority to issue instructions to two or more persons.

(2) A removal packer in the Furniture Warehousing and Removing Industry is a skilled worker who packs china and other articles.

Heavy brakesman and steersman

42. A heavy brakesman and steersman is a person operating the steering and braking equipment of a heavy trailer used for the carriage of abnormal indivisible loads.

Film transport worker

43. A film transport worker is a worker engaged exclusively in the collection and delivery of films for the cinematograph industry:

Provided that a worker shall not cease to be a film transport worker solely by reason of the fact that he collects from and delivers to cinemas cinematograph accessories and equipment which are carried at the same time as the films are normally carried.

Milk Worker

44. A milk worker is a regular worker who is employed on 6 days a week and who is exclusively engaged in the collection of milk from farms and its delivery to dairies:

Provided that a worker shall not cease to be a milk worker solely by reason of the fact that, exceptionally, he is required to work on the duties specified above on the remaining day of the week.

Ordinary working hours

45. The expression "number of hours (excluding overtime) ordinarily worked by the worker on that day of the week" means—

(1) in the case of a regular worker other than a milk worker:—

(a) in respect of a six-day worker (subject to the provisions of paragraph 25), 7¼ hours on any day Monday to Thursday, 7 hours on Friday and 4 hours on Saturday:

Provided that 7¼ hours may be substituted for 7 hours on Friday if 7 hours is substituted for 7¼ hours on one other day from Monday to Thursday.

(b) in respect of a five-day worker, 8 hours on any day Monday to Friday;

(2) in the case of a milk worker, 6 hours 40 minutes.

PART VII

WORKERS TO WHOM THIS SCHEDULE APPLIES

46. Subject to the provisions of this paragraph and to the provisions of paragraph 49 hereof, this Schedule applies to road haulage workers in respect of road haulage work performed in connection with any motor goods vehicle (including a trailer) specified or deemed to be specified in an "A" licence or a "B" licence granted under the Road Traffic Act 1960(a):

Provided that the remuneration specified in this Schedule shall not apply to the following classes of road haulage work, namely, the employment of contractors' men on vehicles hired on a 24-hour stand-by basis by or on behalf of the Secretary of State for Defence in connection with manoeuvres, exercises, training or active service.

47. A person is a road haulage worker and is deemed to be employed on road haulage work if he is employed on all or any of the work described in (1) to (5) below or if his time is occupied as specified in (6) to (9) below, that is to say:—

(1) driving or assisting in the driving or control of the vehicle;

(2) collecting or loading goods to be carried in or on the vehicle;

(3) attending to goods while so carried;

(4) unloading or delivering goods after being so carried;

(5) acting as attendant to the vehicle;

and who is required to travel on or to accompany the vehicle for the purpose of doing any such work;

(6) in doing any work incidental to his employment in work mentioned in sub-paragraphs (1) to (5) hereof;

(7) in travelling in or on or accompanying a goods vehicle in connection with his employment in the work so mentioned;

(8) in holding himself under the orders or at the disposal of his employer while waiting in connection with his employment in the work so mentioned;

(a) 1960 c. 16.

(9) in waiting (whether overnight or otherwise) in accordance with the instructions of his employer as a necessary consequence of his employment in any of the work so mentioned:

Provided that a person employed in loading goods to be carried in or on a goods vehicle or in unloading goods after being so carried and required to travel on or to accompany the vehicle partly for that purpose, shall not be deemed to be a road haulage worker by reason only of that employment, if the main purpose for which he is required to travel on or to accompany the vehicle is that of executing work other than road haulage work after its arrival at his destination.

48. For the purposes of this Schedule road haulage work includes road haulage work performed by a road haulage worker employed by a person carrying on the business of a goods transport clearing house, i.e., the business of arranging for the mechanical transport of goods by road.

49. This Schedule does not apply to workers:—

(1) for whom or in respect of whose work a minimum rate of wages is, for the time being, fixed by or under any other enactment; or

(2) for whom minimum remuneration has been fixed pursuant to proposals of any other Wages Council established under the Wages Councils Act 1959.

EXPLANATORY NOTE

(This Note is not part of the Order.)

This Order, which has effect from 23rd January 1970, sets out the statutory minimum remuneration payable and the holidays to be allowed in substitution for the statutory minimum remuneration and holidays set out in the Wages Regulation (Road Haulage) Order 1968 (Order R.H. (88)), which Order is revoked.

New provisions are printed in italics.

STATUTORY INSTRUMENTS

1969 No. 1719

CUSTOMS AND EXCISE

The Import Duties (General) (No. 4) Order 1969

Made - - - - -	*2nd December* 1969
Laid before the	
House of Commons	*5th December* 1969
Coming into Operation	*1st January* 1970

The Lords Commissioners of Her Majesty's Treasury, by virtue of the powers conferred on them by sections 1, 2 and 13 of the Import Duties Act 1958(a), and of all other powers enabling them in that behalf, on the recommendation of the Board of Trade hereby make the following Order:—

1.—(1) This Order may be cited as the Import Duties (General) (No. 4) Order 1969.

(2) The Interpretation Act 1889(b) shall apply for the interpretation of this Order as it applies for the interpretation of an Act of Parliament.

(3) This Order shall come into operation on 1st January 1970.

2. In Article 1(3) of the Import Duties (General) (No. 3) Order 1969(c) (which includes a saving for instruments under the Import Duties Act 1958, other than those revoked by the Order), for the words " the foregoing paragraph " there shall be substituted the words " this Order ".

Ernest Armstrong,

E. G. Perry,

Two of the Lords Commissioners
of Her Majesty's Treasury.

2nd December 1969.

EXPLANATORY NOTE

(*This Note is not part of the Order.*)

This Order corrects a paragraph reference to the revocation of earlier Orders. The revocation is effected by Article 4.

(**a**) 1958 c. 6.   (**b**) 1889 c. 63.   (**c**) S.I. 1969/1413 (1969 III, p. 4150).

STATUTORY INSTRUMENTS

1969 No. 1720

PENSIONS

The Pensions Increase (Approved Schemes) (Local Government) Amendment Regulations 1969

Made - - -	*2nd December* 1969
Laid before Parliament	*11th December* 1969
Coming into Operation	*22nd December* 1969

The Minister of Housing and Local Government, in exercise of the powers conferred upon him by section 3(2)(b)(ii) and (4) of the Pensions (Increase) Act 1965(a) as extended by section 1(4) of and paragraph 10 of Schedule 2 to the Pensions (Increase) Act 1969(b), and of all other powers enabling him in that behalf, with the consent of the Minister for the Civil Service, hereby makes the following regulations:—

Citation, commencement and interpretation

1.—(1) These regulations may be cited as the Pensions Increase (Approved Schemes) (Local Government) Amendment Regulations 1969, and shall come into operation on 22nd December 1969.

(2) The Pensions Increase (Approved Schemes) (Local Government) Regulations 1968(c) (hereinafter called "the principal regulations") and these regulations may be cited together as the Pensions Increase (Approved Schemes) (Local Government) Regulations 1968 and 1969.

(3) The Interpretation Act 1889(d) shall apply for the interpretation of these regulations as it applies for the interpretation of an Act of Parliament.

Extension of pension increases

2. In regulation 2(1) of the principal regulations (which relates to interpretation) the following shall be inserted after item (v) in the definition of "statutory pension increases"—

"and

(vi) section 1 of the Pensions (Increase) Act 1969".

Employment by nursing associations

3.—(1) After regulation 4(2) of the principal regulations (which defines the persons to whom the regulations are to apply) there shall be added the following paragraph:—

"(3) For the purposes of paragraph (1) (b) (ii) of this regulation (but for no other purpose) a person may aggregate with his reckonable service employment by a county or district nursing association during any period when a local authority had arrangements with that association under section 1 of the Midwives Act 1936(e).".

(a) 1965 c. 78.   (b) 1969 c. 7.
(c) S.I. 1968/1284 (1968 II, p. 3597). (d) 1889 c. 63.
(e) 1936 c. 40.

(2) In paragraph 2(vi) of the schedule to the principal regulations (which defines reckonable service) before the words "district nursing association" there shall be inserted the words "county or".

Effective date of operation

4.—(1) Any allowance, or any increase of an allowance, which becomes payable by virtue of the amendment effected by regulation 2 of these regulations shall be payable in relation to any period beginning on or after 1st April 1969.

(2) Any allowance, or any increase of an allowance, which becomes payable by virtue of an amendment effected by regulation 3 of these regulations shall be payable in relation to any period beginning on or after 1st July 1966.

Given under the official seal of the Minister of Housing and Local Government on 2nd December 1969.

(L.S.)   *Anthony Greenwood,*
                                                           Minister of Housing
                                                     and Local Government.

Consent of the Minister for the Civil Service given under his Official Seal on 2nd December 1969.

(L.S.)   *J. E. Herbecq,*
                                                  Authorised by the Minister
                                                          for the Civil Service.

EXPLANATORY NOTE

(*This Note is not part of the Regulations.*)

The Pensions Increase (Approved Schemes) (Local Government) Regulations 1968 provide for the payment of allowances to certain retired local government employees whose pension rights were secured through insurance policies. The allowances correspond broadly to the increases for which they would have been eligible under pensions increase legislation had they been pensionable as contributory employees in their local government employment. These Regulations authorise new or increased allowances which correspond with the new increases provided by the Pensions (Increase) Act 1969. They also amend the Regulations of 1968 by extending the scope of the nursing association employment which is reckonable for these purposes.

The Regulations are given retrospective effect under the express powers of section 3(4) of the Pensions (Increase) Act 1965 and paragraph 10 of Schedule 2 to the Pensions (Increase) Act 1969.

STATUTORY INSTRUMENTS

1969 No. 1726

WAGES COUNCILS

The Wages Regulation (Industrial and Staff Canteen) (No. 2) Order 1969

Made - - -		*3rd December* 1969
Coming into Operation		*19th January* 1970

Whereas the Secretary of State has received from the Industrial and Staff Canteen Undertakings Wages Council the wages regulation proposals set out in the Schedule hereto ;

Now, therefore, the Secretary of State in exercise of her powers under section 11 of the Wages Councils Act 1959(**a**), and of all other powers enabling her in that behalf, hereby makes the following Order :—

1. This Order may be cited as the Wages Regulation (Industrial and Staff Canteen) (No. 2) Order 1969.

2.—(1) In this Order the expression "the specified date" means the 19th January 1970, provided that where, as respects any worker who is paid wages at intervals not exceeding seven days, that date does not correspond with the beginning of the period for which the wages are paid, the expression "the specified date" means, as respects that worker, the beginning of the next such period following that date.

(2) The Interpretation Act 1889(**b**) shall apply to the interpretation of this Order as it applies to the interpretation of an Act of Parliament and as if this Order and the Order hereby revoked were Acts of Parliament.

3. The wages regulation proposals set out in the Schedule hereto shall have effect as from the specified date and as from that date the Wages Regulation (Industrial and Staff Canteen) Order 1969(**c**) shall cease to have effect.

Signed by order of the Secretary of State.

3rd December 1969.

A. A. Jarratt,
Deputy Under Secretary of State,
Department of Employment and Productivity.

(**a**) 1959 c. 69.   (**b**) 1889 c. 63.
(**c**) S.I. 1969/691 (1969 II, p. 1879).

ARRANGEMENT OF SCHEDULE

PART I

REMUNERATION FOR EMPLOYMENT

PART II

HOLIDAYS AND HOLIDAY REMUNERATION

PART III

DEFINITIONS

PART IV

GENERAL

SCHEDULE

Article 3

The following minimum remuneration and provisions as to holidays and holiday remuneration shall be substituted for the statutory minimum remuneration and the provisions as to holidays and holiday remuneration set out in the Wages Regulation (Industrial and Staff Canteen) Order 1969 (hereinafter referred to as "Order I.S.C. (43)").

PART I

REMUNERATION FOR EMPLOYMENT

WORKERS OTHER THAN NIGHT WORKERS, SHIFT WORKERS AND SPLIT DUTY WORKERS

1. The minimum weekly remuneration for workers (other than night workers, shift workers and split duty workers) who are employed in the circumstances specified in paragraph 6 shall be in accordance with the following Table.

Where an increase in remuneration becomes payable under the provisions of paragraphs 8A, 9A, 10A, 11A or 12A on a day other than the first day of a pay week it shall become effective on the first day of the first full pay week following the date upon which the increase would otherwise become payable under those provisions.

	Column 1 Workers employed in the circumstances specified in Paragraph 6(1)		Column 2 Paragraph 6(2)
	London area	Other areas	All areas
A. FEMALE WORKERS—	s. d.	s. d.	s. d.
CANTEEN ATTENDANT	132 6	130 0	105 2
Provided that where a Canteen Attendant in the course of her duties on any day or night is engaged in the cooking of prepared food she shall receive for that day or night in addition an allowance of 8d.			
Provided also that where a Canteen Attendant is deputed to supervise staff for a minimum consecutive period of one hour, she shall receive in addition for all time during which she is so employed an allowance of 1d. per hour.			
ALL WORKERS UNDER 18 YEARS OF AGE—			
17 and under 18 years of age	107 0	104 6	86 4
16 „ „ 17 „ „	84 6	82 0	70 5
Under 16 years of age	73 0	70 0	60 1
CASHIER	136 6	134 0	109 2
ASSISTANT COOK	142 6	140 0	115 2
COOK	156 6	154 0	129 2
HEAD COOK	171 6	169 0	144 2
CANTEEN SUPERVISOR, MANAGERESS OR STEWARDESS—			
Grade X	161 0	158 6	133 8
Grade A	169 0	166 6	141 8
Grade B	179 0	176 6	151 8
Grade C	189 0	186 6	161 8
Grade D	199 0	196 6	171 8
TWO-YEAR TRAINEE COOKS			
First year of training	79 0	76 6	66 0
Second year of training	98 0	95 6	82 0
FOUR-YEAR TRAINEE COOKS			
First year of training	79 0	76 6	66 0
Second year of training	98 0	95 6	82 0
Third year of training	127 0	124 6	106 6
Fourth year of training	155 0	152 6	130 0

Provided that in the case of a four-year trainee, for the purpose of determining the "year of training" any period by which the 4 years' training is reduced under the proviso to the definition of "TRAINEE COOK" in paragraph 29 shall be treated as a period of training.

	Column 1 Workers employed in the circumstances specified in Paragraph 6(1)		Column 2 Paragraph 6(2)
	London area	Other areas	All areas
	s. d.	s. d.	s. d·
B. MALE WORKERS—			
PORTER OF 21 YEARS OF AGE OR OVER ...	178 6	176 0	151 2
Provided that where a Porter is deputed to supervise staff for a minimum consecutive period of one hour, he shall receive in addition for all time during which he is so employed an allowance of 1d. per hour.			
ASSISTANT COOK	197 6	195 0	170 2
COOK	217 6	215 0	190 2
HEAD COOK	230 6	228 0	203 2
CANTEEN SUPERVISOR, MANAGER OR STEWARD—			
Grade A	225 6	223 0	198 2
Grade B	235 6	233 0	208 2
Grade C	245 6	243 0	218 2
Grade D	255 6	253 0	228 2
APPRENTICE COOKS—			
First year of apprenticeship	92 6	90 0	79 6
Second year of apprenticeship	115 0	112 6	99 0
Third year of apprenticeship	138 0	135 6	119 0
Fourth year of apprenticeship	160 0	157 6	138 0
Fifth year of apprenticeship	182 0	179 6	157 0
Provided that for the purpose of determining the "year of apprenticeship" any period by which the 5 years' apprenticeship is reduced under the proviso to the definition of "APPRENTICE COOK" in paragraph 29 shall be treated as a period of apprenticeship.			
TWO-YEAR TRAINEE COOKS			
First year of training	*92 6*	*90 0*	*79 6*
Second year of training	*115 0*	*112 6*	*99 0*
FOUR-YEAR TRAINEE COOKS			
First year of training	*92 6*	*90 0*	*79 6*
Second year of training	*115 0*	*112 6*	*99 0*
Third year of training	*149 0*	*146 6*	*128 6*
Fourth year of training	*182 0*	*179 6*	*157 0*
Provided that in the case of a four-year trainee, for the purpose of determining the "year of training" any period by which the 4 years' training is reduced under the proviso to the definition of "TRAINEE COOK" in paragraph 29 shall be treated as a period of training.			
ALL OTHER MALE WORKERS aged			
21 years or over	178 6	176 0	151 2
20 and under 21 years	152 6	150 0	125 2
19 „ „ 20 „	137 0	134 6	112 6
18 „ „ 19 „	117 0	114 6	96 10
17 „ „ 18 „	100 6	97 6	83 1
16 „ „ 17 „	81 0	78 6	66 11
Under 16 years	69 6	67 0	57 1

NIGHT WORKERS

2. The minimum remuneration for a night worker who is employed in the circumstances specified in sub-paragraph (1) or (2) of paragraph 6 and who is not a shift worker or a split duty worker is that for the corresponding description of worker in the same area specified in paragraph 1 INCREASED IN EACH CASE BY ONE-FIFTH.

SHIFT WORKERS

3. The minimum remuneration for a shift worker who is employed in the circumstances specified in sub-paragraph (1) or (2) of paragraph 6 is that for the corresponding description of worker in the same area specified in paragraph 1 with the ADDITION OF 1d. per hour.

SPLIT DUTY WORKERS

4. The minimum remuneration for a split duty worker who is employed in the circumstances specified in paragraph 6(2) is that for the corresponding description of worker specified in Column 2 of paragraph 1 with the ADDITION OF 2d. per hour.

WORKERS TEMPORARILY TRANSFERRED TO HIGHER GRADE WORK

5. Where a worker is required temporarily to perform the duties of a worker entitled to a higher minimum remuneration than himself and is engaged on such higher graded duties for four or more hours on any day he shall be paid for the whole of his time on that day not less than the minimum remuneration appropriate to the worker of the higher grade.

WORKERS PROVIDED WITH MEALS OR FULL BOARD AND LODGING, OVERALLS AND HEADWEAR

6.—(1) The minimum remuneration in Column 1 of paragraph 1 is payable to a worker not being a worker to whom sub-paragraph (2) hereof applies who is employed in the circumstances that he is provided by the employer, subject in the case of (b) to the requisite supplies being available, with—

(a) such meals as are available during the time the worker is on duty and as are provided for the persons using the canteen; and

(b) a reasonable supply in good repair of clean overalls and (except in the case of a supervisor, manager, manageress, steward, stewardess or porter) of clean headwear for the use of the worker while at work.

(2) The minimum remuneration in Column 2 of paragraph 1 is payable to a worker employed in the circumstances that he is provided by the employer, subject in the case of (b) to the requisite supplies being available, with—

(a) full board and lodging for 7 days a week; and

(b) a reasonable supply in good repair of clean overalls and (except in the case of a supervisor, manager, manageress, steward, stewardess or porter) of clean headwear for the use of the worker while at work.

WORKERS NOT PROVIDED WITH MEALS, FULL BOARD, LODGING, OVERALLS OR HEADWEAR

7. The minimum remuneration for a worker who is not employed in the circumstances specified in paragraph 6(1) or 6(2) is:—

(1) In the case of a worker who is not provided by his employer with meals as specified in paragraph 6(1)(a) or full board and lodging, the remuneration specified in paragraph 1 (Column 1), 2, 3 or 5 for the corresponding description of worker in the same area INCREASED BY 17s. PER WEEK.

(2) In the case of a worker who is provided by his employer with full board or lodging (but not full board and lodging) the remuneration specified in paragraph 1 (Column 2), 2, 3 or 5 for the corresponding description of worker in the same area increased by the following amounts:—

(a) Where lodging is provided but not full board:—

    (i) Workers 17 years of age or over   ... AN INCREASE of 27s. 5d. per week of seven days or 3s. 11d. per day.

    (ii) Workers under 17 years of age   ... AN INCREASE of 19s. 3d. per week of seven days or 2s. 9d. per day.

(b) Where full board is provided but not lodging:—

    (i) Workers 17 years of age or over   ... AN INCREASE of 15s. 2d. per week of seven days or 2s. 2d. per day.

    (ii) Workers under 17 years of age...   ... AN INCREASE of 8s. 9d. per week of seven days or 1s. 3d. per day.

(3) In the case of any worker who is not provided by his employer with a reasonable supply in good repair of clean overalls and headwear as specified in paragraph 6(1)(b) or (2)(b) the remuneration specified in paragraph 1, 2, 3, 4 or 5 for the corresponding description of worker in the same area INCREASED BY 2s. 6d. PER WEEK.

GUARANTEED WEEKLY REMUNERATION AND OVERTIME RATES

FOR THE PERIOD UP TO AND INCLUDING 29TH JUNE 1970

HOURS ON WHICH REMUNERATION IS BASED

8.—(1) Up to and including 29th June 1970 the weekly remuneration specified in this Schedule except as provided in paragraph 7(2) relates to a week of 41 hours and, except as provided in paragraph 9, is subject to a proportionate reduction according as the number of hours worked is less than 41.

(2) In calculating the remuneration for the purposes of this Schedule recognised breaks for meal times shall be excluded.

GUARANTEED WEEKLY REMUNERATION FOR FULL-TIME WORKERS

9.—(1) Up to and including 29th June 1970, where in any week a full-time worker works for the employer for less than 41 hours he shall, subject to and in accordance with the provisions of this paragraph, be paid in respect of that week not less than the guaranteed weekly remuneration.

(2) The guaranteed weekly remuneration payable in respect of any week to a full-time worker

    (a) who normally works for the employer for less than 40 hours in the week, is the remuneration to which he would be entitled under this Schedule (calculated as in paragraph 8) for 40 hours' work;

    (b) who normally works for the employer for 40 hours or more in the week, is the remuneration to which he would be entitled under this Schedule for 41 hours' work;

    (c) who normally works for the employer for less than 41 hours in the week by reason only of the fact that he does not hold himself out as available for work for more than the number of hours he normally works in the week and who has so informed the employer in writing, is the remuneration (calculated as in paragraph 8) for the number of hours normally worked by the worker for the employer.

(3) Guaranteed weekly remuneration is not payable in respect of any week unless the worker is capable of and available for work (except as respects any time allowed to him as a holiday)

(a) in the case of a worker to whom sub-paragraph (2)(a) applies, for 40 hours in that week, including the hours normally worked by him;

(b) in the case of a worker to whom sub-paragraph (2)(b) applies, for 41 hours in that week, including the hours normally worked by him; and

(c) in the case of a worker to whom sub-paragraph (2)(c) applies, for the number of hours normally worked by him;

and is willing to perform such duties outside his normal occupation as may reasonably be required by the employer when work is not available for him in his normal occupation in the undertaking.

(4) If the employer is prevented from providing employment by reason of strikes or other circumstances outside his control and has given the worker not less than four days' notice of his inability to provide such employment and the notice has expired, the provisions in regard to the guaranteed payment shall not apply and the worker shall be entitled in that week to payment in respect of hours actually worked.

(5) In order to ascertain for the purposes of sub-paragraph (1) of this paragraph whether a full-time worker has worked in any week for less than 41 hours, any day or days allowed and taken as holidays by the worker under Part II of this Schedule shall be treated as a day or days on which the worker worked for the number of hours usually worked by him on that day of the week or those days of the week as the case may be.

(6) Where in any week any day or days have been allowed and taken as holidays by a worker under Part II of this Schedule the guaranteed weekly remuneration which that worker would be entitled to under the preceding sub-paragraphs of this paragraph shall be reduced by the amount of remuneration received or receivable by him in respect of the day or days of holiday aforesaid.

OVERTIME RATES

WORKERS OTHER THAN SHIFT AND SPLIT DUTY WORKERS

10.—(1) Up to and including 29th June 1970 and subject to the provisions of paragraphs 13 and 15, overtime rates shall be paid as follows:—

(a) to workers other than night workers, shift workers and split duty workers:—

For the first 2 hours worked in excess of 8 hours on any of five week-days in the week other than the weekly short day or in excess of 4 hours on the weekly short day	Time-and-a-quarter.
For all time worked thereafter on any of those days ...	Time-and-a-half.
For all time worked on Sunday	Double time.
For all time worked in excess of 41 hours in any week exclusive of any time in respect of which overtime rates are payable under the foregoing provisions of this sub-paragraph	Time-and-a-quarter.

The weekly short day shall be Saturday or any other week-day substituted therefor by agreement between an employer and a worker or his representative:

Provided that in the case of a worker who is customarily required to attend only on five days a week the following overtime rates shall apply:—

For the first 2 hours worked in excess of 9 hours on any week-day on which he is customarily required to attend	Time-and-a-quarter.
For all time worked thereafter on any of such days ...	Time-and-a-half.

For the first 2 hours worked on a sixth day (not including any time worked on Sunday) on which attendance is not customarily required ... ... Time-and-a-quarter.

For all time worked thereafter on that day (not including any time worked on Sunday) ... ... Time-and-a-half.

For all time worked on Sunday ... ... Double time.

For all time worked in excess of 41 hours in any week exclusive of any time in respect of which overtime rates are payable under the foregoing provisions of this proviso ... ... Time-and-a-quarter.

(b) to night workers other than shift workers and split duty workers:—

For the first 2 hours worked in excess of 9 hours on any day from Monday to Friday inclusive ... ... Time-and-a-quarter.

For all time worked thereafter on any of such days ... Time-and-a-half.

For the first 2 hours worked on Saturday ... ... Time-and-a-quarter.

For all time worked thereafter on Saturday ... ... Time-and-a-half.

For all time worked on Sunday ... ... Double time.

For all time worked in excess of 41 hours in any week exclusive of any time in respect of which overtime rates are payable under the foregoing provisions of (b) of this sub-paragraph ... ... Time-and-a-quarter.

(2) The whole of a worker's turn of duty shall be counted for the purpose of ascertaining the overtime rate payable and, where the turn extends beyond midnight, shall be regarded as having been worked on the day upon which it commences.

(3) Notwithstanding the provisions of sub-paragraphs (1) and (2) of this paragraph all time worked between midnight on Saturday and midnight on Sunday shall be paid at double time and all time worked on Monday which is part of a turn of duty which normally commences on Sunday shall be regarded as overtime and paid as follows:—

For such time as is required to complete 2 hours from the commencement of the turn of duty ... ... Time-and-a-quarter.

For the remainder of the time ... ... Time-and-a-half.

The time worked on Monday aforesaid shall not be included in calculating overtime on any turn of duty which commences on Monday.

SHIFT WORKERS

11.—(1) Up to and including 29th June 1970 and subject to the provisions of paragraph 15, overtime rates shall be paid to shift workers as follows:—

(a) to workers whose shift comprises six full turns of duty:—

For the first 2 hours worked in excess of 7½ hours on any of the six turns of duty ... ... Time-and-a-quarter.

For all time worked thereafter on such turns of duty ... Time-and-a-half.

For all time worked on a seventh turn of duty or on the normal rest day ... ... Double time.

For all time worked in excess of 41 hours in any week exclusive of any time in respect of which overtime rates are payable under the foregoing provisions of this sub-paragraph ... ... Time-and-a-quarter.

(b) to workers whose shift comprises five full turns and one short turn of duty:—

For the first 2 hours worked in excess of 8 hours on any of the five full turns of duty or in excess of 4 hours on the one short turn of duty ... ... Time-and-a-quarter.

For all time worked thereafter on any such turns of duty	Time-and-a-half.
For all time worked on a seventh turn of duty or on the normal rest day	Double time.
For all time worked in excess of 41 hours in any week exclusive of any time in respect of which overtime rates are payable under the foregoing provisions of (*b*) of this sub-paragraph	Time-and-a-quarter.

(*c*) to workers whose shift comprises five turns of duty:—

For the first 2 hours worked in excess of 9 hours on any turn of duty	Time-and-a-quarter.
For all time worked thereafter on any turn of duty ...	Time-and-a-half.
For all time worked on the first day of the week on which attendance is not normally required	Time-and-a-quarter.
For all time worked on the second day of the week on which attendance is not normally required	Double time.
For all time worked in excess of 41 hours in any week exclusive of any time in respect of which overtime rates are payable under the foregoing provisions of (*c*) of this sub-paragraph	Time-and-a-quarter.

(2) A shift worker shall in addition to the above be paid an amount calculated at the rate of 1d. per hour for all overtime worked in respect of which an overtime rate is payable as above.

(3) For the purpose of calculating the time worked in any week a shift worker who is allowed and has taken a holiday in any week under Part II of this Schedule shall be treated as having worked on any such day of holiday the number of hours usually worked by him on the turn of duty which he would otherwise have worked if the holiday had not been allowed.

SPLIT DUTY WORKERS

12.—(1) Up to and including 29th June 1970 and subject to the provisions of paragraph 15, overtime rates shall be paid to split duty workers as follows:—

For the first 4 hours worked in excess of 41 hours in any week on days other than the normal rest day ...	Time-and-a-quarter.
For all time worked thereafter on days other than the normal rest day	Time-and-a-half.
For all time worked on a normal rest day	Double time.

(2) A split duty worker shall in addition to the above be paid an amount calculated at the rate of 2d. per hour for all overtime worked in respect of which an overtime rate is payable as above.

(3) For the purpose of calculating the time worked in any week a split duty worker who is allowed and has taken a holiday in any week under Part II of this Schedule shall be treated as having worked on any such day of holiday the number of hours usually worked by him on the turn of duty which he would otherwise have worked if the holiday had not been allowed.

GUARANTEED WEEKLY REMUNERATION AND OVERTIME RATES FOR THE PERIOD ON AND AFTER 30TH JUNE 1970

HOURS ON WHICH REMUNERATION IS BASED

8A.—(1) On and after 30th June 1970 the weekly remuneration specified in this Schedule except as provided in paragraph 7(2) relates to a week of 40 hours and, except as provided in paragraph 9A, is subject to a proportionate reduction according as the number of hours worked is less than 40.

(2) In calculating the remuneration for the purposes of this Schedule recognised breaks for meal times shall be excluded.

GUARANTEED WEEKLY REMUNERATION FOR FULL-TIME WORKERS

9A.—(1) On and after 30th June 1970, where in any week a full-time worker works for the employer for less than 40 hours he shall, subject to and in accordance with the provisions of this paragraph, be paid in respect of that week not less than the guaranteed weekly remuneration.

(2) The guaranteed weekly remuneration payable in respect of any week to a full-time worker

    (a) who normally works for the employer for less than 40 hours in the week, is the remuneration to which he would be entitled under this Schedule (calculated as in paragraph 8A) for 40 hours' work;

    (b) who normally works for the employer for less than 40 hours in the week by reason only of the fact that he does not hold himself out as available for work for more than the number of hours he normally works in the week and who has so informed the employer in writing, is the remuneration (calculated as in paragraph 8A) for the number of hours normally worked by the worker for the employer.

(3) Guaranteed weekly remuneration is not payable in respect of any week unless the worker is capable of and available for work (except as respects any time allowed to him as a holiday)

    (a) in the case of a worker to whom sub-paragraph (2)(a) applies, for 40 hours in that week, including the hours normally worked by him; and

    (b) in the case of a worker to whom sub-paragraph (2)(b) applies, for the number of hours normally worked by him;

and is willing to perform such duties outside his normal occupation as may reasonably be required by the employer when work is not available for him in his normal occupation in the undertaking.

(4) If the employer is prevented from providing employment by reason of strikes or other circumstances outside his control and has given the worker not less than four days' notice of his inability to provide such employment and the notice has expired, the provisions in regard to the guaranteed payment shall not apply and the worker shall be entitled in that week to payment in respect of hours actually worked.

(5) In order to ascertain for the purposes of sub-paragraph (1) of this paragraph whether a full-time worker has worked in any week for less than 40 hours, any day or days allowed and taken as holidays by the worker under Part II of this Schedule shall be treated as a day or days on which the worker worked for the number of hours usually worked by him on that day of the week or those days of the week as the case may be.

(6) Where in any week any day or days have been allowed and taken as holidays by a worker under Part II of this Schedule the guaranteed weekly remuneration which that worker would be entitled to under the preceding sub-paragraphs of this paragraph shall be reduced by the amount of remuneration received or receivable by him in respect of the day or days of holiday aforesaid.

OVERTIME RATES

Workers other than Shift and Split Duty Workers

10A.—(1) On and after 30th June 1970 and subject to the provisions of paragraphs 13 and 15, overtime rates shall be paid as follows:—

    (a) to workers other than night workers, shift workers and split duty workers:—
For the first 2 hours worked in excess of 7½ hours on any of five week-days in the week other than the weekly short day or in excess of 4 hours on the weekly short day   ...   .   Time-and-a-quarter.

For all time worked thereafter on any of those days ...	Time-and-a-half.
For all time worked on Sunday	Double time.
For all time worked in excess of 40 hours in any week exclusive of any time in respect of which overtime rates are payable under the foregoing provisions of this sub-paragraph	Time-and-a-quarter.

The weekly short day shall be Saturday or any other week-day substituted therefor by agreement between an employer and a worker or his representative:

Provided that in the case of a worker who is customarily required to attend only on five days a week the following overtime rates shall apply:—

For the first 2 hours worked in excess of 8 hours on any week-day on which he is customarily required to attend	Time-and-a-quarter.
For all time worked thereafter on any of such days ...	Time-and-a-half.
For the first 2 hours worked on a sixth day (not including any time worked on Sunday) on which attendance is not customarily required	Time-and-a-quarter.
For all time worked thereafter on that day (not including any time worked on Sunday)	Time-and-a-half.
For all time worked on Sunday	Double time.
For all time worked in excess of 40 hours in any week exclusive of any time in respect of which overtime rates are payable under the foregoing provisions of this proviso	Time-and-a-quarter.

(b) to night workers other than shift workers and split duty workers:—

For the first 2 hours worked in excess of 8 hours on any day from Monday to Friday inclusive	Time-and-a-quarter.
For all time worked thereafter on any of such days ...	Time-and-a-half.
For the first 2 hours worked on Saturday	Time-and-a-quarter.
For all time worked thereafter on Saturday	Time-and-a-half.
For all time worked on Sunday	Double time.
For all time worked in excess of 40 hours in any week exclusive of any time in respect of which overtime rates are payable under the foregoing provisions of (b) of this sub-paragraph	Time-and-a-quarter.

(2) The whole of a worker's turn of duty shall be counted for the purpose of ascertaining the overtime rate payable and, where the turn extends beyond midnight, shall be regarded as having been worked on the day upon which it commences.

(3) Notwithstanding the provisions of sub-paragraphs (1) and (2) of this paragraph all time worked between midnight on Saturday and midnight on Sunday shall be paid at double time and all time worked on Monday which is part of a turn of duty which normally commences on Sunday shall be regarded as overtime and paid as follows:—

For such time as is required to complete 2 hours from the commencement of the turn of duty	Time-and-a-quarter.
For the remainder of the time	Time-and-a-half.

The time worked on Monday aforesaid shall not be included in calculating overtime on any turn of duty which commences on Monday.

Shift Workers

11A.—(1) On and after 30th June 1970 and subject to the provisions of paragraph 15, overtime rates shall be paid to shift workers as follows:—

(a) to workers whose shift comprises six full turns of duty:—

For the first 2 hours worked in excess of 7 hours on any of the six turns of duty	Time-and-a-quarter.
For all time worked thereafter on such turns of duty	Time-and-a-half.
For all time worked on a seventh turn of duty or on the normal rest day	Double time.
For all time worked in excess of 40 hours in any week exclusive of any time in respect of which overtime rates are payable under the foregoing provisions of this sub-paragraph	Time-and-a-quarter.

(b) to workers whose shift comprises five full turns and one short turn of duty:—

For the first 2 hours worked in excess of 7½ hours on any of the five full turns of duty or in excess of 4 hours on the one short turn of duty	Time and-a-quarter.
For all time worked thereafter on any such turns of duty	Time-and-a-half.
For all time worked on a seventh turn of duty or on the normal rest day	Double time.
For all time worked in excess of 40 hours in any week exclusive of any time in respect of which overtime rates are payable under the foregoing provisions of (b) of this sub-paragraph	Time-and-a-quarter.

(c) to workers whose shift comprises five turns of duty:—

For the first 2 hours worked in excess of 8 hours on any turn of duty	Time-and-a-quarter.
For all time worked thereafter on any turn of duty ...	Time-and-a-half.
For all time worked on the first day of the week on which attendance is not normally required	Time-and-a-quarter.
For all time worked on the second day of the week on which attendance is not normally required	Double time.
For all time worked in excess of 40 hours in any week exclusive of any time in respect of which overtime rates are payable under the foregoing provisions of (c) of this sub-paragraph	Time-and-a-quarter.

(2) A shift worker shall in addition to the above be paid an amount calculated at the rate of 1d. per hour for all overtime worked in respect of which an overtime rate is payable as above.

(3) For the purpose of calculating the time worked in any week a shift worker who is allowed and has taken a holiday in any week under Part II of this Schedule shall be treated as having worked on any such day of holiday the number of hours usually worked by him on the turn of duty which he would otherwise have worked if the holiday had not been allowed.

Split Duty Workers

12A.—(1) On and after 30th June 1970 and subject to the provisions of paragraph 15, overtime rates shall be paid to split duty workers as follows:—

For the first 4 hours worked in excess of 40 hours in any week on days other than the normal rest day ...	Time-and-a-quarter.
For all time worked thereafter on days other than the normal rest day	Time-and-a-half.
For all time worked on a normal rest day	Double time.

(2) A split duty worker shall in addition to the above be paid an amount calculated at the rate of 2d. per hour for all overtime worked in respect of which an overtime rate is payable as above.

(3) For the purpose of calculating the time worked in any week a split duty worker who is allowed and has taken a holiday in any week under Part II of this Schedule shall be treated as having worked on any such day of holiday the number of hours usually worked by him on the turn of duty which he would otherwise have worked if the holiday had not been allowed.

JEWISH UNDERTAKINGS

13. Where it is, or becomes, the established practice in a Jewish undertaking for the employer to require attendance on Sunday instead of Saturday, the provisions of paragraph 10 or 10A, as the case may be, shall apply in like manner as if in such provisions Sunday were treated as a week-day and as if:—

(1) in sub-paragraph (1) thereof the word "Sunday" were substituted for "Saturday" and the word "Saturday" for "Sunday"; and

(2) in sub-paragraph (3) thereof the word "Friday" were substituted for "Saturday", the word "Saturday" for "Sunday" and the word "Sunday" for "Monday".

WORK ON CUSTOMARY HOLIDAYS

14. Notwithstanding the foregoing provisions of this Schedule where a worker is required to work—

(1) on any day of customary holiday for which he has qualified under Part II of this Schedule; or

(2) a turn of duty which commences on the day preceding any day of customary holiday and extends beyond midnight or a turn of duty which commences on the day of customary holiday and extends into the following day,
he shall, in addition to the minimum remuneration appropriate to him under the foregoing provisions, be paid for all time so worked between midnight and midnight on the day of customary holiday, one-half of the minimum remuneration which would be appropriate to the corresponding description of worker in the same area employed in the circumstances specified in sub-paragraph (1) of paragraph 6.

SPECIAL PROVISIONS RELATING TO WORKERS PROVIDED WITH FULL BOARD AND LODGING

15.—(1) The provisions of this paragraph apply in the case of a worker who is provided by his employer with full board and lodging.

(2) Where a worker to whom this paragraph applies works on a seventh turn of duty or on a normal rest day pursuant to an agreement in writing with his employer that the employer will allow the worker an equivalent time off within a period of one month in lieu of time so worked, the worker shall for the purposes of the provisions of this Part of this Schedule be treated as though during such turn of duty or on that day as the case may be he had performed no work to which the Schedule applies.

(3) Where a worker to whom this paragraph applies is allowed time off pursuant to an agreement as is specified in sub-paragraph (2) of this paragraph he shall be treated for the purposes of the provisions of this Part of this Schedule as though in respect of that time he had been employed by the employer in his usual occupation.

PART II

HOLIDAYS AND HOLIDAY REMUNERATION
CUSTOMARY HOLIDAYS

16. An employer shall (except as provided in paragraph 17) allow to every worker to whom this Schedule applies, who at the date of the holiday has been in his employment for not less than six days and (unless excused by the employer or absent by reason of proved sickness) has worked for the employer the number of hours ordinarily worked by him on the last working day on which work was available to him preceding a holiday, a holiday on each of the following days:—

2r

(1) In England and Wales—Christmas Day (or, if Christmas Day falls on a Sunday, such week-day as may be prescribed by national proclamation or the next following Tuesday), Boxing Day, Good Friday, Easter Monday, Whit Monday (or where another day is substituted therefor by national proclamation, that day), August Bank Holiday and all nationally proclaimed holidays;

(2) In Scotland—

(a) New Year's Day (or the following day if New Year's Day falls on a Sunday), the local Spring holiday, the local Autumn holiday, and all nationally proclaimed holidays;

(b) three other week-days in the course of a calendar year, to be fixed by the employer and notified to the worker not less than three weeks before the holiday, or any other day or days falling within the same calendar year which may be substituted for such day or days by agreement between the employer and the worker or his representative:

Provided that where, in any establishment it is not the custom or practice to observe such days as are specified in sub-paragraph (1) or (2)(a) of this paragraph as holidays, other days not fewer in number may, by agreement between the employer and the worker or his representative, be substituted for the above-mentioned days.

17. A worker may be required to work on any day specified in paragraph 16 above, or on any day substituted therefor under the proviso to that paragraph, and if so required he shall be allowed a day of holiday in lieu thereof within the period of eight weeks from the day on which he is so required to work unless it is agreed in writing between the employer and the worker or his representative that the day in lieu be granted at another date not later than the last day of February next following:

Provided that, in the case of a worker who is ordinarily employed on turns of duty extending beyond midnight, another day of holiday shall not be allowed in lieu of a day of customary holiday if the worker having worked on one turn of duty which finishes or commences on the customary holiday has not been required to work on another turn of duty which he would otherwise be required to work and which would commence or finish on the customary holiday.

REMUNERATION FOR CUSTOMARY HOLIDAYS

18.—(1) Subject to the provisions of sub-paragraph (2) of this paragraph, for each day allowed as a holiday under paragraphs 16 and 17, the worker shall be paid the appropriate statutory minimum remuneration to which he would have been entitled had the day not been a day of holiday and he had worked the number of hours usually worked by him on that day of the week, and

(a) in the case of a worker other than a worker to whom the provisions of (b) of this sub-paragraph apply, AN ADDITION OF 2s. 10d. for each day of holiday, or

(b) in the case of a worker who is employed in the circumstances that he is provided by his employer with full board and lodging or either full board or lodging, AN ADDITION OF—

(i) 6s. 1d. if the worker is 17 years of age or over, or

(ii) 4s. 0d. if the worker is under 17 years of age

for each day of holiday except where board and lodging is available to the worker on that day.

(2) Notwithstanding the provisions of the foregoing sub-paragraph, payment of remuneration in respect of the said holiday is subject to the condition that the worker (unless excused by the employer or absent by reason of proved sickness) worked for the employer the number of hours ordinarily worked by him on the first working day on which work was available to him following the holiday.

ANNUAL HOLIDAY

19.—(1) Subject to the provisions of paragraphs 22 and 23, in addition to the customary holidays provided in paragraphs 16 and 17, an employer shall, between 1st March 1970 and 31st October 1970, and in each succeeding year between 1st March and 31st October, allow a holiday (hereinafter referred to as an "annual holiday") to every worker to whom this Schedule applies who was employed or engaged to be employed by him during the 12 months immediately preceding the commencement of the holiday season (hereinafter referred to as the "qualifying period") for any of the periods of employment set out in the appropriate column of the table below, and the duration of the annual holiday shall, in the case of each such worker, be related to that period as follows:—

Where the worker's normal working week is:—

Period of Employment	Six days		Five days		Four days or less	
	Duration of annual holiday in 12 months commencing 1st March		Duration of annual holiday in 12 months commencing 1st March		Duration of annual holiday in 12 months commencing 1st March	
	1970	1971 and thereafter	1970	1971 and thereafter	1970	1971 and thereafter
	Days	Days	Days	Days	Days	Days
At least 4 weeks	1	1	1	1	—	—
,, 8 ,,	2	2	2	2	1	1
,, 12 ,,	3	3	3	3	2	2
,, 14 ,,	4	4	3	3	2	2
,, 16 ,,	5	5	4	4	3	3
,, 18 ,,	6	6	4	5	3	3
,, 20 ,,	6	7	5	5	4	4
,, 22 ,,	7	8	5	6	4	4
,, 24 ,,	8	8	6	7	5	5
,, 26 ,,	8	9	6	7	6	6
,, 28 ,,	9	10	7	8	7	7
,, 30 ,,	10	11	8	9	7	7
,, 32 ,,	10	12	8	9	8	8
,, 34 ,,	11	13	9	10	8	8
,, 36 ,,	12	14	10	11	9	9
,, 38 ,,	12	15	10	11	9	9
,, 40 ,,	13	16	11	12	10	10
,, 42 ,,	14	17	12	13	10	10
,, 44 ,,	14	18	12	13	11	11
,, 46 ,,	15	17	13	14	11	11
,, 48 ,,	16	18	14	15	12	12

(2) Notwithstanding the provisions of the last foregoing sub-paragraph—

(*a*) the number of days of annual holiday which an employer is required to allow to a worker in respect of a period of employment during the 12 months immediately preceding 1st March 1970 shall not exceed in the aggregate—

in the case of a worker with a normal working week of five days or more, twice the number of days constituting the worker's normal working week, plus four days; and

in the case of a worker with a normal working week of less than five days, three times the number of days constituting the worker's normal working week; and

(*b*) the number of days of annual holiday which an employer is required to allow to a worker in respect of a period of employment during the 12 months immediately preceding 1st March 1971 and during the 12 months immediately preceding 1st March in any succeeding year shall not exceed in the aggregate three times the number of days constituting the worker's normal working week;

(3) In this Schedule the expression "holiday season" means in relation to the year 1970 the period commencing on 1st March 1970, and ending on 31st October 1970, and in each succeeding year, the period commencing on 1st March and ending on 31st October of the same year.

20. For the purpose of calculating any period of employment referred to in paragraph 19, 23 or 27 qualifying the worker for an annual holiday or for any accrued holiday remuneration, a worker shall be treated as having been employed:—

(1) For a week in respect of any week in which he has performed some work for the employer which would entitle him to statutory minimum remuneration.

(2) When absent from work in any of the following circumstances:—

(*a*) on customary holidays and annual holidays as provided in this Part of this Schedule or in the Schedule to Order I.S.C. (43);

(*b*) during proved sickness or accident up to and not exceeding a maximum of eight weeks in the aggregate during any such period as aforesaid;

(*c*) by leave of the employer.

21. An annual holiday shall be allowed on consecutive days and days of holiday shall be treated as consecutive notwithstanding that a Sunday (or in the case of a shift worker or split duty worker the normal day of rest), or a holiday allowed under the provisions of paragraph 16 or 17 intervenes:

Provided that—

(*a*) Where the number of days of annual holiday for which a worker has qualified exceeds the number of days constituting his normal working week, but does not exceed twice that number, the holiday may be allowed in two periods of consecutive working days; so, however, that when a holiday is so allowed, one of the periods shall consist of a number of such days not less than the number of days constituting the worker's normal working week.

(*b*) Where the number of days of annual holiday for which a worker has qualified exceeds twice the number of days constituting his normal working week the holiday may be allowed as follows:—

(i) as to the period comprising twice the number of days constituting the worker's normal working week, in accordance with sub-paragraph (*a*) of this paragraph; and

(ii) as to the additional days, on working days to be fixed by agreement between the employer and the worker or his representative, either during the holiday season or before the beginning of the next following holiday season.

22.—(1) Notwithstanding the provisions of paragraph 19, days of annual holiday may be allowed after the end of the holiday season and before the commencement of the next following holiday season if it is agreed before the end of the holiday season in writing between the employer and the worker or his representative.

(2) Where by agreement in writing between the employer and the worker or his representative at any time during the qualifying period immediately preceding the commencement of the holiday season in any year, the employer allows the worker, in respect of employment within that qualifying period, any day or days of holiday (not being days of customary holiday) and pays him holiday remuneration in respect thereof calculated in accordance with the provisions of paragraph 25, then—

(a) the annual holiday to be allowed in accordance with paragraph 19 in the holiday season in that year shall be reduced by the day or days of holiday so allowed prior to the commencement of that holiday season; and

(b) for the purpose of calculating accrued holiday remuneration under paragraph 27 any day or days of holiday deducted in accordance with (a) hereof shall be treated as if they had been allowed as a day or days of annual holiday.

23. Notwithstanding the provisions of paragraph 19, an employer may make application to the Wages Council to vary the holiday season to meet special circumstances, either by providing for its commencement earlier than 1st March or extending its duration beyond 31st October in any year, provided that any such application is made, in the case of the commencement of the holiday season on an earlier date, not less than six weeks before the date on which it is desired that the holiday season shall commence, and in the case of the extension of the holiday season, before 1st August.

Where the holiday season has been varied under this provision so as to commence earlier than 1st March, the qualifying period in respect of the worker or workers concerned shall be the 12 months immediately preceding the commencement of the holiday season as varied.

24. An employer shall give to a worker reasonable notice of the commencing date or dates and duration of his annual holiday and such notice may be given individually to a worker or by the posting of a notice in the place where the worker is employed.

REMUNERATION FOR ANNUAL HOLIDAY

25.—(1) Subject to the provisions of paragraph 26, a worker qualified to be allowed an annual holiday under this Schedule shall be paid by his employer in respect thereof, on the last pay day preceding such annual holiday, one day's holiday pay in respect of each day thereof.

(2) Where under the provisions of this Schedule an annual holiday is taken in more than one period the holiday remuneration shall be apportioned accordingly.

26. Where in accordance with the provisions of paragraph 27 of this Schedule, or of Order I.S.C. (43), accrued holiday remuneration has been paid by the employer to the worker in respect of any period of employment in the 12 months immediately preceding the holiday season within which an annual holiday is allowed by the employer to the worker in accordance with the provisions of this Schedule, the amount of holiday remuneration payable by the employer in respect of the said annual holiday under the provisions of paragraph 25 shall be reduced by the amount of the said accrued holiday remuneration.

ACCRUED HOLIDAY REMUNERATION PAYABLE ON TERMINATION OF EMPLOYMENT

27. Subject to the provisions of this paragraph, where a worker ceases to be employed by an employer after the provisions of this Schedule become effective, the employer shall, immediately on the termination of the employment, pay to the worker as accrued holiday remuneration:—

(1) in respect of employment in the 12 months up to the commencing date of the current holiday season, a sum equal to the holiday remuneration for any days of annual holiday for which he has qualified, except days of annual holiday which he has been allowed or has become entitled to be allowed before leaving the employment; and

(2) in respect of any employment since the commencing date of the current holiday season, or if no holiday season is then current, the commencing date of the last holiday season, a sum equal to the holiday remuneration which would have been payable to him if he could have been allowed an annual holiday in respect of that employment at the time of leaving it:

Provided that—

(a) the amount of the accrued holiday remuneration payable to a worker who leaves his employment without the consent of his employer before giving one week's notice of termination of employment or before one week has elapsed from the time of giving such notice, shall be the amount payable under the foregoing provisions of this Schedule less an amount equal to the holiday remuneration which would have been payable to him if at the termination of his employment he had been allowed an annual holiday of the number of days constituting his normal working week;

(b) accrued holiday remuneration shall not be payable to a worker if he is dismissed on the grounds of dishonesty and is so informed by his employer at the time of dismissal;

(c) where, during the period or periods in respect of which the said accrued holiday remuneration is payable, the worker has been allowed any day or days of holiday for which he had not qualified under the provisions of this Schedule or of Order I.S.C. (43), not being days of holiday referred to in paragraph 22(2) of this Schedule, any accrued holiday remuneration payable as aforesaid shall be reduced by the amount of any sum paid by the employer to the worker in respect of such day or days of holiday.

PART III

DEFINITIONS

28. For the purposes of paragraphs 8 to 12 of this Schedule the expressions "time-and-a-quarter", "time-and-a-half" and "double time" mean in the case of any worker whether employed as a day worker, a night worker, a shift worker or a split duty worker, respectively, one and a quarter times, one and a half times and twice the hourly rate obtained by dividing by 41 the minimum weekly remuneration specified in paragraph 1 for the corresponding description of worker employed in the same area and in the circumstances specified in sub-paragraph (1) of paragraph 6.

28A. For the purposes of paragraphs 8A to 12A of this Schedule the expressions "time-and-a-quarter", "time-and-a-half" and "double time" mean in the case of any worker whether employed as a day worker, a night worker, a shift worker or a split duty worker, respectively, one and a quarter times, one and a half times and twice the hourly rate obtained by dividing by 40 the minimum weekly remuneration specified in paragraph 1 for the corresponding description of worker employed in the same area and in the circumstances specified in sub-paragraph (1) of paragraph 6.

29. In this Schedule the following expressions have the meanings hereby respectively assigned to them, that is to say:—

"APPRENTICE COOK" is a male worker under the age of 21 years who is employed during the whole of his time under a written contract of apprenticeship which has been duly executed and which contains the provisions set out in (1) and (2) below or provisions substantially to the same effect and no provisions contrary thereto:—

(1) the worker of his own free will and with the consent of his guardian binds himself to serve the employer as his apprentice for a term of not less than five years;

(2) the employer will employ the worker as his apprentice during the said term and to the best of his power, skill and knowledge, instruct the worker or cause him to be instructed by a Head Cook in the underlying principles of cookery including the preparation, cooking and service of fish, meat, poultry, game, vegetables, eggs, pastry, cakes and sauces:

Provided that the minimum period of five years' apprenticeship under sub-paragraph (1) above shall be reduced—

(a) where the worker has after attaining the age of 15 years received a course of instruction in cookery in a technical class at any university, college, school or similar establishment, by a period equal to the duration of such course of instruction subject to a maximum reduction of two years;

(b) where the worker has after attaining the age of 16 years continued to receive at a school full time general education which does not include a course of instruction in cookery in a technical class, by a period equal to the duration of such full time general education received after he attained the age of 16 years subject to a maximum reduction of one year;

but so that the total reduction in the minimum period of any worker's apprenticeship shall not be more than two years.

"ASSISTANT COOK" is a male worker of 21 years of age or over, a female worker of 18 years of age or over or a worker who has completed a period of not less than two years' training as a trainee cook (as defined below), wholly or mainly engaged in assisting in the preparing and cooking of food under the instructions of a cook or a canteen supervisor, manager, manageress, steward or stewardess who is required to perform the duties of a cook.

"CANTEEN ATTENDANT" is a female worker of 18 years of age or over employed as a waitress, counter assistant, service worker, washer-up, cleaner, tea girl, or kitchen assistant whose duties may include vegetable preparation.

"CANTEEN SUPERVISOR", "MANAGER OR MANAGERESS", "STEWARD OR STEWARDESS" is a person of one of the undermentioned grades who is in direct control of the staff of a canteen and immediately responsible for its operation including such a person required to perform the whole or part of the duties of a cook:—

Grade	Staff (exclusive of the supervisor, manager or manageress, steward or stewardess) normally employed in the canteen under his or her direct control
X (Female only)	Not less than 2 and not more than 4 persons
A	„ „ „ 5 „ „ „ „ 10 „
B	„ „ „ 11 „ „ „ „ 20 „
C	„ „ „ 21 „ „ „ „ 30 „
D	„ „ „ 31 „ „ „ „ 40 „

In computing the number of persons normally employed on the staff of the canteen both full-time workers and workers other than full-time workers shall be included except that in the case of workers other than full-time workers the number to be counted shall be the number disregarding fractions obtained by dividing by 36 the aggregate of the hours usually worked in the week by all such workers.

"CASHIER" is a female worker of 18 years of age or over wholly or mainly engaged in taking cash or giving change.

"COOK" is a worker of 21 years of age or over, or a worker who has completed a period of not less than four years' training as a trainee cook (as defined below), wholly or mainly engaged in the preparing and cooking of food requiring the mixing of two or more ingredients and/or the preparing and the cooking of meat, poultry or game.

"HEAD COOK" is a cook experienced in all departments of the kitchen who is capable of training inexperienced staff and has not less than three cooks or assistant cooks under his or her control and whose duties mainly consist in cooking, planning menus, ordering supplies and who may be required to control kitchen staff.

"TRAINEE COOK" *is a worker who is employed during the whole of his time under a written agreement approved by the Hotel and Catering Industry Training Board and which contains the provisions set out in (a) and (b) below or provisions substantially to the same effect and no provisions contrary thereto:—*

(a) *the worker of his own free will and with the consent of his guardian binds himself to serve the employer, or any subsequent employer to whom the agreement is transferred with the approval of the Hotel and Catering Industry Training Board, as his trainee for a period of not less than two years in the case of a two-year trainee cook and not less than four years in the case of a four-year trainee cook;*

(b) *the employer will employ the worker as his trainee during the said term and teach and instruct him to the best of his knowledge and ability or cause him to be taught the business and trade of a cook and all things relating thereto, according to the agreed standard decided upon by the Hotel and Catering Industry Training Board:*

Provided that in the case of a four-year trainee—

(i) *the period under sub-paragraph (a) above shall be reduced where the worker has after attaining the age of 15 years received a course of instruction in cookery approved by the Hotel and Catering Industry Training Board in a technical class at any university, college, school or similar establishment by a period equal to the duration of such a course of instruction subject to a maximum reduction of two years; and*

(ii) *any such period shall be treated as a period of training for the purpose of determining the "year of training" in Sections A and B of paragraph 1 of this Schedule.*

30. In this Schedule the following expressions have the meanings hereby respectively assigned to them, that is to say:—

"AREAS"—

"LONDON AREA" means the Metropolitan Police District, as defined in the London Government Act 1963(a), the City of London, the Inner Temple and the Middle Temple.

"OTHER AREAS" means all areas other than the London area.

"FULL-TIME WORKER" means a worker whose usual hours of employment amount to 36 hours or more per week.

"FULL BOARD" means four meals per day which shall be of good and sufficient quality and quantity and shall consist of dinner and three other meals.

"LODGING" means clean and adequate accommodation and facilities for eating, sleeping, washing and leisure.

"NIGHT WORKER" is a worker whose usual turn of duty includes not less than four hours' work between 8.30 p.m. on one day and 6.30 a.m. on the next day and who is not a shift worker or a split duty worker.

"NORMAL WORKING WEEK" means the number of days on which it has been usual for the worker to work in a week in the employment of the employer during the 12 months immediately preceding the commencement of the holiday season or, where accrued holiday remuneration is payable under paragraph 27 on the termination of the employment, during the 12 months immediately preceding the date of the termination of the employment.

"ONE DAY'S HOLIDAY PAY" means the appropriate proportion of the remuneration which the worker would be entitled to receive from his employer at the date of the annual holiday (or, where the holiday is allowed in more than one period, at the date of the first period) or at the date of termination of the employment as the case may be for one week's work if working his normal working week and the number of daily hours usually worked by him (exclusive of overtime) and if paid at the appropriate rate of statutory minimum remuneration for work for which

(a) 1963 c. 33.

statutory minimum remuneration is payable and at the same rate for any work for the same employer for which such remuneration is not payable with the ADDITION of the following amounts—

(1) in the case of a worker, other than a worker to whom the provisions of (2) apply, an addition of 2s. 10d.;

(2) in the case of a worker who is employed in the circumstances that he is provided by his employer with full board and lodging or either full board or lodging—

(a) 6s. 1d. if the worker is 17 years of age or over; or

(b) 4s. 0d. if the worker is under 17 years of age.

In this definition "appropriate proportion" means—

where the worker's normal working week is six days ... ... one-sixth

where the worker's normal working week is five days ... ... one-fifth

where the worker's normal working week is four days or less ... one-quarter.

"SHIFT WORKER" means a worker employed on a shift system in accordance with which—

(1) a 24-hour period is divided into three turns of duty; or

(2) there is no night turn of duty and the remainder of the day is divided into two or more turns of duty;

and the worker is employed for not less than five out of the seven days in any week on the same turn and changes turns periodically in accordance with a pre-arranged plan.

"SPLIT DUTY WORKER" means a worker who is employed in the circumstances that he is provided by the employer with full board and lodging for seven days in any week and whose normal hours of daily duty are spread over a period exceeding 10 hours inclusive of meal times but not exceeding 14 hours inclusive of meal times.

"STATUTORY MINIMUM REMUNERATION" means minimum remuneration (other than holiday remuneration) which has been fixed by a wages regulation order made by the Secretary of State to give effect to proposals submitted to her by the Wages Council; and

"APPROPRIATE STATUTORY MINIMUM REMUNERATION" means the statutory minimum remuneration payable to the worker at the date of the holiday or the date when the employment ceases, as the case may be, but excluding any part of such remuneration payable thereunder solely by reason of the fact that meals, board, lodging, or overalls and headwear are not provided by the employer.

"WEEK" means "pay week".

PART IV

GENERAL

WORKERS TO WHOM THE SCHEDULE APPLIES

31. The provisions of this Schedule apply to the following workers, that is to say:—
Workers employed in Great Britain by the person or body of persons carrying on an industrial or staff canteen undertaking who are so employed in the said undertaking, and who are engaged on any of the following work, that is to say:—

(a) the preparation of food or drink;

(b) the service of food or drink;

(c) work incidental to such preparation or service;

(d) any work performed on or about premises where food or drink is prepared or served, including work in connection with any service or amenity provided at such premises;

(e) transport work;

(f) work performed at any office, depot, store or similar place;

but excuding transport workers and workers at any office, depot, store or similar place who are employed by the person or body of persons carrying on the undertaking mainly on work not in connection with the undertaking.

DEFINITION OF INDUSTRIAL OR STAFF CANTEEN UNDERTAKING

An industrial or staff canteen undertaking consists of any undertaking or any part of an undertaking which is wholly or mainly engaged in supplying food or drink for immediate consumption and activities incidental or ancillary thereto, and which is carried on for the use of employed persons in connection with their employment:—

(a) by their employer or employers; or

(b) by the employed persons themselves; or

(c) by the employed persons and their employer or employers jointly; or

(d) by any other person or body of persons in pursuance of an arrangement or arrangements with the employer or employers of the employed persons, or with the employed persons themselves, or with the employed persons and their employer or employers jointly; or

(e) by a dock authority or by any person or body of persons under an arrangement with a dock authority;

but excluding any such undertaking carried on:—

(1) directly by the Crown; or

(2) by an employer or by workers and their employer jointly, wholly or mainly for the use of workers employed by the employer:—

(i) in the business of supplying food or drink for immediate consumption by the general public; or

(ii) at or in connection with a shop, if the shop includes a restaurant, café or similar place where meals are served to the general public; or

(iii) at or in connection with an hotel, boarding house, hostel or other similar establishment; or

(iv) at or in connection with any hospital, nursing home or other similar establishment; or

(v) at or in connection with any university, college, school or other similar establishment.

For the purpose of this definition "dock authority" means any person or body of persons whether incorporated or not who are authorised to construct or are owners or lessees of any dock authorised by or under any Act, and "dock" includes a wharf or quay.

32. Nothing in this Schedule shall be construed as authorising the making of any deduction or the giving of any remuneration in any manner which is illegal by virtue of the Truck Acts 1831 to 1940(a) or of any other enactment.

33. *The revocation by this order of Order I.S.C. (43) and the coming into effect of the provisions of this Schedule shall not affect the right of a worker to be allowed, and to receive holiday remuneration for, any such days af annual holiday which his employer was required to allow him before 28th February 1970 under the provisions of paragraph 21(b)(ii) of the Schedule to Order I.S.C.(43).*

(a) 1831 c. 37; 1887 c. 46; 1896 c. 44; 1940 c. 38.

EXPLANATORY NOTE

(*This Note is not part of the Order.*)

This Order, which has effect from 19th January 1970, sets out the statutory minimum remuneration payable and the holidays to be allowed to workers in substitution for the statutory minimum remuneration and holidays set out in the Wages Regulation (Industrial and Staff Canteen) Order 1969 (Order I.S.C. (43)), which Order is revoked.

New provisions are printed in italics.

STATUTORY INSTRUMENTS

1969 No. 1728

CUSTOMS AND EXCISE

The Hydrocarbon Oil Duties (Rebates and Reliefs) (Amendment) Regulations 1969

Made - - -	*4th December* 1969
Laid before Parliament	11*th December* 1969
Coming into Operation	12*th December* 1969

The Commissioners of Customs and Excise in exercise of the powers conferred on them by section 198 of the Customs and Excise Act 1952(a) and section 6(5) of and Part I of Schedule 6 to the Finance Act 1964(b) and of all other powers enabling them in that behalf hereby make the following Regulations:—

1.—(1) These Regulations may be cited as the Hydrocarbon Oil Duties (Rebates and Reliefs) (Amendment) Regulations 1969.

(2) The Interpretation Act 1889(c) shall apply for the interpretation of these Regulations as it applies for the interpretation of an Act of Parliament.

(3) These Regulations shall come into operation on 12th December 1969.

2. The Hydrocarbon Oil Duties (Rebates and Reliefs) Regulations 1964(d) as amended by the Hydrocarbon Oil Duties (Rebates and Reliefs) (Amendment) Regulations 1967(e) and the Hydrocarbon Oil Duties (Rebates and Reliefs) (Amendment) (No. 2) Regulations 1967(f) shall be further amended as follows:—

(a) In regulations 1 and 2 the references to section 6 of the said Finance Act 1964 shall be construed as references to that section as amended by paragraph 4 of Schedule 7 to the Finance Act 1969(g);

(b) In regulation 5(ii) the words "as a material, solvent, extractant, preservative or finish" shall be deleted; and after the words "any article" there shall be inserted the words "or for cleaning plant";

(c) In regulation 8 the reference to section 6(1) of the said Act of 1964 shall be construed as a reference to paragraph 4 of Schedule 7 to the said Act of 1969; and

(d) In regulation 26 paragraph (i) shall be deleted.

R. W. Radford,
Commissioner of Customs
and Excise.

Dated this 4th day
of December 1969.

King's Beam House,
Mark Lane,
London, E.C.3.

(a) 1952 c. 44.   (b) 1964 c. 49.   (c) 1889 c. 63.
(d) S.I. 1964/1349 (1964 II, p. 3065).   (e) S.I. 1967/793 (1967 II, p. 2331).
(f) S.I. 1967/1004 (1967 II, p. 3051).   (g) 1969 c. 32.

EXPLANATORY NOTE

(This Note does not form part of the Regulations.)

Paragraph 4 of Schedule 7 to the Finance Act 1969 replaced section 6(1) of the Finance Act 1964 (under which relief from customs or excise duty could be granted on hydrocarbon oils used or supplied for certain purposes) by new provisions which slightly extended the scope of the relief.

These Regulations amend the Hydrocarbon Oil Duties (Rebates and Reliefs) Regulations 1964 which prescribe the procedure to be followed by persons applying for relief. The amendments are purely consequential upon the change in the law: they introduce no change in practice.

STATUTORY INSTRUMENTS

1969 No. 1731

SAVINGS BANKS

The Trustee Savings Banks (Inspection Committee) Scheme 1969

Made - - - -	3rd December 1969
Laid before —	
House of Commons	5th December 1969
House of Lords	12th December 1969
Coming into Operation	13th December 1969

The Inspection Committee established under section 4 of the Trustee Savings Banks Act 1969(a), with the approval of the National Debt Commissioners, in exercise of the powers conferred upon them by section 4(2) of that Act, hereby make the following scheme:—

Citation and commencement

1. This scheme may be cited as the Trustee Savings Banks (Inspection Committee) Scheme 1969, and shall come into operation on 13th December 1969.

Interpretation

2.—(1) The Interpretation Act 1889(b) shall apply for the interpretation of this scheme as it applies for the interpretation of an Act of Parliament.

(2) The provisions of this scheme are subject to the provisions of the Trustee Savings Banks Act 1969.

Composition of Committee

3. The Inspection Committee of Trustee Savings Banks (in this scheme referred to as "the Committee") shall consist of seven members, of whom four (in this scheme referred to as "the official members") shall be appointed in accordance with paragraph 4(1) of this scheme and three shall be appointed in accordance with paragraph 4(4) thereof.

Appointment of members

4.—(1) Of the official members—

(a) one shall be appointed by the Governor of the Bank of England;

(b) one shall be appointed by the Council of the Institute of Chartered Accountants in England and Wales;

(c) one shall be appointed by the Council of the Law Society; and

(d) one shall be appointed by the Chief Registrar of Friendly Societies.

(a) 1969 c. 50.   (b) 1889 c. 63.

(2) If the holder of any office or any body entitled to appoint an official member fails or refuses to do so, the Committee shall make the appointment.

(3) In 1971 and in every fourth year thereafter the trustees and managers of every trustee savings bank shall not later than 1st October in that year nominate one person to serve as a member of the Committee.

(4) The official members shall hold a meeting after 1st October and before 20th November in 1971 and every fourth year thereafter and, having first appointed from among themselves a person to act as chairman of the meeting, shall at that meeting appoint from the persons nominated under sub-paragraph (3) above three persons to be members of the Committee (hereinafter referred to as the "representative members") and shall transact no other business at that meeting.

Filling of casual vacancies

5.—(1) Where a casual vacancy occurs among the official members, the vacancy shall be filled by the holder of the office or by the body, as the case may be, by whom the member whose office has become vacant was appointed.

(2) Where a casual vacancy occurs among the representative members, the vacancy shall be filled by the Committee either from the remaining persons from whom the person whose office has become vacant was appointed or from those persons and persons nominated in response to a request under sub-paragraph (3) below, as the Committee in its discretion shall decide.

(3) The Committee may for the purpose of filling a casual vacancy occurring among the representative members request the trustees and managers of every trustee savings bank to nominate within three months after receiving the request one person to serve on the Committee.

(4) The Committee shall fill a casual vacancy occurring among the representative members as soon as practicable after the vacancy occurs and, if it makes a request under sub-paragraph (3) above, not later than four months after making the request.

Term of office, etc.

6.—(1) Subject to the provisions of this paragraph, the term of office of members of the Committee shall be four years, except that any member appointed to fill a casual vacancy shall be appointed for the remainder of the term for which his predecessor was appointed.

(2) A member may at any time resign his office.

(3) If any member of the Committee—

    (a) absents himself from three successive meetings of the Committee or, in any period of twelve months ending with 20th November, absents himself from more than six meetings of the Committee, except (in either case) for a reason approved by the Committee, or

    (b) is adjudged bankrupt or makes an arrangement with his creditors, or

    (c) on being convicted of an offence, is sentenced to imprisonment,

the Committee shall declare his office as a member of the Committee to be vacant and thereupon the office shall become vacant.

(4) A person who ceases to be a member of the Committee otherwise than by virtue of sub-paragraph (3) above shall be eligible for re-appointment.

Management of matters connected with filling of vacancies

7.—(1) Subject to the provisions of this scheme, the Committee shall have the conduct and management of all matters connected with the filling of vacancies among its members.

(2) If any dispute arises concerning any such matter, the dispute shall be referred to the National Debt Commissioners whose decision shall be final.

Election of chairman

8.—(1) The Committee shall on, or as soon as may be after, 21st November in each year elect one of its members to be chairman of the Committee.

(2) A member who ceases to be chairman shall be eligible for re-election.

Meetings and procedure

9.—(1) The Committee shall meet twelve times a year or more often if need be.

(2) Subject to sub-paragraph (3) below, the Committee shall, with the approval of the National Debt Commissioners, from time to time frame rules for regulating the procedure of the Committee.

(3) The quorum at meetings of the Committee shall be three.

Revocation and transitional provision

10.—(1) The scheme dated 23rd July 1891 made under section 2 of the Savings Banks Act 1891(a) is hereby revoked.

(2) Any person appointed to be a member of the Committee by virtue of the scheme revoked by sub-paragraph (1) above shall be deemed to have been appointed to be a member of the Committee by virtue of this scheme, and, subject to the provisions of paragraph 6 of this scheme, shall hold office for the remainder of the term for which he was appointed.

Dated 3rd December 1969.

N. E. Sheldon,
Secretary to the Committee.

Approved.

I. de Lisle Radice,
On behalf of the National
Debt Commissioners.

3rd December 1969.

(a) 1891 c. 21.

EXPLANATORY NOTE
(This Note is not part of the Scheme.)

The Inspection Committee of Trustee Savings Banks was originally established under section 2 of the Savings Banks Act 1891, which also provided for the framing of a scheme for the appointment of the Inspection Committee, and for determining the mode in which the members were to be appointed, and their term of office, and their powers, procedure and duties. A scheme was duly framed in July 1891 and the Inspection Committee have continued to operate under it since then.

The scheme contained in this Statutory Instrument supersedes the scheme of 1891. It contains provisions as to the composition of the Committee, the appointment and term of office of members, the filling of vacancies, and the meetings and procedure of the Committee.

Apart from the omission of provisions of the scheme of 1891 which either have become spent, or are now superseded by corresponding provisions in the Trustee Savings Banks Act 1969, the only substantial change is in paragraph 4(3). This provision allows all Trustee Savings Banks to participate in the nomination of persons to serve as members of the Committee, whereas the scheme of 1891 limited such participation to Banks satisfying a financial qualification.

STATUTORY INSTRUMENTS

1969 No. 1733

ROAD TRAFFIC

The Motor Vehicles (Third Party Risks) (Amendment) Regulations 1969

Made - - - -	*3rd December* 1969
Laid before Parliament	*15th December* 1969
Coming into Operation	*16th December* 1969

The Minister of Transport, in exercise of his powers under sections 215 and 226(1) of the Road Traffic Act 1960(a), and under section 23 of the Vehicles (Excise) Act 1962(b) as extended by section 211 of the said Act of 1960, and of all other enabling powers, and after consultation with representative organisations in accordance with the provisions of section 260(2) of the said Act of 1960, hereby makes the following Regulations:—

1. These Regulations shall come into operation on the 16th December 1969 and may be cited as the Motor Vehicles (Third Party Risks) (Amendment) Regulations 1969.

2. The Interpretation Act 1889(c) shall apply for the interpretation of these Regulations as it applies for the interpretation of an Act of Parliament.

3. The Motor Vehicles (Third Party Risks) Regulations 1961(d) shall have effect as though:—

(1) in Regulation 4(1), after the definition of " security ", there were added the following definition:—

" " specified body " means—

(*a*) any of the local authorities referred to in paragraph (*a*) of section 202(2) of the Act ; or

(*b*) a Passenger Transport Executive established under an order made under section 9 of the Transport Act 1968(e), or a subsidiary of that Executive, being an Executive or subsidiary to whose vehicles section 202(2)(*a*) of the Act has been applied ; or

(*c*) the London Transport Executive or a wholly-owned subsidiary of that Executive referred to in paragraph (*e*) of section 202(2) of the Act as amended by section 9(2) of the Transport (London) Act 1969(f). " ;

(2) for Regulation 7(3) there were substituted the following paragraph:—

" (3) in the case of a motor vehicle owned by a specified body, a police authority or the Receiver for the metropolitan police district, a certificate in Form F signed by some person authorised in that behalf by such specified body, police authority or Receiver as the case may be that the said motor vehicle is owned by the said specified body, police authority or Receiver. " ;

(a) 8 & 9 Eliz. 2. c. 16.   (b) 10 & 11 Eliz. 2. c. 13.   (c) 52 & 53 Vict. c. 63.
(d) S.I. 1961/1465 (1961 II, p. 2967).   (e) 1968 c. 73.   (f) 1969 c. 35.

(3) for Regulation 9(1)(*c*)(ii) there were substituted the following:—

"(ii) in the case of a motor vehicle owned by a specified body, a police authority or the Receiver for the metropolitan police district, a certificate in Form F signed by some person authorised in that behalf by such specified body, police authority or Receiver as the case may be that the vehicle in respect of which the application for a licence is made is owned by the said specified body, police authority or Receiver. ";

(4) in Regulation 10(2), for the words "local authority referred to in paragraph (*a*) of sub-section (2) of section 202 of the Act", there were substituted the words "specified body";

(5) in Regulation 10(4), for the words "local authority", there were substituted the words "specified body";

(6) at the end of Regulation 11 the following proviso were added:—

"Provided that such notification need not be made if the certificate relating to the policy or security has been received by the company from the person to whom the certificate was issued on or before the date on which the policy or security ceases to be effective.";

(7) in Part 1 of the Schedule, for Form F there were substituted the following form:—

"FORM F
Road Traffic Act 1960

Certificate of ownership by a Local Authority, Police Authority, Receiver, Passenger Transport Executive, the London Transport Executive or subsidiary of those Executives

We hereby certify that the vehicle of which the registration mark and number are ....
is the property of ....
....
....

Signed on behalf of the authority/
Receiver/Executive/or subsidiary.";

(8) at the end of Part 2 of the Schedule the following paragraph were added:

"8. A certificate in Form F issued by a subsidiary of a Passenger Transport Executive or by a wholly-owned subsidiary of the London Transport Executive shall indicate under the signature that the issuing body is such a subsidiary of an Executive which shall there be specified."

4. Notwithstanding the provisions of these Regulations, a certificate in Form F as prescribed by the Motor Vehicles (Third Party Risks) Regulations 1961 as in force immediately before the coming into operation of these Regulations may continue to be issued by a local authority, police authority or the Receiver for the purposes of the said Regulations of 1961 as amended by these Regulations.

Given under the Official Seal of the Minister of Transport the 3rd December 1969.

(L.S.)   *Fred Mulley*,
                                              Minister of Transport.

EXPLANATORY NOTE

(This Note is not part of the Regulations.)

These Regulations amend the Motor Vehicles (Third Party Risks) Regulations 1961 by:—

1. extending certain provisions relating to exemptions from the requirement to have third party motor insurance, including the issue of a certificate of ownership of exempt vehicles specified as Form F in the Schedule, to

    (a) a Passenger Transport Executive and its subsidiaries ; and

    (b) the London Transport Executive and its wholly-owned subsidiaries ;

2. adding a proviso to Regulation 11 to clarify the requirements in respect of notification to the Minister of Transport of ineffective policies or securities.

STATUTORY INSTRUMENTS

1969 No. 1736

PURCHASE TAX

The Purchase Tax (No. 1) Order 1969

Made - - - - -	*4th December* 1969
Laid before the House of Commons	*8th December* 1969
Coming into Operation -	*1st January* 1970

The Lords Commissioners of Her Majesty's Treasury, by virtue of the powers conferred on them by section 2(3) of the Purchase Tax Act 1963(**a**), and of all other powers enabling them in that behalf, hereby make the following Order:—

1.—(1) This Order may be cited as the Purchase Tax (No. 1) Order 1969.

(2) In the following Articles of this Order, any reference to a Group is to a Group in Part I of Schedule 1 to the Purchase Tax Act 1963 (chargeable and exempt goods and rates of tax), as amended by subsequent Acts and orders.

(3) The Interpretation Act 1889(**b**) shall apply for the interpretation of this Order as it applies for the interpretation of an Act of Parliament.

(4) This Order shall come into operation on 1st January 1970.

2. In Group 6, under the heading " Exempt ", after the words " air cushions " there shall be inserted the words " disposable incontinence pads ".

3. In Group 7, under the heading " Exempt "—

(*a*) in paragraph (1)(v) after the words " bonded fibre fabric " there shall be inserted the words " not put up for retail sale "; and

(*b*) after paragraph (15) there shall be inserted the following paragraph:—

" (16)(*a*) Polyolefin fabrics, that is to say fabrics woven from polyolefin strip (including split film) which, after weaving, is not less than 1 millimetre in width, and having not more than 40 strips (including both warp and weft) per square inch of fabric.

(*b*) Fabrics woven from polyolefin strip (including split film) which, after weaving, is not less than 1 millimetre in width, and jute or flax threads, and having not more than 40 strips or threads (including both warp and weft) per square inch of fabric ".

4. In Group 12, after the words " mechanical lighters " (in the heading) there shall be inserted a semi-colon and the words " elements for electrically operated ceiling, wall or floor heating systems "; and after paragraph (*d*) there shall be inserted the following paragraph:—

" (*e*) Elements for electrically operated ceiling, wall or floor ... $36\frac{2}{3}\%$ heating systems, being elements which consist of electrically

---

(**a**) 1963 c. 9.   (**b**) 1889 c. 63.

conductive or resistive material in strip or sheet form between two layers of insulating material, whether or not supplied in lengths which require to be cut or sealed or fitted with connectors during installation ".

5. In Group 19A, under the heading " Not chargeable under this Group ", after paragraph 2 there shall be inserted the following paragraph:—

" 3.   Instruments which are—
    (i) suitable only for use in a course of instruction; and
    (ii) capable of operation only from mains supply; and
    (iii) incapable of erasing instructional material pre-recorded on magnetic tape or other recording material ".

Walter Harrison,

E. G. Perry,

Two of the Lords Commissioners
of Her Majesty's Treasury

4th December 1969.

EXPLANATORY NOTE

(*This Note is not part of the Order.*)

This Order amends the Schedule of goods chargeable with purchase tax.

It relieves from the tax disposable incontinence pads.

It amends the exemption for bonded fibre fabric so that any that is put up for retail sale is chargeable.

It relieves from the tax certain polyolefin fabrics.

It adds certain elements for electrically operated ceiling, wall or floor heating systems to the goods chargeable with the tax under the Group (Group 12) which includes corresponding complete appliances and apparatus.

It excludes certain instruments for instructional use from charge as tape recorders and reproducers.

STATUTORY INSTRUMENTS

1969 No. 1737

ANIMALS

DISEASES OF ANIMALS

The Exotic Animals (Importation) Order 1969

Made - - - -	*4th December* 1969
Laid before Parliament	*12th December* 1969
Coming into Operation	*15th December* 1969

The Minister of Agriculture, Fisheries and Food and the Secretary of State, acting jointly, in exercise of the powers vested in them under sections 1, 24, 27, 33, 77, 84 and 85 of the Diseases of Animals Act 1950(a), as read with the Transfer of Functions (Animal Health) Order 1955(b) and as adapted to air transport by section 11 of the Agriculture (Miscellaneous Provisions) Act 1954(c) and by Schedule 2 thereto, and of all other powers enabling them in that behalf, hereby order as follows : —

Citation, extent and commencement

1. This order, which may be cited as the Exotic Animals (Importation) Order 1969, applies to Great Britain and shall come into operation on 15th December 1969.

Interpretation

2.—(1) In this order the following expressions have the following meanings respectively, that is to say—

" the Act " means the Diseases of Animals Act 1950 ;

" approved acclimatisation centre " means a centre approved by the Minister in writing for the purposes of this order for the acclimatisation of exotic animals imported from outside Great Britain ;

" approved research establishment " means any establishment from time to time approved by the Minister in writing for the purposes of this order, being an establishment used for the carrying out in relation to imported exotic animals of medical or veterinary research, or for the manufacture or testing in connection with such animals of vaccine or serum or other pharmaceutical products ;

" approved zoological establishment " means a zoological gardens or other establishment from time to time approved by the Minister in writing for the purposes of this order, being gardens or an establishment used for the exhibition of exotic animals ;

" exotic animals " means, in relation to the orders of mammals mentioned in column 1 of Schedule 1 to this order, animals of the families mentioned in column 2 of that Schedule ;

(a) 1950 c. 36. For change of title of the Minister see S.I. 1955/554 (1955 I, p. 1200).
(b) S.I. 1955/958 (1955 I, p. 1184).   (c) 1954 c. 39.

" inspector " has the meaning assigned to it by section 84(4) of the Act ;

" the Minister " means, in the application of this order to England and Wales, the Minister of Agriculture, Fisheries and Food, and in its corresponding application to Scotland, the Secretary of State.

(2) An approved acclimatisation centre, approved research establishment and an approved zoological establishment may be approved either unconditionally or subject to such conditions as may be specified in the document of approval.

(3) For the purposes of the Act and of this order the definition of the expression " animals " in section 84(1) is hereby extended so as to comprise exotic animals.

(4) The Animals (Importation) Order of 1930(**a**) shall not apply to exotic animals imported under this order.

(5) The Interpretation Act 1889(**b**) applies to the interpretation of this order as it applies to the interpretation of an Act of Parliament.

General prohibition of landing of exotic animals

3. Subject to the provisions of this order no exotic animal, being an animal brought from any country outside Great Britain other than Northern Ireland, the Republic of Ireland, the Channel Islands and the Isle of Man, shall be landed in Great Britain ; and accordingly Part I of Schedule 1 to the Act (which requires animals to be slaughtered on landing) shall except in so far as the Minister otherwise directs apply to any such animal.

Control of importation of specified exotic animals for research or exhibition

4.—(1) Notwithstanding article 3 above, an exotic animal to which this article applies may be landed in Great Britain without being subject to the provisions of the said Part I of Schedule 1 ; but subject to the provisions of this order Part II of the said Schedule (which requires animals to be kept in quarantine) and paragraph 1 of Part III thereof (which in the circumstances mentioned negatives any right to compensation) shall apply to any such animal allowed to be landed.

(2) The ports and airports which alone may be used by vessels and aircraft carrying exotic animals imported under this article are the ports and airports respectively prescribed in Parts I and II of Schedule 2 to this order ; and for the purpose of paragraph 1 of Part II of Schedule 1 to the Act (as applied by this order) so much of any such port or airport as is from time to time set apart by the port or airport authority for the reception of exotic animals landed from outside Great Britain shall constitute an imported animals quarantine station.

(3) Nothing in paragraph (2) above shall render it unlawful for an aircraft bringing exotic animals from outside Great Britain to be landed in Great Britain at any other airport to which the aircraft is while airborne ordered to be diverted, or at which it is otherwise expedient for the aircraft to be landed in the interests of air safety ; but no animal shall be unloaded from such an aircraft after landing except with the authority of an inspector.

(4) The exotic animals to which this article applies are animals as mentioned in sub-paragraphs (*a*), (*b*) and (*c*) of this paragraph in respect of which

(a) S.R. & O. 1930/922 (Rev. II, p. 331: 1930, p. 52).   (b) 1889 c. 63.

the Minister has granted a licence authorising them to be imported into Great Britain, that is to say—

(a) exotic animals of the kinds specified in Part I of Schedule 1 to this order, being animals which the Minister is satisfied are intended for general medical or veterinary research or are to be used in connection with the manufacture or testing of vaccine or serum or other pharmaceutical products ; or

(b) exotic animals of the kinds specified in Part II of that Schedule, being animals which it is expedient in the opinion of the Minister as an exceptional measure to authorise their importation into Great Britain for the purposes of research of a kind which cannot be suitably carried out in relation to animals of the kinds specified in Part I of that Schedule ; or

(c) exotic animals (whether of the kinds specified in Part I or Part II of that Schedule) which the Minister is satisfied are intended only for exhibition at an approved zoological establishment.

Control of movement of exotic animals after landing

5.—(1) Subject to article 6 of this order, an exotic animal to which article 4 of this order applies shall not after being landed at an imported animals quarantine station be moved otherwise than subject to the terms of a licence granted under article 7 below and to the conditions respectively applicable to such animal by virtue of paragraphs (2) and (3) of this article.

(2) In the case of exotic animals other than animals intended for exhibition, the animals shall not be moved except—

(a) from an imported animals quarantine station to an approved acclimatisation centre or to an approved research establishment ; or

(b) from an approved acclimatisation centre to another such centre or to an approved research establishment ; or

(c) from an approved research establishment to another such establishment.

(3) In the case of exotic animals intended for exhibition, paragraph (2) above shall have effect with the substitution, for the references to an approved research establishment, of references to an approved zoological establishment.

Export of exotic animals previously imported

6. Notwithstanding anything contained in this order an exotic animal which is landed in Great Britain may at any time be moved in accordance with a licence granted under article 7 below to a port or airport, to be specified in the licence, with a view to the animal being exported from that port or airport.

Licences

7.—(1) A licence granted under any provision of this order shall be granted by the Minister and shall contain such conditions, to be specified in the licence, as in the opinion of the Minister are necessary or expedient for the purpose of in any manner preventing the introduction or spreading of any disease to which the Act applies or is from time to time extended.

(2) Any such licence may at any time be cancelled, or its conditions varied, but without prejudice to anything lawfully done pursuant to the licence before the cancellation or variation took effect.

(3) Any such licence shall accompany the animals to which it relates while the animals are being landed or moved.

(4) Breach of any condition of a licence shall be an offence against the Act.

Records

8.—(1) The person in charge of an approved acclimatisation centre, approved research establishment or of an approved zoological establishment shall adopt such system for the identification of every exotic animal received at such centre or establishment, and shall keep such record in relation to its receipt, treatment and subsequent despatch (or death) and other matters, as may be required by the Minister either generally or in relation to any particular case.

(2) Every entry in such a record shall be made in ink or indelible pencil within 36 hours of the event which is required by this article to be recorded.

(3) Every entry in such a record shall be retained by the person whose duty it is to keep such record for a period of at least twelve months from such event, and shall be produced by him for inspection at all reasonable times on demand to an inspector, who shall be entitled to make a copy of such entry.

(4) A local authority may supply forms of record for the purposes of this article to any person in the district of the local authority.

Detention of exotic animals illegally imported

9.—(1) If any exotic animal is imported into Great Britain in contravention of this order, then without prejudice to the provisions of Part I of Schedule 1 to the Act relating to slaughter (as applied by this order) the Minister or an inspector may serve on any person appearing to him to have the control or custody of the animal a notice in writing requiring him at the expense of the owner of the animal or the person on whom the notice was served to detain or isolate the animal subject to any conditions imposed by the notice and to subject it, or to permit it to be subjected to, such examinations and tests as the Minister or the inspector may require ; and the person on whom such a notice is served shall comply with the requirements thereof.

(2) If any person on whom such a notice is served fails to comply with the requirements thereof it shall be lawful for an inspector, without prejudice to any proceedings for an offence arising out of such default, to seize the animal in respect of which the notice was served, and to detain or isolate it and subject it to such examinations and tests as he may determine.

(3) A person who has failed to comply with the terms of any such notice shall give all necessary facilities to an inspector to enable him to exercise the power conferred on him by paragraph (2) above ; and the reasonable expenses incurred by such an inspector in exercising the said power shall be recoverable as a civil debt from the owner of the animal or the person on whom the notice was served.

(4) A notice under this article may be served in any of the ways authorised under section 77(4) and (5) of the Act.

Transhipment in ports and airports

10. Nothing in this order shall operate to prevent the transhipment in a port or airport in Great Britain of an exotic animal brought from outside Great Britain where such transhipment takes place with the written authority of the Minister or an officer of Customs and Excise and subject to such conditions (if any) as may be specified in such authority.

Enforcement

11. This order shall, except where it is otherwise provided, be executed and enforced by the local authority.

In Witness whereof the Official Seal of the Minister of Agriculture, Fisheries and Food is hereunto affixed on 4th December 1969.

(L.S.)

Cledwyn Hughes,
Minister of Agriculture, Fisheries and Food.

Given under the Seal of the Secretary of State for Scotland on 4th December 1969.

(L.S.)

William Ross,
Secretary of State for Scotland.

SCHEDULE 1

EXOTIC ANIMALS TO WHICH THE ORDER APPLIES

PART I

Exotic animals which may (subject to the terms of the Order) be landed in Great Britain

Order of mammals Column 1	Family Column 2	Common name (see note below)
PRIMATES	Cebidae	Douroucouli (owl monkeys or night apes) Titis Uakaris Sakis Howlers Capuchins Squirrel Monkeys Spider Monkeys Woolly Monkeys Goeldi's Monkeys
	Callithricidae	Marmosets Tamarins
	Cercopithecidae	Macaques Mangabeys Baboons Guenons Langurs Colobus Monkeys, etc.

PART II

Exotic animals generally prohibited (except for exhibition) from being landed in Great Britain

Order of mammals Column 1	Family Column 2	Common name (see note below)
	Tupaiidae	Tree-shrews
	Lemuridae	Lemurs
	Indriidae	Indrises and Sifakas
	Daubentoniidae	Aye-Ayes
PRIMATES	Lorisidae	Lorises Bushbabies, etc.
	Tarsiidae	Tarsiers
	Pongidae	Gibbons Orang-Utans Chimpanzees Gorillas
	Procyonidae	Raccoons Coatis Kinkajous Olingos
CARNIVORES	Mustelidae (except sub-family Lutrinae (otters) and Mustela Vison (American mink))	Stoats Weasels Ferrets Polecats Martens Wolverines Ratels (Honey badgers) Badgers Skunks
	Viverridae	Genets Civets Linsangs Mongooses
MARSUPIALS	Didelphidae	Opossums
	Sciuridae	Squirrels Chipmunks Marmots
RODENTS	Geomyidae	Gophers
	Anomaluridae	Scaly-tailed Squirrels
CHIROPTERA	All families	Bats

NOTE: Some of the common names of animals included in this Schedule are set out opposite the appropriate reference. The list is for guidance only and does not form part of the order. Not all the common names are listed, and some of the listed names can also be applied to animals which are not subject to the order.

SCHEDULE 2

PORTS AND AIRPORTS AT WHICH AUTHORISED LANDINGS OF
EXOTIC ANIMALS MAY TAKE PLACE

PART I
Ports

Port of London   Southampton
Liverpool

PART II
Airports

Heathrow Airport, London   Manchester
Gatwick Airport, London   Prestwick

EXPLANATORY NOTE

(This Note is not part of the Order.)

This order extends the application of the Diseases of Animals Act 1950
so as to include prescribed exotic animals, imposes a general prohibition on
the importation of such animals (other than from Northern Ireland, the
Republic of Ireland, the Channel Islands and the Isle of Man) and thereby
in general requires any such animals which are brought to Great Britain
from overseas in contravention of such prohibition to be slaughtered on
landing. Exceptions are made for certain kinds of prescribed animals (e.g.
monkeys) which may be imported under licence where the importation is
for research purposes ; but such animals may only be landed at prescribed
ports and airports from which they may be moved, again only under licence,
directly or indirectly to approved research establishments. Other exotic
animals, which are prescribed, may also be imported under licence (subject
to the above conditions) where as an exceptional measure it is judged
expedient to allow them to be imported to enable research to be carried out
of a kind for which the first category of exotic animals is considered
unsuitable.

The order also contains provision for the importation under licence (subject
to similar conditions) of exotic animals of both categories where the purpose
of importation is for exhibition in an approved zoo.

The order contains default powers.

STATUTORY INSTRUMENTS

1969 No. 1739

WAGES COUNCILS

The Wages Regulation (Sack and Bag) Order 1969

Made - - -   *4th December* 1969

Coming into Operation   *29th December* 1969

Whereas the Secretary of State has received from the Sack and Bag Wages Council (Great Britain) the wages regulation proposals set out in the Schedule hereto ;

Now, therefore, the Secretary of State in exercise of her powers under section 11 of the Wages Councils Act 1959(**a**), and of all other powers enabling her in that behalf, hereby makes the following Order :—

1. This Order may be cited as the Wages Regulation (Sack and Bag) Order 1969.

2.—(1) In this Order the expression "the specified date" means the 29th December 1969, provided that where, as respects any worker who is paid wages at intervals not exceeding seven days, that date does not correspond with the beginning of the period for which the wages are paid, the expression "the specified date" means, as respects that worker, the beginning of the next such period following that date.

(2) The Interpretation Act 1889(**b**) shall apply to the interpretation of this Order as it applies to the interpretation of an Act of Parliament and as if this Order and the Order hereby revoked were Acts of Parliament.

3. The wages regulation proposals set out in the Schedule hereto shall have effect as from the specified date and as from that date the Wages Regulation (Sack and Bag) Order 1968(**c**) shall cease to have effect.

Signed by Order of the Secretary of State.

4th December 1969.

A. A. Jarratt,
Deputy Under Secretary of State,
Department of Employment and Productivity.

(**a**) 1959 c. 69.   (**b**) 1889 c. 63.
(**c**) S.I. 1968/1357 (1968 II, p. 3771).

SCHEDULE

Article 3

The following minimum remuneration shall be substituted for the statutory minimum remuneration fixed by the Wages Regulation (Sack and Bag) Order 1968 (Order S.B. (65)).

STATUTORY MINIMUM REMUNERATION

PART I

GENERAL

1. The minimum remuneration payable to a worker to whom this Schedule applies for all work except work to which a minimum overtime rate applies under Part IV of this Schedule is:—

(1) in the case of a time worker, the general minimum time rate payable to the worker under Part II or Part III of this Schedule ;

(2) in the case of a male worker employed on piece work, piece rates each of which would yield, in the circumstances of the case, to an ordinary worker at least the same amount of money as the general minimum time rate which would be payable under Part II of this Schedule if he were a time worker ;

(3) in the case of a female worker employed on piece work, piece rates each of which would yield, in the circumstances of the case, to an ordinary worker at least the same amount of money as the piece work basis time rate applicable to the worker under Part III of this Schedule.

PART II

MALE WORKERS

GENERAL MINIMUM TIME RATES

2. The general minimum time rates payable to male workers are as follows:—

Per hour

(1) Workers aged 21 years or over and employed during the whole or part of their time:—

s. d.

(a) as superintendents of packing presses (hand or machine) or as press foremen (hand or machine), or

(b) in setting up or minding, or in setting up and minding, branding or printing machines or both such machines 5 1¼

Provided that the general minimum time rate payable during his first six months' employment in the trade to a worker who enters, or who has entered, the trade for the first time at or over the age of 21 years shall be 5 0½

(2) All other workers aged

								s.	d.
21 years or over	...	...	...	...	...	...	...	4	10½
20 and under 21 years		...	...	...	...	...	...	4	4¾
19 „ „ 20 „	...	...	...	...	...	...	...	4	0¼
18 „ „ 19 „	...	...	...	...	...	...	...	3	8¼
17 „ „ 18 „	...	...	...	...	...	...	...	3	0¼
16 „ „ 17 „	...	...	...	...	...	...	...	2	8
under 16 years	...	...	...	...	...	...	...	2	5½

Provided that the general minimum time rate payable during his first two months' employment in the trade to a worker who enters, or who has entered, the trade for the first time at or over the age of 18 years shall be ½d. per hour less than the minimum rate otherwise payable under this sub-paragraph.

Part III

FEMALE WORKERS

GENERAL MINIMUM TIME RATES

3. The general minimum time rates payable to female workers are as follows:—

	Per hour s. d.
(1) Workers aged 18 years or over and employed as examiners of mended work, allocators, forewomen, hand sewers of heavy twill sacks and bags of 10 porter and upwards, selectors or graders of mixed loads or setters-up on branding machines	3 10
Provided that the general minimum time rate payable during her first six months' employment in the trade to a worker who enters, or who has entered, the trade for the first time at or over the age of 18 years shall be	3 8¼

(2) All other workers aged

	Per hour s. d.
18 years or over	3 8¼
17 and under 18 years	3 0¼
16 „ „ 17 „	2 8
under 16 years	2 5½

Provided that the general minimum time rate payable during her first two months' employment in the trade to a worker who enters, or who has entered, the trade for the first time at or over the age of 16 years shall be ½d. per hour less than the minimum rate otherwise payable under this sub-paragraph.

PIECE WORK BASIS TIME RATES

4. The piece work basis time rates applicable to female workers of any age employed on piece work are as follows:—

	Per hour s. d.
(1) Workers employed as examiners of mended work, allocators, forewomen, hand sewers of heavy twill sacks and bags of 10 porter and upwards, selectors or graders of mixed loads or setters-up on branding machines ...	3 11¾
(2) All other workers	3 10¼

Part IV

OVERTIME AND WAITING TIME

MINIMUM OVERTIME RATES

5. Minimum overtime rates are payable to any worker, not being a male worker employed on piece work, as follows:—

(1) on any day other than a Saturday, Sunday or customary holiday—

    (a) for the first two hours worked in excess of 8½ hours   time-and-a-quarter

    (b) thereafter ... ... time-and-a-half

Provided that, where the employer normally requires the worker's attendance on five days only in the week, the foregoing minimum overtime rates of time-and-a-quarter and time-and-a-half shall be payable after 9 and 11 hours' work respectively.

(2) on a Saturday, not being a customary holiday—

    (a) where the worker is normally required to attend on six days in the week—
        for the first 2 hours worked in excess of 4 hours   ... time-and-a-quarter
        thereafter ... ... time-and-a-half

    (b) where the worker is normally required to attend on five days only in the week—
        for the first 2 hours worked ... ... time-and-a-quarter
        thereafter ... ... time-and-a-half

(3) on a Sunday or a customary holiday—
    for all time worked   ...   .   double time
(4) in any week exclusive of any time for which a minimum overtime rate is payable under the foregoing provisions of this paragraph—
    for all time worked in excess of *40 hours*   ...   ...   time-and-a-quarter.

6. In this Part of this Schedule—

(1) the expressions "time-and-a-quarter", "time-and-a-half" and "double time" mean respectively—

    (*a*) in the case of a time worker, one and a quarter times, one and a half times and twice the general minimum time rate otherwise payable to the worker ;

    (*b*) in the case of a female worker employed on piece work—

        (i) a time rate equal respectively to one-quarter, one-half and the whole of the piece work basis time rate otherwise applicable to the worker under Part III of this Schedule and, in addition thereto—

        (ii) the piece rates otherwise applicable to the worker under paragraph 1 (3).

(2) the expression "customary holiday" means

    (*a*) (i) in England and Wales—
Christmas Day (or, if Christmas Day falls on a Sunday, such weekday as may be appointed by national proclamation, or, if none is so appointed, the next following Tuesday), Boxing Day, Good Friday, Easter Monday, Whit Monday (or where another day is substituted therefor by national proclamation, that day), and August Bank Holiday ;

    (ii) in Scotland—
New Year's Day and the following day:
Provided that if New Year's Day falls on a Sunday the holidays shall be the following Monday and Tuesday, and if New Year's Day falls on a Saturday the holidays shall be New Year's Day and the following Monday ;
the local Spring holiday ;
the local Autumn holiday ; and
two other days (being days on which the worker would normally work) in the course of a calendar year, to be fixed by the employer and notified to the worker not less than three weeks before the holiday ;

or (*b*) in the case of each of the said days (other than a day fixed by the employer in Scotland and notified to the worker as aforesaid) such weekday as may be substituted therefor by the employer being either—

    (i) a day which is by local custom recognised as a day of holiday, or

    (ii) a day (being a day on which the worker would normally work) which falls within three weeks of the day for which it is substituted and is mutually agreed between the employer and the worker.

WAITING TIME

7.—(1) A worker is entitled to payment of the minimum remuneration specified in this Schedule for all time during which he is present on the premises of his employer unless he is present thereon in any of the following circumstances :—

    (*a*) without the employer's consent, express or implied ;

    (*b*) for some purpose unconnected with his work and other than that of waiting for work to be given to him to perform ;

(c) by reason only of the fact that he is resident thereon ;

(d) during normal meal times in a room or place in which no work is being done and he is not waiting for work to be given to him to perform.

(2) The minimum remuneration payable under sub-paragraph (1) of this paragraph to a piece worker when not engaged on piece work is that which would be payable if he were a time worker.

PART V

APPLICATION

8. This Schedule applies to workers in relation to whom the Sack and Bag Wages Council (Great Britain) operates, namely, workers employed in Great Britain in the trade specified in the Schedule to the Trade Boards (Sack and Bag Trade, Great Britain) (Constitution and Proceedings) Regulations 1933(a), that is to say : —

The making from woven fabrics of corn sacks, flour sacks, coal sacks, sugar sacks, cement bags, sand bags, nail bags, potato bags, seed bags and similar sacks or bags, or the repairing thereof :

including : —

(a) the following and similar operations (whether performed by hand or machine) known in the trade as : —

(i) Folding (or hooking), cutting, machining, turning ;

(ii) Brushing, selecting, mending ;

(iii) Branding, tarring, bundling ;

(b) the warehousing of, the packing of, and similar operations in regard to sacks or bags of the kind mentioned above when carried on in association with or in conjunction with the making or repairing thereof ;

(c) the warehousing of, the packing of, and similar operations in regard to any other articles when carried on in or in association with or in conjunction with any business, establishment, branch or department mainly engaged in any of the operations mentioned in paragraph (b) above ;

but excluding : —

(i) any of the operations mentioned above when carried on in association with or in conjunction with the weaving of jute, flax or hemp, or the dyeing, bleaching or finishing of jute, flax or hemp yarn or cloth ;

(ii) any of the operations mentioned above when carried on in or in association with or in conjunction with any business, establishment, branch or department mainly engaged in a business in which the sacks or bags are used as containers for other articles the production or sale of which forms part of the business ;

(iii) the making of rope-bound coal or coke sacks when carried on in association with or in conjunction with any business, establishment, branch or department engaged in the making of made-up textile articles other than sacks or bags, whether rope-bound or not, of the kind mentioned ;

(iv) any of the operations mentioned in paragraph (b) above when carried on in or in association with or in conjunction with any business, establishment, branch or department mainly engaged in the warehousing of, the packing of, and similar operations in regard to made-up textile articles other than sacks or bags, whether rope-bound or not, of the kind mentioned ;

(a) S.R. & O. 1933/1157 (1933, p. 2052).

(v) operations included in the Trade Boards (Waste Materials Reclamation) Order 1920(a).

EXPLANATORY NOTE

(This Note is not part of the Order.)

This Order, which has effect from 29th December 1969, sets out the statutory minimum remuneration payable in substitution for that fixed by the Wages Regulation (Sack and Bag) Order 1968 (Order S.B. (65)), which Order is revoked.

New provisions are printed in italics.

(a) S.R. & O. 1920/305 (1920 II, p. 794).

STATUTORY INSTRUMENTS

1969 No. 1740

WAGES COUNCILS

The Wages Regulation (Sack and Bag) (Holidays) Order 1969

Made	-	-	-	4th December 1969
Coming into Operation			29th December 1969

Whereas the Secretary of State has received from the Sack and Bag Wages Council (Great Britain) (hereinafter referred to as "the Wages Council") the wages regulation proposals set out in the Schedule hereto ;

Now, therefore, the Secretary of State in exercise of her powers under section 11 of the Wages Councils Act 1959(a), and of all other powers enabling her in that behalf, hereby makes the following Order :—

1. This Order may be cited as the Wages Regulation (Sack and Bag) (Holidays) Order 1969.

2.—(1) In this Order the expression "the specified date" means the 29th December 1969, provided that where, as respects any worker who is paid wages at intervals not exceeding seven days, that date does not correspond with the beginning of the period for which the wages are paid, the expression "the specified date" means, as respects that worker, the beginning of the next such period following that date.

(2) The Interpretation Act 1889(b) shall apply to the interpretation of this Order as it applies to the interpretation of an Act of Parliament and as if this Order and the Order hereby revoked were Acts of Parliament.

3. The wages regulation proposals set out in the Schedule hereto shall have effect as from the specified date and as from that date the Wages Regulation (Sack and Bag) (Holidays) Order 1968(c), shall cease to have effect.

Signed by Order of the Secretary of State.
4th December 1969.

A. A. Jarratt,
Deputy Under Secretary of State,
Department of Employment and Productivity.

Article 3

SCHEDULE

The following provisions as to holidays and holiday remuneration shall be substituted for the provisions as to holidays and holiday remuneration set out in the Wages Regulation (Sack and Bag) (Holidays) Order 1968 (hereinafter referred to as "Order S.B. (66)").

(a) 1959 c. 69. (b) 1889 c. 63.
(c) S.I. 1968/1358 (1968 II, p. 3777).

PART I

APPLICATION

1.—(1) This Schedule applies to every worker (other than an outworker) for whom statutory minimum remuneration has been fixed.

(2) For the purposes of this Schedule an outworker is a worker who works in his own home or in some other place not under the control or management of the employer.

PART II

CUSTOMARY HOLIDAYS

2.—(1) An employer shall allow to every worker to whom this Schedule applies a holiday (hereinafter referred to as a "customary holiday") in each year on the days specified in the following sub-paragraph, provided that the worker was in his employment and (unless excused by the employer or absent by reason of the proved illness of, or accident to, the worker) has worked for the employer throughout the last working day on which work was available to him prior to the customary holiday.

(2) The said customary holidays are:—

    (a) (i) In England and Wales—

        Christmas Day (or, if Christmas Day falls on a Sunday, such weekday as may be appointed by national proclamation, or, if none is so appointed, the next following Tuesday), Boxing Day, Good Friday, Easter Monday, Whit Monday (or where another day is substituted therefor by national proclamation, that day), and August Bank Holiday ;

    (ii) In Scotland—

        New Year's Day and the following day:
            Provided that if New Year's Day falls on a Sunday the holidays shall be the following Monday and Tuesday, and if New Year's Day falls on a Saturday the holidays shall be New Year's Day and the following Monday ;
        the local Spring holiday ;
        the local Autumn holiday ; and
        two other days (being days on which the worker would normally work) in the course of a calendar year to be fixed by the employer and notified to the worker not less than three weeks before the holiday ;

or (b) in the case of each of the said days (other than a day fixed by the employer in Scotland and notified to the worker as aforesaid) such weekday as may be substituted therefor by the employer being either—

        (i) a day which is by local custom recognised as a day of holiday, or

        (ii) a day (being a day on which the worker would normally work) which falls within three weeks of the day for which it is substituted and is mutually agreed between the employer and the worker.

(3) Notwithstanding the preceding provisions of this paragraph, where by reason of the circumstances in which the work is carried on in an establishment the allowing of the customary holiday is rendered impracticable, a worker may be required to work on a customary holiday (except where in the case of a woman or young person such a requirement would be unlawful) and, if so required, shall be paid for all time worked thereon the statutory minimum remuneration appropriate to him for work on a customary holiday.

Part III

Annual Holiday

3.—(1) Subject to the provisions of paragraph 4, in addition to the holidays specified in Part II of this Schedule an employer shall between 6th April 1970 and 30th September 1970, and in each succeeding year between 6th April and 30th September allow a holiday (hereinafter referred to as an "annual holiday") to every worker in his employment to whom this Schedule applies who has been employed by him during the 12 months immediately preceding the commencement of the holiday season for any of the periods of employment (calculated in accordance with the provisions of paragraph 10) set out in the *appropriate column of the* table below and the duration of the annual holiday shall, in the case of each such worker, be related to his period of employment during that 12 months as follows:—

Period of employment	Workers with a normal working week of six days				Workers with a normal working week of five days or less			
	Duration of annual holiday				Duration of annual holiday			
	1970	1971	1972	1973	1970	1971	1972	1973
At least 48 weeks	14	15	16	18	12	13	14	15
„ „ 47 „	13	14	15	17	11	12	13	14
„ „ 46 „	13	14	15	17	11	12	13	14
„ „ 45 „	13	14	15	17	11	12	13	14
„ „ 44 „	12	13	14	16	11	12	13	13
„ „ 43 „	12	13	14	16	10	11	12	13
„ „ 42 „	12	13	14	15	10	11	12	13
„ „ 41 „	12	13	13	15	10	11	12	12
„ „ 40 „	11	12	13	15	10	10	11	12
„ „ 39 „	11	12	13	14	9	10	11	12
„ „ 38 „	11	12	12	14	9	10	11	12
„ „ 37 „	10	11	12	14	9	10	11	11
„ „ 36 „	10	11	12	13	9	9	10	11
„ „ 35 „	10	11	11	13	8	9	10	11
„ „ 34 „	9	10	11	12	8	9	10	10
„ „ 33 „	9	10	11	12	8	8	9	10
„ „ 32 „	9	10	10	12	8	8	9	10
„ „ 31 „	9	10	10	11	7	8	9	9
„ „ 30 „	8	9	10	11	7	8	9	9
„ „ 29 „	8	9	9	11	7	7	8	9
„ „ 28 „	8	9	9	10	6	7	8	8
„ „ 27 „	7	8	9	10	6	7	8	8
„ „ 26 „	7	8	9	9	6	6	7	8
„ „ 25 „	7	8	8	9	6	6	7	8
„ „ 24 „	6	7	8	9	5	6	7	7
„ „ 23 „	6	7	8	8	5	6	7	7
„ „ 22 „	6	7	7	8	5	5	6	7
„ „ 21 „	6	7	7	8	5	5	6	6
„ „ 20 „	5	6	7	7	4	5	6	6
„ „ 19 „	5	6	6	7	4	4	5	6
„ „ 18 „	5	6	6	6	4	4	5	5
„ „ 17 „	4	5	6	6	4	4	5	5
„ „ 16 „	4	5	5	6	3	4	5	5
„ „ 15 „	4	5	5	5	3	3	4	4
„ „ 14 „	3	4	5	5	3	3	4	4
„ „ 13 „	3	4	4	5	3	3	4	4
„ „ 12 „	3	4	4	4	2	2	3	4
„ „ 11 „	3	4	4	4	2	2	3	3
„ „ 10 „	2	3	3	3	2	2	3	3
„ „ 9 „	2	3	3	3	2	2	3	3
„ „ 8 „	2	3	3	3	—	—	—	—

(2) *Notwithstanding the provisions of sub-paragraph (1) of this paragraph, the number of days of annual holiday which an employer is required to allow to a worker in the holiday season 6th April to 30th September shall not exceed in the aggregate twice the number of days constituting the worker's normal working week, plus—*

(a) *in the case of workers with a normal working week of 6 days—*

two days in the holiday season in 1970
three days in the holiday season in 1971
four days in the holiday season in 1972
six days in the holiday season in 1973 and in each succeeding holiday season ;

and (b) *in the case of workers with a normal working week of 5 days or less—*

two days in the holiday season in 1970
three days in the holiday season in 1971
four days in the holiday season in 1972
five days in the holiday season in 1973 and in each succeeding holiday season ;

so, however, that in no case shall the number of days of annual holiday which an employer is required to allow to a worker exceed in the aggregate three times the number of days constituting the worker's normal working week.

(3) In this Schedule the expression "holiday season" means in relation to the year 1970 the period commencing on 6th April 1970 and ending on 30th September 1970, and, in each succeeding year, the period commencing on 6th April and ending on 30th September of the same year.

4.—(1) Subject to the provisions of this paragraph, an annual holiday shall be allowed on consecutive working days, being days on which the worker is normally called upon to work for the employer.

(2) Where the number of days of annual holiday for which a worker has qualified exceeds the number of days constituting his normal working week, the holiday may be allowed in two periods of consecutive working days ; so, however, that when a holiday is so allowed, one of the periods shall consist of a number of such days not less than the number of days constituting the worker's normal working week.

(3) For the purposes of this paragraph, days of annual holiday shall be treated as consecutive notwithstanding that a day of holiday allowed to a worker under Part II of this Schedule or a day upon which he does not normally work for the employer intervenes.

(4) Where a day of holiday allowed to a worker under Part II of this Schedule immediately precedes a period of annual holiday or occurs during such a period and the total number of days of annual holiday required to be allowed in the period under the foregoing provisions of this paragraph, together with any such day of holiday allowed under Part II of this Schedule, exceeds the number of days constituting the worker's normal working week then, notwithstanding the foregoing provisions of this paragraph, the duration of that period of annual holiday may be reduced by one day and in such a case one day of annual holiday may be allowed on any working day (not being the worker's weekly short day) in the holiday season.

(5) Subject to the provisions of sub-paragraph (1) of this paragraph, any day of annual holiday under this Schedule may be allowed on a day on which the worker is entitled to a day of holiday or to a half-holiday under any enactment other than the Wages Councils Act 1959.

5. An employer shall give to a worker reasonable notice of the commencing date or dates and duration of the period or periods of his annual holiday. Such notice shall be given at least 21 days before the first day of the annual holiday or before the first day of each period of annual holiday, as the case may be, and may be given individually to the worker or by the posting of a notice in the place where the worker is employed.

PART IV

HOLIDAY REMUNERATION

A.—CUSTOMARY HOLIDAYS

6.—(1) Subject to the provisions of this paragraph, for each day of holiday to which a worker is entitled under Part II of this Schedule he shall be paid by the employer as holiday remuneration whichever of the following sums is the greater, that is to say either:—

(a) a sum equal to the worker's average hourly earnings for the hours worked by him for the employer in the week immediately preceding that in which the holiday occurs ; or

(b) a sum equal to the hourly general minimum time rate (being statutory minimum remuneration) which is applicable to the worker (or which would be applicable to him if he were a time worker) ;

multiplied in either case by the number of hours (exclusive of overtime) normally worked by him for the employer on that day of the week.

(2) Payment of the said holiday remuneration is subject to the condition that the worker presents himself for employment at the usual starting hour on the first working day following the holiday and works throughout that day or, if he fails to do so, failure is by reason of the proved illness of, or accident to, the worker or with the consent of the employer.

(3) The holiday remuneration in respect of any customary holiday shall be paid by the employer to the worker on the pay day on which the wages for the week including the first working day following the customary holiday are paid.

B.—ANNUAL HOLIDAY

7.—(1) Subject to the provisions of this paragraph and of paragraph 8, a worker qualified to be allowed an annual holiday under this Schedule shall be paid as holiday remuneration by his employer in respect thereof, on the last pay day preceding such annual holiday :—

(a) in respect of the annual holiday to be allowed during the holiday season commencing on 6th April 1970 an amount equal to *4.8* per cent. of the total remuneration paid by the employer to the worker during the 12 months immediately preceding the commencement of the holiday season ;

(b) *in respect of the annual holiday to be allowed during the holiday season commencing on*

6th April 1971—5.2 per cent.
6th April 1972—5.6 per cent.
6th April 1973 and on 6th April in each succeeding year—6.0 per cent.
} *of the total remuneration paid by the employer to the worker during the 12 months immediately preceding the commencement of the holiday season aforesaid.*

(2) Where under the provisions of paragraph 4 an annual holiday is allowed in more than one period, the holiday remuneration shall be apportioned accordingly.

8. Where any accrued holiday remuneration has been paid by the employer to the worker (in accordance with paragraph 9 of this Schedule or with Order S.B. (66)), in respect of employment during any of the periods referred to in that paragraph or that Order, the amount of holiday remuneration payable by the employer in respect of any annual holiday for which the worker has qualified by reason of employment during the said period shall be reduced by the amount of the said accrued holiday remuneration unless that remuneration has been deducted from a previous payment of holiday remuneration made under the provisions of this Schedule or of Order S.B. (66).

ACCRUED HOLIDAY REMUNERATION PAYABLE ON TERMINATION OF EMPLOYMENT

9. Where a worker ceases to be employed by an employer after the provisions of this Schedule become effective, the employer shall, immediately on the termination of the employment (hereinafter called "the termination date"), pay to the worker as accrued holiday remuneration:—

(1) in respect of employment in the 12 months up to and including 5th April immediately preceding the termination date, a sum equal to the holiday remuneration for any days of annual holiday for which he has qualified except days of annual holiday which he has been allowed or has become entitled to be allowed before leaving the employment ; and

(2) *in respect of any employment since 5th April immediately preceding the termination date, an amount equal to the holiday remuneration which would have been payable to him if he could have been allowed an annual holiday in respect of that employment at the time of leaving it :*

Provided that no worker shall be entitled to the payment by his employer of accrued holiday remuneration if he is dismissed on the grounds of industrial misconduct and is so informed by the employer at the time of dismissal.

PART V

GENERAL

10. For the purpose of calculating any period of employment qualifying a worker for an annual holiday under this Schedule, the worker shall be treated—

(1) as if he were employed for a week in respect of any week in which—

(a) in the case of a worker other than a part-time worker, he has worked for the employer for not less than 24 hours and has performed some work for which statutory minimum remuneration is payable ;

(b) in the case of a part-time worker, he has worked for the employer and has performed some work for which statutory minimum remuneration is payable ;

(c) (i) in the case of a worker other than a part-time worker, he has worked for the employer for less than 24 hours by reason of the proved illness of, or accident to, the worker or, in the case of any worker, for a like reason he has been absent throughout the week:
Provided that the number of weeks which may be treated as weeks of employment for such reason shall not exceed four in the aggregate in any such period ; or

(ii) in the case of any worker, he has been suspended throughout the week owing to shortage of work:
Provided that the number of weeks which may be treated as weeks of employment for such reason shall not exceed four in the aggregate in any such period ;

(2) as if he were employed on any day of holiday allowed under the provisions of this Schedule, or of Order S.B. (66), and for the purposes of the provisions of sub-paragraph (1) of this paragraph, a worker who is absent on any such holiday shall be treated as having worked thereon for the employer on work for which statutory minimum remuneration is payable for the number of hours normally worked by him on that day of the week.

DEFINITIONS

11. In this Schedule, unless the context otherwise requires, the following expressions have the meanings hereby respectively assigned to them, that is to say:—

"AVERAGE HOURLY EARNINGS" means the total remuneration paid by the employer to the worker in the week preceding the holiday divided by the number of hours (including overtime) worked for the employer in that week:

Provided that where a worker has been allowed any day as holiday in that week he shall be deemed to have worked thereon for the number of hours normally worked by him on that day of the week.

"NORMAL WORKING WEEK" means the number of days on which it has been usual for the worker to work in a week in the employment of the employer in the 12 months immediately preceding the commencement of the holiday season, or, where under paragraph 9 accrued holiday remuneration is payable on the termination of the employment, in the 12 months immediately preceding the termination date:

Provided that—

(1) part of a day shall count as a day;

(2) no account shall be taken of any week in which the worker did not perform any work for which statutory minimum remuneration has been fixed.

"PART-TIME WORKER" means a worker who normally works for the employer for less than 24 hours a week by reason only of the fact that he does not hold himself out as normally available for work for more than the number of hours he normally works in the week.

"STATUTORY MINIMUM REMUNERATION" means minimum remuneration (other than holiday remuneration) fixed by a wages regulation order made by the Secretary of State to give effect to proposals submitted to her by the Wages Council.

"TOTAL REMUNERATION" means any payments paid or payable to the worker under his contract of employment, for time worked or piece work done by him, holiday remuneration, any productivity, long service or other bonus payable to the worker on a weekly, fortnightly or monthly basis and merit payments so payable but does not include any other payments.

"WEEK" means "pay week".

12. The provisions of this Schedule are without prejudice to any agreement for the allowance of any further holidays with pay or for the payment of additional holiday remuneration.

EXPLANATORY NOTE

(This Note is not part of the Order.)

This Order, which has effect from 29th December 1969, sets out the holidays which an employer is required to allow to workers and the remuneration payable for those holidays in substitution for the holidays and holiday remuneration set out in the Wages Regulation (Sack and Bag) (Holidays) Order 1968 (Order S.B. (66)), which Order is revoked.

New provisions are printed in italics.

STATUTORY INSTRUMENTS

1969 No. 1742

ANIMALS

DISEASES OF ANIMALS

The Export of Horses (Excepted Cases) Order 1969

Made - - -	*4th December* 1969
Laid before Parliament	*17th December* 1969
Coming into Operation	*1st January* 1970

The Minister of Agriculture, Fisheries and Food and the Secretary of State, acting jointly, in exercise of the powers conferred on them by sections 1, 37 and 85 of the Diseases of Animals Act 1950(a), as read with the Transfer of Functions (Animal Health) Order 1955(b), as adapted to air transport by section 11 of the Agriculture (Miscellaneous Provisions) Act 1954(c) and as amended by section 1 of the Ponies Act 1969(d), and of all other powers enabling them in that behalf, hereby order as follows :—

Citation and commencement

1. This Order, which may be cited as the Export of Horses (Excepted Cases) Order 1969, shall come into operation on 1st January 1970.

Interpretation

2.—(1) In this Order unless the context otherwise requires—

"the Act" means the Diseases of Animals Act 1950 ;

"horse" means a horse (including an ass and mule) over 14½ hands in height ;

"local authority" means a local authority for the purposes of the Act ;

"master" includes any person having the charge or command of a vessel except the pilot ;

"the Minister", in its application to horses shipped or intended to be shipped from England and Wales, means the Minister of Agriculture, Fisheries and Food, and in its corresponding application to Scotland, means the Secretary of State ;

"permit" means a permit issued by the Minister under the provisions of this Order ;

"pilot", in relation to an aircraft, means the pilot or other person having the command or charge of the aircraft ;

"shipped" means carried by sea or by air and "shipment" shall be construed accordingly ;

"veterinary inspector" means a veterinary inspector appointed by the Minister of Agriculture, Fisheries and Food.

(a) 1950 c. 36. For change of title of the Minister see S.I. 1955/554 (1955 I, p. 1200).
(b) S.I. 1955/958 (1955 I, p. 1184).   (c) 1954 c. 39.
(d) 1969 c. 28.

(2) The Interpretation Act 1889(a) applies to the interpretation of this Order as it applies to the interpretation of an Act of Parliament, and as if this Order and the Order hereby revoked were Acts of Parliament.

Exemption of certain horses from examination before export

3. Section 37(1) of the Act, as adapted to air transport by section 11 of the Agriculture (Miscellaneous Provisions) Act 1954 and as amended by section 1 of the Ponies Act 1969 (which as so adapted and amended requires any horse over 14½ hands in height and a foal travelling with its dam if the dam is over that height shipped from any port or aerodrome in Great Britain to any port or aerodrome outside the United Kingdom, the Channel Islands and the Isle of Man to be examined by a veterinary inspector immediately before being shipped), shall not apply to—

(a) any horse shipped to any port or aerodrome which is in the Republic of Ireland or which is not in Europe, and any foal travelling with its dam if the dam is such a horse ;

(b) any horse which the Minister is satisfied is intended for exhibition, breeding, racing, jumping, riding or polo ; or

(c) a foal travelling with its dam if the dam is any such horse as is referred to in paragraph (b) of this Article.

Provided that in every case in which paragraph (b) or (c) of this Article shall apply, a permit authorising the shipment of the horse shall be obtained before shipment takes place.

Provisions as to permits authorising shipment

4.—(1) An application for a permit authorising shipment of a horse shall be made to the Minister 7 days before the proposed date of shipment (or within such lesser period as the Minister may at his discretion allow), in such form as the Minister may require, and the applicant for the permit shall furnish to the Minister if requested to do so such information and evidence as the Minister may require to satisfy himself that the case falls within the terms of paragraph (b) or (c) of Article 3 of this Order.

(2) A permit shall be delivered at the time of shipment to the master of the vessel or the pilot of the aircraft on which the horse to which the permit relates is shipped, who shall on demand produce the same to any police officer, officer of the Minister or Customs and Excise or an inspector of the local authority and allow such person to take a copy of or extract from the permit, and if the master or pilot fails to do so, or allows the horse to be shipped without delivery of the permit, he shall be guilty of an offence against the Act.

Local Authority to enforce Order

5. This Order shall, except where it is otherwise provided, be executed and enforced by the local authority.

Revocation

6.—(1) The Export of Horses (Excepted Cases) Order 1966(b) is hereby revoked.

(a) 1889 c. 63.   (b) S.I. 1966/508 (1966 I, p. 1074).

(2) Any permit insofar as it relates to a horse as defined by this Order or to a foal travelling with its dam where the dam is such a horse made or having effect under the aforesaid Order, if in force immediately before the coming into operation of this Order, shall thenceforth have effect under and by virtue of this Article.

In Witness whereof the Official Seal of the Minister of Agriculture, Fisheries and Food is hereunto affixed on 4th December 1969.

(L.S.)   *Cledwyn Hughes,*
Minister of Agriculture, Fisheries and Food.

Given under the Seal of the Secretary of State for Scotland on 4th December 1969.

(L.S.)   *William Ross,*
Secretary of State for Scotland.

EXPLANATORY NOTE

(*This Note is not part of the Order.*)

This Order revokes and re-enacts with modifications the Export of Horses (Excepted Cases) Order 1966.

By its terms, there are exempted from examination by a veterinary inspector (as required by section 37(1) (as amended) of the Diseases of Animals Act 1950 for horses over 14½ hands in height intended for export) (1) horses intended for export by sea or air to the Republic of Ireland or to any place outside Europe, (2) horses intended for export to Europe which the Minister of Agriculture, Fisheries and Food or the Secretary of State for Scotland is satisfied are intended for exhibition, breeding or various sporting purposes, and (3) foals travelling with their dams when the dams fall within a category above described.

In all cases, (other than accompanying foals), these exemptions relate to horses over 14½ hands in height.

STATUTORY INSTRUMENTS

1969 No. 1743

ANIMALS

DISEASES OF ANIMALS

The Importation of Dogs and Cats (Amendment) Order 1969

Made	-	-	-	*8th December* 1969
Laid before Parliament				*8th December* 1969
Coming into Operation				*9th December* 1969

The Minister of Agriculture, Fisheries and Food and the Secretary of State, acting jointly, in exercise of the powers vested in them under sections 1, 33 and 85 of the Diseases of Animals Act 1950(**a**), as read with the Transfer of Functions (Animal Health) Order 1955(**b**), and of all other powers enabling them in that behalf, hereby order as follows:—

Citation, extent, commencement and interpretation

1.—(1) This order which may be cited as the Importation of Dogs and Cats (Amendment) Order 1969, applies to Great Britain and shall come into operation on 9th December 1969.

(2) In this order "the principal order" means the Importation of Dogs and Cats Order of 1928(**c**).

(3) The Interpretation Act 1889(**d**) applies to the interpretation of this order as it applies to the interpretation of an Act of Parliament.

Period of detention and isolation for imported dogs and cats

2.—(1) In article 2(1) of the principal order (which requires an imported dog or cat for a period of six calendar months after its landing in Great Britain to be detained and isolated at the expense of its owner upon premises in the occupation or under the control of a veterinary surgeon) for the reference therein to a period of six calendar months there shall be substituted a reference to eight calendar months.

(2) Accordingly—

(*a*) in article 3(iii) of the principal order (which enables rules to be made and conditions to be inserted in licences granted under the principal order for the purpose of regulating the movement of dogs and cats during a period of six calendar months after landing), and

(*b*) in paragraphs (1)(*a*) and (*b*) and (3) of article 4 of the principal order (which in prescribing the action which may be taken in the case of illegal landing or other default refer to periods of six calendar months),

for the references in each case to six calendar months there shall be substituted references to eight calendar months.

(a) 1950 c. 36. For change of title of the Minister see S.I. 1955/554 (1955 I, p. 1200).
(b) S.I. 1955/958 (1955 I, p. 1184).   (c) S.R. & O. 1928/922 (Rev. II p. 399: 1928 p. 177).
(d) 1889 c. 63.

Transitional

3.—(1) This article applies to dogs and cats which on the coming into operation of this order are after landing in Great Britain already undergoing detention and isolation in accordance with article 2 of the principal order.

(2) With effect from the coming into operation of this order the said article 2, in its application to dogs and cats to which this article applies, shall have effect as if—

(*a*) for the period of six calendar months referred to in paragraph (1) of the said article there were substituted a reference to such a period as having regard to the period of detention and isolation already undergone will amount to a total of eight months from the landing ; and

(*b*) in relation to any period occurring after a period of six months from such landing has elapsed, the words in paragraph (1) of the said article " at the expense of its owner " were omitted.

In Witness whereof the Official Seal of the Minister of Agriculture, Fisheries and Food is hereunto affixed on 8th December 1969.

(L.S.)   *Cledwyn Hughes,*
Minister of Agriculture, Fisheries and Food.

Given under the Seal of the Secretary of State for Scotland on 8th December 1969.

(L.S.)   *William Ross,*
Secretary of State for Scotland.

EXPLANATORY NOTE

(*This Note is not part of the Order.*)

This order extends the period of detention and isolation of imported dogs and cats under the Importation of Dogs and Cats Order of 1928 from six months to eight months.

STATUTORY INSTRUMENTS

1969 No. 1746

CIVIL AVIATION

The Civil Aviation (Documentary Evidence) Regulations 1969

Made - - -	*5th December* 1969
Laid before Parliament	*16th December* 1969
Coming into Operation	*1st January* 1970

The Board of Trade, in exercise of the powers conferred upon them by section 6 of the Tokyo Convention Act 1967(a) and of all other powers enabling them in that behalf, hereby make the following Regulations:—

1. These Regulations may be cited as the Civil Aviation (Documentary Evidence) Regulations 1969 and shall come into operation on 1st January 1970.

2. Article 58 of the Air Navigation Order 1966(b), as amended (c), is hereby revoked.

3.—(1) The Interpretation Act 1889(d) shall apply for the interpretation of these Regulations as it applies for the interpretation of an Act of Parliament.

(2) Section 38(2) of the Interpretation Act 1889 (which relates to the effect of repeals) shall apply to these Regulations as if these Regulations were an Act of Parliament and as if Article 58 of the Air Navigation Order 1966 (which is revoked by regulation 2 of these Regulations) were an Act of Parliament thereby repealed.

4. Each of the authorities or persons named in column 1 of the Schedule hereto is hereby designated for the purpose of certifying a document as being, or being a true copy of, or of part of, a document or record of a description appearing opposite their respective names in column 2 of the said Schedule.

5. The Board of Trade and the Secretary of State for Defence are hereby designated for the purposes of section 5(1) of the Civil Aviation (Eurocontrol) Act 1962(e).

Goronwy Roberts,
Minister of State,
Board of Trade.

5th December 1969.

(a) 1967 c. 52.   (b) S.I. 1966/1184 (1966 III, p. 3073).
(c) There are no relevant amending Orders.   (d) 1889 c. 63.   (e) 1962 c. 8.

SCHEDULE

Authorities and persons designated for the purpose of certifying documents

Column 1	Column 2
Authorities and Persons	Documents and Records
The Board of Trade.	All documents issued and records kept by the Board of Trade or by the person for the time being holding the office of Director of Aviation Safety or of deputy to the said Director (being an official of the Board of Trade), in pursuance of an Order in Council made under section 8 of the Civil Aviation Act 1949(a) or in pursuance of the Civil Aviation (Licensing) Act 1960(b).
The person for the time being holding the office of the Secretary or Deputy Secretary of the Air Registration Board.	All documents issued and records kept by the Air Registration Board in pursuance of an Order in Council made under section 8 of the Civil Aviation Act 1949.
The person for the time being holding the office of the Secretary or Deputy Secretary of the Air Transport Licensing Board.	All documents issued and records kept by the Air Transport Licensing Board in pursuance of the Civil Aviation (Licensing) Act 1960.

EXPLANATORY NOTE

(This Note is not part of the Regulations.)

Section 6(1) of the Tokyo Convention Act 1967 provides that a document purporting to be certified by such authority or person as may be designated for the purpose by regulations made by the Board of Trade as being, or being a true copy of, or of part of, a document issued or record kept in pursuance of an Order in Council made under section 8 of the Civil Aviation Act 1949, or in pursuance of the Civil Aviation (Licensing) Act 1960, shall be evidence of the matters referred to in that document. These Regulations designate the authorities and persons who may certify such documents.

The Regulations also designate the Board of Trade and the Secretary of State for Defence for the purposes of section 5(1) of the Civil Aviation (Eurocontrol) Act 1962, which, as amended by section 6(2) of the Tokyo Convention Act 1967, provides for the use as evidence in any legal proceedings of records made by designated authorities and persons which purport to show the position of an aircraft or the terms or content of any message or signal transmitted to or received from an aircraft by such authorities or persons.

The Regulations revoke Article 58 of the Air Navigation Order 1966.

(a) 1949 c. 67.   (b) 1960 c. 38.

STATUTORY INSTRUMENTS

1969 No. 1749

SOCIAL SECURITY

The National Insurance (Industrial Injuries) (Determination of Claims and Questions) Amendment Regulations 1969

Made - - -	*8th December* 1969
Laid before Parliament	*16th December* 1969
Coming into Operation	*5th January* 1970

The Secretary of State for Social Services, in exercise of his powers under sections 42(2) and 50(2) of the National Insurance (Industrial Injuries) Act 1965(**a**) and section 10(5) of the National Insurance Act 1966(**b**) and of all other powers enabling him in that behalf, after consultation with the Council on Tribunals, and after reference to the Industrial Injuries Advisory Council, hereby makes the following regulations :—

Citation, interpretation and commencement

1. These regulations, which may be cited as the National Insurance (Industrial Injuries) (Determination of Claims and Questions) Amendment Regulations 1969, shall be read as one with the National Insurance (Industrial Injuries) (Determination of Claims and Questions) (No. 2) Regulations 1967(**c**) (hereinafter referred to as "the principal regulations") and shall come into operation on 5th January 1970.

Amendment of regulation 17 of the principal regulations

2.—(1) In regulation 17(1) of the principal regulations (which relates to oral hearings of applications, appeals and references from medical appeal tribunals) for the proviso there shall be substituted the following words :—

"Unless after considering the documents in the case and the reasons put forward in such request, the adjudicating authority is satisfied that the application, appeal or reference can properly be determined without a hearing, in which event the adjudicating authority may refuse such request and proceed to determine the application, appeal or reference and the person who made the request shall be informed in writing of such refusal.".

(2) For paragraph (7) of the said regulation 17 (which relates to determination of appeal by consent after application) there shall be substituted the following paragraph :—

"(7) Where the Commissioner, upon consideration of an application made to him in accordance with the provisions of regulation 14 of these regulations, gives leave to appeal he may proceed to determine any question of law stated in the application for leave to appeal as though it were a question of law arising on an appeal and as though the application were an appeal :

Provided that he shall not so proceed unless the consent of the Secretary of State for Social Services and the claimant or the association has been given.".

(a) 1965 c. 52.   (b) 1966 c. 6.   (c) S.I. 1967/1571 (1967 III, p. 4362).

(3) At the end of the said regulation 17 there shall be added the following paragraph : —

"(11) Where on an application for leave to appeal or on an appeal there is before the Commissioner medical advice or medical evidence relating to the claimant which has not been disclosed to him and in the opinion of the Commissioner the disclosure to the claimant of that advice or evidence would be harmful to the claimant's health such advice or evidence shall not be required to be disclosed to the claimant, but the Commissioner shall not by reason of such non-disclosure be precluded from taking it into account for the purpose of his determination of the application or appeal.".

Signed by authority of the Secretary of State for Social Services.

David Ennals,
Minister of State,
Department of Health and Social Security.

8th December 1969.

EXPLANATORY NOTE

(This Note is not part of the Regulations.)

These Regulations amend the National Insurance (Industrial Injuries) (Determination of Claims and Questions) (No. 2) Regulations 1967. The Regulations enable the National Insurance Commissioner to determine an application for leave to appeal on a point of law from the decision of a medical appeal tribunal, or such an appeal, or any question of law referred to him by a medical appeal tribunal, without an oral hearing, if he is satisfied that he can properly do so.

They also enable the Commissioner to proceed to decide a point of law raised on an application without the need for further appeal proceedings if all persons concerned agree, and to take into account certain medical advice or evidence without disclosing it to claimants when it is not in the claimants' interests to disclose it.

STATUTORY INSTRUMENTS

1969 No. 1750 (L.30)

LANDLORD AND TENANT

The Housing (Qualification Certificate and Rights of Entry Proceedings) Rules 1969

Made - - - - -	*4th December* 1969
Coming into Operation	*22nd December* 1969

The Lord Chancellor, in exercise of the powers conferred on him by section 106 of the Rent Act 1968(a) and section 56(2) of the Housing Act 1969(b), hereby makes the following Rules:—

1.—(1) These Rules may be cited as the Housing (Qualification Certificate and Rights of Entry Proceedings) Rules 1969 and shall come into operation on 22nd December 1969.

(2) The Interpretation Act 1889(c) shall apply to the interpretation of these Rules as it applies to the interpretation of an Act of Parliament.

2. Subject to the provisions of these Rules the Rent Restrictions Rules 1957(d) shall apply to appeals and applications to the county court under section 49 or 54 of the Housing Act 1969 as they apply to applications to the county court under the provisions specified in section 106(3) of the Rent Act 1968.

3. Unless the court otherwise directs, the local authority concerned and the tenant of the premises to which the certificate relates shall be made respondents to an application under subsection (1) of section 49 of the Housing Act 1969, and the local authority concerned and the landlord of the premises shall be made respondents to an application under subsection (2) of that section.

4. The forms in the Appendix to these Rules or forms substantially to the same effect shall be used for the purposes of applications under section 49 or 54 of the Housing Act 1969.

Dated 4th December 1969.

Gardiner, C.

(a) 1968 c. 23.　　　　　　　　　　(b) 1969 c. 33.
(c) 1889 c. 63.　　　　　　　　　　(d) S.I. 1957/1137 (1957 I, p. 1310).

APPENDIX

FORM 1

Housing
Act 1969
s. 49 (1), (2)

APPLICATION FOR ORDER TO LOCAL AUTHORITY TO ISSUE QUALIFICATION CERTIFICATE,
OR FOR CANCELLATION OF QUALIFICATION CERTIFICATE

In the   County Court

No. of Application

In the Matter of the Housing Act 1969

Between A.B.   Applicant
    and
    C.D.   Respondent

I,   *[name of applicant]*
of   *[address and occupation of applicant]*
hereby apply to the Court for an order [directing the Council [*name of local authority*]
to issue a qualification certificate in respect of the premises known as
                    of which I am the landlord and
[*name of tenant*] is the tenant. Notice of refusal of my application for a certificate was
served on me by the   Council on
the   day of   .]
[*or* quashing a qualification certificate issued by the   Council
[*name of local authority*] on the   day of   , in respect of
the premises known as   of which I am the tenant
and   [*name and address of landlord*] is the landlord.
A copy of the certificate was served on me on the   day of   .]

The grounds for this application are: [*state the grounds of the application*].

The names and addresses of the persons on whom it is intended to serve this application are: [*state names and addresses of persons intended to be served*].

My address for service is [*state applicant's address for service*].

Dated this   day of

Signed

Applicant.

To the Respondent

If you wish to oppose this application or dispute any allegation contained in it,
you must, within 6 days of its being served on you, inclusive of the day of service,
deliver at the court office an answer together with a copy for the applicant. The
documents may be sent by post so as to arrive at the court office within the time allowed.

In your answer you must state the grounds on which you oppose the application
and specify any allegation which you dispute.

If you do not deliver an answer, or if you deliver your answer out of time, you may
be ordered to pay any costs incurred in consequence of your failure or delay.

You should attend the hearing even if you have delivered an answer.

FORM 2

ORDER ON APPLICATION FOR ORDER TO LOCAL AUTHORITY TO ISSUE QUALIFICATION
CERTIFICATE, OR FOR CANCELLATION OF QUALIFICATION CERTIFICATE

Housing
Act 1969
s. 49 (1), (2)

In the	County Court
No. of Application	

In the Matter of the Housing Act 1969

Between A.B.	Applicant
and	
C.D.	Respondent

(Seal)

Upon hearing
  It is hereby ordered [that the
Council do issue a certificate in respect of the premises known as
          , of which the applicant is the landlord certifying that the premises
satisfy the qualifying conditions under section 43(1) of the Housing Act 1969].
[or that the qualification certificate dated the   day of   and
issued by the   Council under section 45 of the
Housing Act 1969 in respect of the premises known as   ,
of which the applicant is the tenant shall be quashed and deemed never to have had
effect.]

[*Add, if appropriate, order as to costs*]

Dated this   day of

Registrar

To the Applicant and the Respondent.

FORM 3

APPLICATION FOR ORDER EMPOWERING LANDLORD TO ENTER PREMISES AND CARRY OUT WORKS

In the   County Court

No. of Application

In the Matter of the Housing Act 1969

Between A.B.   Applicant
      and
       C.D.   Respondent

I,   [*name of applicant*]
of   [*address and occupation of applicant*]
hereby apply to the Court for an order authorising me to enter the premises known as
                , of which I am the landlord and
[*name of tenant*], is the tenant, in order to carry out works covered by a certificate of
fair rent relating to those premises dated   , being
works required to satisfy the conditions laid down in section 43 of the Housing Act
1969.
And for an order for the costs of this application.
The grounds for this application are: [*state the grounds of the application*].

The names and addresses of the persons on whom it is intended to serve this application are: [*state names and address of persons intended to be served*].

My address for service is [*state applicant's address for service*].

Dated this   day of
        Signed

Applicant.

To the Respondent

If you wish to oppose this application or to dispute any allegation contained in it, you must, within 6 days of its being served on you, inclusive of the day of service, deliver at the court office an answer, together with a copy for the applicant. The documents may be sent by post so as to arrive at the court office within the time allowed.

In your answer you must state the grounds on which you oppose the application and specify any allegation which you dispute.

If you do not deliver an answer, or if you deliver your answer out of time, you may be ordered to pay any costs incurred in consequence of your failure or delay.

You should attend the hearing even if you have delivered an answer.

FORM 4

ORDER EMPOWERING LANDLORD TO ENTER PREMISES AND CARRY OUT WORKS

Housing
Act 1969
s. 54

In the   County Court

No. of Application

In the Matter of the Housing Act 1969

Between A.B.   Applicant
    and
    C.D.   Respondent

(Seal)

Upon hearing
    It is ordered that the applicant, being the landlord of the premises known as
                                                    of which the
respondent is the tenant, or the applicant's duly authorised agent, be entitled to enter
the said premises in order to carry out [the works] [*or* the following works, namely
                            ] which are covered by the certificate of
fair rent relating to the said premises dated
being works required to satisfy the conditions laid down in section 43 of the Housing
Act 1969.

[*Add, if appropriate, order as to costs*]

                            Dated this   day of

                                            Registrar

To the Applicant and the Respondent.

EXPLANATORY NOTE

(This Note is not part of the Rules.)

These Rules apply the Rent Restriction Rules 1957 with minor adjustments
to proceedings in the county court under sections 49 and 54 of the Housing Act
1969 (which relate to the issue or refusal of qualification certificates and to
rights of entry to do works in premises occupied by tenants) and prescribe the
forms to be used in the proceedings.

STATUTORY INSTRUMENTS

1969 No. 1751

CUSTOMS AND EXCISE

The Import Duties (Temporary Exemptions) (No. 9) Order 1969

Made - - - -	*8th December* 1969
Laid before the House of Commons	*16th December* 1969
Coming into Operation	*1st January* 1970

The Lords Commissioners of Her Majesty's Treasury, by virtue of the powers conferred on them by sections 3(6) and 13 of the Import Duties Act 1958(a), and of all other powers enabling them in that behalf, on the recommendation of the Board of Trade hereby make the following Order:—

1.—(1) This Order may be cited as the Import Duties (Temporary Exemptions) (No. 9) Order 1969.

(2) The Interpretation Act 1889(b) shall apply for the interpretation of this Order as it applies for the interpretation of an Act of Parliament.

(3) This Order shall come into operation on 1st January 1970.

2.—(1) Until the beginning of 1st January 1971 or, in the case of goods in relation to which an earlier day is specified in Schedule 1 to this Order, until the beginning of that day, any import duty which is for the time being chargeable on goods of a heading of the Customs Tariff 1959 specified in that Schedule shall not be chargeable in respect of goods of any description there specified in relation to that heading.

(2) In the said Schedule 1—

(*a*) a reference to I.U.P.A.C. numbering, in relation to a compound having a ring structure, is to be taken as a reference to the system of numbering such compounds specified in the rules of the International Union of Pure and Applied Chemistry, as published in the year 1957;

(*b*) a reference to the British Pharmacopoeia or the British Pharmaceutical Codex is to the edition thereof current at the date of this Order, with amendments up to (but exclusive of) that date;

(*c*) an item marked with an asterisk is an item not exempt from import duty at the date of this Order; and

(*d*) an item marked with a dagger is an item appearing under a revised description, as compared with the corresponding description under which exemption from import duty was allowed at the date of this Order.

(3) Any entry in column 2 in the said Schedule 1 is to be taken to comprise all goods which would be classified under an entry in the same terms constituting a sub-heading (other than the final sub-heading) in the relevant heading in the Customs Tariff 1959.

(a) 1958 c. 6.   (b) 1889 c. 63.

(4) For the purposes of classification under the Customs Tariff 1959, in so far as that depends on the rate of duty, any goods to which paragraph (1) of this Article applies shall be treated as chargeable with the same duty as if this Order had not been made.

3. Until the beginning of 2nd July 1970, goods of sub-heading 39.03(A)(2)(*b*) of the Customs Tariff 1959 (which comprises photographic, including cine-matograph, film base of cellulose acetate) shall not be chargeable with import duty of an amount greater than 10 per cent. of their value.

4. The Import Duties (Temporary Exemptions) Orders specified in Schedule 2 to this Order, and the Import Duties (Temporary Exemptions) (Amendment) Order 1969(a) (which made minor amendments of the No. 6 Order of 1968), are hereby revoked.

Walter Harrison,
E. G. Perry,
Two of the Lords Commissioners
of Her Majesty's Treasury.

8th December 1969.

(a) S.I. 1969/315 (1969 I, p. 821).

SCHEDULE 1

Goods Temporarily Exempt from Import Duty

Tariff heading	Description

05.15   Norway Pout (Trisopterus (Gadus) Esmarkii)
Sand eels (ammodytes)

10.05   Flat white maize (until 5th March 1970)

12.01   Castor seed (until 7th May 1970)

15.04   Sperm oil, unrefined

15.17   Residues containing not less than 5 per cent. by weight and not more than 60 per cent. by weight of tocopherols

25.19   Magnesite, dead-burned, containing (a) not less than 90 per cent. by weight of magnesium compounds expressed as MgO, (b) a total of not more than $1 \cdot 0$ per cent. by weight of aluminium compounds and iron compounds expressed as Al_2O_3 and Fe_2O_3, (c) a total of not less than $2 \cdot 5$ per cent. by weight and not more than $5 \cdot 0$ per cent. by weight of calcium compounds and silicon compounds expressed as CaO and SiO_2, and in which the weight of calcium compounds expressed as CaO is not less than $1 \cdot 5$ times the weight of silicon compounds expressed as SiO_2 (until 5th March 1970)

27.07   Anthracene (until 2nd July 1970)
Pyridine bases, having a basicity equivalent to not less than $7 \cdot 0$ millilitres and not more than $12 \cdot 5$ millilitres of $1 \cdot 0$ N sulphuric acid solution when estimated by method No. RB. 1–67 of " Standard Methods for Testing Tar and its Products " published by the Standardisation of Tar Products Test Committee
Pyridine bases, of which, after drying, not less than 70 per cent. by volume distils between $140°$ and $250°$ centigrade at normal pressure

28.13   Hydrogen bromide, anhydrous

28.14   Arsenic trichloride
Boron tribromide
Boron trichloride
Phosphorus pentabromide
Phosphorus pentafluoride
Silicon tetrachloride
Sulphur tetrafluoride
Thionyl chloride

28.15   Carbonyl sulphide
tetraPhosphorus heptasulphide
Phosphorus pentasulphide, containing less than 15 parts per million by weight of arsenic calculated as As_2O_3, and containing less than 35 parts per million by weight of iron calculated as Fe

28.17   Potassium hydroxide, pharmaceutical quality

28.18   Barium oxide
Magnesium oxide, dead-burned but not fused, of a purity not less than 96 per cent., containing (a) a total of not more than $1 \cdot 0$ per cent. by weight of aluminium compounds and iron compounds expressed as Al_2O_3 and Fe_2O_3, (b) a total of not more than $3 \cdot 5$ per cent. by weight of calcium compounds and silicon compounds expressed as CaO and SiO_2, the weight of silicon compounds being not less than $1 \cdot 5$ times and not more than $3 \cdot 0$ times the weight of calcium compounds; and (c) of which not less than 50 per cent. by weight is retained by a sieve having a nominal width of aperture of $\frac{3}{16}$ inch (until 5th March 1970)

Tariff heading   *Description*

28.18 Magnesium oxide, dead-burned but not fused, of a purity not less than 96 per cent., which contains (a) not more than $0 \cdot 05$ per cent. by weight of boron compounds expressed as B_2O_3, (b) a total of not more than $0 \cdot 5$ per cent. by weight of aluminium compounds and iron compounds expressed as Al_2O_3 and Fe_2O_3, and (c) a total of not less than $1 \cdot 0$ per cent. by weight and not more than $3 \cdot 5$ per cent. by weight of calcium compounds and silicon compounds expressed as CaO and SiO_2, the weight of calcium compounds being not less than $1 \cdot 5$ times and not more than $2 \cdot 5$ times the weight of silicon compounds; and (d) of which not less than 35 per cent. by weight is retained by a sieve having a nominal width of aperture of $\frac{3}{16}$ inch (until 5th March 1970)

28.20 Aluminium oxide, not being artificial corundum, being in the form of spheres and containing by weight not more than $0 \cdot 06$ per cent. of acid soluble sulphates expressed as SO_3 and not more than $0 \cdot 005$ per cent. of sodium expressed as Na, and all of which passes a sieve having a nominal width of aperture of $4 \cdot 76$ millimetres and not less than 99 per cent. by weight of which is retained by a sieve having a nominal width of aperture of $1 \cdot 00$ millimetre

28.23 γ-Ferric oxide

28.28 Beryllium hydroxide
       Beryllium oxide
       Hydroxylammonium chloride containing not more than $0 \cdot 0005$ per cent. by weight of heavy metals estimated as Pb
       Hydroxylammonium sulphate

28.29 Potassium fluorosilicate
       Sodium fluoride, which does not contain impurities equivalent to more than 5×10^{-9} grammes of U_3O_8 per gramme, and of which 1 gramme must not contain impurities capable of depressing the estimation of U_3O_8 by more than 1×10^{-8} grammes, when determined fluorimetrically
       Sodium fluorosilicate
       Tungsten hexafluoride

28.30 Beryllium chloride
       Ferric chloride, analytical reagent quality
       Ferrous chloride, analytical reagent quality
       *Nickel chloride (until 2nd July 1970)

28.32 Ammonium perchlorate
       Calcium chlorate
       Sodium perchlorate

28.33 Barium bromide
       Sodium bromide which, in the form in which it is imported, loses not more than 1 per cent. of its weight on drying at 105° centigrade, contains (a) not less than 92 per cent. by weight and not more than 96 per cent. by weight of total bromides estimated as NaBr, (b) aluminosiliceous material equivalent to not less than $0 \cdot 3$ per cent. by weight and not more than $0 \cdot 5$ per cent. by weight of Al_2O_3 and to not less than $1 \cdot 5$ per cent. by weight and not more than $2 \cdot 5$ per cent. by weight of SiO_2, and of which not less than 90 per cent. by weight passes a sieve having a nominal width of aperture of 150 microns (until 5th March 1970)

28.35 Zinc sulphide

28.38 Beryllium sulphate
       Magnesium sulphate, anhydrous, containing not less than $0 \cdot 05$ per cent. by weight and not more than $1 \cdot 0$ per cent. by weight of potassium compounds calculated as K
       Mercuric sulphate
       Nickel sulphate (until 2nd July 1970)
       Potassium hydrogen per*mono*sulphate
       Thallous sulphate

Tariff heading	Description
28.39	Barium nitrate containing not more than $0 \cdot 006$ per cent. by weight of heavy metals calculated as Pb (until 2nd July 1970)
	Beryllium nitrate
	Potassium nitrite
28.40	*tetra*Potassium pyrophosphate
28.42	Magnesium carbonate, light, in rectangular blocks of a weight not less than 25 grammes and not more than 125 grammes and of a cubic capacity not less than 115 cubic centimetres
	Manganous carbonate
	Nickel carbonate, basic
	Potassium hydrogen carbonate
28.43	Potassium ferricyanide
	Sodium nitroprusside
28.44	Ammonium thiocyanate
	Potassium cyanate
	Sodium thiocyanate
28.46	Sodium metaborate tetrahydrate, $Na_2B_2O_4$, $4H_2O$
28.47	Bismuth aluminate containing not less than 52 per cent. by weight and not more than 55 per cent. by weight of bismuth calculated as Bi on the dry anhydrous salt
	Calcium dichromate
	Sodium antimonate
	Sodium tungstate containing not more than $0 \cdot 0003$ per cent. by weight of arsenic compounds calculated as As and not more than $0 \cdot 005$ per cent. by weight of molybdenum compounds calculated as Mo
28.48	*tri*Aluminium sodium tetradecahydrogen octaorthophosphate
	Dihydroxyaluminium sodium carbonate
	Ferric sodium pyrophosphate
28.49	Pyruvic acid enol phosphate, barium silver salt
	Silver protein, mild, which satisfies the requirements of the British Pharmaceutical Codex
	Silver protein, which satisfies the requirements of the British Pharmaceutical Codex
28.50	All goods of this heading other than radium compounds, natural uranium and compounds thereof and nuclear reactor cartridges, spent or irradiated
28.51	Deuterium oxide
	Lithium sulphate, of which the lithium is in the form of a stable isotope either of atomic weight 6 or of atomic weight 7, of a value not less than £1 per gramme
	*di*Sodium tetraborate, of which the boron is in the form of a stable isotope either of atomic weight 10 or of atomic weight 11, of a value not less than £1 per gramme
28.52	Compounds of uranium depleted in uranium-235, the following:—
	Uranium hexafluoride
	Uranium tetrafluoride
	Mixed rare earth compounds containing not less than $3 \cdot 5$ per cent. by weight and not more than $9 \cdot 0$ per cent. by weight of combined fluorine estimated as F, and not less than $0 \cdot 5$ per cent. by weight and not more than $4 \cdot 0$ per cent. by weight of barium compounds estimated as $BaSO_4$; and of which not less than 10 per cent. by weight is retained by a sieve having a nominal width of aperture of 45 microns
	Samarium trioxide
28.57	Aluminium sodium hydride
	Lithium borohydride
	Silane

Tariff heading	Description

28.58　Cyanogen bromide
Lithamide
Trichlorosilane containing not more than 0·002 parts per million by
weight of boron compounds calculated as B

29.01　Acenaphthylene
Allene
Anthracene (until 2nd July 1970)
Azulene
1,2-Benzanthracene
1,2-Benzofluorene
2,3-Benzofluorene
Bicyclo[2,2,1]hepta-2,5-diene
isoButane
n-But-1-ene
cisBut-2-ene
transBut-2-ene
But-2-ene, mixed isomers
isoButylbenzene
But-l-yne
Chrysene
pseudoCumene
trans-trans-trans-Cyclododeca-1,5,9-triene
Cyclo-octa-1,3-diene
Cyclo-octa-1,5-diene
Cyclo-octene
Cyclopentane
p-Cymene
Decahydronaphthalene
n-Decane
n-Dec-1-ene
1,2:3,4-Dibenzanthracene
9,10-Dihydroanthracene
3,3′-Dimethylbiphenyl
1,2-Dimethylcyclohexane
1,6-Dimethylnaphthalene
2,3-Dimethylnaphthalene
2,6-Dimethylnaphthalene
2,7-Dimethylnaphthalene
2,2-Dimethylpropane
n-Docos-1-ene
n-Dodecane
n-Dodec-1-ene
n-Dodecylbenzene
n-Eicosane
n-Eicos-1-ene
5-Ethylidenebicyclo[2,2,1]hept-2-ene
Fluoranthene
Fluorene
n-Hept-1-ene
n-Hept-2-ene
n-Hept-3-ene
n-Hept-1-yne
n-Hexadecane
n-Hexadec-1-ene
Humulene
Indane
Isoprene
Mesitylene
2-Methylbut-2-ene
1-Methylcycloheptene

Tariff heading	Description
29.01	Methylcyclohexane
	4-Methylcyclohexene
	Methylcyclopentane
	1-Methylcyclopentene
	1-Methylnaphthalene
	2-Methylnaphthalene
	Methylnaphthalene, mixed isomers
	2-Methylpentane
	2-Methylpent-1-ene
	4-Methylpent-1-ene
	cis-4-Methylpent-2-ene
	Methylstyrene, mixed isomers
	Myrcene
	Naphthacene
	Nona-1,8-diyne
	n-Nonane
	n-Octadec-1-ene
	Octa-1,7-diene
	n-Oct-1-ene
	n-Oct-2-ene
	n-Oct-1-yne
	n-Penta-1,3-diene
	n-Pent-1-ene
	Perylene
	Phellandrene
	Phenylacetylene
	Picene
	Propyne
	Pyrene
	β-Santalene
	Squalane
	Squalene
	transStilbene
	m-Terphenyl
	p-Terphenyl
	n-Tetracosane
	n-Tetradecane
	n-Tetradec-1-ene
	1,2,3,4-Tetrahydro-1,1,2,4,4,7-hexamethylnaphthalene
	1,2,3,4-Tetrahydronaphthalene
	4,5,9,10-Tetrahydropyrene (I.U.P.A.C. numbering)
	1,2,4,5-Tetramethylbenzene
	Tricyclo[5,2,1,0^{2,6}]decane
	n-Tridecane
	2,2,4-Trimethylpentane
	n-Undecane
	o-Xylene
	m-Xylene
29.02	Aldrin
	Allyl chloride
	Benzotrifluoride
	4-Bromobenzotrifluoride
	2-Bromobut-1-ene
	1-Bromo-3-chloro-2-methylpropane
	4-Bromo-n-heptane
	2-Bromo-n-hexane
	3-Bromo-n-hexane
	2-Bromomesitylene
	2-Bromopropene
	Bromotrifluoroethylene

Tariff heading   *Description*

29.02   Bromotrifluoromethane
         Carbon tetrafluoride
         Chlordane
         2-Chlorobenzotrifluoride
         3-Chlorobenzotrifluoride
         4-Chlorobenzotrifluoride
         2-Chlorobuta-1,3-diene
         1-Chloro-*n*-butane
         1-Chloro-*n*-but-1-ene
         3-Chloro-*n*-but-1-ene
         1-Chloro-*n*-but-2-ene
         1-Chloro-*n*-dodecane
         1-(Chloromethyl)naphthalene
         1-Chloronaphthalene
         1-Chloro-*n*-octane
         Chloropentafluoroethane (until 7th May 1970)
         1-Chloroprop-1-ene
         3-Chloropropyne
         2-Chlorotoluene
         2-Chloro-*p*-xylene
         Decachlorobicyclopenta-2,4-dienyl
         1,4-Dibromobut-2-ene
         2,3-Dibromobut-2-ene
         Dibromodifluoromethane
         1,2-Dibromoethane
         Dibromomethane
         1,2-Dibromo-2-methylpropane
         1,1-Dibromoprop-1-ene
         1,2-Dibromotetrafluoroethane
         1,3-Dichlorobenzene
         2,6-Dichlorobenzylidene chloride
         2,3-Dichlorobuta-1,3-diene
         1,4-Dichlorobutane
         1,3-Dichloro-*n*-but-2-ene
         1,4-Dichlorobut-2-ene
         1,1-Dichloro-2,2-di-(4-chlorophenyl)ethane
         1,1-Dichloro-2,2-di-(4-ethylphenyl)ethane
         1,2-Dichloroethylene
         2,3-Dichlorohexafluorobut-2-ene
         1,2-Dichlorohexafluorocyclopentene
         1,1-Dichloroprop-1-ene
         1,3-Dichloropropene
         2,3-Dichloroprop-1-ene
         2,6-Dichlorotoluene
         3,4-Dichlorotoluene
         2,5-Dichloro-*p*-xylene
         1,1-Difluoroethane
         1,1-Difluoroethylene
         Diphenylchloromethane
         Dodecachloropentacyclo[5,2,1,0^{2,6},0^{3,9},0^{5,8}]decane
         1,6,7,8,9,14,15,16,17,17,18,18-Dodecachloropentacyclo-
             [12,2,1,1^{6,9},0^{2,13},0^{5,10}]octadeca-7,15-diene
         Fluorobenzene
         4-Fluorobenzotrifluoride
         2-Fluoronaphthalene
         Heptachlor
         Heptafluoro-1-iodopropane
         Hexabromobenzene
         1,2,5,6,9,10-Hexabromocyclododecane
         Hexachlorobuta-1,3-diene

Tariff heading	Description

29.02   1,2,3,4,5,6-Hexachlorocyclohexane, mixed isomers, of which either
         (a) the α-isomer content is not more than 50 per cent. by weight, or
         (b) the γ-isomer content is not less than 35 per cent. by weight
         provided that, in a case where the γ-isomer content is not less than
         35 per cent. and not more than 40 per cent. by weight, not less
         than 90 per cent. by weight of the material passes a sieve having a
         nominal width of aperture of 53 microns
         α-1,2,3,4,5,6-Hexachlorocyclohexane
         γ-1,2,3,4,5,6-Hexachlorocyclohexane
         Hexachlorocyclopentadiene
         Hexafluoropropene
         Methallyl chloride
         3-Methylbenzyl bromide
         4-Methylbenzyl bromide
         Octafluorocyclobutane
         Pentachloroethane
         1,1,2,2-Tetrabromoethane
         1,2,4,5-Tetrachlorobenzene
         1,1,2,2-Tetrachloroethane
         1,2,2,3-Tetrachloropropane
         2,3,5,6-Tetrachloro-p-xylene
         Tribromofluoromethane
         1,2,3-Tribromo-2-methylpropane
         1,2,3-Trichlorobenzene
         1,2,4-Trichlorobenzene
         Trichlorobenzene, mixed isomers
         Trifluoroiodomethane
         Vinyl bromide
         Vinyl chloride (until 2nd July 1970)
         Vinyl fluoride

29.03   Benzene-1,3-disulphonic acid
         1-tertButyl-3,4,5-trimethyl-2,6-dinitrobenzene
         Chloropicrin
         1,5-Dinitronaphthalene
         Ethanesulphonyl chloride
         1-Ethyl-2-nitrobenzene
         1-Fluoro-2-nitrobenzene
         Methanesulphonic acid
         Methanesulphonyl chloride
         2-Nitrobiphenyl
         4-Nitrobiphenyl
         Nitroethane
         Nitromethane
         1-Nitronaphthalene
         1-Nitropropane
         2-Nitropropane
         3-Nitro-o-xylene
         2-Nitro-p-xylene
         1,1,3,3,5-Pentamethyl-4,6-dinitroindane
         diSodium benzene-1,3-disulphonate
         Sodium 2-bromoethanesulphonate
         Sodium 4-chlorobenzenesulphonate
         Sodium 3-chloro-n-but-2-ene-1-sulphonate
         Sodium dibunate
         Sodium ethylenesulphonate
         Sodium styrenesulphonate, mixed isomers
         1,3,5-Trinitrobenzene

29.04   Adonitol
         Allyl alcohol

Tariff heading	*Description*
29.04	Amyl alcohol, containing not less than 58 per cent. by weight of *n*-pentan-1-ol and not more than 1 per cent. by weight of aldehydes or ketones calculated as $C_5H_{10}O$

D-Arabitol
3-Bromopropan-1-ol
n-Butane-1,3-diol
Butane-1,4-diol
n-Butane-2,3-diol
Butane-1,2,4-triol
n-Butan-2-ol
But-2-ene-1,4-diol
n-But-2-en-1-ol
But-3-en-2-ol
Butylchloral hydrate
But-2-yne-1,4-diol
But-3-yn-1-ol
But-3-yn-2-ol
4-Chlorobutan-1-ol
2-Chloroethanol
3-Chloropropan-1-ol
Decane-1,10-diol
1,6-Dibromo-1,6-dideoxymannitol
2,3-Dibromopropan-1-ol containing not more than 0·1 per cent. by weight of 1,2,3-tribromopropane (until 5th March 1970)
2,6-Dimethylheptan-4-ol
2,5-Dimethylhexane-2,5-diol
(±)-3,7-Dimethylnona-1,6-dien-3-ol
2,4-Dimethylnonan-4-ol
3,6-Dimethyloctan-3-ol
3,7-Dimethyloctan-3-ol
Dimethyloctanol, mixed 2,6,2- and 3,7,3- isomers
(−)-3,7-Dimethyloct-6-en-1-ol
3,7-Dimethyloct-6-en-1-yn-3-ol
3,6-Dimethyloct-4-yne-3,6-diol
2,4-Dimethylpentan-1-ol
2,2-Dimethylpropanediol
2,2-Dimethylpropanol
*meso*Erythritol
Ethchlorvynol
2-Ethylbutan-1-ol
2-Ethylhexane-1,3-diol
2-Ethyl-2-hydroxymethylpropanediol
2-Ethyl-4-methylpentan-1-ol
Farnesol
Glyoxal sodium bisulphite
n-Heptan-1-ol
n-Hept-1-en-4-ol
Hexadecyl alcohol, mixed isomers, which freezes at a temperature not higher than −40° centigrade
2*H*-Hexafluoropropan-2-ol
Hexane-1,6-diol
n-Hexane-2,5-diol
Hexane-1,2,6-triol
Hexanetriol, mixed isomers
n-Hexan-1-ol
n-Hex-3-en-1-ol
7-Hydroxy-3,7-dimethyloctanal sodium bisulphite
2-Hydroxymethyl-2-methylpropanediol
2-Hydroxymethyl-2-nitropropanediol
Methallyl alcohol
3-Methylbutan-1-ol, of a purity not less than 90 per cent.

Tariff heading	Description
29.04	2-Methylbutan-2-ol
	6-Methylhept-5-en-2-ol
	3-Methylpentyn-3-ol
	2-Methylpropan-2-ol containing not more than 0·007 per cent. by weight of unsaturated compounds calculated as butene
	Nerolidol
	1H,1H,5H-Octafluoropentan-1-ol
	2-n-Octyl-n-dodecan-1-ol
	Pentane-1,5-diol
	n-Pentan-1-ol
	Phytol
	isoPhytol
	Pinacol
	Propane-1,3-diol
	Prop-2-yn-1-ol
	Succinaldehyde di(sodium bisulphite)
	1H,1H,3H-Tetrafluoropropan-1-ol
	2,4,7,9-Tetramethyldec-5-yne-4,7-diol
	3,7,11,15-Tetramethylhexadecane-1,2,3-triol
	Tridecyl alcohol, mixed isomers (until 5th March 1970)
	3,7,9-Trimethyldeca-1,6-dien-3-ol
	2,2,4-Trimethylpentan-1-ol
	n-Undecan-1-ol
	Xylitol
29.05	17α-Allyloestr-4-en-17β-ol
	Borneol
	isoBorneol
	Dicyclopropylmethanol
	Dihydrotachysterol
	2,2-Di-(4-hydroxycyclohexyl)propane
	1,4-Di(hydroxymethyl)cyclohexane
	Ethynodiol
	Fenchyl alcohol
	mesoInositol
	2-Methyl-4-phenylbutan-2-ol
	3-Methyl-1-phenylpentan-3-ol
	3-Nitrobenzyl alcohol
	4-Nitrobenzyl alcohol
	Nopol
	1-Phenylethanol
	α-Terpineol, having a freezing point not less than 20° centigrade
	2,2,2-Trichlorodi-(4-chlorophenyl)ethanol
	4,7,7-Trimethylbicyclo[4,1,0]hept-4-en-3-ylmethanol
29.06	2-Benzylphenol
	2-tertButyl-4-ethylphenol
	2-secButylphenol (until 5th March 1970)
	4-secButylphenol
	2-tertButylphenol
	o-Cresol
	p-Cresol (until 5th March 1970)
	3,5-Ditertbutyl-4-hydroxybenzyl alcohol
	3,5-Ditertbutyl-4-hydroxybiphenyl
	1,1-Di-(3-tertbutyl-4-hydroxy-6-methylphenyl)-n-butane
	2,6-Ditertbutylphenol
	Di-(3,5-ditertbutyl-4-hydroxyphenyl)methane
	2,3-Di-(3,4-dihydroxybenzyl)-n-butane
	2,2'-Dihydroxybiphenyl
	3,4-Dihydroxybiphenyl
	1,3-Dihydroxynaphthalene
	1,5-Dihydroxynaphthalene

Tariff heading	Description

29.06
2,3-Dihydroxynaphthalene
3,4-Di-(4-hydroxyphenyl)-*n*-hexane-3,4-diol
Di-(1-methylbutyl)phenol, mixed isomers
2,4-Di*tert*pentylphenol
2,5-Di*tert*pentylquinol
2,6-Di*iso*propylphenol
2-Hydroxybiphenyl (until 5th March 1970)
4-Hydroxybiphenyl
Indan-5-ol
2-Methylquinol
1-Naphthol
2-Naphthol (until 2nd July 1970)
3-*n*-Pentadecylphenol
4-*tert*Pentylphenol
*iso*Propylcresol, mixed isomers
Resorcinol
Salicyl alcohol
Sodium biphenyl-2-yloxide (until 5th March 1970)
2,4,2′,4′-Tetrahydroxybiphenyl
Thymol
1,1,3-Tri-(5-*tert*butyl-4-hydroxy-2-methylphenyl)-*n*-butane-toluene
　　complex
2,4,6-Tri-(3,5-di*tert*butyl-4-hydroxybenzyl)mesitylene
2,3,5-Trimethylquinol
2,4-Xylenol
3,5-Xylenol (until 7th May 1970)

29.07
3-Chloro-4-hydroxybiphenyl
3-Chlorophenol
Chloro-5-*iso*propyl-*m*-cresol (—OH at 1), mixed isomers
2,3-Dichlorophenol
2,2-Di-(3,5-dichloro-4-hydroxyphenyl)propane
6,7-Dihydroxynaphthalene-2-sulphonic acid
Hexachlorophane
5-Hydroxynaphthalene-1-sulphonic acid
*di*Sodium 1,8-dihydroxynaphthalene-3,6-disulphonate
*Sodium 6,7-dihydroxynaphthalene-2-sulphonate
*Sodium 2,4,5-trichlorophenoxide
2-Trifluoromethylphenol
3-Trifluoromethylphenol
4-Trifluoromethylphenol

29.08
4-Allylanisole
Allyl ethyl ether
Anethole
Batyl alcohol
1-(2-Benzylphenoxy)propan-2-ol
n-Butyl vinyl ether
*iso*Butyl vinyl ether
Chloromethyl methyl ether
Di-*n*-butyldigol
2,5-Di*tert*butylperoxy-2,5-dimethylhexane
1,4-Di-(1-*tert*butylperoxy-1-methylethyl)benzene
1,1-Di*tert*butylperoxy-3,3,5-trimethylcyclohexane
Di-(2-chloroethyl) ether
2,4-Dichlorophenyl 4-nitrophenyl ether
2,2-Di-(4,4-di*tert*butylperoxycyclohexyl)propane
Di-(αα-dimethylbenzyl) peroxide
1,2-Diethoxyethane
Diethyldigol
Di-*n*-hexyl ether
2-[2,2-Di-(2-hydroxyethoxymethyl)-*n*-butoxy]ethanol

Tariff heading   *Description*

29.08   1,2-Dimethoxyethane
Dimethyldigol
Dimethyl ether
Dimethyltetragol
Dimethyltrigol
2,4-Dinitrophenetole
1,4-Dioxan
Di(phenoxyphenoxy)benzene, mixed isomers
Di-(3-phenoxyphenyl) ether
Di*iso*propylbenzene hydroperoxide, mixed 1,3- and 1,4- isomers (until 5th March 1970)
Di-(2,3,3,3-tetrachloropropyl) ether
Ethoxyacetylene
2-Ethoxynaphthalene
Ethyldigol, containing not more than 1 per cent. by weight of ethanediol
13β-Ethyl-17α-ethynyl-3-methoxygona-2,5(10)-dien-17β-ol
Ethyl vinyl ether
n-Hexyldigol
2-*n*-Hexyloxyethanol
p-Menthanyl hydroperoxide
3-Methoxy-*n*-butan-1-ol
Methoxyflurane
4-Methoxy-4-methylpentan-2-ol
2-Methoxynaphthalene
4-Methoxy-1-naphthol
Methyl vinyl ether
Musk ambrette
4-Nitroanisole
4-Nitrophenetole
*iso*Pentyl 2-phenylethyl ether
2-Phenoxyethanol
Potassium guaiacolsulphonate
1,1,1-Trichlorodi-(4-methoxyphenyl)ethane
Trigol containing not more than 0·1 per cent. by weight of digol
1,2,3-Tri-(2-hydroxyethoxy)propane
1,2,3-Tri-(2-hydroxy-*n*-propoxy)propane
Tri-α-propylene glycol *mono*methyl ether

29.09   Allyl glycidyl ether
1-Bromo-2,3-epoxypropane
n-Butyl glycidyl ether
1-Chloro-2,3-epoxypropane
Dicyclopentadiene dioxide
Dieldrin
1,4-Di-(2,3-epoxypropoxy)butane
Endrin
1,2-Epoxy-*n*-butane
Epoxybutane, mixed 1,2- and 2,3- isomers
$\alpha\beta$-Epoxyethylbenzene
3,4-Epoxytricyclo[5,2,1,0^{2,6}]decanol
Glycidol

29.10 α-Anhydroglucochloral
8-*tert*Butyl-1,4-dioxaspiro[4,5]decane
1-Chloro-2,2-diethoxyethane
1,1-Diethoxy-3,7-dimethylocta-2,6-diene
1,1-Diethoxy-*n*-hex-2-ene
1,1-Dimethoxy-3,7-dimethylocta-2,6-diene
*Dimethoxymethane
1,1-Dimethoxy-*n*-octane
1,3-Dioxan
1,3-Dioxolan containing not more than 0·02 per cent. by weight of water
1-Ethoxy-1,3,3-trimethoxypropane

Tariff heading	*Description*
29.10	2-Ethyl-2-methyl-1,3-dioxolan
	Hexahydro-2,3,6,7-tetrahydroxy-1,4,5,8-tetraoxanaphthalene
	Penthrichloral
	4,4a,5,9b-Tetrahydroindeno[1,2-*d*]-1,3-dioxin
	4,4a,9,9a-Tetrahydroindeno[2,1-*d*]-1,3-dioxin
	1,1,3,3-Tetramethoxypropane
29.11	Acrylaldehyde
	β-8′-Apocarotenal
	4-*tert*Butylbenzaldehyde
	3-(4-*tert*Butylphenyl)-2-methylpropionaldehyde
	n-Butyraldehyde
	*iso*Butyraldehyde
	Crotonaldehyde containing not more than 4 per cent. by weight of water
	*iso*Cyclocitral
	2,4-Dihydroxybenzaldehyde
	3,4-Dihydroxybenzaldehyde
	2,3-Dimethoxybenzaldehyde
	2,6-Dimethylhept-5-enal
	3,7-Dimethylnona-2,6-dienal
	2-Ethylhexanal
	Glutaraldehyde (until 2nd July 1970)
	DL-Glyceraldehyde
	Glycidaldehyde
	Glyoxal
	n-Heptanal
	n-Hex-2-enal
	4-Hydroxybenzaldehyde
	4-(4-Hydroxy-4-methylpentyl)cyclohex-3-enaldehyde
	Methacrylaldehyde
	1,2,3,4,5,6,7,8-Octahydro-8,8-dimethyl-2-napthaldehyde
	Terephthalaldehyde
	m-Tolualdehyde
	3,5,5-Trimethylhexanal
	2,6,10-Trimethylundec-10-enal
	n-Valeraldehyde
	*iso*Valeraldehyde
29.12	2-Chlorobenzaldehyde
	4-Chlorobenzaldehyde
	4-Chloro-3-nitrobenzaldehyde
	3,4-Dichlorobenzaldehyde
	2,4-Dinitrobenzaldehyde
	2-Nitrobenzaldehyde
	4-Nitrobenzaldehyde
	5-Nitrosalicylaldehyde
	Sodium 2-formylbenzenesulphonate
29.13	Acetoin
	Acetoin dimer
	Acetonylacetone
	Acetovanillone
	4-Acetyl-6-*tert*butyl-1,1-dimethylindane
	7-Acetyl-6-ethyl-1,2,3,4-tetrahydro-1,1,4,4-tetramethylnaphthalene
	7-Acetyl-2-methyl-5-*iso*propylbicyclo[2,2,2]oct-2-ene
	4-Acetyl-3,7,7-trimethylbicyclo[4,1,0]hept-2-ene
	Benzoin
	p-Bromo-*n*-valerophenone
	Butanedione
	n-Butyrophenone
	(+)-Camphor

Tariff heading	Description
29.13	Canthaxanthin
	L-Carvone
	Chloranil
	p-Chloro-n-butyrophenone
	2-Chlorocyclohexanone
	2-[α-(4-Chlorophenyl)phenylacetyl]indane-1,3-dione
	Cycloheptadecanone
	Cycloheptadec-9-enone
	Cycloheptanone
	Cyclohexane-1,3-dione
	Cyclo-octanone (until 2nd July 1970)
	Cyclopentadecanone
	4-n-Decyloxy-2-hydroxybenzophenone
	Dibenzo[a,i]pyrene-5,8-dione
	2,5-Dichloro-p-benzoquinone
	3,3:20,20-Di(ethylenedioxy)-17α-hydroxypregn-5-en-11-one
	1,3-Dihydroxyacetone
	2,4-Dihydroxyacetophenone
	2,6-Dihydroxyacetophenone
	2,2′-Dihydroxy-4,4′-dimethoxybenzophenone
	2,2′-Dihydroxy-4-methoxybenzophenone
	5,11α-Dihydroxy-6β-methyl-5α-pregnane-3,20-dione
	11β,17α-Dihydroxypregna-1,4-diene-3,20-dione
	11β,21-Dihydroxypregna-4,17(20)-dien-3-one
	3β,17α-Dihydroxy-5β-pregnane-11,20-dione
	11β,21-Dihydroxypregna-1,4,17(20)-trien-3-one
	11β,17α-Dihydroxypregn-4-ene-3,20-dione
	3β,17α-Dihydroxypregn-5-en-20-one
	4,4-Dimethoxybutan-2-one
	2,6-Dimethylheptan-4-one
	6,10-Dimethylundeca-5,9-dien-2-one
	3,17-Dioxoandrost-4-en-19-al
	1,1-Diphenylacetone
	Dydrogesterone
	2-Ethylanthraquinone
	17,17-Ethylenedioxyandrosta-1,4-dien-3-one
	13β-Ethyl-3-methoxygona-2,5(10)-dien-17-one
	Fenchone
	Flumethasone
	Fluorenone
	6α-Fluoro-17α,21-dihydroxy-16α-methylpregn-4-ene-3,20-dione
	6α-Fluoro-21-hydroxy-16α,17α-isopropylidenedioxypregn-4-ene-3,20-dione
	Flurandrenolone
	n-Heptan-2-one
	n-Heptan-3-one
	3H,3H-Hexafluoroacetylacetone
	2-n-Hexylcyclopent-2-enone
	2-n-Hexylidenecyclopentanone
	2-Hydroxyacetophenone
	4-Hydroxyacetophenone
	4-Hydroxybenzophenone
	2-Hydroxy-3-methylcyclopent-2-enone
	2-Hydroxy-4-n-octyloxybenzophenone
	17α-Hydroxypregna-1,4-diene-3,11,20-trione
	17α-Hydroxypregn-4-ene-3,11,20-trione
	3β-Hydroxypregn-5-en-20-one
	4-Hydroxypropiophenone
	17β-Hydroxy-4,5-seco-19-norandrostane-3,5-dione
	Indanetrione hydrate (until 2nd July 1970)
	(±)-isoMenthone

Tariff heading   *Description*

29.13   Mesityl oxide
         Methandienone
         4-Methoxy-4-methylpentan-2-one
         4-(4-Methoxyphenyl)-3-methylbutan-2-one
         p-Methyl-*n*-butyrophenone
         5-Methylheptan-3-one
         5-Methylhexan-2-one
         6-Methyl-α-ionone
         3-Methyl-2-(*n*-pent-2-enyl)cyclopent-2-enone
         4-Methyl-4-phenylpentan-2-one
         4-Methyl-4-*p*-tolylpentan-2-one
         Musk ketone
         1,4-Naphthaquinone
         n-Nonan-2-one
         (±)-Norgestrel
         n-Octan-3-one
         Oestr-5(10)-ene-3,17-dione
         Oestr-4-en-17-one
         3-Oxodinorchol-4-en-22-al
         n-Pentan-2-one
         Pentan-3-one
         4-*tert*Pentylcyclohexanone
         Phenacyl bromide
         Pinacolone
         Pyruvaldehyde
         Sodium 2,2'-dihydroxy-4,4'-dimethoxybenzophenone-5-sulphonate
         2,4,2',4'-Tetrahydroxybenzophenone
         Tetramethylcyclobutane-1,3-dione
         2,5-Toluquinone, having a melting point of not less than $67 \cdot 0°$ centigrade
         1,1,1-Trifluoroacetylacetone, of a purity not less than 99 per cent.
         14α,17α,21-Trihydroxypregn-4-ene-3,20-dione
         n-Undecan-2-one
         n-Valerophenone
         Zerumbone

29.14   Acrylic acid
         Allethrin
         Allyl 3-cyclohexylpropionate
         Allyl methacrylate
         (±)-3-Allyl-2-methyl-4-oxocyclopent-2-enyl
              trans-(+)-chrysanthemum*mono*carboxylate
         Allyl trifluoroacetate
         Aluminium acetate, basic
         Ammonium pentadecafluoro-*n*-octanoate
         Arachidic acid
         Arachidonic acid
         Biphenyl-4-carboxylic acid
         (−)-Bornyl acetate
         4β-Bromo-17α,21-dihydroxy-5β-pregnane-3,11,20-trione 21-acetate
         n-Butane-1,3-diol dimethacrylate
         Butane-1,4-diol dimethacrylate
         *iso*Butyl acrylate
         4-*tert*Butylbenzoic acid
         2-*sec*Butyl-4,6-dinitrophenyl 3-methylcrotonate
         *tert*Butyl 2-ethylperbutyrate
         n-Butyric acid
         *iso*Butyric acid
         Calcium sorbate
         Chloroacetyl chloride
         2-Chlorocinnamic acid
         3-(2-Chloroethoxy)-9α-fluoro-11β,21-dihydroxy-20-oxo-16α,17α-
              *iso*propylidenedioxypregna-3,5-diene-6-carbaldehyde 21-acetate

Tariff heading   *Description*

29.14   2-Chloro-4-nitrobenzoic acid
               4-Chloro-3-nitrobenzoic acid
               Citronellyl 3-methylcrotonate
               Cobaltous acetate (until 5th March 1970)
               Crotonic acid
               Cyclopent-2-enyl cyclohexylacetate
               Cyclopropanecarboxyl chloride
               Decahydro-2-naphthyl acetate
               *tert*Decanoic acid, mixed isomers
               n-Dec-2-enoic acid
               Decyl acrylate, mixed isomers
               Dichloroacetic acid
               Dichloroacetyl chloride
               2,4-Dichlorobenzoyl chloride (until 7th May 1970)
               Dihydrocarveyl acetate
               Dihydrocarveyl propionate
               17α,21-Dihydroxy-16α-methylpregna-1,4,9(11)-triene-3,20-dione
                  21-acetate
               17α,21-Dihydroxypregn-4-ene-3,20-dione 21-acetate
               3β,17α-Dihydroxypregn-5-en-20-one 3-acetate
               3α,20-Dihydroxy-5β-pregn-17(20)-en-11-one diacetate
               3β,11α-Dihydroxy-5α-pregn-16-en-20-one diacetate
               1,1-Dimethyl-5-methylenehept-6-enyl acetate
               (−)-3,7-Dimethyloct-6-enyl acetate
               1,1-Dimethyl-2-phenylethyl *n*-butyrate
               1,1-Dimethyl-3-phenylpropyl acetate
               cis-3,3-(2,2-Dimethyltrimethylenedioxy)-6β-methyl-5α-pregn-17(20)-
                  ene-5,11β,21-triol 21-acetate
               (±)-1,5-Dimethyl-1-vinylhept-4-enyl acetate
               2,5-Dinitrobenzoic acid
               Drostanolone propionate
               Ethanediol dimethacrylate
               Ethyl β-8'-apocarotenoate
               Ethyl fluoroacetate
               2-Ethyl-2-hydroxymethylpropanediol trimethacrylate
               Ethyl methacrylate
               α-Ethyl-3-nitrocinnamic acid
               Ethyl trichloroacetate
               Ethynodiol diacetate
               Fenchyl acetate
               Flumethasone 21-pivalate
               9α-Fluoro-11β,17α-dihydroxypregn-4-ene-3,20-dione 17-acetate
               Geranyl 5,9,13-trimethyltetradeca-4,8,12-trienoate
               Glycerol 1,3-dipropionate
               Glycerol tripropionate
               Glycidyl methacrylate
               Heptafluoro-*n*-butyric acid
               n-Heptanoic acid
               n-Hept-2-enoic acid
               n-Heptyl acrylate
               n-Hex-3-enoic acid
               Lead tetra-acetate
               Linalyl cinnamate
               3-Methoxy-*n*-butyl acetate
               2-Methoxyethyl chloroformate
               Methyl acetate of a purity not less than 98 per cent.
               Methyl 2-chloro-3-(4-chlorophenyl)propionate
               Methyl chloroformate
               3-(4-Methylcyclohex-3-enyl)but-3-enyl acetate
               Methyl cyclopropanecarboxylate

Tariff heading	Description
29.14	Methyl formate
	Methyl 1-methyl-4-*iso*propylbicyclo[2,2,2]oct-2-ene-6-carboxylate
	Methyl *p*-toluate
	3-Methyl-*n*-valeric acid
	4-Methyl-*n*-valeric acid
	1-Naphthoic acid
	(±)-Nerolidyl acetate
	(±)-Nerolidyl *iso*butyrate
	(±)-Nerolidyl formate
	(±)-Nerolidyl propionate
	2-Nitrobenzoic acid
	4-Nitrobenzoic acid
	2-Nitrocinnamic acid
	3-Nitrocinnamic acid
	4-Nitrocinnamic acid
	4-Nitrophenylacetic acid
	n-Nonanoic acid
	n-Non-3-enoic acid
	Nonyl acetate, mixed isomers, having a specific rotation at 20° centigrade to the D line of sodium of between −9° and −13°
	n-Non-2-ynoic acid
	n-Octanoic acid (until 2nd July 1970)
	n-Oct-2-ynoic acid
	Pentadecafluoro-*n*-octanoic acid
	Pentafluoropropionic acid
	Pent-4-enoic acid
	2-Phenyl-*n*-butyric acid
	Phenyl chloroformate
	2-Phenylethyl cinnamate
	1-Phenyl-2-salicyloylvinyl benzoate
	Pivalic acid
	Potassium sorbate
	2-(4-*iso*Propenylcyclohex-1-enyl)ethyl formate
	Propiolic acid
	Propionic anhydride
	n-Propyl acrylate
	*iso*Propyl acrylate
	Sodium fluoroacetate
	Sodium formate
	Sodium pentadecafluoro-*n*-octanoate
	Sodium trichloroacetate
	Tetragol di-(2-ethylhexanoate)
	Tetragol dimethacrylate
	o-Toluic acid (—COOH at 1)
	m-Toluic acid (—COOH at 1)
	p-Toluic acid (—COOH at 1)
	Tricyclo[5,2,1,0^{2,6}]dec-4-en-8-yl acetate
	Tricyclo[5,2,1,0^{2,6}]dec-4-en-8-yl formate
	Triethyl orthoacetate
	Triethyl orthopropionate
	Trifluoroacetic acid
	Trigol di-(2-ethylbutyrate)
	Trigol dimethacrylate
	3β,17α,21-Trihydroxypregn-5-en-20-one 21-acetate
	4,7,7-Trimethylbicyclo[4,1,0]hept-4-en-3-ylmethyl acetate
	Trimethyl orthoformate
	2,2,4-Trimethylpentane-1,3-diol 1-*iso*butyrate
	2,2,4-Trimethylpentane-1,3-diol di*iso*butyrate
	2,4,6-Trinitrobenzoic acid which yields not more than 0·1 per cent. by weight of sulphated ash

Tariff heading	*Description*
29.14	Undec-10-enoic acid
	Vaccenic acid
	*iso*Valeric acid
	Vinyl *n*-butyrate
	Vinyl chloroacetate
	Vinyl decanoate, mixed isomers
	Vinyl *n*-dodecanoate
	Vinyl 2-ethylhexanoate
	Vinyl propionate
29.15	*cis*Aconitic acid
	Ammonium ferric oxalate
	Azelaic acid
	Benzenedicarboxylic acid, mixed isomers
	Benzene-1,2,4-tricarboxylic anhydride
	Bicyclo[2,2,1]hept-5-ene-2,3-dicarboxylic acid
	Bicyclo[2,2,1]hept-5-ene-2,3-dicarboxylic anhydride
	Biphenyl-2,2′-dicarboxylic acid
	n-Butyl hydrogen itaconate
	Calcium malonate
	Cyclohexane-1,2-diacetic acid
	Cyclohexane-1,2-dicarboxylic anhydride
	Di-*n*-butyl itaconate
	Dichloromaleic anhydride
	Dimethyl adipate
	Dimethyl itaconate
	Dimethyl maleate
	Dioctyl 2*H*,3*H*-hexachlorobicyclo[2,2,1]hept-5-ene-2,3-dicarboxylate, mixed isomers
	Di(tridecyl) sodium-sulphosuccinate, mixed isomers
	Dodecane-1,12-dioic acid
	Dodecenylsuccinic acid, mixed isomers
	Ethanediol cyclic brassylate
	Glutaric anhydride
	2*H*,3*H*-Hexachlorobicyclo[2,2,1]hept-5-ene-2,3-dicarboxylic acid
	2*H*,3*H*-Hexachlorobicyclo[2,2,1]hept-5-ene-2,3-dicarboxylic anhydride
	1,8,9,10,11,11-Hexachlorotricyclo[6,2,1,0^{2,7}]undec-9-ene-4,5-dicarboxylic anhydride
	Hexafluoroglutaric acid
	Hexafluoroglutaryl chloride
	Hydroxydione sodium succinate
	Isophthalic acid
	Itaconic anhydride
	Malonic acid
	Methylbicyclo[2,2,1]hept-5-ene-2,3-dicarboxylic anhydride
	Oxalic acid (until 5th March 1970)
	Pimelic acid
	Pyromellitic dianhydride
	Sodium oxalate which, in the form in which it is imported, contains not less than 5·0 per cent. by weight of moisture and which contains in the dried material not more than 98·0 per cent. by weight of oxalates expressed as sodium oxalate, $Na_2C_2O_4$ (until 5th March 1970)
	Suberic acid
	Succinic acid which, in the dry state, contains not more than 97 per cent. by weight of free acid calculated as succinic acid
	4-Sulphophthalic acid
	4-Sulphophthalic acid, diammonium salt
	Terephthaloyl chloride
	Tetrabromophthalic anhydride
	Tetrachlorophthalic anhydride

Tariff heading   *Description*

29.16   Acetone-1,3-dicarboxylic acid
         Aluminium hydroxide di-(*O*-acetylsalicylate)
         Antimony potassium tartrate, which satisfies the requirements of the
             British Pharmacopoeia
         n-Butoxycarbonylmethyl *n*-butyl phthalate
         n-Butyl 4,4-di*tert*butylperoxyvalerate
         n-Butyl glycollate
         4-*n*-Butyryl-2,3-dichlorophenoxyacetic acid
         Calcium bromide lactobionate
         Calcium glucoheptonate, pyrogen free
         Calcium gluconate lactobionate
         Calcium D-saccharate
         Carbenoxolone
         Carbenoxolone, disodium salt
         Cyclandelate
         2,5-Dichloro-6-methoxybenzoic acid
         Diethyl ethoxymethylenemalonate
         2,5-Dihydroxybenzoic acid
         3,4-Dihydroxybenzoic acid
         3,5-Dihydroxybenzoic acid
         2,2-Di(hydroxymethyl)propionic acid
         3,4-Dihydroxyphenylacetic acid
       *3,5-Di-iodosalicylic acid (−COOH at 1)
         2,3-Dimethoxybenzoic acid
         3,5-Dimethoxybenzoic acid
         3,4-Dimethoxyphenylacetic acid
         Dimethyl methoxymethylenemalonate
         Enoxolone
         3,4-Epoxy-6-methylcyclohexylmethyl 3,4-epoxy-6-methylcyclohexane-
             carboxylate
         Ethacrynic acid
         Ethyl diethoxyacetate
         Ethyl 2-hydroxy*iso*butyrate
         Ethyl 2-hydroxy-2-methylbutyrate
         Ethyl pyruvate
         Ethyl sodioacetoacetate
         Galacturonic acid
         Glucuronic acid
         Glycollic acid
         Glyoxylic acid
         2-(4-Hydroxybenzoyl)benzoic acid
         3-Hydroxycinnamic acid
         4-Hydroxy-3,5-dimethoxycinnamic acid
         1-Hydroxy-2-naphthoic acid
         2-Hydroxy-*m*-toluic acid
         Lactobionic acid
         Laevulic acid
         L-Malic acid
         L-Mandelic acid
         Manganese α-D-glucoheptonate
         Methallenoestril
         Mucic acid
         Mucochloric acid
         2-Oxo-2,3:4,6-di*iso*propylidenegulonic acid
         2-Oxoglutaric acid
         Oxydiacetic acid
         Pentaerythritol tetra-3-(3,5-di*tert*butyl-4-hydroxyphenyl)propionate
         3-Phenylsalicylic acid
         Potassium gluconate
         *iso*Propyl 4,4'-dichlorobenzilate
         Pyruvic acid which, in the dry state, contains not more than 97 per cent.
             by weight of free acid calculated as pyruvic acid

Tariff heading	Description
29.16	Quinic acid
	Shikimic acid
	*tri*Sodium (±)-*iso*citrate
	Sodium deoxycholate
	Sodium dihydrogen citrate
	Sodium 2,5-dihydroxybenzoate
	Sodium 2-hydroxy-4-methoxybenzoate
	(−)-Tartaric acid
	*meso*Tartaric acid
	2,4,5-Trichlorophenoxyacetic acid
	Triethyl *O*-acetylcitrate
	3,7,12-Trioxo-5β-cholanic acid
	Vanillic acid
29.17	1-*iso*Butyl-4-ethyloctyl sodium sulphate
	n-Dodecyl sodium sulphate
29.18	Cyclohexyl nitrate
29.19	Barium hydrogen 2-phosphoglycerate
	Barium hydrogen 3-phospho-D-glycerate
	Calcium phytate
	Chloro-1-(2,4-dichlorophenyl)vinyl diethyl phosphate
	1,2-Dibromo-2,2-dichloroethyl dimethyl phosphate
	Di-*n*-butyl 2,2-dichlorovinyl phosphate
	Di-*n*-butyl phenyl phosphate (until 2nd July 1970)
	2,2-Dichlorovinyl dimethyl phosphate
	Di-(2-ethylhexyl) sodium phosphate
	2-Ethylhexyl diphenyl phosphate
	Sodium phytate
	†Tri-(2,3-dibromopropyl) phosphate containing not more than 0·20 per cent. by weight of 2,3-dibromopropanol (until 5th March 1970)
	Triethyl phosphate
29.20	2-*sec*Butyl-4,6-dinitrophenyl *iso*propyl carbonate
	Diallyl digol dicarbonate
	Di-(4-*tert*butylcyclohexyl) peroxydicarbonate
	Diethyl pyrocarbonate
	Diphenyl carbonate
	Ethylene carbonate
	Propylene carbonate
29.21	*O*-4-Bromo-2,5-dichlorophenyl *OO*-diethyl phosphorothioate
	O-4-Bromo-2,5-dichlorophenyl *OO*-dimethyl phosphorothioate
	O-2,4-Dichlorophenyl *OO*-diethyl phosphorothioate
	OO-Diethyl *O*-4-nitrophenyl phosphorothioate
	OO-Diethyl phosphorochloridothioate
	1,3-Di-(4-methyl-1,3,2-dioxaborinan-2-yloxy)-*n*-butane
	OO-Dimethyl *O*-3-methyl-4-nitrophenyl phosphorothioate
	OO-Dimethyl *O*-4-nitrophenyl phosphorothioate
	OO-Dimethyl *O*-2,4,5-trichlorophenyl phosphorothioate
	Di-(4,4,6-trimethyl-1,3,2-dioxaborinan-2-yl) oxide
	1,9,10,11,12,12-Hexachloro-4,6-dioxa-5-thiatricyclo[7,2,1,0^{2,8}]dodec-10-ene 5-oxide
	Phenyl phosphorodichloridate
	4,4′-*iso*Propylidenedicyclohexyl di-(4-[1-(4-hydroxycyclohexyl)-1-methylethyl]cyclohexyl phenyl phosphite)
	Tri-(2-ethylhexyl) phosphite
	Triethyl phosphite
	Trimethyl phosphite
29.22	Allylamine
	2-Aminobiphenyl
	4-Aminobiphenyl
	6-Aminochrysene (I.U.P.A.C. numbering)

Tariff heading	Description
29.22	N-2-Amino-3,5-dibromobenzyl-N-cyclohexylmethylammonium chloride
	4-Amino-1-diethylamino-n-pentane
	2-Amino-4,4´-dinitrobiphenyl
	4-Aminodiphenylamine
	3-Aminomethyl-3,5,5-trimethylcyclohexylamine
	8-Aminonaphthalene-1-sulphonic acid
	8-Aminonaphthalene-2-sulphonic acid
	Amitriptyline embonate
	Amitriptyline hydrochloride
	Benzidine
	Benzidine hydrochloride
	Benzphetamine hydrochloride
	2-Bromo-5-trifluoromethylaniline
	4-Bromo-2-trifluoromethylaniline
	4-Bromo-3-trifluoromethylaniline
	n-Butylamine
	isoButylamine
	secButylamine
	tertButylamine
	2-Chloro-NN-diethyl-4-nitroanilinium chloride zinc chloride
	N-3-Chloropropyldimethylammonium chloride, solid
	2-Chloro-5-trifluoromethylaniline
	4-Chloro-2-trifluoromethylaniline
	4-Chloro-3-trifluoromethylaniline
	3-Cyclohexylaminopropylamine
	N-Cyclohexyldimethylamine
	N-Cyclohexylmethylamine
	Cyclopentamine hydrochloride
	Cyclopentamine 2-(4-hydroxybenzoyl)benzoate
	(Cyclopropylmethyl)ammonium chloride
	N-n-Decyldimethylamine
	Diallylamine
	Di-(4-aminocyclohexyl)methane
	1,2-Diaminoethane (until 5th March 1970)
	1,2-Diaminoethane hydrate
	1,7-Diaminoheptane
	Di-(4-amino-3-methylcyclohexyl)methane
	1,8-Diaminonaphthalene
	1,2-Diaminopropane
	1,3-Diaminopropane
	Di-(3-aminopropyl)amine
	2,4-Diaminotoluene
	1,6-Diaminotrimethylhexane, mixed 2,2,4- and 2,4,4- isomers
	Diamylamine, mixed isomers
	6,8-Dianilinonaphthalene-1-sulphonic acid
	2,6-Dibromoaniline
	Di-n-butylamine
	2,4-Dichloroaniline
	3,4-Dichloroaniline
	2,4-Dichlorobenzylamine
	3,4-Dichlorobenzylamine
	4,5-Dichloro-o-phenylenediamine
	Dicyclohexylamine
	NN´-Dicyclohexyl-p-phenylenediamine
	1,3-Di(dimethylamino)-n-butane
	1,4-Di(dimethylamino)butane
	2-Diethylaminoethylamine
	3-Diethylaminopropylamine
	NN-Diethylaniline (until 2nd July 1970)
	Diethylenetriamine (until 5th March 1970)

Tariff heading	Description
29.22	NN'-Di-(l-ethyl-3-methylpentyl)-p-phenylenediamine
	NN-Diethyl-p-phenylenediamine
	2-Dimethylaminoethylamine
	3-Dimethylaminopropylamine
	3-Dimethylaminopropyne
	NN'-Di-(l-methylheptyl)-p-phenylenediamine
	NN-Dimethyl-n-octylamine
	NN-Dimethyl-p-phenylenediamine
	6,10-Dimethyl-2,6,10,14-tetra-azapentadecane
	2,6-Dinitro-NN-di-n-propyl-4-trifluoromethylaniline
	Di-n-octylamine
	Di-n-propylamine
	Diisopropylamine
	N-n-Dodecyldimethylamine
	Ethamsylate
	2-Ethylaniline
	N-Ethylaniline
	N-Ethyldi-(3-phenylpropyl)ammonium dihydrogen citrate
	N-Ethyl-1-naphthylamine
	N-Ethyl-m-toluidine
	Fencamfamin hydrochloride
	Fenfluramine hydrochloride
	2-Fluoroaniline
	4-Fluoroaniline
	2-Fluoro-5-trifluoromethylaniline
	4-Fluoro-2-trifluoromethylaniline
	n-Heptylamine
	n-Hexylamine
	Mephentermine
	3-Methylaminopropylamine
	N-Methylaniline
	3-Methylbenzylamine
	1-Methylheptylamine
	N-l-Methylheptyl-N'-phenyl-p-phenylenediamine
	N-Methyl-1-methylprop-2-ynylamine
	N-Methyl-4-nitroaniline (until 7th May 1970)
	N-(2-Methyl-2-nitropropyl)-4-nitrosoaniline
	N-Methyltaurine
	N-Methyltaurine, sodium salt
	1-Naphthylamine
	2-Naphthylamine
	4-Nitroaniline
	4-Nitro-m-phenylenediamine
	n-Octylamine
	Pargyline hydrochloride
	NNN'N"N"-Pentamethyldiethylenetriamine
	n-Pentylamine
	isoPentylamine
	Phentermine
	m-Phenylenediamine
	p-Phenylenediamine
	p-Phenylenediamine dihydrochloride
	(±)-1-Phenylethylamine
	Prenylamine lactate
	n-Propylamine
	isoPropylamine
	(−)-Propylhexedrine hydrochloride
	Protriptyline hydrochloride
	Sodium 4-aminonaphthalene-1-sulphonate
	Spermidine

Tariff heading   *Description*

29.22 Spermidine trihydrochloride
     Taurine
     3,4,3′,4′-Tetra-aminobiphenyl tetrahydrochloride
     Tetraethylenepentamine (until 5th March 1970)
     5,6,7,8-Tetrahydro-1-naphthylamine
     1,2,3,4-Tetrahydro-2-naphthylamine
     5,6,7,8-Tetrahydro-2-naphthylamine
     o-Tolidine
     o-Tolidine dihydrochloride
     m-Tolidine dihydrochloride
     m-Tolidine di(hydrogen sulphate)
     Tolpropamine hydrochloride
     8-*p*-Toluidinonaphthalene-1-sulphonic acid
     Triallylamine
     Tri-*n*-butylamine
     2,4,5-Trichloroaniline
     Tri-*n*-decylamine
     Triethylammonium 3β,17β-dihydroxyandrost-5-en-17α-ylpropiolate
     Triethylenetetramine (until 5th March 1970)
     2-Trifluoromethylaniline
     4-Trifluoromethylaniline
     Tri-*n*-hexylamine
     Tri-*n*-octylamine
     Tri-*n*-pentylamine
     Tri*iso*pentylamine
     Tri-*n*-propylamine
     2,3-Xylidine
     2,5-Xylidine
     3,4-Xylidine

29.23 Acetaldehyde ammonia
     D-Alanine
     L-Alanine
     DL-Alanine
     4-Aminoacetophenone
     7-(4-Aminoanilino)-4-hydroxynaphthalene-2-sulphonic acid
     3-Aminobenzoic acid
     4-Aminobenzoic acid
     2-Amino-*n*-butan-1-ol
     4-Aminobutyric acid
     5-Amino-2-chlorobenzoic acid
     2-Amino-5,2′-dichlorobenzophenone
     2-Amino-4,6-dichlorophenol
     1-Amino-3-diethylaminopropan-2-ol
     L-2-Amino-3-(3,4-dihydroxyphenyl)-2-methylpropionic acid
     DL-2-Amino-3-(3,4-dihydroxyphenyl)-2-methylpropionic acid
     2-Amino-1-(3,4-dihydroxyphenyl)propan-1-ol hydrochloride
     2-(2-Aminoethoxy)ethanol
     2-Aminoethyl dihydrogen phosphate
     N-(2-Aminoethyl)ethanolamine
     2-Amino-2-ethylpropane-1,3-diol
     6-Aminohexanoic acid
     2-Amino-2-methylpropane-1,3-diol
     2-Amino-2-methylpropan-1-ol
     5-Amino-1-naphthol
     3-Amino-2-naphthol
     2-Amino-5-nitrophenol
     (−)-2-Amino-1-(4-nitrophenyl)propane-1,3-diol
     3-Aminophenol
     4-Aminophenylacetic acid
     (+)-2-Aminopropan-1-ol

Tariff heading   *Description*
29.23   3-Aminopropan-1-ol
         3-Aminopropionic acid
         4-Aminosalicylic acid (—COOH at 1)
         5-Aminosalicylic acid (—COOH at 1)
         Amylocaine hydrochloride
         7-Anilino-4-hydroxynaphthalene-2-sulphonic acid
         m-Anisidine
         Anthranilic acid
         L-Aspartic acid
         DL-Aspartic acid
         Bamethan sulphate
         Benzocaine
         (—)-2-Benzylaminopropan-1-ol
         (±)-2-Benzylaminopropan-1-ol
         Butacaine sulphate
         2-*tert*Butylaminoethyl methacrylate
         Calcium 3-aminopropionate
         Calcium 4-aminosalicylate (—COOH at 1)
         7-(4-Carboxymethoxyanilino)-4-hydroxynaphthalene-2-sulphonic acid
         Chlophedianol
         Chlophedianol hydrochloride
         5-Chloro-*o*-anisidine (—NH$_2$ at 1)
      *3-Chloro-4-(4-chlorophenoxy)aniline
         4-Chloro-2,5-dimethoxyaniline
         4-(4-Chlorophenoxy)aniline
         3-Chloro-6-phenoxyaniline
         Chlorphenoxamine hydrochloride
         Clorprenaline hydrochloride
         2,4-Diaminoanisole
         2,4-Diaminoanisole *mono*sulphate
         1,2-Diaminocyclohexane-*NNN'N'*-tetra-acetic acid
         1,3-Diaminopropan-2-ol
         1,3-Diaminopropan-2-ol-*NNN'N'*-tetra-acetic acid
         3,9-Di-(3-aminopropyl)-2,4,8,10-tetraoxaspiro[5,5]undecane
         o-Dianisidine
         o-Dianisidine dihydrochloride of a purity not greater than 98·5 per cent.
         1,15-Diaza-5,8,11-trioxapentadecane
         2,6-Di*tert*butyl-4-dimethylaminomethylphenol
         3,3'-Di(carboxymethoxy)benzidine, dipotassium salt
         6,6'-Dichloro-*o*-dianisidine
         1,2-Di[di-(2-hydroxy-*n*-propyl)amino]ethane
         Di-(2-dimethylaminoethyl) ether
         2,2-Diethoxyethylamine
         2-Diethylaminoethyl 4-amino-2-*n*-propoxybenzoate *mono*hydrochloride
         2-Diethylaminoethyl diphenylacetate hydrochloride
         3-Diethylaminopropan-1-ol
         5,5'-Dihydroxy-2,2'-dinaphthylamine-7,7'-disulphonic acid
         3-(3,4-Dihydroxyphenyl)-L-alanine
         3-(3,4-Dihydroxyphenyl)-DL-alanine
         2-(3,4-Dihydroxyphenyl)ethylammonium chloride
         Di-(2-hydroxy-*n*-propyl)amine
         2,5-Dimethoxyaniline
         N-2,2-Dimethoxyethylmethylamine
         1-(3,4-Dimethoxyphenyl)-1-dimethylamino-4-phenylbutane hydro-
           chloride
         2-(3,4-Dimethoxyphenyl)ethylamine
         β-Dimethylamino*iso*butyrophenone hydrochloride
         2-Dimethylaminoethyl methacrylate
         6-Dimethylaminomethyl-2,5-xylenol hydrochloride (—OH at 1)
         1-Dimethylaminopropan-2-ol

Tariff heading	Description
29.23	3-(3-Dimethylaminopropyl)-1,2:4,5-dibenzocycloheptadien-3-ol

1,4-Di-(2,4,6-trimethylanilino)anthraquinone
Embramine hydrochloride
Ethomoxane hydrochloride
Ethyl aminoacetate hydrochloride
2-Ethylaminoethanol, of which not less than 90 per cent. by volume
  distils between 165° and 170° centigrade at normal pressure and which
  contains not more than 0·5 per cent. by weight of water
Ethylenediamine-NN'-diacetic acid
Ethylenediamine-NN'-diacetic acid, cobalt complex
Ethylenediamine-NN'-di-[α-(2-hydroxyphenyl)acetic acid]
Ethylenediamine-NN'-di-[α-(2-hydroxyphenyl)acetic acid], iron complex
N-Ethyl-N-2-hydroxyethyl-m-toluidine
D-Glucosamine hydrochloride
Glutamic acid
Glycine
DL-Homoserine
1-(4-Hydroxyphenyl)-2-methylaminoethanol hydrogen tartrate
1-(4-Hydroxyphenyl)-2-methylaminoethanol tartrate
Iopanoic acid
Isatoic anhydride
Isoetharine mesylate
Isoxsuprine hydrochloride
L-Leucine
DL-Leucine
L-isoLeucine
DL-isoLeucine
L-norLeucine
DL-norLeucine
Levopropoxyphene napsylate
L-Lysine
DL-Lysine dihydrochloride
L-Lysine ethyl ester dihydrochloride
L-Lysine monohydrochloride
DL-Lysine monohydrochloride
Lyxosamine
Magnesium glutamate hydrobromide
Mannomustine dihydrochloride
Mebeverine hydrochloride
Meclofenoxate hydrochloride
Metaraminol hydrogen (+)-tartrate
3-Methoxypropylamine
6-Methoxy-m-toluidine ($-NH_2$ at 1)
2-Methylaminoethanol
3-(3-Methylaminoprop-1-ynyl)-1,2:4,5-dibenzocycloheptadien-3-ol
N-Methyldiethanolamine
Orciprenaline sulphate
DL-Ornithine monohydrochloride
Orphenadrine
Orphenadrine dihydrogen citrate
Orphenadrine hydrochloride
Pentyl 4-dimethylaminobenzoate, mixed isomers
5-tertPentyl-2-phenoxyaniline
o-Phenetidine
m-Phenetidine
p-Phenetidine
L-3-Phenylalanine
DL-3-Phenylalanine
Potassium 4-aminosalicylate ($-COOH$ at 1)
Potassium dimethylaminoacetate

Tariff heading	Description
29.23	Potassium 2-methylaminopropionate
	Procaine
	Procaine hydrochloride
	Protokylol hydrochloride
	Proxymetacaine *mono*hydrochloride
	Sarcosine
	L-Serine
	DL-Serine
	Sodium 4-aminosalicylate (−COOH at 1)
	Sodium hydrogen glutamate
	L-Threonine
	DL-Threonine
	Thymoxamine hydrochloride
	Tri-(2-hydroxy-*n*-propyl)amine
	Trolnitrate phosphate
	Trometamol
	Tyramine hydrochloride
	L-Tyrosine
	DL-Tyrosine
	L-Valine
	DL-Valine
	DL-*nor*Valine
29.24	Benzethonium chloride
	Betaine
	Betaine hydrochloride
	Carbenoxolone, dicholine salt
	Cetalkonium chloride
	1,3-Di(dimethylamino)propan-2-ol dimethiodide
	Edrophonium chloride
	N-2,3-Epoxypropyltrimethylammonium chloride
	Methylbenzethonium chloride
	Oxyphenonium bromide
	Tetraethylammonium chloride
	Tridihexethyl chloride
29.25	8-Acetamido-2-naphthol
	O-Acetyl-4′-chloro-3,5-di-iodosalicylanilide
	N-Acetyl-L-glutamine
	N-Acetyl-L-tyrosine
	Acrylamide
	Ambenonium chloride
	Ambucetamide
	7-(4-Aminobenzamido)-4-hydroxynaphthalene-2-sulphonic acid
	4-Aminohippuric acid
	L-α-Asparagine
	DL-α-Asparagine
	L-β-Asparagine
	Barbitone
	Barbitone sodium
	N-Bromoacetamide
	Bucetin
	N-(*n*-Butoxymethyl)acrylamide
	*sec*Butylurea (until 5th March 1970)
	Carbachol
	O-Carbamoyl-β-methylcholine chloride
	†Carbiphene hydrochloride
	Chloroacetamide
	4-Chlorobut-2-ynyl 3-chlorophenylcarbamate
	N-5-Chloro-2-(4-chloro-2-sulphophenoxy)phenyl-N′-3,4-dichloro-phenylurea
	2-Chloro-2-diethylcarbamoyl-1-methylvinyl dimethyl phosphate
	α-Chloro-2′,6′-diethyl-N-(methoxymethyl)acetanilide

Tariff heading   *Description*

29.25   11a-Chloro-5-hydroxytetracycline 6,12-hemiacetal
               N-4-(4-Chlorophenoxy)phenyl-*N′N′*-dimethylurea
               α-Chloro-*N*-*iso*propylacetanilide
               N-(3-Chloro-*p*-tolyl)-2-methyl-*n*-valeramide
               Chlorphenesin carbamate
               N-Cyclo-octyl-*N′N′*-dimethylurea
               Cyclopropanecarboxyamide
               Diacrylamidomethane
               3′,4′-Dichloromethacrylanilide
               3,3′-Dichloro-5-trifluoromethyl-*NN′*-diphenylurea
            *4,4′-Dichloro-3-trifluoromethyl-*NN′*-diphenylurea
               NN′-Di-(4-chloro-3-trifluoromethylphenyl)urea
               1,2-Di(diacetylamino)ethane
               Diethylcarbamoyl chloride
               2-(2,5-Dihydroxybenzamido)ethanol
               Dimethylcarbamoyl chloride
               NN′-Dimethyl-*NN′*-dinitrosoterephthalamide
               NN-Dimethyl-*N′*-3-trifluoromethylphenylurea
               NN′-Dimethylurea containing not more than 0·005 per cent. by weight
                  of iron calculated as Fe
            *3-(*N′N′*-Dimethylureido)phenyl *tert*butylcarbamate
               3,5-Dinitro-*o*-toluamide (−CONH$_2$ at 1)
               Di-(4-phenoxycarbonylaminophenyl)methane
               Ethosalamide
               Ethotoin
               Ethyl *N*-3-(1,2:5,6-dibenzocycloheptatrien-7-yl)propylmethylcarbamate
               1-Ethyl-1-methylprop-2-ynyl carbamate
               Fluoroacetamide
               Formamide
               L-Glutamine
               DL-Glutamine
               N-Glycyl-L-β-asparagine
               N-Glycyl-DL-β-asparagine
               N-(Hydroxymethyl)acrylamide
               1-Hydroxymethyl-5,5-dimethylhydantoin, solid
               Iodipamide, dimeglumine salt
               Iodoacetamide
               Iothalamic acid
               Isopropamide iodide
               Mebutamate
               Methacrylamide
               Methohexitone
               Methyl 4-acetamido-2-ethoxybenzoate
               Methyl 4-acetamido-5-chloro-2-methoxybenzoate
               Methyl carbamate
               Methyl 3-(*m*-tolylcarbamoyloxy)phenylcarbamate
               Metoclopramide dihydrochloride
               Metoclopramide *mono*hydrochloride
               1-Naphthyl methylcarbamate
               Nealbarbitone
               Niclosamide
               Oxethazaine
               Phenytoin sodium
               Pivalamide
               Procainamide hydrochloride (until 5th March 1970
               2-*iso*Propoxyphenyl methylcarbamate
               Sodium diatrizoate
               Styramate
               Tetramethylurea
               3,4,4′-Trichloro-*NN′*-diphenylurea

Tariff heading	Description
29.25	5,3′,4′-Trichlorosalicylanilide
	N-Vanillyl-n-nonanamide
	Vinbarbitone sodium
29.26	Acetamidinium chloride
	α-(4-Aminophenyl)-α-ethylglutarimide
	L-Arginine
	L-Arginine monohydrochloride
	N^α-Benzoyl-DL-arginine 2-naphthylamide hydrochloride
	Creatine
	3,5-Dichloro-p-benzoquinonechlorimine
	1,2-Di-(1,3-dimethylbutylideneamino)ethane
	Di-[2-(1,3-dimethylbutylideneamino)ethyl]amine
	1-(Di-[2-(1,3-dimethylbutylideneamino)ethyl]amino)-3-phenoxy-propan-2-ol
	Di-(2,6-diisopropylphenyl)carbodi-imine
	3-Dimethylaminomethyleneaminophenyl methylcarbamate hydrochloride
	n-Dodecylguanidinium acetate
	N-(2-Ethylhexyl)bicyclo[2,2,1]hept-5-ene-2,3-dicarboxyimide
	N-Ethylmaleimide
	Gluetethimide
	Guanidinium carbonate
	Guanidinium chloride
	4-Guanidinobutyric acid
	Hexahydro-1,3,5-tri-(2-hydroxyethyl)-1,3,5-triazine
	Hexamine 3-chloroallylochloride
	Phenformin monohydrochloride
	N-Phosphonocreatine, sodium salt
	3,4,5,6-Tetrahydrophthalimidomethyl 2,2-dimethyl-3-(2-methylprop-1-enyl)cyclopropanecarboxylate
	NNN′N′-Tetramethylguanidine
29.27	(—)-2-Acetamido-2-vanillylpropionitrile
	Acrylonitrile (until 2nd July 1970)
	Benzonitrile
	n-Butyronitrile
	Chloroacetonitrile
	3-Chlorophenylacetonitrile
	4-Chlorophenylacetonitrile
	Cyanocyclopropane
	3-Cyano-5-dimethylamino-2-methyl-3-phenylhexane
	3-Cyclohexylaminopropionitrile
	2,6-Dichlorobenzonitrile
	2,3-Dichloro-5,6-dicyanobenzoquinone
	NN-Di-2-cyanoethylformamide
	αα′-Dicyano-o-xylene
	αα′-Dicyano-m-xylene
	αα′-Dicyano-p-xylene
	4-Diethylaminobutyronitrile
	2-Dimethylamino-2,2-diphenyl-n-valeronitrile
	3-Dimethylaminopropionitrile
	2,2-Dimethylpropionitrile
	Diphenylacetonitrile
	4-Di-n-propylaminobutyronitrile
	4-Diisopropylaminobutyronitrile
	Ethyl 2-cyano-3,3-diphenylacrylate
	Ethyl 2-cyano-3-ethoxyacrylate
	2-Ethylhexyl 2-cyano-3,3-diphenylacrylate
	n-Hexanonitrile
	3-Hydroxypropionitrile
	Mandelonitrile
	Methacrylonitrile

Tariff heading   *Description*

29.27   2-Phenylpropionitrile
Phthalonitrile
Propionitrile
Succinonitrile
Tetracyanoethylene
o-Tolunitrile
o-Tolylacetonitrile
p-Tolylacetonitrile
Verapamil hydrochloride

29.28   4-Anilinophenyldiazonium hydrogen sulphate
Azobenzene
4-*N*-Benzylethylaminophenyldiazonium zinc chloride
3,4-Dimethyl-6-D-ribitylaminoazobenzene
Sodium 6-diazo-5-hydroxynaphthalene-1-sulphonate
*tri*Sodium hydrogen 4,5-dihydroxy-3,6-di-(2-sulphophenylazo)-
   naphthalene-2,7-disulphonate
2,5,4′-Triethoxy-4-biphenylyldiazonium zinc chloride

29.29   *p*-Benzoquinone dioxime
p-Benzoquinone dioxime dibenzoate
Benzylideneaminoguanidinium tartrate
N-(4-Bromophenyl)-*N*′-methoxy-*N*′-methylurea
1-(2-Carboxyphenyl)-5-(2-hydroxy-5-sulphophenyl)-3-phenylformazan
N-(4-Chlorobenzoyl)-*N*-(4-methoxyphenyl)hydrazine
N-4-Chlorophenyl-*N*′-methoxy-*N*′-methylurea
2-Chloro-4,6-xylylhydrazinium chloride
Cyclopropanecarboxyhydrazide
Desferrioxamine
Desferrioxamine hydrochloride
Desferrioxamine mesylate
N-3,4-Dichlorophenyl-*N*′-methoxy-*N*′-methylurea
Di(dimethylglyoximato)diamminecobaltic nitrate
NN-Diethylhydroxylamine
Diethyl naphthalimido phosphate
Di-(17*β*-hydroxy-2*α*,17*α*-dimethyl-5*α*-androstan-3-ylidene)hydrazine
NN-Dimethylhydrazine
N-Hydroxyphthalimide
Hydroxyurea
Phenelzine hydrogen sulphate
Pheniprazine *mono*hydrochloride
Phenylhydrazine
1-Phenylsemicarbazide
Procarbazine hydrochloride

29.30   4-*tert*Butyl-2-chlorophenyl methyl methylphosphoramidate
1-Chloro-2-*iso*cyanatobenzene
1-Chloro-3-*iso*cyanatobenzene
1-Chloro-4-*iso*cyanatobenzene
1-Chloro-2-*iso*cyanatoethane
*iso*Cyanatobenzene
*iso*Cyanatocyclohexane
1-*iso*Cyanato-4-fluorobenzene
*iso*Cyanatomethane
1-*iso*Cyanatonaphthalene
1-*iso*Cyanato-*n*-octadecane
1-*iso*Cyanatopropane
3-Cyano-5-dimethylamino-2-methyl-3-phenylhexane cyclamate
1,2-Dichloro-4-*iso*cyanatobenzene
1,4-Dichloro-2-*iso*cyanatobenzene
Di-(4-*iso*cyanatocyclohexyl)methane
4,4′-Di*iso*cyanato-3,3′-dimethoxybiphenyl

Tariff heading	*Description*
29.30	4,4′-Di*iso*cyanato-3,3′-dimethylbiphenyl
	4,4′-Di*iso*cyanatodiphenylmethane of a purity not less than 85 per cent.
	1,6-Di*iso*cyanatohexane
	1,5-Di*iso*cyanatonaphthalene
	2,4-Di*iso*cyanatotoluene
	Dimethylamine-borine
	Hexamethylphosphoramide
	Tetra(dimethylamino)diboron
	4,4′,4″-Tri*iso*cyanatotriphenylmethane
29.31	*N*-Acetyl-L-cysteine
	N-Acetyl-DL-methionine
	Ambazone
	2-Aminobenzenethiol
	Ammonium phenylhydrazinodithioformate
	Benzenethiol
	Bithionol
	*iso*Bornyl thiocyanatoacetate
	Butane-1,4-dithiol
	n-Butane-1-thiol
	4-*tert*Butylbenzenethiol
	Calcium 2-hydroxy-4-(methylthio)butyrate
	S-Carboxymethylcysteine
	Chlordantoin
	2-Chloroallyl diethyldithiocarbamate
	4-Chlorophenylthiomethyl *OO*-diethyl phosphorodithioate
	L-Cystathionine
	DL-Cystathionine
	L-Cysteine
	L-Cysteine hydrochloride
	Cysteine methyl ester hydrochloride
	D-Cystine
	L-Cystine
	Dapsone, of a purity less than 99 per cent.
	n-Decane-1-thiol
	Di-(3-*tert*butyl-4-hydroxy-6-methylphenyl) sulphide
	Di-(2-carboxyphenyl) disulphide
	S-2,3-Dichloroallyl di*iso*propylthiocarbamate
	Di-(4-chlorophenyl) sulphone
	2,5-Dichlorophenylthiomethyl *OO*-diethyl phosphorodithioate
	2,6-Dichlorothiobenzamide
	Di-(2-cyanoethyl) sulphide
	2-Diethylaminoethanethiol hydrochloride
	OO-Diethyl 2-ethylthioethyl phosphorodithioate
	OO-Diethyl *O*-2-ethylthioethyl phosphorothioate
	Diethyl *S*-2-ethylthioethyl phosphorothioate
	OO-Diethyl ethylthiomethyl phosphorodithioate
	Di-(2-ethylhexyl) 4,4′-thiodibutyrate
	Di-(2-hydroxyethyl) sulphide
	Di-(6-hydroxy-2-naphthyl) disulphide
	Dimercaprol
	Dimethyl disulphide
	Dimethyl *S*-2-(1-methylcarbamoylethylthio)ethyl phosphorothioate
	OO-Dimethyl methylcarbamoylmethyl phosphorodithioate
	OO-Dimethyl phthalimidomethyl phosphorodithioate
	Dimethyl sulphide
	Dimethyl sulphoxide
	Dimethylxanthogen disulphide
	Di-(4-nitrophenyl) disulphide
	1,4-Dioxan-2,3-dithiol di-(*OO*-diethyl phosphorodithioate)

Tariff heading   *Description*

29.31   Diphenyl disulphide
Diphenyl sulphide
NN′-Diphenylthiourea
3,6-Dithiaoctane-1,8-diol

†Dithiocyanatomethane having a melting point not less than 100° centigrade (until 5th March 1970)
*Di(trichloromethyl) sulphone
Dodecanethiol, mixed isomers
Ethane-1,2-dithiol
Ethanethiol
D-Ethionine
L-Ethionine
DL-Ethionine
Ethylcarbamoylmethyl *OO*-dimethyl phosphorodithioate
S-Ethyl di-*n*-propylthiocarbamate
Ethylene-1,2-di-(*N′N′*-dimethylthiuram disulphide)
Ethyl methyl sulphide
O-2-Ethylthioethyl *OO*-dimethyl phosphorothioate
S-2-Ethylthioethyl dimethyl phosphorothioate
Glutathione
Glutathione disulphide
Glutathione, *mono*sodium salt
N-Glycyl-DL-methionine
Hexane-1,6-dithiol
n-Hexane-1-thiol
DL-Homocysteine
2-Mercapto*iso*butyric acid
2-Mercaptoethanol
2-Mercaptoethylammonium chloride
3-Mercaptopropane-1,2-diol (until 2nd July 1970)
2-Mercaptopropionic acid
3-Mercaptopropionic acid (until 2nd July 1970)
Mercaptosuccinic acid
Methanethiol
Methionine
2-Methoxyethylcarbamoylmethyl *OO*-dimethyl phosphorodithioate
Methyl phenyl sulphide
2-Methylpropane-2-thiol
Methylsulphonal
4-(Methylthio)-3,5-xylyl methylcarbamate
1-Naphthylthiourea
Noxythiolin
n-Octane-1-thiol
Pentachlorobenzenethiol
n-Pentane-1-thiol
Potassium ethylxanthate
Potassium *n*-pentylxanthate
Propane-1,3-dithiol
Propane-1-thiol
Propane-2-thiol
S-*n*-Propyl *n*-butylethylthiocarbamate
Sodium *sec*butylxanthate
Sodium ethylxanthate
Sodium *iso*propylxanthate
Sodium toluene-4-sulphinate
Sulphonal
2,4,5,4′-Tetrachlorodiphenyl sulphide
2,4,5,4′-Tetrachlorodiphenyl sulphone
N-(1,1,2,2-Tetrachloroethanesulphenyl)cyclohex-4-ene-
1,2-dicarboxyimide
OOO′O′-Tetraethyl methylene di(phosphorodithioate)

Tariff heading   *Description*

29.31
- Thioacetamide
- Thioacetanilide
- Thioacetic acid
- Thiobarbituric acid
- Thiocarlide
- isoThiocyanatobenzene
- isoThiocyanatomethane
- Thiodiacetic acid
- Thiomesterone
- Thiourea
- Tolnaftate
- Toluene-2-thiol
- S-2,3,3-Trichloroallyl diisopropylthiocarbamate
- Trichloromethanesulphenyl chloride
- N-(Trichloromethanesulphenyl)cyclohex-4-ene-1,2-dicarboxyimide
- N-(Trichloromethanesulphenyl)phthalimide
- Zinc di-(2-benzamidophenyl sulphide)
- Zinc di(pentachlorophenyl sulphide)
- Zinc propylenebisdithiocarbamate

29.32
- o-Arsanilic acid
- p-Arsanilic acid (until 3rd September 1970)
- Bismuth N-glycollylarsanilate
- Cacodylic acid
- Phenylarsonic acid
- Sodium cacodylate
- Sodium hydrogen p-arsanilate
- diSodium methylarsonate

29.33
- 4-Chloromercuribenzoic acid of a purity of not less than 98 per cent. and a melting point of not less than 278° centigrade
- 3,2-Mercurioxy-4-nitrotoluene
- Methylmercury hydroxide

29.34
- Allyltrichlorosilane
- 3-Aminopropyltriethoxysilane
- 3-Aminopropyltrimethoxysilane
- n-Butyl-lithium
- secButyl-lithium
- 3-Chloropropyltrimethoxysilane
- Diisobutylaluminium hydride
- Dicyclopentadienyliron
- Diethyl di-(2-hydroxyethyl)aminomethylphosphonate
- Dimethyl 2,2,2-trichloro-1-hydroxyethylphosphonate
- Diphenyldichlorosilane
- Diphenylsilanediol
- 2-(3,4-Epoxycyclohexyl)ethyltrimethoxysilane
- O-Ethyl phenyl ethylphosphonodithioate
- 3-Glycidyloxypropyltrimethoxysilane
- 1-Hydroxyethylidenediphosphonic acid
- 3-Methacryloyloxypropyltrimethoxysilane
- Methylcyclopentadienylmanganese tricarbonyl
- Methylvinyldichlorosilane
- Molybdenum hexacarbonyl
- Nitrilotri(methylphosphonic acid)
- Phenylphosphinic acid
- pentaSodium hydrogen nitrilotri(methylphosphonate)
- Sodium tetraphenylborate
- Tetramethylsilane
- Tri-n-butylaluminium
- *Tri-n-butyl-2,4-dichlorobenzylphosphonium chloride
- Triphenylphosphine

Tariff heading   *Description*

29.34   Triphenyltin acetate
               Tungsten hexacarbonyl
               Vinyltrichlorosilane
               Vinyltriethoxysilane
               Vinyltri-(2-methoxyethoxy)silane

29.35   Acepromazine hydrogen maleate
               Acetoguanamine
               2-Acetothienone
               2-Acetylbenzofuran
               2-Acetyl-1,4-butyrolactone
               3-Acetyl-2,4-dimethylpyrrole
               N-Acetylhistamine
               3-Acetylindole
               5-Acetylindoline
               3-Acetylpyridine
               4-Acetylpyridine
               N^α-Acetyl-DL-tryptophan
               Acridine
               Acridone
               Adenine
               Adenine sulphate
               Adenosine
               Adenosine 3′-(dihydrogen phosphate)
               Adenosine 5′-(dihydrogen phosphate)
               Adenosine 5′-(dilithium hydrogen pyrophosphate)
               Adenosine 5′-(disodium dihydrogen triphosphate)
               Adenosine 5′-(tetrahydrogen triphosphate)
               Adenosine 5′-(tetrasodium triphosphate)
               Adenosine 5′-(trilithium pyrophosphate)
               Adenosine 5′-(trisodium pyrophosphate)
               S-Adenos-5′-yl-L-methionine iodide
               2-Allyloxypyridine
               Ambrettolide
               2-Aminobenzothiazole
               2-Aminobenzothiazole-6-carboxylic acid
               N^α-4-Aminobutyryl-L-histidine sulphate
               5-Amino-4-chloro-2-phenylpyridazin-3-one
               5-Amino-1-di(dimethylamino)phosphinyl-3-phenyl-1,2,4-triazole
               5-Amino-3,4-dimethyl*iso*oxazole
               4-Amino-2,6-dimethylpyrimidine
               2-(1-Aminoethyl)-3,4-di(hydroxymethyl)furan hydrochloride
               4-Amino-5-methoxymethyl-2-*n*-propylpyrimidine
               5-Amino-3-methyl-1-phenylpyrazole
               2-Amino-4-methylpyrimidine
               3-Amino-5-morpholinomethyl-2-oxazolidone
               3-Amino-2-oxazolidone sulphate
               6-Aminopenicillanic acid
               4-Aminophenazone
               5-Amino-1-phenylpyrazole
               3-Amino-1-phenyl-5-pyrazolone
               6-Amino-2-picoline
               2-Amino-3-picoline
               2-Amino-4-picoline
               1-(4-Amino-2-*n*-propyl-5-pyrimidylmethyl)-2-picolinium chloride
                   *mono*hydrochloride
               Aminopterin
               4-Aminopyridine
               2-Aminopyrimidine
               3-Amino-1,2,4-triazole
               Ammonium hydrogen 7-oxabicyclo[2,2,1]heptane-2,3-dicarboxylate

Tariff heading	Description

29.35
*di*Ammonium 7-oxabicyclo[2,2,1]heptane-2,3-dicarboxylate
Angiotensin amide
D-*iso*Ascorbic acid
8-Aza-adenine
Azapetine dihydrogen phosphate
Aziridine
Bamipine *mono*hydrochloride
3,4-Benzacridine
2-[2-(4-Benzhydrylpiperazin-1-yl)ethoxy]ethanol dihydrochloride
2-[2-(4-Benzhydrylpiperazin-1-yl)ethoxy]ethanol 4,4'-methylenedi-
   (3-hydroxy-2-naphthoate)
2-Benzhydrylpyridine
3-Benzhydrylpyridine
4-Benzhydrylpyridine
Benzimidazole
Benziodarone
Benzoguanamine
5,6-Benzoquinoline
N-Benzothiazol-2-yl-*NN'*-dimethylurea
6-Benzylaminopurine
3-Benzyl-1-methyl-2-*n*-undecylimidazolium bromide
Biperiden
Biperiden hydrochloride
4,4'-Biphenyldiyldi-(2,5-diphenyltetrazolium chloride)
2,2'-Biquinolyl
Bisacodyl
5-Bromo-3-*sec*butyl-6-methyluracil
5-Bromo-2'-deoxycytidine
5-Bromo-2'-deoxyuridine
5-Bromoindole
5-Bromoindole-3-aldehyde
5-Bromo-6-methyl-3-*iso*propyluracil
2-Bromothiophen
5-Bromouracil
Brompheniramine hydrogen maleate
Buclizine dihydrochloride
Bupivacaine hydrochloride
Butalamine hydrochloride
2-*n*-Butoxyethyl nicotinate
2-*n*-Butoxypyridine
*N-tert*Butylbenzothiazole-2-sulphenamide
*tert*Butyl 1-(4-chlorobenzoyl)-5-methoxy-2-methylindol-3-ylacetate
3-*tert*Butyl-5-chloro-6-methyluracil
2-(3-*tert*Butyl-2-hydroxy-5-methylphenyl)-5-chlorobenzotriazole
*tert*Butyl 5-methoxy-2-methylindol-3-ylacetate
2-*iso*Butylquinoline
6-*iso*Butylquinoline
6-*tert*Butylquinoline
Butylquinoline, mixed isomers
1,4-Butyrolactone
2-Carbamoyloxymethyl-1-methyl-5-nitroimidazole
Carbinoxamine hydrogen maleate
1-(Carboxymethyl)pyridinium chloride, pyridinium salt
Chlordiazepoxide
Chlordiazepoxide *mono*hydrochloride
1-(4-Chlorobenzyl)-2-methylbenzimidazole hydrochloride
2-(4-Chlorobenzyl)pyridine
6-Chloro-2-chloromethyl-4-phenylquinazoline 3-oxide hydrochloride
5-Chloro-2-(3,5-di*tert*butyl-2-hydroxyphenyl)benzotriazole
7-Chloro-10-(2-dimethylaminoethyl)dibenzo[*b,e*]-1,4-diazepin-11-one-
   *mono*hydrochloride

Tariff heading
29.35

Description

O-3-Chloro-4-methylcoumarin-7-yl OO-diethyl phosphorothioate
(6-Chloro-2-oxobenzoxazolin-3-yl)methyl OO-diethyl
   phosphorodithioate
6-Chloropurine
2-Chloropyridine
2-Chloroquinoline
Chlorprothixene
Chlorthenoxazin
Chlorzoxazone
Cinnarizine
(±)-*iso*Citric acid lactone
Clorazepic acid, dipotassium salt
Cocarboxylase
Coenzyme A
2,4,6-Collidine
Creatinine
Creatinine hydrochloride
o-Cresolphthalein-6,6'-di(methylaminodiacetic acid)
Cumetharol
5-Cyanoindole
3-Cyano-4-methoxymethyl-6-methyl-5-nitro-2-pyridone
4-Cyano-1-methyl-4-phenylazacycloheptane
2-Cyanophenothiazine
Cyanuric acid
Cyanuric chloride
3-Cyclohexyl-1,2,3,4,6,7-hexahydro-2,4-dioxocyclopentapyrimidine
Cyclomethycaine hydrogen sulphate
2-Cyclopentyl-2-(2-thienyl)glycollic acid
Cyproheptadine hydrochloride
Cytidine
Cytidine dihydrogen phosphate, mixed 2'- and 3'- isomers
Cytosine
Cytosine-1 β-D-arabinoside hydrochloride
Debrisoquine sulphate
Decahydro-4a-hydroxy-2,8,8-trimethyl-2-naphthoic acid lactone
Dehydracetic acid of a purity not less than 96 per cent.
2'-Deoxyadenosine
2'-Deoxycytidine 5'-(disodium phosphate)
2'-Deoxycytidine hydrochloride
2'-Deoxyguanosine
2'-Deoxyguanosine 5'-(disodium phosphate)
2'-Deoxyuridine
Dextromethorphan
Dextromethorphan hydrobromide
Dextromoramide hydrogen (+)-tartrate
2,5-Diamino-7-ethoxyacridinium lactate
2,6-Diaminopyridine
Diamthazole
1,4-Diazabicyclo[2,2,2]octane
Diazepam
Diazoxide
Dibenzofuran
NN'-Di(benzothiazol-2-ylthiomethyl)urea
3,5-Dibenzyltetrahydro-1,3,5-thiadiazine-2-thione
2-(3,5-Di*tert*butyl-2-hydroxyphenyl)benzotriazole
1-(2,3-Dichloroallyl)pyridinium chloride
3,5-Dichloro-4-hydroxylutidine
Dichloro-1,3,5-triazinetrione
Dichloro-1,3,5-triazinetrione, potassium derivative
Dichloro-1,3,5-triazinetrione, sodium derivative
1,3-Di-(3-*iso*cyanato-4-methylphenyl)-1,3-diazacyclobutane-2,4-dione

Tariff heading   *Description*

29.35   2,3-Dicyano-1,4-dithia-anthraquinone

NN-Dicyclohexylbenzothiazole-2-sulphenamide

5-(2-Diethylaminoethyl)-3-phenyl-1,2,4-oxadiazole dihydrogen citrate

5-(2-Diethylaminoethyl)-3-phenyl-1,2,4-oxadiazole dihydrogen phosphate

Diethyl phenyl-2-pyridylmethylmalonate hydrochloride

2,4-Diethyl-6-*iso*propoxy-1,3,5-triazine

OO-Diethyl *O*-pyrazin-2-yl phosphorothioate

OO-Diethyl *O*-3,5,6-trichloro-2-pyridyl phosphorothioate

α-(4-[4,4-Di-(4-fluorophenyl)butyl]piperazin-1-yl)acet-2′,6′-xylidide

1-(1-[4,4-Di-(4-fluorophenyl)butyl]-4-piperidyl)benzimidazolin-2-one

Dihydrallazine *mono*sulphate

4,5-Dihydro-2,3:6,7-dibenzazepine

(±)-2,3-Dihydro-4-methyl-2-(2-methylprop-1-enyl)pyran

Dihydronicotinamide-adenine dinucleotide, disodium salt

Dihydronicotinamide-adenine dinucleotide phosphate, tetrasodium salt

2,3-Dihydropyran

3-(3β,17β-Dihydroxyandrost-5-en-17α-yl)propionic acid lactone

2,4-Dihydroxyquinoline

2,4-Dihydroxyquinoline, disodium derivative

2,4-Dihydroxyquinoline, *mono*sodium derivative

Dimethindene hydrogen maleate

Dimethisoquin *mono*hydrochloride

Dimethoxanate *mono*hydrochloride

11-(3-Dimethylaminopropylidene)-6,11-dihydrodibenz[*b,e*]oxepin hydrochloride

11-(3-Dimethylaminopropylidene)-6,11-dihydrobenzo[*b,e*]thiepin hydrochloride

5,6-Dimethylbenzimidazole

OO-Dimethyl morpholinocarbonylmethyl phosphorodithioate

OO-Dimethyl 4-oxobenzotriazin-3-ylmethyl phosphorodithioate

3,6-Dimethyl-1-phenylphosphepan

2,3-Dimethyl-1-phenyl-4-*iso*propyl-5-pyrazolone

4,4-Dimethyl-1-phenyl-3-pyrazolidone

2,5-Dimethylpyrazine

2,4-Dimethylthiophan 1,1-dioxide

1,5-Di-(5-nitro-2-furyl)pentadien-3-one amidinohydrazone hydrochloride

Diosgenin

Diperodon

Diperodon hydrochloride

Diphenoxarsin-10-yl oxide

Diphenoxylate hydrochloride

Diphenylpyraline hydrochloride

NN-Di*iso*propylbenzothiazole-2-sulphenamide

Di-*n*-propyl pyridine-2,5-dicarboxylate

Dipyridamole

1,3-Di-(2-pyridylimino)*iso*indoline

Dipyrone

Di(pyrrobutamine) napadisylate

Distigmine bromide

Dithiazanine iodide

Ellagic acid

Ethionamide

2-Ethoxy-3,4-dihydropyran

7-Ethoxy-4-methylcoumarin

2-Ethylamino-4-methylthio-6-*iso*propylamino-1,3,5-triazine

Ethyl 6,7-di*iso*butoxy-4-hydroxyquinoline-3-carboxylate

2-Ethyl-3-hydroxy-4-pyrone

Ethyl 7-methyl-4-oxo-1,8-naphthyridine-3-carboxylate

Tariff heading	Description
29.35	N-Ethyl-N'-(5-nitrothiazol-2-yl)urea
	5-Ethyl-2-picoline
	2-Ethylpiperidine
	Fentanyl
	Fentanyl dihydrogen citrate
	Flavin-adenine dinucleotide
	Fluanisone
	Fluopromazine monohydrochloride
	Fluorescein-2',7'-di(methylaminodiacetic acid)
	1-[3-(4-Fluorobenzoyl)propyl]-4-hydroxy-4-(3-trifluoromethylphenyl)-piperidine
	1-[3-(4-Fluorobenzoyl)propyl]-4-hydroxy-4-(3-trifluoromethylphenyl)-piperidinium chloride
	1-(1-[3-(4-Fluorobenzoyl)propyl]-4-piperidyl)benzimidazolin-2-one hydrochloride
	1-(1-[3-(4-Fluorobenzoyl)propyl]-1,2,3,6-tetrahydro-4-pyridyl)-benzimidazolin-2-one
	5-Fluorouracil
	Fluphenazine O-n-decanoate
	Fluphenazine dihydrochloride
	Furan
	Furfuraldehyde
	3-(2-Furyl)acrylic acid
	D-Glucuronolactone
	Glycine-6-hydroxy-2H-pyridazin-3-one complex, sodium derivative
	Glycopyrronium bromide
	Guanethidine monosulphate
	2-Guanidinobenzimidazole
	Guanine
	Guanine hydrochloride
	Guanosine 3'-(dihydrogen phosphate)
	Guanosine 5'-(disodium phosphate)
	Haematoporphyrin
	Haematoporphyrin dihydrochloride
	Haloperidol
	Hecogenin
	Hecogenin acetate
	10-(3-[4-(2-n-Heptanoyloxyethyl)piperazin-1-yl]propyl)-2-trifluoro-methylphenothiazine
	N-n-Hexadecyl-N-[2-(N-4-methoxybenzyl-2-pyrimidylamino)ethyl]-dimethylammonium bromide
	1,3,4,6,7,8-Hexahydro-4,6,6,7,8,8-hexamethylindeno[5,6-c]pyran
	Hexahydroisonicotinamide
	Hexa(methoxymethyl)melamine
	1,6-Hexanolactam
	1,4-n-Hexanolactone
	1,6-Hexanolactone
	Hexetidine
	Hexocyclium methylsulphate
	2-n-Hexyl-1,4-butyrolactone
	Histamine acid phosphate
	Histamine di-(3,4-dichlorobenzenesulphonate)
	Histamine dihydrochloride
	L-Histidine
	L-Histidine monohydrochloride
	DL-Histidine monohydrochloride
	Hydrallazine hydrochloride
	2-Hydrazinobenzothiazole
	2-Hydroxycarbazole
	2-Hydroxycarbazole-3-carboxylic acid

Tariff heading   *Description*
29.35   Hydroxychloroquine *mono*sulphate
      1-(2-Hydroxyethyl)-2-*n*-nonylimidazoline
      3-Hydroxy-5-hydroxymethyl-4-methoxymethyl-2-picolinium chloride
      4-Hydroxy-1-methylpiperidine
      7-Hydroxy-7-(1-methyl-4-piperidyl)-1,2:5,6-dibenzocycloheptatriene
        hydrochloride
      8-Hydroxynaphth[1,2-*d*]imidazole
      2-(2-Hydroxyphenyl)benzotriazole
      4-Hydroxypiperidine
      L-Hydroxyproline
      3-Hydroxypyridine
      1-Hydroxypyridine-2-thione, sodium derivative
      5-(α-Hydroxy-α-2-pyridylbenzyl)-7-(α-2-pyridylbenzylidene)bicyclo-
        [2,2,1]hept-5-ene-2,3-dicarboxyimide
      6-Hydroxyquinoline
      4-Hydroxy-3-(1,2,3,4-tetrahydro-1-naphthyl)coumarin
      4-Hydroxy-DL-tryptophan
      5-Hydroxy-DL-tryptophan
      Hydroxyzine dihydrochloride
      Hydroxyzine embonate

      Idoxuridine
      Imidazole
      Imidazol-1-ylacetic acid
      3-(Imidazol-4-yl)propionic acid
      Imperatorin
      Indole
      Indole-3-carboxylic acid
      Indole-5-carboxylic acid
      Indomethacin
      Inosine
      Inosine 5′-(disodium phosphate)
      Inosine 5′-(trisodium pyrophosphate)
      6-Iodopurine
      Iproniazid *mono*phosphate
      Isatin
      Isocarboxazid
      Isoniazid
      Isothipendyl *mono*hydrochloride

      Lepidine
      Leptazol
      Levallorphan hydrogen tartrate
      Levorphanol hydrogen tartrate
      2,3-Lutidine
      2,5-Lutidine
      3,4-Lutidine

      Maltol
      Mebhydrolin napadisylate
      Meclozine dihydrochloride
      Mepenzolate bromide
      2-Mercaptobenzimidazole
      6-Mercaptopurine
      Methapyrilene 2-(4-hydroxybenzoyl)benzoate
      Methdilazine *mono*hydrochloride
      Methixene hydrochloride
      Methotrexate
      2-(Methoxycarbonylhydrazonomethyl)quinoxaline 1,4-dioxide
      5-Methoxyindole
      2-Methoxyphenothiazine
      α-(4-Methoxyphenyl)piperidinoacetamide

Tariff heading	Description
29.35	α-(4-Methoxyphenyl)piperidinoacetonitrile

α-(4-Methoxyphenyl)pyrrolidinoacetamide
α-(4-Methoxyphenyl)pyrrolidinoacetonitrile
8-Methoxypsoralen
6-Methoxyquinoline
Methyl 3-amino-5,6-dichloropyrazine-2-carboxylate
6-Methylaminopurine
2-Methylbenzoselenazole
3-Methylbenzothiazolium toluene-4-sulphonate
*Methyl 1-(n-butylcarbamoyl)benzimidazol-2-ylcarbamate
3-Methylchromone
Methyl 7-diethylamino-4-hydroxy-6-n-propylquinoline-3-carboxylate
6-Methyl-1,3-dithiolo[4,5-b]quinoxalin-2-one
Methylenedi-(1,6-hexanolactam), mixed isomers
2-Methylfuran
1-Methylimidazol-4-ylacetic acid
2-Methylindole
1-Methylindole-2-carboxylic acid
2-Methyl-4-nitroimidazole
3-Methyl-1-(4-nitrophenyl)-5-pyrazolone
Methyl phenidate monohydrochloride
6-Methylpicolinic acid
1-Methylpiperazine
3-(2-Methylpiperidino)propan-1-ol
1-Methyl-4-piperidone
N-Methyl-3-piperidylmethanol
Methyl 2-pyridylacetate
Methyl 4-pyridylacetate
1-Methylpyrrole
1-Methyl-2-pyrrolidone
2-Methylthiophen
3-Methylthiophen
6-Methyl-2-thiouracil
4-Methylumbelliferone
Methyprylone
Metyrapone
4-Morpholinobutyronitrile
2-(Morpholinodithio)benzothiazole
N-(Morpholinomethyl)pyrazinecarboxyamide
α-Morpholinophenylacetamide
α-Morpholinophenylacetonitrile
3-Morpholino-1-phenyl-1-(2-thienyl)propan-1-ol methiodide
3-Morpholinopropionitrile
Nalidixic acid
2-(1-Naphthyl)-5-phenyloxazole
Nialamide
Nicotinamide-adenine dinucleotide
Nicotinamide-adenine dinucleotide phosphate, monosodium salt
Nicotinyl alcohol
isoNicotinyl alcohol
Nifuratel
Nitrazepam
5-Nitroindole
Nitron
2-Nitrothiophen
1,3,4,5,6,7,8,8-Octachloro-1,3,3a,4,7,7a-hexahydro-
    4,7-methanoisobenzofuran
1,4,4a,4b,5,8,8a,8b-Octahydrodibenzofuran-4b-aldehyde
1,8-Octanolactam
7-Oxabicyclo[2,2,1]heptane-2,3-dicarboxylic acid

Tariff heading	Description
29.35	12-Oxa-1,16-hexadecanolactone

Oxazepam
Oxymetazoline hydrochloride
Oxyphencyclimine hydrochloride
Oxyphenisatin diacetate
Pancuronium bromide
(−)-Pantolactone
(±)-Pantolactone, which yields on hydrolysis not more than 5 parts per million by weight of cyanides calculated as CN
Pemoline
1,15-Pentadecanolactone
1,4-n-Pent-2-enolactone
Penthienate hydrochloride
Penthienate methobromide
Phenazone
Phenazopyridine monohydrochloride
Phenbutrazate hydrochloride
Pheniramine hydrogen maleate
Phenmetrazine hydrochloride
Phenodioxin
Phenolphthalein, which satisfies the requirements of the British Pharmacopoeia
Phenoperidine
Phenoperidine hydrochloride
Phenothiazine of a purity not less than 98 per cent., which contains not more than 0·0035 per cent. by weight of total iodine, and which yields not more than 0·05 per cent. by weight of sulphated ash (until 2nd July 1970)
2-Phenoxypyridine
Phenprocoumon
Phentolamine monomesylate
4-(N-Phenylamidino)thiazole hydrochloride
Phenylbutazone
2-Phenylcinchoninic acid
2-Phenylindole
1-Phenylphosphorinan
α-Phenylpiperidinoacetamide
α-Phenylpiperidinoacetonitrile
α-Phenylpyrrolidinoacetamide
2-Picoline
3-Picoline
4-Picoline
Picoline, mixed isomers
Picolinic acid
Pipazethate monohydrochloride
Pipenzolate bromide
4-Piperidinobutyronitrile
Piperidolate hydrochloride
Piritramide
Potassium 4-amino-3,5,6-trichloropicolinate
Potassium hydrogen 7-oxabicyclo[2,2,1]heptane-2,3-dicarboxylate
diPotassium 7-oxabicyclo[2,2,1]heptane-2,3-dicarboxylate
Pramoxine hydrochloride
L-Proline
DL-Proline
Prolintane hydrochloride
Propantheline bromide
1,3-Propiolactone
Propiomazine hydrogen maleate
2-n-Propylpyridine

Tariff heading	Description
29.35	6-*n*-Propylthiouracil

Prothionamide
Prothipendyl *mono*hydrochloride
Pyrazinamide
Pyrazole
Pyridine
Pyridine-2,3-dicarboxylic acid
2-Pyridone
3-Pyridylacetic acid
2-Pyridylacetic acid hydrochloride
4-Pyridylacetic acid hydrochloride
3-Pyridylacetonitrile
3-Pyridyl dimethylcarbamate
1-(4-Pyridyl)pyridinium chloride
Pyrimidine
Pyritinol dihydrochloride
Pyrrobutamine pentahydrogen diphosphate
Pyrrolidine
4-Pyrrolidinobutyronitrile
2-Pyrrolidone
3-Pyrroline
Quinoline (until 2nd July 1970)
*iso*Quinoline
Quinuronium sulphate
Skatole
Sodium D-*iso*ascorbate
Sodium dehydracetate
Sodium deoxyribonucleate
*di*Sodium 7-oxabicyclo[2,2,1]heptane-2,3-dicarboxylate
Sodium 2-phenylcinchoninate
Sodium ribonucleate
Sodium 6,8-thioctamidoacetate
Spironolactone
Tetrabenazine
Tetrachlorothiophen
Tetracosactide hexa-acetate
Tetra(dichloro-1,3,5-triazinetrione)-trichloro-1,3,5-triazinetrione
    complex, tetrapotassium derivative
Tetrahydro-2,5-dimethoxyfuran
Tetrahydro-3,5-dimethyl-1,3,5-thiadiazine-2-thione
Tetrahydrofuran
Tetrahydrofurfuryl alcohol
Tetrahydro-2-methylfuran
(+)-Tetrahydro-4-methyl-2-(2-methylprop-1-enyl)pyran
(−)-Tetrahydro-4-methyl-2-(2-methylprop-1-enyl)pyran
Tetrahydro-4-methyl-6-ureido-2-pyrimidone
2-(Tetrahydro-5-methyl-5-vinyl-2-furyl)propan-2-ol
3-(Tetrahydro-2-*n*-pentyl-3-furyl)-1-[3-(tetrahydro-2-*n*-pentyl-3-
    furyl)propoxy]propan-1-ol
2,3,5,6-Tetrahydro-6-phenylimidazo[2,1-*b*]thiazole hydrochloride
Tetrahydrozoline *mono*hydrochloride
Thenyldiamine *mono*hydrochloride
Thiabendazole
Thiethylperazine di(hydrogen maleate)
6,8-Thioctamide
5,8-Thioctic acid
Thioguanine
Thionaphthen
Thiophen
Thioridazine

Tariff heading	Description
29.35	Thioridazine *mono*hydrochloride
	Thioxolone
	Thymidine
	Thymine
	Thymolphthalein-2,2'-di(methylaminodiacetic acid)
	Tigogenin acetate
	Triallyl cyanurate
	Triaziridin-1-ylphosphine oxide
	2-(3-Trifluoromethylanilino)nicotinic acid
	4,4,4-Trifluoro-1-(2-thienyl)butane-1,3-dione
	Tri-(2-hydroxyethyl)-1,3,5-triazinetrione
	Trimetaphan *mono*-(+)-camphorsulphonate
	Trimetazidine dihydrochloride
	Tri-(2-methylaziridin-1-yl)phosphine oxide
	NN'-Trimethyleneurea
	Tripelennamine citrate
	Tripelennamine *mono*hydrochloride
	Tryptamine hydrochloride
	L-Tryptophan
	DL-Tryptophan
	Uracil
	Uric acid
	Uridine
	Uridine 3'-(dihydrogen phosphate)
	Uridine 5'-(disodium dihydrogen triphosphate)
	Usnic acid
	5-Vinyl-2-picoline (until 2nd July 1970)
	N-Vinyl-2-pyrrolidone
	Viprynium embonate
	Visnadine
	Xanthen-9-carboxylic acid
	Xanthine
	Xanthurenic acid
	Xylometazoline hydrochloride
	Zinc di-(2-thiobenzimidazole)
	Zoxazolamine
29.36	Acetohexamide
	4-Acetylbenzenesulphonamide
	*N*¹-Acetylsulphamethoxypyridazine
	4-Amino-*N*-ethyl-*N*-(2-methanesulphonamidoethyl)-*m*-toluidine sesquisulphate (−NH₂ at 1)
	Benzthiazide
	3-*iso*Butyl-6-chloro-3,4-dihydrobenzo-1,2,4-thiadiazine-7-sulphonamide 1,1-dioxide
	Chloramine T
	5-Chloroaniline-2,4-disulphonamide
	3-Chloro-6-sulphanilamidopyridazine
	Chlorpropamide
	Clopamide
	Cyclopenthiazide
	Cyclothiazide
	N-Dichlorofluoromethylthio-*N'N'*-dimethyl-*N*-phenylsulphamide
	Dichlorphenamide
	Dimethothiazine mesylate
	2-Dimethylsulphamoylphenothiazine
	Epithiazide
	Ethiazide
	Ethyl 4-acetylbenzenesulphonylcarbamate
	N'-Ethyl-*p*-toluidine-3-sulphonanilide (−NH₂ at 1)
	*Glibenclamide

Tariff heading   *Description*

29.36   2-Methoxy-3-sulphanilamidopyrazine
Methyclothiazide
3-Methyl-1-phenyl-5-sulphanilamidopyrazole
Polythiazide
Probenecid
Quinethazone
Sulphadimethoxine
Sulphadimidine esylate, sodium derivative
Sulphamerazine
Sulphamethoxazole
Sulphamethoxypyridazine
Sulphanilamide (until 2nd July 1970)
Sulphormethoxine
Teclothiazide potassium
Thioproperazine dimesylate
Thiothixene
Tolazamide

29.37   *o*-Cresolsulphonephthalein-6,6'-di(methylaminodiacetic acid)
o-Cresolsulphonephthalein-6,6'-di(methylaminodiacetic acid),
    tetrasodium salt
4,5,6,7,3',5',3'',5'''-Octabromophenolsulphonephthalein
1,3-Propanesultone
Sulthiame
Thymolsulphonephthalein-2,2'-di(methylaminodiacetic acid)

29.38   L-Ascorbic acid
Ascorbyl palmitate
D-Biotin
Calciferol
Carotene
Dexpanthenol
Ergosterol
(+)-*N*-(3-Ethoxypropyl)-2,4-dihydroxy-3,3-dimethylbutyramide
Phytomenadione
Pteroylmonoglutamic acid
Pyridoxal 5-(dihydrogen phosphate)
Riboflavine
Sodium D-pantothenate
D-γ-Tocopherol

29.39   (+)-Aldosterone
Chlormadinone acetate
3-Cyclopentyloxy-17α-ethynyloestra-1,3,5(10)-trien-17β-ol
3-Cyclopentyloxy-17α-hydroxypregna-3,5-dien-20-one acetate
3-Cyclopentyloxypregna-3,5-dien-20-one
Deoxycorticosterone acetate
Deoxycorticosterone 21-D-glucoside
Deoxycorticosterone pivalate
*Dexamethasone
Dexamethasone 21-(disodium phosphate)
Dexamethasone 21-*iso*nicotinate
Dexamethasone 21-(3-sodium-sulphobenzoate)
*Edogestrone
17α-Ethyloestr-4-en-17β-ol
Fludrocortisone 21-acetate
Fluocinolone acetonide
6α-Fluoro-11β,21-dihydroxy-16α,17α-*iso*propylidenedioxypregna-1,4-
    diene-3,20-dione
Fluorometholone
9α-Fluoro-11β,17α,21-trihydroxypregna-1,4-diene-3,20-dione
    1-ace ate

Tariff heading   *Description*

29.39   Fluoxymesterone
Follicle stimulating hormone (FSH) and luteinising hormone (LH), mixed
17α-Hydroxypregn-4-ene-3,20-dione n-heptanoate
17α-Hydroxypregn-4-ene-3,20-dione n-hexanoate
Lynoestrenol
Medroxyprogesterone acetate
Methylprednisolone
Methylprednisolone 21-acetate
Nandrolone laurate
(−)-Noradrenaline
(−)-Noradrenaline hydrogen tartrate
Norethandrolone
Norethisterone
Norethisterone acetate
17β-Oestradiol di-n-undecanoate
17β-Oestradiol 17-n-valerate
Oxymesterone
Oxymetholone
Oxytocin
Oxytocin dihydrogen citrate
Paramethasone 21-acetate
Prednisolone 21-pivalate
Prednisolone 21-(3-sodium-sulphobenzoate)
Prednisolone 21-O-stearoylglycollate
Prednylidene
Quinestradol
Testosterone 3-cyclohexylpropionate
Testosterone n-heptanoate
DL-Thyroxine sodium
Triamcinolone
Triamcinolone acetonide
Vasopressin
Vasopressin tannate

29.40   Urokinase

29.41   Aesculin
Digitalin
Digitonin
Digitoxin
Ouabain
Salicin

29.42   18β-Acetoxy-10β,17α-dimethoxy-16β-methoxycarbonyl-3-oxo-2,3-seco-20α-yohimbane
Alcuronium chloride
Arecoline
Arecoline-acetarsol
Arecoline hydrobromide
Bamifylline hydrochloride
Berberine hydrogen sulphate
Bicuculline
2-Bromo-NN-diethyl-D-lysergamide hydrogen tartrate
Bulbocapnine hydrochloride
Cinchonidine
Cinchonidine sulphate
Cinchonine
Cinchonine monohydrochloride
Cinchonine sulphate
Cocaine, of a purity not greater than 97·5 per cent. by weight

Tariff heading   *Description*

29.42   Colchicine
Demecolcine
Deptropine dihydrogen citrate
Deserpidine
Dihydroergocornine
Dihydroergocristine
Dihydroergocryptine
Dihydroergotamine *mono*mesylate
7,8-Dihydro-14-hydroxy-6-methylene-6-deoxymorphine
Dimenhydrinate
*pseudo*Ephedrine
*pseudo*Ephedrine hydrochloride
Ergotamine tartrate
Ethyl quinine carbonate
Galanthamine hydrobromide
Galegine sulphate
Harmalol
Harmine
1-*n*-Hexyltheobromine
Hydromorphone hydrochloride
18β-Hydroxy-10,17α-dimethoxy-20α-yohimbane-16β-carboxylic acid
    lactone
Hyoscine *n*-butylobromide
Lobeline hydrochloride
Lobeline sulphate
(+)-Lysergic acid
Lysergide tartrate-methanol complex
Meralluride
Mescaline hydrochloride
Mescaline sulphate
Methoserpidine
Methylergometrine maleate
Methysergide hydrogen maleate
Papaverine
Papaverine hydrochloride
Papaverine hydrogen sulphate
Phenmetrazine theoclate
Reserpine
Sparteine *mono*sulphate
Syrosingopine
Tomatidine
Vinblastine sulphate
Vincristine sulphate
Xanthinol nicotinate
Yohimbine *mono*hydrochloride

29.43   D-Arabinose
L-Arabinose
D-Erythrose
Fructose 1-(barium phosphate)
Fructose tetranicotinate, mixed isomers
L-Fucose
D-Galactose
Galactose 6-(barium phosphate)
Gentiobiose
Maltose
D-Mannose
Mannose 6-(barium phosphate)
D-Melezitose dihydrate
Methyl α-D-xyloside (until 3rd September 1970)
Methyl β-D-xyloside (until 3rd September 1970)

Tariff heading   *Description*

29.43   Raffinose
           L-Rhamnose
           D-Ribose
           Ribose 5-(barium phosphate)
           Sorbose
           Sucrose benzoate having a benzoyl content of not less than 80 per cent.
              by weight calculated as benzoic acid
           Sucrose diacetate hexa*iso*butyrate
           Turanose
           P1-Uridine-5′ P2-glucose-1 disodium pyrophosphate
           D-Xylose

29.44   Amphotericin B
           Bacitracin methylenedisalicylate
           Bacitracin zinc
           Calcium amphomycin
           Capreomycin disulphate
           Chloramphenicol 3-cinnamate
           Chloramphenicol sodium succinate
           Clindamycin hydrochloride
           Clomocycline, sodium salt
           Colistin sulphate
           Colistin sulphomethate sodium
           Cycloserine
           Diethanolammonium fusidate
           3-[2-(3,5-Dimethyl-2-oxocyclohexyl)-2-hydroxyethyl]glutarimide
           Erythromycin ethyl succinate
           Erythromycin glucoheptonate
           Erythromycin lactobionate
           Framycetin sulphate
           Fumagillin
           Fusafungin
           Gentamicin sulphate
           Gramicidin
           Hygromycin B
           Kanamycin sulphates
           Kojic acid
           Lincomycin hydrochloride
           Lymecycline
           Methacycline
           Methacycline hydrochloride
           3-(4-Methylpiperazin-1-yliminomethyl)rifamycin SV
           Natamycin
           Novobiocin
           Novobiocin calcium
           Novobiocin sodium
           Nystatin
           Oleandomycin *mono*phosphate
           Paromomycin
           Paromomycin sulphates
           Rifamycin B diethylamide, *mono*sodium derivative
           Rolitetracycline nitrate
           Rubidomycin hydrochloride
           Sodium cephalothin (until 5th November 1970)
           Sodium fusidate
           Spectinomycin dihydrochloride
           Spectinomycin sulphate
           Spiramycin
           Thiostrepton
           Triacetyloleandomycin
           Tyrothricin

Tariff heading	Description

29.44   Vancomycin hydrochloride
Viomycin pantothenate sulphate
Viomycin sulphate
Virginiamycin
Xanthocillin

29.45   Boron trifluoride-ethylamine complex
Ferrous sulphate-glycine complex
Potassium *tert*butoxide
Potassium methoxide
Sodium dihydridodi-(2-methoxyethoxy)aluminate
Sodium ethoxide
Sodium methoxide

30.01   Grafts of bone or cartilage, defatted, dried and packed in vacuum

30.03   Digitalin, being a mixture of digitalis glycosides standardised with the addition of lactose or other diluent

Preparations consisting of not less than 3·4 per cent. by weight of 3-cyclopentyloxy-17α-hydroxypregna-3,5-diene-20-one acetate dissolved in fixed vegetable oil

Preparations consisting of not less than 10 per cent. by weight of methenolone *n*-heptanoate dissolved in fixed vegetable oil

Preparations consisting of not less than 0·14 per cent. by weight of quinestradol dissolved in fixed vegetable oil

Preparations containing either (*a*) not less than 0·8 per cent. by weight of thiotepa and not less than 95 per cent. by weight of polyethylene glycol ethers or (*b*) not less than 9·5 per cent. by weight of thiotepa

Preparations containing leucovorin calcium equivalent to not less than 2·7 grammes and not more than 3·6 grammes of leucovorin per litre

Preparations containing not less than 18 per cent. by weight and not more than 58 per cent. by weight of frusemide

Preparations containing not less than 18 per cent. by weight of 2-(4-chloroanilino)-5-(4-chlorophenyl)-3,5-dihydro-3-*iso*propylimino-phenazine

Preparations containing not less than 15 per cent. by weight of *O*-(3-chloro-4-methylcoumarin-7-yl) *OO*-diethyl phosphorothioate

Preparations containing not less than 2·5 per cent. by weight of colistin sulphate

Preparations containing not less than 50 per cent. by weight of fluanisone calculated on the dry material

Preparations containing not less than 0·45 per cent. by weight of fusafungin and not less than 99 per cent. by weight of squalane

Preparations containing not less than 0·18 per cent. by weight of fusafungin and not less than 80 per cent. by weight of volatile propellents

Preparations containing not less than 95 per cent. by weight of lactose and not less than 0·3 per cent. by weight of uramustine

Preparations containing not less than 1·2 per cent. by weight of methylprednisolone

Preparations containing not less than 1 per cent. by weight of orciprenaline sulphate and not less than 96 per cent. by weight of propellent gases liquefied under pressure

Preparations containing not less than 0·13 per cent. by weight of tramazoline hydrochloride, not less than 0·02 per cent. by weight of dexamethasone 21-*iso*nicotinate, and not less than 96 per cent. by weight of volatile propellents

Preparations containing sodium salts of methotrexate equivalent to not less than 20 per cent. by weight and not more than 60 per cent. by weight of methotrexate

Preparations, in the form of capsules, the contents of which include not less than 70 per cent. by weight of acetazolamide

Tariff heading	*Description*
30.03	Preparations, in the form of cream, containing not less than 70 per cent. by weight of water and not less than 0·8 per cent. by weight of chlordantoin
	Preparations, in the form of suppositories, containing not less than 0·25 per cent. by weight of bisacodyl
	Preparations, in the form of tablets, containing aminopterin sodium equivalent to not less than 0·35 per cent. by weight and not more than 0·45 per cent. by weight of aminopterin
	Preparations, in the form of tablets, containing not less than 1·8 per cent. by weight and not more than 2·3 per cent. by weight of methotrexate
	Preparations, in the form of tablets, containing not less than 4 per cent. by weight of orciprenaline sulphate
32.07	Dispersions of carbon black in artificial plastics, containing not less than 6 per cent. by weight of carbon black, not less than 40 per cent. by weight of cellulose acetate butyrate and not less than 35 per cent. by weight of acrylic resin
	Preparations consisting of titanium dioxide dispersed in nylon 6, containing not less than 18 per cent. by weight and not more than 22 per cent. by weight of titanium dioxide
35.04	Protein substances of which, when 20 grammes are shaken for 2 hours at 20° centigrade with ethanol of a strength of 90 per cent. by volume, not more than 0·2 millilitre remains undissolved
37.01	Diazo film in sheets, being film which is capable, when developed by heating at between 105° and 135° centigrade, of producing a positive image consisting of light-scattering cavities in an otherwise transparent coating (until 7th May 1970)
37.02	Diazo film in rolls, being film which is capable, when developed by heating at between 105° and 135° centigrade, of producing a positive image consisting of light-scattering cavities in an otherwise transparent coating (until 7th May 1970)
37.03	Diazo paper, unexposed, being paper which is capable, when developed by heating at between 105° and 135° centigrade, of producing a positive image consisting of light-scattering cavities in an otherwise transparent coating (until 7th May 1970)
38.03	Activated carbon, not being of animal origin, which, in the form in which it is imported, on subjection to extraction with acetic acid of a strength of 30 per cent. by weight at 50° centigrade for 30 minutes, yields (*a*) a total of extractable solids which, when dried at 105° centigrade, does not exceed 0·2 per cent. by weight of the material and (*b*) extractable phosphate, which expressed in terms of phosphorus pentoxide, does not exceed 50 parts per million by weight of the material
38.05	Tall oil, crude
38.11	Preparations containing not less than 0·2 per cent. by weight of 2-[α-(4-chlorophenyl)phenylacetyl]indane-1,3-dione and not less than 95 per cent. by weight of hydrocarbon oil
	Preparations containing not less than 7 per cent. by weight of 2,6-dichlorothiobenzamide and not more than 15 per cent. by weight of materials soluble in diethyl ether
	Preparations, in powder form, containing not less than 17 per cent. by weight of triphenyltin hydroxide
	Preparations, liquid, containing not less than 35 per cent. by weight of 4-chlorophenylthiomethyl *OO*-diethyl phosphorodithioate
	Preparations, liquid, containing not less than 40 per cent. by weight of *OO*-diethyl *O*-pyrazin-2-yl phosphorothioate

Tariff heading	Description

38.11 Preparations, liquid, containing not less than 65 per cent. by weight of S-ethyl di-n-propylthiocarbamate

Preparations, liquid, containing not less than 65 per cent. by weight of S-n-propyl n-butylethylthiocarbamate

Preparations, solid, containing not less than 45 per cent. by weight of OO-dimethyl phthalimidomethyl phosphorodithioate

Preparations, solid, containing not less than 90 per cent. by weight of sodium ethylenebisdithiocarbamate

Prepared cereal baits containing not less than 0·4 per cent. by weight and not more than 1 per cent. by weight of 5-(α-hydroxy-α-2-pyridylbenzyl)-7-(α-2-pyridylbenzylidene)bicyclo[2,2,1]hept-5-ene-2,3-dicarboxyimide

38.14 Prepared oil additives, consisting of hydrocarbon oil and organic compounds of antimony, and containing not less than 6 per cent. by weight and not more than 13 per cent. by weight of antimony calculated as Sb

Prepared oil additives containing not less than 5 per cent. by weight of calcium calculated as Ca when determined by titration with a solution of perchloric acid in acetic acid, and not more than 5·5 per cent. by weight of calcium calculated as Ca when determined by the Institute of Petroleum method No. 111/49T

Prepared oil additives, having a viscosity at 99° centigrade of not less than 20 centistokes, containing not less than 2·5 per cent. by weight and not more than 4·5 per cent. by weight of zinc calculated as Zn, and containing not less than 2 per cent. by weight of phosphorus calculated as P

38.15 Prepared rubber accelerators, being sulphides of alkylphenols, and containing not less than 20 per cent. by weight and not more than 30 per cent. by weight of sulphur in all

Prepared rubber accelerators containing not less than 80 per cent. by weight of NNN'-trimethylthiourea

38.19 Amines, mixed primary aromatic, containing not less than 4·5 per cent. by weight and not more than 5·5 per cent. by weight of nitrogen calculated as N

Chlordane

Cultured crystals, weighing not less than two and a half grammes of barium fluoride

Mixed alkenylsuccinic anhydrides having a saponification value not less than 505

Mixed alkyl selenides containing not less than 14 per cent. by weight and not more than 21 per cent. by weight of combined selenium

Mixed alkyl-substituted benzenesulphonic acids having an acid value not greater than 125

Poly-(3,4-diacetyl-5-thiothien-2-yl) which on ignition yields not more than 10 per cent. by weight of ash

Polyglyoxal

Preparations consisting of acrylamide with not less than 2 per cent. by weight and not more than 12 per cent. by weight of diacrylamido-methane

Preparations consisting of calcium tetrahydrogen diorthophosphate and aluminium compounds, and containing not less than 1·5 per cent. by weight and not more than 2·5 per cent. by weight of aluminium calculated as Al$_2$O$_3$

Preparations consisting of 1-chloro-1,1-difluoroethane and 1,1-difluoroethane, and containing not less than 40 per cent. by weight and not more than 50 per cent. by weight of 1,1-difluoroethane

Preparations consisting of clay and not less than 30 per cent. by weight and not more than 40 per cent. by weight of N-methyl-N,4-dinitro-soaniline

Tariff heading	*Description*
38.19	Preparations containing not less than 85 per cent. by weight of aluminium compounds calculated as Al_2O_3, and not less than 10 per cent. by weight of molybdenum compounds calculated as MoO_3, and of which not more than 10 per cent. by weight is retained by a sieve having a nominal width of aperture of $1 \cdot 2$ millimetres
	Preparations containing not less than 55 per cent. by weight of melamine compounds calculated as melamine and not less than 12 per cent. by weight of peroxides calculated as hydrogen peroxide
	Preparations, gaseous, containing not less than $0 \cdot 002$ per cent. by volume and not more than $1 \cdot 5$ per cent. by volume of antimony compounds calculated as stibine, and having a value not less than £15 per cubic metre at standard temperature and pressure
	Preparations, gaseous, containing not less than $0 \cdot 002$ per cent. by volume and not more than $1 \cdot 5$ per cent. by volume of arsenic compounds calculated as arsine, and having a value not less than £15 per cubic metre at standard temperature and pressure
	Preparations, gaseous, containing not less than $0 \cdot 002$ per cent. by volume and not more than $1 \cdot 5$ per cent. by volume of boron compounds calculated as diborane, and having a value not less than £15 per cubic metre at standard temperature and pressure
	Preparations, gaseous, containing not less than $0 \cdot 002$ per cent. by volume and not more than $1 \cdot 5$ per cent. by volume of phosphorus compounds calculated as phosphine, and having a value not less than £15 per cubic metre at standard temperature and pressure
	Preparations, gaseous, containing not less than $0 \cdot 002$ per cent. by volume and not more than $1 \cdot 5$ per cent. by volume of selenium compounds calculated as hydrogen selenide, and having a value not less than £15 per cubic metre at standard temperature and pressure
	Preparations, gaseous, containing not less than $0 \cdot 5$ per cent. by volume and not more than 6 per cent. by volume of silicon compounds calculated as silane, and having a value not less than £40 per cubic metre at standard temperature and pressure
	Prepared catalysts consisting of phosphoric acids and siliceous earth and containing not less than 55 per cent. by weight and not more than 70 per cent. by weight of phosphates calculated as P_2O_5
	Prepared catalysts, in the form of spheres, containing silver or silver oxide dispersed in, or deposited on, aluminium oxide or silica or other compounds of silicon, and which contain not less than 7 per cent. by weight and not more than 25 per cent. by weight of total silver calculated as Ag
	Prepared catalysts which in the dry state contain not less than 5 per cent. by weight of nickel compounds calculated as Ni and not less than 50 per cent. by weight of phosphate calculated as PO_4
39.01	Nylon 6 in the forms covered by Note 3(*b*) of Chapter 39, containing not more than 2 per cent. by weight of titanium dioxide and not more than $2 \cdot 5$ per cent. by weight of carbon black, but not otherwise compounded
	Phenoxy resins, not plasticised or otherwise compounded, being thermoplastic polyaddition products of 2,2-di-(4-hydroxyphenyl)-propane and 1-chloro-2,3-epoxypropane and having an epoxide content of less than $0 \cdot 8$ per cent. by weight calculated as ethylene oxide
	Poly-[2,2-di-(4-hydroxyphenyl)propane carbonate] moulding compounds, containing glass fibres which amount to not less than 25 per cent. by weight of the product and not more than 45 per cent. by weight of the product
	Poly-[2,2-di-(4-hydroxyphenyl)propane carbonate], uncompounded, or compounded with other materials which do not exceed 3 per cent. by weight of the product

Tariff heading   *Description*

39.01   Polynoxylin

Resins, being products of the condensation of adipic acid with a mixture of propane-1,2-diol and ethanediol of which the ethanediol content is not less than 50 per cent. by weight, and having:—
    (*a*) an acetyl value not less than 34 and not more than 38,
    (*b*) an acid value not more than 1,
    (*c*) a colour not deeper than 50 Hazen units, and
    (*d*) a viscosity at 40° centigrade of not less than 70 seconds and not more than 125 seconds, for a free fall of 20 centimetres of a steel sphere ⅛ inch in diameter, in a tube of internal diameter 3·5 centimetres, when determined by the method of British Standard 188:1957, part 3, as amended up to and including September 1964

39.02   Acrylic sheet, transparent, colourless, of a thickness not less than 1·5 millimetres and not greater than 17·0 millimetres, which, when kept for 24 hours at a temperature of 110° centigrade, undergoes a linear shrinkage of not more than 10 per cent., and which, when kept for 24 hours at a temperature of 145° centigrade, undergoes a linear shrinkage of not less than 40 per cent.

Polystyrene sheet, in rolls, colourless, of a thickness not less than 0·1 millimetre and not greater than 0·9 millimetre and having a light transmission not less than 85 per cent. (until 2nd July 1970)

Poly(vinyl butyral) sheet, of a thickness not greater than 0·8 millimetre and of a width not less than 35 centimetres

Poly(vinyl chloride) having an apparent density of not more than 0·3 grammes per millilitre and a viscosity number of not less than 170 when tested by the methods described in British Standard 2782:1965 and of which not more than 5 per cent. by weight is retained by a sieve having a nominal width of aperture of 150 microns (until 5th March 1970)

39.03   Carboxymethylcellulose, aluminium salt

Cellulose acetate, where the weight of the acetyl content, calculated as acetic acid, is not less than 60 per cent. of the weight of the cellulose acetate, not being cellulose acetate plasticised or otherwise compounded

Cellulose acetate butyrate compounded with other materials which do not exceed 25 per cent. by weight of the product, in the forms covered by Note 3(*b*) of Chapter 39

Cellulose acetate butyrate, not plasticised or otherwise compounded

Cellulose acetate propionate, not plasticised or otherwise compounded

Cellulose propionate, not plasticised or otherwise compounded

Ethylcellulose

Ethylhydroxyethylcellulose

Hydroxyethylcellulose

Hydroxypropylcellulose

Scrap exposed X-ray film

49.11   Identification kits, consisting essentially of a series of transparent slides or foils printed to depict individual characteristics of the human face or head; parts of such kits (until 2nd July 1970)

51.01   Yarn wholly of polytetrafluoroethylene

51.02   Monofil wholly of fluorocarbon polymer

68.13   Asbestos paper, rubber impregnated, in rolls, being not less than 0·75 millimetre and not more than 0·85 millimetre in thickness, weighing not less than 0·71 kilogramme and not more than 0·78 kilogramme per square metre, and which, when heated to a temperature of 1,000° centigrade, has a loss in weight of not less than 28 per cent. and not more than 32 per cent. (until 2nd July 1970)

Tariff heading	Description
69.09	Catalyst carriers in the form of spheres, consisting of aluminium oxide and silica whether or not combined together, and containing not more than 12·5 per cent. by weight of total silica, and of which (a) not less than 99 per cent. by weight passes a sieve having a nominal width of aperture of 2·40 millimetres and (b) not less than 99 per cent. by weight is retained by a sieve having a nominal width of aperture of 1·00 millimetre
70.01	Glass in the mass (other than optical glass) containing not less than 5 per cent. and not more than 11 per cent. by weight of fluorine calculated as F (until 2nd July 1970)
70.03	Amber-coloured tubing of soda glass, not being glass containing 0·25 per cent. or more of cadmium, free or combined, calculated as Cd
	Tubing of neutral glass, in straight lengths and capable of passing a test corresponding with the test for limit of alkalinity of glass prescribed by British Pharmacopoeia, not including (a) glass with a content of more than 85 per cent. of silica and boric oxide together, or (b) glass of fused silica or fused quartz
70.10	Carboys having a capacity of not less than 5 gallons (until 2nd July 1970)
70.18	Optical glass in the form of sheets, slabs or moulded lens blanks, having, with reference to the D line of sodium, a refractive index (n_D) not less than 1·5625 and not greater than 1·5650 and a dispersive power (v_D) not less than 60·0 and not greater than 61·5 (until 2nd July 1970)
	Optical glass in the form of sheets, slabs or moulded lens blanks, having, with reference to the D line of sodium, a refractive index (n_D) not less than 1·612 and not greater than 1·615 and a dispersive power (v_D) not less than 43·5 and not greater than 45·0; having also at a wavelength of 400 nanometres a light transmission for a 25 millimetres path of not less than 83 per cent.; and which acquires no visible stain when kept for 15 minutes at a temperature of 25° centigrade in contact with a buffered sodium acetate solution having a pH value of 4.6 (until 2nd July 1970)
	Optical glass in the mass containing not less than 5 per cent. by weight and not more than 11 per cent. by weight of fluorine calculated as F (until 2nd July 1970)
70.20	Glass fibres, loose, unfelted, having a diameter not greater than 3 microns
73.06	Iron or steel ingots, blocks, lumps and similar forms, other than those manufactured entirely from pig iron smelted wholly with charcoal (until 2nd July 1970)
73.07	Iron or steel blooms, billets, slabs and sheet bars (until 2nd July 1970)
73.08	Iron or steel coils for re-rolling (until 2nd July 1970)
73.12	Strip of iron or steel, coated with tin, of a width not less than 304 millimetres, and not more than 500 millimetres, of a thickness of not less than 0·12 millimetre and not more than 0·5 millimetre, and of a length of not more than 1016 millimetres (until 2nd April 1970)
	†Strip of iron or steel, in coil form, coated with tin, of a width of not less than 140 millimetres, and not more than 500 millimetres, and of a thickness of not less than 0·12 millimetre and not more than 0·5 millimetre (until 2nd April 1970)
73.13	Cold reduced sheets and plates of iron or steel, rectangular or in coils, of a width exceeding 500 millimetres, and of a thickness of less than 3 millimetres, not plated, coated, clad, drilled, punched or otherwise worked (until 2nd April 1970)
	Sheets of iron or steel, coated with tin, of a width exceeding 500 millimetres but not more than 966 millimetres, of a thickness of not less than 0·12 millimetre and not more than 0·5 millimetre, and of a length of not more than 1016 millimetres (until 2nd April 1970)

Tariff heading   *Description*

73.13   Sheets of iron or steel, in coil form, coated with tin, of a width exceeding 500 millimetres but not more than 966 millimetres, and of a thickness of not less than 0·12 millimetre and not more than 0·5 millimetre (until 2nd April 1970)

73.14   †Iron-nickel alloy wire, copper-clad and nickel-plated, having an overall diameter of not less than 400 microns and not more than 450 microns, the nickel plating being not less than 2 microns and not more than 30 microns in thickness; the whole containing not less than 20 per cent. by weight of copper, not less than 25 per cent. by weight of nickel and not less than 40 per cent. by weight of iron, and having, when measured on an 0·20 metre length, a percentage elongation not less than 18 and not more than 25, and a tensile strength not less than 430 newtons per square millimetre and not more than 530 newtons per square millimetre, the rate of straining being 50 millimetres per minute (until 5th March 1970)

Iron or steel wire of a diameter not less than 0·019 inch nor more than 0·200 inch, and having a coating of nickel of not less than 0·0001 inch in thickness (until 2nd July 1970)

73.15   Cold-rolled steel strip, with dressed edges, in coils, the strip being not less than 0·002 inch nor more than 0·007 inch in thickness and not less than ¼ inch nor more than 4 inches in width, containing not less than 16 per cent. by weight nor more than 18 per cent. by weight of chromium, and not less than 6 per cent. by weight nor more than 8 per cent. by weight of nickel and being of a tensile strength of not less than 115 tons per square inch

Cold-rolled steel strip, with dressed edges, in coils, the strip being not less than 0·002 inch nor more than 0·040 inch in thickness and not less than $\frac{1}{16}$ inch nor more than 4 inches in width, containing not less than 16 per cent. by weight nor more than 18 per cent. by weight of chromium, and not less than 6 per cent. by weight nor more than 8 per cent. by weight of nickel, and being of a tensile strength of not less than 120 tons per square inch

Single strand alloy steel wire coated with niobium alloy containing tin and with an outer coating of silver (until 2nd July 1970)

73.19   Hot rolled seamless circular steel tubes of an outside diameter of not less than 19½ inches and not more than 24½ inches, and of a wall thickness of not less than $\frac{7}{16}$ inch and not more than ⅜ inch (until 2nd July 1970)

74.05   Tape consisting of a layer of niobium alloy containing tin, laminated between two layers of copper foil whether or not coated with tin, and being (a) not less than 0·25 inch nor more than 0·75 inch in width and (b) not more than 0·005 inch in thickness (until 2nd July 1970)

76.03   Aluminium discs of a minimum value of 8s. per lb., not less than 6 inches nor more than 18 inches in diameter and not less than 0·033 inch nor more than 0·036 inch in thickness and which, when either face is placed on a flat surface, do not deviate from the flat by more than 0·010 inch at any point (until 2nd July 1970)

81.02   Molybdenum, of a purity not less than 99·8 per cent., in the form of rods (whether or not threaded at the ends) not less than 55 inches nor more than 100 inches in length and not less than $1\frac{7}{32}$ inches nor more than $2\frac{1}{16}$ inches in diameter

Molybdenum, of a purity not less than 99·8 per cent., in the form of rods of not less than 18 inches and not more than 100 inches in length and of not less than 2¼ inches and not more than 4¼ inches in diameter and whether or not threaded at the ends

Tariff heading	Description

81.04   Chromium, electrolytic, in the form of cathode chips, which contains no more than 0·10 per cent. by weight of total oxygen, not more than 0·015 per cent. by weight of total aluminium, and not more than 0·001 per cent. by weight of aluminium compounds insoluble in boiling 5N hydrochloric acid and in boiling fuming perchloric acid, and estimated as Al (until 2nd July 1970)

Hafnium crystal bars consisting of hafnium wire on which hafnium crystals have been deposited

Manganese metal of a purity not less than 96 per cent. and not more than 99·5 per cent. and containing not more than 1·0 per cent. by weight of carbon and not more than 3·0 per cent. by weight of iron (until 7th May 1970)

Vanadium, unwrought, of a purity not less than 99 per cent. and containing not more than 0·1 per cent. by weight of iron calculated as Fe (until 2nd July 1970)

Wrought titanium alloy containing not less than 3 per cent. nor more than 5 per cent. by weight of vanadium, not less than 5 per cent. nor more than 7 per cent. by weight of aluminium, the balance being mainly titanium, in the form of billets of not less than 4 inches nor more than 7 inches in diameter or not less than 4 inches nor more than 7 inches square, in random lengths (until 5th March 1970)

Wrought titanium of a purity exceeding 99·6 per cent. titanium, in the form of slabs of a thickness of not less than 4½ inches nor more than 6 inches, of a width of not less than 36 inches nor more than 48 inches, in random lengths (until 5th March 1970)

Zirconium alloy ingots, surface trimmed, containing not less than 1·0 per cent. by weight nor more than 2·0 per cent. by weight of tin as the major alloying element, of circular cross section of a diameter of not less than 17 inches and not more than 21 inches, and of a length of not less than 40 inches and not more than 50 inches

Zirconium sponge

83.13   Tinplate caps for sealing jars, of an internal diameter on the rim of not less than 1·580 inches and not more than 1·610 inches and a maximum depth of not less than 0·415 inch and not more than 0·425 inch stamped from tinplate of nominal thickness of 0·0055 inch or of 0·0066 inch, with an internal curl, a vinyl coating applied to the internal surface and a plasticised lining compound deposited on the internal side wall and top sealing panel to form a sealing gasket (until 7th May 1970)

84.06   Combined crankcase and cylinder block castings of iron or steel, of a weight exceeding 291 lb. but not exceeding 308 lb., of a kind used in motor vehicle engines of 3 cylinder, direct injection, water-cooled. 2-stroke horizontally opposed piston type

85.14   Microphones, of a kind for incorporation in deaf aids, approximately rectangular in shape, with a maximum thickness not exceeding 0·165 inch and a total of the length and width not exceeding 0·675 inch, exclusive of sound tube

85.15   Loran receivers incorporating direct reading indicators, designed to operate only on frequencies of 1,700 kilocycles per second or more (until 3rd September 1970)

85.18   Tantalum capacitors greater than 10 microfarads in capacitance, of a kind for incorporation in deaf aids, with a maximum length not exceeding 7 millimetres exclusive of leads and with a transverse cross section having a circumference not exceeding 14 millimetres (until 2nd July 1970)

Tantalum capacitors, of a kind for incorporation in deaf aids, with a maximum length not exceeding 7 millimetres exclusive of leads and with a transverse cross section having a circumference not exceeding 10 millimetres (until 2nd July 1970)

Tariff heading	*Description*

85.19 Carbon track volume controls of a kind for incorporation in deaf aids, being of drum type with a cylindrical drum not exceeding 12 millimetres in diameter and 4 millimetres in thickness

85.20 Glass neon discharge lamps, having a metal cap fitted to each end and not exceeding 1 inch in overall length and $\frac{1}{2}$ inch in diameter over the caps (until 2nd July 1970)

85.23 Insulated tape incorporating a layer of niobium alloy containing tin, laminated between two layers of copper foil, whether or not coated with tin and being (*a*) not less than 0·25 inch nor more than 0·75 inch in width and (*b*) not more than 0·005 inch in thickness (until 2nd July 1970)

90.01 Lenses, Fresnel, converging, being composite sheets of artificial plastics, bearing a concentric system of grooves of a uniform density, not less than 18 grooves per centimetre; the lenses being not more than 1·0 centimetres in thickness, not less than 27 centimetres and not more than 29 centimetres square, with chamfered corners and having a focal length not greater than 16 centimetres (until 5th March 1970)
Lenses, prisms, mirrors and other optical elements, not optically worked, of barium fluoride
Lenses, prisms, mirrors and other optical elements, not optically worked, of thallium bromide-iodide (until 7th May 1970)
Material consisting of a polarising film supported on one or both sides by transparent material, and analysers and polarisers made therefrom (until 2nd July 1970)
Optical windows of zinc sulphide, unmounted
Photographic process screens of the contact type, consisting of a base of cellulose acetate or of poly(ethylene terephthalate) on which is a regularly spaced pattern of grey-coloured or magenta-coloured dots (until 2nd July 1970)

90.17 Ampoule injectors consisting of a glass reservoir connected to a flexible plastic tube in which is inserted a hypodermic needle protected by a removable plastic sheath, of a total length not exceeding 10 centimetres (until 5th March 1970)
Endoradiosondes for the measurement of pH; and specialised receiving and recording apparatus therefor

90.19 Aortic heart valves (until 2nd July 1970)
Earphones, of a kind for incorporation in deaf aids, approximately rectangular in shape, with a maximum thickness not exceeding 0·165 inch and a total of the length and width not exceeding 0·675 inch exclusive of sound tube
Mitral heart valves (until 2nd July 1970)

90.20 Beryllium metal windows of a thickness less than 0·004 inch for X-ray tubes (until 2nd July 1970)

SCHEDULE 2

THE IMPORT DUTIES (TEMPORARY EXEMPTIONS) ORDERS REVOKED

Number and year of Order	*Reference*
No. 6 of 1968	S.I. 1968/1948 (1968 III, p. 5263).
No. 1 of 1969	S.I. 1969/232 (1969 I, p. 620).
No. 2 of 1969	S.I. 1969/572 (1969 I, p. 1535).
No. 3 of 1969	S.I. 1969/573 (1969 I, p. 1539).
No. 4 of 1969	S.I. 1969/839 (1969 II, p. 2341).
No. 5 of 1969	S.I. 1969/1215 (1969 II, p. 3554).
No. 6 of 1969	S.I. 1969/1254 (1969 III, p. 3757).
No. 7 of 1969	S.I. 1969/1416 (1969 III, p. 4477).
No. 8 of 1969	S.I. 1969/1519 (1969 III, p, 4942).

EXPLANATORY NOTE

(*This Note is not part of the Order.*)

This Order provides that the goods listed in Schedule 1 shall be exempt, or shall continue to be exempt, from import duty until 1st January 1971, except for items for which an earlier day is specified. Descriptions of goods which were not exempt at the date of this Order are marked *.

Some goods the exemption of which is continued by this Order appear under a modified description. These items are marked †.

The Order also continues until 2nd July 1970 the partial exemption for photographic film base of cellulose acetate.

The more specialist publications referred to in the Order are as follows:—

I.U.P.A.C. rules

Included in a publication entitled " International Union of Pure and Applied Chemistry, Nomenclature of Organic Chemistry, Sections A and B ". Second edition published by Butterworth and Co. (Publishers) Ltd., 88, Kingsway, London, W.C.2.

Standard Methods for Testing Tar and its Products

6th edition published in 1967, by the Standardisation of Tar Products Testing Committee, c/o Coal Tar Research Association, Oxford Road, Gomersal, Cleckheaton, Yorkshire.

Institute of Petroleum Standards for Petroleum and its Products
Part I, Section I

Obtainable from the Institute at 61, New Cavendish Street, London, W.1.

STATUTORY INSTRUMENTS

1969 No. 1752

WEIGHTS AND MEASURES

The Weights and Measures (Jersey) Order 1969

Made - - - - 8th December 1969

Coming into Operation 1st January 1970

Whereas the Board of Trade are satisfied that it is proper, having regard to the law for the time being in force in Jersey,—

(i) to provide that any weighing and measuring equipment of the classes described in Article 2 of this Order which has been duly stamped in accordance with the law of Jersey or which is to be regarded as so stamped for the purposes of that law shall be treated for the purposes of the Weights and Measures Act 1963(**a**) (hereinafter referred to as "the Act") as if it had been duly stamped in Great Britain under section 11 of the Act ; and

(ii) to designate Jersey for the purposes of the provisions of the Act mentioned in Article 3 of this Order:

Now, therefore, the Board of Trade, in pursuance of the powers conferred upon them by sections 11(9) and 58(1) of the Act and all other powers enabling them in that behalf, hereby make the following Order: —

1. This Order may be cited as the Weights and Measures (Jersey) Order 1969, and shall come into operation on 1st January 1970.

2. Weighing and measuring equipment of any class prescribed under section 11 of the Act shall be treated for the purposes of the Act as duly stamped in Great Britain under that section if—

(i) it has been duly stamped under the Weights and Measures (Jersey) Law 1967 ; or

(ii) falls to be treated for the purposes of that Law as so stamped.

3. Jersey shall be a designated country for the purposes of sections 9(2), 21(5)(b), 25(1)(c) and 28(1) of the Act.

Gwyneth Dunwoody,
Parliamentary Secretary to the
Board of Trade.

8th December 1969.

(**a**) 1963 c. 31.

EXPLANATORY NOTE

(This Note is not part of the Order.)

The Weights and Measures Act 1963 does not extend to Jersey, which has its own weights and measures legislation.

A number of the provisions of the 1963 Act relating to the regulation of trade and weighing and measuring equipment used for trade do not apply in relation to goods " for despatch to a destination outside Great Britain and any designated country ".

This Order declares Jersey to be a designated country for the purposes of these provisions and the other sections of the Act which refer to designated countries. The principal effect is that the provisions described above will in future apply in relation to goods intended for despatch to Jersey.

The Order also provides that any weighing and measuring equipment which must be stamped by an inspector of weights and measures before it can be used for trade in Great Britain is to be treated as so stamped if it is to be treated as validly stamped in accordance with the law of Jersey.

STATUTORY INSTRUMENTS

1969 No. 1753

WEIGHTS AND MEASURES

The Weights and Measures (Northern Ireland) Order 1969

Made - - -	*8th December* 1969
Coming into Operation	*1st January* 1970

Whereas the Board of Trade are satisfied that it is proper, having regard to the law for the time being in force in Northern Ireland,—

(i) to provide that any weighing and measuring equipment of the classes described in Article 2 of this Order which has been duly stamped in accordance with that law or which is to be regarded as so stamped for the purposes of that law shall be treated for the purposes of the Weights and Measures Act 1963(a) (hereinafter referred to as "the Act") as if it had been duly stamped in Great Britain under section 11 of the Act; and

(ii) to designate Northern Ireland for the purposes of the provisions of the Act mentioned in Article 3 of this Order:

Now, therefore, the Board of Trade, in pursuance of the powers conferred upon them by sections 11(9) and 58(1) of the Act and all other powers enabling them in that behalf, hereby make the following Order:—

1. This Order may be cited as the Weights and Measures (Northern Ireland) Order 1969 and shall come into operation on 1st January 1970.

2. Weighing and measuring equipment of any class prescribed under section 11 of the Act shall be treated for the purposes of the Act as duly stamped in Great Britain under that section if—

(i) it has been duly stamped under the Weights and Measures Act (Northern Ireland) 1967(b); or

(ii) falls to be treated for the purposes of that Act as so stamped.

3. Northern Ireland shall be a designated country for the purposes of sections 9(2), 21(5) (b), 25(1) (c) and 28(1) of the Act.

Gwyneth Dunwoody,
Parliamentary Secretary to the
Board of Trade.

8th December 1969.

(a) 1963 c. 31.   (b) N.I. 1967 c. 6.

EXPLANATORY NOTE

(This Note is not part of the Order.)

The Weights and Measures Act 1963 does not generally extend to Northern Ireland which has its own weights and measures legislation.

A number of the provisions of the 1963 Act relating to the regulation of trade and weighing and measuring equipment used for trade do not apply in relation to goods "for despatch to a destination outside Great Britain and any designated country".

This Order declares Northern Ireland to be a designated country for the purposes of these provisions and the other sections of the Act which refer to designated countries. The principal effect is that the provisions described above will in future apply in relation to goods intended for the Northern Ireland market.

The Order also provides that any weighing and measuring equipment which must be stamped by an inspector of weights and measures before it can be used for trade in Great Britain is to be treated as so stamped if it is to be treated as validly stamped under the law of Northern Ireland.

STATUTORY INSTRUMENTS

1969 No. 1756 (S.153)

REGISTERS AND RECORDS, SCOTLAND

The Preservation of Sheriff Court Records Regulations 1969

Laid before Parliament in draft

Made - - -		*5th December* 1969
Coming into Operation		*1st January* 1970

I, the Lord President of the Court of Session, in exercise of the powers conferred upon me by section 12 of the Public Records (Scotland) Act 1937(a) and section 5 of the Public Registers and Records (Scotland) Act 1948(b), do hereby make the following Regulations, a draft whereof has lain before each House of Parliament in accordance with section 12(2) of the said Act of 1937 and no address has been presented to Her Majesty by either House against the draft :—

1. The Regulations made by the Lord Justice General and Lord President and the Secretary of State (c) under section 12 of the Public Records (Scotland) Act 1937 relating to the disposal of documents not to be preserved by the Keeper of the Registers and Records of Scotland, in so far only as they relate to sheriff court records, are hereby revoked.

2. In these Regulations "sheriff court records" shall have the same meaning as sheriff court records as defined in section 14(1) of the Public Records (Scotland) Act 1937.

3. These Regulations shall apply to all sheriff court records whether in the custody of the Keeper of the Records of Scotland (hereinafter called "the Keeper") or of any other body or person.

4. No sheriff court record containing an entry of older date than the year 1860 shall be disposed of by destruction or otherwise.

5. Subject to the provisions of Regulations 4 and 6 to 8 hereof the sheriff court records of the sheriff court district named and described in Schedule 1 hereto shall be selected for preservation in accordance with a scheme to be determined by the Lord President after consultation with the Sheriff of the sheriffdom concerned and the Keeper, with a view to preserving a representative sample of records relating to the development of sheriff court procedure and administration.

6. The sheriff court records described in Schedule 2 hereto shall be transmitted to the Keeper in terms of section 2(1) of the Public Records (Scotland) Act 1937, for preservation or for disposal in accordance with Regulations 7 and 8 hereof.

(a) 1937 c. 43. (b) 1948 c. 57.
(c) S.R. & O. 1940/2107 (Rev. XIX, p. 846: 1940 I, p. 917).

7. Subject to the provisions of Regulations 9, 10 and 11 hereof no sheriff court record shall be disposed of by destruction or otherwise until the expiry of twenty-five years from the date of the last interlocutor or other entry made therein or in respect thereof, or until the expiry of such longer period as may be particularly specified in Schedule 3 hereto. No such record shall be disposed of by destruction or otherwise until it has been transmitted to the Keeper, nor shall any such record be destroyed except in accordance with Regulation 8 hereof.

8. The sheriff court records referred to in Regulation 7 hereof and described in Schedule 3 hereto may be destroyed under the directions of the Keeper after the periods specified in the said Schedule. Such directions shall so far as practicable ensure the preservation of such records, or parts thereof, as shall seem to the Keeper to have a value for legal purposes or for historical or other research.

9. Subject to the provisions of Regulations 4 and 5 hereof the sheriff court records referred to in Schedule 4 hereto shall be destroyed forthwith by the person having proper legal custody thereof.

10. Subject to the provisions of Regulations 4 and 5 hereof the person having proper legal custody of the sheriff court records referred to in Schedule 5 hereto shall destroy them after the expiry of ten years from the date of the last entry to be made therein :

Provided that documents falling under the head of administrative records in the said Schedule may be destroyed earlier with the consent in writing of the Queen's and Lord Treasurer's Remembrancer.

11. Subject to the provisions of Regulations 4 and 5 hereof the person having proper legal custody of the sheriff court records referred to in Schedule 6 hereto shall destroy them after the expiry of twenty years from the date of the last entry to be made therein.

12. Except as aforesaid no sheriff court record shall be disposed of by the person having custody thereof, provided that transmission of any record to the custody of the Keeper shall not be a disposal for the purposes of these Regulations. In appropriate cases the Keeper may, with the consent of the Lord President and of the Sheriffs concerned, transfer such records in his custody, which in terms of section 12(1) of the Public Records (Scotland) Act 1937 would more appropriately be in the custody of any person, body or institution other than the Keeper, to such person, body or institution.

13.—(1) These Regulations may be cited as the Preservation of Sheriff Court Records Regulations 1969 and shall come into operation on 1st January 1970.

(2) The Interpretation Act 1889(**a**) shall apply for the interpretation of these Regulations as it applies for the interpretation of an Act of Parliament, and Section 38 of the said Interpretation Act shall apply as if these regulations were an Act of Parliament and as if the regulations revoked (in so far as they relate to sheriff court records) by these Regulations were an Act of Parliament repealed by an Act of Parliament.

J. L. Clyde,
Lord President.

Edinburgh,
5th December 1969.

(**a**) 1889 c. 63.

SCHEDULE 1

Regulation 5

*Sheriff Court District of which the records shall be
selected for preservation in accordance with Regulation 5.*

Name and Description of District:

Linlithgow District of the Sheriffdom of the Lothians and Peebles.

SCHEDULE 2

Regulation 6

*List of sheriff court records to be transmitted to the
Keeper in terms of Regulation 6.*

1.　　　　Ordinary Court, Applications and Appeals:
Processes and miscellaneous applications, including club applications and pro-
　　ductions.
Act Books
Minute Books
"A" Register
"B" Register
Extract Decree Books
Process Inventory Books
Borrowing Books
Register of English and Irish Judgments
Register of Bankruptcy Sequestrations
Register of Appeals
Register of Precepts of Arrestment
Register of Reports of Poinding and Sale
Register of Consignations
Register of Solicitors
Register of Sheriff Officers
Register of Reports of Sequestration Sale
Fiars Court Registers and Proceedings
Adoption of Children Processes and Registers
Register of Clubs

2.　　　　Workmen's Compensation:
Memoranda of Agreement
Special Register
Minute Book of Memoranda
Register of Arbitrations etc.
Processes
Ledgers (sums paid into Court)
Certificates and Reports

3.　　　　Small Debt Court:
Small Debt Court Books

4.　　　　Debts Recovery Court (abolished 1907):
Debt Recovery Court Books

5.　　　　Summary Removing Court:
Court Books

6.　　　　Commissary:
Bonds of Caution
Register of Inventories
Register of Wills
Register of Confirmations
Minute Book of Petitions
Minute Book of Inventories

7.   Sheriff's Criminal, Summary and Juvenile Courts:

Criminal Record and Copy Indictments
Register of Criminal and *quasi* Criminal Cases
Juvenile Court Registers
Juvenile Complaints and related documents

8.   Register of Deeds and Protests:

Recorded Deeds
Recorded Protests
Register of Deeds and Minute Books
Register of Protests and Minute Books
Register of Hornings

9.   Parliamentary Deposits and Plans:

Plans and Books of reference

10.   Miscellaneous:

Registers of Freeholders
Regality Records
Other records prior in date to 1860

Regulations 7 and 8   SCHEDULE 3

*List of sheriff court records which may be disposed of by
the Keeper in terms of Regulations 7 and 8.*

1.   Ordinary Court, Applications and Appeals:

Processes and miscellaneous applications, including club applications and pro-
ductions (after the expiry of twenty-five years from the date of the last interlocutor or other entry made therein or in respect thereof).
Note: This does not apply to adoption processes which must be preserved
permanently.

2.   Workmen's Compensation:

Workmen's Compensation records, as described in Schedule 2 hereof (after the
expiry of seventy-five years).

3.   Sheriff's Criminal, Summary and Juvenile Courts:

Juvenile Complaints and related documents (after the expiry of twenty-five years).

Regulation 9   SCHEDULE 4

List of sheriff court records which shall be destroyed forthwith.

1.   Workmen's Compensation:
Registers of Medical Referees Reports

2.   Debts Recovery Court (abolished 1907):
Complaints

Regulation 10   SCHEDULE 5

*List of sheriff court records to be preserved for ten years from the date of the
last entry made therein.*

1.   Ordinary Court, Applications and Appeals:
Returned Citations Book
Register of Notices of Appearance
Dog Licences—Register of Applications

Fatal Accident Inquiries—Petitions and Minutes of Evidence
Lunacy and Mental Deficiency—Register of Warrants

2.   Small Debt Court:

Returned Citations Book

3.   Summary Removing Court:

Complaints

4.   Commissary:

Printed weekly list of petitions

5.   Sheriff's Criminal, Summary and Juvenile Courts:

Bail Bonds
Bonds of Caution
Road Traffic Offences

6.   Administrative Records:

Routine correspondence files and books, bank books, fine and fee ledgers, and
cash books, extract order books, search order books etc.

SCHEDULE 6   Regulation 11

*List of sheriff court records to be preserved for twenty years from the date of
the last entry made therein.*

1.   Ordinary Court, Applications and Appeals:

Caveat Books
Register of Indorsations
Fatal Accident Inquiries—Notes of Evidence
Registration of Births, Deaths and Marriages—Applications
Sequestrations
Receipts and processes relevant to sums paid into Court

2.   Workmen's Compensation:

Receipts and processes relevant to sums paid into Court

3.   Small Debt Court:

Small Debt Complaints

4.   Commissary:

Petitions
Receipt Book for Wills
Borrowing Receipt Books
Extract Decree Dative Book

5.   Sheriff's Criminal, Summary and Juvenile Courts:

Summary Complaints

EXPLANATORY NOTE

(This Note is not part of the Regulations.)

These Regulations prescribe a new code for the preservation or disposal of
Sheriff Court records.

STATUTORY INSTRUMENTS

1969 No. 1758

SAVINGS BANKS

The Post Office Savings Bank (Amendment) (No. 2) Regulations 1969

Made - - - -	*9th December* 1969
Laid before Parliament	*17th December* 1969
Coming into Operation	*1st January* 1970

The Treasury, in exercise of the powers conferred on them by section 2(1) of the Post Office Savings Bank Act 1954(a), as amended by section 94(2) of, and Part I of Schedule 6 to, the Post Office Act 1969(b), and of all other powers enabling them in that behalf, hereby make the following Regulations:—

1. These Regulations may be cited as the Post Office Savings Bank (Amendment) (No. 2) Regulations 1969, and shall come into operation on 1st January 1970.

2. The Interpretation Act 1889(c) shall apply for the interpretation of these Regulations as it applies for the interpretation of an Act of Parliament.

3. The Post Office Savings Bank Regulations 1966(d), as amended(e), shall be further amended by substituting, in Regulation 21(1) thereof (which provides for the withdrawal on demand of ordinary deposits with the National Savings Bank to an amount not exceeding £10), for the figures "£10", the figures "£20".

> *Ernest Armstrong,*
> *Neil McBride,*
> Two of the Lords Commissioners
> of Her Majesty's Treasury.

9th December 1969.

EXPLANATORY NOTE

(This Note is not part of the Regulations.)

These Regulations amend the Post Office Savings Bank Regulations 1966 so as to increase from £10 to £20 the limit on the amount which may be withdrawn on demand from ordinary deposits in the National Savings Bank.

(a) 1954 c. 62.   (b) 1969 c. 48.   (c) 1889 c. 63.
(d) S.I. 1966/727 (1966 II, p. 1662).
(e) The relevant amending instrument is S.I. 1969/1335 (1969 III, p. 3973).

STATUTORY INSTRUMENTS

1969 No. 1761

ROAD TRAFFIC

The Motor Vehicles (Construction and Use) (Amendment) (No. 4) Regulations 1969

Made - - -	*8th December* 1969
Laid before Parliament	*22nd December* 1969
Coming into Operation	*1st January* 1970

The Minister of Transport, in exercise of his powers under section 64(1) of the Road Traffic Act 1960(a), as amended by section 51 of and Schedule 4 to the Road Traffic Act 1962(b), and as extended by section 8 of the Road Safety Act 1967(c) and of all other enabling powers, and after consultation with representative organisations in accordance with the provisions of section 260(2) of the said Act of 1960, hereby makes the following Regulations:—

1.—(1) These Regulations shall come into operation on the 1st January 1970 and may be cited as the Motor Vehicles (Construction and Use) (Amendment) (No. 4) Regulations 1969.

(2) The Interpretation Act 1889(d) shall apply for the interpretation of these Regulations as it applies for the interpretation of an Act of Parliament.

2. The Motor Vehicles (Construction and Use) Regulations 1969(e), as amended (f), shall have effect as though—

(1) in Regulation 118, after the definition of "Ministry plate" there were inserted the following definition:—

" "Ministry test date disc" means a plate issued by the Minister for a goods vehicle, being a trailer, following the issue of a goods vehicle test certificate for that trailer under the plating and testing regulations and containing the following particulars namely:—

(a) the identification mark allotted to that trailer and shown in that certificate;

(b) the date until which that certificate is valid;

(c) the number of the vehicle testing station shown in the said certificate;";

(2) after Regulation 120, there were inserted the following Regulation:—
"120A. On and after 1st February 1970, every goods vehicle to which this Part of these Regulations applies, being a trailer, shall as from each date (on or after the said 1st February) on which a goods vehicle test certificate is issued for that trailer under the plating and testing regulations (being a test certificate which will expire on or

---

(a) 8 & 9 Eliz. 2. c. 16.
(b) 10 & 11 Eliz. 2. c. 59.
(c) 1967 c. 30.
(d) 52 & 53 Vict. c. 63.
(e) S.I. 1969/321 (1969 I, p. 829).
(f) There is no relevant amending instrument.

after 1st February 1971) carry in the relevant position and in legible condition a Ministry test date disc issued for that trailer following the issue of that test certificate until the date of expiry of that test certificate or the date of issue of a further test certificate for that trailer, whichever date is the earlier, and shall not display that disc after that one of such dates as is the earlier.

In this Regulation "relevant position" means a conspicuous and readily accessible position, being such that the disc is clearly visible by daylight from the nearside of the road.".

Given under the Official Seal of the Minister of Transport the 8th December 1969.

(L.S.)

Fred Mulley,
Minister of Transport.

EXPLANATORY NOTE
(This Note is not part of the Regulations.)

These Regulations further amend the Motor Vehicles (Construction and Use) Regulations 1969 by in general requiring as from the 1st February 1970 trailers, for which goods vehicle test certificates have been issued after that date, to carry a current test date disc in a conspicuous position on the trailer.

STATUTORY INSTRUMENTS

1969 No. 1762

ROAD TRAFFIC

The Goods Vehicles (Plating and Testing) (Amendment) (No. 3) Regulations 1969

Made	- - -	*8th December* 1969
Laid before Parliament		*22nd December* 1969
Coming into Operation		*1st January* 1970

The Minister of Transport, in exercise of his powers under section 9(1) and (6) of the Road Safety Act 1967(a) as amended by section 148 of the Transport Act 1968(b) and of all other enabling powers, and after consultation with representative organisations in accordance with the provisions of section 260(2) of the Road Traffic Act 1960(c), as applied by section 29(6) of the said Act of 1967, hereby makes the following Regulations:—

1.—(1) These Regulations shall come into operation on the 1st January 1970 and may be cited as the Goods Vehicles (Plating and Testing) (Amendment) (No. 3) Regulations 1969.

(2) The Interpretation Act 1889(d) shall apply for the interpretation of these Regulations as it applies for the interpretation of an Act of Parliament.

2. The Goods Vehicles (Plating and Testing) Regulations 1968(e), as amended (f), shall have effect as though—

(1) after Regulation 27A there were inserted the following Regulation:—

"27B.—(1) For the purposes of this Regulation,

"expedited certificate" means a goods vehicle test certificate under these Regulations for a goods vehicle, the date of issue of which falls in a month, being a month at least one month before the month at the end of which another goods vehicle test certificate issued for that vehicle will expire.

(2) Where at any time in a calendar year an expedited certificate is issued under these Regulations for a goods vehicle to which these Regulations apply, being a trailer, then notwithstanding anything to the contrary contained in Regulation 27(4) or (5) or Regulation 27A the goods vehicle shall be submitted for a periodical test not later than the end of the month in each following calendar year in which month falls the anniversary of the date of issue of the expedited certificate last issued for that vehicle.

(a) 1967 c. 30.　　　　　　　　　　(b) 1968 c. 73.
(c) 8 & 9 Eliz. 2. c. 16.　　　　　(d) 52 & 53 Vict. c. 63.
(e) S.I. 1968/601 (1968 I, p. 1372).
(f) The relevant amending instrument is S.I. 1969/1324 (1969 III, p. 3941).

(3) Nothing in the foregoing provisions of this Regulation shall be taken to prevent the Minister from authorising a goods vehicle to which these Regulations apply being submitted for a periodical test on or after the date by which that goods vehicle is required by those provisions to be submitted for such a test.";

(2) In Regulation 29, after the words "or 27A" there were inserted the words "or 27B";

(3) in Regulation 36, after the words "or Regulation 27A" there were inserted the words "or Regulation 27B";

(4) each reference in Regulation 50 to a goods vehicle test certificate included a reference to a Ministry test date disc as defined in Regulation 118 of the Motor Vehicles (Construction and Use) Regulations 1969(a), as amended(b).

Given under the Official Seal of the Minister of Transport the 8th December 1969.

(L.S.)

Fred Mulley,
Minister of Transport.

EXPLANATORY NOTE

(This Note is not part of the Regulations.)

These Regulations further amend the Goods Vehicles (Plating and Testing) Regulations 1968. The main change is to permit the dates, by which trailers are at present required by the 1968 Regulations to be submitted for periodical tests, to be altered.

(a) S.I. 1969/321 (1969 I, p. 829).
(b) The relevant amending instrument is S.I. 1969/1761.

STATUTORY INSTRUMENTS

1969 No. 1764

STATISTICS OF TRADE

The Census of Production (1970) (Returns and Exempted Persons) Order 1969

Made - - -	10*th December* 1969	
Laid before Parliament	18*th December* 1969	
Coming into Operation	31*st December* 1969	

The Board of Trade, in exercise of the powers conferred upon them by sections 2 and 11 of the Statistics of Trade Act 1947(a) and all other powers enabling them in that behalf, hereby order as follows :—

Citation, commencement and interpretation

1.—(1) This Order may be cited as the Census of Production (1970) (Returns and Exempted Persons) Order 1969 and shall come into operation on 31st December 1969.

(2) The Interpretation Act 1889(b) shall apply to the interpretation of this Order in like manner as it applies to the interpretation of an Act of Parliament.

Matters to which returns may relate

2. The matters about which a person carrying on an undertaking may be required to furnish returns for the purposes of the census of production being taken under the said Act by the Board of Trade in 1970 shall be the following matters, being matters included in the Schedule to the Act, that is to say, the nature of the undertaking, the persons employed or normally employed (including working proprietors), stocks and work in progress, the acquisition and disposal of fixed capital assets and plant, and the premises occupied.

Exempted Persons

3. Any person carrying on an undertaking in the field of production of coal, gas, electricity, or crude or refined petroleum shall be exempted from the obligation to furnish returns for the purposes of the said census.

Gwyneth Dunwoody,
Parliamentary Secretary to
the Board of Trade.

10th December 1969.

(a) 1947 c. 39.   (b) 1889 c. 63.

EXPLANATORY NOTE

(This Note is not part of the Order.)

This Order prescribes that the only matters about which a person carrying on an undertaking may be required to furnish returns for the purposes of the Census of Production being taken in 1970 are those matters set out in Article 2.

It also exempts from the obligation to furnish such returns any person carrying on an undertaking in the field of production of coal, gas, electricity, or crude or refined petroleum.

STATUTORY INSTRUMENTS

1969 No. 1767 (S.155)

ROAD TRAFFIC

The Cycle Racing on Highways (Amendment) (Scotland) Regulations 1969

Made - - -	*4th December* 1969
Laid before Parliament	*18th December* 1969
Coming into Operation	*19th December* 1969

In exercise of the powers conferred on me by section 12 of the Road Traffic Act 1960(a) and of all other powers enabling me in that behalf, and after consultation with representative organisations, in accordance with the provisions of section 260(2) of that Act, I hereby make the following regulations:—

1.—(1) These regulations may be cited as the Cycle Racing on Highways (Amendment) (Scotland) Regulations 1969 and shall come into operation on 19th December 1969.

(2) The Interpretation Act 1889(b) shall apply for the interpretation of these regulations as it applies for the interpretation of an Act of Parliament.

(3) The Cycle Racing on Highways (Scotland) Regulations 1960(c) as amended by the Cycle Racing on Highways (Amendment) (Scotland) Regulations 1963(d) shall be further amended by inserting after paragraph 8 the following paragraph:—

"*Exceptions and relaxations*

9. Without prejudice to the foregoing provisions of these regulations, the Secretary of State may relax any prohibition or restriction imposed by the foregoing provisions of these regulations."

William Ross,
One of Her Majesty's Principal
Secretaries of State.

St. Andrew's House,
Edinburgh.
4th December 1969.

(a) 1960 c. 16.
(c) S.I. 1960/270 (1960 III, p. 3053).

(b) 1889 c. 63.
(d) S.I. 1963/1071 (1963 II, p. 1848).

EXPLANATORY NOTE

(*This Note is not part of the Regulations.*)

These regulations amend the Cycle Racing on Highways (Scotland) Regulations 1960 by giving the Secretary of State power to relax any prohibition or restriction included in the 1960 Regulations.

STATUTORY INSTRUMENTS

1969 No. 1771

LANDLORD AND TENANT

The Landlord and Tenant (Notices) Regulations 1969

Made - - - - -	10*th December* 1969
Laid before Parliament	18*th December* 1969
Coming into Operation	1*st January* 1970

The Lord Chancellor, in exercise of the powers conferred on him by section 66 of the Landlord and Tenant Act 1954(a), hereby makes the following Regulations:—

1.—(1) These Regulations may be cited as the Landlord and Tenant (Notices) Regulations 1969 and shall come into operation on 1st January 1970.

(2) The Interpretation Act 1889(b) shall apply to the interpretation of these Regulations as it applies to the interpretation of an Act of Parliament.

2. In these Regulations, unless the context otherwise requires—
"the principal Regulations" means the Landlord and Tenant (Notices) Regulations 1957(c) as amended(d).

3. For Forms 7 and 9 in the Appendix to the Landlord and Tenant (Notices) Regulations 1957 as amended by the Landlord and Tenant (Notices) Regulations 1963 and regulation 6 of the Landlord and Tenant (Notices) Regulations 1967 there shall be substituted the forms so numbered in Appendix I to these Regulations.

4. Form 12 in the Appendix to the principal Regulations shall be amended by the insertion of the following words at the end of Note 4(*f*):—

"but where the landlord opposes the application on this ground, the court can still order the grant of a new tenancy, if

    (i) the tenant agrees to the inclusion in the new tenancy of terms giving the landlord facilities for carrying out the work intended and, given those facilities, the landlord could reasonably carry

---

(a) 1954 c. 56.   (b) 1889 c. 63.
(c) S.I. 1957/1157 (1957 I, p. 1230).
(d) S.I. 1963/795, 1967/1831 (1963 I, p. 1179; 1967 III, p. 4866).

out the work without obtaining possession of the tenant's premises and without interfering to a substantial extent or for a substantial time with the use of the premises for the tenant's business; or

(ii) the tenant is willing to accept a tenancy of part of the premises, which can be let separately without substantially reducing the rental income obtainable from the entire premises, and either the tenant agrees to give the landlord facilities for carrying out work as under paragraph (i) above, or possession of the remainder of the premises would be reasonably sufficient to enable the landlord to carry out the intended work;''

5. The Form in Appendix II to these Regulations shall be added to the Appendix to the principal Regulations and stand as number 16.

6. Nothing in these Regulations shall invalidate any Notice served before 1st July 1970 which complies with the requirements of the principal Regulations.

Dated 10th December 1969.

Gardiner, C.

APPENDIX I

FORM 7
LANDLORD AND TENANT ACT 1954

Landlord's Notice to Terminate Business Tenancy

To   , of   , tenant of premises known as

1. I,   of   , landlord of the See Note 1. above-mentioned premises, hereby give you notice terminating your tenancy on the   day of   , 19 .

2. You are required within two months after the giving of this Notice to See Note 2. notify me in writing whether or not you will be willing to give up possession of the premises on that date.

3. I would not oppose an application to the Court under Part II of the Act See Note 6. for the grant of a new tenancy, *or*

I would oppose an application to the Court under Part II of the Act for the See Note 4. grant of a new tenancy on the ground that [*state ground or grounds*].

4. This Notice is given under the provisions of section 25 of the Landlord and Tenant Act 1954.

Your attention is called to the Notes below.

Dated this   day of   , 19 .

Signed...........................(Landlord)

...........................(Address)

FORM 7

NOTES

1. Under the Landlord and Tenant Act 1954, a tenancy of premises to which Part II of the Act applies continues until it is brought to an end in accordance with the Act. One of the ways in which it can be brought to an end is by a landlord's notice to terminate the tenancy. As a general rule, that notice must be given not more than 12 nor less than 6 months before the date specified in it for the termination of the current tenancy of the premises. This date must not be earlier than the date on which apart from Part II of the Act the current tenancy would expire or could be terminated by notice to quit given by the landlord on the date of the notice.

2. Part II of the Act enables the tenant, on being served with a notice in this form, to apply to the court for an order for the grant of a new tenancy. Such an application, however, will not be entertained unless the tenant has within 2 months after the giving of the notice terminating the tenancy notified the landlord in writing that he will not be willing to give up possession of the premises on the date specified in the notice. The application must be made not less than 2 or more than 4 months after the giving of the notice.

3. Where the rateable value of the premises (excluding any part which is not occupied by the tenant or by an employee in his business) does not exceed £2,000, an application for an order for the grant of a new tenancy must be made to the County Court and in any other case it must be made to the High Court.

4. The court has no power to make an order for the grant of a new tenancy if the landlord, having stated in his notice that he will oppose an application to the court on one of the grounds specified in the Act, establishes that ground to the satisfaction of the court. The grounds specified in the Act are—

(a) where under the current tenancy the tenant has any obligations as respects the repair and maintenance of the premises, that the tenant ought not to be granted a new tenancy in view of the state of repair of the premises which has resulted from the tenant's failure to comply with these obligations;

(b) that the tenant ought not to be granted a new tenancy in view of his persistent delay in paying rent which has become due;

(c) that the tenant ought not to be granted a new tenancy in view of other substantial breaches by him of his obligations under the current tenancy, or for any other reason connected with the tenant's use or management of the premises;

(d) that the landlord has offered and is willing to provide or secure the provision of alternative accommodation for the tenant, that the terms on which the alternative accommodation is available are reasonable having regard to the terms of the current tenancy and to all other relevant circumstances, and that the accommodation and the time at which it will be available are suitable for the tenant's requirements (including the requirement to preserve goodwill) having regard to the nature and class of his business and to the situation and extent of, and facilities afforded by, the premises which he occupies;

(e) where the current tenancy was created by the subletting of part only of the property comprised in a superior tenancy, that the aggregate of the rents reasonably obtainable on separate lettings of the tenant's premises and the remainder of that property would be substantially less than the rent reasonably obtainable on a letting of that property as a whole, and that on the termination of the current tenancy the landlord requires possession of the tenant's premises for the purpose of letting or otherwise disposing of the said property as a whole and therefore the tenant ought not to be granted a new tenancy;

(*f*) that on the termination of the current tenancy the landlord intends to demolish or reconstruct the whole or a substantial part of the premises or to carry out substantial work of construction on the whole or part of them and that he could not reasonably do so without obtaining possession of the premises; but where the landlord opposes the application on this ground, the court can still order the grant of a new tenancy, if

   (i) the tenant agrees to the inclusion in the new tenancy of terms giving the landlord facilities for carrying out the work intended and, given those facilities, the landlord could reasonably carry out the work without obtaining possession of the tenant's premises and without interfering to a substantial extent or for a substantial time with the use of the premises for the tenant's business; or

   (ii) the tenant is willing to accept a tenancy of a part of the premises, which can be let separately without substantially reducing the rental income obtainable from the entire premises, and either the tenant agrees to give the landlord facilities for carrying out work as under paragraph (i) above, or possession of the remainder of the premises would be reasonably sufficient to enable the landlord to carry out the intended work;

(*g*) that on the termination of the current tenancy the landlord intends to occupy the premises for the purposes, or partly for the purposes, of a business to be carried on by him in them or as his residence; but the landlord cannot rely on this ground if his interest was purchased or created less than 5 years before the termination of the current tenancy and at all times since the purchase or creation of the landlord's interest the premises have been let to a tenant occupying them for the purposes of his business.

5. If the only grounds for opposing an application for the grant of a new tenancy stated in paragraph 3 of this notice are grounds set out in (*e*), (*f*) and (*g*) above, the tenant is entitled on leaving the premises to recover compensation from the landlord at the rate specified in the Act. If other grounds are also stated, the tenant is entitled to the compensation if the court on an application for a new tenancy finds that it is precluded from making an order by reason only of any of the grounds set out in (*e*), (*f*) and (*g*).

6. If the landlord states in this notice that he will not oppose an application to the court for the grant of a new tenancy, it will be open to the tenant and the landlord to negotiate on the terms of the tenancy. If all the terms are agreed between them, an application to the court will not be necessary; if some but not all of the terms are agreed, the agreed terms will be incorporated in any tenancy granted by the court and the other terms will be such as the court may determine. A new tenancy, if granted by the court, will not include any part of the property comprised in the current tenancy which is occupied neither by the tenant, nor by a person employed by him for the purposes of his business, unless the landlord requires the new tenancy to include the whole of the property.

7. The term "landlord" in this notice does not necessarily mean the landlord to whom the rent is paid; it means the person who is the landlord for the purposes of Part II of the Act. The term "business" includes a trade, profession or employment and any activity carried on by a body of persons, whether corporate or unincorporate.

FORM 9

LANDLORD AND TENANT ACT 1954

Landlord's Notice to Terminate Business Tenancy where Change Required at Future Date on Grounds of Public Interest

To   , tenant of premises known as

See Note 1.   1. I,   , landlord of the above-mentioned premises, hereby give you notice terminating your tenancy on the day of   , 19   .

See Note 2.   2. You are required within two months after the giving of this Notice to notify me in writing whether or not you will be willing to give up possession of the premises on that date.

See Note 2.   3. A certificate has been given by   that it is requisite for the purposes of the   [*insert name of Government department, local authority, statutory undertakers, development corporation, or as the case may be*] that the use or occupation of the property or of a part of the property shall be changed by the   day of   , 19   , and a copy of the certificate is set out in the schedule to this Notice.

See Note 6.   4. I would not oppose an application to the court under Part II of the Act for the grant of a new tenancy terminating on or before the   day of   , 19   , *or*

See Note 4.   I would oppose an application to the court under Part II of the Act for the grant of a new tenancy on the ground that   [*state ground or grounds*].

5. This Notice is given under the provisions of section 25 and section 57 of the Landlord and Tenant Act 1954.

Your attention is called to the Notes below.
Dated this   day of   , 19   .

Signed..

for...(Landlord)

....(Address)

THE SCHEDULE

[Insert a copy of the relevant certificate]

Form 9

NOTES

1. Under the Landlord and Tenant Act 1954 a tenancy of premises to which Part II of the Act applies continues until it is brought to an end in accordance with the Act. One of the ways in which it can be brought to an end is by a landlord's notice to terminate the tenancy. As a general rule, that notice must be given not more than 12 nor less than 6 months before the date specified in it for the termination of the current tenancy. This date must not be earlier than the date on which apart from Part II of the Act the current tenancy would expire, or could be terminated by notice to quit given by the landlord on the date of the notice.

2. Part II of the Act enables the tenant, on being served with a notice in this form, to apply to the court for an order for the grant of a new tenancy. Such an application, however, will not be entertained unless the tenant has within 2 months after the giving of the notice terminating the tenancy notified the landlord in writing that he will not be willing to give up possession of the premises on the date specified in the notice. The application must be made not less than 2 nor more than 4 months after the giving of the notice.

The notice you are now given contains a copy of a certificate stating that a change in the use or occupation of the premises or part of them is required for the purposes of a Government department or public body. The date on which the change is stated to be required is later than the date of termination of your tenancy specified in paragraph 1 of this notice. Where such a certificate has been given in accordance with the provisions of the Act, any new tenancy granted by the court must expire on or before the date stated in the certificate.

3. Where the rateable value of the premises (excluding any part which is not occupied by the tenant or by an employee in his business) does not exceed £2,000, an application for an order for the grant of a new tenancy must be made to the County Court and in any other case it must be made to the High Court.

4. The court has no power to make an order for the grant of a new tenancy if the landlord has stated in this notice that he will oppose an application to the court on one of the grounds specified in the Act, and establishes that ground to the court's satisfaction. The grounds specified in the Act are—

(a) where under the current tenancy the tenant has any obligations as respects the repair and maintenance of the premises, that the tenant ought not to be granted a new tenancy in view of the state of repair of the premises which has resulted from the tenant's failure to comply with these obligations;

(b) that the tenant ought not to be granted a new tenancy in view of his persistent delay in paying rent which has become due;

(c) that the tenant ought not to be granted a new tenancy in view of other substantial breaches by him of his obligations under the current tenancy, or for any other reason connected with the tenant's use or management of the premises;

(d) that the landlord has offered and is willing to provide or secure the provision of alternative accommodation for the tenant, that the terms on which the alternative accommodation is available are reasonable having regard to the terms of the current tenancy and to all other relevant circumstances, and that the accommodation and the time at which it will be available are suitable for the tenant's requirements (including the requirement to preserve goodwill) having regard to the nature and class of his business and to the situation and extent of, and facilities afforded by, the premises which he occupies;

(*e*) where the current tenancy was created by the subletting of part only of the property comprised in a superior tenancy, that the aggregate of the rents reasonably obtainable on separate lettings of the tenant's premises and the remainder of that property would be substantially less than the rent reasonably obtainable on a letting of that property as a whole, and that on the termination of the current tenancy the landlord requires possession of the tenant's premises for the purpose of letting or otherwise disposing of the said property as a whole and therefore the tenant ought not to be granted a new tenancy;

(*f*) that on the termination of the current tenancy the landlord intends to demolish or reconstruct the whole or a substantial part of the premises or to carry out substantial work of construction on the whole or part of them and that he could not reasonably do so without obtaining possession of the premises; but where the landlord opposes the application on this ground the court can still order the grant of a new tenancy, if

(i) the tenant agrees to the inclusion in the new tenancy of terms giving the landlord facilities for carrying out the work intended and, given those facilities, the landlord could reasonably carry out the work without obtaining possession of the tenant's premises and without interfering to a substantial extent or for a substantial time with the use of the premises for the tenant's business; or

(ii) the tenant is willing to accept a tenancy of a part of the premises, which can be let separately without substantially reducing the rental income obtainable from the entire premises, and either the tenant agrees to give the landlord facilities for carrying out work as under paragraph (i) above, or possession of the remainder of the premises would be reasonably sufficient to enable the landlord to carry out the intended work;

(*g*) that on the termination of the current tenancy the landlord intends to occupy the premises for the purposes, or partly for the purposes, of a business to be carried on by him in them or as his residence; but the landlord cannot rely on this ground if his interest was purchased or created less than 5 years before the termination of the current tenancy and at all times since the purchase or creation of the landlord's interest the premises have been let to a tenant occupying them for the purposes of his business.

5. If no grounds for opposing an application for the grant of a new tenancy are stated in paragraph 4 of this notice or if the only grounds there stated are those set out in (*e*), (*f*) and (*g*) above, the tenant is entitled on leaving the premises to recover compensation from the landlord at the rate specified in the Act. If other grounds are also stated, the tenant is entitled to the compensation if the court on an application for a new tenancy finds that it is precluded from making an order by reason only of any of the grounds set out in (*e*), (*f*) and (*g*). If the court makes an order for a new tenancy, but is precluded from ordering a new tenancy expiring later than the date specified in the Ministerial certificate, the tenant may similarly be entitled to compensation.

6. If the landlord states in this notice that he will not oppose an application to the court for the grant of a new tenancy, it will be open to the tenant and the landlord to negotiate on the terms of the tenancy. If all the terms are agreed between them, an application to the court will not be necessary; if some but not all of the terms are agreed, the agreed terms will be incorporated in any tenancy granted by the court and the other terms will be such as the court may determine. If the court grants a new tenancy it will not include any part of the property comprised in the current tenancy which is occupied neither by the tenant nor by a person employed by him for the purposes of his business, unless the landlord requires the new tenancy to include the whole of the property.

7. The term "landlord" in this notice does not necessarily mean the landlord to whom the rent is paid; it means the person or body who is the landlord for the purposes of Part II of the Act. The term "business" includes a trade, profession or employment and any activity carried on by a body of persons, whether corporate or unincorporate.

APPENDIX II

FORM 16

LANDLORD AND TENANT ACT 1954

Superior Landlord's Notice Withdrawing Notice to Terminate Business Tenancy
To   , of
tenant of premises known as

1. Notice terminating your tenancy of the premises has been given you by a Landlord's Notice to Terminate Business Tenancy dated the
            given by your landlord, [*state name and address*]

2. I,   of   , have now become
the landlord for the purposes of Part II of the Landlord and Tenant Act 1954,   See Note 1.
because—

*your landlord's tenancy will expire by effluxion of time on the   day of   *Delete which-
                    19   ,   ever is not
                                                                              appropriate.
or
I have served a notice on your landlord terminating his tenancy on the
day of   19   .

[*or state for what reason intermediate landlord's interest is coming to an end*]

3. I hereby give you notice that I withdraw the Landlord's Notice referred to
in paragraph 1 above, which shall cease to have effect from the date of this   See Note 2.
Notice.

4. This Notice is given under the provisions of section 44 of and paragraph 6 of the Sixth Schedule to the Landlord and Tenant Act 1954, as amended by section 14 of the Law of Property Act 1969.

Your attention is called to the Notes below.

        Dated this   day of   19   .

            Signed...

            ....(Address)

NOTES

1. The "landlord" who can terminate a business tenancy is not necessarily the landlord to whom the rent is paid; it is, broadly, the person who qualifies as landlord for the purposes of Part II of the Landlord and Tenant Act 1954 because he has an interest in the property which is superior to that of the tenant and has at least 14 months to run.

2. This notice can be given by a superior landlord who becomes the landlord for the purposes of the Act and wishes to withdraw a notice to terminate a business tenancy given by the person who previously qualified as the landlord. When this notice is given the earlier notice ceases to have effect, but the tenant may be given a fresh notice terminating the tenancy by the newly qualified landlord.

EXPLANATORY NOTE

(This Note is not part of the Regulations.)

These Regulations amend Forms 7, 9 and 12 prescribed in the Landlord and Tenant (Notices) Regulations 1957 which by the Landlord and Tenant Act 1954 are required to be used for landlords' notices to terminate business tenancies and for tenants' requests for new business tenancies. A new form is prescribed for use where a superior landlord withdraws a notice to terminate a business tenancy given by an intermediate landlord. The amendments are consequential on the amendment of Part II of the Act of 1954 by the Law of Property Act 1969 (c. 59).

STATUTORY INSTRUMENTS

1969 No. 1774

NATIONAL HEALTH SERVICE, ENGLAND AND WALES

The National Health Service (Welsh Joint Pricing Committee) (Amendment) Order 1969

Made - - -		*9th December* 1969
Coming into Operation		*15th December* 1969

The Secretary of State for Wales, in exercise of his powers under sections 31(4) and 75(4) of the National Health Service Act 1946(a) and of all other powers enabling him in that behalf, hereby orders as follows:—

1.—(1) This Order may be cited as the National Health Service (Welsh Joint Pricing Committee) (Amendment) Order 1969 and shall come into operation on 15th December 1969.

(2) The Interpretation Act 1889(b) applies to the interpretation of this Order as it applies to the interpretation of an Act of Parliament.

2. The National Health Service (Welsh Joint Pricing Committee) Order 1948(c) as amended (d) shall be further amended as follows:—

(1) For Article 12(1) (Application of regulations 10 to 14 of The National Health Service (Executive Councils) Regulations 1947(e)) there shall be substituted the following paragraph:—

"12—(1) The provisions of regulations 12 (Meetings), 13 (Minutes), 14 (Officers), 15 (Committees) and 16 (Power to make Standing Orders) of the National Health Service (Executive Councils) Regulations 1969(f) shall apply for the purposes of this Order as if for any reference therein to a Council there were substituted a reference to the Committee and as if for any reference to a committee of a council there were substituted a reference to a sub-committee."

(2) Articles 15 (Application of the National Health Service (Executive Councils and Dental Estimates Board) Financial Regulations 1948(g), 16 (Annual and Supplementary Estimates, 17 (Books and Accounts) and 18 (Audit) shall cease to have effect.

3. The provisions of Part II (Financial arrangements and audit of accounts) of the National Health Service (Executive Councils and Dental Estimates Board) Financial Regulations 1969(h) shall apply to the Welsh Joint Pricing Committee

---

(a) 1946 c. 81.   (b) 1889 c. 63.
(d) S.I. 1950/354 (1950 I, p. 1319).
(f) S.I.1969/352 (1969 I,p.980).
(h) S.I. 1969/1581 (1969 III,p.5047).
(c) S.I. 1948/1488 (Rev. XV, p. 711: 1948 I,p.2178).
(e) S.R.&O. 1947/889 (Rev.XV,p.505: 1947 I,p.1324).
(g) S.I. 1948/1239 (Rev. XV, p.716: 1948 I,p.2076).

as they apply to Executive Councils as if for any reference therein to a Council there were substituted a reference to the Committee and as if for any reference to the finance committee there were substituted a reference to the finance sub-committee.

Signed by authority of the Secretary of State.

D. G. McPherson,
Assistant Under Secretary of State,
Welsh Office.

9th December 1969.

EXPLANATORY NOTE

(*This Note is not part of the Order.*)

This Order amends the National Health Service (Welsh Joint Pricing Committee) Order 1948 which established a Welsh Joint Pricing Committee for the purpose of exercising the functions of Executive Councils in regard to the pricing of prescriptions for drugs. This Order applies to the Welsh Joint Pricing Committee—

(*a*) the provisions relating to procedure contained in the National Health Service (Executive Councils) Regulations 1969 in place of similar provisions of the National Health Service (Executive Councils) Regulations 1947, and

(*b*) the provisions of Part II of the National Health Service (Executive Councils and Dental Estimates Board) Financial Regulations 1969 in place of some provisions of the National Health Service (Executive Councils and Dental Estimates Board) Financial Regulations 1948 (S.I. 1948/1239) (superseded by the Financial Regulations of 1969) and of the Order of 1948.

STATUTORY INSTRUMENTS

1969 No. 1775 (C. 56)

POLICE

The Police Act 1969 (Commencement No. 1) Order 1969

Made - - - 11*th December* 1969

In exercise of the powers conferred on me by section 7(2) of the Police Act 1969(a), I hereby make the following Order:—

1. This Order may be cited as the Police Act 1969 (Commencement No. 1) Order 1969.

2. The provisions of the Police Act 1969 specified in column 1 of the Schedule to this Order (which relate to the matters specified in column 2 thereof) shall come into operation on 17th December 1969.

James Callaghan,
One of Her Majesty's Principal
Secretaries of State.

Home Office,
Whitehall.
11th December 1969.

SCHEDULE

PROVISIONS COMING INTO OPERATION ON 17th DECEMBER 1969

Provisions of the Act	Subject matter of provisions
Section 1(4)	Extension of powers of the Parliament of Northern Ireland.
Section 2	Members of home police forces who engage for periods of service in the Royal Ulster Constabulary.
Section 5	Power to give retrospective effect to certain police pensions regulations, and Parliamentary control of the power to make them.
Section 6	Orders.
Section 7	Short title and commencement.

(a) 1969 c. 63.

EXPLANATORY NOTE

(*This Note is not part of the Order.*)

This Order brings into operation on 17th December 1969 all the provisions of the Police Act 1969 with the exception of those of section 1(1), (2) and (3) (aid by home police forces of the Royal Ulster Constabulary), section 3 (aid given to a home police force by the Royal Ulster Constabulary) and section 4 (Police Council for the United Kingdom).

1969 No. 1777

EDUCATION, ENGLAND AND WALES

LOCAL GOVERNMENT, ENGLAND AND WALES

The Schools (Qualified Teachers) Regulations 1969

Made - - - -	11*th December* 1969
Laid before Parliament	19*th December* 1969
Coming into Operation	1*st January* 1970

The Secretary of State for Education and Science, in exercise of the powers conferred upon him by section 33 of the Education Act 1944**(a)**, as amended by the Secretary of State for Education and Science Order 1964**(b)**, and by section 3(4) of the Local Government Act 1958**(c)**, hereby makes the following regulations:—

Citation, commencement and interpretation

1.—(1) These regulations may be cited as the Schools (Qualified Teachers) Regulations 1969 and shall come into operation on 1st January 1970.

(2) The Interpretation Act 1889**(d)** shall apply for the interpretation of these regulations as it applies for the interpretation of an Act of Parliament.

Teachers in County and Voluntary Schools

2.—(1) Regulation 16(2) of the Schools Regulations 1959**(e)** as amended**(f)** (which defines the expression "qualified teacher") shall have effect subject to the substitution for everything after the words "that is to say" of—
"any of the following:—

> (*a*) a person who has completed a course of initial training for persons training to be teachers in schools, being a course provided in accordance with regulations made by the Secretary of State, or any other course of training (whether within the United Kingdom or elsewhere) approved by him for the purposes of these regulations as comparable to such a course;
>
> (*b*) a person who possesses a special qualification (acquired, in the case of a teacher in a primary school, before 1st January 1970) approved by the Secretary of State for the purposes of these regulations;
>
> (*c*) a person recognised by, or eligible for recognition by, the Board of Education as an uncertificated teacher who has completed 20 years service as a teacher;

(a) 1944 c. 31.   (b) S.I. 1964/490 (1964 I, p. 800).
(c) 1958 c. 55.   (d) 1889 c. 63.
(e) S.I. 1959/364 (1959 I, p. 1584).
(f) There is no amendment which relates expressly to the subject matter of these Regulations.

(*d*) a supplementary teacher who has completed 20 years service as a teacher;

(*e*) a person who possesses such a qualification, and has completed 10 years (or such shorter period as may for special reasons be approved) of such service as a teacher, as may be approved by the Secretary of State for the purposes of this sub-paragraph;

and (in each case) has been accepted by the Secretary of State as a qualified teacher."

(2) Schedule I to the Schools Regulations 1959**(a)** as amended**(b)** (which specifies courses of training for teachers) is hereby revoked.

Teachers in Special Schools

3. In Regulation 15(2) of the Handicapped Pupils and Special Schools Regulations 1959**(c)** as amended **(d)** (which requires teachers in special schools to be qualified teachers) the reference to regulation 16(2) of the Schools Regulations 1959 shall be construed as if the words "in the case of a teacher in a primary school" in sub-paragraph (*b*) were omitted.

Given under the Official Seal of the Secretary of State for Education and Science on 11th December 1969.

(L.S.)   *E. W. Short,*
                              Secretary of State for Education and Science.

EXPLANATORY NOTE
(*This Note is not part of the Regulations.*)

These regulations amend the definition of the expression "qualified teacher" in the Schools Regulations 1959, so that from 1st January 1970 a person shall be eligible for appointment as a qualified teacher in a maintained primary school or a special school by virtue of a special qualification only if he acquired it before that date.

(a) S.I. 1959/364 (1959 I, p. 1584).
(b) The relevant amending instrument is S.I. 1966/1577 (1966 III, p. 4860).
(c) S.I. 1959/365 (1959 I, p. 1024).
(d) The amending Regulations are not relevant to the subject matter of these Regulations.

STATUTORY INSTRUMENTS

1969 No. 1780

EDUCATION, ENGLAND AND WALES

The Remuneration of Teachers (Farm Institutes) Order 1969

Made - - -	12*th December* 1969	
Coming into Operation	15*th December* 1969	

Whereas—

(1) in pursuance of section 2(2) of the Remuneration of Teachers Act 1965(a) (hereinafter referred to as "the Act") the Committee constituted under section 1 of the Act for the purpose of considering the remuneration of teachers in farm institutes and teachers of agricultural subjects on the staff of local education authorities (hereinafter referred to as "the Committee") have transmitted to the Secretary of State for Education and Science (hereinafter referred to as "the Secretary of State") recommendations agreed on by them with respect to the remuneration of such teachers ;

(2) in pursuance of section 2(3) of the Act, the Secretary of State has prepared a draft document setting out the scales and other provisions required for determining the remuneration of teachers of the description aforesaid in the form in which, in his opinion, those scales and provisions should be so as to give effect to those recommendations ;

(3) the Secretary of State, as required by section 2(4) of the Act, has consulted the Committee with respect to the draft document and made such modifications thereof as were requisite for giving effect to representations made by the Committee ; and

(4) the Secretary of State has arranged for a document setting out the requisite scales and other provisions in the form of the draft as modified as aforesaid to be published by Her Majesty's Stationery Office on 11th December 1969 under the title "SCALES OF SALARIES FOR THE TEACHING STAFF OF FARM INSTITUTES AND FOR TEACHERS OF AGRICULTURAL (INCLUDING HORTICULTURAL) SUBJECTS, ENGLAND AND WALES, 1969".

Now therefore the Secretary of State, in pursuance of section 2(4) of the Act, hereby orders as follows :—

Citation

1. This Order may be cited as the Remuneration of Teachers (Farm Institutes) Order 1969 and shall come into operation on 15th December 1969.

Interpretation

2. The Interpretation Act 1889(b) shall apply for the interpretation of this Order as it applies for the interpretation of an Act of Parliament.

(a) 1965 c. 3.   (b) 1889 c. 63.

Remuneration of Teachers

3. The remuneration payable from 1st April 1969 to full-time teachers employed as members of the teaching staff of farm institutes maintained by local education authorities or as teachers of agricultural subjects (including horticultural and related subjects) on the staff of local education authorities shall be determined in accordance with the scales and other provisions set out in the document published by Her Majesty's Stationery Office as aforesaid.

Revocation

4. The Remuneration of Teachers (Farm Institutes) Order 1968(a) is hereby revoked and section 38(2) of the Interpretation Act 1889 (which relates to the effect of repeals) shall have effect in relation to that Order as if it were an enactment repealed by an Act.

Given under the Official Seal of the Secretary of State for Education and Science on 12th December 1969.

(L.S.)   *Edward Short,*
                          Secretary of State for Education and Science.

EXPLANATORY NOTE

(*This Note is not part of the Order.*)

This Order brings into operation the scales and other provisions relating to the remuneration of full-time teachers in farm institutes and teachers of agricultural subjects on the staff of local education authorities contained in a document published by Her Majesty's Stationery Office. This document contains the recommendations of the Committee constituted under the Remuneration of Teachers Act 1965 for the purpose of considering the remuneration of such teachers.

The Order has effect from 1st April 1969 by virtue of section 7(3) of the Act.

(a) S.I. 1968/345 (1968 I, p. 990).

STATUTORY INSTRUMENTS

1969 No. 1781

NATIONAL HEALTH SERVICE, ENGLAND AND WALES

The National Health Service (Joint Pricing Committee for England) Amendment Order 1969

Made	-	-	*12th December* 1969
Coming into Operation			*29th December* 1969

The Secretary of State for Social Services, in exercise of his powers under sections 31(4) and 75(4) of the National Health Service Act 1946(**a**) and of all other powers enabling him in that behalf, hereby orders as follows :—

1.—(1) This order may be cited as the National Health Service (Joint Pricing Committee for England) Amendment Order 1969 and shall come into operation on 29th December 1969.

(2) The Interpretation Act 1889(**b**) applies to the interpretation of this order as it applies to the interpretation of an Act of Parliament.

2. The National Health Service (Joint Pricing Committee for England) Order 1948(**c**) as amended (**d**) shall be further amended as follows :—

(1) For article 12(1) (Application of regulations 10 to 14 of the National Health Service (Executive Councils) Regulations 1947(**e**)) there shall be substituted the following paragraph :—

"**12.**—(1) The provisions of regulations 12 (Meetings), 13 (Minutes), 14 (Officers), 15 (Committees) and 16 (Power to make standing orders) of the National Health Service (Executive Councils) Regulations 1969(**f**) shall apply for the purposes of this order as if for any reference therein to a council there were substituted a reference to the Committee and as if for any reference to a committee of a council there were substituted a reference to a sub-committee."

(2) Articles 15 (Application of National Health Service (Executive Councils and Dental Estimates Board) Financial Regulations 1948(**g**)), 16 (Annual and Supplementary Estimates), 17 (Books and Accounts) and 18 (Audit) shall cease to have effect.

3. The provisions of Part II (Financial Arrangements and Audit of Accounts) of the National Health Service (Executive Councils and Dental Estimates Board) Financial Regulations 1969(**h**) shall apply to the Joint Pricing Committee for England as they apply to Executive Councils as if for any reference

---

(**a**) 1946 c. 81.   (**b**) 1889 c. 63.
(**c**) S.I. 1948/1301 (Rev. XV, p. 704: 1948 I, p. 2172).
(**d**) The amending orders are not relevant to the subject matter of this order.
(**e**) S.R. & O. 1947/889 (Rev. XV, p. 505: 1947 I, p. 1324).
(**f**) S.I. 1969/352 (1969 I, p. 980)   (**g**) S.I. 1948/1239 (Rev. XV, p. 716: 1948 I, p. 2076).
(**h**) S.I. 1969/1581 (1969 III, p. 5047).

therein to a Council there were substituted a reference to the Committee and as if for any reference to the finance committee there were substituted a reference to the finance sub-committee.

Signed by authority of the Secretary of State for Social Services.

C. L. Bourton,
Assistant Under Secretary of State,
Department of Health and Social Security.

12th December 1969.

EXPLANATORY NOTE

(*This Note is not part of the Order.*)

This Order amends the National Health Service (Joint Pricing Committee for England) Order 1948 which established a Joint Pricing Committee for England for the purpose of exercising the functions of Executive Councils in regard to the pricing of prescriptions for drugs. This Order applies to the Joint Pricing Committee—

(*a*) the provisions relating to procedure contained in the National Health Service (Executive Councils) Regulations 1969 in place of similar provisions of the National Health Service (Executive Councils) Regulations 1947, and

(*b*) the provisions of Part II of the National Health Service (Executive Councils and Dental Estimates Board) Financial Regulations 1969 in place of some provisions of the National Health Service (Executive Councils and Dental Estimates Board) Financial Regulations 1948 (superseded by the Financial Regulations of 1969) and of the Order of 1948.

STATUTORY INSTRUMENTS

1969 No. 1782

ROAD TRAFFIC

The Road Vehicles (Excise) (Prescribed Particulars) (Amendment) Regulations 1969

Made - - - -	*9th December* 1969
Laid before Parliament	*23rd December* 1969
Coming into Operation	*1st January* 1970

The Minister of Transport in exercise of his powers under section 12(1) of the Vehicles (Excise) Act 1962**(a)**, as substituted by section 6(2) of the Finance Act 1969**(b)**, and under section 23 of the said Act of 1962, and of all other enabling powers, hereby makes the following Regulations:—

1.—(1) These Regulations shall come into operation on the 1st January 1970 and may be cited as the Road Vehicles (Excise) (Prescribed Particulars) (Amendment) Regulations 1969.

(2) The Interpretation Act 1889**(c)** shall apply for the interpretation of these Regulations as it applies for the interpretation of an Act of Parliament.

2. The Road Vehicles (Excise) (Prescribed Particulars) Regulations 1966**(d)**, shall have effect as though—

(*a*) in Regulation 7, after the words "the Regulations of 1964" there were inserted the words "as amended by the Road Vehicles (Registration and Licensing) (Amendment) (No. 2) Regulations 1969**(e)**";

(*b*) for form VE. 7 as set out in Schedule 2 to the Regulations there were substituted the following form:—

(a) 1962 c. 13. (b) 1969 c. 32.
(c) 1889 c. 63. (d) S.I. 1966/224 (1966 I, p. 435).
(e) S.I. 1969/1589 (1969 III, p. 5066).

"Form VE. 7

PARTICULARS

PARTICULARS OF PRESENT LICENCE (if any)

Plate number [   ]

I APPLY for a TRADE LICENCE for use on

* ALL CLASSES OF VEHICLE for the
CYCLE CLASS ONLY

⎧ Year ending 31 December 19.........

⎪ Quarter ending 31 March 19.........

*⎨ Quarter ending 30 June 19.........

⎪ Quarter ending 30 September 19......

⎩ Quarter ending 31 December 19......

In the case of an all vehicle licence, are alternative plates for display of the licence on vehicles of the "Cycle" class required?

Duty of

£ ....
enclosed

* YES/NO

DECLARATION

* I DECLARE that I am a MOTOR TRADER and the licence is for use on
VEHICLE TESTER

*mechanically propelled vehicles which are from time to time temporarily in my possession in the course of my business as a motor trader and all recovery vehicles kept by me for the purpose of dealing with disabled vehicles in the course of that business (MOTOR TRADER)

*mechanically propelled vehicles which are from time to time submitted to me for testing in the course of my business as a vehicle tester as defined in Section 12(10) of the Vehicles (Excise) Act 1962 as amended by Section 9 of the Finance Act 1968 (VEHICLE TESTER)

I FURTHER DECLARE that the above business is carried on under the name of

BLOCK ....
CAPITALS at...

....

Full name and address of Applicant

BLOCK Mr/Mrs/Miss...
CAPITALS

....

Date............... Signature ....

State in the case of a partnership, limited company or other legal entity, capacity in which application is signed

....".

*DELETE AS APPROPRIATE

Given under the Official Seal of the Minister of Transport the 9th December 1969.

(L.S.)   *Fred Mulley*,
                                          Minister of Transport.

EXPLANATORY NOTE

(This Note is not part of the Regulations.)

These Regulations amend the Road Vehicles (Excise) (Prescribed Particulars) Regulations 1966 by introducing into those Regulations as from 1st January 1970 a new form containing particulars to be furnished and a declaration to be made by an applicant for a trade licence, which single type of licence will as from the above date replace general trade licences and limited trade licences by reason of section 6(2) of the Finance Act 1969.

STATUTORY INSTRUMENTS

1969 No. 1784

ANIMALS

DISEASES OF ANIMALS

The Export of Horses (Protection) Order 1969

Made - - - - - - *12th December* 1969

Coming into Operation—
Articles 3, 4, 5, 6, 11(1), 11(2),
11(4), 14(2)(*a*)(ii) and
14(2)(*b*)- - - - *1st June* 1970

Remainder - - - - - *1st January* 1970

The Minister of Agriculture, Fisheries and Food and the Secretary of State, acting jointly, in exercise of the powers conferred on them by sections 1, 20, 23 and 85 of the Diseases of Animals Act 1950(a), as read with the Transfer of Functions (Animal Health) Order 1955(b), as extended to horses by the Diseases of Animals (Extension of Definitions) Order 1952(c) and as adapted to air transport by section 11 of the Agriculture (Miscellaneous Provisions) Act 1954(d), and by section 2 of the Ponies Act 1969(e), and of all other powers enabling them in that behalf, hereby order as follows:—

Citation and commencement

1. This order, which may be cited as the Export of Horses (Protection) Order 1969, shall come into operation on 1st January 1970, except for Articles 3, 4, 5, 6, 11(1), 11(2), 11(4), 14(2)(*a*)(ii) and 14(2)(*b*), which shall come into operation on 1st June 1970.

Interpretation

2.—(1) In this order, unless the context otherwise requires—

"the Act" means the Diseases of Animals Act 1950;

"animals" means cattle, sheep and goats, and all other ruminating animals and swine, horses, asses, mules and jennets;

"approved disinfectant" means a disinfectant approved for the time being for the purposes of the Diseases of Animals (Disinfection) Order of 1936(f);

"approved premises" has the meaning assigned to it by Article 3(1) of this order;

"exempted horse" means a horse which is exempted from examination under section 37 of the Act by any of the provisions of the Export of Horses (Excepted Cases) Order 1969(g);

(a) 1950 c. 36.   For change of title of the Minister see S.I. 1955/554 (1955 I, p. 1200).
(b) S.I. 1955/958 (1955 I, p. 1184).   (c) S.I. 1952/1236 (1952 I, p. 128).
(d) 1954 c. 39.   (e) 1969 c. 28.
(f) S.R. & O. 1938/191 (Rev. II, p. 320; 1938 I, p. 303).
(g) S.I. 1969/1742 (1969 III, p. 5470).

"horse" includes pony, ass and mule;

"inspector" means a person appointed to be an inspector for the purposes of the Act by the Minister of Agriculture, Fisheries and Food or by a local authority and, when used in relation to a person appointed by the said Minister, includes a veterinary inspector;

"local authority" means a local authority for the purposes of the Act;

"master" includes any person having the charge or command of a vessel, except the pilot;

"the Minister" in its application to horses shipped or intended to be shipped from England and Wales, means the Minister of Agriculture, Fisheries and Food, and in its corresponding application to Scotland, means the Secretary of State;

"pilot", in relation to an aircraft, means the pilot or other person having the command or charge of the aircraft;

"pony" means any horse not more than 14½ hands in height, except a foal travelling with its dam if the dam is over 14½ hands;

"rest period" has the meaning assigned to it by Article 3(2) of this order;

"shipped" means carried by sea or air and "shipment" shall be construed accordingly;

"veterinary inspector" means a veterinary inspector appointed by the Minister of Agriculture, Fisheries and Food.

(2) The Interpretation Act 1889(a) shall apply to the interpretation of this order as it applies to the interpretation of an Act of Parliament and as if this order and the order hereby revoked were Acts of Parliament.

Provision for the resting of horses before export

3.—(1) Subject to the provisions of this order, it shall be unlawful to ship or attempt to ship or cause or permit to be shipped any horse from any place in Great Britain to any place outside the United Kingdom, the Channel Islands and the Isle of Man, unless immediately before being loaded in the vessel or aircraft in which it is to be carried it has been rested by detention for the rest period defined by the succeeding paragraph of this Article on premises (hereinafter referred to as "approved premises") which are:—

(a) at or near the place of loading;

(b) provided with adequate protection against the weather;

(c) provided with facilities, including adequate lighting, to allow satis-factory supervision of horses throughout the detention period and for each horse to be individually inspected;

(d) provided with suitable facilities for tying horses; and

(e) approved in writing for that purpose, in England and Wales by the Minister of Agriculture, Fisheries and Food or in Scotland by the Secre-tary of State, which approval may be granted subject to such conditions as to the duration of the approval and otherwise as the said Minister or the Secretary of State may see fit to impose, and in particular subject to a condition (in addition to any limitation imposed by Article 4(b)(v) hereof) limiting the total number of horses to be rested on the premises at any one time.

(2) The rest period shall be a period of not less than 10 hours which shall include at least 3 consecutive hours between sunrise and sunset, and in respect of

(a) 1889 c. 63.

any horse detained on approved premises in any pen or enclosure shall commence at the time of entry into such pen or enclosure of the last horse of the group to be rested thereon.

Provided always that if during the rest period of any horses, other horses are introduced into the pen or enclosure where horses already resting are detained, then the rest period of the horses already detained therein shall be deemed to have commenced at the time of the entry of the last of the horses so introduced.

(3) It shall be unlawful to load into any vessel or aircraft any horse required to be rested under this Article unless at the time of loading it is accompanied by a certificate signed by the person having charge of the approved premises on which the horse has been rested in accordance with the requirements of this Article to the effect that it was detained there throughout the whole of the rest period specified in the certificate.

Conditions of use of approved premises

4. No person having the charge or control of any approved premises shall use them or cause or permit them to be used for the rest period of any horses—

(a) except in accordance with such conditions, if any, as the Minister of Agriculture, Fisheries and Food or the Secretary of State may have attached to his approval of the premises, and

(b) unless during the whole of the rest period of any horses—

(i) sufficient clean bedding is provided;

(ii) an adequate supply of wholesome and palatable food suitable for horses is provided in racks or troughs which are easily accessible to the horses and are such as by their number, dimensions and disposition enable all the horses to eat simultaneously;

(iii) an adequate supply of wholesome water is provided in suitable receptacles easily accessible to the horses;

(iv) all animals, other than horses being detained in accordance with the provisions of this order or of any licence granted under it, are excluded from the premises;

(v) not more than 10 horses are detained together in any one pen or enclosure;

(vi) any horse (other than a mare which has a foal at foot) with shod hind feet is either penned by itself or suitably tied by the head in such a manner that it cannot injure any other horse;

(vii) any mare which has a foal at foot is kept separate (with its foal) from any other horse, and any stallion is kept separate from any other horse;

(viii) separate pens or enclosures are provided for horses which are ailing or which disturb other horses detained on the premises and any such horses are placed in such pens and enclosures;

(ix) the horses are supervised by experienced and competent attendants;

(x) all reasonable facilities are afforded to an inspector or to any police officer for observation of the horses during detention.

Cleansing and disinfection

5.—(1) No person shall use any pen, fitting or utensil on approved premises in connection with the detention of horses for a rest period under the provisions of this order unless such pen, fitting or utensil has before each occasion on which it is so used been—

(a) scraped and swept, and any scrapings, dung, litter or other matter removed or burnt; and

(b) thoroughly washed and scrubbed with water and thereafter thoroughly disinfected with an approved disinfectant.

(2) An inspector may give notice in writing to the person having charge of approved premises requiring the cleansing and disinfection of the whole or any part of those premises or of any pen, fitting, utensil or other thing, or prescribing the method of disposal of dung, food, litter or other matter.

(3) When such notice shall have been given the approved premises or such part thereof as may be specified in the notice or such things as are mentioned in the previous paragraph of this Article (as the case may be) shall not be used for horses unless and until the cleansing and disinfection required by the said notice has been carried out to the satisfaction of an inspector, and dung, food, litter or other matter shall not be disposed of otherwise than in accordance with the notice.

Notification of arrival at approved premises

6. It shall be the duty of the person having the charge or control of any approved premises—

(a) to give to an inspector of the Ministry and to the local authority not less than 48 hours notice of the anticipated time of arrival of any consignment of horses to be rested therein, and

(b) to notify with all practicable speed to an inspector of the Ministry and to the local authority at the commencement of the rest period of any consignment of horses—

(i) the number of horses in the consignment;

(ii) the actual time of arrival at the premises of the last horse in the consignment; and

(iii) the place or places from which the consignment was despatched.

Restriction on the export of exempted horses

7. Subject to the provisions of this order, it shall be unlawful to ship or attempt to ship or to cause or permit to be shipped any exempted horse other than a horse of the description mentioned in the proviso to this Article, from any place in Great Britain to any place outside the United Kingdom, the Republic of Ireland, the Channel Islands and the Isle of Man unless immediately before shipment the horse has been inspected in accordance with the provisions of this order by a veterinary inspector and has been certified in writing by him to be capable of being conveyed to the destination to which it is to be shipped and disembarked without unnecessary suffering.

Provided that this Article shall not apply to an exempted horse shipped from any place in Great Britain to any place outside Europe.

Inspection of exempted horses and ponies

8.—(1) Any inspection of an exempted horse for the purposes of this order or of a pony for the purposes of section 37(4A) of the Act (which requires any pony shipped from Great Britain outside the United Kingdom, the Channel Islands and the Isle of Man to undergo veterinary inspection) shall be made immediately before shipment at a place to be approved by a veterinary inspector, and having such facilities for the inspection of horses as may reasonably be required by him.

(2) It shall be the duty of any person exporting any exempted horse required to be inspected under this order or any pony to provide all reasonable assistance to the veterinary inspector making the inspection.

Expiry of certificate of veterinary inspection

9. Any certificate of veterinary inspection issued under this order or pursuant to section 37(4A) of the Act shall specify the date and time of the inspection and shall cease to be valid for the purposes of this order or of the Act (as the case may be) after the expiry of 18 hours from the time at which the inspection was carried out.

Notification by veterinary inspector of unfitness for travel of a horse

10. Where a veterinary inspector is of opinion that any exempted horse inspected under the provisions of this order or any pony inspected pursuant to section 37(4A) of the Act cannot be conveyed to its destination and disembarked without unnecessary suffering, he may—

(*a*) place a mark upon the horse (or pony) and serve a notice on the person in charge of it and also, when practicable, upon the master of the vessel or the pilot of the aircraft (as the case may be) prohibiting the shipment of the horse (or pony), and until such notice is withdrawn by a veterinary inspector, it shall be unlawful to ship the horse (or pony);

(*b*) in the case of a horse (or pony) already loaded into a vessel or aircraft, serve a notice on the master of the vessel or the pilot of the aircraft (as the case may be) in which it is loaded requiring him to unload it;

(*c*) serve a notice on any person having charge of the horse (or pony) requiring him to comply with such conditions as to rest or other treatment of it before it is shipped as the veterinary inspector may specify in the notice.

Exemptions from resting and veterinary inspection

11.—(1) Nothing in this order shall require the resting before shipment of any horse (other than a pony) which is shipped from any place in Great Britain to any place which is in the Republic of Ireland or which is outside Europe.

(2) Nothing in this order shall require the resting before shipment of any horse in respect of which a written certificate has been issued by a steward or the secretary of the Jockey Club pursuant to section 40 of the Act (which relates to thoroughbred horses shipped for the purpose of being run in a race or breeding).

(3) The Minister may grant a licence exempting from the provisions of Article 3 or of Article 7 of this order (or of both of them) any horse (other than a pony) which he is satisfied—

(*a*) is intended for exhibition, jumping, polo or racing;

(*b*) is a thoroughbred horse intended for breeding;

(*c*) by reason of special circumstances does not require resting before shipment, or veterinary inspection; or

(*d*) is a foal travelling with its dam if the dam is a horse exempted under the foregoing provisions of this paragraph.

(4) The Minister may grant a licence exempting from the provision of Article 3 of this order any pony which he is satisfied by reason of special circumstances does not require resting before shipment.

Licences

12.—(1) An application for any licence which may be granted under this order shall be made to the Minister, in such form and manner as the Minister may require, 7 days before the intended date of shipment of the horse to which the application relates (or within such lesser period as the Minister may at his discretion allow), and any licence so granted may have attached thereto such conditions as the Minister may think fit for the prevention of unnecessary suffering in transit.

(2) Failure to comply with any term of a licence issued under this order shall be an offence against the Act.

Requirements in respect of ponies intended for export

13.—(1) In the case of any pony intended for shipment from any port in Great Britain to any port outside the United Kingdom, the Channel Islands and the Isle of Man in respect of which the Minister is required under the provisions of section 37(4A) of the Act to be satisfied that it is intended for breeding, riding or exhibition, and is of not less value than the relevant amount specified in that section, the owner or other person intending to ship the pony shall furnish to the Minister 7 days before the intended date of shipment of the pony (or within such lesser period as the Minister may at his discretion allow) such evidence as the Minister may require—

   (a) as to the purpose for which the pony is intended to be used after export; and

   (b) as to the value of the pony.

(2) Upon receipt of evidence under the foregoing provisions of this Article which he considers satisfactory as to the aforesaid requirements of the said section 37(4A) of the Act the Minister shall issue to the person submitting such evidence a certificate to that effect.

Production of certificates and licences

14.—(1) Any certificate issued under Article 3, Article 7 or Article 13 of this order, and any licence issued under Article 11 thereof shall be delivered at the time of shipment to the master of the vessel or pilot of the aircraft on which the horse or pony to which the certificate or licence relates is loaded, who shall on demand produce the same to any police officer, or any officer of the Minister or of the local authority or Customs and Excise and allow such person to take a a copy or extract from any such certificate or licence.

(2) It shall be unlawful for the master of any vessel or the pilot of any aircraft to permit to be shipped—

   (a) any exempted horse to which Article 7 of this order applies unless there has been delivered to him in respect thereof—

      (i) a certificate under Article 7 of this order or a licence in lieu under Article 11 thereof; and

      (ii) a certificate under Article 3 of this order or a licence in lieu under Article 11 thereof.

   (b) a pony unless there has been delivered to him in respect thereof a certificate under Article 3 of this order or a licence in lieu under Article 11 thereof.

Information to be given about proposed shipment

15. Where under the provisions of this order or of section 37(4A) of the Act any exempted horse or any pony has to be inspected by a veterinary inspector the person making application for such inspection shall if the Minister so requires supply 7 days before the date of shipment (or within such lesser period as the Minister may at his discretion allow), such information in writing as the Minister, having regard to the circumstances of the case, considers necessary for the purpose of ensuring that the horse or pony is properly inspected.

Local Authority to enforce Order

16. This order shall, except where it is otherwise provided, be executed and enforced by the local authority.

Revocation

17.—(1) The Exported Horses Protection Order 1966(a) is hereby revoked.

(2) Any certificate or licence insofar as it relates to a horse over 14½ hands in height or to a foal travelling with its dam where the dam is such a horse made or having effect under the aforesaid order, if in force immediately before the coming into operation of this order, shall thenceforth have effect under and by virtue of this Article.

In Witness whereof the Official Seal of the Minister of Agriculture, Fisheries and Food is hereunto affixed on
12th December 1969.

(L.S.)   *Cledwyn Hughes,*
**Minister of Agriculture, Fisheries
and Food.**

Given under the Seal of the Secretary of State for Scotland on 12th December 1969.

(L.S.)   *William Ross,*
Secretary of State for Scotland.

EXPLANATORY NOTE
(*This note is not part of the Order.*)

This order revokes and re-enacts with amendments the Exported Horses Protection Order 1966.

Horses (other than ponies) exempted from the veterinary examination required by section 37 of the Diseases of Animals Act 1950 and which are exported from Great Britain to any place in Europe outside the United Kingdom, the Republic of Ireland, the Channel Islands and the Isle of Man are required immediately

---

(a) S.I. 1966/509 (1966 I, p. 1077).

before export to undergo inspection by a veterinary inspector and to be certified by him to be capable of being conveyed to their destination and disembarked without unnecessary suffering. In the case of ponies intended for export (further to section 37(4A) of the Diseases of Animals Act 1950) administrative arrangements for a veterinary inspection etc. are also laid down. The order further empowers a veterinary inspector to prohibit the carriage of any horse or to require removal of any horse from a vessel or aircraft if it is likely to be exposed to unnecessary suffering during transit. All these provisions take effect from 1st January 1970.

From 1st June 1970, the order also requires horses (including ponies) exported from Great Britain outside the United Kingdom, the Channel Islands or the Isle of Man to be rested at approved premises for at least 10 hours before loading into the vessel or aircraft in which they are to be exported. It requires the provision of adequate and accessible food and water and shelter and bedding, and limits the number of horses which may be put at one time into any one pen or enclosure. An exemption is made in respect of horses (other than ponies) shipped to the Republic of Ireland or outside Europe.

STATUTORY INSTRUMENTS

1969 No. 1786

POLICE

The Police Cadets (Amendment) (No. 2) Regulations 1969

Made - - -	*11th December* 1969
Laid before Parliament	*22nd December* 1969
Coming into Operation	*1st January* 1970

In exercise of the powers conferred on me by section 35 of the Police Act 1964(**a**), and after consulting the Police Council for Great Britain in accordance with section 45(4) of that Act, I hereby make the following Regulations :—

Citation and operation

1. These Regulations may be cited as the Police Cadets (Amendment) (No. 2) Regulations 1969 and shall come into operation on 1st January 1970.

Interpretation

2. In these Regulations any reference to the principal Regulations is a reference to the Police Cadets Regulations 1968(**b**), as amended(**c**).

Pay

3. For the Table in Schedule 1 to the principal Regulations (which, as set out in Regulation 3 of the Police Cadets (Amendment) Regulations 1969(**c**), contains scales of pay) there shall be substituted the following Table :—

"TABLE

Age	City of London and metropolitan police forces	Other police forces
Under 17 years	£438 a year	£408 a year
17 years	£474 a year	£444 a year
18 years	£531 a year	£501 a year
19 years	£582 a year	£552 a year"

(**a**) 1964 c. 48.   (**b**) S.I. 1968/25 (1968 I, p. 31).
(**c**) S.I. 1969/408 (1969 I, p. 1150).

Charge for board and lodging

4. For paragraph 2 of Schedule 2 to the principal Regulations (which, as set out in Regulation 4 of the said Regulations of 1969, relates to charges for board and lodging) there shall be substituted the following paragraph :—

"2. The annual rate of charge shall be—
   (*a*) in the case of a police cadet attached to the City of London or metropolitan police force, £105 ;

   (*b*) in any other case, £96.".

James Callaghan,
One of Her Majesty's Principal
Secretaries of State.

Home Office,
   Whitehall.

11th December 1969.

EXPLANATORY NOTE

(*This Note is not part of the Regulations.*)

These Regulations amend the Police Cadets Regulations 1968.

Regulation 3 increases the pay of a police cadet by amounts which vary according to his age.

Regulation 4 increases charges payable by police cadets for board and lodging by £1 10s. 0d. a year in the case of cadets attached to the City of London or metropolitan police force and £2 10s. 0d. in the case of other cadets.

The Regulations come into operation on 1st January 1970.

STATUTORY INSTRUMENTS

1969 No. 1787

POLICE

The Police Federation Regulations 1969

Made - - - -	11*th December* 1969
Laid before Parliament	23*rd December* 1969
Coming into Operation	1*st January* 1970

ARRANGEMENT OF REGULATIONS

PART I

GENERAL

PART II

ORGANISATION

PART III

FINANCIAL ARRANGEMENTS

SCHEDULES

Schedule 1: Regulations revoked.

Schedule 2: Proceedings.

Schedule 3: Elections, etc.

Schedule 4: Delegates to central conferences.

    Part I—Men.

    Part II—Women.

Schedule 5: Regions.

In exercise of the powers conferred on me by section 44 of the Police Act 1964(a), and after consultation with the three Central Committees of the Police Federation for England and Wales sitting together as a Joint Committee, I hereby make the following Regulations:—

PART I

GENERAL

Citation, commencement and extent

1.—(1) These Regulations may be cited as the Police Federation Regulations 1969 and shall come into operation on 1st January 1970.

(2) These Regulations shall not extend to Scotland.

Interpretation

2.—(1) In these Regulations the expression "division", in relation to a police force, has the same meaning as in the regulations for the time being in force under section 33 of the Police Act 1964 but, for the purposes of these Regulations, a member of a specialist branch of a police force shall be deemed not to belong to a division of that force.

(2) In these Regulations the expression "specialist branch", in relation to a police force, means—

    (*a*) the criminal investigation department thereof,

    (*b*) the traffic branch thereof, or

    (*c*) the branch attached to the headquarters thereof,

however styled, except that, in relation to the metropolitan police force, the said expression means the criminal investigation department thereof or the A, B and D departments, attached to the office of the commissioner of police of the metropolis, taken together.

(3) In these Regulations, unless the context otherwise requires, a reference to a Regulation shall be construed as a reference to a Regulation contained in these Regulations, a reference to a Schedule shall be construed as a reference to a Schedule to these Regulations and a reference to a paragraph shall be construed as a reference to a paragraph in the same Regulation, the same Schedule or the same Part of a Schedule, as the case may be.

(4) In these Regulations any reference to any enactment is a reference to that enactment as amended or extended by or under any subsequent enactment.

(5) The Interpretation Act 1889(b) shall apply for the interpretation of these Regulations as it applies for the interpretation of an Act of Parliament.

    (a) 1964 c. 48.   (b) 1889 c. 63.

Revocations and transitional provisions

3.—(1) The Regulations set out in Schedule 1, that is to say the Police Federation Regulations 1965**(b)** and the Regulations amending those Regulations, are hereby revoked.

(2) Anything done under, or for the purposes of, any provision of the Regulations revoked by this Regulation shall have effect as if done under, or for the purposes of, the corresponding provision of these Regulations.

PART II

ORGANISATION

Membership of Police Federation and branches thereof

4.—(1) The Police Federation for England and Wales (hereinafter referred to as "the Federation") shall be known as the Police Federation.

(2) There shall be a branch of the Federation for each police force, consisting of the following persons—

  (*a*) every member of that force below the rank of superintendent, and

  (*b*) every police cadet undergoing training with a view to becoming a member of that force,

and every such person shall be a member of the Federation.

Proceedings of branches

5.—(1) General meetings of the members of a branch of the Federation, or of such members belonging to a particular division or specialist branch of a police force, may be held in accordance with arrangements made by—

  (*a*) a board or joint board of that branch, or

  (*b*) a central committee or the joint central committee of the Federation.

(2) The chief officer of police of the force in whose area such a meeting is to be held shall be given at least fourteen days' notice of the date of the meeting.

(3) The arrangements referred to in paragraph (1) may provide for the attendance at a meeting of members of the police authority and of other members of the Federation but shall not permit the attendance of other persons except to such extent, and subject to such conditions, as may be determined—

  (*a*) by the chief officer of police, where the arrangements are made under paragraph (1)(*a*);

  (*b*) by the Secretary of State, where the arrangements are made under paragraph (1)(*b*).

(4) The arrangements referred to in paragraph (1) shall not permit the passing of a resolution at a meeting for submission to a chief officer of police, a police authority or the Secretary of State.

(5) Subject to the provisions of the arrangements referred to in paragraph (1), Schedule 2 shall have effect in relation to the proceedings of a meeting held under this Regulation.

Branch boards

6.—(1) In each branch of the Federation there shall be constituted, in accordance with this Regulation, an inspectors', a sergeants' and a constables' branch board.

(a) S.I. 1965/619 (1965 I, p. 1928).

(2) Where a police force consists of fewer than five divisions, the men belonging to those divisions holding the rank of inspector, sergeant or, as the case may be, constable in that force shall elect, from among their number, five members of the appropriate branch board.

(3) Where a police force consists of five or more divisions, the men belonging to each division and holding the rank of inspector, sergeant or, as the case may be, constable therein shall elect from among their number one member of the appropriate branch board.

(4) The men belonging to each specialist branch of a police force and holding the rank of inspector, sergeant or, as the case may be, constable therein shall elect from among their number one member of the appropriate branch board except that in the case of the two specialist branches of the metropolitan police force—

> (*a*) five members shall be elected by the criminal investigation department, and

> (*b*) three members shall be elected by the A, B and D departments.

(5) The women holding the rank of inspector, sergeant or, as the case may be, constable in a police force shall elect one member of the appropriate branch board from among their own number or, in the case of the metropolitan police force, from among the members thereof elected as delegates to the appropriate central conference in accordance with Regulation 9(4).

(6) The police cadets undergoing training with a view to becoming members of a police force may elect, from among their number, one member of the constables' branch board; but, where they do not so elect a member, they shall designate to represent their interests a member of the constables' branch board elected in accordance with the preceding provisions of this Regulation.

(7) Schedule 3 shall have effect in relation to a branch board, so however that in any election thereto—

> (*a*) if only one person is qualified to take part therein, that person shall be deemed to be elected;

> (*b*) if only two persons are qualified to take part therein, subject to any agreement to the contrary between them, the senior of those two shall be deemed to be elected.

(8) Annual elections shall be held for the purposes of this Regulation in such month in each year as the Secretary of State may determine at the request of the joint central committee of the Federation.

(9) A person becoming a member of a branch board shall, subject to any rules made under paragraph 5(1)(*b*) of Schedule 3, become such on the first day of the month following that in which annual elections are held and, subject to paragraph (10), shall remain a member until the end of the month in which annual elections are held in the next following year.

(10) A person shall cease to be a member of an inspectors', sergeants' or constables' branch board if—

> (*a*) he ceases to hold the rank of inspector, sergeant or, as the case may be, constable;

> (*b*) he ceases to be a member of the police force or, in the case of a police cadet, ceases to undergo training with a view to becoming such a member, or

> (*c*) in the case of a person elected in accordance with paragraph (3) or (4),

he ceases to belong to the division or specialist branch by which he was elected;

but, where a person who is the secretary of a joint branch board ceases to be a member of a branch board in accordance with sub-paragraph (c) of this paragraph, he shall, by virtue of this paragraph and without prejudice to the filling of the casual vacancy, become an additional member of that board and shall remain such for the period for which he would have remained a member but for the said sub-paragraph (c).

(11) Where a member of a branch board has been chosen as such a central officer of the Federation as is hereinafter mentioned he shall, by virtue of this paragraph and without prejudice to the filling of the casual vacancy, become an additional member of that board and, subject to paragraph (10), shall remain such until some other person is chosen for the office in question.

In this paragraph the reference to a central officer of the Federation is a reference to—

(a) a person chosen by the joint central committee as the chairman, secretary or treasurer thereof, or

(b) a person chosen by a central committee as the secretary thereof.

(12) A reference in any provision of this Regulation to a person holding a rank in a police force shall be construed as excluding a reference to such a person who is a member of the first class of the police reserve.

Proceedings of branch boards

7.—(1) Each branch board may hold quarterly meetings, each lasting one day and, with the consent of the chief officer of police, additional meetings of the branch board and meetings of committees thereof.

(2) Each branch board shall hold a quarterly meeting in the month following that in which annual elections are held, which meeting is in these Regulations referred to as the annual meeting, and where more than one meeting is held in that month the first meeting so held shall be the annual meeting.

(3) In any branch of the Federation the three or any two of the branch boards may, by agreement, sit together as a joint branch board, either generally or for a special purpose.

(4) Without prejudice to any arrangements for informal consultation, a branch board or joint branch board may make written representations to the chief officer of police or the police authority and, if it thinks fit, submit a copy thereof to the Secretary of State; and in matters of importance a deputation may be appointed to make oral representations to the chief officer of police or the police authority.

(5) Schedule 2 shall have effect in relation to the proceedings of any branch board or joint branch board.

Liaison committees

8.—(1) In each branch of the Federation there shall be constituted, by the constables' branch board and in accordance with this Regulation, a liaison committee to represent the women members of the branch holding the rank of constable and consisting of a representative from each division of the force to which such members belong elected by the members in question belonging to that division.

(2) In each branch of the Federation there may, with the consent of the chief officer of police, be constituted by the sergeants' or constables' branch board,

and in accordance with this Regulation, such other liaison committees as appear to them expedient having regard to the size and organisation of the police force.

(3) Members of a branch who hold the rank of constable or are police cadets may be represented by the same or separate liaison committees constituted under paragraph (2) but members who hold the rank of sergeant may only be represented by a sergeants' liaison committee.

(4) Subject to the preceding provisions of this Regulation, a liaison committee constituted under paragraph (1) or (2) shall be constituted in accordance with arrangements made by the appropriate branch board with the approval of the chief officer of police and any such arrangements—

(a) shall provide that the committee shall consist of members of the branch who are not members of the appropriate branch board, and

(b) without prejudice to the generality of this paragraph, may apply, subject to appropriate modifications, the provisions of Schedule 2 to the proceedings of the committee and the provisions of Schedule 3 to the committee.

(5) In each year, a liaison committee constituted under paragraph (1) may hold two ordinary meetings and a liaison committee constituted under paragraph (2) may hold four ordinary meetings, each lasting half a day.

(6) A liaison committee constituted under paragraph (1) or (2) may, with the consent of the chief officer of police, hold additional meetings.

Central conferences

9.—(1) There shall be constituted, in accordance with this Regulation, an inspectors', a sergeants' and a constables' central conference.

(2) Each branch board, at their annual meeting, shall elect from among the men holding the rank of inspector, sergeant or, as the case may be, constable in the police force, such number of delegates to the appropriate central conference as is provided in Part I of Schedule 4:

Provided that a woman member of a branch board shall not vote in an election held for the purposes of this paragraph.

(3) The women members of the inspectors', sergeants' and constables' branch boards for the branches of the Federation in each of the regions mentioned in Schedule 5 shall elect, from among the women holding the rank of inspector, sergeant or, as the case may be, constable in a police force in the region in question, such number of delegates to the appropriate central conference as is provided in Part II of Schedule 4.

(4) The women holding the rank of inspector, segeant or, as the case may be, constable in the metropolitan police force or the City of London police force shall elect, from among their number, four delegates to the appropriate central conference.

(5) A person shall cease to be a delegate to a central conference if he ceases to hold the rank of inspector, sergeant or, as the case may be, constable or ceases to be a member of the branch from which he is a delegate or, in the case of a woman, of a branch in the region from which she is a delegate or, as the case may be, of the metropolitan police force or the City of London police force.

(6) Where a member of a branch board has been chosen as such a central officer of the Federation as is mentioned in Regulation 6(11), he shall, by virtue of this paragraph and without prejudice to the filling of any casual vacancy among the delegates elected by that board to the appropriate central conference,

become an additional delegate from that board to that conference and, subject to paragraph (5), shall remain such until some other person is chosen for the office in question.

(7) Schedule 3 shall have effect in relation to each of the central conferences.

Proceedings of central conferences

10.—(1) Each central conference shall meet each year at such times as the Secretary of State shall determine after consultation with the joint central committee of the Federation and shall hold an annual meeting lasting not more than three days or, with the consent of the Secretary of State, four days.

(2) The three, or any two, of the central conferences may, by agreement, sit together for the purpose of discussing matters of common interest.

(3) The three central conferences sitting together shall be known as the joint central conference.

(4) Schedule 2 shall have effect in relation to the proceedings of each of the central conferences.

Conferences arrangements committee

11.—(1) There shall be constituted, in accordance with this Regulation, a conferences arrangements committee charged with the making of arrangements for such meetings as are referred to in Regulation 10.

(2) The conferences arrangements committee shall consist of—

(a) three men holding the rank of inspector,

(b) three men holding the rank of sergeant,

(c) three men holding the rank of constable, and

(d) one woman holding the rank of inspector, sergeant or constable,

not being members of a central committee; and of the three men holding each rank, one shall be a London member, that is to say, a member of the City of London or the metropolitan police force, and the other two shall be provincial members, that is to say, members of other police forces.

(3) The men who are members of the conferences arrangements committee shall be elected by the men who are delegates to the appropriate central conference from the City of London and metropolitan police forces, in the case of the London members, or by the men who are such delegates from other forces, in the case of the provincial members; and the woman member of the said committee shall be elected by the delegates to the joint central conference who are women.

(4) A person shall cease to be a member of the conferences arrangements committee on ceasing to be qualified for membership by reason of his ceasing to hold a particular rank or to be a member of a particular police force or by reason of his becoming a member of a central committee.

(5) The conferences arrangements committee may, each year, hold four ordinary meetings each lasting one day, and such additional meetings as appear to them necessary.

(6) Any expenses incurred by the conferences arrangements committee with the approval of the joint central committee shall be defrayed by the joint central committee.

(7) Notwithstanding anything in Regulation 9, each member of the conferences arrangements committee shall, by virtue of this paragraph, be an additional delegate to the appropriate central conference and on a person becoming a

member of the committee and such an additional delegate he shall, if he has been elected a delegate to the conference under Regulation 9, cease to be a delegate so elected.

(8) Schedule 2 shall have effect in relation to the proceedings of the conferences arrangements committee and Schedule 3 shall have effect in relation to that committee.

Central committees

12.—(1) There shall be constituted, in accordance with this Regulation, an inspectors', a sergeants' and a constables' central committee of the Federation.

(2) Each central committee shall be elected by the delegates to the inspectors', sergeants' or, as the case may be, constables' central conference in the manner following:—

- (a) two members shall be elected by the men who are delegates from the metropolitan police force or the City of London police force;
- (b) one member shall be elected in respect of each region mentioned in Schedule 5 by the men who are delegates from police forces in the region in question, and
- (c) one member shall be elected by the delegates who are women,

in each case, from among their number.

(3) Schedule 3 shall have effect in relation to each of the central committees.

Proceedings of central committees

13.—(1) Each central committee may hold—

- (a) an ordinary meeting once in two months, each meeting lasting not more than three days;
- (b) an ordinary meeting once a year with the corresponding central committee of the Scottish Police Federation, lasting not more than two days, and
- (c) additional meetings called with the consent of the Secretary of State.

(2) The three or any two of the central committees may, by agreement, sit together as a joint committee either for all purposes of common interest or for any special purpose.

(3) The three central committees shall, at the request of the Secretary of State, sit together as a joint committee for the purpose of considering any question referred to them by him.

(4) The three central committees sitting together shall be known as the joint central committee of the Federation.

(5) A central committee, the joint central committee or a joint committee of any two central committees may make written representations to the Secretary of State and, in matters of importance, a deputation may be appointed to make oral representations to him.

(6) Schedule 2 shall have effect in relation to the proceedings of each central committee, the joint central committee and a joint committee of any two central committees.

Women's regional conferences

14.—(1) In each of the regions mentioned in Schedule 5 two women's conferences, each lasting not more than one day, may be held each year in accordance with arrangements made by the joint central committee of the Federation.

(2) The women members of all the branch boards of the Federation in the region in question shall be delegates to a conference held under this Regulation.

(3) Schedule 2 shall have effect in relation to the proceedings of a women's regional conference.

PART III

FINANCIAL ARRANGEMENTS

Emoluments etc. of secretary of Federation

15.—(1) The Federation shall make such contribution to the police authority maintaining the police force of which the secretary of the joint central committee is a member, in respect of the pay, pension or allowances payable to or in respect of him, as may be agreed between the joint central committee and the police authority or, in default of agreement, as may be determined by the Secretary of State.

(2) The Regulations for the time being in force under—

(*a*) section 33 of the Police Act 1964(**a**), in so far as they relate to leave, pay and allowances, and

(*b*) the Police Pensions Act 1948(**b**), except in so far as they relate to compulsory retirement on account of age,

shall have effect in relation to the secretary of the joint central committee as if he held the rank of chief inspector in the City of London police force so, however, that nothing in this paragraph shall be construed as transferring any rights or liabilities to the police authority maintaining that force.

Subscriptions etc.

16.—(1) The Federation may raise funds by—

(*a*) the collection of voluntary subscription from the members thereof;

(*b*) the acceptance of donations from such members, from central police officers, reversionary members of home police forces or servicemen within the meaning of the regulations from time to time in force under the Police Pensions Act 1948 or from persons with a contingent right of reversion to a home police force under section 2 of the Police Act 1969(**c**), or

(*c*) the sale of periodicals and other articles,

but not otherwise.

(2) Voluntary subscriptions shall be collected by the appropriate branch boards and the normal amount of such subscriptions (including additional subscriptions) shall be determined by the joint central committee, subject to the approval of the joint central conference.

(3) Out of the sum collected by way of subscriptions in each year a branch board shall pay to the appropriate central committee such sum in respect of each subscribing member as the joint central committee shall have determined should be paid by branch boards in that year but, subject to the next following paragraph, the balance of the sum so collected shall be retained by the branch board.

(**a**) 1964 c. 48.   (**b**) 1948 c. 24.
(**c**) 1969 c. 63.

(4) If at the end of any year the funds held by a branch board exceed—

(a) £200, where the number of subscribing members is less than a hundred;

(b) £2 for each subscribing member, where the number of such members is a hundred or more but less than five hundred or, in the case of the metropolitan police force, a hundred or more but less than four thousand;

(c) £1,000 or, in the metropolitan police force £4,000, where the number of subscribing members is five hundred or more or, as the case may be, four thousand or more,

the board shall pay the excess to the appropriate central committee and, after making such payment, may pay such sum as they think fit to the joint branch board.

Expenses of joint central committee

17.—(1) There shall be paid to the joint central committee, out of Federation funds held by the central committees, such sums as the joint central committee determine.

(2) Subject to Regulation 19 any expenses incurred by or for the purposes of the joint central committee shall be defrayed out of Federation funds held by that committee except that, to the extent that the Secretary of State has agreed with the joint central committee that such expenses should be defrayed by him, they shall be so defrayed.

Accounts

18.—(1) This Regulation shall have effect in relation to every branch board or joint branch board, each central committee and the joint central committee.

(2) Every such board and committee shall, in relation to Federation funds held by the board or committee in question, keep accounts showing all monies received or paid out and shall cause the accounts for each year to be audited by an independent auditor.

(3) The independent auditor shall be a person who is a member, or a firm all of the partners wherein are members, of one or more of the following bodies, that is to say:—

(a) the Institute of Chartered Accountants in England and Wales;

(b) the Institute of Chartered Accountants in Scotland;

(c) the Association of Certified and Corporate Accountants;

(d) the Institute of Chartered Accountants in Ireland;

(e) any other body of accountants established in the United Kingdom and for the time being recognised for the purposes of section 161(1)(b) of the Companies Act 1948(a) by the Board of Trade.

(4) After the end of each year a summary of the accounts for that year, together with a copy of the independent auditor's report thereon, shall—

(a) in the case of the accounts of a branch board or joint branch board, be made available to the subscribing members and sent to the chief officer of police and the appropriate central committee or, as the case may be, the joint central committee which shall, if so requested in a particular case by the Secretary of State, transmit copies to him;

(a) 1948 c. 38.

(b) in the case of the accounts of a central committee or the joint central committee, be made available to the appropriate central conference or, as the case may be, the joint central conference, sent to the Secretary of State and published, in a manner approved by the committee in question, to members of the Federation.

Use of Federation funds

19.—(1) Federation funds shall not without the consent of the Secretary of State be used otherwise than for the purposes mentioned in paragraphs (3) and (4) and, notwithstanding anything in those paragraphs, shall not be used—

(a) to promote directly or indirectly a person's candidature in a parliamentary or local government election;

(b) to contribute to the funds of a trade union, political party or other body or organisation not connected with the police service or its welfare, or

(c) in connection with the defence of a member or former member of the Federation against whom civil, criminal or disciplinary proceedings are brought, except as authorised by paragraph (4)(h).

(2) Subject as aforesaid the joint central committee shall, subject to the approval of the joint central conference, determine the purposes for which Federation funds held by the branch boards or joint branch boards and by the central committees, respectively, may be used.

(3) Federation funds may be used to defray expenses lawfully incurred for the purpose specified in section 44(1) of the Police Act 1964, namely for the purpose of representing members of the police forces and police cadets in England and Wales in all matters affecting their welfare and efficiency, other than questions of discipline and promotion affecting individuals.

(4) Without prejudice to the generality of the preceding paragraph, Federation funds may be used to defray—

(a) expenses arising under these Regulations or arising out of anything done in accordance therewith;

(b) the administrative expenses of the Federation, including expenses in connection with the provision of office accommodation and the remuneration of persons outside the police service employed or consulted in an administrative, professional or advisory capacity;

(c) the payment of honoraria to members of the central committees and of branch boards;

(d) the payment of subsistence and similar allowances to such members as aforesaid and to delegates to conferences held in accordance with these Regulations in respect of expenses incurred by them as such members and delegates;

(e) expenses in connection with the publication and distribution of reports and other documents, including a journal (whether or not a charge is made therefor) and the purchase of publications for use by branch boards and the central committees;

(f) expenses incurred for benevolent or charitable purposes connected with the police service or its welfare;

(g) expenses lawfully incurred in connection with a claim made by a member or former member of the Federation, his widow or child (including legal proceedings arising therefrom) where the claim relates to—

(i) a question of general principle or importance which is of special concern to the members of the Federation or a substantial class thereof,

(ii) the emoluments of a member of the Federation or the pension or other award payable to or in respect of a former member of the Federation,

(iii) an injury or disease alleged to have been received or contracted by a member of the Federation, or

(iv) the compulsory retirement of a member of a police force or of a police cadet, otherwise than as an alternative to dismissal, and

(h) legal charges incurred by a member or former member of the Federation or by a central police officer, within the meaning of the regulations from time to time in force under the Police Pensions Act 1948, entitled at the end of his period of central service to revert to his police force in a rank below that of superintendent, in connection with criminal proceedings brought against him for an offence under the Road Traffic Act 1960(a) or any other enactment relating to road traffic, other than an offence under section 6 or 11 of the Road Traffic Act 1960 or section 12 of the Licensing Act 1872(b) (driving or being in charge when impaired by drink or drugs), section 1, 2 or 3 of the Road Safety Act 1967(c) (driving etc. with an undue proportion of alcohol in the blood) or section 12 of the Theft Act 1968(d) (taking a motor vehicle or other conveyance without authority) committed in, or founded upon something done in, the performance or purported performance of his duties as a member of a police force (including an offence committed on any occasion in respect of which an allowance is payable under regulations made under section 33 of the Police Act 1964 for the use of a motor vehicle or bicycle owned by the member) or as a police cadet, or as such a central police officer, as the case may be.

Trustees of Federation property and funds

20.—(1) Federation property and funds held by a branch board or joint branch board shall be vested in not more than three trustees appointed in such manner as may be determined by the board in question.

(2) Federation property and funds held by a central committee or the joint central committee shall be vested in three trustees appointed by the committee in question.

(3) Where any Federation funds are vested in trustees in accordance with this Regulation those trustees shall not invest the funds or vary any investment except in pursuance of the powers of investment conferred on trustees generally by the Trustee Investment Act 1961(e) and in accordance with the directions of the appropriate board or committee.

(4) Where any Federation property or funds are vested in three trustees in accordance with this Regulation, any two of those trustees shall have the like

(a) 1960 c. 16.   (b) 1872 c. 94.
(c) 1967 c. 30.   (d) 1968 c. 60.
(e) 1961 c. 62.

powers to deal with that property or those funds as they would have had if they had been the sole trustees thereof.

James Callaghan,
One of Her Majesty's Principal
Secretaries of State.

Home Office,
Whitehall.

11th December 1969.

SCHEDULE 1
REGULATIONS REVOKED

Regulations	References
The Police Federation Regulations 1965	S.I. 1965/619 (1965 I, p. 1928).
The Police Federation (Amendment) Regulations 1966	S.I. 1966/542 (1966 II, p. 1119).
The Police Federation (Amendment) Regulations 1967	S.I. 1967/94 (1967 I, p. 199).
The Police Federation (Amendment) Regulations 1968	S.I. 1968/24 (1968 I, p. 29).
The Police Federation (Amendment) (No. 2) Regulations 1968	S.I. 1968/2044 (1968 III, p. 5513).

SCHEDULE 2
PROCEEDINGS

1. This Schedule shall have effect in relation to the proceedings of the following bodies (hereafter in this Schedule referred to as "specified bodies"):—

any branch meeting, including a meeting of members belonging to a particular division or specialist branch of a police force;

any branch board or joint branch board;

each central conference;

the conferences arrangements committee;

each central committee, the joint central committee and a joint committee of any two central committees;

any women's regional conference.

2. Each specified body shall choose its chairman and secretary from among its members.

3. The chairman at any meeting of a specified body shall have a second or casting vote.

4. Subject as aforesaid, each specified body shall regulate its own procedure and may provide for the appointment of committees and sub-committees and for their procedure.

5. Where a police authority can make available to a specified body accommodation in premises provided for police purposes, the specified body shall be under no obligation to make payment for the use of such accommodation.

SCHEDULE 3
ELECTIONS, ETC.

1. This Schedule shall apply in relation to the following bodies (hereafter in this Schedule referred to as "specified bodies"):—

    any branch board;

    each central conference;

    the conferences arrangements committee;

    each central committee.

2. An election to a specified body shall be by secret ballot.

3. At any such election each person qualified to take part therein shall be entitled to give the like number of votes as there are vacancies to be filled but shall not give more than one vote for any one candidate.

4. Where at any such election an equality of votes is found to exist between any candidates and the addition of a vote would entitle any of those candidates to be declared elected, the decision between those candidates shall be reached by lot and the candidate on whom the lot falls shall be declared elected.

5.—(1) Subject to the provisions of these Regulations, rules may be made by the appropriate rule-making body mentioned in sub-paragraph (2) as respects—

    (a) the conduct of elections to a specified body, and

    (b) the circumstances and manner in which casual vacancies thereon are to be filled, whether the vacancy occurs as a result of the death or resignation of a person or in consequence of any provision of these Regulations.

(2) The appropriate rule-making body shall be—

    (a) in relation to a branch board, that board;

    (b) in relation to the election of male delegates to a central conference by a particular branch board and to casual vacancies among those delegates, that board;

    (c) in relation to the election of female delegates to a central conference and casual vacancies among those delegates, the joint central committee;

    (d) in relation to the conferences arrangements committee, the joint central conference;

    (e) in relation to the election of members of a central committee by a central conference and casual vacancies among those members, that central conference.

SCHEDULE 4
DELEGATES TO CENTRAL CONFERENCES

PART I
MEN

1.—(1) Except in the metropolitan police force, there shall be elected to the appropriate central conference under Regulation 9(2), by each inspectors', sergeants' and constables' branch board, two delegates together with a further delegate for each five hundred men included in the authorised establishment.

(2) In this paragraph the reference to the authorised establishment for a police force is a reference to the number of men of all ranks included in the authorised establishment.

2. In the metropolitan police force the inspectors', sergeants' and constables' branch boards shall, under Regulation 9(2), each elect to the appropriate central conference—

    (a) two delegates from each division;

    (b) five delegates from the criminal investigation department, and

    (c) six delegates from A, B and D departments.

PART II
WOMEN

1. The number of delegates to be elected, under Regulation 9(3), by women members of inspectors', sergeants' or constables' branch boards in a region to the appropriate central conference shall be determined by reference to the aggregate authorised establishment for the police forces in the region, as hereafter in this Part of this Schedule provided.

2. Where the aggregate authorised establishment is less than two hundred women, there shall be one delegate.

3. Where the aggregate authorised establishment is two hundred women or more, there shall be two delegates with a further delegate for each five hundred women included in the aggregate authorised establishment.

4. In this Part of this Schedule a reference to the authorised establishment for a police force is a reference to the number of women of all ranks included in the authorised establishment.

SCHEDULE 5
REGIONS

For the purposes of these Regulations there shall be the following seven regions:—

    (a) No. 1 (North-West) Region, comprising the combined police areas known as the Cheshire, Cumbria, Lancashire, Liverpool and Bootle and Manchester and Salford police areas;

    (b) No. 2 (North-East) Region, comprising the county boroughs of Bradford, Kingston-upon-Hull, Leeds and Teesside and the combined police areas known as the Durham, Northumberland, Sheffield and Rotherham, York and North-East Yorkshire and West Yorkshire police areas;

    (c) No. 3 (Midlands) Region, comprising the county borough of Birmingham and the combined police areas known as the Staffordshire County and Stoke-on-Trent, Warwickshire and Coventry, West Mercia and West Midlands police areas;

    (d) No. 4 (Eastern) Region, comprising the combined police areas known as the Derby county and borough, Leicester and Rutland, Lincolnshire, Northampton and County, Mid-Anglia and Suffolk police areas, the Norfolk joint police area and the Nottinghamshire combined police area;

    (e) No. 5 (South-East) Region, comprising the counties of Hertfordshire and Surrey and the combined police areas known as the Bedfordshire and Luton, Hampshire, Kent, Sussex and Thames Valley police areas and the Essex and Southend-on-Sea joint police area;

    (f) No. 6 (South-West) Region, comprising the counties of Gloucestershire and Wiltshire, the county borough of Bristol and the combined police areas known as the Devon and Cornwall, Dorset and Bournemouth and Somerset and Bath police areas.

    (g) No. 7 (Wales) Region, comprising the combined police areas known as the Dyfed-Powys, Gwent, Gwynedd and South Wales police areas.

EXPLANATORY NOTE

(This Note is not part of the Regulations.)

These Regulations consolidate, with amendments, the Regulations set out in Schedule 1, that is to say the Police Federation Regulations 1965 and the Regulations amending those Regulations.

The principal changes are described below.

Regulation 5 permits the holding of branch meetings on a divisional basis.

Regulation 8 provides for liaison committees.

Regulation 11 provides for a conferences arrangements committee.

Regulations 16(4) and 17(1) provide for the holding of Federation funds by joint branch boards and by the joint central committee and Regulations 18 and 20 apply to funds so held.

For the purposes of the Regulations Schedule 5 establishes seven regions; these replace the eight districts provided for in the Regulations revoked.

STATUTORY INSTRUMENTS

1969 No. 1791

CUSTOMS AND EXCISE

The Import Duties (General) (No. 5) Order 1969

Made - - - -	15*th December* 1969
Laid before the House of Commons - -	18*th December* 1969
Coming into Operation -	1*st January* 1970

The Lords Commissioners of Her Majesty's Treasury, by virtue of the powers conferred on them by sections 1, 2 and 13 of the Import Duties Act 1958(a), and of all other powers enabling them in that behalf, on the recommendation of the Board of Trade hereby make the following Order:—

1.—(1) This Order may be cited as the Import Duties (General) (No. 5) Order 1969.

(2) The Interpretation Act 1889(b) shall apply for the interpretation of this Order as it applies for the interpretation of an Act of Parliament.

(3) This Order shall come into operation on 1st January 1970.

2. In Schedule 1 to the Import Duties (General) (No. 3) Order 1969(c) (which Schedule by reference to the Customs Tariff 1959 sets out the import duties chargeable under the Import Duties Act 1958), in heading 03.01 (fish, fresh (live or dead), chilled or frozen) the rate of duty shown in column 3 against sub-heading (C)(1) and prefixed by the letter " E " shall be omitted.

E. G. Perry,
Joseph Harper,

Two of the Lords Commissioners
of Her Majesty's Treasury

15th December 1969

EXPLANATORY NOTE
(*This Note is not part of the Order*)

This Order removes the import duty on imports from the European Free Trade Area of chilled or frozen fish fillets and of certain chilled or frozen portions prepared by cutting blocks of fillets.

(a) 1958 c. 6.   (b) 1889 c. 63.   (c) S.I. 1969/1413 (1969 III, p. 4150).

STATUTORY INSTRUMENTS

1969 No. 1796 (C.57) (S.156)

POLICE
The Police (Scotland) Act 1967 (Commencement) Order 1969

Made - - - -	11*th December* 1969
Laid before Parliament	23*rd December* 1969
Coming into Operation	1*st January* 1970

In exercise of the powers conferred on me by section 53(3) of the Police (Scotland) Act 1967(a), I hereby make the following order:—

1. This Order may be cited as the Police (Scotland) Act 1967 (Commencement) Order 1969 and shall come into operation on 1st January 1970.

2. Section 39 of the Police (Scotland) Act 1967 shall come into operation on 1st January 1970.

William Ross,
One of Her Majesty's Principal Secretaries of State.

St. Andrew's House,
Edinburgh.
11th December 1969.

EXPLANATORY NOTE
(*This Note is not part of the Order.*)

This Order brings into force on 1st January 1970 section 39 of the Police (Scotland) Act 1967 which relates to liability for the wrongful acts of constables and is the only provision of the said Act which is not already in operation.

(a) 1967 c. 77.

STATUTORY INSTRUMENTS

1969 No. 1797

CUSTOMS AND EXCISE

The European Free Trade Association (Drawback) (Amendment) Regulations 1969

Made - - -	*16th December* 1969
Laid before the House of Commons	*23rd December* 1969
Coming into Operation	*1st January* 1970

The Board of Trade, in pursuance of the powers conferred upon them by section 2 of the European Free Trade Association Act 1960(a), hereby made the following Regulations :—

1. These Regulations may be cited as the European Free Trade Association (Drawback) (Amendment) Regulations 1969 and shall come into operation on 1st January 1970.

2. The European Free Trade Association (Drawback) Regulations 1966(b), as amended (c), shall have effect as if for the reference in Regulation 3(*h*) to £30 there were substituted a reference to £50.

3. The European Free Trade Association (Drawback) (Amendment) Regulations 1968(c) are hereby revoked.

Gwyneth Dunwoody,
Parliamentary Secretary to
16th December 1969. the Board of Trade.

EXPLANATORY NOTE

(This Note is not part of the Regulations.)

These Regulations further amend the European Free Trade Association (Drawback) Regulations 1966.

The 1966 Regulations generally debar goods of E.F.T.A. origin from E.F.T.A. tariff treatment on importation into the United Kingdom if they have been the subject of a claim for drawback or equivalent relief on exportation from the E.F.T.A. country in which they underwent their last process of production. Regulation 3(*h*) provides an exception where the f.o.b. value of the goods does not exceed a specified amount. These Regulations increase that amount from £30 to £50.

(a) 1960 c. 19. (b) S.I. 1966/1481 (1966 III, p. 4088).
(c) The relevant amending Regulations are S.I. 1968/100 (1968 I, p. 298).

STATUTORY INSTRUMENTS

1969 No. 1798

CLEAN AIR

The Smoke Control Areas (Authorised Fuels) Regulations 1969

Made - - - -	16*th December* 1969
Laid before Parliament	23*rd December* 1969
Coming into Operation	31*st December* 1969

The Minister of Housing and Local Government, in exercise of the powers conferred on him by section 34(1) of the Clean Air Act 1956(**a**), and of all other powers enabling him in that behalf, hereby makes the following regulations: —

Title and commencement

1. These regulations may be cited as the Smoke Control Areas (Authorised Fuels) Regulations 1969 and shall come into operation on 31st December 1969.

Interpretation

2. The Interpretation Act 1889(**b**) shall apply for the interpretation of these regulations as it applies for an Act of Parliament.

Authorised fuels for the purposes of the Clean Air Act 1956

3. The following fuels are hereby declared to be authorised fuels for the purposes of the Clean Air Act 1956: —

" Coziglo " nuts manufactured by British Benzol and Coal Distillation Limited from a blend of Thoresby, Bedwas and anthracite fuels by a high temperature carbonisation process.

" Rexco Ovoids " manufactured by the National Carbonising Company Limited having Rexco breeze as a main constituent which has been subjected to a heating process.

Given under the official seal of the Minister of Housing and Local Government on 16th December 1969.

(L.S.)

Anthony Greenwood,
Minister of Housing and
Local Government.

EXPLANATORY NOTE

(This Note is not part of the Regulations.)

Section 11 of the Clean Air Act 1956 makes it an offence to emit smoke from a chimney of a building within a smoke control area unless it can be shown that the emission of smoke was not caused by the use of any fuel other than an authorised fuel. These Regulations declare the fuels mentioned in Regulation 3 to be authorised fuels for the purposes of the Act.

(**a**) 1956 c. 52.   (**b**) 1889 c. 63.

STATUTORY INSTRUMENTS

1969 No. 1799

ROAD TRAFFIC

The Goods Vehicles (Carriers' and Operators' Licences) (Fees) Regulations 1969

Made - - -	*15th December* 1969
Laid before Parliament	*23rd December* 1969
Coming into Operation	*31st December* 1969

The Minister of Transport in exercise of his powers under sections 182 and 190 of the Road Traffic Act 1960(a) as amended by section 22 of the Road Traffic Act 1962(b), sections 89(1) and 91(1) of the Transport Act 1968(c), and of all other enabling powers, and after consultation with representative organisations in accordance with the provisions of section 260(2) of the said Act of 1960 and section 91(8) of the said Act of 1968, hereby makes the following Regulations:—

Commencement and citation

1. These Regulations shall come into operation on the 31st December 1969 and may be cited as the Goods Vehicles (Carriers' and Operators' Licences) (Fees) Regulations 1969.

Interpretation

2.—(1) In these Regulations the expression "the Regulations of 1960" means the Goods Vehicles (Licences and Prohibitions) Regulations 1960(d), as amended (e).

(2) The Interpretation Act 1889(f) shall apply for the interpretation of these Regulations as it applies for the interpretation of an Act of Parliament.

Amendment of the Goods Vehicles (Licences and Prohibitions) Regulations 1960

3. The Regulations of 1960 shall have effect as if Regulation 13 (*Fees*) were omitted, and as if the reference in Regulation 14 thereof to the said Regulation 13 were a reference to Regulation 4 of these Regulations.

Fees for and in respect of carriers' licences

4.—(1) Subject to the provisions of this Regulation, fees for carriers' licences, except licences granted for a shortened currency period under Regulation 25 of the Regulations of 1960, shall be the following in respect of each vehicle authorised:

(a) 1960 c. 16.
(b) 1962 c. 59.
(c) 1968 c. 73.
(d) S.I. 1960/1505(1960 III, p. 3020).
(e) S.I. 1969/1638 (1969 III, p. 5159).
(f) 1889 c. 63.

			Licences coming into force before the 1st March 1970 £ s. d.	Licences coming into force on or after the 1st March 1970 £ s. d.
A licence	...	...	10 0 0	2 10 0
B licence	...	...	5 0 0	1 0 0
C licence	...	...	1 10 0	1 0 0

(2) Where vehicles on hire or loan are authorised to be used under a carrier's licence the amount of the fee shall be reckoned on the basis of the maximum number of such vehicles specified in the licence.

(3) Where a carrier's licence authorises the use of vehicles to be acquired by the licensee an extra fee shall be paid when a vehicle is acquired which shall be computed at the following rate for each such vehicle and shall be calculated as from the date on which the identity certificate for that vehicle is issued for each period of 6 months (or part of such period) of the unexpired period of a licence coming into force—

    (a) before the 1st March 1970

				£	s.	d.
(i) in the case of an A licence ...	...	...		1	0	0
(ii) in the case of a B licence ...	...	...		1	5	0

    (b) on or after the 1st March 1970 in the case of an A or B licence, 5s.

(4) Where on an application to which the provisions of paragraph (c) of section 173(1) of the Act apply the licensing authority grants a carrier's licence to expire not later than an existing licence under which the vehicles concerned are authorised to be used for the purpose of a business which the applicant has acquired or intends to acquire, the fee to be paid shall be calculated as from the date on which the first-mentioned licence is expressed to have effect and shall be that for a licence for the full currency period less an amount computed at the following rate in respect of each complete period of 6 months by which the currency period is shortened in respect of each vehicle authorised :—

			Licences coming into force before the 1st March 1970 £ s. d.	Licences coming into force on or after the 1st March 1970 £ s. d.
A licence	...	...	1 0 0	0 5 0
B licence	...	...	1 5 0	0 5 0

(5) On the variation of an A, B or C licence being a variation which has the effect of reducing the total number of vehicles authorised by the licence (including any vehicle intended to be acquired by the holder of the licence and any vehicle to the use of which section 164 of the Act does not apply by virtue of section 93(2) of the Transport Act 1968, but not including any vehicle to the use of which section 164 of the Act does not apply by virtue of section 93(1) of the Transport Act 1968) the licensing authority shall, if an application in writing is made to him in that behalf by the holder of the licence within 3 months of the licence being so varied, refund to the holder of the licence an amount computed at the following rate in respect of each vehicle by which the total number of vehicles is reduced in respect of each complete period of one year of the period of the currency of the licence which is unexpired at the date of the variation :—

			Licences coming into force before the 1st March 1970			Licences coming into force on or after the 1st March 1970		
			£	s.	d.	£	s.	d.
A licence	...	...	2	0	0	0	10	0
B licence	...	...	2	10	0	0	10	0
C licence	...	...	0	6	0	0	4	0

Provided that no refund shall be made in respect of vehicles for which no fee has been paid or in the case of a C licence in respect of any period before the 1st March 1970.

(6) Except in the case of a licence which authorises the use of a vehicle brought temporarily into Great Britain no carrier's licence shall be granted until the applicant shall have paid to the licensing authority the appropriate fee in respect thereof.

(7) Except in the case of a licence which authorises the use of a vehicle brought temporarily into Great Britain no identity certificate shall be issued in respect of any vehicle until the applicant shall have paid to the licensing authority any fee in respect of the carrier's licence under which such vehicle is authorised.

(8) In this Regulation, unless the context otherwise requires, "carrier's licence" has the same meaning as the word "licence" in the Regulations of 1960, except that it does not include a short-term licence, and any other expression which is also used in those Regulations has the same meaning as in those Regulations.

Fees for and in respect of operators' licences

5.—(1) Whenever a motor vehicle is specified in an operator's licence the holder of the licence shall pay a fee at the rate of—

(a) £4 in respect of each motor vehicle so specified for each whole year of the unexpired term of the licence, calculated from the date when the vehicle is so specified, and

(b) one-twelfth of the said amount in respect of each motor vehicle so specified for each whole month (any part of a month counting as a whole month for this purpose) in any period less than a whole year which remains in the unexpired term of the licence when the whole years have been deducted.

(2) Whenever the number of motor vehicles specified in an operator's licence is reduced the licensing authority shall, if an application in writing is made to him in that behalf by the holder of the licence within 3 months of the reduction, refund to the holder of the licence an amount at the rate specified in paragraph (1)(b) of this Regulation in respect of each vehicle by which the total number of specified vehicles is reduced for each whole month of the unexpired term of the licence calculated from the date of the reduction :
Provided that :—

(i) no refund shall be made in respect of any period of less than 3 months ; and

(ii) for the purposes of this paragraph any part of a month at the end of such term ending on the 24th March in any year, in the case of a licence which expires on the 24th March in that year, shall count as a whole month.

(3) (*a*) No identity disc shall be issued in respect of any vehicle until the applicant shall have paid to the licensing authority any fee for specifying the vehicle in the operator's licence in which such vehicle is specified.

(*b*) No refund shall be paid under this Regulation in respect of any vehicle until the applicant shall have returned to the licensing authority the identity disc or any copy thereof issued in respect of that vehicle.

(4) On and after the day appointed for the beginning of the transitional period for the purposes of the Decimal Currency Act 1969(**a**) if any fee or refund payable under this Regulation is made in the new currency as defined in section 16(1) of that Act any remaining amount of such fee or refund of less than one new penny shall be disregarded.

(5) In this Regulation, unless the context otherwise requires, —
"month" means a calendar month running from any date ;
"operator's licence" means an operator's licence within the meaning of Part V of the Transport Act 1968 other than an interim licence granted under section 67(5) of that Act ;
"year" means a calendar year running from any date ;
and any expression not defined above which is also used in the Goods Vehicles (Operators' Licences) Regulations 1969 has the same meaning as in those Regulations.

Given under the Official Seal of the Minister of Transport the 15th December 1969.

(L.S.)   *Fred Mulley*,
                 Minister of Transport.

EXPLANATORY NOTE

(*This Note is not part of the Regulations.*)

These Regulations prescribe new fees payable for the grant of a carrier's licence to use a goods vehicle for hire or reward or for business on own account under Part IV of the Road Traffic Act 1960, and make new provision for the refund of such fees in certain circumstances. (Regulation 4)

These Regulations also prescribe the fees payable for the grant or variation of an operator's licence to use a goods vehicle for hire or reward or for business on own account under Part V of the Transport Act 1968, and for the refund of such fees in certain circumstances. (Regulation 5)

(a) 1969 c. 19.

STATUTORY INSTRUMENTS

1969 No. 1800

ROAD TRAFFIC

The Road Vehicles (Registration and Licensing) (Amendment) (No. 3) Regulations 1969

Made - - -	*12th December* 1969
Laid before Parliament	*31st December* 1969
Coming into Operation	*1st January* 1970

The Minister of Transport in exercise of his powers under subsections (1) to (5) of section 12 of the Vehicles (Excise) Act 1962(**a**), as substituted by section 6(2) of the Finance Act 1969(**b**), under section 16(2) of the said Act of 1962 as amended by paragraph 3 in Part II of Schedule 12 to the said Act of 1969, under section 23 of the said Act of 1962, and of all other enabling powers, hereby makes the following Regulations :—

1.—(1) These Regulations shall come into operation on the 1st January 1970 and may be cited as the Road Vehicles (Registration and Licensing) (Amendment) (No. 3) Regulations 1969.

(2) The Interpretation Act 1889(**c**) shall apply for the interpretation of these Regulations as it applies for the interpretation of an Act of Parliament.

2. The Road Vehicles (Registration and Licensing) Regulations 1964(**d**), as amended (**e**), shall have effect as though—

(1) in Regulation 3(1)—

(*a*) in the definition of "prescribed" for the words "the Road Vehicles (Excise) (Prescribed Particulars) Regulations 1957(**f**)" there were substituted the words "the Road Vehicles (Excise) (Prescribed Particulars) Regulations 1966(**g**), as amended by the Road Vehicles (Excise) (Prescribed Particulars) (Amendment) Regulations 1969(**h**)";

(*b*) in the definition of "trade plates" for the words "in Regulation 34" there were substituted the words "in Regulation 35";

(2) in Part V, as substituted by the Road Vehicles (Registration and Licensing) (Amendment) (No. 2) Regulations 1969, the Regulation in that Part numbered "43" were renumbered "42A."

Given under the Official Seal of the Minister of Transport the 12th December 1969.

(L.S.)

Fred Mulley,
Minister of Transport.

(**a**) 1962 c. 13.   (**b**) 1969 c. 32.
(**c**) 1889 c. 63.   (**d**) S.I. 1964/1178 (1964 II, p. 2722).
(**e**) The relevant amending instrument is S.I. 1969/1589 (1969 III, p. 5066).
(**f**) S.I. 1957/702 (1957 II, p. 2128).   (**g**) S.I. 1966/224 (1966 I, p. 435).
(**h**) S.I. 1969/1782(1969 III, p. 5579)

EXPLANATORY NOTE

(This Note is not part of the Regulations.)

These Regulations further amend the Road Vehicles (Registration and Licensing) Regulations 1964 by making certain minor amendments of a drafting nature.

STATUTORY INSTRUMENTS

1969 No. 1806

LOCAL GOVERNMENT, ENGLAND AND WALES

The Rate Support Grant (Increase) Order 1969

Made - - -		*21st November* 1969
Laid before the House of Commons		*26th November* 1969
Coming into Operation		*16th December* 1969

The Minister of Housing and Local Government, with the consent of the Treasury and after consultation with the associations of local authorities appearing to him to be concerned and with the local authority with whom consultation appeared to him to be desirable, in exercise of his powers under section 3 of the Local Government Act 1966(a) and of all other powers enabling him in that behalf, hereby makes the following order :—

Title, commencement and interpretation

1.—(1) This order may be cited as the Rate Support Grant (Increase) Order 1969 and shall come into operation on the day following the day on which it is approved by a resolution of the Commons House of Parliament.

(2) In this order any reference to a numbered section shall be construed as a reference to the section bearing that number in the Local Government Act 1966 and any reference to a numbered paragraph shall be construed as a reference to the paragraph bearing that number in Part I of Schedule 1 to that Act.

Amendment of Rate Support Grant Order 1968

2. For the items set out in column (2) of the following table, prescribed by the Rate Support Grant Order 1968(b) for the purposes of rate support grants for the years 1969-70 and 1970-71 in respect of the matters indicated in column (1), there shall be substituted the items specified in column (3).

(a) 1966 c. 42.　　　　　　　　　　(b) S.I. 1968/1956 (1968 III, p. 5356).

Relevant matter (1)	Existing item (2)	Substituted item (3)
	£	£
For the year 1969–70— As the aggregate amount of the rate support grants—	1,528,000,000	1,612,000,000
As the amount of the needs element—	1,230,000,000	1,302,000,000
As the amount of the resources element—	225,000,000	237,000,000
For the year 1970–71—		
As the aggregate amount of the rate support grants—	1,633,000,000	1,744,000,000
As the amount of the needs element—	1,297,000,000	1,394,000.000
As the amount of the resources element—	236,000,000	250,000,000
In relation to the basic payment under paragraph 2		
As the sum to be multiplied by the population—		
For the year 1969–70:	14.70	15.59
For the year 1970–71:	15.03	16.24
As the sum to be multiplied by the estimated number of persons under 15 years of age in the population—		
For the year 1969–70:	1.15	1.22
For the year 1970–71:	1.17	1.26
In relation to the supplementary payment under paragraph 3		
As the sum to be multiplied by the estimated number of persons under 5 years of age in the population—		
For the year 1969–70:	1.04	1.10
For the year 1970–71:	1.05	1.13
In relation to the supplementary payment under paragraph 4		
As the sum to be multiplied by the estimated number of persons over 65 years of age in the population—		
For the year 1969–70:	1.04	1.10
For the year 1970–71:	1.05	1.13

Relevant matter (1)	Existing item (2)	Substituted item (3)
In relation to the supplementary payment under paragraph 5	£	£
As the sum to be multiplied by the excess and by the population to determine the amount of the payment—		
For the year 1969–70:	0.079	0.083
For the year 1970–71:	0.081	0.087
In relation to the supplementary payment under paragraph 8		
As the sum by which the road-mileage of the area of the authority (excluding trunk roads) is to be multiplied—		
For the year 1969–70:	262	277
For the year 1970–71:	268	289
As the sum by which the road-mileage of the roads in the area of the authority classified as principal roads under section 27 (hereinafter called "the prescribed sum") is to be multiplied—		
For the year 1969–70:	1,281	1,354
For the year 1970–71:	1,311	1,414
As the sum by which the prescribed sum is to be reduced for each 100 persons in the short-fall—		
For the year 1969–70:	24.75	26.15
For the year 1970–71:	25.35	27.35
As the sum by which the prescribed sum is to be increased for each 100 persons in the excess—		
For the year 1969–70:	32.28	34.14
For the year 1970–71:	33.04	35.63
As the sum below which the prescribed sum shall not be reduced—		
For the year 1969–70:	786	831
For the year 1970–71:	804	867

Given under the official seal of the Minister of Housing and Local Government on 21st November 1969.

(L.S.)   *Anthony Greenwood,*

                              Minister of Housing and Local
                                     Government.

We consent to this Order.

                               Neil McBride,

                              Walter Harrison,

                    Two of the Lords Commissioners of
                        Her Majesty's Treasury.
21st November 1969.

EXPLANATORY NOTE

(This Note is not part of the Order.)

This Order came into operation on 16th December 1969 and (under the powers of section 3(1) of the Local Government Act 1966) relates to the financial years 1969-70 and 1970-71. It—

(*a*) increases the aggregate amounts of the rate support grants payable under Part I of the Local Government Act 1966 to councils of counties, county boroughs and county districts in England and Wales, the Greater London Council, the councils of London Boroughs, the Common Council of the City of London and the Council of the Isles of Scilly ;

(*b*) increases two of the constituent elements of the rate support grants, namely the needs element (which is not payable to councils of county districts or, subject to the provision to the contrary by regulations under the Act, to the Greater London Council) and the resources element ; and

(*c*) varies certain of the matters prescribed by the Rate Support Grant Order 1968 in relation to the distribution of the needs element.

STATUTORY INSTRUMENTS

1969 No. 1807 (S.157)

SHERIFF COURT, SCOTLAND

Act of Sederunt (Sheriff Court Witnesses' Fees) 1969

Made - - -		12*th December* 1969
Laid before Parliament		2*nd January* 1970
Coming into Operation		6*th January* 1970

The Lords of Council and Session, under and by virtue of the powers conferred upon them by section 40 of the Sheriff Courts (Scotland) Act 1907(**a**) as amended by section 39 of, and the Schedule to, the Administration of Justice (Scotland) Act 1933(**b**) and of all other powers competent to them in that behalf, do hereby enact and declare as follows :—

1. The Table of Witnesses' Fees, contained in Chapter IV of the Act of Sederunt of 7th May 1935(**c**) as substituted by the Act of Sederunt (Sheriff Court Witnesses' Fees) 1953(**d**) shall be amended by the deletion of section (*a*) and the following words of section (*b*) namely "(*b*) Witnesses whose attendance entails loss of wages or payment of substitutes" ; and by the substitution of the following :—

"(*a*) Professional persons, persons in managerial or like executive positions, and officers in H.M. Services or in the Mercantile Marine, per day

Such sum not exceeding £15 15/- as the Auditor may determine, plus, in the case of a witness in the medical profession, such expenses (if any) as the Auditor may determine to have been necessarily incurred by the witness in employing a substitute or substitutes.

"(*b*) Witnesses whose attendance entails loss of wages or payment of substitutes (except the payment of a substitute to a witness to whom a fee is allowed under section (*a*) hereof)."

2. This Act of Sederunt may be cited as the Act of Sederunt (Sheriff Court Witnesses' Fees) 1969, and shall come into operation on 6th January 1970.

And the Lords appoint this Act of Sederunt to be inserted in the Books of Sederunt.

J. L. Clyde,
I.P.D.

Edinburgh,
12th December 1969.

EXPLANATORY NOTE

(This Note is not part of the Act of Sederunt.)

This Act of Sederunt revises the Table of Witnesses' Fees in the Sheriff Court so far as it relates to professional and certain other persons.

(**a**) 1907 c. 51. (**b**) 1933 c. 41.
(**c**) S.R. & O. 1935/488 (Rev. XX, p. 880: 1935 p. 1588).
(**d**) S.I. 1953/1832 (1953 II, p. 1935).

STATUTORY INSTRUMENTS

1969 No. 1811

REGISTRATION OF BIRTHS, DEATHS, MARRIAGES, ETC.

ENGLAND AND WALES

The Registration of Births, Deaths and Marriages (Amendment) Regulations 1969

Made - - - *17th December* 1969

Coming into Operation *1st January* 1970

The Registrar General in exercise of his powers under section 20 of the Registration Service Act 1953(**a**), section 9, section 10 (as amended by section 27 of the Family Law Reform Act 1969(**b**)), section 39 of the Births and Deaths Registration Act 1953(**c**), section 2 of the Welsh Language Act 1967(**d**) and all other powers enabling him in that behalf, with the approval of the Secretary of State for Social Services hereby makes the following regulations :—

PART I

RE-REGISTRATION OF BIRTHS

Title and commencement

1.—(1) These regulations may be cited as the Registration of Births, Deaths and Marriages (Amendment) Regulations 1969 and shall come into operation on 1st January 1970.

(2) These regulations and the Registration of Births, Deaths and Marriages Regulations 1968(**e**) shall be construed as one and may be cited together as the Registration of Births, Deaths and Marriages Regulations 1968 and 1969.

Interpretation

2.—(1) The Interpretation Act 1889(**f**) shall apply to the interpretation of these regulations as it applies to the interpretation of an Act of Parliament.

(2) In these regulations—

"the principal regulations" means the Registration of Births, Deaths and Marriages Regulations 1968 ;

"the Act of 1969" means the Family Law Reform Act 1969.

Officers before whom written statements may be made

3. The officer before whom a written statement for the purposes of section 27(4) of the Act of 1969 may be made shall be—

(*a*) in a case where not more than 3 months have elapsed since the date of the birth of the child, any registrar of births and deaths other than the registrar of births and deaths for the sub-district in which the birth occurred ; or

(*b*) in any other case, any superintendent registrar.

(**a**) 1953 c. 37. (**b**) 1969 c. 46.
(**c**) 1953 c. 20. (**d**) 1967 c. 66.
(**e**) S.I. 1968/2049 (1968 III, p. 5522). (**f**) 1889 c. 63.

Re-registration on joint information of parents

4. Where under section 27(2)(*a*) of the Act of 1969 the Registrar General authorises the re-registration of the birth of an illegitimate child at the joint request of the mother and the person acknowledging himself to be the father of the child—

(*a*) if the parents attend, pursuant to the authority of the Registrar General, before the registrar for the sub-district in which the birth occurred, within 3 months after the date of the birth, to give information for the re-registration of the birth, the registrar shall—

    (i) ascertain from the parents the particulars to be registered concerning the birth and enter them in spaces 1 to 13 in the register in the presence of the parents in accordance with the authority of the Registrar General ;

    (ii) call upon the parents to verify the particulars entered and to sign the entry in space 14 ;

    (iii) enter the date on which the entry was made and add the words "On the authority of the Registrar General" ;

    (iv) sign the entry in space 16 and add his official description.

(*b*) if the parents attend, pursuant to the authority of the Registrar General, within 3 months after the date of the birth before any other registrar, or after 3 months have elapsed since the date of the birth, before any superintendent registrar, that officer shall—

    (i) call upon the parents to make and sign a declaration in the form of Schedule 1 ;

    (ii) attest the declaration and deliver it to the registrar of the sub-district in which the birth occurred.

(*c*) upon receiving the authority of the Registrar General to re-register a birth under paragraph (*b*) of this regulation and the declaration made in pursuance thereof, the registrar for the sub-district in which the birth occurred shall—

    (i) copy the particulars recorded in the spaces of the declaration into the corresponding spaces of the entry and shall call upon the parents to sign the entry in space 14 of the register or, if they are not present, shall enter in space 14 the names of the parents in the form in which they are signed in the declaration and shall add the words "by declaration dated......" inserting the date on which the declaration was made and signed ;

    (ii) enter the date on which the entry was made and add the words "On the authority of the Registrar General" ;

    (iii) if not more than 3 months have elapsed since the date of birth of the child, sign the entry in space 16 of the register and add his official description ;

    (iv) if more than 3 months have elapsed since the date of birth of the child, make the entry in the presence of the superintendent registrar of the district in which the birth occurred and the superintendent registrar and the registrar shall sign the entry and add their official descriptions.

Re-registration on mother's information and father's statutory declaration

5.—(1) Where under section 27(2)(*b*) of the Act of 1969 the Registrar General authorises the re-registration of the birth of an illegitimate child at the request of the mother of the child—

   (*a*) a declaration in the form of Schedule 2 shall be made by the mother before one of the officers specified in regulation 3 or, if not more than 3 months have elapsed since the date of the birth of the child, before the registrar of the sub-district in which the birth occurred ;

   (*b*) the declaration shall be attested by the officer before whom it was made ;

   (*c*) where the declaration is attested by a superintendent registrar, or a registrar other than the registrar for the sub-district in which the birth occurred, the officer who attested it shall deliver it to that registrar together with the authority of the Registrar General and a statutory declaration made by the person who is to be shown in the register as the father, acknowledging himself to be the father of the child.

(2) Upon receiving the documents specified in the foregoing sub-paragraph the registrar for the sub-district in which the birth occurred shall—

   (*a*) copy the particulars recorded in the spaces of the declaration made by the mother into the corresponding spaces in the register ;

   (*b*) call upon the mother to verify the particulars as entered and to sign the entry in space 14 or, if she is not present, shall enter her name in space 14 in the form in which it is signed in the declaration made by her and add the words "by declaration dated........." inserting the date on which her declaration was made and signed ;

   (*c*) add in space 14 the words "Statutory declaration made by......... on ...." inserting the full name of the person acknowledging himself to be the father and the date on which the statutory declaration was made and signed by him ;

   (*d*) enter the date on which the entry was made and add the words "On the authority of the Registrar General" ;

   (*e*) if not more than 3 months have elapsed since the date of birth of the child, sign the entry in space 16 and add his official description ;

   (*f*) if more than 3 months have elapsed since the date of the birth, make the entry in the presence of the superintendent registrar of the district in which the birth occurred and the superintendent registrar and registrar shall sign the entry and add their official descriptions.

Noting of entries

6. The superintendent registrar or registrar having custody of the register in which the birth was previously registered shall, when so directed by the Registrar General, note the previous entry relating to the birth with the words "Re-registered under section 27 of the Family Law Reform Act 1969 on......" inserting the date of the re-registration and make a certified copy of that entry, including a copy of the note, and send the copy to the Registrar General.

Welsh version

7.—(1) Where a regulation specified in column (1) of Schedule 5 to these regulations requires the use of a form of words set out in column (2), the form of words set out opposite thereto in column (3) shall be used in any Welsh version.

(2) In relation to a birth registered or re-registered in Wales or Monmouthshire references in these regulations to Schedules 1 and 2 shall have effect as if they were references to Schedules 3 and 4 respectively.

PART II

AMENDMENT OF THE PRINCIPAL REGULATIONS

Signatures

8. There shall be substituted for regulation 20(2) of the principal regulations (signatures), the following paragraph :—

"(2) If, in pursuance of section 10 of the Act as amended, an entry has been made of the name of the person acknowledging himself to be the father, and that person is present, the registrar shall call first upon that person and then upon the mother to sign the entry ; if that person is not present and there is produced to the registrar a statutory declaration and declaration in pursuance of the said section 10, the registrar shall call upon the mother to sign the entry in space 14, and shall add after her signature the words "Statutory declaration made by ...... on ......" inserting the full name of the person acknowledging himself to be the father and the date on which the statutory declaration was made and signed by him".

Declarations

9.—(1) There shall be substituted for regulation 24(6)(*b*) of the principal regulations (making of declaration under section 9 of the Act), the following paragraph—

"(*b*) with respect to space 14 (signature of informant)—

(i) any name of a declarant in a declaration required by this sub-paragraph to be written in space 14 shall be written in the form in which it is signed by the declarant in the declaration ;

(ii) if the declaration was made by one informant only the registrar shall write the name of that informant and shall add the words "by declaration dated ......" inserting the date on which the declaration was made and signed ;

(iii) if the declaration was made by the father and mother of an illegitimate child, the registrar shall write the names of the father and mother and shall add the words "by declaration dated ......" inserting the date on which the declaration was made and signed ;

(iv) if the declaration was made in pursuance of section 10 of the Act by the mother and by a statutory declaration by the person acknowledging himself to be the father of the child, the registrar shall write the name of the mother and shall add the words "by declaration dated ......" inserting the date on which her declaration was made and signed and shall add the words "Statutory declaration made by ...... on ......" inserting the full name of the person acknowledging himself to be the father and the date on which the statutory declaration was made and signed.".

(2) Paragraphs (7) and (8) of regulation 24 and the references to those paragraphs in paragraph (6), shall be re-numbered (8) and (9) respectively and the following paragraph shall be inserted—

"(7) If not more than 3 months have elapsed since the date of the birth of the child, the registrar shall sign the entry and add his official description."

Signature in entry after declaration

10. In regulation 30(1) of the principal regulations there shall be inserted between the words "space 14" and "the words" the words "the name of the declarant in the form in which it is signed in the declaration and shall add".

SCHEDULE 1

DECLARATION FOR THE REGISTRATION OF A BIRTH

Regulation 4(*b*)(i)

Births and Deaths Registration Act 1953, *ss*.6 *and* 9
Family Law Reform Act 1969, *s*. 27

CHILD	
1. Date and place of birth	
2. Name and surname	3. Sex
FATHER	
4. Name and surname	
5. Place of birth	
6. Occupation	
MOTHER	
7. Name and surname	
8. Place of birth	
9. (*a*) Maiden surname	(*b*) Surname at marriage if different from maiden surname
10. Usual address (if different from place of child's birth)	
INFORMANT	
11. Name and surname (if not the mother or father)	12. Qualification
13. Usual address (if different from that in 10 above)	

For use (a) where the informants give information out of the sub-district of the child's birth or (b) in any case where more than 3 months have elapsed since the date of birth of the child.

We................, being qualified under the Births and Deaths Registration Act 1953 to give information for the registration of the birth of the above-named child, DO SOLEMNLY DECLARE that the particulars above are those which are required to be registered concerning such birth, according to the best of our knowledge and belief, and request that the name of the father of the child be entered in the register of births as in space 4 above.

Signatures.............................   .... Date.........................

Signed and declared by the above-named declarants in the presence of...

Registrar of Births and Deaths/Superintendent Registrar

..............................Sub-district   ....District

REGISTRATION OF BIRTHS, DEATHS
MARRIAGES, ETC.

SCHEDULE 2

DECLARATION FOR THE REGISTRATION OF A BIRTH

Regulations 5(1)(*a*),8.   *Family Law Reform Act* 1969, *s*. 27

CHILD	
1. Date and place of birth	
2. Name and surname	3. Sex
FATHER	
4. Name and surname	
5. Place of birth	
6. Occupation	
MOTHER	
7. Name and surname	
8. Place of birth	
9. (*a*) Maiden surname	(*b*) Surname at marriage if different from maiden surname
10. Usual address (if different from place of child's birth)	
INFORMANT	
11. Name and surname (if not the mother or father)	12. Qualification
13. Usual address (if different from that in 10 above)	

For use where the child is illegitimate and the mother produces a statutory declaration of paternity made by the father

I,..DO SOLEMNLY DECLARE that I am the mother of the child the particulars of whose birth are specified above and that the person named in space 4 above is the father of the child; and I request that his name should be recorded as such in the register of births.

Signature..   Date......................................

Signed and declared by the above-named declarant in the presence of.....................
................................Registrar of Births and Deaths/Superintendent Registrar

....Sub-district   ....District

SCHEDULE 3

DECLARATION FOR THE REGISTRATION OF A BIRTH

Regulation 7(2)   *Births and Deaths Registration Act* 1953
                                             Family Law Reform Act 1969

CHILD—Y PLENTYN

1. Date and place of birth

....

   Dyddiad a lle y ganwyd

---

2. Name and surname
   Enw a chyfenw

3. Sex
   ....
   Rhyw

FATHER—TAD

4. Name and surname
   Enw a chyfenw

---

5. Place of birth   Lle y ganwyd

---

6. Occupation   Gwaith

MOTHER—MAM

7. Name and surname
   Enw a chyfenw

---

8. Place of birth   Lle y ganwyd

---

9. (a) Maiden surname   (b) Surname at marriage if different
        Cyfenw morwynol   from maiden surname
                                       Cyfenw adeg priodi os yn wahanol
                                       i'r cyfenw morwynol

---

10. Usual address (if different from   Cyfeiriad arferol (os yn wahanol i le
    place of child's birth)   geni'r plentyn)

INFORMANT—HYSBYSYDD

11. Name and surname (if not the mother or father) | 12. Qualification
    Enw a chyfenw (os nad y tad neu'r fam)   ....
                                                      Cymhwyster

---

13. Usual address (if different from that in 10 above) Cyfeiriad arferol (os yn
                                                         wahanol i'r hyn sydd yn 10
                                                         uchod)

---

*For use (a) where the informants give information out of the sub-district of the
child's birth or (b) in any case where more than 3 months have elapsed since the
date of birth of the child.*

I'w ddefnyddio (a) lle bo'r sawl sy'n cyflwyno hysbysiaeth yn gwneud hynny y tu allan i'r is-ddosbarth lle ganwyd y plentyn, neu (b) mewn unrhyw achos pan fo mwy na thri mis wedi mynd heibio oddi ar ddyddiad geni y plentyn.

We ⎱
Yr ydym ni ⎰ ....

being qualified under the Births and Deaths Registration Act 1953 to give information for the registration of the birth of the above-named child, DO SOLEMNLY DECLARE that the particulars above are those which are required to be registered concerning such birth, according to the best of our knowledge and belief, and request that the name of the father of the child be entered in the register of births as in space 4 above.

gan ein bod yn gymwys dan Births and Deaths Registration Act 1953, i roi gwybodaeth ar gyfer cofrestru genedigaeth y plentyn a enwyd uchod YN CYHOEDDI YMA O DDIFRIF mai'r manylion uchod yw'r rhai y mae'n rhaid eu cofrestru ynglŷn â'r enedigaeth hon, hyd eithaf ein gwybodaeth a'n cred, a dymunwn i enw tad y plentyn gael ei gofnodi yn y gofrestr genedigaethau fel yn 4 uchod.

Signatures.. Date ....
Llofnodau.. Dyddiad..............................

Signed and declared by the above-named ⎫
declarants in the presence of   ⎪
Wedi ei lofnodi a'i ddatgan gan y personau ⎬ ....
a enwyd uchod fel datganwyr ac yng ngŵydd ⎭

Superintendent Registrar/Cofrestrydd Arolygol

Registrar of Births and Deaths/Cofrestrydd Genedigaethau a Marwolaethau
                              ⎰ Sub-district   ⎰ District
..............................⎱ Is-ddosbarth ....⎱ Dosbarth

SCHEDULE 4

DECLARATION FOR THE REGISTRATION OF A BIRTH

Regulation 7(2)   *Births and Deaths Registration Act* 1953
Family Law Reform Act 1969

CHILD—Y PLENTYN		
1. Date and place of birth		
Dyddiad a lle y ganwyd		
2. Name and surname Enw a chyfenw		3. Sex Rhyw

FATHER—TAD
4. Name and surname Enw a chyfenw
5. Place of birth   Lle y ganwyd
6. Occupation   Gwaith

MOTHER—MAM	
7. Name and surname Enw a chyfenw	
8. Place of birth Lle y ganwyd	

9. (*a*) Maiden surname
       Cyfenw morwynol
	(*b*) Surname at marriage if different
	      from maiden surname
	      Cyfenw adeg priodi os yn wahanol
	      i'r cyfenw morwynol

10. Usual address (if different from place of child's birth)	Cyfeiriad arferol (os yn wahanol i le geni'r plentyn.

INFORMANT—HYSBYSYDD	
11. Name and surname (if not the mother or father) Enw a chyfenw (os nad y tad neu'r fam)	12. Qualification Cymhwyster
13. Usual address (if different from that in 10 above)	Cyfeiriad arferol (os yn wahanol i'r hyn sydd yn 10 uchod)

*For use where the child is illegitimate and the mother produces a statutory declaration
of paternity made by the father*

I'w ddefnyddio lle bo'r plentyn yn anghyfreithlon a'r fam yn cyflwyno datganiad statudol a wnaied gan y tad i'r perwyl mai ef yw'r tad

I,
Yr wyf i, } ....

DO SOLEMNLY DECLARE that I am the mother of the child the particulars of whose birth are specified above and that the person named in space 4 above is the father of the child; and I request that his name should be recorded as such in the register of births.

YN CYHOEDDI YMA O DDIFRIF mai myfi yw mam y plentyn y rhoddwyd uchod fanylion am ei enedigaeth, ac mai'r person a enwyd yn 4 uchod yw tad y plentyn; a dymunaf i'w enw gael ei gofnodi felli yn y gofrestr genedigaethau.

Signature }
Llofnod } ....

Date ....
Dyddiad...............................

Signed and declared by the above-named }
declarant in the presence of }
Wedi ei lofnodi a'i ddatgan gan y person }
a enwyd uchod fel datganwr ac yng ngŵydd }

....
Superintendent Registrar/Cofrestrydd Arolygol

Registrar of Births and Deaths/
Cofrestrydd Genedigaethau a
Marwolaethau

.... { Sub-district
{ Is-ddosbarth

.... { District
{ Dosbarth

SCHEDULE 5

Regulation 7(1)

(1) Regulation	(2) Form of words required	(3) Welsh Version
Reg 4(a)(iii)	"On the authority of the Registrar General"	Dan awdurdod y Cofrestrydd Cyffredinol
Reg 4(c)(i)	"by declaration dated"	trwy ddatganiad dyddiedig y...............
Reg 4(c)(ii)	"On the authority of the Registrar General"	Dan awdurdod y Cofrestrydd Cyffredinol
Reg 5(2)(b)	"by declaration dated"	trwy ddatganiad dyddiedig y...............
Reg 5(2)(c)	"Statutory declaration made by......on......"	Datganiad Statudol a wnaethpwyd gan ....ar y......................
Reg 5(2)(d)	"On the authority of the Registrar General"	Dan awdurdod y Cofrestrydd Cyffredinol
Reg 6	"Re-registered under Section 27 of the Family Law Reform Act 1969 on............"	Ail-gofrestrwyd dan Adran 27 Family Law Reform Act 1969 ar y..................

Given under my hand on 17th December 1969.

Michael Reed,
Registrar General.

I approve.

R. H. S. Crossman,
Secretary of State for Social Services.

17th December 1969.

EXPLANATORY NOTE

(This Note is not part of the Regulations.)

Section 27 of the Family Law Reform Act 1969 makes further provision for the entry in a register of births of the name of the person acknowledging himself to be the father of an illegitimate child. Part I of these Regulations provides for the re-registration of the birth of such a child and prescribes the manner in which that person's name shall be entered. The forms to be used for this purpose are also prescribed (Schedules 1 to 4).

Part II, by amendment of the principal regulations, makes similar provisions for the initial registration of the birth of an illegitimate child.

Regulation 7 and Schedules 3, 4 and 5 provide for the entry of particulars in Welsh in registrations and re-registrations in Wales and Monmouthshire.

STATUTORY INSTRUMENTS

1969 No. 1812

AGRICULTURE

The Milk Marketing Scheme (Amendment) Order 1969

Made - - - 16*th December* 1969

Whereas the Milk Marketing Board duly submitted to the Minister of Agriculture, Fisheries and Food an amendment of the Milk Marketing Scheme 1933(a) as amended (b) which amendment is set forth in the Schedule hereto:

And Whereas the Minister of Agriculture, Fisheries and Food and the Secretary of State for Wales (hereinafter called "the Ministers") laid before each House of Parliament the amendment set forth in the said Schedule and the House of Commons resolved on 8th December 1969 and the House of Lords resolved on 18th November 1969 that it should be approved:

Now, therefore, the Ministers in pursuance of section 2 of the Agricultural Marketing Act 1958(c) and the First Schedule to that Act, as read with the Transfer of Functions (Wales) Order 1969(d), acting jointly, hereby make the following order:—

1. This order may be cited as the Milk Marketing Scheme (Amendment) Order 1969.

2. The amendment of the Milk Marketing Scheme 1933, as amended, which is set forth in the Schedule hereto is hereby approved and shall come into operation on 31st December 1969.

In Witness whereof the Official Seal of the Minister of Agriculture, Fisheries and Food is hereunto affixed on 15th December 1969.

(L.S.) *Cledwyn Hughes*,
Minister of Agriculture, Fisheries and Food.
Given under my hand on 16th December 1969.

George Thomas,
Secretary of State for Wales.

(a) S.R. & O. 1933/789 (Rev. I, p. 224: 1933, p. 20).
(b) S.R. & O. 1936/767, 1937/228, 744, 1939/324 (Rev. I, at p. 225: 1936 I, p. 22; 1937, pp. 1, 2; 1939 I, p. 30); S.I. 1950/1029, 1955/946 (1950 I, p. 43; 1955 I, p. 128).
(c) 1958 c. 47.
(d) S.I. 1969/388 (1969 I, p. 1070).

SCHEDULE

The Milk Marketing Scheme 1933, as amended, shall be further amended by substituting in paragraph 51(2) thereof for the words "one farthing" the words "one halfpenny".

EXPLANATORY NOTE

(This Note is not part of the Order.)

This order approves a further amendment to the Milk Marketing Scheme 1933, as amended.

The amendment, which is set out in the Schedule to the order, increases the maximum total sum which a registered producer may be required by prescriptive resolution to contribute under paragraph 51(2) of the Scheme to the fund administered and controlled by the Board from the equivalent of one farthing per gallon on all milk produced and sold by him during a year to the equivalent of one halfpenny on such production and sale.

STATUTORY INSTRUMENTS

1969 No. 1816 (L. 31)

MATRIMONIAL CAUSES
COUNTY COURTS

The Divorce County Courts (Amendment) Order 1969

Made - - -	*16th December* 1969
Coming into Operation	*2nd February* 1970

The Lord Chancellor, in exercise of the powers conferred on him by section 1(1) of the Matrimonial Causes Act 1967(a), hereby makes the following Order:—

1.—(1) This Order may be cited as the Divorce County Courts (Amendment) Order 1969, and shall come into operation on 2nd February 1970.

(2) The Interpretation Act 1889(b) shall apply to the interpretation of this Order as it applies to the interpretation of an Act of Parliament.

2. The Divorce County Courts Order 1968(c), as amended (d), which designates certain courts as divorce county courts and courts of trial for undefended matrimonial causes, shall have effect as further amended by this Order, and a reference in either of the following paragraphs to a schedule by number means the schedule so numbered in that Order.

3. The Salford County Court shall be a divorce county court and court of trial for the purposes of the Matrimonial Causes Act 1967, and accordingly the following entry shall be inserted in Schedule 1 immediately below the reference to Saint Helens and Widnes:—

"Salford (T)".

4. The Wrexham County Court shall be a court of trial for the purposes of the Matrimonial Causes Act 1967, and accordingly that court shall be marked "T" in Schedule 1.

Gardiner, C.

Dated 16th December 1969.

(a) 1967 c. 56. (b) 1889 c. 63.
(c) S.I. 1968/314 (1968 I, p. 940). (d) S.I. 1968/1934 (1968 III, p. 5244).

EXPLANATORY NOTE
(*This Note is not part of the Order.*)

This Order amends the Divorce County Courts Order 1968 by designating the Salford County Court as a divorce county court, and adding the Salford and Wrexham County Courts to the list of those at which undefended matrimonial causes may be tried.

STATUTORY INSTRUMENTS

1969 No. 1817

FOOD AND DRUGS

COMPOSITION AND LABELLING

The Artificial Sweeteners in Food Regulations 1969

Made - - -	17*th December* 1969
Laid before Parliament	30*th December* 1969
Coming into Operation	1*st January* 1970

The Minister of Agriculture, Fisheries and Food and the Secretary of State for Social Services, acting jointly, in exercise of the powers conferred on them by sections 4, 7 and 123 of the Food and Drugs Act 1955(**a**), as read with the Secretary of State for Social Services Order 1968(**b**), and of all other powers enabling them in that behalf, hereby make the following regulations after consultation with such organisations as appear to them to be representative of interests substantially affected by the regulations and reference to the Food Hygiene Advisory Council under section 82 of the said Act (insofar as the regulations are made in exercise of the powers conferred by the said section 7) :—

PART I

PRELIMINARY

Citation and commencement

1. These regulations may be cited as the Artificial Sweeteners in Food Regulations 1969, and shall come into operation on 1st January 1970.

Interpretation

2.—(1) In these regulations, unless the context otherwise requires—

"the Act" means the Food and Drugs Act 1955 ;

"artificial sweetener" means any chemical compound which is sweet to the taste, but does not include any sugar or any polyhydric alcohol ;

"artificial sweetening tablet" means any tablet which contains an artificial sweetener and which is intended for sale with a view to its use in the preparation of food ;

"carbohydrate" means a substance containing carbon, hydrogen and oxygen only in which the hydrogen and oxygen occur in the same proportion as in water ;

(**a**) 4 & 5 Eliz. 2. c. 16.   (**b**) S.I. 1968/1699 (1968 III, p. 4585).

"food" means food intended for sale for human consumption and includes drink, chewing gum and other products of a like nature and use, and articles and substances used as ingredients in the preparation of food or drink or of such products, but does not include—

(*a*) water, live animals or birds,

(*b*) fodder or feeding stuffs for animals, birds or fish, or

(*c*) articles or substances used only as drugs ;

"food and drugs authority" has the meaning assigned to it by section 83 of the Act ;

"full strength tablets" means artificial sweetening tablets which comply with the requirements as to composition set out in paragraph 1 of Schedule 2 to these regulations ;

"half strength tablets" means artificial sweetening tablets which comply with the requirements as to composition set out in paragraph 2 of Schedule 2 to these regulations ;

"human consumption" includes use in the preparation of food for human consumption ;

"permitted artificial sweetener" means saccharin, saccharin calcium or saccharin sodium ;

"polyhydric alcohol" means an alcohol with three or more free hydroxyl groups ;

"saccharin" means the substance conforming to the description, specifications and requirements for saccharin contained in the British Pharmacopoeia 1968 ;

"saccharin calcium" means the substance conforming to the description, specifications and requirements for saccharin calcium contained in Schedule 1 to these regulations ;

"saccharin sodium" means the substance conforming to the description, specifications and requirements for saccharin sodium contained in the British Pharmacopoeia 1968 ;

"sell" includes offer or expose for sale or have in possession for sale ; and

"sale" and "sold" shall be construed accordingly ;

"sugar" means any soluble carbohydrate sweetening matter ;
AND other expressions have the same meaning as in the Act.

(2) For the purposes of these regulations, the supply of any artificial sweetener or any food containing any artificial sweetener, otherwise than by sale, at, in or from any place where artificial sweeteners or such food are or is supplied in the course of a business shall be deemed to be a sale of that artificial sweetener or that food, as the case may be ; and references to purchasing and purchaser shall be construed accordingly.

(3) For the purposes of the Labelling of Food Order 1953(**a**), as amended (**b**), these regulations, insofar as they prescribe requirements as to composition for artificial sweetening tablets, shall be taken to prescribe standards for such tablets.

(4) Any reference in these regulations to a label borne on a container shall be construed as including a reference to any legible marking on the container however effected.

(**a**) S.I. 1953/536 (1953 I, p. 665).
(**b**) The relevant amending instruments are S.I. 1953/1889, 1959/471, 1967/1864 (1953 I, p. 685; 1959 I, p. 1326; 1967 III, p. 5013).

(5) The Interpretation Act 1889(**a**) shall apply to the interpretation of these regulations as it applies to the interpretation of an Act of Parliament, and as if these regulations and the regulations hereby revoked were Acts of Parliament.

Exemptions

3. The provisions of these regulations shall not apply to any food or artificial sweetener intended at the time of sale, consignment, delivery or importation, as the case may be, for exportation to any place outside the United Kingdom.

PART II

REQUIREMENTS RELATING TO ARTIFICIAL SWEETENERS

Sale, etc. of artificial sweeteners

4. No person shall sell, consign, deliver or import into England and Wales any artificial sweetener for human consumption which is not a permitted artificial sweetener.

Requirements as to composition for tablets containing artificial sweeteners

5.—(1) Every artificial sweetening tablet containing saccharin or saccharin calcium or saccharin sodium or a mixture of two or all of those substances shall conform to the requirements as to composition set forth in relation thereto in the appropriate paragraph of Schedule 2 to these regulations.

(2) No person shall sell, consign, deliver or import into England and Wales any artificial sweetening tablet which does not comply with this regulation.

Labelling of containers of artificial sweetening tablets

6.—(1) No person shall sell, consign, deliver or import into England and Wales any artificial sweetening tablets in a container unless such container bears a label on which there appears such one of the following descriptions as may be appropriate—

(*a*) the words "saccharin tablets" or "half strength saccharin tablets" for full strength or half strength tablets respectively, containing no permitted artificial sweetener other than saccharin or a mixture of saccharin and saccharin calcium and saccharin sodium or of any two of those substances;

(*b*) the words "saccharin calcium tablets" or "half strength saccharin calcium tablets" for full strength or half strength tablets respectively, containing no permitted artificial sweetener other than saccharin calcium;

(*c*) the words "saccharin sodium tablets" or "soluble saccharin tablets" for full strength tablets, or the words "half strength saccharin sodium tablets" or "half strength soluble saccharin tablets" for half strength tablets, containing in each case no permitted artificial sweetener other than saccharin sodium:

Provided that any word of similar meaning may be substituted for the word "tablets" in any of the foregoing descriptions.

(**a**) 1889 c. 63.

(2) Every letter in every word appearing on a label on a container which is required so to appear by virtue of this regulation shall appear conspicuously and legibly in a dark colour upon a light coloured ground or in a light colour upon a dark coloured ground and shall be of uniform colour and size.

Sales by description

7. No person shall sell any food under such a description as to lead an intending purchaser to believe that he is purchasing a permitted artificial sweetener or artificial sweetening tablet if the food does not conform to the appropriate description, specifications and requirements prescribed by these regulations.

8. Where a person sells any article or substance to a purchaser in response to a request for an artificial sweetener to which these regulations apply, he shall be deemed to sell such article or substance as such an artificial sweetener and under such a description as is specified in relation to such an artificial sweetener in these regulations unless he clearly notifies the purchaser at the time of sale that the article or substance is not such an artificial sweetener.

PART III

REQUIREMENTS RELATING TO FOOD CONTAINING ARTIFICIAL SWEETENERS

Sale, etc. of food containing artificial sweeteners

9.—(1) No food shall contain any artificial sweetener other than a permitted artificial sweetener.

(2) No person shall sell, consign, deliver or import into England and Wales any food which does not comply with this regulation.

PART IV

ADMINISTRATIVE PROVISIONS

Condemnation of food

10. Where any artificial sweetener or any other food is certified by a public analyst as being food which it is an offence against regulation 4 or 9 hereof to sell, consign, deliver or import into England and Wales, it may be treated for the purposes of section 9 of the Act (under which food may be seized and destroyed on the order of a justice of the peace) as being unfit for human consumption.

Penalties and enforcement

11.—(1) If any person contravenes or fails to comply with any of the foregoing provisions of these regulations he shall be guilty of an offence and shall be liable to a fine not exceeding one hundred pounds or to imprisonment for a term not exceeding three months, or to both, and, in the case of a continuing offence, to a further fine not exceeding five pounds for each day during which the offence continues after conviction.

(2) Each food and drugs authority shall enforce and execute such provisions in their area:

Provided that each port health authority shall enforce and execute in their district the provisions of regulations 4, 5, 6 and 9 hereof insofar as these regulations relate to importation.

(3) The requirements of section 109(3) of the Act (which requires notice to be given to the Minister of Agriculture, Fisheries and Food of intention to institute proceedings for an offence against any provisions of these regulations relating to labelling or marking) shall not apply as respects any proceedings instituted by a council for an offence against any such provisions of these regulations.

Application of various sections of the Act

12.—(1) Sections 108(3) and (4) (which relate to prosecutions), 110(1), (2) and (3) (which relate to evidence of analysis), 112 (which relates to the power of a court to require analysis by the Government Chemist), 113 (which relates to a contravention due to some person other than the person charged), 115(2) (which relates to the conditions under which a warranty may be pleaded as a defence) and 116 (which relates to offences in relation to warranties and certificates of analysis) of the Act shall apply for the purposes of these regulations as if references therein to proceedings, or a prosecution, under or taken or brought under the Act included references to proceedings, or a prosecution as the case may be, taken or brought for an offence under these regulations and as if the reference in the said section 112 to subsection (4) of section 108 included a reference to that subsection as applied by these regulations.

(2) Paragraph (*b*) of the proviso to section 108(1) of the Act shall apply for the purposes of these regulations as if the reference therein to section 116 of the Act included a reference to that section as applied by these regulations.

Revocation

13. The Artificial Sweeteners in Food Regulations 1967(**a**) are hereby revoked.

In Witness whereof the Official Seal of the Minister of Agriculture, Fisheries and Food is hereunto affixed on 15th December 1969.

(L.S.)

Cledwyn Hughes,
Minister of Agriculture, Fisheries and Food.

R. H. S. Crossman,
Secretary of State for Social Services.

17th December 1969.

SCHEDULE 1   Regulation 2(1)

Saccharin calcium

Saccharin calcium is the calcium derivative of 2-sulphobenzoic imide with $3\frac{1}{2}$ molecules of water of crystallisation. It contains not less than 98 per cent. of $C_{14}H_8$ Ca $N_2O_6S_2$ calculated with reference to the substance dried to constant weight at 105°C.

Description	White crystals or white crystalline powder, odour faintly aromatic, taste intensely sweet.
Solubility	1 g. dissolves in 1·5 g. water.

(**a**) S.I. 1967/1119 (1967 II, p. 3274).

Loss on drying	...	...	...	When dried to constant weight at 105 °C. loses not less than 11 per cent. and not more than 15 per cent. of its weight.
Ammonium Compounds		...	...	Complies with the test given under Saccharin in the British Pharmacopoeia 1968.
4-Sulphamoylbenzoates		...	...	Complies with the test given under Saccharin Sodium in the British Pharmacopoeia 1968.

Regulations 2(1)
SCHEDULE 2 and 5

Requirements as to composition for tablets containing permitted artificial sweeteners

1. *Full strength tablets*

An artificial sweetening tablet containing saccharin or saccharin calcium or saccharin sodium or a mixture of two or all of those substances shall, when dried to constant weight at 105 °C., have a total quantity of saccharin free and combined calculated as $C_7H_5NO_3S$, which shall be not less than 11 milligrams and not more than 14 milligrams.

2. *Half strength tablets*

An artificial sweetening tablet containing saccharin or saccharin calcium or saccharin sodium or a mixture of two or all of those substances shall, if sold in a container bearing a label upon which there appears the description "half strength", have when dried to constant weight at 105 °C. a total quantity of saccharin free and combined calculated as $C_7H_5NO_3S$, which shall be not less than 5·5 milligrams and not more than 7 milligrams.

EXPLANATORY NOTE

(*This Note is not part of the Regulations.*)

These regulations, which apply to England and Wales only, supersede the Artificial Sweeteners in Food Regulations 1967 and come into operation on 1st January 1970.

The principal change is that cyclamic acid, calcium cyclamate and sodium cyclamate are no longer permitted artificial sweeteners or permitted ingredients in artificial sweetening tablets.

STATUTORY INSTRUMENTS

1969 No. 1818

FOOD AND DRUGS

COMPOSITION AND LABELLING

The Soft Drinks (Amendment) Regulations 1969

Made	-	-	-	17*th December* 1969
Laid before Parliament				30*th December* 1969
Coming into Operation				1*st January* 1970

The Minister of Agriculture, Fisheries and Food and the Secretary of State for Social Services, acting jointly, in exercise of the powers conferred on them by sections 4, 7 and 123 of the Food and Drugs Act 1955(**a**), as read with the Secretary of State for Social Services Order 1968(**b**), and of all other powers enabling them in that behalf, hereby make the following regulations after consultation with such organisations as appear to them to be representative of interests substantially affected by the regulations and reference to the Food Hygiene Advisory Council under section 82 of the said Act (insofar as the regulations are made in exercise of the powers conferred by the said section 7) :—

Citation and commencement

1. These regulations may be cited as the Soft Drinks (Amendment) Regulations 1969, and shall come into operation on 1st January 1970.

Interpretation

2.—(1) In these regulations the expression "the principal regulations" means the Soft Drinks Regulations 1964(**c**) and, unless the context otherwise requires, any reference herein to a numbered regulation or schedule shall be construed as a reference to the regulation or schedule bearing that number in the principal regulations.

(2) The Interpretation Act 1889(**d**) shall apply to the interpretation of these regulations as it applies to the interpretation of an Act of Parliament.

Amendment of the principal regulations

3. Regulation 2(1) shall be amended—

(*a*) by deleting the definition of cyclamic acid ;

(*b*) by deleting from the definition of permitted artificial sweetener the words "or cyclamic acid".

(**a**) 4 & 5 Eliz. 2. c. 16. (**b**) S.I. 1968/1699 (1968 III, p. 4585).
(**c**) S.I. 1964/760 (1964 II, p. 1605). (**d**) 1889 c. 63.

4. Regulation 5(2) shall be amended by substituting in sub-paragraph (*a*) of the proviso thereto for the words and figures "columns 4 and 5" the word and figure "column 4" and by deleting from that sub-paragraph the words "(calculated as therein required)".

5. Regulation 12 shall be amended by adding at the end thereof the following proviso :—

"Provided that the said description or descriptive name need not be included in the said declaration if a label on a container of the soft drink dispensed from the vending machine, or an exact facsimile of such label, bearing the said description, where applicable, and otherwise the said descriptive name is conspicuous and legible to an intending purchaser on or through the outside of the vending machine.".

6. The following regulation shall be substituted for regulation 13 :—

"**13.** Subject to the provisions of these regulations, no person shall sell, consign or deliver in any container any soft drink to which any permitted artificial sweetener has been added unless that container bears a label on which there appears the expression 'saccharin added' or 'contains saccharin' or, where appropriate, any one of the following expressions :—

    (*a*) 'saccharin and sugar added' ;

    (*b*) 'sugar and saccharin added' ;

    (*c*) 'contains saccharin and sugar' ;

    (*d*) 'contains sugar and saccharin' ;

    (*e*) 'sweetened with sugar and saccharin' ;

    (*f*) 'sweetened with saccharin and sugar' :

Provided that as respects any sale, consignment or delivery of a soft drink on or before 31st December 1970, it shall be a sufficient compliance with the requirements of this regulation if the words 'permitted artificial sweetener' are substituted for the word 'saccharin' in any of the foregoing expressions.".

7. Regulation 14 shall be amended by inserting immediately after the word "container" the words "or required by virtue of regulation 12 hereof to appear on a vending machine" and by inserting immediately before the word "requirements" the word "appropriate".

8. The Schedule to these regulations shall be substituted for Schedule 1 to the principal regulations.

9. Schedule 2 shall be amended—

    (*a*) by deleting from the words preceding the table in Parts I and II respectively the words following the words "Table below" ;

    (*b*) by deleting from Parts I and II respectively column 5 and all the figures and words contained within the said column ;

    (*c*) by deleting Part III.

10. Schedule 3 shall be amended—

(*a*) by deleting from the words preceding the table in Parts I and II respectively the words following the words "Table below" ;

(*b*) by deleting from Parts I and II respectively column 5 and all the figures and words contained within the said column ;

(*c*) by deleting Part III.

11. Schedule 4 shall be amended by substituting in paragraph 3 for the words "and shall be not less than half an inch in height" the following words:—

"and—

(*a*) if it is part of the description or descriptive name referred to in regulation 12, shall be not less than half an inch in height ;

(*b*) if it is part of any expression specified in regulation 13, shall be not less than one quarter of an inch in height.".

In Witness whereof the Official Seal of the Minister of Agriculture, Fisheries and Food is hereunto affixed on 15th December 1969.

(L.S.)   *Cledwyn Hughes,*
Minister of Agriculture, Fisheries and Food.

                              R. H. S. Crossman,
Secretary of State for Social Services.

17th December 1969.

SCHEDULE   Regulation 8

PERMITTED ARTIFICIAL SWEETENERS

1. Saccharin

Saccharin is the substance conforming to the description, specifications and requirements for saccharin contained in the British Pharmacopoeia 1968.

2. Saccharin calcium

Saccharin calcium is the calcium derivative of 2-sulphobenzoic imide with $3\frac{1}{2}$ molecules of water of crystallisation. It contains not less than 98 per cent. of $C_{14}H_8$ Ca $N_2O_6S_2$ calculated with reference to the substance dried to constant weight at 105°C.

Description	White crystals or white crystalline powder, odour faintly aromatic, taste intensely sweet.
Solubility	1 g. dissolves in 1·5 g. water.
Loss on drying	When dried to constant weight at 105°C. loses not less than 11 per cent. and not more than 15 per cent. of its weight.
Ammonium Compounds	Complies with the test given under Saccharin in the British Pharmacopoeia 1968.
4-Sulphamoylbenzoates	Complies with the test given under Saccharin Sodium in the British Pharmacopoeia 1968.

3. Saccharin sodium

Saccharin sodium is the substance conforming to the description, specifications and requirements for saccharin sodium contained in the British Pharmacopoeia 1968.

EXPLANATORY NOTE

(This Note is not part of the Regulations.)

These amending regulations, which come into operation on 1st January 1970—

    (*a*) amend the definition of "permitted artificial sweetener" in the principal regulations so that saccharin, saccharin calcium and saccharin sodium (as defined in the Schedule to these regulations) are the only permitted artificial sweeteners ;

    (*b*) amend the requirements in regulation 12 of the principal regulations as to declarations on the sale of soft drinks in or from vending machines ;

    (*c*) make changes in the forms of expressions, specified in regulation 13 of the principal regulations, for labels of containers of soft drinks containing any permitted artificial sweetener ;

    (*d*) amend the specifications for saccharin, saccharin calcium and saccharin sodium in Schedule 1 to the principal regulations.

STATUTORY INSTRUMENTS

1969 No. 1819 (S.159)

COURT OF SESSION, SCOTLAND

Act of Sederunt (Rules of Court Amendment No. 5) 1969

| Made | - | - | - | 16th December 1969 |
| Coming into Operation | | | 6th January 1970 |

The Lords of Council and Session, under and by virtue of the powers conferred upon them by section 16 of the Administration of Justice (Scotland) Act 1933(a) and of all other powers competent to them in that behalf, do hereby enact and declare as follows :—

1. In the case of any decree or extract in an action commenced on or after 6th January 1970, the provisions of Rule 66 of the Rules of Court (b) shall not apply. Instead there shall be substituted a new Rule 66 as follows :—

"Where interest is included in or exigible under a decree or extract, it shall be deemed to be at the rate of seven per centum per annum, unless otherwise stated."

2. The Appendix to the Rules of Court (b) shall be amended by deleting in each of Examples (1), (8) and (16) of Form 2 the word "five", and by leaving a blank space in place thereof.

3. This Act of Sederunt may be cited as the Act of Sederunt (Rules of Court Amendment No. 5) 1969, and shall come into operation on 6th January 1970.

And the Lords appoint this Act of Sederunt to be inserted in the Books of Sederunt.

J. L. Clyde,
I.P.D.

Edinburgh.
16th December 1969.

EXPLANATORY NOTE

(This Note is not part of the Act of Sederunt.)

This Act of Sederunt prescribes that in the case of a decree or extract in an action commenced on or after 6th January 1970, the rate of interest shall be deemed to be 7% unless otherwise stated.

(a) 1933 c. 41.   (b) S.I. 1965/321 (1965 1, p. 803).

STATUTORY INSTRUMENTS

1969 No. 1820 (S.160)

POLICE

The Police Cadets (Scotland) Amendment (No. 2) Regulations 1969

Made - - -	*17th December* 1969	
Laid before Parliament	*31st December* 1969	
Coming into Operation	*1st January* 1970	

In exercise of the powers conferred on me by section 27 of the Police (Scotland) Act 1967(a), and of all other powers enabling me in that behalf, and after consulting (i) the Police Advisory Board for Scotland in accordance with section 26(9) of the said Act, and (ii) the Police Council for Great Britain in accordance with section 26(8) of the said Act, I hereby make the following regulations :—

Citation, commencement and interpretation

1.—(1) These regulations may be cited as the Police Cadets (Scotland) Amendment (No. 2) Regulations 1969.

(2) These regulations shall come into operation on 1st January 1970 and shall have effect as from that date.

(3) In these regulations any reference to the principal regulations is a reference to the Police Cadets (Scotland) Regulations 1968(b), as amended (c).

Medical examination

2. For regulation 10 of the principal regulations (which relates to medical examination) there shall be substituted the following regulation :—

"**10.** Every police cadet shall be medically examined, as near as may be 6 months after appointment and thereafter as near as may be at 12-monthly intervals, in accordance with arrangements made by the police authority, but subject to the proviso that a medical examination shall be arranged by the police authority on every occasion that—

(*a*) a cadet returns to duty from sick leave attributable to other than a trivial or short illness ;

(*b*) a superior officer of the rank of superintendent or above considers it necessary ; and

(*c*) a cadet requests it on the grounds that he feels unable to carry out his duties."

(a) 1967 c. 77.
(b) S.I. 1968/208 (1968 I, p. 557).
(c) S.I. 1969/493 (1969 I, p. 1402).

Pay

3. For the Table in Schedule 1 to the principal regulations (which contains scales of pay) there shall be substituted the following Table :—

"TABLE

Age	Annual Pay
Under 17 years	£408
17 years	£444
18 years	£501
19 years	£552

"

Charge for board and lodging

4. In Schedule 2 to the principal regulations (which relates to charges for board and lodging) there shall be substituted the sum of "£96" for the sum of "£93 10s.".

William Ross,
One of Her Majesty's Principal
Secretaries of State.

St. Andrew's House,
Edinburgh.
17th December 1969.

EXPLANATORY NOTE

(This Note is not part of the Regulations.)

These Regulations amend the Police Cadets (Scotland) Regulations 1968. Regulation 2 changes the conditions for medical examination to provide, with certain exceptions, for medical examination of police cadets six months after appointment and thereafter once a year.

Regulation 3 provides for increases in pay.

Regulation 4 increases charges for board and lodging by £2 10s. a year.

STATUTORY INSTRUMENTS

1969 No. 1821

LANDLORD AND TENANT

The Rent Regulation (Forms etc.) (England and Wales) (Amendment) Regulations 1969

Made - - - -	*18th December* 1969
Laid before Parliament	*31st December* 1969
Coming into Operation	*1st January* 1970

The Minister of Housing and Local Government, in relation to England other than Monmouthshire, in exercise of the powers conferred on him by section 37(1) of the Rent Act 1968(a) and of all other powers enabling him in that behalf, and the Secretary of State, in relation to Wales and Monmouthshire, in exercise of the powers conferred on him by sections 37(1) and 114(1) of the said Act and of all other powers enabling him in that behalf, hereby make the following regulations:—

1. These regulations may be cited as the Rent Regulation (Forms etc.) (England and Wales) (Amendment) Regulations 1969 and shall come into operation on 1st January 1970.

2.—(1) In these regulations "notice of increase" means a notice of increase under section 22(2) of the Rent Act 1968.

(2) The Interpretation Act 1889(b) applies for the interpretation of these regulations as it applies for the interpretation of an Act of Parliament.

3. Schedule 1 to the Rent Regulation (Forms etc.) (England and Wales) Regulations 1969(c) shall be amended as follows—

(1) in the heading of Form No. 3 after the words "Housing Act 1969" there shall be inserted the words "or the Rent (Control of Increases) Act 1969"; and

(2) immediately after Form No. 5 there shall be inserted the Form No. 5A set out in the Schedule to these regulations as the form prescribed for a notice of increase served consequent upon the registration of a rent under Part IV of the Rent Act 1968 where there is a period of delay under section 5 of the Rent (Control of Increases) Act 1969(d).

(a) 1968 c. 23.	(b) 1889 c. 63.
(c) S.I. 1969/1184 (1969 II, p. 3483).	(d) 1969 c. 62.

SCHEDULE

FORM NO. 5A

RENT ACT 1968

(RENT (CONTROL OF INCREASES) ACT 1969)

Rent Act, section 22

Notice of Increase of Rent where there are restrictions on rent increases under the Rent (Control of Increases) Act 1969 (Note 1)

Date....................

To .... tenant of

....

Strike out words in square brackets if they do not apply

1. A rent of £.   s.   d.   per......... was registered on..............
as the fair rent for the above-mentioned premises (Notes 2 and 3) [of which £.   s.   d.   per........ was noted in the register as the amount apportioned to services provided by the landlord or a superior landlord (Note 4)].

2. Where a rent for a dwelling which is subject to a regulated tenancy is registered in 1970 or 1971, the entitlement of the landlord to increase the rent payable for a statutory period of the tenancy is, by virtue of Section 5 of, and the Schedule to, the Rent (Control of Increases) Act 1969, subject to certain limits (Note 5).

[3. It is noted in the register that the rates for the above-mentioned premises are paid by the landlord. These are currently £.   s.   d.   per [half-year] [year] and the landlord is entitled to add this amount to the rent he is otherwise permitted to obtain (Note 6)].

4. I hereby give you notice that your rent will be increased as follows:

Present rent	Increase in rent	New rent	Date of new rent
per............	per............	per............	as from (Note 7)
£. s. d.	£. s. d.	£. s. d.	

5. The rental period for which the rent is being increased by this notice begins in the [first] [second] year of the period of delay (Note 8), and the following information is relevant to the calculation of the increase.

Previous limit (Note 9)   ..   ..   ..   £.   s.   d.   per........
[Services apportionment (Note 4)]   ..   £.   s.   d.   per........

[6. The new rent includes the sum of £.   s.   d.   per..........in respect of rates paid by the landlord or a superior landlord].

Signature of [landlord] [agent authorised to serve this notice] ....

[Name of landlord if notice served by agent ....]

Address of landlord ....

....

[Address of agent] ....

....

NOTES

1. This notice of increase is needed where a dwelling-house is let on a tenancy—

   (*a*) which is regulated under the Rent Act 1968 ; and

   (*b*) which either has become a statutory tenancy or will become one under Section 26(3) of that Act (Note 10) ; and

   (*c*) for which a rent is registered under that Act in the year 1970 or 1971, other than :

   (i) a rent to which the restrictions on rent increases under the Housing Act 1969 apply ; or

   (ii) a rent registered in accordance with a Certificate of Fair Rent (except in the case of a rent so registered which is in substitution for a rent where there is a period of delay under the Rent (Control of Increases) Act 1969) ; or

   (iii) a rent registered under Section 49 of the Rent Act in accordance with a rent condition attached by a local authority to an improvement grant ; or

   (iv) a rent in the case of a regulated tenancy which arose under Part I of the Landlord and Tenant Act 1954 on the termination of a long tenancy which was registered (or is deemed to have been registered) while the rent payable continued to be that last payable under the long tenancy.

2. If there is still a contract of tenancy between the landlord and tenant the registration of a rent which is higher than the rent payable under that contract does not allow the landlord to increase the rent unless the terms of the contract permit him to do so. In the case of a registration where there is a period of delay under the Rent (Control of Increases) Act 1969 the limits under the Act continue to apply notwithstanding any agreement purporting to entitle the landlord to charge a higher rent.

3. If a contractual tenancy has come to an end and the tenant is holding over as a statutory tenant under the Rent Act, the landlord may increase the rent to the extent permitted by the Rent (Control of Increases) Act 1969 by the service of Notice(s) of Increase.

4. The amount apportioned to services (the 'services apportionment') is that part of the increase in rent which is treated as representing an increase in the cost of any services provided by the landlord or a superior landlord. The services apportionment can be added in full and is not subject to phasing.

5. (i) For rents registered in 1970, one-third of the net increase (or 7s. 6d. per week if one-third is less than this) can be added from the commencement of the first rental period following registration, one-third (or 7s. 6d. per week if one-third is less than this) on the corresponding date in 1971 and one-third (or the balance) on the corresponding date in 1972.

   (ii) For rents registered in 1971, one-third (or 7s. 6d. per week if one-third is less than this) can be added from the first rental period following registration, and the balance on the corresponding date in 1972.

6. The phasing restrictions do not apply to any changes in rent resulting from changes in rates borne by the landlord or a superior landlord.

7. This date must be a date which is not earlier than :

   (i) the date of registration, or

   (ii) four weeks before the service of this Notice, or

   (iii) the commencement of the first rental period beginning during the first or second year of the period of delay as the case may be.

8. The appropriate proportion by which the rent for any rental period may be increased is:

(a) one-third (or 7s. 6d. per week if one-third is less than this) if the rental period begins in the first year of the period of delay ; and

(b) (in a case where the period of delay is two years) two-thirds (or 15s. per week if two-thirds is less than this) if the rental period begins in the second year of the period of delay.

The period of delay with respect to any rent is:

(a) if the rent is registered in 1970, two years ;

(b) if the rent is registered in 1971, one year ;

from the date on which the rent is registered.

9. The previous limit of rent is the amount which the landlord could have charged immediately before the registration in question, on the assumption that he had served all permissible notices of increase. It is the base from which the phasing calculation starts.

10. If this Notice is served while the regulated tenancy is still a contractual one and the landlord, by serving a notice to quit at the same time as this Notice, could bring the tenancy to an end before the date specified in this Notice for the increased rent to take effect, this Notice will operate to convert the tenancy into a statutory tenancy as from that date.

Given under the official seal of the Minister of Housing and Local Government on 18th December 1969.

(L.S.)

Denis H. Howell,
Minister of State,
Ministry of Housing and
Local Government.

Given under my hand

George Thomas,
One of Her Majesty's Principal
Secretaries of State,
18th December 1969.
Welsh Office.

EXPLANATORY NOTE

(This Note is not part of the Regulations.)

These regulations, which apply throughout England and Wales, amend slightly the heading of Form No. 3 in Schedule 1 to the Rent Regulation (Forms etc.) (England and Wales) Regulations 1969. They also prescribe a new form of notice of increase of rent to be served in cases where a rent is registered under Part IV of the Rent Act 1968 and there is a period of delay under the Rent (Control of Increases) Act 1969.

STATUTORY INSTRUMENTS

1969 No. 1822

SEA FISHERIES

The Foreign Sea-Fishery Officers (North-East Atlantic Fisheries Commission Scheme) Order 1969

Made - - -	*17th December* 1969
Laid before Parliament	*31st December* 1969
Coming into Operation	*1st January* 1970

The Minister of Agriculture, Fisheries and Food and the Secretaries of State for Scotland and the Home Department (being the Secretaries of State respectively concerned with the sea-fishing industry in Scotland and Northern Ireland) in exercise of the powers conferred on them by section 7(4) of the Sea Fisheries Act 1968(**a**) and of all other powers enabling them in that behalf hereby make the following Order :—

Citation and Commencement

1. This Order may be cited as the Foreign Sea-Fishery Officers (North-East Atlantic Fisheries Commission Scheme) Order 1969 and shall come into operation on 1st January 1970.

Interpretation

2.—(1) in this Order :—

"the Act" means the Sea Fisheries Act 1968 ;

"the Commission" means the North-East Atlantic Fisheries Commission established under the Convention ;

"the Convention" means the North-East Atlantic Fisheries Convention signed in London on 24th January 1959(**b**) ;

"the Convention area" means the area to which the Convention applies, comprising the waters described in Part II of Schedule 1 to this Order ;

"the Scheme" means the Scheme of Joint Enforcement of the Commission which is set out in Part I of Schedule 1 to this Order, being a Recommendation of the Commission which takes effect as an international arrangement by virtue of the agreement thereto of the member states of the Commission, subject to the Reservations mentioned in the said Part I of Schedule 1.

(2) The Interpretation Act 1889(**c**) shall apply for the interpretation of this Order as it applies for the interpretation of an Act of Parliament.

(**a**) 1968 c. 77. (**b**) Cmnd. 2190.
(**c**) 1889 c. 63.

Foreign Sea-Fishery Officers

3. In relation to the Scheme there are hereby specified as foreign sea-fishery officers, entitled to exercise in relation to British fishing boats anywhere within the Convention area outside the fishery limits of the British Islands, the powers referred to in section 9 of the Act, officers of the countries referred to in Schedule 2 to this Order, who are duly appointed by the government of their respective countries as inspectors under the terms of the Scheme and who hold a document of identity in the form approved under the Scheme.

In witness whereof the Official Seal of the Minister of Agriculture, Fisheries and Food is hereunto affixed on 9th December 1969.

(L.S.)
Cledwyn Hughes,
Minister of Agriculture,
Fisheries and Food.

Given under the Seal of the Secretary of State for Scotland on 11th December 1969.

(L.S.)
William Ross,
Secretary of State for
Scotland.

Given under the Hand of the Secretary of State for the Home Department on 17th December 1969.

James Callaghan,
Secretary of State for
the Home Department.

SCHEDULE 1

PART I

Scheme of Joint Enforcement

Recommendation

Pursuant to Article 13(3) of the Convention the Commission recommends the establishment of the following arrangements for international control outside territorial waters and fishery limits for the purpose of ensuring the application of the Convention and the measures in force thereunder:—

(1) Control shall be carried out by inspectors of the fishery control services of Contracting States. The names of the inspectors appointed for that purpose by their respective governments shall be notified to the Commission.

(2) Ships carrying inspectors shall fly a special flag or pennant approved by the Commission to indicate that the inspector is carrying out international inspection duties. The names of the ships so used for the time being, which may be either special inspection vessels or fishing vessels, shall be notified to the Commission.

(3) Each inspector shall carry a document of identity supplied by the authorities of the flag state in a form approved by the Commission and given him on appointment stating that he has authority to act under the arrangements approved by the Commission.

(4) Subject to the arrangements agreed under paragraph (9), a vessel of any Contracting State employed for the time being in fishing for sea fish or in the treatment of sea fish in the Convention area shall stop when given the appropriate signal in the International Code of Signals by a ship carrying an inspector unless actually fishing, shooting or hauling, in which case it shall stop immediately it has finished hauling. The master of the vessel shall permit the inspector, who may be accompanied by a witness, to board it. The master shall enable the inspector to make such examination of catch, nets or other gear and any relevant documents as the inspector deems necessary to verify the observance of the Commission's recommendations in force in relation to the flag state of the vessel concerned and the inspector may ask for any explanations that he deems necessary.

(5) On boarding the vessel an inspector shall produce the document described in (3) above. Inspections shall be made so that the vessel suffers the minimum interference and inconvenience. An inspector shall limit his enquiries to the ascertainment of the facts in relation to the observance of the Commission's recommendations in force in relation to the flag state of the vessel concerned. In making his examination an inspector may ask the master for any assistance he may require. He shall draw up a report of his inspection in a form approved by the Commission. He shall sign the report in the presence of the master of the vessel who shall be entitled to add or have added to the report any observations which he may think suitable and must sign such observations. Copies of the report shall be given to the master of the vessel and to the Inspector's Government who shall transmit copies to the appropriate authorities of the flag state of the vessel and to the Commission. Where any infringement of the recommendations is discovered the inspector should where possible also inform the competent authorities of the flag state, as notified to the Commission, and any inspection ship of the flag state known to be in the vicinity.

(6) Resistance to an inspector or failure to comply with his directions shall be treated by the flag state of the vessel as if the inspector were an inspector of that state.

(7) Inspectors shall carry out their duties under these arrangements in accordance with the rules set out in this recommendation but they shall remain under the operational control of their national authorities and shall be responsible to them.

(8) Contracting States shall consider and act on reports of foreign inspectors under these arrangements on the same basis as reports of national inspectors. The provisions of this paragraph shall not impose any obligation on a Contracting State to give the report of a foreign inspector a higher evidential value than it would possess in the inspector's own country. Contracting States shall collaborate in order to facilitate judicial or other proceedings arising from a report of an inspector under these arrangements.

(9) (i) Contracting States shall inform the Commission by 1st March each year of their provisional plans for participation in these arrangements in the following year and the Commission may make suggestions to Contracting States for the co-ordination of national operations in this field including the number of inspectors and ships carrying inspectors.

(ii) The arrangements set out in this Recommendation and the plans for participation shall apply between Contracting States unless otherwise agreed between them; and such agreement shall be notified to the Commission:

Provided, however, that implementation of the scheme shall be suspended between any two Contracting States, if either of them has notified the Commission to that effect, pending completion of an agreement.

(10) (i) When nets are inspected the meshes of the cod-end are to be examined with a flat gauge with parallel sides, a thickness of 2 mm. and the appropriate width made of any durable material that will retain its shape and constructed with a wedge shaped section or sections have a taper of 2 cm. in 8 cm. calibrated to measure the width of the meshes in which the section or sections are inserted. An illustration of such a gauge is appended.

(ii) The appropriate width is the appropriate width prescribed in the Commission's recommendations for the type of net inspected and the area on which the inspection takes place which are in force in relation to the flag state of the vessel concerned.

(iii) At least 20 consecutive meshes of the cod-end running parallel to its long axis, starting at least ten meshes from the lacings, are to be examined, or the maximum number if less than 20.

(iv) The gauge should be inserted into the meshes when wet so as to measure the long axis of the mesh when stretched diagonally lengthwise. If the section of the gauge with parallel sides passes easily through a mesh it is not undersized. If the inspector has any doubt as to whether the gauge passes easily through, he shall insert the gauge in the mesh held horizontally and attach a weight of 5 kilogrammes to the gauge and if the section in the gauge with parallel sides passes through the mesh the mesh is not undersized.

(v) The number of undersized meshes and the width of each mesh examined shall be entered in the inspector's report, together with the average width of the meshes examined.

(vi) Inspectors shall have authority to inspect all nets other than those which are dry and stowed away below deck.

(11) The inspector shall affix an identification mark approved by the Commission, to any net which appears to have been used in contravention of the Commission's recommendations in force in relation to the flag state of the vessel concerned and shall record this fact in his report.

(12) The inspector may photograph the net in such a way that the identification mark and the measurement of the net is visible, in which case the subjects photographed should be listed in the report and copies of the photographs should be attached to the copy of the report to the flag state.

(13) The inspector shall so far as reasonably practicable examine the catch and may take such measurements as he deems necessary to establish whether and to what extent undersized fish of protected species are present in the part of the catch inspected. He shall report his findings including the number of fish measured and the size of any fish which are undersized to the authorities of the flag state of the inspected vessel as soon as possible.

RESERVATIONS

(a) As between the Union of Soviet Socialist Republics and other Contracting States the provisions of the Scheme relating to inspection of gear below deck and of catch do not apply.

(b) As between Poland and other Contracting States the provisions of the Scheme relating to inspection of gear or catch below deck do not apply.

(c) As between Sweden and other Contracting States the provisions of the Scheme relating to inspection of gear or catch below deck do not apply.

PART II

Convention Area

All waters which are situated

(a) within those parts of the Atlantic and Arctic Oceans and their dependent seas which lie north of 36° north latitude and between 42° west longitude and 51° east longitude, but excluding

(i) the Baltic Sea and Belts lying to the south and east of lines drawn from Hasenore Head to Gniben Point, from Korshage to Spodsbierg and from Gilbierg Head to the Kullen, and

(ii) the Mediterranean Sea and its dependent seas as far as the point of intersection of the parallel of 36° north latitude and the meridian of 5° 36' west longitude.

(b) within that part of the Atlantic Ocean north of 59° north latitude and between 44° west longitude and 42° west longitude.

SCHEDULE 2

Foreign Countries which are parties to the Scheme

1. Belgium
2. Denmark
3. France
4. Iceland
5. Norway
6. Poland
7. Portugal
8. Spain
9. Sweden
10. Union of Soviet Socialist Republics

EXPLANATORY NOTE

(This Note is not part of the Order.)

This Order specifies the class of persons who are to be foreign sea-fishery officers for the purposes of the Scheme of Joint Enforcement of the North-East Atlantic Fisheries Commission. Copies of the illustration of the net measuring gauge referred to in the Scheme (which is scheduled to this Order) may be obtained from the Ministry of Agriculture, Fisheries and Food, Whitehall Place, London, S.W.1, from the Department of Agriculture and Fisheries for Scotland, Argyle House, 3 Lady Lawson Street, Edinburgh EH3 9DR and from the Ministry of Agriculture for Northern Ireland, Dundonald House, Newtownards Road, Belfast BT4 3SB.

STATUTORY INSTRUMENTS

1969 No. 1823

SEA FISHERIES

BOATS AND METHODS OF FISHING

The Fishing Nets (North-East Atlantic) Order 1969

Made - - -	*17th December* 1969	
Laid before Parliament	*31st December* 1969	
Coming into Operation	*1st January* 1970	

The Minister of Agriculture, Fisheries and Food and the Secretaries of State for Scotland and the Home Department (being the Secretaries of State respectively concerned with the sea-fishing industry in Scotland and Northern Ireland) in exercise of the powers conferred upon them by sections 3 and 15 of the Sea Fish (Conservation) Act 1967(a) as the latter section is amended by section 22 of, and paragraph 38 of Schedule 1 (Part II) to, the Sea Fisheries Act 1968(b) and of all other powers enabling them in that behalf hereby make the following Order :—

Citation and Commencement

1. This Order may be cited as the Fishing Nets (North-East Atlantic) Order 1969 and shall come into operation on 1st January 1970.

Interpretation

2.—(1) In this Order—

"the area dividing line" means a line drawn east from the meridian of 44° west longitude along the parallel of 59° north latitude to the meridian of 42° west longitude, thence south to the parallel of 48° north latitude, thence east to the meridian of 18° west longitude, thence north to the parallel of 60° north latitude, thence east to the meridian of 15° west longitude, thence north to the parallel of 62° north latitude, thence east to the meridian of 10° west longitude, thence north to the parallel of 63° north latitude, thence east to the meridian of 4° west longitude, thence south to the parallel of 62° north latitude, thence east to the meridian of 51° east longitude ;

"British Sea-Fishery Officer" means any person who is for the time being a British Sea-Fishery Officer by virtue of section 7 of the Sea Fisheries Act 1968 ;

"the Faroes Area" means the area bounded by a line drawn east from the meridian of 15° west longitude along the parallel of 60° north latitude

---

(a) 1967 c. 84.   (b) 1968 c. 77.

to the meridian of 5° west longitude, thence north to the parallel of 60° 30′ north latitude, thence east to the meridian of 4° west longitude, thence north to the parallel of 63° north latitude, thence west to the meridian of 10° west longitude, thence south to the parallel of 62° north latitude, thence west to the meridian of 15° west longitude, thence south to the parallel of 60° north latitude ;

"foreign fishing boat" has the meaning assigned to it by the Fishery Limits Act 1964(a) ;

"fishing boat" means a vessel of whatever size and in whatever way propelled which is for the time being employed in sea-fishing or in the sea-fishing service ;

"the Irish Sea" means the area bounded on the north by the parallel of 54° 38′ north latitude, on the east by the western coasts of England and Wales, on the south by the parallel of 51° north latitude and on the west by the meridian of 7° west longitude and the eastern coasts of the Republic of Ireland and Northern Ireland ;

"net" means any net constructed to take fish whilst being towed or hauled at or near the bottom of the sea by or from a fishing boat ;

"topside chafer" means a piece of netting attached to the upperside of the cod-end of a net for the purpose of preventing or reducing wear and tear.

(2) The Interpretation Act 1889(b) shall apply for the interpretation of this Order as it applies for the interpretation of an Act of Parliament, and as if this Order and the Order hereby revoked were Acts of Parliament.

Revocation of Previous Orders

3. The Fishing Nets (North-East Atlantic) Order 1968(c) is hereby revoked.

Areas in relation to which this Order has application

4. This Order has application in relation to those areas of the Atlantic and Arctic Oceans and seas adjacent to those oceans which lie north of the parallel of 36° north latitude, between the meridians of 42° west longitude and 51° east longitude and north of 59° north latitude between 44° west longitude and 42° west longitude (but excluding the Mediterranean and Baltic Seas and Belts lying to the south and east of lines drawn from Hasenore Head, Denmark, to Gniben Point, Denmark, from Korshage, Denmark, to Spodsbierg, Denmark and from Gilbierg Head, Denmark, to Kullen, Sweden).

Sizes of Mesh of Nets

5.—(1) Except as hereinafter provided, there shall not be carried, in any British fishing boat registered in the United Kingdom for the purpose of fishing for sea-fish in any of the waters referred to in the first column of Schedule 1 to this Order, any net or part of a net of a type specified in the second column of Schedule 1 opposite the reference to the said waters unless it has in all its parts meshes of such dimensions that when any mesh is stretched diagonally length-wise of the net a flat gauge 2 millimetres thick, and of a width specified in the third column of Schedule 1 opposite the reference to that type of net, will pass easily through the mesh whether the net is wet or dry.

(a) 1964 c. 72.　　(b) 1889 c. 63.
(c) S.I. 1968/2075 (1968 III, p. 5610).

(2) Except as hereinafter provided, there shall not be carried, by any foreign fishing boat within the fishery limits of the British Islands adjacent to the United Kingdom for the purpose of fishing for sea-fish in any of the waters in relation to which this Order has application, any net or part of a net of a type specified in the first column of Schedule 2 to this Order unless it has in all its parts meshes of such dimensions that when any mesh is stretched diagonally lengthwise of the net a flat gauge 2 millimetres thick, and of a width specified in the second column of Schedule 2 opposite the reference to that type of net, will pass easily through the mesh whether the net is wet or dry.

Obstruction of nets

6.—(1) Except as hereinafter provided, there shall not be carried in

(a) any British fishing boat registered in the United Kingdom, or

(b) any foreign fishing boat in any waters adjacent to the United Kingdom, and within the fishery limits of the British Islands

for the purposes of fishing for sea-fish in any waters to which this Order has application, any net having a covering of canvas or other material attached to it, or in respect of which any artifice may have been employed in such a manner that the mesh in any part of the net is obstructed or otherwise diminished in effect.

(2) Nothing in this Order shall be deemed to prohibit the attachment to the underside of the cod-end of a net of any canvas, netting or other material for the purpose of preventing or reducing wear and tear.

Topside Chafers

7.—(1) There shall not be carried in any British fishing boat registered in the United Kingdom any net to which a topside chafer is attached unless the net in question is a trawl net, the attachment is made for the purpose of fishing in waters north of the area dividing line, and the chafer complies with one of the following specifications :—

(a) a piece of netting, rectangular in shape, having in all its parts meshes the dimensions of which are not less than those of the meshes of the cod-end whether the netting and the cod-end respectively be wet or dry ; being in width at least one and a half times the width of the part of the cod-end which is covered by it, (such widths being measured at right angles to the long axis of the cod-end) ; and fastened to the cod-end only along the forward and lateral edges of the piece of netting in such a way that—

(i) if there is a splitting strop, the piece of netting begins at a distance of not more than four of the meshes to which it is attached forward of the splitting strop and ends at a distance of not less than four of such meshes forward of the cod-line mesh, or

(ii) if there is no splitting strop, the piece of netting extends for not more than one-third of the length of the cod-end and ends at a distance of not less than four of the meshes of the net to which it is attached forward of the cod-line mesh ; or

(b) pieces of netting having in all their parts meshes the dimensions of which are not less than those of the meshes of the cod-end whether the netting and the cod-end respectively be wet or dry ; each piece being

(i) fastened by its forward edge only across the cod-end at right angles to the long axis of the cod-end ;

(ii) of a width of at least the width of the cod-end (such width being measured at right angles to the long axis of the cod-end at the point of attachment) and

(iii) of not more than ten meshes long ;

and the said pieces having an aggregate length when so attached not exceeding two-thirds of the length of the cod-end ; or

(c) a piece of netting made of the same material as the cod-end, having in all its parts meshes whereof the dimensions are twice the dimensions of the meshes of the cod-end, whether the netting and the cod-end respectively be wet or dry, and fastened to the cod-end along the forward, lateral and rear edges only of the netting, in such a way that each mesh of the piece of netting coincides with four meshes of the cod-end.

(2) The provisions of this Article shall be without prejudice to the provisions of Article 7 of the Fishing Nets (North West Atlantic) Order 1969(a) and the carrying of any net to which a topside chafer is attached in accordance with the provisions of that Article shall be deemed not to be a contravention of the provisions of this Article.

Defences—British Fishing Boats

8. In any proceedings in respect of a contravention of Article 5(1) of this Order it shall be a sufficient defence to prove that the net to which the proceedings relate :—

(1) was being carried solely for the purpose of fishing in waters situated north of the area dividing line for mackerel, clupeoid fish, sand-eels (Ammodytes), Norway pout (Gadus esmarkii), smelts, eels, great weevers (Trachinus draco), capelin (Mallotos villosus), blue whiting (Gadus poutassou), horse mackerel (Trachurus trachurus), Polar Cod (Boreogadus saida), shrimps, prawns, nephrops or molluscs other than squid ; or

(2) had in no part of its cod-end meshes of such dimensions that when any mesh was stretched diagonally lengthwise of the net a flat gauge of 50 mm. broad and 2 mm. thick would pass easily through it whether the net was wet or dry and was being carried solely for the purpose of fishing :—

(a) for mackerel, clupeoid fish, sand-eels (Ammodytes), Norway pout (Gadus esmarkii), smelts, eels, great weevers (Trachinus draco), capelin (Mallotus villosus), Polar cod (Boreogadus saida), shrimps, prawns or molluscs other than squids in waters south of the area dividing line, or

(b) for horse mackerel (Trachurus trachurus) in waters south of the area dividing line and north of the parallel of 48° north latitude, or

(c) for blue whiting (Gadus poutassou) in waters south of the area dividing line and north of the parallel of 48° north latitude other than such part of those waters as lies between the parallels of 52° 30′ north latitude and 48° north latitude and between the meridians of 7° west longitude and 18° west longitude, or

(d) for Nephrops norvegicus (commonly known as Norway lobster or Dublin Bay prawn) in the Irish Sea, and that none of the sea-fish taken in the course of the voyage on which the net to which the proceedings relate was carried, was landed, or was to be landed, at a place other than one bordering upon the Irish Sea ; or

(a) S.I. 1969/628 (1969 I, p. 1734).

(3) (a) had in all its parts meshes of such dimensions that when any mesh was stretched diagonally lengthwise of the net a flat gauge 60 mm. broad and 2 mm. thick would pass easily through it whether the net was wet or dry, and

(b) was carried solely in that part of the Irish Sea which lies between the parallels of 53° and 54° 30′ north latitude and west of the meridian of 5° 15′ west longitude for the purpose of fishing for whiting, and

(c) was carried in a fishing boat operating from and landing its catch at a port or place bordering upon the said part of the Irish Sea.

Defences—Foreign Fishing Boats

9. In any proceedings in respect of a contravention of Article 5(2) of this Order it shall be a sufficient defence to prove that the net to which the proceedings relate :—

(a) had in no part of its cod-end meshes of such dimensions that when any mesh was stretched diagonally lengthwise of the net a flat gauge 50 mm. broad and 2 mm. thick would pass easily through it whether the net was wet or dry, and that it was being carried solely for the purpose of fishing for mackerel, clupeoid fish, sand-eels (Ammodytes), Norway pout (Gadus esmarkii), smelts, eels, great weevers (Trachinus draco), capelin (Mallotus villosus), horse mackerel (Trachurus trachurus), blue whiting (Gadus poutassou), Polar Cod (Boreogadus saida), shrimps, prawns, nephrops or molluscs, or

(b) being a net of a type specified in the first column of Schedule 3, had in all its parts meshes of such dimensions that when any mesh was stretched diagonally lengthwise of the net a flat gauge 2 mm. thick and of a width specified in the second column of Schedule 3 opposite the reference to that type of net would pass easily through the mesh whether the net was wet or dry, and that it was being carried solely for the purpose of fishing south of the parallel of 48° north latitude.

Powers of British Sea-Fishery Officers

10.—(1) For the purpose of enforcing the provisions of this Order any British sea-fishery officer may exercise in relation to any fishing boat in any waters adjacent to the United Kingdom and within the fishery limits of the British Islands, and in relation to any British fishing boat registered in the United Kingdom anywhere outside those limits, the following powers :—

(a) He may go on board the boat with or without persons assigned to assist him in his duties, and for that purpose may require the boat to stop and to do anything else which will facilitate the boarding of the boat.

(b) He may require the attendance of the master and other persons on board the boat and may make any examination and inquiry which appears to him to be necessary for the purpose of enforcing this Order, and in particular : —

(i) may examine any fish and fishing gear on the boat and require persons on board the boat to do anything which appears to him to be necessary for facilitating the examination, and

(ii) may require any person on board the boat to produce any documents relating to the boat or the persons on board which are in his custody or possession and may take copies of such documents.

(2) In relation only to any foreign fishing boat in any waters adjacent to the United Kingdom and within the fishery limits of the British Islands, if it appears to a British sea-fishery officer that a contravention of Article 5(2) or of Article 6 of this Order has at any time taken place, he may take the boat in relation to which the contravention took place and the crew of the boat to the port which appears to him to be the nearest convenient port and detain the boat and the crew in the port until the completion of proceedings for the contravention.

In witness whereof the Official Seal of the Minister of Agriculture, Fisheries and Food is hereunto affixed on 11th December 1969.

(L.S.)

Cledwyn Hughes,
Minister of Agriculture, Fisheries and Food.

Given under the seal of the Secretary of State for Scotland on 12th December 1969.

(L.S.)

William Ross,
Secretary of State for Scotland.

Given under the hand of the Secretary of State for the Home Department on 17th December 1969.

James Callaghan,
Secretary of State for the Home Department.

Article 5(1)

SCHEDULE 1

Column 1	Column 2	Column 3
Waters	Net	Appropriate width of gauge
(a) Waters of the areas north of the area dividing line	(1) Seine net	110 millimetres
	(2) Such part of any trawl net as is made of cotton hemp, polyamide fibres or polyester fibres	120 millimetres
	(3) Such part of any trawl net as is made of any other material	130 millimetres
(b) Waters of the Faroes area	(1) Seine net	105 millimetres
	(2) Such part of any trawl net as is made of manila or sisal	110 millimetres
	(3) Such part of any trawl net as is made of any other material	105 millimetres
(c) All other waters of the areas in relation to which this Order has effect	(1) Seine net, or such part of any trawl net as is made of single twine and contains no manila or sisal	70 millimetres
	(2) Such part of any trawl net as is made of double twine and contains no manila or sisal	75 millimetres
	(3) Such part of any trawl net as is made of manila or sisal	80 millimetres

Article 5(2)

SCHEDULE 2

Column 1	Column 2
Net	Appropriate width of gauge
(1) Seine net, or such part of any trawl net as is made of single twine and contains no manila or sisal	70 millimetres
(2) Such part of any trawl net as is made of double twine and contains no manila or sisal	75 millimetres
(3) Such part of any trawl net as is made of manila or sisal	80 millimetres

Article 9

SCHEDULE 3

Column 1	Column 2
Net	Appropriate width of gauge
(1) Such part of any net as is made of single twine synthetic fibre	60 millimetres
(2) Such part of any net as is made of double twine synthetic fibre	65 millimetres
(3) Such part of any net as is made of manila or sisal	70 millimetres

EXPLANATORY NOTE

(*This Note is not part of the Order.*)

This Order supersedes the Fishing Nets (North-East Atlantic) Order 1968. It prescribes minimum sizes of mesh for the fishing nets carried by registered British fishing boats for fishing in areas specified in the Order and by foreign fishing boats within the fishery limits of the British Islands adjacent to the United Kingdom.

The principal change is that the minimum sizes of mesh prescribed for nets of various descriptions carried for use in the Faroes area are increased in each case by 10 millimetres.

STATUTORY INSTRUMENTS

1969 No. 1824

TRANSPORT

PENSIONS AND COMPENSATION

The British Transport (Pensions of Employees) (No. 1) Order 1969

Made	- - -	*17th December* 1969
Laid before Parliament		*30th December* 1969
Coming into Operation		*31st December* 1969

The Minister of Transport and the Secretary of State, acting jointly, make this Order in exercise of their powers under section 74 of the Transport Act 1962(**a**), as read with section 136 of the Transport Act 1968(**b**) and section 18 of the Transport (London) Act 1969(**c**), and of all other enabling powers :—

PART I

PRELIMINARY

Commencement, citation and interpretation

1.—(1) This Order shall come into operation on the 31st December 1969 and, except as mentioned in paragraph (2) of this Article, shall have effect from the 30th October 1969.

(2) Article 7 of this Order shall have effect from the 1st January 1969, and Articles 10 and 12 to 14 of this Order shall have effect from the 31st December 1969.

(3) This Order may be cited as the British Transport (Pensions of Employees) (No. 1) Order 1969.

(4) In this Order, unless the context otherwise requires—

"the Act of 1962" means the Transport Act 1962 ;

"the Act of 1968" means the Transport Act 1968 ;

"the Act of 1969" means the Transport (London) Act 1969 ;

"beneficiary", in relation to a pension scheme, means a person who has pension rights thereunder by virtue of the pensionable service of a member who has died or whose pension rights under the scheme have otherwise terminated ;

"the Commission" means the British Transport Commission which was dissolved under the Act of 1962 ;

"the designated company" means the company (being a wholly owned subsidiary of the National Bus Company) designated under section 16(2) of the Act of 1969 ;

(**a**) 1962 c. 46.   (**b**) 1968 c. 73.
(**c**) 1969 c. 35.

"employing body" means—

 (a) for a present member of an established scheme, the publicly owned transport body employing him,

 (b) for a past member of an established scheme, the publicly owned transport body in which is vested under such one or more of the following Acts as may be relevant, that is to say, the Transport Act 1947(a), the Act of 1962, the Act of 1968 and the Act of 1969, the particular undertaking, or the particular part of an undertaking (as the case may be), in connection with which he was employed immediately before his pensionable service ended,

 (c) for a beneficiary under an established scheme, the publicly owned transport body which would have been the employing body under the foregoing provisions of this definition for the member by virtue of whose pensionable service the pension rights of the beneficiary have arisen, if that member had not died or if his pension rights under the scheme had not otherwise terminated ;

"established scheme" has the meaning given to that expression in Article 2(1) of this Order ;

"the Executive" means the London Transport Executive established under section 4 of the Act of 1969 ;

"the London Board" means the London Transport Board ;

"the Minister" means—

 (a) for the purposes of matters relating only to the Scottish Transport Group (including any subsidiary of that group), the Secretary of State,

 (b) for the purposes of matters relating both to the Scottish Transport Group (including any subsidiary as aforesaid) and to other publicly owned transport bodies, the Minister of Transport and the Secretary of State acting jointly, and

 (c) for all other purposes, the Minister of Transport ;

"member", in relation to a pension scheme, means a person who has pension rights thereunder by virtue of his pensionable service, whether or not he is a participant therein, and "membership" shall be construed accordingly ;

"national transport authority" means any of the following—

 (a) the British Railways Board,

 (b) the London Board,

 (c) the British Transport Docks Board,

 (d) the British Waterways Board,

 (e) the Transport Holding Company,

 (f) the National Freight Corporation,

 (g) the National Bus Company,

 (h) the Scottish Transport Group,

 (i) a subsidiary of any of the above bodies ;

"past member", in relation to a pension scheme, means a member whose pensionable service has ceased ;

"pensionable service", in relation to a member of a pension scheme, means service in respect of which pension rights accrue or have accrued under that scheme ;

(a) 1947 c. 49.

"present member", in relation to a pension scheme, means a member whose pensionable service has not ceased;

"publicly owned transport body" means a national transport authority, the Executive, or a subsidiary of the Executive;

"relevant Transfer Order", in relation to a transfer of liabilities or functions, means whichever of the following Orders is an Order under which the liabilities or functions in question have been or are transferred, that is to say, the No. 2 Order of 1962, the No. 3 Order of 1962, the No. 1 Order of 1968 and this Order;

"responsible body", in relation to an established scheme, means—

(i) where the scheme is one in relation to which the rights, liabilities and functions of the London Board are transferred by Part IV of this Order, the publicly owned transport body to which they are so transferred,

(ii) where the scheme is one in relation to which the property, rights and liabilities of the Transport Holding Company were transferred by Part IV of the No. 1 Order of 1968, the national transport authority to which they were so transferred,

(iii) where the scheme does not fall within (i) or (ii) above but is a scheme in relation to which the responsibility for making payments was placed, or the rights, liabilities and functions of the Commission were transferred, by the No. 2 or the No. 3 Order of 1962 (as the case may be), the national transport authority (or if more than one, any one of those authorities) on which that responsibility rests, or in which those rights, liabilities and functions are vested, immediately after the 1st January 1970,

(iv) where the scheme does not fall within (i), (ii) or (iii) above but is a scheme in which employees of a body which is a subsidiary of a national transport authority specified in any of the heads (a) to (h) of the definition of that expression in this Article are participating immediately before the 1st January 1970, whichever of the said national transport authorities is the authority of which the said body is a subsidiary immediately after the 1st January 1970,

(v) in all other cases, the national transport authority which has established the scheme;

"subsidiary", in relation to a national transport authority, has the same meaning as in the Act of 1962, and in this connection no account shall be taken of the provisions of section 51(5) of the Act of 1968;

"term", in relation to a pension scheme, includes any rule or provision of the scheme, or of any statutory provision relating to the scheme, or of any deed or other instrument made for the purposes of the scheme;

"transport pension scheme" means a pension scheme which relates in whole or in part to the provision of pensions in respect of service rendered in the employment of a publicly owned transport body.

(5) References in this Order to the No. 1, 2, 3 or 4 Order of 1962, the No. 1 Order of 1964, or the No. 1 or 2 Order of 1968 are respectively references—

(*a*) in the case of an Order of 1962 or 1964, to the British Transport Reorganisation (Pensions of Employees) Order so numbered of the year in question (**a**), and

(*b*) in the case of an Order of 1968, to the British Transport (Pensions of Employees) Order so numbered of that year (**b**).

(6) Unless the context otherwise requires, references in this Order to the provisions of any enactment or instrument shall be construed as references to those provisions as amended, re-enacted or modified by or under any subsequent enactment or instrument.

(7) The Interpretation Act 1889(**c**) shall apply for the interpretation of this Order as it applies for the interpretation of an Act of Parliament, and as if for the purposes of section 38 of that Act this Order were an Act of Parliament and the provisions revoked by Article 5 of this Order were provisions of an Act of Parliament thereby repealed.

Application of the Order

2.—(1) This Order applies to every established scheme, that is to say, to every transport pension scheme which is in existence on the 1st January 1970 and which is either—

(*a*) an existing scheme within the meaning of the No. 1 Order of 1964, or

(*b*) a pension scheme established under section 74 of the Act of 1962, or

(*c*) a pension scheme which does not fall within (*a*) or (*b*) above but is a scheme in which employees of, or of a subsidiary of, the British Railways Board or the Transport Holding Company were participating immediately before the 1st January 1969, or

(*d*) a pension scheme which does not fall within (*a*), (*b*) or (*c*) above but is a scheme in which employees of, or of a subsidiary of, the London Board are participating immediately before the 1st January 1970.

(2) Every established scheme shall, subject to the provisions of paragraph (3) of this Article, be construed and have effect as if the provisions of this Order were terms of the scheme, any other term thereof, whether express or implied, to the contrary notwithstanding, and each publicly owned transport body shall, for the purposes of giving effect to this Order, be bound by the terms of every such scheme.

(3) The rights to continue to participate in an established scheme given by this Order shall be additional to any similar rights existing under the terms of that scheme apart from the provisions of this Order and nothing in this Order shall derogate from such rights where they subsist.

PART II

REPLACEMENT, ADAPTATION AND EXTENSION OF PROVISIONS OF CERTAIN ORDERS

Obligations of employing bodies

3.—(1) Where in consequence of a statutory provision specified in paragraph (4) of this Article the employing body for any present member of an

(**a**) No. 1 Order 1962—S.I. 1962/2714 (1962 III, p. 3688); No. 2 Order 1962—S.I. 1962/2715 (1962 III, p. 3692); No. 3 Order 1962—S.I. 1962/2758 (1962 III, p. 3866); No. 4 Order 1962—S.I. 1962/2793 (1962 III, p. 4020); No. 1 Order 1964—S.I. 1964/1329 (1964 II, p. 3034).
(**b**) No. 1 Order 1968—S.I. 1968/2011 (1968 III, p. 5450); No. 2 Order 1968—S.I. 1968/2012 (1968 III, p. 5462).　　　　　　　　　　　(**c**) 1889 c. 63.

established scheme is not the responsible body, or one of the responsible bodies, for that scheme, then—

(*a*) any sums required by the terms of that scheme to be paid by that member as his contributions to the scheme shall be deducted by the employing body from his salary or wages and shall be paid by that body in accordance with those terms to the trustees of, or persons administering, the scheme ; and

(*b*) any sums required by the terms of that scheme to be paid in respect of that member by his employer as the employer's contributions to the scheme shall be paid by the employing body in accordance with those terms to the trustees of, or persons administering, the scheme.

(2) Where in consequence of a statutory provision specified in paragraph (4) of this Article the employing body for any present members or past members of, or beneficiaries under, an established scheme is not the responsible body, or one of the responsible bodies, for that scheme, then—

(*a*) the employing body shall make such payments to the responsible body or bodies by way of contributions towards the administrative expenses of the scheme or (subject to the provisions of paragraph (3) of this Article) towards any payments which the responsible body in question is obliged to make in the discharge of the liabilities, or in performance of the functions, transferred to it under a relevant Transfer Order in relation to the scheme, or to implement any guarantee given by such responsible body or binding upon it by virtue of the provisions of such Transfer Order in relation to the scheme, as may be equitable having regard to all the circumstances of the case, including the number of present members, past members and beneficiaries involved, and to any obligations or benefits (including past or prospective obligations or benefits) of the employing body or of, or in relation to, such present members, past members and beneficiaries as aforesaid, and in the case of any disagreement between the employing body and any responsible body or between any responsible bodies themselves, as to their obligations under this paragraph, the matter shall on the application of any of the bodies concerned be determined by the Minister, whose decision shall be final ;

(*b*) the Minister may, on the application of the employing body or of any responsible body, and after consultation with any other body concerned, direct that any power in relation to that scheme (whether a power of appointing trustees, amending rules, approving the admission of members, or otherwise howsoever in relation to that scheme) exercisable by the responsible body or bodies for the scheme shall be exercisable by the employing body to such extent (whether instead of the responsible body or bodies or jointly with such body or bodies) and in such manner as may appear to the Minister to be appropriate, and where any such direction is so given the terms of the scheme shall, whilst the direction remains in force, have effect subject to the provisions of the direction.

(3) Except in pursuance of an agreement made, with the consent of the Minister, between the employing body and the responsible body or bodies concerned, the employing body shall not by virtue of paragraph (2) of this Article be required to make any payment to any responsible body by way of a contribution towards any payments which the responsible body is obliged to make in discharge of any liability transferred to it by a relevant Transfer Order, being a liability in connection with any pension fund monies which were deposited with the Commission before the 1st January 1963 for the purposes of any established scheme.

(4) The statutory provisions referred to in paragraphs (1) and (2) of this Article are any provision of—

    (*a*) the Act of 1962,

    (*b*) the Act of 1968,

    (*c*) the Act of 1969,

    (*d*) any order or scheme made under any of the said Acts.

Persons having pension rights under an established scheme and becoming members or directors of a publicly owned transport body

4. Where a person who has pension rights under an established scheme by virtue of his employment by the Commission or a publicly owned transport body is on the 30th October 1969 or becomes on or after that date, a member or director of a publicly owned transport body and holds his office as such a member or director full time and at a salary, he shall be entitled to be treated for the purposes of that scheme as if his service as such a member or director were service in the employment of such a body, and as if, where that service immediately precedes or follows other service which is, or is to be treated as, service in the employment of a publicly owned transport body, the two periods of service were continuous.

Revocation of provisions

5. Articles 13 and 14 of the No. 3 Order of 1962 and Articles 7 and 8 of the No. 1 Order of 1964 (which make provision corresponding to Article 3 of this Order), Article 16 of the No. 3 Order of 1962 (which makes provision corresponding to Article 4 of this Order) and Article 4 of the No. 1 Order of 1968 (which adapts and extends Articles 13, 14 and 16 of the No. 3 Order of 1962) are hereby revoked.

Interavailability of pension schemes

6.—(1) The No. 1 Order of 1964 (which enables employees of one national transport authority to continue to participate in or to re-enter pension schemes of another national transport authority), (except Article 5 thereof), as amended by Article 3 of the No. 1 Order of 1968, shall have effect as if—

    (*a*) (except in relation to the cases mentioned in paragraph (2) of this Article) the expression "Board" in the said Order of 1964 included the Executive, and

    (*b*) the expression "existing scheme" in that Order included any established scheme as defined in this Order.

(2) The cases referred to in paragraph (1) of this Article are—

    (*a*) where a member of a pension scheme specified in Part 1 of the Schedule to this Order ceases, after the 1st January 1970, to be in the employment of the Executive or of a subsidiary of the Executive (otherwise than by reason of a transfer under section 21 or 22 of the Act of 1969) and enters the employment of a national transport authority ;

    (*b*) where a member of an established scheme (not being a pension scheme specified in Part 1 of the Schedule to this Order or referred to in Article 12(2) of this Order) ceases, after the 1st January 1970, to be in the employment of a national transport authority (otherwise than as aforesaid) and enters the employment of the Executive or of a subsidiary of the Executive.

Amendment of No. 1 *Order of* 1968

7. In Article 11 of the No. 1 Order of 1968 (which makes provision as to the transfer of property, rights and liabilities of the Transport Holding Company relating to pension schemes) there shall be inserted after paragraph (2) the following paragraph :—

"(2A) Without prejudice to the foregoing provisions of this Article, the following provisions shall have effect in relation to the Railway Clearing System Superannuation Fund Scheme on and after the 1st January 1969 :—

(*a*) the Freight Corporation shall be regarded as an Assenting Contributing Body within the meaning of, and for all the purposes of, that scheme, and

(*b*) the Freight Corporation shall be regarded for the purposes of that scheme as the employer of every member thereof who becomes, or is, employed by a subsidiary of that Corporation on or at any time after the 1st January 1969.".

PART III

ELIGIBILITY TO PARTICIPATE IN PENSION SCHEMES

Preservation of eligibility

8. Any person who, immediately before the 1st January 1970, is a present member of a pension scheme specified in Part 1 of the Schedule to this Order but who does not on or before that date become employed by the Executive or by a subsidiary of the Executive shall not in consequence of the transfer to the Executive of the rights, liabilities and functions of the London Board relating to that scheme provided for in Part IV of this Order cease to be eligible to be a member of that scheme.

Persons having no pension rights under an established scheme and becoming employees of the Executive or the designated company before 1st January 1970

9. Where a person who has no pension rights under an established scheme enters before the 1st January 1970 the employment of the Executive or the designated company after leaving the employment of the London Board or a subsidiary of that Board, he shall be eligible to become a member of that established scheme to the same extent and on the same basis as he would have been so eligible if, instead of entering the employment of the Executive or the designated company, he had been continuing in comparable employment of the London Board and if the transfer of the property, rights and liabilities of the London Board under section 16 of the Act of 1969 were not taking place.

Certain transfers not to affect eligibility to join pension schemes

10. Where by reason of a transfer under section 16, 21(3) or 22(2) of the Act of 1969 a person ceases to be employed by one publicly owned transport body and becomes employed by another such body, or the employer of a person ceases to be a subsidiary of one publicly owned transport body and becomes a subsidiary of another such body, and that person is not, immediately before the transfer, a member of an established scheme, then he shall, notwithstanding the transfer, be eligible to become a member of that established scheme to the same extent and on the same basis as he would have been so eligible if the transfer had not occurred.

Designation of pension schemes for employees of subsidiaries of the Executive, if no other pension schemes are available

11. Where on or after the 30th October 1969 a person enters employment by a subsidiary of the Executive (whether by reason of becoming an employee of that subsidiary or by reason of a change in the terms and conditions of his existing employment by that subsidiary) and apart from the provisions of this Article that person would not be eligible to become a member of a transport pension scheme appropriate to the employment which he is entering, then he shall be eligible to become a member of the London Transport (Administrative and Supervisory) Staff Superannuation Fund or the London Transport Pension Fund according as the terms and conditions of that employment would have created eligibility for membership of the Fund in question, if the employment entered had been that of the Executive.

PART IV

TRANSFER OF RIGHTS AND LIABILITIES OF LONDON BOARD

Transfer of property, rights and liabilities

12.—(1) The rights, liabilities and functions of the London Board relating to, and any property held by that Board on trust for, the established schemes which are specified in Parts 1 and 2 of the Schedule to this Order shall be respectively transferred to the Executive and the designated company.

(2) The rights, liabilities and functions of the London Board (including any property held on trust by that Board) relating to the London Borough of Newham Superannuation Fund (so far as regards persons who were formerly members of the West Ham Corporation Superannuation Fund) or to the Railway Clearing System Superannuation Fund Scheme which were transferred to the London Board by the No. 3 Order of 1962 shall be transferred to the Executive or the designated company according as those rights, liabilities, functions and property relate to persons (whether present members, or past members of, or beneficiaries under, the pension scheme in question) for whom the Executive or the designated company (as the case may be) is, or becomes, the employing body on the 1st January 1970.

(3) Any rights, liabilities and functions of the London Board relating to pensions or pension schemes, which are not transferred under the foregoing provisions of this Article or under Article 13 of this Order, shall be transferred to the Executive.

Transfer of certain liabilities

13.—(1) The liabilities of the London Board to make payments or contributions to some other national transport authority under any of the provisions mentioned in paragraph (2) of this Article shall be transferred to the Executive or the designated company according as those liabilities relate to persons (whether present members or past members of, or beneficiaries under, a pension scheme) for whom the Executive or the designated company (as the case may be) is, or becomes, the employing body on the 1st January 1970.

(2) The provisions referred to in paragraph (1) of this Article are the provisions of—

(a) Article 5 of the No. 1 Order of 1962,

(b) Articles 13 and 14 of the No. 3 Order of 1962,

(c) Article 10 of the No. 4 Order of 1962,

(d) Articles 7 and 8 of the No. 1 Order of 1964.

General provisions as to transfers

14.—(1) All the transfers of rights, liabilities, functions and property of the London Board provided for in this Part of this Order shall take place on the 1st January 1970 and shall be transfers subject to the provisions of this Order, and the rights, liabilities, functions and property hereby transferred shall by virtue of this Order vest on that date in the bodies to which they are respectively transferred.

(2) The provisions of paragraphs 8 to 13 of Schedule 2 to the Act of 1969 (so far as relevant) shall apply in relation to the transfers provided for in this Part of this Order but subject to the following modifications, that is to say,

(a) the word "agreement" in those paragraphs shall include any trust deed, rules or other instrument relating to an established scheme,

(b) the references to property, rights or liabilities in those paragraphs shall include references to functions,

(c) nothing in those paragraphs shall, in relation to the cases mentioned in paragraph (2) of Article 6 to this Order, have the effect of applying the No. 1 Order of 1964 to the Executive as if it were the London Board.

(3) Without prejudice to the foregoing provisions of this Article, the following provisions shall have effect in relation to the Railway Clearing System Superannuation Fund Scheme on and after the 1st January 1970 : —

(a) the Executive and the designated company shall be regarded as Assenting Contributing Bodies within the meaning of, and for all the purposes of, that scheme, and

(b) the Executive and the designated company shall respectively be regarded for the purposes of that scheme as the employer of every present member thereof for whom a subsidiary of the Executive or of that company (as the case may be) becomes, or is, the employing body at any time after the 1st January 1970.

(4) Nothing in this Part of this Order shall affect the tenure of office of any person appointed or nominated by the London Board before the 1st January 1970 in the exercise of any power conferred on that Board by any term of any established scheme or otherwise exercisable by that Board in relation to an established scheme.

Given under the Official Seal of the Minister of Transport the 15th December 1969.

(L.S.)
Fred Mulley,
Minister of Transport.

Given under the Seal of the Secretary of State for Scotland on 17th December 1969.

(L.S.)
William Ross,
Secretary of State for Scotland.

THE SCHEDULE

PART 1

ESTABLISHED SCHEMES—THE EXECUTIVE

British Electrical Endowment Fund.

Greater London Council Superannuation Fund.

London Borough of Bexley Superannuation Fund.

London Borough of Croydon Superannuation Fund.

London Borough of Newham Superannuation Fund (in relation to persons who were formerly members of the East Ham Corporation Superannuation Fund).

London Borough of Redbridge Superannuation Fund.

London Borough of Waltham Forest Superannuation Fund.

London Transport (Administrative and Supervisory) Staff Superannuation Fund.

London Transport (Male Wages Grades) Pension Scheme.

London Transport Pension Fund.

Metropolitan Railway Pension Fund.

Metropolitan Railway Supplementary Pension Fund (Wages Staff).

Allowances and supplementation of pensions of the former London Passenger Transport Board in pursuance of customary obligations which became obligations of the Commission under section 99(2) of the Transport Act 1947.

Allowances and supplementation of pensions of the Commission in pursuance of customary obligations which became obligations of the London Board under section 75 of, and Schedule 7 to, the Act of 1962.

Allowances and supplementation of pensions of the London Board in pursuance of schemes established with the consent of the Minister under Article 17 of the No. 3 Order of 1962.

PART 2

ESTABLISHED SCHEMES—THE DESIGNATED COMPANY

London Transport (Country Buses and Coaches) Employees' Friendly Society.

EXPLANATORY NOTE

(*This Note is not part of the Order.*)

This Order makes provision for certain changes in connection with established pension schemes in the public sector of the transport industry consequent on the establishment of the London Transport Executive by the Transport (London) Act 1969 and the establishment of a new subsidiary of the National Bus Company for the purposes of that Act.

Articles 3 and 4 replace, in an amended form, provisions which appeared in the British Transport Re-organisation (Pensions of Employees) (No. 3) Order 1962 and (No. 1) Order 1964. These provisions relate to the obligations of employing bodies to deduct employees' pension contributions from their salaries and to pay such contributions, together with employers' pension contributions and contributions towards administrative expenses, to the bodies responsible for the pension schemes in question. They also relate to the preservation of pension rights of certain persons who become members or directors of publicly owned transport bodies. The superseded provisions are revoked by Article 5.

Article 6 enables employees of one national transport authority to continue to participate in or to re-enter pension schemes of another national transport authority and Article 7 amends the British Transport (Pensions of Employees) (No. 1) Order 1968 by making further provisions as to the transfer of the rights and liabilities of the Transport Holding Company under the Transport Act 1968.

Provision is made in Articles 8 to 11 to confer on staff of the national transport authorities (and their subsidiaries) additional eligibility to join or to remain in pension schemes.

In Articles 12 to 14 the Order provides for the transfer to the London Transport Executive and the new subsidiary of the National Bus Company of the property, rights and liabilities of the London Transport Board in relation to certain established pension schemes for which the Board is at present responsible.

By virtue of section 74(7) of the Transport Act 1962 Article 7 of the Order has effect from 1st January 1969 and the rest of the Order (except for Articles 10, 12, 13 and 14) has effect from 30th October 1969.

STATUTORY INSTRUMENTS

1969 No. 1825

TRANSPORT

PENSIONS AND COMPENSATION

The British Transport (Pensions of Employees) (No. 2) Order 1969

Made - - -	*17th December* 1969
Laid before Parliament	*30th December* 1969
Coming into Operation	*31st December* 1969

The Minister of Transport and the Secretary of State, acting jointly, make this Order in exercise of their powers under section 74 of the Transport Act 1962(a), as read with section 136 of the Transport Act 1968(b) and section 18 of the Transport (London) Act 1969(c), and of all other enabling powers :—

Commencement, citation and interpretation

1.—(1) This Order shall come into operation on the 31st December 1969 and shall have effect from the 30th October 1969.

(2) This Order may be cited as the British Transport (Pensions of Employees) (No. 2) Order 1969.

(3) In this Order, unless the context otherwise requires—

"accrued pension rights" has the meaning assigned to that expression in paragraph (4) of this Article ;

"an actuary" means a Fellow of the Institute of Actuaries or of the Faculty of Actuaries in Scotland ;

"the Commission" means the British Transport Commission which was dissolved under the Transport Act 1962 ;

"discharged officer" means an officer who loses his employment as an officer by reason of a relevant event (the cause of the loss having arisen not later than the end of 10 years after the date of the event in question) and who does not thereupon enter the employment of another publicly owned transport body, and "discharge" in relation to a discharged officer means such loss of employment ;

"the Executive" means the London Transport Executive established under section 4 of the Transport (London) Act 1969 ;

"funded scheme" means a scheme, not being an insurance scheme, which relates in whole or in part to providing pensions in respect of service rendered in the employment of a publicly owned transport body, such pensions being payable out of a fund held by any person for the purposes of the scheme ;

"general scheme" means a scheme, not being a funded scheme or an insurance scheme, which relates in whole or in part to providing pensions in respect of service rendered in the employment of a publicly owned transport body ;

(a) 1962 c. 46.   (b) 1968 c. 73.
(c) 1969 c. 35.

"insurance scheme" means a scheme for providing pensions in respect of service rendered in the employment of a publicly owned transport body by way of contracts or policies made or effected with an insurance company carrying on life assurance business within the meaning of the Insurance Companies Act 1958(a) (including contracts or policies made with such a company for the purpose of implementing any form of private superannuation fund) ;

"member", in relation to a pension scheme, means a person who has pension rights thereunder whether or not he is a participant therein, and "membership" shall be construed accordingly ;

"the Minister" means the Minister of Transport ;

"national transport authority" means any of the following—

    (a) the British Railways Board,

    (b) the London Transport Board,

    (c) the British Transport Docks Board,

    (d) the British Waterways Board,

    (e) the Transport Holding Company,

    (f) the National Freight Corporation,

    (g) the National Bus Company,

    (h) the Scottish Transport Group,

    (i) a subsidiary of any of the above bodies ;

"non-participating employment" has the meaning assigned to it by section 56(1) of the National Insurance Act 1965(b) ;

"normal retiring age" means—

    (a) in relation to a discharged officer who immediately before his discharge was, by virtue of the terms of his employment or the terms of the pension scheme associated with that employment, subject to a requirement to retire from that employment before attaining the age of 65 years (if a man) or 60 years (if a woman), the age at which he would have been required by those terms to retire if he had not been discharged,

    (b) in relation to a discharged officer who immediately before his discharge had the right of continuing in his employment as an officer beyond the age of 65 years (if a man) or 60 years (if a woman), the minimum age at which he could, by the terms of his employment or the terms of his pension scheme, be required to retire or, if there is no such age, his actual age at the time when he could have been required by those terms to retire if he had not been discharged, and

    (c) in all other cases, 65 years for men and 60 years for women ;

"officer" means a person employed (whether as a member, director or holder of some other office or appointment, or as a servant) by any of the following bodies, that is to say—

    the British Railways Board,

    the London Transport Board,

    the National Bus Company,

    the Executive,

(a) 1958 c. 72.   (b) 1965 c. 51.

a subsidiary of any of the foregoing bodies,

and "employment as an officer" means such employment by any of those bodies ;

"pensionable service", in relation to a person having pension rights, means service ranking for benefit under his pension scheme ;

"publicly owned transport body" means a national transport authority, the Executive or a subsidiary of the Executive ;

"relevant event" means any one of the events specified in paragraph (a), (b) or (c) of section 37(1) of the Transport (London) Act 1969 ;

"responsible body", in relation to a pension scheme under which pensions are provided in respect of service rendered in the employment of a publicly owned transport body, means—

(i) where the scheme is one in relation to which the rights, liabilities and functions of the London Transport Board are transferred by the British Transport (Pensions of Employees) (No. 1) Order 1969(a), the publicly owned transport body to which they are so transferred,

(ii) where the scheme is one in relation to which the property, rights and liabilities of the Transport Holding Company were transferred by Part IV of the British Transport (Pensions of Employees) (No. 1) Order 1968(b), the national transport authority to which they were so transferred,

(iii) where the scheme does not fall within (i) or (ii) above but is a scheme in relation to which the responsibility for making payments was placed, or the rights, liabilities and functions of the Commission were transferred, by the British Transport Reorganisation (Pensions of Employees) (No. 2) Order 1962(c), or the British Transport Reorganisation (Pensions of Employees) (No. 3) Order 1962(d) (as the case may be), the national transport authority (or if more than one, any one of those authorities) on which that responsibility for the time being rests, or in which those rights, liabilities and functions are for the time being vested,

(iv) where the scheme does not fall within (i), (ii) or (iii) above but is a scheme in which employees of a body which is a subsidiary of a national transport authority specified in any of the heads (a) to (h) of the definition of that expression in this Article are participating immediately before the 1st January 1970, whichever of the said national transport authorities is the authority of which the said body is a subsidiary immediately after the 1st January 1970,

(v) in all other cases, the publicly owned transport body which has established the scheme ;

"subsidiary", in relation to a publicly owned transport body, has the same meaning as in the Transport Act 1962 (the provisions of section 51(5) of the Transport Act 1968 being disregarded) ; and

"tribunal" means a tribunal established under section 12 of the Industrial Training Act 1964(e).

(a) S.I. 1969/1824 (1969 III, p. 5668).   (b) S.I. 1968/2011 (1968 III, p. 5450).
(c) S.I. 1962/2715(1962 III, p.3692).   (d) S.I. 1962/2758 (1962 III, p. 3866).
(e) 1964 c. 16.

(4) In this Order the expression "accrued pension rights", in relation to a discharged officer, means any right to the payment on or after his reaching normal retiring age or on or after the happening of any other contingency (which expression includes the exercise of any right to receive a pension on retirement before reaching normal retiring age) carrying entitlement to pension under his scheme—

(a) if his scheme is an insurance scheme, of the pension which would have been payable to or in respect of him by virtue of any premiums paid by or in respect of him under the scheme up to the date of his discharge; or

(b) if his scheme is a funded scheme or a general scheme and the scheme is a scheme under which the pension rights are related by some specific proportion to pensionable service and pensionable emoluments, of a pension payable to or in respect of him calculated at such fraction or fractions of his pensionable emoluments in respect of each year or part of a year of his pensionable service as would have been applicable under that scheme in the calculation of the pension, if he had at the date of his discharge reached normal retiring age, or, as the case may be, if the other contingency had then happened and there had been no requirement of the scheme as to a minimum qualifying period of service ; or

(c) if his scheme is a funded scheme or a general scheme and the scheme is a scheme under which the pension rights are not related by some specific proportion to pensionable service and pensionable emoluments, of a pension payable to or in respect of him calculated on reaching normal retiring age or, as the case may be, on the happening of the other contingency, as follows : —

(i) on reaching normal retiring age, the pension which would have been payable under the scheme had he continued to be a member of the scheme until that age without increase of emoluments, but reduced in the proportion which the number of years of pensionable service under the scheme before the date of his discharge bears to the number of years of pensionable service which he would have rendered had he continued to be a member of the scheme until normal retiring age ; or

(ii) on the happening of the other contingency, the pension which would have been payable under the scheme if the contingency had happened on the date of his discharge with the corresponding emoluments and length of service and there had been no requirement of the scheme as to a minimum qualifying period of service:

Provided that for the purpose of ascertaining the amount of any pension under sub-paragraphs (b) and (c) of this paragraph no account shall be taken of any right to payments of pension on account of temporary periods of incapacity which exceed in total amount or total period of payment the maximum amount or period laid down in the relevant scheme.

(5) Unless the context otherwise requires, references in this Order to the provisions of any Act of Parliament or instrument made thereunder shall be construed as references to those provisions as amended, re-enacted or modified by or under any subsequent Act or instrument.

(6) The Interpretation Act 1889(a) shall apply for the interpretation of this Order as it applies for the interpretation of an Act of Parliament.

(a) 1889 c. 63.

Return of contributions

2. Where a discharged officer is entitled under his pension scheme, on his discharge, to receive any payment by way of a return of contributions paid by or in respect of him, with or without interest thereon, he may, at any time within three months of the date of his discharge exercise his right to receive such a payment ; and where such a right is exercised by any person the subsequent provisions of this Order shall not apply to him, and the persons administering the scheme, the persons in whom any fund held for the purposes of the scheme is vested, and the responsible body shall be discharged from all other liability under the scheme to or in respect of that officer or to any other person by reason of that right having been exercised.

Funded schemes

3.—(1) Subject to the provisions of this Order, this and the next two succeeding Articles shall apply to every discharged officer who at the date of his discharge has accrued pension rights under a funded scheme.

(2) In respect of a discharged officer to whom this Article applies, the responsible body may, not later than 3 months after the date of his discharge, make such arrangements with the persons administering the scheme as shall secure to him his accrued pension rights.

(3) Any arrangements made under the last foregoing paragraph may be terminated by the responsible body at any time upon giving to the persons administering the scheme 3 months' previous notice in writing.

(4) Notwithstanding anything to the contrary in any such scheme as aforesaid or any statutory provisions relating thereto or trust deeds, rules or other instruments made for the purposes thereof, the persons administering the scheme shall be authorised to make such arrangements (including the disposal of funds held for the purposes of the scheme) as are referred to in paragraph (2) of this Article and the said scheme, statutory provisions, trust deeds, rules and other instruments shall be construed accordingly and as though provision was duly made in the scheme for any arrangements so made.

4.—(1) Where no such arrangements as are mentioned in Article 3 of this Order are made in relation to a discharged officer to whom this Article applies, or where such arrangements, if made, have been duly terminated, the persons in whom any funds held for the purposes of the scheme are vested shall transfer to the responsible body a sum which equals in amount either—

(*a*) the transfer value at the date of his discharge or the date on which the arrangements are terminated, as the case may be, of his pension rights as defined for the purposes of the scheme, or

(*b*) in the absence of such a definition, the estimated capital value at that date of his accrued pension rights,

with compound interest from the date of his discharge or the date on which the arrangements are terminated, as the case may be, until such sum is transferred to the responsible body; and upon such sum being transferred, the responsible body shall indemnify the persons in whom the said sum is vested against any liability for the payment of income tax in respect of the sum transferred to that body, and, without prejudice to their liability under arrangements made in accordance with Article 3 of this Order or under the preceding provisions of this Article, as from the date of the discharge of such discharged officer, the persons administering the scheme, and the persons in whom the said fund is vested, shall be discharged from all liability under the scheme to or in respect of that discharged officer or to any other person by reason of the transfer.

(2) The reference in paragraph (1) of this Article to compound interest shall be construed as a reference to compound interest at the same rate and with the same rests as were applied—

(a) in a case where the sum to be transferred is that referred to in sub-paragraph (a) of the said paragraph, for the purposes of the last periodical actuarial valuation of the fund held for the purposes of the scheme; and

(b) in any other case, for the purposes of calculating the estimated capital value of the accrued pension rights referred to in that paragraph.

(3) The sum to be transferred to the responsible body under the provisions of paragraph (1) of this Article shall be transferred within 6 months after the date of the discharge of the officer concerned or, where any such arrangements as are referred to in paragraph (2) of the last preceding Article have been made, the date on which the arrangements are duly terminated, as the case may be.

(4) The sum referred to in paragraph (1)(b) of this Article shall be determined by an actuary appointed by the responsible body and the fees of any actuary so appointed shall be defrayed by the responsible body.

5.—(1) Subject to the provisions of this Article, where in relation to a discharged officer to whom this Article applies a sum has been transferred to the responsible body under the provisions of the last preceding Article, the responsible body shall pay to or in respect of that officer:—

(a) as from his reaching normal retiring age, or as from the happening of any other contingency carrying entitlement to pension under the scheme, the payment or payments comprised in his accrued pension rights; or

(b) at the option of the responsible body in any case where the sum does not exceed £250 and where the officer concerned has not at any time before his discharge been in non-participating employment or, if he has so been, a payment in lieu of graduated contributions has been made in respect of his non-participating employment in accordance with section 58 of the National Insurance Act 1965, (such option to be exercised not later than 6 months after the date of his discharge), a lump sum equal in amount to the estimated capital value of his accrued pension rights at the date when the option is exercised, as determined by an actuary appointed by the responsible body, reduced by the aggregate of—

(i) any sum which the persons in whom the fund held for the purposes of that scheme is vested may become liable to pay by way of income tax in respect of the amount transferred by way of transfer value or estimated capital value, and

(ii) in a case where a payment in lieu of graduated contributions has been made under section 58 of the National Insurance Act 1965 on the discharge of the officer concerned and the period taken into account in fixing the amount of that payment includes any period of his pensionable service under that scheme, the smaller of the following two sums—

(A) one-half of so much of that payment in lieu of graduated contributions as is referable to that period of pensionable service, and

(B) the estimated capital value (determined as aforesaid) of the pension rights which have accrued to him under that scheme in respect of that period of pensionable service:

Provided that for the purposes of this paragraph, the expression "accrued pension rights" excludes any pension payable during the period for which any such arrangements as are referred to in Article 3(2) of this Order are in force.

(2) Except as provided in paragraph (1)(b) of this Article, the payment or payments comprised in the accrued pension rights of a discharged officer to whom this Article applies shall not be capable of surrender, commutation or assignment otherwise than in accordance with the rules of his pension scheme.

(3) The responsible body may discharge its liability under paragraph (1)(a) of this Article by making such arrangements with a life assurance company as will secure to or in respect of the discharged officer concerned, as from his reaching normal retiring age or as from the happening of any other contingency carrying entitlement to pension under his pension scheme, the payment or payments comprised in his accrued pension rights.

(4) Except as aforesaid, the responsible body shall be under no liability to or in respect of the discharged officer concerned by reason of any rights under or arising out of his membership of the scheme.

Insurance schemes

6.—(1) Subject to the provisions of this Order, this Article shall apply to every discharged officer who at the date of his discharge has accrued pension rights under an insurance scheme.

(2) In respect of a discharged officer to whom this Article applies, the responsible body shall, not later than 3 months after the date of his discharge, make such arrangements with the persons administering the scheme and the life assurance company concerned as shall secure to or in respect of that discharged officer on his reaching normal retiring age, or on the happening of any other contingency carrying entitlement to pension under the scheme, the payment or payments comprised in his accrued pension rights.

(3) Any arrangements made under paragraph (2) of this Article shall, in any case where the payments to be secured thereunder to or in respect of a discharged officer on his reaching normal retiring age do not exceed £13 per annum and where the officer concerned has not at any time before his discharge been in non-participating employment or, if he has so been, a payment in lieu of graduated contributions has been made in respect of his non-participating employment in accordance with section 58 of the National Insurance Act 1965, provide that the life assurance company may, at any time within 3 months of the making of the arrangements, discharge its liability thereunder by paying to or in respect of the discharged officer concerned a lump sum equal in amount to the estimated capital value of his accrued pension rights as at the date on which the arrangements are made, determined in such manner as may be provided by the arrangements so made, and adjusted, in such manner as may be provided by the arrangements, in respect of the aggregate of:—

(a) any sum which the persons administering the scheme may become liable to pay by way of income tax in consequence of the payment of the said lump sum, and

(b) in a case where a payment in lieu of graduated contributions has been made under section 58 of the National Insurance Act 1965 on the discharge of the officer concerned and the period taken into account in fixing the amount of that payment includes any period of his pensionable service under that scheme, the smaller of the following two sums—

(i) one-half of so much of that payment in lieu of graduated contributions as is referable to that period of pensionable service, and

(ii) the estimated capital value (determined as aforesaid) of the pension rights which have accrued to him under that scheme in respect of that period of pensionable service.

(4) Notwithstanding anything to the contrary in such scheme as aforesaid or any statutory provisions relating thereto or trust deeds, rules or other instruments made for the purposes thereof, the persons administering the scheme and the life assurance company concerned shall be authorised to make such arrangements (including the disposal of any funds held for the purposes of the scheme) as are referred to in paragraph (2) of this Article and the said scheme, statutory provisions, trust deeds, rules and other instruments shall be construed accordingly and as though provision was duly made in the scheme for any arrangements so made.

(5) Except as provided in paragraph (3) of this Article, the arrangements aforesaid shall ensure that the payment or payments comprised in the accrued pension rights of the officer concerned shall not be capable of surrender, commutation or assignment otherwise than in accordance with the rules of his pension scheme.

General schemes

7.—(1) Subject to the provisions of this Order, this Article shall apply to every discharged officer who at the date of his discharge has accrued pension rights under a general scheme.

(2) The responsible body shall pay to or in respect of a discharged officer to whom this Article applies—

    (a) as from his reaching normal retiring age, or as from the happening of any other contingency carrying entitlement to pension under the scheme, the payment or payments comprised in his accrued pension rights; or

    (b) at the option of the responsible body in any case where the sum does not exceed £250 and where the officer concerned has not at any time before his discharge been in non-participating employment or, if he has so been, a payment in lieu of graduated contributions has been made in respect of his non-participating employment in accordance with section 58 of the National Insurance Act 1965, (such option to be exercised not later than 6 months after the date of his discharge), a lump sum equal in amount to the estimated capital value of his accrued pension rights at the date when the option is exercised, as determined by an actuary appointed by the responsible body, reduced by the aggregate of—

        (i) any sum payable by way of income tax in consequence of the payment of the said lump sum, and

        (ii) in a case where a payment in lieu of graduated contributions has been made under section 58 of the National Insurance Act 1965 on the discharge of the officer concerned and the period taken into account in fixing the amount of that payment includes any period of his pensionable service under that scheme, the smaller of the following two sums:—

           (A) one-half of so much of that payment in lieu of graduated contributions as is referable to that period of pensionable service, and

           (B) the estimated capital value (determined as aforesaid) of the pension rights which have accrued to him under that scheme in respect of that period of pensionable service.

(3) Except as provided in paragraph (2)(*b*) of this Article, the payment or payments comprised in the accrued pension rights of the officer concerned shall not be capable of surrender, commutation or assignment otherwise than in accordance with the rules of his pension scheme.

(4) The responsible body may discharge its liability under paragraph (2)(*a*) of this Article by making such arrangements with a life assurance company as will secure to or in respect of the discharged officer concerned as from his reaching normal retiring age or as from the happening of any other contingency carrying entitlement to pension under the scheme, the payment or payments comprised in his accrued pension rights.

(5) Except as aforesaid, the responsible body shall be under no liability to or in respect of the discharged officer concerned by reason of any rights under or arising out of his membership of the scheme.

Transfer of pension rights

8.—(1) Subject to the provisions of this Order, this Article shall apply to (and only to) every discharged officer who at the date of his discharge is a participant in a funded scheme, or who, having immediately before entering the employment of the Commission been a participant in a funded scheme, is at the date of his discharge a member of a general scheme by virtue of regulations made by the Minister under section 98 of the Transport Act 1947(**a**).

(2) In respect of any discharged officer to whom this Article applies, and who, within a period of 12 months from the date of his discharge, obtains other employment in connection with which he has pension rights under another pension scheme (being a scheme approved in whole or in part by the Commissioners of Inland Revenue under section 379 of the Income Tax Act 1952(**b**) or otherwise approved by them for the purposes of this Article), the responsible body may, subject to the provisions of this Article, make arrangements with the persons administering that other scheme and, in the case of a participant in a funded scheme, with the persons administering that scheme, for the transfer to the persons administering that other scheme of a sum which equals in amount either—

(*a*) the transfer value at the date on which the arrangements are made of his pension rights as defined for the purposes of his existing scheme, or

(*b*) in the absence of such a definition, the estimated capital value at that date of his accrued pension rights,

with compound interest from the date on which the arrangements are made until such transfer is made:

Provided that no such arrangements shall be concluded unless and until the responsible body has communicated the terms thereof to the discharged officer concerned, has furnished him with a copy of a certificate given by the actuary of that other pension scheme certifying that the pension rights to be conferred on him under the arrangements, if made, will be actuarially equivalent to his accrued pension rights under his former scheme, and has obtained his consent to the making of the arrangements.

(a) 1947 c. 49.   (b) 1952 c. 10.

(3) Except as provided in paragraph (2)(b) of this Article, the payment or payments comprised in the accrued pension rights of the officer concerned shall not be capable of surrender, commutation or assignment otherwise than in accordance with the rules of his pension scheme.

(4) The responsible body may discharge its liability under paragraph (2)(a) of this Article by making such arrangements with a life assurance company as will secure to or in respect of the discharged officer concerned as from his reaching normal retiring age or as from the happening of any other contingency carrying entitlement to pension under the scheme, the payment or payments comprised in his accrued pension rights.

(5) Except as aforesaid, the responsible body shall be under no liability to or in respect of the discharged officer concerned by reason of any rights under or arising out of his membership of the scheme.

Transfer of pension rights

8.—(1) Subject to the provisions of this Order, this Article shall apply to (and only to) every discharged officer who at the date of his discharge is a participant in a funded scheme, or who, having immediately before entering the employment of the Commission been a participant in a funded scheme, is at the date of his discharge a member of a general scheme by virtue of regulations made by the Minister under section 98 of the Transport Act 1947(a).

(2) In respect of any discharged officer to whom this Article applies, and who, within a period of 12 months from the date of his discharge, obtains other employment in connection with which he has pension rights under another pension scheme (being a scheme approved in whole or in part by the Commissioners of Inland Revenue under section 379 of the Income Tax Act 1952(b) or otherwise approved by them for the purposes of this Article), the responsible body may, subject to the provisions of this Article, make arrangements with the persons administering that other scheme and, in the case of a participant in a funded scheme, with the persons administering that scheme, for the transfer to the persons administering that other scheme of a sum which equals in amount either—

(a) the transfer value at the date on which the arrangements are made of his pension rights as defined for the purposes of his existing scheme, or

(b) in the absence of such a definition, the estimated capital value at that date of his accrued pension rights,

with compound interest from the date on which the arrangements are made until such transfer is made:

Provided that no such arrangements shall be concluded unless and until the responsible body has communicated the terms thereof to the discharged officer concerned, has furnished him with a copy of a certificate given by the actuary of that other pension scheme certifying that the pension rights to be conferred on him under the arrangements, if made, will be actuarially equivalent to his accrued pension rights under his former scheme, and has obtained his consent to the making of the arrangements.

(a) 1947 c. 49.   (b) 1952 c. 10.

(3) An officer to whom this Article applies as a result of a change in the nature or terms of his employment, the change being such as would terminate his membership of the pension scheme, shall have the right, if he gives notice in writing to that effect to the persons administering the scheme within 3 months of the date of such change, to continue to be a member of the scheme so long as he remains in the employment of a publicly owned transport body and to be treated as having been such from the date of such change and as subject to the like conditions as to payment of premiums or contributions and otherwise in all respects as if that change had not taken place; and notwithstanding anything to the contrary contained therein, every such scheme and any statutory provisions relating thereto and all trust deeds, rules and other instruments made for the purposes thereof, shall be construed accordingly and as though the provisions of this paragraph were a term of the scheme.

(4) Where an officer who is entitled to give notice under paragraph (3) of this Article to the persons administering a pension scheme does not give that notice within the time prescribed thereby, the provisions of this Order (other than Article 2) shall apply in respect of him as if he were a discharged officer and as if the date of the change in the nature or terms of his employment which entitles him to give the said notice were the date of his discharge.

Payment of contributions towards liability of responsible body

10.—(1) Where by reason of any provision of this Order any liability falls upon the responsible body for a pension scheme in respect of a discharged officer or an officer to whom Article 9 of this Order applies and—

(*a*) in the case of a discharged officer, he was not an officer of, or of any subsidiary of, that body immediately before his discharge, and

(*b*) in the case of an officer to whom Article 9 of this Order applies, he was not an officer of, or of any subsidiary of, that body immediately before the occurrence of the diminution of his emoluments or the change in the nature or terms of his employment,

then the body specified in paragraph (2) of this Article as the appropriate body shall make such payment by way of contribution to the liability of the responsible body as may be just in all the circumstances; and if there is any disagreement between the bodies concerned as to the obligations of any such body as aforesaid under this Article, the matter shall, on the application of either body, be referred for decision to the Minister and the Secretary of State jointly, in a case involving the Scottish Transport Group, or to the Minister in all other cases, and the decision of the Minister and the Secretary of State or the decision of the Minister (as the case may be) shall be final.

(2) For the purposes of paragraph (1) of this Article the appropriate body shall be—

(*a*) where the officer in question was employed by the London Transport Board immediately before his discharge or the occurrence of the diminution of his emoluments or the change in the nature or terms of his employment, the publicly owned transport body to which is transferred under the Transport (London) Act 1969 that part of the undertaking of the London Transport Board in connection with which he was then employed, (*b*) where the officer in question was employed by a subsidiary of the London Transport Board immediately before the discharge or occurrence aforesaid, the publicly owned transport body to the control of which the said subsidiary is transferred under the said Act of 1969,

(*c*) in all other cases, whichever of the following bodies, that is to say, the British Railways Board, the National Bus Company and the Executive, is the body by which, or by the subsidiary of which, the officer in question was employed immediately before the discharge or occurrence aforesaid.

Determination of disputes

11. Without prejudice to the provisions of Article 10 of this Order any question arising between the responsible body and any person as to whether that person is a member of a pension scheme, and any question arising between the responsible body and a member of a pension scheme as to the application or effect of any of the provisions of Articles 3(2), 5(1)(*a*), 5(3), 6(2), 7(2)(*a*) or 7(4) of this Order shall in default of agreement between the parties concerned be referred to a tribunal.

Given under the Official Seal of the Minister of Transport the 15th December 1969.

(L.S.)

Fred Mulley,
Minister of Transport.

Given under the Seal of the Secretary of State for Scotland on 17th December 1969.

(L.S.)

William Ross,
Secretary of State for Scotland.

EXPLANATORY NOTE

(*This Note is not part of the Order.*)

This Order deals with the preservation of the pension rights of persons who because of changes brought about as provided for in the Transport (London) Act 1969 either lose their employment or suffer diminution of emoluments or a change in the nature or terms of their employment.

In the case of a person who loses his employment, the pension accrued up to the date on which he was discharged is normally to be paid to him at age 65 (age 60 for a woman) or at such time as, by the terms of his employment or of his pension scheme, he would have been entitled to receive a pension (Articles 3(2), 5(1)(*a*), 6(2) and 7(2)(*a*)). A discharged person may, however, elect within 3 months of his discharge to have a return of contributions if the rules of his pension scheme permit this; but, if he does so, he will have no other rights under the Order (Article 2). Where the value of the accrued pension rights is small, the responsible body as defined in Article 1(3) (or in the case of an insurance scheme, the life assurance company) may, in certain circumstances and at their option, commute their liability by an immediate lump sum payment (Articles 5(1)(*b*), 6(3) and 7(2)(*b*)).

The responsible body may discharge its liability to preserve a discharged person's accrued pension rights by arranging for a life assurance company to make the payments at the appropriate time (Articles 5(3) and 7(4)).

In certain cases, where the new employment obtained by a discharged person is pensionable, the responsible body may, with the prior agreement of the discharged person, pay or arrange for the payment to that person's new pension scheme of the sum representing the value of that person's rights in his former scheme (Article 8).

A person who does not lose his employment but who suffers a reduction in pay may be allowed to continue to contribute to, and benefit from, his pension scheme on the basis of his former pay. Similarly, if such a person is transferred from a pensionable to a non-pensionable grade he can, within 3 months, choose to remain in his pension scheme, though if he does not choose to do this his pension rights will be preserved in the same way as if he had been discharged (Article 9).

Provision is made for contributions between the responsible transport bodies defined in the Order (Article 10) and for the settlement of disputes (Article 11).

The Order has effect from 30th October 1969 by virtue of section 74(7) of the Transport Act 1962.

STATUTORY INSTRUMENTS

1969 No. 1826

OPTICIANS

The General Optical Council (Disciplinary Committee) (Procedure) Order of Council 1969

Made - - - - - 18*th December* 1969

At the Council Chamber, Whitehall, the 18th day of December 1969

By the Lords of Her Majesty's Most Honourable Privy Council

Whereas in pursuance of section 15(2) of the Opticians Act 1958(a) the General Optical Council have made rules entitled "The General Optical Council Disciplinary Committee (Procedure) Rules 1969":

And whereas by subsection (4) of the said section such rules shall not come into force until approved by Order of the Privy Council:

Now, therefore, Their Lordships, having taken the said rules into consideration, are hereby pleased to approve the same as set out in the Schedule to this Order.

This Order may be cited as the General Optical Council (Disciplinary Committee) (Procedure) Order of Council 1969.

W. G. Agnew.

SCHEDULE

THE GENERAL OPTICAL COUNCIL DISCIPLINARY COMMITTEE (PROCEDURE) RULES 1969

The General Optical Council, having complied with the provisions of section 15(3) of the Opticians Act 1958, in exercise of their powers under section 15(2) of the Act hereby make the following rules:—

PART I

CITATION AND INTERPRETATION

1.—(1) These rules may be cited as the General Optical Council Disciplinary Committee (Procedure) Rules 1969.

(2) In these rules, unless the context otherwise requires:

"the Act" means the Opticians Act 1958;

"the Chairman" means the Chairman or the Acting Chairman of the Committee;

"the Committee" means the Disciplinary Committee set up by the Council in pursuance of section 10(1) of the Act;

"the complainant" means a person or body by whom a complaint has been made to the Council in a case to which these rules apply; a complainant shall not be deemed to appear in any proceeding if he takes part therein only as a witness;

(a) 1958 c. 32.

"conviction" means a conviction by any Court in the United Kingdom of any criminal offence, not being an offence which, owing to its trivial nature or the circumstances under which it was committed, does not render a registered optician unfit to have his name on the register;

"the Council" means the General Optical Council;

"disciplinary case" means a disciplinary case as defined in section 9(1) of the Act which the Investigating Committee decide ought to be referred to the Disciplinary Committee pursuant to section 9(2) of the Act;

"inquiry" means the proceedings at which the Committee consider and determine any disciplinary case or other case to which these rules apply;

"the Investigating Comittee" means the Committee set up by the Council in pursuance of section 9(1) of the Act for the preliminary consideration of disciplinary cases;

"the Legal Assessor" means an assessor appointed by the Council or the Committee for the purposes of section 16 of the Act;

"party to the inquiry" means the complainant (if any), the Solicitor and any person on whom a notice of inquiry has been served in accordance with these rules: provided that if the complainant does not appear at the inquiry he shall not thereafter be included in the said phrase;

"register" and "list" have the meanings given to them by section 30(1) of the Act;

"the Registrar" means the registrar of the Council;

"the respondent" means any person or body corporate whose name has been entered in a register or list under the provisions of the Act and in respect of whom a case to which these rules apply has been referred to the Committee for inquiry;

"the Solicitor" means a solicitor nominated by the Council to act as their solicitor for the purposes of these rules, and in relation to an inquiry includes counsel instructed by the Solicitor to act on his behalf.

(3) The Interpretation Act 1889(a) shall apply for the interpretation of these rules as it applies for the interpretation of an Act of Parliament.

PART II
PRELIMINARY PROCEEDINGS

Notice of Inquiry

2.—(1) The Solicitor shall, as soon as may be after a disciplinary case has been referred to the Committee, serve upon the respondent a notice of inquiry as nearly as may be in the form set out in the Appendix to these rules stating the charge or charges and specifying the alleged convictions or other facts relied on in relation to each charge and the provision of section 11 of the Act under which any charge is brought, and stating also the day, time and place at which the Committee will hold an inquiry into these matters, and enclosing a copy of these rules and of the Act. The said notice and copies shall be sent by post in a registered letter addressed to the respondent in accordance with the provisions of section 11(8) of the Act as though it were a notification to which that sub section applies.

(2) If there is a complainant the Solicitor shall send him a copy of the notice of inquiry and a copy of these rules.

(3) The Committee shall not hold an inquiry unless a notice of inquiry has been served upon the respondent in accordance with the foregoing provisions of this rule.

(4) Except with the agreement of the respondent the inquiry shall not be held within twenty-eight days after the date of posting the notice of inquiry.

Postponement or Cancellation of Inquiry

3.—(1) The Chairman, of his own motion or upon the application of any party thereto, may postpone the hearing of an inquiry, or may refer a disciplinary case to the Investigating Committee for further consideration as to whether an inquiry should be held.

<hr/>

(a) 1889 c. 63.

(2) Where before the inquiry opens it appears to the Chairman, or at any stage of the proceedings it appears to the Committee, that a notice of inquiry is defective, he or they shall cause the notice to be amended, unless it appears to him or them that the required amendment cannot be made without injustice, or, if he or they consider that the circumstances in which an amendment is made require it, he or they may direct that the amended notice shall be served on the respondent and that the inquiry shall be postponed.

(3) The Solicitor shall, as soon as may be, give to all parties to whom a notice of inquiry has been sent notification of any decision to postpone or not to hold an inquiry, and inform them of any date fixed for the hearing of a postponed inquiry.

Access to Documents

4. Upon application by any party to the inquiry the Solicitor shall send to that party a copy of any statutory declaration, complaint, answer, admission, explanation or other similar document received by the Council from any party to the inquiry.

PART III

DISCIPLINARY CASES

The Reading of the Charge or Charges

5.—(1) The charge or charges shall be read in the presence of the respondent, and of the complainant if one appears:

Provided that if the respondent does not appear at the inquiry but the Committee nevertheless decide that the inquiry shall proceed the charge or charges shall be read in his absence.

(2) As soon as the charge or charges have been read the respondent may, if he so desires, object to the charge or charges, or to any part thereof, in point of law, and any other party may reply to any such objection; and, if any such objection is upheld, no further proceedings shall be taken on a charge or on a part of a charge to which the objection relates.

Proof of the facts alleged

6.—(1) If the respondent has appeared at the inquiry the Chairman shall ask if all or any of the convictions or other facts alleged in the charge or charges are admitted.

(2) The complainant or, if no complainant appears, the Solicitor shall then open the case and may call witnesses and adduce evidence of any such convictions or other facts not admitted by the respondent and of any matter connected with the facts alleged which may be relevant.

The respondent may cross-examine any such witness and the witness may thereafter be re-examined.

(3) The respondent may then submit that the evidence called by the Solicitor does not establish the charge alleged or does not justify the erasure of his name from the register. The Committee shall consider and determine any such submission, and the Chairman shall thereupon announce their determination.

(4) If no such submission is made, or if any such submission is not upheld, the respondent may then call witnesses and adduce evidence; such witnesses may be cross-examined and re-examined, and the respondent may address the Committee either before or after such evidence but not more than once save with the leave of the Committee. The Complainant or, if no complainant appears, the Solicitor may address the Committee on any point of law raised by the respondent.

(5) Where the respondent adduces evidence the complainant or, if no complainant appears, the Solicitor may address the Committee thereon and may call witnesses and adduce evidence in rebuttal and such witnesses may be cross-examined and re-examined. The respondent shall have the right to address the Committee upon such address or evidence in rebuttal.

(6) The Committee shall then deliberate, and decide in relation to each charge which remains outstanding whether the facts alleged in such charge have been proved and in relation to any facts found by the Committee to have been proved whether they are such as to substantiate such charge, and the Chairman shall announce their findings:

Provided that if the Committee find that any charge under section 11 of the Act is not proved a finding to that effect shall be recorded.

7.—(1) Where the Committee find that a charge is proved the Chairman shall invite the complainant or, if no complainant appears, the Solicitor to adduce evidence of the circumstances leading up to the facts found proved and as to the character and antecedents of the respondent.

(2) The respondent may then address the Committee in mitigation and adduce any relevant evidence.

(3) The Committee shall then deliberate and decide whether they can properly reach a decision forthwith not to erase the name of the respondent from the register or list or, in a case to which section 11(6) of the Act applies, not to issue a direction under that subsection.

(4) If the Committee decide the question under the last foregoing paragraph in the negative they shall then decide whether to postpone judgement or forthwith to direct the Registrar to erase the name of the respondent from the register or list, or, in a case to which section 11(6) of the Act applies, forthwith to issue a direction under that subsection.

(5) If the Committee decide under the last foregoing paragraph to postpone judgement, they shall specify either a period for which judgement is postponed, or a further meeting of the Committee at which they will further consider the judgement.

(6) Any decision of the Committee under this rule shall be announced by the Chairman in such terms as the Committee may approve.

Procedure upon postponement of judgement

8.—(1) Where under the foregoing provisions of these rules the judgement of the Committee in any case stands postponed, the procedure shall be as follows:—

(a) The Solicitor shall, not less than six weeks before the day fixed for the resumption of proceedings, send to the respondent a notice which shall

    (i) specify the day, time and place at which the proceedings are to be resumed and invite him to appear thereat,

    (ii) unless the Chairman otherwise directs, invite the respondent to furnish the Registrar with the names and addresses of persons to whom reference may be made confidentially or otherwise concerning his character and conduct, and

    (iii) invite the respondent to send to the Solicitor, not less than three weeks before the day fixed for the resumption of proceedings, a copy of any statement or statutory declaration, whether made by the respondent or not, relating to his conduct or setting out any material facts which have arisen since that hearing.

(b) A copy of the notice and of any statement or statutory declaration sent in accordance with the provisions of the last foregoing sub-paragraph shall be sent to the complainant, if any, if he is then a party to the inquiry and he may in turn, if he so desires, send to the Solicitor a statement or statutory declaration, whether made by himself or not, as to the matters mentioned in that sub-paragraph, or as to any other material facts which have arisen since the hearing. A copy of any such statement or statutory declaration shall thereupon be supplied to the respondent.

(c) At the meeting at which the proceedings are resumed the Chairman shall first invite the Solicitor to recall, for the information of the Committee, the position in which the case stands, and the Committee may then receive further oral or documentary evidence as to the conduct of the respondent or any material facts which may have arisen since the hearing, and shall hear any party to the inquiry who desires to be heard.

(*d*) The Committee shall than consider their decision, and paragraphs (3) to (6) of Rule 7 shall apply to their procedure.

(2) At any resumed proceedings any new charge alleged against the respondent in accordance with these rules shall first be dealt with in accordance with such of the provisions of Rules 5 to 7 as may be applicable, and the Committee may apply paragraphs (3) to (6) of Rule 7 simultaneously to the new charge and to the charge in respect of which they had postponed judgement.

(3) Nothing in the last foregoing paragraph shall prevent the Committee from receiving evidence at any resumed proceedings of any conviction recorded against the respondent which has not been made the subject of a charge under these rules.

(4) Subject to the provisions of the Act, the validity of any resumed proceedings shall not be called into question by reason only that members of the Committee who were present at any former meeting were not present at the resumed meeting or that members present at the resumed meeting were not present at any former meeting.

(5) The Chairman, of his own motion or upon the application of any party thereto, may postpone the resumption of proceedings, and in that case the Solicitor shall so soon as may be inform all parties to whom notice of the resumption of proceedings has been given of the postponement and of any date now fixed for the resumption of proceedings.

PART IV

REMOVAL OF NAME OF BODY CORPORATE FROM THE LIST UNDER SECTION 11(5) OF THE ACT

9.—(1) This Part of these rules applies to proceedings brought for the purpose of removing the names of a body corporate from the list, under section 11(5) of the Act, or, if the Committee so decide, of issuing a direction under section 11(6).

(2) Where:—

   (i) the name of a director of an enrolled body corporate is erased from the register under section 11 of the Act or

   (ii) a director of an enrolled body corporate is convicted of an offence under the Act or

   (iii) the name of a registered optician employed by an enrolled body corporate is erased from the register (unless the Committee have stated that they are satisfied that the act or omission constituting the ground on which it was erased was not instigated or connived at by a director of the body corporate or, if the act or omission was a continuing act or omission, that a director of the body had not nor was reasonably required to have had knowledge of the continuance thereof)

and the period within which proceedings might be brought by way of appeal under section 14 of the Act has expired, or any such appeal has been dismissed, withdrawn or struck out, the provisions of Rule 10 shall apply.

10.—(1) The Solicitor shall send to the respondent body corporate and to the complainant (if any) a notice of inquiry in accordance with Rule 2, the charges and facts to be specified being the circumstances falling under Rule 9 which are relevant to the case.

(2) A copy of the notice shall be sent to every director of or registered optician employed by the respondent who is named therein. The Chairman may direct that a copy of the notice shall also be sent to any other person or body.

(3) Any other person or body may with the leave of the Chairman or of the Committee appear at the inquiry as an additional respondent.

(4) Any erasure from the register shall be proved by a certificate to that effect signed by the Registrar.

(5) Subject to the provisions of this rule the provisions of Parts II (except as regards reference to the Investigating Committee) and III of these rules shall apply to any proceedings to which this rule applies.

PART V

CASES UNDER SECTION 13 OF THE ACT RELATING TO FRAUDULENT OR INCORRECT ENTRIES IN REGISTER OR LIST

11.—(1) Where any question, whether an entry in the register or list has been fraudulently or incorrectly made, has been referred to the Committee, the Solicitor shall send to the respondent (being the person or body corporate in relation to whom the entry was made) a notice of inquiry specifying the nature of the fraud or mistake alleged, stating the day, time and place at which the Committee will hold an inquiry into the question, inviting his attendance thereat, and containing such further information as the nature of the case may require.

(2) Subject to the provisions of this rule, the provisions of Part II of these rules (except as regards reference to the Investigating Committee) shall apply to any proceedings to which this rule applies.

(3) Where the question is whether the entry in the register or list has been fraudulently made a copy of the notice shall be sent to any person who is alleged to have been a party to the fraud and to such other persons (if any) as the Chairman may direct. Any such person may with the leave of the Chairman or of the Committee appear at the inquiry as an additional party thereto.

(4) The inquiry shall proceed as though the question were a charge contained in a notice of inquiry in a disciplinary case and the provisions of Rule 6 shall accordingly apply thereto so far as may be.

(5) If the Committee determine that the entry has been proved to their satisfaction to have been fraudulently or incorrectly made, they shall make an order in writing, signed by the Chairman, that the entry having been proved to the satisfaction of the Committee to have been fraudulently or incorrectly made (as the case may be) shall be erased from the register or list, and the Chairman shall announce the determination in terms indicating whether in the view of the Committee the entry was made fraudulently or was made incorrectly but not fraudulently.

(6) Where an inquiry relates to two or more entries, the Committee may proceed under the foregoing provisions of this rule to consider the allegations in respect of those entries either separately or taken together, as the Committee may think fit; and where an inquiry relates to an entry specifying two or more particulars, the Committee may proceed thereunder in respect of so much of the entry as specifies each of those particulars as if it were a separate entry.

PART VI

RESTORATION OF NAMES AFTER ERASURE

12. Where an application is made:

    (a) in accordance with section 12 of the Act by a person or body whose name has been erased from a register or list in pursuance of a direction made under section 11 of the Act; or

    (b) in accordance with section 13(2) of the Act by a person or body whose name has been erased from a register or list on the ground of fraud in pursuance of a direction by the Committee under section 13(1); or

    (c) in accordance with section 11(6) of the Act by a body corporate that a direction made in respect of it by the Committee under that subsection should not remain in force;

the following provisions shall have effect:—

    (i) the Committee shall afford the applicant an opportunity of being heard by the Committee and of adducing evidence;

    (ii) the Committee may require such evidence as they think necessary concerning the identity or character of the applicant, or his conduct since his name was erased from the register or list, and for this purpose may receive written or oral evidence;

    (iii) subject to the foregoing provisions of this rule, and to Part VII of these rules, the procedure of the Committee in connection with the application shall be such as they may determine.

PART VII

GENERAL

Hearing and Adjournment

13.—(1) Subject to the provisions of section 16(3) of the Act, and of any rules made thereunder, the Committee may deliberate in camera (with or without the Legal Assessor) at any time and for any purpose during or after the hearing of any proceedings.

(2) Save as aforesaid all proceedings before the Committee shall take place in the presence of all parties thereto who appear therein and shall be held in public except as provided by the next following paragraph of this rule.

(3) Where in the interests of justice it appears to the Committee that the public should be excluded from any proceedings or part thereof, the Committee may direct that the public shall be so excluded; but a direction under this paragraph shall not apply to the announcement in pursuance of any of these rules of a determination of the Committee.

(4) The Committee may adjourn their proceedings from time to time as they think fit.

Evidence

14.—(1) Where a respondent or an applicant under Rule 12 has supplied to the Committee or to the Registrar on their behalf the name of any person to whom reference may be made confidentially as to his character or conduct, the Committee may consider any information received from such person in consequence of such reference without disclosing the same to the respondent or applicant.

(2) The Committee may receive oral, documentary or other evidence of any fact which appears to them relevant to the inquiry into the case before them:

Provided that, where a fact which it is sought to prove, or the form in which any evidence is tendered, is such that it would not be admissible in criminal proceedings in a court of law the Committee shall not receive evidence of the fact or in that form, unless after consultation with the Legal Assessor they are satisfied that it is desirable in the interests of justice to receive it having regard to the difficulty and expense of obtaining evidence which would be so admissible.

(3) The Committee may cause any person to be called as a witness in any proceedings before them whether or not the parties consent thereto. Questions may be put to any witness by the Committee through the Chairman or by the Legal Assessor with the leave of the Chairman.

Voting

15.—(1) Any question put to the vote shall be put in the form of a motion. The Chairman shall call upon members present to vote for or against the motion and shall declare that the motion appears to him to have been carried or not carried as the case may be.

(2) Where the result so declared is challenged by any member, the Chairman shall call upon the Registrar to read the roll, and as his name is read every member present including the Chairman (who shall be called last) shall say "For" or "Against" according to whether his vote is given for or against the motion. The Chairman shall thereupon declare the number of members who have voted for the motion and the number who have voted against the motion, and whether the motion has been carried or not carried.

(3) Where on any question the votes are equal, the question shall be deemed to have been resolved in favour of the respondent or of the applicant under Rule 12, as the case may be.

Procedure where there is more than one respondent

16. Nothing in this Part of these rules shall prevent one inquiry being held into charges against two or more respondents, and where such an inquiry is held the foregoing rules shall apply with the necessary adaptations and subject to any directions given by the Committee as to the order in which proceedings shall be taken under any of these rules by or in relation to the several respondents, so however that any of the rights of a respondent under these rules shall be exercised separately by each of the respondents who desires to invoke that right.

Supplementary

17.—(1) Any party being an individual may appear either in person or by counsel or solicitor, or if the party so elects by any officer or member of any organisation of which he is a member, or by any member of his family.

(2) Any party being a body corporate or an unincorporated body of persons may appear by their secretary or other officer duly appointed for the purpose or by counsel or solicitor.

18. A shorthand-writer shall be appointed by the Committee to take shorthand notes of proceedings before them (except that the Committee may dispense with a shorthand-writer in proceedings under Part VI of these rules) and any party to an inquiry shall, on application to the Solicitor and on payment of the proper charge on a scale fixed by the Committee, be furnished by the Solicitor with a transcript of the shorthand notes of any part of the inquiry at which the party was entitled to be present.

Operation of rules

19. These rules shall come into operation on the 1st day of January 1970, and the General Optical Council Disciplinary Committee (Procedure) Rules 1961, scheduled to the General Optical Council (Disciplinary Committee) (Procedure) Order of Council 1961(a), shall cease to have effect on that date.

Sealed on the 22nd day of October 1969

Attested by:

G. R. Rougier,
Member of Council.

L.S.

Ronald Russell
Member of Council.

A. T. Gerard,
Registrar.

APPENDIX

Form of Notice Under Rule 2

Sir/Madam,

On behalf of the General Optical Council notice is hereby given to you that in consequence of (a complaint made against you to the Council) [*or*] (information received by the Council) an inquiry is to be held into the following charges, on which evidence will be placed before the Committee at the meeting referred to below.

[Here set out the charge or charges, numbering them consecutively where there is more than one charge. State the section, subsection and paragraph of the Act under which each charge is brought and the convictions or other facts constituting the basis of such charge.]

(a) S.I. 1961/1933 (1961 III, p. 3639).

You are hereby invited to send me an answer in writing, to the above-mentioned charge(s), stating whether you admit or deny it (them) and also specifying which, if any, of the facts set out above you admit. Any answer, admission, or other statement or communication which you may desire to make with respect to the said charge(s) should be addressed to me at the above address.

Notice is further given to you that on [day of the week], the.................
day of.................. 19...., a meeting of the Disciplinary Committee of the Council will be held at ....(address)......................
at ....(time)........ to consider the above mentioned charge(s) against you and to determine whether or not they should direct the Registrar to erase your name from the register (list) pursuant to section 11 of the Opticians Act 1958, or give any other direction provided for in that section. You are invited to appear before the Committee at the place and time specified above for the purpose of answering the charge(s). The Committee have power, if you do not appear, to hear and decide upon the said charge(s) in your absence.

If you desire to make an application that the inquiry should be postponed you should send it to me at the above address as soon as may be, stating the grounds upon which you desire a postponement. Any such application will be considered by the Chairman of the General Optical Council in accordance with the General Optical Council Disciplinary Committee (Procedure) Rules 1969, a copy of which is sent herewith for your information, along with a copy of the Opticians Act 1958.

Your attention is drawn to the provisions of Rule 17 of these rules with regard to your right to be represented by counsel, solicitor or other persons.

I am, Sir/Madam,

Your obedient servant,

Solicitor to the General Optical Council.

EXPLANATORY NOTE
(*This Note is not part of the Order.*)

The rules approved by this Order supersede the existing rules prescribing the procedure to be followed and the rules of evidence to be observed in proceedings before the Disciplinary Committee of the General Optical Council.

The principal changes include the institution of a common set of rules for the proof of alleged facts applicable to all types of disciplinary cases, and new provisions governing the sequence of the decisions to be made by the Disciplinary Committee upon finding a charge proved.

STATUTORY INSTRUMENTS

1969 No. 1829

PLANT BREEDERS' RIGHTS

The Plant Varieties and Seeds (Isle of Man) Order 1969

Made	-	-	-	19*th December* 1969
Coming into Operation				1*st January* 1970

At the Court at Buckingham Palace, the 19th day of December 1969

Present,

The Queen's Most Excellent Majesty in Council

Her Majesty, in pursuance of the power conferred upon Her by section 40 of the Plant Varieties and Seeds Act 1964(a), is pleased, by and with the advice of Her Privy Council, to order, and it is hereby ordered, as follows:—

1. This Order may be cited as the Plant Varieties and Seeds (Isle of Man) Order 1969 and shall come into operation on 1st January 1970.

2. The provisions of Part I (Plant Breeders' Rights), and of Part IV (General) in its application to the said Part I, of the Plant Varieties and Seeds Act 1964, as extended by the Plant Varieties and Seeds (Northern Ireland) Order 1964(b) and as amended by section 43 of, and the first entry in Schedule 7 to, the Agriculture (Miscellaneous Provisions) Act 1968(c), shall extend to the Isle of Man subject to the exceptions, adaptations and modifications specified in the Schedule to this Order.

W. G. Agnew.

SCHEDULE

EXCEPTIONS, ADAPTATIONS AND MODIFICATIONS IN THE EXTENSION
OF THE PLANT VARIETIES AND SEEDS ACT 1964 TO THE ISLE OF MAN

1. In section 4(1)(*b*) and (2) for the words "Great Britain" wherever they occur there shall be substituted the words "the Isle of Man".

2. In section 5A(2) for the words "Great Britain" there shall be substituted the words "the Isle of Man".

3. Section 8 shall be omitted.

4. In section 10(5)(*a*) for the words "in which part of Great Britain" there shall be substituted the words "where in the Isle of Man".

5. Section 14(2) and (3) shall be omitted.

6. Section 35(2) shall be omitted.

(a) 1964 c. 14.　　(b) S.I. 1964/1574 (1964 III, p. 3543).　　(c) 1968 c. 34.

7. In section 36(*b*) the words "Minister or" shall be omitted.

8. Section 37 shall be omitted.

9. In section 38(1) for the definitions of "the Minister" and "the Ministers" there shall be substituted the following definition:—

' "the Ministers" means the Minister of Agriculture, Fisheries and Food and the Secretary of State acting jointly;'.

10. Section 41(2) shall be omitted.

11. In Schedule 1, in paragraph 1(2) for the words "United Kingdom" there shall be substituted the words "Isle of Man".

12. In Part I of Schedule 2, in paragraph 2(2) after the words "United Kingdom" there shall be inserted the words "and the Isle of Man" and in paragraph 2(7) after the words "United Kingdom" in the first place where they occur there shall be inserted the words "and the Isle of Man" and after those words in the second place where they occur there shall be inserted the words ", the Isle of Man".

13. In Part II of Schedule 2, in paragraph 2(1) and in paragraph 2(2) before the proviso after the words "United Kingdom" there shall be inserted the words ", the Isle of Man" and after those words in the proviso there shall be inserted the words "and the Isle of Man".

14. In Schedule 3, in paragraph 1(1) for the words "Great Britain" there shall be substituted the words "the Isle of Man".

15. In Schedule 4, in paragraph 8(7) for the words "Great Britain" there shall be substituted the words "the Isle of Man".

EXPLANATORY NOTE

(*This Note is not part of the Order.*)

This Order extends Part I of the Plant Varieties and Seeds Act 1964 (plant breeders' rights) and the general provisions relating to that Part to the Isle of Man with exceptions, adaptations and modifications.

STATUTORY INSTRUMENTS

1969 No. 1830

PRICES AND INCOMES

The Prices and Incomes Act 1966 (Continuation of Part II) Order 1969

Laid before Parliament in draft

Made - - - *19th December* 1969

At the Court at Buckingham Palace, the 19th day of December 1969

Present,

The Queen's Most Excellent Majesty in Council

Whereas Her Majesty by Order in Council(a) made under section 6 of the Prices and Incomes Act 1966(b) brought into force sections 7 to 22 (inclusive) of Part II of the said Act of 1966 for a period of twelve months beginning with the 12th August 1967, which sections were continued in force by section 1 of the Prices and Incomes Act 1968(c):

And whereas it is provided by section 13(4) of the said Act of 1968 that section 1 of that Act shall cease to have effect at the end of the year 1969:

And whereas it is provided by paragraph 1 of Schedule 3 to the said Act of 1968, as applied by the said section 13(4), that the provision made by section 6(1) of the Act of 1966 in relation to extension of a period specified in an Order in Council under that section for the bringing into force of sections 7 to 22 of that Act shall have effect in like manner on the expiration of section 1 of the said Act of 1968:

And whereas the Secretary of State in pursuance of section 6(1) of the Act of 1966 has laid copies of the draft of this Order before Parliament, having first consulted with such organisations appearing to her to represent to a substantial extent the interests of those particularly concerned with the Order:

And whereas the said draft has been approved by a resolution of each House of Parliament:

Now, therefore, Her Majesty, in pursuance of the power conferred upon Her by section 6(1)(b) of the said Act of 1966, and of all other powers enabling Her in that behalf is pleased, by and with the advice of Her Privy Council, to order, and it is hereby ordered, as follows:—

1.—(1) This Order may be cited as the Prices and Incomes Act 1966 (Continuation of Part II) Order 1969.

(2) The Interpretation Act 1889(d) shall apply for the interpretation of this Order as it applies for the interpretation of an Act of Parliament.

(a) S.I. 1967/1142 (1967 II, p. 3372).   (b) 1966 c. 33.   (c) 1968 c. 42.
(d) 1889 c. 63.

2. The period during which the provisions of Part II of the Prices and Incomes Act 1966, that is to say, sections 7 to 22 (inclusive) thereof, continue in force shall be extended by a further period of twelve months beginning on 1st January 1970.

W. G. Agnew

EXPLANATORY NOTE

(This Note is not part of the Order.)

This Order continues in force for a further period of 12 months, beginning with 1st January 1970, those provisions of Part II of the Prices and Incomes Act 1966 (relating to notices and standstills) which were first brought into force by Order in Council on 12th August 1967 and further continued in force until the end of the year 1969 by virtue of section 1 of the Prices and Incomes Act 1968.

STATUTORY INSTRUMENTS

1969 No. 1831

PACIFIC ISLANDS

The British Solomon Islands (Electoral Provisions) Order 1969

Made - - - -	*19th December* 1969
Laid before Parliament	*22nd December* 1969
Coming into Operation	*23rd December* 1969

At the Court at Buckingham Palace, the 19th day of December 1969

Present,

The Queen's Most Excellent Majesty in Council

Whereas it is proposed that in due course there shall be established a new Constitution for the British Solomon Islands Protectorate making provision for, among other things, a Governing Council (in this Order referred to as "the proposed Governing Council") comprising seventeen elected members as well as certain other members:

Now, therefore, Her Majesty, by virtue and in exercise of the powers in that behalf by the Foreign Jurisdiction Act 1890(a) or otherwise in Her Majesty vested, is pleased, by and with the advice of Her Privy Council, to order, and it is hereby ordered, as follows:—

1.—(1) This Order may be cited as the British Solomon Islands (Electoral Provisions) Order 1969.

(2) This Order shall come into operation on 23rd December 1969.

(3) The provisions of section 2 (Interpretation) of the British Solomon Islands Order 1967(b) shall apply in relation to the provisions of this Order as they apply in relation to the provisions of the said Order of 1967.

2.—(1) The High Commissioner may by regulations make provision for the election of the elected members of the proposed Governing Council, and in particular, and without prejudice to the generality of the foregoing power, may provide for—

(a) the qualifications and disqualifications of voters;

(b) the registration of voters;

(c) the nomination of candidates for election (including the number of persons required to support nominations);

(d) the ascertainment of the qualifications of voters and of candidates for election;

(e) the division of the Protectorate into constituencies for the purpose of elections, and the division of such constituencies for any purpose connected with elections;

(f) the holding of elections;

(g) the establishment, composition and procedure of electoral colleges;

(a) 1890 c. 37.   (b) S.I. 1967/477 (1967 I, p. 1449).

(*h*) the determination of any question whether any person has been validly elected an elected member of the proposed Governing Council or whether an elected member of the proposed Governing Council has vacated his seat therein ; and

(*i*) the definition and trial of offences connected with elections and the imposition of penalties therefor, including disqualification for membership of the proposed Governing Council, or for registration as a voter, or for voting at elections, of any person concerned in any such offence.

(2) No election of members to the proposed Governing Council shall be held under regulations made under this section until provision has been made by Order of Her Majesty in Council for the establishment of that Governing Council ; but constituencies may be established, registration of voters may take place and all other things necessary or expedient to prepare for such elections may be done in pursuance of such regulations at any time after the commencement of this Order.

(3) Regulations made under this section shall be published by exhibition at the Public Office of the High Commissioner and shall be printed in the Gazette as soon as may be after the date of such publication.

W. G. Agnew

EXPLANATORY NOTE

(This Note is not part of the Order.)

This Order empowers the High Commissioner for the Western Pacific to make regulations providing for the election of the elected members of a Governing Council for the British Solomon Islands Protectorate, which it is proposed should be established in due course.

STATUTORY INSTRUMENTS

1969 No. 1832

BRITISH NATIONALITY

The British Protectorates, Protected States and Protected Persons Order 1969

Made - - - - 19*th December* 1969
Coming into Operation 1*st January* 1970

At the Court at Buckingham Palace, the 19th day of December 1969

Present,

The Queen's Most Excellent Majesty in Council

Her Majesty, in exercise of the powers conferred on Her by sections 29(5), 30 and 32(1) of the British Nationality Act 1948(**a**), section 5 of the British Nationality (No. 2) Act 1964(**b**) and of all other powers enabling Her in that behalf, is pleased, by and with the advice of Her Privy Council, to order, and it is hereby ordered, as follows :—

1. This Order may be cited as the British Protectorates, Protected States and Protected Persons Order 1969 and shall come into operation on 1st January 1970. *Citation and commencement.*

2. The Orders specified in Schedule 1 to this Order are revoked. *Revocation.*

3.—(1) In this Order, unless the context otherwise requires— *Interpretation.*

" the Act " means the British Nationality Act 1948 as from time to time amended (whether before or after the commencement of this Order) ;

" British protected person " means a British protected person by virtue of any provision of this Order or, in relation to any time before the commencement of this Order, by virtue of any provision of the British Protectorates, Protected States and Protected Persons Order in Council 1949(**c**) or the British Protectorates, Protected States and Protected Persons Order 1965(**d**) (as those Orders were from time to time amended) or of any enactment mentioned in the second column of Schedule 3 to this Order ;

" former Arabian protectorate " means Kamaran or the Protectorate of South Arabia ;

" former protectorate " means a territory named in the first column of Part I of Schedule 3 to this Order and accordingly does not include a former Arabian protectorate ;

" former trust territory " means a territory named in the first column of Part II of Schedule 3 to this Order ;

" High Commissioner " includes acting High Commissioner ;

" protectorate " means a territory referred to in article 6(1) of this Order ;

" protected state " means a territory referred to in article 6(2) of this Order.

(a) 11 & 12 Geo. 6. c. 56.   (b) 1964 c. 54.
(c) S.I. 1949/140 (1949 I, p. 522).   (d) S.I. 1965/1864 (1965 III, p. 5649).

(2) A person shall, for the purposes of this Order, be of full age if he has attained the age of eighteen years or if, being a woman under that age, she has been married, and shall be of full capacity if he or she is not of unsound mind.

(3) The Interpretation Act 1889(a) shall apply, with the necessary adaptations, for the purpose of interpreting this Order and otherwise in relation thereto as it applies for the purpose of interpreting and otherwise in relation to Acts of Parliament of the United Kingdom.

Legitimated children.

4.—(1) A person born out of wedlock and legitimated by the subsequent marriage of his parents shall, as from the date of the marriage or 28th January 1949, whichever is later, be treated, for the purpose of determining whether he is a British protected person under article 10, 11, 12(1), 13(2) or, where the relevant parent is the father, article 15 (1) of this Order, as if he had been born legitimate.

(2) A person shall be deemed for the purposes of this article to have been legitimated by the subsequent marriage of his parents if by the law of the place in which his father was domiciled at the time of the marriage the marriage operated immediately or subsequently to legitimate him, and not otherwise.

Posthumous children.

5. Any reference in this Order to the status or description of the father of a person at the time of that person's birth shall, in relation to a person born after the death of his father, be construed as a reference to the status or description of the father at the time of the father's death ; and if that death occurred before 28th January 1949 and the birth occurred on or after that date, the status or description which would have been applicable to the father had he died after 28th January 1949 shall be deemed to be the status or description applicable to him at the time of his death.

Protectorates and protected states.

6.—(1) The British Solomon Islands Protectorate, being a territory under the protection of Her Majesty through Her Government in the United Kingdom, is a protectorate for the purposes of the Act.

(2) The states or territories named in the first column of Schedule 2 to this Order, being states or territories under the protection of Her Majesty as aforesaid, are protected states for the purposes of the Act.

New Hebrides and Canton Island.

7. The provisions of the Act and of section 1(5) of the British Nationality Act 1964(b) shall apply to the New Hebrides and to Canton Island as if they were protected states.

Extension to protected states of references in British Nationality Acts to protectorates.

8. The references to protectorates contained in sub-paragraphs (b) and (e) of paragraph 1 of Schedule 2 to the Act and in paragraph 3(6) of the Schedule to the British Nationality (No. 2) Act 1964(c) shall be construed as including references to all the protected states set out in the first column of Schedule 2 to this Order, to the New Hebrides and to Canton Island ; and references in the Act, in the British Nationality Act 1958(d), in section 1(5) of the British Nationality Act 1964 and in this Order to the Governor shall be construed as including references, in relation to the said protected states, to the authorities specified in the second column of Schedule 2 to this Order, and in relation to the New Hebrides and Canton Island to the High Commissioner for the Western Pacific, and to the persons for the time being exercising their functions.

(a) 52 & 53 Vict. c. 63.   (b) 1964 c. 22.   (c) 1964 c. 54.   (d) 6 & 7 Eliz. 2. c. 10.

9.—(1) The references to protectorates contained in sections 8(1), 10(2), 22 and 29(3) and in the definition of "person naturalised in the United Kingdom and Colonies" in section 32(1) of the Act, in paragraph 4 of Schedule 2 to the Act and in section 3 of the British Nationality Act 1958 shall be construed as including references to Brunei.

Extension to Brunei, the New Hebrides and Canton Island of references to protectorates in British Nationality Acts.

(2) The references to protectorates contained in section 10(2) and in the definition of "person naturalised in the United Kingdom and Colonies" in section 32(1) of the Act and in paragraph 4 of Schedule 2 to the Act shall be construed as including references to the New Hebrides and to Canton Island.

10. Subject to the provisions of article 21 of this Order, a person shall be a British protected person by virtue of his connection with a protectorate—

British protected persons by virtue of connection with a protectorate.

(a) if he was born (whether before or after the commencement of this Order) in that protectorate ; or

(b) in the case of a person born elsewhere than in a protectorate before 28th January 1949, if his father was born in that protectorate ; or

(c) in the case of a person born elsewhere than in a protectorate on or after 28th January 1949, if his father was born in that protectorate and was a British protected person at the time of that person's birth.

11. Subject to the provisions of article 21 of this Order, a person shall be a British protected person by virtue of his connection with Canton Island—

British protected persons by virtue of connection with Canton Island.

(a) if he was born there before 28th January 1949 and at the time of his birth the territory in which his father was born was a protectorate, protected state, trust territory or mandated territory ; or

(b) if he was born there on or after 28th January 1949 and his father was a British subject or a British protected person at the time of that person's birth.

12.—(1) A person shall be a British protected person by virtue of his connection with a former Arabian protectorate—

British protected persons by virtue of connection with a former Arabian protectorate.

(a) if immediately before 30th November 1967 (being the date upon which the former Arabian protectorates ceased to be territories under Her Majesty's protection) he was, in accordance with the provisions of the British Protectorates, Protected States and Protected Persons Order 1965, a British protected person by virtue of his connection with one of those territories ; or

(b) if he was born on or after 30th November 1967 and his father was born in a former Arabian protectorate and is (or would but for his death have been) a British protected person by virtue of sub-paragraph (a) of this paragraph.

(2) A person shall not be a British protected person under paragraph (1) of this article if he is or has at any time been a national of the People's Republic of Southern Yemen.

British protected persons by virtue of connection with a former protectorate or trust territory.

13.—(1) A person shall be a British protected person by virtue of his connection with a former protectorate or trust territory if he was a British protected person immediately before the commencement of this Order by virtue of section 3(2) of the Botswana Independence Act 1966(**a**) or by virtue of article 12(1) of the British Protectorates, Protected States and Protected Persons Order 1965 and any other enactment mentioned in the second column of Schedule 3 to this Order.

(2) Subject to the provisions of paragraph (3) of this article, a person shall be a British protected person by virtue of his connection with a former protectorate or trust territory if his father was born there and, at the time of that person's birth, was (or would but for his death have been) such a British protected person by virtue of paragraph (1) of this article or by virtue of any such provisions as are mentioned in that paragraph.

(3) A person shall not be a British protected person under paragraph (2) of this article by virtue of his connection with a former protectorate or trust territory if he is, or has at any time been, a citizen of a country mentioned in section 1(3) of the Act which is constituted by that former protectorate or trust territory or of which that former protectorate or trust territory forms part.

Additional grounds for status of British protected person by birth.

14.—(1) For the purposes of this Order, a person born aboard a ship or aircraft which is registered in a protectorate, a former protectorate or trust territory or a former Arabian protectorate, or aboard an unregistered ship or aircraft of the government of a protectorate, or a former protectorate or trust territory or a former Arabian protectorate shall be deemed to have been born in that protectorate, former protectorate or trust territory or former Arabian protectorate.

(2) Where a new-born infant is found on or after 29th October 1965 abandoned in a protectorate, a former protectorate or trust territory or a former Arabian protectorate or in Canton Island, that infant shall, unless the contary is shown, be deemed for the purposes of this Order to have been born in the territory where he was so found.

(3) In paragraph (1) of this article any reference to a ship shall include a reference to a hovercraft within the meaning of the Hovercraft Act 1968(**b**).

Registration of stateless persons as British protected persons by virtue of connection with a protectorate or one of certain other territories.

15.—(1) A person shall be entitled, on making application in the prescribed manner, to be registered as a British protected person if he satisfies the authority to whom application is made that he is and always has been stateless and that he has the following connection with a protectorate or a former protectorate or trust territory, that is to say—

(a) if he was born before 28th January 1949, that his father or mother became (or would but for his or her death have become) a British protected person on 28th January 1949 by virtue of his or her connection with that protectorate or that former protectorate or trust territory ;

(b) if he was born on or after 28th January 1949, that his father or mother was (or would but for his or her death have been) a British

---

(**a**) 1966 c. 23.   (**b**) 1968 c. 59.

protected person at the time of his birth by virtue of his or her connection with that protectorate or that former protectorate or trust territory.

(2) A person shall be entitled, on making application in the prescribed manner, to be registered as a British protected person if he satisfies the authority to whom application is made that he is and always has been stateless and that he has a connection with a former Arabian protectorate by reason that his father or mother is (or would but for his or her death have been) a British protected person by virtue of paragraph (1)(*a*) of article 12 of this Order.

(3) An application for the registration under this article of a person who is not of full age may be made by his parent or guardian or, if he has attained the age of sixteen years, by that person himself or by his parent or guardian.

(4) The provisions of paragraph (1) and of paragraph (2) of this article shall apply, where the relevant parent is the mother, to persons born illegitimate as well as to persons born legitimate.

16.—(1) Subject to the provisions of paragraph (2) of this article, a woman may, on making application in the prescribed manner, be registered as a British protected person if she satisfies the authority to whom the application is made that she has been married to a person who, at the time of the application is, or but for his death would be, a British protected person by virtue of his connection with— *(margin: Registration of women married to British protected persons.)*

(*a*) a protectorate or Canton Island ; or

(*b*) a former protectorate, a former trust territory or a former Arabian protectorate.

(2) A woman shall not be registered under this article—

(*a*) where the connection is with a former protectorate or a trust territory, if she is a citizen of a country mentioned in section 1(3) of the Act which is constituted by that former protectorate or trust territory or of which that former protectorate or trust territory forms part ; or

(*b*) where the connection is with a former Arabian protectorate, if she is, or has at any time been, a national of the People's Republic of Southern Yemen.

17. A person registered under article 15 or 16 of this Order shall be a British protected person by registration as from the date on which he is registered. *(margin: Effect of registration as a British protected person.)*

18.—(1) A person who, by virtue of his connection with a former protectorate or trust territory, is a British protected person by or under any provision of article 13, 15 or 16 of this Order shall cease to be such if he becomes a citizen of a country mentioned in section 1(3) of the Act which is constituted by that former protectorate or trust territory or of which that former protectorate or trust territory forms part. *(margin: Loss of status of British protected person in certain cases.)*

(2) A person who, by virtue of his connection with a former Arabian protectorate, is a British protected person by or under any provision of article 12, 15(2) or 16 of this Order shall cease to be such if he becomes a national of the People's Republic of Southern Yemen.

British
protected
person by
virtue of
connection
with a
protected
state.

19.—(1) A person who, under any law providing for citizenship or nationality in force in any protected state, is a citizen or national of that state shall be a British protected person by virtue of his connection with that state.

(2) If in any protected state no law providing for citizenship or nationality of that state is in force, the provisions of articles 10, 14, 15 and 16 of this Order shall have effect in relation to that state as if it were a protectorate.

(3) If any question arises whether any such law as is mentioned in paragraphs (1) and (2) of this article is in force, a certificate of the Secretary of State on the question shall be conclusive.

Renunci-
ation of
status
of British
protected
person.

20.—(1) Notwithstanding any other provision of this Order, any person of full age and capacity who is a British protected person by or under any provision, other than article 19(1), of this Order and—

(*a*) is also a citizen of any country mentioned in section 1(3) of the Act or of the Republic of Ireland or a national of a foreign country as defined in section 32(1) of the Act ; or

(*b*) satisfies the authority to whom the declaration of renunciation is submitted that after registration of the declaration he will become such a citizen or national,

may by declaration renounce his status as a British protected person.

(2) The authority to whom the declaration is submitted shall cause it to be registered, and upon registration the declarant shall cease to be a British protected person ; but if he is a person who made the declaration in pursuance of the provisions of paragraph (1)(*b*) of this article and he does not become such a citizen or national within six months from the date of registration he shall be, and be deemed to have remained, a British protected person notwithstanding the registration.

(3) The authority to whom a declaration of renunciation under this article is submitted may withhold registration thereof if it is made during any war in which Her Majesty may be engaged.

Enemy
aliens.

21. A person who was an enemy alien on 28th January 1949 shall not be a British protected person under article 10 or 11 of this Order unless the authority specified in article 22 of this Order, on application made to him by that person, so orders.

Authority to
whom
applications
or declar-
ations are
to be made
or submitted.

22. An application for registration as a British protected person under article 15 or 16, a declaration of renunciation of the status of British protected person under article 20, and an application for an order under article 21, of this Order, shall be made or submitted,—

(*a*) where a connection is claimed with a protectorate or Canton Island, to the Governor thereof ;

(*b*) where a connection is claimed with a former protectorate or trust territory which constitutes or is comprised in a country mentioned in section 1(3) of the Act, in which there is a High Commissioner for Her Majesty's Government in the United Kingdom, to the High Commissioner in that country ;

(*c*) in any other case, to the Secretary of State ;

and the authority to whom the application is made or the declaration is submitted may prescribe the form thereof and the manner of making it.

23. Any application, declaration, order or registration made, given Transition or effected before the commencement of this Order in accordance with any of the provisions of the British Protectorates, Protected States and Protected Persons Order 1965 or of any Order revoked by that Order shall continue to have effect as if made, given or effected in accordance with the corresponding provision of this Order, subject to any such modification or exception as may be necessary to bring it into conformity with that provision.

W. G. Agnew

SCHEDULE 1

Article 2

ORDERS REVOKED

Title	Number
The British Protectorates, Protected States and Protected Persons Order 1965.	S.I. 1965/1864 (1965 III, p. 5649).
The British Protectorates, Protected States and Protected Persons (Amendment) Order 1967.	S.I. 1967/247 (1967 I, p. 950).
The British Protectorates, Protected States and Protected Persons (Amendment No. 2) Order 1967.	S.I. 1967/1271 (1967 II, p. 3700).

SCHEDULE 2

Article 6

Protected States	*Authority*
Brunei	The High Commissioner for Brunei.
Tonga	The British Commissioner and Consul in Tonga.
The Persian Gulf States, viz: Bahrain Qatar The Trucial States, viz. : Abu Dhabi Ajman Dubai Fujairah Ras al Khaimah Sharjah Umm al Qaiwain	The Political Resident in the Persian Gulf.

SCHEDULE 3
Article 3

PART I

FORMER PROTECTORATES

Bechuanaland Protectorate	Botswana Independence Act 1966, section 3(2)	1966 c. 23.
Gambia Protectorate ...	Gambia Independence Act 1964, section 2(2)	1964 c. 93.
Kenya Protectorate ...	Kenya Independence Act 1963, section 2(1)	1963 c. 54.
Nigeria Protectorate ...	Nigeria Independence Act 1960, section 2(1)	8 & 9 Eliz. 2. c. 55.
Northern Rhodesia ...	Zambia Independence Act 1964, section 3(2)	1964 c. 65.
Northern Territories of the Gold Coast	Ghana Independence Act 1957, section 2	5 & 6 Eliz. 2. c. 6.
Nyasaland Protectorate ...	Malawi Independence Act 1964, section 2(2)	1964 c. 46.
Sierra Leone Protectorate	Sierra Leone Independence Act 1961, section 2(1)	9 & 10 Eliz. 2. c. 16.
Uganda Protectorate ...	Uganda Independence Act 1962, section 2(1)	10 & 11 Eliz. 2. c. 57.

PART II

FORMER TRUST TERRITORIES

Tanganyika	Tanganyika Independence Act 1961, section 2(1)	10 & 11 Eliz. 2. c. 1.
Cameroons under United Kingdom Trusteeship	Nigeria Independence Act 1960, section 2(1)	8 & 9 Eliz. 2. c. 55.
Togoland under United Kingdom Trusteeship	Ghana Independence Act 1957, section 2	5 & 6 Eliz. 2. c. 6.

EXPLANATORY NOTE

(This Note is not part of the Order.)

This Order, made under the British Nationality Act 1948 and the British Nationality (No. 2) Act 1964, supersedes the British Protectorates, Protected States and Protected Persons Orders 1965 and 1967. It makes provision, as in the Orders it supersedes, which specifies the territories which are protectorates or protected states for the purposes of the Acts or to which provisions of the Acts are applied as if they were one or the other, defines who are to be British protected persons for the purposes of the Acts by virtue of their connection with a protectorate, a protected state or a former protectorate or trust territory, and provides for the registration as British protected persons of certain categories of persons who are stateless. The Order includes provision under which the status of British protected person will be restored to certain persons who lost that status when Kamaran and the Protectorate of South Arabia became independent.

STATUTORY INSTRUMENTS

1969 No. 1835

CIVIL AVIATION

The Tokyo Convention (Certification of Countries) Order 1969

Made - - - 19*th December* 1969

At the Court at Buckingham Palace, the 19th day of December 1969

Present,

The Queen's Most Excellent Majesty in Council

Her Majesty, in exercise of the powers conferred upon Her by section 7(1) of the Tokyo Convention Act 1967(a) (which provides that Her Majesty may by Order in Council certify which countries are Convention countries, that is to say countries in which the Convention on Offences and certain other Acts Committed on board Aircraft signed in Tokyo on 14th September 1963 is for the time being in force) and of all other powers enabling Her in that behalf is pleased, by and with the advice of Her Privy Council, to order, and it is hereby ordered, as follows:

1. It is hereby certified that the countries listed in the Schedule hereto are Convention countries.

2. This Order may be cited as the Tokyo Convention (Certification of Countries) Order 1969.

W. G. Agnew

SCHEDULE

The United Kingdom of Great Britain and Northern Ireland
    The Channel Islands
    The Isle of Man
    Bahamas
    Bermuda
    British Antarctic Territory
    British Honduras
    British Indian Ocean Territory
    British Solomon Islands Protectorate
    British Virgin Islands
    Cayman Islands
    Central and Southern Line Islands
    The Sovereign Base Areas of Akrotiri and Dhekelia in the island of Cyprus

(a) 1967 c. 52.

SCHEDULE *(continued)*

    Falkland Islands and Dependencies
    Fiji
    Gibraltar
    Gilbert and Ellice Islands Colony
    Hong Kong
    Montserrat
    Pitcairn
    St. Helena and Dependencies
    St. Vincent
    Seychelles
    Turks and Caicos Islands

Denmark and the Faroe Islands

Israel

Italy

Mexico

Niger

Norway and all territories subject to the sovereignty or authority of Norway

The Philippines

Portugal and all territories (including overseas provinces) subject to the sovereignty or authority of Portugal

Sweden

The United States of America and all territories subject to the sovereignty or authority of the United States of America

Upper Volta

EXPLANATORY NOTE
(This Note is not part of the Order.)

This Order certifies in which countries the Convention on Offences and certain other Acts Committed on board Aircraft, signed in Tokyo on 14th September 1963, is for the time being in force. Under section 7(1) of the Tokyo Convention Act 1967 this Order is conclusive evidence of the matters certified.

STATUTORY INSTRUMENTS

1969 No. 1836

STRATEGIC GOODS
MERCHANT SHIPPING
The Defence Powers (Continuance) Order 1969

Laid before Parliament in draft

Made	- - -	19th December 1969
Coming into Operation		31st December 1969

At the Court at Buckingham Palace, the 19th day of December 1969

Present,

The Queen's Most Excellent Majesty in Council

Whereas a draft of this Order has been approved by resolution of each House of Parliament:

Now, therefore, Her Majesty, in exercise of the powers conferred upon Her by sections 3 and 16 of the Emergency Laws (Re-enactments and Repeals) Act 1964(a), is pleased, by and with the advice of Her Privy Council, to order, and it is hereby ordered, as follows:—

1. This Order may be cited as the Defence Powers (Continuance) Order 1969, and shall come into operation on 31st December 1969.

2. Sections 3 and 16 of the Emergency Laws (Re-enactments and Repeals) Act 1964 shall continue in force for a further period of 5 years from the end of 1969.

W. G. Agnew

EXPLANATORY NOTE

(This Note is not part of the Order.)

This Order continues for a further 5 years from the end of 1969 powers to exercise control, for defence purposes, over strategic goods, the construction of ships, the transfer and mortgage of ships and the transfer of their registry.

(a) 1964 c. 60.

STATUTORY INSTRUMENTS

1969 No. 1837

MARRIAGE

Hong Kong (Non-Domiciled Parties) Divorce Rules 1969

Made	-	-	-	17*th December* 1969
Coming into Operation				1*st January* 1970

In exercise of his powers under subsection (4) of section 1 of the Indian and Colonial Divorce Jurisdiction Act 1926(**a**), as amended by article 2 of, and Part II of the Schedule to, the Government of India (Adaptation of Acts of Parliament) Order 1937(**b**) and paragraph (*d*) of section 1 of the Colonial and Other Territories (Divorce Jurisdiction) Act 1950(**c**), and subsection (1) of section 2 of the said Act of 1926 as amended by the said article 2 and Part II of the Schedule to the said Order of 1937, and as applied by articles 2 and 3 of the Hong Kong Divorce Jurisdiction Order in Council 1935(**d**) as amended by article 2 of the Hong Kong Divorce Jurisdiction (Amendment) Order 1969(**e**), the Secretary of State for Foreign and Commonwealth Affairs, with the concurrence of the Lord Chancellor, hereby makes the following Rules:—

Citation and commencement

1. These Rules may be cited as the Hong Kong (Non-Domiciled Parties) Divorce Rules 1969, and shall come into operation on 1st January 1970.

Interpretation

2. In these Rules, unless the context otherwise requires—

" court " means the Supreme Court of Hong Kong ;

" Matrimonial Causes Ordinance " means the Matrimonial Causes Ordinance of Hong Kong (**f**) and any rules made thereunder and also means any Ordinance or rules for the time being amending or replacing such Ordinance or rules ;

" the Act of 1926 " means the Indian and Colonial Divorce Jurisdiction Act 1926 ;

" the Act of 1940 " means the Indian and Colonial Divorce Jurisdiction Act 1940(**g**) ;

" the Acts " means the Colonial and Other Territories (Divorce Jurisdiction) Acts 1926 to 1950 and any Act amending or replacing the same.

Appointment of judges

3.—(1) The Chief Justice of Hong Kong may, from time to time, submit to the Lord Chancellor, through the Secretary of State for Foreign and

---

(a) 1926 c. 40.
(b) S.R. & O. 1937/230 (Rev. Vol. X, p. 545).
(c) 1950 c. 20.
(d) S.R. & O. 1935/836 (Rev. Vol. VI, p. 18; 1935 p. 585).
(e) S.I. 1969/1060 (1969 II, p. 3106).
(f) Laws of Hong Kong, Chapter 179.
(g) 1940 c. 35.

Commonwealth Affairs, the names of such judges of the court (including himself) as he may consider necessary for the purpose of exercising jurisdiction under the Acts and these Rules.

(2) Upon the approval of the Lord Chancellor of any nomination so submitted being signified to the Chief Justice by the Secretary of State for Foreign and Commonwealth Affairs, the Chief Justice shall cause the names so approved to be notified in the Hong Kong Government Gazette as judges appointed to exercise jurisdiction under the Acts, and the judges whose names shall have been so notified shall thereupon have power to exercise jurisdiction accordingly.

(3) Any judge who has been appointed to exercise jurisdiction in accordance with the provisions in that behalf contained in the Hong Kong (Non-Domiciled Parties) Divorce Rules 1936 (a) shall be deemed to have been appointed under this Rule.

Hearing of petitions

4. Every petition under the Acts shall be heard and determined by one judge nominated and approved under Rule 3, sitting without a jury.

Appeals to two judges

5. An appeal shall lie to a bench of two other judges who have been nominated and approved under Rule 3 against any decree or order made by a judge under Rule 4 which could have been appealed against if it had been made in proceedings under the Matrimonial Causes Ordinance.

Appeals to Privy Council

6. An appeal shall lie from the determination of a bench of two such judges to Her Majesty in Council in any case where an appeal would lie in England from a similar decision of the Court of Appeal to the House of Lords.

Form of petition

7. In addition to any provisions as to the form of petitions in matrimonial causes specified in the rules for the time being in force in Hong Kong relating to matrimonial causes, every petition under the Acts shall state—

(a) the nationality of the parties to the marriage ;

(b) the address at which the parties to the marriage last cohabited ;

(c) whether there have been in any court of competent jurisdiction in any part of the United Kingdom any, and if so what, previous proceedings (including any application under Rule 5 or 6 of the Matrimonial Causes Rules 1968 (b)) with reference to the marriage, or with reference to any children of the family, the date and effect of any decree or order made in such proceedings, and, in the case of proceedings with reference to the marriage, whether there has been any resumption of cohabitation since the making of such decree or order ;

(a) S.R. & O. 1936/30 (Rev. VI, p. 992).
(b) S.I. 1968/219 (1968 I, p. 665).

(*d*) in the case of a wife's petition in which the court is alleged to have jurisdiction by virtue of section 3 of the Act of 1940, the domicile of the husband immediately before the alleged desertion, and the date when and circumstances in which the alleged desertion began ;

(*e*) the places at which the matrimonial offences charged are alleged to have been committed ;

(*f*) the grounds upon which the petitioner claims that in the interests of justice it is desirable that the suit should be determined in Hong Kong.

Limitation where proceedings pending in United Kingdom

8.—(1) Where it appears to the court that proceedings for the dissolution of the marriage have been instituted in any part of the United Kingdom before the date upon which the petition was filed in Hong Kong, the court shall either dismiss the petition or stay further proceedings thereon until the proceedings in the United Kingdom have terminated, or until the court shall otherwise direct.

(2) Where it appears to the court that such proceedings were instituted after the filing of the petition in Hong Kong, the court may, subject to the provisions of the Acts, proceed with the trial of the suit.

Appointment of Proctor

9. The Attorney General of Hong Kong shall, under the designation of Proctor, exercise within the jurisdiction of the court the duties assigned to Her Majesty's Proctor by the law for the time being applying to matrimonial causes in England.

Court not to order secured provision where parties domiciled in Scotland

10. Where a decree is made for the dissolution of a marriage the parties to which are domiciled in Scotland, the court shall not make an order for the securing of a gross or annual sum of money.

Court not to modify, etc. orders in certain circumstances

11. The court shall not entertain an application for the modification or discharge of an order unless the person on whose petition the decree for the dissolution of the marriage was pronounced is resident in Hong Kong at the time such application is made.

Certificates to be signed by Registrar of court

12. A certificate referred to in subsection (2) of section 1 of the Act of 1926 (as substituted by subsection (1) of section 4 of the Act of 1940 and as amended by paragraph (*c*) of section 1 of the Colonial and Other Territories (Divorce Jurisdiction) Act 1950) shall be in the form set out in the Schedule hereto and shall be signed by the Registrar of the court and sealed with the seal of the court.

Procedure generally

13. Subject to the provisions of these Rules, all proceedings under the Acts shall be regulated by the Matrimonial Causes Ordinance with such modifications as the circumstances require.

Revocation

14. The Hong Kong (Non-Domiciled Parties) Divorce Rules 1936 are revoked.

Given under my hand this 17th day of December 1969.

Michael Stewart,
Secretary of State for Foreign
and Commonwealth Affairs.

I concur.
Gardiner, C.

SCHEDULE
(See Rule 12)

I, *A.B.*, Registrar of the Supreme Court of Hong Kong, at the Courts of Justice, Hong Kong, hereby certify that the foregoing is a true copy of $\frac{\text{a decree}}{\text{an order}}$ made by the aforesaid Supreme Court acting in exercise of the matrimonial jurisdiction conferred by or under the Colonial and Other Territories (Divorce Jurisdiction) Acts 1926 to 1950 in

Divorce Jurisdiction Action No. .... of ....

Appeal No. .... of ....

from judgment and decree in Divorce Jurisdiction Action No. .... of

.....................in which the abovenamed *C.D.* was petitioner and the abovenamed

E.F. was respondent and the abovenamed *G.H.* was co-respondent/intervener.

Dated this   day of   19 .

(Signed)

Registrar.

EXPLANATORY NOTE
(*This Note is not part of the Rules.*)

These Rules are made under section 1 of the Indian and Colonial Divorce Jurisdiction Act 1926, as amended by the Indian and Colonial Divorce Jurisdiction Act 1940 and the Colonial and Other Territories (Divorce Jurisdiction) Act 1950. That section has been applied to Hong Kong by the Hong Kong Divorce Jurisdiction Order in Council 1935 as amended by the Hong Kong Divorce Jurisdiction (Amendment) Order 1969. The Rules make provision for the manner in which proceedings shall be conducted before the Supreme Court of Hong Kong in the exercise of divorce jurisdiction in certain cases where the parties are domiciled in the United Kingdom, and also revoke the Hong Kong (Non-Domiciled Parties) Divorce Rules 1936.

STATUTORY INSTRUMENTS

1969 No. 1841

WAGES COUNCILS

The Wages Regulation (Flax and Hemp) (Holidays) Order 1969

Made	-	-	-	-	18*th December* 1969
Coming into Operation					15*th January* 1970

Whereas the Secretary of State has received from the Flax and Hemp Wages Council (Great Britain) the wages regulation proposals set out in the Schedule hereto;

Now, therefore, the Secretary of State in exercise of her powers under section 11 of the Wages Councils Act 1959(a), and of all other powers enabling her in that behalf, hereby makes the following Order:—

1. This Order may be cited as the Wages Regulation (Flax and Hemp) (Holidays) Order 1969.

2.—(1) In this Order the expression "the specified date" means the 15th January 1970, provided that where, as respects any worker who is paid wages at intervals not exceeding seven days, that date does not correspond with the beginning of the period for which the wages are paid, the expression "the specified date" means, as respects that worker, the beginning of the next such period following that date.

(2) The Interpretation Act 1889(b) shall apply to the interpretation of this Order as it applies to the interpretation of an Act of Parliament and as if this Order and the Order hereby revoked were Acts of Parliament.

3. The wages regulation proposals set out in the Schedule hereto shall have effect as from the specified date and as from that date the Wages Regulation (Flax and Hemp) (Holidays) Order 1968(c), shall cease to have effect.

Signed by order of the Secretary of State.

A. A. Jarratt,
Deputy Under Secretary of State,
Department of Employment
18th December 1969. and Productivity.

Article 3
SCHEDULE

The following provisions as to holidays and holiday remuneration shall be substituted for the provisions as to holidays and holiday remuneration set out in the Wages Regulation (Flax and Hemp) (Holidays) Order 1968 (hereinafter referred to as "Order F.H. (118)").

(a) 1959 c. 69.   (b) 1889 c. 63.
(c) S.I. 1968/1485 (1968 III, p. 4234).

PART I

APPLICATION

1. This Schedule applies to every worker for whom statutory minimum remuneration has been fixed.

PART II

CUSTOMARY HOLIDAYS

2.—(1) An employer shall allow to every worker to whom this Schedule applies a holiday (hereinafter referred to as a "customary holiday") in each year on the days specified in the next following sub-paragraph, provided that the worker has been in his employment for a period of not less than four weeks immediately preceding the customary holiday and has worked for the employer during the whole or part of that period and (unless excused by the employer or absent by reason of the proved incapacity of the worker due to sickness or injury) has worked for the employer throughout the last working day on which work was available to him prior to the customary holiday.

(2) The said customary holidays are:—

(a) (i) In England and Wales—

Christmas Day (or, if Christmas Day falls on a Sunday, such week-day as may be appointed by national proclamation, or, if none is so appointed, the next following Tuesday), Boxing Day, Good Friday, Easter Monday, Whit Monday (or where another day is substituted therefor by national proclamation, that day) and August Bank Holiday:

Provided that in the case of workers who normally work on each week-day except Saturday if Christmas Day falls on a Saturday the holiday shall be the next following Tuesday;

(ii) In Scotland—

New Year's Day and the following day:

Provided that if New Year's Day falls on a Sunday the holidays shall be the following Monday and Tuesday; if New Year's Day falls on a Saturday then in the case of workers who normally work on each week-day except Saturday the holidays shall be the following Monday and Tuesday and in the case of all other workers, New Year's Day and the following Monday;

the local Spring holiday;

the local Autumn holiday;

and two other days (being days on which the worker normally works for the employer) in the course of a calendar year to be fixed by the employer in consultation with the worker or his representative and notified to the worker not less than three weeks before the holiday;

or (b) in the case of each of the said days (other than a day fixed by the employer in Scotland and notified to the worker as aforesaid) a day substituted by the employer therefor, being a day recognised by local custom as a day of holiday in substitution for the said day.

(3) Notwithstanding the preceding provisions of this paragraph, an employer may (except where in the case of a woman or young person such a requirement would be unlawful) require a worker who is otherwise entitled to any customary holiday under the foregoing provisions of this Schedule to work thereon and, in lieu of any such holiday on which he so works, the employer shall allow to the worker a day's holiday (hereinafter referred to as a "holiday in lieu of a customary holiday") on a week-day on which he would normally work for the employer within the period of four weeks immediately following the customary holiday.

(4) A worker who is required to work on a customary holiday shall be paid:—

(a) for all time worked thereon at the minimum rate then appropriate to the worker for work on a customary holiday; and

(b) in respect of the holiday in lieu of the customary holiday, holiday remuneration in accordance with paragraph 6.

Part III

ANNUAL HOLIDAY

3.—(1) Subject to the provisions of this paragraph and of paragraph 4, in addition to the holidays specified in Part II of this Schedule an employer shall between 6th April 1970 and 30th September 1970 and between 6th April and 30th September in each succeeding year, allow a holiday (hereinafter referred to as an "annual holiday") to every worker in his employment to whom this Schedule applies who has been employed by him during the 12 months immediately preceding the commencement of the holiday season for any of the periods of employment (calculated in accordance with the provisions of paragraph 10) set out in the appropriate part of the following table and the duration of the annual holiday shall, in the case of each such worker, be related to his period of employment during that 12 months as follows:—

A. DURATION OF ANNUAL HOLIDAY IN 12 MONTHS COMMENCING 6th APRIL 1970		B. DURATION OF ANNUAL HOLIDAY IN 12 MONTHS COMMENCING 6th APRIL 1971 AND THEREAFTER	
Period of employment	Duration of annual holiday	Period of employment	Duration of annual holiday
At least 48 weeks	13 days	At least 48 weeks ...	15 days
„ „ 45 „	12 „	„ „ 45 „ ...	14 „
„ „ 41 „	11 „	„ „ 42 „ ...	13 „
„ „ 37 „	10 „	„ „ 39 „ ...	12 „
„ „ 34 „	9 „	„ „ 36 „ ...	11 „
„ „ 30 „	8 „	„ „ 32 „ ...	10 „
„ „ 26 „	7 „	„ „ 29 „ ...	9 „
„ „ 23 „	6 „	„ „ 26 „ ...	8 „
„ „ 19 „	5 „	„ „ 23 „ ...	7 „
„ „ 15 „	4 „	„ „ 20 „ ...	6 „
„ „ 12 „	3 „	„ „ 16 „ ...	5 „
„ „ 8 „	2 „	„ „ 13 „ ...	4 „
„ „ 4 „	1 day	„ „ 10 „ ...	3 „
		„ „ 7 „ ...	2 „
		„ „ 4 „ ...	1 day

(2) Notwithstanding the provisions of sub-paragraph (1) of this paragraph :—

(a) the number of days of annual holiday which an employer is required to allow to a worker in respect of a period of employment during the 12 months immediately preceding 6th April 1970 shall not exceed in the aggregate—

in the case of a worker with a normal working week of four days or more, twice the number of days constituting the worker's normal working week, plus three days; and

in the case of a worker with a normal working week of less than four days, three times the number of days constituting the worker's normal working week;

(b) the number of days of annual holiday which an employer is required to allow to a worker in respect of a period of employment during the 12 months immediately preceding 6th April 1971 and during the 12 months immediately preceding 6th April in each succeeding year shall not exceed in the aggregate three times the number of days constituting the worker's normal working week.

(3) In this Schedule the expression "holiday season" means in relation to the year 1970 the period commencing on 6th April 1970 and ending on 30th September 1970, and, in each succeeding year, the period commencing on 6th April and ending on 30th September of the same year.

4.—(1) Subject to the provisions of this paragraph, an annual holiday shall be allowed on consecutive working days, being days on which the worker is normally called upon to work for the employer.

(2)(a) Where the number of days of annual holiday for which a worker has qualified exceeds the number of days constituting his normal working week, days of holiday not exceeding twice that number may, by agreement in writing between the employer and the worker or his representative, be allowed in two periods of consecutive working days; so, however, that when a holiday is so allowed, one of the periods shall consist of a number of such days not less than the number of days constituting the worker's normal working week.

(b) *Where the number of days of annual holiday for which a worker has qualified exceeds twice the number of days constituting his normal working week the holiday may be allowed as follows:—*

    (i) *as to the period comprising twice the number of days constituting the worker's normal working week, in accordance with sub-paragraph (a) of this paragraph; and*

    (ii) *as to any additional days, on working days which need not be consecutive, to be fixed by agreement between the employer and the worker or his representative on any working day or days in the holiday season or before the beginning of the next following holiday season.*

(3) For the purposes of this paragraph, days of annual holiday shall be treated as consecutive notwithstanding that a day of holiday allowed to a worker under Part II of this Schedule or a day upon which he does not normally work for the employer intervenes.

(4) Where a day of holiday allowed to a worker under Part II of this Schedule immediately precedes a period of annual holiday or occurs during such a period and the total number of days of annual holiday required to be allowed in the period under the foregoing provisions of this paragraph, together with any such day of holiday allowed under Part II of this Schedule, exceeds the number of days constituting the workers' normal working week then, notwithstanding the foregoing provisions of this paragraph, the duration of that period of annual holiday may be reduced by one day and in such a case one day of annual holiday may be allowed on any working day in the holiday season *or before the beginning of the next following holiday season.*

(5) Subject to the provisions of sub-paragraph (1) of this paragraph, any day of annual holiday under this Schedule may be allowed on a day on which the worker is entitled to a day of holiday or to a half-holiday under any enactment other than the Wages Councils Act 1959.

5. An employer shall give to the worker reasonable notice of the commencing date or dates and duration of the period or periods of his annual holiday. Such notice may be given individually to the worker or by the posting of a notice in the place where the worker is employed.

PART IV

HOLIDAY REMUNERATION

A—CUSTOMARY HOLIDAYS AND HOLIDAYS IN LIEU OF

CUSTOMARY HOLIDAYS

6.—(1) Subject to the provisions of this paragraph, for each day of holiday to which a worker is entitled under Part II of this Schedule he shall be paid by the employer holiday remuneration as follows:—

(*a*) in the case of a piece worker, an amount equal to the worker's average hourly earnings for the hours worked by him for the employer (exclusive of overtime) in the week immediately preceding that in which the holiday occurs multiplied by the number of hours normally worked by him (exclusive of overtime) on that day of the week;

(*b*) in the case of a time worker, an amount equal to the sum which would be payable to him by the employer if that day were not a holiday and he worked thereon the number of hours normally worked by him (exclusive of overtime) on that day of the week and if he were paid at the hourly rate payable to him under his contract of employment immediately before the holiday.

(2) Payment of the said holiday remuneration is subject to the condition that the worker presents himself for employment at the usual starting hour on the first working day following the holiday and works throughout that day or, if he fails to do so, failure is by reason of the proved incapacity of the worker due to sickness or injury or with the consent of the employer.

(3) The holiday remuneration in respect of any customary holiday shall be paid by the employer to the worker on the pay day on which the wages for the week including the first working day following the customary holiday are paid.

(4) The holiday remuneration in respect of any holiday in lieu of a customary holiday shall be paid on the pay day on which the wages are paid for the week including the first working day following the holiday in lieu of a customary holiday:

Provided that the said payment shall be made immediately upon the termination of the worker's employment in the case where he ceases to be employed before being allowed a holiday in lieu of a customary holiday to which he is entitled, and in that case sub-paragraph (2) of this paragraph shall not apply.

B—ANNUAL HOLIDAY

7.—(1) Subject to the provisions of this paragraph and of paragraph 8, a worker qualified to be allowed an annual holiday under this Schedule shall be paid as holiday remuneration by his employer—

(*a*) in respect of the annual holiday to be allowed during the holiday season commencing on 6th April 1970, an amount equal to *5.2 per cent* of his total remuneration determined in accordance with paragraph 11 during the 12 months immediately preceding the commencement of the holiday season;

(*b*) in respect of the annual holiday to be allowed during the holiday season commencing on 6th April 1971 and during the holiday season in each succeeding year, an amount equal to *6 per cent* of his total remuneration determined in accordance with paragraph 11 during the 12 months immediately preceding the commencement of the holiday season.

(2) Holiday remuneration shall be paid by the employer to the worker—

(*a*) in respect of a holiday allowed on consecutive days, the number of such days being not less than the number of days constituting the worker's normal working week, on the last pay day preceding the holiday; and

(*b*) *in respect of a day or days of holiday allowed within a week in which the worker also works for the employer, on the first pay day following the holiday.*

(3) Where under the provisions of paragraph 4 an annual holiday is allowed in more than one period the holiday remuneration shall be apportioned accordingly.

8. Where any accrued holiday remuneration has been paid by the employer to the worker (in accordance with paragraph 9 of this Schedule or with Order F.H. (118)) in respect of employment during any of the periods referred to in that paragraph or that Order, the amount of holiday remuneration payable by the employer in respect of any annual holiday for which the worker has qualified by reason of employment during the said period shall be reduced by the amount of the said accrued holiday remuneration unless that remuneration has been deducted from a previous payment of holiday remuneration made under the provisions of this Schedule.

ACCRUED HOLIDAY REMUNERATION PAYABLE ON TERMINATION OF EMPLOYMENT

9. Where a worker ceases to be employed by an employer after the provisions of this Schedule become effective, the employer shall, immediately on the termination of the employment (hereinafter called "the termination date"), pay to the worker as accrued holiday remuneration:—

(1) in respect of employment in the 12 months up to and including 5th April immediately preceding the termination date, a sum equal to the holiday remuneration for any days of annual holiday for which he has qualified except days of annual holiday which he has been allowed or has become entitled to be allowed before leaving the employment; and

(2) in respect of any employment of at least four weeks duration since the said 5th April, a sum equal to the holiday remuneration which would have been payable to him if he could have been allowed an annual holiday in respect of that employment at the time of leaving it.

PART V

GENERAL

10. For the purpose of calculating any period of employment qualifying a worker for an annual holiday under this Schedule, the worker shall be treated—

(1) as if he were employed for a week in respect of any week during the qualifying period in which—
    (a) in the case of a worker other than a part-time worker, he has worked for the employer for not less than 20 hours and has performed some work for which statutory minimum remuneration is payable;
    (b) in the case of a part-time worker, he has worked for the employer and has performed some work for which statutory minimum remuneration is payable;
    (c) in the case of a worker other than a part-time worker, he has worked for the employer for less than 20 hours by reason of proved incapacity due to sickness or injury or, in the case of any worker, for a like reason he has been absent throughout the week or has been suspended throughout the week owing to shortage of work:

    Provided that the number of weeks which may be so treated as weeks of employment shall not exceed:—

      (i) 26 weeks in the case of proved incapacity in respect of which the worker is entitled to injury benefit under the National Insurance (Industrial Injuries) Acts 1965 to 1967; and

      (ii) four weeks in the case of any other proved incapacity or of suspension owing to shortage of work.

(2) as if he were employed on any day of holiday allowed under the provisions of this Schedule, or of Order F.H. (118), and for the purposes of the provisions of sub-paragraph (1) of this paragraph, a worker who is absent on any such holiday shall be treated as having worked thereon for the employer on work for which statutory minimum remuneration is payable for the number of hours normally worked by him on that day of the week.

11. A worker's total remuneration shall include:—
(1) all payments paid or payable to the worker by the employer in respect of his employment except:—
    (a) payments by way of annual holiday remuneration;
    (b) payments by way of accrued holiday remuneration;
    (c) payments in respect of overtime; and

(*d*) payments in respect of any period of absence from work by reason of incapacity due to sickness or injury or by reason of suspension owing to shortage of work; and

(2) in respect of any period of absence which under the provisions of sub-paragraph (1)(*c*) of paragraph 10 is to be treated as a period of employment, the amount to which he would have been entitled if he had worked during that period as a time worker for the number of daily hours (exclusive of overtime) normally worked by him.

DEFINITIONS

12. In this Schedule, unless the context otherwise requires, the following expressions have the meanings hereby respectively assigned to them, that is to say:—

"NORMAL WORKING WEEK" means the number of days on which it has been usual for the worker to work in a week in the employment of the employer in the 12 months immediately preceding the commencement of the holiday season, or, where under paragraph 9 accrued holiday remuneration is payable on the termination of the employment, in the 12 months immediately preceding the termination date: Provided that—

(1) part of a day shall count as a day;

(2) no account shall be taken of any week in which the worker did not perform any work for which statutory minimum remuneration has been fixed.

"PART-TIME WORKER" means a worker who normally works for the employer for less than 20 hours a week by reason only of the fact that he does not hold himself out as normally available for work for more than the number of hours he normally works in the week.

"STATUTORY MINIMUM REMUNERATION" means minimum remuneration (other than holiday remuneration) fixed by a wages regulation order made by the Secretary of State to give effect to proposals submitted to her by the Flax and Hemp Wages Council (Great Britain).

"WEEK" in paragraphs 3, 6 and 10 and in this paragraph means "pay week".

13. The provisions of this Schedule are without prejudice to any agreement for the allowance of any further holidays with pay or for the payment of additional holiday remuneration.

EXPLANATORY NOTE
(This Note is not part of the Order.)

This Order, which has effect from 15th January 1970, sets out the holidays which an employer is required to allow to workers and the remuneration payable for those holidays in substitution for the holidays and holiday remuneration set out in the Wages Regulation (Flax and Hemp) (Holidays) Order 1968 (Order F.H. (118)), which Order is revoked.

New provisions are printed in italics.

STATUTORY INSTRUMENTS

1969 No. 1842

RESTRICTIVE TRADE PRACTICES

The Restrictive Trade Practices (Information Agreements) Order 1969

Laid before Parliament in draft

Made   -   -   -   *18th December* 1969

Coming into Operation   *1st February* 1970

Whereas a notice has been published complying with the terms of section 5(5) of the Restrictive Trade Practices Act 1968(**a**) and all the representations made with respect thereto have been taken into consideration :

And Whereas a draft of this Order has been laid before, and approved by a resolution of, each House of Parliament :

Now, therefore, the Secretary of State in exercise of her powers under section 5(2) of the Restrictive Trade Practices Act 1968 as having effect by virtue of the Transfer of Functions (Monopolies, Mergers and Restrictive Trade Practices) Order 1969(**b**) hereby makes the following Order :—

1. This Order may be cited as the Restrictive Trade Practices (Information Agreements) Order 1969 and shall come into operation on 1st February 1970.

2.—(1) In this Order "the Act of 1956" and "the Act of 1968" mean, respectively, the Restrictive Trade Practices Act 1956(**c**) and the Restrictive Trade Practices Act 1968.

(2) The Interpretation Act 1889(**d**) shall apply for the interpretation of this Order as it applies for the interpretation of an Act of Parliament.

3.—(1) It is directed that the provisions of Part I of the Act of 1956 (including sections 7 and 8 thereof) shall apply in relation to the following class of information agreements, that is to say, agreements (other than agreements described in Part I of the Schedule hereto) which relate to any of the matters specified in paragraph (2) of this Article, whether or not they relate to any other matters.

(2) The matters referred to in paragraph (1) are as follows :—

(*a*) the prices charged or quoted or to be charged or quoted otherwise than to any of the parties to the relevant agreement for goods which have been or are to be supplied or offered or for the application of any process of manufacture to goods ;

(**a**) 1968 c. 66.   (**b**) S.I. 1969/1534 (1969 III, p. 4991).
(**c**) 1956 c. 68.   (**d**) 1889 c. 63.

(*b*) the terms or conditions on or subject to which goods have been or are to be supplied otherwise than to any such party or any such process has been or is to be applied to goods otherwise than for any such party.

Signed by order of the Secretary of State.

Edmund Dell,
Minister of State,
Department of Employment and Productivity.

18th December 1969.

Article 3(1)

SCHEDULE

Part I

Agreements to which the Order does not apply

1. An agreement particulars of which would, but for the provisions of this paragraph, be required to be furnished to the Secretary of State by virtue of section 31 (provisions relating to export agreements) of the Act of 1956.

2. An agreement which, insofar as it contains provisions for or in relation to the furnishing of information with respect to the matters mentioned in Article 3(2), contains only provisions of one or more of the following kinds, that is to say, —

(*a*) provision for or in relation to the furnishing of such information by parties to the agreement whereby each such party is to furnish such information separately and directly to a specified authority ;

(*b*) provision for or in relation to the furnishing of such information by parties to the agreement whereby each such party is to furnish such information separately and directly to a person who does not carry on such a business as is mentioned in section 6(1) of the Act of 1956 or, where the parties are members of an unincorporated trade association, to a person employed by them solely for the purposes of the association, and under which neither that information nor information based thereon is to be furnished directly or indirectly by that person to any party to the agreement except—

(i) information which does not relate to any party other than the party to whom it is furnished ; or

(ii) information which has been furnished to a specified authority at the written request of the authority, and then only in a form that prevents any information being identified, except by the party to whom the information relates, as being information relating to any particular party ;

(*c*) provision for or in relation to the furnishing of such information which at the time it is to be furnished is information which has already been published in such manner that it is readily available to persons who are or may be purchasing goods or who are or may be requiring the application of processes of manufacture to goods, being goods or processes of descriptions to which the information relates ; including, but without prejudice to the generality of the foregoing, the furnishing of particulars of prices charged for goods at any market or other place at which such goods are regularly offered for sale by a substantial number of sellers ;

(*d*) provision for or in relation to the furnishing of such information by parties to the agreement whereby each such party is to furnish such information separately and directly to a person who does not carry on such a business as is mentioned in section 6(1) of the Act of 1956 or, where the parties are members of an unincorporated trade association, to a person employed by them solely for the purposes of the association, and under which neither that information nor information based thereon is to be furnished directly or indirectly by that person to any party before the information or, as the case may be, the information based thereon has been published in the manner described in head (c) of this paragraph.

3. An agreement—

(a) of which the terms, by virtue of which it is an information agreement to which Part I of the Act of 1956 would but for this paragraph apply by virtue of this Order, are incidental to other terms of the agreement, and

(b) of which those other terms are terms by virtue of which, apart from this Order, the said Part I would apply to the agreement but for the provisions of section 7 or section 8 of the said Part I.

4.—(1) An agreement, made before the date on which this Order comes into operation, in respect of which the Minister certifies before that date that it is an agreement in relation to which the provisions of section 45(2) of the Agriculture (Miscellaneous Provisions) Act 1968(a) would have applied if this Order, apart from this paragraph, had been in force at all relevant times, and that had notice of the proposed terms thereof been served on him he would not have objected to those terms.

(2) An agreement, whenever made, of a kind mentioned in paragraph (a) or paragraph (b) of subsection (5) of the said section 45 and which is made as the result of the making of an agreement, between a board and a trade association, which is excluded from the operation of this Order by virtue of sub-paragraph (1) of this paragraph.

(3) In this paragraph "Minister" and "board" have the meanings respectively assigned to them in subsection (7) of the said section 45.

5.—(1) An agreement to which the only parties are bodies carrying on the business of the production and supply of gas under national ownership.

(2) An agreement to which the only parties are bodies carrying on the business of the generation and supply of electricity under national ownership.

6. In this Part "specified authority" means any of the bodies mentioned in Part II of this Schedule.

PART II

1. Any Government Department (including any Department of the Government of Northern Ireland) and any Committee established by any such Department.
2. The National Economic Development Council and any of its Economic Development Committees.
3. The National Board for the Review of Government Contracts.
4. The National Board for Prices and Incomes.
5. The Industrial Reorganisation Corporation.
6. The Monopolies Commission.
7. Any local authority as defined in section 66 of the Finance Act 1965(b).
8. The White Fish Authority.
9. The Herring Industry Board.
10. The Home-Grown Cereals Authority.
11. The Meat and Livestock Commission.
12. The Northern Ireland Livestock Marketing Commission.
13. The Central Council for Agricultural and Horticultural Co-operation.

(a) 1968 c. 34.   (b) 1965 c. 25.

14.   The National Seed Development Organisation.
15.   The Sugar Board.
16.   The Shipbuilding Industry Board.
17.   The National Research Development Corporation.
18.   The Metrication Board.
19.   Any development council established under the Industrial Organisation and Development Act 1947(a).
20.   Any Royal Commission.
21.   Any consultative council or committee or consumers' council established by Act of Parliament in relation to an industry carried on under national ownership.

EXPLANATORY NOTE
(This Note is not part of the Order.)

This Order applies Part I of the Restrictive Trade Practices Act 1956 (which relates to the registration and judicial investigation of agreements) to information agreements (other than those described in Part I of the Schedule to this Order) which provide for the furnishing of information about prices and the terms and conditions in connection with the sale of goods or the application of any process of manufacture to goods.

The agreements described in Part I of the Schedule to this Order which are excluded from the class of agreements made subject to registration and judicial investigation are those, subject to the conditions laid down therein,—

(a) which relate to exports,

(b) which relate to information furnished to a Government Department or other authority specified in Part II of the Schedule,

(c) which relate to the furnishing of information already published or to be made public,

(d) which relate to the furnishing of information as an incidental matter in agreements already excluded from registration and judicial investigation by virtue of sections 7 or 8 of the Act of 1956,

(e) which are entered into by an agricultural marketing board and are of a kind referred to in section 45 of the Agriculture (Miscellaneous Provisions) Act 1968,

(f) where the only parties are the nationalised gas industries or the nationalised electricity industries.

Agreements existing at the date of operation of this Order must be registered within three months from that date, and other agreements must be registered before they become effective and in any event within three months of their making.

(a) 1947 c. 40.

STATUTORY INSTRUMENTS

1969 No. 1843

COMMON

The Commons Registration (New Land) Regulations 1969

Made - - -	*19th December* 1969
Laid before Parliament	*2nd January* 1970
Coming into Operation	*3rd January* 1970

The Minister of Housing and Local Government and the Secretary of State, in exercise of their respective powers under paragraphs (*a*) and (*b*) of section 13, paragraphs (*a*), (*b*), (*g*), (*i*) and (*k*) of subsection (1), and subsections (2) and (4) of section 19 of the Commons Registration Act 1965(**a**), as read with the Ministry of Land and Natural Resources (Dissolution) Order 1967(**b**), and of all other powers enabling them in that behalf, hereby make the following Regulations :—

Title and commencement

1. These Regulations may be cited as the Commons Registration (New Land) Regulations 1969, and shall come into operation on 3rd January 1970.

Interpretation

2.—(1) The Interpretation Act 1889(**c**) applies for the interpretation of these Regulations as it applies for the interpretation of an Act of Parliament.

(2) In these Regulations, unless the context otherwise requires,—

"the Act" means the Commons Registration Act 1965 ;

"application" means an application under these Regulations ;

"concerned authority", in relation to an application to a registration authority, means a local authority (other than the registration authority) in whose area any part of the land affected by the application lies ;

"Form 6" means the form so numbered in the General Regulations or a form to substantially the same effect, and "Form" followed by a number above 28 means the form so numbered in the Schedule to these Regulations, or a form to substantially the same effect ;

"the General Regulations" means the Commons Registration (General) Regulations 1966(**d**) as amended (**e**), and "General Regulation" followed by a number means the regulation so numbered in the General Regulations ;

"Model Entry" followed by a number means the specimen entry so numbered in Part 1 of Schedule 2 to the General Regulations, and "Standard Entry" followed by a number means the specimen entry so numbered in Part 2 of that Schedule, or an entry to substantially the same effect ;

(**a**) 1965 c. 64. (**b**) S.I. 1967/156 (1967 I, p. 258).
(**c**) 1889 c. 63.
(**d**) S.I. 1966/1471 (1966 III, p. 3978).
(**e**) The amending instruments are S.I. 1968/658, 1968/989 (1968 I, p. 1490; 1968 II, p. 2615).

"provisional registration" means a registration under section 4 of the Act which has not become final ;

"substituted land" and, in relation to any substituted land, "the taken land", bear the same meanings as in General Regulation 28.

(3) A requirement upon a registration authority to publish a document in any area is a requirement to cause the document to be published in such one or more newspapers circulating in that area as shall appear to the authority sufficient to secure adequate publicity for it.

(4) A requirement to display a document or copies thereof is a requirement to treat it, for the purposes of section 287 of the Local Government Act 1933(a) (public notices), as if it were a public notice within that section.

(5) Where the day or the last day on which anything is required or permitted by or in pursuance of these Regulations to be done is a Sunday, Christmas Day, Good Friday, bank holiday or a day appointed for public thanksgiving or mourning, the requirement or permission shall be deemed to relate to the first day thereafter which is not one of the days before-mentioned.

(6) Any requirement (however expressed) that a registration authority shall send anything to "the applicant" shall, where a solicitor has been instructed for the purposes of an application, be deemed to be satisfied by sending it to the solicitor, or, where two or more persons are concerned together in an application and no solicitor has been instructed, to that one of them whose name appears first in the application form.

(7) A requirement upon a registration authority to stamp any document is a requirement to cause an impression of its official stamp as described in General Regulation 3 to be affixed to it, and that the impression shall bear the date mentioned in the requirement or (where no date is mentioned) the date when it was affixed.

(8) An indication in any form in the Schedule to these Regulations that the form shall bear the official stamp of a registration authority is a requirement upon the authority to stamp it.

Land becoming common land or a town or village green

3.—(1) Where, after 2nd January 1970, any land becomes common land or a town or village green, application may be made subject to and in accordance with the provisions of these Regulations for the inclusion of that land in the appropriate register and for the registration of rights of common thereover and of persons claiming to be owners thereof.

(2) Where any land is for the time being registered under the Act, no application shall be entertained for its registration under these Regulations, and, where any land is for the time being registered under section 4 of the Act (whether or not the registration has become final) no application shall be entertained for the registration of rights of common over it.

(3) No person shall be registered under these Regulations as the owner of any land which is registered under the Land Registration Acts 1925 to 1966(b) and no person shall be registered under these Regulations as the owner of any other land unless the land itself is registered under these Regulations.

(4) An application for the registration of any land as common land or as a town or village green may be made by any person, and a registration authority

---

(a) 1933 c. 51.   (b) 1925 c. 21; 1936 c. 26; 1966 c. 39.

shall so register any land in any case where it registers rights over it under these Regulations.

(5) An application for the registration of a right of common over land which is registered, or which is capable of being registered, under these Regulations, may be made by the owner of the right, or by any person entitled by law to act, in relation to the right, on the owner's behalf or in his stead, or, where the right belongs to an ecclesiastical benefice of the Church of England which is vacant, by the Church Commissioners.

(6) An application for the registration of a claim to the ownership of any land registered under these Regulations may be made by the owner of the land, or by any person entitled by law to act, in relation to the land, on the owner's behalf or in his stead, or, where the land belongs to an ecclesiastical benefice of the Church of England which is vacant, by the Church Commissioners.

(7) An application must be—

(a) in Form 29, 30, 31 or 32 as appropriate ;

(b) signed by or on behalf of every applicant who is an individual, and by the secretary or some other duly authorised officer of every applicant which is a body corporate or unincorporate ;

(c) accompanied by such documents (if any) as may be requisite under regulation 4 below ;

(d) supported—

(i) by a statutory declaration as set out in the appropriate form of application, with such adaptations as the case may require, to be made by the applicant, or by one of the applicants if there is more than one, or by his or their solicitor, or, if the applicant is a body corporate or unincorporate, or charity trustees, by its or their solicitor or by the person who signed the application ; and

(ii) by such further evidence, if any, as, at any time before finally disposing of the application, the registration authority may reasonably require.

Documents to accompany applications

4.—(1) Subject to paragraph (2) below, every application must be accompanied by, or by a copy or sufficient abstract of, every document relating to the matter which the applicant has in his possession or under his control, or of which he has a right to the production.

(2) In the case of an application for the registration of any rights of common, or of a claim to the ownership of any land, the applicant shall not be obliged to furnish to the registration authority, or to disclose the existence of, any document which he would not be obliged to abstract or produce to a purchaser under a contract for the sale by the applicant of the rights or the land made otherwise than by correspondence and containing no stipulations as to title.

Disposal of applications

5.—(1) On receiving an application, the registration authority shall allot a distinguishing number to it, and shall mark the application form with that number.

(2) Where a registration authority receives an application for the registration of a right of common affecting any coal or anthracite it shall, before entertain-

ing the application, serve notice in writing to that effect upon the National Coal Board, giving the name and address of the applicant and particulars of the right of common, of the land over which it is exercisable and of the land (if any) to which it is attached.

(3) The registration authority shall send the applicant a receipt for his application containing a statement of the number allotted thereto; and Form 6, if used for that purpose, shall be sufficient.

(4) Subject to paragraph (7) below, a registration authority shall, on receipt of an application,—

(*a*) send a notice in Form 33, 34 or 35, as appropriate, to every person (other than the applicant) whom the registration authority has reason to believe (whether from information supplied by the applicant or otherwise) to be an owner, lessee, tenant or occupier of any part of the land affected by the application, or to be likely to wish to object to the application ;

(*b*) publish in the concerned area, and display, such a notice as aforesaid, and send the notice and a copy of the application to every concerned authority ;

(*c*) affix such a notice to some conspicuous object on any part of the land which is open, unenclosed and unoccupied, unless it appears to the registration authority that such a course would not be reasonably practicable.

(5) The date to be inserted in any notice under paragraph (4) above by which statements in objection to an application must be submitted to the registration authority shall be such as to allow an interval of not less than six weeks from the latest of the following dates, that is to say, the date on which the notice is displayed by the registration authority, or is published, or may reasonably be expected to be delivered in due course of post or to be displayed under paragraph (6) below.

(6) Every concerned authority receiving, under this regulation, a notice and a copy of an application shall forthwith display copies of the notice, and shall keep the copy of the application available for public inspection at all reasonable times until informed by the registration authority of the disposal of the application.

(7) Where an application appears to a registration authority after preliminary consideration not to be duly made, the authority may reject it without complying with paragraph (4) above, but where it appears to the authority that any action by the applicant might put the application in order, the authority shall not reject the application under this paragraph without first giving the applicant a reasonable opportunity of taking that action.

(8) In this regulation "concerned area" means, in the case of a registration authority which is the council of a county borough, an area including the area of the county borough and the area of every concerned authority, and in any other case, an area including the area of every concerned authority.

Consideration of objections

6.—(1) As soon as possible after the date by which statements in objection to an application have been required to be submitted, the registration authority shall proceed to the further consideration of the application, and the consideration of statements (if any) in objection thereto, in accordance with the following provisions of this regulation.

(2) The registration authority shall not consider any statement in objection to an application unless it is in writing and signed by or on behalf of the person making it, but, subject as aforesaid, the authority shall consider every statement in objection to an application which it receives before the date on which it proceeds to the further consideration of the application under paragraph (1) above, and may consider any such statement which it receives on or after that date and before the authority finally disposes of the application.

(3) The registration authority shall send the applicant a copy of every statement which it is required under paragraph (2) above to consider, and of every statement which it is permitted under that paragraph to consider and intends to consider, and shall not reject the application without giving the applicant a reasonable opportunity of dealing with the matters contained in the statements of which copies are sent to him under this paragraph and with any other matter in relation to the application which appears to the authority to afford prima facie grounds for rejecting the application.

Method of registration

7.—(1) Where a registration authority accepts an application, it shall make the necessary registration, following as closely as possible whichever of the Model Entries 4 and 7 to 12 may be applicable, with such variations and adaptations as the circumstances may require, but with the substitution, for the words "(Registration provisional.)", of the words "(Registration under section 13 of the Act.)".

(2) The provisions of paragraphs (2) to (7) of General Regulation 10 shall apply to registrations under these Regulations as they apply to provisional registrations.

(3) The provisions of regulation 9 of the Commons Registration (Objections and Maps) Regulations 1968(a) (changes as to provisional register maps) shall apply for the purposes of section 13 of the Act as they apply for the purposes of section 4 thereof, and, accordingly, the following shall be substituted for the definition of "registration" in regulation 2(2) of the said regulations :—

‘ "registration", except in regulation 9 below, means registration under section 4 of the Act, and "registered" shall be construed accordingly ;’.

(4) Where a registration authority has made a registration under this regulation, it shall file the application form and any plan thereto which is not required for the purpose of General Regulation 20 (supplemental maps) and shall return all other documents which accompanied the application form to the applicant.

Information about disposal of applications, and procedure on rejection

8.—(1) When a registration authority has disposed of an application and, if it has accepted the application, has made the necessary registration, it shall give written notice of the fact to every concerned authority, to the applicant and to every person whose address is known to the registration authority and who objected to the application, and such notice shall include, where the registration authority has accepted the application, details of the registration, and, where it has rejected the application, the reasons for the rejection.

(2) A person shall be taken to have objected to an application for the purposes of paragraph (1) above if he submitted a statement in objection to the

---

(a) S.I. 1968/989 (1968 II, p. 2615).

application which the registration authority was required to consider under paragraph (2) of regulation 6 above or which it did consider under that paragraph.

(3) Where a registration authority has rejected an application, it shall return the application form and all accompanying documents to the applicant.

Substituted land

9.—(1) Where under these Regulations a registration authority registers any substituted land in a register, and the taken land is registered in that register, then—

> (*a*) if no application has been duly made under General Regulation 27 for the removal of the taken land from the register, the authority shall nevertheless amend the register in relation to the taken land as shown in Standard Entry 6 ;

> (*b*) if such an application has been duly made, the registration authority shall not be required to comply with paragraphs (5) to (8) of General Regulation 27 (except so much of paragraph (7) thereof as requires the register to be amended in accordance with Standard Entry 6).

(2) In General Regulation 28(1) (which prohibits the removal of any taken land from a register until the substituted land has been registered under the Act, unless the substituted land is exempt from registration under section 11 of the Act) the words "unless it is exempt from registration under section 11 thereof" are hereby revoked, but without prejudice to their effect in relation to applications and registrations under section 4 of the Act.

Land descriptions

10.—(1) Land must be described for the purposes of any application—

> (*a*) by a plan accompanying the application and referred to therein ; or

> (*b*) in the case of land already registered under the Act, by a reference to the register sufficient to enable the land to be identified ; or

> (*c*) in the case of land to which rights of common are attached, by reference to the numbered parcels on the most recent edition of the ordnance map (quoting the edition).

(2) Any plan accompanying an application must—

> (*a*) be drawn to scale ;

> (*b*) be in ink or other permanent medium ;

> (*c*) be on a scale of not less, or not substantially less, than six inches to one mile ;

> (*d*) show the land to be described by means of distinctive colouring ; and

> (*e*) be marked as an exhibit to the statutory declaration in support of the application.

SCHEDULE   Regulation 2

FORMS

FORM 29

	Official stamp of registration	Application No.
	authority indicating date	
	of receipt	Register unit No(s):
		CL
This section for		
official use only		CL

COMMONS REGISTRATION ACT 1965, SECTION 13

APPLICATION FOR THE REGISTRATION OF LAND WHICH BECAME COMMON LAND AFTER 2nd JANUARY 1970

IMPORTANT NOTE:—Before filling in this form, read carefully the notes at the end. An incorrectly completed application form may have to be rejected.

[1]*Insert name of registration authority*

To the[1]

Application is hereby made for the registration as common land of the land described below, which became so registrable after 2nd January 1970.

Part 1.

(Give Christian names or forenames and surname or, in the case of a body corporate or unincorporate, the full title of the body. If part 2 is not completed all correspondence and notices will be sent to the first-named applicant.)

Name and address of the applicant or (if more than one) of every applicant.

Part 2.

(This part should be completed only if a solicitor has been instructed for the purposes of the application. If it is completed, all correspondence and notices will be sent to the solicitor.)

Name and address of solicitor, if any.

Part 3.

Particulars of the land to be registered, i.e. the land claimed to have become common land.

Name by which usually known

Locality

Colour on plan herewith

Part 4.

On what date did the land become common land?

Part 5.

How did the land become common land?

Part 6.

Name and address of every person whom the applicant believes to be an owner, lessee, tenant or occupier of any part of the land claimed to have become common land. (If none are known, write "none".)

Part 7.

For applications to register substituted land (see Note 5); to be disregarded in other cases.

Particulars of the "taken land", i.e. the land which ceased to be common land when the land described in part 3 became common land.

Name by which usually known

Locality

Colour on plan herewith (if any)

If registered under the 1965 Act, register unit No(s).

Part 8.

List of supporting documents sent herewith, if any. (If none are sent, write "none".)

Part 9.

If there are any other facts relating to the application which ought to be brought to the attention of the registration authority (in particular if any person interested in the land is believed to dispute the claim that it has become common land) full particulars should be given here.

[2]*The application must be signed by or on behalf of each individual applicant, and by the secretary or some other duly authorised officer of any applicant which is a body corporate or unincorporate.*

Date ....19 .

Signatures[2]..

....

....

(See Note 10)

STATUTORY DECLARATION IN SUPPORT

To be made by the applicant, or by one of the applicants, or by his or their solicitor, or, if the applicant is a body corporate or unincorporate, by its solicitor or by the person who signed the application.

[1]Insert full name (and address if not given in application form).
[2]Delete and adapt as necessary.
[3]Insert name if applicable.

I[1],
solemnly and sincerely declare as follows:—

1.[2] I am ((the person) (one of the persons) who (has) (have) signed the foregoing application)) ((the solicitor to (the applicant) ([3]   one of the applicants)).

2. I have read the Notes to the application form.

3. The facts set out in the application form are to the best of my knowledge and belief fully and truly stated and I am not aware of any other fact which should be brought to the attention of the registration authority as likely to affect its decision on this application, nor of any document relating to the matter other than those (if any) mentioned in parts 8 and 9 of the application.

[4]Insert "marking" as on plan.

4. The plan now produced and shown to me marked [4]"   " is the plan referred to in part 3 of the application.

[5]Delete this paragraph if there is no plan referred to in part 7.

5.[5] The plan now produced and shown to me marked [4]"   " is the plan referred to in part 7 of the application.

And I make this solemn declaration, conscientiously believing the same to be true, and by virtue of the Statutory Declarations Act 1835(a).

Declared by the said..⎫
....⎪
at ....⎬ *Signature of Declarant*
in the...........................of..⎪
this.......................day of...............................19 .⎭

Before me,

Signature ....

Address ....

....

Qualification ....

REMINDER TO OFFICER TAKING DECLARATION:
Please initial all alterations and mark any plan as an exhibit.

(a) 1835 c. 62.

NOTES

1. Registration authorities

The applicant should take care to submit his application to the correct registration authority. This depends on the situation of the land which is claimed to have become common land. The registration authority for land in an administrative county is the county council; for land in a county borough, it is the county borough council, and for land in Greater London, it is the Greater London Council. However, if the land in question is partly in the area of one registration authority and partly in that of another, the authorities may by agreement have provided for one of them to be the registration authority for the whole of the land. An applicant concerned with land lying close to the boundary of an administrative area, or partly in one area and partly in another, should therefore enquire whether such an agreement has been made and, if so, which authority is responsible for the land.

2. Who may apply for registration

An application for the registration of any land which has become common land after 2nd January 1970 may be made by any person, but a person who wishes to apply for the registration of rights of common over land which became common land after 2nd January 1970 should use C.R. Form 31 and not this form, whether or not the land itself has been registered under the Act.

3. No double registration

If the land is already registered under the Act, whether in the Register of Common Land or in the separate Register of Town or Village Greens, and whether the registration is provisional, final, or under section 13 of the Act (which relates to land becoming common land or a town or village green after 2nd January 1970), an application for registration cannot be entertained, but this does not prevent the submission of an application later on, should the existing registration cease for any reason to be effective (as, for example, by the land being removed from the register under section 13 or by a provisional registration being cancelled or failing to achieve finality). If an earlier registration is believed to exist a search of the register may be obtained by means of C.R. Form 21 (a separate form must be used for each register).

4. Meaning of "common land"

For the purpose of an application after 2nd January 1970, common land may be taken to mean either—

    (a) land which, after 2nd January 1970, became subject to rights of common (see Note 6 below) whether those rights are exercisable at all times or only during limited periods; or

    (b) land which, after 2nd January 1970, became "substituted land", whether or not subject to rights of common (this category is explained in Note 5 below).

It does not include a town or village green or any land forming part of a highway. (There is a separate form available for applying for the registration under the Act of land which became a town or village green after 2nd January 1970.) "Land" includes land covered with water, so that common land can, for instance, include ponds and lakes.

5. How land can become common land

Land can become common land after 2nd January 1970 in any of the following ways:—

    (1) By or under an Act of Parliament otherwise than as substituted land (as to substituted land, see category (4) below).

    (2) By a grant by the owner of the land of rights of common over it.

    (3) By rights of common being acquired over it by prescription.

    (4) By substitution or exchange for other land which has ceased to be common land under—

        (a) sections 147 and 148 of the Inclosure Act 1845(a); or

        (b) paragraph 11 of Schedule 1 to the Acquisition of Land (Authorisation Procedure) Act 1946(b); or

        (c) any other enactment providing, on the exchange of land, for the transfer of rights, trusts or incidents attaching to the land given in exchange from that land to the land taken in exchange and vice versa.

(a) 1845 c. 118.   (b) 1946 c. 49.

Land in category (4) is referred to in this form as "substituted land", and the land for which it is substituted, and which has ceased to be common land, is referred to as "the taken land". If this application is accepted for registration, and the taken land is registered in the Register of Common Land maintained by the same registration authority, the taken land will be removed from the register automatically provided the registration authority is satisfied as to the exact areas of both the substituted and the taken land. No separate application in regard to the latter is necessary in such a case.

6. Meaning of "rights of common"

There are many different kinds of rights of common, some existing only in particular areas. This is why there is no exhaustive list or definition of rights of common in the Act. However, it may be said that a right of common is a right which a person has (generally in common with others including the owner of the soil) to take part of the natural produce of another man's land. Examples are: a right to turn out sheep or other animals to graze (common of pasture, called in the Act a right to graze animals); a right to turn out pigs to eat acorns and beechmast (pannage); a right to take tree loppings, gorse, furze, bushes or underwood (estovers); a right to take turf or peat (turbary); a right to take fish (piscary). There is also a right of common in the soil, as it is called, which consists of the right of taking sand, gravel, etc. from another man's land. These are only a few of the most frequently encountered rights of common; there are many others, and any person in doubt should seek legal advice. On the other hand, many rights connected with land are not rights of common and are not subject to the Act; for example, rights of way (public or private), and rights to water cattle, horses or other animals on the land of another.

The Act provides that cattlegates or beastgates (by whatever name known) and rights of sole or several vesture or herbage or of sole or several pasture are to be considered as rights of common. These are in essence various kinds of rights of pasture normally enjoyed to the exclusion of the owner of the land.

Rights held for a term of years or from year to year are not registrable under the Act, and, accordingly, land subject to such rights does not qualify for registration on that account, although it may do so in some other way, e.g. as substituted land.

7. Land descriptions

In addition to the particulars asked for at part 3 of the form, a plan of the land claimed to have become common land must accompany the application. The particulars in part 3 are necessary to enable the registration authority to identify the land concerned, but the main description of the land will be by means of the plan. This must be drawn to scale, in ink or other permanent medium, and be on a scale of not less, or not substantially less, than six inches to one mile. It must show the land by means of distinctive colouring (a coloured edging inside the boundary will usually suffice) and it must be marked as an exhibit to the statutory declaration (see Note 10 below). If the land to be registered is substituted land (see Note 5 above), then a description of the taken land must be given in part 7, and a plan of this area, too, may have to be provided. If the taken land has already been registered under the Act (as it will have been in most cases) and comprises the whole of the land in one or more register units, a plan is unnecessary provided the register unit number(s) are quoted. If the taken land comprises only part of the land in a register unit a plan may be dispensed with if the land can be described by reference to some physical feature such as a road, river or railway; the description might, for example, read: "The land in register unit No. . . . . lying to the south of the road from A to B". Where this method is not practicable, or the taken land is not registered under the Act, it must be described by a plan which must conform to the requirements mentioned above. Where two plans accompany the application, a different colour should be used in each.

8. Grounds of application: evidence

In part 5 should be set out, as concisely as possible, a statement of the facts relied on to show that the land became common land on the date stated in part 4; this date must be after 2nd January 1970, otherwise the application cannot be entertained. The statement should include particulars of every Act of Parliament, statutory order, order of court, deed or other instrument, and of every act or event, which is material for the purpose. The registration authority has power to call for such further evidence in support of the application as it may reasonably require. If the land is substituted land (see Note 5 above) there should be included in part 5 particulars of the enactment and of the compulsory purchase order, order of exchange or other instrument authorising the exchange or substitution, and of the instrument (if any) under which the exchange or substitution actually took place.

9. Supporting documents

The application must be accompanied by the original or (preferably) by a copy or sufficient abstract of every document relating to the matter which the applicant has in his possession or under his control, or of which he has a right to the production. The following are examples of documents which, under this rule, may normally be expected to be among the documents accompanying applications in the particular cases mentioned:—

(1) Where the land is stated to have become common land by virtue of a private or local Act or of a statutory instrument, the award or other instrument of allotment (if any) made thereunder.

(2) Where the land is stated to have become common land by a grant of rights of common, a copy of the deed of grant.

(3) Where the land is stated to have become common land by the acquisition of rights of common over it by prescription, and there is a declaration by a court of competent jurisdiction to that effect, an office copy of the order embodying that declaration. (In the absence of such a declaration, a claim based solely on the Prescription Act 1832(a) cannot be admitted, and a claim based on prescription otherwise than under that Act is unlikely to be admitted if any objection is received by the registration authority.)

(4) Where the land is stated to be substituted land (see Note 5 above), the original or a duly authenticated copy (a) of the compulsory purchase order, order of exchange or other instrument authorising the exchange or substitution, and (b) of the instrument (if any) under which the exchange or substitution actually took place.

The foregoing list is not exhaustive and in special cases the applicant may need to consult the registration authority. Applicants are strongly recommended NOT to forward the original of any deed or other private document. Instead, a copy should be supplied, preferably indorsed with a certificate signed by a solicitor that it has been examined against the original. The applicant should indicate, either on the copy itself or in part 8 of the application, as convenient, who has the original and where it may be inspected. If any document relating to the matter is believed to exist, but neither the original nor a copy can be produced, the fact should be mentioned in part 9 of the application, where particulars of the missing document should be given and its non-production accounted for.

The registration authority has power to call for such further evidence as it may reasonably require.

10. Statutory Declaration

The statutory declaration must be made before a justice of the peace, commissioner for oaths or notary public. The plan (or each plan) accompanying the application and referred to in the statutory declaration must be marked as an exhibit and signed by the officer taking the declaration (initialling is insufficient). A plan is marked by writing on the face in ink an identifying symbol such as the letter 'A'. If there is more than one plan a different identifying letter must be used for each. On the back of the plan should appear these words:

This is the exhibit marked 'A' referred to in the statutory declaration of (*name of declarant*) made this (*date*)   19   before me,

....
(*Signature and qualification*)

11. Action by registration authority

The registration authority will on receipt of the application send an acknowledgment. If this is not received within 10 days the applicant should communicate with the authority. Unless the application has to be rejected after preliminary consideration, the registration authority will give publicity to it and will consider it further in the light of any objections which may be received. The applicant will be supplied with copies of all objections which fall to be considered and will have an opportunity of answering them. Later, the applicant will be informed whether the application has been accepted or rejected. If it is accepted, the land will be registered as common land, and the applicant will be supplied with particulars of the registration. If it is rejected, the applicant will be notified of the reasons for the rejection.

12. False statements

The making of a false statement for the purposes of this application may render the maker liable to prosecution.

(a) 1832 c. 71.

FORM 30

This section for official use only

Official stamp of registration authority indicating date of receipt

Application No.

Register unit No(s):

VG

VG

COMMONS REGISTRATION ACT 1965, SECTION 13

APPLICATION FOR THE REGISTRATION OF LAND WHICH BECAME A TOWN OR VILLAGE GREEN AFTER 2nd JANUARY 1970

IMPORTANT NOTE:—Before filling in this form, read carefully the notes at the end. An incorrectly completed application form may have to be rejected.

¹*Insert name of registration authority*

To the¹

Application is hereby made for the registration as a town or village green of the land described below, which became so registrable after 2nd January 1970.

Part 1.

(Give Christian names or forenames and surname or, in the case of a body corporate or unincorporate, the full title of the body. If part 2 is not completed all correspondence and notices will be sent to the first named applicant.)

Name and address of the applicant or (if more than one) of every applicant.

Part 2.

(This part should be completed only if a solicitor has been instructed for the purposes of the application. If it is completed, all correspondence and notices will be sent to the solicitor.)

Name and address of solicitor, if any.

Part 3.   **Particulars of the land to be registered, i.e. the land claimed to have become a town or village green.**

Name by which usually known

Locality

Colour on plan herewith

Part 4.   **On what date did the land become a town or village green?**

Part 5.   **How did the land become a town or village green?**

Part 6.   **Name and address of every person whom the applicant believes to be an owner, lessee, tenant or occupier of any part of the land claimed to have become a town or village green. (If none are known, write "none".)**

Part 7.   **For applications to register substituted land (see Note 5); to be disregarded in other cases.**

Particulars of the "taken land", i.e. the land which ceased to be a town or village green (or part thereof) when the land described in part 3 became a town or village green (or part).

Name by which usually known

Locality

Colour on plan herewith (if any)

If registered under the 1965 Act, register unit No(s).

Part 8.   **List of supporting documents sent herewith, if any. (If none are sent, write "none".)**

Part 9.

If there are any other facts relating to the application which ought to be brought to the attention of the registration authority (in particular if any person interested in the land is believed to dispute the claim that it has become a town or village green) full particulars should be given here.

[2] *The application must be signed by or on behalf of each individual applicant, and by the secretary or some other duly authorised officer of any applicant which is a body corporate or unincorporate.*

Date ....19 .

Signatures[2]..

....

....

(See Note 9)   STATUTORY DECLARATION IN SUPPORT

To be made by the applicant, or by one of the applicants, or by his or their solicitor, or, if the applicant is a body corporate or unincorporate, by its solicitor or by the person who signed the application.

[1]*Insert full name (and address if not given in the application form).*
[2]*Delete and adapt as necessary.*
[3]*Insert name if applicable.*

I[1],

solemnly and sincerely declare as follows:—

1.[2] I am ((the person) (one of the persons) who (has) (have) signed the foregoing application)) ((the solicitor to (the applicant) ([3]   one of the applicants)).

2. I have read the Notes to the application form.

3. The facts set out in the application form are to the best of my knowledge and belief fully and truly stated and I am not aware of any other fact which should be brought to the attention of the registration authority as likely to affect its decision on this application, nor of any document relating to the matter other than those (if any) mentioned in parts 8 and 9 of the application.

[4]*Insert "marking" as on plan.*

4. The plan now produced and shown to me marked [4]"   " is the plan referred to in part 3 of the application.

[5]*Delete this paragraph if there is no plan referred to in part 7.*

5.[5] The plan now produced and shown to me marked [4]"   " is the plan referred to in part 7 of the application.

And I make this solemn declaration, conscientiously believing the same to be true, and by virtue of the Statutory Declarations Act 1835.

Declared by the said..⎫

....⎪

at ....⎬ *Signature of Declarant*
                                                                             ⎪
in the ....of..⎪

this................................day of...........................19...⎭

Before me,

Signature ....

Address ....

....

Qualification ....

REMINDER TO OFFICER TAKING DECLARATION:

Please initial all alterations and mark any plan as an exhibit.

NOTES

1. Registration authorities

The applicant should take care to submit his application to the correct registration authority. This depends on the situation of the land which is claimed to have become a town or village green. The registration authority for land in an administrative county is the county council; for land in a county borough, it is the county borough council, and for land in Greater London, it is the Greater London Council. However if the land in question is partly in the area of one registration authority and partly in that of another, the authorities may by agreement have provided for one of them to be the registration authority for the whole of the land. An applicant concerned with land lying close to the boundary of an administrative area, or partly in one area and partly in another, should therefore enquire whether such an agreement has been made and, if so, which authority is responsible for the land.

2. Who may apply for registration

An application for the registration of any land which has become a town or village green after 2nd January 1970 may be made by any person.

3. No double registration

If the land is already registered under the Act, whether in the Register of Town or Village Greens or in the separate Register of Common Land, and whether the registration is provisional, final, or under section 13 of the Act (which relates to land becoming common land or a town or village green after 2nd January 1970), an application for registration cannot be entertained, but this does not prevent the submission of an application later on, should the existing registration cease for any reason to be effective (as, for example, by the land being removed from the register under section 13 or by a provisional registration being cancelled or failing to achieve finality). If an earlier registration is believed to exist a search of the register may be obtained by means of C.R. Form 21 (a separate form must be used for each register).

4. Meaning of "town or village green"

"Town or village green" is defined in the Commons Registration Act 1965 as land—

    (a) which has been allotted by or under any Act for the exercise or recreation of the inhabitants of any locality, or

    (b) on which the inhabitants of any locality have a customary right to indulge in lawful sports and pastimes, or

    (c) on which the inhabitants of any locality have indulged in such sports and pastimes as of right for not less than twenty years.

While a town or village green can be subject to rights of common, it does not include land which is registered as common land in the separate Register of Common Land maintained under the Act. (There is a separate form available for applying for the registration under the Act of land which became common land after 2nd January 1970.) "Land" includes land covered with water so that a town or village green can, for instance, include a pond.

5. How land can become a town or village green

Land can become a town or village green after 2nd January 1970 in one of the following ways:—

    (1) By or under an Act of Parliament otherwise than as substituted land (as to substituted land, see category (4) below).

    (2) By customary right established by judicial decision.

    (3) By the actual use of the land by the local inhabitants for lawful sports and pastimes as of right for not less than 20 years.

    (4) By substitution or exchange for other land which has ceased to be a town or village green under—

        (a) sections 147 and 148 of the Inclosure Act 1845; or

        (b) paragraph 11 of Schedule 1 to the Acquisition of Land (Authorisation Procedure) Act 1946; or

        (c) any other enactment providing, on the exchange of land, for the transfer of rights, trusts or incidents attaching to the land given in exchange from that land to the land taken in exchange and vice versa.

Land in category (4) is referred to in this form as "substituted land", and the land for which it is substituted, and which has ceased to be a town or village green, is referred to as "the taken land". If this application is accepted for registration, and the taken land is registered in the Register of Town or Village Greens maintained by the same registration authority, the taken land will be removed from the register automatically provided the registration authority is satisfied as to the exact areas of both the substituted and the taken land. No separate application in regard to the latter is necessary in such a case.

6. Land descriptions

In addition to the particulars asked for at part 3 of the form, a plan of the land claimed to have become a town or village green must accompany the application. The particulars in part 3 are necessary to enable the registration authority to identify the land concerned, but the main description of the land will be by means of the plan. This must be drawn to scale, in ink or other permanent medium, and be on a scale of not less, or not substantially less, than six inches to one mile. It must show the land by means of distinctive colouring (a coloured edging inside the boundary will usually suffice) and it must be marked as an exhibit to the statutory declaration (see Note 9 below). If the land to be registered is substituted land (see Note 5 above), then a description of the taken land must be given in part 7, and a plan of this area, too, may have to be provided. If the taken land has already been registered under the Act (as it will have been in most cases) and comprises the whole of the land in one or more register units, a plan is unnecessary provided the register unit number(s) are quoted. If the taken land comprises only part of the land in a register unit a plan may be dispensed with if the land can be described by reference to some physical feature such as a road, river or railway; the description might, for example, read "The land in register unit No................lying to the south of the road from A to B". Where this method is not practicable, or the taken land is not registered under the Act, it must be described by a plan which must conform to the requirements mentioned above. Where two plans accompany the application, a different colour should be used in each.

7. Grounds of application: evidence

In part 5 should be set out, as concisely as possible, a statement of the facts relied on to show that the land became a town or village green on the date stated in part 4; this date must be after 2nd January 1970, otherwise the application cannot be entertained. The statement should include particulars of every Act of Parliament, statutory order, order of court, deed or other instrument, and of every act or event, which is material for the purpose. The registration authority has power to call for such further evidence in support of the application as it may reasonably require. If the land is substituted land (see Note 5 above) there should be included in part 5 particulars of the enactment and of the compulsory purchase order, order of exchange or other instrument authorising the exchange or substitution, and of the instrument (if any) under which the exchange or substitution actually took place.

8. Supporting documents

The application must be accompanied by the original or (preferably) by a copy or sufficient abstract of every document relating to the matter which the applicant has in his possession or under his control, or of which he has a right to the production. The following are examples of documents which, under this rule, may normally be expected to be among the documents accompanying applications in the particular cases mentioned:—

(1) Where the land is stated to have become a town or village green by virtue of a private or local Act or of a statutory instrument, the award or other instrument of allotment (if any) made thereunder.

(2) Where the land is stated to have become a town or village green by customary right, an office copy of an order of a court of competent jurisdiction embodying a declaration to that effect.

(3) Where the land is stated to have become a town or village green by the actual use of the land by the local inhabitants for lawful sports and pastimes as of right for not less than 20 years, and there is a declaration by a court of competent jurisdiction to that effect, an office copy of the order embodying that declaration.

(4) Where the land is stated to be substituted land (see Note 5 above), the original or a duly authenticated copy (a) of the compulsory purchase order, order of exchange or other instrument authorising the exchange or substitution, and (b) of the instrument (if any) under which the exchange or substitution actually took place.

The foregoing list is not exhaustive and in special cases the applicant may need to consult the registration authority. Applicants are strongly recommended NOT to forward the original of any deed or other private document. Instead, a copy should be supplied, preferably indorsed with a certificate signed by a solicitor that it has been examined against the original. The applicant should indicate, either on the copy itself or in part 8 of the application, as convenient, who has the original and where it may be inspected. If any document relating to the matter is believed to exist but, neither the original nor a copy can be produced, the fact should be mentioned in part 9 of the application, where particulars of the missing document should be given and its non-production accounted for.

The registration authority has power to call for such further evidence as it may reasonably require.

9. Statutory Declaration

The statutory declaration must be made before a justice of the peace, commissioner for oaths or notary public. The plan (or each plan) accompanying the application and referred to in the statutory declaration must be marked as an exhibit and signed by the officer taking the declaration (initialling is insufficient). A plan is marked by writing on the face in ink an identifying symbol such as the letter 'A'. If there is more than one plan a different identifying letter must be used for each. On the back of the plan should appear these words:

This is the exhibit marked 'A' referred to in the statutory declaration of (*name of declarant*) made this (*date*) 19 before me,

....

(*Signature and qualification*)

10. Action by registration authority

The registration authority will on receipt of the application send an acknowledgment. If this is not received within 10 days the applicant should communicate with the authority. Unless the application has to be rejected after preliminary consideration, the registration authority will give publicity to it and will consider it further in the light of any objections which may be received. The applicant will be supplied with copies of all objections which fall to be considered and will have an opportunity of answering them. Later, the applicant will be informed whether the application has been accepted or rejected. If it is accepted, the land will be registered as a town or village green, and the applicant will be supplied with particulars of the registration. If it is rejected, the applicant will be notified of the reasons for the rejection.

11. False statements

The making of a false statement for the purposes of this application may render the maker liable to prosecution.

FORM 31

This section for official use only

Official stamp of registration authority indicating date of receipt

Application No.

Register Unit No(s):

COMMONS REGISTRATION ACT 1965, SECTION 13

APPLICATION FOR THE REGISTRATION OF A RIGHT OF COMMON OVER LAND, WHERE BOTH THE RIGHT AND THE LAND BECAME REGISTRABLE AFTER 2nd JANUARY 1970

IMPORTANT NOTE:—Before filling in this form, read carefully the notes at the end. An incorrectly completed application may have to be rejected.

[1]*Insert name of registration authority.*

To the[1]

Application is hereby made for the registration of the right of common of which particulars are set out below.

Part 1.

(Give Christian names or forenames and surname or, in the case of a body corporate, the full title of the body.   If part 2 is not completed all correspondence and notices will be sent to the first-named applicant.)

Name and address of the applicant or (if more than one) of every applicant, and the capacity in which he applies.

Part 2.

(This part should be completed only if a solicitor has been instructed for the purposes of the application.   If it is completed, all correspondence and notices will be sent to the solicitor.)

Name and address of solicitor, if any.

Part 3.

Particulars of the land over which the right of common is exercisable.

(*a*)　Name by which usually known

(*b*)　Locality

(*c*)　Colour on plan herewith (if any)

If the land is registered under the 1965 Act, registration particulars—

[2]*Insert "Common Land" or "Town or Village Greens".*

(*d*)　Register[2]

(*e*)　Register unit No(s).

Part 4.   Description of the right of common, including, if it is exer-
                           cisable only during limited periods, full particulars of the
                           periods, and, if it is a right to graze animals, details of the
                           number(s) and kind(s) of animals.

Part 5.   Description of the farm, holding or other land to which the right
                           is attached, if any.   (If the right is not attached to any land, the
                           fact should be stated here.)

                           Name by which usually known

                           Locality, O.S. Nos. and reference to ordnance map (if given),
                           and any further description

                           Colour on plan herewith (if any)

Part 6.   On what date did the right first become exercisable over the
                           land described in part 3 above?

Part 7.   How did the right first become exercisable over the land des-
                           cribed in part 3 above?

Part 8.   Name and address of every person whom the applicant believes to
                           be an owner, lessee, tenant or occupier of any part of the land
                           described in part 3 above.   (If none are known, write "none".)

Part 9.   List of supporting documents sent herewith, if any.   (If none are
                           sent, write "none".)

Part 10.   If there are any other facts relating to the application which
                           ought to be brought to the attention of the registration authority
                           (in particular if any person interested in the land described in
                           part 3 above is believed to dispute the claim that it is subject
                           to rights of common) full particulars should be given here.

---

3 *The application must*   Date 19   .
be signed by or on
behalf of each indi-   Signatures[3]   ....
vidual applicant, and
by the secretary or some   ....
other duly
authorised officer of   ....
any applicant which is
a body corporate or   ....
charity trustees.

(See Note 12)

STATUTORY DECLARATION IN SUPPORT

To be made by the applicant, or by one of the applicants, or by his or their solicitor, or, if the applicant is a body corporate or charity trustees, by its or their solicitor or by the person who signed the application.

¹*Insert full name (and address if not given in the application form).*

I,¹
solemnly and sincerely declare as follows:—

²*Delete and adapt as necessary.*
³*Insert name if applicable.*

1.² I am ((the person) (one of the persons) who (has) (have) signed the foregoing application)) ((the solicitor to (the applicant) (³   one of the applicants)).

2. I have read the Notes to the application form.

3. The facts set out in the application form are to the best of my knowledge and belief fully and truly stated and I am not aware of any other fact which should be brought to the attention of the registration authority as likely to affect its decision on this application, nor of any document which ought to be submitted or disclosed to the authority other than those (if any) mentioned in parts 9 and 10 of the application.

⁴*Insert "marking" as on plan.*

4. The plan now produced and shown to me marked ⁴"   " is the plan referred to in part 3 of the application.

⁵*Delete this paragraph if there is no plan referred to in part 5.*

5.⁵ The plan now produced and shown to me marked ⁴"   " is the plan referred to in part 5 of the application.

And I make this solemn declaration, conscientiously believing the same to be true, and by virtue of the Statutory Declarations Act 1835.

Declared by the said..

....

at ....

in the..............................of.......................................

this ....day of........................19

Before me,

Signature ....

Address ....

....

Qualification ....

⎫
⎬ *Signature of Declarant*
⎭

REMINDER TO OFFICER TAKING DECLARATION:

Please initial all alterations and mark any plan as an exhibit.

NOTES

1. Registration authorities

The applicant should take care to submit his application to the correct registration authority. This depends on the situation of the land over which the right of common is claimed. The registration authority for land in an administrative county is the county council; for land in a county borough, it is the county borough council, and for land in Greater London, it is the Greater London Council. However, if the land over which the right is claimed is partly in the area of one registration authority and partly in that of another, the authorities may by agreement have provided for one of them to be the registration authority for the whole of the land. An applicant concerned with land lying close to the boundary of an administrative area, or partly in one area and partly in another, should therefore enquire whether an agreement has been made and, if so, which authority is responsible for the land.

2. When to use this form

This form should not be used in cases where a right of common has been shifted from one piece of land to another in the circumstances mentioned in category (4) of Note 5 below, and both pieces of land are in the area of one registration authority. In such cases, re-registration of the right of common is automatic on registration of the substituted land. The matter is fully explained in Note 5. Nor should it be used where a right of common which has already been registered has been apportioned or varied, or, in the case of a registered right in gross (that is, not attached to any land), has been transferred. In such cases amendment of the register should be applied for on C.R. Form 19. In all other cases within Note 9 below this form should be used to apply to register a right of common whether or not the land over which the right is claimed to be exercisable has itself been registered, since it is not necessary for the land over which a right of common is exercisable to be registered before an application for the registration of the right itself is made: see Note 13 below.

3. Who may apply for registration

An application for the registration of a right of common may be made by the owner of the right or, where the right belongs to an ecclesiastical benefice of the Church of England which is vacant, by the Church Commissioners.

In certain cases a person may be entitled by law to apply on behalf of the owner of the right or in his stead. Examples are:

(a) a receiver appointed under section 105 of the Mental Health Act 1959(a);

(b) charity trustees where the right of common is vested in the Official Custodian for Charities;

(c) trustees for the purposes of the Settled Land Act 1925(b) authorised by order under section 24 of that Act.

In all cases the applicant should state in part 1 the capacity in which he applies (e.g. as owner of the right). If he applies on behalf of, or instead of, another person he should also state in part 1:—

(a) the Act of Parliament, statutory instrument, order of court or other authority under which he claims to be entitled to apply;

(b) the name and address of the person on whose behalf or in whose stead the application is made; and

(c) the capacity of that person (who will normally be the owner of the right).

Where the Church Commissioners apply with respect to a right of common belonging to a vacant benefice, the fact should be stated, and the name of the benefice given, in part 1. Where charity trustees apply the fact should be stated, and the name of the charity given, in part 1.

4. Meaning of "rights of common"

There are many different kinds of rights of common, some existing only in particular areas. This is why there is no exhaustive list or definition of rights of common in the Act. However, it may be said that a right of common is a right which a person has (generally in common with others including the owner of the soil) to take part of the natural produce of another man's land. Examples are: a right to turn out sheep or other animals to graze (common of pasture, called in the Act a right to graze animals); a right to turn out pigs to eat acorns and beechmast (pannage); a right to take tree loppings, gorse, furze, bushes or underwood (estovers); a right to take turf or peat (turbary); a right to take fish (piscary). There is also a right of

---

(a) 1959 c. 72.　　　　　　　　　　　(b) 1925 c. 18.

common in the soil, as it is called, which consists of the right of taking sand, gravel, stone, etc. from another man's land. These are only a few of the most frequently encountered rights of common; there are many others, and any person in doubt should seek legal advice. On the other hand, many rights connected with land are not rights of common and are not subject to the Act; for example, rights of way (public or private), and rights to water cattle, horses or other animals on the land of another.

The Act provides that cattlegates or beastgates (by whatever name known) and rights of sole or several vesture or herbage or of sole or several pasture are to be considered as rights of common. These are in essence various kinds of rights of pasture normally enjoyed to the exclusion of the owner of the land.

Rights held for a term of years or from year to year are not registrable under the Act.

5. How land can become subject to rights of common

Land can become subject to rights of common after 2nd January 1970 in one of the following ways:—

(1) By or under an Act of Parliament, otherwise than as substituted land (as to substituted land, see category (4) below).

(2) By a grant by the owner of the land of rights of common over it.

(3) By rights of common being acquired over it by prescription.

(4) By substitution or exchange for other land which has ceased to be common land under—

(a) sections 147 and 148 of the Inclosure Act 1845; or

(b) paragraph 11 of Schedule 1 to the Acquisition of Land (Authorisation Procedure) Act 1946; or

(c) any other enactment providing, on the exchange of land, for the transfer of rights trusts or incidents attaching to the land given in exchange from that land to the land taken in exchange and vice versa.

Land in category (4) is referred to in this form as "substituted land", and the land for which it is substituted, and which has ceased to be subject to rights of common, is referred to as "the taken land". If both the taken and the substituted land are in the area of one registration authority, then when the substituted land is registered under the Act, a note will appear in the register to the effect that rights of common (if any) which subsisted over the taken land at the date of the substitution or exchange have shifted over to the substituted land, and no application for the re-registration of these rights will be necessary. Inquiry should be made of the registration authority whether the substituted land has been registered, and whether a note about the shifting of the rights appears in the register.

6. Land descriptions

(a) For purposes of part 3. Except where the land has already been registered under the Act (see Note 7 below), the particulars asked for at (a), (b) and (c) of part 3 of the form must be given, and a plan must accompany the application. The particulars at (a) and (b) of part 3 are necessary to enable the registration authority to identify the land concerned, but the main description of the land will be by means of the plan. This must be drawn to scale, in ink or other permanent medium, and be on a scale of not less, or not substantially less, than six inches to one mile. It must show the land to be described by means of distinctive colouring (a coloured edging inside the boundary will usually suffice), and it must be marked as an exhibit to the statutory declaration (see Note 12 below).

Where the land has already been registered (see Note 7 below) and comprises the whole of the land in one or more register units, a plan is unnecessary provided the register and register unit number(s) are quoted at (d) and (e) of part 3 of the form. If the application concerns only part of the land in a register unit a plan may be dispensed with if the land can be described by reference to some physical feature such as a road, river or railway; the description might, for example, read "The land in register unit No....... lying to the south of the road from A to B". Where this method is not practicable the land must be described by a plan prepared as mentioned above. Where the procedure of reference to an existing register unit is adopted, part 3 of the form should be adapted accordingly.

(b) For purposes of part 5. If the right is attached to any farm, holding or other land, that land must be described in part 5. This may be done either by a plan prepared as explained in (a) above, or, alternatively, by reference to the numbered parcels on the most recent edition of the ordnance map (quoting the edition), supplemented, where necessary to describe part of a parcel, or any land not numbered on the ordnance map, by a plan prepared in accordance with (*a*) above. Sufficient particulars of the locality must in any case be given to enable the land to be identified on the ordnance map. Where two plans accompany the application, a different colour should be used in each.

If the right is held in gross, that is, not attached to any land, that fact should be stated in part 5.

7. Inspection and search of registers

To ascertain whether land has been registered under the Act, anyone may inspect the registers free of charge at the office of the registration authority. Alternatively, an official certificate of search may be obtained from the registration authority. A requisition for such search must be made in writing on C.R. Form No. 21, a separate requisition being required for each register. If the land is registered, the certificate will reveal the register unit number(s) and whether any rights of common and claims to ownership are registered.

8. Rights for limited periods: grazing rights

Certain rights of common (usually grazing rights) are not exercisable at all times but only during limited periods. In the case of a right of common to which this applies, full particulars must be given in part 4 of the period or periods during which the right is exercisable. Further, if the right (by whatever name it may be known) consists of or includes a right to graze animals, or animals of any class, the applicant must state at part 4 the number of animals, or the numbers of animals of different classes, to be entered in the register.

9. Date for part 6

The date to be entered in part 6 is the date on which the right of common first came into existence and became registrable as exercisable over the land described in part 3. If this date is before 3rd January 1970 the application cannot be entertained by the registration authority. Moreover, the land over which the right is exercisable must have become registrable under the Act after 2nd January 1970, whether it has in fact been so registered or not. If either the right or the land was registrable under the Act before 3rd January 1970 it is now too late to apply for the registration of either.

10. Grounds of application: evidence

In part 7 should be set out, as concisely as possible, a statement of the facts relied on to show that the right of common came into existence and became registrable on the date stated in part 6 (as to this date, see Note 9 above). The statement should include particulars of every Act of Parliament, statutory order, order of court, deed or other instrument, and of every act or event, which is material for the purpose. The registration authority has power to call for such further evidence in support of the application as it may reasonably require.

11. Supporting documents

The application must be accompanied by the original or (preferably) by a copy or sufficient abstract of every document relating to the matter which the applicant has in his possession or under his control, or of which he has a right to the production, with the exception of documents which he would not be obliged to abstract or produce to a purchaser under a contract for the sale of the right of common made otherwise than by correspondence and containing no stipulations as to title. The following are examples of documents which, under this rule, may normally be expected to be among the documents accompanying applications in the particular cases mentioned:—

(1) Where the right is stated to have become exercisable by virtue of a private or local Act or of a statutory instrument, the award or other instrument of allotment (if any) made thereunder.

(2) Where the right is stated to have become exercisable by a grant of rights of common, a copy of the deed of grant.

(3) Where the right is stated to have become exercisable by prescription, and there is a declaration by a court of competent jurisdiction to that effect, an office copy of the order embodying that declaration. (In the absence of such a declaration, a claim based solely on the Prescription Act 1832 cannot be admitted, and a claim based on prescription otherwise than under that Act is unlikely to be admitted if any objection is received by the registration authority.)

The foregoing list is not exhaustive and in special cases the applicant may need to consult the registration authority. Applicants are strongly recommended NOT to forward the original of any deed or other private document. Instead, a copy should be supplied, preferably indorsed with a certificate signed by a solicitor that it has been examined against the original. The applicant should indicate, either on the copy itself or in part 9 of the application, as convenient, who has the original and where it may be inspected.

If for any reason a document cannot be produced, the fact should be mentioned in part 10 of the application, where particulars of the missing document should be given and its non-production accounted for.

The registration authority has power to call for such further evidence as it may reasonably require.

12. Statutory declaration

The statutory declaration must be made before a justice of the peace, commissioner for oaths or notary public. Any plan referred to in the statutory declaration must be marked as an exhibit and signed by the officer taking the declaration (initialling is insufficient). A plan is marked by writing on the face in ink an identifying symbol such as the letter 'A'. On the back of the plan should appear these words:—

This is the exhibit marked 'A' referred to in the statutory declaration of (*name of declarant*) made this (*date*)   19   before me,

....

(*Signature and qualification*)

If there is more than one plan care should be taken to choose a different letter for each.

13. Action by registration authority

The registration authority will on receipt of the application send an acknowledgment. If this is not received within 10 days the applicant should communicate with the authority. Unless the application has to be rejected after preliminary consideration, the registration authority will give publicity to it and will consider it further in the light of any objections which may be received. The applicant will be supplied with copies of all objections which fall to be considered and will have an opportunity of answering them. Later, the applicant will be informed whether the application has been accepted or rejected. If the application is accepted, and the land over which the right is exercisable is not already registered under the Act, this will be done, and, whether or not the land is already registered, the right of common will be registered and the applicant will be supplied with particulars of the registration. If the application is rejected, the applicant will be notified of the reasons for the rejection.

14. False statements

The making of a false statement for the purposes of this application may render the maker liable to prosecution.

FORM 32

This section for official use only

Official stamp of registration authority indicating date of receipt

Application No.

Register unit No.

COMMONS REGISTRATION ACT 1965, SECTION 13

APPLICATION FOR THE REGISTRATION OF A CLAIM TO OWNERSHIP OF LAND REGISTERED UNDER SECTION 13 OF THE ACT

IMPORTANT NOTE:—Before filling in this form, read carefully the notes at the end. An incorrectly completed application form may have to be rejected.

[1] *Insert name of registration authority maintaining the register containing the registration of the land.*

To the[1]

Application is hereby made for the registration, in accordance with the particulars set out below, of a claim to the ownership of the under-noted land, which is registered under the Act, having become so registrable after 2nd January 1970.

Part 1.

(Give Christian names or forenames and surname or, in the case of a body corporate, the full title of the body. If part 2 is not completed all correspondence and notices will be sent to the first-named applicant.)

Name and address of the applicant or (if more than one) of every applicant, and the capacity in which he applies.

Part 2.

(This part should be completed only if a solicitor has been instructed for the purposes of the application. If it is completed, all correspondence and notices will be sent to the solicitor.)

Name and address of solicitor, if any.

Part 3.

(Insert "Common Land" or "Town or Village Greens.")

Register containing the registration of the land of which ownership is claimed.

Part 4.

Register unit number.

Part 5.

(Answer " Yes" or "No".)

Is ownership claimed of the whole of the land comprised in the above-mentioned register unit?

Part 6.

If the answer to part 5 is "yes", leave this part blank. Otherwise describe the portion of the land of which ownership is claimed. Where a plan is used the fact should be mentioned here, and the colouring used on the plan stated.

Part 7.

Does any person dispute the applicant's title to the land described above or claim any title to that land inconsistent with the applicant's title? If so, give the name and address of that person, or, if there is more than one, of every such person. (If there are none, write "none".)

Part 8.

List of supporting documents sent herewith, if any. (If none are sent, write "none".)

Part 9.

If there are any other facts relating to the application which ought to be brought to the attention of the registration authority full particulars should be given here.

Date 19   .

²The application must be signed by or on behalf of each individual applicant, and by the secretary or some other duly authorised officer of any applicant which is a body corporate or charity trustees.

Signatures² ....

....

(See Note 7)

STATUTORY DECLARATION IN SUPPORT

To be made by the applicant, or by one of the applicants, or by his or their solicitor, or, if the applicant is a body corporate or charity trustees, by its or their solicitor or by the person who signed the application.

[1] *Insert full name (and address if not given in the application form).*
[2] *Delete and adapt as necessary.*
[3] *Insert name if applicable.*

I,[1]
solemnly and sincerely declare as follows:—

1.[2] I am ((the person) (one of the persons) who (has) (have) signed the foregoing application)) ((the solicitor to (the applicant) ([3]   one of the applicants)).

2. I have read the Notes to the application form.

3. The facts set out in the application form are to the best of my knowledge and belief fully and truly stated and I am not aware of any other fact which should be brought to the attention of the registration authority as likely to affect its decision on this application, nor of any document which ought to be submitted or disclosed to the authority other than those (if any) mentioned in parts 8 and 9 of the application.

[4] *Delete this paragraph if there is no plan.*
[5] *Insert "marking" as on plan.*

4.[4] The plan now produced and shown to me marked[5] "   "
is the plan referred to in part 6 of the application.

And I make this solemn declaration, conscientiously believing the same to be true, and by virtue of the Statutory Declarations Act 1835.

Declared by the said...

....

at ....

in the...............................of...

this ....day of........................19   .

Signature of Declarant

Before me,

Signature ....

Address ....

....

Qualification ....

REMINDER TO OFFICER TAKING DECLARATION:
Please initial all alterations and mark any plan as an exhibit.

NOTES

1. Who may apply for registration

An application for the registration of a claim to the ownership of any land registered under the Act may be made by the owner of the land, or where the land belongs to an ecclesiastical benefice of the Church of England which is vacant, by the Church Commissioners.

In certain cases a person may be entitled to apply on behalf of the owner of the land or in his stead. Examples are:—

(a) a receiver appointed under section 105 of the Mental Health Act 1959;

(b) charity trustees where the land is vested in the Official Custodian for Charities;

(c) trustees for the purposes of the Settled Land Act 1925 authorised by order under section 24 of that Act.

In all cases the applicant should state in part 1 the capacity in which he applies (e.g. as owner of the land). If he applies on behalf of, or instead of, another person he should also state in part 1:—

(a) the Act of Parliament, statutory instrument, order of court or other authority under which he claims to be entitled to apply;

(b) the name and address of the person on whose behalf or in whose stead the application is made; and

(c) the capacity of that person (who will normally be the owner of the land).

Where the Church Commissioners apply with respect to land belonging to a vacant benefice, the fact should be stated, and the name of the benefice given, in part 1. Where charity trustees apply the fact should be stated, and the name of the charity given, in part 1.

The ownership of any land, for the purposes of the Act, means the ownership of the legal estate in fee simple in that land. It follows that applications made by, on behalf or instead of persons not having the legal estate in fee simple cannot be entertained. Thus, for example, an application by or on behalf of a lessee, mortgagee, or person having only an equitable interest in the land must be rejected. Anyone who is not sure whether he is entitled to apply should obtain legal advice.

2. Effect of registration at H.M. Land Registry

Where the freehold title to land is registered at H.M. Land Registry under the Land Registration Acts 1925 to 1966 registration of claims to the ownership thereof under the Commons Registration Act 1965 is not permitted. The registration authority will, on receipt of this application, inquire of the District Land Registry whether the freehold title to the land is registered under the Land Registration Acts, and, if this is the case, the registration authority will note the register accordingly and reject this application. An intending applicant who is uncertain whether the freehold title is registered under those Acts should therefore himself inquire of the District Land Registry, whose address may be obtained from the registration authority.

3. The land itself must be registered under section 13

Two separate registers are maintained under the Commons Registration Act 1965 by each registration authority—a Register of Common Land and a Register of Town or Village Greens. Before a claim to the ownership of land can be registered the land must itself have been registered under section 13 of the Act. This condition can only be satisfied in relation to land which became registrable under the Act after 2nd January 1970; if it became registrable on or before this date then (whether or not it was in fact so registered) the time for making application for the registration of a claim to its ownership has expired. (Where the land became registrable after 2nd January 1970 but has not yet been registered the owner may, if he wishes, himself apply for its registration as common land or as a town or village green, and, if the land is so registered, thereafter apply on this form to register his ownership.) The ownership application must be submitted to the registration authority maintaining the register which contains the registration of the land. For land in an administrative county this will normally be the county council; for land in a county borough, the county borough council, and for land in Greater London, the Greater London Council. Where land lies partly in the area of one registration authority and partly in that of another, the authorities may by agreement have provided for one of them to be the registration authority for the whole of the land. An applicant concerned with land lying close to the boundary of an administrative area, or partly in one area and partly in another, should therefore enquire whether an agreement has been made and, if so, which authority is responsible for the land.

4. Inspection and search of registers

To ascertain whether land has been registered under the Act, anyone may inspect the registers at the office of the registration authority. Alternatively, an official certificate of search may be obtained from the registration authority. A requisition for such search must be made in writing on C.R. Form No. 21, a separate requisition being required for each register. If the land is registered, the certificate will reveal the register unit number(s) and whether any rights of common and claims to ownership are registered.

5. Scope of application: land descriptions

An application must relate to land comprised in one register unit and no more. If land in two or more register units is concerned, a separate application form must be used for each. In part 4, the register unit number should be quoted; the applicant should keep a note of this number, which will be used by the registration authority for reference. If the application relates to the whole of the land comprised in the register unit no further description than the register unit number is needed. If not, the land which is the subject of the application must be clearly identified. This can sometimes be done by reference to some physical feature such as a road, river or railway, so that the description might, for example, read "The land in register unit No.................lying to the south of the road from A to B". Where this cannot be done the land must be described by a plan, which must be drawn to scale, in ink or other permanent medium, and be on a scale of not less, or not substantially less, than six inches to one mile. It must show the land to be described by means of distinctive colouring (a coloured edging inside the boundary will usually suffice), and it must be marked as an exhibit to the statutory declaration (see Note 7 below).

6. Evidence of ownership: supporting documents

The application must be accompanied by the original or (preferably) by a copy or sufficient abstract of every document relating to the matter which the applicant has in his possession or under his control, or of which he has a right to the production, with the exception of documents which he would not be obliged to abstract or produce to a purchaser under a contract for the sale of the land made otherwise than by correspondence and containing no stipulations as to title. The registration authority has power to call for such further evidence in support of the application as it may reasonably require. In special cases the applicant may need to consult the registration authority before formally applying for registration.

Applicants are strongly recommended NOT to forward the original of any deed or other private document. Instead, a copy should be supplied, preferably indorsed with a certificate signed by a solicitor that it has been examined against the original. The applicant should indicate, either on the copy itself or in part 8 of the application, as convenient, who has the original and where it may be inspected. If for any reason a document cannot be produced, the fact should be mentioned in part 9 of the application where particulars of the missing document should be given and its non-production accounted for.

7. Statutory declaration

The statutory declaration must be made before a justice of the peace, commissioner for oaths or notary public. Any plan referred to in the statutory declaration must be marked as an exhibit and signed by the officer taking the declaration (initialling is insufficient). A plan is marked by writing on the face in ink an identifying symbol such as the letter 'A'. On the back of the plan should appear these words:

This is the exhibit marked 'A' referred to in the statutory declaration of (*name of declarant*) made this (*date*)   19   before me,

....

(*Signature and qualification*)

8. Action by registration authority

The registration authority will on receipt of the application send an acknowledgment. If this is not received within 10 days the applicant should communicate with the authority. Unless the application has to be rejected after preliminary consideration, the registration authority will give publicity to it and will consider it further in the light of any objections which may be received. The applicant will be supplied with copies of all objections which fall to be considered and will have an opportunity of answering them.

Later, the applicant will be informed whether the application has been accepted or rejected. If it is accepted, the applicant will be registered as owner and particulars of the registration will be supplied to him. If the application is rejected, the applicant will be notified of the reasons for the rejection.

9. False statements

The making of a false statement for the purposes of this application may render the maker liable to prosecution.

FORM 33

(*Name of registration authority*)

COMMONS REGISTRATION ACT 1965

Notice of application for registration of land claimed to have become
(common land) (a town or village green)[1] after 2nd January 1970

To every reputed owner, lessee, tenant or occupier of any part of the land described
below, and to all others whom it may concern.

Application has been made to the registration authority, the (*name and address of
registration authority*) by (*name and address of applicant*) under section 13 of the
Commons Registration Act 1965 for the inclusion in the Register of (Common Land)
(Town or Village Greens)[1] of the land described (at Annex A)[2] below, which it is
claimed became (common land) (a town or village green)[1] on (*date given in part 4 of
Form 29 or 30*) (in substitution for the land described at Annex B below, which, it is
claimed, ceased to be (common land) (a town or village green)[1] on that date)[2], under
and by virtue of (*account of circumstances, etc., summarised from part 5 of Form 29
or 30*).

The application, which includes a plan of(   ),[3] may be inspected at (*address
where application available*) (and copies of the application and plan(s) may be inspected
at the following local authority offices (*insert names and addresses of concerned local
authorities, if any*))[1].

If the registration authority is satisfied that the land described (at Annex A)[2] below
has become (common land) (a town or village green)[1] as claimed, it will so register the
land, and such registration will be conclusive evidence of the status of the land as at
the date of registration. (The land described at Annex B below will then be removed
from the register).[2]

Any person wishing to object to the registration of the land as (common land) (a
town or village green)[1] (or to the removal from the register of the land described at
Annex B below)[2] should send a written and signed statement of the facts on which he
bases his objection to (*name and address of registration authority*) so as to arrive not
later than[4]

Dated   19   .

(*Signature on behalf of registration authority*).

(ANNEX A)[2]

Description of the land claimed to have become (common land) (a town or village
green)[1]

(ANNEX B)[2]

(Description of the land claimed to have ceased to be (common land) (a town or village
green)[1] *including a reference to the register unit number if the land is registered*)[2]

---

[1]Delete as necessary.   [2]For substituted land cases only.

[3]Insert "the land proposed for registration" or, in a substituted land case where a plan of the
taken land is also provided, "both areas".

[4]Insert date in accordance with regulation 5(5).

FORM 34

(Name of registration authority)

COMMONS REGISTRATION ACT 1965

Notice of application for registration of rights of common over land (registered) (claimed to be registrable)[1] under section 13 of the Act

To every reputed owner, lessee, tenant or occupier of any part of the land lastly described below, and to all others whom it may concern.

Application has been made to the registration authority, the *(name of registration authority)* for the registration under section 13 of the Commons Registration Act 1965 of the right(s) of common specified in Annex A below which (is) (are)[1] claimed by the (person) (persons respectively)[1] named in the said Annex to be exercisable over the land described in Annex B below. The alleged origin of the right(s) is as stated in Annex A.

The application, (which includes a plan of) (and register unit No......................... in the Register of (Common Land) (Town or Village Greens)[1] which (comprises) (includes)[1])[1] the land over which the right(s) (is)(are) claimed to be exercisable (and a plan or other description of the land to which they are attached)[1] may be inspected at *(insert address where application etc. available)* (and copies of the application and plan(s) may be inspected at the following local authority offices *(insert names and addresses of concerned local authorities, if any)*)[1].

If the registration under the Act of (any of)[1] the said right(s) of common is effected, it will be conclusive evidence of the matters registered as at the date of registration.

(If any of the said rights are registered, the land over which the rights are exercisable will be registered also, and such registration will be conclusive evidence of the matters registered as at the date of registration.)[2]

Any person wishing to object to the registration of (any of)[1] the said right(s) of common (or to the registration of the said land)[2] should send a written and signed statement of the facts on which he bases his objection to *(name and address of registration authority)* so as to arrive not later than[3]

Dated   19   .

(Signature on behalf of registration authority)

ANNEX A

Description of the claimed right(s) of common

Name and address of claimant	Particulars of the claimed right of common	Particulars of the land (if any) to which the right is alleged to be attached	Alleged origin of the right

[1]Delete or adapt as necessary.   [2]For use only where the land has not yet been registered under section 13.
[3]Insert date in accordance with regulation 5(5).

ANNEX B

Description of the land over which the claimed rights are alleged to be exercisable

FORM 35

(Name of registration authority)

COMMONS REGISTRATION ACT 1965

Notice of application for registration of a claim to the ownership of land registered under section 13 of the Act

To every reputed owner, lessee, tenant or occupier of any part of the land described below, and to all others whom it may concern.

Application has been made to the registration authority, the *(name of registration authority)* for the registration in the Register of (Common Land) (Town or Village Greens)[1] of *(name and address)* as owner of the land described below, which was registered as (common land) (a town or village green)[1] under Register unit No..............
on *(date of registration)* under section 13 of the Act.

The application, and the register unit affected, may be inspected at *(insert address where register maintained)* (and copies of the application alone may be inspected at the following local authority offices *(insert names and addresses of concerned local authorities, if any))*[1].

Any person wishing to object to the application should send a written and signed statement of the facts upon which he bases his objection to *(name and address of registration authority)* so as to arrive not later than[2]

Dated   19   .

(Signature on behalf of registration authority)

DESCRIPTION OF THE LAND referred to above

---

[1]Delete as necessary.   [2]Insert date in accordance with regulation 5(5).

Given under the official seal of the Minister of Housing and Local Government on 19th December 1969.

(L.S.)   *Denis H. Howell,*
                                             Minister of State.
                     Ministry of Housing and Local Government.

Given under my hand

George Thomas,
One of Her Majesty's Principal
Secretaries of State,
Welsh Office.

19th December 1969.

EXPLANATORY NOTE

(*This Note is not part of the Regulations.*)

These Regulations provide for the inclusion, in the registers of common land and of town or village greens maintained under the Commons Registration Act 1965, of any land which becomes common land or a town or village green after 2nd January 1970, and for the registration of rights of common over such land and of claims to the ownership thereof.

STATUTORY INSTRUMENTS

1969 No. 1845 (S. 161)

AGRICULTURE

AGRICULTURAL GRANTS, GOODS AND SERVICES

The Winter Keep (Scotland) Scheme 1969

Laid before Parliament in draft

Made - - - 18*th December* 1969

Coming into Operation 1*st January* 1970

In exercise of the powers conferred on me by sections 10 and 12 of the Agriculture (Miscellaneous Provisions) Act 1963(**a**), as amended by section 44 of the Agriculture Act 1967(**b**), and of all other powers enabling me in that behalf, and with the approval of the Treasury, I hereby make the following scheme, a draft of which has been laid before Parliament and has been approved by resolution of each House of Parliament:—

Citation and commencement

1. This scheme may be cited as the Winter Keep (Scotland) Scheme 1969 and shall come into operation on 1st January 1970.

Interpretation

2.—(1) In this scheme, unless the context otherwise requires—

"the Act" means the Agriculture (Miscellaneous Provisions) Act 1963;

"agricultural unit" means land, other than land occupied by any person as a crofter or as an eligible occupier, which is occupied as a unit for agricultural purposes, together with any other land, including land held in common, used in connection with such land for the purpose of grazing;

"crofter" means a crofter within the meaning of the Crofters (Scotland) Acts 1955 and 1961(**c**);

"eligible occupier" means a person who is for the time being an eligible occupier within the meaning of the Crofting Counties Agricultural Grants (Scotland) Scheme 1961(**d**), the Crofting Counties Agricultural Grants (Scotland) Scheme 1963(**e**) or the Crofting Counties Agricultural Grants (Scotland) Scheme 1965(**f**) and, except in the case of a person who is a sub-tenant as is mentioned in section 14(1)(*c*) of the Crofters (Scotland) Act 1961, who has been offered a grant under any of the said schemes;

"grass" includes rye grass and other rotational grasses, clover and permanent grass;

(**a**) 1963 c. 11.	(**b**) 1967 c. 22.
(**c**) 1955 c. 21; 1961 c. 58.	(**d**) S.I. 1961/2266 (1961 III, p. 3973).
(**e**) S.I. 1963/1294 (1963 II, p. 2240).	(**f**) S.I. 1965/1519 (1965 II, p. 4399).

"livestock rearing purposes" means the breeding, rearing and maintenance of sheep or cattle, and includes other activities carried on in connection therewith;

"occupier" in relation to any land, means the person who has the right to use that land for growing any such crops as are specified in Schedule 1 to this scheme; and the word "occupation" shall be construed accordingly;

"year" means a year commencing with 1st January and ending with 31st December.

(2) In this scheme "livestock rearing land" has the meaning assigned to it by section 10(3) of the Act, that is to say—

(a) land situated in an area consisting predominantly of mountains, hills or heath, being land which is, or by improvement could be made, suitable for use for the breeding, rearing and maintenance of sheep or cattle but not for the carrying on, to any material extent, of dairy farming, the production, to any material extent, of fat sheep or fat cattle or the production of crops in quantity materially greater than that necessary to feed the number of sheep or cattle capable of being maintained on the land, and

(b) any land suitable for use with such land for livestock rearing purposes.

(3) Any reference in this scheme to any other scheme shall be construed as a reference to that scheme as amended by any subsequent scheme, and if any scheme referred to in this scheme is replaced by a subsequent scheme the reference shall be construed as a reference to that subsequent scheme.

(4) The Interpretation Act 1889(a) shall apply for the interpretation of this scheme as it applies for the interpretation of an Act of Parliament.

Winter keep grants

3.—(1) Subject to the provisions of this scheme, the Secretary of State may pay annual grants, to be known as winter keep grants, for each year in the period commencing with 1st January 1970 and ending with 31st December 1974 in respect of livestock rearing land which in the year to which the grant relates is—

(a) comprised in an agricultural unit which appears to the Secretary of State to consist predominantly of such land as is described in paragraph 2(2)(a) of this scheme, being a unit used predominantly for livestock rearing purposes, and

(b) used for growing any such crops for the winter feeding of livestock as are specified in Schedule 1 to this scheme.

(2) The rate of grant payable in respect of any such land shall be the rate specified in column 2 of Schedule 2 to this scheme in relation to the class of land into which that land falls, being one of the classes of land specified in column 1 of the said Schedule:

Provided that—

(a) for the purposes of this subparagraph the class of land into which any such land falls shall be such one of the said classes as is determined by the Secretary of State;

(b) in calculating the amount of a grant fractions of an acre shall be rounded down to the nearest quarter of an acre.

(a) 1889 c. 63.

(3) The person to whom such a grant may be made shall be the occupier of the land on 4th June in the year to which the grant relates:

Provided that where after 4th June in the year to which the grant relates there is a change in the occupation of the land and the land is used for growing a crop, or in the case where the crop is grass, for setting aside of grass for mowing, after such change and then for the first time in that year, the person to whom the grant may be made shall be the occupier of the land who grew the crop or set aside the grass for mowing.

(4) A grant shall not be paid under this scheme in respect of less than one acre of land.

Withholding or restriction of grant for bad work, etc.

4. Where in the opinion of the Secretary of State—

    (a) any operation relevant to the payment of a grant under this scheme has been inefficiently carried out; or

    (b) adequate facilities have not been given for the inspection of any land in respect of which a grant may be made, or of the crop grown thereon, or of any sheep or cattle on the agricultural unit of which the land forms part,

payment of the grant may be withheld or the amount of the grant may be restricted to such amount as the Secretary of State considers reasonable.

Restriction of grant for inadequate crops

5. Where the Secretary of State is of the opinion, after making allowance for the weather and other natural conditions, that a crop is unduly small in relation to the acreage of land on which it has been grown, the amount of any grant payable under this scheme in respect of that land shall be restricted to the amount which would have been so payable if the crop had been grown on a part of that land reasonably sufficient in the opinion of the Secretary of State to produce a crop of the kind and quantity actually grown.

Restriction of grant for excess winter keep

6. The total grant payable under this scheme for any year in respect of land comprised in an agricultural unit shall be restricted to the amount payable in respect of such acreage of land as would, in the opinion of the Secretary of State, have been reasonably sufficient to provide adequate crops for the winter feeding of the numbers of sheep and cattle likely to be maintained by the occupier on the unit throughout the following winter.

Other conditions of payment

7. Payment of grant under this scheme in respect of any land used for growing a crop shall be subject to the following conditions—

    (a) an application for the grant shall be submitted to the Secretary of State in writing by the person to whom the grant may be made in such form and within such time as the Secretary of State may require;

    (b) the person to whom the grant may be made shall, on being requested to do so by the Secretary of State, give to him such information as he may require to enable him to verify the application;

    (c) the land shall, in the opinion of the Secretary of State, be suitable for growing the crop.

Withholding or restriction of grant where land has been grant-aided under other schemes

8. Where in the opinion of the Secretary of State the carrying out on any land of any operation relevant to the payment of grant under this scheme appears to frustrate the purposes served by any expenditure in respect of which, within the period of seven years immediately preceding the date of application for the grant, there has been made for the benefit of that land a grassland renovation grant under section 11 of the Act or a grant towards the cost of improvement of hill land under section 41 of the Agriculture Act 1967, the Secretary of State may withhold the grant under this scheme or restrict it to such amount as in the circumstances appears to him to be appropriate.

William Ross,
One of Her Majesty's Principal
Secretaries of State.

St. Andrew's House,
Edinburgh.
17th December 1969.

We approve.

Joseph Harper,
Walter Harrison,
Two of the Lords Commissioners
of Her Majesty's Treasury.

18th December 1969.

SCHEDULE 1 Paragraphs 2(1) and 3(1)
Crops for the winter feeding of livestock

(1) Grass for drying, hay or silage, set aside for mowing by being kept ungrazed for a substantial part of the growing season.

(2) Other crops grown exclusively for silage.

(3) Oats, turnips, swedes, kale, cabbage, rape, mangolds, fodder beet, fodder radish, beans, peas, kohlrabi, vetches, tares and any mixture of 2 or more of these crops.

SCHEDULE 2 Paragraph 3(2)
Rate of grant

Column 1 Classes of land	Column 2 Rate of grant

CLASS A
Land comprised in an agricultural unit normally possessing most of the following natural characteristics:—
  (*a*) good grazings, capable of carrying the less hardy types of sheep or cattle;
  (*b*) a not unduly restricted grazing season;
  (*c*) the capacity to carry a reasonably high rate of stocking;
  (*d*) arable land of fair quality and sufficient in area for the production of crops in reasonable relationship to the stock carrying capacity of the unit ..   ..   ..
	£2 10s. per acre.

Column 1 Classes of land	Column 2 Rate of grant
CLASS B Land comprised in an agricultural unit normally possessing natural characteristics intermediate to those specified in Classes A and C respectively in this Column	£3 10s. per acre.
CLASS C Land comprised in an agricultural unit normally possessing most of the following natural characteristics:— (a) poor grazings, capable of carrying only the hardier types of sheep and cattle; (b) a short grazing season; (c) the capacity to carry only a low rate of stocking due to poor or insufficient arable land	£5 per acre.

EXPLANATORY NOTE

(This Note is not part of the Scheme.)

This Scheme provides for the payment of annual winter keep grants at different rates to occupiers of different classes of livestock rearing land which is used in the years 1970 to 1974 to grow specified crops (including grass set aside for mowing) for the winter feeding of livestock. The land must be part of an agricultural unit consisting predominantly of livestock rearing land and being used predominantly for livestock rearing purposes. Grant may be reduced or withheld where the land used for growing the crops has been improved with the aid of grassland renovation grant or a hill land improvement grant within the preceding seven years. Restrictions are imposed on the payment of grant where work is inefficiently carried out, where adequate facilities for inspection are not given, where inadequate crops are grown and where more winter keep is grown than is likely to be needed for sheep and cattle on the unit in the following winter. The Scheme provides for the making of applications for grant. The Scheme does not apply to croft land or to other land occupied by persons eligible for grant under the Crofting Counties Agricultural Grants (Scotland) Schemes.

The Scheme is materially the same as the previous scheme, the Winter Keep (Scotland) Scheme 1966, but operates for 5 instead of 3 years and provides for the obtaining of information to verify applications.

STATUTORY INSTRUMENTS

1969 No. 1846 (S.162)

LANDLORD AND TENANT

RENT CONTROL, ETC (SCOTLAND)

The Rent Regulation (Forms etc.) (Scotland) (Amendment) Regulations 1969

Made - - -	18*th December* 1969
Laid before Parliament	31*st December* 1969
Coming into Operation	1*st January* 1970

In exercise of the powers conferred upon me by section 46 of the Rent Act 1965(**a**), section 6(4) of the Rent (Control of Increases) Act 1969(**b**), and of all other powers enabling me in that behalf, I hereby make the following regulations :—

1. These regulations may be cited as the Rent Regulation (Forms etc) (Scotland) (Amendment) Regulations 1969 and shall come into operation on 1st January 1970.

2. The Interpretation Act 1889(**c**) shall apply for the interpretation of these regulations as it applies for the interpretation of an Act of Parliament.

3. Schedule 2 to the Rent Regulations (Forms etc) (Scotland) Regulations 1969(**d**) shall be amended as follows :—

    (*a*) in the List of Forms there shall be added at the end of the title of Form No. 3 the words "or under the Rent (Control of Increases) Act 1969" ;

    (*b*) in the List of Forms there shall be added the title of Form No. 4A as set out in Schedule 1 hereto ;

    (*c*) in the heading to Form No. 3 there shall be inserted after the words "Act 1969" the words "or under the Rent (Control of Increases) Act 1969" ;

    (*d*) after Form No. 4 there shall be inserted Form No. 4A as set out in Schedule 2 hereto, as the form prescribed for a notice of increase served consequent upon the registration of a rent under Part II of the Rent Act 1965 where there is a period of delay under section 5 of the Rent (Control of Increases) Act 1969.

William Ross,
One of Her Majesty's Principal
Secretaries of State.

St. Andrew's House,
  Edinburgh.
18th December 1969.

(**a**) 1965 c. 75.   (**b**) 1969 c. 62.
(**c**)1889 c. 63.   (**d**) S.I. 1969/1419 (1969 III, p. 4478).

SCHEDULE 1

Form Number	Purpose	Reference to sections or schedules
4A	Form of notice of increase of rent under section 7(b) of the Rent Act 1965 where a rent has been registered and there are restrictions on rent increases under the Rent (Control of Increases) Act 1969.	7(b)1

SCHEDULE 2

FORM No. 4A

RENT ACT 1965

RENT (CONTROL OF INCREASES) ACT 1969

Form of Notice of Increase of Rent under section 7(b) of the Rent Act 1965 where a rent has been registered and there are restrictions on rent increases under the Rent (Control of Increases) Act 1969 (Note 1).

Date...

To...................................tenant of...............................

1. A rent of £   per   was registered on as the fair rent for the above mentioned dwelling (Note 2) [of which £ per   was noted in the Register as the amount apportioned to services provided by the landlord (Note 3)].

Strike out words in square brackets if they do not apply.

2. Where a rent for a dwelling which is subject to a regulated tenancy is registered in 1970 or 1971 there is, by virtue of section 5 of the Rent (Control of Increases) Act 1969, a period of delay determined in accordance with the Schedule to that Act and the rent payable for any statutory period of the tenancy (Note 4) may only be increased in such stages as are permitted in that Schedule (Note 5).

3. [It is noted in the register that the rates for the above mentioned premises are paid by the landlord. These are currently £   per year and the landlord is entitled to add this amount to the rent he is otherwise permitted to obtain (Note 6)].

4. I hereby give you notice that your rent will be increased from your present rent of £   per   by an increase of £   per to the new rent of £   per   and the date from which such increase is to take effect is   (Note 7).

5. The rental period for which the rent is being increased by this notice begins in the first [first] [second] year of the period of delay (Note 5) and the following information is relevant to the calculation of the increase.

    a. The amount of the previous limit (Note 8) £   per

    b. The amount apportioned to services (Note 3) £   per

    c. The appropriate proportion of the difference between the registered rent and the sum of *a.* and *b.* (Note 9)   £

6. [The new rent includes the sum of £   per   in respect of rates paid by the landlord].

Signature of [landlord] [agent authorised to serve this notice]

....

[Name of landlord if notice served by agent...

....]

Address of landlord..

....

[Addres of agent ....

....]

NOTES

1. This Notice of Increase is needed where a dwelling house is let on a tenancy

(*a*) which is regulated under the Rent Act 1965; and

(*b*) which either has become a statutory tenancy or will become one under section 9(3) of that Act (Note 3); and

(*c*) for which a fair rent is registered under that Act in the year 1970 or 1971 other than:

(i) a rent to which the restrictions on rent increases under the Housing (Scotland) Act 1969 apply; or

(ii) a rent registered in accordance with a certificate of fair rent (except in the case of a rent so registered which is in substitution for a rent with respect to which there is a period of delay under the Rent (Control of Increases) Act 1969).

2. The Rent Register may be inspected at the office of the Rent Officer.

3. The amount apportioned to services is that part of the increase in rent which is regarded as representing an increase in the cost of any services provided by the landlord and the amount so noted is excluded from the restrictions on increases in rent (Note 9).

4. If there is still a contract of tenancy between the landlord and tenant the registration of a fair rent which is higher than the rent payable under that contract does not allow the landlord to increase the rent unless there is a provision to that effect in the contract. In a case where there is a period of delay under the Rent (Control of Increases) Act 1969 the limits under that Act continue to apply notwithstanding any agreement purporting to entitle the landlord to charge a higher rent.

If however a contractual tenancy has come to an end and the tenant is holding over as a statutory tenant under the Rent Acts, the landlord may increase the rent by the service of notice(s) of increase to the extent permitted by the Rent (Control of Increases) Act 1969.

If this Notice is served while the regulated tenancy is still a contractual one and the landlord, by serving a notice to quit at the same time as this Notice could bring the tenancy to an end before the date specified in this Notice for the increase in rent to take effect, this Notice will operate, by virtue of section 9(3) of the Rent Act 1965, to convert the tenancy into a statutory tenancy as from that date.

5. The Schedule to the 1969 Act provides for a two year or one year period of delay with respect to the rent registered beginning with the date of registration, according as to whether it was registered in 1970 or 1971.

For rents registered in 1970 one-third of the net increase (or 7s 6d per week if one-third is less than this) can be added from the commencement of the first rental period following registration, one-third (or 7s 6d per week if one-third is less than this) on the corresponding date in 1971 and one-third (or the balance) on the corresponding date in 1972.

For rents registered in 1971, one-third (or 7s 6d per week if one-third is less than this) can be added from the first rental period following registration, and the balance on the corresponding date in 1972.

6. The phasing restrictions do not apply to any changes in rent resulting from changes in rates borne by the landlord.

7. This date must be a date which is not earlier than:

    (i) the date of registration or

    (ii) four weeks before the service of this Notice, or

    (iii) the commencement of the first rental period beginning during the first or second year of the period of delay as the case may be.

If this Notice is served while the regulated tenancy is still contractual then the date must be one later than the date on which the tenancy could be brought to an end by a notice to quit served at the same time as this notice (Note 4).

8. The previous limit of rent is the amount which the landlord could have charged immediately before the registration in question, on the assumption that he had served all permissible notices of increase.

9. The amount of increase permitted is the appropriate proportion, calculated according to the year of the period of delay (Note 5), of the difference between the registered rent and sum of

    (a) the amount of the previous limit (Note 8) and

    (b) the amount apportioned to services (Note 3).

The appropriate proportion by which the rent for any rental period may be increased is

    (a) one-third (or 7s 6d per week if one-third is less than this) if the rental period begins in the first year in the period of delay and

    (b) (in a case where the period of delay is two years) two-thirds (or 15s 0d per week if two-thirds is less than this) if the rental period begins in the second year of the period of delay.

EXPLANATORY NOTE

(*This Order is not part of the Regulations.*)

These Regulations prescribe a new form of notice of increase of rent to be served in cases where a rent is registered under Part II of the Rent Act 1965 and there is a period of delay under the Rent (Control of Increases) Act 1969. They also amend the heading of Form No. 3 in Schedule 2 to the Rent Regulation (Forms etc.) (Scotland) Regulations 1969.

STATUTORY INSTRUMENTS

1969 No. 1847 (S.163)

FOOD AND DRUGS

COMPOSITION AND LABELLING—SCOTLAND

The Soft Drinks (Scotland) Amendment Regulations 1969

Made - - -		18*th December* 1969
Laid before Parliament		31*st December* 1969
Coming into Operation		1*st January* 1970

In exercise of the powers conferred on me by sections 4, 7 and 56 of the Food and Drugs (Scotland) Act 1956(**a**), and of all other powers enabling me in that behalf, and after consultation with such organisations as appear to me to be representative of interests substantially affected by these regulations and after reference to the Scottish Food Hygiene Council under section 25 of the said Act (in so far as the regulations are made in exercise of the powers conferred by the said section 7), I hereby make the following regulations :—

Citation and commencement

1. These regulations may be cited as the Soft Drinks (Scotland) Amendment Regulations 1969, and shall come into operation on 1st January 1970.

Interpretation

2.—(1) In these regulations the expression "the principal regulations" means the Soft Drinks (Scotland) Regulations 1964(**b**) and, unless the context otherwise requires, any reference herein to a numbered regulation or schedule shall be construed as a reference to the regulation or schedule bearing that number in the principal regulations.

(2) The Interpretation Act 1889(**c**) shall apply for the interpretation of these regulations as it applies for the interpretation of an Act of Parliament.

Amendment of the principal regulations

3. Regulation 2(1) shall be amended—

  (*a*) by deleting the definition of cyclamic acid ;

  (*b*) by deleting from the definition of permitted artificial sweetener the words "or cyclamic acid".

4. Regulation 6(2) shall be amended by substituting in sub-paragraph (*a*) of the proviso thereto for the words and figures "columns 4 and 5" the word and figure "column 4" and by deleting from that sub-paragraph the words "(calculated as therein required)".

(a) 1956 c. 30.   (b) S.I. 1964/767 (1964 II, p. 1634).
(c) 1889 c. 63.

5. Regulation 13 shall be amended by adding at the end thereof the following proviso :—

"Provided that the said description or descriptive name need not be included in the said declaration if a label on a container of the soft drink dispensed from the vending machine, or an exact facsimile of such label, bearing the said description, where applicable, and otherwise the said descriptive name is conspicuous and legible to an intending purchaser on or through the outside of the vending machine.".

6. The following regulation shall be substituted for regulation 14 :—

"**14.** Subject to the provisions of these regulations, no person shall sell, consign or deliver in any container any soft drink to which any permitted artificial sweetener has been added unless that container bears a label on which there appears the expression 'saccharin added' or 'contains saccharin' or, where appropriate, any one of the following expressions :—

    (*a*) 'saccharin and sugar added' ;

    (*b*) 'sugar and saccharin added' ;

    (*c*) 'contains saccharin and sugar' ;

    (*d*) 'contains sugar and saccharin' ;

    (*e*) 'sweetened with sugar and saccharin' ;

    (*f*) 'sweetened with saccharin and sugar':

Provided that as respects any sale, consignment or delivery of a soft drink on or before 31st December 1970, it shall be a sufficient compliance with the requirements of this regulation if the words 'permitted artificial sweetener' are substituted for the word 'saccharin' in any of the foregoing expressions.".

7. Regulation 15 shall be amended by inserting immediately after the word "container" the words "or required by virtue of regulation 13 hereof to appear on a vending machine" and by inserting immediately before the word "requirements" the word "appropriate".

8. The Schedule to these regulations shall be substituted for Schedule 1 to the principal regulations.

9. Schedule 2 shall be amended—

    (*a*) by deleting from the words preceding the table in Parts I and II respectively the words following the words "Table below" ;

    (*b*) by deleting from Parts I and II respectively column 5 and all the figures and words contained within the said column ;

    (*c*) by deleting Part III.

10. Schedule 3 shall be amended—

    (*a*) by deleting from the words preceding the table in Parts I and II respectively the words following the words "Table below" ;

    (*b*) by deleting from Parts I and II respectively column 5 and all the figures and words contained within the said column ;

    (*c*) by deleting Part III.

11. Schedule 4 shall be amended by substituting in paragraph 3 for the words "and shall be not less than half an inch in height." the following words :—
"and—

> (*a*) if it is part of the description or descriptive name referred to in regulation 13, shall be not less than half an inch in height ;
> (*b*) if it is part of any expression specified in regulation 14, shall be not less than one quarter of an inch in height.".

William Ross,
One of Her Majesty's Principal
Secretaries of State.

St. Andrew's House,
   Edinburgh.
18th December 1969.

Regulation 8

SCHEDULE

PERMITTED ARTIFICIAL SWEETENERS

  1. *Saccharin*

Saccharin is the substance conforming to the description, specifications and requirements for saccharin contained in the British Pharmacopoeia 1968.

  2. *Saccharin calcium*

Saccharin calcium is the calcium derivative of 2-sulphobenzoic imide with $3\frac{1}{2}$ molecules of water of crystallisation. It contains not less than 98 per cent. of $C_{14}H_8Ca\,N_2O_6S_2$ calculated with reference to the substance dried to constant weight at 105°C.

Description	... ...	White crystals or white crystilline powder, odour faintly aromatic, taste intensely sweet.
Solubility ...	... ...	1 g. dissolves in 1·5 g. water.
Loss on drying	... ...	When dried to constant weight at 105°C. loses not less than 11 per cent. and not more than 15 per cent. of its weight.
Ammonium Compounds ...		Complies with the test given under Saccharin in the British Pharmacopoeia 1968.
4-Sulphamoylbenzoates ...		Complies with the test given under Saccharin Sodium in the British Pharmacopoeia 1968.

  3. *Saccharin sodium*

Saccharin sodium is the substance conforming to the description, specifications and requirements for saccharin sodium contained in the British Pharmacopoeia 1968.

EXPLANATORY NOTE

(This Note is not part of the Regulations.)

These amending Regulations, which come into operation on 1st January 1970—

(*a*) amend the definition of "permitted artificial sweetener" in the principal Regulations so that saccharin, saccharin calcium and saccharin sodium (as defined in the Schedule to these Regulations) are the only permitted artificial sweeteners ;

(*b*) amend the requirements in Regulation 13 of the principal Regulations as to declarations on the sale of soft drinks in or from vending machines;

(*c*) make changes in the forms of expressions, specified in Regulation 14 of the principal Regulations, for labels of containers of soft drinks containing any permitted artificial sweetener ;

(*d*) amend the specifications for saccharin, saccharin calcium and saccharin sodium in Schedule 1 to the principal Regulations.

STATUTORY INSTRUMENTS

1969 No. 1848 (S.164)

FOOD AND DRUGS

COMPOSITION AND LABELLING—SCOTLAND

The Artificial Sweeteners in Food (Scotland) Regulations 1969

Made - - -	*18th December* 1969
Laid before Parliament	*31st December* 1969
Coming into Operation	*1st January* 1970

In exercise of the powers conferred upon me by sections 4, 7 and 56 of the Food and Drugs (Scotland) Act 1956(a), and of all other powers enabling me in that behalf, and after consultation with such organisations as appear to me to be representative of interests substantially affected by these regulations and after reference to the Scottish Food Hygiene Council under section 25 of the said Act (in so far as the regulations are made in exercise of the powers conferred by the said section 7), I hereby make the following regulations:—

PART I

PRELIMINARY

Citation and commencement

1. These regulations may be cited as the Artificial Sweeteners in Food (Scotland) Regulations 1969, and shall come into operation on 1st January 1970.

Interpretation

2.—(1) In these regulations, unless the context otherwise requires—

"the Act" means the Food and Drugs (Scotland) Act 1956;

"artificial sweetener" means any chemical compound which is sweet to the taste, but does not include any sugar or any polyhydric alcohol;

"artificial sweetening tablet" means any tablet which contains an artificial sweetener and which is intended for sale with a view to its use in the preparation of food;

"carbohydrate" means a substance containing carbon, hydrogen and oxygen only in which the hydrogen and oxygen occur in the same proportion as in water;

"food" means food intended for sale for human consumption and includes drink, chewing gum and other products of a like nature and use, and articles and substances used as ingredients in the preparation of food or drink or of such products, but does not include—

(*a*) water, live animals or birds,

(*b*) fodder or feeding stuffs for animals, birds or fish, or

(*c*) articles or substances used only as drugs;

(a) 1956 c. 30.

"full strength tablets" means artificial sweetening tablets which comply with the requirements as to composition set out in paragraph 1 of schedule 2 to these regulations;

"half strength tablets" means artificial sweetening tablets which comply with the requirements as to composition set out in paragraph 2 of schedule 2 to these regulations;

"human consumption" includes use in the preparation of food for human consumption;

"permitted artificial sweetener" means saccharin, saccharin calcium or saccharin sodium;

"polyhydric alcohol" means an alcohol with three or more free hydroxyl groups;

"saccharin" means the substance conforming to the description, specifications and requirements for saccharin contained in the British Pharmacopoeia 1968;

"saccharin calcium" means the substance conforming to the description, specifications and requirements for saccharin calcium contained in schedule 1 to these regulations;

"saccharin sodium" means the substance conforming to the description, specifications and requirements for saccharin sodium contained in the British Pharmacopoeia 1968;

"sell" includes offer or expose for sale or have in possession for sale; and "sale" and "sold" shall be construed accordingly;

"sugar" means any soluble carbohydrate sweetening matter;

and other expressions have the same meaning as in the Act.

(2) For the purposes of these regulations, the supply of any artificial sweetener or any food containing any artificial sweetener otherwise than by sale, at, in or from any place where artificial sweeteners or such food are or is supplied in the course of a business, shall be deemed to be a sale of that artificial sweetener or that food, as the case may be; and references to purchasing and purchaser shall be construed accordingly.

(3) For the purposes of the Labelling of Food Order 1953(a), as amended(b), these regulations, in so far as they prescribe requirements as to composition for artificial sweetening tablets, shall be taken to prescribe standards for such tablets.

(4) Any reference in these regulations to a label borne on a container shall be construed as including a reference to any legible marking on the container however effected.

(5) The Interpretation Act 1889(c) shall apply for the interpretation of these regulations as it applies for the interpretation of an Act of Parliament.

Exemptions

3. The provisions of these regulations shall not apply to any food or artificial sweetener intended at the time of sale, consignment, delivery or importation, as the case may be, for exportation to any place outside the United Kingdom.

(a) S.I. 1953/536 (1953 I, p. 665).
(b) The relevant amending instruments are S.I. 1953/1889, 1959/571 (1953 I, p. 685; 1959 I, p. 1328).   (c) 1889 c. 63.

PART II

REQUIREMENTS RELATING TO ARTIFICIAL SWEETENERS

Sale, etc. of artificial sweeteners

4. No person shall sell, consign, deliver or import into Scotland any artificial sweetener for human consumption which is not a permitted artificial sweetener.

Requirements as to composition for tablets containing artificial sweeteners

5.—(1) Every artificial sweetening tablet containing saccharin or saccharin calcium or saccharin sodium or a mixture of two or all of those substances shall conform to the requirements as to composition set forth in relation thereto in the appropriate paragraph of schedule 2 to these regulations.

(2) No person shall sell, consign, deliver or import into Scotland any artificial sweetening tablet which does not comply with this regulation.

Labelling of containers of artificial sweetening tablets

6.—(1) No person shall sell, consign, deliver or import into Scotland any artificial sweetening tablets in a container unless such container bears a label on which there appears such one of the following descriptions as may be appropriate—

(*a*) the words "saccharin tablets" or "half strength saccharin tablets" for full strength or half strength tablets respectively, containing no permitted artificial sweetener other than saccharin or a mixture of saccharin and saccharin calcium and saccharin sodium or of any two of those substances;

(*b*) the words "saccharin calcium tablets" or "half strength saccharin calcium tablets" for full strength or half strength tablets respectively, containing no permitted artificial sweetener other than saccharin calcium;

(*c*) the words "saccharin sodium tablets" or "soluble saccharin tablets" for full strength tablets, or the words "half strength saccharin sodium tablets" or "half strength soluble saccharin tablets" for half strength tablets, containing in each case no permitted artificial sweetener other than saccharin sodium;

Provided that any word of similar meaning may be substituted for the word "tablets" in any of the foregoing descriptions.

(2) Every letter in every word appearing on a label on a container which is required so to appear by virtue of this regulation shall appear conspicuously and legibly in a dark colour upon a light-coloured ground or in a light colour upon a dark-coloured ground and shall be of uniform colour and size.

Sales by description

7. No person shall sell any food under such a description as to lead an intending purchaser to believe that he is purchasing a permitted artificial sweetener or artificial sweetening tablet if the food does not conform to the appropriate description, specifications and requirements prescribed by these regulations.

8. Where a person sells any article or substance to a purchaser in response to a request for an artificial sweetener to which these regulations apply, he shall be deemed to sell such article or substance as such an artificial sweetener and under such a description as is specified in relation to such an artificial sweetener in these regulations unless he clearly notifies the purchaser at the time of sale that the article or substance is not such an artificial sweetener.

PART III

REQUIREMENTS RELATING TO FOOD CONTAINING ARTIFICIAL SWEETENERS

Sale, etc. of food containing artificial sweeteners

9.—(1) No food shall contain any artificial sweetener other than a permitted artificial sweetener.

(2) No person shall sell, consign, deliver or import into Scotland any food which does not comply with this regulation.

PART IV

ADMINISTRATION AND GENERAL

Condemnation of food

10. Where any artificial sweetener or any other food is certified by a public analyst as being food which it is an offence against regulation 4 or 9 of these regulations to sell, consign, deliver or import into Scotland it may be treated for the purposes of section 9 of the Act (under which food may be seized and destroyed on the order of a justice of the peace) as being unfit for human consumption.

Enforcement

11.—(1) The local authority of any area shall, subject to the provisions of the next following paragraph, enforce and execute the provisions of these regulations within their area.

(2) Where any part of the area of a local authority lies within the area of a port local authority such of the functions of the local authority under these regulations in relation to any food imported into that part shall, in so far as these functions fall to be exercised by the port local authority by virtue of any order made under section 172 of the Public Health (Scotland) Act 1897(a), be exercised by that port local authority.

(3) In this regulation "local authority" means the council of a county or of a large burgh within the meaning of the Local Government (Scotland) Act 1947(b); and any small burgh within the meaning of that Act shall, for the purposes of these regulations, be included in the county in which it is situated; and "port local authority" includes a joint port local authority.

Penalties

12.—(1) If any person contravenes or fails to comply with any of the foregoing provisions of these regulations he shall be guilty of an offence under these regulations.

(a) 1897 c. 38.   (b) 1947 c. 43.

(2) Any person who is guilty of an offence under these regulations shall be liable—

(a) on summary conviction to—

(i) a fine not exceeding £100 or to imprisonment for a term not exceeding 6 months or to both such fine and imprisonment; and

(ii) in the case of a continuing offence, to a further fine not exceeding £10 for every day during which the offence is continued; or

(b) on conviction on indictment to—

(i) a fine not exceeding £500 or to imprisonment for a term not exceeding one year or to both such fine and imprisonment; and

(ii) in the case of a continuing offence, to a further fine not exceeding £50 for every day during which the offence is continued.

Application of various sections of the Act

13.—(1) Sections 41(2) and (5) (which relates to proceedings), 42(1), (2) and (3) (which relates to evidence of certificates of analysis), 44 (which relates to the power of a court to require analysis by the Government Chemist), 46(2) (which relates to the conditions under which a warranty may be pleaded as a defence) and 47 (which relates to offences in relation to warranties and certificates of analysis) of the Act shall apply for the purposes of these regulations as if references therein to proceedings, or a prosecution, under or taken under the Act included references to proceedings, or a prosecution as the case may be, taken for an offence against these regulations and in addition as if—

(a) in the case of section 44(1) of the Act, the reference therein to section 41(5) of the Act included a reference to said section 41(5) as applied by these regulations; and

(b) in the case of section 47(1) and (2) of the Act, the references therein to an offence against the Act included references to an offence against these regulations.

(2) Section 41(4) of the Act shall apply for the purposes of these regulations as if the reference therein to section 47 of the Act included a reference to said section 47 as applied by these regulations.

Revocation

14.—(1) The Artificial Sweeteners in Food (Scotland) Regulations 1967**(a)** are hereby revoked.

(2) Section 38 of the Interpretation Act 1889 shall apply as if these regulations were an Act of Parliament and as if the regulations revoked by these regulations were an Act of Parliament repealed by an Act of Parliament.

William Ross,
One of Her Majesty's
Principal Secretaries of State.

St. Andrew's House,
Edinburgh.

18th December 1969.

(a) S.I. 1967/1203 (1967 II, p. 3526).

SCHEDULE 1

Regulation 2(1)

Saccharin calcium

Saccharin calcium is the calcium derivative of 2-sulphobenzoic imide with $3\frac{1}{2}$ molecules of water of crystallisation. It contains not less than 98 per cent. of $C_{14}H_8Ca\ N_2O_6S_2$ calculated with reference to the substance dried to constant weight at 105°C.

Description	White crystals or white crystalline powder, odour faintly aromatic, taste intensely sweet.
Solubility	1g. dissolves in 1·5g. water.
Loss on drying	When dried to constant weight at 105°C. loses not less than 11 per cent. and not more than 15 per cent. of its weight.
Ammonium Compounds	Complies with the test given under Saccharin in the British Pharmacopoeia 1968.
4-Sulphamoylbenzoates ...	Complies with the test given under Saccharin Sodium in the British Pharmacopoeia 1968.

SCHEDULE 2

Regulations 2(1) *and* 5

Requirements as to composition for tablets containing permitted artificial sweeteners

1. *Full strength tablets*

An artificial sweetening tablet containing saccharin or saccharin calcium or saccharin sodium or a mixture of two or all of those substances shall, when dried to constant weight at 105°C., have a total quantity of saccharin free and combined calculated as $C_7H_5NO_3S$, which shall be not less than 11 milligrams and not more than 14 milligrams.

2. *Half strength tablets*

An artificial sweetening tablet containing saccharin or saccharin calcium or saccharin sodium or a mixture of two or all of those substances shall, if sold in a container bearing a label upon which there appears the description "half strength", have when dried to constant weight at 105°C. a total quantity of saccharin free and combined calculated as $C_7H_5NO_3S$, which shall be not less than 5·5 milligrams and not more than 7 milligrams.

EXPLANATORY NOTE

(This Note is not part of the Regulations.)

These regulations, which apply to Scotland only, supersede the Artificial Sweeteners in Food (Scotland) Regulations 1967 and come into operation on 1 January 1970. The principal change is that cyclamic acid, calcium cyclamate and sodium cyclamate are no longer permitted artificial sweeteners or permitted ingredients in artificial sweetening tablets.

STATUTORY INSTRUMENTS

1969 No. 1849

POLICE

The Police Pensions (Amendment) (No. 3) Regulations 1969

Laid before Parliament in draft

Made - - - *19th December* 1969

Coming into Operation *1st January* 1970

In exercise of the powers conferred on me by sections 1 and 3 of the Police Pensions Act 1948(a) (read with Article 2(1) of the Minister for the Civil Service Order 1968(b)), as extended and amended by section 43 of the Reserve and Auxiliary Forces (Protection of Civil Interests) Act 1951(c), section 5(3) of the Overseas Service Act 1958(d) and Schedule 2 thereto, section 1(1) of the Police Pensions Act 1961(e), sections 40, 43(4), 45(4) and 63 of the Police Act 1964(f) and Schedules 6 and 9 thereto, and sections 35 and 38(4) of the Police (Scotland) Act 1967(g), and after consultation with the Police Council for Great Britain, I hereby, with the consent of the Minister for the Civil Service, make the following Regulations, a draft of which has been laid before Parliament and has been approved by resolution of each House of Parliament :—

1. These Regulations may be cited as the Police Pensions (Amendment) (No. 3) Regulations 1969 and shall come into operation on 1st January 1970.

2. For Regulation 14(1) of the Police Pensions Regulations 1966(h), as amended (i), (which relates to a widow's augmented award where her husband's death results from an attack or an injury received in effecting an arrest or preventing an escape or rescue) there shall be substituted the following provision :—

"**14.**—(1) This Regulation shall apply to a widow of a member of a police force whose death is the result of an injury received without his own default in the execution of his duty where—

(a) he was attacked by a person or persons in a manner which, in the opinion of the police authority, was intrinsically likely to cause death and death ensued. on or after 5th July 1948, as a result of the attack, or

(a) 1948 c. 24.   (b) S.I. 1968/1656 (1968 III, p. 4485).
(c) 1951 c. 65.   (d) 1958 c. 14.
(e) 1961 c. 35.   (f) 1964 c. 48.
(g) 1967 c. 77.   (h) S.I. 1966/1582 (1966 III, p. 4894).
(i) The relevant amending instrument is S.I. 1968/530 (1968 I, p. 1269).

(*b*) the injury was received in the course of duties performed, in the opinion of the police authority, for the immediate purpose of effecting an arrest or of preventing an escape or rescue from legal custody and death ensued on or after 1st August 1964, or

(*c*) the injury was received in the course of duties performed, in the opinion of the police authority—

  (i) for the immediate purpose of saving the life of another person or of preventing loss of human life, and

  (ii) in circumstances in which there was an intrinsic likelihood of his receiving a fatal injury,

and death ensued on or after 1st January 1970.".

James Callaghan,
One of Her Majesty's Principal
Secretaries of State.

19th December 1969.

Consent of the Minister for the Civil Service given under his Official Seal on 19th December 1969.

(L.S.)

K. H. McNeill,
Authorised by the
Minister for the Civil Service.

EXPLANATORY NOTE

(This Note is not part of the Regulations.)

These Regulations amend Regulation 14 of the Police Pensions Regulations 1966, under which a widow qualifies for an augmented award where her husband's death results from an attack or an injury received in specified circumstances, to cover the case in which the husband's death results from an injury received while saving, or preventing loss of, human life.

STATUTORY INSTRUMENTS

1969 No. 1850

POLICE

The Special Constables (Pensions) (Amendment) (No. 3) Regulations 1969

Made - - -	*19th December* 1969
Laid before Parliament	*31st December* 1969
Coming into Operation	*1st January* 1970

In exercise of the powers conferred on me by section 34 of the Police Act 1964(**a**) (read with section 1(2) of the Police Pensions Act 1961(**b**)), I hereby make the following Regulations :—

1. These Regulations may be cited as the Special Constables (Pensions) (Amendment) (No. 3) Regulations 1969 and shall come into operation on 1st January 1970.

2. In these Regulations any reference to the Instrument of 1966 is a reference to the Special Constables (Pensions) Regulations 1966(**c**), as amended (**d**).

3. For Regulation 3(1) of the Instrument of 1966 (which relates to a widow's augmented award where her husband's death results from an attack or an injury received in effecting an arrest or preventing an escape or rescue) there shall be substituted the following provision :—

"(1) This Regulation shall apply to a widow of a special constable whose death is the result of an injury received without his own default in the execution of his duty where—

(*a*) he was attacked by a person or persons in a manner which, in the opinion of the police authority, was intrinsically likely to cause death and death ensued on or after 11th April 1949, as a result of the attack, or

(*b*) the injury was received in the course of duties performed, in the opinion of the police authority, for the immediate purpose of effecting an arrest or of preventing an escape or rescue from legal custody and death ensued, on or after 1st August 1964, or

(*c*) the injury was received in the course of duties performed, in the opinion of the police authority—

(i) for the immediate purpose of saving the life of another person or of preventing loss of human life, and

(ii) in circumstances in which there was an intrinsic likelihood of his receiving a fatal injury,

and death ensued on or after 1st January 1970.".

(**a**) 1964 c. 48.   (**b**) 1961 c. 35.
(**c**) S.I. 1966/1590 (1966 III, p. 5008).
(**d**) The relevant amending instrument is S.I. 1969/1514 (1969 III, p. 4920).

4.—(1) In the application of the Police Pensions Regulations 1966(**a**) to the calculation of an award in respect of a special constable under the Instrument of 1966, those Regulations shall apply as amended by the Police Pensions (Amendment) (No. 3) Regulations 1969(**b**) (which amendments relate to awards payable on death resulting from an injury received in the performance of life-saving duties).

(2) In accordance with paragraph (1) of this Regulation, for Regulation 15(1) of the Instrument of 1966 (which, as set out in the Special Constables (Pensions) (Amendment) (No. 2) Regulations 1969(**c**), defines the expression "the principal Regulations") there shall be substituted the following provision :—

'(1) In these Regulations the expression "the principal Regulations" means the Police Pensions Regulations 1966, as amended by the Police Pensions (Amendment) (No. 2) Regulations 1967(**d**), the Police Pensions (Amendment) Regulations 1968(**e**), the Police Pensions (Amendment) Regulations 1969(**f**), the Police Pensions (Amendment) (No. 2) Regulations 1969(**g**) and the Police Pensions (Amendment) (No. 3) Regulations 1969.'.

James Callaghan,
One of Her Majesty's Principal
Secretaries of State.

Home Office,
Whitehall.

19th December 1969.

EXPLANATORY NOTE

(This Note is not part of the Regulations.)

These Regulations amend the Special Constables (Pensions) Regulations 1966 which give to special constables and their dependants certain pension benefits for which members of police forces and their dependants are eligible.

The Police Pensions (Amendment) (No. 3) Regulations 1969 provide that a widow of a member of a police force shall qualify for an augmented award where her husband's death results from an injury received while saving, or preventing loss of, human life.

These Regulations make similar provision as respects the widow of a special constable.

(a) S.I. 1966/1582 (1966 III, p. 4894).   (b) S.I. 1969/1849 (1969 III, p. 5788).
(c) S.I. 1969/1514 (1969 III, p. 4920).   (d) S.I. 1967/1500 (1967 III, p. 4204).
(e) S.I. 1968/530 (1968 I, p. 1269).   (f) S.I. 1969/723 (1969 II, p. 1952).
(g) S.I. 1969/1484 (1969 III, p. 4748).

STATUTORY INSTRUMENTS

1969 No. 1851 (S. 165)

CLEAN AIR

The Smoke Control Areas (Authorised Fuels) (Scotland) Regulations 1969.

Made - - - -	*19th December* 1969
Laid before Parliament	*30th December* 1969
Coming into Operation	*31st December* 1969

In exercise of the powers conferred on me by section 34(1) of the Clean Air Act 1956(a), and of all other powers enabling me in that behalf, I hereby make the following regulations :—

Citation and commencement

1. These regulations may be cited as the Smoke Control Areas (Authorised Fuels) (Scotland) Regulations 1969 and shall come into operation on 31st December 1969.

Interpretation

2. The Interpretation Act 1889(b) shall apply for the interpretation of these regulations as it applies for the interpretation of an Act of Parliament.

Authorised fuels for the purposes of the Clean Air Act 1956

3. In Scotland the following fuel is hereby declared to be an authorised fuel for the purposes of the Clean Air Act 1956 :—

"Rexco Briquettes" manufactured by Scottish Rexco Limited having Rexco breeze as a main constituent which has been subjected to a heating process.

William Ross,
One of Her Majesty's Principal
Secretaries of State.

St. Andrew's House,
Edinburgh.

19th December 1969.

EXPLANATORY NOTE

(*This Note is not part of the Regulations.*)

Section 11 of the Clean Air Act 1956 makes it an offence to emit smoke from a chimney of a building within a smoke control area unless it can be shown that the emission of smoke was not caused by the use of any fuel other than an authorised fuel. These regulations declare the fuel mentioned in regulation 3 to be an authorised fuel for the purposes of the Act in Scotland.

(a) 1956 c. 52.	(b) 1889 c. 63.

STATUTORY INSTRUMENTS

1969 No. 1852

SAVINGS BANKS

The Savings Banks (Fees) (Amendment) Warrant 1969

Laid before Parliament in draft

Made - - -		*21st December* 1969
Coming into Operation		1*st January* 1970

The Treasury, in exercise of the powers conferred on them by section 9 of the Post Office Savings Bank Act 1954(a), section 88 of the Trustee Savings Banks Act 1969(b), and the said section 9 as applied by Regulation 27(4) of the Savings Certificates Regulations 1933(c) and Regulation 18(4) of the Premium Savings Bonds Regulations 1956(d), and of all other powers enabling them in that behalf, hereby direct as follows:—

1. This Warrant may be cited as the Savings Banks (Fees) (Amendment) Warrant 1969, and shall come into operation on 1st January 1970.

2. The Interpretation Act 1889(e) shall apply for the interpretation of this Warrant as it applies for the interpretation of an Act of Parliament.

3.—(1) The Treasury Warrant dated 9th April 1921(f), as amended (g), fixing certain fees of the Registrar of Friendly Societies in relation to savings banks and savings certificates shall have effect as if:—

  (*a*) in table II in article 1 thereof (as substituted by the Savings Bank (Fees) (Amendment) Warrant 1953(h)), in the item specifying the fees for an award, order or determination where the savings bank deposit does not exceed £10, for the figures "2s. 6d." there were substituted the figures "3s. 0d.";

  (*b*) in table III in article 1 thereof (as substituted by the said Warrant of 1953), in the item specifying the fees for an award where the value of the savings certificates does not exceed £10, for the figures "2s. 6d." there were substituted the figures "3s. 0d.".

(a) 1954 c. 62.
(b) 1969 c. 50.
(c) S.R. & 0.1933/1149 (Rev. XV, p. 309; 1933, p. 1406).
(d) S.I. 1956/1657 (1956 I, p. 1489).
(e) 1889 c. 63.
(f) S.R. & O. 1921/622 (Rev. XX, p. 606; 1921, p. 1149).
(g) The relevant amending instrument is S.I. 1953/365 (1953 II, p. 1926).
(h) S.I. 1953/365 (1953 II, p. 1926).

(2) The Premium Savings Bonds (Fees) Warrant 1959(a) shall have effect as if in article 1 thereof, in the item specifying the fees where the number of unit bonds does not exceed 10, for the figures "2s. 6d." there were substituted the figures "3s. 0d.".

Joseph Harper,
Walter Harrison,

Two of the Lords Commissioners
of Her Majesty's Treasury.

21st December 1969.

EXPLANATORY NOTE

(This Note is not part of the Warrant.)

This Warrant alters from 2s. 6d. to 3s. 0d. the fees in certain cases for awards made by the Registrar of Friendly Societies in respect of disputes relating to savings bank deposits, savings certificates and premium savings bonds. The fees in question were fixed in relation to savings bank deposits and savings certificates by the Savings Bank (Fees) (Amendment) Warrant 1953, and in relation to premium savings bonds by the Premium Savings Bonds (Fees) Warrant 1959.

(a) S.I. 1959/1123 (1959 I, p. 305).

STATUTORY INSTRUMENTS

1969 No. 1853

SAVINGS BANKS

The Savings Contracts (Registrar's Awards) (Fees) Warrant 1969

Laid before Parliament in draft

Made - - -	*21st December* 1969
Coming into Operation	*1st January* 1970

The Treasury, in exercise of the powers conferred on them by section 9 of the Post Office Savings Bank Act 1954(a), as applied by Regulation 18(4) of the Savings Contracts Regulations 1969(b), and of all other powers enabling them in that behalf, hereby direct as follows:—

1. This Warrant may be cited as the Savings Contracts (Registrar's Awards) (Fees) Warrant 1969, and shall come into operation on 1st January 1970.

2.—(1) In this Warrant, unless the context otherwise requires—

"the amount in question" means, in relation to the savings contract or contracts in question in a dispute referred to the Chief Registrar, the total amount (including any bonus or interest) which would have been repayable (if repayment had been demanded) in respect of the savings contract or contracts in question on the date of the award, or, in a case where the sum in question in the dispute is less than that total amount, that lesser sum;

"the Chief Registrar" means—

(a) in relation to England and Wales, the Chief Registrar of Friendly Societies,

(b) in relation to Scotland, the Assistant Registrar of Friendly Societies for Scotland, and

(c) in relation to Northern Ireland, the Chief Registrar of Friendly Societies or a deputy appointed by him;

"savings contract" has the meaning assigned to it by Regulation 2(1) of the Savings Contracts Regulations 1969.

(2) The Interpretation Act 1889(c) shall apply for the interpretation of this Warrant as it applies for the interpretation of an Act of Parliament.

(a) 1954 c. 62.   (b) S.I. 1969/1342 (1969 III, p. 3984).   (c) 1889 c. 63.

3. There shall be charged on any award made by the Chief Registrar under Regulation 18 of the Savings Contracts Regulations 1969 a fee calculated in accordance with the following scale:—

	s.	d.
Where the amount in question does not exceed £10	3	0
Where the amount in question exceeds £10 but does not exceed £20	5	0
Where the amount in question exceeds £20 but does not exceed £30	10	0
Where the amount in question exceeds £30 but does not exceed £50	15	0
Where the amount in question exceeds £50, for every £50 or part of £50	15	0

4. The Chief Registrar upon making any award may order that any fee payable under the provisions of this Warrant shall be deducted from the amount repayable (including any bonus or interest) in respect of the savings contract or contracts in question, or shall be paid by such person as he may direct, and any fee so directed to be paid by any such person shall be recoverable from him as a debt due to Her Majesty:

Provided that the Chief Registrar may remit such fee or any part thereof in any case where in his opinion it would be unjust that the fee or part thereof should be deducted or paid.

Joseph Harper,
Walter Harrison,

Two of the Lords Commissioners
of Her Majesty's Treasury.

21st December 1969.

EXPLANATORY NOTE
(*This Note is not part of the Warrant.*)

This Warrant prescribes the fees payable for awards made by the Registrar of Friendly Societies in respect of disputes relating to savings contracts administered under the Save As You Earn scheme operated by the Department for National Savings, the Trustee Savings Banks and the Birmingham Municipal Bank.

STATUTORY INSTRUMENTS

1969 No. 1858

TRANSPORT

PENSIONS AND COMPENSATION

The British Transport (Alteration of Pension Schemes) Order 1969

Made - - -	*19th December* 1969
Laid before Parliament	*30th December* 1969
Coming into Operation	*31st December* 1969

The Minister of Transport, in exercise of his powers under section 74 of the Transport Act 1962**(a)** and of all other enabling powers, hereby makes the following Order:—

Commencement, citation and interpretation

1.—(1) This Order shall come into operation on the 31st December 1969 and may be cited as the British Transport (Alteration of Pension Schemes) Order 1969.

(2) In this Order unless the context otherwise requires—

"the Act of 1939" means the London and North Eastern Railway (Superannuation Fund) Act 1939**(b)**;

"the Board" means the British Railways Board;

"the Fund" means the London and North Eastern Railway Superannuation Fund established by the Act of 1939;

"the Minister" means the Minister of Transport;

"term", in relation to the Fund, includes any rule or provision of the Fund, or of any statutory provision relating to the Fund, or of any instrument made for the purposes of the Fund.

(3) The Interpretation Act 1889**(c)** shall apply for the interpretation of this Order as it applies for the interpretation of an Act of Parliament.

Application of the Order

2. This Order shall apply to the London and North Eastern Railway Superannuation Fund which shall be construed and have effect as if the provisions of this Order were terms thereof, any other term thereof, whether express or implied, to the contrary notwithstanding.

(a) 1962 c. 46. (b) 1939 c. xxii. (c) 1889 c. 63.

Alterations in terms of Fund

3. The following alterations shall be made to the terms of the Fund namely:—

(*a*) In addition to the powers to invest moneys of the Fund contained in subsection (4) of section 5 of the Act of 1939, the Board may invest property forming part of the Fund in any manner specified in the Schedule to this Order.

(*b*) In exercising the powers to invest moneys of the Fund contained in the Act of 1939 as extended by paragraph (*a*) of this Article the Board shall ensure that at the time of such investment not less than one-quarter in value of the Fund shall be invested in any manner specified in Parts I and II of the First Schedule to the Trustee Investments Act 1961(a) as read with Part IV of that Schedule, or applied by the Board to the general purposes of their undertaking pursuant to paragraph (*a*) of subsection (4) of section 5 of the Act of 1939.

(*c*) The Board shall at intervals of not more than 6 months commencing with a period calculated from 1st January 1970 credit the Fund with interest at a rate of not less than four per centum per annum on all moneys applied by the Board to the general purposes of their undertaking pursuant to paragraph (*a*) of subsection (4) of section 5 of the Act of 1939, but such interest shall not be credited at a rate higher than four per centum per annum without the consent of the Minister.

(*d*) Any interest credited by the Board under paragraph (*c*) of this Article shall be taken into account in the calculation of any sum to be credited to the Fund by the Board under the provisions of subsection (5) of section 5 of the Act of 1939.

(*e*) The Board may charge the assets of the Fund as security for money borrowed for the purposes of the Fund.

(*f*) As to all immovable property held by the Fund (whether situate in England or any other part of the United Kingdom, the Isle of Man or the Channel Islands and whether purchased alone or jointly or in common with any other person or corporation), the Board shall have and may exercise or join in exercising except as provided in the next following paragraph all the powers of management, or superintending the management thereof, referred to in section 102 of the Settled Land Act 1925(b), and also generally all the powers conferred upon a tenant for life or the trustees of a settlement under the said Act, and, by way of extension of such powers, power to carry out with moneys forming part of the Fund any improvements of any kind to land or buildings (whether referred to in the said Act or not and including the erection, demolition and reconstruction of any buildings), and may grant or join in granting leases of any kind for any term not exceeding 999 years and on such terms and conditions as may be thought desirable, and may grant or join in granting options.

(*g*) Nothing in the last preceding paragraph of this Article shall be construed or have effect so as to enable the Board to borrow money otherwise than in accordance with section 19 of the Transport Act 1962.

Sealed with the Official Seal of the Minister of Transport the 19th December 1969.

(L.S.)

Fred Mulley,
Minister of Transport.

(a) 1961 c. 62.   (b) 1925 c. 18.

SCHEDULE

1. In the purchase, whether alone or jointly or in common with any other person or corporation, of immovable property of any tenure or kind in the United Kingdom, the Isle of Man or the Channel Islands or of any share or interest in such immovable property, including any interest in such immovable property comprised in a building agreement providing for the grant of a lease of such property contingently on the erection and completion of the building specified in such agreement.

2. In the advance of money upon the security of
   (*a*) immovable property of any tenure or kind in the United Kingdom, the Isle of Man or the Channel Islands or
   (*b*) any interest in such immovable property comprised in a building agreement, as specified in paragraph 1 hereof

and in any such case whether the security be taken by a separate and distinct mortgage or security made exclusively to or in trust for the Fund or by a mortgage or security made to or in trust for the Board jointly with any other person or corporation who may contribute to the total amount advanced on such mortgage or security and although the Fund may not obtain the whole or any portion of the estate or interest in such immovable property therein comprised.

3. In the purchase of or the advance of money upon the security of debentures, debenture stock, bonds or other obligations, of any company, public or private, incorporated with limited liability in the United Kingdom.

4. In the purchase of shares of any company incorporated in the United Kingdom which has the acquisition and development of immovable property as a main object.

5. In the purchase of or the advance of money upon the security of preference, preferred or ordinary stock or shares of any Public Company incorporated with limited liability in the United Kingdom, the shares of which are quoted on a stock exchange in the United Kingdom or permission has been granted to deal in them.

6. In the placing of money on loan or on deposit or on current account with any bank or banking house in Great Britain or on deposit with any building society as defined in section 1(4) of the Building Societies Act 1962(a).

7. In the purchase of, or the advance of money upon the security of, investments outside the United Kingdom being
   (*a*) investments of the kind specified, in relation to the United Kingdom, in paragraph 5 of this Schedule, or
   (*b*) units, or other shares in the investments subject to the trusts, of a unit or similar trust scheme:

Provided that such investments are dealt in under the rules of the London Stock Exchange.

8. In any units, or other shares of the investments subject to the trusts of a unit trust scheme, in the case of which there is in force at the time of investment an Order of the Board of Trade under section 17 of the Prevention of Fraud (Investments) Act 1958(b).

9. In any units of a unit trust which has the acquisition and development of immovable property as a main object.

EXPLANATORY NOTE

(*This Note is not part of the Order.*)

The Order provides for the widening of the powers of investment in respect of the London and North Eastern Railway Superannuation Fund and for the British Railways Board to pay interest on moneys forming part of the Fund held by the Board.

(a)   1962 c. 37.   (b)   1958 c. 45.

STATUTORY INSTRUMENTS

1969 No. 1859

CIVIL AVIATION

The Rules of the Air and Air Traffic Control (Second Amendment) Regulations 1969

Made - - - -			*19th December* 1969
Coming into Operation			*31st December* 1969

The Board of Trade, in exercise of their powers under Article 59(1) of the Air Navigation Order 1966(a), as amended(b), and of all other powers enabling them in that behalf, hereby make the following Regulations.

1. These Regulations may be cited as the Rules of the Air and Air Traffic Control (Second Amendment) Regulations 1969 and shall come into operation on 31st December 1969.

2. The Interpretation Act 1889(c) applies for the purpose of the interpretation of these Regulations as it applies for the purpose of the interpretation of an Act of Parliament.

3. The Schedule to the Rules of the Air and Air Traffic Control Regulations 1969(d), as amended(e), shall be further amended as follows:—

(1) In Rule 5 for paragraph (3) there shall be substituted the following paragraphs:

"(3) Nothing in this Rule shall prohibit an aircraft from flying in such a manner as is necessary for the purpose of saving life.

(3A) Nothing in this Rule shall prohibit any aircraft from flying in accordance with normal aviation practice, for the purpose of taking off from, landing at or practising approaches to landing at, or checking navigational aids or procedures at, a Government or licensed aerodrome in the United Kingdom or at any aerodrome in any other country:

Provided that the practising of approaches to landing shall be confined to the airspace customarily used by aircraft when landing or taking off in accordance with normal aviation practice at the aerodrome concerned.";

(2) In Rule 28(1) for "enters" there shall be substituted "otherwise flies within";

(3) In Rule 45:

(*a*) after the heading "*Marshalling Signals*" there shall be added "(*from a marshaller to an aircraft*)";

(a) S.I. 1966/1184 (1966 III, p. 3073).
(b) There is no relevant amending instrument.
(c) 1889 c. 63.   (d) S.I. 1969/216 (1969 I, p. 557).
(e) S.I. 1969/974 (1969 II, p. 2861).

(b) in the first sentence for "paragraphs (a) to (u)" there shall be substituted "paragraphs (a) to (x)";

(c) at the end of Table B there shall be added the provisions set out in the Schedule hereto.

(4) After Rule 45 there shall be added the following Rule 45A:

"*Marshalling Signals* (*from a pilot of an aircraft to a marshaller*)

45A. The following signals made by a pilot in an aircraft to a marshaller on the ground shall respectively have the following meanings:—

Description of Signal	Meaning of Signal
(a) Raise arm and hand with fingers extended horizontally in front of face, then clench fist.	Brakes engaged.
(b) Raise arm with fist clenched horizontally in front of face, then extend fingers.	Brakes released.
(c) Arms extended palms facing outwards, move hands inwards to cross in front of face.	Insert chocks.
(d) Hands crossed in front of face, palms facing outwards, move arms outwards.	Remove chocks.
(e) Raise the number of fingers on one hand indicating the number of the engine to be started. For this purpose the aircraft engines shall be numbered in relation to the marshaller facing the aircraft, from his right to his left, for example, No. 1 engine shall be the port outer engine, No. 2 engine shall be the port inner engine, No. 3 engine shall be the starboard inner engine, and No. 4 engine shall be the starboard outer engine."	Ready to start engines.

Robert Burns,
A Second Secretary
of the Board of Trade.

19th December 1969.

(b) in the first sentence for "paragraphs is (a) to (w)" there shall be substituted "paragraphs (a) to (x)";

(c) at the end of Table d there shall be added the provisions set out in the Schedule hereto.

(4) After Rule 453 there shall be added the following Rule 454.

"Marshalling Signals (from a pilot of an aircraft to a marshaller)

454. The following signals made by a pilot in aircraft to a marshaller on the ground shall respectively have the following meanings:—"

THE SCHEDULE

Description of Signal	Meaning of Signal	In Daylight
(v) Raise arm and hand, with fingers extended, horizontally in front of body, then clench fist.	Engage brakes	
Raise arm, with fist clenched, horizontally in front of body, then extend fingers.	Release brakes	

Description of Signal	Meaning of Signal	In Daylight
(w) Left hand overhead with the number of fingers extended, to indicate the number of the engine to be started, and circular motion of right hand at head level.	Start engine(s)	

Description of Signal	Meaning of Signal	In Daylight	By Night
(x) Point left arm down, move right arm down from overhead, vertical position to horizontal forward position, repeating right arm movement	Back aircraft's tail to starboard		
Point right arm down, move left arm down from overhead, vertical position to horizontal forward position, repeating left arm movement.	Back aircraft's tail to port		

EXPLANATORY NOTE

(This Note is not part of the Regulations.)

These Regulations amend the Schedule to the Rules of the Air and Air Traffic Control Regulations 1969 as previously amended. In addition to some drafting amendments the following change is made:—

Three additional marshalling signals from a marshaller to an aircraft are prescribed (Rule 45) and three marshalling signals from a pilot to a marshaller are prescribed (Rule 45A).

STATUTORY INSTRUMENTS

1969 No. 1860 (C.58)

DEFENCE

The Ulster Defence Regiment Act 1969 (Commencement) Order 1969

Made - - -	*23rd December* 1969
Laid before Parliament	*31st December* 1969
Coming into Operation	*1st January* 1970

The Secretary of State, in exercise of the powers conferred on him by section 6(2) of the Ulster Defence Regiment Act 1969(a) and all other powers enabling him, hereby makes the following Order :—

1. The Ulster Defence Regiment Act 1969 shall come into operation on 1st January 1970.

2. This Order may be cited as the Ulster Defence Regiment Act 1969 (Commencement) Order 1969 and shall come into operation on 1st January 1970.

Dated 23rd December 1969.

Denis Healey,
One of Her Majesty's Principal
Secretaries of State.

EXPLANATORY NOTE

(*This Note is not part of the Order.*)

This Order brings the Ulster Defence Regiment Act 1969 into force on 1st January 1970.

(a) 1969 c. 65.

STATUTORY INSTRUMENTS

1969 No. 1861

INJURIES IN WAR COMPENSATION

The Injuries in War (Shore Employments) Compensation (Second Amendment) Scheme 1969

Made - - - - *22nd December* 1969

The Defence Council, in exercise of the powers conferred on them by section 1 of the Injuries in War Compensation Act, 1914 (Session 2)(a) (as amended by the Defence (Transfer of Functions) (No. 1) Order 1964(b)) and section 1(1) and (3) of the Defence (Transfer of Functions) Act 1964(c) and of all other powers enabling them in that behalf, hereby make the following Scheme:—

1. The Injuries in War (Shore Employments) Compensation Scheme 1914 as amended(d) shall be further amended as follows:—

In paragraph (3) thereof for the figures " 152s. 0d.", wherever they occur, there shall be substituted the figures " 168s. 0d.".

2. This Scheme shall have effect as from 5th November 1969 so, however, that no payment shall be made thereunder in respect of any period before that date.

3. This Scheme may be cited as the Injuries in War (Shore Employments) Compensation (Second Amendment) Scheme 1969 and the Injuries in War (Shore Employments) Compensation Schemes 1914 to 1969 and this Scheme may be cited together as the Injuries in War (Shore Employments) Compensation Schemes 1914 to 1969.

Roy Hattersley.
G. H. Baker.

Dated 18th December 1969.

Consent of the Minister for the Civil Service given under his Official Seal.

K. H. McNeill,
Authorised by the Minister
for the Civil Service.

Dated 22nd December 1969.

(a) 5 & 6 Geo. 5. c. 18.   (b) S.I. 1964/488 (1964 I, p. 769).   (c) 1964 c. 15.
(d) The relevant amending instrument is S.I. 1969/1053 (1969 II, p. 3101).

EXPLANATORY NOTE

(This Note is not part of the Scheme.)

The Injuries in War (Shore Employments) Compensation Schemes 1914 to 1969 provide for the payment of weekly allowances to small numbers of ex-members of the Women's Auxiliary Forces who suffered disablement from their service overseas during the 1914-18 war. The amending scheme provides that the maximum weekly allowance payable shall be increased from 152s. 0d. to 168s. 0d. and that other allowances shall be increased proportionately. The increases will take effect as from 5th November 1969 in accordance with section 1(5) of the Injuries in War Compensation Act, 1914 (Session 2) (5 & 6 Geo. 5 c. 18).

1969 No. 1864

DEFENCE

The Armed Forces (Discharge by Purchase) (Amendment) Regulations 1969

Made - - -	*23rd December* 1969
Laid before Parliament	*31st December* 1969
Coming into Operation	*1st January* 1970

The Defence Council, in exercise of the powers conferred upon them by section 2 of the Armed Forces Act 1966(a) and of all other powers enabling them in that behalf, hereby make the following Regulations:—

1.—(1) These Regulations may be cited as the Armed Forces (Discharge by Purchase) (Amendment) Regulations 1969 and shall come into operation on 1st January 1970.

(2) The Interpretation Act 1889(b) shall apply to the interpretation of these Regulations as it applies to the interpretation of an Act of Parliament.

2. Regulations 3(1) and 4(1) of the Armed Forces (Discharge by Purchase) Regulations 1968(c) (which confer rights on certain persons who join the armed forces to claim their discharge) shall, in relation to persons who enter the Royal Navy or who enlist in the Royal Marines, the regular army or the regular air force on or after 1st January 1970, have effect as if, for the references (wherever they occur) to the age of 17 years and 6 months, 17 years and 3 months and 17 years and 9 months, there were respectively substituted references to the age of 18 years, 17 years and 9 months and 18 years and 3 months.

On behalf of the Defence Council.

Roy Hattersley,

Charles Harington,

23rd December 1969.

Members of the Defence Council.

(a) 1966 c. 45.   (b) 1889 c. 63.   (c) S.I. 1968/1801 (1968 III, p. 4816).

EXPLANATORY NOTE
(*This Note is not part of the Regulations.*)

These Regulations amend the Armed Forces (Discharge by Purchase) Regulations 1968 (which confer rights on certain persons who join the armed forces to claim their discharge) in the case of persons who join on or after 1st January 1970, by extending by 6 months the age limits applicable for making such a claim.

STATUTORY INSTRUMENTS

1969 No. 1865

FOREIGN COMPENSATION

The Foreign Compensation Commission (Union of Soviet Socialist Republics) (Amendment) Rules Approval Instrument 1969

Made - - -	*22nd December* 1969
Laid before Parliament	*2nd January* 1970
Coming into Operation	*14th January* 1970

Whereas the Foreign Compensation Commission have, in exercise of their powers under section 4 of the Foreign Compensation Act 1950(**a**), made rules of procedure and submitted them to the Lord Chancellor for his approval :

Now, therefore, the Lord Chancellor, in exercise of the powers conferred on him by sections 4 and 8 of the said Act hereby approves the said rules in the form set out in the Schedule hereto.

This instrument may be cited as the Foreign Compensation Commission (Union of Soviet Socialist Republics) (Amendment) Rules Approval Instrument 1969 and shall come into operation on 14th January 1970.

Dated 22nd December 1969.

Gardiner, C.

SCHEDULE

The Foreign Compensation Commission in exercise of their powers under section 4 of the Foreign Compensation Act 1950, hereby make the following Rules : —

1.—(1) These Rules may be cited as the Foreign Compensation Commission (Union of Soviet Socialist Republics) (Amendment) Rules 1969.

(2) The Interpretation Act 1889(**b**) shall apply to the interpretation of these Rules as it applies to the interpretation of an Act of Parliament.

2. The Foreign Compensation Commission (Union of Soviet Socialist Republics) Rules 1969(**c**) shall be amended by the deletion of the proviso to Rule 33 and the substitution of the following proviso : —

"Provided that the time for completing and delivering to the Commission any relevant application form or appendix referred to in either of the provisos (*b*) and (*c*) to paragraph (1) of Rule 7 shall not be extended so as to expire more than two months after 31st December 1969 except by leave of not less than two Commissioners which shall not be granted unless they are satisfied that it was not reasonably practicable for the form or appendix to be delivered to the Commission within such time."

(**a**) 1950 c. 12.　　(**b**) 1889 c. 63.　　(**c**) S.I. 1969/842 (1969 II, p. 2359).

The Seal of the Foreign Compensation Commission was hereunto affixed this 18th day of December 1969.

(L.S.)

C. Montgomery White,
Chairman of the Commission.

H. Walsh,
Secretary.

EXPLANATORY NOTE

(This Note is not part of the Rules.)

These Rules amend the proviso to rule 33 of the Foreign Compensation Commission (Union of Soviet Socialist Republics) Rules 1969 to enable two Commissioners to extend the time for delivering full particulars of claims for compensation so that it will expire more than two months after 31st December 1969 if they are satisfied that it was not reasonably practicable for the particulars to be delivered earlier.

STATUTORY INSTRUMENTS

1969 No. 1869 (L.32)

LONDON CITY

The Mayor's and City of London Court Funds (Amendment No. 2) Rules 1969

Made	- - -	*22nd December* 1969
Laid before Parliament		*5th January* 1970
Coming into Operation		*15th January* 1970

The Lord Chancellor, in pursuance of the powers contained in section 169 of the County Courts Act 1959(**a**), as modified by section 11 of the Administration of Justice Act 1965(**b**), hereby makes the following Rules :—

1. These Rules may be cited as the Mayor's and City of London Court Funds (Amendment No. 2) Rules 1969 and shall come into Operation on 15th January 1970.

2. The Mayor's and City of London Court Funds Rules 1965(**c**), as amended (**d**), shall have effect subject to the amendments set out in the Schedule to these Rules.

Dated 22nd December 1969.

Gardiner, C.

SCHEDULE

AMENDMENTS TO MAYOR'S AND CITY OF LONDON COURT FUNDS RULES 1965

1. In Part IV of the Arrangement of Rules, after the words "By post" and "By cheque", where they respectively occur, there shall be added the words "or through the National Giro".

2. For rule 3 (which relates to the payment of suitors' money into court), there shall be substituted the following rule :—

"3. Suitors' money to be paid into court may be so paid either—

(*a*) through the National Giro, or

(*b*) by post or otherwise into the office of the registrar, in which case payment may be made during office hours on any day on which the office is open and the registrar shall give a receipt therefor".

3. For rule 4 (which relates to suitors' money paid into court), there shall be substituted the following rule :—

"4. Money received pursuant to the last preceding rule which is not required for making authorised payments shall be paid by the registrar into the bank to the credit of his official account (or into the court's Giro account, as the registrar may determine) on the day of receipt or, if that is not practicable, on the next working day".

(**a**) 1959 c. 22.
(**c**) S.I. 1965/1707 (1965 III, p. 4821).

(**b**) 1965 c. 2.
(**d**) There are no relevant amendments.

4. In rule 6 (which relates to the transmission of money from the court to a county court), after the word "transmitted", where it appears for the second time, there shall be inserted the words:—

"through the National Giro or".

5. The following amendments shall be made to rule 8 (which relates to the payment of suitors' money out of court):—

(a) in paragraph (3)(b), after the words "crossed cheque", there shall be inserted the words "or through the National Giro".

6. The following amendments shall be made to rule 10 (which relates to the transmission of suitors' money by post):—

(a) at the end of paragraph (1), there shall be inserted the words "or through the National Giro";

(b) in paragraph (2)(b), after the words "crossed cheque", there shall be inserted the words "or through the National Giro";

(c) in paragraph (2)(c), after the words "sufficiently stamped", there shall be inserted the words "for the return of the proof of title and, where appropriate,";

(d) in paragraph (3), for the words "forward the money", there shall be substituted the words "pay the money through the National Giro or forward it".

7. At the end of rule 11 (which relates to payment of suitors' money out of court), there shall be inserted the words "or pay that sum through the National Giro".

8. In rule 12(1) (which relates to the payment of funds into court), after subparagraph (a), there shall be inserted the following subparagraph:—

"(aa) transmit the money through the National Giro, or".

9. In rule 23 (which relates to the payment of funds out of court) after the words "crossed cheque" in paragraph (3), there shall be inserted the words "or through the National Giro".

EXPLANATORY NOTE

(This Note is not part of the Rules.)

These Rules amend the Mayor's and City of London Court Funds Rules 1965 by providing for the payment of money into, or out of, the court through accounts opened with the National Giro.

The Rules come into operation on 15th January 1970.

1969 No. 1871

INDUSTRIAL TRAINING

The Industrial Training (Road Transport Board) Order 1969 (Amendment) Order 1969

Made - - - -	23rd December 1969
Laid before Parliament	5th January 1970
Coming into Operation	7th January 1970

The Secretary of State after consultation with the Road Transport Industry Training Board and with organisations and associations of organisations appearing to be representative respectively of substantial numbers of employers engaging in the activities hereinafter mentioned and of substantial numbers of persons employed in those activities and with the bodies established for the purpose of carrying on under national ownership industries in which the said activities are carried on to a substantial extent and in exercise of her powers under section 9 of the Industrial Training Act 1964(a) and of all other powers enabling her in that behalf hereby makes the following Order:—

Citation, commencement and interpretation

1.—(1) This Order may be cited as the Industrial Training (Road Transport Board) Order 1969 (Amendment) Order 1969 and shall come into operation on 7th January 1970.

(2) In this Order—

(*a*) "the Act" means the Industrial Training Act 1964;

(*b*) "the Board" means the Road Transport Industry Training Board;

(*c*) "Levy Order" includes the Industrial Training Levy (Road Transport) Order 1967(b), the Industrial Training Levy (Road Transport) Order 1968(c) and the Industrial Training Levy (Road Transport) Order 1969(d);

(*d*) "the 1969 Order" means the Industrial Training (Road Transport Board) Order 1969(e);

(*e*) "the principal Order" means the Industrial Training (Road Transport Board) Order 1966(f).

(3) The Interpretation Act 1889(g) shall apply to the interpretation of this Order as it applies to the interpretation of an Act of Parliament and as if this Order, the principal Order and the 1969 Order were Acts of Parliament.

Amendment of the 1969 Order

2. The 1969 Order (which substituted the Schedule to that Order for Schedule 1 to the principal Order) shall be amended in accordance with the Schedule to this Order, and accordingly the activities in relation to which the Board exercises

(a) 1964 c. 16.
(c) S.I. 1968/1835 (1968 III, p. 4841).
(e) S.I. 1969/879 (1969 II, p. 2495).
(g) 1889 c. 63.
(b) S.I. 1967/1309 (1967 III, p. 3939).
(d) S.I. 1969/880 (1969 II, p. 2503).
(f) S.I. 1966/1112 (1966 III, p. 2712).

the functions conferred by the Act upon industrial training boards shall, in lieu of the activities specified in the Schedule to the 1969 Order, be the activities specified in that Schedule as amended by the Schedule to this Order.

Transitional provisions

3.—(1) The chairman and other members of the Board on the day upon which this Order comes into operation shall continue to be members of the Board and to hold and vacate their offices in accordance with the terms of the instruments appointing them to be members.

(2) The provisions of this Order shall not—

(a) extend the operation of a Levy Order;

(b) affect the operation of a Levy Order in relation to the assessment of an employer within the meaning of that Order in respect of an establishment that was engaged in the relevant levy period wholly or mainly in activities included in the Schedule to the 1969 Order as amended by the Schedule to this Order;

(c) affect the operation of any assessment notice served by the Board under the provisions of a Levy Order before the date upon which this Order comes into operation or any appeal or other proceedings arising out of any such notice.

Signed by order of the Secretary of State,
23rd December 1969.

Edmund Dell,
Minister of State,
Department of Employment and Productivity.

Article 2

SCHEDULE

AMENDMENTS TO THE 1969 ORDER

1. In this Schedule the expression "the Schedule" means the Schedule to the 1969 Order.

2.—(1) Paragraph 1 of the Schedule shall be amended as follows.

(2) Immediately after sub-paragraph (d) there shall be inserted as sub-paragraph (da) the following:—

"(da) the manufacture or fitting out of vehicle bodies;".

(3) At the end of sub-paragraph (e) there shall be added the words "or the repair of vehicle bodies;".

3.—(1) Paragraph 2 of the Schedule shall be amended as follows.

(2) In sub-paragraph (c) head (ii) shall be omitted and immediately after head (iii) there shall be inserted as heads (iv) and (v) the following:—

"(iv) in the manufacture or fitting out of vehicle bodies where the employer is engaged in the manufacture of motor vehicles or where the vehicle bodies are manufactured or fitted out to the order of an employer engaged in the manufacture of motor vehicles; or

(v) in the manufacture, fitting out or repair of caravans not being motor vehicles;".

(3) Sub-paragraph (*d*) (which relates to certain establishments engaged wholly or mainly in the repair of vehicle bodies) shall be omitted.

(4) In head (vii) of sub-paragraph (*e*) before the words "the United Kingdom Atomic Energy Authority" there shall be inserted the words "the Post Office or".

(5) In sub-paragraph (*f*) for the expression "the London Transport Board" there shall be substituted the expression "the London Transport Executive".

4.—(1) Paragraph 3 of the Schedule shall be amended as follows.

(2) Immediately after sub-paragraph (*i*) there shall be inserted as sub-paragraph (*ia*) the following:—

"(*ia*) 'manufacture' includes assembly and any process or operation incidental or appertaining to manufacture or assembly;".

(3) In head (iv) of sub-paragraph (*p*) (which sub-paragraph defines the expression "related activities") for the words "at office premises or laboratories" there shall be substituted the words "at booking offices, other office premises or laboratories".

(4) In sub-paragraph (*q*) (which defines the expression "repair") immediately after the word "reconditioning" there shall be inserted the words "painting, paint spraying,".

(5) In sub-paragraph (*v*) (which defines the expression "vehicle bodies") the words "invalid carriages and bodies for caravans" shall be omitted.

5.—(1) The Appendix to the Schedule shall be amended as follows.

(2) The following entries shall be substituted for the corresponding entries in the said Appendix—

Column 1	Column 2	Column 3
The iron and steel industry	The Industrial Training (Iron and Steel Board) Order 1964 as amended by the Industrial Training (Iron and Steel Board) Order 1969(a)	Schedule 1 Paragraph 1(*k*)
The engineering industry	The Industrial Training (Engineering Board) Order 1964 as amended by the Industrial Training (Engineering Board) Order 1968 and the Industrial Training (Engineering Board) Order 1968 (Amendment) Order 1969(b)	Schedule 1 Paragraph 1(*m*)
The furniture and timber industry	The Industrial Training (Furniture and Timber Industry Board) Order 1965 as amended by the Industrial Training (Furniture and Timber Industry Board) Order 1969(c)	Schedule 1 Paragraph 1(*x*)
The man-made fibres producing industry	The Industrial Training (Man-made Fibres Producing Industry Board) Order 1966 as amended by the Industrial Training (Man-made Fibres Producing Industry Board) Order 1969(d)	Schedule 1 Paragraph 1(*e*)
The hotel and catering industry	The Industrial Training (Hotel and Catering Board) Order 1966 as amended by the Industrial Training (Hotel and Catering Board) Order 1969(e)	Schedule 1 Paragraph 1(*e*)

(a) S.I. 1964/949, 1969/884 (1964 II, p. 2127; 1969 II, p. 2157).
(b) S.I. 1964/1086, 1968/1333, 1969/1376 (1964 II, p. 2402; 1968 II, p. 3694; 1969 III, p. 4103).
(c) S.I. 1965/2028, 1969/1290 (1965 III, p. 5998; 1969 III, p. 3820).
(d) S.I. 1966/143, 1969/1210 (1966 I, p. 257; 1969 II, p. 3545).
(e) S.I. 1966/1347, 1969/1405 (1966 III, p. 3669; 1969 III, p. 4132).

(3) At the end of the said Appendix there shall be added the entries following—

Column 1	Column 2	Column 3
The clothing and allied products industry	The Industrial Training (Clothing and Allied Products Board) Order 1969(a)	Schedule 1 Paragraph 1(j)
The hairdressing and allied services industry	The Industrial Training (Hairdressing and Allied Services Board) Order 1969(b)	Schedule 1 Paragraph 1(g)

EXPLANATORY NOTE

(This Note is not part of the Order.)

This Order amends the Schedule to the Industrial Training (Road Transport Board) Order 1969 which specifies the activities in relation to which the Road Transport Industry Training Board exercises its functions.

The principal changes are the inclusion in the road transport industry of—

(a) the manufacture or fitting out of vehicle bodies;

(b) the repair of vehicle bodies.

There will be excluded from the industry the activities of an establishment engaged wholly or mainly in—

(i) the manufacture or fitting out of vehicle bodies where the employer is a motor vehicle manufacturer or where the vehicle bodies are manufactured or fitted out to the order of a motor vehicle manufacturer; or

(ii) the manufacture, fitting out or repair of caravans not being motor vehicles.

The activities of the Post Office are excluded from the road transport industry.

(a) S.I. 1969/1375 (1969 III, p. 4094).   (b) S.I. 1969/1634 (1969 III, p. 5133).

STATUTORY INSTRUMENTS

1969 No. 1878 (S. 166)

PENSIONS

The Pensions Increase (Approved Schemes) (National Health Service) (Scotland) Amendment Regulations 1969

Made - - - -	*23rd December* 1969
Laid before Parliament	*31st December* 1969
Coming into Operation	*1st January* 1970

In exercise of the powers conferred upon me by section 3(2)(*b*)(i) and (4) of the Pensions (Increase) Act 1965(**a**) as extended by section 1(4) and paragraph 10 of schedule 2 to the Pensions (Increase) Act 1969(**b**), and of all other powers enabling me in that behalf, and with the consent of the Minister for the Civil Service, I hereby make the following regulations :—

Citation and commencement

1. These regulations may be cited as the Pensions Increase (Approved Schemes) (National Health Service) (Scotland) Amendment Regulations 1969, and shall come into operation on 1st January 1970.

Interpretation

2.—(1) The Interpretation Act 1889(**c**) shall apply for the interpretation of these regulations as it applies for the interpretation of an Act of Parliament.

(2) In these regulations, unless the context otherwise requires, references to an enactment or regulations shall be construed as references, to that enactment or those regulations as amended or extended by any other enactment or regulations.

Amendment of the Pensions Increase (Approved Schemes) (National Health Service) (Scotland) Regulations 1968

3. The Pensions Increase (Approved Schemes) (National Health Service) (Scotland) Regulations 1968(**d**) shall be amended as follows :—

in regulation 2(1) in the definition of " statutory pension increases " after the words " (v) section 1 of the Act of 1965 " there shall be added the words " (vi) section 1 of the Pensions (Increase) Act 1969 ".

Effective date of new benefits

4. Any allowance, or any increase of an allowance, payable by virtue of these regulations shall be payable in respect of any period beginning on or after 1st April 1969.

William Ross,
One of Her Majesty's Principal
Secretaries of State.

St. Andrew's House,
Edinburgh.
18th December 1969.

(a) 1965 c. 78.   (b) 1969 c. 7.   (c) 1889 c. 63.   (d) S.I. 1968/1299 (1968 II p. 3619).

Consent of the Minister for the Civil Service given under his Official Seal on 23rd December 1969.

(L.S.)

J. E. Herbecq,
**Authorised by the Minister
for the Civil Service.**

EXPLANATORY NOTE

(This Note is not part of the Regulations.)

Certain persons who retired from employment in the National Health Service in Scotland elected to secure their superannuation benefits through schemes which operated by way of insurance policies to produce lump sums or annuities, or both, upon retirement. The Pensions Increase (Approved Schemes) (National Health Service) (Scotland) Regulations 1968 provide for the payment of allowances corresponding broadly to the increases for which they would have been eligible under the Pensions (Increase) Acts 1952, 1956, 1959, 1962 and 1965 had they been pensionable under the National Health Service Superannuation Scheme.

These regulations authorise additional allowances corresponding to the increases provided by section 1 of the Pensions (Increase) Act 1969 and have retrospective effect from 1st April 1969 (the date when increases payable under that Act took effect) by virtue of section 3(4) of the Pensions (Increase) Act 1965 and paragraph 10 of Schedule 2 to the Pensions (Increase) Act 1969.

STATUTORY INSTRUMENTS

1969 No. 1880 (S.168)

POLICE

The Special Constables (Pensions) (Scotland) Amendment (No. 3) Regulations 1969

Made	- - -	*26th December* 1969
Laid before Parliament		*31st December* 1969
Coming into Operation		*1st January* 1970

In exercise of the powers conferred on me by section 26 of the Police (Scotland) Act 1967(**a**) (as read with section 1(2) of the Police Pensions Act 1961(**b**)), and of all other powers enabling me in that behalf, and after consultation with the Joint Central Committee and such bodies and associations as are mentioned in section 26(9)(*b*) of the said Act of 1967, I hereby make the following regulations:—

1. These regulations may be cited as the Special Constables (Pensions) (Scotland) Amendment (No. 3) Regulations 1969 and shall come into operation on 1st January 1970.

2. In these regulations any reference to the Instrument of 1966 is a reference to the Special Constables (Pensions) (Scotland) Regulations 1966(**c**), as amended (**d**).

3. For regulation 5(1) of the Instrument of 1966 (which relates to a widow's augmented award where her husband's death results from an attack or an injury received in effecting an arrest or preventing an escape or rescue) there shall be substituted the following provision:—

"**5.**—(1) This regulation shall apply to a widow of a special constable whose death is the result of an injury received without his own default in the execution of his duty where—

(*a*) he was attacked by a person or persons in a manner which, in the opinion of the police authority, was intrinsically likely to cause death and death ensued on or after 2nd June 1949, as a result of the attack, or

(*b*) the injury was received in the course of duties performed, in the opinion of the police authority, for the immediate purpose of effecting an arrest or of preventing an escape or rescue from legal custody and death ensued on or after 1st August 1964, or

(*c*) the injury was received in the course of duties performed, in the opinion of the police authority—

(i) for the immediate purpose of saving the life of another person or of preventing loss of human life, and

(ii) in circumstances in which there was an intrinsic likelihood of his receiving a fatal injury,

and death ensued on or after 1st January 1970."

(**a**) 1967 c. 77. (**b**) 1961 c. 35. (**c**) S.I. 1966/1625 (1966 III, p. 5066).
(**d**) The relevant amending instrument is S.I. 1969/1529 (1969 III, p. 4960).

4.—(1) In the application of the Police Pensions Regulations 1966(**a**) to the calculation of an award in respect of a special constable under the Instrument of 1966, those regulations shall apply as amended by the Police Pensions (Amendment) (No. 3) Regulations 1969(**b**) (which amendments relate to awards payable on death resulting from an injury received in the performance of life-saving duties).

(2) In accordance with paragraph (1) of this regulation, for regulation 2(1) of the Instrument of 1966 (which, as set out in the Special Constables (Pensions) (Scotland) Amendment (No. 2) Regulations 1969(**c**), defines the expression "the principal regulations") there shall be substituted the following provision :—

"(1) In these regulations the expression "the principal regulations" means the Police Pensions Regulations 1966 as amended by the Police Pensions (Amendment) (No. 2) Regulations 1967(**d**), the Police Pensions (Amendment) Regulations 1968(**e**), the Police Pensions (Amendment) Regulations 1969(**f**), the Police Pensions (Amendment) (No. 2) Regulations 1969(**g**) and the Police Pensions (Amendment) (No. 3) Regulations 1969."

William Ross,
One of Her Majesty's Principal
Secretaries of State.

St. Andrew's House,
Edinburgh.
26th December 1969.

EXPLANATORY NOTE

(This Note is not part of the Regulations.)

These Regulations amend the Special Constables (Pensions) (Scotland) Regulations 1966 which give to special constables and their dependants certain pension benefits for which members of police forces and their dependants are eligible. The Police Pensions (Amendment) (No. 3) Regulations 1969 provide that a widow of a member of a police force shall qualify for an augmented award where her husband's death results from an injury received while saving, or preventing loss of, human life.

These Regulations make similar provisions as respects the widow of a special constable.

(**a**) S.I. 1966/1582 (1966 III, p.4894).   (**b**) S.I. 1969/1849(1969 III, p. 5788).
(**c**) S.I. 1969/1529 (1969 III, p.4960).   (**d**) S.I. 1967/1500 (1967 III, p. 4204).
(**e**) S.I. 1968/530 (1968 I, p. 1269).   (**f**) S.I. 1969/723 (1969 II, p. 1952).
(**g**) S.I. 1969/1484 (1969 III, p.4745).

STATUTORY INSTRUMENTS

1969 No. 1881 (S. 169)

PENSIONS

The Pensions Increase (Approved Schemes) (Local Government) (Scotland) Amendment Regulations 1969

Made - - - -	*23rd December* 1969
Laid before Parliament	*9th January* 1970
Coming into Operation	*15th January* 1970

In exercise of the powers conferred on me by section 3(2)(*b*)(ii) and (4) of the Pensions (Increase) Act 1965(a) as extended by section 1(4) of and paragraph 10 of Schedule 2 to the Pensions (Increase) Act 1969(b), and of all other powers enabling me in that behalf, and with the consent of the Minister for the Civil Service, I hereby make the following regulations:—

Citation, commencement and interpretation

1.—(1) These regulations may be cited as the Pensions Increase (Approved Schemes) (Local Government) (Scotland) Amendment Regulations 1969, and shall come into operation on 15th January 1970.

(2) The Pensions Increase (Approved Schemes) (Local Government) (Scotland) Regulations 1968(c) (hereinafter called "the principal regulations") and these regulations may be cited together as the Pensions Increase (Approved Schemes) (Local Government) (Scotland) Regulations 1968 and 1969.

(3) The Interpretation Act 1889(d) shall apply for the interpretation of these regulations as it applies for the interpretation of an Act of Parliament.

Extension of pension increases

2. In regulation 2(1) of the principal regulations (which relates to interpretation) the following shall be inserted after item (v) in the definition of " statutory pension increases "—

" and

(vi) section 1 of the Pensions (Increase) Act 1969 ".

Employment by nursing associations

3.—(1) After regulation 4(2) of the principal regulations (which defines the persons to whom the regulations are to apply) there shall be added the following paragraph:—

" (3) For the purposes of paragraph (1)(*b*)(ii) of this regulation (but for no other purpose) a person may aggregate with his reckonable service employment by a county or district nursing association during any period when a local authority had arrangements with that association under section 1 of the Maternity Services (Scotland) Act, 1937(e)."

(2) In paragraph 2(vi) of the Schedule to the principal regulations (which defines reckonable service) before the words " district nursing association " there shall be inserted the words " county or ".

(a) 1965 c. 78.   (b) 1969 c. 7.   (c) S.I. 1968/1298 (1968 II, p. 3614).
(d) 1889 c. 63.   (e) 1937 c. 30.

Effective date of operation

4.—(1) Any allowance, or any increase of an allowance, which becomes payable by virtue of the amendment effected by regulation 2 of these regulations shall be payable in relation to any period beginning on or after 1st April 1969.

(2) Any allowance, or any increase of an allowance, which becomes payable by virtue of an amendment effected by regulation 3 of these regulations shall be payable in relation to any period beginning on or after 1st July 1966.

William Ross,
One of Her Majesty's Principal
Secretaries of State.

St. Andrew's House,
 Edinburgh,
18th December 1969.

, Consent of the Minister for the Civil Service given under his Official Seal on 23rd December 1969.

(L.S.)   *J. E. Herbecq,*
Authorised by the Minister
for the Civil Service.

EXPLANATORY NOTE

(This Note is not part of the Regulations.)

The Pensions Increase (Approved Schemes) (Local Government) (Scotland) Regulations 1968 provide for the payment of allowances to certain retired local government employees whose pension rights were secured through insurance policies. The allowances correspond broadly to the increases for which they would have been eligible under pensions increase legislation had they been pensionable as contributory employees in their local government employment. These Regulations authorise new or increased allowances which correspond with the new increases provided by the Pensions (Increase) Act 1969. They also amend the Regulations of 1968 by extending the scope of the nursing association employment which is reckonable for these purposes.

The Regulations are given retrospective effect under the express powers of section 3(4) of the Pensions (Increase) Act 1965 and paragraph 10 of Schedule 2 to the Pensions (Increase) Act 1969.

STATUTORY INSTRUMENTS

1969 No. 1883

EXCHANGE CONTROL

The Exchange Control (Import and Export) (Amendment) Order 1969

Made	-	-	-	*29th December* 1969
Laid before Parliament				*1st January* 1970
Coming into Operation				*2nd January* 1970

The Treasury, in exercise of the powers conferred upon them by sections 31 and 36(5) of the Exchange Control Act 1947(**a**), hereby make the following Order:—

1.—(1) This Order may be cited as the Exchange Control (Import and Export) (Amendment) Order 1969, and shall come into operation on 2nd January 1970.

(2) The Interpretation Act 1889(**b**) shall apply for the interpretation of this Order as it applies for the interpretation of an Act of Parliament.

2. The Exchange Control (Import and Export) Order 1966(**c**) shall be amended as follows:—

(*a*) in article 5(1)(i) by substituting " £25 " for " £15 "; and

(*b*) in article 5(1)(ii) by substituting " £300 " for " £50 ".

3. This Order shall extend to the Channel Islands, and any reference in this Order to the Exchange Control Act 1947 includes a reference to that Act as extended by the Exchange Control (Channel Islands) Order 1947(**d**).

Joseph Harper,
E. G. Perry,

Two of the Lords Commissioners of
Her Majesty's Treasury.

29th December 1969.

(a) 1947 c. 14.   (b) 1889 c. 63.   (c) S.I. 1966/1351 (1966 III, p. 3681).
(d) S.R. & O. 1947/2034 (Rev. VI, p. 1001: 1947 I, p. 660).

EXPLANATORY NOTE

(This Note is not part of the Order.)

This Order amends the Exchange Control (Import and Export) Order 1966. Travellers to destinations outside the United Kingdom, the Channel Islands and the Republic of Ireland may now take with them out of the United Kingdom up to £25 worth of sterling notes or currency notes of other scheduled territories, instead of £15 worth. They may also take with them up to £300 worth of foreign currency notes, instead of £50 worth.

STATUTORY INSTRUMENTS

1969 No. 1887

CUSTOMS AND EXCISE

The Export of Goods (Control) (Amendment No. 3) Order 1969

Made	-	-	-	*22nd December* 1969	
Coming into Operation				*5th January* 1970	

The Board of Trade, in exercise of the powers conferred on them by section 1 of the Import, Export and Customs Powers (Defence) Act 1939(a), hereby order as follows :—

1.—(1) This Order may be cited as the Export of Goods (Control) (Amendment No. 3) Order 1969 and shall come into operation on 5th January 1970.

(2) The Interpretation Act 1889(b) shall apply to the interpretation of this Order as it applies to the interpretation of an Act of Parliament.

2. The Export of Goods (Control) Order 1967(c), as amended (d), shall have effect as if in Schedule 1, Part I, Group 8, there were included the following entry :—

"Potatoes   ...   .   A".

R. Fell,
An Under Secretary of
the Board of Trade.

22nd December 1969.

EXPLANATORY NOTE

(This Note is not part of the Order.)

This Order further amends the Export of Goods (Control) Order 1967 by including potatoes among the goods of which the export is controlled.

(a) 1939 c. 69.   (b) 1889 c. 63.
(c) S.I. 1967/675 (1967 I, p. 2080).
(d) The relevant amending Order is S.I. 1968/132 (1968 I, p. 353).

STATUTORY INSTRUMENTS

1969 No. 1888

PENSIONS

The Pensioners' Declarations (Amendment) Rules 1969

Made - - -		30*th December* 1969
Coming into Operation		7*th January* 1970

The Minister for the Civil Service, in exercise of the powers conferred upon him by section 6 of the Appropriation Act 1957(a) (hereafter in these Rules referred to as "the Act") and article 2(1)(c) of the Minister for the Civil Service Order 1968(b), and of all other powers enabling him in that behalf, hereby makes the following Rules:—

1. These Rules may be cited as the Pensioners' Declarations (Amendment) Rules 1969, and shall come into operation on 7th January 1970.

2. The Interpretation Act 1889(c) shall apply for the interpretation of these Rules as it applies for the interpretation of an Act of Parliament.

3. The Pensioners' Declarations Rules 1958(d), as amended (e), shall be further amended as follows:—

    (*a*) by substituting for Rule 3(1) (which, subject as therein mentioned, provides an exemption from the requirement of a declaration under section 6 of the Act in relation to a payment falling due within 12 months of a previous declaration under that section) the following paragraphs:—

"(1) It shall not be necessary for a person to make a declaration under section 6 of the Act in relation to any payment in respect of a pension if he has made a declaration under that section in respect of that pension within the relevant period ending on the day on which that payment falls due:

Provided that the authority responsible for the payment of a pension may from time to time require the person receiving payments in respect of that pension to make a declaration in relation to the payment falling due on a specified day in each year, and, if they so require, the person receiving the payment shall first comply with the requirement in relation to the payment falling due on the day specified by the authority, notwithstanding that he has made a declaration within the relevant period ending on the day so specified.

(1A) In paragraph (1), the expression 'relevant period' means a period of 1 year, or such longer period not exceeding 3 years as the authority responsible for payment may from time to time specify in relation to any particular pension or class of pensions, as the case may be."; and

---

(a) 1957 c. 63.   (b) S.I. 1968/1656 (1968 III, p. 4485).   (c) 1889 c. 63.
(d) S.I. 1958/1041 (1958 II, p. 1803).   (e) S.I. 1959/1343 (1959 II, p. 2011).

(*b*) by inserting at the end of Rule 3 the following paragraph:—

"(6) An authority responsible for the payment of pensions may, in respect of any particular case or class of cases, dispense with the requirement contained in Rule 1(1)(*d*) that the declaration under section 6 of the Act shall state the place of residence of the pensioner."

Given under the Official Seal of the Minister for the Civil Service on 30th December 1969.

(L.S.)

K. H. McNeill,
Authorised by the Minister
for the Civil Service.

30th December 1969.

EXPLANATORY NOTE

(This Note is not part of the Rules.)

Section 6 of the Appropriation Act 1957 provides that, subject to such exemptions as may be provided by or under Rules made by the Minister for the Civil Service by statutory instrument, a person shall not receive any payment out of moneys provided by Parliament for half-pay or for the Navy, Army, Air Force or Civil non-effective Services unless the declaration prescribed by Rules made by the Minister for the Civil Service has been made.

These rules make two changes in the Pensioners' Declaration Rules 1958 which prescribe the declaration to be made and provide for certain exemptions. The first change provides that instead of making annual declarations, the declaration to be made by the pensioner may be either annually or such longer period, not exceeding 3 years, as may be specified by the authority responsible for payment of the pension. The second change enables the pension paying authority to dispense with the requirement that the pensioner shall state his place of residence.

STATUTORY INSTRUMENTS

1969 No. 1889

AGRICULTURE

The Price Stability of Imported Products (Rates of Levy No. 25) Order 1969

Made	-	-	-	*30th December* 1969
Coming into Operation		-		*31st December* 1969

The Minister of Agriculture, Fisheries and Food, in exercise of the powers conferred upon him by section 1(2), (4), (5), (6) and (7) of the Agriculture and Horticulture Act 1964(a) and of all other powers enabling him in that behalf, hereby makes the following order:—

1. This order may be cited as the Price Stability of Imported Products (Rates of Levy No. 25) Order 1969, and shall come into operation on 31st December 1969.

2.—(1) In this order—

" the Principal Order " means the Price Stability of Imported Products (Levy Arrangements) Order 1966(b) as amended(c) and as amended by any subsequent order, and if any such order is replaced by any subsequent order the expression shall be construed as a reference to such subsequent order;

AND other expressions have the same meaning as in the Principal Order.

(2) The Interpretation Act 1889(d) shall apply to the interpretation of this order as it applies to the interpretation of an Act of Parliament.

3. In accordance with and subject to the provisions of Part II of the Principal Order (which provides for the charging of levies on imports of certain specified commodities), and notwithstanding the provisions of Article 3(a) of the Price Stability of Imported Products (Rates of Levy No. 24) Order 1969(e), the rate of general levy for such imports into the United Kingdom of any specified commodity as are described in column 2 of the Schedule to this order in relation to a tariff heading indicated in column 1 of that Schedule shall on and after 31st December 1969 be the rate set forth in relation thereto in column 3 of that Schedule.

In Witness whereof the Official Seal of the Minister of Agriculture, Fisheries and Food is hereunto affixed on 30th December 1969.

(L.S.)

R. J. E. Taylor,
Assistant Secretary.

(a) 1964 c. 28.   (b) S.I. 1966/936 (1966 II, p. 2271).
(c) S.I 1969/758, 1564 (1969 II, p. 2137; III, p. 5018).   (d) 1889 c. 63.
(e) S.I. 1969/1677 (1969 III, p. 5300).

SCHEDULE

1. Tariff Heading	2. Description of Imports	3. Rate of General Levy
		per ton £ s. d.
	Imports of:—	
11.01	Wheat flours	2 0 0

EXPLANATORY NOTE

(*This Note is not part of the Order.*)

This order, which comes into operation on 31st December 1969, increases on and after that date the general levy on imports of wheat flours to 40s. per ton.

STATUTORY INSTRUMENTS

1969 No. 1891

PRICES AND INCOMES

The Prices and Incomes (General Considerations) Order 1969

Made - - -	*30th December* 1969
Laid before Parliament	*7th January* 1970
Coming into Operation	*8th January* 1970

The Secretary of State, in exercise of the powers conferred on her by section 4 of the Prices and Incomes Act 1966(**a**) and after consultation, in accordance with subsection (3) of that section, with organisations appearing to her to represent to a substantial extent the interests of those particularly concerned, hereby makes the following Order :—

1.—(1) This Order, which may be cited as the Prices and Incomes (General Considerations) Order 1969, shall come into operation on 8th January 1970.

(2) The Interpretation Act 1889(**b**) shall apply for the interpretation of this Order as it applies for the interpretation of an Act of Parliament and as if this Order and the Order hereby revoked were Acts of Parliament.

2. The considerations set out in the Schedule to this Order (which reproduces certain sections of a memorandum entitled "Productivity, Prices and Incomes Policy after 1969"(**c**) which was presented to Parliament by the Secretary of State by Command of Her Majesty in December 1969) shall be substituted for the considerations set out in Schedule 2 to the said Act of 1966 (as substituted by the Schedule to the Prices and Incomes (General Considerations) Order 1968(**d**)) as the considerations to which the National Board for Prices and Incomes are to have regard in accordance with section 4 of that Act.

3. The Prices and Incomes (General Considerations) Order 1968 is hereby revoked.

Signed by order of the Secretary of State.

30th December 1969.

Edmund Dell,
Minister of State,
Department of Employment and Productivity.

(**a**) 1966 c. 33.	(**b**) 1889 c. 63.
(**c**) Cmnd. 4237.	(**d**) S.I. 1968/616 (1968 I, p. 1425).

Article 2

SCHEDULE

A. The Aims of the Policy

1. From the beginning, the policy has tried to give the community an opportunity of achieving three aims:—

to keep prices more stable than in the past;

to achieve faster growth in the real standard of living;

to get a more rational and fair relationship between the incomes of various groups, and in particular to improve the position of low paid workers.

2. Stopping prices rising as much as in the past means relating increases in money incomes to the rise in output. But it also means seeing that producers of goods and services do not exploit their market power at the expense of other sections of the community.

3. Raising the real standard of living of the country means more capital investment in industry and more rapid adoption of new techniques. But it also means making much more effective use of the time workers spend on the job, and persuading them to accept links between increases in their pay and increases in their productivity.

4. To secure a fairer distribution of incomes means that some of us must accept a little smaller increase in our incomes over the years in order that those who are worse off can have more. There is no magic fund out of which we can improve the position of low paid workers.

5. In all these aims, the community has a choice which the Government cannot make for it. If we want price stability, then we cannot all have large increases in pay every year regardless of the rise in productivity. If we want our real standard of living to rise, we must be prepared to change the way in which work is organised and carried out. If we want to improve the position of those who are worse off, the rest of us must be prepared to accept a little less ourselves.

6. The Green Paper "The Task Ahead" suggested that the rise in output per worker over the next few years would be of the order of 3% a year. In 1968, there was a particularly large increase in output per worker. But this does not appear to have been repeated in 1969; and it would be most imprudent, and totally at variance with past experience, to base policy on the hope that there will be an early change in the rate of increase of output per worker. So if incomes rise by an average of more than about 3% a year, the result will inevitably be a rise in prices caused by higher labour costs.

7. Over the past decade, incomes have in fact risen by much more than 3% a year. The average increase in earnings has been 6 or $6\frac{1}{2}\%$ a year. The simple and inevitable result of this has been a rise in prices year by year averaging something like 3%. Everyone objects to rising prices. The lowest paid workers and those on small fixed incomes suffer most from them. Yet the country as a whole has not been prepared to accept that stable prices are simply incompatible with large increases in incomes year by year which have not been earned by higher productivity.

8. Moreover, the evils flowing from a rise in money incomes faster than the rise in output are not confined to a rise in prices. It reduces the incentive to save. Our export position deteriorates and this requires deflationary measures to put the balance of payments right.

9. The Government believes that what the community as a whole really wants is a steady rise in real incomes coupled with a broad measure of price stability. This is what the policy aims at giving the community a chance to achieve over the next few years. Whether it succeeds depends not just on what the Government does, but on what choices individual men and women make. People can have large increases in pay—but with inflation which takes away much of the benefit. Or they can have smaller

money increases whose real value is greater because prices are kept stable and steady expansion is possible. In this sense any incomes policy is essentially a voluntary policy operating through the decisions of employers and trade unions.

10. None of these aims can be achieved by a prices and incomes policy narrowly conceived or operated in isolation from the other measures the Government is taking to strengthen the economy, increase industrial efficiency, improve the structure of the labour market and create a just society. But within this wider strategy, a prices and incomes policy is essential to achieve the following aims:—

> establishing on a firm and continuing basis the principle of links between pay increases and the more effective use of labour;

> securing fundamental improvements in the methods of pay negotiation and settlement;

> creating wage and salary structures which will avoid successive leap-frogging settlements and eliminate friction;

> improving the position of low paid workers, particularly by reorganisations which will make better use of their efforts, and by the introduction of equal pay for women;

> raising the efficiency with which labour and capital equipment are used in all sectors of the economy—private industry, publicly owned industry, and the public services;

> ensuring that the larger industrial units now being brought into existence use their resources efficiently and to the benefit of the consumer, and do not use their increased market power to operate pricing policies or pay policies which fail to take proper account of the wider public interest.

B. Guidance for Pay Negotiations

General Character of Pay Settlements

11. To keep prices as stable as possible has been an objective of the policy since the Joint Statement of Intent was signed by representatives of employers, unions, and the Government in December 1964. The cost of living can be affected by a number of factors including the level of import prices and of indirect taxation. During 1968 prices were unavoidably inflated by the effects of devaluation and the measures necessary to make it work. But price rises due to these influences are now levelling out and the main determinant of price levels in the coming months will be how far we are successful in relating increases in money incomes to increases in output.

12. In the next few years output per worker is likely to go up by about 3% a year. Therefore if we are to avoid a steep increase in the cost of living money incomes should only rise at about this rate. This was the basis of the "norm" of 3-3½% for pay increases which formed the starting point of the policy in 1965. If productivity rises faster than expected then so can incomes. The princple was accepted in 1965. It is still true today.

13. This means that most wage and salary settlements need to fall in the range of 2½-4½% increase in a year if this aim of greater price stability is to be achieved. A range within which most settlements need to fall has been given because no single figure can be appropriate to the circumstances of all negotiations. Nor indeed will the average figure be the same from one year to the next. The appropriate level for a particular settlement within this range will depend on a variety of factors affecting the firm or industry, including the rate of increase in labour productivity, the extent to which low paid or women workers are involved and the labour market situation. Opportunities must be given for changes in the relative pay of different groups of workers.

14. Special care must be taken where basic rates are negotiated at the national level but a substantial part of total earnings springs from payments of various kinds fixed by individual employers. If these local elements tend to rise faster than the basic rates—as they do in some industries—then increases in the national basic rates need

to be kept at a lower level than in settlements which effectively determine the real level of earnings. In the former cases a national settlement needs to be in the lower part of the range if it is not to be inflationary. This principle is recognised by the TUC in its own guidance to unions on pay claims contained in its 1969 Economic Review.

15. If the other objectives of incomes policy are to be achieved—encouraging a more rapid rise in productivity and securing a better relationship between the pay of various groups of workers—some settlements in any year will come above the top of the normal range. But such settlements need to be exceptional, not normal, if there is to be reasonable price stability.

16. In the rest of this section, the main factors which come under consideration in individual pay negotiations are reviewed. In most cases what needs to be considered is their bearing on the point *within the range* of $2\frac{1}{2}$-$4\frac{1}{2}$% at which a settlement should fall. This section also reviews the exceptional circumstances in which it might be appropriate for a settlement to be concluded for a group of workers at a level outside the normal range.

17. The factors considered are:—

Productivity and Efficiency Agreements

Reorganisation of Pay Structures

Low Paid Workers

Equal Pay for Women

Labour Market Requirements

Pay in the Public Services.

18. The various reasons which may exist for increasing pay should be considered together. For example, there is no logic in arguing that an increase in pay of x% is needed in order to recruit an adequate labour force, and then in addition paying an extra y% as the workers' share of a productivity deal. The y% increase may well in itself raise pay sufficiently to recruit the necessary labour. All increases in pay, in any industry or firm, including those within the range, should, as far as possible, be covered by an increase in output per worker in that industry or firm if unit costs are not to rise.

Productivity and Efficiency Agreements

19. A central feature of the productivity, prices and incomes policy throughout its development has been to encourage management and workers together to find ways of increasing productivity and to relate pay to performance. And under the stimulus of the policy, productivity bargaining has in the past four years spread widely through industry. Over 6 million workers have been involved in over 3,500 productivity agreements.

20. The rapid spread of productivity bargaining has not occurred without raising some doubts, and indeed criticism. Some have felt that productivity deals represented little more than the sale of restrictive practices ("selling the rule-book") which should never have been allowed to develop. This is too narrow a view of most productivity agreements. But more fundamental criticisms were also made.

21. Productivity agreements usually provided for changes in working practices to be accepted by the workers concerned in return for higher pay. But what then of the position of workers who had never placed any restrictions on changes in working practice, and readily accepted the role of management to organise work in the most effective way? Would not the trend to productivity bargaining encourage such workers in future to demand a price for their acquiescence in change?

22. Other critics argued that the real scope for productivity bargaining was relatively narrow; that many productivity agreements would have little effect in raising output per worker; that some agreements were "phoney", designed simply to comply with the

form of incomes policy and not its substance; that there were some workers for whom it was inappropriate to specify changes in working practice; and that increases in one firm led to claims from those doing similar work in other firms with no similar justification.

23. Thirdly, concern was growing at the possible repercussions of productivity agreements covering particular groups of workers rather than all workers in a firm or industry. Specially large increases might be earned by a particular group in return for a change in working practices. But this tended to lead in due course to consequential increases to other workers in the establishment (supervisors, maintenance workers, office staff) in order to maintain what was regarded as a sound pay structure. Moreover, specially large increases in one year might raise expectations of similar increases in later years, when no similar increases in productivity would be possible.

24. In these circumstances, the Government decided it would be helpful if the NBPI carried out a fresh review of the situation. The following conclusions emerge from the Board's Report No. 123, "Productivity Agreements" (Cmnd. 4136) of August 1969:—

> productivity agreements have on the whole promoted good industrial relations;

> productivity bargaining has reduced costs: its effect was that productivity rose more than earnings;

> productivity agreements should not be once-for-all affairs: negotiations linking pay and productivity are a continuing possibility: efficiency should be constantly raised on the basis of close and continuing co-operation between managements and workers;

> non-manual workers can contribute as effectively as manual workers to a more economical use of all the factors of production: and forms of agreement are needed which can be used for their particular circumstances.

25. The NBPI concluded that the kind of points raised in paragraphs 20-23 above required that its earlier guidelines for effective productivity agreements should be revised and broadened. In particular the Board wished to formulate them in terms clearly applicable to all types of workers, both manual and non-manual, including those workers for whom is it not appropriate to specify changes in working practices. The revised guidelines for efficiency agreements, including productivity agreements, are set out in Appendix 1.

26. In all cases there must be clear links between increased efficiency and increased pay. In some cases it may be possible to achieve this in a national or industry-wide agreement. This may be so, for example, in the nationalised industries. In the private sector it will be more common for efficiency agreements to be concluded at the level of the company. It is then important to ensure that companies' agreements are not impeded as a result of national agreements and the process of collective bargaining itself taking forms more appropriate to the days when the aim was to reach all the important decisions about pay at industry level. In these industries both sides need to look again at their arrangements. Sometimes it would be right to concentrate nationally on setting adequate minimum standards and providing a proper framework within which efficiency agreements can be concluded at company level. Guidance from the centre, both by employers' associations and by trade unions, can greatly help efficiency bargaining to develop on sound lines.

27. In the next phase of the policy pay increases should wherever practicable be negotiated in the context of an efficiency agreement, which should aim at increasing the efficiency with which use is made of the capital equipment and labour in the undertaking. The principles set out in Appendix 1 are clearly applicable to most workers—maintenance workers as well as production workers, office staff as well as factory workers, supervisory and professional staff as much as any other workers, workers in the public sector as well as those in private industry and commerce. This overcomes the difficulty previously experienced in applying a more narrowly conceived "productivity bargaining" in respect of many groups of workers.

28. More thorough costing and monitoring of agreements is needed in many cases. The NBPI in its report drew attention to the shortcomings of many firms in this respect. Full account must be taken of possible consequential pay increases to other workers in the establishment, and full allowance made for an adequate return on extra capital employed.

29. Consumers must share in the benefits of higher productivity through stable or lower prices if all sections of the community are to share in rising national prosperity. In most cases rising productivity does not spring entirely from major changes in working practice or working methods. In some parts of the economy modern technology enables output per worker to be increased specially rapidly and without extra effort. In these cases particularly it would be quite wrong for all the benefits of increased productivity to be enjoyed by workers and shareholders in the enterprise. So a reasonable share must be used for the benefit of the community as a whole.

30. Incomes policy has always accepted that workers who have contributed by their efforts to a rise in productivity are entitled to share in its benefits through higher pay. In some cases a reasonable share for the workers concerned may permit a pay increase higher than the normal range for settlements. But in many cases the rise in productivity will be no more than sufficient to enable pay increases within the normal range to be made. Increases in productivity should not in any case be treated as an isolated element in pay settlements divorced from other grounds for raising pay.

Reorganisation of Pay Structures

31. The efficient use of labour and other resources can be made impossible by out of date—even chaotic—pay structures which have grown up over years, even decades, and which bear little relation to the realities of present day working methods. Where such a state of affairs has developed there may be no alternative to a thorough-going rationalisation of the whole grading and pay structure and where necessary of the distribution of duties amongst the workers.

32. Such a fundamental reorganisation may well involve increases in pay which, on average, work out above the normal range. This may be justified both for the employer and for the community at large if it opens the way to substantial improvements in the efficiency with which labour is used. A more rational pay structure based on job evaluation may also reduce the risks of leap-frogging pay claims amongst the various groups of workers, and eliminate causes of dissatisfaction among workers. The NBPI has produced a valuable report on Job Evaluation (Cmnd. 3772).

33. The full gains from such a reorganisation will however only be realised in the long term. This makes it particularly important to associate a fundamental reorganisation of pay structure with the conclusion of an efficiency agreement through which the gains expected from the reorganisation are achieved.

34. Of course all pay systems and structures need to be kept in line with changes in the methods of work and systems of organisation. But this should be a continuous process, and there should be no need for exceptionally large pay increases to be given in connection with such limited changes. Major reorganisations should become necessary only infrequently—perhaps once in a decade.

35. Major reorganisations of pay structure have been carried through in many firms and industries in the past five years. But others also require major changes. Some have already been examined by the NBPI, or in other ways. The Government accepts the responsibility for carrying through changes which become necessary in the public services with which it is concerned. It will give all the help it can to those trying to achieve reforms in other sectors of the economy.

Low Paid Workers

36. One of the weaknesses of the system of free collective bargaining has been its inability to solve the problem of the low paid. Many of them are poorly organised, and even where they are well organised they do not command economic power. That is one of the reasons why they are low paid. Under a system where wage increases go to

the strong, the low paid have difficulty in holding their own, let alone improving their position.

37. One of the main aims of any productivity, prices and incomes policy must be to remedy this failure of a free-for-all system. Since 1965 the policy has offered opportunities for improving the relative position of the low paid. (For instance, under the criteria laid down in the policy for 1968-69, low pay was held to be sufficient justification for increases up to the ceiling—and indeed above the ceiling if other workers in the group were willing to let the low paid have priority). But the decision whether to take these opportunities was left to the employers and unions concerned; and although the gap between low paid and higher paid industries narrowed slightly it was not greatly reduced.

38. The challenge which faces us as a socially just society is what steps we can now take to improve the lot of the low paid in an increasingly affluent society. This will call for a conscious, deliberate effort by all those involved—Government, employers and trade unions. The first step must be to identify who are the low paid and why they are low paid. The initiative taken by the Department of Employment and Productivity in launching a new Earnings Survey in September 1968 covering all industries and occupations now enables us to discover the exact distribution of earnings behind the averages, by occupation, age and region, and thus to locate the lower paid groups. It has also sought to identify some reasons for low pay: whether for example it is associated with any particular age level, with payments in kind or with mental or physical disability.

39. The survey shows that in September 1968 1 in every 12 adult male workers in this country had total earnings before tax for a full week of less than £15, and nearly 1 in 30 less than £13 a week, at a time when the average adult male worker earned more than £25. The position of women was much worse; one in every 4 adult women had earnings for a full week of £10 a week or less, and nearly 1 in 12 less than £8 a week. The survey shows that certain industries have a particularly large proportion of workers below these levels (farming, catering, and retail distribution are obvious examples). But detailed analysis reveals that the great majority of low paid workers are scattered throughout industries whose workers, taken as a whole, are well paid. It shows too, that the reasons for low pay vary from group to group, almost from individual to individual. In some cases the reasons for their low pay would be difficult to overcome. For example, some people are low paid because they are young and inexperienced; others because they have passed the productive peak. Some workers prefer low paid jobs because they are less exacting and more suited to their abilities, and therefore offer them their best hope of having a job. Earnings are also affected in some cases by the number of hours worked or by the existence of tips or payments in kind. All this means that no single figure can represent a general definition of "low pay" applicable to workers in all circumstances. And the problem is in many cases too complex to be met by blanket increases covering a whole industry, or even a whole occupation.

40. In recent years it has been suggested that the inequalities of a system of free collective bargaining could be redressed by introducing a statutory national minimum wage or minimum earnings level. The Government set up an inter-departmental working party to study the implications of a national minimum wage and its report* was published for the purpose of providing a factual basis for informed discussion which the Government hopes will now take place. The study shows the complexity of the problem of helping the low income groups. For instance about two-thirds of the households in the country with an income of less than £15 a week would not benefit from a national minimum wage as they do not contain any wage earners. Again, a national minimum wage would have a very uneven effect in relieving poverty because it could not take account of family circumstances. The question of low pay cannot therefore be separated from social service policy. But an even greater difficulty arises from the fact that by far the greater number of low paid workers are scattered through industries where the general level of pay is relatively high. If, therefore, other wage earners in these industries merely took the establishment of a national minimum as a new base on which to rebuild their existing differentials, the cost of living

*National Minimum Wage. Report of an Inter-Departmental Working Party. HMSO 1969

would rise sharply; and the low paid would in the end be no better off. Unfortunately there is at present little evidence that higher paid workers would not take advantage for their own purposes of the attempt to help the low paid through the establishment by law of a national minimum.

41. How, then, can the problem of low pay be tackled? The first need is to strengthen trade union organisation among these low paid groups and this will be one of the aims of the Industrial Relations Bill. Many of the occupations where low pay predominates are at present covered by Wages Councils and it is arguable that this protection, which was once essential, is actually a hindrance today to the development of effective voluntary collective bargaining. The Industrial Relations Bill will make it easier to dismantle the Wages Council machinery in those industries where this has become desirable in the workers' interests.

42. Secondly, many groups of workers are low paid simply because their productivity is low. Much could be done by employers, with the co-operation of unions, to change working methods and so help the low paid to achieve higher earnings by sharply raising their productivity. Here again the Government has given a lead by the emphasis it has laid on the productivity aspects of the policy. The NBPI has spelt out the possibilities for improving the earnings potential of low paid workers in such activities as clothing manufacture, local government and the National Health Service. In some cases good progress has been made in applying the Board's suggestions; in others management still seems unaware of, or indifferent to, the new techniques required. One of the tasks of the recently created Manpower and Productivity Service of the DEP has been to help management and unions to follow up the possibilities opened up by the Board's reports. The Government intends that the MPS shall play an increasingly active role in seeing that the proposals of the Board (and later the CIM) for improving the productivity—and therefore the earnings—of the low paid are followed up urgently.

43. But when all this has been done the solution of this problem will still depend primarily on the attitude of negotiators in industry. The only hope of the low paid lies in a conscious decision by their fellow workers that they will accept a reassessment of differentials both between different industries and within an industry. Some differentials are of course fully justified, properly reflecting additional responsibility or rewarding the acquisition of new skills. But this is by no means true in every case; and that is why the Government has welcomed the increasing use of job evaluation, not only in manufacturing industry but for such groups as local government manual workers and ancillary workers in the National Health Service, in order to establish the worth of jobs on an objective basis. This can often lead to a reappraisal of the worth of jobs which are at present low paid.

44. One way of helping many low paid workers is to give priority to the improvement of minimum earnings levels, as has been done in engineering, rubber manufacturing, food manufacturing and the motor vehicle retail and repairing trade. This enables much larger increases to be given to the low paid workers than to the rest of the workers in the industry.

45. But neither job evaluation nor minimum earnings levels nor any other techniques will succeed in improving the real position of low paid workers unless employers and unions wish to do so. There can be no lasting improvement in the position of the low paid, either relatively or in real terms, if every increase they win becomes a new "floor" on which the existing spread of rates of pay is re-erected automatically, thus engendering not social justice but inflation. Recent wage claims by dustmen and firemen aroused a good deal of public sympathy in the belief that the pay of these groups of essential workers had fallen behind those of workers in manufacturing industry. Yet once substantial increases had been granted, others—many of whom are on higher levels of pay—promptly began to argue that these settlements entitled them to similar increases. It is this attitude of mind which, if it continues, will stultify the Government's efforts to improve the position of the low paid.

46. What is needed is a real improvement in the position of those who are low paid in the context of particular situations, of particular needs, and of particular systems of

pay negotiation. To do this the Government intends to ask the NBPI (and later the CIM) to initiate investigations in depth into those cases where low pay is a major problem and to suggest the means by which progress can be made case by case, industry by industry.

47. Where low paid workers form comparatively small pockets in more highly paid industries, it should be possible to improve their position as part of a pay settlement falling within the normal range. In a few industries, however, the general pay level is low; here any radical improvement in the position of the low paid can only be achieved by a settlement above the normal range, and the Government recognises that in these cases such a settlement may be appropriate, particularly in association with measures to increase efficiency. That is why the Government accepted as justified in February 1969 a wage increase above the ceiling for farm workers. However, the numbers involved in these generally low paid industries form a very small part of the national labour force; and increases above the normal range in such industries should not mean an intolerable addition to the national wages bill *provided that workers in other better paid industries do not take this as a signal to step up their own claims.*

48. The Government will be guided by the approach in this White Paper in dealing with its own employees. But here too the unions will have the responsibility of deciding whether, and to what extent, they are prepared to co-operate in giving priority to the low paid.

49. The Government invites unions and employers to join with it in working out, within the context of the policy outlined above, solutions to the problems of those low paid workers who have been unjustifiably left behind in the scramble of wage bargaining. Only in this way can social justice be achieved without imperilling our economic recovery.

Equal Pay for Women

50. As the national minimum wage report points out, women comprise the great majority of low paid workers. Any policy designed to lift the levels of low pay will therefore be concerned to a very great extent with women.

51. There are many reasons why women earn less than men. Women may be employed in the less skilled jobs or may work little or no overtime. But women also earn less because their rates of pay, including Wages Council rates, are commonly only four-fifths of the corresponding men's rates, and because industries where very low pay is found tend to have a relatively high proportion of women who are employed in small firms, and whom the trade unions find it very difficult to organise.

52. It is for these reasons, as well as on grounds of natural justice, that the Government has decided to legislate on equal pay. It has announced its intention to introduce legislation which would make discrimination in remuneration on grounds of sex illegal by the end of 1975. The full implementation of equal pay means that there will be a statutory obligation to give many women substantial increases over the next six years to bring their rates up to the level of men's rates. In negotiations between now and 1975 there will therefore need to be increases in many women's rates substantially greater than those in men's rates.

53. Overall, the Government estimates that the introduction of equal pay will increase the national wage and salary bill by between 3% and 4% between now and the end of 1975. This is not a large amount in comparison with the increase of perhaps 20% in output per head which is likely to occur during that period. Overall it should be possible to accomodate it without raising significantly the average yearly increase in money incomes throughout the economy. Indeed in many individual firms it should be possible to move towards equal pay without taking pay settlements outside the normal range.

54. The cost of introducing equal pay will however be spread unevenly over the economy, and will fall particularly on firms employing a high proportion of women at rates well below those of men doing similar work. In such cases the Government recognises that the introduction of equal pay will be possible only through pay settlements which on average work out about the normal range.

55. As with low paid workers generally women workers are, in many cases, used less efficiently than they might be. Indeed low rates of pay have in the past reduced the incentive to use women's labour more productively. Surveys in many industries have revealed the opportunities for reorganising women's work so as to raise their productivity. And if these opportunities are taken this in itself will cover at least part of the cost of introducing equal pay.

56. By definition moves towards equal pay for women cannot be used as arguments for increasing men's rates of pay; nor should they be used as arguments for increases in the pay of those women who already enjoy equality in rates. Equal pay for women is one move towards a fairer and more rational structure of pay. Like all such moves it involves changes in traditional pay differentials. The community must accept these changes—as a necessary consequence of accepting the principle of equal pay.

Labour Market Requirements

57. Many pay increases are defended by employers on the grounds that they are necessary to keep their pay in line with "market rates" and so enable them to retain their workers or recruit additional labour. These arguments are not confined to situations where there is an immediate labour supply problem. Employers often argue that they need to increase the pay of their workers either to match rates paid in other undertakings, or changes in rates or earnings elsewhere, because otherwise labour supply difficulties would soon emerge. They argue that it is both foolish, and unfair to their workers, to wait until the situation deteriorates visibly. For their part, unions often place great weight in negotiations on changes in the pay of other groups of workers who have had increases since their last settlement.

58. Without doubt some weight must be given in pay negotiations to the effects of pay on the maintenance of an adequate labour force. Clearly for this purpose some account must be taken of comparisons with the pay of workers doing similar jobs in the same area, or with the pay for different jobs to which workers could move. And in jobs requiring special skills or training, pay has got to be kept at levels which will encourage an adequate rate of recruitment in the long term.

59. The question which needs to be asked in terms of incomes policy is how much weight should be attached to these factors, as compared with the linking of pay to performance, or with producing a stable and equitable pay structure. In practice arguments based on so-called labour market requirements and, therefore, on comparisons with the pay of others have often played—and continue to play—too large a role in pay negotiations; when this happens they are an inflationary element in pay settlements.

60. In national negotiations immediate labour supply difficulties will rarely constitute a sound argument for an increase in pay above the normal range. The labour supply situation differs from one part of the country to another—often from one firm to another. No single increase in pay is likely to be apt for all. An individual employer may however find himself unable to recruit enough labour to meet an expansion of his buisness; or may face an increase in labour turnover, and in particular may find some of his best workers leaving for other jobs where they can get higher pay.

61. However, simple comparisons with levels of pay in other firms or with changes in rates paid by other firms are usually so over-simplified as to give only poor guidance as to the case for a pay increase on labour supply grounds. As regards *absolute levels of pay* there is now ample evidence of the fact that quite large differences in earnings by the same type of worker between one firm and another in the same area can exist for long periods of time without leading to a loss of labour by the firms with lower pay. In such cases the differences probably reflect other factors making it preferable to work for one employer rather than another. Many factors may influence an individual worker's choice of employer and job. A case for a pay increase on the grounds that rates or earnings in a particular enterprise are below those of similar jobs in other enterprises demands (even if other conditions are satisfied) a most careful analysis of all the facts about the conditions of employment, the job itself and actual earnings.

Jobs which, on the face of it, appear to be the same may be found under detailed examination to have significant differences; or earnings may turn out to be much the same, although rates differ.

62. Simple comparisons made with *changes in pay* in other jobs are also unlikely in themselves to provide clear grounds for any particular increase. In the first place, all depends on the assumption that at some previous date the relationship with pay in the other jobs was appropriate, and there is seldom much evidence of this. In the second place, comparisons are only too often with changes in some general index of wage rates or earnings and not with the changes in pay of jobs in the same area to which the workers concerned could move.

63. In any case, an effort to deal with actual or impending labour supply difficulties simply by increasing pay is seldom likely to be the solution. Employers need to consider with their workers whether:—

an efficiency agreement (or a revision of an earlier one) would meet the situation by both reducing the labour requirement and increasing the rewards for the job;

full advantage has been taken of all possible scope for internal transfers, training and retraining of the existing work force;

the causes of any excessive overtime, absenteeism or labour turnover have been established and appropriate action taken;

methods of attracting and recruiting labour are themselves adequate.

64. Such measures are particularly important since straight increases in pay are often unlikely permanently to secure extra labour or to prevent a loss of labour. A labour shortage in a particular firm is often no more than a reflection of a general shortage of that kind of labour in the area. In such cases an increase in pay by one firm is likely simply to be copied by other firms; in the end the pay increases will not have helped significantly to meet the labour shortage concerned.

65. All this means that too much weight must not be placed simply on keeping rates of pay in line with those of other workers as a means of maintaining an adequate labour force. Nevertheless, it is one factor which employers need to consider; and it may well affect the level of pay increase within the normal range which is appropriate in a particular case. But to make pay increases above the normal range merely on labour supply grounds is something which needs very strong justification indeed. And it should only be contemplated if, after taking account of the considerations mentioned in paragraphs 63 and 64:—

detailed information is available about comparative pay and earnings for clearly similar jobs; and

the discrepancy revealed is so substantial that even with an increase in pay at the top of the normal range the employer is still likely to be left with serious labour supply difficulties.

66. Even when no special problems of labour supply exist, comparisons with the level of pay in similar occupations, or with average increases in pay of all workers, often assume a crucial role (either implicit or explicit) in pay negotiations. This springs perhaps from a widespread, and no doubt natural, feeling that when the national wealth is increasing year by year the increase should be shared throughout the working population. No doubt it also springs from an equally widespread, if less admirable, feeling that each worker is entitled to have as large an increase as the next man or woman.

67. If the general level of pay increases were no greater than the increase in national production, the use of comparisons as the basis for pay increases might not be positively harmful, although it would obstruct many desirable changes. But in present circumstances, general use of the "comparability" argument as a basis for pay increases is a recipe for inflation. This is particularly true of claims based on:—

the mere maintenance of traditional relationships which have no economic justification;

the restoration of differentials between higher and lower paid workers following an increase given deliberately to improve the position of the lower paid;

the restoration of pay relativities which have altered over the years as a result of changes in the social structure;

the matching of pay increases earned by other workers under efficiency agreements.

68. This is not to say that comparisons with changes in the pay of other workers are wholly irrelevant in considering pay. Supervisors need to be paid more than line workers, and craftsmen should normally earn more than unskilled workers in the same plant. Chaotic pay structures can only lead to future trouble. Moreover, in skilled occupations the question of future recruitment may be highly relevant. But in these cases, as elsewhere, it is necessary to seek continually to raise efficiency, and to ensure that wherever possible there is a link between rising efficiency and increased pay.

Pay in the Public Services

69. Subject to what is said below, the guidance set out in this White Paper applies to the settlement of pay in the public services as much as to the settlement of pay in the private sector and in the nationalised industries. The Government's continuing policy is that workers in the public services should be treated on the same basis as workers in these other sectors of the economy.

70. Some special problems always arise in settling pay in the public services. In the first place, the nature of the jobs done by many workers in the public services (e.g. teachers, doctors and nurses) makes it impracticable to measure their output for the purpose of making a direct link between efficiency and pay. This does not mean their efficiency cannot be raised, but it has to be done by other means. Secondly, though the cost of labour can be measured as readily as elsewhere, a market price cannot normally be assigned to the value of its output because the output is not sold in a competitive market. This removes one of the major factors which bear on pay in other sectors of the economy. Thirdly, movement in and out of the public services tends to be re-stricted not only by the career nature of much of the employment, but also by the limited opportunities for employment elsewhere in the same kind of job for some occupations in the public services. This means that an unduly low level of pay in a public service, if it were allowed to develop, might take a relatively long time to show itself in labour supply difficulties. Finally, since the Government is directly or in-directly involved in all pay settlements in most of the public services, there are strong pressures for broad uniformity of treatment, in spite of the large numbers and varied occupations involved.

71. These problems mean that, for many public servants, more reliance has to be placed in determining pay on the closest comparisons possible with the pay of workers doing similar jobs in the private sector. In some cases, of which the police are an example, there are no counterparts in the private sector. In other cases, such as nurses and teachers, the public sector is the dominant employer, and there are too few counterparts in private employment for their pay to be useful as a guide. Where close comparisons with similar jobs in the private sector are not possible, or are of limited value, regard will have to be paid to more generalised comparisons with pay elsewhere as well as to other relevant considerations. Special considerations also apply to the Armed Forces, for whom the present arrangements for regular review under the standing reference to the NBPI will continue.

72. The use of comparisons as a basis for determining pay does not mean, however, that work measurement or method improvement are not applicable in the public services. Even where these techniques cannot be used to create a direct link between efficiency and pay, they are a guide to all concerned with pay negotiations as to whether labour in these cases is being used as effectively as possible. Indeed, where comparisons are used in determining the pay of public servants the results may be inflationary unless every possible step is taken to maximise the efficency with which their labour is used; and this places a special responsibility on employers, unions and workers to ensure that this is done.

73. The Government will continue its practice of asking the NBPI—and later the CIM —to consider particular pay issues arising in the public services in relation to the guid-ance set out in this White Paper. But even more important, the Government intend to

use the Board and its successor to make periodic reviews of the pay structures in various parts of the public services and, in particular, to advise on ways in which changes in pay structures and the organisation of the work can increase the efficiency of the service concerned.

Some General Considerations

74. The guidance set out in the previous parts of this section has been related primarily to pay settlements. It is mainly concerned therefore with increases in rates of pay, whether at the national or local level, whether of wage or salary earners, rather than with individual earnings, which will be affected by the number of hours worked; by levels of output under payment by results schemes; by pay increments or merit awards within pay scales; by pay increases on promotion to more responsible jobs. These factors, if under proper control, do not increase labour costs per unit of output.

75. However, increases in rates of pay need to take account of some other major factors affecting earnings. For example, a reduction in normal hours or an increase in the length of holidays must be treated on all fours with an increase in rates of pay. Such changes will increase unit costs of production just as much as a pay increase.

76. Although increases in rates of pay above the normal range represent the biggest inflationary risk, other elements in pay can easily be handled in an inflationary manner by employers, as enquiries by the NBPI have repeatedly shown. Overtime can be used simply as a way of raising earnings rather than because it is essential. Payment by results schemes can easily get out of control or posts may be upgraded or merit pay given as an alternative to raising basic rates. Some types of incremental scale may be found in practice to cost more year by year, creating a kind of "salary drift" corresponding to "wage drift"*. In such cases the resultant increase in earnings can well be seriously inflationary. There is no virtue in an employer keeping a pay settlement within the normal range if increases in average earnings far exceed the range in these ways.

77. It is wholly undesirable for pay settlements to be reached at intervals shorter than twelve months. If one pay settlement follows another at an interval of less than a year it is impossible to assess properly the effects of the earlier one in achieving what it set out to do. Time is needed to assess the working out of the costs and benefits of an efficiency agreement, or to see whether a rise in pay has had the effect expected on recruitment or labour turnover. Moreover, increases at short intervals for workers in one industry are disturbing to those who work in other industries. In many cases, pay agreements covering periods longer than twelve months would be appropriate.

78. Where an agreement takes effect after an interval of more than a year from the last one, the normal range can be adjusted proportionately to take account of the longer period. But there is no reason why a settlement whose operative date is more than twelve months after the last one should, merely on this account, be above $4\frac{1}{2}\%$.

C. GUIDANCE FOR DETERMINING PRICES AND CHARGES

79. An effective prices policy forms an essential part of any attempt to secure steady expansion without the inflation which usually accompanies it. In a modern industrial society in which many industries are dominated by a small number of firms it is increasingly difficult to rely on traditional competitive market forces alone to protect consumers. Indeed, there are many parts of the economy where conditions of even near perfect competition do not exist. In this situation continuing vigilance over prices is needed.

80. Such vigilance is the more important because price rises inevitably tend to intensify the pressure of wage demands. Unnecessary price rises will therefore exacerbate the problem of keeping the rise in incomes in line with the rise in output.

---

*This possibility is discussed fully in the NBPI Report "Salary Structures" (Cmnd. 4178).

If workers are to be persuaded not to press inflationary wage claims, they must have confidence that greater price stability will follow. They must be confident also that their co-operation in increasing productivity, and technological developments in industry, will be reflected not simply in higher profits but also in a reduction in prices as costs are reduced.

81. The need for a positive prices policy grows as the movement towards larger industrial units proceeds. Market power is being concentrated in a smaller number of firms. The Government recognises the need for this concentration. If industry is to make full use of technological development, and is to command the resources needed for modern research and development, production must in many cases become concentrated in fewer units. That is why the Government established the Industrial Reorganisation Corporation. That is why it has itself brought forward proposals for rationalisation in certain industries. That is why it has raised no objections to the great majority of industrial mergers.

82. Production in many industries will therefore be concentrated in a few large firms. But the Government has always recognised that this greater size and greater concentration may involve risks to the public interest against which proper safeguards must be created. That was one reason why the Government in 1965 extended the monopolies legislation to cover service industries and mergers. That is one reason why the NBPI has been asked to examine proposed price increases in several industries where production is concentrated in a small number of firms. That is one reason why it is proposed to establish the new Commission for Industry and Manpower.

83. The possible dangers from the creation of oligopoly in many manufacturing and service industries have been clearly recognised. Concentration is intended to yield economies of scale in production and marketing which should be reflected in lower prices. But where an industry is dominated by a small group of firms their actions must be influenced to a greater extent by the likely reactions of their few main competitors. In such a situation the significance of price competition may be lessened and other forms of competition assume greater importance. Or a highly efficient firm may set prices at a level above that which would yield an adequate return on capital, thus taking the pressure off the less efficient firms in the industry.

84. Another danger is that the pressure to explore all possible methods of reducing costs may be lessened by the relative ease with which prices can be raised. This is a particular problem in relation to labour costs. There is a risk that a dominant firm, or a small group of firms, may not consider it worthwhile to try to secure productivity-based pay settlements rather than inflationary ones if it seems not too difficult to pass on the resultant costs through higher prices. In some cases a further stimulus may be needed to achieve fully efficient use of labour and other resources, to ensure that pay structures and negotiating procedures are designed to relate pay to performance and to avoid leap-frogging settlements. For example, the development of plant bargaining as against national pay agreements could have inflationary effects unless there are adequate incentives to avoid such inflationary settlements.

85. Enlightened management can and does ensure that these dangers in industrial concentration are avoided, and its advantages secured. The principles underlying the prices policy are widely accepted by industry. Moreover as import tariffs are being reduced British industry has to take greater account of competition from firms abroad, and this provides a new protection to the consumer in some parts of the economy. But the need will remain for machinery through which the community can be satisfied that the principles are being applied in particular cases.

86. The conditions to be satisfied before price increases are made were first set out in the White Paper of April 1965 on Prices and Incomes Policy (Cmnd. 2639). They are reproduced in Appendix 2. Two major points are involved. First, there can be no question of simply passing on in higher prices particular increases in costs of labour, materials or capital. The economic and financial position of the enterprise must be considered as a whole. An increase in labour costs or material costs may well be offset by reductions in other costs. Any attempt automatically to pass on particular increases in costs is quite contrary to this principle.

87. The second major point is that full and realistic account must be taken in considering price levels of the possibilities of cost savings to offset cost increases in whole or part throughout the activities of the enterprise. This must include not only savings already achieved but also the opportunities that exist to reduce costs in the future. This is the principle which has been applied by the NBPI in considering proposals for price increases in both the private and public sectors.

88. Taking the economy as a whole, labour costs are overwhelmingly the largest single element in the final prices of the goods and services bought by consumers. However, the upward trend in productivity means that unit labour costs will not be rising as fast as wage and salary rates. Proposals for price increases which include any element to cover increases in labour costs therefore need the most careful scrutiny. Most firms ought to be able to absorb all, or most, of the cost of pay settlements which fall within the normal range. Firms will be expected to show good grounds for not absorbing at least this amount of the cost of any pay settlements. The cost of any pay increases arising from an efficiency or productivity agreement should automatically be met—indeed more than met—from the savings flowing from the agreement.

89. The prices of some products—particularly foodstuffs and raw materials—are much affected by changes in the supplies available for seasonal or other reasons. Increased prices will then be unavoidable; but where prices rise for these reasons they should fall again when supplies are plentiful.

90. Decisions on price levels inevitably involve decisions on the appropriate level of return on the capital employed in the business. No single figure can be appropriate either for all industries, or for all firms in a particular industry. Exceptional efficiency, rapid technical innovation or a high degree of risk may properly be associated with a higher return on capital in a particular firm or industry than would be appropriate for others. The return on capital achieved in recent years in a particular firm is however not something sacrosanct. It requires to be examined in the light of changing circumstances, and is always relevant to the consideration of price increases. In some cases increases in costs can and should be absorbed in whole or in part by a reduction in profit margins. The Government will continue to examine with special care proposed price increases where the return on capital has been maintained at a high level in a situation where price competition is weak. On the other hand, price increases may sometimes be essential if firms are to secure, either by ploughing back profits or by attracting capital in the open market, resources essential to enable them to modernise and expand their production and to reduce costs. Indeed in some efficient enterprises the return on capital may over a period for special reasons have fallen to so low a level as to jeopardise their long-term future. The Government does not believe that any general reduction in the level of return on capital invested in British industry, whether privately or publicly owned, would be helpful in the context of the essential modernisation of the economy. But what is true in the case of the average level is not necessarily true of individual enterprises.

91. In short, the aim of prices policy is not to keep all prices low at any cost. It is to ensure in each enterprise that changes in prices genuinely reflect unavoidable costs and take account of the possibility of cost savings. General price stability can be achieved only if in certain sectors price reductions occur to offset inevitable increases elsewhere. In these sectors of the economy, where technical innovation or rationalisation of facilities offers opportunities for cost reductions well in excess of the national average, this needs to be reflected in price reductions. A prices and incomes policy which works fairly for the whole community requires that the whole benefit of the cost reductions in these sectors should not go to the workers and shareholders in the firms concerned. The circumstances in which price reductions are called for are set out in Appendix 2.

D. Guidance in Relation to Dividends

92. From the outset of the policy in 1964 the Government has emphasised its intention to use its fiscal powers, or other appropriate means, to correct any excessive growth in aggregate profits, whether distributed or not, as compared with the growth of total wages and salaries, after allowing for short-term fluctuations in profit levels.

Total company profits, as well as the profits of individual companies, may fluctuate considerably from year to year, whereas the total of wages and salaries increases year by year. The *trend* in profits and dividends is therefore normally more relevant to prices and incomes policy than the figures for particular years for individual companies.

93. In 1968 the Government introduced a $3\frac{1}{2}$% ceiling on increases in individual company dividends as a necessary reinforcement of the more general policy of restraint. It was always intended as a short-term measure associated with the stringent powers over other incomes and prices introduced at that time. Although the policy provided for increases in the dividends of individual companies the total of dividends paid on ordinary shares in 1968 was in fact less than the amounts paid in either 1965 or 1966. The figures are given in the following table:—

Dividends on Ordinary Shares
£ million

1965	..	..	1,735
1966	..	..	1,687
1967	..	..	1,576
1968	..	..	1,630

Source: CSO

94. On general grounds a ceiling for dividends paid out by individual companies is undesirable as a long-term policy, and it involves substantial disadvantages in particular cases. For example, fixed dividend limits can affect the ability of companies to raise in the open market additional capital needed for the efficient functioning of their business. A fixed limit may expose firms to take-over bids on terms which do not fairly reflect the value of the undertaking to be acquired. In time also, fixed limits would impede the flow of capital into the most productive channels.

95. Moreover, a rigid control of dividend payments by individual companies may not in itself reduce in the long term the share of the national product accruing to owners of capital. Enforced retention by companies of profits may to some extent be reflected in the long term in capital gains which can be realised. Although therefore limitation of dividends may be helpful as a short term measure, it is not necessarily in the long term an effective instrument of greater social equity, which is better achieved by taxation and other means.

96. For these reasons the $3\frac{1}{2}$% ceiling scheme for dividends will come to an end on 31 December 1969. However, the need for moderation in the distribution of profits to shareholders remains as a proper counterpart to the other elements of the prices and incomes policy. Under Part II of the Prices and Incomes Act 1966, the Government will continue to have the power to require notification of individual dividend increases if this seems desirable. It will also continue to have the power to refer to the NBPI—and later to the CIM—cases where the growth of profits and dividends appears to be based on price levels made possible by excessive market power; and will do so in appropriate cases.

E. Rents and Rates

Rents

97. Rent affects the household budget of millions of families. During 1968 and 1969 the Government successfully prevented undue increases in rents.

98. In the private sector, the great majority of unfurnished tenancies other than those which are still controlled are subject to the rent regulation system set up by the Rent Act 1965. In general the rent of such tenancies can be increased only as the result of the determination of a fair rent by a rent officer or rent assessment committee. In some cases the rent will previously have been low, and the determination of the new rent can involve sharp increases. Under Part III of the Prices and Incomes Act 1968 the Housing Ministers have ensured that such increases occurring during the latter half of 1968 and in 1969 will have been spread out, or "phased", in annual stages.

99. Part III of this Act also required local authorities to obtain the consent of the Housing Ministers to any increase in the rents of council houses. Many local authorities followed the Government's advice and voluntarily refrained from making avoidable rent increases. But in some cases the Housing Ministers had to use their powers to prevent rent increases which were not justified by rising costs or which an authority could avoid by, for example, using housing account balances. In addition the Government adopted the recommendation of the National Board for Prices and Incomes that the rents of any Council should not be increased by more than 7s. 6d. on average in a twelve-month period. Ministers have also been unwilling to authorise increases of more than 10s. a week for any individual house in any year.

100. The powers in the 1968 Act governing rent increases expire at the end of 1969. The Government considers that restraint in rent increases must continue to be an integral part of prices and incomes policy. Measures are therefore being taken to continue the restriction of sharp rent increases for a further period, and a Bill is before Parliament.

101. For regulated tenancies, the Government has brought forward legislation under which phasing of rent increases is to continue for two more years. This will apply to rents registered up to the end of 1971, and will complement the phasing arrangements already introduced under the Housing Acts of 1969 for rent increases resulting from the conversion from rent control to rent regulation of houses in good repair, or from grant-aided improvements.

102. As regards council rents, the Government believes that the principles justifying increases are now well established and understood, and should as far as possible be applied by the local authorities themselves. The Housing Ministers have accordingly agreed with the local authority associations that rents should be increased only to meet unavoidable increases in costs on the basis of guidelines which are being recommended to their members for observance during the period 1 January 1970 to 30 June 1971.

103. The legislation provides that any increase which in any twelve-month period exceeds 7s. 6d. a week on average, or 10s. a week for any individual house, will require the prior consent of the appropriate Minister. This is unlikely to be given save in the most exceptional circumstances.

104. Ministers will continue to ensure under the existing arrangements that restraint in rent increases is applied to houses owned by New Towns and the Scottish Special Housing Association.

Rates

105. Rates, as a form of taxation, are outside the scope of prices and incomes policy: they are necessary to help pay for the range of services provided by local authorities. Better services are bound to cost more money. The Government has taken steps to reduce the impact of rates on householders by providing special grants which have reduced the amount in the £ they have to pay. In England and Wales the reduction has been 5d. in the £ in 1967/68, 10d. in the £ in 1968/69 and 1s. 3d. in the £ this year; the reduction in 1970/71 will be 1s. 8d. in the £. As a result of this, and of the savings made by local authorities, domestic rates were held steady, on average, in 1967/68 and 1968/69, and went up by only 4¼% in 1969/70. In addition the income limits for rate rebates were raised from October 1968 and this has helped many householders with small incomes, particularly those with large families. In Scotland, where rate poundages are higher than in England and Wales, special grants have reduced the amount which householders would otherwise have had to pay by 10d. in the £ in 1967/68, 1s. 8d. in the £ in 1968/69 and 2s. 6d. in the £ this year. With this assistance, domestic rates increased on average by only 7d. in the £ between 1966/67 and 1968/69. It is not yet possible to say what the position will be in 1969/70, because of the later rating year in Scotland.

APPENDIX 1

NATIONAL BOARD FOR PRICES AND INCOMES GUIDELINES FOR EFFICIENCY AGREEMENTS (INCLUDING PRODUCTIVITY AGREEMENTS)

The following guidelines are reproduced from paragraph 133 of NBPI Report No. 123, "Productivity Agreements" (Cmnd. 4136). Each guideline is accompanied by a brief note intended by the Board to clarify its meaning and intended practical application.

1st Guideline

It should be shown that the workers are contributing towards the achievement of constantly rising levels of efficiency. Where appropriate, major changes in working practice or working methods should be specified in the agreement.

The objective of efficiency agreements is to make possible the constant raising of efficiency; this will require close and continuing co-operation between managements and workers so as to achieve and maintain the highest standards in the use of both equipment and manpower. The second sentence has special reference to agreements which specify major changes in working practice to which workers have agreed. Such changes should always be spelled out if there is any possibility that commitments in more general terms will lead to difficulties of interpretation or will not be given full expression in practice.

2nd Guideline

Measurements of efficiency should be based on the application of relevant indices of performance or work standards.

Managements should devise and use appropriate yardsticks for measuring the contribution of workers of all kinds towards achieving rising levels of efficiency and develop an information system which makes full use of the data obtained as a result. For many manual operations work-studied standards are applicable and should be used, but work measurement can also be applied to a wide range of clerical and other non-manual work. For other workers in other situations it will be necessary to use more broadly-based indicators of performance, if necessary on a group basis.

3rd Guideline

A realistic calculation of all the relevant costs of the agreement and of the gains attributable to the workers' contribution should normally show that the effect is to reduce the total cost of output or the cost of providing a given service.

"Relevant costs" may include, for example, the cost of redundancy payments or a proportion of consultants' fees where they are an integral part of an agreement, and these should be apportioned as necessary over a reasonable period rather than charged only to the first year following the agreement. The "gains attributable to the workers' contribution" may result from more effective working methods, the fuller utilisation of existing capital equipment, the adaptation of working practices to enable full and prompt use to be made of new equipment and reduced capital investment (if for example revised scheduling and shift-working make possible a smaller transport fleet). The reference to a reduction in costs assumes a calculation for the purpose of which unrelated costs, e.g. the price of raw materials, are left out of account.

4th Guideline

There should be effective controls to ensure that projected increases in efficiency are achieved and that higher pay or other improvements are made only when such increases are assured.

In order to observe this guideline managements must operate effective controls, including an information system which makes it possible to estimate in advance and subsequently monitor the extent to which increases in efficiency are in fact being achieved. In so far as the information system shows that progress exceeds or falls short of the original projection, some adjustment may need to be made. In any case due allowance should be made for the accrual of some of the achieved gain to the consumer. Particular care also needs to be taken to distinguish the contribution of workers from other sources of more efficient working.

5th Guideline

There should be clear benefits to the consumer by way of a contribution to stable or lower prices.

This guideline is of particular importance in areas of rapid economic expansion, since the most needs to be made of opportunities to reduce prices in these areas in order to contribute as much as possible to raising the real incomes of the community as a whole. In some cases the community may benefit by an improvement in quality while prices remain unchanged or by the use of the gains to compete more effectively in export markets.

6th Guideline

An agreement applying to one group of workers only should bear the cost of consequential increases to other groups, if any have to be granted.

An example would be if supervisors have to be given a pay increase to prevent the disappearance of a differential as a result of a pay increase granted to the workers whom they supervise. The need for consequential increases unrelated to increases in efficiency should, however, be reduced as much as possible by enabling other groups of workers to conclude their own efficiency agreements or by including them within the scope of the original agreement.

7th Guideline

Negotiators should avoid setting levels of pay or conditions which might have undesirable repercussions elsewhere.

Where large increases in pay are shown to be justified negotiators should consider the possibility of staging the increases over a period of time or, alternatively, of a non-recurring lump sum payment. Failure to do so might raise expectations for future increases which could not be fulfilled and might also because of the exceptional size of the increases have repercussions which would eventually rebound on the undertaking granting the original increase.

APPENDIX 2

CRITERIA FOR PRICE INCREASES AND REDUCTIONS

1. Circumstances in one or more of which price increases may be necessary were first set out in April 1965 in the White Paper "Prices and Incomes Policy" (Cmnd. 2639): they are as follows:—

    (i) if output per employee cannot be increased sufficiently to allow wages and salaries to increase at a rate consistent with the guidance on incomes without some increase in prices, and no offsetting reductions can be made in non-labour costs per unit of output or in the return sought on investment;

(ii) if there are unavoidable increases in non-labour costs such as materials, fuel, services or marketing costs per unit of output which cannot be offset by reductions in labour or capital costs per unit of output or in the return sought on investment;

(iii) if there are unavoidable increases in capital costs per unit of output which cannot be offset by reductions in non-capital costs per unit of output or in the return sought on investment;

(iv) if, after every effort has been made to reduce costs, the enterprise is unable to secure the capital required to meet home and overseas demand.

2. The circumstances in one or more of which price reductions are called for were also first set out in Cmnd. 2639: they are as follows:—

(i) if output per employee is increasing faster than the rate of increase in wages and salaries which is consistent with the guidance on incomes, and there are no offsetting and unavoidable increases in non-labour costs per unit of output;

(ii) if the costs of materials, fuel or services per unit of output are falling and there are no offsetting and unavoidable increases in labour or capital costs per unit of output;

(iii) if capital costs per unit of output are falling and there are no offsetting and unavoidable increases in non-capital costs per unit of output;

(iv) if profits are based on excessive market power.

EXPLANATORY NOTE

(*This Note is not part of the Order.*)

This Order sets out the considerations to which the National Board for Prices and Incomes are required to have regard in examining questions relating to prices, incomes and other matters referred to them under section 2 of the Prices and Incomes Act 1966 and in complying with instructions to keep such questions under continuous review under section 3.

The Order provides that, from 8th January 1970, the said considerations shall be those set out in the Schedule to this Order (which reproduces certain sections of the White Paper "Productivity, Prices and Incomes Policy after 1969"—Cmnd. 4237) in substitution for those set out in the Schedule to the Prices and Incomes (General Considerations) Order 1968.

STATUTORY INSTRUMENTS

1969 No. 1894 (L.33)

SUPREME COURT OF JUDICATURE, ENGLAND

PROCEDURE

The Rules of the Supreme Court (Amendment No. 2) 1969

Made - - -	*23rd December* 1969
Laid before Parliament	*6th January* 1970
Coming into Operation	
Rules 1, 2, 3, 4(2), 5, 6, 7	*10th January* 1970
Rules 4(1), 8	*16th February* 1970

We, the Rule Committee of the Supreme Court, being the authority having for the time being power under section 99(4) of the Supreme Court of Judicature (Consolidation) Act 1925(**a**) to make, amend or revoke rules regulating the practice and procedure of the Supreme Court of Judicature, hereby exercise those powers and all other powers enabling us in that behalf as follows:—

1.—(1) These Rules may be cited as the Rules of the Supreme Court (Amendment No. 2) 1969.

(2) In these Rules an Order referred to by number means the Order so numbered in the Rules of the Supreme Court 1965(**b**), as amended (**c**).

(3) The Interpretation Act 1889(**d**) shall apply to the interpretation of these Rules as it applies to the interpretation of an Act of Parliament.

2. In Order 14, rule 2(3), for the words "4 clear days" there shall be substituted the words "10 clear days".

3. Order 20 shall be amended as follows :—

(1) At the end of rule 1(3) there shall be added the words "unless the amendment is made before service of the writ on any party to the action."

(2) In rule 4(1) after the words "on a party" there shall be inserted the words "of a writ amended under rule 1(1) or".

(3) In rule 4(2) after the words "was made under" there shall be inserted the words "rule 1(1) or".

4. Order 22 shall be amended as follows :—

(1) In rule 10(2) the words "on his written authority" and "or, if the Court so orders, to his solicitor without such authority" shall be omitted.

(2) Rule 13 shall be amended by inserting at the beginning the words

---

(**a**) 1925 c. 49.   (**b**) S.I. 1965/1776 (1965 III, p. 4995).
(**c**) There are no relevant amending instruments.   (**d**) 1889 c. 63.

"(1) Subject to paragraph (2)" and by adding at the end the following paragraph :—

"(2) Nothing in paragraph (1) shall restrict the manner of investment of cash transferred to and held by the Public Trustee under a declaration of trust approved by the Court."

5. For paragraph (4) of Order 42, rule 7, there shall be substituted the following paragraph :—

"(4) Every interlocutory order made by a Chancery master or district registrar and required to be drawn up, not being an order to be acted upon by the Accountant General, shall—

(*a*) if the party having the carriage of the order so requests at the time of the making of the order and unless the master or district registrar otherwise directs, be drawn up by that party within 7 days after the order was made and be passed by the master or district registrar before being entered ;

(*b*) in any other case or in case of default by a party in drawing up the order pursuant to sub-paragraph (*a*), be drawn up by or under the direction of a Chancery registrar or the district registrar, as the case may be, and be settled, passed and entered without notice to the parties affected unless the master, the Chancery registrar or district registrar directs that it shall be settled with such parties."

6. Order 65 shall be amended as follows :—

(1) In rule 7 for the words "after twelve noon on a Saturday" there shall be substituted the words "between twelve noon on a Saturday and midnight on the following day".

(2) At the end there shall be added the following rule :—

"Service of process on Sunday

10.—(1) No process shall be served or executed within the jurisdiction on a Sunday except, in case of urgency, with the leave of the Court.

(2) For the purposes of this rule 'process' includes a writ, judgment, notice, order, petition, originating or other summons or warrant."

7. Order 75 shall be amended as follows :—

(1) In rule 10 paragraph (7) shall be omitted and paragraph (8) shall stand as paragraph (7).

(2) At the end of rule 11 there shall be added the following paragraph :—

"(3) Order 65. rule 10, shall not apply in relation to a warrant of arrest or writ in rem."

8. Order 92, rule 5(3), shall be amended as follows :—

(1) For the words "£200 in value" there shall be substituted the words "£500 in value".

(2) The words "by affidavit" shall be omitted.

(3) At the end there shall be added the following paragraph :—

"Unless otherwise directed, an ex parte application under this paragraph shall be made by affidavit".

9. Rules 1, 2, 3, 4(2), 5, 6 and 7 of these Rules shall come into operation on 10th January 1970 and Rules 4(1) and 8 on 16th February 1970.

Dated 23rd December 1969.

Gardiner, C.
Parker of Waddington, C.J.
Denning, M.R.
J. E. S. Simon, P.
Cyril Salmon, L.J.
Denys B. Buckley, J.
John R. Willis, J.
Nigel Bridge, J.
E. S. Fay.
Oliver Lodge.
W. O. Carter.
Arthur J. Driver.

EXPLANATORY NOTE

(This Note is not part of the Rules.)

These Rules amend the Rules of the Supreme Court in a number of respects. The period which must elapse between the service of a summons under Order 14 and the return day is extended from 4 clear days to 10 clear days (Rule 2). It will no longer be necessary to obtain leave for any amendment to a writ which has not yet been served (Rule 3). Order 22 is amended, first, to abolish the need for a solicitor to have his client's express authority to receive money out of court and, secondly, to enable the management of a fund under the control of the court to be entrusted to the Public Trustee under a declaration of trust (Rule 4). The classes of Chancery masters' orders which, instead of being drawn up by or under the authority of a Chancery registrar, may be drawn up by a party's solicitor are widened to include all interlocutory orders, and other changes are made in relation to the drawing up of Chancery orders (Rule 5). Section 6 of the Sunday Observance Act 1677 (C.7), which is repealed by the Statute Law (Repeals) Act 1969 (C.52), is replaced by a new rule (Order 65, rule 10) forbidding the service or execution of process on a Sunday, except, in case of urgency, with the leave of the court (Rule 6), and consequential amendments are made in other rules (Rule 7). The sum which can be paid out of court on an ex parte application to the Chief Chancery Master is raised from £200 to £500 and power is given to dispense with an affidavit (Rule 8).

STATUTORY INSTRUMENTS

1969 No. 1900

TAXES

The Selective Employment Tax (Payments to Public Bodies) (Variation) (No. 2) Order 1969

Made - - -	*31st December* 1969
Laid before Parliament	*9th January* 1970
Coming into Operation	*12th January* 1970

The Treasury, in exercise of the powers conferred on them by section 9(2) of the Selective Employment Payments Act 1966(**a**) and of all other powers enabling them in that behalf, hereby make the following Order :—

1. This Order may be cited as the Selective Employment Tax (Payments to Public Bodies) (Variation) (No. 2) Order 1969, and shall come into operation on 12th January 1970.

2. The Interpretation Act 1889(**b**) shall apply for the interpretation of this Order as it applies for the interpretation of an Act of Parliament.

3.—(1) Part I of Schedule 1 to the Selective Employment Payments Act 1966, as amended (**c**) (which sets out the bodies to which section 3 of that Act applies), shall be further amended by inserting in the said Part I, after paragraph 19, the following paragraph :—

"19A. BEA Airtours Ltd."

(2) Part II of the said Schedule 1, as amended (**d**) (which sets out the excepted parts of the undertakings of bodies to which the said section 3 applies), shall be further amended by adding at the end of the said Part II the following words :—

"NCB Computer Power.

The National Data Processing Service of the Post Office."

E. G. Perry,
Joseph Harper,
Two of the Lords Commissioners
of Her Majesty's Treasury.

31st December 1969.

(**a**) 1966 c.32.
(**b**) 1889 c.63.
(**c**) S.I. 1968/1388 (1968 II, p.3956).
(**d**) S.I. 1968/1388 1622, 1969/1255 (1968 II, p. 3956; III, p.4445; 1969 III, p.3759).

EXPLANATORY NOTE

(This Note is not part of the Order.)

This Order amends Schedule 1 to the Selective Employment Payments Act 1966, which relates to payments to certain public bodies. The Order

adds BEA Airtours Ltd. to the list of undertakings in respect of which refunds of selective employment tax may be made, and

adds NCB Computer Power and The National Data Processing Service of the Post Office to the list of parts of undertakings in respect of which refunds of selective employment tax may not be made.

APPENDIX
OF CERTAIN INSTRUMENTS
NOT REGISTERED AS S.I.

Orders in Council,
Letters Patent
and Royal Instructions

relating to the Constitutions etc. of
Overseas Territories or to appeals to the Judicial
Committee,

Royal Proclamations, etc.

BY THE QUEEN

A PROCLAMATION

ALTERING CERTAIN DAYS FOR BANK HOLIDAYS IN THE YEAR 1970

ELIZABETH R.

Whereas We consider it inexpedient that the Monday in Whitsun week or the first Monday in August should be a bank holiday in England and Wales in the year 1970, or that the first Monday in May should be a bank holiday in Scotland in that year:

Now, therefore, We, in exercise of the powers conferred on Us by section 5 of the Bank Holidays Act 1871(**a**), section 3 of the Holidays Extension Act 1875(**b**), section 1 of the Revenue Offices (Scotland) Holidays Act 1880(**c**), and section 3(3) of the Customs and Excise Act 1952(**d**), do hereby, by and with the advice of Our Privy Council, declare and appoint as follows:—

1. In England and Wales, in the year 1970—

(*a*) the Monday in Whitsun week shall not be a bank holiday, and instead the twenty-fifth day of May shall be a bank holiday ;

(*b*) the first Monday in August shall not be a bank holiday, and instead the thirty-first day of August shall be a bank holiday.

2. In Scotland, in the year 1970, the first Monday in May shall not be a bank holiday, and instead the twenty-fifth day of May shall be a bank holiday.

3. In this Proclamation the expression " bank holiday " shall include a public holiday in the Inland Revenue Offices and a holiday in the Customs and Excise.

Given at Our Court at Buckingham Palace, this twenty-second day of October in the year of our Lord one thousand nine hundred and sixty-nine, and in the eighteenth year of Our Reign.

GOD SAVE THE QUEEN

(**a**) 34 & 35 Vict. c. 17.   (**b**) 38 & 39 Vict. c. 13.
(**c**) 43 & 44 Vict. c. 17.   (**d**) 15 & 16 Geo. 6 & 1 Eliz. 2. c. 44.

SEYCHELLES

The Seychelles (Amendment) Order 1969

At the Court at Buckingham Palace the 22nd day of October 1969

Present,

The Queen's Most Excellent Majesty in Council

Her Majesty, by virtue and in exercise of the powers in Her Majesty vested, is pleased, by and with the advice of Her Privy Council, to order, and it is hereby ordered, as follows:—

1.—(1) This Order may be cited as the Seychelles (Amendment) Order 1969.

(2) This Order shall be construed as one with the Seychelles Order 1967(a) and both Orders may be cited together as the Seychelles Orders 1967 and 1969.

(3) This Order shall be published in the Gazette and shall come into operation on the day on which it is so published.

2. Section 67 of the Seychelles Order 1967 is amended by the deletion of proviso (b) from subsection (1) and the substitution of the following:—

"(b) a person who has attained the age of sixty-two years may be appointed as a judge of the Supreme Court for such period as may be prescribed in the instrument by which he is appointed or a person who has not attained that age may be so appointed for such period (not being less than seven years) as may be so prescribed, in which case he shall vacate his office at the expiration of the period for which he was appointed."

W. G. Agnew.

EXPLANATORY NOTE

(This Note is not part of the Order.)

This Order amends the provisions of the Seychelles Order 1967 relating to the tenure of office of judges of the Supreme Court.

(a) S.I. 1967 Part III, p. 5423.

PACIFIC ISLANDS

The Gilbert and Ellice Islands (Amendment) Order 1969

At the Court at Buckingham Palace the 28th day of November 1969

Present,

The Queen's Most Excellent Majesty in Council

Her Majesty, by virtue and in exercise of the powers in Her Majesty vested, is pleased, by and with the advice of Her Privy Council, to order, and it is hereby ordered, as follows :—

1.—(1) This Order may be cited as the Gilbert and Ellice Islands (Amendment) Order 1969.

(2) This Order shall be construed as one with the Gilbert and Ellice Islands Order in Council 1915(a) and the Gilbert and Ellice Islands Order 1967(b), and those Orders and this Order may be cited together as the Gilbert and Ellice Islands Orders 1915 to 1969.

(3) This Order shall be published in the Colony by exhibition at the Public Office of the Resident Commissioner and printed in the Gazette as soon as may be after the date of such publication and shall come into operation on the date of such publication.

2. Until the next dissolution of the House of Representatives after this Order comes into operation, section 60(2) of the Gilbert and Ellice Islands Order 1967 shall have effect as if for the words " two years " there were substituted the words " four years ".

W. G. Agnew.

EXPLANATORY NOTE

(This Note is not part of the Order.)

This Order extends the life of the present House of Representatives for a maximum period of two years from the date on which it would otherwise have to be dissolved (i.e. 8th December 1969).

(a) Rev. IX, p. 655 (1915 III, p. 315).   (b) S.I. 1967 II, p. 3872.

CLASSIFIED LIST

OF THE

LOCAL
STATUTORY INSTRUMENTS

REGISTERED DURING

1969

TABLE OF CONTENTS

NOTES

1. In the following list the number in brackets after the description of each instrument is the S.I. number of that instrument in the 1969 series.

2. Instruments indicated with an asterisk were not printed and sold by H.M.S.O. Copies will usually be obtained from the local authority or Government Department concerned.

3. The list does not show ministerial orders (including special procedure orders) which are not statutory instruments. Information as to any such orders may be obtained from the local authority or Government Department concerned.

CLASS 1—ROADS, BRIDGES, ROAD TRAFFIC AND RIGHTS OF WAY

(1) *Bridges and tunnels*
(2) *Establishment as highways*
(3) *Parking places*

(4) *Rights of way (extinguishment, stopping up, diversion, re-opening, retention of pipes in highways, etc.)*
(5) *Traffic regulation*

(1) Bridges and tunnels

Minister of Transport—Confirmation Instruments under Highways (Miscellaneous Provisions) Act 1961 (c. 63), s. 3.

Borough of Wallsend (Willington Gut Bridge) Scheme 1968 ... (828).
City of Lincoln (Brayford Head New Bridge) Scheme 1965 ... (455).
County of Lincoln—Ports of Lindsey Crowle Overbridge Scheme 1968 ... (228).
Durham County Council (River Derwent Bridge) Scheme 1968 ... (766).

*BIDEFORD BRIDGE O., made by Minister of Transport under Highways Act 1959 (c. 25), s. 99 ... (720).

TAY ROAD BRIDGE (SCHEME) APPROVAL O., made by Secretary of State under Tay Road Bridge O. Confirmation Act 1962 (c. xxxiii), s. 76 ... (1119).

(2) Establishment as highways

(a) TRUNK ROADS

Restriction of traffic on trunk roads—*see* (5) below.
Trunk roads in built-up areas—*see* (5) below.

(i) England and Wales

Minister of Transport—Orders under Highways Act 1959 (c. 25), s. 7†.

Barons Cross—Skirsgill Section (Trunking) (1033).
Birmingham–Great Yarmouth Trunk Road (Hinckley Road, Leicester) (156).
Coventry–Leicester Trunk Road (Hinckley Road Roundabout, Ansty) (712).
Exeter–Leeds Trunk Road (Stourton Junction) (1863).
Leeds–East of Preston Trunk Road (Whitehall Road Diversion) (578).
Liverpool–Skegness Trunk Road—
  (A.57/M.1 Todwick Junction) (260).
  (Gateford Road, Worksop Diversion) (345).
  (Retford Road) (910).
London–Fishguard Trunk Road—
  (Ffynnon Bridge near Commercial) (926).
  (Wheatley By-Pass Slip Roads, Trunking) (509).
London–Inverness Trunk Road (A.6/M.1 Junction, Kegworth) (28).
London–Thurso Trunk Road (Balderton Diversion Slip Roads) (1468).
North of Oxford–South of Coventry Trunk Road (North of Tackley Turn, De-trunking) (87).
North-West of Wolverhampton–Oakengates Trunk Road (Diversion at Cosford Pumping Station) (313).
West of Maidenhead–Oxford Trunk Road (Crowmarsh Gifford, De-trunking) (281).

Secretary of State—Orders under Highways Act 1959 (c. 25), s. 7†.

Fishguard–Bangor (Menai Suspension Bridge) Trunk Road (Vaynol Junction, Port Dinorwic) 4 Mar. (303).
Neath–Abergavenny Trunk Road (Cefn-Coed-y-Cymmer Link Road) (1242).
Newport–Shrewsbury Trunk Road (East of Hall's Bridge, Llangua) (72).

---

*Not printed for sale in the S.I. series.
†Orders made under this section are liable to special Parliamentary procedure.

Class 1—Roads, Bridges, Road Traffic and Rights of Way—*cont.*

(2) Establishment as highways—*cont.*

(a) TRUNK ROADS—*cont.*

(i) England and Wales—*cont.*

Minister of Transport—Orders under Highways Act 1959 (c. 25), ss. 7†, 44.

Folkestone–Honiton Trunk Road (Cadnam Improvement) (1043).
London–Bristol Trunk Road (Theale Diversion) (99).
London–Edinburgh–Thurso Trunk Road (Eaton Socon Western By-Pass) (Slip Roads) (42).
London–Fishguard Trunk Road (Oxford Northern By-Pass, Connecting Roads) (496).
North West of Doncaster–Kendal Trunk Road (Harden Bridge Diversion) (1648).
Sunderland By-Pass Trunk Road (Connecting Roads) (609).

LONDON–FISHGUARD TRUNK ROAD (LON LAS DIVERSION) O., made by Secretary of State under Highways Act 1959 (c. 25), ss. 7, 44 … (73).

NORMAN CROSS–GRIMSBY TRUNK ROAD (CITY OF PETERBOROUGH NEW TRUNK ROAD (VARIATION) AND WALPOLE STREET/LINCOLN ROAD GYRATORY SYSTEM) O., made by Minister of Transport under Highways Act 1959 (c. 25), ss. 7, 44, 286 … (390).

SWANSEA–MANCHESTER TRUNK ROAD (WREXHAM BY-PASS VARIATION AND SLIP ROADS) O., made by Secretary of State under Highways Act 1959 (c. 25), ss. 7, 44, 286 … (1627).

Minister of Transport—Orders under Highways Act 1959 (c. 25), ss. 7†, 286.

East of London–Southend Trunk Road (Warley Street Improvement Slip Roads) (1474).
Exeter–Leeds Trunk Road (Lichfield By-Pass) (Variation) (132),
Widmerpool–Nottingham–Bawtry–Goole–Howden Trunk Road (Thorne By-Pass) (Revn.) (1220).

LONDON–GREAT YARMOUTH TRUNK ROAD—

(LOWESTOFT INNER HARBOUR BRIDGE TEMPORARY DIVERSION TRUNKING) O., made by Minister of Transport under Highways Act 1959 (c. 25), ss. 7, 20 … (968).

(LOWESTOFT INNER HARBOUR BRIDGE DIVERSION) (No. 2) O., made by Minister of Transport under Highways Act 1959 (c. 25), ss. 7, 20, 286 … (946).

SUNDERLAND BY-PASS TRUNK ROAD O., made by Minister of Transport under Highways Act 1959 (c. 25), ss. 7, 20, 44 … (608).

Minister of Transport—Orders under Highways Act 1959 (c. 25), s. 7†; Local Government Act 1966 (c. 42), s. 27.

Exeter–Leeds Trunk Road (Broadway and Other Roads, Bridgewater) (1009).
London–Cambridge–King's Lynn Trunk Road (High Street, Downham Market, De-trunking) (287).
Norman Cross–Grimsby Trunk Road (Grimsby) (523).
Oxford–Market Deeping Trunk Road (Duddington By-Pass) (347).

Secretary of State—Orders under Highways Act 1959 (c. 25), s. 7†; Local Government Act 1966 (c. 42), s. 27.

Fishguard–Bangor (Menai Suspension Bridge) Trunk Road (Dolbenmaen By-Pass) (92).
London–Fishguard Trunk Road (Llangyfelach to County Borough Boundary De-trunking) (943).

†Orders made under this section are liable to special Parliamentary procedure.

Class 1—Roads, Bridges, Road Traffic and Rights of Way—*cont.*

(2) Establishment as highways—*cont.*

(a) TRUNK ROADS—*cont.*

(i) *England and Wales—cont.*

Minister of Transport—Orders under Highways Act 1959 (c. 25), ss. 7†, 44; Local Government Act 1966 (c. 42), s. 27.

King's Lynn–Newark Trunk Road (Gedney Diversion) (1535).
Levens Bridge–Broughton-in-Furness–Workington–Aspatria–Carlisle Trunk Road (Grizebeck Diversion) (8).
London–Cambridge–King's Lynn Trunk Road (Puckeridge By-Pass) (1439).
London–Fishguard Trunk Road (Britannia Inn Diversion) (346).
London–Great Yarmouth Trunk Road (Margaretting By-Pass) (1620).
London–Norwich Trunk Road (Red Lodge, Freckenham By-Pass) (1557).
London–Penzance Trunk Road—
  (Blackford Hollow Diversion) (172).
  (Haldon Hill, Kenn, Diversion) (56).
  (Linhay Hill, Near Ashburton, Diversion) (171).
  (Maperton Ridge and Dancing Cross Diversion) (827).
London–Portsmouth Trunk Road (Esher By-Pass Slip Roads) (1884).
Nottingham–Stoke-on-Trent Trunk Road (Sudbury By-Pass) (1239).
West of Dishforth–Thirsk Trunk Road (Topcliffe and Asenby Diversion) (625).

LONDON–FISHGUARD TRUNK ROAD (OVER BRIDGE–WESTGATE BRIDGE, GLOUCESTER) O., made by Minister of Transport under Highways Act 1959 (c. 25), ss. 7, 20, 44; Local Govt. Act 1966 (c. 42), s. 27 ... (1639).

LONDON–NORWICH TRUNK ROAD (WYMONDHAM BY-PASS (VARIATION) AND AVENUE ROAD AND NORWICH ROAD, WYMONDHAM DETRUNKING) O., made by Minister of Transport under Highways Act 1959 (c. 25), ss. 7, 286; Local Govt. Act 1966 (c. 42), s. 27 ... (1198).

NOTTINGHAM RING ROAD TRUNK ROAD (CLIFTON BRIDGE AND SLIP ROADS) O., made by Minister of Transport under Highways Act 1959 (c. 25), ss. 7, 20, 44, 286; Local Govt. Act 1966 (c. 42), s. 27 ... (74).

TRUNK ROAD (NORTH CIRCULAR ROAD, BRENT) (PRESCRIBED ROUTE) O., made by Minister of Transport under Road Traffic Regulation Act 1967 (c. 76), s. 6; as amended by Transport Act 1968 (c. 73), Part IX ... (1653).

(ii) *Scotland*

Secretary of State—Orders under Trunk Roads Act 1946 (c. 30), s. 1(2)†.

Connel–Glencoe Trunk Road (South Approach to Connel Bridge Diversion) ... (662).
Edinburgh–Carlisle Trunk Road (Newfaan Isle Diversion) (1186).
Edinburgh–Glasgow Trunk Road (Drumpark, Shawhead and Newhouse Industrial Estate Junctions Slip Roads) (Trunking) (109).
Glasgow–Greenock–Monkton Trunk Road (Langbank and other Diversions) (1882).
Gretna–Stranraer–Glasgow–Stirling Trunk Road—
  (Brae, Bogrie and Deanside Diversions) (877).
  (Kilmarnock Eastern Bypass Slip Roads) (1213).
  (Nether Culzean Diversion) (30).
  (North Drummurran and Other Diversions) (31).
Invergarry–Kyle of Lochalsh Trunk Road (Shiel Bridge–Inverinate Diversion) (223).

---

†Orders made under this section are liable to special Parliamentary procedure.

Class 1—Roads, Bridges, Road Traffic and Rights of Way—*cont*.

(2) Establishment as highways—*cont*.

(*a*) TRUNK ROADS—*cont*.

(*ii*) Scotland—*cont*.

Inverkeithing–Perth Trunk Road (Southfield Diversion) (1568).
London–Carlisle–Glasgow–Inverness Trunk Road—
    (Beattock, Lockerbie, Ecclefechan and Kirtlebridge Junctions Slip Roads)
      (Trunking) (341).
    (Blackwood and Lesmahagow Junctions Slip Roads) (Trunking) (110).
London–Edinburgh–Thurso Trunk Road (Windy House Diversion, Berriedale)
    (102).

Secretary of State—Orders under Trunk Roads Act 1946 (c. 30), ss. 1(2)†, 2(3).

Edinburgh–Glasgow Trunk Road—
    (Dechmont to Whitburn Detrunking) (1629).
    (Newbridge to Dechmont Detrunking) (1630).
Edinburgh–Thurso Trunk Road (Edinburgh to Lathallan Detrunking) (1631).
London–Carlisle–Glasgow–Inverness Trunk Road (Fort William Relief Road)
    (1610).
Newcastle upon Tyne–Edinburgh Trunk Road (Jedburgh Relief Road) (492).
West of Biggar and North of Abington (Trunking and Detrunking) (678).

*Secretary of State—Orders under Trunk Roads Acts 1936 (c. 5), s. 13(2); 1946
(c. 30), ss. 1(2), 11(4).*

Gretna–Stranraer–Glasgow–Stirling Trunk Road (Kilmarnock Eastern By-Pass)
    (Variation) (1212).
London–Edinburgh–Thurso Trunk Road (Granthouse and other Diversions)
    (Variation) (1760).

LONDON–EDINBURGH–THURSO TRUNK ROAD—

(DALMAGARRY DIVERSION) O., made by Secretary of State under Trunk Roads
    Act 1946 (c. 30), s. 1(2); Special Roads Act 1949 (c. 32), s. 14(5) ... (239).

(CONONBRIDGE AND MARYBURGH BY-PASS) (REVN.) O., made by Secretary of State
    under Trunk Roads Acts 1936 (c. 5), s. 13(2); 1946 (c. 30), s. 11(4) ... (1271).

(*b*) SPECIAL ROADS

(*i*) *England and Wales*

*Minister of Transport—Special Roads Schemes under Highways Act 1959 (c. 25),
ss. 11†, 12, 14, 286.*

Bradford (Oakenshaw–Staygate) Motorways Scheme 1968 Confirmation (1769).
Edgware Road and North Circular Road Flyovers Special Roads (817).
Gloucestershire County Council Special Road Schemes (Revn.) Scheme 1969
    ... (1245).
Greater London Council (Eastway to Grand Union Canal) Motorway Scheme 1968
    Confirmation (1539).
Lancashire County Council—
    Liverpool Outer Ring Road (Netherton to Kirkby) Special Roads Scheme 1968
      Confirmation (852).
    (Manchester Outer Ring Road Northern Section Middleton Link to the
      Lancashire/Yorkshire Motorway) Special Roads Scheme 1968 Confirmation
      (1387).

---

†Orders made under this section are liable to special Parliamentary procedure.

Class 1—Roads, Bridges, Road Traffic and Rights of Way—*cont.*

(2) Establishment as highways—*cont.*

(*b*) SPECIAL ROADS—*cont.*

(*i*) *England and Wales*—*cont.*

Leeds (Inner Ring Road Stage IIA) Special Roads Scheme 1969 Confirmation
(1660).
M.4 Motorway—
(Wickham to Theale Section) Connecting Roads (284).
(Theale to Winnersh Section) Connecting Roads (No. 2) (70).
M.5 Motorway (Cribbs Causeway–South of Almondsbury) (1150).
M.25 South Orbital Motorway (Merstham Interchange) Connecting Roads (1192).
M.62—
(Lancashire–Yorkshire) Motorway (River Calder, Clifton–Gildersome Street)
Connecting Roads (582).
Lancashire–Yorkshire Motorway (Tarbock to Croft Section) Connecting Roads
(1892).
Newcastle upon Tyne Central Motorway East Scheme 1966 Confirmation (669).
South of Fiveways Corner–North Circular Road, Hendon, Special Roads (818).
West of Slough–West of Maidenhead Special Road (Variation) (No. 2) … (1122).
West Riding (Cleckheaton–Oakenshaw) Motorways Scheme 1968 Confirmation
(1770).

EAST OF LLANSAMLET–LLANGYFELACH SPECIAL ROADS SCHEME; made by Secretary
of State under Highways Act 1959 (c. 25), ss. 11, 12, 14 … (71).

(*ii*) *Scotland*

KINROSS AND MILNATHORT BY-PASS (CONNECTING ROADS) SPECIAL ROAD SCHEME,
made by Secretary of State under Special Roads Act 1949 (c. 32), ss. 1, 2, 9 (1567).

(*c*) METROPOLITAN ROADS*

*London Government (Metropolitan Roads) Orders made by Minister of Transport
under London Government Act 1963 (c. 33), s. 17.*

(210).
(No. 2) (657).
(No. 3) (789).
(No. 4) (1224).
(No. 5) (1463).

(*d*) COUNTY ROADS*

*County Roads Cesser Orders made by Minister of Transport under Highways Act
1959 (c. 25), s. 22.*

Hertford—
(No. 1) (192).
(No. 2) (1094).
Leicester (No. 1) (666).
Salop (No. 1) (1207).

(3) Parking places

PARKING PLACES AND CONTROLLED PARKING ZONE (MANCHESTER) (1966) (VARIA-
TION) O., made by Minister of Transport under Road Traffic Regulation Act 1967
(c. 76), s. 35(6) … (138).

---

*Not printed for sale in the S.I. series.

Class 1—Roads, Bridges, Road Traffic and Rights of Way—*cont.*

(4) Rights of way (extinguishment, stopping up, etc.)

Stopping up of Highways Orders made by Secretary of State under Town and Country Planning (S.) Act 1947 (c. 53), s. 46†.

Coatbridge (1663).
Edinburgh—
(Carrington Crescent) (160).
(Giles Street, Leith) (577).
(Porterfield Road) (956).
(St. Leonards) (No. 2) (1776).
Glasgow—
(Cowcaddens)—
(No. 1) (1097).
(No. 2) (1403).
(Townhead No. 2) (1546).

Johnstone (969).
Kirkcaldy—
(1458).
Dysart (1584).
Links Street/Esplanade (795).
Sinclairtown (1623).
Stirling (1507).

(5) Traffic regulation

(a) England and Wales   (b) Scotland

(a) ENGLAND AND WALES*

(i) General Regulation

Minister of Transport—Order under Road Traffic Regulation Act 1967 (c. 76), ss. 1, 2, 3, 6, 9, 10, 84D; as amended by Transport Act 1968 (c. 73), Part IX.

BOX JUNCTIONS—
Blyth Level Crossing (1131).
Broxbourne, High Road (1298).
Cheadle (1417).
Guildford, Woodbridge Road (1465).
Malton Level Crossing (775).

BOX JUNCTIONS—*cont.*
Redhill, London Road (12).
Salisbury, High Street, Wilton Road and Rampart Road (123).
Stroud, Merrywalks (751).
Turnhead and York Road Level Crossings (891).

TRUNK ROAD (MANCHESTER ROAD, DENTON) (CLOSURE OF GAPS) O., made by Minister of Transport under Road Traffic Regulation Act 1967 (c. 76), s. 1 ... (1300).

ONE WAY—
Cheltenham (1839).
Cullompton By-Pass (1524).
Hoddesdon Various Roads (1010).
Macclesfield, Mill Street (1088).
Rawtenstall, Queen's Square (332).
Slough, Bath Road Service Road (190).
Upton, Long Lane (1783).
PRESCRIBED ROUTES—
Enfield, Great Cambridge Road (140).
Exeter (405).
Maidenhead, High Street (1314).
PROHIBITION OF CYCLING—
Braunstone, Leicestershire (391).
Bromsgrove (982).
PROHIBITION OF DRIVING—
Askham Bryan, Junction with Mill Lane (25).
Beeston, Derby Road (139).
Birstall, Leicestershire (241).
Borrowash By-Pass (229).
Camberley, London Road (681).
Cheshunt, Great Cambridge Road (1788).
Crawley—
Cycle Tracks (1619).
London Road (106).
Egham By-Pass (14).
Honiton, Ottery Moor Lane (983).
Ingleby Arncliffe, Yorkshire (1158).
Lowton, East Lancashire Road (750).
Rugby, London Road, Junction with—
Freeboard Lane (515).
Rugby Lane (516).
Ryton-on-Dunsmore, London Road, Junctions with Church Road and High Street (1885).
Sawtry, Ermine Street, Junctions with Toft Hill and Slough Lane (726).
Stannington (981).
Washbrook By-Pass, East Suffolk (765).

PROHIBITION OF ENTRY AND EXIT—
Dartford, Princes Road (685).
Egham, Egham Hill (916).
Long Eaton, Tamworth Road (57).
South Mimms By-Pass, Hertfordshire (249).
PROHIBITION OF LEFT TURNS—
Egham By-Pass (960).
PROHIBITION OF RIGHT TURNS—
Allesley, Junction with Oak Lane (422).
Alveston, Gloucestershire (1040).
Bingham, Nottinghamshire (1464).
Bletchley, Bucks. (300).
Chatham (5).
Folkestone (991).
Gillingham and Chatham, Rainham Road (1249).
High Wycombe, Oxford Road (563).
Hothfield Cross Roads (627).
London–Carlisle–Glasgow–Inverness (331).
Mirfield, Slipper Lane (82).
Nottingham, Western Boulevard (124).
Sale, Sibson Road and School Road (815).
PROHIBITION OF THROUGH TRAFFIC—
Atcham, Nesscliffe (1123).
Gobowen, Chirk Road (198).
PROHIBITION OF U TURNS—
Enfield and Cheshunt, Great Cambridge Road (1789).
Golden Valley By-Pass, Gloucestershire (1350).
PROHIBITION OF WAITING—
Addington, Kent, East of Aldon Road (1221).
Andover, Weyhill Road (1041).
Barham, Kent (1356).
Bath–Cheltenham–Evesham–Coventry–Leicester–Lincoln (1421); (1857).
Belford, High Street and Church Street (1525).
Blyth, Darsham Railway Station (1159).
Boreham, Main Road (1838).

*Not printed for sale in the S.I. series.
†Orders made under this section are liable to special Parliamentary procedure.

Class 1—Roads, Bridges, Road Traffic and Rights of Way—*cont.*

(5) Traffic regulation—*cont.*

(a) ENGLAND AND WALES*—*cont.*

(i) General regulation—*cont.*

PROHIBITION OF WAITING—*cont.*
Broadoak, Gloucestershire (113).
Castlegate, Cockermouth (13).
Cheltenham, Hewlett Road (162).
Dymchurch, Hythe Road (836).
Exeter–Leeds, Clearways (476).
Fenny Stratford, High Street and Denbigh Road; 14 July (959).
Flemingate, Beverley (622).
Gosforth, High Street and Great North Road (952).
Harbledown, Kent, London Road and Church Hill (431).
Horndean, London Road (802).
Leominster, High Street and Broad Street (1606).
Lexden, London Road (1431).
Liphook, Hampshire (711).
Liverpool, Walton Hall Avenue and East Lancashire Road (334).
Liverpool–Preston–Leeds, Clearways (1289).
London–Aylesbury–Warwick–Birmingham, Clearways (1854).
London–Bristol, Clearways (1157).
London–Cambridge–Kings Lynn Trunk Road, Clearways—
(157).
(Amdt.) (564).
London–Folkestone–Dover, Clearways (957).
London–Great Yarmouth, Clearways (1694).
London–Holyhead, Clearways (1576).
London–Norwich, Clearways—
(1898).
(Amdt.) (565).
London–Portsmouth, Clearways (112).
Lowdon, East Lancashire Road Service Road (706).
Lymm, Higher Lane (1218).
Melbourn, High Street (1840).
Newcastle-upon-Tyne–Edinburgh (Newcastle Airport) (1223).
North Hykeham, Newark Road (787).
Northchurch, High Street (650).
Norton, Commercial Street (10).
Nottingham, Western Boulevard (114).
Old Stratford and Potterspury (1802).
Poynton, London Road (1287).
Pyecombe, Cuckfield, East Sussex (607).
Rushden, Higham Road and High Street South (704).
Sittingbourne, London Road (1056).
Spalding, Various Roads (107).
Stratton St. Margaret, Wiltshire, Various Roads (1649).
Tamworth Road (1160).
Taunton, Various Streets—
(50).
Amdt. No. 2 (308).
Thatcham, Chapel Street (393).
West of Maidenhead–Oxford, Clearways (1301).
Winchester–Preston, Clearways—
(774).
No. 2 (823).
PROHIBITION AND RESTRICTION OF WAITING—
Arundel, Sussex, High Street and Queen Street (673).
Berwick-upon-Tweed, Golden Square, Marygate and Castlegate (718).
Beverley, Various Roads (6).
Bideford (1477).
Brampton (649).
Duffield, Derbyshire (248).
Epping, High Street (914).
Henley-on-Thames, Various Roads—
(780).
Variation (1283).
Lancaster, Various Roads (120).
Matlock, Various Roads (333).
Otley, Various Roads (1593).
Penwortham, Liverpool Road (824).
Rye, Winchelsea Road, The Strand Quay and South Undercliff (623).

PROHIBITION AND RESTRICTION OF WAITING—*cont.*
Saxmundham, North Entrance, High Street and South Entrance (49).
Shifnal, Victoria Road, Market Place and Park Street (719).
Stafford, Various Roads (531).
Winborne Minster, Dorset (569).
Wrentham, High Street (796).
PROHIBITION OF WAITING, LOADING AND UNLOADING—
Boston, High Street, Strait Bargate and Wide Bargate (786).
Hatfield, Yorkshire (514).
Larkfield, Kent, London Road (652).
Little Hulton, Manchester Road West and Manchester Road East (343).
Plympton, Plymouth, The Ridgeway (725).
Ripley, Surrey, High Street (1251).
Rochester—
City (917).
Star Hill (1590).
Salfords, Surrey (1763).
PROHIBITION AND RESTRICTION OF WAITING, LOADING AND UNLOADING—
Brownhills, High Street (683).
Cambridge, Mitchams Corner (950).
Evesham, Various Streets (485).
Hereford, Various Roads (1124).
Salisbury, Various Roads (801).
Warminster, Various Roads (853).
Wellington, Mantle Street, Fore Street and High Street (24).
Whitefield, Bury New Road (392).
PROHIBITION AND RESTRICTION OF WAITING AND ONE-WAY TRAFFIC—
Abingdon, Various Roads (58).
PROHIBITION AND RESTRICTION OF WAITING, LOADING AND UNLOADING AND ONE-WAY—
Worksop, Various Roads (406).
PROHIBITION OF WAITING AND RESTRICTION OF WAITING, LOADING AND UNLOADING—
Hazel Grove, London Road, Buxton Road and Macclesfield Road (426).
RESTRICTION OF WAITING—
Beeston, Various Roads (755).
Bury St. Edmunds, Various Roads (66).
Carlton, High Street (444).
Clitheroe, Various Streets (1228).
Cross Gates, Leeds Ring Road and Station Road (119).
Dover, Folkestone Road (1355).
Hayle, Various Roads (932).
Hemel Hempstead, London Road—
(1002).
Amdt. (1625).
Hoddesdon, Various Roads (993).
King's Lynn, Wisbech Road and Hardwick Road (335).
Lowestoft, Various Roads (65).
Morley, Various Roads (1280).
Shipley, Bradford Road and Bingley Road (1225).
Spilsby, Church Street and Boston Road (1222).
Tring (1554).
RESTRICTION OF WAITING, LOADING AND UNLOADING—
Cambridge, Mitcham's Corner (404).
Peterborough (961).
Prestwick, Bury New Road (1182).
Swinton and Pendlebury, Chorley Road—
(301).
Amdt. (1408).
Walton-le-Dale, Victoria Road and Chorley Road (1856).
Warmsworth (1466).
Worsbrough, Park Road (394).
TRAFFIC REGULATION—
Alnwick, Various Streets (908).
Kendal, Various Roads (1279).
Maidenhead, High Street and Bridge Street (1667).
WEIGHT RESTRICTION—
Beverley, North Bar (282).
Lowestoft Swing Bridge (992).

*Not printed for sale in the S.I. series.

Class 1—Roads, Bridges, Road Traffic and Rights of Way—*cont.*

(5) Traffic regulation—*cont.*

(a) ENGLAND AND WALES*—*cont.*

(i) General regulation—*cont.*

Secretary of State— Orders under Road Traffic Regulation Act 1967 (c. 76), ss. 1, 3, 108.

NO RIGHT TURN—
  Llanfoist Refuse Tip (1435).
ONE-WAY—
  Pembroke, Various Slip Roads (1899).
PRESCRIBED ROUTES—
  Dixon By-Pass, Monmouth (1166).
PROHIBITION OF WAITING—
  Chester–Bangor, Clearways, Wales No. 1 (900).
  Colwyn Bay, Conway Road (447).

PROHIBITION OF WAITING—*cont.*
  Llandudno Junction Flyover (1051).
  Newport – Monmouth – Ross-on-Wye – Worcester,
    Clearways, Wales No. 1 (587).
  Ruabon, Bridge Street (188).
PROHIBITION AND RESTRICTION OF WAITING—
  Portmadoc, Various Roads (116).
  Builth Wells, Brecon (1266).
RESTRICTION OF WAITING—
  Pontardulais, St. Teilo Street (130).

Miscellaneous restrictions

Trunk Roads (Restricted Roads) Orders made by Minister of Transport under Road Traffic Regulation Act 1967 (c. 76), ss. 72(3), 73(1)(4)(5), 74(1)(6).

No. 1.	A.428.	Bromham (125).		No. 6.	A.339.	Kingsclere (1438).
No. 2.	A.1.	Morpeth (307).		No. 7.	A.361.	Swimbridge (1545).
No. 3.	A.69.	Lemington (603).		No. 8.	A.4.	Calne (1615).
No. 4.	A.49.	Bromfield (1217).		No. 9.	A.12.	Colchester (1722).
No. 5.	A.339.	Kingsclere (1281).		No. 10.	A.10.	Turnford (1768).

BOROUGH OF STALYBRIDGE (RESTRICTED ROADS) O., made by Minister of Transport under Road Traffic Regulation Act 1967 (c. 76), ss. 72(3), 73(1), 84D(i); as amended Transport Act 1968 (c. 73), Part IX ... (1176).

Trunk Roads (Restricted Roads) Orders made by Secretary of State under Road Traffic Regulation Act 1967 (c. 76), ss. 72(3), 73(1), 84D, 108; as amended by Transport Act 1968 (c. 73) Pt. IX.

No. 1.	A.48.	Groes, Wales (977).		No. 2.	A.483.	Penllergaer (1895).
No. 1.	Amdt.	(1267).				

Trunk Roads (40 m.p.h. Speed Limit) Orders made by Minister of Transport under Road Traffic Regulation Act 1967 (c. 76), s. 74.

No. 1.	A.428.	Bromham (133).		No. 15.	A.435.	Greehill (965).
No. 2.	A.12.	Blythburgh (134).		No. 16.	A.2.	River (990).
No. 3.	A.560.	Longdondale (135).		No. 17.	A.2.	Dartford (1031).
No. 4.	A.40.	Churchdown (230).		No. 18.	A.435.	Cheltenham (1111).
No. 5.	A.12.	Yoxford (237).		No. 19.	A.41.	Handley (1142).
No. 6.	A.58.	Brighouse (306).		No. 20.	A.41.	Aylesbury (1208).
No. 7.	A.4.	Hungerford (443).		No. 21.	A.595.	Cummersdale (1282).
No. 8.	A.34.	Newbold-on-Stour (497).		No. 22.	A.27.	Lewes (1299).
No. 9.	A.69.	Lemington (602).		No. 23.	A.11.	Woodford Green (1412).
No. 10.	A.38.	Bittaford (626).		No. 24.	A.570.	Scarisbrick (1480).
No. 11.	A.34.	Abingdon and Wantage (773).		No. 25.	A.6.	Milton Ernest (1489).
No. 12.	A.3.	Guildford (947).		No. 26.	A.449.	Broadwaters (1577).
No. 13.	A.435.	Bishops Cleeve (948).		No. 27.	A.146.	Bracondale (1748).
No. 14.	A.41.	Christleton (949).		No. 28.	A.34.	Hockley Heath (1897).

Trunk Roads (40 m.p.h. Speed Limit) Orders made by Secretary of State under Road Traffic Regulation Act 1967 (c. 76), ss. 74(1), 108.

No. 1.	A.48.	Pwllmeryric (220).		No. 3.	A.487.	Tremadon and Penmorfa (1197).
No. 2.	A.492.	Llanidloes (221).		No. 4.	A.483.	Bonllwyn (1655).

CITY OF WORCESTER (40 M.P.H. SPEED LIMIT) O., made by Minister of Transport under Road Traffic Regulation Act 1967 (c. 76), s. 74(1)(2) ... (1540).

---

*Not printed for sale in the S.I. series.

Class 1—Roads, Bridges, Road Traffic and Rights of Way—*cont.*

(5) Traffic regulation—*cont.*

(a) ENGLAND AND WALES*—*cont.*

(i) General regulation—cont.

LONDON TRAFFIC (40 M.P.H. SPEED LIMIT) (NO. 1) REGULATIONS (VARIATION) O., made by Minister of Transport under Road Traffic Regulation Act 1967 (c. 76), ss. 74(1), 84D(1); as amended Transport Act 1968 (c. 73), Part IX ... (1200).

Trunk Roads (50 m.p.h. Speed Limit) Orders made by Minister of Transport under Road Traffic Regulation Act 1967 (c. 76), s. 74(1).

No. 1.	A.11.	Buckhurst Hill (136).		No. 4.	A.41.	Colne Way, Watford (1656).
No. 2.	A.23.	Sayers Common (1422).		No. 5.	A.631.	Tinsley Viaduct (1855).
No. 3.	A.12.	Colchester (1723).				

Trunk Roads (50 m.p.h. Speed Limit) (England) (Variation) Orders made by Minister of Transport under Road Traffic Regulation Act 1967 (c. 76), s. 74(1)(6), 84D(1).

No. 1.	A.60.	Leapool (11).		No. 3.	A.4019.	Coombe Hill (958).
No. 2.	A.45.	Bury St. Edmunds (48).		No. 4.	A.1.	Hatfield (1199).
	B.108.	Kentford.				

TRUNK ROADS (50 M.P.H. SPEED LIMIT) (WALES) (NO. 1) O., made by Secretary of State under Road Traffic Regulation Act 1967 (c. 76), s. 74(1), 108; as amended by Transport Act 1968 (c. 73), Part IX ... (745).

(ii) Temporary restrictions

Minister of Transport—Orders under Road Traffic Regulation Act 1967 (c. 76), s. 12.

ONE-WAY—
 Hereford, Edgar Street (236).
 Huntingdon, High Street (811).
 Norwich, King Street (263).
 Slough, Sussex Place (1193).
PRESCRIBED ROUTES—
 East Ham and Barking By-Pass, Newham (1112).
 Kingston-upon-Thames, Hook Rise (100).
 Redbridge, Eastern Avenue (1716).
 Rochester Way, Bexley (651).
 Watford Way, Barnet (1250).
PROHIBITION OF RIGHT-HAND TURN—
 Cheshunt, Cambridge Road—
  (262).
  (No. 2) (617).
PROHIBITION OF TRAFFIC—
 Alnwick By-Pass (524).
 Altrincham, Durham Road (498).
 Bamber Bridge Station Level Crossing, Walton-le-Dale (1650).
 Banbury, Southam Road (772).
 Barnet, Great North Way (803).
 Beckingham, Sleaford Road (266).
 Bere Regis, North Street (265).
 Beverley, North Bar (1183).
 Birmingham–Preston Motorway, M.6 (234).
 Blythe Bridge Level Crossing (9).
 Cannock, Walsall Road (1455).
 Carlton-on-Trent and Sutton-on-Trent (525).
 Cheshunt, Great Cambridge Road—
  (809).
  (No. 2) (933).
 Colne Way, Watford (1288)
 Cromwell By-Pass (797).
 Ealing, Western Avenue (1258).
 Eamont Bridge (645).
 Enderby, Narborough Road South (771).
 Fareham, Hampshire (616).
 Foston Cross Roads (656).
 Grantham By-Pass—
  (88).
  (1400).
  Variation (1556).

PROHIBITION OF TRAFFIC—*cont.*
 Holbeach, Washway Road—
  (1555).
  (No. 2) (1862).
 Ketley Level Crossing (445).
 Kildwick Level Crossing—
  (396).
  No. 2 (1668).
 Kingston-upon-Thames—
  Hook Rise and Tolworth Rise—
   (141).
  No. 2 (684).
  Hook Rise South (199).
  Malden Way—
   (446).
  No. 2 (837).
  No. 3 (984).
 Lancaster By-Pass M.6 (264).
 Lichfield Road (788).
 Llanymynech Railway Bridge, Salop (1418).
 Lowestoft Swing Bridge (181).
 Long Bennington, Great North Road (1357).
 Newark By-Pass (1313).
 Northampton, St. Peters Bridge (1616).
 Quinton (951).
 Stoke-on-Trent, Newcastle Road (186).
 Teesside, Wolviston Road (1790).
 Whitefield Station Bridge (267).

PROHIBITION OF TRAFFIC AND ONE-WAY—
 Chippenham, The Causeway (529).
 Hereford, Various Streets (816).
 Whitfield, Gloucestershire—
  (548).
  No. 2 (1358).

PROHIBITION AND RESTRICTION OF TRAFFIC—
 Altrincham Level Crossing (1692).
 Doublebois Bridge, Cornwall (1693).
 Hounslow, Hogarth Roundabout (604).
 Kingston-upon-Thames, Tolworth Rise (358).

---

*Not printed for sale in the S.I. series.

Class 1—Roads, Bridges, Road Traffic and Rights of Way—*cont.*

(5) Traffic regulation—*cont.*

(a) ENGLAND AND WALES*—*cont.*

(ii) Temporary restrictions—cont.

RESTRICTION OF TRAFFIC—
  Barnet—
    Fiveways Corner (1057).
    Watford Way and Hall Lane—
      (754).
      (No. 2) (1248).
      (No. 3) (1490).
  Bideford Long Bridge (1252).
  Bodmin, Fore Street (1032).
  Cheltenham, Various Roads (1669).
  Chiswick–Langley–Maidenhead—
    (1238).
    (No. 2) (1381).
    (No. 3) (1657).
  Chiswick–North of Harmondsworth (966).
  Claydon Bridge, East Suffolk (1718).

RESTRICTION OF TRAFFIC—*cont.*
  Dirt House Hill (1893).
  Fareham, Titchfield Road (1553).
  Kingston-upon-Thames (Malden Way)—
    (33).
    (No. 2) (967).
    (No. 3) (1491).
  M.4 Motorway (1640).
  Newport Canal Bridge (1801).
  Preston By-Pass Motorway (M.6) ... (183).
  Redbridge, Various Roads (43).
  Shrewsbury, Castle Street and Castle Gates (1286).
  Slough, Various Roads (1411).
  Whitefield Station Bridge—
    (Phase I) (182).
    (Phase III) (579).

Secretary of State—Orders under Road Traffic Regulation Act 1967 (c. 76), ss. 12, 108.

PROHIBITION OF TRAFFIC—
  Cardiff, St. Athans Road (93).
  Cross Hands Railway Bridge (661).
  Chain Bridge, Llandovery (782).
  River Elwy Bridge, St. Asaph (1698).

  Ruthin, Rhos Street (1608).
  Taffs Well (1318).
  Trefechan Railway Bridge (44).

REGULATION OF TRAFFIC ON ALTERNATIVE ROADS—
  River Ely Bridge, Cowbridge Road West, Cardiff (885).

WEIGHT RESTRICTION—
  River Ely Bridge, Cowbridge Road West, Cardiff (615).

RESTRICTION OF TRAFFIC—
  Holy Island, Anglesey (1363).

TRUNK ROAD (BRIDGE STREET AND WHITEHART STREET, THETFORD) (TEMPORARY TRAFFIC REGULATION) O., made by Minister of Transport under Road Traffic Regulation Act 1967 (c. 76), s. 12 ... (261).

TRUNK ROAD (DOCK ROAD BRIDGE) (TEMPORARY 20 M.P.H. SPEED LIMIT) O., made by Minister of Transport under Road Traffic Regulation Act 1967 (c. 76), s. 12 ... (235).

TRUNK ROAD (M.5 MOTORWAY NEAR BROMSGROVE) (TEMPORARY PROHIBITION OF TRAFFIC AND PROHIBITION OF OVERTAKING) O., made by Minister of Transport under Road Traffic Regulation Act 1967 (c. 76), s. 12 ... (395).

TRUNK ROAD (ROCHESTER WAY, BEXLEY) (TEMPORARY SPEED LIMIT) O., made by Minister of Transport under Road Traffic Regulation Act 1967 (c. 76), s. 12 ... (605).

TRUNK ROAD (ST. PETER'S BRIDGE, NORTHAMPTON) (TEMPORARY WEIGHT RESTRICTION) O., made by Minister of Transport under Road Traffic Regulation Act 1967 (c. 76), s. 12 ... (1666).

TRUNK ROAD (WESTERN AVENUE, EALING) (TEMPORARY SUSPENSION OF RESTRICTION) O., made by Minister of Transport under Road Traffic Regulation Act 1967 (c. 76), s. 12 ... (606).

---

*Not printed for sale in the S.I. series.

Class 1—Roads, Bridges, Road Traffic and Rights of Way—*cont.*

(5) Traffic regulation—*cont.*

(*a*) ENGLAND AND WALES*—*cont.*

(iii) Experimental traffic schemes

Minister of Transport—Orders under Road Traffic Regulation Act 1967 (c. 76), ss. 9, 10, 84(1)(D), 108.

PRESCRIBED ROUTES—
Barnet—
  Edgware Road (1467).
  Edgware Way—
    (1151).
    (No. 2) (1747).
Enfield, North Circular Road—
  (283).
  Variation (1886).
Havering—
  New Road (1717).
  Southend Arterial Road (810).

PROHIBITION OF RIGHT-HAND TURN—
  Bodicote, Oxfordshire (421).
PROHIBITION AND RESTRICTION OF WAITING—
  Lewes, High Street and Western Road (342).
  Ross-on-Wye, Gloucester Road (717).
PROHIBITION AND RESTRICTION OF WAITING, LOADING
  AND UNLOADING—
  Maidenhead, High Street and Bridge Road (336).
RESTRICTION OF WAITING—
  Aylesbury, High Street (1284).
TRAFFIC REGULATION—
  Lewes, Various Roads (994).

TRUNK ROAD (CONWAY ROAD, COLWYN BAY) (RESTRICTION OF WAITING) (EXPERIMENTAL) O., made by Secretary of State under Road Traffic Regulation Act 1967 (c. 76), ss. 9, 108 … (448).

(*b*) SCOTLAND*

(i) General regulation

Secretary of State—Orders under Road Traffic Regulation Act 1967 (c. 76), ss. 1, 3, 12, 84D.

BOXED CROSSING—
  Gollanfield Level Crossing, Inverness-shire (1442).
CLEARWAYS—
  Kincardine–Kirkcaldy (40).
PROHIBITION OF WAITING—
  Auchinleck (1394).
  Balannan Railway Bridge, A.75 (7).
  Carluke (1561).
  Castle Douglas (530).
  Glasgow–Inverness, Loch Lomond (1147).
  Inveraray (561).
  Lochgilphead (576).

PROHIBITION OF WAITING—*cont.*
  Newton Mearns, Broom Shops (899).
  Tain (1148).
PROHIBITION OF WAITING AND LOADING—
  Cumnock (526).
  Jedburgh, High Street (527).
  Irvine (1727).
RESTRICTION OF WAITING—
  Galashiels—
    (467).
    Amdt. (1395).
  Maybole (934).
  Thurso (643).

Miscellaneous restrictions

Trunk Roads (Restricted Roads) Orders made by Secretary of State under Road Traffic Regulation Act 1967 (c. 76), ss. 72, 73.

No. 1. A.1.   Macmerry (75).

No. 2. A.985.   Kincardine-on-Forth, Toll Road (1562).

Trunk Roads (40 m.p.h. Speed Limit) Orders made by Secretary of State under Road Traffic Regulation Act 1967 (c. 76), s. 74.

No. 1. A.977.   Blairgone, Kinross (1448).

No. 2. A.92.   Arbroath, Angus (1098).

TRUNK ROAD (THE COUNTY OF ROSS AND CROMARTY (SPEED LIMIT) O., 1945) (REVN.) O., made by Secretary of State under Road Traffic Regulation Act 1967 (c. 76), ss. 74, 84 as amended Transport Act 1968 (c. 73), Part IX … (1560).

(ii) Temporary restrictions

Secretary of State—Orders under Road Traffic Regulation Act 1967 (c. 76), ss. 12, as amended Transport Act 1968 (c. 73), Part IX.

PROHIBITION OF TRAFFIC—

  Kirkcaldy–St. Andrews (1320).
  Motorways (M90), Duloch–Masterton (1191).

---

*Not printed for sale in the S.I. series.

Class 1—Roads, Bridges, Road Traffic and Rights of Way—*cont.*

(5) Traffic regulation—*cont.*

(*b*) SCOTLAND*—*cont.*

(*ii*) *Temporary restrictions*—*cont.*

SPEED LIMIT—

Carlisle–Glasgow–Inverness (Route A.82) (30 m.p.h.)—
   (1755).
   (No. 2) (1901).
Edinburgh–Glasgow (Route A.8) (30 m.p.h.) ... (1163).
Fort William–Mallaig (Route A.830 at East of Achdalieu Bridge) (40 m.p.h.) ...
   (1724).
Glasgow–Inverness (Route A.82) (30 m.p.h.) ... (566).
Kincardine Bridge (30 m.p.h.) ... (545).

(*iii*) *Experimental traffic schemes*

TRUNK ROADS (UDDINGSTON) (PROHIBITION OF WAITING AND LOADING) EXPERI-
MENTAL O., made by Secretary of State under Road Traffic Regulation Act 1967
(c. 76), s. 9 ... (499).

CLASS 2—RAILWAYS, TRAMWAYS AND TROLLEY VEHICLES

*Light Railway Orders made by Minister of Transport under Light Railways Act
1896 (c. 48), ss. 7, 9, 10, 18 as amended by Light Railways Act 1912 (c. 19) and Railways
Act 1921 (c. 55).*

British Railways Bd. (Seaton and Beer) Light Railway (835).
Corringham Light Railway (Transfer) (1401).

BRITISH RAILWAYS BD. (TOTNES AND ASHBURTON) LIGHT RAILWAY (TRANSFER) O.,
made by Minister of Transport under Light Railways Act 1896 (c. 48), s. 24; Light
Railways Act 1912 (c. 19); Railways Act 1921 (c. 55), Pt. V (508).

Minister of Transport—Orders under Transport Act 1968 (c. 73), s. 17.

Merseyside Passenger Transport Area (Transfer of Undertakings) (1402).
South East Lancashire and North East Cheshire Passenger Transport Area (Transfer
of Undertakings) (1264).
Tyneside Passenger Transport Area (Transfer of Undertakings) (1580).
West Midlands Passenger Transport Area (Transfer of Undertakings) (1175).

CLASS 3—RIVERS AND INLAND WATERWAYS

(1) *Land drainage schemes and orders*   (3) *Salmon and freshwater fisheries*
(2) *River authorities*

(1) Land drainage schemes and orders

*Minister of Agriculture, Fisheries and Food—Orders under Land Drainage Act 1930
(c. 44), ss. 4†, 14 as applied by Water Resources Act 1963 (c. 38).*

Essex River Authority (Abolition of the East Ham, the Ilford Bridge to Loughton,
the Abridge to Hallsford Bridge, and the Chipping Ongar to Canfield Internal
Drainage Districts) (350).
Great Ouse River Authority—
   (Reconstitution of the Sawtry Internal Drainage Bd.) (423).
   (Warboys, Somersham and Pidley Internal Drainage District) (1680).

---

*Not printed for sale in the S.I. series.
†Orders made under this section are liable to special Parliamentary procedure.

Class 3—Rivers and Inland Waterways—*cont.*

(1) Land drainage schemes and orders—*cont.*

Lincolnshire River Authority—
(Black Sluice Internal Drainage District) (1260).
(Transfer of Powers to the Black Sluice Internal Drainage Bd.) (1259).

EAST SUFFOLK AND NORFOLK RIVER AUTHORITY (TRANSFER OF POWERS OF THE WHERSTEAD AND SHOTLEY INTERNAL DRAINAGE BD.) O., made by Minister of Agriculture, Fisheries and Food under Drainage Act 1930 (c. 44), s. 11 as applied by Water Resources Act 1963 (c. 38) ... (682).

VARIATION OF NAVIGATION RIGHTS (RIVER TONE) O., made by Minister of Agriculture, Fisheries and Food under Land Drainage Act 1930 (c. 44), s. 41 ... (1604).

GENERAL DRAINAGE CHARGE O., made by Minister of Agriculture, Fisheries and Food under Agriculture (Miscellaneous Provisions) Act 1968 (c. 34), s. 22(2) ... (324).

(2) River authorities

LUNE VALLEY WATER BD. O., made by Minister of Housing and Local Government under Water Resources Act 1963 (c. 38), s. 133 ... (1773).

USK RIVER AUTHORITY (SENNI SITE INVESTIGATION) O., made by Secretary of State under Water Resources Act 1963 (c. 38), s. 67 ... (1303).

WREXHAM AND EAST DENBIGHSHIRE WATER O., made by Secretary of State under Water Resources Act 1963 (c. 38), s. 133 ... (1745).

(3) Salmon and freshwater fisheries

(*a*) ENGLAND AND WALES

BRISTOL AVON RIVER AUTHORITY (FISHERIES) O., made by Minister of Agriculture, Fisheries and Food under Salmon and Freshwater Fisheries Act 1923 (c. 16), ss. 37†, 38† as applied by Water Resources Act 1963 (c. 38), s. 5 ... (1473).

DISEASES OF FISH (INFECTED AREA) No. 1 O., made by Minister of Agriculture, Fisheries and Food under Diseases of Fish Act 1937 (c. 33), s. 2 ... (26).

(*b*) SCOTLAND

DISTRICT OF THE RIVER ANNAN (ANNUAL CLOSE TIME) O., made by Secretary of State under Salmon Fisheries (S.) Act 1868 (c. 123), s. 9 ... (79).

CLASS 4—SHIPPING, HARBOURS, DOCKS, PORTS, &c.

(1) *Dockyard ports*
(2) *Harbour development and improvement*
(3) *Pilotage*
(4) *Port health authorities*
(5) *Revision of charges*

(1) Dockyard ports

DOCKYARD PORT OF PLYMOUTH O. IN C., made under Dockyard Ports Regulation Act 1865 (c. 125), ss. 3, 5; as amended by Defence (Transfer of Functions) Act 1964 (c. 15), s. 3; Criminal Justice Act 1967 (c. 80), s. 92(2), Pt. II, sch. 3 (1684).

(2) Harbour development and improvement

Harbour Revision Orders made by Minister of Transport under Harbours Act 1964 (c. 40), s. 14†.

Aberdeen (477).
Dover (1578).
Dundee (1488).

---

†Orders made under this section are liable to special Parliamentary procedure.

Class 4—Shipping, Harbours, Docks, Ports, &c.—*cont.*

(2) Harbour development and improvement—*cont.*

Emsworth (180).
Exmouth (103).
Gillingham, Borough of (1734).
Ipswich (1521).
King's Lynn Conservancy Bd. (829).
Mersey Docks and Harbour Bd. (1522).
Milford Haven Conservancy (478).
Southampton (323).
Sutton Harbour (1735).
Tetney Marine Terminal (1044).

SCARBOROUGH HARBOUR REVISION O., made by Minister of Agriculture, Fisheries
and Food under Harbours Act 1964 (c. 40), s. 14† (658).

MEDWAY PORTS REORGANISATION SCHEME 1968 CONFIRMATION O., made by Minister
of Transport under Harbours Act 1964 (c. 40), s. 18, sch. 4. (1045).

(3) Pilotage

Bd. of Trade—Orders under Pilotage Act 1913 (c. 31), s. 7.

Forth (1462).
Inverness (1273).
Liverpool (41).
Milford (748).

(4) Port health authorities

HARWICH PORT AMENDMENT O., made by Secretary of State under Public Health
Act 1936 (c. 49), s. 9† (1415).

(5) Revision of charges*

*Minister of Transport—Orders under Transport Charges &c. (Miscellaneous
Provisions) Act 1954 (c. 64), s. 6.*

Middlesbrough Transporter Bridge (730).
Port of Tyne Authority (Market Place Ferry) (1087).

BLYTH HARBOUR (AMDT. OF LOCAL ACT) O., made by Minister of Transport
under Harbours Act 1964 (c. 40), s. 60; Blyth Harbour Act 1957 (c. vi), s. 13 (1652).

CLASS 5—LOCAL GOVERNMENT

(1) *Accounts and audit*
(2) *Adaptation of enactments*
(3) *Clean air*
(4) *Licensing*
(5) *Local government areas*
(6) *Pensions*
(7) *Police*
(8) *Powers and duties of local authorities*
(9) *Sunday cinematograph entertainments*
(10) *Miscellaneous*

(1) Accounts and audit*

*Amalgamation of Funds Orders made by Minister of Housing and Local Government
under Local Government (Miscellaneous Provisions) Act 1953 (c. 26), s. 1.*

Dudley (1566).
Exeter (1471).
Grimsby (4).

---

*Not printed for sale in the S.I. series.
†Orders made under this section are liable to special Parliamentary procedure.

Class 5—Local Government—*cont.*

(1) Accounts and audit*—*cont.*

Walsall (1302).
West Bromwich (1309).
Wolverhampton (893).

(2) Adaptation of enactments*

HALIFAX (REPEAL OF LOCAL ENACTMENTS) O., made by Minister of Housing and Local Government under General Rate Act 1967 (c. 9), s. 40 … (490).

(3) Clean air*

Suspension of Smoke Control—Orders made by Minister of Housing and Local Government under Clean Air Acts 1956 (c. 52), s. 11; 1968 (c. 62), s. 9.

Chesterfield (1874).
Knottingley (1866).
Lancaster, City of (1873).
Pontefract, Borough of (1872).
Wombwell, urban district (1867).

HARROW (SUSPENSION OF SMOKE CONTROL) (REVN.) O., made by Minister of Housing and Local Government under Clean Air Act 1956 (c. 52), s. 11 … (51).

BURGH OF DUMBARTON (SUSPENSION OF SMOKE CONTROL) O., made by Secretary of State under Clean Air Act 1956 (c. 52), s. 11 … (1542).

(4) Licensing *

Secretary of State—Orders under the Licensing Act 1964 (c. 26), s. 120.

Sheffield (1359).
Southampton (1268).

(5) Local government areas

(a) ENGLAND AND WALES

(i) County electoral divisions

County (Electoral Divisions)—Orders made by Secretary of State under Local Government Act 1933 (c. 51), s. 11 as amended by Local Government Act 1958 (c. 55), sch. 8 para. 3.

Berkshire (311).
Cambridgeshire, Isle of Ely (1392).
Derbyshire (1827).
Lincoln, County of, Parts of Holland—
  (1364).
  (1390).

North Riding of Yorkshire (1360).
Staffordshire (1386).
West Suffolk (1391).
West Riding of Yorkshire (194).
Westmorland (1725).

(ii) Alteration of areas

Minister of Housing and Local Government—Orders under Local Government Act 1933 (c. 51), s. 143 as amended by Local Government Act 1958 (c. 55), sch. 8 para. 9.

Leicester (340).
Northamptonshire and Northampton (494).

Warwickshire and Worcestershire (361).

---

*Not printed for sale in the S.I. series.

Class 5—Local Government—*cont.*

(5) Local government areas—*cont.*

(*b*) SCOTLAND*

Local Government (S.) Orders made by Secretary of State under Local Government (S.) Act 1947 (c. 43).

(*i*) *County councils and electoral divisions (ss. 13, 361, 372)*

Lanarkshire Electoral Divisions (1877).
Midlothian Electoral Divisions (1449).

(*ii*) *Burgh councils and wards (ss. 21, 361)*

Burgh of Saltcoats Wards (247).

(6) Pensions

*SOUTH-EAST LANCASHIRE (LOCAL AUTHORITIES) SUPERANNUATION SCHEME APPROVAL INSTRUMENT, made by Minister of Housing and Local Government under Local Government Superannuation Act 1937 (c. 68), ss. 2(4), 36(1); Local Government Superannuation Act 1953 (c. 25), s. 26(2) ... (1317).

JUSTICES' CLERKS AND ASSISTANTS (SUPERANNUATION) (CITY OF LONDON) REGS., made by Minister of Housing and Local Government under Local Government Superannuation Act 1953 (c. 25), sch. 3 para. 6 ... (1563).

*PENSIONS INCREASE (COLLEGE OF DOMESTIC ARTS OF SOUTH WALES AND MONMOUTHSHIRE) (AMDT.) REGS., made by Secretary of State under Pensions (Increase) Act 1965 (c. 78), s. 3(2)(*a*)(ii), (4) as amended by Pensions (Increase) Act 1969 (c. 7), sch. 2 para. 10 ... (470).

*MR. SPEAKER MORRISON'S RETIREMENT ACT 1959 (PENSIONS INCREASE) REGS., made by Pensions (Increase) Act 1969 (c. 7), s. 1(4), sch. 2 paras. 12, 14 ... (1512).

(7) Police

NORTHERN POLICE (AMALGAMATION) O., made by Secretary of State under Police (S.) Act 1967 (c. 77), s. 20 ... (305).

Police (Amalgamation) Orders made by Secretary of State under Police Act 1964 (c. 48), ss. 21, 22.

Northumberland (189).   Warwickshire and Coventry (728).
South Wales (484).

POLICE (ADAPTATION OF ENACTMENTS) (CHESHIRE, LIVERPOOL AND BOOTLE) O., made by Secretary of State under Police Act 1964 (c. 48), s. 24 ... (2).

(8) Powers and duties of local authorities

(*a*) GENERAL POWERS

(*i*) *Borough and district councils*

**Minister of Housing and Local Government—Orders under Public Health Act 1875 (c. 55), s. 276.*

Louth (644).   Tiverton (1156).
Northallerton (495).

**Secretary of State—Orders under Public Health Act 1875 (c. 55), s. 276.*

Chepstow (1114).   Gwyrfai (633).

---

*Not printed for sale in the S.I. series.

Class 5—Local Government—*cont.*

(8) Powers and duties of local authorities—*cont.*

(*a*) GENERAL POWERS—*cont.*

(*i*) *Borough and district councils—cont.*

*Minister of Housing and Local Government—Orders under Public Health Act 1875 (c. 55), s. 276; Public Health Act 1925 (c. 71), s. 4(2).

Beaminster (1237).
Bradfield (1379).
Hambledon (1729).
Salisbury and Wilton (1559).

Southwell (1278).
Tendring (1180).
Williton (898).

*Minister of Housing and Local Government—Orders under Public Health Act 1875 (c. 55), s. 276; Local Government Act 1933 (c. 51), s. 190.

Loddon (1814).

Newton Abbot (971).

*PRESTON RURAL DISTRICT (URBAN POWERS) O., made by Minister of Housing and Local Government under Public Health Act 1875 (c. 55), s. 276; Local Government Act 1933 (c. 51), s. 148(1), Parish Councils Act 1957 (c. 42), s. 3(4) ... (272).

*Secretary of State—Declarations under Public Health Acts Amdt. Act 1890 (c. 59), s. 5.

Calne and Chippenham (126).
Camelford (1759).
Cannock (1691).
Cheadle (634).
Ceiriog (1741).

Chepstow (1662).
Newcastle-under-Lyme (819).
Stone (1482).
Tutbury (825).

*Pleasure Boats Orders made by Secretary of State under Public Health Acts Amdt. Act 1907 (c. 53), s. 3.

O. (36).
O. (1520).

No. 2 (1690).
Promenade Byelaws and Pleasure Boats (Queens-borough-in-Sheppey) (1548).

*Minister of Housing and Local Government—Orders under Public Health Act 1936 (c. 49), s. 13.

Dursley (935).

Wing (792).

*NEATH RURAL DISTRICT (URBAN POWERS) O., made by Secretary of State under Public Health Act 1936 (c. 49), s. 13.

*Minister of Housing and Local Government—Orders under the Highways Act 1959 (c. 25), s. 290.

Poulton-le-Fylde (729).

Torbay (1715).

EAST SUFFOLK (ADVANCE PAYMENTS FOR STREET WORKS) O., made by Minister of Housing and Local Government under Highways Act 1959 (c. 25), sch. 14 para. 6 ... (191).

(*ii*) *Special expenses*

*Minister of Housing and Local Government—Orders under Local Government Act 1933 (c. 51), s. 190.

Biggleswade (452).
Northallerton (1538).

Tutbury (1744).
Winslow (69).

*Secretary of State—Orders under Local Government Act 1933 (c. 51), s. 190.

Chepstow (1113).

Twrcelyn (1319).

(*b*) EXTENSION OF POWERS

*Minister of Housing and Local Government—Orders under Local Government Act 1933 (c. 51), s. 271.

Dronfield (271).
Huyton-with-Roby (1450).

Padiham (185).
Thornton Cleveleys (277).

*Not printed for sale in the S.I. series.

Class 5—Local Government—*cont.*

(9) Sunday cinematograph entertainments*

Secretary of State—Orders under Sunday Entertainments Act 1932 (c. 51), s. 1.

Burnham-on-Crouch (1844).   Derwent (631).

(10) Miscellaneous

Water Undertaking (Valuation) Orders made by Minister of Housing and Local Government under General Rate Act 1967 (c. 9), sch. 4 para. 10.

Claro (1571).   Craven—
                                       O. (457).
                                       No. 2 O. (996).

Water Undertaking (Valuation) Orders made by Secretary of State under General Rate Act 1967 (c. 9), sch. 4 para. 10.

Cardiff (1337).   Conway Valley (389).

LOCAL GOVERNMENT (ALLOWANCES TO MEMBERS) (PRESCRIBED BODIES) REGS., made by Minister of Housing and Local Government under Local Government Act 1948 (c. 26) ss. 115, 117 ... (1712).

CUMBERLAND COUNTY COUNCIL ACT 1964 (EXTENSION OF OPERATION) O., made by Minister of Housing and Local Government under Cumberland County Council Act 1964 (c. xxxiv), s. 19(2) ... (1810).

WEST RIDING COUNTY COUNCIL (GENERAL POWERS) ACT 1964 (EXTENSION OF OPERATION) O., made by Minister of Housing and Local Government under West Riding County Council (General Powers) Act 1964 (c. xxxix), s. 9(2) ... (1809).

CLASS 6—PUBLIC HEALTH

(1) *Authorities*   (3) *National Health Service*
(2) *Food and drugs*

(1) Authorities

*SOUTH-WEST SALOP UNITED DISTRICTS (MEDICAL OFFICER OF HEALTH) REVN. O., made by Secretary of State under Local Government Act 1933 (c. 51), s. 112 ... (614)

MID-CALDER AND HYNDBURN JOINT SEWERAGE O., made by Ministe. of Housing and Local Government under Public Health Act 1936 (c. 49), ss. 6, 9; Rivers (Prevention of Pollution) Act 1951 (c. 51), s. 9 ... (1757).

*WEST HERTFORDSHIRE MAIN DRAINAGE (AMDT.) O., made by Minister of Housing and Local Government under Hertfordshire County Council (Colne Valley Sewerage &c.) Act 1937 (c. lxxxix), s. 11 ... (1194).

SKELMERSDALE NEW TOWN SEWERAGE (AMDT.) O., made by Minister of Housing and Local Government under New Towns Act 1965 (c. 59), s. 34 ... (1291).

(2) Food and drugs

*COUNTY BOROUGH OF HASTINGS (REGISTRATION OF FOOD PREMISES) DECLARATION, made by Secretary of State under Food and Drugs Act 1955 (c. 15), s. 16(5) ... (427).

MILK (SPECIAL DESIGNATIONS) (SPECIFIED AREAS) (S.) O., made by Secretary of State under Milk (Special Designations) Act 1949 (c. 34), s. 5 ... (1721).

---

*Not printed for sale in the S.I. series.

Class 6—Public Health—*cont.*

(3) National Health Service

(*a*) ENGLAND AND WALES

National Health Service—Orders made by Secretary of State under National Health Service Act 1946 (c. 81), s. 11.

Birmingham Regional Hospital (218).
East Cornwall Hospitals (160).
East End Maternity Hospital (89).
Epsom and West Park Hospital (1469).
Frenchay Hospital (337).
Grendon Hospital (98).
Heathfield Hospital (491).

Highland Ct. (90).
North Hampshire Group Hospital (1793).
Oak Lane Hospital (108).
Sherborne House (91).
Standish Hospital (1378).
Swindon, Cirencester and District Hospital (338).
Wakefield Hospital (435).

*National Health Service—Orders made by Secretary of State under National Health Service Act 1946 (c. 81), s. 11(9).

Cardiff and Cardiff North and District Hospital (461).

Mid-Glamorgan and Morgannwg Hospital (462).

(*b*) SCOTLAND

ROYAL EDINBURGH AND ASSOCIATED HOSPITALS ENDOWMENTS SCHEME CONFIRMATION O., made by Secretary of State under National Health Service (S.) Act 1947 (c. 27), s. 8 ... (1617).

Secretary of State—Orders under National Health Service (S.) Act 1947 (c. 27), ss. 8, 11.

Dundee General and Dundee Northern Hospitals Endowments (454).
Greenock and District Hospitals Endowments (450).
Paisley and District Hospitals Endowments (449).

*NATIONAL HEALTH SERVICE (APPOINTMENT OF BOARDS OF MANAGEMENT—CONSEQUENTIAL PROVISIONS) (S.) O., made by Secretary of State under National Health Service (S.) Act 1947 (c. 27), s. 11(10) ... (1340).

CLASS 7—TOWN AND COUNTRY PLANNING, OPEN SPACES, ACCESS TO THE COUNTRYSIDE

(1) Byelaws under Military Lands Act 1892
(2) Designation of New Town Sites
(3) Determination of schemes (Town and Country Planning Act 1932)

(4) Open spaces
(5) Planning permission

(1) Byelaws under Military Lands Act 1892*

Range Byelaws made by Secretary of State under Military Lands Act 1892 (c. 43), Pt. II.

Chilcomb Range (533).
Perham Down Range (1902).

(2) Designation of New Town Sites*

Minister of Housing and Local Government—Orders under New Towns Act 1965 (c. 59), ss. 1, 53.

Newington Amdt. (1730).
Skelmersdale Amdt. (127).

---

*Not printed for sale in the S.I. series.

Class 7—Town and Country Planning, Open Spaces, Access to the Countryside
—*cont.*

(3) Determination of schemes (Town and Country Planning Act 1932)*

Minister of Housing and Local Government—Orders under Town and Country Planning Act 1947 (c. 51), sch. 10 para. 7; Town and Country Planning Act 1962 (c. 38), sch. 13 para. 1.

Blackpool (53).
Croydon (East)—
(674).
(No. 2) (675).
Hornsea (1004).

(4) Open spaces

WAKEHURST PLACE REGS., made by Minister of Agriculture, Fisheries and Food under Parks Regulation (Amdt.) Act 1926 (c. 36), ss. 2, 3 as amended by Agriculture (Miscellaneous Provisions) Act 1968 (c. 34), s. 48 ... (1000).

(5) Planning permission

CONTROL OF OFFICE DEVELOPMENT (DESIGNATION OF AREAS) (VARIATION) O., made by Board of Trade under Control of Office and Industrial Development Act 1965 (c. 33), ss. 1(2)(b), 23 ... (173).

CLASS 8—WATER SUPPLY

Minister of Housing and Local Government—Orders made under one or more of the following sections of Water Act 1945 (c. 42), Water Act 1948 (c. 22) and Compulsory Purchase Act 1965 (c. 56).

1945: ss. 9†, 10†, 19, 23†, 32†, 33†, 40, 50.
1948: ss. 2†, 3, 14.
1965: s. 33.

Ardleigh Reservoir (746).
Bournemouth and District (Water Charges) (1804).
Bradford (Water Charges) (360).
Brighton—
Corporation (Water Charges) (1434).
(Extension of Operation of Byelaws)—
(441).
(No. 2) (1328).
Bristol Waterworks—
Oldford (1628).
(No. 2) (1813).
Bucks—
Bd. (Extension of Operation of Byelaws) (222).
(Radnage Pumping Station) (1673).
Cambridge—
(1766).
(Lintor.) (1393).
Central Nottinghamshire Water Bd.—
(29).
(Chequer House Boreholes) (442).
(Financial Provisions) (938).
Chester (Borrowing Powers) (1409).
Claro Water Bd. (Glasshouse Springs) (1102).
Colchester and District Water Bd. (196).
Colne Valley (Extension of Operation of Byelaws)—
(671).
(No. 2) (1558).
Cotswold Water Bd. (Bibury) (777).

Craven Water Bd.—
(Acquisition of Mains) (416).
(Amdt.) (925).
(Charges) (1226).
(Extension of Operation of Byelaws) (1354).
Cromer Urban District (424).
Derwent Valley (1526).
Durham County Water Bd. (325).
East Cornwall Water Bd. (1428).
East Shropshire Water Bd. (Shiffords Bridge Borehole) (1602).
East Surrey (Water Charges) (68).
Eden Water Bd. (920).
Ely, Mildenhall and Newmarket Water Bd. (1618).
Herefordshire Water Bd. (601).
Huddersfield (502).
Kesteven Water Bd.—
(486).
(Aswarby) (348).
Lakes and Lune (Burneside Water Mains) (1792).
Makerfield Water Bd. (Variation of Limits) (1815).
Metropolitan Water Bd. (Queen Mary Reservoir) (3).
Mid Southern (1754).
Mid-Sussex—
(304).
(No. 2) (1050).
Mid-Wessex (1670).

*Not printed for sale in the S.I. series.
†Orders made under this section are liable to special Parliamentary procedure.

Class 8—**Water Supply**—*cont.*

Newcastle and Gateshead—
  (Financial Provisions) (1201).
  (Transfer of Works) (1143).
North and Mid Cornwall—
  (1671).
  (Hallworthy Borehole) (821).
North Derbyshire Water Bd. (Charges) (489).
North-West Norfolk Water Bd. (104).
North West Sussex—
  (Lodsworth Borehole) (1233).
  (Water Charges) (1870).
North West Worcestershire Water Bd. (1012).
Norwich (Ketteringham Waterworks) (714).
Oxfordshire and District Water Bd.—
  (121).
  (No. 2) (503).
  (Charges) (480).
Plymouth (23).
River Dove Water Bd. (1013).
Royal Tunbridge Wells (Extension of Operation of
  Byelaws) (1005).
Rugby Joint Water Bd. (1227).
St. Helens (907).
Sevenoaks and Tonbridge (1049).
Sevenoaks and Tonbridge and Mid Kent (Variation
  of Limits) (1410).
Sheffield (Extension of Operation of Byelaws)—
  (302).
  (No. 2) (1129).
South Essex—
  (Extension of Operation of Byelaws) (397).
  Waterworks—
    (Borrowing Powers) (1572).
    (Water Charges) (1868).
South Norfolk Water Bd. (55).
South Staffordshire (Water Charges) (764).
South Warwickshire Water Bd.—
  (919).
  and Coventry (Variation of Limits) (1672).
  (Charges) (166).
  (Offchurch) (1483).

South West Devon Water Bd. (439).
South West Suburban (Water Charges) (892).
South Wilts Water Bd.—
  (Amdt.) (749).
  (Amdt.) (No. 2) (1485).
Southend—
  (1048).
  (No. 2) (1890).
Spenborough (Extension of Operation of Byelaws)
  (781).
Stafford (768).
Staffordshire Potteries Water Bd. (1185).
Sunderland and South Shields (Financial Provisions)
  (1047).
Tendring Hundred—
  (1596).
  (Charges) (1533).
  (Extension of Operation of Byelaws)—
    (814).
    (No. 2) (1803).
Thames Valley (705).
Wessex Water Bd. (122).
West Cumberland Water Bd. (118).
West Lancashire Water Bd. (1398).
West Pennine (Royal Air Force Heywood Pipeline)
  (46).
West Shropshire Water Bd.—
  (Charges) (1805).
  (Eyton Borehole) (202).
West Somerset Water Bd.—
  (642).
  (No. 2) (831).
West Suffolk Water Bd.—
  (Barrow Heath) (1599).
  (Charges) (504).
  (Ixworth Pumping Station) (1404).
  (Wixoe) (432).
West Surrey and Woking (Variation of Limits) (1144).
Woking (Financial Provisions) (1601).
York (1661).

*Secretary of State—Orders made under one or more of the following sections of the
Water Act 1945 (c. 42) and Water Act 1948 (c. 22).*
  1945: ss. 9†, 19, 23†, 32†, 33, 40, 50.
  1948: ss. 2, 14.

Blaenavon Urban District (21).
Cardiff Corporation—
  (Barry Docks Waterworks) (612).
  (Water Charges) (624).
Cardiganshire (Llechryd) Water Bd. (298).
Conway Valley Water Bd. (27).
Eryri Water Bd. (Bwrdd Dwr Eryri) (Marchlyn Bach
  Reservoir) (1202).

Gwent Water Bd. (1475).
Mid-Glamorgan Water Bd. (847).
Pembrokeshire Water Bd. (Charges) (846).
Taf Fechan Water Bd.—
  (22).
  (No. 2) (845).

**Drought Orders made by Minister of Housing and Local Government under Water
Act 1958 (c. 67), s. 1(1).*

Craven Water Bd.—
  (1384).
  (No. 2) (1573).
Huddersfield—
  (1433).
  (No. 2) (1583).

North Derbyshire Water Bd. (1794).
North Devon Water Bd.—
  (1011).
  (No. 2) (1253).
Wakefield and District Water Bd. (1530).

**Drought Orders made by Secretary of State under Water Act 1958 (c. 67), s. 1(1).*

Abertillery and District Water Bd. (1828).
Newport and South Monmouthshire Water Bd.
  (1738).

West Glamorgan Water Bd.—
  (No. 1) (1681).
  (No. 2) (1697).

---

*Not printed for sale in the S.I. series.
†Orders made under this section are liable to special Parliamentary procedure.

Class 8—Water Supply—*cont.*

Secretary of State—Orders made under one or more of the following sections of the Water (S.) Act 1946 (c. 42), as amended by Water (S.) Act 1949 (c. 31) and Water (S.) Act 1967 (c. 78).
1946: ss. 21†, 44†, 75.
1949: s. 23.

Argyll Water Bd.—
  (Drumore Burn, Bellochantay) (1879).
  (Loch Nell) (1459).
  (Loch Righeachan and Steallaire Ban Loch) (830).
  (Scallastle River, Craignure) (812).
Ayrshire and Bute Water Bd. (Loch Spallander) (246).
Inverness-shire Water Bd. (Loch Bealach Na Gaoithe) (193).

Lower Clyde Water Bd. (Kelly Dam) (540).
North-East of Scotland Water Bd.—
  (Culvie, Banffshire) (539).
  (Deveron) (1808).
Ross and Cromarty Water Bd. (River Glass) (534).
South-East of Scotland Water Bd. (Galashiels Mill Lade) (945).

*Secretary of State—Orders under Water Act 1958 (c. 67), s. 1.

Lower Clyde Water Bd. (Water of Gryfe) (Emergency) (1436).

North East of Scotland Water Bd.—
  (River Deveron) (Emergency) (1785).
  (River Nairn) (Emergency) (1351).

LANARKSHIRE AND MID-SCOTLAND WATER BDS. (ALTERATION OF REGIONS) O., made by Secretary of State under Water (S.) Act 1967 (c. 78), s. 5 ... (54).

MID-SCOTLAND WATER BD. (CONSTITUTION ETC.) AMDT. O., made by Secretary of State under Water (S.) Act 1967 (c. 78), ss. 8, 33(5) ... (1678).

CENTRAL SCOTLAND WATER DEVELOPMENT BD. (REVN. ETC. OF LOCAL ENACTMENTS) O., made by Secretary of State under Water (S.) Act 1967 (c. 78), s. 32 ... (581).

CLASS 9—EDUCATION

Endowment Scheme Orders in Council under Education (S.) Act 1962 (c. 47), s. 127(1).

Aberlour Trust (381).
Bute Educational Trust (Amdt.) (1834).
Esdaile Trust (149).
Highlands and Islands Educational Trust (1687).

James G. H. Glass Trust (382).
Montague Burton Chair of International Relations (Amdt.) (600).

CLASS 10—LIGHTING, POWER AND HEATING

(1) *Mines and quarries*
(2) *Coal industry*

(3) *Electricity*

(1) Mines and quarries*

(a) SPECIAL REGULATIONS

Minister of Power—regulations under Mines and Quarries Act 1954 (c. 70), ss. 141, 143 revoking special mines regs.

Bagworth (Pass Byes) (727).

Westoe (Electric Lighting) (244).

Mines—Special Regulations made by Minister of Power under Mines and Quarries Act 1954 (c. 70).

regs. relating to bye-pits (made under ss. 141, 143):

Newmarket Silkstone (285).

---

*Not printed for sale in the S.I. series.
†Orders made under this section are liable to special Parliamentary procedure.

Class 10—Lighting, Power and Heating—*cont.*

(1) Mines and quarries*—*cont.*

(a) SPECIAL REGULATIONS—*cont.*

regs. relating to friction winding (made under ss. 141, 143):

Bedlay (Amdt.) (1635).
Brodsworth (Amdt.) (1246).

Seafield (Amdt.) (1029).

regs. relating to shafts (made under ss. 141, 143):

Bentley (No. 2) (1055).
Camborne (No. 1) (1030).
Hatfield/Thorne (No. 1) (1181).

Lynemouth (No. 4) (1722).
Sutton Manor (No. 1) (274).

regs. relating to cinematograph lighting (made under ss. 68, 141, 143):

Bagworth (154).
Barony (555).
Bilston Glen (556).
Cadley Hill (159).
Craghead (255).
Dawdon (1016).
Easington (979).
Killoch (557).
Lady Victoria/Lingerwood (613).
Manton (1165).
Mansvers (924).

Monktonhall (316).
Polkemmet (580).
Rawdon (1017).
Seafield (243).
Silverwood (1128).
Snibston (317).
Wearmouth (558).
Whittle (1778).
Williamthorpe/Grassmoor (256).
Wolstanton (629).

regs. relating to electric lighting (made under ss. 68, 141, 143):

Bagworth (184).
Betteshanger (1591).
Bilston Glen (1145).
Boldon (242).
Calverton (1531).
Coventry (1486).
Daw Mill (215).
Eppleton (1875).

Hucknall (1544).
Kellingley (838).
Lea Hall (980).
Markham (273).
Measham (1779).
Monktonhall (1146).
Snibston (328).
South Kirkby (874).

regs. relating to storage battery locomotives (made under ss. 68, 83, 141):

Blackdene (1876).
Camborne (570).

Levant (1236).
Whiteheaps (1592).

regs. relating to cable reel shutter cars (made under ss. 40, 68, 141, 143):

Ellington (800).

Lynemouth (799).

regs. relating to locomotives and diesel vehicles (made under ss. 40, 83, 141, 143):

Prince of Wales (1377).

Cotgrave (744).

regs. relating to rope haulage (made under ss. 47, 141, 143):

Brenkley (559).

(b) STOPPING UP AND REOPENING OF RIGHTS OF WAY

*OPENCAST COAL (HIGHWAY) ORDERS (REVN.) O., made by Minister of Technology under Opencast Coal Act 1958 (c. 69), sch. 10 para. 49 ... (1595).

Blue Lodge Site.
City Site.
Coney Warren Site.
Esh Site.

Gawthorpe—
    Hall.
    Hall Site.
Maish End Site.
Owl Wood.
Starvehimvalley Site.

---

*Not printed for sale in the S.I. series.

Class 10—Lighting, Power and Heating—*cont.*

(2) Coal Industry*

Coal Industry Nationalisation (Variation of Trusts) Orders made by Minister of Power under Coal Industry Nationalisation Act 1946 (c. 59), as amended by Miners' Welfare Act 1952 (c. 23), s. 11.

Lynemouth Miners' Welfare Institute and Hall (83).
Miners' Welfare National Scholarship Endowment Fund and Miners' Welfare National Students Exhibitions Fund (928).

(3) Electricity

NORTH OF SCOTLAND HYDRO-ELECTRIC BD. (CONSTRUCTIONAL SCHEME NO. 40) CONFIRMATION O., made by Secretary of State under Hydro-Electric Development (S.) Act 1943 (c. 32), s. 5(4) … (169).

CLASS 11—ADMINISTRATION OF JUSTICE

(1) *Coroners' districts*
(2) *Fixed penalty areas*
(3) *Petty sessional divisions*
(4) *Prisons*
(5) *Probation areas*

(1) Coroners' districts*

Coroners' Districts—Orders made by Secretary of State under Coroners' (Amdt.) Act 1926 (c. 59), s. 12.

Devon (Amdt.) (1896).
West Sussex (Amdt.) (872).

York, North Riding (Amdt.) (560).

(2) Fixed penalty areas

Fixed Penalty (Areas)—Orders made by Secretary of State under Road Traffic Regulation Act 1967 (c. 76), s. 80.

(715).
(No. 2) (1292).

(No. 3) (1574).
(No. 4) (1732).

(3) Petty sessional divisions

(*a*) PETTY SESSIONS GENERALLY

Petty Sessional Divisions—Orders made by Secretary of State under Justices of the Peace Act 1949 (c. 101), s. 18.

Buckinghamshire (621).
Denbighshire (1247).

Herefordshire—
(62).
(No. 2) (1385).
West Suffolk (63).

SOUTH STAFFORDSHIRE AND STAFFORDSHIRE POTTERIES STIPENDIARY MAGISTRATES O., made by Secretary of State under Justices of the Peace Act 1968 (c. 69), sch. 3 para. 11(1) … (357).

SOUTH STAFFORDSHIRE AND STAFFORDSHIRE POTTERIES STIPENDIARY JUSTICE COMMISSIONERS REGS., made by Secretary of State under Justices of the Peace Act 1968 (c. 69), sch. 3 para. 14 … (356).

(*b*) JUVENILE COURT PANELS*

Juvenile Court Panel—Orders made by Secretary of State under Children and Young Persons Act 1933 (c. 12), sch. 2 paras. 6, 21.

Carlisle (227).

Denbighshire (653).

---

*Not printed for sale in the S.I. series.

Class 11—Administration of Justice—*cont.*

(4) Prisons

DISCONTINUANCE OF LEGALISED POLICE CELLS (S.) RULES, made by Secretary of State under Prisons (S.) Act 1952 (c. 61), s. 14 ... (986).

(5) Probation areas*

Probation and After-Care Area—Orders made by Secretary of State under Criminal Justice Act 1948 (c. 58), s. 76, sch. 5 paras. 1, 2.

Bedfordshire (197).
Cheshire (1054).
Durham (37).
Essex (Amdt.) (38).

Manchester and Salford (525).
Newcastle and Northumberland (268).
Suffolk (165).

CLASS 12—AGRICULTURE, FISHERIES AND FORESTRY

(1) *Diseases of animals*
(2) *Forestry*

(3) *Protection of birds*
(4) *Sea fisheries*

(1) Diseases of animals*

CONTROL OF IMPORTS

IMPORTATION OF PEDIGREE ANIMALS (NO. 1) O., made by Minister of Agriculture, Fisheries and Food under Diseases of Animals Act 1950 (c. 36), ss. 24, 26 ... (663).

(2) Forestry

BEDGEBURY PINETUM BYELAWS made by Forestry Commissioners under Forestry Act 1967 (c. 10), s. 46 ... (312).

(3) Protection of birds

WILD BIRDS (BURRY ESTUARY SANCTUARY) O., made by Secretary of State under Protection of Birds Act 1954 (c. 30), s. 3(1) ... (1795).

(4) Sea fisheries

OVERY CREEK MUSSEL AND COCKLE FISHERY O., made by Minister of Agriculture, Fisheries and Food under Sea Fisheries (Shellfish) Act 1967 (c. 83), s. 1 ... (1651).

CLASS 13—MISCELLANEOUS

(1) Aerodrome Roads

Minister of Transport—Orders under Airports Authority Act 1965 (c. 16), s. 12; Civil Aviation Act 1968 (c. 61), s. 10.

Gatwick (647).
Heathrow (646).

Stansted (648).

AERODROME TRAFFIC (PRESTWICK) O., made by Secretary of State under Airports Authority Act 1965 (c. 16), s. 12; Civil Aviation Act 1968 (c. 61), s. 10 ... (970).

(2) Banks and Banking

BARCLAYS BANK ACT 1969 (APPOINTED DAY) O., made by Board of Trade under Barclays Bank Act 1969 (c. xiii), s. 2(3) ... (1164).

NATIONAL WESTMINSTER BANK ACT 1969 (APPOINTED DAY) O., made by Board of Trade under National Westminster Bank Act 1969 (c. xxii), s. 3(1) ... (1705).

---

*Not printed for sale in the S.I. series.

Class 13—Miscellaneous—*cont.*

(3) Charities

CHARITIES (SIR JOHN SOANE'S MUSEUM) O., made by Charities Act 1960 (c. 58), s. 19(2)(9) ... (468).

(4) Civil Aviation

Air Navigation (Restriction of Flying)—Regulations made by Board of Trade under Air Navigation O. 1966(a), art. 60.

(Investiture Ceremony) (Caernarvon Castle) (832).　　(Torbay Naval Review) (985).
(Naval Review) (Spithead) (574).

AERODROMES (DESIGNATION) (FACILITIES FOR CONSULTATION) O., made by Board of Trade under Civil Aviation Act 1968 (c. 61), s. 8 ... (721).

BRITISH OVERSEAS AIRWAYS CORPORATION (BORROWING POWERS) O., made by Board of Trade under Air Corporations Act 1967 (c. 33), s. 16 ... (1765).

SOUTHAMPTON AIRPORT (DESIGNATION) (BYELAWS) O., made by Civil Aviation Act 1968 (c. 61), s. 4 ... (883).

(5) Continental Shelf

Protection of Installations—Orders made by Minister of Power under Continental Shelf Act 1964 (c. 29), s. 2.

(No. 3) (195).　　(No. 4) (1322).

(6) Landlord and Tenant*

FURNISHED LETTINGS (RENT CONTROL) (WANDSWORTH DISTRICT) O., made by Minister of Housing and Local Government under Rent Act 1968 (c. 23), s. 68 ... (238).

(7) National Gallery and Tate Gallery

NATIONAL GALLERY (LENDING OUTSIDE THE UNITED KINGDOM No. 1) O., made by Secretary of State under National Gallery and Tate Gallery Act 1954 (c. 65), s. 4(2) ... (798).

(8) Theatres

THEATRES (ADAPTATION OF ENACTMENTS) O., made by Secretary of State under Theatres Act 1968 (c. 54), s. 19 ... (1478).

---

*Not printed for sale in the S.I. series.
(a) S.I. 1966/1184 (1966 III, p. 3073).

TABLES OF EFFECT
of the Statutory Instruments of 1969
(With certain additional information)

Table A

A CHRONOLOGICAL TABLE OF ACTS OF PARLIAMENT
WHOSE OPERATION WAS AFFECTED BY
STATUTORY INSTRUMENTS OF 1969
Public General Acts

Table B

A CHRONOLOGICAL TABLE OF SUBORDINATE LEGISLATION
(S.R. & O. AND S.I. AND CERTAIN PREROGATIVE INSTRUMENTS)
WHOSE OPERATION WAS AFFECTED BY
LEGISLATION OF 1969 (ACTS AND INSTRUMENTS)

TABLE A

NOTES

1. For List of Abbreviations used in this Table, see p. ix.

2. A comprehensive table showing the effect of Acts, Measures and S.I. of 1969 on Acts and Measures is printed in the *Annual Volume of Public General Acts.*

EFFECT ON PUBLIC GENERAL ACTS

Short Title	How affected and Instrument by which affected
1867 Lyon King of Arms Act 1867 (c. 17) ...	sch. B am., 1969/1454.
1887 Sheriffs Act 1887 (c. 55)	sch. 2 **am.** (W.), 1969/1276.
1898 Merchant Shipping (Mercantile Marine Fund) Act 1898 (c. 44)	sch. 2 scale of payments **replaced,** rules 1, 7 proviso **am.,** Exemptions **am.,** 1969/386.
1913 Ancient Monuments Consolidation and Amdt. Act 1913 (c. 32)	*see* 1969/388.†
1919 Ministry of Health Act 1919 (c. 21) ...	s. 5 **rep.,** 1969/388. *see* 1969/388.*
1923 Salmon and Freshwater Fisheries Act 1923 (c. 16)	*see* 1969/388.‡
1930 Land Drainage Act 1930 (c. 44)	*see* 1969/388.‡
Reservoirs (Safety Provns.) Act 1930 (c. 51)	Functions transfd. to Secy of State and Minister of Housing and Local Govt., ss. 2, 8, 10 **am.,** 1969/1067
1931 Ancient Monuments Act 1931 (c. 16) ...	*see* 1969/388.*
1932 Destructive Imported Animals Act 1932 (c. 12)	*see* 1969/388.‡
1935 Herring Industry Act 1935 (c. 9)	*see* 1969/388.‡
1937 Physical Training and Recreation Act 1937 (c. 46)	Functions of Secy. of State for Education and Science transfd. to Min. of Housing and Local Govt., 1969/1497.
Agriculture Act 1937 (c. 70)	*see* 1969/388.‡
1938 Herring Industry Act 1938 (c. 42)	*see* 1969/388.‡
1940 Agriculture (Miscellaneous War Provns.) Act 1940 (c. 14)	*see* 1969/388.‡
1941 Agriculture (Miscellaneous Provns.) Act 1941 (c. 50)	*see* 1969/388.‡
1944 Agriculture (Miscellaneous Provns.) Act 1944 (c. 28)	*see* 1969/388.‡

* Functions as to Wales transferred to Secy. of State.
† Certain functions as to Wales transferred to Secy. of State.
‡ Certain functions as to Wales transferred to Secy. of State and Minister of Agriculture, Fisheries and Food.

Short Title	How affected and Instrument by which affected
1945 Ministry of Fuel and Power Act 1945 (c. 19)	s. 1 **am.**, 2, 3 **rep.**, 5 **rep.** (saving), 1969/1498.
1946 Acquisition of Land (Authorisation Procedure) Act 1946 (c. 49)	see 1969/388.†
Hill Farming Act 1946 (c. 73)	see 1969/388.‖
National Health Service Act 1946 (c. 81)...	see 1969/388.†
1947 Statistics of Trade Act 1947 (c. 39) ...	s. 17 **am.**, 1969/1498.
Industrial Organisation and Development Act 1947 (c. 40)	Certain functions of Bd. of Trade transfd. to Min. of Technology, 1969/1498.
Agriculture Act 1947 (c. 48)	see 1969/388.‡
Town and Country Planning (S.) Act 1947 (c. 53)	s. 12(4) functions of Bd. of Trade transfd. to Min. of Technology, 1969/1498.
1948 Radioactive Substances Act 1948 (c. 37) ...	ss. 3, 4, 12 **am.**, 1969/388.
Agricultural Holdings Act 1948 (c. 63) ...	see 1969/388.‡
Monopolies and Mergers Act 1948 (c. 66)	functions of Bd. of Trade transfd. to Secy. of State, 1969/1534.
1949 Patents Act 1949 (c. 87)	s. 40 **am.**, 1969/1534.
National Health Service (Amdt.) Act 1949 (c. 93)	see 1969/388.*
1951 Sea Fish Industry Act 1951 (c. 30)... ...	see 1969/388.‡
National Health Service Act 1951 (c. 31)...	see 1969/388.* sch. **am.**, (E. and W.) 1969/906, (S.) 1969/918.
1952 Agriculture (Fertilisers) Act 1952 (c. 15) ...	see 1969/388.‖
National Health Service Act 1952 (c. 25) ...	see 1969/388.* s. 2 **am.**, (E. and W.) 1969/906, (S.) 1969/918.
Agriculture (Ploughing Grants) Act 1952 (c. 35)	see 1969/388.‖
Agriculture (Calf Subsidies) Act 1952 (c. 62)	see 1969/388.‖
1953 White Fish and Herring Industries Act 1953 (c. 17)	see 1969/388.‡

* Functions as to Wales transferred to Secy. of State.
† Certain functions as to Wales transferred to Secy. of State.
‖ Functions as to Wales transferred to Secy. of State and Minister of Agriculture, Fisheries and Food.
‡ Certain functions as to Wales transferred to Secy. of State and Minister of Agriculture, Fisheries and Food.

	Short Title	How affected and Instrument by which affected
1953	Post Office Act 1953 (c. 36)...	**rep.** (exc. ss. 50, 60, 61, 64, 65, 65A) (Jersey) 1969/1366, (Guernsey) 1969/1367. ss. 16, 17, 70, 87 **am.,** 1969/1368.
	Historic Buildings and Ancient Monuments Act 1953 (c. 49)	*see* 1969/388.†
1954	Protection of Birds Act 1954 (c. 30) ...	*see* 1969/388.‡
	Landlord and Tenant Act 1954 (c. 56) ...	s. 60 functions of Bd of Trade transfd. to Min. of Technology, 1969/1498.
	Pests Act 1954 (c. 68)	*see* 1969/388.‡
1955	Fisheries Act 1955 (c. 7)	*see* 1969/388.‡
1956	Therapeutic Substances Act 1956 (c. 25) ...	ss. 4, 8, 9 **am.,** 1969/388.
	Finance Act 1956 (c. 54)	*see* 1969/388.†
	Restrictive Trade Practices Act 1956 (c. 68)	Pt. I (ss. 1–23) and certain functions in Pt. III transfd. from Bd. of Trade to Secy. of State, 1969/1534.
1957	House of Commons Disqualification Act 1957 (c. 20)	sch. 2 **am.,** 1969/1498.
	White Fish and Herring Industries Act 1957 (c. 22)	*see* 1969/388.‡
	Dentists Act 1957 (c. 28)	sch. 1 para. 14 **am.,** 1969/388.
	Agriculture Act 1957 (c. 57)	*see* 1969/388.‡
	Coal-Mining (Subsidence) Act 1957 (c. 59)	*see* 1969/388.†
1958	Agricultural Marketing Act 1958 (c. 47) ...	*see* 1969/388.‡
1959	Agriculture (Small Farmers) Act 1959 (c. 12)	*see* 1969/388.‖
	Agricultural Improvement Grants Act 1959 (c. 31)	*see* 1969/388.‖
	Licensing (S.) Act 1959 (c. 51)	sch. 1 Pt. II **am.** 1969/1019.
	Weeds Act 1959 (c. 54)	*see* 1969/388.‖
1960	Local Employment Act 1960 (c. 18) ...	Pts. I (ss. 1–15), II (ss. 16–20), Pt. III ss. 26(2), 27, 28(2)(3)(*a*) functions of Bd. of Trade transfd. to Min. of Technology, 1969/1498.
	Horticulture Act 1960 (c. 22)	*see* 1969/388.‡
	Professions Supplementary to Medicine Act 1960 (c. 66)	sch. 1 para. 1 **am.,** 1969/388.

† Certain functions as to Wales transferred to Secy. of State.
‖ Functions as to Wales transferred to Secy. of State and Minister of Agriculture, Fisheries and Food.
‡ Certain functions as to Wales transferred to Secy. of State and Minister of Agriculture, Fisheries and Food.

	Short Title	How affected and Instrument by which affected
1961	National Health Service Act 1961 (c. 19) ...	*see* 1969/388.*
1962	Commonwealth Immigrants Act 1962 (c. 21)	s. 16 am., 1969/388.
	Health Visiting and Social Work (Training) Act 1962 (c. 33)	s. 7 am., 1969/388.
	Town and Country Planning Act 1962 (c. 38)	ss. 38, 39 functions of Bd. of Trade transfd. to Min. of Technology, 1969/1498.
1963	Betting, Gaming and Lotteries Act 1963 (c. 2)	sch. 5 para. 3 **am.**, 1969/1605.
	Purchase Tax Act 1963 (c. 9)	sch. 1 groups 6, 7, 12, 19A **am.**, 1969/1736.
	Agriculture (Miscellaneous Provns.) Act 1963 (c. 11)	*see* 1969/388.‡
	Weights and Measures Act 1963 (c. 31) ...	s. 10 am., 1969/388.
	Water Resources Act 1963 (c. 38)	*see* 1969/388.‡
1964	Television Act 1964 (c. 21)	s. 13 am., 1969/875.
	Agriculture and Horticulture Act 1964 (c. 28)	*see* 1969/388.‡
	Harbours Act 1964 (c. 40)	*see* 1969/388.‡
	Shipping Contracts and Commercial Documents Act 1964 (c. 87)	s. 2 am., 1969/1498.
	Ministers of the Crown Act 1964 (c. 98) ...	sch. 2 Pt. II **am.**, 1969/1498.
1965	Science and Technology Act 1965 (c. 4) ...	s. 5 **am.**, 1969/1498.
	Ministerial Salaries and Members' Pensions Act 1965 (c. 11)	sch. 4 **am.**, 1969/1498.
	Cereals Marketing Act 1965 (c. 14) ...	*see* 1969/388.‡
	Dangerous Drugs Act 1965 (c. 15)... ...	sch. Pt. I am., 1969/738.
	Teaching Council (S.) Act 1965 (c. 19) ...	sch. 1 am., 1969/586.
	Finance Act 1965 (c. 25)	*see* 1969/388.‡
	Control of Office and Industrial Development Act 1965 (c. 33)	Pt. I functions of Bd. of Trade transfd. to Min. of Housing and Local Govt. and Secy. of State, Pt. II functions of Bd. of Trade transfd. to Min. of Technology, 1969/1498.
	Monopolies and Mergers Act 1965 (c. 50)	Functions of Bd. of Trade transfd. to Secy. of State, sch. 1 para. 6 **am.**, 1969/1534.
	National Insurance Act 1965 (c. 51) ...	s. 49 am., 1969/289.

* Functions as to Wales transferred to Secy. of State.
   ‡ Certain functions as to Wales transferred to Secy. of State and Minister of Agriculture, Fisheries and Food.

Short Title	How affected and Instrument by which affected
1965 National Health Service Contributions Act 1965 (c. 54)	s. 1 **am.,** 1969/388.
Ministerial Salaries Consolidation Act 1965 (c. 58)	s. 2, sch. 1 **am.,** 1969/1498.
Superannuation Act 1965 (c. 74)	sch. 8 **am.,** 1969/349, 665.
1966 Mines (Working Facilities and Support) Act 1966 (c. 4)	see 1969/388.†
National Health Service Act 1966 (c. 8) ...	s. 4 **am.,** 1969/388. see 1969/388.*
Ministry of Social Security Act 1966 (c. 20)	sch. 2 Pt. II **am.,** 1969/1036.
Docks and Harbours Act 1966 (c. 28) ...	sch. 1 **am.,** 1969/1209.
Selective Employment Payments Act 1966 (c. 32)	ss. 1, 2 **am.,** 1969/867. sch. 1 Pt. II **am.,** 1969/255. sch. 1 Pts. I, II **am.,** 1969/1900.
Prices and Incomes Act 1966 (c. 33) ...	sch. 2 **replaced,** 1969/1891.
Industrial Development Act 1966 (c. 34) ...	Pts. I–III functions of Bd. of Trade transfd. to Min. of Technology, s. 18 **am.,** 1969/1498.
Sea Fisheries Regulation Act 1966 (c. 38)...	see 1969/388.‡
Industrial Reorganisation Corporation Act 1966 (c. 50)	Functions of Secy. of State transfd. to Min. of Technology, 1969/1498.
1967 Parliamentary Commissioner Act 1967 (c. 13)	sch. 2 **am.,** 1969/1498.
Agriculture Act 1967 (c. 22)	see 1969/388.‡ s. 9 am., 1969/1534.
Housing Subsidies Act 1967 (c. 29)... ...	s. 28 **mod.,** 1969/1626.
Air Corporations Act 1967 (c. 33) ...	s. 16 **am.,** 1969/1765. (Local S.I.).
National Health Service (Family Planning) Act 1967 (c. 39)	see 1969/388.*
Finance Act 1967 (c. 54)	s. 40 **am.,** 1969/535. s. 3 functions of Secy. of State transfd. to Treasury, 1969/1498.
Sea Fisheries (Shellfish) Act 1967 (c. 83) ...	see 1969/388.‡
Abortion Act 1967 (c. 87)	s. 2 **am.,** 1969/388.
1968 Administration of Justice Act 1968 (c. 5)...	s. 1 **am.,** 1969/862.
National Loans Act 1968 (c. 13)	s. 4 **am.,** 1969/998.
New Towns (S.) Act 1968 (c. 16)	ss. 38, 39 **am.,** 1969/453.

* Functions as to Wales transferred to Secy. of State.
  † Certain functions as to Wales transferred to Secy. of State.
  ‡ Certain functions as to Wales transferred to Secy. of State and Minister of Agriculture, Fisheries and Food.

Short Title	How affected and Instrument by which affected
1968 Firearms Act 1968 (c. 27)	sch. 4 para. 4 **replaced** (E. and W.) 1969/1219, (S.) 1969/1453.
Industrial Expansion Act 1968 (c. 32) ...	s. 1 **am.,** 1969/1498.
Agriculture (Miscellaneous Provns.) Act 1968 (c. 34)	*see* 1969/388.†‡
Health Services and Public Health Act 1968 (c. 46)	*see* 1969/388.* ss. 59, 61 **am.,** 1969/388.
Restrictive Trade Practices Act 1968 (c. 66)	s. 2 **am.,** 1969/1498. Certain functions of Bd. of Trade transfd. to Secy. of State, s. 3 **am.,** 1969/1534.
Medicines Act 1968 (c. 67)	ss. 1, 5 **am.,** 1969/388.
Town and Country Planning Act 1968 (c. 72)	*see* 1969/388.† ss. 83(1) functions of Bd. of Trade transfd. to Min. of Technology, 88(2) functions of Bd. of Trade transfd. to Min. of Housing and Local Govt., 1969/1498.
Transport Act 1968 (c. 73)	Pt. V ss. 59–94 **mod.,** 1969/1636.
Customs (Import Deposits) Act 1968 (c. 74)	sch. 1 **am.,** 1969/240.
Sea Fisheries Act 1968 (c. 77)	*see* 1969/388.‡
1969 Town and Country Planning (S.) Act 1969 (c. 30)	s. 84(1) functions of Bd. of Trade transfd. to Min. of Technology, 1969/1498.
Iron and Steel Act 1969 (c. 45)	s. 11(1) functions of Bd. of Trade transfd. to Min. of Technology, 1969/1498.
Post Office Act 1969 (c. 48)...	ss. 12, 13, 20, 23 **rep.,** 28, 29 **am.,** 30 64, 73, 79 **rep.,** 80 **am.,** 84 **rep.,** sch. 9 **am.,** (Jersey) 1969/1366, (Guernsey) 1969/1367. ss. 30, 133, sch. 5 **am.,** 1969/1368. sch. 9 para. 36 functions of Bd. of Trade transfd. to Min. of Technology, 1969/1498.

* Functions as to Wales transferred to Secy. of State.
† Certain functions as to Wales transferred to Secy. of State.
‡ Certain functions as to Wales transferred to Secy. of State and Minister of Agriculture, Fisheries and Food.

TABLE B

A Chronological Table of Subordinate Legislation

(S.R. & O. and S.I. and certain Prerogative Instruments)

whose operation was affected by

Legislation of 1969 (Acts and Instruments)

Notes

1. For List of Abbreviations used in this Table, see p. ix.

2. In Col. 2, Volume references given in brackets after the titles of instruments have the following significance:—

    " Rev., 1903 " indicates *Statutory Rules and Orders Revised* (2nd Edition, to 31 Dec. 1903).

    " Rev." indicates *Statutory Rules and Orders and Statutory Instruments Revised* (3rd Edition, to 31 Dec. 1948).

    Where neither of these appears, the reference is to the Annual Volume of S.R. & O. (1890 to 1947) or S.I. (1948 onwards) for the year shown (in heavy type) in col. 1.

    The Roman numeral indicates the Volume or Part number of the Edition or year concerned.

Year and Number (or date)	Title or Description	How affected and Act or Instrument by which affected
1839 13 Feb.	St. Helena, Supreme Ct. and appeals to H.M. in Council—O. in C. 1839 (Rev. XX, p. 559)	r., 1969/857.
1852 5 Apr.	St. Helena, Powers of Governor—O. in C. 1852 (Rev. XX, p. 570)	r., 1969/857.
1871 29 June	Trial of the Pyx O. in C. 1871 (Rev. IV, p. 537)	am., 1969/148.
1878 22 Feb.	Wording of Crown Office documents and publication of Royal Proclam.— O. in C. (Rev. III, p. 1009)	sch. rules 1 **am.**, 2 **r.**, 4 **am.**, 1969/1070.
29 June	St. Helena Supreme Ct., Assessors— O. in C. 1878 (Rev. XX, p. 571)	r., 1969/857.
1910 10 Jan.	St. Helena, summoning of justices as assessors in civil or criminal trials— O. in C. 1910 (Rev. XX, p. 572)	r., 1969/857.
1912 69	Irish Land (Finance) Rules 1912 (1912, p. 405)	rule 16 **am.**, 1969/851.
1862	British Solomon Is. Maritime O. in C. 1912 (Rev. XIV, p. 28)	art. 9A **inserted**, 1969/1061.

Year and Number (or date)	Title or Description	How affected and Act or Instrument by which affected
1917 1018	New Hebrides Maritime O. in C. 1917 (Rev. XIV, p. 36)	art. 9A **inserted,** 1969/1062.
14 Feb.	Hong Kong R. Instructions 1917	cl. II, X, XIII, XIX, XXIV **am.,** Addnl. Instructions 11.3.69 (1969 I, p. 1748).
1920 803	Victory Bonds (Post Office Issue), drawing—Regs. 1920 (Rev. XV, p. 439)	regs. 2, 3, 4 **r.,** 5 **replaced,** 1969/1326.
1921 622	Fees for certificates of Savings Bank Rules, Awards, etc.—Warrant 1921 (Rev. XX, p. 606)	art. 1 **am.,** 1969/1852.
1925 788	Post Office Register Regs. 1925 (Rev. XV, p. 448)	regs. 2, 4, 6, 13, 15, 26, 38, 39, 41, 42 **am.,** sch. 2 **replaced,** 1969/1310.
1093	Land Registration Rules 1925 (Rev. XII, p. 81)	rules 88, 138, 292, 293, 294 sch. forms 18, 79, 81 **r.,** 1969/1179.
1927 1184	Supreme Ct. Funds Rules 1927 (1927, p. 1638)	rule 78 **am.,** 1969/206.
1928 133	Foot and Mouth Disease O. 1928 (Rev. II, p. 499)	arts. 1, 3, 5, 6, 10, 11, 13, 14, 16, 17, 20 **am.,** 22, 23 **r.,** 26 sch. 1 forms A, C **am.,** D **replaced,** E **am.,** 1969/1444.
922	Importation of Dogs and Cats O. 1928 (Rev. II, p. 399)	art. 2–4 **am.,** 1969/1743.
1929 831	Companies (Bd. of Trade) Fees O. 1929 (Rev. IV, p. 749)	**r.,** 1969/519.
1048	Trustee Savings Banks Regs. 1929 (Rev. XX, p. 584)	regs. 2, 16, 29 **am.,** 1969/1700.
1930 40	Post Office Register (Trustee Savings Banks) Regs. 1930 (Rev. XV, p. 473)	gen. **am.,** regs. 4 **am.,** 6 **replaced,** 10 **am.,** 1969/1311.
211	Land Registration Rules 1930 (Rev. XII, p. 167)	**r.,** 1969/1179.
220	Land Registration Fee O. 1930 (Rev. XII, p. 172)	First Registrations—para. XII **am.,** Abatement of Fees—No. 10 **r.,** 1969/1441.
1064	Companies (Bd. of Trade) Fees O. 1930 (Rev. IV, p. 749)	**r.,** 1969/519.
1931 1140	Asbestos Industry Regs. 1931 (Rev. VII, p. 181)	**r.,** 1969/690.
1932 560	Agricultural Marketing (Facilities Ctee.) Regs. 1932 (Rev. I, p. 160)	reg. 9 functions transfd. 1969/388.

Year and Number (or date)	Title or Description	How affected and Act or Instrument by which affected
1932 715	Agricultural Marketing (Consumers' Ctee.) Regs. 1932 (Rev. I, p. 158)	reg. 13 functions transfd. 1969/388.
1933 774	Approved School Rules 1933 (Rev. III, p. 788)	rule 30A am., 1969/1304.
789	Milk Marketing Scheme (Approval) O. 1933 (Rev. 1, p. 224)	scheme— paras. 59(c), 60 functions transfd. 1969/388. para. 51 am., 1969/1812.
1149	Savings Certificates Regs. 1933 (Rev. XV, p. 309)	reg. 4 am., 1969/541. gen. am., regs. 1 am., 3 r., 6, 26, 32 am., 35 replaced, 37 am., 38 r., 40 am., sch. 1 r., 1969/1334.
1935 488	Sheriff Ct., solicitors', etc. fees—A.S. 1935 (Rev. XX, p. 880)	c. IV am., 1969/1807.
836	Hong Kong Divorce Jurisdiction O. in C. 1935 (Rev. VI, p. 18)	art. 3 am., 1969/1060.
Instrt. not S.I. 3 Oct.	St. Helena, Administration of Justice O. in C. 1839—Amdg. O. in C. 1935 (Rev. XX, p. 568)	r., 1969/857.
1936 30	Hong Kong (Non-Domiciled Parties) Divorce Rules 1936 (Rev. VI, p. 992)	r., 1969/1837.
626	County Ct. Rules 1936 (1936 I, p. 282)	O. 2, 8, 11, 15, 16, 25, 35, 37, 46, 47 am., Appx. A forms am., 1969/585.
1244	Heavy Goods Vehicles (Driver's Licences) Regs. 1936 (Rev. XX, p. 478)	r., 1969/903.
1302	Land Registration Rules 1936 (Noted Rev. XII, p. 167)	r., 1969/1179.
1937 250	Firearms Rules 1937 (Rev. II, p. 763)	r., 1969/1219.
309	Firearms (S.) Rules 1937 (Rev. II, p. 775)	r., 1969/1453.
1217	Indian Civil Service Family Pension Fund Rules (Rev. X, p. 715)	rules 26A, 26C am., sch. 7 replaced, 1969/1149.
1226	Indian Military Service Family Pension Fund Rules 1937 (Rev. X, p. 632)	rule 14 am., 14B inserted, 1969/400.
1938 451	Heavy Goods Vehicles (Driver's Licences) (Amdt.) Regs. 1938 (Rev. XX, p. 478)	r., 1969/903.
661	Trade Marks Rules 1938 (Rev. XXIII, p. 3)	sch. 1 replaced, 1969/522.

Year and Number (or date)	Title or Description	How affected and Act or Instrument by which affected
1938 1434	Foot and Mouth Disease (Infected Areas Restrictions) O. 1938 (Rev. II, p. 528)	gen. am., arts. 2—7 am., 7A–7C inserted, 9, 11 am., 13 replaced, 14 inserted, 17, 21 sch. 1 am., 1969/1445.
1435	Foot and Mouth Disease (Controlled Areas Restrictions) General O. 1938 (Rev. II, p. 520)	gen. am., arts. 4—7, 11, 15 sch. am., 1969/1446.
1940 2107	Keeper of the Registers and Records of Scotland, disposal of documents— Regs. 1940 (Rev. XIX, p. 846)	r. (Sheriff Cts.), 1969/1756.
1945 698	Provision of Milk and Meals Regs. 1945 (Rev. VI, p. 380)	r., 1969/483.
1946 137	Family Allowances (Making of Claims and Payments) Regs. 1946 (Rev. VII, p. 616)	regs. 1 am., 10A inserted, 13 am., 1969/288. regs. 1 am., 8 replaced, 9, 10A am., 1969/1135.
138	Family Allowances (Qualifications) Regs. 1946 (Rev. VII, p. 607)	r., 1969/212.
1708	Pensions Appeal Tribunals (E. and W.) (Amdt.) Rules 1946 (Rev. XVII, p. 733)	sch. 2 am., 1969/931.
1709	Pensions Appeal Tribunals (S.) Rules 1946 (Rev. XVII, p. 752)	sch. 2 am., 1969/1585.
2105	Isles of Scilly (Housing) O. 1946 (Rev. XII, p. 572)	art. 3 am., 1969/637.
1947 1245	National Insurance (Modification of Local Govt. Superannuation Schemes) Regs. 1947 (Rev. XVI, p. 273)	r., 1969/793.
1421	Trial of the Pyx O. 1947 (Rev. IV, p. 541)	r., 1969/148.
1531	Federated Superannuation System for Universities (Pensions Increase) Regs. 1947 (Rev. XVII, p. 628)	regs. 2, 3 am., 1969/1321.
1675	National Insurance (Modification of Local Govt. Superannuation Schemes) Amdt. Regs. 1947 (1947 I, p. 1507)	r., 1969/793.
1778	Double Taxation Relief (Taxes on Income) (Seychelles) O. 1947 (Rev. X, p. 486)	sch. paras. 1, 6, 13 am., 1969/379.
1948 55	National Insurance (Pensions, Existing Beneficiaries and Other Persons) (Transitional) Regs. 1948 (Rev. XVI, p. 36)	regs. 9, 10 am., schs. 1–3 replaced, 1969/1361.

Year and Number (or date)	Title or Description	How affected and Act or Instrument by which affected
1948		
60	National Health Service (Functions of Regional Hospital Bds, etc.) Regs. 1948 (Rev. XV, p. 541)	r., 1969/297.
167	Isles of Scilly (National Health Service) O. 1948 (Rev. XV, p. 807)	sch. **am.**, 1969/355.
185	Agriculture (Calculation of Value for Compensation) Regs. 1948 (Rev. I, p. 821)	r., 1969/1704.
594	National Health Service (Functions of Regional Hospital Bds.) (S.) Regs. 1948 (Rev. XV, p. 841)	regs. 2, 4 **am.**, 1969/437.
612	National Insurance (Pensions, Existing Contributors) (Transitional) Regs. 1948 (Rev. XVI, p. 18)	reg. 11 **am.**, sch. 2 **replaced**, 5 **am.**, 1969/1361.
944	Teachers Pensions (National Insurance Mod.) (S.) Regs. 1948 (Rev. VI, p. 823)	regs. 2, 3 r., 1969/77.
1041	National Insurance (Claims and. Payments) Regs. 1948 (Rev. XVI, p. 313)	regs. 12 **replaced**, 18 **am.**, 1969/289. sch. 2 Pt. II **am.**, 1969/339. regs. 1, 9, 10, 12 sch. 2 Pt. II **am.**, 1969/1135.
1225	National Insurance (Mod. of Local Govt. Superannuation Schemes) Amdt. Regs. 1948 (Rev. XVI, p. 284)	r., 1969/793.
1239	National Health Service (Executive Councils and Dental Estimates Bd.) Financial Regs. 1948 (Rev. XV, p. 716)	r., 1969/1581.
1261	National Insurance (Widow's Benefit and Retirement Pensions) Regs. 1948 (Rev. XVI, p. 207)	sch. **replaced**, 1969/1361.
1274	National Insurance and Industrial Injuries (Collection of Contributions) Regs. 1948 (Rev. XVI, p. 148)	regs. 10A, 11 **am.**, 1969/1362.
1301	National Health Service (Joint Pricing Cttee. for E.) O. 1948 (Rev. XV, p. 704)	arts. 12 **am.**, 15–18 r., 1969/1781.
1390	National Health Service (Appointment of Medical and Dental Officers) (S.) Regs. 1948 (Rev. XV, p. 854)	regs. 5, 6 **am.**, 1969/257.
1414	National Health Service (Hospital Accounts and Financial Provns.) Regs. 1948 (Rev. XV, p. 734)	r., 1969/1582.
1417	National Insurance (Contributions) Regs. 1948 (Rev. XVI, p. 164)	r., 1969/1696.

Year and Number (or date)	Title or Description	How affected and Act or Instrument by which affected
1948		
1425	National Insurance (Classification) Regs. 1948 (Rev. XVI, p. 95)	sch. 1 paras. 9 **am.**, 33, 36 **r.**, 39 **replaced**, 1969/1135. sch. 1 paras. 8 **am.**, 11 **inserted**, 32, 34–44A, 46–53 **am.**, 1969/1362.
1488	National Health Service (Welsh Joint Pricing Cttee.) O. 1948 (Rev. XV, p. 711)	art. 12 **am.**, 15–18 **r.**, 1969/1774.
1494	National Health Service (Finance of Executive Councils and Scottish Dental Estimates Bd.) (S.) Regs. 1948 (Rev. XV, p. 996)	**r.**, 1969/1612.
1596	National Health Service (Drug Accounts Cttee.) (S.) O. 1948 (Rev. XV, p. 989)	arts. 10 **am.**, 13–16 **r.**, 1969/1641.
2038	National Health Service (Hospital Accounts and Financial Provns.) (S.) Regs. 1948 (Rev. XV, p. 1003)	**r.**, 1969/1611.
2361	Air Corporations (Pensions) Regs. 1948 (Rev. I, p. 1275)	sch. **am.**, 1969/834.
2595	Voluntary Homes (Registration) (S.) Regs. 1948 (Rev. III, p. 806)	**r.**, 1969/1622.
2677	Horse Breeding Rules 1948 (Rev. II, p. 707)	rule 13 sch. 2 forms A, F **am.**, 1969/1137.
1949		
316	Enrolment of Deeds (Change of Name) Regs. 1949 (1949 I, p. 3997)	reg. 8 **replaced**, 1969/1432.
330	Companies (Winding-up) Rules 1949 (1949 I, p. 789)	rule 72 **am.**, 1969/1177.
352	National Insurance (New Entrants Transitional) Regs. 1949 (1949 I, p. 2737)	reg. 5 **am.**, sch. 2 **am.**, 1969/1361.
632	National Insurance (Mod. of Local Govt. Superannuation Schemes) (Amdt.) Regs. 1949 (1949 I, p. 2750)	**r.**, 1969/793.
850	Companies (Bd. of Trade) Fees O. 1949 (1949 I, p. 930)	**r.**, 1969/519.
1461	National Insurance (Hospital In-Patients) Regs. 1949 (1949 I, p. 2718)	regs. 3—6A **am.**, 1969/1361.
1464	Superannuation (Local Govt. and Public Bds.) Interchange Rules 1949 (1949 I, p. 3075)	**r.**, 1969/997.
1466	National Insurance (Mod. of Local Govt. Superannuation Schemes) (Amdt. No. 2) Regs. 1949 (1949 I, p. 2752)	**r.**, 1969/793.

Year and Number (or date)	Title or Description	How affected and Act or Instrument by which affected
1949		
1668	National Assistance (Registration of Homes) (S.) **Regs.** 1949 (1949 I, p. 2582)	**r.**, 1969/1622.
1912	Livestock (Licensing of Boars) (S.) Regs. 1949 (1949 I, p. 482)	regs. 2, 7 **am.**, 12 **replaced**, sch. 1, 2 **am.**, 1969/1155.
2058	County Cts. Districts O. 1949 (1949 I, p. 955)	sch. 1 **am.**, 1969/295, 1178, 1397.
2199	Double Taxation Relief (Taxes on Income) (Swaziland) O. 1949 (1949 I, p. 2309)	**superseded**, 1969/380.
2368	Designs Rules 1949 (1949 I, p. 1417)	sch. 1 **replaced**, 1969/481.
2441	Business Names Rules 1949 (1949 I, p. 531)	rule 9, Appx. forms R.B.N. I, 1A, 1B, 1C, 3, 3A, 3B **am.**, 1969/1330.
2452	Agricultural Marketing (Ctee, of Investigation) Regs. 1949 (1949 I, p. 32)	reg. 19 functions transfd. 1969/388.
1950		
330	National Insurance (Contributions) Amdt. Regs. 1950 (1950 II, p. 15)	**r.**, 1969/1696.
392	Patents Appeal Tribunal Rules 1950 (1950 II, p. 201)	rule 5A **am.**, 1969/500.
1195	Double Taxation Relief (Taxes on Income) (Denmark) O. 1950 (1950 I, p. 1019)	sch. arts. I, II, **am.**, V **r.**, VII, VIII **replaced**, VIIIA **inserted**, XVI **replaced**, XVII, XIX **am.**, XXII **replaced**, 1969/1068.
1250	Representation of the People (S.) Regs. 1950 (Rev XX, p. 56)	**r.** (saving), 1969/912.
1254	Representation of the People Regs. 1950 (Rev. XX, p. 7)	**r.** (saving), 1969/904.
1255	Representation of the People (N.I.) Regs. 1950 (Rev. XX, p. 105)	**r.** (saving), 1969/905.
1539	Superannuation (Transfers between the Civil Service and Public Bds.) Rules 1950 (1950 II, p. 291)	sch. **am.**, 1969/1382.
1544	Industrial Assurance (Deposits etc.) Rules 1950 (1950 I, p. 1102)	**r.**, 1969/1654.
1869	Agricultural Marketing (Re-organisation Commn.) Regs. 1950 (1950 I, p. 16)	reg. 14 functions transfd. 1969/388.
1947	National Insurance (Contributions) Amdt. (No. 2) Regs. 1950 (1950 II, p. 20)	**r.**, 1969/1696.
1951		
266	Rural District Council Election Rules 1951 (1951 II, p. 361)	**r.**, 1969/757.

Year and Number (or date)	Title or Description	How affected and Act or Instrument by which affected
1951 267	Urban District Council Election Rules 1951 (1951 II, p. 385)	r., 1969/756.
309	Superannuation (English Local Govt. and Is. of Man) Interchange Rules 1951 (1951 II, p. 148)	rules 1, 2, 4 **am.**, 7 **r.**, 12—14 **inserted**, 1969/710.
377	Enrolment of Deeds (Change of Name) (Amdt.) Regs. 1951 (Noted Rev. XXII, p. 258)	**superseded**, 1969/1432.
843	National Health Service (Charges for Appliances) Regs. 1951 (1951 I, p. 1389)	reg. 3 **replaced**, 1969/906.
861	National Health Service (General Dental and Supplementary Ophthalmic Services) (S.) Regs. 1951 (1951 I, p. 1412)	reg. 5 **am.**, 1969/918.
862	National Health Service (Charges for Appliances) (S.) Regs. 1951 (1951 I, p. 1411)	reg. 2 **replaced**, 1969/918.
1653	Civil Aviation (Investigation of Accidents) Regs. 1951 (1951 I, p. 234)	r., 1969/833.
1952 170	Agriculture (Calculation of Value for Compensation) Amdt. Regs. 1952 (1952 I, p. 40)	r., 1969/1704.
868	Colonial Civil Aviation (Application of Act) O. 1952 (1952 I, p. 565)	r. (certain territories), 1969/592.
900	Public Service Vehicles (Licences and Certificates) Regs. 1952 (1952 III, p. 2907)	regs. 10, 17, 24, 41 **am.**, Pt. VIII (regs. 49—51) **inserted**, 1969/32.
937	Superannuation (English Local Govt. and N.I.) Interchange Rules 1952 (1952 II, p. 2354)	rules 1, 2, 4 **am.**, 7 **r.**, 12—15 **inserted**, 1969/710.
938	National Insurance (Mod. of Local Govt. Superannuation Schemes) (Amdt.) Regs. 1952 (1952 II, p. 2192)	r., 1969/793.
1032	Civil Aviation Act (Is. of Man) O. 1952 (1952 I, p. 561)	sch. **am.**, 1969/594.
1046	Licensing of Bulls (S.) Regs. 1952 (1952 I, p. 158)	regs. 2, 7 **am.**, 15 **replaced**, sch. 2 **am.**, 1969/1154.
1393	National Insurance (Contributions) Amdt. Regs. 1952 (1952 II, p. 2140)	r., 1969/1696.
1457	Family Allowances (Conditions for Increase of Allowance) Regs. 1952 (1952 I, p. 996)	reg. 3 **r.**, 1969/212.
1469	Firearms Rules 1952 (1952 I, p. 176)	r., 1969/1219.

Year and Number (or date)	Title or Description	How affected and Act or Instrument by which affected
1952		
1617	Agriculture (Calculation of Value for Compensation) Amdt. (No. 2) Regs. 1952 (1952 I, p. 41)	r., 1969/1704.
1792	Firearms (S.) Rules 1952 (1952 I, p. 179)	r., 1969/1453.
1894	Representation of the People (N.I.) Regs. 1952 (1952 III, p. 2821)	r. (saving), 1969/905.
1900	Wireless Telegraphy (Channel Is.) O. 1952 (1952 III, p. 3414)	sch. **am.**, 1969/1369.
1999	Family Allowances (Qualifications) Amdt. Regs. 1952 (1952 I, p. 1001)	r., 1969/212.
2113	Bankruptcy Rules 1952 (1952 I, p. 213)	rule 123 **am.**, 1969/1007. rule 70 **am.**, 1969/1162.
2117	Companies (Bd. of Trade) Fees O. 1952 (1952 I, p. 624)	r., 1969/519.
1953		
121	Federated Superannuation System for Universities (Pensions Increase) Regs. 1953 (1953 II, p. 1527)	regs. 2, 3 **am.**, 1969/1321.
456	Agriculture (Calculation of Value for Compensation) Amdt. Regs. 1953 (1953 I, p. 2)	r., 1969/1704.
495	National Insurance (Contributions) Amdt. Regs. 1953 (1953 I, p. 1371)	r., 1969/1696.
591	Colonial Civil Aviation (Application of Act) (Amdt.) O. 1953 (1953 I, p. 275)	r. (certain territories), 1969/592.
1059	Family Allowances (Qualifications) Amdt. Regs. 1953 (1953 I, p. 746)	r., 1969/212.
1107	Representation of the People Regs. 1953 (1953 II, p. 1757)	r. (saving), 1969/904.
1108	Representation of the People (N.I.) Regs. 1953 (1953 II, p. 1760)	r. (saving), 1969/905.
1109	Representation of the People (S.) Regs. 1953 (1953 II, p. 1763)	r. (saving), 1969/912.
1544	National Insurance (Contributions) Amdt. (No. 2) Regs. 1953 (1953 I, p. 1372)	r., 1969/1696.
1669	Colonial Civil Aviation (Application of Act) (Amdt.) (No. 2) O. 1953 (1953 I, p. 277)	r. (certain territories), 1969/592.
1671	Aliens O. 1953 (1953 I, p. 94)	arts. 30, 32, 33 **am.**, 1969/388.
1954		
14	Coroners' Records (Fees for Copies) Rules 1954 (1954 I, p. 514)	r., 1969/1511.

Year and Number (or date)	Title or Description	How affected and Act or Instrument by which affected
1954 189	National Insurance (Maternity Benefit and Miscellaneous Provns.) Regs. 1954 (1954 I, p. 1387)	regs. 3, 13 **am.**, 1969/1361. reg. 20 **r.**, sch. 1 **am.**, 1969/1696.
224	National Health Service (Executive Councils) Regs. 1954 (1954 I, p. 1270)	**r.**, 1969/352.
370	Pedestrian Crossing Regs. 1954 (1954 II, p. 1948)	reg. 2 **am.**, 1969/888.
498	Representation of the People Regs. 1954 (1954 II, p. 1921)	**r.** (saving), 1969/904.
499	Representation of the People (N.I.) Regs. 1954 (1954 II, p. 1923)	**r.** (saving), 1969/905.
515	Representation of the People (S.) Regs. 1954 (1954 II, p. 1922)	**r.** (saving), 1969/912.
641	National Insurance and Industrial Injuries (Switzerland) O. 1954 (1954 I, p. 1422)	**r.**, 1969/384.
796	Non-Contentious Probate Rules 1954 (1954 II, p. 2202)	rules 2, 3, 21, 38 **am.**, 1969/1689.
830	Colonial Civil Aviation (Application of Act) (Amdt.) O. 1954 (1954 I, p. 463)	**r.** (certain territories), 1969/592.
1048	Local Govt. Superannuation (Benefits) Regs. 1954 (1954 II, p. 1537)	regs. 2, 20, sch. 3 **am.**, 1969/793.
1192	Local Govt. Superannuation (Administration) Regs. 1954 (1954 II, p. 1570)	regs. 2, 6 **am.**, 13A **inserted**, 16 **am.**, 1969/793.
1207	National Insurance (Mod. of Local Govt. Superannuation Schemes) (Amdt.) Regs. 1954 (1954 I, p. 1408)	**r.**, 1969/793.
1212	Local Govt. Superannuation (Transfer Value) Regs. 1954 (1954 II, p. 1723)	Pt. IV, sch. 5 **r.**, 1969/793.
1224	Local Govt. Superannuation (Actuarial Valuations) Regs. 1954 (1954 II, p. 1537)	regs. 5, 7 **am.**, sch. 2 form A **replaced**, form H **am.**, 1969/793.
1484	Rural District Council Election Rules 1954 (1954 II, p. 1919)	**r.**, 1969/757.
1485	Urban District Council Election Rules 1954 (1954 II, p. 1920)	**r.**, 1969/756.
1616	Firearms Rules 1954 (1954 I, p. 160)	**r.**, 1969/1219.
1955 75	Firearms (S.) Rules 1955 (1955 I, p. 223)	**r.**, 1969/1453.
120	Midwives Rules 1955 (1955 I, p. 1145)	annex s. D **r.**, 1969/1440.
709	Colonial Civil Aviation (Application of Act) (Amdt.) O. 1955 (1955 I, p. 458)	**r.** (certain territories), 1969/592.

Year and Number (or date)	Title or Description	How affected and Act or Instrument by which affected
1955		
1125	Cinematograph (Safety) (S.) Regs. 1955 (1955 I, p. 326)	reg. 8 **am.**, 31A **inserted**, 1969/1575.
1494	Superannuation (Local Govt. and National Health Service) Interchange Rules 1955 (1955 II, p. 1758)	rules 2–4 **am.**, 8 **r.**, 13–15 **inserted**, 1969/710.
1546	Superannuation (Local Govt. and Public Bds.) Interchange (Amdt.) Rules 1955 (1955 II, p. 1782)	**r.**, 1969/997.
1602	National Insurance (Contributions) Amdt. Regs. 1955 (1955 I, p. 1629)	**r.**, 1969/1696.
1956		
162	Rules of Procedure (Army) 1956 (1956 I, p. 213)	rules 5, 62, schs. 1, 3, 4 **am.**, 1969/680.
163	Rules of Procedure (Air Force) 1956 (1956 II, p. 2020)	rule 62, schs. 3, 4 **am.**, 1969/679.
715	Ulster and Colonial Savings Certificates (Income Tax Exemption) Regs. 1956 (1956 I, p. 1086)	reg. 3 **am.**, 1969/542.
1048	Conveyance in Harbours of Govt. Explosives and Explosives of Visiting Forces Regs. 1956 (1956 I, p. 841)	**r.**, 1969/18.
1049	Conveyance by Rail of Govt. Explosives and Explosives of Visiting Forces Regs. 1956 (1956 I, p. 886)	**r.**, 1969/19.
1050	Conveyance by Road of Govt. Explosives and Explosives of Visiting Forces Regs. 1956 (1956 I, p. 896)	**r.**, 1969/20.
1075	National Health Service (Executive Councils) Amdt. Regs. 1956 (1956 I, p. 1552)	**r.**, 1969/352.
1077	National Health Service (Service Ctees. and Tribunal) Regs. 1956 (1956 I, p. 1554)	regs. 2–4, 20–22, 48, schs. 1, 3 **am.**, 1969/354.
1078	National Health Service (Supplementary Ophthalmic Services) Regs. 1956 (1956 I, p. 1524)	gen. **am.**, regs. 2, 4, 6, 7, 11, 18 **am.**, 21 **r.**, sch. 3 **am.**, 1969/351. reg. 14, sch. 3 **am.**, 1969/906.
1427	Licensing of Bulls (E. and W.) Regs. 1956 (1956 I, p. 196)	**r.**, 1969/1139.
1428	Licensing of Boars (E. and W.) Regs. 1956 (1956 I, p. 188)	regs. 3, 8 **am.**, 14 **replaced**, schs. 1, 2 **am.**, 1969/1138.
1657	Premium Savings Bonds Regs. 1956 (1956 I, p. 1489)	generally **am.**, regs. 1, 4, 17, 23 **am.**, 26 **replaced**, 1969/1333.
1669	Post Office Register (Amdt.) (No. 2) Regs. 1956 (1956 I, p. 1485)	reg. 2 **r.**, 1969/1310.

Year and Number (or date)	Title or Description	How affected and Act or Instrument by which affected
1956 1793	National Health Service (Functions of Regional Hospital Bds. etc.) Amdt. Regs. 1956 (1956 I, p. 1512)	r., 1969/297.
1938	Federated Superannuation System for Universities (Pensions Increase) Regs. 1956 (1956 II, p. 1725)	regs. 2, 3 **am.**, 1969/1321
2020	National Insurance (Contributions) Amdt. Regs. 1956 (1956 I, p. 1639)	r., 1969/1696.
1957 356	Teachers (Superannuation) (S.) Regs. 1957 (1957 I, p. 733)	r., 1969/77.
467	Importation of Horses, Asses and Mules O. 1957 (1957 I, p. 159)	r., 1969/915.
485	Public Trustee (Fees) O. 1957 (1957 II, p. 2578)	r., 1969/513.
525	Road and Rail Traffic Act (Exemption) Regs. 1957 (1957 II, p. 2148)	r., 1969/1349.
777	Representation of the People (S.) Regs. 1957 (1957 II, p. 1949)	r. (saving), 1969/912.
855	National Insurance (Cyprus) O. 1957 (1957 I, p. 1649)	r., 1969/1494.
1074	Motor Vehicles (International Circulation) O. 1957 (1957 II, p. 2154)	art. 5 **am.**, 1969/1086.
1155	Superannuation (English Local Govt. and N.I. Civil Service) Interchange Rules 1957 (1957 II, p. 1774)	rules 2, 3, 5 **am.**, 6, 9 **r.**, 13–16 **inserted**, 1969/710.
1157	Landlord and Tenant (Notices) Regs. 1957 (1957 I, p. 1230)	appx. forms 7, 9 **replaced**, 12 **am.**, 16 **inserted**, 1969/1771.
1299	National Insurance (Contributions) Amdt. Regs. 1957 (1957 I, p. 1635)	r., 1969/1696.
1835	National Insurance (Child's Special Allowance) Regs. 1957 (1957 I, p. 1523)	sch. **am.**, 1969/1696.
2176	National Insurance (Contributions) Amdt. (No. 2) Regs. 1957 (1957 I, p. 1642)	r., 1969/1696.
2197	Superannuation (English Local Govt. and N.I. Health Service) Interchange Rules 1957 (1957 II, p. 1783)	rules 2–4, 6 **am.**, 8 **r.**, 12–14 **inserted**, 1969/710.
2224	Judicial Cttee. Rules 1957 (1957 I, p. 1205)	sch. Arrangement of Rules, rule 11 **am.**, 11A **inserted**, 22–24, 29, 34 **am.**, 1969/365.
1958 101	Royal Irish Constabulary (Widows' Pensions) Regs. 1958 (1958 I, p. 354)	regs. 1, 2 **am.**, 1969/1517.

Year and Number (or date)	Title or Description	How affected and Act or Instrument by which affected
1958 426	Federation of Malaya (Appeals to Privy Council) O. in C. 1958 (1958 I, p. 1322)	art. 5, sch. 2 **am.**, 1969/369.
744	Licensing of Bulls (E. and W.) Amdt. Regs. 1958 (1958 I, p. 196)	**r.**, 1969/1139.
1041	Pensioners' Declarations Rules 1958 (1958 II, p. 1803)	rule 3 **am.**, 1969/1888.
1181	Govt. Annuities Payment Regs. 1958 (1958 I, p. 1232)	reg. 6 **am.**, 1969/1327.
1402	Superannuation (Local Govt. and Overseas Employment) Interchange (S.) Rules 1958 (1958 II, p. 1857)	**r.** (saving), 1969/1642.
1416	Superannuation (Local Govt. and Overseas Employment) Interchange Rules 1958 (1958 II, p. 1845)	**r.** (saving), 1969/975.
1514	Colonial Civil Aviation (Application of Act) (Amdt.) O. 1958 (1958 I, p. 303)	**r.** (certain territories), 1969/592.
1595	Teachers (Superannuation) (S.) (Amdt. No. 1) Regs. 1958 (1958 I, p. 1077)	**r.**, 1969/77.
1778	Agriculture (Spring Traps) (S.) O. 1958 (1958 I, p. 159)	spent on enactment of Agriculture (Spring Traps) (S.) Act 1969 (c. 26).
1976	Import Duty Reliefs (No. 4) O. 1958 (1958 I, p. 797)	**r.** (saving), 1969/1339.
2191	International Sugar Council (Immunities and Privileges) O. 1958 (1958 I, p. 956)	**r.**, 1969/734.
1959 277	Milk and Dairies (General) Regs. 1959 (1959 I, p. 1351)	sch. Pt. I functions transfd., 1969/388.
364	Schools Regs. 1959 (1959 I, p. 1584)	reg. 12 **am.**, 1969/231 6 **r.**, 20 **am.**, 1969/1174 16 **am.**, sch. 1 **r.**, 1969/1777
365	Handicapped Pupils and Special Schools Regs. 1959 (1959 I, p. 1024)	reg. 15 **am.**, 1969/1777.
366	Special Schools and Establishments (Grant) Regs. 1959 (1959 I, p. 1051)	reg. 5 **r.**, 1969/410.
393	Further Education (Local Education Authies.) Regs. 1959 (1959 I, p. 1577)	**r.**, 1969/403.
394	Further Education (Grant) Regs. 1959 (1959 I, p. 1041)	**r.**, 1969/403.
409	Provision of Milk and Meals Amdg. Regs. 1959 (1959 I, p. 1029)	**r.**, 1969/483.
430	Rural District Council Election Rules 1959 (1959 II, p. 2310)	**r.**, 1969/757.
467	National Insurance (Industrial Injuries) (Prescribed Diseases) Regs. 1959 (1959 II, p. 1943)	sch. 1 **am.**, 1969/619.

Year and Number (or date)	Title or Description	How affected and Act or Instrument by which affected
1959		
476	Abolition of the Education (S.) Fund (Consequential Provns.) Regs. 1959 (1959 I, p. 1095)	reg. 13 **r.**, 1969/77.
496	Agriculture (Calculation of Value for Compensation) Regs. 1959	**r.**, 1969/1704.
748	National Health Service (Designation of Teaching Hospitals) O. 1959 (1959 I, p. 1813)	sch. 1 **am.**, 1969/759.
833	Grant-Aided Secondary Schools (S.) Grant Regs. 1959 (1959 I, p. 1104)	reg. 4 **am.**, sch. **replaced,** 1969/506.
847	National Insurance (Contributions) Amdt. Regs. 1959 (1959 II, p. 1882)	**r.**, 1969/1696.
890	Standards for School Premises Regs. 1959 (1959 I, p. 1006)	regs. 2, 3, 5, 15–17, 30–32, 51, 52, 56 **am.**, 1969/433.
961	Public Trustee (Fees) O. 1959 (1959 II, p. 2704)	**r.**, 1969/513.
1035	Bahrain O. 1959 (1959 I, p. 250)	arts. 14, 15 **am.**, 1969/855.
1038	Quatar O. 1959 (1959 II, p. 2252)	arts. 14, 15 **am.**, 1969/856.
1039	Trucial States O. 1959 (1959 II, p. 2676)	arts. 4, 14, 15, 17, 25 **am.**, 1969/859.
1052	Colonial Civil Aviation (Application of Act) (Amdt.) O. 1959 (1959 I, p. 684)	**r.** (certain territories), 1969/592.
1123	Premium Savings Bonds (Fees) Warrant 1959 (1959 I, p. 305)	art. 1 **am.**, 1969/1852.
1169	Family Allowances (Qualifications) Amdt. Regs. 1959 (1959 I, p. 1276)	**r.**, 1969/212.
1226	Fishing Nets (Northwest Atlantic) O. 1959 (1959 II, p. 2469)	**r.**, 1969/628.
1334	Postal Order Warrant 1959 (1959 II, p. 2201)	regs. 1, 2, 10 **am.**, (P.O. scheme 18.9.69).*
1388	Air Navigation (Investigation of Combined Military and Civil Air Accidents) Regs. 1959 (1959 I, p. 671)	**r.**, 1969/1437.
1573	Superannuation (Local Govt. Social Workers and Health Education Staff) Interchange Rules 1959 (1959 II, p. 2015)	rules 2–4, 7 **am.**, 8 **r.**, 13–15 **inserted,** 1969/710.
1609	Federated Superannuation System for Universities (Pensions Increase) Regs. 1959 (1959 II, p. 2004)	regs. 1, 3–5 **am.**, 1969/1321.
1803	National Insurance (Contributions) Amdt. (No. 2) Regs. 1959 (1959 II, p. 1891)	**r.**, 1969/1696.
2108	Aliens (Approved Ports) O. 1959 (1959 I, p. 225)	**r.**, 1969/840.

*[Not S.I. *see* London Gazette 18-9-69; p. 15.]

Year and Number (or date)	Title or Description	How affected and Act or Instrument by which affected
1959		
2117	Mines (Notification of Dangerous Occurrences) O. 1959 (1959 I, p. 1786)	arts. 3, 4 **am.,** 1969/963.
2118	Quarries (Notification of Dangerous Occurrences) O. 1959 (1959 I, p. 1789)	arts. 3, 4 **am.,** 1969/964.
2201	Saint Vincent (Constitution) O. in C. 1959 (1959 I, p. 479)	**r.,** 1969/1500.
2245	Public Path Orders Regs. 1959 (1959 II, p. 2343)	**r.,** 1969/269.
1960		
270	Cycle Racing on Highways (S.) Regs. 1960 (1960 III, p. 3053)	reg. 5 **am.,** 1969/850. reg. 9 **inserted,** 1969/1767.
630	Public Trustee (Fees) O. 1960 (1960 III, p. 3310)	**r.,** 1969/513.
695	Town and Country Planning (Control of Advertisements) Regs. 1960	**r.,** 1969/1532.
764	Control of Hiring (Rebates) O. 1960 (1960 I, p. 1321)	**r.,** 1969/1307.
782	National Insurance (Contributions) Amdt. Regs. 1960 (1960 II, p. 2228)	**r.,** 1969/1696.
779	Savings Banks (Deposits) (Limits) O. 1960 (1960 III, p. 3062)	**r.,** 1969/939.
870	Detention Centre (S.) Rules 1960 (1960 I, p. 1176)	rule 24 **replaced,** 1969/253.
1064	National Insurance (Switzerland) O. 1960 (1960 II, p. 2340)	**r.,** 1969/384.
1210	National Insurance (Graduated Contributions and Non-participating Employments—Miscellaneous Provns.) Regs. 1960 (1960 II, p. 2234)	regs. 7–9, 11, 12 **r.,** 1969/1696.
1240	National Health Service (Functions of Regional Hospital Bds. etc.) Amdt. Regs. 1960 (1960 II, p. 2072)	**r.,** 1969/297.
1270	National Insurance (Mod. of the Superannuation Acts) Regs. 1960 (1960 II, p. 2297)	reg. 4 **am.,** 1969/1549.
1268	Meat (Staining and Sterilization) Regs. 1960 (1960 II p. 1523)	**r.,** 1969/871.
1285	National Insurance (Contributions) Amdt. (No. 2) Regs. 1960 (1960 II, p. 2230)	**r.,** 1960/1696.
1322	Trustee Savings Banks (Special Investments) (Limits) O. 1960 (1960 III, p. 3067)	art. 1 **am.,** 1969/941.

Year and Number (or date)	Title or Description	How affected and Act or Instrument by which affected
1960		
1444	Conveyance in Harbours of Govt. Explosives and Explosives of Visiting Forces (Amdt.) Regs. 1960 (1960 I, p. 1385)	r., 1969/18.
1445	Conveyance by Rail of Govt. Explosives and Explosives of Visiting Forces (Amdt.) Regs. 1960 (1960 I, p. 1390)	r., 1969/19.
1446	Conveyance by Road of Govt. Explosives and Explosives of Visiting Forces (Amdt.) Regs. 1960 (1960 I, p. 1396)	r., 1969/20.
1471	Legal Aid (Assessment of Resources) Regs. 1960 (1960 II, p. 1749)	reg. 1 am., 1969/922.
1505	Goods Vehicles (Licences and Prohibitions) Regs. 1960 (1960 III, p. 3020)	reg. 8 am., 1969/420. regs. 4, 8, 9 am., 14 replaced, 16, 18, 20 21, sch. 2 forms GV 5, GV 7 am., 1969/1638.
1526	Air Navigation (Investigation of Combined Military and Civil Air Accidents) (Amdt.) Regs. 1960 (1960 I, p. 708)	r., 1969/1437.
1695	National Insurance (Non-Participation —Teachers Superannuation) (S.) Regs. 1960 (1960 II, p. 2281)	r., 1969/77.
1932	Shipbuilding and Ship-repairing Regs. 1960 (1960 II, p. 1427)	regs. 3, 76, 77 am., 1969/690.
2409	Indian Civil Service Family Pension Fund (Amdt.) Rules 1960 (1960 II, p. 1711)	superseded, 1969/1149.
1961		
21	National Insurance (Modification of Local Govt. Superannuation Schemes) Regs. 1961	r., 1969/793.
34	National Health Service (Functions of Regional Hospital Bds. etc.) Regs. 1961	r., 1969/297.
124	A.S. (Sheriff Ct. Betting and Gaming Act Appeals) 1961	r., 1969/1452.
209	Motor Vehicles (Tests) (Exemption) Regs. 1961	r., 1969/419.
260	Importation of Horses, Asses and Mules (African Horse Sickness) (Prohibition) O. 1961	r., 1969/915.
316	Superannuation (English Local Govt. and Jersey) Interchange Rules 1961	rules 2, 3, 5 am., 7 r., 11—14 inserted, 1969/710.
405	National Insurance (Modification of Local Govt. Superannuation Schemes) No. 2 Regs. 1961	r., 1969/793.

Year and Number (or date)	Title or Description	How affected and Act or Instrument by which affected
1961 411	Parking Places Orders (Procedure) (E. and W.) Regs. 1961	r., 1969/463.
471	National Insurance (Non-Participation —Teachers Superannuation) (S.) Regs. 1961	r., 1969/77.
505	Parking Places Orders (Procedure) (S.) Regs. 1961	r., 1969/487.
669	Traffic Regulation Orders (Procedure) (S.) Regs. 1961	r., 1969/487.
692	A.S. (Fees of Clerks to Appropriate Authies.) 1961	r., 1969/1452.
770	Superannuation (Local Govt. and Overseas Employment) Interchange (Amdt.) Rules 1961	r. (saving), 1969/975.
1012	Irish Land (Finance) (Amdt.) Rules 1961	rule 1 am., 1969/851.
1091	Victory Bonds (Post Office Issue) (Amdt.) Regs. 1961	regs. 1 r., 2 am., 1969/1326.
1156	Superannuation (Local Govt. and Overseas Employment) Interchange (S.) Amdt. Rules 1961	r. (saving), 1969/1642.
1242	Street Playground Orders (Procedure) (E. and W.) Regs. 1961	r., 1969/463.
1322	Street Playgrounds Orders (Procedure) (S.) Regs. 1961	r., 1969/487.
1465	Motor Vehicles (Third Party Risks) Regs. 1961	regs. 4, 7, 9—11 am., sch. Pts. 1, 2 am., 1969/1733
1470	Ionising Radiations (Sealed Sources) Regs. 1961	r., 1969/808.
1519	Enrolled Nurses Rules, Approval Instrt., 1961	r. (excl. sch. Pt. V), 1969/1674 sch. Pt. V. r. (22-9-70), 1969/1674.
1520	Nurses Rules, Approval Instrt., 1961	r., 1969/1675
1566	Superannuation (Teaching and Public Bds.) (S.) Rules 1961	r. (saving), 1969/1046.
1582	Further Education (Local Education Authies.) Amdg. Regs. 1961	r., 1969/403
1933	General Optical Council (Disciplinary Cttee.) (Procedure) O. in C. 1961	r., 1969/1826.
2108	Motor Vehicles (Tests) (Exemption) (Amdt.) Regs. 1961	r., 1969/419
2317	Colonial Civil Aviation (Application of Act) (Amdt.) O. 1961	r. (certain territories), 1969/592.

Year and Number (or date)	Title or Description	How affected and Act or Instrument by which affected
1961 2412	Savings Banks (Deposits) (Limits) (Amdt.) O. 1961	r., 1969/939.
1962 12	National Insurance (Consequential Provns.) Regs. 1962	reg. 6, sch. 4 r., 1969/1696
25	Family Allowances (Qualifications) Amdt. Regs. 1962	r., 1969/212.
148	Legal Aid (General) Regs. 1962	reg. 1 **am.**, 1A **r.**, 1969/923. reg. 24 **am.**, 1969/1346.
300	National Insurance (Contributions) Amdt. Regs. 1962	r., 1969/1696
347	Drainage Charges (Forms) Regs. 1962	r., 1969/469
562	Public Trustee (Fees) O. 1962	r., 1969/513.
623	Approved Schools (Contribution by Local Authies.) Regs. 1962	reg. 1 **am.**, 1969/501.
790	Wages Regulation (Hair, Bass and Fibre) (Holidays) O. 1962	r., 1969/641.
987	National Insurance (Contributions) Amdt. (No. 2) Regs. 1962	r., 1969/1696.
1058	Public Service Vehicles (Licences and Certificates) (Amdt.) (No. 2) Regs. 1962	**superseded,** 1969/32.
1084	West Indies (Dissolution and Interim Commissioner) O. in C. 1962	art. 2 **am.**, 1969/1502.
1127	Motor Vehicles (Production of Test Certificates) Regs. 1962	r., 1969/418.
1268	Rural District Council Election Rules 1962	r., 1969/757.
1269	Urban District Council Election Rules	r., 1969/756.
1287	Food and Drugs (Legal Proceedings) Regs. 1962	reg. 5 **r.**, 1969/871.
1504	Enrolled Nurses Cttee. (Election Scheme) Rules, Approval Instrt. 1962	r., 1969/1676.
1633	Representation of the People (N.I.) Regs. 1962	**r.** (saving), 1969/905.
1669	Salmon and Migratory Trout (Prohibition of Drift-net Fishing) O. 1962	art. 3 **am.**, 1969/167.
2352	Double Taxation Relief (Taxes on Income) (South Africa) O. 1962	r., 1969/864.
2758	British Transport Reorganisation (Pensions of Employees) (No. 3) O. 1962	arts. 13, 14, 16 **r.**, 1969/1824.

Year and Number (or date)	Title or Description	How affected and Act or Instrument by which affected
1962 2489	National Assistance (Registration of Homes) (S.) (Amdt.) Regs. 1962	r., 1969/1622.
2785	International Coffee Organisation (Immunities and Privileges) O. 1962	r., 1969/733.
1963 133	A. S. (Alteration of Sheriff Ct. Fees) 1963	annex: Pt. I s. A am., 1969/464.
382	Wages Regulation (Brush and Broom) (Holidays) O. 1963	r., 1969/209.
436	Motor Vehicles (International Motor Insurance Card) Regs. 1963	r., 1969/668.
467	Companies (Bd. of Trade) Fees O. 1963	r., 1969/519.
501	National Insurance (Contributions) Amdt. Regs. 1963	r., 1969/1696.
523	Public Trustee (Fees) O. 1963	r., 1969/513.
569	Eggs (Guaranteed Prices) O. 1963	r., 1969/401.
709	Town and Country Planning General Development O. 1963	arts. 2 am., 5 replaced, 5A inserted, 6, 8, 9 am., 11A inserted, 13 am., 14 replaced, 14A inserted, 16 am., schs. 2, 3 replaced, 4 am., 5 renumbered 7, new 5, 6 inserted, 1969/276.
757	Federated Superannuation System for Universities (Pensions Increase) Regs. 1963	regs. 1, 4, 5 am., 1969/1321.
792	Location of Offices Bureau O. 1963	Functions of Bd. of Trade transfd. to Min. of Housing and Local Govt. 1969/1498.
934	National Insurance (Industrial Injuries) (Colliery Workers Supplementary Scheme) Amdt. and Consolidation O. 1963	sch. 1 art. 12 am., 1969/716, 1646.
935	Exchange of Securities (General) Rules 1963	generally am., rules 2, 7 am., 1969/1325.
1004	Zebras (Control of Importation) O. 1963	r., 1969/915.
1017	National Health Service (Functions of Regional Hospital Bds. etc.) Regs. 1963	r., 1969/297.
1026	Motor Vehicles (Driving Licences) Regs. 1963	regs. 3, 13 am., 18 replaced, sch. 5 am., 1969/252. reg. 7 am., 1969/1614.
1132	Education Authy. Bursaries (S.) Regs. 1963	r. (saving), 1969/841.
1223	State Awards Regs. 1963	regs. 2, 3 am., 6, 7 mod., 1969/554.

Year and Number (or date)	Title or Description	How affected and Act or Instrument by which affected
1963		
1342	Nurses (Regional Nurse-Training Ctees.) (S.) O. 1963	sch. 2 Pts. II, III **am.**, 1969/849.
1571	Milk (Special Designation) Regs. 1963	sch. 4 Pt. I function transfd., 1969/388.
1658	Wages Regulation (General Waste Materials Reclamation) (Holidays) O. 1963	**r.**, 1969/762.
1710	Weights and Measures Regs. 1963	regs. 8, 46 **am.**, 1969/81.
1871	Aliens (Approved Ports) O. 1963	**r.**, 1969/840.
1919	Patents Etc. (Central African Republic, Chad, Laos, Upper Volta and Roumania) (Convention) O. 1963	art. 1 **am.**, 1969/865.
2060	National Insurance (Modification of Local Govt. Superannuation Schemes) Regs. 1963	**r.**, 1969/793.
2084	Bahama Is. (Constitution) O. in C. 1963	**r.** (prosp.), 1969/590.
2093	Qatar (Amdt.) O. 1963	**superseded,** 1969/856.
2111	National Insurance (Modification of Teachers Superannuation) (S.) Regs. 1963	**r.**, 1969/77.
20 Dec.	Bahama Is. R. Instructions 1963 (1963 III, p. 4840)	**r.** (prosp.), 1969/590.
1964		
73	National Insurance (Industrial Injuries) (Claims and Payments) Regs. 1964	regs. 20 **replaced,** 25 **am.**, 1969/291. regs. 1, 15, 16, 20 **am.**, 1969/1135.
81	Weights and Measures (Equivalents for dealings with drugs) Regs. 1964	**r.** (1.1.70) (as to manufacturers), (1.4.70) (as to wholesalers), (1.1.71) (as to retailers), 1969/101.
127	Licensing of Bulls (E. and W.) Amdt. Regs. 1964	**r.**, 1969/1139.
346	Greater London (Elections) O. 1964	art. 3 **r.** (as to 1950/1254), 1969/904. art. 4, 7 **r.**, 1969/904.
359	Motor Vehicles (Approved Driving Instructors) Regs. 1964	**r.**, 1969/85.
409	Importation of Potatoes (Health) (G.B.) O. 1964	sch. 3 **am.**, 1969/521.
462	Eggs (Guaranteed Prices) (Amdt.) O. 1964	**r.**, 1969/401.
504	National Insurance (Industrial Injuries) (Benefit) Regs. 1964	regs. 4, 7 **am.**, 18 **replaced,** 44 **am.**, schs. 3, 4 **replaced,** 1969/1168.
561	British Sugar Corporation Limited (Incentive Agreement) (No. 2) O. 1964	annex—sch. paras. 3, 5 **am.**, 1969/1312.

Year and Number (or date)	Title or Description	How affected and Act or Instrument by which affected
1964		
632	Road and Rail Traffic Act (Exemption) (Amdt.) Regs. 1964	r., 1969/1349.
760	Soft Drinks Regs. 1964	regs. 2, 5, 12 am., 13 replaced, 14 am., schs. 1 replaced, 2–4 am., 1969/1818.
767	Soft Drinks (S.) Regs. 1964	regs. 2, 6, 13 am., 14 replaced, 15 am., schs. 1 replaced, 2–4 am., 1969/1847.
840	Cereals (Guaranteed Payments) O. 1964	arts. 2, 3 am., 4 replaced, 1969/672.
942	Hire-Purchase and Credit Sale Agreements (Control) O. 1964	r., 1969/1308.
943	Control of Hiring O. 1964	r., 1969/1307.
949	Industrial Training (Iron and Steel Bd.) O. 1964	sch. 1 replaced, 1969/884.
1071	Civil Aviation (Navigation Services Charges) Regs. 1964	reg. 2 am., 1969/510.
1107	Justices of the Peace (Size and Chairmanship of Bench) Rules 1964	rule 4 am., 1969/1272.
1116	Civil Aviation (Licensing) Regs. 1964	reg. 13 am., 1969/1374.
1144	Weights and Measures (Equivalents for dealings with drugs) Amdt. Regs. 1964	r. (1.1.70) (as to manufacturers), (1.4.70) (as to wholesalers), (1.1.71) (as to retailers), 1969/101.
1178	Road Vehicles (Registration and Licensing) Regs. 1964	regs. 3, 4, 11, 22, 24, 25, 43, 44, sch. 2 Pt. II paras. 2, 3, 4, 5 am., 1969/1331. regs. 2, 7 am., 32–43 replaced, 1969/1589. regs. 3 am., 43 renumbered 42A, 1969/1800.
1202	Television Act 1964 (Channel Is.) O. 1964	sch. paras. 1 am., 1A inserted, 4, 9 am., 1969/1370.
1216	Police (Appeals) (S.) Rules 1964	r., 1969/1632.
1217	Governors' Pensions (Maximum Amounts) O. 1964	r., 1969/1211.
1309	Further Education (Local Education Authies.) Amdg. Regs. 1964	r., 1969/403.
1310	Further Education (Grant) Amdg. Regs. 1964	r., 1969/403.
1329	British Transport Reorganisation (Pensions of Employees) (No. 1) O. 1964	mod., arts. 7, 8 r., 1969/1824.
1336	Designs (Amdt. No. 2) Rules 1964	r., 1969/481.
1349	Hydrocarbon Oil Duties (Rebates and Reliefs) Regs. 1964	regs. 1, 2, 5, 8, 26 am., 1969/1728.
1382	Town and Country Planning General Regs. 1964	r., 1969/286.

Year and Number (or date)	Title or Description	How affected and Act or Instrument by which affected
1964 1393	Federated Superannuation System for Universities (Pensions Increase) (No. 2) Regs. 1964	regs. 1–3 **am.**, 1969/1321.
1514	Further Education (Grant) Second Amdg. Regs. 1964	**r.**, 1969/403.
1515	Further Education (Local Education Authies.) Second Amdg. Regs. 1964	**r.**, 1969/403.
1664	Admiralty Jurisdiction (St. Helena) O. 1964	**r.**, 1969/858.
1771	London Govt. (Executive Councils) O. 1964	sch. 2 **am.**, 1969/353.
1835	Trade Marks (Amdt. No. 2) Rules 1964	**r.**, 1969/522.
1848	Overseas Solicitors (Admission) O. 1964	art. 3, sch. 2 **am.**, 1969/1503.
1851	Enrolled Nurses (Amdt.) Rules Approval Instrt. 1964	**r.**, 1969/1674.
1857	Traffic Signs Regs. 1964	regs. 7 **replaced,** 11A **inserted,** 12, 31, 34, sch. 1 **am.**, 1969/1269
1858	Traffic Signs (Disqualification for Offences) Regs. 1964	**r.**, 1969/1270.
1898	Indian Civil Service Family Pension Fund (Amdt.) Rules 1964	**superseded,** 1969/1149.
1966	European Free Trade Assocn. (Origin of Goods) Regs. 1964	reg. 6 **am.**, sch. 1 c. 84, 85, 86, 90, sch. 2 note 6 **am.**, 1969/1347.
1971	General Nursing Council (Election Scheme) Rules, Approval Instrt. 1964.	**r.**, 1969/1676.
1972	Mental Nurses Cttee. (Election Scheme) Rules, Approval Instrt. 1964	**r.**, 1969/1676.
1990	Nurses (Regional Nurse-Training Ctees.) (S.) Amdt. O. 1964	**superseded,** 1969/849.
2041	Bahama Is. (Constitution) (Amdt.) O. 1964.	**r.** (prosp.), 1969/590.
2077	Personal Injuries (Civilians) Scheme 1964.	arts. 12 **am.** (15.2.71), 17, 59, 65 **am.,** 73 **am.** (15.2.71), schs. 3, 4 **replaced** (temp.), 3, 4 **replaced** (15.2.71), 1969/1035.
19 Sept.	Disablement and Death Pensions, etc. (Military), 1914 World War Service and Service subsequent to Sept. 1939, R. Warrant 1964 (1964 III, p. 5257).	arts. 12 **am.** (15.2.71),* 17 **am.,** 48, 52, 55 **am.** (15.2.71)*, 61 **am.,** 66 **am.** (15.2.71).* schs. 2 **replaced** (temp.), **replaced** (15.2.71),* 3 **am.,** 4 **replaced, am.** (15.2.71),* 6, 7 **replaced** (temp.), **replaced,** (15.2.71),* R. Warrant 28.7.69 (II p. 3652).

* Appointed day under Decimal Currency Act 1969 (c. 19).

Year and Number (or date)	Title or Description	How affected and Act or Instrument by which affected
1964 24 Sept.	Disablement and Death Pensions, etc. (Air Forces), 1914 World War Service, and Service subsequent to 2 Sept. 1939, O. 1964/1964 III, p. 5361)	arts. 12 **am.** (15.2.71),* 17 **am.,** 55 **am.,** (15.2.71),* 61 **am.,** 66 **am.** (15.2.71),* schs. 2 **replaced** (temp.), **replaced** (15.2.71),* 3 **am.,** 4 **replaced, am.** (15.2.71),* 6, 7 **replaced** (temp.), **replaced** (15.2.71),* O. 29.7.69 (II p. 3682).
25 Sept.	Disablement and Death Pensions; etc., (Naval Forces), 1914 World War Service and Service subsequent to 2 Sept. 1939, O. in C. 1964 (1964 III, p. 5466)	arts. 12 **am.** (15.2.71),* 17 **am.,** 52, 55 **am.** (15.2.71),* 61 **am.,** 66 **am.** (15.2.71),* schs. 2 **replaced** (temp.), **replaced** (15.2.71),* 3 **am.,** 4 **replaced, am.** (15.2.71),* 6, 7 **replaced** (temp.), **replaced** (15.2.71),* O. in C. 31.7.69 (II p. 3712).
1965 2	Further Education (Local Education Authies) Amdg. Regs. 1965	**r.,** 1969/403.
65	Plant Breeder's Rights Regs. 1965	**r.,** 1969/1021.
308	Provision of Milk and Meals Amdg. Regs. 1965	**r.,** 1969/483.
321	A.S. (Rules of Ct. consolidation and amdt.) 1965	rule 166 **am.,** 1969/474. rules 169 **am.,** 346 **replaced,** 347 **am.,** appx. forms 22 24, 26 **am.,** 1965/475. rule 347 **am.,** 1969/1703. rule 66 **replaced** (actions after 6.1.70), appx. form 2 **am.,** 1969/1819.
329	Motor Vehicles (International Circulation) Regs. 1965	regs. 1, 5 **r.,** 6, 7 **am.,** sch. **r.,** 1969/667.
473	Town and Country Planning (Inquiries Procedure) Rules 1965	**r.,** 1969/1092.
499	Town and Country Planning General (Amdt). Regs. 1965	**r.,** 1969/286.
516	Income Tax (Employments) Regs. 1965	reg. 17 **am.,** 1969/170. regs. 19, 29 **am.,** 1969/688.
527	National Health Service (Regional Hospital Areas) O. 1965	sch. 1 **am.,** 1969/451.
542	River Authies. (Precepts) Regs. 1965	**r.,** 1969/438.
555	Town and Country Planning (Control of Advertisements) (Amdt.) Regs. 1965	**r.,** 1969/1532.
574	Trustee Savings Banks (Current Account Deposits) (Limits) O. 1965	art. 1 **am.,** 1969/942.
601	Television Act 1964 (Is. of Man) O. 1965	sch. **am.,** 1969/1372.
619	Police Federation Regs. 1965	**r.,** 1969/1787.
621	London Authies. (Superannuation) O. 1965	arts. 14, 15, 21 **am.,** 1969/413.
717	Elections (Welsh Forms) Regs. 1965	sch. forms 1, 4, 5 **r.,** 1969/1407.

* Appointed day under Decimal Currency Act 1969 (c. 19).

Year and Number (or date)	Title or Description	How affected and Act or Instrument by which affected
1965		
980	Colonial Civil Aviation (Application of Act) (Amdt.) O. 1965	r. (certain territories), 1969/592.
1105	Merchant Shipping (Life-Saving Appliances) Rules 1965	rule 9, sch. 12 **am.**, 1969/409.
1107	Merchant Shipping (Radio) Rules 1965	rules 15, 19, 24, 27, sch. 1–3, 5 **am.**, 1969/1315.
1108	Merchant Shipping (Radio) (Fishing Boats) Rules 1965	rules, 14, 17, 22, 25, 27 sch. 1–3, 11 **am.**, 1969/1316.
1164	National Health Service (Functions of Regional Hospital Bds. etc.) Amdt. Regs. 1965	r., 1969/297.
1166	Teachers (Superannuation) (S.) (Amdt.) Regs. 1965	r., 1969/77.
1167	Teachers (Superannuation) (S.) Rules 1965	r., 1969/77.
1168	A.5 (Betting, Gaming and Lotteries Act Appeals) 1965	paras. 1–3 r., 1969/1537.
1298	Education Authy. Bursaries (S.) (Amdt. No. 1) Regs. 1965	r. (saving), 1969/841.
1373	Building Regs. 1965	regs. A2, A9, B3 **am.**, B5 **replaced**, D14, E1, E9–E11 **am.**, E11A **inserted**, E14 **am.**, E14A **inserted**, H1, L1, L2, L6, L8, L14, L16–L18, M1, M4, sch. 1 Pts. A, B, sch. 2 rules A, C, F, sch. 4, sch. 6 rule 2 **am.**, 1969/639.
1400	Motor Vehicles (Competitions and Trials) (E.) Regs. 1965	r., 1969/414.
1412	Milk (N.I.) O. 1965	art. 3 **am.**, sch. **replaced**, 1969/973.
1414	Motor Vehicles (Competitions and Trials) (W.) Regs. 1965	r., 1969/414.
1426	Importation of Plants and Plant Produce (Health) (G.B.) O. 1965	sch. 1 pts. 1A, 1C, IIIA **am.**, 1969/677.
1471	Hire-Purchase and Credit Sale Agreements (Control) (Amdt. No. 3) O. 1965	r., 1969/1308.
1485	Nurses (Amdt.) Rules, Approval Instrt. 1965	r., 1969/1675.
1500	County Ct. Funds Rules 1965	rule 24 **am.**, 1969/204. rules 2 **am.**, 3, 4 **replaced**, 6, 8, 10–13 **am.**, 14 replaced, 16, 26, 28, heading Pt. X, rules 33, 35 **am.**, 1969/1547.
1537	Double Taxation Relief (Taxes on Income) (Jamaica) O. 1965	sch. arts. VI, XVIII **am.**, XVIIIA **inserted**, 1969/1069.
1551	Designs (Amdt.) Rules 1965	rule 1 **am.**, sch. 1 r., 1969/481.

Year and Number (or date)	Title or Description	How affected and Act or Instrument by which affected
1965		
1572	Companies (Winding-up) (Amdt.) Rules 1965	**superseded** 1969/1177.
1590	Town and Country Planning General (Amdt. No. 2) Regs. 1965	**r.**, 1969/286.
1621	Injuries in War (Shore Employments) Compensation (Amdt.) Scheme 1965	**superseded**, 1969/1053.
1622	Bankruptcy Fees O. 1965	sch. Table B **am.**, 1969/520.
1676	Superannuation (Local Govt. and Public Transport Services) Interchange Rules 1965	rules 2–6 **am.**, 8 **r.**, 12–14 **inserted**, 1969/710.
1707	Mayor's and City of London Ct. Funds Rules 1965	rule 21 **am.**, 1969/205. arrangement of rules **am.**, rules 3, 4 **replaced**, 6, 8, 10–12, 23 **am.**, 1969/1869.
1734	British Commonwealth and Foreign Parcel Post Regs. 1965	sch. 1 **replaced**, 1969/784. regs. 1, 22 **am.**, sch. 4 **am.**, (P.O. scheme 18.9.69)*.
1735	British Commonwealth and Foreign Post Regs. 1965	schs. 2 **am.**, 3 Pt. 2 **am.**, 1969/783. regs. 1, 41 **am.**, schs. 4, 7 **am.**, (P.O. scheme 18.9.69)*.
1743	Public Trustee (Fees) O. 1965	**r.**, 1969/513.
1753	British Nationality Regs. 1965	**r.**, 1969/760.
1776	Rules of the Supreme Ct. 1965	Arrangement of orders O.18, 24, 25, 27, 38, 42, 63, 75, 94 **am.**, 105 **r**, 1969/1105. O. 14, 20, 22, 42, 65, 75, 92, **am.**, 1969/1894.
1815	Measuring Instruments (Intoxicating Liquor) Regs. 1965	regs. 4 **replaced**, 13, 18 **am.**, 1969/67.
1823	Nuclear Installations (Insurance Certificate) Regs. 1965	reg. 3 **am.**, 1969/64.
1861	Turks and Caicos Is. (Constitution) O. in C. 1965	**r.**, 1969/736.
1864	British Protectorates, Protected States and Protected Persons O. 1965	**r.**, 1969/1832.
1976	Rent Regulations (Forms etc.) (E. and W.) Regs. 1965	**r.**, 1969/1184.
2028	Industrial Training (Furniture and Timber Industry Bd.) O. 1965	sch. 1 **replaced**, 1969/1290.
2042	Rent Regulations (Forms etc.) (S.) Regs. 1965	**r.** (saving), 1969/1419.
2090	Wages Regulation (Perambulator and Invalid Carriage) (Holidays) O. 1965	sch. para. 2 **am.**, 1969/562.
2169	Wages Regulation (Baking) (E. and W.) O. 1965	**r.**, 1969/901.
2179	National Insurance (National Health Service Superannuation Scheme—Mod. and Non-participation) Regs. 1965	regs. 2, 19 **am.**, 1969/1472.

*[Not S.I. *see* London Gazette 18.9.69, p 15.]

Year and Number (or date)	Title or Description	How affected and Act or Instrument by which affected
1965		
2196	National Ports Council Provision of Funds Scheme 1965 (Confirmation) O. 1965	scheme, sch. **am.**, 1969/1348.
1966		
10	Witnesses' Allowances Regs. 1966	regs. 2, 11A **am.**, 1969/214.
11	Coroners (Fees and Allowances) Rules 1966	rules 1, 2 **am.**, 1969/213.
24	Increase of Pensions (Injury Warrant Pensions) Regs. 1966	reg. 3 **r.**, 1969/584.
66	Postal Packets (Customs and Excise) Regs. 1966	**r.**, 1969/1399.
113	Hire-Purchase and Credit Sales Agreements (Control) (Amdt. No. 4) O. 1966	**r.**, 1969/1308.
132	Police Federation (S.) Regs. 1966	reg. 11, sch. 2 **am.**, 1969/1679.
143	Industrial Training (Man-made Fibres Producing Industry Bd.) O. 1966	sch. 1 **replaced**, 1969/1210.
151	Federated Superannuation System for Universities (Pension Increase) Regs. 1966	regs. 1–4 **am.**, 1969/1321.
159	Overseas Service (Pensions Supplement) Regs. 1966	**r.**, 1969/553.
164	Pneumoconiosis, Byssinosis and Miscellaneous Diseases Benefit Scheme 1966	art. 2, sch. 1 **am.**, 6 **inserted**, 1969/722. arts. 4, 22 **am.**, 1969/1196.
165	Workmen's Compensation (Supplementation) Scheme 1966	arts. 7, 10, sch. 1 **am.**, 1969/1195.
188	Aircraft (Exemption from Seizure on Patent Claims) O. 1966	**r.**, 1969/150.
224	Road Vehicles (Excise) (Prescribed Particulars) Regs. 1966	reg. 7 **am.**, sch. 2 form VE. 7 **replaced**, 1969/1782.
255	Nurses (Amdt.) Rules, Approval Instrt. 1966	**r.**, 1969/1675.
310	Plant Varieties (Index) Regs. 1966	**r.**, 1969/1027.
431	Aliens (Approved Ports) O. 1966	**r.**, 1969/840.
479	Eggs (Guaranteed Prices) (Amdt.) O. 1966	**r.**, 1969/401.
491	Traffic Signs (Disqualification for offences) (Amdt.) Regs. 1966	**r.**, 1969/1270.
505	Therapeutic Substances (Manufacture of Antibiotics) Regs. 1966	regs. 19, 25, 32, 37, 43, 48, 60, 71 **am.**, 1969/1707.
508	Export of Horses (Excepted Cases) O. 1966	**r.**, 1969/1742.
509	Exported Horses Protection O. 1966	**r.**, 1969/1784.

Year and Number (or date)	Title or Description	How affected and Act or Instrument by which affected
1966		
542	Police Federation (Amdt.) Regs. 1966	**r.**, 1969/1787.
545	Enrolled Nurses (Admt.) Rules Approval Instrt. 1966	**r.**, 1969/1674.
564	Overseas Service (Pensions Supplement) (Special Provns.) Regs. 1966	**r.**, 1969/553.
569	National Health Service (Appointment of Consultants) Regs. 1966	**r.**, 1969/163.
579	Local Land Charges Rules 1966	rules 3, 11 **am.**, 13 **replaced**, sch. 2 form D **am.**, 1969/1152.
597	Judicial Officers (Salaries) O. 1966	**r.**, 1969/1008.
637	Wages Regulation (Coffin Furniture and Cerement-making) O. 1966	**r.**, 1969/610.
638	Coffin Furniture and Cerement-making (Holidays) O. 1966	**r.**, 1969/611.
669	Wages Regulation (Holloware) (Holidays) O. 1966	**r.**, 1969/929.
701	Victory Bonds (Post Office Issue) (Admt.) Regs. 1966	**r.**, 1969/1326.
727	Post Office Savings Bank Regs. 1966	generally **am.**, regs. 1 **replaced**, 17, 20–22, 25, 38, 53 **am.**, 55 **r.**, 61 **am.**, 1969/1335. reg. 2 **am.**, 1969/1758.
734	Savings Banks (Deposits) (Limits) O. 1966	**r.**, 1969/940.
750	Trustee Savings Banks (Special Investments) (Limits) (Amdt.) O. 1966	**r.**, 1969/941.
785	Air Navigation (Investigation of Combined Military and Civil Air Accidents) (Second Amdt.) Regs. 1966	**r.**, 1969/1437.
821	Wages Regulation (Paper Box) (Holi-	**r.**, 1969/1173.
887	Hire-Purchase and Credit Sale Agreements (Control) (Amdt. No. 5) O. 1966	**r.**, 1969/1308.
936	Price Stability of Imported Products (Levy Arrangements) O. 1966	sch. 1 **am.**, 1969/758. sch. 2 **am.**, 1969/1564.
952	National Insurance (Mod. of the Superannuation Acts) (Amdt.) Regs. 1966	**r.**, 1969/1549.
1010	National Insurance (Miscellaneous Consequential Amdts. and Transitional Provns.) Regs. 1966	reg. 4 **r.**, 1969/1696.
1014	Plant Varieties (Performance Trials) Regs. 1966	**r.**, 1969/1028.
1045	Firemen's Pension Scheme O. 1966	Appx. 2—arts. 9, 11A **am.**, 27 **replaced**, 31, 40 **am.**, 1969/1001.

Year and Number (or date)	Title or Description	How affected and Act or Instrument by which affected
1966		
1063	Agriculture (Poisonous Substances) Regs. 1966	regs. 3, 5, sch. 1 Pt. II, sch. 2 Pt. III **am.**, 1969/843.
1065	Supplementary Benefit (General) Regs. 1966	reg. 5 **am.**, 1969/294.
1067	Supplementary Benefit (Claims and Payments) Regs. 1966	regs. 9 **replaced**, 13 **am.**, 1969/293. regs. 1 **am.**, 8 **replaced**, 9, 12 **am.**, 1969/1169.
1069	Motor Vehicles (Competitions and Trials) (S.) Regs. 1966	**r.**, 1969/414.
1102	Gaming Machine (Licence Duty) Regs. 1966	**r.**, 1969/1101.
1112	Industrial Training (Road Transport) O. 1966	sch. 1 **replaced**, 1969/879. **am.**, 1969/1871.
1129	National Insurance (Modification of Local Govt. Superannuation Schemes) (Amdt.) Regs. 1966	**r.**, 1969/793.
1174	Botswana (Procedure in Appeals to Judicial Ctee. of Privy Council) O. 1966	s. 3, sch. 1 **am.**, 1969/376.
1176	Lesotho (Procedure in Appeals to Judicial Ctee. of Privy Council) O. 1966	s. 3, sch. 1 **am.**, 1969/368.
1182	Republic of Singapore (Appeals to Judicial Ctee.) O. 1966	art. **5 am.**, 1969/370 .
1184	Air Navigation O. 1966	arts. 2, 16, 17, 26, 83 **am.**, 1969/1082. art. 58 **r.**, 1969/1746.
1189	District Registries O. in C. 1966	sch. **am.**, 1969/1232.
1210	National Health Service (General Medical and Pharmaceutical Services) Regs. 1966	sch. 4 Pt. I para. 1 **am.**, 1969/217.
1214	National Insurance (National Health Service Superannuation Scheme—Mod. and Non-participation) (Amdt.) Regs. 1966	**r.**, 1969/1472.
1229	National Insurance (Mod. of Teachers Superannuation) (S.) Amdt. Regs. 1966	**r.**, 1969/77.
1233	National Health Service (General Medical and Pharmaceutical Services) (S). Regs. 1966	sch. 4 Pt. I para. 1 **am.**, 1969/254.
1256	Air Navigation (General) Regs. 1966	reg. 11, sch. **am.**, 1969/583.
1240	Motor Vehicles (Tests) (Exemption) (Amdt.) Regs. 1966	**r.**, 1969/419.
1257	Rules of the Air and Air Traffic Control Regs. 1966	**r.**, 1969/216.

Year and Number (or date)	Title or Description	How affected and Act or Instrument by which affected
1966		
1282	A.S. (Betting, Gaming and Lotteries Act Appeals Amdt.) 1966	**superseded,** 1969/1537.
1288	Motor Vehicles (Construction and Use) Regs. 1966	**r.,** 1969/321.
1289	Motor Vehicles (Authorisation of Special Types) General O. 1966	**r.,** 1969/344.
1327	Importation of Horses, Asses and Mules (Amdt.) (No. 2) O. 1966	**r.,** 1969/915.
1347	Industrial Training (Hotel and Catering Bd.) O. 1966	sch. 1 **replaced,** 1969/1405.
1349	Importation of Horses, Asses and Mules (African Horse Sickness) (Amdt.) O. 1966	**r.,** 1969/915.
1351	Exchange Control (Import and Export) O. 1966	art. 5 **am.,** 1969/1883.
1377	Rules of the Air and Air Traffic Control (Amdt.) Regs. 1966	**r.,** 1969/216.
1432	Further Education (Local Education Authies.) Amdg. Regs. 1966	**r.,** 1969/403.
1449	National Health Service (General Dental Services) (S.) Regs. 1966	regs. 2, 6, 22, 24, sch. 1 paras. 10, 11, 15 **am.,** para. 16 **replaced,** sch. 3 **r.,** 4 Pt. I, 5 Pt. VII **am.,** 1969/254, reg. 27 **am.** (1.4.69) (contracts before 1.7.66), 30 **r.,** sch. 5 Pts. I–VI **replaced,** 1969/436.
1481	European Free Trade Assocn. (Drawback) Regs. 1966	reg. 3 **am.,** 1969/1797.
1518	Wages Regulation (Paper Bag) (Holidays) O. 1966	**r.,** 1969/1188.
1519	Wages Regulation (Retail Newsagency, Tobacco and Confectionery) (E. and W.) O. 1966	**r.,** 1969/35.
1548	County Cts. (Bankruptcy and Companies Winding-up Jurisdiction) O. 1966	schs. 1, 2 **am.,** 1969/1170.
1582	Police Pensions Regs. 1966	regs. 1, 66, 73, 93 **am.,** 94A **inserted,** 95, sch. 2 Pts. I, II **am.,** 3 Pts. I, III **am.,** 1969/723. regs. 12, 15, 17, sch. 3 Pt. III **am.,** 1969/1484. reg. 14 **am.,** 1969/1849.
1590	Special Constables (Pensions) Regs. 1966	reg. 15 **am.,** 1969/724, 1514. regs. 3, 15 **am.,** 1969/1850.
1625	Special Constables (Pension (S.) Regs. 1966	reg. 2 **am.,** 1969/1529. regs. 2, 5 **am.,** 1969/1880.

Year and Number (or date)	Title or Description	How affected and Act or Instrument by which affected
1967		
18	Southern Rhodesia (Prohibited Trade and Dealings) (Overseas Territories) O. 1967	**r.** (Dominica) (prosp.), 1969/593.
19	Southern Rhodesia (Prohibited Trade Dealings) (Channel Is.) O. 1967	**r.**, 1969/860.
20	Southern Rhodesia (Prohibited Trade and Dealings) (Is. of Man) O. 1967	**r.**, 1969/861.
29	Teachers (Colleges of Education) (S.) Regs. 1967	sch. 1 paras. 1–10 **am.**, 1969/1460
94	Police Federation (Amdt.) Regs. 1967	**r.**, 1969/1787.
135	Salmon and Migratory Trout (Prohibition of Drift-net Fishing) (Extension) O. 1967	**superseded,** 1969/167.
163	Double Taxation Relief (Taxes on Income) (Denmark) O. 1967	**superseded,** 1969/1068.
176	Motor Vehicles (Competitions and Trials) (W.) (Amdt.) Regs. 1967	**r.**, 1969/414.
178	Pedestrian Crossing (Push Button Control) Regs. and General Directions 1967	**r.** (10.7.71), 1969/888.
232	Saint Vincent Constitution (Amdt.) O. 1967	**r.**, 1969/1500.
240	Saint Vincent Electoral Provns. O. 1967	**r.**, 1969/1064.
247	British Protectorates, Protected States and Protected Persons (Amdt.) O. 1967	**r.**, 1969/1832.
248	Southern Rhodesia (Prohibited Trade and Dealings) (Overseas Territories) (Amdt.) O. 1967	**r.** (Dominica) (prosp.), 1969/593.
252	Goods Vehicles (Temporary Use in G.B.) Regs. 1967	**r.**, 1969/1423.
261	Motor Vehicles (Tests) (Exemption) (Amdt.) Regs. 1967	**r.**, 1969/419.
270	Rate Support Grant (S.) O. 1967	**superseded,** 1969/233.
278	National Health Service (Executive Councils) Amdt. Regs. 1967	**r.**, 1969/352.
284	Public Trustee (Fees) O. 1967	**r.**, 1969/513.
330	National Insurance (Unemployment and Sickness Benefit) Regs. 1967	regs. 6, 15, sch. 3 **am.**, 1969/292. sch. 2 **replaced,** 1969/1361.
363	Rate Support Grant Regs. 1967	sch. **am.**, 1969/105.
385	Food (Control of Irradiation) Regs. 1967	reg. 4 **replaced,** 1969/1039.

Year and Number (or date)	Title or Description	How affected and Act or Instrument by which affected
1967		
386	National Insurance (Mariners) Regs. 1967	regs. 5, 18, 21 **am.**, 22A **r.**, schs. 1, 2 **replaced,** 1969/1277.
388	Food (Control of Irradiation) (S.) Regs. 1967	reg. 4 **replaced,** 1969/1038.
415	Motor Vehicles (Competitions and Trials) (E.) (Amdt.) Regs. 1967	**r.,** 1969/414.
439	Motor Vehicles (Competitions and Trials) (W.) (Amdt.) (No. 2) Regs. 1967	**r.,** 1969/414.
455	Milk (G.B.) O. 1967	art. 3 **am.**, schs. 1, 2 **replaced,** 1969/972.
467	Rate Support Grants (Pooling Arrangements) Regs. 1967	reg. 2 **am.,** 1969/403, 1107.
471	Virgin Is. (Constitution) O. 1967	s. 51A **inserted,** 1969/1065.
480	Carriage by Air Acts (Application of Provisions) O. 1967	sch. 1 Pts. II, IIIB, **am.,** 1969/1083.
488	National Insurance and Industrial Injuries (Stamps) Regs. 1967	**r.,** 1969/1603.
489	Teachers' Superannuation Reg. 1967	reg. 24 **am.,** 1969/80.
533	Rules of the Air and Air Traffic Control (Second Amdt.) Regs. 1967	**r.,** 1969/216.
547	Saint Vincent Constitution (Amdt. No. 2) O. 1967	**r.,** 1969/1500.
587	Saint Vincent Constitution (Amdt. No. 3) O. 1967	**r.,** 1969/1500.
593	Plant Varieties (Index) (Amdt.) Regs. 1967	**r.,** 1969/1027.
628	Wages Regulation (Rubber Proofed Garment) (Holidays) O. 1967	sch. para. 2 **am.,** 1969/131.
640	Wages Regulation (Boot and Shoe Repairing) O. 1967	**r.,** 1969/428.
641	Wages Regulation (Boot and Shoe Repairing) (Holidays) O. 1967	sch. Pt. II **am.,** 1969/428.
643	Rules of the Air and Air Traffic Control (Third Amdt.) Regs. 1967	**r.,** 1969/216.
645	Wages Regulation (Licensed Non-residential Establishment) (Managers and Club Stewards) O. 1967	**r.,** 1969/655.
675	Export of Goods (Control) O. 1967	sch. 1 Pt. 1 group 5 **am.,** 1969/988, 1479. sch. 1 Pt. 1 group 8 **am.,** 1969/1887.

Year and Number (or date)	Title or Description	How affected and Act or Instrument by which affected
1967		
706	Motor Vehicles (Competitions and Trials) (S.) (Amdt.) Regs. 1967	r., 1969/414.
714	Game Licences and Gamedealers' Licences (S.) O. 1967	art. 3 **am.**, 4 **r.**, 1969/1396.
715	Rate Support Grant (S.) Regs. 1967	reg. 4 **am.**, 1969/670.
757	Wages Regulation (Rope, Twine and Net) O. 1967	r., 1969/654.
792	Training of Teachers Regs. 1967	reg. 12 **am.**, 1969/848.
801	Money Order Regs. 1967	regs. 1, 18 **am.**, (P.O. scheme 18.9.69)*.
815	Commonwealth Countries and Republic of Ireland (Immunities) (No. 2) O. 1967	sch. 1 Pt. 1 **am.**, 1969/142.
844	National Insurance (Assessment of Graduated Contributions) Regs. 1967	regs. 2, 3, 9 **am.**, schs. 1, 2 **replaced,** 1969/1133.
901	Teachers Superannuation (Family Benefits) (S.) Regs. 1967	r., 1969/78.
937	National Health Service (General Dental Services) Regs. 1967	regs. 2, 4, 7, 23, 25, sch. 1 Pt. I paras. 10, 11 **am.**, Pt. II paras. 14, 15 **am.**, 16 **replaced**, sch. 3 **r.**, sch. 4 Pt. I, sch. 5 Pt. VII **am.**, sch. 6 paras. 1, 3 **replaced,** 4 **am.**, 1969/217. reg. 31 **r.**, sch. 1 para. 8 **am.**, sch. 5 Pts. I–VI **replaced,** 1969/399.
939	Wages Regulation (Industrial and Staff Canteen) O. 1967	r., 1969/691.
968	Nurses (Regional Nurse-Training Ctees.) (S.) Amdt. O. 1967	**superseded,** 1969/849.
977	Turks and Caicos Is. (Constitution) (Amdt.) O. 1967	r., 1969/736.
988	Wages Regulation (Perambulator and Invalid Carriage) O. 1967	r., 1969/562.
1018	Army Terms of Service Regs. 1967	reg. 4 **am.**, sch. 1 **r.**, 1969/245.
1019	Grading of Produce (Pears) Regs. 1967	schs. 2, 3 **am.**, 1969/937.
1020	Grading of Produce (Apples) Regs. 1967	schs. 2, 3 **am.**, 1969/936.
1078	Sausage and Other Meat Product (S.) Regs. 1967	regs. 4, 6 **am.**, 1969/327.
1079	Canned Meat Product (S.) Regs. 1967	regs. 6, 7, 9 **am.**, 1969/326.
1081	Rules of the Air and Air Traffic Control (Fourth Amdt.) Regs. 1967	r., 1969/216.
1087	Control of Office Development (Exemption Limit) O. 1967	art. 1 **am.**, 1969/174.

* [Not S.I. *see* London Gazette 18.9.69; p. 15]

Year and Number (or date)	Title or Description	How affected and Act or Instrument by which affected
1967		
1119	Artificial Sweeteners in Food Regs. 1967	r., 1969/1817.
1139	Turks and Caicos Is. (Constitution) (Amdt.) (No. 2) O. 1967	r., 1969/736.
1162	Teachers (Education, Training and Registration) (S.) Regs. 1967	sch. 2 am., 1969/77. sch. 1 para. 2 am., 1969/1341.
1188	Wages Regulation (Retail Newsagency, Tobacco and Confectionery) (E. and W.) (Amdt.) O. 1967	r., 1969/35.
1203	Artificial Sweeteners in Food (S.) Regs. 1967	r., 1969/1848.
1241	Town and Country Planning General (Amdt.) Regs. 1967	r., 1969/286.
1265	National Insurance (Increase of Benefit and Miscellaneous Provns.) Regs. 1967	sch. 1 am., 1969/1696.
1270	Motor Vehicles (Construction and Use) (Amdt.) Regs. 1967	r., 1969/321.
1271	British Protectorates, Protected States and Protected Persons (Amdt. No. 2) O. 1967	r., 1969/1832.
1279	Wireless Telegraphy (Channel Is.) O. 1967	sch. para. 12 inserted, 1969/1369.
1292	Control of Hiring (Amdt. No. 6) O. 1967	r., 1969/1307.
1293	Hire-Purchase and Credit Sale Agreements (Control) (Amdt. No. 8) O. 1967	r., 1969/1308.
1294	A.S. (Alteration of Sheriff Ct. Fees) 1967	sch.—General Regs., reg. 4 replaced. Table of Fees, chapter I am., IV replaced, 1969/1203.
1305	Remuneration of Teachers (Primary and Secondary Schools) O. 1967	r., 1969/618.
1312	National Assistance (Charges for Accommodation) Regs. 1967	r., 1969/1265.
1322	Goods Vehicles (Temporary Use in G.B.) (No. 2) Regs. 1967	r., 1969/1423.
1324	Goods Vehicles (Temporary Use in G.B.) (No. 3) Regs. 1967	r., 1969/1423.
1330	London Authies. (Superannuation) (Amdt.) O. 1967	art. 8 replaced, 1969/413.
1366	Trade Marks (Amdt.) Rules 1967	r., 1969/522.
1369	Road and Rail Traffic Act (Exemption) (Amdt.) Regs. 1967	r., 1969/1349.

Year and Number (or date)	Title or Description	How affected and Act or Instrument by which affected
1967		
1390	National Assistance (Charges for Accommodation) (S.) Regs. 1967	r., 1969/1443.
1406	Plant Varieties (Performance Trials) (Amdt.) Regs. 1967	r., 1969/1028.
1468	National Insurance (Contributions) Amdt. Regs. 1967	r., 1969/1696.
1489	Double Taxation Relief (Taxes on Income) (South Africa) O. 1967	r., 1969/864.
1513	Wages Regulation (Linen and Cotton Handkerchief etc.) O. 1967	r., 1969/868.
1514	Wages Regulation (Linen and Cotton Handkerchief etc.) (Holidays) O. 1967	r., 1969/869.
1522	Mines (Notification of Dangerous Occurrences) (Amdt.) O. 1967	r., 1969/963.
1523	Quarries (Notification of Dangerous Occurrences) (Amdt.) O. 1967	r., 1969/964.
1530	Plant Breeder's Rights (Amdt.) Regs. 1967	r., 1969/1021.
1555	Beef Cow (E. and W.) Scheme 1967	para. 4 am., 1969/693.
1556	Rules of the Air and Air Traffic Control (Fifth Amdt.) Regs. 1967	r., 1969/216.
1559	Beef Cow Subsidy Payment (E. and W.) O. 1967	art. 3 am., 1969/694.
1561	Beef Cow Subsidy Payment (S.) O. 1967	art. 3 am., 1969/708.
1570	National Insurance (Determination of Claims and Questions) (No. 2) Regs. 1967	reg. 15 am., 1969/290.
1571	National Insurance (Industrial Injuries) (Determination of Claims and Questions) (No. 2) Regs. 1967	reg. 17 am., 1969/1749.
1611	Merchant Shipping (Fees) Regs. 1967	sch. Pts. 12, 13 **replaced**, 1969/692.
1648	Rent Regulation (Forms etc.) (E. and W.) (Amdt.) Regs. 1967	r., 1969/1184.
1653	National Health Service (Functions of Regional Hospital Bds. etc.) Regs. 1967	r., 1969/297.
1665	Motor Vehicles (Construction and Use) (Amdt.) (No. 2) Regs. 1967	r., 1969/321.
1666	Motor Vehicles (Construction and Use) (Amdt.) (No. 3) Regs. 1967	r., 1969/321.
1683	Carriage of Goods by Road (Parties to Convention) O. 1967	sch. am., 1969/385.

Year and Number (or date)	Title or Description	How affected and Act or Instrument by which affected
1967 1699	Local Review Ctee. (S.) Rules 1967	rules 3, 4 **am.**, 1969/1256.
1702	Control of Hiring (Amdt. No. 7) O. 1967	**r.**, 1969/1307.
1703	Hire-Purchase and Credit Sale Agreements (Control) (Amdt. No. 9) O. 1967	**r.**, 1969/1308.
1704	Nurses (Amdt.) Rules, Approval Instrt. 1967	**r.**, 1969/1675.
1715	Betterment Levy (Waiver of Interest) (No. 2) Regs. 1967	reg. 4 **inserted**, 1969/532.
1736	Teachers Superannuation (S.) (Amdt.) Regs. 1967	**r.**, 1969/77.
1753	Motor Vehicles (Construction and Use) (Amdt.) (No. 4) Regs. 1967	**r.**, 1969/321.
1759	Wages Regulation (Brush and Broom) O. 1967	sch. 1 Pts. II, III, VI **replaced**, 1969/208. sch. 2 **r.**, 1969/209. sch. 1 Pts. II, III, VI, VII **am.**, 1969/909.
1768	Leasehold Reform (Notices) Regs. 1967	appx.—Form 1 **am.**, 1969/1481.
1806	Wages Regulation (Rubber Proofed Garment) (No. 2) O. 1967	**r.**, 1969/131.
1819	Registration of Births (Amdt.) Regs. 1967	regs. 1–8 **r.**, 1969/203.
1839	Foot and Mouth Disease (Infected Areas Restrictions) (Amdt.) O. 1967	**r.**, 1969/1445.
1853	Acquisition of Land (Rate of Interest after Entry) (S.) (No. 3) Regs. 1967	**r.**, 1969/459.
1854	Acquisition of Land (Rate of Interest after Entry) (No. 3) Regs. 1967	**r.**, 1969/458.
1855	Opencast Coal (Rate of Interest on Compensation) (No. 4) O. 1967	**r.**, 1969/460.
1869	Hill Sheep (E. and W.) Scheme 1967	para. 9 **am.**, 1969/697.
1890	Traffic Signs (Speed Limits) Regs. and General Directions 1967	**r.**, 1969/1487.
1898	Wages Regulation (Boot and Shoe Repairing) (Amdt.) O. 1967	**r.**, 1969/428.
1933	Road Vehicles (Headlamps) Regs. 1967	**r.**, 1969/1647.
1976	Beef Cow (N.I.) Scheme 1967	para. 4 **am.**, 1969/698.
1977	Beef Cow Subsidy Payment (N.I.) O. 1967	art. 3 **am.**, 1969/699.
23 Aug.	Gilbert and Ellice Is. O. 1967 (1967 II, p. 3872)	s. 60 **am.** (temp.), O. in C. 28.11.69.
13 Nov.	Seychelles O. 1967 (1967 III, p. 5423)	s. 67 **am.**, O. 22.10.69.

Year and Number (or date)	Title or Description	How affected and Act or Instrument by which affected
1968		
8	Wages Regulation (General Waste Materials Reclamation) O. 1968	r., 1969/761.
21	Shot Guns Rules 1968	r., 1969/1219.
24	Police Federation (Amdt.) Regs. 1968	r., 1969/1787.
25	Police Cadets Regs. 1968	reg. 14, schs. 1, 2 **am.**, 1969/408, 1786.
26	Police Regs. 1968	reg. **40 am.**, schs. 3, 4 **replaced**, 1969/137. sch. **6 am.**, 1969/911.
54	Wages Regulation (Licensed Residential Establishment and Licensed Restaurant) O. 1968	r., 1969/753.
100	European Free Trade Assocn. (Drawback) (Amdt.) Regs. 1968	r., 1969/1797.
105	Mayor's and City of London Ct. Funds (Amdt.) Rules 1968	**superseded**, 1969/205.
106	Supreme Ct. Funds (Amdt.) Rules 1968	**superseded**, 1969/206.
133	Wages Regulation (Hair, Bass and Fibre) O. 1968	r., 1969/640.
135	Shot Guns (S.) Rules 1968	r., 1969/1453.
172	Traffic Regulation Orders (Procedure) (E. and W.) Regs. 1968	r., 1969/463.
176	Personal Injuries (Civilians) (Amdt.) Scheme 1968	**superseded**, 1969/1035.
189	Town and Country Planning (Grants) Regs. 1968	reg. 5 **am.**, 1969/1594.
196	Approved Schools (Contributions by Education Authies.) (S.) Regs. 1968	r., 1969/224.
197	Remuneration of Teachers (Further Education) O. 1968	r., 1969/1713.
208	Police Cadets (S.) Regs. 1968	reg. 15, schs. 1, 2 **am.**, 1969/493.
		reg. 10 **replaced**, schs. 1, 2 **am.**, 1969/1820.
219	Matrimonial Causes Rules 1968	rules 44, 115, Appx. 1 **am.**, 1969/763.
255	Plant Breeder's Rights (Amdt.) Regs. 1968	r., 1969/1021.
260	Wages Regulation (Paper Box) O. 1968	r., 1969/1172.
282	Agricultural and Horticultural Improvements (Standard Costs) Regs. 1968	schs. 1, 2 Pt. I work 14, 15, 64, 65, 71, 91, 106 **am.**, 1969/1430.
296	Foreign Compensation (Financial Provns.) O. 1968	**expired** (24.3.69).

Year and Number (or date)	Title or Description	How affected and Act or Instrument by which affected
1968		
314	Divorce County Cts. O. 1968	sch. 1 **am.**, 1969/1816.
327	Wages Regulation (Baking) (E. and W.) (Amdt.) O. 1968	**r.**, 1969/901.
328	Wages Regulation (Paper Bag) O. 1968	**r.**, 1969/1187.
344	Land Registration (District Registries) O. 1968	**r.**, 1969/115.
345	Remuneration of Teachers (Farm Institutes) O. 1968	**r.**, 1969/1780.
362	Motor Vehicles (Construction and Use) (Amdt.) Regs. 1968	**r.**, 1969/321.
375	Remuneration of Teachers (Primary and Secondary Schools) Amdg. O. 1968	**r.**, 1969/618.
378	Agriculture (Calculation of Value for Compensation) Amdt. Regs. 1968	**r.**, 1969/1704.
390	Abortion Regs. 1968	reg. 4 **replaced**, 5, sch. 2 **am.**, 1969/636.
400	Sugar Beet (Research and Education) O. 1968	**expired** (31.3.69).
407	Approved Schools (Contributions by Local Authies.) Regs. 1968	**r.**, 1969/501.
425	Savings Certificates (Amdt.) Regs. 1968	**r.**, 1969/541.
426	Motor Vehicles (Construction and Use) (Amdt.) (No. 2) Regs. 1968	**r.**, 1969/321.
427	Welfare Foods (N.I.) O. 1968	**expired** (1.7.69).
428	Ulster and Colonial Savings Certificates (Income Tax Exemption) (Amdt.) Regs. 1968	**r.**, 1969/542.
438	Motor Vehicles (Authorisation of Special Types) (Amdt.) O. 1968	**r.**, 1969/344.
443	National Health Service (General Dental Services) Amdt. Regs. 1968	**r.**, 1969/217.
448	British Nationality (Amdt.) Regs. 1968	**r.**, 1969/760.
454	Non-Residents' Transitional Relief from Income Tax on Dividends (Extension of Period) O. 1968	**superseded**, 1969/319.
455	Transitional Relief for Interest and Royalties paid to Non-Residents (Extension of Period) O. 1968	**superseded**, 1969/320.

Year and Number (or date)	Title or Description	How affected and Act or Instrument by which affected
1968 457	Milk (G.B.) (Amdt.) O. 1968	**r.**, 1969/972.
523	Motor Vehicles (Construction and Use) (Amdt.) (No. 3) Regs. 1968	**r.**, 1969/321.
525	Wages Regs. (Milk Distributive) (E. and W.) O. 1968	**r.**, 1969/1476.
534	Provision of Milk and Meals Amdg. Regs. 1968	**r.**, 1969/483.
552	Police (Amdt.) Regs. 1968	**superseded,** 1969/137.
580	Merchant Shipping (Light Dues) O. 1968	**r.**, 1969/386.
601	Goods Vehicles (Plating and Testing) Regs. 1968	regs. 2, 4, 15, 16 **am.**, sch. 3 **replaced,** 1969/322. reg. 2 **am.**, 3 **replaced,** 8, 9 **am.**, 10A, 12A **inserted,** 19, 23, 27 **am.**, 27A **inserted,** 29 **replaced,** 32, 36, 52, 53, schs. 1, 3 Pts. I, II **am.**, 4 Pts. IV, V **inserted,** 1969/1324. regs. 27B **inserted,** 29, 36 **am.**, 1969/1762.
602	Motor Vehicles (Construction and Use) (Amdt.) (No. 4) Regs. 1968	**r.**, 1969/321.
616	Prices and Incomes (General Considerations) O. 1968	**r.**, 1969/1891.
619	Plant Breeder's Rights (Fees) Regs. 1968	sch. 2 **am.**, 1969/1022.
622	Plant Breeder's Rights (Amdt. No. 2) Regs. 1968	**r.**, 1969/1021.
626	Wages Regulation (Hollow-ware) O. 1968	**r.**, 1969/930.
679	Import Duties (General) (No. 4) O. 1968	**r.**, 1969/1413.
716	Police (S.) Regs. 1968	reg. 42 **am.**, schs. 3, 4 **replaced,** 1969/137. regs. 18 **am.**, 55 **replaced,** 1969/505. sch. 6 **am.**, 1969/927. sch. 5 **am.**, 1969/1586.
728	Turks and Caicos Is. (Constitution) (Amdt.) O. 1968	**r.**, 1969/736.
742	Wages Regulation (Button Manufacturing) O. 1968	**r.**, 1969/894.
745	Overseas Service (Pensions Supplement) (Amdt.) Regs. 1968	**r.**, 1969/553.
751	Wages Regulation (Aerated Waters) (S.) O. 1968	**r.**, 1969/546.
752	Wages Regulation (Aerated Waters) (S.) (Holidays) O. 1968	**r.**, 1969/547.

Year and Number (or date)	Title or Description	How affected and Act or Instrument by which affected
1968 765	Trustee Savings Banks (Rate of Interest) O. 1968	**r.,** 1969/687.
827	National Insurance (Members of the Forces) Regs. 1968	reg. 5 **am.,** schs. 3–5 **replaced,** 5A **inserted,** 1969/1508.
830	Hill Sheep (N.I.) Scheme 1968	para. 9 **am.,** 1969/702.
839	Motor Vehicles (Authorisation of Special Types) (Amdt.) (No. 2) O. 1968	**r.,** 1969/344.
850	Milk (N.I.) (Amdt.) O. 1968	**r.,** 1969/973.
875	Hill Cattle (Breeding Herds) (E. and W.) Scheme 1968	para. 10 **am.,** 1969/695.
876	Hill Cattle Subsidy (Breeding Herds) (E. and W.) Payment O. 1968	art. 3 **am.,** 1969/696.
931	Postal Packets (Customs and Excise) Amdt. (No. 1) Regs. 1968	**r.,** 1969/1399.
937	Fees of Appointed Factory Doctors O. 1968	**r.,** 1969/1633.
950	Import Duties (General) (No. 5) O. 1968	**r.,** 1969/1413.
955	Housing (Forms) (S.) Regs. 1968	**r.** (saving), 1969/1420.
965	Hill Cattle (Breeding Herds) (N.I.) Scheme 1968	para. 9 **am.,** 1969/700.
966	Hill Cattle Subsidy (Breeding Herds) (N.I.) Payment O. 1968	art. 3 **am.,** 1969/701.
967	Beef Cow Subsidy Payment (E. and W.) (Amdt.) O. 1968	**superseded,** 1969/694.
968	Beef Cow Subsidy Payment (N.I.) (Amdt.) O. 1968	**superseded,** 1969/699.
982	Hill Cattle Subsidy Payment (S.) O. 1968	art. 2 **am.,** 1969/707.
983	Beef Cow Subsidy Payment (S.) (Amdt.) O. 1968	**superseded,** 1969/908.
989	Commons Registration (Objections and Maps) Regs. 1968	reg. 2 **am.,** 1969/1843.
991	Irish Land (Finance) (Amdt.) Rules 1968	**r.,** 1969/851.
1030	Import Duties (General) (No. 6) O. 1968	**r.,** 1969/1413.
1047	Offices, Shops and Railway Premises Act 1963 (Exemption No. 5) O. 1968	**r.,** 1969/1323.
1051	Wages Regulation (Rope, Twine and Net) (Holidays) O. 1968	sch. paras. 6, 11 **am.,** 1969/654.

Year and Number (or date)	Title or Description	How affected and Act or Instrument by which affected
1968 1080	Prices and Incomes (Regulated Rents) (E. and W.) Regs. 1968	regs. 3–5 **am.**, 9 sch. Pt. II **r.**, 1969/1184.
1081	Prices and Incomes (Regulated Rents) (S.) Regs. 1968	regs. 3, 5 **am.**, 9 **r.** (saving), 1969/1419.
1093	Saint Vincent Constitution (Amdt.) O. 1968	**r.**, 1969/1500.
1111	Motor Vehicles (International Circulation) (Amdt.) O. 1968	**r.**, 1969/1086.
1130	Wages Regulation (Road Haulage) O. 1968	**r.**, 1969/1714.
1147	Selective Employment Payments Variation O. 1968	arts. 1, 2 **am.**, 1969/867.
1158	Import Duties (General) (No. 7) O. 1968	**r.**, 1969/1413.
1168	Goods Vehicles (Temporary Use in G.B.) Regs. 1968	**r.**, 1969/1423.
1205	Family Allowances, National Insurance and Industrial Injuries (Consequential) (No. 2) Regs. 1968	reg. 2 **r.** (saving), 1969/1361.
1207	Police (Amdt.) (No. 3) Regs. 1968	**superseded**, 1969/137.
1235	White Fish and Herring Subsidies (U.K.) Scheme 1968	para. 13 **r.**, sch. 2 Pt. I **am.**, 1969/471.
1248	Motor Vehicles (Construction and Use) (Amdt.) (No. 5) Regs. 1968	**r.**, 1969/321.
1251	Provision of Milk and Meals (Amdt. No. 2) Regs. 1968	**r.**, 1969/483.
1253	Inland Post Regs. 1968	regs. 1 **am.**, 10A, 10B **inserted**, 18, 21 **replaced**, 22 **r.**, 28, 55 **am.**, 55A **inserted**, (P.O. scheme 18.9.69).*
1284	Pensions Increase (Approved Schemes) (Local Govt.) Regs. 1968	regs. 2, 4, sch. **am.**, 1969/1720.
1285	Pensions Increase (Approved Schemes) (National Health Service) Regs. 1968	reg. 2 **am.**, 1969/1447.
1298	Pensions Increase (Approved Schemes) (Local Govt.) (S.) Regs. 1968	regs. 2, 4, sch. **am.**, 1969/1881.
1299	Pensions Increase (Approved Schemes) (National Health Service) (S.) Regs. 1968	reg. 2 **am.**, 1969/1878.
1333	Industrial Training (Engineering Bd.) O. 1968	sch. paras. 1–3, appx. **am.**, 1969/1376.
1355	Wages Regulation (Cotton Waste Reclamation) O. 1968	**r.**, 1969/632.

*Not S.I. *see* London Gazette 18-9-69, p. 15.

Year and Number (or date)	Title or Description	How affected and Act or Instrument by which affected
1968		
1357	Wages Regulation (Sack and Bag) O. 1968	r., 1969/1739.
1358	Wages Regulation (Sack and Bag) (Holidays) O. 1968	r., 1969/1740.
1366	Public Health (Infectious Diseases) Regs. 1968	regs. 2, 6, 10 am., 1969/844.
1383	Import Duties (General) (No. 8) O. 1968	r., 1969/1413.
1389	Patents Rules 1968	sch. 1 replaced, 1969/482. sch. 1 am., 1969/1706.
1448	Nurses (Regional Nurse-Training Ctees.) (S.) Amdt. O. 1968	superseded, 1969/849.
1484	Wages Regulation (Flax and Hemp) O. 1968	r., 1969/1261.
1485	Wages Regulation (Flax and Hemp) (Holidays) O. 1968	r., 1969/1841.
1502	Housing (Forms) (S.) (No. 2) Regs. 1968	sch. form A am., 1969/1424.
1509	Import Duties (General) (No. 9) O. 1968	r., 1969/1413.
1510	Import Duties (General) (No. 10) O. 1968	r., 1969/1413.
1513	British Sugar Corporation Limited (Incentive Agreement) (Variation) O. 1968	superseded, 1969/1312.
1534	Wages Regulation (Laundry) O. 1968	r., 1969/1344.
1535	Wages Regulation (Laundry) (Holidays) O. 1968	r., 1969/1345.
1591	Betterment Levy (Rate of Interest) (No. 2) O. 1968	r., 1969/440.
1598	Wages Regulation (Licensed Non-residential Establishment) (Managers and Club Stewards) (Amdt.) O. 1968	r., 1969/655.
1632	Motor Vehicles (Construction and Use) (Amdt.) (No. 6) Regs. 1968	r., 1969/321.
1634	Exchange Control (Authorised Dealers and Depositories) O. 1968	r., 1969/517.
1677	Control of Hiring (Amdt. No. 8) O. 1968	r., 1969/1307.
1678	Hire-Purchase and Credit Sale Agreements (Control) (Amdt. No. 10) O. 1968	r., 1969/1308.

Year and Number (or date)	Title or Description	How affected and Act or Instrument by which affected
1968 1714	Motor Vehicles (Tests) Regs. 1968	regs. 3, 4, 10, 15 **am.**, schs. 2 **replaced**, 3, 5, **am.**, 1969/1171.
1736	Control of Hiring (Amdt. No. 9) O. 1968	**r.**, 1969/1307.
1737	Hire-Purchase and Credit Sale Agreements (Control) (Amdt. No. 11) O. 1968	**r.**, 1969/1308.
1771	Fees of Appointed Factory Doctors (Amdt.) O. 1968	**r.**, 1969/1633.
1778	Import Duties (General) (No. 11) O. 1968	**r.**, 1969/1413.
1798	Remuneration of Teachers (Further Education) (Amdt.) O. 1968	**r.**, 1969/1713.
1799	Remuneration of Teachers (Primary and Secondary Schools) (Amdt. No. 2) O. 1968	**r.**, 1969/618.
1801	Armed Forces (Discharge by Purchase) Regs. 1968	regs. 3, 4 **am.** (enlistments after 1.1.70), 1969/1864.
1837	Rules of the Air and Air Traffic Control (Sixth Amdt.) Regs. 1968	**r.**, 1969/216.
1880	Import Duties (General) (No. 12) O. 1968	**r.**, 1969/1413.
1881	Import Duty Drawbacks (No. 10) O. 1968	schs. 2, 3 **am.**, 1969/1034. schs. 1, 2 **am.**, 1969/1658.
1885	Anti-Dumping (Provisional Charge to Duty) O. 1968	**r.**, 1969/60.
1896	National Insurance (Industrial Injuries) (Colliery Workers Supplementary Scheme) Amdt. (No. 2) O. 1968	**superseded**, 1969/716.
1919	Magistrates' Cts. (Forms) Rules 1968	sch. forms 29 **am.**, 98A **inserted**, 1969/1710.
1920	Magistrates' Cts. Rules 1968	rules 16, 28 **am.**, 88A **inserted**, 1969/1711.
1930	Road Vehicles (Headlamps) Regs. 1968	**r.**, 1969/1647
1939	Price Stability of Imported Products (Rates of Levy No. 13) O. 1968	**r.**, 1969/45.
1948	Import Duties (Temporary Exemptions) (No. 6) O. 1968	**r.**, 1969/1751.
1953	Town and Country Planning (Inquiries Procedure) (Amdt.) Rules 1968	**r.**, 1969/1092.
1954	Building Societies (Accounts and Annual Return etc.) Regs. 1968	regs. 6A **inserted**, 7 **am.**, sch. **am.**, 1969/1587.
1956	Rate Support Grant O. 1968	reg. 3 **mod.** (temp.), 1969/1806.

Year and Number (or date)	Title or Description	How affected and Act or Instrument by which affected
1968		
1963	Police (S.) Amdt. (No. 2) Regs. 1968	**superseded,** 1969/927.
1986	Eggs (Protection of Guarantees) O. 1968	**r.,** 1969/187.
2009	Sugar (Surcharge Remission) O. 1968	sch. **am.,** 1969/1509.
2011	British Transport (Pensions of Employees) (No. 1) O. 1968	arts. 4 **r.,** 11 **am.,** 1969/1824.
2015	Sugar (Rates of Surcharge and Surcharge Repayments) (No. 8) O. 1968	**superseded,** 1969/178.
2016	Composite Sugar Products (Surcharge and Surcharge Repayments—Average Rates) (No. 8) O. 1968	**superseded,** 1969/179.
2019	Exchange Control (Authorised Dealers and Depositories) (Amdt.) (No. 4) O. 1968	**r.,** 1969/517.
2044	Police Federation (Amdt.) (No. 2) Regs. 1968	**r.,** 1969/1787.
2049	Registration of Births, Deaths and Marriages Regs. 1968	**mod.** (W.), 1969/203. regs. 20, 24, 30 **am.,** 1969/1811.
2050	Birth Certificate (Shortened Form) Regs. 1968	reg. 4 **mod.** (W.), 1969/203.
2052	Justices (Supplemental List) Rules 1968	rule 3 **am.,** 1969/76.
2063	Anti-Dumping Duty (No. 2) O. 1968	suspended as to Portugal until 1.3.70, 1969/1216.
2070	Rules of the Air and Air Traffic Control (Seventh Amdt.) Regs. 1968	**r.,** 1969/216.
2075	Fishing Nets (North-East Atlantic) O. 1968	**r.,** 1969/1823.
1969		
39	A.S. (Sessions of Ct.) 1969	**r.,** 1969/1536.
45	Price Stability of Imported Products (Rates of Levy No. 1) O. 1969	**r.,** 1969/211.
52	Motor Vehicles (Construction and Use) (Amdt.) Regs. 1969	**r.,** 1969/321.
77	Teachers Superannuation (S.) Regs. 1969	reg. 78 **am.,** 1969/659.
85	Motor Cars (Driving Instruction) Regs. 1969	sch. **replaced,** 1969/713.
129	Exchange Control (Authorised Dealers and Depositories) (Amdt.) O. 1969	**r.,** 1969/517.
178	Sugar (Rates of Surcharge and Surcharge Repayments) O. 1969	**superseded,** 1969/279.

Year and Number (or date)	Title or Description	How affected and Act or Instrument by which affected
1969		
179	Composite Sugar Products (Surcharge and Surcharge Repayments—Average Rates) O. 1969	**superseded,** 1969/280.
208	Wages Regulation (Brush and Broom) (Amdt.) O. 1969	**r.,** 1969/909.
211	Price Stability of Imported Products (Rates of Levy No. 2) O. 1969	**r.,** 1969/314.
216	Rules of the Air and Air Traffic Control Regs. 1969	sch. rules 38, 45, sch. Table B **am.,** 1969/974. sch. rules 5, 28, 45 **am.. 45A inserted,** 1969/1859.
232	Import Duties (Temporary Exemptions) (No. 1) O. 1969	**r.,** 1969/1751.
278	Exchange Control (Authorised Dealers and Depositaries) (Amdt.) (No. 2) O. 1969	**r.,** 1969/517.
279	Sugar (Rates of Surcharge and Surcharge Repayments) (No. 2) O. 1969	**superseded,** 1969/362.
280	Composite Sugar Products (Surcharge and Surcharge Repayments—Average Rates) (No. 2) O. 1969	**superseded,** 1969/363.
314	Price Stability of Imported Products (Rates of Levy No. 3) O. 1969	**r.,** 1969/329.
315	Import Duties (Temporary Exemptions) (Amdt.) O. 1969	**r.,** 1969/1751.
318	Price Stability of Imported Products (Rates of Levy No. 4) O. 1969	**r.,** 1969/329.
321	Motor Vehicles (Construction and Use) Regs. 1969	regs. 12A, 12B **inserted,** 1969/1042. reg. 4 **am.,** 1969/1456. reg. 75A **inserted,** 1969/1456. sch. 2 Pts. II, III **am.,** 1969/1456. regs. 118 **am.,** 120A **inserted,** 1969/1761.
329	Price Stability of Imported Products (Rates of Levy No. 5) O. 1969	**r.,** 1969/407.
344	Motor Vehicles (Authorisation of Special Types) General O. 1969	art. 20 **am.,** 1969/1457.
362	Sugar (Rates of Surcharge and Surcharge Repayments) (No. 3) O. 1969	**superseded,** 1969/588.
363	Composite Sugar Products (Surcharge and Surcharge Repayments—Average Rates) (No. 3) O. 1969	**superseded,** 1969/589.
407	Price Stability of Imported Products (Rates of Levy No. 6) O. 1969	**r.,** 1969/473.
440	Betterment Levy (Rate of Interest) O. 1969	**r.,** 1969/536.

Year and Number (or date)	Title or Description	How affected and Act or Instrument by which affected
1969		
458	Acquisition of Land (Rate of Interest after Entry) Regs. 1969	r., 1969/896.
459	Acquisition of Land (Rate of Interest after Entry) (S.) Regs. 1969	r., 1969/897.
460	Opencast Coal (Rate of Interest on Compensation) O. 1969	r., 1969/1513.
473	Price Stability of Imported Products (Rates of Levy No. 7) O. 1969	r., 1969/571.
483	Provision of Milk and Meals Regs. 1969	sch. 1 **am.**, 1969/1093.
511	Bacon Curing Industry Stabilisation Scheme 1969	para. 3 **am.** (temp.), 1969/999.
517	Exchange Control (Authorised Dealers and Depositories) O. 1969	sch. 2 **am.**, 1969/1414, 1624.
537	Price Stability of Imported Products (Rates of Levy No. 8) O. 1969	r., 1969/571.
546	Wages Regulation (Aerated Waters) (S.) O. 1969	r., 1969/1645.
571	Price Stability of Imported Products (Rates of Levy No. 9) O. 1969	r., 1969/664.
572	Import Duties (Temporary Exemptions) (No. 2) O. 1969	r., 1969/1751.
573	Import Duties (Temporary Exemptions) (No. 3) O. 1969	r., 1969/1751.
588	Sugar (Rates of Surcharge and Surcharge Repayments) (No. 4) O. 1969	**superseded,** 1969/889.
589	Composite Sugar Products (Surcharge and Surcharge Repayments—Average Rates) (No. 4) O. 1969	**superseded,** 1969/890.
591	Turks and Caicos Is. (Constitution) (Amdt.) O. 1969	r., 1969/736.
664	Price Stability of Imported Products (Rates of Levy No. 10) O. 1969	r., 1969/779.
676	Price Stability of Imported Products (Rates of Levy No. 11) O. 1969	r., 1969/779.
691	Wages Regulation (Industrial and Staff Canteen) O. 1969	r., 1969/1726.
716	National Insurance (Industrial Injuries) (Colliery Workers Supplementary Scheme) Amdt. O. 1969	**superseded,** 1969/1646.
724	Special Constables (Pensions) (Amdt.) Regs. 1969	**superseded,** 1969/1514.
770	Anti-Dumping (Provisional Charge to Duty) O. 1969	r., 1969/1136.

Year and Number (or date)	Title or Description	How affected and Act or Instrument by which affected
1969		
779	Price Stability of Imported Products (Rates of Levy No. 12) O. 1969	r., 1969/878.
813	Fees of Appointed Factory Doctors (Amdt.) O. 1969	r., 1969/1633.
822	Price Stability of Imported Products (Rates of Levy No. 13) O. 1969	r., 1969/878.
839	Import Duties (Temporary Exemptions) (No. 4) O. 1969	r., 1969/1751.
842	Foreign Compensation Commn. (U.S.S.R.) Rules 1969	rule 33 am., 1969/1865.
878	Price Stability of Imported Products (Rates of Levy No. 14) O. 1969	r., 1969/1020.
879	Industrial Training (Road Transport Bd.) O. 1969	sch. paras. 1–3, appx. am., 1969/1871.
889	Sugar (Rates of Surcharge and Surcharge Repayments) (No. 5) O. 1969	superseded, 1969/1120.
890	Composite Sugar Products (Surcharge and Surcharge Repayments—Average Rates) (No. 5) O. 1969	superseded, 1969/1121.
939	Savings Banks (Ordinary Deposits) (Limits) O. 1969	gen. am., art. 3 am., 1969/1699.
940	Post Office Savings Banks (Investment Deposits) (Limits) O. 1969	gen. am., 1969/1701.
989	Special Constables (Pensions) (S.) Amdt. Regs. 1969	superseded, 1969/1529.
1020	Price Stability of Imported Products (Rates of Levy No. 15) O. 1969	r., 1969/1244.
1053	Injuries in War (Shore Employments) Compensation (Amdt.) Scheme 1969	superseded, 1969/1861.
1120	Sugar (Rates of Surcharge and Surcharge Repayments) (No. 6) O. 1969	superseded, 1969/1189.
1121	Composite Sugar Products (Surcharge and Surcharge Repayments—Average Rates) (No. 6) O. 1969	superseded, 1969/1190.
1126	Price Stability of Imported Products (Rates of Levy No. 16) O. 1969	r., 1969/1167.
1167	Price Stability of Imported Products (Rates of Levy No. 17) O. 1969	r., 1969/1244.
1184	Rent Regulation (Forms etc.) (E. and W.) Regs. 1969	sch. 1 forms 3 am., 5A inserted, 1969/1821.
1189	Sugar (Rates of Surcharge and Surcharge Repayments) (No. 7) O. 1969	superseded, 1969/1204.

Year and Number (or date)	Title or Description	How affected and Act or Instrument by which affected
1969		
1190	Composite Sugar Products (Surcharge and Surcharge Repayments—Average Rates) (No. 7) O. 1969	**superseded,** 1969/1205.
1204	Sugar (Rates of Surcharge and Surcharge Repayments) (No. 8) O. 1969	**superseded,** 1969/1229.
1205	Composite Sugar Products (Surcharge and Surcharge Repayments—Average Rates) (No. 8) O. 1969	**superseded,** 1969/1230.
1214	Import Duties (General) (No. 1) O. 1969	r., 1969/1413.
1215	Import Duties (Temporary Exemptions) (No. 5) O. 1969	r., 1969/1751.
1229	Sugar (Rates of Surcharge and Surcharge Repayments) (No. 9) O. 1969	**superseded,** 1969/1426.
1230	Composite Sugar Products (Surcharge and Surcharge Repayments—Average Rates) (No. 9) O. 1969	**superseded,** 1969/1427.
1244	Price Stability of Imported Products (Rates of Levy No. 18) O. 1969	r., 1969/1294.
1254	Import Duties (Temporary Exemptions) (No. 6) O. 1969	r., 1969/1751.
1275	Price Stability of Imported Products (Rates of Levy No. 19) O. 1969	r., 1969/1294.
1294	Price Stability of Imported Products (Rates of Levy No. 20) O. 1969	r., 1969/1518.
1329	Price Stability of Imported Products (Rates of Levy No. 21) O. 1969	r., 1969/1518.
1338	Import Duties (General) (No. 2) O. 1969	r., 1969/1413.
1413	Import Duties (General) (No. 3) O. 1969	art. 1 **am,** 1969/1719. sch. 1c, 5, 12, 15, 27–30, 32, 35, 37–39, 49, 51, 68–70, 73, 74, 76, 81, 83–85, 90 **am.** (temp.), 1969/1751. sch. 3 **am.,** 1969/1791.
1416	Import Duties (Temporary Exemptions) (No. 7) O. 1969	r., 1969/1751.
1419	Rent Regulation (Forms etc.) (S.) Regs. 1969	sch. 2 List of Forms, Form 3 **am.,** 4A **inserted,** 1969/1846.
1426	Sugar (Rates of Surcharge and Surcharge Repayments) (No. 10) O. 1969	**superseded,** 1969/1505.
1427	Composite Sugar Products (Surcharge and Surcharge Repayments—Average Rates) (No. 10) O. 1969	**superseded,** 1969/1506.

Year and Number (or date)	Title or Description	How affected and Act or Instrument by which affected
1969 1505	Sugar (Rates of Surcharge and Surcharge Repayments) (No. 11) O. 1969	**superseded**, 1969/1527.
1506	Composite Sugar Products (Surcharge and Surcharge Repayments—Average Rates) (No. 11) O. 1969	**superseded**, 1969/1528.
1518	Price Stability of Imported Products (Rates of Levy No. 22) O. 1969	**r.**, 1969/1550.
1519	Import Duties (Temporary Exemptions) (No. 8) O. 1969	**r.**, 1969/1751.
1527	Sugar (Rates of Surcharge and Surcharge Repayments) (No. 12) O. 1969	**superseded**, 1969/1664.
1528	Composite Sugar Products (Surcharge and Surcharge Repayments—Average Rates) (No. 12) O. 1969	**superseded**, 1969/1665.
1550	Price Stability of Imported Products (Rates of Levy No. 23) O. 1969	**r.**, 1969/1677.

NUMERICAL

LIST

1969

NUMERICAL LIST
of those Statutory Instruments of 1969
which were printed and sold under the
Statutory Instruments Act 1946

[*Note.*—With respect to each instrument listed, two dates are shown; the first is the date on which it is made, and the second, which is in square brackets, is the date on which it was first issued by Her Majesty's Stationery Office.]

No.	Subject		Part	Page
1	Industrial Training Levy (Iron and Steel), 2 Jan. [13 Jan.]		I,	1
2	Police (Adaptation of Enactments) (Cheshire, Liverpool and Bootle), 2 Jan. [10 Jan.]	(n) III,	5878
3	Metropolitan Water Bd. (Queen Mary Reservoir), 6 Jan. [16 Jan.]	(n) III,	5882
8	Levens Bridge–Broughton-in-Furness–Workington–Aspatria–Carlisle Trunk Road (Grizebeck Diversion), 1 Jan. [20 Jan.]	(n) III,	5865
16	Town and Country Planning Act 1968 (Commencement), 7 Jan. [15 Jan.]	I,	5
17	Town and Country Planning (Tree Preservation), 7 Jan. [15 Jan.]	I,	7
18	Conveyance in Harbours of Military Explosives, 6 Jan. [17 Jan.]	I,	19
19	Conveyance by Rail of Military Explosives, 6 Jan. [17 Jan.]	I,	42
20	Conveyance by Road of Military Explosives, 6 Jan. [17 Jan.]	I,	68
21	Blaenavon Urban District Water, 8 Jan. [20 Jan.]	(n) III,	5883
22	Taf Fechan Water Bd., 8 Jan. [21 Jan.]	(n) III,	5883
23	Plymouth Water, 8 Jan. [21 Jan.]	(n) III,	5883
26	Diseases of Fish (Infected Area), 7 Jan. [17 Jan.]...	(n) III,	5875
27	Conway Valley Water Bd., 9 Jan. [20 Jan.] ...	(n) III,	5883
28	London–Inverness Trunk Road (A.6/M.1 Junction, Kegworth), 8 Jan. [24 Jan.]	(n) III,	5863
29	Central Nottinghamshire Water, 10 Jan. [22 Jan.]	(n) III,	5882
30	Gretna–Stranraer–Glasgow–Stirling Trunk Road (Nether Culzean Diversion), 7 Jan. [23 Jan.] ...	(n) III,	5865
31	Gretna–Stranraer–Glasgow–Stirling Trunk Road (North Drammwuran and Other Diversions), 7 Jan. [23 Jan.]	(n) III,	5865

(n) Instrument classified as local, noted in the Classified List of Local S.I. at the page shown above, but not set out in full.

(n) Instrument classified as local, noted in the Classified List of Local S.I. at the page shown above, but not set out in full.

(n) Instrument classified as local, noted in the Classified List of Local S.I. at the page shown above but not set out in full.

(n) Instrument classified as local, noted in the Classified List of Local S.I. at the page shown above, but not set out in full.

(n) Instrument classified as local, noted in the Classified List of Local S.I. at the page shown above, but not set out in full.

(n) Instrument classified as local, noted in the Classified List of Local S.I. at the page shown above, but not set out in full.

(n) Instrument classified as local, noted in the Classified List of Local S.I. at the page shown above, but not set out in full.

(n) Instrument classified as local, noted in the Classified List of Local S.I. at the page shown above, but not set out in full.

(n) Instrument classified as local, noted in the Classified List of Local S.I. at the page shown above, but not set out in full.

(n) Instrument classified as local, noted in the Classified List of Local S.I. at the page shown above, but not set out in full.

(n) Instrument classified as local, noted in the Classified List of Local S.I. at the page shown above, but not set out in full.

No.	Subject	Part	Page
440	Betterment Levy (Rate of Interest), 21 Mar. [31 Mar.]	I,	1296
441	Brighton Water (Extension of Operation of Bye-laws), 24 Mar. [2 Apr.]	(n) III,	5882
442	Central Nottinghamshire Water Bd. (Chequer House Boreholes), 24 Mar. [2 Apr.]	(n) III,	5882
449	Paisley and District Hospitals Endowments, 18 Mar. [31 Mar.]	(n) III,	5881
450	Greenock and District Hospitals Endowments, 18 Mar. [31 Mar.]	(n) III,	5881
451	National Health Service (Regional Hospital Areas), 24 Mar. [31 Mar.]	I,	1297
453	New Towns (S.) Act 1968 National Loans Fund Substitution, 25 Mar. [31 Mar.]	I,	1298
454	Dundee General and Dundee Northern Hospitals Endowments, 24 Mar. [31 Mar.]	(n) III,	5881
455	City of Lincoln (Brayford Head New Bridge), 21 Mar. [8 Apr.]	(n) III,	5863
456	Superannuation (Local Govt. and National and Local Govt. Officers Association) Interchange, 25 Mar. [31 Mar.]	I,	1300
457	Craven Water Undertaking (Valuation), 24 Mar. [31 Mar.]	(n) III,	5880
458	Acquisition of Land (Rate of Interest after Entry), 24 Mar. [2 Apr.]	I,	1315
459	Acquisition of Land (Rate of Interest after Entry) (S.), 24 Mar. [2 Apr.]	I,	1316
460	Opencast Coal (Rate of Interest on Compensation), 24 Mar. [2 Apr.]	I,	1317
463	Local Authorities' Traffic Orders (Procedure) (E. and W.), 25 Mar. [3 Apr.]	I,	1318
464	A.S. (Alteration of Sheriff Ct. Fees), 25 Mar. [1 Apr.]	I,	1331
465	Clean Air (Height of Chimneys) (Exemption) (S.), 25 Mar. [1 Apr.]	I,	1333
466	Clean Air (Height of Chimneys) (Prescribed Form) (S.), 25 Mar. [1 Apr.]	I,	1335
468	Charities (Sir John Soane's Museum), 26 Mar. [2 Apr.]	(n) III,	5888
469	Drainage Charges (Forms), 24 Mar. [3 Apr.] ...	I,	1339
471	White Fish and Herring Subsidies (U.K.), 17 Feb. [2 Apr.]	I,	1349
472	White Fish Subsidy (Deep Sea Vessels) (U.K.), 17 Feb. [2 Apr.]	I,	1351
473	Price Stability of Imported Products (Rates of Levy), 25 Mar. [28 Mar.]	I,	1358
474	A.S. (Rules of Ct.), 14 Feb. [16 June]	I,	1361
475	A.S. (Rules of Ct.), 25 Mar. [16 June]	I,	1362
477	Aberdeen Harbour Revision, 17 Dec. 1968 [2 Apr.]	(n) III,	5875
478	Milford Haven Conservancy Revision, 24 Jan. [2 Apr.]	(n) III,	5876

(n) Instrument classified as local, noted in the Classified List of Local S.I. at the page shown above, but not set out in full.

(n) Instrument classified as local, noted in the Classified List of Local S.I. at the page shown above, but not set out in full.

(n) Instrument classified as local, noted in the Classified List of Local S.I. at the page shown above, but not set out in full.

(n) Instrument classified as local, noted in the Classified List of Local S.I. at the page shown above, but not set out in full.

(n) Instrument classified as local, noted in the Classified List of Local S.I. at the page shown above, but not set out in full.

(n) Instrument classified as local, noted in the Classified List of Local S.I. at the page shown above, but not set out in full.

(n) Instrument classified as local, noted in the Classified List of Local S.I. at the page shown above, but not set out in full.

(n) Instrument classified as local, noted in the Classified List of Local S.I. at the page shown above, but not set out in full.

(n) Instrument classified as local, noted in the Classified List of Local S.I. at the page shown above, but not set out in full.

(n) Instrument classified as local, noted in the Classified List of Local S.I. at the page shown above, but not set out in full.

(n) Instrument classified as local, noted in the Classified List of Local S.I. at the page shown above, but not set out in full.

(n) Instrument classified as local, noted in the Classified List of Local S.I. at the page shown above, but not set out in full.

(n) Instrument classified as local, noted in the Classified List of Local S.I. at the page shown above, but not set out in full.

(n) Instrument classified as local, noted in the Classified List of Local S.I. at the page shown above, but not set out in full.

(n) Instrument classified as local, noted in the Classified List of Local S.I. at the page shown above, but not set out in full.

(n) Instrument classified as local, noted in the Classified List of Local S.I. at the page shown above, but not set out in full.

(n) Instrument classified as local, noted in the Classified List of Local S.I. at the page shown above, but not set out in full.

(n) Instrument classified as local, noted in the Classified List of Local S.I. at the page shown above, but not set out in full.

(n) Instrument classified as local, noted in the Classified List of Local S.I. at the page shown above, but not set out in full.

(n) Instrument classified as local, noted in the Classified List of Local S.I. at the page shown above, but not set out in full.

(n) Instrument classified as local, noted in the Classified List of Local S.I. at the page shown above, but not set out in full.

No.	Subject	Part	Page
1366	Postal Services (Jersey), 24 Sept. [30 Sept.] ...	III,	4074
1367	Postal Services (Guernsey), 24 Sept. [30 Sept.] ...	III,	4078
1368	Postal Services (Channel Islands Consequential Provisions), 24 Sept. [30 Sept.]	III,	4082
1369	Wireless Telegraphy (Channel Islands), 24 Sept. [30 Sept.]	III,	4085
1370	Television Act 1964 (Channel Islands), 24 Sept. [30 Sept.]	III,	4086
1371	Wireless Telegraphy (Isle of Man), 24 Sept. [30 Sept.]	III,	4087
1372	Television Act 1964 (Isle of Man), 24 Sept. [30 Sept.]	III,	4088
1373	Justices of the Peace Act 1968 (Commencement), 24 Sept. [30 Sept.]	III,	4089
1374	Civil Aviation (Licensing), 22 Sept. [30 Sept.] ...	III,	4092
1375	Industrial Training (Clothing and Allied Products Bd.), 22 Sept. [6 Oct.]	III,	4094
1376	Industrial Training (Engineering Bd.), 22 Sept. [6 Oct.]	III,	4103
1378	National Health Service (Standish Hospital Management Committee), 23 Sept. [1 Oct.]	(n) III,	5881
1380	Programme Distribution Systems (Exceptions), 24 Sept. [29 Sept.]	III,	4107
1382	Superannuation (Transfers between the Civil Service and Public Bds.), 24 Sept. [30 Sept.] ...	III,	4111
1383	Baking and Sausage Making (Christmas and New Year), 24 Sept. [3 Oct.]	III,	4113
1385	Petty Sessional Divisions (Herefordshire), 22 Sept. [20 Oct.]	(n) III,	5886
1386	County of Staffordshire (Electoral Divisions), 24 Sept. [2 Oct.]	(n) III,	5877
1387	Lancashire County Council (Manchester Outer Ring Road Northern Section Middleton Link to the Lancashire/Yorkshire Motorway) Special Roads Scheme 1968 Confirmation Instrument, 22 Sept. [2 Oct.]	(n) III,	5866
1388	Clean Air (Arrestment Plant) (Exemption) (S.) 25 Sept. [30 Sept.]	III,	4115
1389	Clean Air (Emission of Dark Smoke) (Exemption) (S.), 25 Sept. [30 Sept.]	III,	4119
1390	County of Lincoln, Parts of Holland (Electoral Divisions), 23 Sept. [3 Oct.]	(n) III,	5877
1391	County of West Suffolk (Electoral Divisions), 23 Sept. [3 Oct.]	(n) III,	5877
1392	County of Cambridgeshire and Isle of Ely (Electoral Divisions), 23 Sept. [3 Oct.]	(n) III,	5877
1393	Cambridge Water (Linton), 25 Sept. [3 Oct.] ...	(n) III,	5882
1396	Game Licences and Gamedealers' Licences (S.) 25 Sept. [30 Sept.]	III,	4122
1397	County Court Districts (Wisbech and March), 25 Sept. [3 Oct.]	III,	4124
1398	West Lancashire Water Bd. (Charges), 26 Sept. [6 Oct.]	(n) III,	5883

(n) Instrument classified as local, noted in the Classified List of Local S.I. at the page shown above, but not set out in full.

(n) Instrument classified as local, noted in the Classified List of Local S.I. at the page shown above, but not set out in full.

(n) Instrument classified as local, noted in the Classified List of Local S.I. at the page shown above, but not set out in full.

(n) Instrument classified as local, noted in the Classified List of Local S.I. at the page shown above, but not set out in full.

(n) Instrument classified as local, noted in the Classified List of Local S.I. at the page shown above, but not set out in full.

(n) Instrument classified as local, noted in the Classified List of Local S.I. at the page shown above, but not set out in full.

(n) Instrument classified as local, noted in the Classified List of Local S.I. at the page shown above, but not set out in full.

(n) Instrument classified as local, noted in the Classified List of Local S.I. at the page shown above, but not set out in full.

(n) Instrument classified as local, noted in the Classified List of Local S.I. at the page shown above, but not set out in full.

(n) Instrument classified as local, noted in the Classified List of Local S.I. at the page shown above, but not set out in full.

(n) Instrument classified as local, noted in the Classified List of Local S.I. at the page shown above, but not set out in full.

(n) Instrument classified as local, noted in the Classified List of Local S.I. at the page shown above, but not set out in full.

No.	Subject	Part	Page
1868	South Essex Waterworks (Water Charges), 23 Dec. [9 Jan.]	(n) III,	5883
1869	Mayor's and City of London Ct. Funds, 22 Dec. [5 Jan.]	III,	5813
1870	North West Sussex (Water Charges), 23 Dec. [6 Jan.]	(n) III,	5883
1871	Industrial Training (Road Transport Bd.) 23 Dec. [5 Jan.]	III,	5815
1878	Pensions Increase (Approved Schemes) (National Health Service) (S.), 23 Dec. [2 Jan.]	III,	5819
1879	Argyll Water Bd. (Drumore Burn, Bellochantuy) Water, 24 Dec. [6 Jan.]	(n) III,	5884
1880	Special Constables (Pensions) (S.), 26 Dec. [6 Jan.]	III,	5821
1881	Pensions Increase (Approved Schemes) (Local Govt.) (S.), 23 Dec. [9 Jan.]	III,	5823
1882	Glasgow–Greenock–Monkton Trunk Road (Langbank and other Diversions), 9 Dec. [9 Jan.] ...	(n) III,	5865
1883	Exchange Control (Import and Export), 29 Dec. [1 Jan.]	III,	5825
1884	London–Portsmouth Trunk Road (Esher By-Pass Slip Roads), 29 Dec. [2 Jan.]	(n) III,	5865
1887	Export of Goods (Control), 22 Dec. [5 Jan.] ...	III,	5827
1888	Pensioners' Declarations, 30 Dec. [7 Jan.]	III,	5828
1889	Price Stability of Imported Products (Rates of Levy), 30 Dec. [1 Jan.]	III,	5830
1890	Southend Water, 30 Dec. [9 Jan.]	(n) III,	5883
1891	Prices and Incomes (General Considerations), 30 Dec. [6 Jan.]	III,	5832
1892	M. 62 Lancashire–Yorkshire Motorway (Tarbock to Croft Section) Connecting Roads, 29 Dec. [20 Jan.]	(n) III,	5867
1894	Rules of the Supreme Ct., 23 Dec. [6 Jan.] ...	III,	5852
1900	Selective Employment Tax (Payments to Public Bodies) (Variation), 31 Dec. [9 Jan.]	III,	5855

(n) Instrument classified as local, noted in the Classified List of Local S.I. at the page shown above, but not set out in full.

Index to Parts I, II and III

Volume
Reference

ROAD TRANSPORT BOARD. *See* INDUSTRIAL TRAINING.

ROAD TRANSPORT TRAINING LEVY. *See* INDUSTRIAL TRAINING.

ROPE, TWINE AND NET TRADE. *See* WAGES COUNCILS.

ROYAL AIR FORCE. *See* DEFENCE; PENSIONS.